INSECT BIOLOGY IN THE FUTURE
"VBW 80"

Academic Press Rapid Manuscript Reproduction

INSECT BIOLOGY IN THE FUTURE

"VBW 80"

Edited by

Michael Locke

Department of Zoology
University of Western Ontario
London, Ontario, Canada

David S. Smith

Department of Medicine
University of Miami School of Medicine
Miami, Florida

ACADEMIC PRESS   1980

A Subsidiary of Harcourt Brace Jovanovich, Publishers

New York   London   Toronto   Sydney   San Francisco

ACADEMIC PRESS, INC.
111 Fifth Avenue, New York, New York 10003

United Kingdom Edition published by
ACADEMIC PRESS, INC. (LONDON) LTD.
24/28 Oval Road, London NW1 7DX

LIBRARY OF CONGRESS CATALOG CARD NUMBER: 8024526

ISBN: 0-12-454340-5

PRINTED IN THE UNITED STATES OF AMERICA

80 81 82 83   9 8 7 6 5 4 3 2 1

CONTENTS

CONTRIBUTORS

Numbers in parentheses indicate the pages on which authors' contributions begin.

J. W. L. Beament (1), *Department of Agriculture, University of Cambridge, Cambridge, England*

M. J. Berridge (463), *Department of Zoology/ARC Group, University of Cambridge, Cambridge, England*

D. Blest (705), *Department of Behavioral Biology, Research School of Biological Sciences, The Australian National Academy, Canberra, A.C.T. 2601, Australia*

W. Bowers (613), *New York State Agricultural Experimental Station-Entymology-Plant Pathology, Geneva, New York*

P. Bryant (517), *Developmental Biology Laboratory, University of California, Irvine, California*

E. Bursell* (905), *Department of Biology, University College of Rhodesia, Zimbabwe, Salisbury, Zimbabwe*

S. Caveney (565), *Department of Zoology, University of Western Ontario, London, Ontario, Canada*

K. G. Davey (325), *Department of Biology, York University, Downsview, Ontario, Canada*

C. Duranceau (479), *Developmental Biology Center and Department of Developmental and Cell Biology, University of California, Irvine, California*

E. Edney (39), *Department of Zoology, University of British Columbia, Vancouver, British Columbia, V6T 2A*

J. Edwards (667), *Department of Zoology, University of Washington, Seattle, Washington*

*Present address: % Tsetse Research Laboratories, Department of Veterinary Medicine, Langford, Bristol, BS187DU, England.

ix

T. Eisner (847), *Section of Neurobiology and Behavior, Langmuir Laboratory, Cornell University, Ithaca, New York 14850*

M. Elliott (879), *Insecticides and Fungicides Department, Rothamsted Experimental Station, Harpenden, Herts, A15 2JQ United Kingdom*

F. Engelmann (311), *Department of Zoology, University of California, Los Angeles, California*

B. Filshie (59), *CSIRO, Division of Entomology, Canberra City, A.C.T. 2601, Australia*

L. Gilbert (439), *Department of Biological Sciences, Northwestern University, Evanston, Illinois*

J. Girton (517), *Developmental Biology Center and Department of Developmental and Cell Biology, University of California, Irvine, California*

S. Glenn (479), *Developmental Biology Center and Department of Developmental and Cell Biology, University of California, Irvine, California*

W. R. Harvey (105), *Department of Biology, Temple University, Philadelphia, Pennsylvania, 19140*

P. Hayes (543), *Department of Genetics, University of Alberta, Edmonton, Alberta, Canada*

A. Horridge (705), *Department of Behavioral Biology, Research School of Biological Sciences, The Australian National Academy, Canberra, A.C.T. 2601, Australia*

G. Hoyle (635), *Department of Biology, University of Oregon, Eugene, Oregon 97403*

A. M. Jungreis (273), *Department of Zoology, University of Tennessee, Knoxville, Tennessee 37916*

K. Katula (439), *Department of Biological Sciences, Northwestern University, Evanston, Illinois*

J. Küppers (125, 735), *Institute of Zoology, University of Münster, Hufferstrasse, 1D-4400 Münster, Germany*

N. Lane (765), *Department of Zoology, Cambridge University, Cambridge, England*

J. H. Law (295), *Department of Biochemistry, University of Chicago, Chicago, Illinois 60637*

M. Locke (227), *Department of Zoology, University of Western Ontario, London, Ontario, Canada*

J. Machin (79), *Department of Zoology, University of Toronto, Toronto, Ontario, Canada*

S. Maddrell (179), *Department of Zoology, University of Cambridge, Cambridge, England*

P. Martin (517), *Developmental Biology Center and Department of Developmental Cell Biology, University of California, Irvine, California*

P. Miller (819), *Department of Zoology, University Museum, Parks Road, Oxford, England*

K. Nakanishi (603), *Department of Chemistry, Columbia University, New York, New York 10027*

K. R. Norris (19), *CSIRO, Canberra, A.C.T. 2601, Australia*

H. Oberlander (423), *Insect Attractants, Behavior, and Basic Biology Research Laboratory, U.S. Department of Agriculture, Gainesville, Florida 32601*

J. Phillips (145), *Department of Zoology, University of British Columbia, Vancouver, British Columbia V6T 1W5*

J. W. S. Pringle (925), *F.R.S. Department of Zoology, University Museum, Oxford, England*

L. Riddiford (403), *Department of Zoology, University of Washington, Seattle, Washington 98105*

W. Roelofs (583), *New York State Agricultural Experimental Station-Entymology, Geneva, New York*

M. Russell (543), *Department of Genetics, University of Alberta, Edmonton, Alberta, Canada*

D. S. Smith (797), *University of Miami School of Medicine, Miami, Florida 33101*

D. Schneider (685), *Max-Planck-Institut für Verhaltensphysiologie, Abteilung Schneider, 8131 Seeweisen, West Germany*

H. A. Schneiderman (479), *Monsanto Company, St. Louis, Missouri 63166*

S. Sridhara (439), *Department of Biological Sciences, Northwestern University, Evanston, Illinois*

J. E. Steele (253), *Department of Zoology, University of Western Ontario, London, Ontario, Canada*

R. A. Steinbrecht (685), *Max-Planck-Institut für Verhaltensphsiologie, Abteilung Schneider, 8131 Seeweisen, West Germany*

U. Thurm (125, 735), *Institute of Zoology, University of Münster, Hufferstrasse, ID-4400, Münster, Germany*

S. Tobe (345), *Department of Zoology, University of Toronto, Toronto, Ontario, Canada*

J. Treherne (765), *Department of Zoology, Cambridge University, Cambridge, England*

J. Truman (385), *Department of Zoology, University of Washington, Seattle, Washington 98105*

D. F. Waterhouse (19), *FRS, CSIRO, Canberra, A.C.T. 2601, Australia*

C. M. Williams (369), *The Biological Laboratories, Harvard University, Cambridge, Massachusetts*

G. Wyatt (201), *Department of Biology, Queen's University, Kingston, Ontario, Canada*

PREFACE

Léon Dufour (1833) used the word for 'bug' in the strict entomological sense when he assured his readers that

> The gigantic baobab, the prodigious whale, the massive elephant, the proud human race, are not more valued by the Creator than the impalpable mussel . . . the earthworm and the bug . . . each shows unnumbered marvels to the eye of the naturalist and all are appropriate subjects for our studies.

While it is difficult to fault Dufour on a point of principle, it is noteworthy that he left whales and baobabs to others and shrewdly concentrated his efforts on the Hemiptera, and indeed probably knew more about the anatomy of these animals than anyone prior to Sir Vincent's picking up the functional challenge a century later.

The contributions in this volume underline the value of insect material in approaching a wide spectrum of biological questions. Practical problems attending less judicious selection are hinted at in Topsell's (1658) figure of the cetacean dissection (1). By the early nineteenth century, a variety of insects had been examined with skill and scientific profit, and while Dufour did not, apparently, have access to *Rhodnius prolixus* (a reduviid that until Wigglesworth's works was noted only as the vector of Chagas disease), he provided excellent figures of the anatomy of other Heteroptera, including that of the tracheal system of the water scorpion *Nepa* (2).

Two figures from Wigglesworth's work (1940b) on *Rhodnius* (3 and 4) need no caption in the present context, but epitomize the experimental approach and incidentally emphasize to the mammalian physiologist and the surgeon the extremes of duress (the clinical term is "insult") that insects will survive in the interests of elucidation of basic physiological and developmental questions—and without the complications of tissue typing and rejection. We may even be reasonably sure that these radical operations were painless as discussed in the most recent work (Wigglesworth, 1980) that has come to our attention.

Each of the authors in this volume has been, one way or another, beguiled by insects. Some no doubt arrived via an often-reported empathy with these animals

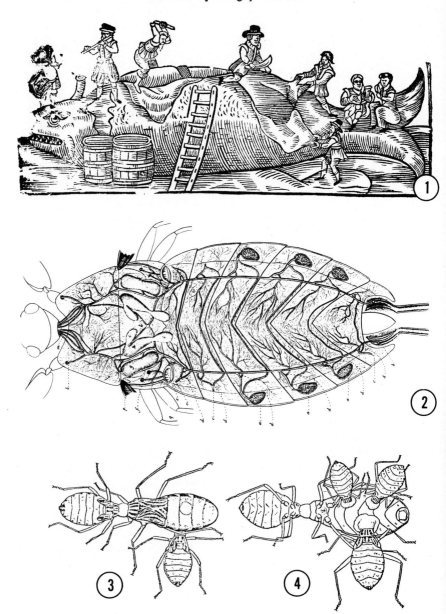

The manner of cutting up the Whale.

sometimes expressed at a very early age, by later appreciation of their many advantages as experimental subjects, or because of their less desirable attributes as competitors in food production and consumption or as vectors of disease.

These essays are presented to Sir Vincent, during his eightieth year. We hope that they will show where many of his ideas have led, and how they have multiplied.

The editors thank Jane Sexsmith for secretarial help above the call of duty.

Michael Locke
David S. Smith

REFERENCES

Dufour, L. (1833). "Récherches Anatomiques et Physiologiques sur les Hémiptères." Paris.
Topsell, E. (1658). "The History of Four-Footed Beasts and Serpents." London.
Wigglesworth, V. B. (1940b). The determination of characters at metamorphosis in *Rhodnius prolixus* (Hemiptera), *J. Exp. Biol.* **17,** 201–222.
Wigglesworth, V. B. (1980). Do insects feel pain? *Antenna (Bull. R. Soc. London)* **4,** 8–9.

WIGGLESWORTH'S CONTRIBUTION TO INSECT BIOLOGY AND THE STATE OF THE ART

Sir James Beament

Department of Applied Biology
University of Cambridge
U.K.

I. INTRODUCTION

Others answer for their special expertise: my apparent crime for which I have to write to this most difficult of titles is that, so far as is known, I was Sir Vincent's first research student and from then on saw him almost daily for some 26 years. To most people a scientist is his published papers, and in the metaphor of an enthusiasm of many of his Cambridge colleagues, which he certainly did not share, 234 not out (latest score) is a formidable achievement. Yet while we all wish him to achieve that distinction for which he wrote the address of congratulations to Sir Rickard Christophers (Wigglesworth, 1973h), this article cannot avoid giving him an inkling of the feelings of Mark Twain on reading his own obituary; for this, and for other things which I must say if this is not simply to be a paean of praise, I trust he will forgive me. Likewise, most of the now distinguished contributors to this volume, and many others who were occupants of the 'top floor' of the Cambridge Zoological Department during his long reign, would not forgive me if I referred to him in any other way than 'VBW' for so he is to everyone (except to his face of course surnames always being the order of the day). Every contribution to science must be judged in the context of the time when it is made. Helmholtz' (1877) theory of hearing may today be totally discredited, but his was the only acceptable theory for 60 years. VBW's scientific contributions to date span almost 60 years: a period in which remarkable advances have been made in the

1

technology of scientific investigation and in the general
understanding of biological mechanisms. Indeed, many of the
more recent contributions to, for example, developmental or
neural biology of apparently much wider implication than to
the insects alone, would have been unthinkable 40 years ago,
yet owe their origins to the demonstration of phenomena, and
to the belief in underlying principle, which stems from VBW's
earlier work.

Maybe it is no longer true, as an examination candidate
once confided to me in an oral that "if you don't know the
reference you put down 'Wigglesworth' and have a 50-50 chance
of being right." More often the problem for the teacher
today is, on the one hand, to persuade students that papers
written before 1970 are by no means out of date, and on the
other, to make the present generation of research workers
acknowledge the people who actually discovered the phenomena
they now re-describe. But inevitably - and to use such a
word implies singular distinction - those who are now leaders
in the various aspects of insect biology will be obliged in
the papers which follow to take account of VBW's contributions,
topic by topic.

II. THE LONDON SCHOOL

VBW was destined by his parents for family medical
practice, but, after demonstrating his insight into the
behaviour of animals (and possibly being put off the subject
permanently) at an early age - by becoming the champion
muleteer of his regiment in the first World War, he completed
his medical training, and came under the influence of the
father of another major scientific discipline in its infancy:
Frederick Gowland Hopkins. He published his first research
papers (1-7), including collaboration with another remarkable
physiologist, J.B.S. Haldane, in biochemistry. The influence
of Hopkins, both personal and subjectwise, is plain to see in
that early work, but more important, repeatedly arises in so
many of his publications in the form of histochemistry.
Thus, in reviewing his main thrust: the adding of the third
dimension of physiology to the taxonomy and natural history
of insects, we should not overlook the fact that over a couple
of generations of mankind, VBW has few rivals in classical
light-microscope histology to the methodology of which he has
contributed substantially.

The origin of the purposeful attack on the physiology of
insects is well substantiated. To Patrick Buxton, professor
of entomology at the London School of Hygiene and Tropical
Medicine, we owe the foresight that progress in medical

entomology was held back by lack of proper physiological knowledge of the insects themselves; VBW was appointed to the lectureship Buxton created to perform this task, and the foundations of insect physiology as a concerted subject may be said to have been laid in the years from 1927-45, which saw the publication of a number of classical papers, and perhaps in some ways more significantly, of papers such as those on respiration (Wigglesworth, 1930b) cuticle (Wigglesworth, 1933d) and hormones (Wigglesworth, 1936d) which signposted the challenging subjects of the post-war years.

But although the appearance in 1934 of the smaller *Insect Physiology* had indicated the nature and tidiness of the new subject, the great landmark of this period was the publication in 1939 of *The Principles* with which it might be said that the subject - and unquestionably also its author - had arrived; it was the year of his election to the Royal Society and the following two were, it is said, exceedingly uncomfortable in the London School until his Head of Department had been accorded the same honour. There is a story that VBW set himself to do one piece of research in each of the areas designated by the chapter headings of *The Principles*: the standard headings into which any physiological text might be divided, in order to familiarise himself with the subject matter. The truth of this may be seen from a brief glance at his own bibliography; at least he did not make a major contribution on locomotion, the sense-organs or nervous coordination.

On the other hand, all science has its origins in previous science. The immense bibliography which he assembled, containing gleanings of physiological significance from papers whose authors had no such pretentions, indicates that a great deal of material physiological knowledge existed from work of the previous 50 years or so but remained buried, waiting for someone to bring it together in a form in which it could be assimilated as a cohesive whole. There was indeed enough material in 1931 on respiration to make this the subject of a review (Wigglesworth, 1931c).

The *Principles of Insect Physiology* must be recognised as one kind of a great achievement of a scientist: seen in perspective of a period when it was, just, possible for one person who started at the right moment to assimilate as well as accumulate the knowledge which spanned the whole subject, to an extent that probably only he, and his arch-rival the late Howard Hinton, ever achieved. The book made it possible for people like myself, entering university a year after it was published, and devouring it in my third year (despite having no less a classical entomologist than A.D. Imms as one of my teachers) to get a bird's-eye view of what the subject was about. I should add that it was to the inspiring

philosophy of my other two main teachers, Carl Pantin and
Eric Smith, who made one look beyond the facts to the horizons
of ideas, that we owe the climate in which so many things
subsequently happened in Cambridge.

Few books have been less aptly named in respect of their
actual mode of approach, or more prophetically named for the
period to which they gave rise. The *Principles* is a superb
accumulation and ordering of scrupulously referenced fact.
It relies on the assumption upon which all science ultimately
must rely, that scientists observe and report accurately and
truthfully. If author 'A' said something increased, and
author 'B' said it decreased, they are thus recorded by VBW,
and it is left to the reader to conclude that more work is
needed to reconcile the two observations. Time and again
when some point was raised, during the quarter-century I
spent in his company, VBW would tell one or other of us 'its
all in the book if you look,' and he was always right in the
sense that the facts were there. He offers enough structure
to hang the facts on, and I strongly suspect his vision is
such that underlying principles, the coordination of facts
into a synthesis, was and is to him so obvious that they do
not need stating; each reader is left to construct his own
picture of how it all fits together to make a concept of a
working insect - and perhaps he did this intentionally in
order to prevent stagnation through reliance on a set of
ideas rather than facts.

Perhaps 'theory' is a young man's word; it occurs only
twice in the 234 titles of his papers, when VBW was under the
age of 30. But if that is so, some of us have remained
immature for a very long time! Science unquestionably is
concerned with facts, and truth is a matter for philosophers.
Scientific investigation is said to proceed (perhaps more
often in public expositions than actually occurs in our
laboratories) by developing theory from fact, and from the
testing of theory to new fact. The problem about 'it all
being in the book,' is that it was hardly possible for the
undergraduate of 30 years ago to command a sufficient
over-view of the physiology of insects to obtain any concept
of principles. Today, as I shall suggest later in this
essay, the mass of fact and detail which has been
accumulated is such that unless the teacher is prepared to
summarise and theorise, perhaps even to make a convincing
story where no story actually exists, it will not be possible
to bring to bear the fruits of all this sophisticated science.
It will indeed only be possible to display one or other area,
large in itself, but small in general physiological terms, and
drive the next generation down the narrow paths which appear
to be radiating further and further away from the road on
which insect physiology set out, and further and further apart

from each other.

In the first phase of insect physiology, which ended at the London School with the end of World War II, VBW never lost sight of the reason why Buxton made it all possible – applied medical entomology. There are ten papers specifically on medical problems, while the physiological research embraced topics of obvious relevance to lice, mosquitoes, bedbugs, tse-tse and other biting flies. In particular there is his first specific investigation (Wigglesworth, 1931f) on *Rhodnius prolixus*.

Rhodnius of course has every right to be included in any list of medically important insects, a blood-sucking reduviid bug, carrying Chagas' disease in South America. Undoubtedly it has also made a bigger contribution to insect physiology than some of the people who have worked on the subject, because, for example, of the extreme convenience with which it can be held for months without feeding, at any particular instar, to provide a bank of material; it requires one large blood meal only per instar, which triggers moulting on a consistently precise timetable. Once acclimatised to its surroundings (Cambridge proved more infective than London) it withstands major surgery with the minimum of aseptic precaution. It is indeed the veritable clockwork insect. A few insects were brought from Brazil to the Pasteur Institute in Paris in the early 1920s, sub-cultured to the London School and to Cambridge and from there were established in many places.

So far as I know, this experimental animal has been inbred, in this particular population, for something like 50 years and continues to show high fertility. And while we pay tribute to VBW, it is appropriate that he and many of us pay tribute to *Rhodnius*, without whose remarkable tolerance and properties insect physiology would certainly have proceeded very much more slowly; whether we really ought to have looked upon such a remarkable beast as the typical insect – the model to which we referred 750,000 other insect species – is another matter. But it would be of singular interest to compare what we have in the laboratory today with some wild specimens lurking in the armadillo burrows of the banks of the Amazon, after perhaps a hundred generations of artificial selection from the jars in the incubator of the best-looking specimens for experimental sacrifice.

With the onset of hostilities, Buxton's vision became of even greater value. There had been feverish stockpiling of materials grown overseas, including the sources of the insecticides nicotine and pyrethrin. The discovery that the pyrethrin store had a limited shelf-life, coupled with the smuggling (so it is said) of 6 kilograms of a magic white powder later called DDT to beleaguered Britain, gave a

particular impulse to the need to understand how insecticides
got into insects: especially how materials penetrated the
cuticle (Wigglesworth, 1941a,b; 1942c; 1944d; 1945c) and,
incidentally, launched me into the area of surface chemistry,
permeability and water relations. We walked around feeding
hundreds of lice on ourselves for 16 hours a day, tried to
recover army shirts heavily impregnated with DDT from vagrants
– or rather tried to recover the vagrants for long enough to
discover whether the DDT had been effective against their
ectopopulations; they got the shirts as a reward for their
cooperation. The London School lost a wing to bombing. And
Buxton, with great humanity, gave each of us in rotation an
undisturbed night's sleep out at Gerrards Cross and, with
considerable sacrifice in the days of food rationing, a good
breakfast.

III. THE AGE OF PRINCIPLES

     The end of hostilities coincided with the retirement of
Imms from the Readership in Entomology at Cambridge
University, to which VBW was appointed, and the Agricultural
Research Council agreed to re-form around him there, the Unit
of Insect Physiology which had just been started in London.
The Unit was traditionally small: Anker David, Tony Lees and
myself were invited out of those who had worked at the London
School, shortly afterwards to be joined by John Kennedy. I
think Lees was probably the nearest of any of us to being a
'real' entomologist in the classical sense, but, whether it
was fortuitous or not, between us we covered a remarkable
range of sciences, and in retrospect, almost as remarkable a
range of temperament and personality.
     The accommodation and the circumstances in the immediate
post-war years in Cambridge made it possible for the Unit to
attract superb research students both locally and from all
over the world. The competition was brutal. As one
distinguished commonwealth contributor to this volume
remarked then, "This place is Mecca. If you get accepted to
work here, you're already a somebody; if you don't you might
as well throw in your chips." Not that anyone was
feather-bedded. Research students were given their project,
and thrown in at the deep end; the success rate was high, the
productivity was prodigious. There were usually as many
working in the lab at 10 p.m. as at 10 a.m. In addition,
VBW would invite young workers in whom he detected promise,
for a few months, presumably exercising some magic influence
over their sponsors to release them, and when the 'top floor'
was full, physiology and its attendant chemistry invaded the

Museum to the discomfort and distaste of the Curator.

I have chosen to call the first ten or so years of the Cambridge period the Age of Principles, and alluded earlier to the prophetically named *Principles*, in the following context. There were (I believe there still are) two aims in studying insect physiology. One, the value to which this knowledge can be put in the applied fields where the impact of insects upon man and his endeavours remains gigantic: the other is the hope and expectation that in the detailed study of a few insects one would arrive at principles applicable to many if not all insects, and begin to obtain a synthesis, an understanding of this remarkable feature of life, as an integrated entity. The second aim is vital to the first, particularly if future generations are not to spend most of their lives trying to assimilate the detail of physiology, taxonomy and ecology. We have to provide principles, so that they can do something, even perhaps something useful, with the knowledge.

What I believed in 1945, and I have every reason to believe VBW and the rest of us believed, was that the cuticle of *Rhodnius* was the cuticle of insects; that all insects would excrete like *Rhodnius* and have their entire development growth and functioning controlled by just two hormones. Probably it was as well that we did believe it. People today are daunted from entering certain fields - like the mechanism of the human brain - however great the challenge, and if he had known the morasse that insect hormones were destined for, perhaps even VBW would have been daunted. But the golden age of any science is the age when it just takes off - when you believe, and perhaps more important everyone else believes, that you have made discoveries of wide implication and application, when you can skim off the cream, when as much as 30% of the time spent at the bench actually appears in published paper (some of us believed in VBW's case it was nearer 90%) instead of the currently accepted figure of around ten.

Here perhaps, in the period of VBW's greatest productivity and influence, one ought to note with all humility his great gift for seeing how to attack a problem: maybe more significantly how to select a problem for attack, so that exciting results would flow from every experiment. When a field is beginning to yield, most experiments have nuggets in them if you are a sufficiently good observer, provided you have dug in the right place to start with. VBW is a remarkably fine observer. As with Helmholtz, new theories will come and go, but like the goldmine of facts in the appendices to Helmholtz (1877) the facts which VBW reported will stand up to any reinvestigation, and that is the hallmark of great experimental science.

But just as VBW had a remit in London to produce
physiology helpful to medical entomology, so also his ARC
Unit in Cambridge was to carry out the similar mission with
respect to agricultural pests. And though specifically one
finds in his publications (e.g. Wigglesworth, 1951b; 1954a;
1955d; 1956b; 1957f) in this period only the occasional direct
reference to this aim, the other members of his Unit, who
devoted years to ticks, red spider mite, aphids, locusts, and
to insecticides, were fulfilling this remit in no uncertain
terms. That apart, and I don't think we had any feelings of
reluctance that we were being directed to work on these
particular subjects, we were encouraged very much to follow
our noses, develop the kind of research that each of us was
particularly good at - for we were a most heterogeneous crew -
and be thoroughly individualistic. There was a strong feeling
of working as a team, but in no way as a group in the modern
sense; we worked for a Director who, be it said, while counting his every second precious would drop everything if you
wanted to discuss your research problem with him.

It was undoubtedly the combination of the stage of
development of the subject, the ripeness of the methodology,
the superb quality of the research students - and an attitude
perhaps engendered in part in the aftermath of war that every
minute of life should be used, and that the laboratory was one
of the exciting places to use it.

IV. THE TURNING POINT

Amongst the sudden transitions which came in 1945, the
teaching of undergraduates in zoology in Cambridge was
switched almost violently. A number of teachers who
themselves have made significant contributions to insect
physiology, amongst whom must particularly be mentioned John
Pringle, Arthur Ramsay and the late Mark Pryor, returned from
war service and with experience of technologies, especially in
electronics, which the war itself had developed apace. But
the teaching of entomology suddenly changed overnight too,
from the classical tradition of Imms to the new physiology of
Wigglesworth. It was therefore Cambridge which attracted
the flower of potential biological scientists (as if it does
not now!) which instilled the new outlook on entomology into
hundreds who, in their turn, in the great expansion of
universities fifteen years later, have handed on the gospel.

All stories have a turning point, often far more
difficult to recognise than the signpost planted by VBW
himself, in the form of the famous Croonian Lecture to the
Royal Society (1948e) "The Insect as a Medium for the

Study of Physiology." Here was the coming-of-age of the new
science, almost exactly 21 years after the first paper
published from the London School; before us, the vista of
peace and affluence - and the original purpose of insect
physiology turned upside-down. VBW demonstrated that
insects were now an ideal vehicle for the study of physiology
for its own sake. And indeed thus it proved to be. The
insect was in almost every sense superior and more convenient
as a laboratory test-bed for the new ideas of the post-war
period, than the previously conventional frog and rat. It
also happened to be far more easy and economic to breed and
culture. Since no centre of learning has been more
dedicated to the pursuit of knowledge for its own sake and
the intellectual satisfaction of the pursuer than Cambridge
itself, which it must be admitted, it has done for centuries
with singular distinction, it needed no second bidding.

Much of what has stemmed, and predictions of what might
stem further, from this turning point, and from the
succeeding generations of VBW's original disciples, is set
out in the following articles to which this volume is devoted.
Much of the modern sciences of developmental biology,
biochemistry, nerve and muscle physiology and so on can be
traced back to this point. They were, and are, great
scientific developments, worked out with insects, and to some
degree therefore contributing to that desired knowledge of
the insects. The state of the Art, its hundreds, indeed
thousands of adherents, and its contribution to mankind's fund
of pure knowledge, stands very high in the esteem of
scientific assessment and patronage.

Fortunately we cannot, like science fiction authors,
reverse the course of time. So it is safe to ponder what
might have happened, had VBW's ARC Unit been transferred to
the Rothamsted Agricultural Research Station, the oldest and
most distinguished centre for scientific research devoted to
agriculture in the world. This was actually under consideration until Imm's Readership became open. Would the flower of
two generations of English-speaking biological scientists
have gone headlong down the pathways to such new knowledge
derived from insects we have today: knowledge which is deep
and heady, sophisticated and full of great thoughts and
puzzles about the very nature of life and the living
machinery - and how much of it is really about the insects
themselves? Because even in 1945 it was possible to make
what proved to be really fundamental discoveries about this
dominant group of living things, without knowing enough about
insects to realise how fundamental they were: indeed without
being able to classify the experimental animal into anything
more precise than its Order. Today one is certain that many
who are adding to the fund of man's knowledge not only could

not identify the animal on which they work, but further, are
hardly familiar with the biology of its life in the culture
room, let alone in the real world where insects actually live.

Let us be abundantly clear that this is no criticism of
VBW. He went into the field to see agricultural problems and
made members of his Unit do so. And he was expounding the
virtues of biological control, and the problems of synthetic
insecticides, in a statesmanlike way long before the
ecological crisis was launched on us by sensation seeking
journalists. But the path our Art has taken gives me great
cause for concern, and VBW did more than anyone to dislodge
the stone, not knowing in which direction it would roll down
the hill, gathering momentum as it went.

V. THE MATERIAL CONTRIBUTION

It would be impossible even if it were appropriate, to
attempt an assessment of VBW's many specific pieces of
research, more particularly because every paper can be held
up to a student as a beautiful example of the way to do
experiments and present a publication. I must be content
with a few of the landmarks which I think had most influence.
Respiration was the subject of classical discoveries
(Wigglesworth, 1930b; 1931 with E.K. Sikes; 1931h) and with
the exception of the controversial business of movement of
'fluid' in the tracheoles for which no convincing explanation
has been advanced, has proceeded from his foundations to a
satisfying cohesive picture today of the mechanisms. His
study of excretion started even before the London School era
(Wigglesworth, 1924a) and led to another early landmark
(Wigglesworth, 1931d,e,f,g). It is a cautionary example. VBW
has never really returned to the topic, his description of
the process in *Rhodnius* was taken as the model for years, and
much later it became apparent that *Rhodnius* was not at all
typical.

But in 1933 there appeared the first paper on cuticle and
moulting (Wigglesworth, 1933d) followed shortly afterwards
(Wigglesworth, 1934b; 1936d) by those on factors controlling
moulting and metamorphosis, and the function of the corpus
allatum, which, if one were forced to choose, must be
regarded as the ultimate classics, the works of greatest
portent, out of so many outstanding papers VBW has produced.
In later years he has said repeatedly that 'the understanding
of cuticle depends on knowing how it is formed' to which one
must add, and how it is formed depends on how it is
controlled. The cuticle became the indicator of hormonal
activity, and led us to the important but we now see simple

concept that cuticle and cells, the integument, are a single
living entity, instead of regarding cuticle as a mechanical
box containing an insect.

How much scientific knowledge, from VBW and hundreds of
others subsequently, owes its origin to these papers it would
be difficult to assess, in fields today far removed from
entomology. And in demonstrating the role of neurosecretory
cells within the nervous system and the transmission of
hormonal material directly to its target along the core of
axons, a major new approach to the controlling mechanisms of
the central nervous system was begun. This work was
characterised by extreme simplicity and elegance of
experimental approach, which belies the masterly command of
histology and of micro-dissection. Is it too much to say
that before his establishment of the elements of this growth
and control machinery, culminating with the (Wigglesworth,
1948a) paper, the whole of man's firm ideas about hormones
had been based on the mammalian system with its complex of
many hormones, determining what happened in all the tissues?
Here he demonstrated a completely different system in which
just two hormones appeared to control the expression of
particular genes in the respective tissues which were
affected.

As this area of research developed, as ever more things
were attributed to just these two hormones - remember that
this was before the mechanisms of RNA and protein synthesis
became understood - one has to confess that it became more
and more difficult to believe that the system was as simple
and all pervasive as it seemed to be: was the goal of a
'principle' beginning to disappear?

Historically, it may prove important that whereas some of
the aspects of insect physiology which VBW initiated
attracted each only a small number of adherents, many
scientists, including some of considerable eminence, entered
the field of insect hormones, not least biochemists intent on
discovering the chemical nature of the materials concerned.

VBW has never been a slouch; his output of papers in the
past ten years alone can be envied by many a worker in the
prime of his scientific youth. But this was the one time we
saw VBW under pressure, anxious to capture the prize in the
race he had himself started, in his characteristic way
single-handed against the assembled teams of Germany, Japan
and the USA. It is an irony of fate that sufficient of the
answer - farnesol (Wigglesworth, 1961d) was in a bottle on the
shelves of his laboratory throughout the search.

VI. THE STATE OF THE PRINCIPLES

I salute the achievements of those who have developed
Arts in other fields, using insects and capitalising on
earlier discoveries about them, but that is no longer insect
physiology in my understanding of the term. I have
discussed insect endocrinology as but one example of the
present state of our Art, seen by one who tries to understand
and, perhaps more challenging, one who wants to and has to
teach insect biology. Whatever research may unveil, the
future of our subject depends on teachers, and on the things
in which we endeavour to arouse the enthusiasm of our pupils,
not least by the example we set them. One of many examples
VBW has set us, in addition to knowing the insects and being
concerned about the application of knowledge to the real
world, has been the way in which he has ranged over many
areas of insect physiology. While others were pursuing the
chemical nature of juvenile hormone with single purpose, he
combined his search with producing some three dozen papers on
a whole range of other subjects too. Today, how many people
are able to break out of the little area in which they do
their Ph.D.? If anyone tries, he is likely to find that
other narrow experts in other tiny fields attempt to damn
anyone who dares make an observation by looking over the
fence at their tiny corn patch. If science goes on in this
manner, with groups ever more proscribed by need to justify
their sophisticated equipment, their thinking limited by what
their machines can do, of course they are going to lose sight
of the original object of insect physiology.
    It is no-one's fault that, as research on insect hormones
mushroomed, the wonderful principle faded, and as more and
more hormones have been found, our picture of the natural
machinery becomes a morasse. Novak (1975) in the second
edition of *Insect Hormones*, lists over 3,000 papers published
in the previous decade and says, understandibly, that the
previous literature is listed in his first edition. There
seems almost to be an anti-experiment for every experiment,
let alone an anti-hormone for every hormone. Maybe it is
not more complicated than the impressive wall-chart which
sets out the biochemical equations of intermediary metabolism;
but where is any semblance of the insect hormone wall chart to
be found? When insect physiology came of age in 1939 it may
have been best for VBW to call his book *The Principles,* and
set out the facts with an implied framework, but the facts
have now expanded to the stage where, if we are to make sense
of them and obtain credulity then, like putting realism into
quarks and coloured ultimate particles, they have to be linked
up with reality. VBW set an example with *Insect Hormones*

(1970) and the obligation must be on, not only the endocrinologists, but also the fine-structuralists, the neuro-muscular biologists and so on, to make their material cohesive and accessible to those who want to build on their discoveries, not merely to those who want to go further into the minutiae, but particularly those who want to obtain a perspective towards understanding the far bigger subject - insects.

What does now seem to be clear at least, is that the insect hormonal system is quite as complicated as the mammalian one, with the added difficulty, belying the claim of the Croonian Lecture, that the orders of magnitude of the materials concerned themselves push technology to the limits of inconvenience; the latest range of hormones must occur and act in quantities comparable with the pheromones, where at least we have the advantage of observing whole insects free of the unknown effects of operative interference. New principles of a kind are certainly emerging. One, quite obviously, is that we are dealing with a multitude of complexly interwoven feed-back loops at which the most advanced theorist in electronic circuitry would shudder to have to predict the outcome of modifying any particular bit. Another, more salutory and mundane, is that unless the researcher investigates the effect of a wide range of hormone concentrations, and relates this to an understanding of the range of biological states of a particular insect, we shall increasingly get conflicting experimental results. A third principle is indeed anti-principle; for example, one field of our Art which appears in great chaos is 'diapause'. Is it not because we have been so obsessed by trying to force it into a single pattern, a single set of principles, that we have failed for lack of true biological understanding to see that it is not one phenomenon, not one common physiological mechanism, but a convergence: a consequence of the great advantage of programming the variety of insects to the great variety of environmental circumstances?

VII. THE STATE OF THE ART

Physiology triumphs in the generalisation and the prize we all sought was the principle, the mechanism, the discovery which is widely applicable in pure terms. But 'what every real biologist knows' is that the domination of the insects, and their unparalleled role in the biology of our planet and of man, does not depend on their likenesses but lies in their differences. There are over three-quarters of a million species because of their ability to capitalise each

micro-habitat, each fragment of biological productivity, to
specialise and speciate, to meet chemical defence of plant
and attack by man with resistance and transformation to their
own advantage: to expand their populations, given half a
chance as if by magic. The things which link them with their
environment in this remarkably detailed way are their cuticle
and senses, their hormones, and behaviour. And we shall not
make real sense of any of these until enough people who study
their biology: whether in pure or applied ecology, are
enabled to acquire a familiarity with such physiological ideas,
in a fashion which intrigues them, rather than frightens them.

The reverse is also true. Many of the puzzles in insect
ecology are now finding adequate explanation because
ecologists are studying water and energy balance, for food
and nutrition is the other main factor which links the insect
with its environment. This area was the first which
attracted VBW, then a young biochemist; his series of papers
(Wigglesworth, 1927a,b; 1928b; 1929d; 1930c; 1931a) ended
abruptly in 1931, with subseqeuntly only the occasional assay
into what might more broadly be called nutrition. Of that
later research I would single out his neglected but splendid
paper (Wigglesworth, 1942b) on the role of the fat body -
unfashionable in all the exciting topics of the 1940s and 50s,
but an example of what only a histologist of VBW's ability
can do. In our current obsession with enzymes and substrates,
one is apt to forget it goes on in that 'ill-organised messy
stuff which makes dissections so difficult' which is at the
centre of the most flexible adaptable machine nature has
devised. Again, the detail of the machine is bewildering,
but perhaps ecology can provide the example we should follow.
The detail of an ecosystem is equally bewildering. The big
step in our understanding came when we looked overall at the
input and output in energetic terms.

To make use of physiology and biochemsitry, to recreate
insect biology as an integrated subject, will require a
different outlook, a different mainspring. It is most likely
to come from capitalising a love of natural history, or a wish
to do something useful with knowledge. Both are values VBW
holds dear and has expounded. It will require a different
technology too. Nowadays science is said to depend on
pushing technology to its limits. In some areas it is true,
though one rarely finds greater credit given to the
technologists than to those completely dependent on them and
on the huge sums of money necessary. The greatest fear we
have for the future of that kind of science is that society
will refuse to provide the cost of the technology against the
yield. But one cannot take that kind of technology into the
field (nor would it be any use there), to the place where one
will learn to understand insects, whether for the intrigue

Wigglesworth, V.B. (1941a). Permeability of insect cuticle. *Nature 147*, 116.

Wigglesworth, V.B. (1941b). The effect of pyrethrum on the spiracular mechanism of insects. *Proc. R. Ent. Soc. Lond. (A) 16*, 11-14.

Wigglesworth, V.B. (1942b). The storage of protein fat, glycogen and uric acid in the fat body and other tissues of mosquito larvae. *J. Exp. Biol. 19*, 56-77.

Wigglesworth, V.B. (1942c). Some notes on the integument of insects in relation to the entry of contact insecticides. *Bull. Ent. Res. 33*, 205-218.

Wigglesworth, V.B. (1944d). Action of inert dusts on insects. *Nature 153*, 493.

Wigglesworth, V.B. (1945c). Transpiration through the cuticle of insects. *J. Exp. Biol. 21*, 91-114.

Wigglesworth, V.B. (1948a). The functions of the corpus allatum in *Rhodnius prolixus* (Hemiptera). *J. Exp. Biol. 25*, 1-14.

Wigglesworth, V.B. (1948e). The insect as a medium for the study of physiology. *Proc. Roy. Soc. B 135*, 430-446.

Wigglesworth, V.B. (1951b). Insects and human affairs. *Essex Farmers' Journal 30*, 25.

Wigglesworth, V.B. (1954a). Organo-phosphorus insecticides. *Chemistry and Industry*, 477-478.

Wigglesworth, V.B. (1955d). The contribution of pure science to applied biology. *Ann. Appl. Biol. 42*, 34-44.

Wigglesworth, V.B. (1956b). Insect physiology in relation to insecticides. *J. Roy. Soc. Arts 104*, 426-438.

Wigglesworth, V.B. (1957f). Insects and the farmer. (The fourth Middleton Memorial Lecture). *Agric. Progress 32*, 1-8.

Wigglesworth, V.B. (1961d). Some observations on the juvenile hormone effect of farnesol in *Rhodnius prolixus* Stal (Hemiptera). *J. Ins. Physiol. 7*, 73-78.

Wigglesworth, V.B. (1973b). Haemocytes and basement membrane formation in *Rhodnius*. *J. Insect Physiol. 19*, 831-844.

INSECTS AND INSECT PHYSIOLOGY IN THE SCHEME OF THINGS

D.F. Waterhouse
K.R. Norris

CSIRO Division of Entomology
Canberra, Australia

As most of this volume is devoted to specialized aspects of insect physiology the present essay is intended to provide an overview of the Insecta. We offer brief comments on the evolution of insects, since their origin(s) and uniformity of descent have obvious bearings on their physiology, and we discuss also the extraordinary exploitation by insect species of the terrestrial environment, possible reasons for their dominance, and why they have not gone even further along some avenues. We also take brief stock of progress in studying insect physiology, and the relevance of the latter to the control of insect pests.

I. ORIGINS

The Class Insecta (from which we here exclude the entognathous hexapods, the Collembola, Protura and Diplura) is known with certainty in fossil form only from the upper Carboniferous onwards, about 300 million years. Most of the orders represented then were already winged and, from their diversity, it seems certain that the power of flight had originated very much earlier. Moreover, as the advent of winged insects must have been preceded by a lengthy period when only apterous insects occurred, the true origins must lie even further back. Perhaps the Insecta have had more than 400 million years (from the Silurian) to achieve their present remarkable diversity. This is a long period indeed, during which groups of comparable antiquity have failed to radiate in comparable fashion, and others have become extinct.

It seems most likely that the insects originated on land. The oceans are quite inimical to nearly all modern insects, for considerations which will be discussed later and, for this and other reasons, a marine origin can be ruled out. The ancestral insects may well have required a rather moist habitat, but it is very doubtful whether they were truly aquatic. To substantiate this one can point to the truly terrestrial nature of the related groups Symphyla and Diplura and of the Archaeognatha and Thysanura, and to the complete absence of evidence for an aquatic stage in the evolution of the ancient Blattoid-Orthopteroid orders, the immature stages of which retain all spiracles. As Hinton (1977) suggests, the insects almost certainly evolved as terrestrial animals, and the tracheal system is an adaptation to life on land.

II. EXPLOITATION OF ENVIRONMENT

In whatever environment they may have originated, the Insecta have achieved a remarkably successful conquest of the non-marine parts of the globe. It is estimated that they may number as many as three million species of which only about one third have been described so far. Thus there are five to ten times as many species of insects as there are of all the rest of the Animal Kingdom put together. The habitats they have come to occupy range from desert to humid, tropical rain-forest, from ice-cold water to hot springs at 51°C, from sea-level to high alpine regions, and from the equator to the polar ice caps.

The failure of insects to colonize the seas effectively has been the cause of much speculation (e.g. Buxton 1926, Mackerras 1950, Usinger 1957), but the critical reasons have not yet been clearly elucidated. However, Hinton (1977) points out that there is an even more marked paucity of insect species inhabiting unit lengths of flowing fresh water than unit lengths of the marine littoral. Thus it seems likely that, contrary to the view of Cheng (1976), osmotic factors play a negligible part in determining the scarcity of marine insects. In fact, halophilous insects have evolved quite a variety of mechanisms for controlling the concentration of salts in their haemolymph. Some have a hydrofuge covering or a cuticle impermeable to ions, and others have effective mechanisms for reducing uptake of salts from the gut, coupled with the ability to excrete hypertonic solutions from the malpighian tubules and rectal sac.

Buxton (1926) and Mackerras (1950) concluded that turbulence of the sea contributes heavily to the limitation of the marine insect fauna, and Hinton (1977) is in agreement with this, but extends the idea to cover the even more marked deficit of insects in turbulent fresh water. Usinger (1957) pointed out that the deficit extends to deep waters, both marine and fresh. There, turbulence is negligible, and an important factor may be the need that almost all adult insects have for access to free oxygen.

Insects that have colonized the marine littoral and the open ocean do not include any giants, so that increase in body size appears not to afford a solution to the problem of turbulence. They tend to a modification or loss of wings, especially in the Chironomidae, important among marine organisms; thus these organs, so valuable to the Insecta on land, may be an impediment in marine life. The only really ocean-going insects known, five species of *Halobates* (Hemiptera: Gerridae) which live on the surface (Anderson and Polhemus 1976), are wingless. Insect colonists of turbulent fresh water do not show any corresponding tendency to loss of wings.

The range of food exploited by insects is unparalleled by any other metazoan group. There are species that attack the fruits, leaves, stems, roots and by-products of almost all sorts of plants. There are numerous intricate and specific relationships with plants which betoken long periods of co-evolution. Some insects, such as certain aphids, exploit two botanically unrelated hosts alternately. Utilization of plants as food and shelter is often based on the ability of insects to react to token chemical substances, blossom "colours", or to structural or other features, and the plants in turn exploit their insect visitors to achieve pollination. The digestive capacities of host-specific insects have also become adapted to the efficient exploitation of the particular plant's tissues, even though these may contain chemicals which are highly toxic to other forms of life. Man finds to his cost that there are many important economic effects from the plant viruses which have become adapted to transmission by sucking insects.

Over recent decades it has been found that many species of phytophagous insects can be cultured on alien substances. This may be because antifeeding compounds are absent or because specific token chemicals that are critical have been incorporated into a balanced artificial diet. This is an important field of research in relation to the application of certain types of control measure.

As another food resource, the animal kingdom has also come in for a generous share of patronage by the Insecta. Many species are predators upon other invertebrates, and a few even of small vertebrates. There are vast numbers of insects which are parasites, parasitoids or predators of other insects or other arthropods, molluscs and annelids. Again, host specificity is often highly developed. Many insect species have become ecto- or endoparasites of vertebrates, often with a high degree of specificity, and there are important groups that suck the blood of vertebrates, sometimes assuming great significance on account of the extreme nuisance they constitute, or seriously affecting human welfare in countless millions of hectares of land, if they are involved in the transmission of such diseases as malaria or sleeping sickness.

A most unusual feat in adaptation of some insects is the ability to digest keratin, the sulphur-containing protein which is the main constituent of wool, hair, horns, hoofs and feathers, occurring also in mammalian skin, reptilian scales, tortoise shell and elsewhere. Clothes moths, dermestid beetles and feather lice are the only animals that have been shown to possess mechanisms for the digestion of these freely available but refractory materials (Waterhouse 1958).

III. REASONS FOR DOMINANCE

The success of an animal group may be judged on such grounds as the number of its species, the number of its individuals in the environment, its biomass or its capacity to control its environment. On the last criterion man wins easily ('though in some cases one might substitute the word "destroy" for "control"). Insects, on the other hand, are clearly the winners on the first criterion and, overall, also on the second and third, so far as the terrestrial environment is concerned. Clearly, however, not all insects are equally successful by the second criterion since, in a particular countryside there are a few species with a very large number of individuals but many more that are comparatively rare (Wigglesworth 1964). Many people have examined possible reasons for the success of the Insecta, as judged by the first of the above criteria, and this almost certainly results from the combination of a number of features, the more important of which are discussed below.

A useful survey of features leading to evolutionary success in the Insecta is given by Hinton (1977) who lists four critical stages in their history. The first was their development of a tracheal system which involved the invagination of a relatively enormous surface area permeable to both oxygen and water. In this system, water loss, so critical to small terrestrial animals, can be greatly reduced because contact with the external environment is only via the relatively small spiracles which, in many cases, can be closed in the face of adverse conditions.

The second major advance (see also Wigglesworth 1945c) is complementary to the first. It concerns the acquisition of a more or less impermeable outer cuticle which enabled the group to invade dry terrestrial environments. A similar capacity has also been developed in some terrestrial arachnids, but not in other land arthropods (Cloudsley-Thompson 1958).

As Hinton (1977) pointed out, a superior mechanism would have
been a cuticle that is less permeable to water than to oxygen,
but such a system may be unattainable, *inter alia* because the
oxygen molecule is larger than the water molecule, and so
gaseous oxygen diffuses through biological membranes less
rapidly.

The third critical point was the development of wings
(see later section), which brought a new dimension to the
location of food supplies and mates, and to both escape and
predation.

The fourth advance occurred in the upper Carboniferous
or lower Permian when, in some forms, the developing wings
were invaginated into the body of the larva (nymph), and one
or more of the penultimate life history stages became a pupa.
The resulting differentiation, in form and function of the
larva as a feeding stage, from the adult as the reproductive
and dispersal stage, permitted the exploitation of a much
wider range of environments. Indeed the success of this
development is reflected in the fact that 88 per cent of known
species of insects are endopterygotes.

Diapause (arrested development), as distinct from cold
quiescence, is a characteristic and enormously valuable adaptation to fluctuating environments of one or more of the stages
of many poikilothermic animals and reaches its peak of
sophistication in the Insecta. During diapause, metabolism
and development is minimised, enabling stocks to tide over
sometimes lengthy periods when the habitat is inhospitable or,
more importantly, favourable for metabolism for periods too
brief for the completion of development. Effective diapause
mechanisms have undoubtedly contributed much to the success
of the Insecta.

The power of flight has been an obvious asset to the
insects in establishing their dominance over other terrestrial invertebrates of comparable size. The history of
theories about the origin of insect wings was summarized by
Wigglesworth (1976a) and Kukalova-Peck (1978). Until recent
times, Crampton (1916) enjoyed almost universal support for
his view that the paranotal lobes, evident on the thoracic
segments of some fossil forms, were the precursors of insect
wings. These broad-based flaps were considered to have
offered certain Paleozoic insects the ability to achieve at
least attitude control when falling, so that they were
suitably poised for a quick escape on reaching the ground,
and were also able to perform gliding flight if they jumped
from the ground, or launched themselves from high places.
Subsequently, through the development of appropriate musculature, innervation, etc., and an extreme narrowing and the
jointing of the base of the lobe, they evolved the capacity
for controlled flight at will.

Wigglesworth (1963a, 1963e) suggested that winged flight
originated in insects of small size that had been borne up into the air to become components of the "aerial plankton",
which has been shown to be so abundant and diverse up to
thousands of metres above the earth's surface. This interesting suggestion was based at the time on the paranotal lobe
theory of the origin of wings. Later, however, basing his
arguments partly on Tower's (1903) studies on the origins of
wing rudiments, he showed that the paranotal lobe theory was
untenable (Wigglesworth 1976a). He postulated that flying
insects originated from forms with secondarily aquatic larvae,
parts of whose meso- and metathoracic gills, which in turn
were derived from parts of biramous limbs, offered a basis
for selection of flapping wings. Such structures would have
been of value initially in bearing their owners to other
bodies of water if their immediate environment showed signs of
drying up. The gill (leg) component in question was held to
be homologous with the coxal styles of modern Archaeognatha.
This theory was condemned by Hinton (1977) on the grounds that
the insect leg was never biramous, and that the styles of the
Archaeognatha are secondary, adaptive structures, which do not
appear in the early instars. However, irrespective of the
homologies of the organs involved, it is still possible that
frequent incorporation of individuals into the aerial plankton
would be a selective agency for improved flight in winged
insects.

Kukalova-Peck (1978) questioned Wigglesworth's theory on
anatomical and evolutionary grounds and drew attention to the
hard facts of fossil evidence. All known primitive Palaeozoic insect nymphs had "wings" on the meso- and metathorax -
that is, articulated, freely movable, thin lobes stiffened
with veins in a corrugated pattern. Moreover, from the
presence also of prothoracic wings and of winglets on all ten
abdominal segments in some Palaeozoic fossils, Kukalova-Peck
concluded that the nymphs of ancestral Pterygota had "wings"
on all body segments. She consistently called these nymphal
structures wings, but expressed an open mind about their
function, which could have been to close spiracles during
submersion or during water-robbing excursions on land, to
protect gills either in or out of water, to irrigate gills, to
act as lateral tactile organs, or to assist in aquatic locomotion by performing a sculling action. She did not postulate
that these fossil insects were either aquatic or terrestrial,
but suggested they may have been amphibious. Whatever the
function of the primitive winglet there is no longer any need
for ingenious theories about the origin of wings. Paradoxi-
cally, we have to turn about and face the fact that the
earliest tentative insect astronauts had to disembarrass them-

selves of eleven pairs of unwanted wings, or put them to uses other than locomotion, keeping only those of the meso- and metathorax, which were most suitably placed for flying.

Kukalova-Peck suggested that the apterygote insects originated among the moisture-loving terrestrial plants (Psilophyta) in the humid upper Silurian swamps. By the middle and upper Devonian, taller forests had evolved, and the phytophagous pre-pterygote insects would have tended to seek the succulent growing tissues in the upper levels. From these heights, those which had come "to possess flapping lateral appendages had a distinct selective advantage in their ability to escape, to break a fall, and to disperse". Early Neoptera, moreover, must have had a distinct capacity for soaring flight.

Kukalova-Peck cited a study of neuromuscular mechanisms by Ewer (1963) which showed that the wing beat in early pterygotes must have been of very much lower frequency than in the majority of today's insects. She suggested that the well-known large wing areas of Palaeozoic insects (Handlirsch 1906) reflect a temporary compensation for this. Perhaps these insects used their powers of flight chiefly on generally downward journeys, and only later, through reduction of body and wing size, development of resilin, improvement in the resilience of the thorax, and emergence of more advanced neuromuscular mechanisms did the "positive" flight of modern insects evolve.

Regrettably the fossil record of the necessarily long period of pterygote history preceding the late Carboniferous is lacking. However, Kukalova-Peck's conclusion from the study of early wing venation and blood sinuses in modern wings that the Pterygota are monophyletic is important to all students of the Insecta. The doubts raised by Mackerras (1967) and others in relation to the Odonata are due to a misreading of secondary, adaptive characters in wing venation and other features.

The acquisition of wings undoubtedly gave the insects an enormous evolutionary boost. Cogent reasons have also been advanced as to why the differentiation of the insect body into head, rigid thorax and legless abdomen is a particularly favourable arrangement for a terrestrial arthropod. The mobility of the head, in contrast with its fusion into a cephalothorax as in the Arachnida, may have facilitated the development of varied types of mouthparts (and hence of varied feeding habits) and also better orientation during flight and landing.

The consolidation of the insect thorax confers a distinct advantage on the group in affording rigid attachment for the legs, and a firm but yet appropriately flexible base for the

insertion of the wings. The interior of the thorax is occupied
largely by the muscles that move the appendages, so that the
thorax is developed as a highly specialized unit for locomotion. Other functions in relation to digestion, excretion
and reproduction have, with advantage, been relegated to the
usually distensible and flexible abdomen. If secondary
rigidity of the abdomen occurs, as in many Coleoptera, an
equivalent of distensibility is brought about by the presence
of large, compressible air-sacs inside the abdomen.

The hexapod gait is another feature of insects which has
probably contributed substantially to their success. Manton
(1952) pointed out that this is a highly efficient form of
locomotion which allows minimal interference of any leg with
the action of its neighbour. It also makes for great stability on the substratum, because the six legs act, in effect,
as two interlocking tripods (Wigglesworth 1964). The fore
and hind legs of the left side and the mid of the right move
forward more or less in unison and are then firmly planted on
the substratum, whereupon the fore and the hind of the right
side and the mid of the left are moved forward, and in turn
planted. With such a gait the insect always has a stable,
three-point support.

IV. THE SIZE OF INSECTS

Insects range in size from small parasitoid wasps (such
as the trichogrammatid *Megaphragma mymaripenne* Timberlake,
0.18 mm in length, which is parasitic on thrips eggs (Doutt
and Viggiani 1968), through bulky dynastid beetles some 16
cm in length (Wigglesworth 1964) to the moth *Coscinocera
hercules* Miskin about 26 cm in wingspan (Oberthur 1916), the
birdwing butterfly, *Ornithoptera alexandrae* Rothschild, about
27 cm in wingspan (Wilson and Trebilcock 1978), and stick
insects in some of which the body length exceeds 30 cm (Key
1970). The smallest insects are considerably smaller than
the largest Protozoa, and the largest far exceed in size the
smallest members of each of the classes of vertebrates (Folsom
1922). As for weight, some insects are lighter than the
nucleus of a large protozoan, but it seems that the heaviest
living insects weigh no more than 100 g. The heaviest invertebrate known is the giant squid *(Architeuthis*, 3,000 kg) and
the heaviest arthropod, a spider crab (30 kg). These marine
forms are far heavier than the heaviest terrestrial invertebrates, which are snails and earthworms that nevertheless
range from 1 to 4 kg (Cloudsley-Thompson 1970), much heavier
than the biggest insects.

Considering the number of species in the Insecta and their diversity of form and habitat, it is interesting to speculate why, at least in special circumstances, they do not achieve greater sizes. It is not unreasonable to expect a general tendency during evolution for the upper and lower ends of the size range of an animal group to increase or to decrease to values at which the benefits of larger or smaller size respectively are offset by their attendant disadvantages. It is possibly easier to set the lower size limit as being that which is sufficient to accommodate the number and diversity of cells - certainly many thousands - necessary to provide for the degree of structural and physiological complexity required by an insect. But what of the upper end of the size range of insects, and what advantages and disadvantages would be conferred if some insects were very much bigger than extant forms? It is of interest to examine biological and physical factors that seem relevant to the problem.

The effects of physical factors such as gravity, surface to volume ratio and oxygen diffusion all vary according to the size of the animal. In particular it would appear that physical problems associated with the insect exoskeleton tend strongly to limit body size.

A comparatively inextensible exoskeleton, such as that of most Arthropoda, confers both advantages and disadvantages. Tubular structures are very resistant to twisting and bending, but above a certain size they become disproportionately heavy in relation to their strength. On the engineering analogy of tubular structures being most useful for scaffolding, but girders for great weights, it can be argued that an exoskeleton is more efficient for smaller animals and solid bones better for larger ones (Cloudsley-Thompson 1970).

The necessity to moult at intervals exposes all arthropods to hazards. Not only may they die if moulting does not go exactly right, but they are extremely vulnerable to enemies until the new cuticle has hardened. A problem during moulting of terrestrial insects that mounts progressively in significance as body size and weight increases is the maintenance of shape of the soft tissues immediately after moulting. In the absence of structural support large insects would tend to flatten increasingly as the size increases. Hanging from some object during the process of moulting may offset this factor up to a certain size, but after a critical point has been reached, problems due to gravity may prove insuperable during moulting.

Another feature of the insect exoskeleton which may contribute to size limitation is the remarkably efficient waterproofing mechanism. This has undoubtedly been of major importance in the evolutionary success of the insects, but it may, however, contribute to the limitation of their size, as it severely restricts the extent to which the body can be cooled by evaporation (Hinton 1977). Under hot conditions, internal temperatures of active insects may build up until they are near critical limits. Consideration of surface-volume ratios would therefore suggest that smaller insects would be less exposed to this risk.

Where there is a need to adapt to rapidly changing conditions, an organism with a large population size and a short generation time provides far greater opportunities for evolutionary forces to operate rapidly than does an organism with a low population size and/or a long generation time. This applies even if the inherent variability in both organisms is the same. Compared with most other animals - even other Arthropoda - the Insects are very advantageously placed in both these respects. Body size is related to generation time, smaller organisms in general having shorter generation times than larger organisms.

Body size is also related to the quantity of food required and, although large animals require proportionately less food per unit body weight than their smaller relatives, a large animal must nevertheless eat more than a smaller one. Because there are times of food shortage for all animals this factor would seem to favour smaller over larger animals, all other things being equal.

Hinton (1977) drew attention to the fact that, with few exceptions, insects are small enough to fall from any height without risk of serious injury, but this would seem to be a side effect of size limitation rather than a cause of it, as risks of shattering would offer no bar to the development of giants among exclusively terrestrial insects.

The importance of the tracheal system in the evolutionary success of the Insecta has been alluded to earlier, but though quite vital to their success, this mode of respiration may well contribute to limiting the maximum size they can attain. True, Day (1950) formed the opinion that the tracheal system of insects is efficient enough to serve larger insects than exist, especially if gaseous diffusion is supplemented by forced ventilation, and there is an adequate system of air sacs, and the distances to be covered by diffusion via tracheae and tracheoles are not too great. Nevertheless there are features of large insects which seem to indicate that respiration may be a factor limiting size. Thus large, active insects such as dragonflies and butterflies tend to have their bulk reduced by their bodies being long and slender, and large bulky beetles,

such as the 20 cm cerambycid, *Titanus giganteus* (Linnaeus)
tend to be very sluggish (Reitter 1961). The insect respiratory system thus serves small species admirably at all levels
of activity, but is relatively less effective in large forms.
In these, however, it has the saving grace of permitting
sustained activity. In contrast with this are large spiders
and scorpions, whose respiratory system consists of book
lungs supplying oxygen to the tissues via the respiratory
blood pigment haemocyanin. These organisms are capable of
short bursts of violent activity, but must then rest for
several minutes while fresh oxygen is stored in the haemocyanin
(Cloudsley-Thompson 1970).

The efficiency of the insect tracheal system has virtually
eliminated a function that blood has in many other organisms,
namely the transport of respiratory gases. Thus the circulatory system has not become elaborate, and this may be an
additional factor limiting body size, through its bearing on
the efficiency of other organ systems. Thus insects seem to
have a requirement for a much longer excretory tubule length
per unit of body weight than vertebrates (*Blatta* 300 cm per
g (Henson 1944), *Lucilia* 250 cm per g (Waterhouse 1950), man
7 cm per g (Cowdry 1938).

Overall, it is probable that the essential features of
the anatomy and physiology of modern insects, which serve
them so well, operate at their best only in organisms of
rather small size. There is a special problem, however, in
that a number of upper Carboniferous insects were relatively
gigantic, the dragonfly, *Meganeura monyi* Brongniart, having a
wingspan of about 68 cm (Tillyard 1917). Admittedly, as
pointed out by Kukalova-Peck (1978), the gigantism ran
principally to a high wing area/body size ratio, which may be
regarded as a necessary step in the evolution of flight, but
why were not all upper Carboniferous insects subject to the
same limitations as modern ones? An answer to this must
await further reconstruction of the habitat they occupied,
including the vital question of the composition of the
atmosphere.

V.   ENVIRONMENTAL EXPLOITATION IN RELATION TO BEHAVIOUR AND
     PHYSIOLOGY

The diversity in life histories of insects mentioned
earlier lends particular zest to the study of insect physiology, but taken in conjunction with the enormous number of
species and the vast range of environmental niches they occupy,
it may tend to leave one with a feeling of having to wrestle
with the infinite. Consider, for example, the contrasts
between some aphid life cycles, with their complex poly-

morphism and host alternation, the curious migrations of warble fly larvae from the heels of cattle through the body tissues to the skin of the host's dorsal surface, the lengthy underground life cycle of the root-sucking cicada nymphs, the inquiline life of predaceous butterfly larvae in ant nests, and the ocean-going existence of lice parasitic on pinnipeds.

It is appropriate to consider whether the somewhat bizarre life cycles listed above are exceptional, rather than closer to the norm. Perhaps they are, and the task of completing the study of the Insecta may not be as enormous and complex as the examples might suggest. However, a word of caution is necessary, and this may be illustrated by reference to the Australian plague locust, *Chortoicetes terminifera* (Walker). This insect differs from the average in that it is usually far from scarce, and we now know that it possesses special characteristics that help it to achieve that status. However, a vast amount of research has been necessary to elucidate the special features of its life cycle and population dynamics.

Superficially this locust appears to be a clumsy beast which, when disturbed, indulges in an untidy evasive flight, finishing in a seemingly unplanned landing. Close observation has shown, however, that in reality the insect displays a considerable capacity for controlled local flight and landing, and for avoiding obstacles. Furthermore, it has been found to have remarkable powers for sustained long-distance flight, and to have numerous other adaptations which fit it nicely to the exploitation of some millions of hectares of grassland in eastern Australia where rainfall is erratic and only patches of habitat are temporarily suitable for it at any one time.

Individual adult locusts in the pre-reproductive stage, whether they come from swarms (where they are in the gregarious phase) or from dispersed populations (where they are in the solitary phase), may make long distance flights at night, usually in disturbed weather. Such flights commence after sunset and persist for several hours under favourable temperatures, during which time the locusts may attain a height of 100 to 500 m. Individuals may be carried downwind in pre-frontal meterological systems for several hundred kilometres to areas where rain is likely to fall. These flights enable the locusts to locate areas likely to be favourable in the future for the development and survival of both eggs and hoppers, irrespective of the contemporary condition of the vegetation (Clark 1972, Farrow 1977, 1979, Johnson 1969). Quite remarkably, night-flying locusts generally arrive in grassland habitats of preferred types though it is still unknown how they achieve this;   no

mechanism has yet been described whereby they could assess the
potential value of grassland by night from the air, but seemingly their biology is geared to their being able to do so.

The aggregation of egg pods in egg beds, and subsequently
hoppers into bands, and adults into swarms, occurs as a result
of an initial concentration of adults in the preceding
generation and of multiplication. Both concentration and
multiplication usually follow a sequence of substantial,
drought-breaking rains and coincide with the availability of
abundant and widespread food supplies (Clark 1972, Farrow
1979). Marching and swarming of gregarious locusts occur by
day and cohesion of individuals is achieved by visual means.
The gregarious behaviour of the bands and swarms is thought
to result in a better utilization of resources than by the
same number of solitary locusts behaving independently of
one another, as they do under less favourable conditions.

In addition to the development of phases, the Australian
plague locust exhibits other phenomena that fit it admirably
to its highly erratic environment. Unlike species in other
climatic zones, its eggs are not adapted to survive long
periods of desiccation, but are geared to hatching when
sufficient water has been taken up, provided that the temperature is high enough for development. Heavy losses may
therefore result during dry summers, as a result of this
opportunistic strategy, but some locusts get through and lay
eggs. Of the eggs laid in summer, only some hatch in autumn,
even when conditions are suitably moist. The remainder
enter a complex diapause which is broken only by exposure to
winter temperatures, and so they are tided over the changeable
conditions of autumn (Wardhaugh 1972). Any eggs which do
hatch in autumn produce nymphs which enter a diapause in the
third instar. Thus the insect overwinters both as diapausing
eggs and as nymphs, and the adults, which are less well suited
to overwintering (Wardhaugh 1980) do not appear until spring.
Ovarian development is then retarded in the adult female if
conditions become unfavourable for growth and reproduction,
which are resumed only when better pasture conditions return
(Clark 1972).

There is a touch of irony in the fact that really long-
range displacements during massive outbreaks may result in
invasion of regions that are only favourable for locusts for
a season or two (Farrow 1975), but many human populations
have made similar mistakes in land use, and the overall
picture is one of finely tuned adaptation to areas prone to
periods of widely fluctuating favourability for survival.

It is a sobering thought that it has taken more than
forty years of research in Australia by successive entomologists to establish this body of knowledge. It would have

taken longer had it not been for the stimulus provided by
similar studies in Africa, the Middle East and elsewhere, and
the development of radar techniques to confirm the occurrence
of night flights. How many other life cycles are not as
simple as they seem? And how many ecological studies and
their associated behavioural and physiological investigations
must therefore have been abandoned prematurely in the mistaken
belief that they were complete?

VI.   IMPACT OF RESEARCH INTO INSECT PHYSIOLOGY

     The contribution of physiological studies to the under-
standing of the biology and population dynamics of insects has
been enormous. To take just one field, the effects of
temperature on the rate of development and other physiological
processes, we can indicate an all-pervading factor in the
biology of these exothermic animals that is examined almost
routinely to give meaning to ecological studies. So it is
with responses to other factors, such as water relationships.
     At one time it was hoped that research into insect physio-
logy and biochemistry would give the key to many practical
problems in insect control, especially as regards the penetration and mode of action of toxicants, but there have been
disappointments along several lines that might have been
expected to yield practical results. Much effort has been
devoted, for instance, to the study of the mechanisms for egg
shell and cuticular waterproofing, partly in the expectation
that the results would enable more specific or more effective
penetration of toxicants. However, to date only marginal
practical advantage has resulted from these studies. Similarly, much effort has been devoted to studying the mechanisms
of insecticide resistance, with which our insect enemies keep
confronting us in a telescoped demonstration of evolution, but,
in effect, no way has yet been found along this avenue for
retaining for long the usefulness of any chemical to which
insects have become resistant. It is true that, in theory,
some forms of genetic manipulation could achieve this, but it
has not yet been achieved in practice.
     One of the more fruitful lines has been the study of
insect hormones, which eventually resulted in the availability
of several pesticides that function as insect growth regulators. The impact of this line of research may have been wider
than often suspected, as it probably contributed substantially
to the development of new ways of thinking about insect
control with chemicals. Conventional methods of testing
insecticides involve application of a range of dosages to
insects that have been reared in as standard a manner as

possible, and judging the value of the substance from the mortality occurring in a relatively short time. However, this method teaches little or nothing about other ways in which a chemical may affect the survival or impact of a pest. For example, cattle ticks (not insects, we know, but traditionally one of the burdens of the economic entomologist!) suffer a toxicosis when treated with formamidines, but they are also stimulated to retract their mouthparts from the host. By doing so they become vulnerable to destruction by the self-grooming of the host or, in their impaired physical condition, may fall to the ground and perish. So a special test had to be devised for screening chemicals to find whether they induce this important behavioural response (Stone and Knowles 1973).

In Australia, at present, tests for the control of the Australian sheep blowfly are in progress on three types of chemical that differ completely in their mode of action from conventional contact toxicants and hence hold more than usual interest. One is an oviposition deterrent, another an inhibitor of chitin synthesis and a third a desiccant. Also there has recently come on the market for sheep blowfly control a triazine (well known as a class of herbicide) which is claimed by the vendors to act on maggots by interfering with moulting, and causing retardation of growth, malformation and death. Third generation pesticides may indeed become increasingly more numerous, even if they don't arise as a result of purposeful design stemming from a knowledge of insect physiology or biochemistry.

It has proved somewhat risky in the past to speculate whether some modes of action may avoid the risk that resistance will develop, but this possibility should always be borne in mind. Wharton and Norris (1980), for instance, suggest that selection for resistance to formamidines may involve pressures on two separate modes of action, one behavioural and the other toxicological, so, dependent on the mechanism of resistance involved, this may slow the development of resistance.

In addition to the impact of hormone studies in the pesticide field we must point to the increasing practical use of insect pheromones. Unless one draws a firm line of demarcation between physiology and behaviour, which would be unrealistic, the contribution in this field has been real, and is potentially very considerable.

VII. INSECT PHYSIOLOGY IN THE FUTURE

Sir Vincent Wigglesworth, to whom this book is dedicated, may fairly be designated as the founding father and doyen of

the science of insect physiology, and the frequency of references to his numerous papers throughout the volume testifies
to the magnitude and importance of his contributions. To him
much credit must be given for the present healthy state of the
science, and for the extent of the contribution it has made
both to general knowledge and to progress in applied entomology. We may forecast with confidence that studies in insect
physiology will continue to flourish. Optimism about future
progress is also evoked simply by recalling the laborious days,
not so long ago, when chemical studies were carried out almost
without instrumentation, and comparing them with the present
situation, in which researchers in many establishments have
access to various forms of spectrophotometry, chromatography
and mass spectrometry. One must also recall how light microscopy, operating only to a few thousand diameters (when the
shaky images created temptation to interpret by the "eye of
faith"), has been superseded by electron microscopy capable
of huge magnifications and great resolving power, and how
light microscopy of solid objects has been assisted and
extended by the extraordinary contributions of the scanning
electron microscope. Further advances in instrumentation
are certain to emerge and to open up new vistas in research.

Physiological investigations of greater precision and
understanding will be extended into groups of insects as yet
little studied, to help round out our knowledge of the Class.
Methods will be found for establishing more insect species in
culture for convenience of study (bearing in mind, we hope,
the mounting evidence that cage-adaptation develops in stocks
with astonishing rapidity). We also exhort the practitioners
of research into insect physiology to pay heed to integrating
the advances they make with those of other fields in order
that the knowledge gained will play an even greater role in
solving problems of concern to man.

REFERENCES

Anderson, N.M., and Polhemus, J.T. (1976). Waterstriders
    (Hemiptera: Gerridae, Veliidae, etc.) *In* "Marine Insects"
    (L. Cheng, ed.) pp. 187-224. North Holland/American
    Elsevier: Amsterdam.
Buxton, P.A. (1926). On the colonization of the sea by
    insects: with an account of the habits of *Pontomyia*, the
    only known submarine insect. *Proc. Zool. Soc. London*
    807-814.
Clark, D.P. (1972). The plague dynamics of the Australian
    plague locust, *Chortoicetes terminifera* (Wlk.).
    *Proc. Int. Study Conf. Current and Future Problems of
    Acridology, London 1970.* pp. 275-87.

Cheng, L. (1976). Insects in Marine Environments. *In* "Marine Insects". pp. 1-4. North Holland/American Elsevier: Amsterdam.

Cloudsley-Thompson, J.L. (1958). "Spiders, Scorpions, Centipedes and Mites". xv + 278. Pergamon: Oxford.

Cloudsley-Thompson, J.L. (1970). The size of animals. *Sci. J. 6*, 24-30.

Cowdry, E.V. (1938). "A Textbook of Histology". 2nd Edition. Lea & Febinger: Philadelphia.

Crampton, G. (1916). The phylogenetic origin and the nature of the wings of insects according to the paranotal theory. *J. N.Y. Entomol. Soc. 24*, 267-301.

Day, M.F. (1950). The histology of a very large insect, *Macropanesthia rhinocerus* Sauss. (Blattidae). *Aust. J. Sci. Res. Ser. B. 3*, 61-75.

Doutt, R.L., and Viggiani, G. (1968). The classification of the Trichogrammatidae (Hymenoptera: Chalcidoidea). *Proc. Calif. Acad. Sci. 35*, 477-586.

Ewer, D.W. (1963). On insect flight. *J. Entomol. Soc. S. Afr. 30*, 18-33.

Farrow, R.A. (1975). Offshore migration and the collapse of outbreaks of the Australian plague locust, *Chortoicetes terminifera* (Wlk.) in south east Australia. *Aust. J. Zool. 23*, 569-595.

Farrow, R.A. (1977). Origin and decline of the 1973 plague locust outbreak in central western New South Wales. *Aust. J. Zool. 25*, 455-489.

Farrow, R.A. (1979). Population dynamics of the Australian plague locust, *Chortoicetes terminifera* (Wlk.) in central western New South Wales. 1. Reproduction and migration in relation to weather. *Aust. J. Zool. 27 (5)*, (in press).

Folsom, J.W. (1922). "Entomology". Blakiston & Sons & Co. Philadelphia.

Handlirsch, A. (1906). Die fossilen Insekten und die Phylogenie der rezenen Formen. *In* "Ein Handbuch für Paläontologen und Zoologen". Lief. 1-4, Leipzig.

Henson, H. (1944). The development of the malpighian tubules of *Blatta orientalis* (Orthoptera). *Proc. R. Ent. Soc. London Ser. A. 19*, 73-91.

Hinton, H.E. (1977). Enabling mechanisms. *Proc. XV Int. Cong. Entomol. Washington D.C. 1*, 71-83.

Johnson, C.G. (1969). "Migration and Dispersal of Insects by Flight". pp. 763. Methuen: London.

Key, K.H.L. (1970). Phasmatodea. *In* "Insects of Australia" Melbourne University Press, Melbourne. pp. 348-359

Kukalova-Peck, J. (1978). Origin and evolution of insect
    wings and their relation to metamorphosis, as documented
    by the fossil record. *J. Morphol. 156*, 53-126.
Mackerras, I.M. (1950). Marine insects. *Proc. R. Soc.
    Queensl. 61*, 19-29.
Mackerras, I.M. (1967). Grades in the evolution and
    classification of insects. *J. Aust. Entomol. Soc. 6*,
    135-144.
Manton, S.M. (1952). The evolution of arthropodan locomotory
    mechanisms. Part 2. General introduction to the
    locomotory mechanisms of the Arthropoda. *Zool. J. Linn.
    Soc. 62*, 93-117.
Oberthur, C. (1916). Notes bibliographiques et figuration de
    Coscinocera hercules. In "Etudes de lepidopterologie
    comparée. Fasc. 11: Contributions a l'étude des grands
    Lepidoptères d'Australie (genres *Coscinocera* et *Xyleutes*)
    pp. 21-23. Rennes, Imprimerie Oberthur.
Reitter, E. (1961). "Beetles". Hamlyn, London.
Stone, B.F., and Knowles, C.O. (1973). A laboratory method
    for evaluation of chemicals causing the detachment of
    the cattle tick, *Boophilus microplus. J. Aust. Entomol.
    Soc. 12*, 165-172.
Tillyard, R.J. (1917). "The Biology of Dragonflies".
    Cambridge University Press, London. p. 396.
Tower, W.L. (1903). The origin and development of the wings
    of Coleoptera. *Zool. Jahrb. Abt. Anat. 17*, 517-572.
Usinger, R.L. (1957). Marine insects. *Geol. Soc. Am. Mem.
    67(1)*, 1177-1182.
Wardhaugh, K.G. (1972). The development of eggs of the
    Australian plague locust in relation to temperature and
    moisture. *Proc. Int. Study Conf. Current and Future
    Problems of Acridology, London 1970*, pp. 261-72.
Wardhaugh, K.G. (1980). Photoperiod as a factor in the
    development of overwintering nymphs of the Australian
    plague locust, *Chortoicetes terminifera* (Wlk.)
    (Orthoptera: Acrididae). *J. Aust. Entomol. Soc.*
    (in press).
Waterhouse, D.F. (1950). Studies of the physiology and
    toxicology of blowflies. The composition, formation
    and fate of the granules in the malpighian tubules of
    Lucilia cuprina larvae. *Aust. J. Sci. Res. Ser. B. 3*,
    76-112.
Waterhouse, D.F. (1958). Wool digestion and mothproofing.
    Adv. Pest Control Res. 2, 207-262.
Wharton, R.H., and Norris, K.R. (1980). Control of
    parasitic arthropods. *Vet. Parasitol. 6*, 135-164.

Wigglesworth, V.B. (1964). "The Life of Insects".
    Weidenfeld and Nicolson, London. xii + 360.
Wilson, D., and Trebilcock, G. (1978). A monograph of the
    Birdwing Butterflies. Vol. 1 Pt. 1. Scandinavia Sci.
    Press Ltd: Klampenborg, Denmark. p. 81.

THE COMPONENTS OF
WATER BALANCE

Eric Edney[1]

Laboratory for Nuclear Medicine
and Radiation Biology,
University of California,
Los Angeles, California

I. INTRODUCTION

The aim of this essay is to consider the various avenues of water loss and gain as interrelated components of overall water balance in land arthropods and to suggest possible areas for further research mainly at the whole animal level. The study of water balance in arthropods was initially stimulated in part by the very practical concerns of medical and agricultural entomology. As long ago as 1912, Babcock was publishing on the role of metabolic water in insects of agricultural importance, while Bacot (1914) was interested in the bionomics of fleas in relation to climate and hence to the occurrence of plague. In the 30's too, Buxton (1930) and Mellanby (1932) drew attention to the importance of understanding the parts played by transpiration and metabolic water in the lives of stored products pests such as *Tenebrio* and *Tineola*, and insects of medical importance such as *Pediculus*, *Cimex* and *Glossina*.

One of the assumptions that lay behind much of this early work was that, because of their small size, the overall water problem for most insects was to obtain and conserve as much as possible. This is reflected in the fact that two of the early leaders in the field - Buxton and Williams, whose interests

[1]*Present address: Zoology Department, University of British Columbia, Vancouver, Canada.*

lay in medical and agricultural entomology respectively -
both wrote about the insect life in hot dry deserts where
water problems were most acute (Buxton, 1924; Williams,
1924).

However, it soon became clear that although water indeed
plays a prominent part in the abundance and distribution of
arthropods, the relationships are complex and variable. There
is neither one general problem nor one solution, and general
statements about the relative importance of particular
avenues of gain or loss are apt to mislead, since rates vary
both absolutely and relatively, sometimes over very wide
ranges.

Nevertheless, one of the tasks of water balance studies
in the future will be to search for unifying principles
relating physiological facts to ecological situations. Such
principles will probably concern the nature, functions and
limits of control mechanisms, several of which are already
known or proposed in the context of "excretion", but few of
which have been adequately specified in relation to other
forms of water exchange, or to overall water balance. Fig. 1
shows the main avenues of water gain and loss by arthropods
and identifies those that are known or believed to be under
physiological control.

II. THE AVENUES OF WATER LOSS

A. Integumental Water Loss

It was recognised early on that information about
transpiration and the effects of ambient conditions on this
would be vital for understanding problems of water balance.
Gunn (1933) was the first to measure the effects of
temperature on water loss in an insect. In cockroaches he
observed that the rate of loss increased above 30°C even
though the effect of saturation deficit was allowed for. He
attributed this to respiratory ventilation. But something
else was also involved, for Ramsay (1935) found a similar
increase even in dead insects with blocked spiracles. Ramsay
suggested that this apparent change in permeability could
result from a phase change, akin to melting, of a fatty
substance in the cuticle. This focussed attention on the
cuticle itself as an avenue of water loss, and there the
matter rested until Wigglesworth (1945b), recognising the
importance of cuticular properties in relation to the action
of inert dust insecticides and the chlorinated hydrocarbons
then becoming available, made a detailed study of cuticular

LOSS   GAIN

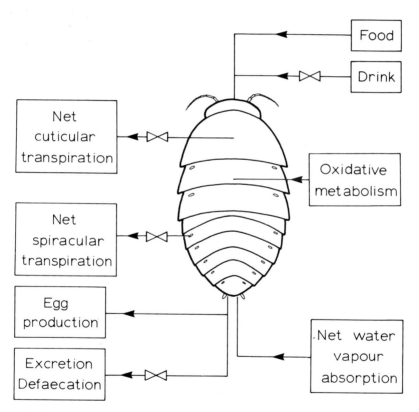

FIGURE 1. The main components of water balance in a
terrestrial arthropod. The symbol ━▷◁━ indicates that the
process is either known, or believed, to be controllable by
the animal. Both absolute and relative amounts passing
through each channel vary greatly, and any component may be
of preponderant importance in particular circumstances.
Water vapour, shown here as entering by the rectum, enters
by the mouth in some species.

water loss and the barriers to it. This work and that of his
associates, particularly Beament (1945) and Lees (1947)
showed that a large part of the resistance to water loss
resides in lipids near the outer surface, and is decreased by
high ambient temperatures. These discoveries stimulated a
great deal of research over the years, and work in the area
still continues (e.g. Wigglesworth, 1975a,b) because the
problems involved are numerous and the difficulties of
interpretation great. The present position is described by
Machin in this volume, and I will make only the following
general comments.

   1. Cuticle Structure and Transpiration. Firstly, work in
this area has been useful in two respects: it has thrown
light on the complex structure of arthropod cuticles and on
transpiration as a factor in arthropod ecology. In the
former context, permeability is the main concern; in the
latter, the rate of loss in relation to total flux and to
total water reserves is the chief interest. Permeability may
be expressed as the mass of water movement across unit area of
barrier under unit concentration gradient, e.g.
$mg \cdot cm^{-2} \cdot h^{-1} \cdot mmHg^{-1}$. If, in isothermal conditions, ambient
relative humidity (R.H.), which is a linear function of the
chemical activity of water vapour (a_v), affects permeability,
this is an indication that R.H. affects the integument as a
water barrier. If in a constant concentration gradient
temperature affects permeability, an effect of temperature on
integumental structure is indicated. In both cases it is of
course essential that the model of expected change in water
flux in the absence of change in permeability be physically
reliable so that deviations therefrom can be rightly ascribed
to the integument itself.
   For measurements in different humidities the model is
simple - if all else is equal, the net rate of loss should be
proportional to ambient R.H. For temperature, the model is
not so simple and the interpretation of data is difficult.
According to most interpretations, even when the effect of
vapour pressure difference (ΔP) is taken into account, the
rate of loss increases more or less abruptly at a particular
temperature or temperature range, and continues to increase
steeply at still higher temperatures. The position and slope
of the curves and the abruptness of the transition vary
greatly, not only among different species, but within species
in different physiological conditions. The original concept
of an oriented monolayer of lipid molecules may have to be
modified, but certainly lipids are involved, and progress is
being made towards relating particular lipids with particular
resistances and transition temperatures (Hadley and Jackson,

1977; Toolson and Hadley, 1977; and others reviewed by Hadley, 1979), and further exploration along these lines will be rewarding. However, there is still an unresolved problem as to the precise nature of the transcuticular water movement, and this must be resolved if interpretation of the effects of temperature on cuticular structure is to be firmly based. Recently Toolson (1978, 1980) has questioned the validity of the model in general use - that which sees a vapour pressure gradient as the driving force for transpiration. He would use gradients in the chemical potential of water, in which case the expected values and therefore the interpretation of experimental data would be different. Some tricky biophysical questions are involved here (see Montieth and Campbell, 1980), and the jury is still out.

   2. Ecological Significance. Secondly, if the details of epicuticular structure in relation to transpiration are still unclear, there is at least no doubt that many arthropod surfaces are extremely well waterproofed, and the relevance of this to ecology is interesting. Measured permeabilities of arthropod cuticles range from several hundreds to less than one $\mu g \cdot cm^{-2} \cdot h^{-1} \cdot mmHg^{-1}$ (for butterfly larvae, and tsetse fly pupae respectively), and in general the lower permeabilities occur in more xeric animals or stages (e.g. desert scorpions or exposed eggs). Over and above this lie considerations of size - and this is why, for ecological purposes, neither cuticle permeability nor transpiration rate (in $mass \cdot length^{-2}$) tell the whole story. A 10 g tarantula (*Eurypelma*) with a cuticle permeability of 10 $\mu g \cdot cm^{-2} \cdot h^{-1} \cdot mmHg^{-1}$ is one hundred times less vulnerable to desiccation on this account (in terms of loss rate in proportion to total water reserves) than a tsetse fry weighing 10 mg with the same cuticle permeability. Because of the very large variation in both size and permeability, statements about the importance of cuticular transpiration in relation to other water fluxes are to be treated with caution.

   3. Adaptive Changes in Cuticle Permeability. Thirdly, there is accumulating evidence that cuticular permeability, even at constant temperature, is not as constant as had been thought. Loveridge (1968) found that in *Locusta* permeability fell with decreasing ambient humidity. Humphreys (1975) found the same thing for a spider, *Geolycosa*, and so did Yokota (1979) for a scorpion, *Paruroctonus*. It has also been widely reported that cuticular water loss decreases with duration of exposure. Examples of this have been found in all classes of land arthropods (refs. in Edney, 1977) and it may be universal. No doubt initially high rates of water loss may reflect a drying out of the cuticle, but longer term effects,

connected with, but not necessarily caused by, a decrease in
body water, need further explanation. For these reasons both
internal and external conditions may obscure a simple linear
relation between R.H. and water loss and the deviations from
expectation are adaptive for water conservation in all cases
so far reported. Locusts weighing about 1.25 g "save" in this
way up to 4 mg·g^{-1}·h^{-1} (Loveridge, 1968) when permeability
falls by about 40% in dry air. In this connection, the report
by Treherne and Willmer (1975) that cuticular permeability in
Periplaneta is affected by hormones is interesting.
Decapitated insects, they found, lost more water than intact
ones, but impermeability was restored by the injection of
brain extracts. These results have been essentially
confirmed in another cockroach, *Leucophaea*, by Franco
(unpublished) and the next step will be to identify the
hormones responsible and to find whether their concentration
in the blood changes appropriately with the insects' water
status. As regards the mode of action, Berridge (1970)
suggested that cuticular resistance to water loss may depend
in part on the apical membranes of epidermal cells. The
properties of a living cell may be affected much more rapidly
than those of a cuticle by circulating hormones, so the
suggestion is attractive, and will no doubt receive further
attention.

B. *Respiratory Water Loss*

    Cuticular water loss may have been wrongly thought of as
an immutable hazard, but loss through the gas exchange
apparatus has for long been recognised as being
physiologically controllable. There is abundant evidence that
occlusible spiracles play a vital part in water conservation,
and some evidence about how they do it. In fact spiracles
provide a good example of the interrelatedness of water
balance mechanisms. Spiracular valves in several insects
including locusts (Hoyle, 1960), dragon flies (Miller, 1964),
mosquitos (Krafsur, 1971) and silk-worm pupae (Beckel, 1958)
are known to respond directly to local CO_2, and the
concentration of CO_2 necessary to open the valves is higher
if the insects are dehydrated or hot, lower if they are
flying. The effect of such control is important. In tsetse
flies, for example, fully 90% of the spiracular water loss
that would occur in dry air is saved by normal spiracular
function (Bursell, 1970), and since respiratory loss may in
these circumstances be a significant fraction of total loss,
such savings are important. The figures for *Locusta*
(Loveridge, 1968) are comparable.

The proportion of total water loss that is respiratory
varies greatly as the following two examples show. In
locusts Loveridge measured spiracular water losses of 2.9 and
11.9 $mg \cdot g^{-1} \cdot h^{-1}$ in resting and flying insects respectively,
while the cuticular loss was about 5.4 $mg \cdot g^{-1} \cdot h^{-1}$. In tsetse
flies, resting insects lost 0.09 and 0.03 $mg \cdot fly^{-1} \cdot h^{-1}$ from
the cuticle and spiracles respectively, while in partially
active flies, spiracular loss rose to 0.12 $mg \cdot fly^{-1} \cdot h^{-1}$. In
other words, the relative importance of the two avenues of
water loss depends greatly on the state of activity and
probably on the degree of hydration and other factors.
Ventilation in those insects where it occurs enhances water
loss, but in locusts at least, low ambient R.H. and low body
water content both inhibit ventilation, and this is clearly
adaptive.

Nevertheless, respiratory loss is in most situations a
significant part of total loss, and would probably be
intolerable were it not for control devices. Whether or not
the presence of sub-elytral cavities in desert tenebrionid
and other beetles, or of sunken or spine-beset spiracles (in
buprestids) reduce water loss in relation to O_2 uptake is a
moot point that will be settled when further evidence is
available. It has also been proposed (Buck, 1958) that the
intermittent release of CO_2 in diapausing saturniid pupae,
very fully described by Schneiderman and his associates (e.g.
Levy and Schneiderman, 1966), conserves water, but direct
evidence is lacking, and on theoretical grounds this seems
rather unlikely. Barnhart (personal communication) points out
that according to Levy and Schneiderman's measurements the
gradient of P_{O_2} across the spiracle is 2.5 times greater than
the maximum gradient for P_{CO_2}. Thus the minimum opening
sufficient for CO_2 release is more than sufficient for O_2
uptake. Water loss is therefore linked with CO_2 output and
anything that reduces the extent of spiracular opening for CO_2
elimination will reduce water loss. This state of affairs is
true only because the insect is able to reduce P_{O_2} in the
tracheae to as low as 3.5 vol. %, and this, rather than cyclic
release should probably be looked upon as the water
conservation adaptation. In Man, for comparison, P_{O_2} may be
reduced from 19.7 vol. % in inspired air only to 15.5 vol. %
in expired air. The question is interesting, and for its
solution further experimental data are required.

C. Water Loss by Excretion

Research into excretion (including defaecation) in
arthropods has uncovered some very striking adaptations, many
of which have to do with water affairs, and it is in this area
that one becomes immediately aware of the fact that water
balance may involve the elimination as well as the
conservation of water, according to particular circumstances.
In insects, and probably in most arthropods, Malpighian
tubules produce a watery urine which is usually isosmotic with
the blood. The function of converting this primary urine into
a state which, by its elimination, restores the osmotic and
ionic norm, falls to the ileum and rectum where ions and water
are adjusted appropriately. The mechanisms involved are the
subject of a later chapter, and my purpose here is only to
consider some general aspects with a bias towards those which
concern the animal as a whole.

Excretion and defaecation are of course both necessary
processes, but they also provide the main vehicle in most
cases for osmotic regulation. Some water, or H^+, is
necessarily lost when N or inorganic ions are excreted, but
the extent of this is minimised firstly by excreting uric
acid, although significant quantities of urea and ammonia have
also been found (refs. in Edney, 1977). Uric acid has a
hydrogen/nitrogen ratio of only 1, and is very poorly soluble
in water, so that it exerts little osmotic pressure.
Secondly, many arthropods have the ability, when necessary, to
reduce the water content of faeces to low levels: equivalent
to a water vapour activity (a_v) of 0.9 in Tenebrio larvae
(which have a cryptonephric system) and 0.5 a_v in Thermobia
(which does not) (Noble-Nesbitt, 1970). Even locusts can
achieve similar levels of faecal dehydration (Loveridge,
1974). The effect of these adaptations is to permit a very
wide range within which the rate of water loss may be
adjusted. In tsetse flies, for example, egested material
varies from nearly 100% water immediately after a blood meal
to only 40% water later in the hunger cycle, and in Locusta
faecal water varies between 85% and 20% according to the water
content of the food and the body (Loveridge, 1974).

However, the significance of this becomes apparent only
when absolute loss rates are considered. In locusts at 50%
R.H., cuticular and spiracular water loss are about
4-5 $mg \cdot g^{-1} \cdot h^{-1}$ each in a 1.6 g insect, so that if both are
reduced by 50% as a result of permeability changes and of
ventilation control, this would mean a saving of 4-5 $mg \cdot g^{-1} \cdot h^{-1}$. Faecal water loss is about 21.6 $mg \cdot g^{-1} \cdot h^{-1}$, and is
reducible to about 1.6 $mg \cdot g^{-1} \cdot h^{-1}$ by lowering faecal water
content - a much greater saving of 20 $mg \cdot g^{-1} \cdot h^{-1}$ (calculated
from Loveridge, 1968, 1975). In tsetse flies the situation is

equally striking. Spiracular water loss is reduced by dry air
and by low body water content by some 40-50% to give savings
of about 3.4 mg·insect^{-1}·h^{-1}. Excretory water loss on the
other hand may be reduced from about 20 mg·insect^{-1} in the
first 3 h after feeding to almost zero later in the hunger
cycle when the fly is short of water. In this case, and in
that of the locust referred to above, absolute water loss is
reduced not only by decreasing faecal water content, but also
by strongly reducing the rate of faecal output.

Tsetse flies and other blood feeders such as *Rhodnius* and
ticks have to cope with too much water only from time to time,
but plant sap feeders such as cercopids or cicadellids have to
face the problem more or less continuously. Here again the
solution lies mainly with the excretory system, which is
adapted by the formation of filter chambers - structures which
in effect separate useful organic molecules from the dilute
food and permit the watery remainder to by-pass the mid-gut
and go directly to the rectum for elimination. The function
of these interesting structures has been described by Saini
(1964), Gouranton (1968) and Marshall and Cheung (1974), but
much remains to be discovered about them and their
relationships to the standard excretory systems of other
insects. Filter chambers are reminiscent of cryptonephridia,
which have been shown to be concerned with water retention in
some species (Grimstone, Mullinger and Ramsay, 1968) as
Wigglesworth (1934) first suggested. However Ramsay (1976)
believes that they may originally have functioned in salt
regulation in some insects such as lepidopteran larvae with a
large food intake, so that the functions of the two systems
may be less disparate than might at first appear.

III. AVENUES OF WATER GAIN

A. *Uptake Through the Mouth*

If excretion in the broad sense is generally the largest
and most controllable component of water loss, drinking stands
in a similar relation to total water gain. There are,
however, interesting exceptions.

Most arthropods if dehydrated will drink water if this is
available (refs. in Edney, 1977) and both blood volume and
osmotic pressure are known to be involved in the control of
this process (Dethier, 1976; Barton Browne and Dudzinski,
1968; Bernays and Chapman, 1974). Certainly drinking is

regulatory inasmuch as insects drink to adjust their body
water, and perhaps to store water. *Tenebrio* larvae, for
example, if dehydrated drink about their own weight of water,
thereby increasing their blood volume greatly (Mellanby and
French, 1958). In this insect, the extent of drinking is
related to two other factors: ambient humidity and the nature
of the food. Murray (1968) found that when these insects are
reared on bran containing 16% water (in equilibrium with 80%
R.H.), optimal development is possible only if they can drink.
However, if the food is whole meal flour, larvae develop well
down to 50% R.H. without drinking, probably because this food
yields much more metabolic water than bran. Rather
surprisingly, beetles that live in desert sand dunes may
maintain their body water by drinking fog water which they
condense either on themselves (*Onymacris*) (Hamilton and
Seely, 1976) or on sand ridges (*Lepidochora*) (Seely and
Hamilton, 1976).

Drinking, then, plays an important and sometimes
necessary part in the lives of some arthropods and provides
for the effective control of body water over wide ranges.
Water in the food may also provide a large and necessary
source, and an interesting question is whether or not, as in
drinking, food is taken solely for the water it contains.
Insects are known to restrict their intake of food if the
latter contains less than a certain proportion of water.
Locusts, for example, gain 32 $mg \cdot g^{-1} \cdot h^{-1}$ by feeding on fresh
grass which contains about 85% water (in which case they do
not drink), but if the food contains only 5% water,
unrestricted feeding would lead to a net loss of water
because the faecal water content is too high, and feeding is
then reduced to a minimum (1.5 $mg \cdot g^{-1} \cdot h^{-1}$ compared with
3.7 $mg \cdot g^{-1} \cdot h^{-1}$ dry weight).

But the question remains as to whether, if water is short,
an insect will eat more moist food than is necessary to
satisfy its energy requirements. Most of the data are
equivocal because the effect of dehydration or low R.H. on
activity has not been specified, and increased activity would
itself lead to increased energy needs and perhaps to greater
food intake. The rice weevil, *Sitophilus oryzae*, does appear
to eat more and thus to gain more water from food at
intermediate than at very high humidities, even though the
metabolic rate is constant (Arlian, 1979). This is an
interesting lead which could be tested by further measurements
of metabolism - particularly in feeding rather than fasting
insects - and extended to other arthropods. But a clear,
convincing answer to this question still remains to be found.

rly work
ints to
d out.
ydrated
fat.
 much
t on an
 fact
ise much
e likely
r weight
tential.
iter
ie
ue in
 both
tained
ncreased

lic rate.
inism
ells
 the
 it seems
led by
 point

idation is obligatory and water so
e general water pool. Questions
metabolic water contribution in
omponents (whether or not it is
e same question), and whether it has a
or insects feeding on dry food,
large and necessary component. Larvae
ia may develop in very dry food and
water content at pupation can have
d as preformed water. The remainder
metabolically. In locusts, metabolic
ut 0.4 mg$\cdot$g$^{-1}\cdot$h^{-1}. This is small
from moist food (32 mg$\cdot$g$^{-1}\cdot$h^{-1}), but
lable the amount eaten is reduced, the
se lower, and the water so derived is
l, which is less than that from
974).
ion about metabolic water so far comes
doubtless because of the difficulty of
field conditions. Recently the use of
^{18}O) has permitted field measurements
future will probably see an
ique to arthropods. Beginnings have
and Hadley (1979), Yokota (1979)
r (in preparation) on beetles. For
ds to overestimate oxygen
with other techniques in the
s are uncomfortably large. But the
nciple and it will assuredly become
re.   For his work on desert beetles
isure total water in and total water
measure metabolism; other
from laboratory data. He found that
cold, dry winter when the beetles
ater was 1.2 mg$\cdot$g$^{-1}\cdot$ day^{-1}, which
, while in the summer, when the
ve, metabolic water was larger -
only 6% of the total input of
y (summer) water in the food
day^{-1}, and net transpiration was

guing of
pods is
 The
d to
achnids,
es and
77;
ll
lways
inable.
cases -
d termite

 long
brio
he
it turns

arly of great importance for some
under their control? Since a gram
water yields nearly twice as much
rate, it would seem that switching
a metabolic substrate would be

adaptive for an animal short of water. Some of the ea
seemed to support this hypothesis. However, theory po
a contrary conclusion as Schmidt-Nielsen (1964) pointe
Loveridge and Bursell (1975) found that fasted and del
locusts did indeed metabolise a greater proportion of
But for an equal weight, fat yields more than twice a
energy as carbohydrate does, and calculations show th
equal energy basis, a locust metabolising fat would i
derive less water than if carbohydrate was used, beca
less fat would be required. Overall it seems much mo
that fats are used as energy stores on account of the
economy rather than their biochemical water storage p

There remains the possibility that an animal in w
shortage may increase its metabolic rate (in which ca
carbohydrates would be the best fuel). This may be t
some circumstances. Buxton (1930) and Mellanby (1932
found that at lower humidities fasting mealworms mai
their dry/wet weight ratio and they ascribed this to
metabolism in dry air. If low humidity causes great
activity, this would in turn call for a higher metab
But except for such increased energy demands the mec
seems unlikely on general biochemical grounds since
usually stop producing energy in the form of ATP whe
energy charge reaches a particular level. At presen
that the production of metabolic water is not contro
arthropods in relation to their water needs - but th
deserves further study.

C. The Absorption of Water Vapour

1. *Occurrence and Limits*. Perhaps the most intr
all processes involved in the water balance of arthr
that whereby water is absorbed from unsaturated air,
ability to do so is well documented, but is restric
certain groups including ticks and mites among the
and firebrats, lice, psocids, fleas and certain bee
cockroaches among insects (refs. in Noble-Nesbitt,
Edney, 1977). Arthropods that have the ability are
wingless, usually immature if they are insects, and
live in places where liquid water is virtually unob
But the ability to absorb does not occur in all suc
for example, I was unable to demonstrate it in dryw
workers, where it might have been expected.

The existence of the process has been known for
time, since Mellanby (1932) first reported it in Te
molitor larvae, and although early workers favoured
tracheal system or the cuticle as the site of uptal

B. *Metabolic Water*

Gain of water by oxidation is obligatory and water so gained forms part of the general water pool. Questions concern the size of the metabolic water contribution in relation to the other components (whether or not it is essential is part of the same question), and whether it has a regulatory function. For insects feeding on dry food, metabolic water forms a large and necessary component. Larvae of the flour moth *Ephestia* may develop in very dry food and then only 7.6% of their water content at pupation can have come from the larval food as preformed water. The remainder must have been produced metabolically. In locusts, metabolic water is produced at about 0.4 $mg \cdot g^{-1} \cdot h^{-1}$. This is small compared with the input from moist food (32 $mg \cdot g^{-1} \cdot h^{-1}$), but if only dry food is available the amount eaten is reduced, the water content is of course lower, and the water so derived is only about 0.1 $mg \cdot g^{-1} \cdot h^{-1}$, which is less than that from metabolism (Loveridge, 1974).

Most of the information about metabolic water so far comes from laboratory studies doubtless because of the difficulty of measuring metabolism in field conditions. Recently the use of doubly labelled water ($HT^{18}O$) has permitted field measurements for vertebrates, and the future will probably see an application of this technique to arthropods. Beginnings have already been made by King and Hadley (1979), Yokota (1979) on scorpions and by Cooper (in preparation) on beetles. For arthropods the method tends to overestimate oxygen consumption in comparison with other techniques in the laboratory, and the errors are uncomfortably large. But the method is valuable in principle and it will assuredly become more reliable in the future. For his work on desert beetles Cooper used tritium to measure total water in and total water out separately, and ^{18}O to measure metabolism; other components were estimated from laboratory data. He found that for *Eleodes armata* in the cold, dry winter when the beetles were inactive, metabolic water was 1.2 $mg \cdot g^{-1} \cdot day^{-1}$, which was 21% of the total input, while in the summer, when the insects were warm and active, metabolic water was larger — 3.2 $mg \cdot g^{-1} \cdot day^{-1}$, but now only 6% of the total input of 50.3 $mg \cdot g^{-1} \cdot day^{-1}$. In July (summer) water in the food accounted for 36.4 $mg \cdot g^{-1} \cdot day^{-1}$, and net transpiration was 24 $mg \cdot g^{-1} \cdot day^{-1}$.

Metabolic water is clearly of great importance for some species, but is this source under their control? Since a gram of fat oxidised to CO_2 and water yields nearly twice as much water as a gram of carbohydrate, it would seem that switching from carbohydrate to fat as a metabolic substrate would be

adaptive for an animal short of water. Some of the early work
seemed to support this hypothesis. However, theory points to
a contrary conclusion as Schmidt-Nielsen (1964) pointed out.
Loveridge and Bursell (1975) found that fasted and dehydrated
locusts did indeed metabolise a greater proportion of fat.
But for an equal weight, fat yields more than twice as much
energy as carbohydrate does, and calculations show that on an
equal energy basis, a locust metabolising fat would in fact
derive less water than if carbohydrate was used, because much
less fat would be required. Overall it seems much more likely
that fats are used as energy stores on account of their weight
economy rather than their biochemical water storage potential.

There remains the possibility that an animal in water
shortage may increase its metabolic rate (in which case
carbohydrates would be the best fuel). This may be true in
some circumstances. Buxton (1930) and Mellanby (1932) both
found that at lower humidities fasting mealworms maintained
their dry/wet weight ratio and they ascribed this to increased
metabolism in dry air. If low humidity causes greater
activity, this would in turn call for a higher metabolic rate.
But except for such increased energy demands the mechanism
seems unlikely on general biochemical grounds since cells
usually stop producing energy in the form of ATP when the
energy charge reaches a particular level. At present it seems
that the production of metabolic water is not controlled by
arthropods in relation to their water needs - but the point
deserves further study.

C. The Absorption of Water Vapour

1. *Occurrence and Limits*. Perhaps the most intriguing of
all processes involved in the water balance of arthropods is
that whereby water is absorbed from unsaturated air. The
ability to do so is well documented, but is restricted to
certain groups including ticks and mites among the arachnids,
and firebrats, lice, psocids, fleas and certain beetles and
cockroaches among insects (refs. in Noble-Nesbitt, 1977;
Edney, 1977). Arthropods that have the ability are all
wingless, usually immature if they are insects, and always
live in places where liquid water is virtually unobtainable.
But the ability to absorb does not occur in all such cases -
for example, I was unable to demonstrate it in drywood termite
workers, where it might have been expected.

The existence of the process has been known for a long
time, since Mellanby (1932) first reported it in *Tenebrio
molitor* larvae, and although early workers favoured the
tracheal system or the cuticle as the site of uptake it turns

out that either the rectum or the mouth is involved (refs. in Edney, 1977, and various authors in Schmidt-Nielsen et al., 1978). The process is limited by R.H. or a_v rather than vapour pressure difference (ΔP), but the limit varies greatly among species, from 45% R.H. for Thermobia to around 90% for ticks. The process is certainly regulatory since above the critical equilibrium humidity (C.E.H.) it is switched on by dehydration and is generally switched off when the optimum water content of the animal has been restored. Tenebrio may be exceptional in this respect (Machin, 1975), and in certain ticks, mites and flea larvae the equilibrium body water content depends on the ambient humidity (Rudolph and Knulle, 1978; Solomon, 1966).

2. Mechanisms. Interest centres on the mechanisms of the process and on its significance for the animals concerned. Although the site of absorption has recently been reliably identified in several cases, the precise mechanism at the biophysical level has not been finally determined. A valuable discussion of this and other aspects of water vapour absorption is contained in several chapters by various contributors in Schmidt-Nielsen et al. (1978).

Work in this field has directed attention to the components of water flux in arthropods, because of the relevance of this both to the range of the process (e.g. does it operate below the C.E.H.?) and to the site and mechanism. Knulle and Devine (1972) used tritiated water to measure influx and efflux separately in a tick, Dermacentor, and found that efflux (gross transpiration) was constant over the whole humidity range while passive influx was linearly related to ambient R.H. The combined effect of these two processes is that net transpiration is inversely related to ambient R.H. They also found that only above 85% R.H. was passive inward diffusion enhanced by an active uptake amounting to about 0.044 µg out of a total of 0.200 µg·tick^{-1}·h^{-1}. A similar analysis by Franco (in preparation) of the situation in a desert beetle larva, Eleodes armata (whose C.E.H. is about 92% R.H.), showed a constant transpiration rate of 6 mg·g^{-1}·h^{-1} over the range from 0-85% R.H. and a rising influx rate from 0 in dry air to 5.3 mg at 85% R.H. Above 90% R.H., however, both efflux and influx increased strongly, influx climbing to a higher level (19 mg) than efflux (16 mg·g^{-1}·h^{-1}), giving a net absorption of water. These data suggest that above the C.E.H. a second avenue for water flux is opened (presumably in the rectum) and that this has a much lower resistance to the passage of water than the remainder of the exchange surface (the cuticle and tracheae). These and other results indicate that the uptake mechanism is inoperative below the C.E.H.

3. Energetics. Several authors have calculated the energy cost of water vapour absorption and concluded that this is negligible (refs. in Edney, 1977; Wharton, 1978). Further consideration suggests that some of these calculations may have been in error. Water absorption has been equated with net water gain, but active absorption is in fact the sum of net gain and what would appear as net transpiration were it not for active absorption. For example, in *Arenivaga* if net transpiration is 1.4 mg·day^{-1} at 90% R.H. (calculated from Edney, 1966) and net gain is 0.6 mg·day^{-1}, active absorption must account for 2.0 mg·day^{-1}. For insects actively absorbing from high R.H. this error may not be serious. In *Arenivaga*, gross active absorption from 90% R.H. would require 0.12 rather than the 0.036 cal·day^{-1} needed for net absorption alone; but for insects such as *Thermobia*, absorbing from 45% R.H., when net transpiration would be high (*Thermobia* cuticle is about 1.25 times as permeable as that of *Arenivaga*) the difference may be important. Even so, the energy cost is well within the capacities of the animals concerned and the process is evidently highly adaptive in all the cases so far recorded. In stored products mites, for example, the C.E.H. corresponds closely with the minimum humidity at which they survive. Lees (1946) described how a questing tick at the top of a grass stem descends periodically to the moister air near the soil and replenishes its body water by vapour absorption; and *Arenivaga*, living in desert sand dunes and feeding on dry detritus, goes to deeper levels where the humidity is above the critical level.

IV. CONCLUSIONS

This essay has been concerned almost exclusively with physiological processes. In real life, behaviour, in the sense of dispersal within a heterogeneous environment both in space and time, is often of great importance in relation to water balance. Behaviour is not another *avenue* of water flux although it does of course affect rates of exchange through several avenues, and apart from noting its relevance I do not propose to consider it here.

Besides the main avenues of flux referred to above there are others, including uptake through special water absorbing areas (Weyda, 1974), loss by defensive and other secretions, salivation, and the production of gametes. While each of these may be important for some species from time to time, the main avenues affect most species for most of the time. Cuticular permeability is very strongly "controlled"

morphologically in relation to habitat - it is relatively
poorly controlled physiologically; respiratory water loss is
controlled both morphologically and physiologically. Intake
of water by drinking is physiologically controlled, but this
is probably not true for metabolic water or the uptake of
preformed water with the food. Absorption of water vapour is
controlled physiologically: it is highly advantageous to
those species that show it, and in view of the apparently
small energy cost it is difficult to understand why the
ability is not more widespread that it is. Finally the
excretory system deals with large absolute amounts of water
and exercises control over a very wide range of water
situations.

There are many unsolved problems in these fields as the
following chapters show, and important advances, particularly
with regard to control mechanisms may be confidently expected
in the future. But there is another aspect of water balance
to which I will refer in these concluding remarks. There is
now, in my view, sufficient information about each of the
avenues for water exchange separately to warrant a synthetic
approach and even an application to real ecological
situations. For some time physiological, and more recently
ecological, processes and problems have been thought about in
terms of energy, and this is indeed legitimate and valuable,
but there are some situations, particularly in arid
environments, where water may be more important than energy
as a *limiting* factor, and the application of water balance
theory to such situations would be helpful.

Some encouraging steps have already been taken. The
theoretical calculations of Weis-Fogh (1967), in which ambient
humidity, temperature, radiation, internal water reserves and
the production of metabolic water are integrated into a
general picture of water balance during the flight of locusts,
provide a good example, albeit a simplified and theoretical
one, of the kind of approach needed. Cooper's work on
Eleodes and Yokota's on scorpions are both useful approaches
to synthesis and integration, and Crawford (in preparation)
also includes water balance and its components in his
treatment of the community ecology of arthropods in desert
ecosystems.

Most ecological problems are concerned not with the
relatively short term effects of ambient conditions on water
balance, but rather with their long term effects on abundance
and distribution. The effects of humidity on the rate of
birth (oviposition and development) and the rate of death are
examples of this kind of relationship, and for several reasons
the problems are tough, as Bursell (1964) and others have
pointed out. In the first place, as we know from laboratory

work, both humidity and temperature affect life processes in complex and unpredictable ways, so that each species has to be considered as a special case. Secondly, it is very difficult to measure continuously varying parameters in the immediate environment of a free running animal. And thirdly, even if such measurements can be made, all too little is known about their integrated effects on the processes concerned. The challenge has existed ever since medical and agricultural entomologists recognised the relevance of water balance to some of their problems. Progress has been slow, not only because of the difficult technical problems but also because it is rare to find good physiologists who are also good ecologists, and such a combination of talents is essential. However, there have been one or two successes (in relation to locust outbreaks, for example) and it is not unreasonable to hope that in the future we shall understand the role of water in ecological contexts, including those harmful man-made ones that result in outbreaks and infestations.

ACKNOWLEDGMENTS

I am grateful to Chris Barnhart, Paul Cooper, Cliff Crawford, Paul Franco and Stan Yokota for permission to refer to their unpublished work.

REFERENCES

Arlian, L. G. (1979). Significance of passive sorption of atmospheric water vapor and feeding in water balance of the rice weevil, *Sitophilus oryzae*. *Comp. Biochem. Physiol. 62A*, 725-733.

Bacot, A. W. (1914). A study of the bionomics of the common rat fleas and other species associated with human habitations, with special reference to the influence of temperature and humidity at various periods of the life history of the insect. *J. Hyg. Plague Sup. 3*, 447-654.

Barton Browne, L. B. and Dudzinski, A. (1968). Some changes resulting from water deprivation in the blowfly, *Lucillia cuprina*. *J. Insect Physiol. 14*, 1423-1434.

Beament, J. W. L. (1945). The cuticular lipoids of insects. *J. Exp. Biol. 21*, 115-131.

Beckel, W. E. (1958). The morphology, histology and physiology of the spiracular regulatory apparatus of *Hyalophora cecropia* (L.). *Proc. 10th Intern. Conf. Entomol. 2*, 87-115.

Bernays, E. A. and Chapman, R. F. (1974). The regulation of food intake by acridids. *In* "Experimental Analysis of Behaviour" (L. Barton Browne, ed.), pp. 48-59. Springer, Berlin.

Berridge, M. J. (1970). Osmoregulation in terrestrial arthropods. *In* "Chemical Zoology 5, Arthropods Part A" (M. Florkin and B. T. Scheer, ed.), pp. 287-320. Academic Press, New York.

Buck, J. (1958). Possible mechanisms and rationale of cyclic CO_2 retention by insects. *Proc. 10th Intern. Conf. Entomol. 2*, 339-342.

Bursell, E. (1964). Environmental aspects: humidity. *In* "Physiology of Insecta 1" (M. Rockstein, ed.), pp. 323-361. Academic Press, New York.

Bursell, E. (1970). "An Introduction to Insect Physiology". Academic Press, New York. 276 pp.

Buxton, P. A. (1924). Heat, moisture and animal life in deserts. *Proc. Roy. Soc. (London) Ser. B. 96*, 123-131.

Buxton, P. A. (1930). Evaporation from the mealworm (*Tenebrio*:Coleoptera) and atmospheric humidity. *Proc. Roy. Soc. (London) Ser. B. 106*, 560-577.

Crawford, C. S. "The Biology of Desert Invertebrates" (In preparation).

Dethier, V. G. (1976). "The Hungry Fly." Harvard U. P., Cambridge, Mass.

Edney, E. B. (1966). Absorption of water vapour from unsaturated air by *Arenivaga* sp. (Polyphagidae: Dictyoptera). *Comp. Biochem. Physiol. 19*, 387-408.

Edney, E. B. (1977). "Water Balance in Land Arthropods." Springer, Heidelberg. 288 pp.

Gouranton, J. (1968). Ultrastructures en rapport avec un transit d'eau. Etude de la 'chambre filtrante' de *Cicadella viridis* L. (Homoptera:Jassidae). *J. Microscopie 7*, 559-574.

Grimstone, A. V., Mullinger, A. M., and Ramsay, J. A. (1968). Further studies on the rectal complex of the mealworm, *Tenebrio molitor* L. (Coleoptera:Tenebrionidae). *Phil. Trans. Roy. Soc. (London) Ser. B. 253*, 343-382.

Gunn, D. L. (1933). The temperature and humidity relations of the cockroach *Blatta orientalis*. I. Desiccation. *J. Exp. Biol. 10*, 274-285.

Hadley, N. F. (1979). Recent developments in ecophysiological research on desert arthropods. *J. Arid Environments 2*, 211-218.

Hadley, N. F., and Jackson, L. L. (1977). Chemical composition of the epicuticular lipids of the scorpion, *Paruroctonus mesaensis*. *Insect Biochem. 7*, 85-90.

Hamilton, W. J., and Seely, M. K. (1976). Fog basking by the Namib desert beetle *Onymacris unguicularis*. *Nature 262*, 284-285.

Hoyle, G. (1960). The action of carbon dioxide gas on an insect spiracular muscle. *J. Insect Physiol. 4*, 63-79,

Humphreys, W. F. (1975). The influence of burrowing and thermoregulatory behaviour in the water relations of *Geolycosa godeffroyi* (Araneae:Lycosidae), an Australian wolf spider. *Oecologia 21*, 291-311.

King, W. W., and Hadley, N. F. (1979). Water flux and metabolic rates of free-roaming scorpions using the doubly-labeled water technique. *Physiol. Zool. 52*, 176-189.

Knulle, W., and Devine, T. L. (1972). Evidence for active and passive components of sorption of atmospheric water vapour by larvae of the tick *Dermacentor variabilis*. *J. Insect Physiol. 18*, 1653-1664.

Krafsuf, E. S. (1971). Behaviour of thoracic spiracles of *Aedes* mosquitoes in controlled relative humidities. *Ann. Entomol. Soc. Am. 64*, 93-97.

Lees, A. D. (1947). Transpiration and the structure of the epicuticle of ticks. *J. Exp. Biol. 23*, 379-410.

Levy, R. I., and Schneiderman, H. A. (1966). Discontinuous respiration in insects. IV. Changes in intratracheal pressure during the respiratory cycle of silkworm pupae. *J. Insect Physiol. 12*, 465-492.

Loveridge, J. P. (1968). The control of water loss in *Locusta migratoria migratorioides* R. & F. I. Cuticular water loss. *J. Exp. Biol. 49*, 1-29.

Loveridge, J. P. (1974). Studies on the water relations of adult locusts. II. Water gain in the food and loss in the faeces. *Trans. Rhodesia Sci. Assoc. 56*, 1-30.

Loveridge, J. P. (1975). Studies on the water relations of adult locusts. III. The water balance of non-flying locusts. *Zoologica Africana 10*, 1-28.

Loveridge, J. P., and Bursell, E. (1975). Studies on the water relations of the adult locust (Orthoptera, Acrididae). I. Respiration and the production of metabolic water. *Bull. Entomol. Res. 65*, 13-20.

Machin, J. (1975). Water balance in *Tenebrio molitor* L. larvae: the effect of atmospheric water absorption. *J. Comp. Physiol. 101,* 121-132.

Marshall, A. T., and Cheung, W. W. K. (1974). Studies on water and ion transport in homopteran insects: Ultrastructure and cytochemistry of the cicadoid and cercopoid Malpighian tubules and filter chamber. *Tissue and Cell 6,* 153-171.

Mellanby, K. (1932). The effect of atmospheric humidity on the metabolism of the fasting mealworm *Tenebrio molitor* (Coleoptera). *Proc. Roy. Soc. (London) Ser. B. 111,* 376-390.

Mellanby, K., and French, R. A. (1958). The importance of drinking water to larval insects. *Entomol. Exp. Appl. 1,* 116-124.

Miller, P. L. (1964). Factors altering spiracle control in adult dragonflies: water balance. *J. Exp. Biol. 41,* 331-343.

Monteith, J. C., and Campbell, G. S. (1980). Diffusion of water vapour through integuments - potential confusion. *J. Thermal Biol.* (in press).

Murray, D. R. P. (1968). The importance of water in the normal growth of larvae of *Tenebrio molitor*. *Entomol. Exp. Appl. 11,* 149-168.

Noble-Nesbitt, J. (1970). Water balance in the firebrat, *Thermobia domestica* (Packard). The site of uptake of water from the atmosphere. *J. Exp. Biol. 52,* 193-200.

Noble-Nesbitt, J. (1977). Active transport of water vapour. *In* "Transport of Ions and Water in Animals" (B. Gupta, R. B. Morton, J. L. Oschman and B. J. Wall, ed.), pp. 571-597.

Ramsay, J. A. (1935). The evaporation of water from the cockroach. *J. Exp. Biol. 12,* 373-383.

Ramsay, J. A. (1976). The rectal complex of the larvae of Lepidoptera. *Phil. Trans. Roy. Soc. (London) Ser. B. 274,* 203-226.

Rudolph, D., and Knulle, W. (1978). Uptake of water vapour from the air: process, site and mechanism in ticks. *In* "Comparative Physiology: Water, Ions and Fluid Mechanics" (K. Schmidt-Nielsen, L. Bolis and S. H. P. Maddrell, ed.), pp. 97-113. Cambridge U. P., England.

Saini, R. S. (1964). Histology and physiology of the cryptonephric system in insects. *Trans. Roy. Entomol. Soc. (London) 116,* 347-392.

Schmidt-Nielsen, K. (1964). "Desert Animals." Oxford, England. 277 pp.

Schmidt-Nielsen, K., Bolis, L., and Maddrell, S. H. P. (ed.) (1978). "Comparative Physiology: Water, Ions and Fluid Mechanics." Cambridge U. P., England. 360 pp.

Seely, M. K., and Hamilton, W. J. (1976). Fog catchment sand trenches constructed by tenebrionid beetles, *Lepidochora*, from the Namib desert. *Science 193*, 484-486.

Solomon, M. E. (1966). Moisture gains, losses and equilibria of flour mites, *Acarus siro* L., in comparison with larger arthropods. *Entomol. Exp. Appl. 9*, 25-41.

Toolson, E. C. (1978). Diffusion of water through arthropod cuticles: thermodynamic consideration of the transition phenomenon. *J. Therm. Biol. 3*, 69-73.

Toolson, E. C. (1980). Thermodynamic and kinetic aspects of water flux through the arthropod cuticle. *J. Therm. Biol.* (in press).

Toolson, E. C., and Hadley, N. F. (1977). Cuticular permeability and epicuticular lipid composition in two Arizona vehovid scorpions. *Physiol. Zool. 50*, 323-330.

Treherne, J. E., and Willmer, P. G. (1975). Hormonal control of integumentary water loss: evidence for a novel neuroendocrine system in an insect (*Periplaneta americana*). *J. Exp. Biol. 63*, 143-159.

Weis-Fogh, T. (1967). Respiration and tracheal ventilation in locusts and other flying insects. *J. Exp. Biol. 47*, 561-587.

Weyda, F. (1974). Coxal vesicles of Machilidae. *Pedobiologia 14*, 138-141.

Wharton, G. W. (1978). Uptake of water vapour by mites and mechanisms utilized by the Acaridei. *In* "Comparative Physiology: Water, Ions and Fluid Mechanics" (K. Schmidt-Nielsen, L. Bolis and S. H. P. Maddrell, ed.), pp. 79-95. Cambridge U. P., England.

Wigglesworth, V. B. (1934). "Insect Physiology." Methuen, London. 134 pp.

Williams, C. B. (1924). Bioclimatic observations in the Egyptian desert in March 1923. *Tech. Sci. Service Bull. Min. Agr. Egypt 37*, 1-18.

Yokota, S. (1979). Water, energy and nitrogen metabolism in the desert scorpion *Paruroctonus mesaensis*. Ph.D. Dissertation, University of California, Riverside, California.

INSECT CUTICLE THROUGH THE ELECTRON MICROSCOPE -
DISTINGUISHING FACT FROM ARTIFACT

B.K. Filshie

CSIRO Division of Entomology
Canberra, Australia

I. INTRODUCTION

Over the past fifteen years, the major advances in our
knowledge of cuticle structure have come from its study under
the electron microscope (e.m.). However the interpretation
of images so-obtained has led to some controversy so that we
are still far from knowing the basic form of the cuticle if,
indeed, such a basic form, or general model, exists.

Subdivision of the cuticle into two major layers appears
to be common to all insects. These layers are the epicuticle
and the procuticle, as defined by Richards (1951). The
epicuticle is very thin - frequently at the limit of resolution of the light microscope - and is assumed to be free
from chitin. The procuticle is composed essentially of chitin
and protein. In sclerotized cuticle, protein of the outer
part of the procuticle becomes tanned and this region is then
known as the exocuticle. The inner part remains soft and is
then called the endocuticle (Fig. 1). The procuticle may, in
fact, be completely absent, as in the lining of tracheoles
and some glandular ducts, so perhaps one should say that there
is only one major layer common to all cuticles (I don't know
of any instance where the epicuticle has been shown definitely
to be absent). Traversing many insect cuticles are canal
systems and filaments which appear to provide a link between
the underlying epidermis, the procuticle, the epicuticle and
the surface. The existence of filaments and canals is well
documented from the results of light microscopy but have been
shown, under the electron microscope, to be diverse in structure within different cuticular layers and between different
insect species.

Problems in interpreting electron microscopic images began when attempts were made to correlate them with those known from the light microscope, when in practice these images bear little resemblence to one another. There are several methods of examining insect cuticles in the electron microscope. Thin specimens were examined as whole mounts (Anderson and Richards, 1942 a,b; Richards and Korda, 1947, 1948, 1950) in the pioneering days before plastic embedding and ultrathin sectioning were developed. More recently, freeze fracturing and scanning electron microscopy have been used to examine artificially revealed or natural surfaces.

With the progressive improvement in microscope instrumentation and techniques of specimen preparation, the quality of electron micrographs has shown a continued improvement, but there is still a need for caution in their interpretation as I will demonstrate in the discussion which follows.

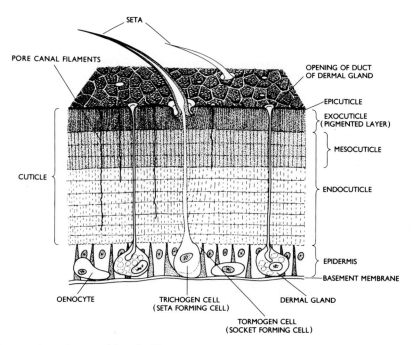

Figure 1. Generalized diagram of the structure of the insect integument (from Hackman, 1971).

II. THE EPICUTICLE

A. *Four Layers From Light Microscopy*

From the results of light microscopy, Wigglesworth
(1933d, 1947a, 1948b) sub-divided the epicuticle into four
layers which, from the inside are the cuticulin, polyphenol,
wax and cement layers. The cuticulin and polyphenol layers
were not seen as discrete entities in the intact cuticle;
their presence was inferred from the results of histochemical
tests, a point which Wigglesworth (1970b) has himself
stressed. It has not been possible to relate with certainty
any of these layers to those seen in normal preparations for
electron microscopy (Fig. 2). Terminology became confused
because, in electron micrographs, the outer, thin, dense
membrane has been called cuticulin and the thicker inner
layer the protein epicuticle (alternatively known as the
dense layer) (Locke 1966, 1974), although no information is
available about their chemical compositions. Weis-Fogh (1970)
suggested that these terms be replaced by "outer" and "inner"
epicuticle. Both terminologies are still in use and there
seems to be little point in pressing for the adoption of one
or the other as long as it is realized that a distinction
exists between layers determined by histochemistry and fine
structural entities.

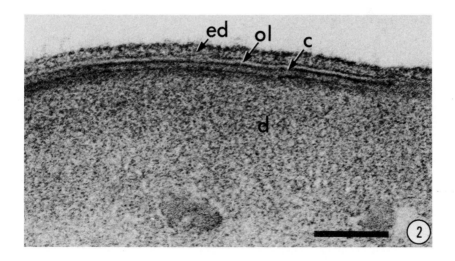

*Figure 2. Epicuticle of a pharate 3rd instar larva of
Lucilia cuprina. Ecdysial membrane, ed; "oriented lipid
layer", ol; cuticulin, c; dense layer, d. Bar = 0.1μ*

B.   *Waterproofing Layers*

There is an additional thin, unstained layer on the
outside of the cuticulin (*sensu* Locke) which Locke (1965a,
1966) suggested, in *Calpodes*, may correspond with a lipid
monolayer. This layer is unlikely to be a simple lipid,
because it has been shown to be resistant to lipid
solvents (Filshie 1970a). In *Lucilia cuprina*, which lacks
a surface wax, the layer occupying this position is much
thicker (Filshie 1970b). Despite its chemical resistance,
the so-called lipid monolayer has one of the properties of
a typical lipid membrane. It was shown recently by Noirot
et al. (1978) that in freeze-fracture preparations, a
preferred cleavage plane exists at the "lipid monolayer" -
cuticulin interface, a phenomenon common to the lipoprotein
membranes of all biological cells.

The wax layer is not seen in its entirety in normal
e.m. preparations, but two methods have been developed for
demonstrating it. Locke (1966) soaked cuticle in lead
nitrate, so converting esters into insoluble lead salts.
When this was done, dense deposits indicated the presence
of lipid. Wigglesworth (1975a) introduced unsaturated
hydrocarbons into the cuticle which he suggested combined
with saturated lipids on and within the cuticle. The
complex lipid deposits then became reactive to osmium
tetroxide and were thus rendered electron dense. Both of
these methods demonstrated electron opaque layers on the
outside of the epicuticle formed before ecdysis, in the
region one would expect to find a wax layer.

Without special fixation or staining methods, laminated
structures are seen sometimes on the outside of the epicuticle for example, in ticks (Figs 3, 4). The alternating
electron lucent and dense layers may indicate alternating
lipid and protein layers (see Neville, 1975).

C.   *Cement Layer*

The cement layer has never been definitely located in
e.m. sections (but see Wigglesworth, 1976c, Figs 27, 28) and,
indeed, is seen in the light microscope only after rather
drastic chemical degradation (Wigglesworth, 1947a). Unlike
the wax layer, which is secreted from the epidermus via
the transverse canal system (see following section), the
cement layer, if present, is secreted from dermal glands.
The structure of the cement layer and the concomitant cyclical
activity of dermal glands (Lai Fook, 1970) deserves further
study.

D.   Does The Epicuticle Contain Chitin?

The epicuticle always reacts negatively to chitin tests, but, as pointed out by Richards (1951) these tests may not be sensitive enough.   Chitin occurs in the procuticle as microfibrils approximately 30Å in diameter (see following section), so it would be reasonable to expect to find similar microfibrils in the epicuticle if chitin were present. Until recently, microfibrils have not been seen in arthropod epicuticle.   However the cattle tick (*Boophilus microplus*) epicuticle contains 30Å microfibres (Hackman and Filshie, in press) which, unlike those of the procuticle are oriented strictly perpendicular to the cuticle surface.

III.   THE PROCUTICLE

A.   Chitin Microfibrils - The Fibrous Elements

The ability to visualize chitin microfibrils in the procuticle is one of the most significant benefits that has been gained by the increased resolution available by electron microscopy.   As long ago as 1948, Richards and Korda recognized microfibres of chitin under

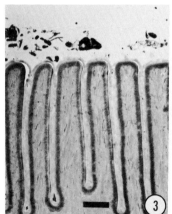
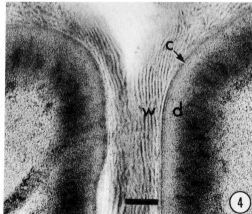

FIGURE 3.   T.S. unfed adult female cattle tick showing folded epicuticle (e). Bar = 1μ.
FIGURE 4.   Higher magnification of the same section as Figure 3, showing the epicuticle and, in particular, the laminated "wax" layer (w). Cuticulin, c; dense layer, d. Bar = 0.1μ.

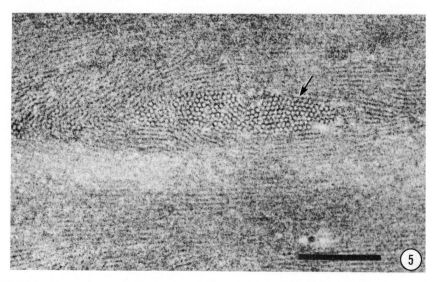

FIGURE 5. T.S. _Tenebrio molitor_ adult sternite exocuticle
showing microfibrillar substructure. Arrow shows bundle of
microfibrils cut in cross section. Bar = 0.1μ.

the electron microscope from whole mounts of disrupted
tracheae. It took almost twenty years before sectioning
and staining techniques were refined to the extent that
microfibrils could be resolved clearly in sections of
cuticle (Rudall, 1965, 1967, Filshie, 1966).

Because of its chemical nature, chitin does not react
with the heavy metals used to introduce contrast into e.m.
sections. Microfibrils are therefore always seen in
negative contrast against a background of the electron
dense protein matrix in which they are embedded (Fig. 5).
In order to visualize chitin microfibrils in sections we
must be able to stain the surrounding matrix, a goal that is
sometimes very difficult to achieve (Filshie and Smith,
in press). Microfibrils from many different arthropod
cuticles have been examined and they all have about the
same diameter (ca 30Å) and have a minimum centre-to-centre
separation of about 60Å when close-packed in the cuticle
(Neville, 1975).

B.   Microfibrillar Architecture

The study of the ways in which the chitin microfibrils
pack together in the protein matrix is fascinating. It
has received much attention in recent years but is far
from complete at this time.   There appear to be two

main types of packing - helicoidal and unidirectional.

The helicoidal model proposed by Bouligand (1965) provided a convincing explanation for the arcuate patterns of microfibrils which are seen in oblique sections of lamellate insect cuticle.   Actually, Bouligand proposed the model to explain the packing of macrofibres in a crustacean cuticle where individual fibres were distinguished clearly.   The subsequent application of the helicoidal model to microfibrillar packing has led to conflicting inter- pretations.   According to this model the fibrils are arranged in sheets oriented parallel to the cuticular surface and the fibrillar orientation of successive sheets is rotated by a constant amount.   Observed parabolic patterns do not then represent single, continuous fibrils joining one lamella with the next;   they are made up of small sections of microfibrils from successive sheets.   Neville (1975) equated helicoidal cuticle with lamellate cuticle, that is, he suggested that lamellate cuticle always contains helicoidally arranged layers of microfibrils, at least when first laid down.   Subsequent ecdysial expansion is likely to distort the arrangement.

Some authors (Dennell, 1973, 1974, 1976; Mutvei, 1974; Dalingwater, 1975) did not accept the helicoidal model. They suggested that the arcuate patterns represented real inter-laminar fibres, as originally proposed by Drach (1953). I do not believe that the published light micrographs and scanning electron micrographs of these authors allow indivi- dual continuous interlaminar fibres to be resolved with any more certainty than one can interpret these patterns as being made up of short sections of straight microfibrils.   There are other observations that do not fit a simple helicoidal model. For example, the exocuticle of the adult meal worm *Tenebrio molitor* is distinctly lamellate in oblique sections but it also contains numerous thick columns of parallel microfibrils oriented perpendicular to the cuticle surface (Delachambre, 1971) (Figs. 6, 7).   To accommodate these vertical columns in a helicoidal packing of microfibrils would require a very complex curvature of microfibrillar orientation within sheets.   Also, these microfibrils seem to occur in bundles of up to a hundred or more, not confined to a single plane and sometimes 8-10 layers thick (e.g. Fig. 5).   A similar impression of microfibrillar bundles is also gained from sections parallel with the surface (Figs 6, 7).

Helicoidal architecture has been established beyond doubt in some biological structures, particularly those in which the fibrous units are large and easily resolved

by the electron microscope, even by the light microscope.
One example is the twisted "plywood" structure of
coelacanth scales (Giraud *et al.* 1978), which is
composed of collagen bundles of diameter 2600Å, easily
visible in the light microscope and nearly 100 times
thicker than chitin microfibrils.

I believe the uncertainties that exist regarding the
detailed fibrous arrangement of insect cuticles result
from placing too much reliance on the interpretation of
thin sections. Some of the disadvantages of using thin
sections for this study are -

(a)   microfibrils of chitin are not stained and their
      visualization depends upon staining the surrounding
      matrix (Neville and Luke, 1969).

(b)   the best known staining method involves the
      use of a strong oxidizing agent, potassium
      permanganate, on the section prior to lead
      staining. This can lead to extraction of protein

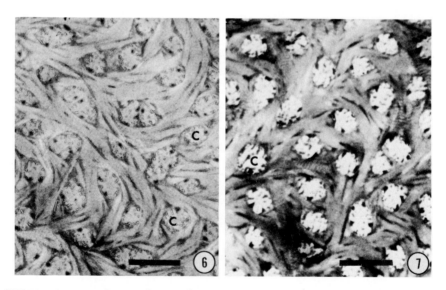

FIGURE 6.   Horizontal section of Tenebrio molitor *adult
sternite showing cross sections of vertical columns of microfibrils (c) and bundles of horizontally oriented microfibrils.
Section is stained with uranyl acetate and lead citrate.
Bar = 1µ.*
*FIGURE 7.   Section similar to Figure 8 but stained instead
with potassium permanganate and lead citrate. Note extraction
of matrix from the vertical columns. Bar = 1µ.*

from sections and uneven staining which, to an extent, depends on the orientation of microfibrils in the section. If Figs 6 and 7 are compared it can be seen that upon permanganate treatment, extraction of the matrix occurs where microfibrils are oriented vertically.

(c)   the microfibril diameter is about one tenth the thickness of the thinnest sections cut for electron microscopy. Transverse sections of micro-fibrils are therefore seen only when the microfibrils are oriented strictly parallel to the electron beam. At all other orientations, images of micro-fibrils throughout the thickness of the section are confused, one with another. Recent improvements in the quality of tilting stages used in the e.m. has allowed some analyses to be made of the relative orientations of microfibrils in sections, but the method is tedious and probably has limited application to dense structures like insect cuticle where confusion of microfibrillar images occurs.

(d)   the sectioning process can itself produce artifacts that are difficult to detect and analyse. For instance, sections transverse to the axes of "bumps" in lamellate cuticle produce a single spiral image, whereas a double spiral is predicted from the helicoidal model. Gordon and Winfree (1978) suggested that the interaction of the microtome knife with microfibrils of different orientations causes this artifact.

C.   *Future Methods For Determining Fibrous Structure?*

What, then, are the likely alternatives to sectioning, that will be applied in the future?

Mechanical disruption of the cuticle to produce frag-ments small enough for whole-mount negative staining is not likely to be fruitful for 3-dimensional analysis. The technique of freeze-fracture replication, on the other hand, is very useful and informative, particularly when microfibrils cannot be revealed in sections by staining of the matrix. Filshie and Smith (in press) applied this technique to a study of lobster gill cuticle, in which the microfibrils cannot be seen in sections. Replicas demonstrate, not only the helicoidally arranged sheets of microfibrils (Fig. 9), but also transverse rows of particles which are the source of the layers of vertical bands seen in transverse sections (Fig. 8).

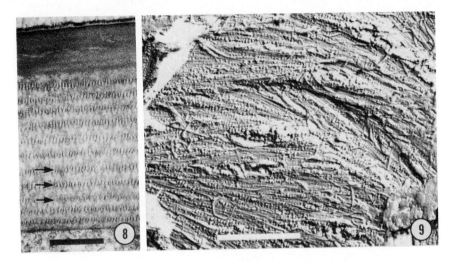

FIGURE 8. *T.S. lobster gill cuticle showing layers of vertically-oriented bands (arrows).*
FIGURE 9. *Horizontal freeze-fracture replica of lobster gill cuticle showing laminae of microfibrils and rows of small particles. Bar = 0.5μ.*

Additional advantages of freeze-fracturing are firstly, that only a single surface is viewed so that the problem of image confusion encountered with sectioning is eliminated, and secondly that where the fracture plane passes obliquely through the cuticle the relative orientations of structures at different levels are revealed clearly, particularly in stereo pairs of micrographs.   A serious disadvantage of freeze-fracture replication is that, for cuticle, the replicas obtained are very fragile because of the jagged nature of the fracture plane. The method is therefore very tedious and analyses are confined to small samples.

The logical extension of freeze-fracture replication (followed by examination of the replica by transmission electron microscopy), is the direct examination of bulk frozen-fractured cuticle in the scanning electron microscope. With suitably cooled specimen stages and the best available resolution (at present about 40Å), the scanning microscope is likely to become a very valuable tool in the further investigation of this intriguing problem.

IV.   CUTICULAR ARCHITECTURE - UNDER EPIDERMAL CONTROL OR
      SELF ASSEMBLING?

The assembly of the proteins, lipids and polysaccharides
that largely comprise the substance of the insect cuticle
occurs extracellularly. A recurring question in recent
literature concerns the extent to which the assembly of
these components into such a complex structure is controlled
by the epidermis or by intrinsic or spontaneous phenomena.
The electron microscope can at best provide only circumstantial evidence to support either hypothesis, so again
opposing views have been put forward.
      Early research into the study of cuticle deposition
was dominated by Wigglesworth (1933d, 1934, 1935a, 1936d,
1939b, 1947b, 1948a,b,c, 1961c, 1963c). More recently our
knowledge of the subcellular events of the moulting process
has been enhanced largely by the meticulous work of Locke
and his co-workers (Locke, 1958, 1965b, 1966, 1967, 1969a,b,
1974, 1976; Locke and Krishnan, 1971, 1973; Condoulis and
Locke, 1966; Locke and Huie, 1979).
      Secretion of all cuticular layers and components,
except the cement, occurs through the apical plasma membrane
of the epidermis. Cuticle precursors pass from the cells
in one of two ways, either through specialized regions of
the apical plasma membrane, the plasma membrane plaques,
which are usually located on the tips of short microvilli,
or by the exocytosis of secretory vesicles arising from
the Golgi complex.   Those components that are secreted
by or assembled at the plasma membrane plaques are the
cuticulin (Locke, 1966) and the chitin microfibres (Locke,
1967), whilst cuticular phenolases (Locke and Krishnan, 1971),
peroxidase (Locke, 1969b), the inner epicuticle (= protein
epicuticle or dense layer (Locke, 1969a) and the ecdysial
droplets (Locke and Krishnan, 1973) all apparently originate
from the Golgi complex.
      The two aspects of cuticle deposition that I will
discuss here are the formation of surface patterns and the
assembly of the fibrous chitin framework. The latter
subject has been reviewed extensively by Neville (1975).

A.   Formation of Surface Patterns

Surface patterns are determined very early in the
moulting cycle when the first layers of the epicuticle, the
cuticulin and protein layers are being produced. At this
time the future cuticular surface and the apical surface
of the epidermis are juxtaposed. The cuticulin layer is
always folded initially. Being inextensible, it is

always produced in sufficient amount to allow for
post-ecdysial expansion and, in the case of soft cuticles
(e.g. larvae of diptera and lepidoptera), to allow for
continued growth and expansion of the procuticle throughout
the instar. Superimposed on this folding are often found
pleats, tubercles and other regular or semi-regular
structures that form microscopic patterns on the completed
surface of the cuticle. Some of these patterns are subcellular in their dimensions such as the taenidial folds
of tracheae (Locke, 1957), or the tubercular patterns on
the specialized wax secreting cuticle of *Calpodes* fifth
instar larvae (Locke, 1960). Other patterns are larger,
reflecting the disposition of cell boundaries of the underlying epidermis (Filshie and Waterhouse, 1969). In *Rhodnius*,
the stellate folding of the cuticle was at one time thought to
be spontaneous and the result of epicuticle production
in excess of that required to cover the cuticular surface.
(Wigglesworth, 1933d). Locke (1974) was able to simulate
these patterns with models of expanding rubber latex, an
analogy that appeared to support the idea that simple,
physical buckling of the cuticulin as it expands is the
cause of the stellate folds.

Wigglesworth (1973e) has since revised his original
hypothesis and suggested that the final pattern is determined
by moulding of the surface by the underlying epidermis.
The apices of the folds frequently occur at the junctions of
several cells and are associated with large intercellular
vacuoles. Locke (1966, 1967) suggested that the influence
of the epidermal cells in moulding of cuticulin patterns of
Calpodes is limited to the initial shape of the cells (before
cuticulin deposition), the rate at which the cuticulin grows
and the final increase in surface area produced by this
growth. The wax-secreting cuticle of *Calpodes* has two orders
of pattern formation which differ in their times of occurrence. The larger pattern is one of polygonal areas with
depressed centres, each area representing secretion of
cuticulin from a single cell. Superimposed on this is a much
finer pattern of crater-shaped tubercles (Locke, 1959),
numbering about 150 per polygonal area (Filshie 1970a). There
are no intracellular components, such as microtubules or
microfibres, with a regular distribution reflecting the
surface pattern and Locke (1966) suggested, therefore, that
the tubercles arise spontaneously from physical buckling of
the cuticulin. Although there are no cellular organelles
apparently involved in the formation of this pattern,
Locke (1966) observed that the epicuticular filaments,
which are confined only to the rims of the tubercles, arise
at the precise time that the craters begin to form. I

suggested (Filshie, 1969a) that these filaments might serve
to reinforce the cuticulin in localized areas until
subsequent stabilization of the epicuticle takes place by
addition of the underlying dense layer. One can even
imagine that the filaments mould the cuticulin into its
tuberculate form as they extend in length from the epidermal
cell surface.

There have been two theories proposed to explain the
moulding of the taenidial folds in tracheae. Locke (1958)
favoured the spontaneous expansion and buckling theory
whilst Wigglesworth (1973e) believed that local extension of
the cuticulin at the site of the taenidial folds is an
active growth process "controlled by the epidermal cells
in conformity with the instructions latent in the pattern".

Some of the most fascinating and regular surface
patterns are to be found on butterfly and moth scales which
have been the subject of several e.m. investigations
(Overton, 1966; Greenstein, 1972; Ghiradella, 1974;
Ghiradella and Radigan, 1976). These studies have shown
that some features such as the longitudinal ribs are
associated with intracellular bundles of cytoskeletal fibres
(Overton, 1966) whilst others, such as the regular laminae
on the ridges of iridescent scales may be produced by
spontaneous expansion and buckling of the cuticulin
(Ghiradella, 1974).

More structural data are required on the formation
of patterns of subcellular dimensions before generalizations
can be made about their production. It is possible that
the conventional embedding and sectioning techniques that
have been employed so far have not revealed all the
relevant features of the pattern forming systems. The
freeze-fracturing technique may, therefore, be of use in
searching for possible cellular organelles or fibres that
are invisible in sections.

B.   *Factors Determining Microfibrillar Orientation*

No papers have been published concerning the possible
relationships between chitin orientation in the cuticle
and epidermal cell polarity since Neville's book was
published in 1975. His review of this subject and his
discussion of unsolved problems still stands. A brief summary
of this is relevant to the present discussion.

As elaborated earlier in this chapter, the two-system
model for cuticle architecture predicts that the two major
kinds of microfibrillar orientation are helicoidal and unidirectional. If this is true and if the cuticle is self-
assembled then, in cuticles in which both helicoidal and

unidirectional layers occur, only three commands (presumably coming from the epidermal cell) are required to control the pattern. These commands are to construct either unidirectional or helicoidal cuticle and, in the case of unidirectional cuticle, to orient the direction. Neville (1975 and refs therein) further suggested that cuticle precursors pass through a liquid crystalline phase immediately after secretion from the epidermis, nematic crystals producing unidirectional orientation and cholesteric crystals producing helicoidal orientation of microfibrils. It is possible, therefore, for the epidermal cell to control the type of cuticle produced by the secretion of a single substance which converts the nematic phase into a cholesteric one. The control of the direction of unidirectional layers of microfibrils may be related to the gradient organization of epidermal cells which is primarily responsible for the polarity of surface patterns on the cuticle (see Lawrence, 1970, for review).

It must be stressed (as did Neville, 1975) that there is no <u>direct</u> evidence in support of the above models for the control of microfibrillar orientation. Furthermore, it is difficult to predict how such evidence could ever be obtained using e.m. techniques alone. If, as Neville suggested, there are chemical substances secreted in cycles into the deposition zone of the cuticle, these might be identified and characterized by sensitive chemical methods, perhaps in association with histochemical staining techniques applied to e.m. sections. This deposition zone was first recognized as a special layer, with different histochemical properties, by Schmidt (1956), who called it the <u>subcuticle</u>. In the electron microscope it is usually more electron dense (using conventional staining techniques) than the overlying, fully formed cuticle. Further careful study of the structure of the subcuticle is needed to establish, for instance, whether or not there are any differences in its staining properties between times of lamellate and of unidirectional cuticle production.

V.   CONCLUDING REMARKS

In a review of cuticle physiology written over twenty years ago, Wigglesworth (1948f) wrote of the observations of the preceding years, that most had been questioned, many had been confirmed, others had been proved incorrect and on still others the last word had yet to be written. The same could be said today of the results of electron microscopy of the insect cuticle in recent years.

Wigglesworth later wrote in reference to modern science in general: "A body of classified knowledge is being built up, held together and summarized by laws and theories which make possible an almost infinite number of predictions from a minimum of brief generalizations. We professional scientists know that all these generalizations are only provisional. They represent summaries of current opinion, some of which may endure for a thousand years or more, ...; while yet others, which we ordinary folk formulate, are destined to be current for no more than a few years at the most". ("Insects and the Life of Man", Chapter 4).

There is an inherent danger, however, in attempting to formulate generalizations based largely on circumstantial evidence as, to a degree, they have been with electron microscopic studies of insect cuticle. Theories so founded will, I submit, often be incorrect and instead of providing "tools of thought" may well stifle original thinking and delay the emergence of a correct interpretation of the observations. Reverting to the title of this chapter, correct interpretation is, in part, the ability to distinguish real structures from artifacts. In e.m. specimens there is little remaining of the original specimen, because its native atoms and molecules are greatly modified during preparation. In a sense, therefore, nearly everything one sees in the electron microscope is "artifact", if one accepts the Oxford Dictionary's definition of the word as "an artificial product". The most informative studies of the future will be those that use a variety of preparative techniques and methods of microscopic examination to analyse a particular cuticle. The elements common to images obtained from all methods may then be selected with confidence as those that represent real structures and used as the bases for the construction of more accurate models of arthropod cuticles.

REFERENCES

Anderson, T.F., and Richards, A.G. (1942a). Nature through the electron microscope. *Sci. Monthly 55*, 187-192.

Anderson, T.F., and Richards, A.G. (1942b). An electron microscopic study of some structural colors in insects. *J. Appl. Physics 13*, 748-758.

Bouligand, Y. (1965). Sur une architecture torsadée répandue dans de nombreuses cuticules d'arthropodes. *C.R. Acad. Sci., Paris 261*, 3665-3668.

Condoulis, W.V., and Locke, M. (1966). The deposition of endocuticle in an insect, *Calpodes ethlius*, Stoll. Lepidoptera, Hesperiidae. *J. Insect Physiol. 12*, 311-323.

Dalingwater, J.E. (1975). SEM observations on the cuticles of some decapod crustaceans. *Zool. J. Linn. Soc. 56*, 327-330.

Delachambre, J. (1971). La formation des canaux cuticulaires chez l'adulte de *Tenebrio molitor* L. Étude ultra-structurale et remarques histochemiques. *Tissue and Cell 3*, 499-520.

Dennell, R. (1973). The structure of the cuticle of the shore crab *Carcinus maenas* (L.). *Zool. J. Linn. Soc. 56*, 159-163.

Dennell, R. (1974). The cuticle of the crabs *Cancer pagurus* L. and *Carcinus maenas* (L.). *Zool. J. Linn. Soc. 54*, 241-245.

Dennell, R. (1976). The fine structure of the cuticle of some Phasmida. *In* "The Insect Integument" (H.R. Hepburn, ed.), pp. 177-192. Elsevier, London.

Drach, P. (1953). Structure des lamelles cuticulaires chez les Crustacés. *C. r. Lebd. Séanc. Acad. Sci. Paris 237*, 1772-1774.

Filshie, B.K. (1966). "The structure and development of insect cuticle and associated structures". Ph.D. Thesis Australian National University, Canberra.

Filshie, B.K. (1970a). The resistance of epicuticular components of an insect to extraction with lipid solvents. *Tissue and Cell 2*, 181-190.

Filshie, B.K. (1970b). The fine structure and deposition of the larval cuticle of the sheep blowfly *(Lucilia cuprina)*. *Tissue and Cell 2*, 479-489.

Filshie, B.K., and Smith, D.S. (in press). A proposed solution to a fine-structural puzzle: the organization of gill cuticle in a crayfish *(Panulirus)*. *Tissue and Cell*.

Filshie, B.K., and Waterhouse, D.F. (1969). The structure and development of a surface pattern on the cuticle of the green vegetable bug *Nezara viridula*. *Tissue and Cell 1*, 367-385.

Ghiradella, H. (1974). Development of ultraviolet-reflecting butterfly scales: how to make an interference filter. *J. Morphol. 142*, 395-410.

Ghiradella, H., and Radigan, W. (1976). Development of butterfly scales. II. Struts, lattices and surface tension. *J. Morphol. 150*, 279-297.

Giraud, M.M., Castanet, S., Meunier, F.J., and Bouligand, Y. (1978). The fibrous structure of coelacanth scales: A twisted 'plywood'. *Tissue and Cell 10*, 671-686.

Gordon, H., and Winfree, A.T. (1978). A single spiral artefact in arthropod cuticle. *Tissue and Cell 10*, 39-50.

Greenstein, M.E. (1972). The ultrastructure of developing
    wings in the giant silkmoth, *Hyalophora cecropia*. II.
    Scale-forming and socket-forming cells. *J. Morphol. 136*,
    23-52.
Hackman, R.H. (1971). The integument of arthropoda. *In*
    "Chemical Zoology" (M. Florkin and B.T. Scheer, eds),
    6, pp. 1-62.
Hackman, R.H., and Filshie, B.K. (in press). The tick
    cuticle. *In* "The Physiology of Ticks" (F.D. Obenchain,
    ed.) Pergamon Press, London.
Lai-Fook, J. (1970). The fine structure of developing type
    'B' dermal glands in *Rhodnius prolixus*. *Tissue and
    Cell 2*, 119-138.
Lawrence, P.A. (1970). Polarity and patterns in the post-
    embryonic development of insects. *Adv. Insect Physiol.
    7*, 197-266.
Locke, M. (1957). The structure of insect tracheae. *Quart.
    J. Micr. Sci. 98*, 487-492.
Locke, M. (1958). The formation of tracheae and tracheoles
    in *Rhodnius prolixus*. *Quart. J. Micr. Sci. 99*, 29-46.
Locke, M. (1960). Cuticle and wax secretion in *Calpodes
    ethlius* (Lepidoptera, Hesperiidae). *Quart. J. Micr.
    Sci. 101*, 333-338.
Locke, M. (1965a). Permeability of insect cuticle to water
    and lipids. *Science, Wash. 147*, 295-298.
Locke, M. (1965b). The hormonal control of wax secretion
    in an insect, *Calpodes ethlius* Stoll. (Lepidoptera,
    Hesperiidae). *J. Insect Physiol. 11*, 641-658.
Locke, M. (1966). The structure and formation of the cuti-
    culin layer in the epicuticle of an insect, *Calpodes
    ethlius* (Lepidoptera, Hesperiidae). *J. Morph. 118*,
    461-494.
Locke, M. (1967). The development of patterns in the inte-
    gument of insects. *In* "Advances in Morphogenesis"
    (M. Abercrombie and J. Brachet, eds), *6*, 33-88.
Locke, M. (1969a). The structure of an epidermal cell during
    the development of the protein epicuticle and the
    uptake of moulting fluid in an insect. *J. Morphol. 127*,
    7-40.
Locke, M. (1969b). The localization of a peroxidase
    associated with hard cuticle formation in an insect,
    Calpodes ethlius Stoll, Lepidoptera, Hesperiidae.
    Tissue and Cell 1, 555-575.
Locke, M. (1974). The structure and formation of the
    integument in insects. *In* "Physiology of Insecta",
    Vol. VI, 2nd edition (M. Rockstein, ed), Academic Press,
    New York pp. 123-213.

Locke, M. (1976). The role of plasma membrane plaques and Golgi complex vesicles in cuticle deposition during the moult/intermoult cycle. *In* "The Insect Integument". (H.R. Hepburn, ed.) Elsevier, London, pp. 237-258.

Locke, M., and Huie, P. (1979). Apolysis and the turnover of plasma membrane plaques during cuticle formation in an insect. *Tissue and Cell 11*, 277-291.

Locke, M., and Krishnan, N. (1971). The distribution of phenol oxidases and polyphenols during cuticle formation. *Tissue and Cell 3*, 103-126.

Locke, M., and Krishnan, N. (1973). The formation of ecdysial droplets and the ecdysial membrane in an insect. *Tissue and Cell 5*, 441-450.

Mutvei, H. (1974). SEM studies on arthropod exoskeletons, Pt. 1: Decapod crustaceans, *Homarus gammarus* L. and *Carcinus maenas* (L.). *Bull. geol. Instn. Univ. Uppsala: NS., 4*, 73-80.

Neville, A.C. (1975). "Biology of the Arthropod Cuticle" Springer-Verlag, Berlin.

Neville, A.C., and Luke, B.M. (1969). A two-system model for chitin-protein complexes in insect cuticles. *Tissue and Cell 1*, 689-707.

Noirot, C., Noirot-Timothée, C., Smith, D.S., and Cayer, M.L. (1978). Cryofracture de la cuticule des Insectes: mise en évidence d'un plan de clivage dans l'epicuticule externe; implications structurales et fonctionelles. *C.R. Acad. Sci. Paris, D. 287*, 503-505.

Overton, J. (1966). Microtubules and microfibrils in morphogenesis of the scale cells in *Ephestia kuhniella*. *J. Cell Biol. 29*, 293-305.

Richards, A.G. (1951). "The Integument of Arthopods" University of Minnesota Press, Minneapolis.

Richards, A.G., and Korda, F.H. (1947). Electron micrographs of centipede setae and microtrichia. *Ent. News 58*, 141-145.

Richards, A.G., and Korda, F.H. (1948). Studies on arthropod cuticle. 2. Electron microscope studies of extracted cuticles. *Biol. Bull. 94*, 212-235.

Richards, A.G., and Korda, F.H. (1950). Studies on arthropod cuticle. 4. An electron microscope survey of the intima of arthropod tracheae. *Ann. Ent. Soc. Amer. 43*, 49-71.

Rudall, K.M. (1965). Skeletal structures in insects. *In* "Aspects of Insect Biochemistry". *Biochem. Soc. Symp. 25*, 83-92.

Rudall, K.M. (1967). Conformation in chitin-protein complexes.
    In "Conformation of Biopolymers". (G.N. Ramachandren,
    ed.) *2*, 751-765. Academic Press, London.
Schmidt, E.L. (1956). Observations on the subcuticular layer
    in the insect integument. *J. Morphol.* *99*, 211-231.
Weis-Fogh, T. (1970). Structure and formation of insect
    cuticle. *Symp. R. ent. Soc. Lond.* *5*, 165-185.
Wigglesworth, V.B. (1976). "Insects and the Life of Man"
    Chapman and Hall, London.

CUTICLE WATER RELATIONS: TOWARDS A NEW
CUTICLE WATERPROOFING MODEL

John Machin

Department of Zoology
University of Toronto
Toronto, Canada

I. INTRODUCTION

This essay continues the theme, "lipid layers and
membrane models" by Professor J.W.L. Beament, which appeared
in 1968 in a volume published to mark Sir Vincent
Wigglesworth's retirement. Beament's article chronicles
the development of ideas which became the orientated
monolayer theory we know today, attributing its origin to
Sir Vincent's hunch that temperature-transpiration curves
represented a "real" transition phenomenon.
In recent years there have been an increasing number
of studies whose results are inconsistent with the
monolayer model. In addition, in over a decade of presenting
arguments supporting the theory to my students and illustrating its salient features in classroom experiments, I have
become increasingly aware that the behaviour of cockroach
cuticle was not always consistent with the theory. On the
basis of personal experience and the published work of others
I offer this alternative account of cuticle waterproofing.

II. DEVELOPMENT OF ORIENTATED MONOLAYER MODEL

By the end of the war it became increasingly clear to
Wigglesworth, from the action of detergents, solvents and
abrasive dusts that the principal barrier to water in the
cuticle lay in its superficial waxy or greasy layer. These
experiments combined with Ramsay's (1935) technique of
observing changes in water loss rate with temperature
eventually led Wigglesworth to suggest in 1945c that water
loss in insects was regulated by a thin layer of oriented
wax on the outer surface of the lipoprotein epicuticle.
Beament (1945) strengthened this conclusion by being able
to recreate the low permeabilities of intact cuticle by the
reapplication of extracted lipid to wax-free membranes.
Beament also showed (1955) that cuticular extracts from
Periplaneta cuticle formed stable monolayers on water
surfaces. It was the series of papers (1958; 1959; 1961a)
in which Beament reinvestigated the effects of temperature
on cuticle permeability with vastly improved techniques to
overcome the problems of temperature and humidity gradients,
which led to the final acceptance of his ideas. Alternative
proposals (Edney, 1957; Holdgate, 1956; Holdgate and Seal,
1956) that the rise in permeability with temperature
represented no more than a smooth exponential increase
without abrupt transitions were rejected in favour of the
orientated monolayer model.
Although Beament's own reviews (1954; 1961b; 1964; 1965;
1968; 1976) and those of many others (Ebeling, 1964; 1974;
Edney, 1967a; b; 1977; Hackman, 1964; 1971; Locke, 1964;
1974; Neville, 1975; Schmidt-Nielsen, 1969) have ensured
that the properties of insect cuticle predicted by the
monolayer model are now widely known, I summarize them here
to serve as the starting point for my argument.

A. *The Model*

(1) Respiratory water loss is controlled by spiracular
closing mechanisms in insects. Tracheal cuticle is readily
permeable to water lacking significant regulatory power of
its own (Beament, 1964).
(2) The principal barrier to water in the cuticle is a
lipid monolayer orientated by polar attraction to the tanned
lipoprotein of the outer epicuticle (Beament, 1958; 1959;
1960; 1961a; b; 1964; 1965). The remaining waterproofing
lies mostly in the unorientated wax or grease outside the
orientated monolayer (Beament, 1958).

(3) At certain "critical temperatures" angular displacement of molecules in the orientated layer bring about spacing changes giving rise to abrupt increases in permeability (Beament, 1964; 1965). Alternatively water permeability changes are due to phase changes of lipid-water crystals being brought to the surface through the epicuticle (Locke, 1964; 1965; 1974).

(4) Cuticles are more permeable to net inward water flow because elevated external water concentrations causes a breakdown of lipid layers sealing water channels (Beament, 1964).

(5) Wettable areas in some aquatic cuticles are caused by lipid reversal on untanned outer epicuticle (Beament, 1960; 1961b; 1964; 1965).

(6) Cuticle water activities are significantly lower than haemolymph levels presumably due to active withdrawal by epidermal cells (Beament, 1964; 1965; Winston, 1967; Winston and Beament, 1969).

(7) Some arthropods absorb water from liquid or vapour states into the haemolymph against massive activity gradients. The mechanism is non-solute coupled, dependent on flow asymmetries and reduced activities described in 4 and 6, respectively (Beament, 1954; 1964; 1965; Wharton and Kanungo, 1962).

It is apparent from the above that Beament's interest in cuticle properties went far beyond its role as a water retarding barrier and the presence or absence of an orientated monolayer. Modern integumental physiology, particularly that of terrestrial animals owes much to his work. The functional analysis of a structure whose component barriers are arranged both in series and parallel anticipated similar approaches with other epithelia by many years. For example the significance of water vapour gradients in air (Beament, 1961b) and their masking effect of true cuticular permeability in permeable insects, predated the "unstirred layer" paper of Dainty and House (1966). Impressed by studies in which water exchange in certain arthropods appeared not to be dictated by water activity differences between haemolymph and environment (Buxton, 1930; Mellanby, 1932; Lees, 1946) Beament proposed that the cuticle might also function as a novel type of water pump. Much effort went into explaining how the cuticle could act as a water barrier in one direction while encouraging water transport without the net movement of solutes in the other.

III. EVIDENCE AGAINST THE ORIENTATED MONOLAYER MODEL

A. *Lipid Films and Cuticle Extracts*

1. Chemistry. The only animal for which there is any
direct evidence of a lipid monolayer is *Periplaneta*. Gilby
and Cox (1963) found that the majority of extractable
cuticular lipids were non-polar hydrocarbons (75% by weight)
whereas the potentially orientatable polar compounds, fatty
acids and aldehydes made up only 18% of the extract. Long
chain alcohols postulated by Beament (1955) to form the
orientated impermeable layer were undetected. Despite
Gilby and Cox's misgivings about whether an orientated layer
existed in *Periplaneta* cuticle, Lockey (1976) pointed out
that Cook and Ries (1959) had produced stable monolayers of
mixtures of stearic acid and n-hexadecane, including the
same 1:3 proportions of polar to non-polar compounds
extracted from *Periplaneta*. There is disagreement however,
about whether or not the complex mixtures extracted from
insect cuticles, which include compounds both with branched
and bent unsaturated hydrocarbon chains, are as tightly
bound to water or as impermeable as pure stearic acid or
simple mixtures of straight chain compounds. Beament's
(1955) surface balance measurements showed that *Periplaneta*
cuticular extract formed an essentially stable, compression
resistant monolayer, whereas Lockey (1976) found the extract
hardly resisted compression at all.

2. Water Drops. There are also conflicting views about
the stability and impermeability of cuticular lipid layers
on water drops. Ramsay (1935) was first to discover that
water drops placed on intact *Periplaneta* cuticle apparently
became coated with a layer of low permeability so that the
drops persisted for prolonged periods. Beament (1958)
obtained long lived drops on a silicone coated metal surface
by applying cuticular compounds from cockroach cuticle with
a needle. My own observations based on large numbers of
observations however, indicate that coats of low permeability
are formed comparatively rarely. Drops lasting longer than
100 min occurred 12% of the time on intact cockroaches,
with 28% frequency when drops on glass were coated with
hexane extracts and with 40% frequency with chloroform
extracts.

There seems to be two reasons why experiments with
cuticular extract monolayers on water surfaces give
conflicting answers about their permeability and stability.
It has long been known that the permeabilities of monolayers
of pure compounds or simple mixtures of lipids are highly

susceptible to trace chemical contamination and consistent results are obtainable only if stringent precautions to avoid contamination are employed (La Mer and Barnes, 1959). Even if acceptable standards of cleanliness are observed in surface balance and water drop experiments, it is not possible to take the same precautions when the source of the experimental material is a living insect. Gilby and McKellar (1970) suggest for example that extract may be contaminated with body lipids of non-cuticular origin. In addition a certain amount of selection occurs and the extracted mixture may differ from that in the intact cuticle. It has been observed that cold, as opposed to hot chloroform-methanol produces different extracts from the same species (Hadley and Filshie, 1979) and the extract of polar compounds is increased by chloroform-methanol compared with hexane (Hadley, 1977).

   3. Cuticle Layers. Although it is an established fact that cuticular extracts can sometimes form impermeable layers on water surfaces, I am far from convinced that they invariably exist on the surface of the intact cuticle. Beament argued that lipids were orientated by the outer epicuticle surface and the remaining lipids formed an unbound, unorientated layer above. Recognizing the difficulties of measuring the thickness of this wax (grease) layer directly, the practice was developed of calculating it indirectly by dividing the volume of extracted lipids by the animal's surface area. For *Periplaneta*, values of 0.52 μm for females and 0.41 μm for males (Dennell and Malek, 1956) 0.25 μm (Beament, 1958) and 0.11 μm based on measurements of surface area determined by gaseous adsorption (Lockey, 1960) have been obtained. These methods are clearly erroneous because it has been well established by Wigglesworth (1947a; 1970b; 1975b; 1976c) and others, that lipids are found within other layers of the cuticle, notably the lipoprotein outer epicuticle. Wigglesworth (1975c) himself pointed out that extracted lipids from *Rhodnius* exceeded the amount calculated to occupy the wax layer. In class experiments where H_2S killed *Periplaneta* are washed in a volume of clean water with a thin layer of *Lycopodium* spores on the surface, I have never seen films equivalent to more than one or two times the total surface area of the cockroach. Of course the films are not necessarily monolayers, but it seems likely that there is much less free lipid on the surface of *Periplaneta* than the tens of layers suggested by Beament.

4. Contact Angles. The contact angles formed by water drops on the cuticle have always been used to indicate molecular orientation in intact *Periplaneta* cuticle. Beament (1964) claimed that water drops on intact cuticle have initial contact angles of about 80°, indicating the lipid is unorientated and that the subsequent reduction in contact angle to 30° is due to the induced molecular orientation with hydrophilic groups towards the drop. My own experiments confirm these observations but they may be interpreted in a different way. In a large number of measurements initial contact angles varied between 68° and 110° with a mean of 91°. The time course of contact angle decrease depended only on the rate of disappearance of the drop as it evaporated. Contrary to the above the base of drops was never observed to creep outwards to bring about a reduction in contact angle. For long periods the area of contact remained constant, then diminished in steps when the drops were very small, temporarily returning them to more spherical proportions and a higher contact angle.

Beament (1964) went on to suggest that low contact angles recorded after the cuticle had been washed by lipid solvents indicated that the cuticle surface was hydrophilic, thus providing the force for binding and orientating the lipid layer. Yet how can low contact angles be considered to reflect the polarity of intact outer epicuticle normally containing lipids if the layer has just been subjected to lipid solvents? I am also doubtful that the proteinaceous outer epicuticle could ever provide, at the molecular level, the surface of water-like smoothness necessary to form the parallel packed layer.

B. *Temperature Transitions*

Studies of the effects of increasing temperatures on cuticular permeability have always been central to understanding cuticle water relations because they provide information about the intact cuticle. The widely used method of analyzing water loss data developed by Beament and the dependent interpretation of transition phenomena has recently been criticized by Toolson (1977). He argues that the correction for concentration gradient across the cuticle in different temperatures must be made in thermo-dynamic terms of chemical potential instead of the traditional vapour pressures or saturation deficits. Chemical potential differences are given by

$$\mu_w - \mu_{wv} = RT \left(\ln X_w - \ln \frac{P_{wv}}{P_{sat}} \right) \tag{1}$$

where μ = partial molar free energy, X_w = water activity in the animal and P_{wv}/P_{sat} the corresponding ambient water vapour value. R is the gas constant and T absolute temperature.

Dramatically different effects are obtained by dividing water loss rates by chemical potential differences, which are proportional to temperature in $^{\circ}K$, rather than an exponential function in $^{\circ}C$, as in the case of vapour pressure. Toolson suggests that the diminished range of the divisor makes the differences between cuticular and air temperatures unimportant and reduces abrupt changes in permeability, previously interpreted as temperature transitions, to minor departures from otherwise smooth curves. He proposes that these curves fit Boltzmann functions of the general form

$$P = K.e^{1/T} \tag{2}$$

where P = cuticle permeability per unit chemical potential difference in $mg.cm^{-2}.h^{-1}.Joule^{-1}$, K = a constant at T = absolute temperature in $^{\circ}K$.

The conformation of permeability with a Boltzmann function suggests that the flow of water through the cuticle depends on the number of molecules having sufficient activation energy for penetration. Toolson further suggests that divergences of points from this relationship at temperatures corresponding to the melting points of cuticular lipids might indicate a progressive permeability transition associated with this change of physical state.

I have applied Toolson's method of permeability analysis to Beament's (1958) data for intact *Periplaneta* nymphs and cuticular extract coated water drops and the data for *Tenebrio* pupae of Holdgate and Seal (1956). It is possible in the *Periplaneta* data to calculate back to the particular humidity at which each determination was made. For the remainder it is not possible to do so for *Tenebrio* and I have assumed a reasonable, uniformly low value of 5% R.H.

The results of these calculations are presented using a semi-log plot of the data. If permeability against the reciprocal of absolute temperature falls in a straight line of negative slope, it conforms to a Boltzmann function. It can be seen in Fig. 1 that there is general linear conformation for both intact nymphs and coated water drops but Beament's "critical temperature" discontinuities are still apparent. There is evidence also that similar discontinuities persist in Toolson's own *Hadrurus arizonensis* data but their divergence from an exponential function is much less. I have noticed in my own calculations that small differences in the ambient humidity term give rise to large differences in chemical potential. It is

possible therefore that the residual scatter in my
recalculated points originate from errors in the ambient
humidity values used. Toolson's values on the other hand
were not reconstructed and gave less scatter.

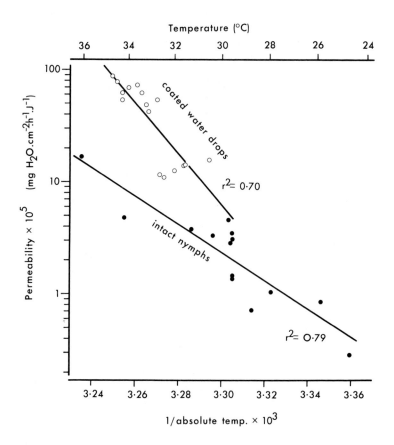

*Fig. 1. Temperature-permeability characteristics of
Periplaneta nymphs and water drops coated with cuticle
extracts. Data calculated from Beament (1958).*

The contrast between the plots in Fig. 1 for an animal
with "greasy" cuticular lipids and that of a "waxy" cuticle
in Fig. 2 may be more significant. Elevated permeabilities
do appear to correspond with the zone of lipid melting
points determined in Holdgate and Seal (1956) by surface
X-ray diffraction. Linear plots obtained with "greasy"
cuticles (Fig. 1) provide convincing support to this

conclusion because transitions at melting point would not be expected in cuticles composed largely of unsaturated hydrocarbons having melting points below zero °C. In the case of *Periplaneta americana*, 50% of the extracted "grease" is composed of double unsaturated cis, cis-6,9 heptacosadiene (Atkinson and Gilby, 1970). Beament's (1961a) data for *Dytiscus*, designated by him as another insect with a "greasy" cuticle also fell on a single straight line when reanalyzed.

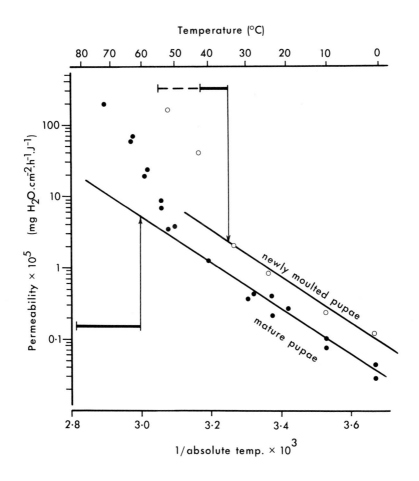

Fig. 2. Temperature-permeability characteristics of newly moulted and mature Tenebrio pupae, compared with the melting point ranges (horizontal bars) of their cuticle waxes. Data from Holdgate and Seal (1956).

I venture to suggest that the presence or absence of temperature transitions is related to the form of the permeability-temperature curves, divided by Beament (1961b) into two types: "Z" shaped of "greasy" cuticles and "L" shaped in "waxy" cuticles. Thus all greasy cuticles with "Z" shaped curves may become straight lines with the new semi-log plots while waxy cuticles with "L" curves remain biphasic.

C. Water Absorption

1. *Site of Water Vapour Uptake.* The cuticular water pump part of the model received its first major setback when Noble-Nesbitt (1970a; b), despite some obscure earlier claims to the contrary, discovered that blocking the anus of *Thermobia domestica* (= *Lepismodes iniquilinus*) and *Tenebrio molitor* larvae prevented atmospheric absorption. Okasha's (1971) contention that the blocking might only have inhibited sensory processes necessary for uptake to occur was subsequently shown to be invalid by improved techniques. Reversible exposure, apparently independently developed by Noble-Nesbitt (1975) and Rudolph and Knülle (1978) showed that weight gain in *Thermobia* only occurred when the anus had access to high humidity whereas ixodid ticks only gained weight when the humidity in a chamber enclosing the head was elevated. A second technique (Ramsay, 1964) involving the weighting of faecal pellets to determine water activities in the rectal lumen was employed by Machin (1976) to establish unambiguously a rectal site of water vapour absorption in *Tenebrio* larvae while O'Donnell (1977a; 1978) used both methods to establish a non-rectal site of uptake in *Arenivaga*. All recent studies, with acarines as well as a variety of insects, clearly associate water vapour uptake with specialized structures restricted to specific parts of the body surface.

2. *Mechanism.* Although Noble-Nesbitt (1970b) initially proposed that water vapour uptake by the rectum was driven by a local cuticular pump, more recent studies support more conventional mechanisms involving transporting epithelia (Machin, 1979a). An analysis of the distribution of osmotic pressures within the rectal complex of *Tenebrio* (Machin, 1979b) lead to the conclusion that atmospheric uptake process is driven by extremely high osmotic pressures (4.3 to 7.0 osmol.kg^{-1}) generated by the Malpighian tubules. Water containing compartments between the tubules and the rectal lumen, particularly the rectal cuticle and the perirectal space, appear to act passively in the inward transmission of water.

Although direct evidence bearing on the nature of the
mechanism is lacking in any other animal, I have argued
(Machin, 1979a) that all of the examples of water vapour
uptake published so far can be interpreted in terms of some
form of solute coupled mechanism. These arguments extend
even to minute grain and house mites weighing only a few
micrograms, whose pattern of net uptake and loss in different
conditions, resembles in some respects the behaviour of a
non-living hygroscopic object undergoing wide fluctuations of
internal water content (Knülle, 1965; 1967). These complex
exchange kinetics can be explained by the large surface to
volume ratios of these tiny animals which increase the
animals' difficulties in balancing uptake and losses to
maintain stable body weights.

It has been further argued that the capacity to absorb
water vapour in species whose lower threshold is below the
solubilities of the biologically common electrolytes
(*Liposcelis* (threshold 55%), *Xenopsylla* (52%) and *Thermobia*
(40%)) need not be considered as evidence for a unique
cuticular water pump functioning without solutes. It is
entirely possible that highly soluble, non-toxic organic
solutes such as glycerol or the amino acid proline could be
used to generate the necessary osmotic gradients for uptake
(Machin 1979a).

3. Absorption of Water Drops. A second group of
experimental observations were used to support the active
involvement of the cuticle in water exchanges across the
integument. Beament (1964; 1965) interpreted the disappearance of drops of iso-osmotic saline placed on *Periplaneta*
cuticle, as evidence of the cuticle developing suction forces
of several hundreds of atmospheres, because precipitated salt
was left behind. Although I have been able to repeat the
basic observations, significantly higher weight loss rates
in the presence of the drops compared to the cockroach alone
can only mean that the drops disappear by evaporation, not
absorption. This was confirmed by experiments which
demonstrated that humidity had a marked effect on the
longevity of cuticle applied drops (Fig. 3).

4. Cuticular Water Content. In my view experiments
attempting to demonstrate lowered cuticular water activities
(Winston, 1967; 1969; Winston and Hoffmeier, 1968; Winston
and Beament, 1969) which would support the existence of
driving forces for water absorption, are unconvincing
because they do not adequately discount the passive hydration
of deficits caused by keeping the experimental subjects in
sub-saturated atmospheres. Furthermore the determination of

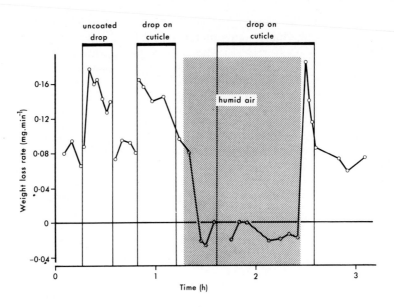

Fig. 3. Weight loss rates in living Periplaneta together with 1 mg water drops placed sequentially beside the animal (uncoated control) or on the cuticle (coated drops). Note that loss rates at an ambient R.H. of 30% (about 0.08 mg.min^{-1} for the cockroach alone) are elevated even in the presence of the coated drop. Note also that the coated drop which persisted for 50 min in humid air, rapidly disappeared on return to ambient conditions.

differences between cuticles of living and dead animals in these studies, which would have distinguished between active and passive phenomena, were not rigorous enough. Winston and Beament's (1969) own data clearly demonstrate that haemolymph osmotic pressure in *Periplaneta* is both subject to considerable individual variability and susceptible to dehydration by comparatively short exposures (7 h) to sub-saturated atmospheres. In spite of this haemolymph concentrations were not measured in the animals actually used in the experiments to counter the possibility of non-random sampling or non-controlled post-mortem changes. It is also unfortunate that water exchange measurements were not made in high enough humidities to represent adequately haemolymph in *Locusta* because this species did show consistency in haemolymph concentration.

Even if Winston and Beament's (1969) cuticular water
activities for *Periplaneta* were accepted, 0.985 (0.42 M NaCl)
is nowhere near the 0.75 value required to absorb water from
a NaCl solution to the point of dryness. Furthermore
cuticular water activities at the level claimed by Winston
and Beament (1969) would not account for the marked
differences in transpiration rate between living and killed
specimens observed by Winston and Nelson (1965) and Winston
(1967; 1969). In a related series of experiments by
Treherne and Willmer (1975a; b), transpiration rates in
Periplaneta double following decapitation or head ligaturing,
even after the usual controls of spiracle blocking or opening
in high CO_2 were applied. Changes in water activity however
cannot be the direct cause of altered transpiration rates
because cuticular water content is lowered following
decapitation. These observations suggest a mechanism in
which water loss is modulated through alterations in cuticle
permeability initiated perhaps, by changing levels of
hormone from the head.

IV. TOWARDS A NEW CUTICULAR MODEL

Even though there is great chemical variability, insect
and acarine cuticular extracts share the common feature of
being composed largely of non-polar compounds with a minor
polar fraction (Hackman, 1971; Neville, 1975). There seems
hope, therefore, that a general theory of cuticular waterproofing applicable to most arthropods will be developed.
The suggestion by Davis (1974b) that the water barrier extends
deeper than the superficial wax layer to the lipoprotein of
the outer epicuticle seems an appropriate starting point for
a new synthesis. Beament's original (1958) analysis of the
water barrier of *Periplaneta* in terms of two layers, seemed
acceptable because the calculated diffusion coefficient for
the unorientated lipid (1.85×10^{-8} ml H_2O vapour at
N.T.P. $sec^{-1}.cm^{-2}.mm$ $Hg^{-1}.mm^{-1}$) agreed with values for bulk
wax (2.0 to 2.1×10^{-8}) in the literature. However, if
grease thickness based on Lockey's (1960) more accurate
surface area values are used, the calculated unorientated
diffusion coefficient (7.3×10^{-9}) is less convincing. The
impression gained by expressing permeabilities per unit
thickness is that the orientated lipid layer is of unique
importance in regulating water loss. This is misleading.
If all the cuticular lipid was unorientated it would only
have to have a diffusion coefficient of 1.65×10^{-8}, which
is still in range of the value for wax. Making the point

another way, it requires only 0.04 μm more unorientated
lipid to account for the properties of the orientated layer,
an addition of 13% to the total thickness. Clearly the new
non-orientated model need not depend on the existence of
novel structures with exceptional properties.

Fig. 4 presents a new arrangement of barriers for
Periplaneta cuticle. Only a few lipid layers are on the
surface, outside the epicuticle, the remaining amount
forming a superficial barrier within the structure of the
epicuticle itself. I have assumed that all lipid is
unoriented, with the water conducting properties of bulk
wax. The remaining cuticle waterproofing I have assigned
to lower layers of epicuticle, of the order of 2 μm in
thickness (Dennell and Malek, 1956). The calculated
diffusion coefficient of this layer is 2.0 X 10^{-7}.

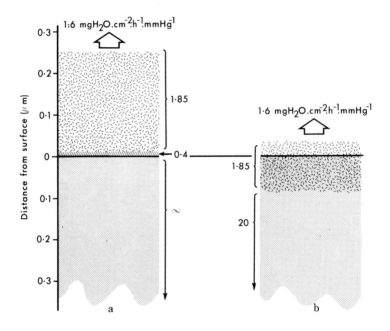

*Fig. 4. Diagrammatic sections of Periplaneta cuticle,
together with calculated diffusion coefficients of the
constituent layers (in ml H_2O vapour at N.T.P. $sec^{-1}.cm^{-2}.
mm Hg^{-1}.mm^{-1}. X 10^8$). Model a) after Beament (1958), model
b) is proposed in the text.*

2. *Other Insects and Acarines.* I am convinced that a
general understanding of cuticle water relations in the
future will come from experimental tests of the unorientated
bulk lipid hypothesis. Techniques are required which
separate the effects of lipid amount (thickness), chemistry
(molecular organization and binding) and parallel pathways
to overall water exchange. The correlation of natural
biological variations in cuticular chemistry, differences
between species (Jackson, 1970; Lockey, 1978), developmental
stage (Armold *et al.*, 1969; Davis, 1974a), seasonal and
acclimatory effects (Hadley, 1977) and with permeability
changes associated with moulting, pioneered by Wigglesworth
(1933d) is the first step. Once more experiments with
temperature as the variable will have a central role in
understanding the "new cuticle". With improved techniques
it may be possible to resolve gradual temperature transitions
into a series of discrete steps, corresponding to the
transition of the component epicuticular lipids. The
preparation and separation of extracted lipids and their
application to artificial substrates may again come into its
own in helping to identify and characterize the functional
components of the water barrier. Current attempts (Filshie,
1970; Hadley and Filshie, 1979) to obtain information about
the distribution and organization of lipids within both wax
and outer epicuticular layers by electron microscopic
examination before and after lipid extraction have been
rather unsuccessful. However a chemical variation of
Wigglesworth's (1945c) abrasion technique, the progressive
removal of lipid layers employing the principles of
differential solubility and mobility, used in chromatography,
might be more successful.

3. *Lower Limits to Permeability.* Research with exotic
desert dwelling arthropods whose cuticle permeabilities are
among the lowest recorded, prompts new speculation about
the lower limits to waterproofing the arthropod integument.
Of particular interest are a number of desert scorpions
(Hadley, 1970; Toolson and Hadley, 1977) among which *Hadrurus
arizonensis* has the lowest overall value (1.0 to 2.5 X 10^{-3}
mg.cm^{-2}.h^{-1}.mm Hg^{-1}, between 20 and 30 °C), about half the
permeability of *Tenebrio molitor* larvae (6.7 X 10^{-3} mg.cm^{-2}.
h^{-1}.mm Hg^{-1} at 25 °C; Beament, 1959) and an order of
magnitude less permeable than *Periplaneta americana*
(1.6 X 10^{-2} mg.cm^{-2}.h^{-1}.mm Hg^{-1} at 25 °C; Beament, 1958).
Inverse correlations between the total amount of extracted
lipid per unit surface area, and average carbon chain length
within related scorpion species (Toolson and Hadley, 1977)
is a promising discovery since it implicitly supports the

bulk lipid model. The correlation does not extend, however,
to general comparisons between similarly adapted insects and
arachnids and further understanding of cuticle waterproofing
must take into account more complex differences of chemistry
and structural organization.

When the sclerite permeability is reduced, parallel
routes of transpiration, joints, intersegmental membranes
and spiracles, become increasingly significant to the overall
water loss from the animal. Hadley and Filshie (1979)
were aware of this, pointing out that it is the inner layers
of the cuticle that are reduced in the interests of
flexibility, whereas outer waterproof layers of the epicuticle
are increased in thickness. In a related study of the
reasons for low overall permeability in adult desert
tenebrionid beetles, Aherne (1970) stresses the important
role of the sub-elegtral cavity in reducing respiratory
water loss. The studies of peripheral structures and
mechanisms of water loss regulation are an important but
underdeveloped avenue of research in arthropod water balance.

4. *Asymmetry*. If it is shown that waterproofing is due
to a bulk layer of non-orientated lipids, a new explanation
for the asymmetry of cuticle permeability will have to be
developed since the Beament (1961b; 1964; 1965) explanation
depends on the valve-like effect of the oriented monolayer
responding to local water concentrations, would be no longer
tenable. It is interesting that the original explanation
of the phenomenon proposed by Hartley (1948) and rejected
by Beament, seems more in line with the new understanding
of cuticle impermeability. The Hartley theory depends on
there being at least two component layers in series having
sufficient bulk for their permeabilities to change with
water content. For the cuticle to be more permeable to net
inward flow than in the reverse direction, water content and
hence permeability must change more rapidly with water
activity in the functional outer layer than in the inner
part of the cuticle. It is significant that Toolson's
(1977) thermodynamic analysis of cuticle permeability also
emphasizes the cuticle water content be known and the forces
determining it be understood.

5. *The Cuticle in Water Vapour Absorption*. Much of this
essay has stressed the role of the cuticle in retarding
water loss. As a student of mechanisms of water vapour
absorption I have been struck by the varied role to which
cuticle has been put in what now seem to be several
independently evolved water condensing and transporting
systems (Machin, 1979a). In *Tenebrio* the rectum is involved,

not external cuticle. Rectal cuticle acts as a condensing surface and to enhance the flow of water to the Malpighian tubules (Machin, 1979b). The cuticle acts as an osmotic coupling system so that water passes passively along osmotic gradients established by the accumulation principally of KCl by the tubules. The impermeable perinephric membrane composed of the compressed membranes of many cell layers (Ramsay, 1964) prevents hydration of the tubular fluid by the haemolymph. By contrast, the permeable nature of the rectal cuticle, which Phillips and Dockrill (1968) suggest is incompletely coated with a monolayer, enhances water flow from the lumen to the tubules. A 5:1 permeability asymmetry (Machin, 1978) minimizes loss in the event of a sudden lowering of humidity below absorption threshold. In fluctuating ambient humidities inward water flow is affected by the efficiency of the osmotic coupling which is enhanced by low proportion of water to solids characteristic of all cuticles (Machin, 1979b). In water vapour absorption in ixodid ticks, on the other hand, the normal impermeability of external cuticle is exploited. Concentrated electrolyte solutions are apparently secreted on to the body surface in the region of the mouth, it is the cuticle which must serve as the barrier preventing hydration from the haemolymph.

Recent discoveries with *Arenivaga* strongly indicate a critical but entirely different involvement of the cuticle in the animal. During absorption a complex system of hairs and plates of hypopharyngeal cuticle conduct a layer of fluid from a pair of frontal glands to the oesophagus (O'Donnell, 1977b). Since the bulk activity of this fluid is similar to that of the haemolymph, lowering sufficient to account for the observed condensation of water vapour for humidities as low as 70% R.H. must be due to surfactant properties of the cuticular hairs and plates. It is too early to speculate on the nature of the forces by which flow to the haemolymph is maintained. Measurements on hypopharyngeal cuticle indicate a remarkably high affinity for water and the capacity to absorb and hold it in large quantities. It appears that the absorption mechanism involves the flow of water along the cuticle rather than through it. This is a tremendously important distinction as there is no necessity to postulate the molecular valves within the cuticle structure. Flow along the cuticle also means that valves, if they exist, need not be at the molecular level and can be spacially separated and mechanically operated.

V. CONCLUSIONS

The principal arguments against the orientated monolayer theory of cuticle waterproofing are that the majority of lipids extracted from arthropod cuticle are non-polar and that a thermodynamic analysis of temperature effects on permeability indicates that temperature transitions at sub-melting point critical temperatures are artifacts. Permeability asymmetry, uptake of liquid and gaseous water by the cuticle and water drop contact angle changes, all previously thought to depend on the model may be explained by mechanisms not involving orientated monolayers.

It is proposed that a new synthesis will emerge from a fuller understanding of internal cuticle structure with particular emphasis on water content and the bulk properties of bound, unorientated lipid. The presently underemphasized study of parallel water pathways and of regional differences in cuticle permeability will greatly contribute to the understanding of water balance in exceptionally waterproof species.

REFERENCES

Aherne, G.A. (1970). The control of water loss in desert tenebrionid beetles. *J. exp. Biol. 53*, 573-595.

Armold, M.T., Blomquist, G.J., and Jackson, L.L. (1969). Cuticular lipids of insects. III. The surface lipids of the aquatic and terrestrial life forms of the big stonefly *Pteronarcys californica* Newport. *Comp. Biochem. Physiol. 31*, 685-692.

Atkinson, P.W., and Gilby, A.R. (1970). Autoxidation of insect lipids: inhibition on the cuticle of the american cockroach. *Science 168*, 992.

Beament, J.W.L. (1945). The cuticular lipoids of insects. *J. exp. Biol. 21*, 115-131.

Beament, J.W.L. (1954). Water transport in insects. *Symp. Soc. exp. Biol. 8*, 94-117.

Beament, J.W.L. (1955). Wax secretion in the cockroach. *J. exp. Biol. 32*, 514-538.

Beament, J.W.L. (1958). The effect of temperature on the water-proofing mechanism of an insect. *J. exp. Biol.* *35*, 494-519.

Beament, J.W.L. (1959). The waterproofing mechanisms of arthropods. I. The effect of temperature on cuticle permeability in terrestrial insects and ticks. *J. exp. Biol.* *36*, 391-422.

Beament, J.W.L. (1960). Wetting properties of insect cuticle. *Nature, Lond. 186*, 408-409.

Beament, J.W.L. (1961a). The waterproofing mechanism of arthropods. II. The permeability of the cuticle of some aquatic insects. *J. exp. Biol. 38*, 277-290.

Beament, J.W.L. (1961b). The water relations of insect cuticle. *Biol. Rev. 36*, 281-320.

Beament, J.W.L. (1964). The active transport and passive movement of water in insects. *In* "Advances in Insect Physiology" (J.W.L. Beament, J.E. Treherne, and V.B. Wigglesworth, eds.), *2*, pp. 67-129. Academic Press, New York and London.

Beament, J.W.L. (1965). The active transport of water: evidence, models and mechanisms. *Symp. Soc. exp. Biol. 19*, 273-298.

Beament, J.W.L. (1968). Lipid layers and membrane models. *In* "Insects and Physiology" (J.W.L. Beament and J.E. Treherne, eds.), pp. 303-314. Elsevier, New York.

Beament, J.W.L. (1976). The ecology of cuticle. *In* "The Insect Integument" (H.R. Hepburn, ed.), pp. 359-374. Elsevier, New York.

Buxton, P.A. (1930). Evaporation from the meal-worm (*Tenebrio*: Coleoptera) and atmospheric humidity. *Proc. R. Soc., Lond. B. 106*, 560-577.

Cook, H.D., and Ries, H.E. (1959). Adsorption of radiostearic acid and radiostearyl alcohol from n-hexadecane onto solid surfaces. *J. Phys. Chem., Ithaca 63*, 226-230.

Davis, M.T.B. (1974a). Changes in cuticle temperature during nymphal and adult development in the rabbit tick, *Haemaphysalis leporispalustris* (Acari: Ixodides: Ixodidae). *J. exp. Biol. 60*, 85-94.

Davis, M.T.B. (1974b). Critical temperature and changes in cuticular lipids in the rabbit tick, *Haemaphysalis leporispalustris*. *J. Insect Physiol. 20*, 1087-1100.

Dainty, J., and House, C.R. (1966). "Unstirred layers" in frog skin. *J. Physiol. 182*, 66-78.

Dennell, R., and Malek, S.R.A. (1956). The cuticle of the cockroach, *Periplaneta americana*. *Proc. R. Soc., Lond. B. 143*, 239-256.

Ebeling, W. (1964). The permeability of insect cuticle. *In* "The Physiology of Insecta" (M. Rockstein, ed.), *3*, pp. 507-556. Academic Press, New York and London.

Ebeling, W. (1974). Permeability of insect cuticle. *In* "The Physiology of Insecta" (M. Rockstein, ed.), *6*, pp. 271-343. Academic Press, New York and London.

Edney, E.B. (1957). "The Water Relations of Terrestrial Arthropods". Cambridge University Press.

Edney, E.B. (1967a). Water balance in desert arthropods. *Science 156*, 1059-1066.

Edney, E.B. (1967b). The impact of the atmospheric environment on the integument of insects. *Proc. Int. Biometerol. Congr. 4*, 71-81.

Edney, E.B. (1977). "Water Balance in Land Arthropods". Springer-Verlag, New York, Heidelberg and Berlin.

Filshie, B.K. (1970). The resistance of epicuticular components of an insect to extraction with lipid solvents. *Tissue and Cell 2*, 181-190.

Gilby, A.R., and Cox, M.E. (1963). The cuticular lipids of the cockroach, *Periplaneta americana* (L.). *J. Insect Physiol. 9*, 671-681.

Gilby, A.R., and McKellar, J.W. (1970). The composition of the empty puparia of a bluefly. *J. Insect Physiol. 9*, 1517-1531.

Hackman, R.H. (1964). Chemistry of the insect cuticle. *In* "The Physiology of Insecta" (M. Rockstein, ed.), *3*, pp. 471-502. Academic Press, New York and London.

Hackman, R.H. (1971). The integument of arthropods. *In* "Chemical Zoology" (M. Florkin and B.T. Scheer, eds.), *6*, pp. 1-62. Academic Press, New York and London.

Hadley, N.F. (1970). Water relations of the desert scorpion, *Hadrurus arizonensis*. *J. exp. Biol. 53*, 547-558.

Hadley, N.F. (1977). Epicuticular lipids of the desert tenebrionid beetle, *Eleodes armata*: seasonal and acclimatory effects on chemical composition. *Insect Biochem. 7*, 277-283.

Hadley, N.F., and Filshie, B.K. (1979). Fine structure of the epicuticle of the desert scorpion, *Hadrurus arizonensis*, with reference to location of lipids. *Tissue and Cell 11*, 263-275.

Hartley, G.S. (1948). Contribution to a discussion on asymmetry. *Disc. Faraday Soc. 3*, 223.

Holdgate, M.W. (1956). Transpiration through the cuticles of some aquatic insects. *J. exp. Biol. 33*, 107-118.

Holdgate, M.W., and Seal, M. (1956). The epicuticular wax layers of the pupa of *Tenebrio molitor* L. *J. exp. Biol. 33*, 82-106.

Jackson, L.L. (1970). Cuticular lipids of insects. II. Hydrocarbons of the cockroaches *Periplaneta australasiae*, *Periplaneta brunnea*, and *Periplaneta fuliginosa*. *Lipids 5*, 38-41.

Knülle, W. (1965). Die sorption und transpiration des wasserdampfes bei der mehlmilbe *(Acarus siro* L.). *Z. vergl. Physiol. 49*, 586-604.

Knülle, W. (1967). Physiological properties and biological implications of the water vapour sorption mechanism in larvae of the oriental rat flea, *Xenopsylla cheopis* (Roths.). *J. Insect Physiol. 13*, 333-357.

La Mer, V.K., and Barnes, G.T. (1959). The effects of spreading technique and purity of sample on the evaporation resistance of monolayers. *Proc. natn. Acad. Sci. U.S.A. 45*, 1274-1280.

Lees, A.D. (1946). The water balance in *Ixodes ricinus* L. and certain other species of ticks. *Parasitology 37*, 1-20.

Locke, M. (1964). The structure and formation of the integument in insects. *In* "Physiology of Insecta" (M. Rockstein, ed.), *3*, pp. 379-470. Academic Press, New York and London.

Locke, M. (1965). Permeability of insect cuticle to water
    and lipids. *Science 147*, 295–298.

Locke, M. (1974). The structure and formation of the integu-
    ment in insects. *In* "The Physiology of Insecta" (M.
    Rockstein, ed.), *6*, 123–213. Academic Press, New York
    and London.

Lockey, K.H. (1960). The thickness of some insect epicuti-
    cular wax layers. *J. exp. Biol. 37*, 316–329.

Lockey, K.H. (1976). Cuticular hydrocarbons of *Locusta,
    Schistocerca,* and *Periplaneta*, and their role in water-
    proofing. *Insect Biochem. 6*, 457–472.

Lockey, K.H. (1978). The adult cuticular hydrocarbons of
    Tenebrio molitor L. and *Tenebrio obscurus* F. (Coleoptera:
    Tenebrionidae). *Insect Biochem. 8*, 237–250.

Machin, J. (1976). Passive exchanges during water vapour
    absorption in mealworms (*Tenebrio molitor*): a new
    approach to studying the phenomenon. *J. exp. Biol. 65*,
    603–615.

Machin, J. (1978). Water vapour uptake by *Tenebrio*: a new
    approach to studying the phenomenon. *In* "Comparative
    Physiology – Water, Ions and Fluid Mechanics" (L. Bolis,
    K. Schmidt-Nielsen and S.H.P. Maddrell, eds.), pp. 67–77.
    Cambridge University Press, Cambridge.

Machin, J. (1979a). Atmospheric water absorption in
    arthropods. *In* "Advances in Insect Physiology" (J.E.
    Treherne, M.J. Berridge and V.B. Wigglesworth, eds.), *14*,
    pp. 1–48. Academic Press, New York and London.

Machin, J. (1979b). Compartmental osmotic pressures in the
    rectal complex of *Tenebrio* larvae: evidence for a single
    tubular pumping site. *J. exp. Biol. 82*, 123–137.

Mellanby, K. (1932). The effect of atmospheric humidity on
    the metabolism of the fasting mealworm (*Tenebrio molitor*
    L., Coleoptera). *Proc. R. Soc., Lond. B. 111*, 376–390.

Neville, A.C. (1975). "Biology of the Arthropod Cuticle".
    Springer-Verlag, New York, Heidelberg and Berlin.

Noble-Nesbitt, J. (1970a). Water uptake from subsaturated
    atmospheres: its site in insects. *Nature, Lond. 225*,
    753–754.

Noble-Nesbitt, J. (1970b). Water balance in the firebrat, *Thermobia domestica* (Packard). The site of uptake of water from the atmosphere. *J. exp. Biol. 52*, 193-200.

Noble-Nesbitt, J. (1975). Reversible arrest of uptake of water from subsaturated atmospheres by the firebrat, *Thermobia domestica* (Packard). *J. exp. Biol. 62*, 657-669.

O'Donnell, M.J. (1977a). Site of water vapour absorption in the desert cockroach, *Arenivaga investigata*. *Proc. natn. Acad. Sci. U.S.A. 74*, 1757-1760.

O'Donnell, M.J. (1977b). Hypopharyngeal bladders and frontal glands: novel structures involved in water vapour absorption in the desert cockroach, *Arenivaga investigata*. *Am. Zool. 17*, 902.

O'Donnell, M.J. (1978). The site of water vapour absorption in *Arenivaga investigata*. *In* "Comparative Physiology - Water, Ions, and Fluid Mechanics" (L. Bolis, K. Schmidt-Nielsen and S.H.P. Maddrell, eds.), pp. 115-121. Cambridge University Press, Cambridge.

Okasha, A.Y.K. (1971). Water relations in an insect, *Thermobia domestica*. I. Water uptake from sub-saturated atmospheres as a means of volume regulation. *J. exp. Biol. 55*, 435-448.

Phillips, J.E., and Dockrill, A.A. (1968). Molecular sieving of hydrophilic molecules by the rectal intima of the desert locust (*Schistocerca gregaria*). *J. exp. Biol. 48*, 521-532.

Ramsay, J.A. (1935). The evaporation of water from the cockroach. *J. exp. Biol. 12*, 373-383.

Ramsay, J.A. (1964). The rectal complex of the mealworm *Tenebrio molitor* L. (Coleoptera, Tenebrionidae). *Phil. Trans. R. Soc., Lond. B. 248*, 279-314.

Rudolph, D., and Knülle, W. (1978). Uptake of water vapour from the air: process, site and mechanism in ticks. *In* "Comparative Physiology - Water, Ions and Fluid Mechanics" (L. Bolis, K. Schmidt-Nielsen and S.H.P. Maddrell, eds.), pp. 97-113. Cambridge University Press, Cambridge.

Schmidt-Nielsen, K. (1969). The neglected interface: the
    biology of water as a liquid gas system. *Q. Rev.
    Biophys.* 2, 283-304.

Toolson, E.C. (1977). Diffusion of water through the arthro-
    pod cuticle: thermodynamic consideration of the transi-
    tion phenomenon. *J. Thermal Biol. 3,* 69-73.

Toolson, E.C., and Hadley, N.F. (1977). Cuticular permea-
    bility and epicuticular lipid composition in two Arizona
    vejovid scorpions. *Physiol. Zool. 50,* 323-330.

Treherne, J.E., and Willmer, P.G. (1975a). Evidence for
    hormonal control of integumentary water loss in
    cockroaches. *Nature, Lond. 254,* 437-439.

Treherne, J.E., and Willmer, P.G. (1975b). Hormonal control
    of integumentary water loss: evidence for a novel
    neuroendocrine system in an insect (*Periplaneta americana*).
    J. exp. Biol. 63, 143-159.

Wharton, G.W., and Kanungo, K. (1962). Some effects of
    temperature and relative humidity on water-balance in
    females of the spiny rat mite, *Echinolaelaps echidninus*
    (Acarina: Laelaptidae). *Ann. ent. Soc. Am. 55,* 483-492.

Wigglesworth, V.B. (1933d). The physiology of the cuticle
    and of ecdysis in *Rhodnius prolixus* (Triatomidae,
    Hemiptera); with special reference to the function of
    the oenocytes and of the dermal glands. *Quart. J. Micr.
    Sci. 76,* 269-318.

Wigglesworth, V.B. (1945c). Transpiration through the cuticle
    of insects. *J. exp. Biol. 21,* 97-114.

Wigglesworth, V.B. (1947a). The epicuticle in an insect,
    Rhodnius prolixus (Hemiptera). *Proc. R. Soc., Lond. B.
    134,* 163-181.

Wigglesworth, V.B. (1970b). Structural lipids in the insect
    cuticle and the function of the oenocytes. *Tissue and
    Cell 2,* 155-179.

Wigglesworth, V.B. (1975b). Distribution of lipid in the
    lamellate endocuticle of *Rhodnius prolixus*. *J. Cell Sci.
    19,* 439-457.

Wigglesworth, V.B. (1975c). Incorporation of lipid into the epicuticle of *Rhodnius* (Hemiptera). *J. Cell Sci. 19*, 459–485.

Wigglesworth, V.B. (1976c). The distribution of lipid in the cuticle of *Rhodnius*. *In* "The Insect Integument" (H.R. Hepburn, ed.), pp. 89–106. Elsevier, New York.

Winston, P.W. (1967). Cuticular water pump in insects. *Nature, Lond. 214*, 383–384.

Winston, P.W. (1969). The cuticular water pump and its physiological and ecological significance in the Acarina. *In* "Proceedings of the 2nd International Congress of Acarology" (G.O. Evans, ed.), pp. 461–468. Akademiai Kiado, Budapest.

Winston, P.W., and Beament, J.W.L. (1969). An active reduction of water level in insect cuticle. *J. exp. Biol. 50*, 541–546.

Winston, P.W., and Hoffmeier, P. (1968). The active control of cuticular water content in *Leucophaea maderae* L. *Am. Zool. 8*, 391.

Winston, P.W., and Nelson, V.E. (1965). Regulation of transpiration in the clover mite *Bryobia praetiosa* Koch (Acarina: Tetranychidae). *J. exp. Biol. 43*, 257–269.

WATER AND IONS IN THE GUT[1]

William R. Harvey

Department of Biology
Temple University
Philadelphia, Pennsylvania

I. BIOLOGICAL VS PHYSIOLOGICAL ANALYSIS

Sir Vincent Wigglesworth's faith in the value of insects as objects of physiological analysis (Wigglesworth, 1948) led him almost single-handedly to found the discipline of Insect Physiology (VBW 1934. Insect Physiology). The success of Insect Endocrinology justified his faith. However, the present status of Insect Gastroenterology falls short of the promise implied in the success of Sir Vincent and of Arthur Ramsay in early studies on digestion, ion regulation and excretion by the gut and Malpighian tubules (Wigglesworth, 1931f, 1932; Ramsay, 1953). The central theme of the present essay is that the membrane physiology of the gut and its associated structures requires both biological and physiological analysis and that the comparatively limited success in this field is due in part to difficulties in communication between workers with a biological rationale and those with a physiological rationale (see Ussing, 1977). It is not that the insect gut is an unfavorable object of study but rather than the analysis of the gut has been uneven.

The biological dogma is that organisms are not all alike but are adapted to their niches and that they are best studied

[1]The writing of this chapter was supported in part by a research grant (AI-09503) from the National Institute of Allergy and Infectious Diseases, National Institutes of Health.

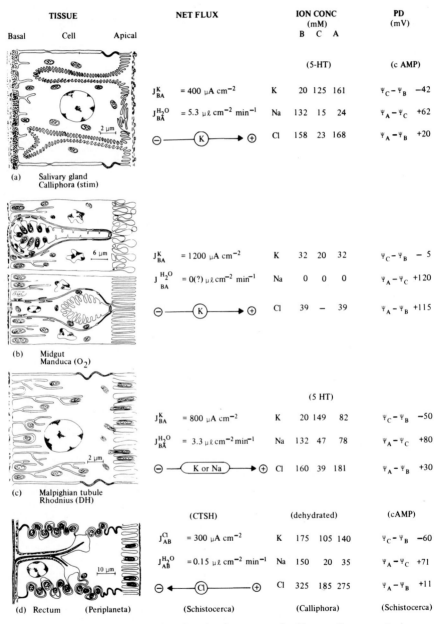

| TISSUE | NET FLUX | ION CONC (mM) | PD (mV) |

Basal   Cell   Apical   **B   C   A**

(a) Salivary gland Calliphora (stim)

(5-HT)   (c AMP)

J_{BA}^{K} = 400 µA cm^{-2} K   20 125 161 $\Psi_C - \Psi_B$ −42

$J_{BA}^{H_2O}$ = 5.3 µℓ cm^{-2} min^{-1} Na 132 15 24 $\Psi_A - \Psi_C$ +62

⊖ — (K) → ⊕   Cl 158 23 168 $\Psi_A - \Psi_B$ +20

(b) Midgut Manduca (O₂)

J_{BA}^{K} = 1200 µA cm^{-2} K   32 20 32 $\Psi_C - \Psi_B$ − 5

$J_{BA}^{H_2O}$ = 0(?) µℓ cm^{-2} min^{-1} Na 0   0   0 $\Psi_A - \Psi_C$ +120

⊖ — (K) → ⊕   Cl 39 − 39 $\Psi_A - \Psi_B$ +115

(c) Malpighian tubule Rhodnius (DH)

(5 HT)

J_{BA}^{K} = 800 µA cm^{-2} K   20 149 82 $\Psi_C - \Psi_B$ −50

$J_{BA}^{H_2O}$ = 3.3 µℓ cm^{-2} min^{-1} Na 132 47 78 $\Psi_A - \Psi_C$ +80

⊖ — (K or Na) → ⊕   Cl 160 39 181 $\Psi_A - \Psi_B$ +30

(d) Rectum (Periplaneta)

(CTSH)   (dehydrated)   (cAMP)

J_{AB}^{Cl} = 300 µA cm^{-2} K   175 105 140 $\Psi_C - \Psi_B$ −60

$J_{AB}^{H_2O}$ = 0.15 µℓ cm^{-2} min^{-1} Na 150 20 35 $\Psi_A - \Psi_C$ +71

⊖ ← (Cl) — ⊕   Cl 325 185 275 $\Psi_A - \Psi_B$ +11

(Schistocerca)   (Calliphora)   (Schistocerca)

Figure 1. The principal characteristics of some transporting epithelia of insects (from Harvey, 1980 with permission from Marcel Dekker).

under conditions which mimic the living state as closely as
possible. The physiological dogma is that organisms are fundamentally alike and that one is entitled to disregard all
complications in the attempt to discover basic physical mechanisms and to isolate the molecules responsible for function.
There is nothing mutually exclusive between the two dogmas but
the theoretical assumptions and technical complexities associated with each have tended to restrict any single person from
working freely in both spheres. The recent success of the
Cambridge group in applying the electron microprobe to problems of insect ion and water regulation demonstrates the value
of a cooperative approach.

II. SUMMARY OF TRANSPORT PHYSIOLOGY

A. *Malpighian Tubule - Rectum Theory of Excretion*

Ramsay (1958) proposed that Malpighian tubules function
like vertebrate glomeruli in that their wall is permeable to
most molecules smaller than proteins and that such small molecules are swept into the tubular lumen from the blood along
with the fluid which follows active potassium and sodium
transport. He proposed that the rectum functions like kidney
tubules in that it selectively reabsorbs certain molecules and
like kidney collecting ducts in that it has the capacity to
reabsorb water or let it pass out depending on specific adaptations and conditions. According to this view the Malpighian
tubule - rectal system is the primary regulator of the composition of the blood. This theory has been widely accepted
(reviews include those by Maddrell (1971), Stobbart and Shaw
(1974), and Phillips (1977). However, there is growing evidence that some reabsorption occurs in Malpighian tubules
(Irvine, 1969), that other organs such as the midgut may be
involved in both secretion and reabsorption, and that insect
organs may have a greater capacity for self regulation than
was originally thought (see Section III. A.)

B. *Ion Pumps*

The principal active transport systems of insects are the
alkali metal ion pump (potassium pump), the classical sodium-
potassium exchange pump, calcium and magnesium pumps, the
chloride pump, and a generalized anion pump (reviews by
Maddrell, 1977; Zerahn, 1978; Harvey, 1980).

An electrogenic alkali metal ion pump (potassium pump) is
located on the apical plasma membrane of the secretory cells
of the salivary glands of *Calliphora* (Fig. 1a; Oschman and
Berridge, 1970; Berridge et al., 1975; Gupta et al., 1978), on
the apical membrane of the goblet cells of Lepidopterous larvae (Fig. 1b: Anderson and Harvey, 1966; Wood et al., 1969;
Blankemeyer and Harvey, 1978), and on the apical membrane of
Malpighian tubule cells of *Carausius, Calliphora,* and *Rhodnius*
(Fig. 1c; Berridge and Oschman, 1969; Maddrell, 1977. It is
also present in the rectum of *Schistocerca* (Williams et al.,
1978). This pump was originally demonstrated in Malpighian
tubules of *Carausius (Dixippus)* by Ramsay (1954) and was confirmed by flux measurements in short circuited midgut preparations of *Hyalophora cecropia* by Harvey and Nedergaard (1964).
A potassium pump with similar properties is found in the
labial glands of adult *Antheraea pernyi* (Kafatos, 1968) and in
the integument of *H. cecropia* during moulting (Jungreis and
Harvey, 1975).

In each case, except the rectum, potassium is transported
from basal to apical sides rendering the apical side electrically positive to the basal side. The rate of transport in
the fully active state is of the order of 1 milliampere per
cm^2. The relationship of the active potassium transport to
the electrochemical gradients and to epithelial structure is
diagrammed in Figure 1. The pump is sometimes called an alkali metal ion pump rather than a potassium pump because it
transports sodium in the Malpighian tubules of *Glossina,
Rhodnius, Calliphora,* and *Carausius* and can be induced to
transport sodium in the presence of low potassium concentration and the absence of calcium in salivary glands of *Calliphora* and the midgut of *Lepidoptera*. Unlike the classical
Na-K pump the alkali pump is not inhibited by ouabain (review
by Jungreis, 1977) and it pumps both potassium and sodium in
the same direction.

The classical Na-K exchange pump has been demonstrated by
ouabain sensitivity of organ function or by the identification
of an Na-K stimulated, ouabain inhibited, ATPase in insect
nerve cord, muscle, brain tissue, and rectum, in some but not
most Malpighian tubules, and possibly in salivary glands and
cockroach midgut (references in Harvey, 1980). However, the
role of the Na-K exchange pump in the absorption of amino
acids and sugars by the gut has not been studied in insects as
much as it has in vertebrates (Treherne, 1967; Nedergaard,
1977; see Phillips, Chapter 7).

Active secretion of magnesium by Malpighian tubules in
Calliphora and *Aedes campestris*, and of calcium by isolated
Malpighian tubules and salivary glands of *Calliphora* have been
reported. Active reabsorption of calcium and magnesium was
demonstrated by measurements of tracer fluxes under short circuit conditions in isolated midguts of *Hyalophora cecropia*
(references in Harvey, 1980). Active extrusion of calcium by
salivary gland cells is implied in Berridge's hypothesis for
the mechanism of action of 5-hydroxytryptamine via intracellular changes in levels of calcium and cyclic AMP (Berridge,
Chapter 22). It is possible that these instances of transepithelial active calcium transport are simply manifestations
of the active extrusion of calcium which is probably characteristic of all cells, the asymmetry of apical and basal membranes of epithelial cells leading almost invariably to net
transepithelial calcium transport (Wood and Harvey, 1976).
The active secretion of calcium by *Calliphora* salivary glands
would then be the result of the very much larger rate of calcium pumping out of the cells across the apical membranes than
across the basal membranes as observed by Berridge (personal
communication) whereas the active reabsorption of calcium by
Hyalophora midgut would be the result of a postulated larger
rate of calcium pumping out of the cells across the basal membranes than across the apical membranes.

Active chloride transport from lumen side to blood side
of the isolated rectum of *Schistocerca gregaria* (Fig. 1d) was
demonstrated by measurements of fluxes of ^{36}chloride under
short circuit conditions by Williams et al., (1978). This
important advance and other aspects of ion transport by the
insect rectum are discussed in Chapter 7 by Phillips.

Finally, the active transport of sulfate and phosphate
and that of many organic anions has been reviewed by Maddrell
(1977) who argues that Malpighian tubules may possess a pump
which can not only handle sulfate and phosphate but a variety
of organic anions as well. An hypothesis regarding such a
non-specific anion active transport is proposed in Section VI.

C. Fluid transport

Fluid transport is a prominent feature of the physiology
of salivary glands (and labial glands), of Malpighian tubules,
and of rectum. Curiously it has not even been studied in midgut (see Section III. B). The widely accepted idea that fluid
transport is accomplished by osmotic coupling of water movement to that of actively transported ions, chiefly sodium and

potassium (Oschman and Berridge, 1970) has been criticized by Hill (1977) who suggests instead that the coupling is by electroosmosis in which active electrogenic potassium or sodium transport is electrostatically coupled to chloride movement which in turn is frictionally coupled to water movement. See essays by Küppert and Thurm (Chapter 6), by Phillips (Chapter 7), and Maddrell (Chapter 8). If it turns out that chloride and water movement do indeed depend on electrogenic cation transport then interest in the alkali metal ion pump of insects, which appears to be one of the few electrogenic pumps which is not primarily a proton pump (review by Wolfersberger and Harvey, 1980), will be enhanced.

III. PERSISTENT PROBLEMS

A. *Regulation of Blood Ionic Composition*

     The argument for a role of midgut in potassium regulation of the blood is that despite the large electrochemical potential driving potassium toward the blood, and the known permeability of the midgut to potassium (references in Harvey and Zerahn, 1972) the blood potassium concentration is constant (Quatrale, 1966). This constancy implies that an equal flux of potassium from blood to lumen in some gut-related structure must be present. The Malpighian tubules of Lepidopterous larvae do transport potassium from blood to lumen in the distal part but reabsorb it in the proximal part and so could not do the job (Irvine, 1969). Potassium transport by the rectum in general is toward the blood i.e. in the wrong direction and in *Manduca* K transport is via the cryptonephridial system which apparently provides a mechanism for potassium (and other solute movement) from rectum directly to Malpighian tubular lumen without mixing with the blood (Ramsay, 1976). The salivary glands are modified to form silk glands in Lepidopterous larvae and do not secrete potassium. However, the midgut, with its large surface area which *in vivo* leaks potassium from gut contents to blood driven by an electrochemical gradient of approximately 180 mV, has been demonstrated *in vitro* to pump potassium across this identically large surface area from blood to lumen side with an equal intensity of approximately 180 mV. On the other hand it must be acknowledged that no direct test of this hypothesis on a living larva has yet been conducted. The argument that the midgut has a major role in the regulation of blood ionic composition can be extended beyond potassium regulation because the midgut actively absorbs magnesium and calcium and amino acids at a rate in the range of 1 to 2 μEquivalents per cm^2 per hour (see Section II. B).

B. *Fluid Transport by Midgut*

The role of the midgut in water regulation has been little studied *in vitro*. Wigglesworth has argued that the goblet cell may be involved in water movement (VBW 1972. The Principles of Insect Physiology, p 527). If the condition for electroosmosis is the presence of an electrogenic pump moving cations toward the lumen, electrostatically coupled to chloride movement, with the chloride frictionally coupled to water (Hill, 1977) and if an enclosed space is important for such transport then examination of Figure 1 reveals that the midgut possesses the necessary properties.

C. *Scarcity of Kinetic and Pharmacological Data*

An apparent K_m of 16 mM and an apparent V_{max} which is two times the rate in 32 mM K has been estimated for potassium transport by the isolated midgut of *H. cecropia* by Wood and Harvey (unpublished data) and similar values can be calculated from the rate vs concentration curve in the review by Harvey and Zerahn (1972). Even such approximations of the apparent K_m and V_{max} are not available for the alkali metal ion pump in salivary glands or in Malpighian tubules. Moreover, the validity of such constants, based as they are on the solute concentrations in external bathing solutions, is open to question. What is required are kinetic constants expressed in terms of the concentrations in the transport pool within the cells. Kinetic constants have enormous value e.g. as markers for pump proteins in efforts to isolate and reconstitute transport systems. The electron microprobe work of Gupta and the Cambridge group shows that it is possible to determine ionic concentrations adjacent to the transporting membrane in *Calliphora* salivary glands (Gupta et al., 1978) and in other transporting epithelia and thereby has provided a method for expressing constants in terms of the correct pool. An alternate and promising method is to determine kinetic constants by analysis of the fluctuations (noise) in the short circuit current or in some other continuously measureable parameter of transport function (Hoshiko and Moore, 1978).

The Pharmacology of insect ion transport is also unsatisfactory. For the alkali metal ion pump we desperately need a specific inhibitor analagous to ouabain. The endotoxin from

Bacillus thuringiensis holds some promise but it apparently
acts on only a part of the active potassium transport in
Manduca midgut (Harvey and Wolfersberger, 1979).

D. *Transport Proteins and Phospholipids*

Considering the ease of isolating membrane proteins and
the voluminous literature on this subject in other systems it
is remarkable that no such analysis for any of the major insect transporting epithelia is known. Until recently the same
could be said of membrane phospholipids but Berridge and Fain
(1979) have now characterized the phospholipids of the salivary glands of *Calliphora*.

IV. PROBLEMS WITH ALKALI PUMP MODEL

A. *Apical location of pump*

The principal evidence that the alkali metal ion pump is
located on the apical plasma membrane of the secretory cells
(containing canaliculi) of *Calliphora* salivary glands is that
this membrane uniquely contains transport particles (Oschman
and Berridge, 1970) and that the apical resistance is not only
much greater than the basal resistance but it changes in the
expected way when the pump is stimulated with 5-hydroxytrypta-
mine (Berridge et al., 1975). This location receives strong
support from potassium selective microelectrode and electron
microprobe evidence that the alkali ion concentration is low
on the cellular side and high on the lumen side of the apical
membrane during transport (Gupta et al., 1978). Evidence for
an apical location of the potassium pump in the midgut is that
the fluxes there occur against a large thermodynamic gradient
(Wood et al., 1969), that particles are uniquely present there
(Anderson and Harvey, 1966; Cioffi, 1979), and that the apical
resistance of the goblet cells increases when the pump is
stopped in nitrogen. Changes in the kinetic pool size when
the cells are coupled and uncoupled (Blankemeyer and Harvey,
1978) and differences in the kinetic pool size of anterior,
middle, and posterior regions of the midgut (Cioffi, unpublished data) are consistent with an apical location. In Malpighian tubules, fluxes against a thermodynamic gradient
(Maddrell, 1977) and the unique presence of particles
(Berridge and Oschman, 1969) suggest strongly that the alkali
pump is located on the apical membrane. On the other hand
Zerahn 1977, 1978) argues that a transport route between the
epithelial cells or one through special channels within the

cells cannot be ruled out and therefore that the location of
the alkali pump on the apical membrane of transporting cells
(in midgut at least) cannot be regarded as being established.
The best prospect for unequivocal demonstration of an alkali
pump located on the apical membrane appears to be to isolate
that membrane cleanly and to demonstrate that vesicles prepared from it can actively transport potassium.

B. Kinetic Pool Location

Cioffi (unpublished data) analysed the transport properties of anterior, middle, and posterior regions of isolated
Manduca midgut and presented evidence that most of the goblet
cell pool is a transported pool located in the goblet cavity.
This argument is supported by the demonstration of Moffett
(1979) that the concentration of potassium is low in the cytoplasm of the transporting goblet cells. Since the total cytoplasmic volume of the goblet cells is small, the low concentration means that only a small portion of the kinetic pool
could be in the cytoplasm of the goblet cells.

C. Basal Entry Step

How does potassium enter the transporting cells from the
basal bathing solution? In both midgut (Wood et al., 1969)
and salivary gland (Berridge and Prince, 1972) the cell interior was sufficiently negative to compensate for the elevated potassium concentration and entry was believed to be
passive. The ion selective microelectrode data of Moffett
(1979) confirm this belief. On the other hand Maddrell (1977),
noting the 50 mV negative interior of the cells of Rhodnius
Malpighian tubules, realized that chloride could not enter the
cells passively, and proposed an active chloride transport
from basal solution to cells to which potassium would be coupled electrostatically. He then had to propose synchroniza-
tion of the apical and basal pumps to account for the constant
cell K level.

V. PORTASOMES

Particles, 7 to 15 nM in diameter are found on the cytoplasmic surface of the apical plasma membrane of potassium
transporting cells in salivary glands, midgut, Malpighian tubules, and rectum of insects from both larval and adult stages

TABLE I. *Particle Studded Apical Plasma Membranes of Insect Transporting Epithelial Cells and Their Close Association with Mitochondria*

Insect	Tissue	Cell	Mito.	Reference
Calliphora erythrocephala	Sal gl	Sec	No	Oschman & B., 1970
Calliphora erythrocephala	Sal gl	Reab	No	Oschman & B., 1970
Hyalophora cecropia	Midgut	Gob	Yes	Anderson & H., 1966
Ephestia kühniella	Midgut	Gob	Yes	Smith et al., 1969
Manduca sexta	Midgut Ant, Mid Post	Gob	Yes No	Cioffi, 1979
Microtermes edentatus	Mal tub	Epi	Yes	Noirot et al., 1967
Cephalotermes rectangularis	Mal tub	Epi	Yes	Noirot et al., 1967
Calliphora erythrocephala	Mal tub	Epi	Yes	Berridge & O., 1969
Calpodes ethlius	Mal tub	Epi	Yes	Ryerse, 1977
Amara eurynota	Rectum	Epi	No	Noirot & N., 1970
6 species of termites	Rectum	Epi	Yes	Noirot & N., 1970
Blabera craniifer	Rectum	Epi	Yes	Noirot & N., 1970
Thermobia domestica	Rectum	Epi	Yes	Noirot & N., 1970
Calliphora erythrocephala	Rectum	Pap	No	Gupta & B., 1966
Aedes campestris	Rectum	Epi	No	Merideth & P., 1973
Periplaneta americana	Rectum	Pad	Yes	Oschman & Wall, 1969
Lepismodes inquillinus	Anal sac	Epi	Yes	Noirot & N., 1971
Calliphora erythrocephala	Haltere	Epi	Yes	Smith, 1969

and from both primitive and highly specialized insect orders.
We suggest the name "portasomes" to describe these particles
and propose that they contain the molecular machinery required
for the active transport of potassium and the other alkali
metal ions.

A. *Distribution of portasomes in relation to transport*

Portasomes were first reported on the apical membrane of
the cortical epithelial cells in the rectal papillae of *Calliphora erythrocephala* by Gupta and Berridge (1966) who suggested that they may be involved in active ion transport. Later,
Berridge and Gupta (1968) showed that ATPase activity was localized on the particle studded apical membrane only when the
incubation medium contained potassium, in contrast to the
ATPase of the particle free lateral membrane stacks which did
not require potassium. Anderson and Harvey (1966) found similar particles on the apical plasma membrane of midgut goblet
cells of *H. cecropia* and proposed that they might be involved
in the massive potassium transport reported by Harvey and
Nedergaard (1964). Recently, Wolfersberger (1979) has identified a membrane bound, potassium modulated ATPase from a midgut preparation (see Wolfersberger and Harvey, 1980).

In *H. cecropia* midgut the portasome-containing apical
membrane is closely associated with mitochondria but such an
association does not appear to be generally necessary for
active potassium transport because the portasome-bearing membrane is not closely associated with mitochondria in the
foldings bordering the apical canaliculi of the secretory
cells in salivary glands of *Calliphora* (Oschman and Berridge,
1970). Recently, Cioffi (1979) showed that mitochondria are
closely associated with the portasome-bearing membrane in
anterior and middle midgut of *Manduca sexta* but not in posterior midgut which nevertheless can transport potassium.
From this work on salivary glands and midgut it appears that
the portasomes alone may provide the structural basis for
active K transport.

The distribution of the portasomes and their relationship
to mitochondria are summarized in Table I. In all cases they
are found on the apical membrane. Mitochondria are associated
with the portasome-studded membranes in all cases except six,
namely the secretory and reabsorptive cells of *Calliphora*
salivary glands, the goblet cells of posterior *Manduca* midgut,
and the rectum of *Amura, Calliphora,* and *Aedes.* Evidently,
even though mitochondria need not be closely associated with

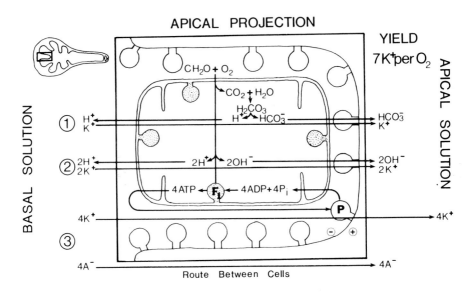

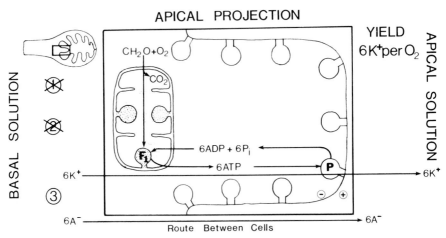

Figure 2. Diagram of multiple K pump hypothesis. Upper diagram - anterior and middle midgut. Lower diagram - posterior midgut. (1) K^+, H^+ exchange and K^+ HCO_3^- active transport driven by metabolically produced CO_2. (2) K^+, H^+ exchange and K^+ OH^- active transport driven by chemiosmotic proton gradient. (3) K^+ electrogenic active transport driven by portasome ATPase reaction. Mechanisms (1) and (2) require a close association of mitochondria with portasome-containing apical membrane, whereas mechanism (3) does not.

portasome-bearing apical membranes for transport to occur
there seems to be some selective advantage for such an association, possibly as a mechanism for alkalinization as suggested
in Section VI. In all cases where it has been examined the
lumen is electrically positive to the cells and the blood side
when potassium transport is dominating, even in the *Schisto-
cera* rectum where the potassium transport is toward the blood.
In the rectum it has not been conclusively demonstrated that
the apical membrane is the site of active potassium transport.

B. Isolation of portasomes

This body of evidence implicating portasomes in potassium
transport suggests that it would be worthwhile to isolate them
and to test directly their potassium transporting capabilities. They are similar in size to the F1 ATPase particles of
mitochondria, for which isolation methods are well known.
Taking advantage of the abundant portasomes in the absence of
closely associated mitochondria in posterior *Manduca* midgut,
Cioffi and Wolfersberger (unpublished data) were able to prepare fractions containing just the apical plasma membrane from
goblet cells with particles intact and the basal plasma membranes from both goblet and columnar cells. K-modulated ATP-
ase activity was enriched in this fraction. Further purification and characterization of the portasomes is under way.

VI. MULTIPLE POTASSIUM PUMP HYPOTHESIS

The working hypothesis diagrammed as Figure 2 utilizes
the facts that mitochondria are closely associated with portasomes in the transporting cells of anterior and middle midgut,
Malpighian tubules, and many rectal epithelial cells whereas
no such close association occurs in posterior midgut, salivary
glands, and rectal papillae (Table 1). Three mechanisms for
active K transport, all located in the apical membrane are
postulated. Mechanism (1) A K^+, H^+ exchange across the basal
membrane coupled to an active K^+, HCO_3^- active transport
driven by metabolically produced CO_2. The bicarbonate ions
leave the mitochondria via the closely associated portasomes
and diffuse into the goblet cavity bringing K^+ ions along
electrostatically. Mechanism (2) A K^+, H^+ exchange across the
basal membrane coupled to an active K^+, OH^- active transport
driven by a chemiosmotically produced proton gradient. The
hydroxyl ions leave the mitochondria via the closely associated portasomes and diffuse into the goblet cavity bringing
K^+ ions along electrostatically. These two mechanisms can

only occur in anterior and middle midgut and in other cases in which mitochondria are closely associated with a portasome-studded membrane. Both would make the lumen either negative or neutral to the cell and both render the lumen alkaline to the blood side without affecting cellular pH. Mechanism (3) A K^+, electrogenic active transport utilizing an ATPase reaction in the portasome. The mitochondria need not be close to the portasome, the ATP being able to diffuse from mitochondria to portasome and the ADP and Pi to diffuse back. The potassium movement renders the lumen positive to the cell enabling potassium to enter replacing that pumped out. It also renders the lumen positive to the blood side, electrostatically attracting anions via the easiest route, probably between the cells.

The following observations are explained by the hypothesis. (1) The contents of anterior and middle midgut are more alkaline than those of posterior midgut (Harvey and Cioffi, unpublished data). In general the midgut contents of plant eating insects is highly alkaline whereas the blood is mildly acidic (VBW 1972. The Principles of Insect Physiology). The potassium rich fluid secreted by labial glands is alkaline (Kafatos, 1968). The fluid secreted by Malpighian tubules is alkaline. However the lumen of the rectum (in which potassium is transported toward the blood) is highly acidic (Ramsay, 1956). (2) The apical plasma membrane is impermeable to potassium (Harvey & Zerahn, 1969) and probably to protons (lumen pH 10 - 11, cell pH probably 6 - 7) and the portasome provides a polar pathway for K^+ and HCO_3^- in the bicarbonate route and for K^+ and OH^- in the chemiosmotic proton route. In the ATPase route the portasome also constitutes an ATPase with a polar head to react with the polar ATP and an apolar tail to insert into the membrane, as well as providing a route for the potassium ion through the apical membrane. (3) The bicarbonate route accounts for the inhibition of the short circuit current by carbonic anhydrase inhibitors (Haskell et al., 1965) and utilizes the carbonic anhydrase of the midgut (Jungreis, personal communication). (4) The hypothesis explains why an F1 ATPase can be separated from the K ATPase in posterior midgut but not in anterior and middle midgut (Wolfersberger, 1979).

The remaining observations are explained by the ATPase route alone but are compatible with a multiple route. (5) The hypothesis accounts for the six to eight potassium ions transported per oxygen molecule deduced by Harvey et al. (1967). (6) It accounts for the large, lumen positive, PD of the midgut in oxygen, its tight coupling to oxygen consumption, and its rapid loss in nitrogen since the ATPase propels K^+ across the membrane and the neutralizing ion follows. The lag between cytochrome reduction and K pump shut-down in nitrogen is accounted for by the measured ATP pool (Mandel et al., 1980). (7) The hypothesis accounts for a generalized anion pump (Maddrell, 1977) because whatever anion is able to cross the epithelium most easily will neutralize the electrogenically transported potassium. If phosphate moves most easily then the preference of midgut, salivary glands, and Malpighian tubules for this ion (references in Harvey, 1980) is explained. (8) The hypothesis also explains basal K entry into the cells and may eliminate the need to consider chloride entry into the cells against an electrochemical gradient if the anion movement turns out to be extracellular. (9) Finally, the hypothesis suggests that the portasome must contain both a K-ionphore (Jungreis and Blondin, 1977) and an anion-ionophore, a K-affinity site, and a K-modulated, oligomycin-insensitive ATPase (Wolfersberger, 1979).

ACKNOWLEDGEMENTS

    I thank Dr. Moira Cioffi for many critical discussions, for the literature search for Table 1, and for assistance in preparing the figures, Dr. Michael G. Wolfersberger for his critical reading of the manuscript, and Mrs. Emily Feinberg for preparation of the "camera ready" draft.

REFERENCES

Anderson, E. and Harvey, W.R. (1966). Active transport by
    the *Cecropia* midgut. II. Fine structure of the midgut
    epithelium. *J. Cell Biol. 31:* 107-134.
Berridge, M.J. and Fain, J.N. (1979). Inhibition of phospha-
    tidylinositol synthesis and the inactivation of calcium
    entry after prolonged exposure of the blowfly salivary
    gland to 5-hydroxytryptamine. *Biochem. J. 178:* 59-69.
Berridge, M.J. and Gupta, B.L. (1968). Fine structural lo-
    calization of adenosine triphosphatase in the rectum of
    Calliphora. J. Cell Sci. 3: 17-32.
Berridge, M.J., Lindley, B.D., and Prince, W.T. (1975). Mem-
    brane permeability changes during stimulation of iso-
    lated salivary glands of *Calliphora* by 5-hydroxytrypt-
    amine. *J. Physiol. 244:* 549-567.
Berridge, M.J. and Oschman, J.L. (1969). A structural basis
    for fluid secretion by Malpighian tubules. *Tissue &
    Cell 1:* 247-272.
Berridge, M.J. and Prince W.T. (1972). Transepithelial po-
    tential changes during stimulation of isolated salivary
    glands with 5-hydroxytryptamine and cyclic AMP. *J. Exp.
    Biol. 56:* 139-153.
Blankemeyer, J.T. and Harvey, W.R. (1978). Identification of
    active cell in potassium transporting epithelium. *J.
    Exp. Biol. 77:* 1-13.
Cioffi, M. (1979). The morphology and fine structure of the
    larval midgut of a moth *(Manduca sexta)* in relation to
    active ion transport. *Tissue and Cell 11:* 467-479.
Gupta, B.L. and Berridge, M.J. (1966). Fine structural
    organization of the rectum in the blowfly, *"Calliphora
    erythrocephala"* (Meig.) with special reference to con-
    nective tissue, tracheae and neurosecretory innervation
    in the rectal papillae. *J. Morphol. 20:* 23-82.
Gupta, B.L, Berridge, M.J., Hall, T.A., and Moreton, R.B.
    (1978). Electron microprobe and ion-selective micro-
    electrode studies of fluid secretion in the salivary
    glands of *Calliphora. J. Exp. Biol. 72:* 261-284.
Harvey, W.R. (1980). Membrane physiology of insects. In
    Membrane Physiology of Invertebrates, R.P. Podesta and
    S.F. Timmers (Eds.). Marcel Dekker, New York (In press).
Harvey, W.R., Haskell, J.A., and Zerahn, K. (1967). Active
    transport of potassium and oxygen consumption in the
    isolated midgut of *Hyalophora cecropia. J. Exp. Biol.
    46:* 235-248.

Harvey, W.R. and Nedergaard, S. (1964). Sodium independent active transport of potassium in the isolated midgut of the *Cecropia* silkworm. *Proc. Nat. Acad. Sci. USA 51:* 757-765.

Harvey, W.R. and Wolfersberger, M.G. (1979). Mechanism of inhibition of active potassium transport in isolated midgut of *Manduca sexta* by *Bacillus thuringiensis* endotoxin. *J. Exp. Biol. 83:* 293-304.

Harvey, W.R. and Zerahn, K. (1969). Kinetics and route of active K-transport in the isolated midgut of *Hyalophora cecropia*. *J. Exp. Biol. 50:* 297-306.

Harvey, W.R. and Zerahn, K. (1972). Active transport of potassium and other alkali metals by the isolated midgut of the silkworm. In *Current Topics in Membranes and Transport,* vol. III, F. Bronner and A. Kleinzeller (Eds.). Academic Press, New York and London, pp. 367-410.

Haskell, J.A., Clemons, R.D., and Harvey, W.R. (1965). Active transport by the *Cecropia* midgut. I. Inhibitors, stimulants, and potassium transport. *J. Cell. Comp. Physiol. 65:* 45-55.

Hill, A.E. (1977). General mechanisms of salt-water coupling in epithelia. In *Transport of Ions and Water in Animals.* B.L. Gupta, J.L. Oschman, R.B. Moreton and B.J. Wall (Eds.). Academic Press, London, New York, pp. 183-214.

Hoshiko, T. and Moore, L.E. (1978). Fluctuation analysis of epithelial membrane kinetics. In *Membrane Transport Processes,* Vol. I., J.F. Hoffman (Ed). Raven Press, New York, pp. 179-198.

Irvine, H.B. (1969). Sodium and potassium secretion by isolated insect Malpighian tubules. *Amer. J. Physiol. 217:* 1520-1527.

Jungreis, A.M. (1977). Comparative aspects of invertebrate epithelial transport. In *Water Relations in Membrane Transport in Plants and Animals,* A.M. Jungreis, T.K. Hodges, A. Kleinzeller and S.G. Schultz (Eds.). Academic Press, New York and London, pp. 89-96.

Jungreis, A.M. and Blondin, G.A. (1977). Presence of electrogenic potassium specific intrinsic ionophore in plasma membranes of larval Lepidopteran midgut epithelium. *Fed. Proc. 36:* 484a.

Jungreis, A.M. and Harvey, W.R. (1975). Role of active potassium transport by integumentary epithelium in secretion of larval-pupal moulting fluid during silk moth development. *J. Exp. Biol. 62:* 357-366.

Kafatos, F.C. (1968). The labial gland: a salt-secreting organ of saturniid moths. *J. Exp. Biol. 48:* 435-453.

Maddrell, S.H.P. (1971). The mechanisms of insect excretory systems. In *Advances in Insect Physiology 8*, J.W.L. Beament, J.E. Treherne, and V.B. Wigglesworth (Eds.). Academic Press, London & New York, pp. 199-331.

Maddrell, S.H.P. (1977). Insect Malpighian tubules. In *Transport of Ions and Water in Animals*, B.L. Gupta, R.B. Moreton, J.L. Oschman, and B.J. Wall (Eds.). Academic Press, London, pp. 541-569.

Mandel, L.J., Riddle, T.G., and Storey, J.M. (1980). Role of ATP in respiratory control and active transport in tobacco hornworm midgut. *Amer. J. Physiol.* (In press).

Merideth, J. and Phillips, J.E. (1973). Rectal ultrastructure in salt- and freshwater mosquito larvae in relation to physiological state. *Z. Zellforsch. 138:* 1-22.

Moffett, D.F. (1979). Potassium activity of single insect midgut cells. *Amer. Zoologist 19:* 996.

Nedergaard, S. (1977). Amino Acid Transport. In *Transport of Ions and Water in Animals*, B.L. Gupta, R.B. Moreton, J.L. Oschman and B.J. Wall (Eds.). Academic Press, London, New York, San Francisco, pp. 239-264.

Noirot, C. and Noirot-Timothée, C. (1970). Revêtement particulaire de la membrane plasmique et absorption dans le rectum des insectes. *7° Congrès Int. Microsc. Electronique Grenoble,* Vol *3:* 37-38.

Noirot, C. and Noirot-Timothée, C. (1971). Ultrastructure du proctodeum chez le Thysanoure *Lepismodes inquillinus* Newman *(Thermobia domestica Packard)* II. Le sac anal. *J. Ultrastruct. Res. 37:* 335-350.

Noirot, C., Noiret-Timothée, C., and Kovoor, J. (1967). Revêtement particulaire de la membrane plasmatique en rapport avec l'excretion dans une région specialisie de l'intestin moyen des Termites superieurs. *C. R. Acad. Sci. Paris 264:* 722-725.

Oschman, J.L. and Berridge, M.J. (1970). Structural and functional aspects of salivary fluid secretion in *Calliphora. Tissue & Cell 2:* 281-310.

Oschman, J.L. and Wall, B.J. (1969). The structure of the rectal pads of *Periplaneta americana* L. with regard to fluid transport. *J. Morphol. 127:* 475-509.

Phillips, J.E. (1977). Excretion in insects: function of gut and rectum in concentrating and diluting the urine. *Fed. Proc. 36:* 2480-2486.

Quatrale, P.R. (1966). Cation concentration charges during development of the silkworm, *Hyalophora cecropia.* Ph.D. thesis, University of Massachusetts.

Ramsay, J.A. (1953). Active transport of potassium by the Malpighian tubules of insects. *J. Exp. Biol. 30:* 358-369.

Ramsay, J.A. (1954). Active transport of water by the Malpig-
    hian tubules of the stick insect, *Dixippus morosus*
    (Orthoptera, Phasmidae). *J. Exp. Biol. 31:* 104-113.
Ramsay, J.A. (1956). Excretion by the Malpighian tubules of
    the stick insect, *Dixippus morosus* (Orthoptera, Phas-
    midae): calcium, magnesium, chloride, phosphate and
    hydrogen ions. *J. Exp. Biol. 33:* 697-708.
Ramsay, J.A. (1958). Excretion by the Malpighian tubules of
    the stick insect, *Dixippus morosus,* (Orthoptera, Phas-
    midae): amino acids, sugars and urea. *J. Exp. Biol. 35:*
    871-891.
Ramsay, J.A. (1976). The rectal complex in the larvae of
    Lepidoptera. *Phil. Trans. Roy. Soc. Lon. 274:* 203-226.
Ryerse, J.S. (1977). Control of mitochondrial movement during
    development of insect Malpighian tubules. *Proc. Microsc.*
    Soc. Can. 4: 48-49.
Smith, D.S. (1969). The fine structure of haltere sensilla in
    the blowfly, *Calliphora erythrocephala* with scanning
    electron microscopic observations on the haltere surface.
    Tissue & Cell 1: 443-484.
Smith, D.S. Compher, K., Janners, M., Lipton, C., and Wittle,
    L.W. (1969). Cellular organization and ferritin uptake
    in the midgut epithelium of a moth *Ephestia kühniella.*
    J. Morphol. 127: 41-72.
Stobbart, R.H. and Shaw, J. (1974). Salt and water balance;
    Excretion. In *The Physiology of Insecta* 2nd Edition,
    Vol. V, M. Rockstein (Ed.). Academic Press, Inc., New
    York and London, pp. 361-446.
Treherne, J.E. (1967). Gut absorption. *Annu. Rev. Entomol.*
    12: 43-58.
Ussing, H.H. (1977). Prelude. In *Transport of Ions and Water*
    in Animals, B.L. Gupta, R.B. Moreton, J.L. Oschman, and
    B.J. Wall (Eds.). Academic Press, London, New York, San
    Francisco, pp. 9-11.
Williams, D., Phillips, J.E., Prince, W.T., and Meredith, J.
    (1978). The source of short-circuit current across
    locust rectum. *J. Exp. Biol. 77:* 107-122.
Wigglesworth, V.B. (1931f). The physiology of excretion in a
    blood-sucking insect, *Rhodnius prolixus* (Hemiptera,
    Reduviidae). *J. Exp. Biol., 8:* 428-442.
Wigglesworth, V.B. (1932). On the function of the so-called
    'rectal glands' of insects. *Quart. J. Microsc. Sci. 75:*
    131-150.
Wigglesworth, V.B. (1934). *Insect Physiology.* Methuen,
    London, 134 pp.
Wigglesworth, V.B. (1948). The insect as a medium for the
    study of physiology. *Proc. Roy. Soc. London B. 23:*
    430-446.

Wigglesworth, V.B. (1972). *The Principles of Insect Physio-
    logy*. Chapman and Hall, London, Halsted Press, New York,
    827 pp.
Wolfersberger, M.G. (1979). A potassium-modulated plasma
    membrane adenosine triphosphatase from the midgut of
    Manduca sexta larvae. *Fed. Proc. 38:* 242.
Wolfersberger, M.G. and Harvey, W.R. (1980). Transepithelial
    potassium transport in insect midgut by an electrogenic
    alkali metal ion pump. In *Current Topics in Membranes
    and Transport*, F. Bronner and A. Kleinzeller (Eds.)
    Academic Press, New York and London (In press).
Wood, J.L., Farrand, P.S., and Harvey, W.R. (1969). Active
    transport of potassium by the *Cecropia* midgut VI. Micro-
    electrode potential profile. *J. Exp. Biol. 50:* 169–178.
Wood, J.L. and Harvey, W.R. (1976). Active transport of cal-
    cium across the isolated midgut of *Hyalophora cecropia*.
    J. Exp. Biol. 65: 347–360.
Zerahn, K. (1977). Potassium transport in insect midgut. In
    Transport of Ions and Water in Animals, B.L. Gupta, R.B.
    Moreton, J.L. Oschman, and B.J. Wall (Eds.). Academic
    Press, London, New York, San Francisco, pp. 381–401.
Zerahn, K. (1978). Transport across insect gut epithelium.
    In *Membrane Transport in Biology III, Transport Across
    Multimembrane Systems*, G. Giebisch, D.C. Tosteson, H.H.
    Ussing (Eds.). Springer-Verlag, Berlin, Heidelberg, New
    York, pp. 273–306.

WATER TRANSPORT BY ELECTROOSMOSIS

Josef Küppers
Ulrich Thurm

Department of Zoology
University of Münster
Münster, FR Germany

I. INTRODUCTION

Water has been observed to move against an osmotic gradient (hyposmotic transport) in numerous terrestrial insects.
In extreme cases such water transport may be capable of gaining water vapour from the air at a relative humidity (r.h.)
below 50 %, which means the surmounting of an osmotic gradient
of more than 10^8 Pa (1000 bar). General reviews of this ability of insects and other arthropods and its significance for
conservation of body water have been presented recently by
Noble-Nesbitt (1977), Edney (1977), and Machin (1979 a).
Isosmotic fluid transport, especially as observed in vertebrate epithelia, led to the formulation of the "double membrane" model (Curran, 1960) and the "standing gradient osmotic
flow" model (Diamond and Bossert, 1967). The latter especially
gave rise to several detailed mathematical analyses and evoked
an intense and partly controversial discussion (Diamond, 1971;
Hill, 1975, 1977; Skadhauge, 1977). Attempts to apply the
"standing gradient" theory also to the hyposmotic water transport in insects did not lead to a complete and consistent concept (Wall, 1977).
Our own approach to the problem of hyposmotic transport
was stimulated by the remarkably simple as well as extremely
specialized organization of the epithelium which builds the
posterior rectum of Lepismatidae as described by Noirot and
Noirot-Timothée (1971). The structural organization of its
single type of cells relates this epithelium to the tormogen
cells of insect sensilla which we studied for their ion-trans-

port contribution to receptor physiology. This rectal epithelium promised to be a model for the functional properties of
the tormogen cells (see Thurm and Küppers, this volume).

The same epithelium had been clearly demonstrated by
Noble-Nesbitt (1969, 1970, 1975) to be capable of one of the
most powerful uphill transports of water known, as it sur-
mounts a chemical potential difference of about $1.1 \cdot 10^8$ Pa
taking up water from $\geq$ 45 % r.h.. However, no satisfying concept was known to explain this extreme capability. From the
physiological and morphological reasons illustrated below it
seems evident that no mechanism based on local osmosis could
account for this uphill water flux (cf. Noble-Nesbitt, 1977;
Phillips, 1977).

If the structural analogies to tormogen cells hold true,
the apical membrane configuration of these rectal epithelial
cells suggests an intense electrogenic K^+-outward transport
(see below). The structural conditions of this transport
appear to be most appropriate to generate an extremely high
apical membrane voltage and thus a very high transepithelial
potential difference, as judged again from our experience in
sensilla (cf. Thurm, 1974). This electrical feature therefore
could be expected to be functionally significant as well as
experimentally salient.

Following these suggestions, we arrived at a model of
electroosmotic water transfer, a model which, in addition to
these electrical consequences of a special ion-transport, in
principle only needs the presence of ion selective channels
as they are known to occur in biomembranes. Our experimental
work, which was encouraged by this model and which is reported
here, has indeed revealed the presence of a powerful voltage
generating ion-transport and of appropriate ion-water coupling
pores. *)

Lepisma saccharina was used for the experiments (which ran
at night around the experimental setup). In addition to the
morphological description of the posterior rectum (= anal sac)
of *Thermobia* reported by Noirot and Noirot-Timothée (1971) we
needed some quantitative structural data and had to check upon
the morphological predictions following from the model. We
therefore performed a systematic morphological study of the
anal sac of *Lepisma* parallel to the physiological measurements
(Neuhaus et al., 1978; Thurm and Neuhaus, in prep.). As in
Thermobia, the morphology of the anal sac proves to be simple
when compared to the water absorbing recta of other insects,
e.g. that of the cockroach (Oschman and Wall, 1969) or, parti-

*) *Short reports of the results have been published by Plage-
mann, Küppers and Thurm (1978) and Küppers, Plagemann and
Thurm (1979).*

cularly, the complex cryptonephric system of *Tenebrio*
(Ramsay, 1964; Saini, 1964; Grimstone et al., 1968).

II. STRUCTURE

As in *Thermobia* the posterior rectum of *Lepisma* is constituted by a folded monolayered epithelium (E) (Fig. 1). The extended subcuticular space (Sc) is anteriorly and posteriorly
closed by tight contact between the cuticle (C) and specialized epithelial cells, called sheath cells by Noirot et al.
(1979). A tightly closing sphincter (S) separates the narrow
air-filled lumen (L) from the anterior rectum (R).

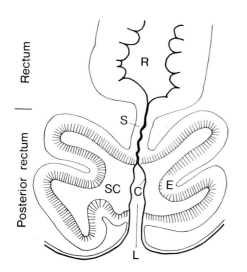

Fig. 1
Scheme of a longitudinal
section through the termi-
nal region of the gut of
Lepisma *(R: rectum, S:*
sphincter, E: epithelium
of the posterior rectum,
C: cuticle, SC: subcuticu-
lar space, L: lumen of the
posterior rectum).

The water transporting epithelium is composed of a single
type of cells (Fig. 2). The intercellular spaces are closed
by highly convoluted septate junctions (sj). The baso-lateral
membrane facing the haemolymph has no special differentiations.
Basal infoldings are poorly developed, and never associated
with mitochondria. Lateral complexes, the close association between mitochondria and folds of the lateral membrane (often
found within other insect recta and so suggestive of a standing gradient flow), are completely lacking.
The apical membrane is deeply folded and closely associated with elongated mitochondria. As a result of folding, the
apical membrane area is about 180 times that of the basal membrane, and the membrane-mitochondria complex accounts for about
80 % of the cell volume. A subcuticle covers the apical mem-

brane and a glycocalyx fills the narrow clefts between the lamellae. Both are high in polyanions as is the thin cuticle of
the posterior rectum (ruthenium red staining).

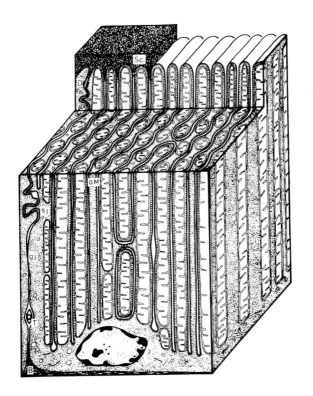

*Fig. 2
Ultrastructural or-
ganization of the
epithelial cells of
the posterior rec-
tum of* Lepisma
*(drawing by G. Neu-
haus) (aM: particle
coated apical mem-
brane, B: basement
membrane, D: desmo-
some, sj: septate
junction, gj: gap
junction, Sc: sub-
cuticle, T: trache-
ole).*

A cross section through the lamellae (Fig. 3) reveals
that mitochondria and folded membrane are associated in a maximally dense arrangement; the extracellular space between the
leaflets has a width of about 10 nm. The cytoplasmic surface
of the membrane is coated with 12 nm particles. This special
membrane configuration has been found in various organs of insects known to transport potassium (Gupta and Berridge, 1966;
Oschman and Wall, 1969; Anderson and Harvey, 1966; Smith, 1969;
Thurm 1970; Jungreis, 1977, and others). In studies of lepidopteran goblet cells (Harvey and Nedergaard, 1964; Wood et
al., 1969; Blankemeyer and Harvey, 1978) and cockroach tormogen cells (Thurm, 1974; Küppers and Thurm, 1979; Küppers, unpublished measurements, see Thurm and Küppers, this volume) it
has been demonstrated that this is the type of membrane which
bears a ouabain insensitive cation pump. This pump transfers

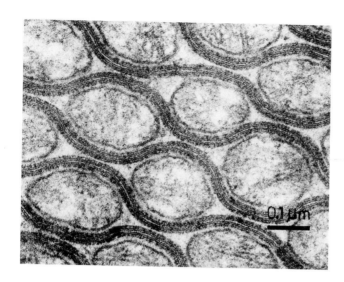

*Fig. 3
Cross-section
through the
folds of the
apical mem-
brane of the
posterior
rectum of
Lepisma (elec-
tron micro-
graph by G.
Neuhaus.*

potassium ions in a purely electrogenic manner from the cytoplasm to the extracellular space. Since the specifity of this
pump is low, it may also be responsible for sodium transport
in some situations as Maddrell (1977) suggests.

III. MODEL

From both the structure and the performance of the posterior rectum of *Lepisma*, some general postulates can be deduced
which an adequate hypothesis concerning the underlying mechanism has to satisfy (cf. Fig. 4).

A water potential gradient which may be up to 10^8 Pa (water potential of air at 48 % r.h. $\cong -10^8$ Pa minus water potential of haemolymph $\cong -1.4 \cdot 10^6$ Pa) exists across the whole
system. Against this gradient, water flow is to be observed.

At the border between air and subcuticular space, i.e.
across the cuticle, only a downhill flow of water should be expected. This means that within the subcuticular space and perhaps the cuticle a hygroscopic material is to be expected, condensing water from the air, and thus supplying water in the
liquid phase to the active step.

The uphill transfer itself should occur across the apical
membrane, since further passive flow would imply that the cytoplasm of the cells, or at least a part of it, has to be in equilibrium with air of less than 50 % r.h., hardly imaginable for

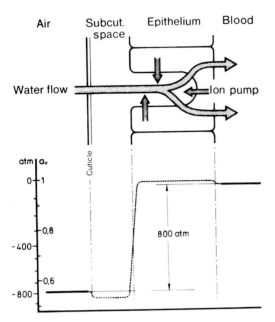

Fig. 4
Suggested course of
water potential across
the epithelium of the
anal sac.

Profile of water potential

a metabolically active tissue. This localization of the site
of water transport is corroborated too by the arrangement of
the mitochondria. At the baso-lateral membrane, we assume a
passive flow, since mitochondria or other characteristic morphological differentiations are lacking at this site.

The following model of the active step of water transfer
has been developed (for illustration cf. Fig. 5), taking into
account the considerations above and the morphological features
of the organ.

The apical membrane of the epithelium is assumed to bear
a cation pump of the type outlined above, transferring cations
(probably potassium) into the subcuticular space and thus generating a voltage across the apical membrane and the epithelium (subcuticular space positive). Since the paracellular
pathways between subcuticular space and haemolymph seem to be
of high resistance, the final consequence of the ion pump will
be the circulation of the transported ion species through the
apical membrane, rather than a transepithelial current. We suggest that the voltage driven cation-flow from the subcuticular
space back into the cell may be coupled with water flow by
electroosmosis.

For a general and detailed mathematical description of
electroosmotic phenomena see Hill (1975) or Rosenberg and Finkelstein (1978). In this context we may confine ourselves to a

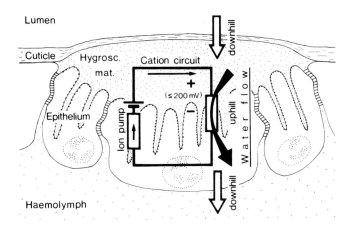

Fig. 5
Illustration
of the elec-
troosmotic
model pro-
posed.

few basic relations which describe electroosmotic water flow
through narrow ion-selective channels. A current (I) passing
such channels will induce an electroosmotic volume flow (J_{ve})
which depends on the concentration of the permeating charges
(c_pF; c_p = ion concentration, F = Faraday constant) within the
lumen of the pore: $J_{ve} = I/c_pF$. A (hydrostatic or osmotic)
pressure difference represents a driving force for ions which
generates an electrokinetic potential (E) given by $E = P/c_pF$.
Reciprocally, a driving voltage generates a pressure according
to $P = Ec_pF$.

   At the posterior rectum of Lepisma, the coupling ratio between ions and water $I/J_{ve} = c_pF$ may be determined by electroosmotic experiments. In order to examine whether electroosmotic phenomena will account for the gradient surmounted and the
volume flow observed, this coupling ratio has to be related to
the driving force generated by the animal and the ionic current
which may be expected.

IV. EXPERIMENTAL *)

A. The Water Uptake Capabilities of Lepisma

   Weighing experiments, similar to those reported by Noble-
Nesbitt for Thermobia (1970), were performed at Lepisma to
establish that this species is able to absorb water from sub-

*) Methods and the most essential results are reported only
   briefly. More detailed information will be given by Küppers,
   Plagemann and Thurm (in prep.).

saturated air and to obtain quantitative data on the uptake
rate *in vivo*.

A representative result is demonstrated in Fig. 6. Animals
dehydrated at 32 % r.h. for three days without access to food
loose about 20 % of their body weight during this period by
starvation and transpiration. Replaced to air of about 70 %
r.h. (Fig. 6 A), they gain within two days 95 % of their initial weight. Weight loss by starvation and (reduced) transpiration, however, further continues when the anus is sealed
with silicone rubber (Fig. 6 B). From the difference of both
curves and the average weight of the animals ($\cong$ 9 mg) the rate
of water uptake is calculated to be 50-60 nl/h ($\cong 1.5 \cdot 10^{-15} m^3/s$)
during the first day.

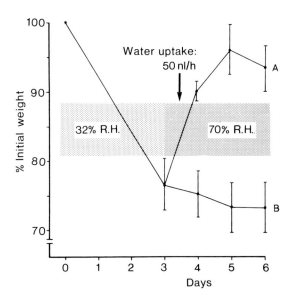

Fig. 6
*Weight loss and gain
of* Lepisma *at 32 % r.h.
and 70 % r.h., resp.,
with anus open: A, and
anus sealed: B.*

Against the background of the more sophisticated investigations of Noble-Nesbitt (1975) with the nearly related species
Thermobia domestica, we read these results as evidence that the
posterior rectum is the site of water uptake by *Lepisma*. Further evidence on this topic follows from experiments reported
below.

B. On the Subcuticular Material

The physical properties and chemical nature of the material filling the subcuticular space are being investigated.

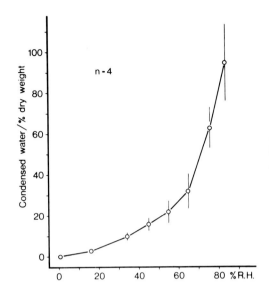

Fig. 7
Water absorption by the
subcuticular material.

There are some preliminary results obtained in collaboration
with M. Volbers for the genus *Thermobia*.

A fluid material was obtained from the subcuticular space
by piercing the internal cuticle of the posterior rectum with
a bevelled micro-pipette. The samples weighed 10^{-8} to 10^{-7} g.
Their hygroscopic properties were examined by means of a conventional quartz-fiber balance (cf. Neuhoff, 1973), modified
by mounting an inlet- and an outlet-nozzle onto the cage. A
stream of air, equilibrated with saturated solutions of various
electrolytes, allowed defined changes to the relative humidity.

The relative weight change of the subcuticular material
versus relative humidity is plotted in Fig. 7. Water absorption
starts from zero humidity and resembles closely that of glycerol though the material is certainly not identical with it, as
revealed by gas chromatography. It generally contains some cry-
stallizing material and it may be that its composition and its
hygroscopic properties change with the adaptation of the animal to different humidities.

Two conclusions can already be drawn from these results: A
substance is present within the subcuticular space which is
well suited to absorb water vapour. It is apparently not the
solubility of this material that determines the critical equilibrium humidity of water uptake in *Thermobia* (45 %).

C. *Electrical Parameters and Electroosmotic Measurements*

According to the model, the voltage at the apical membrane
is the driving force for the water uptake, and the current
across that membrane determines the volume flow. Both parameters are only accessible by intracellular measurements which
would also allow the determination of the conductance of the
apical membrane and by this a description of the mechanism in
terms of quantitative flux coefficients.

For the first experimental examination of the model we
chose the much simpler method of transepithelial measurements,
which centered around two main topics: (i) measurements of the
voltage (TEV) and short circuit current (SCC) at the epithelium
of the posterior rectum to yield some evidence for the presence
of a potent electrogenic transport mechanism driving the cation
circuit and (ii) observation of transepithelial water flow in
relation to an exogenous transepithelial current to reveal the
occurence and the properties of ion-water coupling channels.

1. *Methods*. A scheme of the experimental setup designed for
that purpose is presented in Fig. 8. Double barrelled electrodes were inserted into the lumen of the posterior rectum and
into the haemolymph space. They allowed voltage and current
measurements and the application of an exogenous current. Water
flow was indicated by the movement of an air bubble within a
calibrated cannula connected to one barrel of the different
electrode. The lumen of the posterior rectum was filled with
electrolyte from the electrodes (0.5 mol/l KCl) before sealing
the system at the anus with silicone rubber. The animal was enclosed in a small perspex chamber; substituting air by CO_2 or
N_2, the oxidative metabolism could be reversibly blocked.

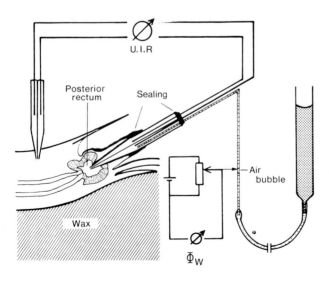

*Fig. 8
Scheme of the ex-
perimental setup.*

2. Voltage and Current. The transepithelial voltage at the beginning of the experiments was usually between 100 and 200 mV, the lumen being positive; the average TEV was 155 ± 25 mV (disregarding those animals which were in the moulting phase and exhibited no significant voltage). It ordinarily declined during the first hour of experiments to values around 100 mV. The dependence of the measured voltage on electrode position reveals that it is generated by the epithelium of the posterior rectum. When the TEV was clamped to zero a SCC was recorded with a mean of 4 ± 1 µA (maximum 9 µA); its time course resembled that of the voltage.

TEV and SCC acutely depend on oxidative metabolism. Substitution of air by N_2 or CO_2 causes a reversible decay of both parameters to values near zero. The rapid increase of TEV and SCC at the end of anoxia especially suggests an electrogenic transport mechanism to be the voltage source rather than a diffusion potential (cf. Thurm and Küppers, this volume).

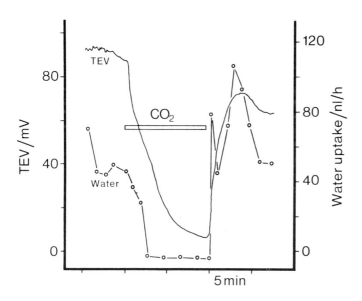

Fig. 9 Dependence of transepithelial voltage (TEV) and of water uptake on oxidative metabolism.

3. Water Uptake. The rate of water uptake during unclamped TEV averaged 55 ± 12 nl/h ($\cong$ (1.5 ± 0.3) · 10^{-15} m³/s); it corresponds to that calculated from weighing experiments. From experiments using electrolyte stained by Procion blue we conclude that this volume flow takes place across the epithelium of the anal sac and that the sphincter remains closed at least for most of the time during these experiments since the dye accumulates in the lumen (Procion blue does not pass cyto-membranes).

As with the TEV, water uptake also depends on metabolism
(Fig. 9). This behaviour demonstrates that the flow observed
is an active one depending on metabolism. Furthermore it yields
the most direct evidence that the posterior rectum bears a potent water transport mechanism.

If - as *in vivo* - volume flow represents the flow of pure
water, it follows that the concentration of the electrolyte
within the lumen will increase. From uptake rate, diffusion
constants and geometry of the electrode tip, it is calculated
that a 0.5 mol/l KCl solution should be concentrated to saturation within the first few minutes of the experiment. That means
that the water flow observed occurred against a constant osmotic gradient corresponding to 84 % r.h..

4. Electroosmosis. Spontaneous water uptake can be increased and decreased by an exogenous transepithelial current
(TEC). The relation between water flow and TEC is shown in
Fig. 10. At an outward current of about 10 μA, volume flow
ceases. On average the slope of this relation is 5.5 ± 1 nl/μAh
($\cong$ (1.5 ± 0.3) $\cdot$ 10^{-9} m^3/As). This corresponds to the flow of
7 water molecules together with one ion or to the flow of a
fluid with a charge concentration of 7 eq/l ($\cong$ 7 $\cdot$ 10^8 As/m^3).

The slope measured in the state of metabolic block when
spontaneous uptake has ceased is not significantly different.
In other words: with respect to water uptake, metabolic activity can be replaced by an inward current of about 10 μA.

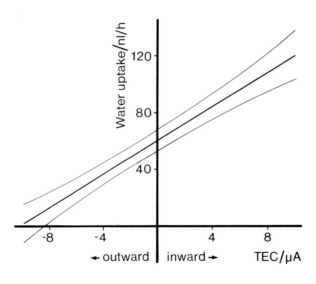

Fig. 10
Relation between
an exogenous
transepithelial
current (TEC) and
volume flow
(95 % confidence
interval given).

V. EVALUATION

The arrangement of the mitochondria (cf. Fig. 2) and the magnitude of the SCC leave little doubt that the source of the high TEV is located in the large area of the deeply folded apical membrane of the rectal epithelium. Since the voltage is most likely generated by an electrogenic ion transport mechanism (suggested by the response of the TEV to anoxia and by the structural analogies mentioned above), the driving force for an electroosmotic water transfer will correspond to the metabolism dependent part of the TEV, that means it may be up to 200 mV.

The transepithelial SCC indicates a rather powerful transport mechanism. But this transepithelially measured value must be much lower than a SCC measured across the apical membrane would be, since the cuticle and especially the resistance and voltage of the basal membrane prevent the adjustment of short circuit conditions at the apical membrane. The cation inward current *in vivo* cannot be calculated since the conductance of the ion channels of the apical membrane system is unknown. One can expect, however, that it exceeds a value of 10 μA.

Water flow observed in electroosmotic experiments is certainly not an artifact caused by "transport number effects" (Barry and Hope, 1969): by selective cation permeability of the apical membrane, an inward current will elevate the concentration in the cell. An estimate of the size of this effect on the basis of the current density in the mitochonria-free plasm of the lamellae and on a restricted diffusion constant for potassium, suggests that it should not exceed some ten mosm. This increase reduces the outward directed water gradient by only a negligible amount.

The coupling ratio revealed by electroosmotic experiments is close to that found for cation selective gramicidin A channels. Rosenberg and Finkelstein (1978) demonstrated by electrokinetic and electroosmotic experiments that the coupling ratio in such channels is 5 - 6 H_2O/cation ($\cong 10^9$ As/m^3). From a completely different approach Schagina et al. (1978) obtained a rather similar result. (As fixed charges or dipoles are essential for ion selectivity of membrane channels, one might expect that the charge concentration within a channel would in general be rather high.) Our assumption that the ion water coupling structures found in the posterior rectum of *Lepisma* are constituents of the apical membrane instead of the cuticle or the basal membrane derives from the plausibility of the model; electroosmotic experiments as performed yield no direct information on this topic.

From the coupling ratio determined for these structures, it follows according to $P = Ec_DF$ (see above) that a water gradient of 10^8 Pa ($\cong 50$ % r.h.) will be surmounted by a driving force of about 140 mV, and that an inward current of > 10 µA might account for the water uptake rate observed *in vivo*. The real size of the inward current required to maintain net volume flow against the osmotic gradient - i.e. the efficiency of the transport mechanism in terms of power - depends on the pressure induced water outflow via the hydraulic permeability of the cell membrane. (In adequate terms that would apply to any other kind of water pump situated in the apical membrane.)

In this context we see a special significance in the deep membrane folds and the narrow extracellular clefts: assuming a usual conductance for the postulated cation channels, it turns out that their number will be in a range allowing their arrangement at the apices of the membrane folds. The interfold clefts could then equilibrate with the cytoplasm. At a given membrane area required for sufficient electrical energy supply, this unstirred layer effect would reduce the membrane area exposed to the huge osmotic gradient by orders of magnitude.

To sum up: We hold that the model outlined agrees with the known facts of water vapour uptake, the structural features of the organ, and the experimental results obtained so far; it is based on known and general phenomena and requires no extraordinary assumptions.

VI. COMPARATIVE CONSIDERATIONS

Ionic currents and ion selective channels are generally met with cell membranes. Since water may enter the hydrophilic lumen of ion channels, some degree of ion water coupling should be expected in any case, which means that electroosmotic or electrokinetic phenomena should be rather common. Whether they may become effective or not at a membrane or an epithelium depends on several parameters: on the voltage or pressure gradient, on the current density, and especially on the hydraulic permeability in parallel to ion channels.

For isosmotic cases of fluid transport, electroosmosis has been discussed and rejected by Diamond (1965). He calculated from streaming potentials that electroosmotic effects should be too small and, compared to the transepithelial voltage, in the wrong direction to account for the water flow observed.

Hill (1975), however, pointed out that a transepithelial voltage may not be that parameter which determines electroosmosis. The complex model he proposed for isosmotic water transport is based on electroosmotic coupling of water to the coun-

ter-ion accompanying an electrogenic transport. To achieve iso-
tonicity, however, a rather high coupling ratio between water
and ions has to be assumed.

In any case, some alternative to the standing gradient flow
seems to be needed, for instance, in the Malpighian tubules and
salivary glands of insects. These organs secrete a nearly isotonic fluid, but neither the structure nor the ionic concentrations within the channels between the microvilli of the brush
border are consistent with solute solvent coupling by this
mechanism (Gupta et al., 1976). The participation of electroosmosis in isosmotic fluid transport is a matter of current
discussions (cf. Skadhauge, 1977).

As first suggested by Wigglesworth (1932a) the resorption of
water seems to be a common function of the recta of terrestrial
insects. Regarding this water transport, which usually seems to
be a hyposmotic one, we expect that an electroosmotic water
pump of the type described is of quite general significance.
This expectation is explained by the following considerations.

According to Noirot et al. (1979), structural features of
rectal epithelia common to the least and the most complicated
cases of organization are (i) a particle coated apical membrane - folded and associated with mitochondria to a smaller
or greater degree, (ii) convoluted septate junctions at the
apical pole which suggest complete closure of the intercellular spaces, and (iii) a more or less extended, but always
closed subcuticular space. This common morphological aspect,
which attracted very little attention of physiologists to date,
represents a sufficient basis for electroosmotic water transfer.

Comparing the osmotic gradient surmounted and the structural organization of the recta of *Calliphora, Periplaneta,* and
Lepisma or *Thermobia,* for example, we cannot agree with Berridge and Oschman (1972) that "The structural complexity of the
rectal epithelium ... seems to be related to the extent to
which water can be absorbed ...", because in that sequence of
instances, just the inverse relation seems to be right. However, between the elaboration of an apical membrane-mitochondria complex and water uptake capabilities one finds a rather
close correlation.

Also physiological data corroborate an electroosmotic mechanism.
a. The observation that water uptake by insect recta is independent of net solute transfer (Phillips, 1964; Grimstone et
al., 1968) follows as a simple consequence of the model presented, without the need of additional recycling mechanisms.
b. Both the cells of cockroach rectal pads (where extended intercellular spaces with high osmotic concentrations seem to corroborate a standing gradient flow (Wall, 1971, 1977; Oschman

and Wall, 1969)) and the rectal tissue of locusts (cf. Phillips, 1977) are hyposmotic to the rectal lumen. In view of the tight appearance of the intercellular clefts, water flow by local osmosis is hardly consistent with this fact. An apical electroosmotic water pump, however, would solve that problem.
c. In the cryptonephric complex of *Tenebrio,* electroosmosis seems a probable candidate for the unknown mechanism at the rectal epithelium which moves water (vapour) from the feces into the perirectal space against a high osmotic gradient (Ramsay, 1964; Maddrell, 1971). (We hold the view that the functional concept proposed by Machin (1979 b) possibly has to be revised. This applies also to some aspects of the model developed by Grimstone et al. (1968).)

As demonstrated, electroosmotic water transport can be performed by a rather simple organization of the organ. If it represents the general basis for rectal water uptake, the question arises of what else the function of the complex compartmentalization of many rectal systems may be. We tentatively suggest that these compartments may be related to the extent to which solutes are absorbed from the feces. They may play a part in the control of solute flow since they allow the establishment of controlled electro-chemical gradients across the rectal epithelium.

Besides its function in water uptake, electroosmosis is an appropriate mechanism for the generation of those water gradients which may be used for the uphill transport of solutes by solvent drag. One example illustrates this: The rectal epithelium of the saline-water mosquito *Aedes taeniorhynchus* produces a hyperosmotic fluid (Bradley and Phillips, 1975) by which Na^+, K^+, Mg^{2+}, and Cl^- are excreted against their electro-chemical gradients. The structure of this organ (Meredith and Phillips, 1973) is in principle very similar to that of the posterior rectum of *Lepisma*. Encouraged by this structural analogy, we presume that it would not be difficult to design a working hypothesis - by the assumption of ion specific channels and by the appropriate setting of the corresponding ion water coupling ratios - which describes the secretion of such hyperosmotic fluid as a consequence of outward solvent drag with the water gradient maintained by electroosmotic water absorption. Such a mechanism would reduce the number of transport enzymes required to a single one.

Generally speaking, we think that a number of the numerous unsolved problems regarding insect rectal functions, as they have been set forth by Phillips (1977), can be solved if electroosmotic water flow maintained by an electrogenic cation transport is taken into consideration as a functional module.

Besides rectal function, we see a possible significance for electroosmotic phenomena in epidermal insect sensilla: The electrogenic potassium transport we have found there may allow - in addition to other functions - some water potential gradient across the apical membranes within the sensilla (see Thurm and Küppers, this volume).

ACKNOWLEDGMENTS

This work has been supported by grants of the Deutsche Forschungsgemeinschaft. The cooperation of Mrs. A. Plagemann, Mrs. G. Peterseim-Neuhaus, and Miss M. Volbers is gratefully acknowledged. We are indebted to Mrs. I. Beständig for typing the manuscript and to Miss I. Bunse for drawing several figures.

REFERENCES

Anderson, E., and Harvey, W.R. (1966). Active transport by the Cecropia midgut. II. Fine structure of the midgut epithelium. *J. Cell Biol.* *31*, 107-134.

Barry, P.H., and Hope, A.B. (1969). Electroosmosis in membranes: effects of unstirred layers and transport numbers. I. Theory. *Biophys. J.* *9*, 700-728.

Berridge, M.J., and Oschman, J.L. (1972), "Transporting Epithelia". Academic Press, London.

Blankemeyer, J.T., and Harvey, W.R. (1978). Identification of active cell in potassium transporting epithelium. *J. exp. Biol.* *77*, 1-13.

Bradley, T.J., and Phillips, J.E. (1975). The secretion of hyperosmotic fluid by the rectum of a saline-water mosquito larva, *Aedes taeniorhynchus*. *J. exp. Biol.* *63*, 331-342.

Curran, P.F. (1960). Na, Cl, and water transport by rat ileum *in vitro*. *J. Gen. Physiol.* *43*, 1137-1148.

Diamond, J.M. (1965). The mechanism of isotonic water absorption and secretion. *Sym. Soc. Exp. Biol.* *19*, 329-348.

Diamond, J.M. (1971). Standing-gradient model of fluid transport in epithelia. *Fed. Proc.* *30*, 6-13.

Diamond, J.M., and Bossert, W.H. (1967). Standing-gradient osmotic flow. A mechanism for coupling of water and solute transport in epithelia. *J. Gen. Physiol.* *50*, 2061-2083.

Edney, E.B. (1977). Water balance in land arthropods. *In* "Zoophysiology and Ecology" *9*, Springer-Verlag, Berlin.

Grimstone, A.V., Mullinger, A.M., and Ramsay, J.A. (1968). Further studies on the rectal complex of the mealworm *Tene-*

brio molitor, L. (Coleoptera, Tenebrionidae). *Phil. Trans. Roy. Soc. Lond. B. 253*, 343-382.

Gupta, B.L., and Berridge, M.J. (1966). Fine structural organization of the rectum in the blowfly *Calliphora erythrocephala* (Meig.) with special reference to connective tissue, tracheae, and neurosecretory innervation in the rectal papillae. *J. Morphol. 120*, 23-82.

Gupta, B.L., Hall, T.A., Maddrell, S.H.P., and Moreton, R.B. (1976). Distribution of ions in a fluid-transporting epithelium determined by electron-probe X-ray microanalysis. *Nature, 264*, 284-287.

Harvey, W.R., and Nedergaard, S. (1964). Sodium independent active transport of potassium in the isolated midgut of the Cecropia silkworm. *Proc. Nat. Acad. Sci. US 51*, 757-765.

Hill, A.E. (1975). Solute-solvent coupling in epithelia: an electro-osmotic theory of fluid transfer. *Proc. Roy. Soc. Lond. B. 190*, 115-134.

Hill, A.E. (1977). General mechanisms of salt-water coupling in epithelia.*In* "Transport of Ions and Water in Animals." (B.L. Gupta, R.B. Moreton, J.L. Oschman, and B.J. Wall,eds.) pp. 183-214. Academic Press, London.

Jungreis,A.M.(1977). Comparative aspects of invertebrate epithelial transport. *In* "Water Relations in Membrane Transport in Plants and Animals" (A.M. Jungreis, T.K. Hodges, A. Kleinzeller, and S.G. Schultz, eds.), pp. 89-96. Academic Press, London.

Küppers, J., and Thurm, U. (1979). Active ion transport by a sensory epithelium. I. Transepithelial short circuit current, potential difference, and their dependence on metabolism. *J. Comp. Physiol. 134*, 131-136.

Küppers, J., Plagemann, A., and Thurm, U. (1979). Electroosmotic uptake of water vapour by *Lepisma. In* "Animals and Environmental Fitness". Abstracts of the first ESCPB conference. (R. Gilles, ed.), pp. 33-34. Pergamon Press, Oxford.

Küppers, J., Plagemann, A., and Thurm, U. Uphill transport of water by electroosmosis. (in preparation).

Machin, J. (1979a). Atmospheric water absorption in arthropods. *In* "Advances in Insect Physiology" (J.E. Treherne, M.J. Berridge, and V.B. Wigglesworth, eds.) *14*, pp. 1-48. Academic Press, London.

Machin, J. (1979b). Compartmental osmotic pressures in the rectal complex of *Tenebrio* larvae: evidence for a single tubular pumping site. *J. exp. Biol. 82*, 123-137.

Maddrell, S.H.P. (1971). The mechanisms of insect excretory systems. *In* "Advances in Insect Physiology" (J.W.L. Beament, J.E. Treherne, and V.B. Wigglesworth, eds.) *8*, pp. 199-331. Academic Press, London.

Maddrell, S.H.P. (1977). Insect Malpighian tubules. *In* "Transport of Ions and Water in Animals" (B.C. Gupta, R.B. Moreton,

J.C. Oschman, and B.J. Wall, eds.), pp 541-569. Academic
Press, London.

Meredith, J., and Phillips, J.E. (1973). Rectal ultrastructure
in salt- and freshwater mosquito larvae in relation to physiological state. Z. Zellforsch. 138, 1-22.

Neuhaus, G., Siebler, H., and Thurm, U. (1978). Ein zur Aufnahme atmosphärischen Wassers befähigtes Organ (Analsack von
Lepisma) Verh. Dtsch. Zool. Ges. 71, 295.

Neuhoff, V. (1973), "Micromethods in Molecular Biology". Springer-Verlag, Berlin.

Noble-Nesbitt, J. (1969). Water balance in the firebrat, Thermobia domestica (Packard). Exchanges of water with the atmosphere. J. exp. Biol. 50, 745-769.

Noble-Nesbitt, J. (1970). Water balance in the firebrat, Thermobia domestica (Packard). The site of uptake of water from
the atmosphere. J. exp. Biol. 52, 193-200.

Noble-Nesbitt, J. (1975). Reversible arrest of uptake of water
from subsaturated atmospheres by the firebrat, Thermobia
domestica (Packard). J. exp. Biol. 62, 657-669.

Noble-Nesbitt, J. (1977). Active transport of water vapour. In
"Transport of Ions and Water in Animals" (B.L. Gupta, R.B.
Moreton, J.C. Oschman, and B.J. Wall, eds.), pp. 571-597.
Academic Press, London.

Noirot, C. and Noirot-Timothée, C. (1971). Ultrastructure du
proctodeum chez les Thysanure Lepismodes inquilinus Newman
(= Thermobia domestica Packard). II. Le sac anal. J. Ultrastruct. Res. 37, 335-350.

Noirot, C., Smith, D.S., Cayer, M.L., and Noirot-Timothée, C.
(1979). The organization and isolating function of insect
rectal sheath cells: a freeze-fracture study. Tissue & Cell,
11, 325-336.

Oschman, J.L., and Wall, B.J. (1969). The structure of rectal
pads of Periplaneta americana L. with regard to fluid transport. J. Morphol. 127, 475-509.

Phillips, J.E. (1964). Rectal absorption in the desert locust,
Schistocerca gregaria Forskål. I. Water. J. exp. Biol. 41,
15-38.

Phillips, J.E. (1977). Problems of water transport in insects.
In "Water Relations in Membrane Transport in Plants and
Animals" (A.M. Jungreis, T.K. Hodges, A. Kleinzeller, and
S.G. Schultz, eds.), pp. 333-353. Academic Press, London.

Plagemann, A., Küppers, J., and Thurm, U. (1978). Elektroosmose:
Grundlage aktiver Aufnahme atmosphärischen Wassers bei Lepisma. Verh. Dtsch. Zool. Ges. 71, 298.

Ramsay, J.A. (1964). The rectal complex of the mealworm Tenebrio molitor L. (Coleoptera, Tenebrionidae). Phil. Trans.
Roy. Soc. Lond. B. 248, 297-314.

Rosenberg, P.A., and Finkelstein, A. (1978). Interaction of ions
and water in gramicidin A channels. Streaming potentials

across lipid bilayer membranes. *J. Gen. Physiol. 72*, 327–340.

Saini, R.S. (1964). Histology and physiology of the cryptone-phridial system in insects. *Trans. Roy. Enthomol. Soc. Lond. 116*, 347–392.

Schagina, L.V., Grinfeldt, A.E., and Lev, A.A. (1978). Interaction of cation fluxes in gramicidin A channels in lipid bilayer membranes. *Nature 273*, 243–245.

Skadhauge, E. (1977). Analysis of computer models. *In* "Transport of Ions and Water in Animals" (B.L. Gupta, R.B. Moreton, J.L. Oschman, and B.J. Wall, eds.), pp. 145–165. Academic Press, London.

Smith, D.S. (1969). The fine structure of haltere sensilla in the blowfly, *Calliphora erythrocephala* (Meig.), with scanning electron microscopic observations on the haltere surface. *Tissue & Cell 1*, 443–484.

Thurm, U. (1970). Untersuchungen zur funktionellen Organisation sensorischer Zellverbände. *Verh. Dtsch. Zool. Ges. 64*, 79–88.

Thurm, U. (1974). Basics of the generation of receptor potentials in epidermal mechanoreceptors of insects. *In* "Mechanoreception" (J. Schwartzkopff, ed.) pp. 355–385. Abh. Rhein. Westf. Akad. Wiss., Opladen.

Thurm, U.,and Neuhaus, G. The structural basis for active uptake of water vapour in an insect (*Lepisma*). (in preparation).

Wall, B.J. (1971). Local osmotic gradients in the rectal pads of an insect. *Fed. Proc. 30*, 42–48.

Wall, B.J. (1977). Fluid transport in the cockroach rectum. *In* "Transport of Ions and Water in Animals" (B.L. Gupta, R.B. Moreton, J.L. Oschman, and B.J. Wall, eds.) pp. 599–612. Academic Press, London.

Wigglesworth, V.B. (1932a) On the function of the so-called "rectal glands" of insects. *Quart. J. Micr. Sci. 75*, 131–150.

Wood, J.L.,Farrand, P.S., and Harvey, W.R. (1969). Active transport of potassium by the Cecropia midgut. VI. Microelectrode potential profile. *J. exp. Biol. 50*, 169–178.

EPITHELIAL TRANSPORT AND CONTROL
IN RECTA OF TERRESTRIAL INSECTS

John E. Phillips

Department of Zoology
University of British Columbia
Vancouver, Canada

I. INTRODUCTION

Wigglesworth (1932) first reported that the gut contents often become very dry as they pass through the rectum and he proposed that this organ was a major site of water conservation in most terrestrial insects. Investigators of rectal function have since been preoccupied with the mechanism whereby water is reabsorbed from the lumen against large differences in osmotic concentration (reviewed by Maddrell, 1971, 1977; Phillips, 1970, 1977a,b; Wall, 1971, 1977), and with the ultrastructure of this organ (reviewed by Wall and Oschman, 1975). Remarkably, this "active" absorption of water can proceed from the vapour phase in two types of rectum: the cryptonephridial complex of the mealworm (reviewed by Machin, 1978, 1979) and the anal sac of the firebat (reviewed by Noble-Nesbitt, 1978). One consequence of this preoccupation with water conservation is that the mechanisms for solute reabsorption in the papillate rectum of terrestrial insects have received limited attention, even though the importance of these processes in the regulation of haemolymph composition has long been recognized.

The classical experiments of Ramsay (reviewed by Maddrell, 1971; Stobbart and Shaw, 1974) demonstrated that the excretory process in most insects consisted of two major steps: relatively non-selective secretion of most hemolymph constituents by the Malpighian tubules, followed by selective reabsorption in the hindgut-rectum of solutes and water in amounts required to maintain hemolymph composition. The first direct measurements of ion and water reabsorption, and of

145

their regulation under different physiological states, were
made by the author using ligated locust recta *in vivo*
(Phillips, 1964a-c). More recently, Goh and Phillips (1978)
have provided direct physiological evidence that prolonged
fluid absorption by locust rectum *in vitro* is secondarily
coupled to active absorption of monovalent ions from the
lumen. Analysis of fluid from intercellular spaces by
micropuncture (Wall, 1971, 1977) suggest that active
recycling of unknown organic solutes may also help to drive
water absorption in papillate recta which are found in such
insects as *Periplaneta*, *Calliphora* and *Schistocerca*.

This organ probably has other important functions,
including regulation of hemolymph metabolites (e.g. amino
acids) and pH. Mullins and Cochran (1972; also Cochran,
1975) have reported that ammonia is a major excretory product
in the cockroach, thereby raising the possibility that the
hindgut-rectum might play an active role in elimination of
this nitrogenous waste. This is certainly true for the
maggot of *Sarcophaga* (Prusch, 1975).

These various observations suggest that future research on
the papillate rectum will focus increasingly on mechanisms of
solute transport, their characteristics (e.g. kinetics and
energy coupling) and biochemical nature, their localization
within the epithelium, and their neural and hormonal control.
Such detailed studies have recently become feasible with the
development of good *in vitro* preparations (e.g. Leader and
Green, 1978). In the case of the locust these preparations
include everted, cannulated rectal sacs (Goh and Phillips,
1978; Balshin and Phillips, 1971) and also short-circuited
recta which are mounted as flat sheets between two "Ussing"
chambers (Williams *et al.*, 1978). After an initial rapid
decline in activity over the first hour, these two
preparations exhibit near steady-state rates of ion transport
and fluid absorption, and relatively constant electrical
parameters (I_{SC}, PD, Ω) for several hours. The "steady-state"
values for these parameters *in vitro* compare favourably with
those previously measured *in situ* (Phillips, 1964a-c). The
remainder of this article summarizes the limited information
which is presently available on solute transport in papillate
recta of terrestrial insects. The very tentative and
speculative nature of this account should emphasize and
identify many specific questions which require investigation.

II. IDENTIFICATION OF SOLUTE TRANSPORT PROCESSES

Harvey (1980) has reviewed the thermodynamic criteria which provide *rigorous* proof that a specific solute is actively transported. If either the steady-state distribution or the net flux of a solute across a permeable membrane cannot be accounted for by simple physical forces such as a concentration difference, an electrical difference (PD), or solvent drag (i.e. as described by the Ussing flux equation), then cell metabolism must supply the necessary energy for uphill movement of that substance. This metabolic input may be direct (primary transport) by means of a coupled biochemical reaction (e.g. Na-K ATPase), or indirect (secondary transport) through use of potential energy stored in ion activity gradients across membranes and with coupling of the two solute transfers achieved through a common carrier protein (e.g. Na-gradient hypothesis; Crane, 1977). In practice, three experimental approaches are commonly used to demonstrate active transport: a) comparison of solute concentration ratios with the PD across a permeable membrane, when there is no net flux; b) demonstration of net transfer of a solute against the summed electrical and concentration differences when fluid movement is prevented; and c) use of radiotracers to show that influx exceeds efflux of a substance when electrical and concentration differences are abolished, using the short-circuit current (I_{sc}) method of Ussing and Zerahn (1951). Methods a) and b) provide only qualitative proof for a transport mechanism (pump) because net diffusion (leak) of the substance also occurs. Since net diffusion is eliminated by method c), this technique provides a quantitative and continuous measure of the transepithelial transport rate.

Using these widely accepted criteria, relatively few specific transport processes have been rigorously demonstrated in the insect hindgut-rectum, and these are restricted to only 4 species. The papillate rectum of the desert locust actively absorbs Cl^-, Na^+, and K^+ (methods a, b, c; Phillips, 1964b,c; Phillips, 1977a; Goh and Phillips, 1978; Williams *et al.*, 1978), inorganic phosphate (method b; Andrusiak, 1974), glycine, proline, alanine, serine and threonine (method b; Balshin and Phillips, 1971; Balshin, 1973), and acetate (Baumeister; reported by Spring and Phillips, 1980b). Bicarbonate is presumed to be actively absorbed, or H^+ secreted into the lumen, to explain the rapid acidification of rectal contents. This proceeds against both electrical and concentration differences in the locust and continues when microbial activity is inhibited (Phillips, 1961; Speight,

1967). Measured rates of active transport, and the highest concentration ratios which these processes have been observed to develop across the locust rectum, are shown in Table I.

Amongst strictly fresh-water species, active absorption of both Na^+ and Cl^- has been convincingly demonstrated by method c) in recta of dragonfly larvae (Leader and Green, 1978). In two species which inhabit hyperosmotic water, portions of the hindgut secrete very concentrated salt solutions into the lumen: larvae of *Aedes taeniorhynchus* living in seawater actively transport Na^+, K^+, Mg^{2+} and Cl^- in the posterior rectal segment (reviewed by Phillips, Bradley and Maddrell, 1978). Maggots of the horsefly, which live in decaying meat, actively secrete NH_4^+, K^+ and Cl^-, but not Na^+, in the unsegmented hindgut (Prusch, 1975). The nature of the energy coupling mechanism is not known for any solute transport processes in the rectum, with the exception of amino acid reabsorption in locusts.

There is partial evidence (including ultrastructural specializations) for KCl, NaCl and amino acid absorption against large concentration differences in the hindgut and rectum of several other fresh-water and terrestrial insects (reviewed by Stobbart and Shaw, 1974; Maddrell, 1971), particularly *Periplaneta* (Wall, 1970a,b, 1977), *Calliphora* (Phillips, 1969) and *Pieris* (Nicholson; reported by Maddrell, 1978). Since PD measurements have not been reported in these species, nor the effect of solvent drag evaluated, it is not yet possible to propose specific ion pumps. Given the great variety of diets on which different insects feed, and the diverse environments in which they live, it would be imprudent at this time to assume that the same reabsorptive mechanisms predominate in the hindgut-rectum of various terrestrial insects. For example, an attempt to demonstrate Cl^- transport in *Calliphora* rectum was unsuccessful (Phillips, 1969) and the data suggest that considerable reabsorption of this ion occurs in the hindgut. Unfortunately insect proctologists, including this author, have not avoided the temptation to extrapolate observations from one species to another. A more extensive survey of different insect recta is required, using acceptable physiological criteria, to identify specific transport processes.

TABLE I. *Rates of Active Transport by Rectum of Schistocerca and Maximum Concentration Ratios Developed across this Epithelium*

Solute	Solute conc. (mM) in lumen	Mean rate of transport[d] ($\mu Mol \cdot h^{-1} \cdot cm^{-2}$)	Conc. ratio (hemo:lumen)
Cl^- stimulated	114	10.5[a]	20:1[c]
unstimulated	80	3.8[a]	-
Na^+ unstimulated	70	4.4[a]	10:1[c]
K^+ unstimulated	200	1.3[b]	50:1[c]
Phosphate	18	0.1[b]	2.8:1[b]
Acetate	200	3.5[a]	-
Glycine	10	0.15[b]	10:1[b]
Proline	10	0.13[b]	7.5:1[b]
Serine	10	0.06[b]	4.5:1[b]
Alanine	10	0.06[b]	3.5:1[b]
Threonine	10	0.03[b]	2.5:1[b]
H^+/HCO_3^-	10^{-4}	1.4[c]	100:1[c]

Methods: [a]*Net flux under short-circuit conditions.* [b]*Net absorption by everted rectal sacs (i.e. less than true rate).* [c]*Net movement across ligated recta in situ.* [d]*Conversion factor: 1 $\mu Mol \cdot h^{-1} \cdot rectum^{-1} =$ 1.5 $\mu Mol \cdot h^{-1} \cdot cm^{-2}$.*

III. AN ULTRASTRUCTURAL FRAMEWORK FOR TRANSPORT STUDIES

The location of specific solute pumps in the rectal wall, and an appreciation of how various passive and active transport processes are organized to cause fluid transport, will only be possible when several ultrastructural and physiological techniques are applied to the same rectal epithelium. The required methods are available: glass micro-electrodes and ion-sensitive electrodes to measure intracellular PD and ion activities respectively; short-circuited recta to control experimental conditions, to monitor transport rates quantitatively with time and to investigate energy coupling and kinetics; transmission electron microscopy to localize carrier enzymes in specific membranes by histochemistry or autoradiography; and electron probe X-ray microanalysis to measure ion concentrations in

tissue compartments. Unfortunately these techniques have been
applied individually to different recta so that firm
conclusions are difficult. Gupta et al. (1978) have made very
detailed and valuable measurements of ion concentrations in
various tissue compartments of rectal papillae from starved
and recently fed Calliphora (Fig. 1), but net transport of
specific ions has not yet been demonstrated in this tissue.
Elegant micropuncture studies by Wall (1971, 1977) have
suggested a detailed model to explain fluid transport across
the rectal pads of Periplaneta, but again evidence for
specific ion transport mechanisms is incomplete. A critical
review of supportive data for this model (Fig. 1) is
presented below.

When a solution of sugar and salt is injected into the
rectal lumen of Periplaneta, large intercellular sinuses
located apically in the tissue can be observed (under a
dissecting microscope) to swell within minutes (Wall et al.,
1970). This indicates that at least part, and perhaps all, of
the fluid absorbed from the rectal lumen first moves into
these intercellular sinuses. This fluid might then flow
across the remainder of the epithelium through elaborate
intercellular channels which ultimately exit at a few points
on the hemocoel (basal) side where tracheae penetrate into
the tissue (Fig. 1). Fluid obtained by micropuncture from the
swollen apical sinuses is hyperosmotic to saline in the rectal
lumen; therefore, water is probably drawn into these tissue
spaces by local osmosis. These experiments were conducted
under transient rather than steady-state conditions; i.e. the
tissue sinuses were previously in equilibrium with fecal
material (>1000 mOsm) which was twice as concentrated as the
experimental solution (500 mOsm) injected into the rectal
lumen (Wall, 1977). Consequently it is uncertain whether the
observed fluid movement was caused by transport of ions,
especially Na^+ from the lumen, or largely by residual solute
(mostly organic) which was originally present in the tissue
sinuses. Under steady-state conditions, ion concentrations
in the fluid entering the apical sinuses might be higher than
those measurements of Wall et al. (1970). Answers to these
questions could be obtained by further micropuncture studies:
in particular it will be definitive if it can be shown, by
ion substitutions and PD measurements, that this local fluid
movement is coupled to transport of specific ions.

The lateral membranes adjacent to the apical sinuses are
highly folded and are closely associated with many
mitochondria in Periplaneta, Calliphora and Schistocerca
(reviewed by Wall and Oschman, 1975). These ultrastructural
features and current models for fluid transport across
vertebrate epithelia would both favour transport of ions into

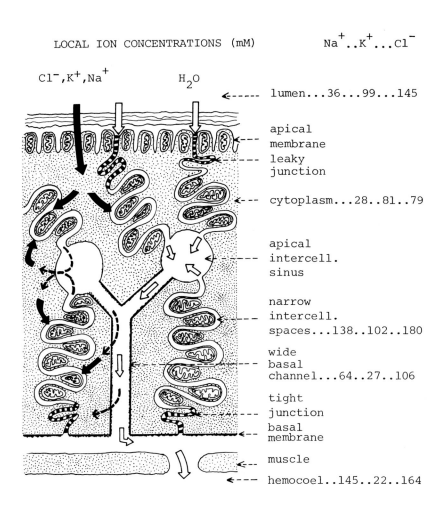

LOCAL ION CONCENTRATIONS (mM) $Na^+ .. K^+ ... Cl^-$

Cl^-, K^+, Na^+ H_2O

lumen...36...99...145

apical
membrane
leaky
junction

cytoplasm...28..81..79

apical
intercell.
sinus

narrow
intercell.
spaces...138..102..180

wide
basal
channel...64..27..106

tight
junction
basal
membrane

muscle

hemocoel..145..22..164

FIGURE 1. *Structure of rectal pad epithelium in Periplaneta (modified from Wall and Oschman, 1975), but general scheme is similar for Schistocerca and Calliphora. Local ion concentrations for Calliphora (from Gupta et al., 1977). Solute transport (solid arrows), site of solute recovery (broken arrows), route of water movement (open arrows).*

the intercellular spaces at this location. In support of this
hypothesis, measurements by electron probe X-ray microanalysis
indicate that concentrations of Cl^-, Na^+ and K^+ are all much
greater in these narrow intercellular spaces than in the
adjacent cytoplasm (Fig. 1). Clearly, either anions or
cations must be transported actively, depending on the local
membrane PD and assuming that net salt transfer actually does
occur across membranes at this location.

Physiological studies with everted rectal sacs of the
desert locust are consistent with this model and provide
direct proof that water transport is secondarily coupled to
ion transport in papillate recta (reviewed by Phillips,
1977a,b; Goh and Phillips, 1978). These sacs continue to
absorb water at near steady rates for at least 5 h and against
small osmotic concentration differences if *any one* of Na^+, K^+
or Cl^- (200 mM with NO_3^- or choline) is present on the lumen
side. The mean rates of fluid transport were 5.2, 4.5 and
2.4 $\mu l \cdot h^{-1} \cdot rectum^{-1}$ in the presence of K^+, Na^+ or Cl^-
respectively, compared to the control value of 6.5 $\mu l \cdot h^{-1} \cdot$
$rectum^{-1}$ when all three ions were provided. All other minor
constituents of the saline (with sucrose) did not sustain
fluid transport after the first hour, nor did the major
monovalent ions if they were only available on the hemocoel
side. This suggests that the active transport processes for
Na^+, K^+ and Cl^- are relatively independent of one another, at
least in unstimulated recta (see Chloride). All three ion
pumps are likely to be at the basolateral membrane in order to
explain how transport of each ion can cause prolonged fluid
movement into the hemocoel compartment.

Fluid absorbed from the rectum (i.e. absorbate) of
dehydrated *Schistocerca* (Phillips, 1964a,c), *Periplaneta*
(Wall, 1967) and *Calliphora* (Phillips, 1969) is hyposmotic to
the lumen contents, which is not the case for vertebrate
epithelia. It has been repeatedly suggested that absorbate
hyposmosity is due to ion reabsorption (Phillips, 1965),
specifically in more distal sections of the intercellular
channels (Berridge and Gupta, 1967; Wall, 1971). In support
of this view, micropuncture studies by Wall (1970b) on
Periplaneta indicated lower concentrations of monovalent ions
in the subepithelial spaces than in apical sinuses. Electron
probe microanalysis studies on *Calliphora* rectal papillae show
much higher ion concentration in the narrow intercellular
spaces compared to the enlarged channels downstream from these
sites (Fig. 1). This ion-recycling hypothesis assumes that
fluid does not continue to enter the more basal intercellular
channels to dilute their contents and that the route for fluid
transport is largely paracellular.

Direct measurements on absorbate collected from everted rectal sacs of the desert locust are consistent with this model (Phillips, 1977a,b). The "steady-state" concentrations of K^+, Na^+, Cl^- and total solutes (osmoles) in absorbate are 81, 78, 50 and 80% respectively of those on the lumen side. When 110 mM KCl + 110 mM NaCl is placed on the lumen side, the absorbate contains (mM) 90 Na^+, 70 K^+ and 100 Cl^-. If the total salt concentration is reduced from 220 to 30 mM using an isosmotic sucrose solution, the rate of fluid transport and the absorbate concentration of K^+ decrease by less than 50%, and in the case of Cl^-, Na^+ and osmolarity, hardly at all (Phillips, 1977a,b; Cl^- values previously unpublished). These results can be readily explained if all three ion pumps are nearly saturated when ion concentrations in the lumen are above 30 mM. It then follows that the rate of fluid entry into apical intercellular spaces will also be relatively independent of external salinity and therefore so will ion reabsorption (i.e. recycling) in the more basal intercellular spaces. There is a deficit of anions compared to cations in absorbate (see above); probably, phosphate and bicarbonate account for much of the deficit, since there is evidence that both of these anions may be transported. On this assumption, inorganic ions can account for 90% of the absorbate osmolarity in locusts (Phillips, 1977b).

There is no evidence that the whole rectal tissue, and hence the large columnar cells which form the bulk of the rectal pads, is hyperosmotic to the lumen content in *Periplaneta* (Wall, 1977) or *Schistocerca* (Phillips, 1970, 1977b; Balshin, 1973). Consequently, there may not be a favourable osmotic gradient to cause water movement into rectal cells from the lumen. The intracellular activity of water has yet to be measured directly. Phillips (1977a) has suggested that this problem would be eliminated if water moved from the lumen to apical intercellular sinuses through apical junctional complexes between the cells. There is increasing evidence for such a paracellular route in various vertebrate epithelia (Fischbarg, 1978; Hill, 1978).

Information on the permeability properties of the junctional complexes in insect recta is fragmentary. Using electron microscopy and freeze-fracture techniques, Lane (1979) showed that lanthanum moves freely through the apical septate junctions from the lumen to intercellular spaces of *Periplaneta* rectum, but this marker does not cross tight junctions between the cells on the hemocoel side (Fig. 1). These observations are consistent with a totally extracellular route for fluid movement across this epithelium. Various electrical and physiological parameters have been used to classify epithelia into two categories, "tight" or "leaky".

These terms indicate the permeability of intercellular
junctions to ions and water (Frömter and Diamond, 1972). The
required parameters are known for locust rectum (Phillips,
1964a-c; Williams *et al.*, 1978). These values are compared
with those for some vertebrate epithelia in Table II. Locust
rectum is clearly of intermediate tightness. Inclusion of
Krebs cycle intermediates and amino acids in the external
saline increases the transepithelial resistance of locust
rectum by 2 to 3 times *in vitro* (Spring and Phillips, 1980b;
Hanrahan, personal comm.). These organic acids might
influence junctional tightness directly, or they might act by
stimulating synthetic events in the cell. More detailed
physiological studies on junctional complexes of insect recta
should prove rewarding.

   Having summarized information which correlates structure
and function in the papillate recta, individual solute
transport processes are considered in more detail in the
following sections.

IV. SPECIFIC SOLUTE TRANSPORT MECHANISMS

A. *Sodium*

   In most absorptive epithelia, sodium is thought to enter
the cell passively, by virtue of a lower intercellular
concentration of this cation and a favourable PD across the
apical membrane. Sodium is then pumped from cells across the
basolateral plasma membrane against large electrochemical
differences by means of a Na-K-ATPase which is specifically
inhibited by ouabain (reviewed by Giebisch *et al.*, 1978).

   Na-K-ATPase has recently been found in the hindgut and,
at much higher concentrations, in the recta of *Locusta,
Schistocerca, Periplaneta,* and other insects (reviewed by
Anstee and Bowler, 1979; also Peacock, 1979). Its
biochemical properties are similar to those observed in a wide
variety of animal tissues, the ionic requirements for maximal
activation being 100 mM Na^+ + 20 mM K^+. Unfortunately,
localization of this enzyme within the epithelial rather than
the muscle cells of papillate recta has not been demonstrated.
Using histochemical methods, Berridge and Gupta (1968)
demonstrated a Mg-ATPase in the lateral membrane stacks, and
a K-Mg-ATPase in the apical membranes of *Calliphora* rectal
papillae, but neither of these enzymes could be stimulated by
Na^+. More recently, Komnick and Achenbach (1979) have shown

TABLE II. *Physiological Parameters Used to Classify Epithelia with "Tight" and "Leaky" Cell Junctions*[a]

Epithelium	R $(ohm \cdot cm^{-2})$	P_{osm} $(ml \cdot cm^{-2} \cdot s^{-1} \cdot osmolar^{-1})$	Transport PD (mV)	Ion transport rate $(\mu Mol \cdot h^{-1} \cdot cm^{-2})$	Max. conc. ratio
TIGHT					
Frog skin	2000	$\{1 \times 10^{-5}$	100	1.5	10,000
Toad bladder	800	$^{no\ ADH}$	35	1.6	>30
INTERMEDIATE					
Locust rectum[b] (unstimulated)	200	6×10^{-6}	15	2.5	10-50
LEAKY					
Rat gall bladder	28	4×10^{-5}	0	13	12
Rat prox. tubule	6	4×10^{-3}	0	55	1.3

[a] Parameters and values for vertebrate epithelia described by Frömter and Diamond (1972). [b]Values mostly from Williams et al. (1978); also Goh and Phillips (1978); Phillips (1964b,c). Note some corrections from Phillips (1977b) due to previous mathematical error.

that fixation for electron microscopy drastically reduces Na^+-stimulation of Na-K-ATPase. These workers used ^3H-ouabain and autoradiography to localize a Na-K-ATPase along the whole basolateral membrane of rectal epithelia from dragonfly larvae. There is some indirect physiological evidence that this enzyme is involved in rectal absorption in terrestrial insects. Ouabain (1 mM) inhibits net Na^+ absorption (Irvine and Phillips, 1970) and also fluid transport (by 50%; Goh and Phillips, 1978) across rectal sacs of *Schistocerca*.

The concentrations of Na^+ in tissue compartments of
Calliphora rectal papillae, as seen by electron probe
microanalysis (Fig. 1), are consistent with passive entry and
active extrusion of this cation, assuming that the PD profile
is like that in *Schistocerca* (Fig. 2). Physiological studies
on *Schistocerca* clearly support this model. The interior of
rectal pad cells is strongly negative to both lumen and
hemocoel by 70 and 60 mV respectively (Spring *et al.*, 1978;
also Phillips, 1964b; Vietinghoff *et al.*, 1969). The
intracellular concentration of Na^+ must be lower than the
value observed for whole rectal tissue (55 - 73 mM $Na^+ \cdot kg$
tissue H_2O^{-1}; Phillips, 1964b), because all of the
extracellular fluids (including absorbate, 85 mM Na^+)
normally have higher levels of this cation. Clearly both
electrical and concentration differences favour passive entry
of Na^+ into the rectal epithelium of *Schistocerca*, whereas
removal of this cation to the hemocoel requires an energy
input. An experiment by Goh (1971; also Goh and Phillips,
1978) using everted rectal sacs demonstrated this active exit
of Na^+. When sacs were bathed on the lumen side in isosmotic
sucrose solution, they continued to transport a hyposmotic
absorbate containing 120 mM Na^+ to the hemocoel side for 1 h.
This occurred at the expense of tissue Na^+ and water, which
both declined by about 30%. This net secretion of Na^+ from
rectal tissue clearly occurred against a concentration
difference and an unfavourable PD.

The Na^+ pump can maintain a flux ratio of 4:1 when
short-circuited recta are bathed in a complex saline
containing 70 mM Na^+ (Williams *et al.*, 1978). The kinetics of
this process have not been studied. In summary, there is no
reason at present to suppose that the mechanism of Na^+
transport across the rectal wall differs from that proposed
for various vertebrate epithelia, with the important
exception that some of this cation is recycled within the
rectal tissue.

Part of the passive entry of Na^+ into rectal cells of
Schistocerca is coupled to the absorption of neutral amino
acids, suggesting that influx of these solutes is facilitated
by specific protein carriers in the apical membrane (see
Amino Acids). Balshin (1973) has calculated that this
mechanism might account for 20% of net Na^+ absorption.
Likewise, phosphate is co-transported with Na^+ at the apical
border of rat proximal tubules. If the active absorption of
phosphate in locust rectum (Andrusiak, 1972) occurs by a
similar process, this mechanism would account for another 10%
of Na^+ net influx. Absorption of Na^+ by coupled exchange for
cellular H^+ or NH_4^+ should also be investigated. H^+/Na^+

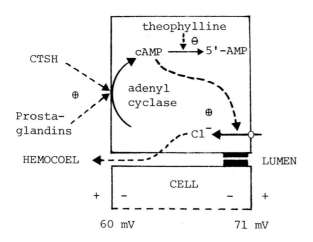

FIGURE 2. A model for the cellular mode of action of stimulants on electrogenic Cl⁻ transport across locust rectum. PD measurements from Spring et al. (1978).

counter-transport, which can be inhibited with amiloride, is well established for other epithelia (Liedtke and Hopfer, 1977). It might explain the acidification of the rectal contents in *Schistocerca*. Similarly, an apical exchange of NH_4^+ for Na^+ might give rise to the ammonia found in excreta from *Periplaneta*.

B. Potassium

Considerably more K^+ than Na^+ enters the rectum from the hindgut in most insects, as a consequence of selective secretion by the Malpighian tubules (Maddrell, 1978). To compensate for this, greater reabsorption of K^+ occurs in the rectum of water-fed *Schistocerca in situ* (5 µMol·h^{-1}·$rectum^{-1}$; Phillips, 1964b,c). Unfortunately we do not know what proportion of this reabsorption is achieved by the K-pump, rather than by a passive movement of cations which accompanies electrogenic transport of Cl⁻. The properties, location and mechanism of K^+ transport have not been studied. When short-circuited recta of *Schistocerca* were bathed in saline containing 8 mM K^+, the ^{42}K flux ratio was 5:3, resulting in only a small net transport of this cation to the hemocoel side

(Williams *et al.*, 1978). However a K^+ concentration of 140 mM
is more typical of hindgut fluid entering the rectum of this
species.

An electrogenic K^+ pump which is insensitive to ouabain
has been well characterized in *Cecropia* midgut (Harvey, this
volume). This is the predominant ion transport process in
several other insect epithelia, including Malpighian tubules
and salivary glands. In all these tissues, the pump is
apparently located in the apical plasma membrane, where it
moves K^+ from the cell into the lumen. This location is
inappropriate to explain K^+ absorption in papillate recta,
but conceivably a similar K^+ pump is present in the
basolateral membranes of this organ. The K^+ pump in midgut
and Malpighian tubules is apparently capable of transporting
Na^+ from the cell, when the basal plasma membrane is made
permeable to Na^+ by lowering external Ca^{2+} levels (Maddrell,
1977). Is it possible that Na^+ and K^+ compete for a single
transport mechanism of this type in locust rectum?
Inhibition of Na^+ absorption in this organ by ouabain
suggests that this may not be the case (see Sodium).

Phillips (1964b; 1965) has suggested that the large PD
across the apical plasma membrane of locust rectum (lumen
positive) is largely a potassium diffusion potential. The
high permeability of this membrane to K^+ was confirmed by Goh
(1973). When he bathed rectal sacs in an isosmotic sucrose
solution or choline chloride saline, over 85% of the tissue
K^+ was lost to the lumen side, while most of the Na^+ was
transported to the hemocoel side, as previously discussed.
Some K^+ transport across the apical border into the rectal
pad cells may be necessary to explain the very large K^+
concentration ratios which may be maintained at this border
in water-fed locusts (Phillips, 1964b, 1965). In support of
this suggestion, Berridge and Gupta (1968) observed a K-Mg
ATPase at this location in *Calliphora* using histochemistry.
Simultaneous measurements of both intracellular K^+ activities
and PD will be necessary to prove existence of an apical K^+
pump. A current model for gastric mucosa (Lee *et al.*, 1979)
proposes an apical K-ATPase which exchanges K^+ (absorption)
for H^+ (secretion). A similar mechanism would explain
acidification of rectal contents in *Schistocerca*.

C. *Chloride*

Rectal absorption of Cl^- is under hormonal control in
Schistocerca (Spring, Hanrahan and Phillips, 1978; Hanrahan,
1978; Spring and Phillips, 1980a,b). When short-circuited
recta are stimulated with cAMP, transport of this anion
greatly exceeds that of Na^+ and probably K^+ (Table I). In

this respect the papillate rectum differs from most other insect epithelia, which transport K^+ preferentially. Stimulation of the Cl^- pump causes the hemocoel side to become even more negative to the lumen than usual, and this larger PD presumably enhances net diffusion of cations from the rectal lumen. The K_t for the stimulated component of I_{sc} is approximately 23 mM Cl^- (Hanrahan, personal comm.). Before discussing the control of this process, let us first consider the nature of the Cl^- pump.

Two mechanisms for secondary transport of Cl^- are now widely accepted for various vertebrate epithelia: 1) Na-coupled co-transport of Cl^-, and 2) $HCO_3^-:Cl^-$ exchange (reviewed by Frizzell et al., 1979). Primary transport of Cl^- in animal tissues by means of a membrane-bound, anion-sensitive ATPase is not widely accepted, in spite of isolated claims to the contrary (e.g. De Renzis and Bornancin, 1977). Chloride transport in locust rectum does not conform to this current dogma, because absorption of this anion is clearly not coupled secondarily to either Na^+ or HCO_3^- fluxes (Hanrahan and Phillips, 1980). Evidence for this conclusion is summarized below.

Everted rectal sacs continue to transport Cl^- and water for more than 5 h when Na^+ is completely absent on the lumen side (Goh, 1973; Phillips, 1977a,b). Moreover, when net flux of $^{36}Cl^-$(J^{Cl}_{net}) is stimulated 2- to 3-fold under short-circuited conditions, both unidirectional and net fluxes of ^{22}Na (J^{Na}_{net}) remain unchanged (Spring and Phillips, 1980b). This independence of J^{Na}_{net} and J^{Cl}_{net} is also apparent over the first 2 h after dissecting recta from locusts; i.e. both I_{sc} and J^{Cl}_{net} fall dramatically from 8-12 $\mu Equiv \cdot h^{-1} \cdot cm^{-2}$ to 2-4 $\mu Equiv \cdot h^{-1} \cdot cm^{-2}$ over this period, whereas J^{Na}_{net} (2-4 $\mu Equiv \cdot h^{-1} \cdot cm^{-2}$) does not change with time (Williams et al., 1978; Spring and Phillips, 1980b). Over the next several hours, I_{sc}, J^{Cl}_{net}, and PD can all be restored to their original high levels by addition of 1 mM cAMP to the external saline. Since ΔJ^{Cl}_{net} can account for all of ΔI_{sc} in such experiments, Cl^- transport cannot be tightly coupled to net transfer of another ion (e.g. Na^+), otherwise ΔJ^{Cl}_{net} should have greatly exceeded ΔI_{sc}. All of the experimental evidence indicates that the cAMP-stimulated component of Cl^- transport is electrogenic.

It might be argued that Cl^- transport is coupled to active recycling of Na^+ or HCO_3^- across part of the rectal wall, so that there is no net transfer of the latter ions to contribute to I_{sc}. Such a model is proposed to explain Na^+-dependent, electrogenic transport of Cl^- across several vertebrate epithelia (Frizzell et al., 1979). This proposal can be excluded in the case of locust rectum (Hanrahan and

Phillips, 1980). Short-circuited recta were bathed in a
Na-free, choline-saline for at least 5 h to deplete the
tissues of Na^+. This treatment did not prevent subsequent
stimulation of I_{sc} and J^{Cl}_{net} by more than 4-fold when cAMP was
added. Likewise, exposure of recta to a NaCl-saline
containing 1 mM ouabain for 6 h did not prevent normal
stimulation of I_{sc} and J^{Cl}_{net} with cAMP.

As an alternative hypothesis to Na^+ recycling, the uphill
entry of Cl^- into rectal pad cells at the apical border might
be driven by passive efflux of HCO_3^- into the lumen (i.e.
$HCO_3^-:Cl^-$ counter-transport). The HCO_3^- might be derived from
metabolic CO_2, with carbonic anhydrase as catalyst.
Inhibition of this enzyme with acetazolamine does cause a 40%
reduction in I_{sc} across unstimulated locust recta (Spring et
al., 1980a; also Herrera et al., 1977) but the increase in
I_{sc} is normal when recta are subsequently stimulated with
cAMP. This would seem to exclude dependence of J^{Cl}_{net} on
metabolically generated HCO_3^-. This leaves the possibility
that a high intracellular concentration of HCO_3^- might be
maintained by a HCO_3-ATPase in the apical membrane, which
pumps HCO_3^- from the lumen (thereby acidifying its contents).
Membrane-bound HCO_3-ATPases have been isolated and
characterized biochemically for several plasma membranes.
This enzyme is inhibited by thiocyanate, which also inhibits
various anion transport processes in animal tissues.
HCO_3-ATPases have been reported recently in several insect
tissues (midgut, Malpighian tubules), including the rectum of
dragonfly larvae (Komnick et al., 1980). In our laboratory,
K. Black has recently shown that 30 mM SCN^- inhibits I_{sc}
across cAMP-stimulated recta of Schistocerca by 50-60%,
whereas 10 mM SCN^- has a negligible effect (Spring and
Phillips, 1980a). Based on these observations, it seemed
plausible that active recycling of HCO_3^- at the apical border
might drive secondary transport of Cl^- across locust rectum.
This possibility can now be excluded, because cAMP causes a
10-fold increase in I_{sc} and J^{Cl}_{net} when locust recta are bathed
in a CO_2/HCO_3^--free saline containing acetazolamide and
buffered at pH 7 with amino acids (Hanrahan and Phillips,
1980). In summary, Cl^- transport across locust recta does
not appear to be secondarily coupled to either Na^+ or HCO_3^-
transport. It is perhaps not surprising then that this
process is not affected by furosemide or SITS (Table III),
agents which inhibit Na- and HCO_3-coupled transport of Cl^-
respectively in vertebrate tissues (Frizzell et al., 1979).

Electrogenic transport of Cl^- is greatly reduced (70%) by
removing the small amount of K^+ (8 mM) in NaCl-salines bathing
short-circuited recta (Hanrahan and Phillips, 1980). The

TABLE III. *Pharmacology of the CTSH-Stimulated Component of I_{SC} and Cl^- Transport in Locust Rectum.[a]*

Stimulants	Inhibitors	No effect
cAMP	cyanide	seratonin
cGMP	azide	epinephrine
theophylline	thiocyanate	dopamine
arachidonic acid		octopamine
Prostaglandins		acetylcholine
$(E_1E_2, F_{2\alpha})$		glutamate
		GABA
		glycine
		proctolin
		DH (locust)
		AKH (locust)
		ouabain
		acetazolamine
		furosemide[b]
		SITS[b]
		Ca^{++} ionophore
		(A23187)[b]

[a]*References in text.* [b]*Hanrahan (personal comm.).*

K-dependence of Cl^- transport obeys Michaelis-Menten kinetics, with an apparent K_t of 4-9 mM K^+. Very high K^+ concentrations (140 mM) are inhibitory (Hanrahan, personal comm.). This partial coupling of K^+ and Cl^- reabsorption is interesting because these are the two major ions which enter the rectum in the Malpighian tubule secretion. Unlike the situation in the latter organs, the concentration differences across the rectal wall favour considerable passive reabsorption of K^+, but not of Cl^-. (This may explain why anion rather than cation transport has been selected for dominance in insect rectum.) The nature of the K^+/Cl^- interaction remains unclear: (1) Chloride transport could be secondarily coupled to active recycling of K^+. (2) The presence of a Cl-stimulated ATPase in papillate recta should be considered. Such an enzyme has been reported recently in dragonfly larvae (Komnick et al., 1980). This ATPase might be K^+ dependent. (3) However, the coupling could be less direct; that is, high

external K^+ concentrations might lower the electrical
gradient against which the Cl^- pump must work. Hanrahan
(personal comm.) recently observed a 50% decrease in
transepithelial resistance when short-circuited locust recta
were stimulated with cAMP, and there is evidence that both K^+
and Cl^- conductances are increased. Phillips (1964b) also
observed that Cl^- absorption was several times more rapid if
KCl rather than NaCl was injected into locust recta *in situ*.

Spring *et al.* (1978) propose that the Cl^- pump is located
in the apical membrane of locust rectum because entry of this
anion into the cell occurs against a very large PD (Fig. 2),
and possibly also against a concentration difference (e.g.
Fig. 1). However, it is difficult to explain how a Cl^- pump
at this location would drive prolonged fluid transport to the
hemocoel when external Na^+ and K^+ are replaced by choline, as
previously discussed. The exact location of this anion pump
will only be resolved by measuring the intracellular activity
of Cl^-.

This account of Cl^- transport in locust rectum has
concentrated on the cAMP-stimulated component. The
unstimulated component is obviously less sensitive to K^+ (e.g.
fluid transport studies) and is possibly not electrogenic.
For example, when NO_3^- or SO_4^{2-} are substituted for Cl^- in a
complex saline used to bathe short-circuited recta, the
steady-state (unstimulated) I_{SC} does not change (Williams *et
al.*, 1978). The same anion substitutions greatly reduce the
stimulation of I_{SC} with cAMP (Spring and Phillips, 1980b;
Hanrahan, 1978). One explanation is that the unstimulated
component of Cl^- transport occurs by a neutral exchange for
HCO_3^-, whereas the stimulated component does not. This
situation has been reported for some vertebrate epithelia
(Sachs, 1977). The alternate explanation is that electrogenic
transport of other ions (e.g. absorption of HCO_3^- and organic
acids, or H^+ secretion) increases to compensate for loss of
Cl^- absorption in Cl-free salines (Williams *et al.*, 1978).
Both stimulated and unstimulated I_{SC} and PD across locust
rectum are rapidly abolished by metabolic inhibitors such as
cyanide and azide.

D. *Phosphate, Calcium and Magnesium*

Malpighian tubules of various insects secrete inorganic
phosphate at relatively high rates and against large
concentration differences (reviewed by Maddrell, 1971, 1977).
This is much less pronounced for the Malpighian tubule
secretion of *Schistocerca*, which contains 12 mM (*in vitro*;
Maddrell and Klunsuwan, 1973) to 15 mM phosphate (*in vivo*;
Speight, 1968) when tubules are bathed in hemolymph or saline

containing 6-7 mM of this anion. While most of this secreted phosphate is reabsorbed in the rectum, the level of this anion can become quite high in the excreta of fed locusts (42 mM; Speight, 1967). The rectal cuticle is quite permeable to $H_2PO_4^-$ ($P=1.7$ cm·sec^{-1}x10^6) but much less so to the divalent form of this anion (0.13 cm·sec^{-1}x10^6; Speight, 1967), because of the latter's greater hydrated size and negative charge. It follows that acidification of the rectal contents facilitates reabsorption of phosphate.

Andrusiak (1974) in our laboratory has studied net absorption of $^{32}PO_4$ by everted rectal sacs of the locust under steady-state conditions. In the absence of fluid movement, absorption of this anion leads to a substantial concentration ratio across the rectal wall (Table I) even though the PD (Fig. 2) opposes net accumulation. This movement is inhibited by 2 mM KCN and iodoacetate. Net absorption of radiophosphate exhibits saturation kinetics with a K_t of 5 mM and a V_{max} of 80-100 nMol·h^{-1}·rectum^{-1}. It is independent of fluid transport rate except when very high concentrations of $^{32}PO_4$ are present in the lumen. Interestingly the V_{max} for rectal reabsorption is just sufficient to recover all of the phosphate secreted by Malpighian tubules of starved locusts (i.e. 8 μl secreted·h^{-1} containing 12 mM PO_4 = 96 nM PO_4 secreted·h^{-1}). However this value may be below the rate at which phosphate enters the rectum of recently fed locusts; consequently, the content of this anion in the excreta rises.

While 75% of the $^{32}PO_4$ entering rectal tissue from the lumen is converted into organic forms, these are not released to the hemocoel side. When 8 mM PO_4 is placed on the lumen side, the rectal tissue content of inorganic phosphate is maintained at 12 mM and the cell interior is negative to the lumen (Fig. 2). This suggests that the entry of $^{32}PO_4$ into the cell is an energy-requiring and carrier-mediated step. In support of this hypothesis, 8 mM arsenate, a competitive inhibitor of PO_4 transport, greatly reduced entry of $^{32}PO_4$ into the tissue. Facilitated, uphill entry of this anion into the cell might be driven by passive influx of Na$^+$, as previously suggested (see Sodium). There is probably a favourable electrochemical gradient for net diffusion of this anion from cell to hemocoel.

The mechanisms of Ca^{2+} and Mg^{2+} reabsorption in the insect rectum are still unknown. What has been clearly established is that these divalent ions can cross the rectal cuticle some 80 times more rapidly than predicted from their large hydrated size (Lewis, 1971; reported by Phillips, 1977). This is made possible by the presence of fixed negative charges (pK=4) which appear to line fluid-filled pores in the cuticle, as demonstrated by both streaming and the diffusion potentials across this membrane. When the external pH was lowered experimentally so that these fixed charges were undissociated, permeability of the cuticle to these divalent cations was reduced by 80-fold. This ion exchange process tends to saturate when external concentrations of Ca^{2+} and Mg^{2+} are high (ca. 40 mM); conceivably, this property of the cuticle may automatically prevent excess resorption of divalent cations should they be ingested in great excess.

E. Amino Acids

Insects have unusually high titres of free amino acids (FAA) in their hemolymph and their total concentration is closely regulated in some insects (e.g. *Chortoicetes*; Djajakusumah and Miles, 1966). For example, when *Schistocerca* are starved and desiccated for 2 days, the hemolymph volume, as measured by ^{3}H-inulin dilution, falls to one-third of that in hydrated animals (Chamberlin and Phillips, 1979). Total FAA (40 mM) and concentrations of the 20 individual FAA in the hemolymph (mostly proline, 10 mM, and glycine, 12 mM) are similar in both groups of locusts. During dehydration, FAA appear in the excreta from *Schistocerca* and this accounts for 50% of the proline lost from the hemolymph. When dehydrated animals are rehydrated by feeding on lettuce, hemolymph volume increases rapidly to its original volume within 8 h. During this recovery, the hemolymph concentration of FAA rises temporarily to 65-70 mM at 3 h, but by 8 h it has returned to 40 mM (Chamberlin and Phillips, 1979). A similar regulation of FAA was observed following injection of an isosmotic NaCl solution into the hemocoel. Clearly large quantities of FAA are removed and re-added to the hemolymph during dehydration-hydration (starvation-feeding) cycles. During hydration and starvation, secretion of fluid (and supposedly FAA) by Malpighian tubules is much reduced (reviewed by Gee, 1977); therefore, it is necessary to postulate a controlled reduction in amino acid resorption in the rectum to explain the increased levels of FAA which appear in the excreta. Regulation of FAA recovery in insect recta has not been studied, but the transport mechanism has been investigated in some detail in *Schistocerca*.

Using everted rectal sacs, Balshin and Phillips (1971) and Balshin (1973) showed that five neutral amino acids (glycine, proline, L-serine, L-alanine, L-theonine) were absorbed against large electrochemical differences when net water movement was prevented (Table I). These five amino acids account for 65% of the total hemolymph FAA concentration in *Schistocerca*. Rates of transport are adequate to explain recovery of most of the FAA secreted by Malpighian tubules (Balshin, 1973). The properties of this transport mechanism, which are summarized below, are generally similar to those for FAA in other animal tissues.

Entry of neutral L-amino acids into rectal pad cells from the lumen is apparently the energy requiring step, because tissue concentrations of these organic acids exceed those on both lumen and hemolymph sides by several fold during absorption. Other permeant, ^{14}C-labelled molecules (e.g. urea, O-methylglucose, D-serine, D-alanine, and GABA) do not accumulate in the tissue or hemocoel compartment above initial levels on the lumen side. Clearly L-amino acid transport is not caused by a general entrainment of solutes in a local flow of fluid within the rectal wall, as suggested by Berridge (1970). The stereospecificity of ^{14}C-serine and ^{14}C-alanine entry into rectal cells indicates that a carrier-mediated process is located in the apical membrane. The transported L-amino acids may share a common carrier, because ^{14}C-glycine influx is competitively inhibited by the presence of L-serine on the lumen side. Proline also reduces glycine influx but the form of inhibition is still obscure. As expected for a carrier-mediated process, ^{14}C-glycine influx obeys Michaelis-Menten kinetics with a K_t of 22 mM when the external Na$^+$ concentration is 174 mM. Replacing all of this Na$^+$ with choline causes drastic reduction in both the lumen-to-cell influx (K_t = 43 mM) and the transepithelial absorption of glycine. However, a small Na-independent component of glycine transport persists and this can cause the hemocoel concentration of this amino acid to rise 1.8x above the level in the lumen. Replacing all the K$^+$ (8 mM) or Cl$^-$ (185 mM) in the bathing saline with Na$^+$ and NO$_3^-$ respectively causes much smaller reductions in glycine transport. In summary, the data are reasonably consistent with the Na-gradient model for amino acid transport (Crane, 1977).

Interestingly, the relative rates at which individual FAA are transported by locust rectum (Table I) corresponds roughly with their relative concentrations in the hemolymph. This suggests that hemolymph FAA composition may be explained in part by the relative affinity of a common carrier mechanism in the rectum for individual FAA. The selectivity sequence suggests that additional methyl groups on amino acids decrease, while hydroxyl groups increase, binding to the carrier.

F. Other Solutes, Acetate

There is evidence for electrogenic transport of unknown anions across short-circuited locust recta (Williams *et al.*, 1978; Spring and Phillips, 1980b). When external Cl^- is completely replaced by NO_3^- or SO_4^{2-}, the I_{sc} across unstimulated recta does not change as long as a complex saline containing Krebs cycle intermediates and amino acids is used. The same anion substitutions for Cl^- cause I_{sc} to fall by 50% if a simple inorganic saline, containing only glucose and glutamate as energy sources, is used. Obviously, some organic constituent of complex saline is itself transported, or it may provide an energy source for increased transport of other ions when Cl^- is absent (e.g. HCO_3^- and organic anion absorption, or H^+ secretion).

At least one organic acid, acetate, can be actively transported by locust rectum. When all of the Cl^- in the bathing saline is replaced by acetate, I_{sc}, PD, and transepithelial resistance all increase 50 to 200% above values observed for unstimulated recta in NaCl saline. Since Cl^- transport is abolished by this treatment, while I_{sc} is increased, the rectal tissue must switch to alternate electrogenic transport processes. T. Baumeister in our laboratory has found that most of the ΔI_{sc} can be accounted for by a net flux of ^{14}C-acetate to the hemocoel side. This acetate transport has an apparent K_t of 70 mM and a V_{max} of 4 $\mu Equiv \cdot h^{-1} \cdot cm^{-2}$. The ΔI_{sc} is rapidly inhibited by cyanide. Propionate, citrate, malate, fumarate, and oxaloacetate do not stimulate I_{sc} when they are substituted for Cl^-. This suggests that acetate is not absorbed by a non-specific transfer process for organic acids, as proposed for vertebrate intestine (Jackson and Dudek, 1979).

Why should locust recta actively absorb acetate? Perhaps this solute is moved by a carrier which normally transports another organic molecule, possibly one involved with fluid transport (see Wall, 1977). Alternatively, insect physiologists may have overlooked an important end product of microbial digestion, which is perhaps produced in large amounts during starvation when the last meal is retained within the gut for 3-4 days. Volatile fatty acids (acetate, butyrate and propionate) are major products of digestion in most vertebrate herbivores, and these species (e.g. cow, rabbit, horse) possess reabsorptive mechanisms for acetate in the rumen and colon (reviewed by Prosser, 1973). The rectum might also retrieve acetate which is produced by lipid

metabolism during flight (Tulp and Van Kam, 1970) and which
is lost from the hemolymph in the Malpighian tubule
secretion. Acetate (2 to 9 mM) has been detected in body
fluids of *Schistocerca* by Baumeister in our laboratory.

V. CONTROL OF REABSORPTION

Hemolymph composition, but not volume, remains
relatively constant when terrestrial insects are starved and
dehydrated, or are fed solutions of diverse ionic
composition (reviewed by Shaw and Stobbart, 1972; also
Nicholson *et al.*, 1974). Concentrations of monovalent ions
in excreta of *Schistocerca, Periplaneta* and *Calliphora* range
from a few millimolar in hydrated individuals to several
hundred millimolar in animals which are salt-loaded or
dehydrated (Phillips, 1964b,c; Stobbart and Shaw, 1974).
Over this range of conditions, the Malpighian tubules
continue to produce an isosmotic fluid of relatively constant
ionic composition, even though the rate of fluid secretion
may be increased several fold by release of diuretic hormone
(DH; Maddrell, 1971, 1977). Clearly regulation of hemolymph
composition, and restoration of its volume after feeding, is
achieved by control of reabsorptive processes in the rectum
and hindgut. The precise nature of the endocrine and neural
mechanisms which control rectal reabsorption *in situ* are
still unclear; however, several factors have been identified
which influence these events *in vitro*.

A. Water

A diuretic factor (DH) which inhibits, and an
antidiuretic factor (ADH) which increases, net water
absorption by isolated rectal sacs are present in various
neurosecretory tissues of *Periplaneta, Schistocerca, Locusta*
and other insects (reviewed by Mordue, 1972; Gee, 1977).
Many of these assays were carried out on recta soon after
they were dissected from insects. During the first 1-2 h,
transport rates decrease rapidly with time and the rectal
tissue swells dramatically because recta are usually
transferred from a hyperosmotic environment on the lumen side
in vivo to an isosmotic one *in vitro* (Goh and Phillips, 1978;
Williams *et al.*, 1978). These rapid initial changes in
rectal activity may also reflect an inadequacy of the
external saline and its oxygenation, and removal of recta
from natural hormonal and neural influences. Consequently,
these earlier reports of factors which influence water

absorption deserve confirmation with well-characterized *in
vitro* preparations of insect recta, under steady-state
conditions. They require further confirmation *in situ* to
exclude the possibility that the *in vitro* effects are
strictly pharmacological.

B. *Ions*

Recently, short-circuited recta of *Schistocerca* have been
used as an assay system to identify agents which might
normally control ion reabsorption in this insect (Spring *et
al*., 1978; Hanrahan, 1978; Spring, 1979; Spring and Phillips,
1980a,b; Hanrahan and Phillips, 1980). A list of substances
which stimulate, or inhibit, or have no effect on steady-
state I_{sc} and J^{Cl}_{net} is given in Table III.
Corpora cardiaca (CC), hemolymph of recently fed locusts,
and cyclic nucleotides all stimulate electrogenic transport
of Cl^- by several fold. Cockroach CC also stimulates I_{sc}
across locust rectum. Other agents which are known to
elevate intracellular levels of cAMP in animal tissues
(prostaglandins and their precursor, arachidonic acid;
theophylline) do likewise. Linear log-dose response curves
were observed and maximum stimulation was achieved with
0.3 mM cAMP or 0.1 pair of CC in 5 ml of bathing saline.
Whole brain and ventral ganglia have slight stimulatory
effects but the concentration of activity in these tissues is
less than 0.5% of that in CC. The active factor in CC is
presumably released into the hemocoel of fed locusts because
cardiatectomy reduces the stimulatory effect of hemolymph
from such animals by 85% (Spring, 1979).

An hypothesis for the cellular mode of action of the
chloride transport stimulating hormone (CTSH) from CC is
shown in Fig. 2. In support of this model, addition of CC to
the hemocoel side of rectal sacs caused whole tissue levels
of cAMP to increase by 2- to 3-fold. In turn, externally
applied cAMP causes a 9 mV hyperpolarization of the PD across
the apical membrane (cell negative) as measured with glass
microelectrodes. This increase in the apical PD does not
occur if SO_4^{2-} is substituted for external Cl^-. Only a slight
depolarization of the basolateral border occurs following
stimulation with cAMP. These observations suggest that
intracellular cAMP stimulates Cl^- entry into the rectal pad
cells against a large PD. A higher intracellular level of
Cl^- may result, causing increased efflux of this anion down a
favourable PD gradient to the hemocoel.

There is evidence that CTSH is a peptide. Large
quantities of flight muscle have no effect on rectal I_{sc},
which indicates that the CC stimulant is not a general

metabolite. Known or putative neurotransmitter substances have been excluded (Table III). The action of CC hemogenate on rectal I_{sc} is mimicked by cAMP, the second messenger of peptide hormones in many animals; moreover CC increases tissue cAMP levels. The active factor is somewhat heat stable and is soluble in 80% methanol, which implies that it is not a large protein.

Phillips et al. (1979) have isolated the active factor in CC by gel filtration on Sephadex G75. A single peak of CTSH activity was observed by this and other methods (e.g. cellulose acetate electrophoresis at several pH values; thin-layer chromatography). By comparison with marker molecules, CTSH is estimated to have a molecular weight of 8-12,000. It is destroyed by trypsin and has a net negative charge over a wide pH range (5-10), but it is most stable at alkaline pH.

Is CTSH activity due to a known hormone from the CC (e.g. AKH, DH or ADH) or is it caused by a new peptide? CTSH is present in both glandular and storage lobes of locust CC, but 80% of the activity is in the latter (Phillips et al., 1979). This distribution would seem to exclude AKH and ADH, which are restricted to the glandular lobe in locust CC (Mordue, 1972; Stone et al., 1976). Moreover, excessive doses of synthetic AKH did not stimulate rectal I_{sc}. While DH and CTSH are both concentrated in the storage lobe, they can be distinguished on the basis of molecular weight determinations, thin-layer chromatography and stability in saline at room temperature (Phillips et al., 1979; Mordue and Phillips, unpublished observations). Moreover, reciprocal bioassays with semi-purified DH and CTSH from locusts were negative. Finally, CTSH stimulates salt transport and this would enhance water absorption from the lumen, whereas DH reduces fluid movement in the rectum. In summary, the available data indicate that CTSH is a new hormone.

The open-circuit PD across the rectal wall of *Melanopus* also increases when cAMP is added. However, recta of *Periplaneta* and *Acheta* did not respond to this treatment (Hanrahan, personal comm.), suggesting that somewhat different control processes may be operative in these species.

C. Integrative Studies on Whole Insects

To understand changes in rectal function during hydration-dehydration and feeding-starvation cycles, it is necessary to have detailed and comparable information on other events in insects: e.g. changes in tissue and hemolymph composition and volume; water loss across the body surface; rates of solute and water assimilation in the midgut; and rates of secretion by Malpighian tubules under different physiological conditions. This type of integration has been attempted for *Rhodnius* (Maddrell, 1976), *Schistocerca* (Shaw and Stobbart, 1972), and *Periplaneta* (Tucker, 1977), but it is clear that much additional information is still required on individual organs. Some observations and speculations on rectal function in whole *Schistocerca* are presented in this section.

Chloride transport in the locust rectum must proceed against large electrochemical gradients, but there are additional reasons why this reabsorptive process may have been selected for predominance in herbivorous insects which have a NaCl-rich hemolymph. When dehydrated individuals restore their hemolymph volume after feeding, Cl^- is often the monovalent ion in shortest supply. For example, a lettuce meal contains an excess of K^+ (114 mM) and organic anions compared to Na^+ (15 mM) and Cl^- (34 mM). But there is possibly an additional source of Na^+ available. *Periplaneta* store hemolymph Na^+ as urates in the fat body when the volume of this body fluid is reduced during dehydration, but the excess Cl^- is presumably excreted (Wall, 1970; Tucker, 1977). Perhaps CTSH or DH initiates release of Na^+ from the fat body after feeding? Hanrahan (1978) found that the Cl^- concentration in hemolymph declined temporarily by 40% within 3 h of feeding lettuce to dehydrated *Schistocerca*. This decline was completely due to dilution by the midgut absorbate, because the total Cl^- content in the hemocoel remained unchanged. Since feeding also stimulates Malpighian tubules in this species to secrete a KCl-rich fluid 3x more rapidly (Mordue, 1972), Cl^- recovery in the rectum must also be stimulated by CTSH to explain the complete retention of body Cl^- at this time. As previously discussed, CTSH may also raise rectal permeability to K^+ so that reabsorption of KCl is increased to compensate for greater Malpighian tubule secretion. The net result is probably an increased recycling of fluid through the whole excretory system, serving to rid the insect of toxic products which are ingested or produced by metabolism of the meal.

After feeding, the rate of Na^+ resorption may also be raised in the rectum temporarily to help increase the volume of NaCl-rich hemolymph. Undoubtedly the ratio of NaCl to KCl reabsorption must change with time to meet these different demands and to ensure a constant $Na^+:K^+$ ratio in the hemolymph. An obvious additional advantage of a powerful chloride pump that can be stimulated hormonally is that it may permit regulation of total salt reabsorption independent of $Na^+:K^+$ ratios in the absorbate. This presupposes the existence of unidentified hormones or neural mechanisms which modulate cation resorption in the rectum. Finally DH or ADH may alter permeability of the rectal wall to water and hence determine the osmolarity of the absorbate (Mordue, 1972). A temporary increase in water reabsorption after feeding might be required to aid in recovery of hemolymph volume and to balance increased Malpighian tubule secretion; however a reduction in the recovery of water may be appropriate if feeding is prolonged. After feeding for 20 minutes the feces become quite wet. Stimulation of salt resorption by CTSH might be expected to draw some additional water from the lumen without the intervention of an ADH to increase water permeability. The true situation in the intact locust is definitely unclear. In particular, it is still not known what activities are controlled by neurosecretory nerve endings which are present in papillate recta. In conclusion, the author wishes to re-emphasize that many of the views expressed in this article are simply working hypotheses, which hopefully will indicate promising topics for future research.

REFERENCES

Andrusiak, E. W. (1974). Resorption of phosphate, calcium, and magnesium in the *in vitro* locust rectum. M.Sc. thesis, University of British Columbia, Vancouver, Canada.

Anstee, J. H., and Bowler, K. (1979). Ouabain-sensitivity of insect epithelial tissues. *Comp. Biochem. Physiol.* *62A*, 61-69.

Balshin, M. (1973). Absorption of amino acids *in vitro* by the rectum of the desert locust (*Schistocerca gregaria*). Ph.D. thesis, University of British Columbia, Vancouver, Canada.

Balshin, M., and Phillips, J. E. (1971). Active absorption of amino acids in the rectum of the desert locust (*Schistocerca gregaria*). *Nature New Biol. 233*, 53-55.

Berridge, M. J. (1970). A structural analysis of intestinal absorption. *Symp. Roy. Entomol. Soc. London 5*, 135-153.

Berridge, M. J., and Gupta, B. L. (1967). Fine-structural changes in relation to ion and water transport in the rectal papillae of the blowfly, *Calliphora*. *J. Cell. Sci. 2*, 89-112.

Berridge, M. J., and Gupta, B. L. (1968). Fine-structural localization of adenosine triphosphatase in rectum of *Calliphora*. *J. Cell. Sci. 3*, 17-32.

Chamberlin, M., and Phillips, J. E. (1979). Regulation of
    hemolymph amino acids in the desert locust. *Federation
    Proc. 38*, 970.
Cochran, D. G. (1975). Excretion in insects. *In* "Insect
    Biochemistry and Function" (D. J. Candy, B. A. Kilby,
    eds.), pp. 179–281. Chapman and Hall, London.
Crane, R. K. (1977). The gradient hypothesis and other
    models of carrier mediated active transport. *Rev.
    Physiol. Biochem. Pharmacol. 78*, 99–159.
De Renzis, G., and B ornancin, M. (1977). A Cl^-/HCO_3^--ATPase
    in the gills of *Carassius auratus*. Its inhibition by
    thiocyanate. *Biochim. Biophys. Acta 467*, 192–207.
Djajakusumah, T., and Miles, P. W. (1966). Changes in the
    relative amounts of soluble protein and amino acids in
    the hemolymph of the locust, *Chortoicetes terminifera*
    Walker (Orthoptera:Acrididae), in relation to
    dehydration and subsequent hydration. *Aust. J. biol.
    Sci. 19*, 1081–1094.
Fischbarg, J. (1978). Fluid transport by corneal
    endothelium. *In* "Comparative Physiology: Water, Ions and
    Fluid Mechanics" (K. Schmidt-Nielsen, L. Bolis, S. H. P.
    Maddrell, eds.), pp. 21–39. University Press, Cambridge,
    England.
Frizzell, R. A., Field, M., and Schultz, S. G. (1979).
    Sodium-coupled chloride transport by epithelial tissues.
    Am. J. Physiol.:Renal Fluid Electrolyte Physiol. 5(1),
    F 1–8.
Frömter, E., and Diamond, J. (1972). Route of passive ion
    permeation in epithelia. *Nature New Biol. 235*, 9–13.
Gee, J. D. (1977). The hormonal control of excretion.
    In "Transport of Ions and Water in Animals" (B. L. Gupta,
    R. B. Moreton, J. L. Oschman, B. J. Wall, eds.),
    pp. 265–284. Academic Press, London.
Giebisch, G., Tosteson, D. C., and Ussing, H. H., eds. (1978).
    "Membrane Transport in Biology", vol. III. Springer-
    Verlag, Berlin.
Goh, S. L. (1971). Mechanism of water and salt absorption in
    the *in vitro* locust rectum. M.Sc. thesis, University of
    British Columbia, Vancouver, Canada.
Goh, S., and Phillips, J. E. (1978). Dependence of prolonged
    water absorption by *in vitro* locust rectum on ion
    transport. *J. exp. Biol. 72*, 25–41.
Gupta, B. L., Hall, T. A., and Moreton, R. B. (1977).
    Electron probe X-ray microanalysis. *In* "Transport of Ions
    and Water in Animals" (B. L. Gupta, R. B. Moreton, J. L.
    Oschman, B. J. Wall, eds.), pp. 83–164. Academic Press,
    London.

Hanrahan, J. W. (1978). Hormonal regulation of chloride in locusts. *The Physiologist 21*, 50.

Hanrahan, J. W., and Phillips, J. E. (1980). Na-independent Cl$^-$ transport in an insect. *Federation Proc.*, In press.

Harvey, W. R. (1980). Membrane physiology of insects. *In* "Membrane Physiology in Invertebrates" (R. P. Podesta, S. F. Timmers, eds.), In press. Academic Press, New York.

Herrera, L., Jordana, R., and Ponz, F. (1977). Effect of inhibitors on chloride-dependent transmural potential in the rectal wall of *Schistocerca gregaria*. *J. Insect Physiol. 23*, 677-682.

Hill, A. E. (1978). Fluid transport across *Necturus* gallbladder epithelium. *In* "Comparative Physiology: Water, Ions and Fluid Mechanics" (K. Schmidt-Nielsen, L. Bolis, S. H. P. Maddrell, eds.), pp. 41-42. University Press, Cambridge, England.

Irvine, H. B., and Phillips, J. E. (1970). Effects of respiratory inhibitors and ouabain on water transport by isolated locust rectum. *J. Insect Physiol. 17*, 381-393.

Jackson, M. J., and Dudek, J. A. (1979). Epithelial transport of weak electrolytes. *Federation Proc. 38*, 2043-2047.

Komnick, H., and Achenbach, U. (1979). Comparative biochemical, histochemical and autoradiographic studies of Na$^+$/K$^+$-ATPase in the rectum of dragonfly larvae (Odonata, Aeshnidae). *European J. Cell. Biol. 20*, 92-100.

Komnick, H., Schmitz, M. H., and Hinssen, H. Biochemischer Nachweis von HCO$_3^-$- und Cl$^-$-abhängigen ATPase-Aktivitäten im Rectum von anisopteren Libellenlarven und Hemmung der rectalen Chloridaufnahme durch Thiocyanat. *European J. Cell. Biol.*, In press.

Lane, N. (1979). Tight junctions in a fluid-transporting epithelium of an insect. *Science 204*, 91-93.

Leader, J. P., and Green, L. B. (1978). Active transport of chloride and sodium by the rectal chamber of the larvae of the dragonfly, *Uropetala carovei*. *J. Insect Physiol. 24*, 685-692.

Lee, H., Breitbart, H., Bergman, M., and Forte, J. G. (1979). K-stimulated ATPase activity and H$^+$ transport in gastric microsomal vesicles. *Biochim. Biophys. Acta 553*(1), 107-131.

Lewis, S. A. (1971). Charge properties and ion selectivity of the rectal intima of the desert locust. M.Sc. thesis, University of British Columbia, Vancouver, Canada.

Liedtke, C. M., and Hopfer, U. (1977). Anion transport in brush border membranes isolated from rat small intestine. *Biochem. Biophys. Res. Commun. 76*, 579-585.

Machin, J. (1978). Water vapour uptake by Tenebrio: a new approach to studying the phenomenon. *In* "Comparative Physiology: Water, Ions, and Fluid Mechanics" (K. Schmidt-Nielsen, L. Bolis, S. H. P. Maddrell, eds.), pp. 67-77. University Press, Cambridge, England.

Machin, J. (1979). Compartmental osmotic pressures in the rectal complex of *Tenebrio* larvae: evidence for a single tubular pumping site. *J. exp. Biol. 82*, 123-237.

Maddrell, S. H. P. (1971). The mechanisms of insect excretory systems. *Adv. Insect Physiol. 8*, 199-331.

Maddrell, S. H. P. (1976). Functional design of the neurosecretory system controlling diuresis in *Rhodnius prolixus*. *Am. Zoologist 16*, 131-139.

Maddrell, S. H. P. (1977). Insect Malpighian tubules. *In* "Transport of Ions and Water in Animals" (B. L. Gupta, R. B. Moreton, J. L. Oschman, B. J. Wall, eds.), pp. 541-570. Academic Press, London.

Maddrell, S. H. P. (1978). Transport across insect excretory epithelia. *In* "Membrane Transport in Biology" vol. III (G. Giebisch, D. C. Tosteson, H. H. Ussing, eds.), pp. 239-272. Springer-Verlag, New York.

Mordue, W. (1972). Hormones and excretion in locusts. *Gen. comp. Endocr. Suppl. 3*, 289-298.

Mullins, D. E., and Cochran, D. G. (1972). Nitrogen excretion in cockroaches: uric acid is not a major product. *Science 177*, 699-701.

Noble-Nesbitt, J. (1978). Absorption of water vapour by *Thermobia domestica* and other insects. *In* "Comparative Physiology: Water, Ions and Fluid Mechanics" (K. Schmidt-Nielsen, L. Bolis, S. H. P. Maddrell, eds.), pp. 53-66. University Press, Cambridge, England.

Peacock, A. J. (1979). A comparison of two methods for preparation of Mg^{2+}-dependent, $(Na^+ + K^+)$-stimulated ATPase from locust rectum. *Insect Biochem. 9*, 481-484.

Phillips, J. E. (1961). Rectal absorption of water and salts in the locust and blowfly. Ph.D. thesis, University of Cambridge, England.

Phillips, J. E. (1964a). Rectal absorption in the desert locust, *Schistocerca gregaria* Forskål. I. Water. *J. exp. Biol. 41*, 15-38.

Phillips, J. E. (1964b). Rectal absorption in the desert locust, *Schistocerca gregaria* Forskål. II. Sodium, potassium and chloride. *J. exp. Biol. 41*, 39-67.

Phillips, J. E. (1964c). Rectal absorption in the desert locust, *Schistocerca gregaria* Forskål. III. The nature of the excretory process. *J. exp. Biol. 41*, 69-80.

Phillips, J. E. (1965). Rectal absorption and renal function in insects. *Trans. Roy. Soc. Can. 3*, 237-254.

Phillips, J. E. (1969). Osmotic regulation and rectal absorption in the blowfly, *Calliphora erythrocephala*. *Can. J. Zool. 47*, 851-863.

Phillips, J. E. (1970). Apparent water transport by insect excretory systems. *Am. Zoologist 10*, 413-436.

Phillips, J. E. (1977a). Excretion in insects: function of gut and rectum in concentrating and diluting the urine. *Federation Proc. 32*, 2480-2486.

Phillips, J. E. (1977b). Problems of water transport in insects. *In* "Water Relations in Membrane Transport in Plants and Animals" (A. M. Jungreis, T. Hodges, A. M. Kleinzeller, S. G. Schultz, eds.), pp. 333-353. Academic Press, New York.

Phillips, J. E., Bradley, T., and Maddrell, S. H. P. (1978). Mechanisms of ionic and osmotic regulation in saline-water mosquito larvae. *In* "Comparative Physiology: Water, Ions and Fluid Mechanics" (K. Schmidt-Nielsen, L. Bolis, S. H. P. Maddrell, eds.), pp. 151-171. University Press, Cambridge, England.

Phillips, J. E., Mordue, W., Meredith, J., and Spring, J. (1979). Isolation of a chloride-transport stimulating hormone from locusts. *Am. Zoologist 19*, 936.

Prosser, C. L. (1973). "Comparative Animal Physiology." Saunders, Philadelphia.

Prusch, R. D. (1975). Unidirectional ion movements in the hindgut of larval *Sarcophaga bullata* (Diptera: Sarcophagidae). *J. exp. Biol. 64*, 89-99.

Sachs, G. (1977). Cation and anion transport mechanisms. *In* "Transport of Ions and Water in Animals" (B. L. Gupta, R. B. Moreton, J. L. Oschman, B. J. Wall, eds.), pp. 215-224. Academic Press, London.

Speight, J. (1967). Acidification of rectal fluid in the locust, *Schistocerca gregaria*. M.Sc. thesis, University of British Columbia, Vancouver, Canada.

Spring, J. H. (1979). Studies on the hormonal regulation of ion resorption in *Schistocerca gregaria*. Ph.D. thesis, University of British Columbia, Vancouver, Canada.

Spring, J., Hanrahan, J., and Phillips, J. E. (1978). Hormonal control of chloride transport across locust rectum. *Can. J. Zool. 56*, 1879-1882.

Spring, J. H., and Phillips, J. E. (1980a). Studies on locust rectum: I. Stimulants of electrogenic ion transport. *J. exp. Biol.*, In press.

Spring, J. H., and Phillips, J. E. (1980b). Studies on locust rectum: II. Identification of specific ion transport processes regulated by corpora cardiaca and cyclic-AMP. *J. exp. Biol.*, In press.

Stobbart, R. H., and Shaw, J. (1974). Salt and water balance: excretion. *In* "The Physiology of Insecta" (M. Rockstein, ed.), Vol. 5, pp. 362-446. Academic Press, New York.

Stone, J. V., Mordue, W., Batley, K. E., and Morris, H. R. (1976). Structure of locust adipokinetic hormone, a neurohormone that reulates lipid utilization during flight. *Nature 263*, 207-211.

Tucker, L. E. (1977). Regulation of ions in the hemolymph of the cockroach, *Periplaneta americana* during dehydration and rehydration. *J. exp. Biol. 71*, 95-110.

Tulp, A., and van Kam, K. (1970). The formation of acetate from pyruvate in housefly flight muscle mitochondria. *FEBS Letters 10*(5), 292-294.

Vietinghoff, U., Olszewska, A., and Janieszewski, L. (1969). Measurements of the bioelectric potentials in the rectum of *Locusta migratoria* and *Carausius morosus* in *in vitro* preparations. *J. Insect Physiol. 15*, 1273-1277.

Ussing, H. H., and Zerahn, K. (1951). Active transport of sodium as the source of electric current in the short-circuited isolated frog skin. *Acta Physiol. Scand. 23*, 110-127.

Wall, B. J. (1967). Evidence for antidiuretic control of rectal water absorption in the cockroach *Periplaneta americana* L. *J. Insect Physiol. 13*, 565-578.

Wall, B. J. (1970a). Effects of dehydration and rehydration on *Periplaneta americana*. *J. Insect Physiol. 16*, 1027-1042.

Wall, B. J. (1970b). Water and solute uptake by rectal pads of *Periplaneta americana*. *Am. J. Physiol. 218*, 1208-1215.

Wall, B. J. (1971). Local osmotic gradients in the rectal pads of an insect. *Federation Proc. 30*, 42-48.

Wall, B. J. (1977). Fluid transport in the cockroach rectum. *In* "Transport of Ions and Water in Animals" (B. L. Gupta, R. B. Moreton, J. L. Oschman, B. J. Wall, eds.), pp. 599-612. Academic Press, London.

Wall, B. J., and Oschman, J. L. (1975). Structure and function of the rectum in insects. *Fortschrifte der Zoologie 23*, 193-222.

Wall, B. J., Oschman, J. L., and Schmidt-Nielsen, B. (1970). Fluid transport: concentration of the intercellular compartment. *Science 167*, 1497-1498.

Wigglesworth, V. B. (1932). On the function of the so-called 'rectal glands' of insects. *Quart. J. Micro. Sci. 75*, 131-150.

Williams, D., Phillips, J. E., Prince, W. T., and Meredith, J. (1978). The source of short-circuit current across locust rectum. *J. exp. Biol. 77*, 107-122.

THE CONTROL OF WATER RELATIONS
IN INSECTS

Simon Maddrell

A.R.C. Unit of Invertebrate Chemistry & Physiology
Department of Zoology
University of Cambridge
Cambridge, U.K.

I. INTRODUCTION

In spite of their small size, insects survive very well in a variety of environments, nearly all of them characterised by a high degree of osmotic stress. In addition, conditions in their habitats are usually very variable. We should therefore expect to find in insects highly developed systems for the control of osmotic and ionic balance. The object of this essay is briefly to summarize the evidence that insect osmoregulatory systems are controlled, to review the most recent discoveries in the field, to illustrate the advantages of some of the ways in which changes are affected, and then finally to highlight several areas where more research is needed because little or nothing is known of whether or how control is carried out.

Most of this article is directly concerned with the control of water movements but since this is so intimately bound up with ion movements reference is also made to how relevant ion movements are regulated.

II. EVIDENCE FOR THE CONTROL OF INSECT OSMOREGULATORY SYSTEMS

The first clues that insects might have their water balance under hormonal control came from work on *Apis mellifera* where Altmann (1956) showed that injection of corpora cardiaca extracts led to decreased water excretion and to increased blood viscosity. A still clearer pointer was Nuñez' pioneering

179

study of the effects of ligation on the beetle larva, *Aniso-tarsus cupripennis* (Nuñez, 1956). He found that if the circulation of haemolymph between the head and the rest of the body is hindered or if the nervous connections between the brain and the rest of the nervous system are cut, then normal exretion stops and the animal swells enormously. He demonstrated that this swelling was due to uptake of water, by showing that the osmotic pressure, chloride concentration and the concentration of non-protein nitrogen had all fallen. Extirpation of the dorsal part of the brain and corpora cardiaca also interrupted excretion. If he repeatedly injected extracts of the brain and corpora cardiaca into such inflated animals, rapid excretion began. Similar extracts of the sub-oesophageal ganglion had no effect. Although these studies gave clear indications that the water balance of these insects were under some form of hormonal control, they did little to throw light on the mechanisms involved.

III. CONTROL OF MALPIGHIAN TUBULE FUNCTION

Using the techniques developed by Ramsay (1954) for making *in vitro* preparations of isolated Malpighian tubules, it has since been possible to assay insect haemolymph for hormones affecting tubule function. This has proved a very powerful tool and many such hormones have now been discovered. Appropriately for this volume, the first and perhaps the most dramatic case concerned the diuretic hormone of *Rhodnius*, the insect scarcely any of whose secrets have survived fifty years of Sir Vincent Wigglesworth's wide ranging and skilful investigation. This bloodsucking insect can survive many months without water yet within moments of one of its gigantic blood meals it can excrete dilute watery fluid at a very high rate (Wigglesworth, 1931a). It turns out that this dramatic reversal of policy is achieved by the release of a potent diuretic hormone into the haemolymph (Maddrell, 1963). The rate of fluid secretion by the Malpighian tubule is accelerated about one thousand fold within two to three minutes.

Following these investigations, a wide variety of insects have now been shown to be able to regulate the rates at which their Malpighian tubules secrete fluid when triggered by hormones. These hormones are usually referred to as diuretic hormones. In many cases, however, because water reabsorption is also accelerated there is no diuresis in the sense of rapid fluid elimination. A list of insects known to use hormones to regulate fluid transport by their Malpighian tubules is shown in Table 1. An example of the effect of one hormone on fluid secretion rate is shown in Fig. 1.

TABLE I. Insects for which there is evidence that the rate of fluid transport by their Malpighian tubules is regulated by hormones

Order	Species	Reference
Hymenoptera	Apis mellifera	Altmann (1956)
Diptera	Calliphora vomitoria	Knowles (1976)
	Calliphora erythrocephala	Schwartz & Reynolds (1979)
	Glossina morsitans	Gee (1975)
	Aedes taeniorhynchus	Maddrell & Phillips (1978)
	Anopheles freeborni	Nijhout & Carrow (1978)
Lepidoptera	Pieris brassicae	Nicolson (1976)
	Calpodes ethlius	Ryerse (1978)
	Danaus plexippus	Dores, Dallman & Herman (1979)
Coleoptera	Anisotarsus cupripennis	Nuñez (1956)
Hemiptera	Rhodnius prolixus	Maddrell (1962)
	Triatoma infestans	Maddrell (unpublished results)
	Triatoma phyllosoma	" " "
	Dipetalogaster maxima	" " "
	Dysdercus fasciatus	Berridge (1966)
Orthoptera	Periplaneta americana	Mills (1967)
	Locusta migratoria	Cazal & Girardie (1968)
	Schistocerca gregaria	Mordue (1969)
	Carausius morosus	Pilcher (1970)

The details of how the acceleration of fluid secretion is achieved is, in most cases, not known. However, in some insects, bathing the tubules in solutions containing 3',5'-cyclic adenosine monophosphate (cylic AMP) will stimulate rapid fluid secretion. The tubules appear to be more sensitive to external cyclic AMP than many other tissues; Rhodnius'tubules are half maximally stimulated when they are exposed to 8×10^{-5} M cyclic AMP in their bathing medium. This sensitivity may

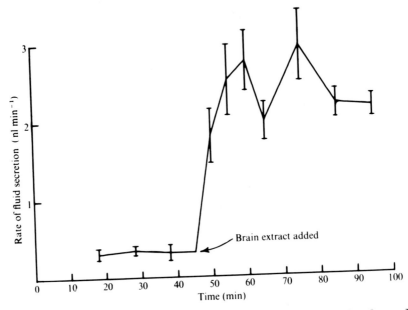

FIGURE 1. *Hormonal stimulation of fluid secretion by larval Malpighian tubules of* Aedes taeniorhynchus *(from Maddrell and Phillips, 1978).*

well be due not to greater intrinsic permeability of the cell membranes but to the relatively larger area of membrane that Malpighian tubule cells expose to their bathing media; this would allow relatively faster entry of cyclic AMP to the cell interior so that enzymic destruction there would more easily be swamped by incoming cyclic AMP. It seems likely from this, of course, that one element in the response of insect Malpighian tubule cells to circulating hormones is a change in the intracellular level of cyclic AMP. In *Rhodnius* this level has been measured and it does indeed increase following treatment with the insect's diuretic hormone (Aston, 1975; Fig. 2). Transport across an epithelium, especially rapid transport, is very likely to involve changes at both apical and basal cell membranes and the use of intracellular second messengers such as cyclic AMP would seem to be essential if the changes are to be coordinated in an effective manner.

In *Rhodnius*, not only is the rate of fluid secretion affected by hormone stimulation, but the composition of the fluid changes as well. Fig. 3 shows how the composition of the fluid secreted by *Rhodnius* Malpighian tubules differs according to whether or not fast fluid secretion has been stimulated. When stimulated, the tubules produce a fluid much richer in sodium than when they secrete fluid slowly. This makes good

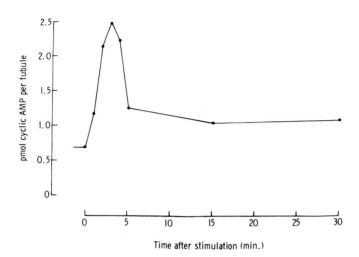

FIGURE 2.   Changes in the intracellular level of cyclic AMP
following hormonal stimulation of Malpighian tubules of
Rhodnius (redrawn from Aston, 1975).

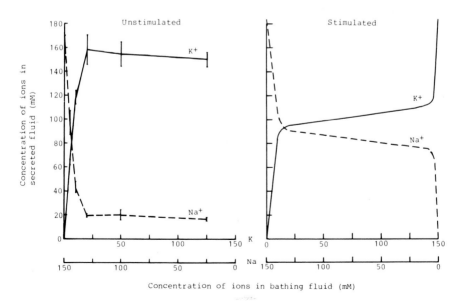

FIGURE 3.   Ion levels in the fluid secreted by Malpighian
tubules of Rhodnius before (left-hand graph) and after stimulation (right-hand graph).

sense as the main function of accelerated fluid secretion is to
eliminate most of the sodium-rich plasma from the blood meal.
After diuresis, when the blood meal is slowly digested, potassium from the blood cells has to be excreted and the tubules
then slowly secrete a fluid suitably rich in potassium.

A. *The function of hormones controlling fluid secretion by*
   Malpighian tubules

Given that so many insects can regulate the rate of fluid
secretion by their Malpighian tubules, there arises the question of the advantages such an ability confers on an insect.
The most obvious use of accelerating fluid secretion by the
Malpighian tubules is that this allows the insect rapidly to
eliminate unwanted fluid. Such an ability is, however, likely
to be useful to insects only under relatively rare circumstances; most terrestrial insects, at least, live most of their
lives under conditions of water lack. Nonetheless blood-
sucking insects such as mosquitoes and *Rhodnius* and its relatives do need rapid diuresis after a blood meal and use diuretic
hormones to achieve this. A further instance, probably of wide
occurrence, concerns newly emerged adult flying insects. Adults
of *Pieris brassicae* using a diuretic hormone rapidly eliminate
fluid after emergence; within 3 h they lose 40% of their body
weight and the volume of haemolymph may fall from 95 to 25 µl,
a decline of close to 75% (Nicolson, 1976). Such weight loss
is clearly of use to an insect about to enter a flying phase.
Apart from these instances where fluid loss is of evident
advantage, the uses of accelerated tubule fluid secretion have
more subtle explanations. One consequence of faster fluid
secretion is that substances, other than the ions and water of
the secreted fluid, will be diluted in the tubule lumen. This
will steepen the concentration gradient for the passive entry
of such substances and it will reduce the tendency for substances actively concentrated in the lumen to leak out. In
both cases it would seem that removal of the substances from
the haemolymph would be accelerated. Enough is now known of
the passive permeability of Malpighian tubules and of the rates
at which they actively transport a variety of substances into
the tubule lumen to be able to examine this expectation.
Figures 4 and 5 show the results of calculations done for the
Malpighian tubules of *Calliphora* to demonstrate how the active
and passive removal of substances from the bathing medium
would be expected to vary with the rate of fluid secretion in
the range 0–30 nl min^{-1}. Unstimulated tubules of *Calliphora*
secrete fluid at about 4 nl min^{-1} (Berridge, 1968) and it has
been recently shown that *Calliphora* Malpighian tubules can,
under stimulation, secrete fluid at rates of the order of 30 nl

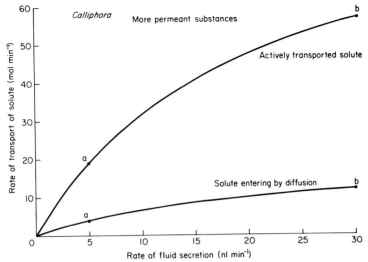

FIGURE 4. Calculated rates of elimination of relatively permeant substances by Malpighian tubules secreting at different
rates. Note that elimination at 30 nl min^{-1} (b) is much faster
than at 5 nl min^{-1} (a), both for substances actively transported across the wall (upper line) and for substances crossing
passively by diffusion.

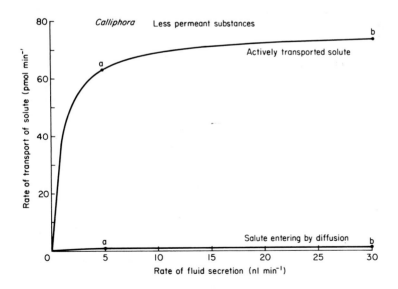

FIGURE 5. As for Figure 4 but for substances to which the
tubule is less permeable. Changes in fluid secretion have
less effect; compare (b) with (a).

min^{-1} (Schwartz and Reynolds, 1979). The calculations have
been done both for substances to which the tubule walls are
relatively permeable (Fig. 4) and for substances to which the
walls are less permeable (Fig. 5). The bases for these calculations are given in Maddrell *et al* (1974) and Maddrell and
Gardiner (1974). The calculations show:

  (i) that changes in the rate of fluid secretion in the
      range 5-30 nl min^{-1} (i.e. stimulated rates) have
      relatively greater effects on the removal of permeable
      substances than they have on substances to which the
      tubules are relatively impermeable (compare Fig. 4
      and Fig. 5).

 (ii) that active and passive entry of substances to which
      the tubule wall is equally permeable are affected in
      a similar way by changes in fluid transport (compare
      the upper and lower line in Fig. 4). However, the
      extra amount of material removed from the haemolymph
      on stimulation is higher in the case of a substance
      subject to active transport, especially where the
      tubule is not very permeable to the substance
      (compare the upper lines in Figs. 4 and 5 with the
      lower lines).

That this analysis is indeed indicative of what might happen
in real circumstances is underlined by comparing the analytical
predictions with measurements actually made on *Calliphora* Malpighian tubules. Such a comparison is shown in Fig. 6 where
actual measurements on dye transport by *Calliphora* tubules are
compared with the theoretical predictions.

  This analysis reveals that changes in fluid secretion have
most effect on substances which the tubule cells actively transport into the lumen. Since these substances are, of course,
the ones which the insect wishes most to eliminate, this makes
very good sense. In addition it provides a reason for the very
existence of a so-called diuretic hormone in insects where no
rapid elimination of water follows the appearance of the hormone in circulation.

  An excellent example of this concerns the 'diuretic' hormone of the locust. It appears that the Malpighian tubules of
the locust are stimulated to secrete fluid faster during flight,
but faster fluid reabsorption in the hindgut means that no
fluid is lost (Mordue, 1969). It has been suggested that this
would result in faster elimination of waste products appearing
in the haemolymph as a result of the intense metabolic activity
during flight. From the analysis given above it can now be
seen that acceleration of fluid secretion by the tubules does
not affect passive excretion very much but does greatly increase elimination of actively transported materials. Since

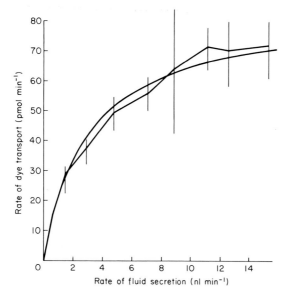

FIGURE 6.   The dependence of net dye transport on rate of fluid secretion in Calliphora Malpighian tubules.   *The smooth curve shows calculated values and the points   show actual measurements (from Maddrell* et al *1974).*

evolution is bound to have favoured the production of active transport mechanisms for the more toxic materials that appear in the haemolymph, it follows that increased circulation of fluid through the locust excretory system will, appropriately, increase most   the excretion of potentially damaging substances.   On the other hand the loss of useful substances which are not actively transported into the lumen will be less affected and so energy is saved in not having to provide for their more rapid reabsorption.

Although these conclusions provide a satisfying rationale for the way in which the excretory system operates during changes in its rate of operation, it has to be admitted that the experimental evidence supporting the main points is still thin.   The few available facts support the interpretation given but much more work needs to be done to put these ideas on a really firm foundation.

B. Advantages of high speed fluid excretion

Before leaving this area there are some remarks to be made about diuresis in *Rhodnius*.   This insect takes enormous meals of blood (up to twelve times its own body weight) and then

excretes the excess fluid at an extraordinarily high rate.   The
rate of excretion can be as high as 1.2 μl min^{-1} which is
equivalent to excreting a volume of fluid equivalent to its
whole haemolymph volume in 15 min.   This goes on until a weight
of fluid equal to 40-45% of the meal has been excreted.   Why is
fluid excreted so fast?   Apart from the advantages of rapidly
recovering its shape and increasing its manoeuvrability, it has
become clear that such very rapid fluid excretion drains less
useful solutes from the haemolymph.   *Rhodnius* haemolymph contains more than 30 mM of amino acids (Maddrell and Gardiner,
1980).   The tubules have a permeability to amino acids of about
0.15 nl min^{-1} mm^{-2} (Maddrell and Gardiner, 1980).   One can
calculate the fraction of the haemolymph content of amino acids
that would be passively lost at, say, an excretory rate of 1.2
μl min^{-1} (that actually observed) and compare it with the loss
that would occur at 80 nl min^{-1} (equivalent to the stimulated
rate of fluid secretion by the tubules in other insects).   If
the insect took a blood meal of 330 μl and excreted 140 μl of
fluid, calculation shows that at 1.2 μl min^{-1} only 3% of the
haemolymph amino acids would be lost (actual measurements agree
with this figure); at 80 nl min^{-1}, more than 30% of the amino
acids would be lost.   It is evidently an advantage to the insect
to excrete fluid as fast as possible.   This may help explain
why it is that the tubules of blood-sucking insects secrete
fluid at the highest rates known for any tissue.

   It can be seen from Fig. 7 that very fast fluid secretion
offers no advantage to insects using accelerated fluid secretion as a means of hastening elimination of actively transported substances.   Once faster fluid secretion has decreased
the luminal concentration of transported material to a level
not much above that of the bathing medium, further increases
in the rate of fluid secretion speed the elimination of actively transported substances relatively little and would of course
require the more rapid expenditure of energy.   The differences
in the rates of fluid secretion by the tubules of blood sucking
insects and of other insects seem to be appropriate.

   The advantages of using hormones to control fluid secretion
by the Malpighian tubules can be summarised:
   (1) Fluid elimination can be greatly increased.   This is
       useful at the pupal/flying adult moult or after large
       meals of dilute fluid.
   (2) The haemolymph can be more rapidly filtered through the
       excretory system.   This leads to much faster elimina-
       tion of permeant substances especially those which are
       actively transported by the tubules.   These are likely
       to be potentially damaging substances and their excre-
       tion can thus be hastened when appropriate.

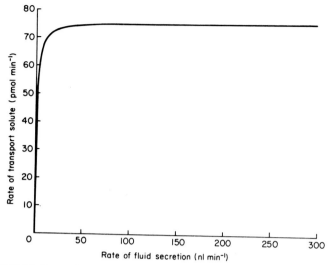

FIGURE 7. The calculated dependence of elimination of transported solute on high rates of Malpighian tubule fluid secretion. The calculation assumed the solute was transported into
the lumen at a rate of 75 pmol min⁻¹ and that the wall had a
permeability to the transported solute of 0.75 nl min⁻¹ mm⁻².

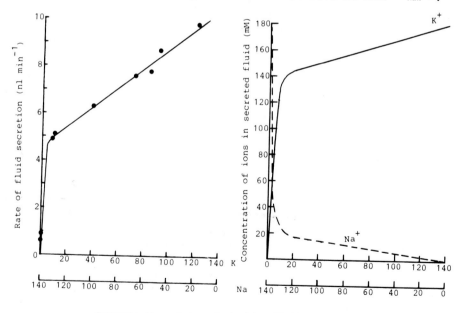

Concentration of ions in bathing fluid (mM)

FIGURE 8. The effects of increasing potassium concentration in
the bathing fluid on the rate of secretion and composition of
fluid secreted by Malpighian tubules (based on Berridge, 1968).

(3) Where fluid elimination is essential, a further advantage results from making the elimination as rapid as
possible. In this way the time during which useful
substances from the haemolymph can enter the primary
excretory fluid is reduced. The fluid can then be
eliminated with little modification without incurring
significant losses of valuable material.

C. Autonomous changes in Malpighian tubule function

Malpighian tubules have as their main function the regulation and control of haemolymph composition and volume. In
carrying out this function it turns out that they respond in
appropriate ways to changes in haemolymph composition, not
only as directed by circulating hormones, but also autonomously.
Regulation of a tissue by a hormone involves a chain of neurones
which monitor some parameter and stimulate suitable hormone
release. A more economical system might be one where the
tissue itself directly responded in an appropriate way to a
change in the composition of its environment. Just such behaviour is seen in some insect Malpighian tubules.

Many insects are phytophagous and in consequence face the
problem of an excess of potassium in the diet. Most insects
seem to absorb the constituents of their diet into the haemolymph in a surprisingly unselective way. Potassium levels in
the haemolymph are known to be strongly affected by the nature
of the diet (Florkin and Jeuniaux, 1964). The Malpighian
tubules of many insects respond appropriately to increasing
levels of potassium in the haemolymph.

Fig. 8 shows how the composition and rate of secretion of
the fluid produced by isolated insect Malpighian tubules changes
with the potassium concentration in their environment. Over
the physiological range, below 20 mM, it is clear that potassium excretion increases rapidly with increasing bathing concentrations and that this does not rely on hormonal regulation.

In recently fed blood-sucking insects the problem is a
different one. We have seen how it is to their advantage to
eliminate fluid at high rates. However, the ingested plasma
contains only 5 mM potassium. If the tubules were to secrete
potassium-rich fluid at a rate dependent on the potassium level,
as do other insects, they would soon not only exhaust the
haemolymph potassium but would be forced to secrete fluid at
very low rates. Significantly the rate of fluid secretion in
the tubules of those blood-sucking insects so far examined is
not dependent on the potassium concentration. Furthermore, in
the tsetse fly, Glossina, the tubules secrete fluid rich in
sodium and containing only low levels of potassium (Fig. 9).

Rhodnius' tubules, however, secrete fluid containing 10-20 times as much potassium as the haemolymph (Fig. 3). The situation is rescued by the activity of the lower region of the Malpighian tubule, where potassium chloride is rapidly returned to the haemolymph leaving a suitably hypo-osmotic, potassium-poor, sodium-rich fluid to be excreted (Maddrell and Phillips, 1975). The potassium concentration of the bathing fluid directly affects the avidity with which the lower tubule recovers potassium from the lumen (Fig. 10). Since potassium transport into the lumen by the upper tubule is also sensitive to potassium, the performance of the whole tubule acts so as to regulate the haemolymph potassium level. If the haemolymph level falls, the upper tubule produces fluid containing less potassium (Fig. 3) and the lower tubule recovers more potassium from the fluid passed to it. Opposite changes follow rises in potassium level. All these changes occur autonomously without alteration of hormone stimulation.

IV. CONTROL OF REABSORPTIVE MECHANISMS IN THE HINDGUT

We have dealt so far only with the control of Malpighian tubule function. Of at least equal importance to the insect is its ability to regulate the extent and quality of reabsorption from the primary excretory fluid delivered from the Malpighian tubules. However, compared with the wealth of information on the regulation of tubule function, rather little is known of how hindgut function is controlled.

In the locust it has been known for some time that rectal reabsorption of ions and water is regulated; locusts fed sea water eliminate a markedly hypertonic fluid while locusts fed distilled water excrete a dilute fluid containing less than 1-2 mM of the common ions (Phillips, 1964). The evidence is that water absorption is under hormonal control (Cazal and Girardie, 1968; Mordue, 1969) as is the rate of chloride uptake (Spring and Phillips, 1980a,b).

Very little is known of how other insects control the vital reabsorptive activities of the hindgut. There is a clear need for more research in this area.

V. COORDINATION OF ACTIVITY OF EPITHELIA INVOLVED IN WATER BALANCE

In the locust, flight elicits both increased fluid secretion by the Malpighian tubules and fluid reabsorption by the rectum,

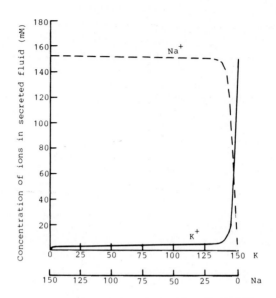

FIGURE 9.   The composition of the fluid secreted by Malpighian
tubules of **Glossina** *(based on Gee, 1976)*.

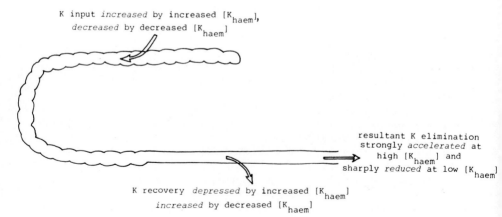

FIGURE 10.   The influence of the potassium concentration of the
haemolymph, [K_{haem}], on the elimination of potassium by the
Malpighian tubule of **Rhodnius.**

so that no water is actually lost (Mordue, 1969). Provided
that the potential for water recovery in the rectum is higher
than the rate at which it is removed from the haemolymph by
the tubules, the locust will remain in water balance.

A somewhat different problem arises during diuresis in
Rhodnius. Excess fluid from the meal is first transported
into the haemolymph and then eliminated through the Malpighian
tubules. The problem here is that the fluid movements are so
rapid and extensive; fluid of 5-10 times the volume of the
haemolymph passes through in the space of 2-3 h. The danger
is that if the activity of the midgut wall and that of the
tubules are not closely matched, the haemolymph volume could
change drastically and produce unacceptable changes in the
concentration of some haemolymph solutes. Coordination of
these epithelia has been shown particularly clearly in experiments in which some of the Malpighian tubules are removed
prior to feeding. Under these conditions, fluid transport by
the midgut is reduced in rate so that it exactly matches the
rate of fluid elimination by the remaining Malpighian tubules
(Maddrell and Gardiner, unpublished results). Evidence is
accumulating that the midgut is as much under hormonal control
as are the tubules. It now seems very likely that the same
hormone controls both epithelia and it is possible to suggest
a way in which the rates of fluid transport by the two epithelia might be matched accurately and automatically. If the
maximum rate of fluid uptake by the midgut is higher than the
possible rate of fluid elimination by the tubules, and if the
concentration of the circulating hormone is such that the midgut is not maximally stimulated and the Malpighian tubules are
more than maximally stimulated, then the situation is stable
with changes in haemolymph volume automatically altering the
hormone concentration so that the original haemolymph volume
is restored. Fig. 11 illustrates this idea. If the haemolymph volume should tend to increase, this will slightly dilute
the hormone controlling the epithelia; as a result, midgut
absorption will be slowed and with fluid removal from the
haemolymph remaining at a high level, the haemolymph volume
will decrease. Conversely a reduction in haemolymph volume
will increase the hormone level so increasing midgut absorption and restoring the situation. Several of the elements in
this proposed scheme have now been established. For example,
during the whole period of diuresis, the haemolymph always
contains more hormone than that required to stimulate the
Malpighian tubules maximally. Furthermore, hormone released
from the neurohaemal areas on the abdominal nerves (Maddrell,
1966) by treatment with K-rich saline (Maddrell and Gee, 1974)
affect Malpighian tubule fluid secretion at concentrations two
to three times lower than that required to stimulate the midgut epithelium (Maddrell and Wakefield, unpublished). Current

research is directed towards establishing whether the haemolymph
contains submaximal doses of the hormone controlling the midgut
and establishing finally that this hormone is identical with
the diuretic hormone regulating fluid secretion by the Malpighian tubules.

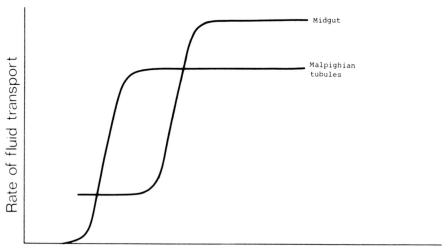

Concentration of diuretic hormone in the haemolymph

FIGURE 11. *Dose/response curves for fluid transport by the
midgut and Malpighian tubules of* **Rhodnius** *under hormonal
control.*

VI. CONTROL OF WATER PERMEABILITY OF THE CUTICLE

     Insect cuticle on the general body surface is usually
practically impermeable to water. Indeed were it not so it is
arguable that insects could not survive on land as they expose
a surface area relatively to their volume which on average is
about 100 times higher than their main terrestrial competitors,
the vertebrates (terrestrial insects range in weight from about
10^{-6} to 10^{2}g, while terrestrial vertebrates range from 1 to 10^{7}
g). The surprising discovery has recently been made (Treherne
and Willmer, 1975) that the water permeability of the cockroach,
Periplaneta americana, may be under hormonal control. Decapitated insects rapidly lose water through their external surface
but implantation of the brain and corpora cardiaca reverses
this. The significance of this discovery is debatable but it
is clear that if the insect needs to eliminate water it could
do it most cheaply and effectively by allowing it to evaporate
through the body wall. Such a method would not involve the

inevitable slight loss of ions and metabolically expensive reabsorption that would be involved if water were eliminated via
the excretory system.

VII. ELIMINATION OF WATER THROUGH THE SALIVARY GLANDS

Emerging adult saturniid moths often produce very large
volumes of saliva. In some cases this is used to provide the
correct operating conditions for the enzyme cocoonase which is
used to soften the cocoon enabling the moth to extricate itself
prior to wing expansion (Kafatos and Williams, 1964). In other
cases there is no cocoon but extensive salivary fluid production
is retained and appears to be largely responsible for the weight
reduction required to prepare the adult for flight (Edwards,
1964). Most insects achieve such weight reduction via greatly
accelerated fluid loss through the Malpighian tubules and hindgut.

VIII. AREAS FOR FUTURE RESEARCH

It is a striking feature of moulting in insects that a
large fraction of the fluid in the haemolymph, as much as 50%,
in some cases (Nicolson, 1975; Jungreis, 1979), is temporarily
transferred across the body wall to form the moulting fluid.
Just before ecdysis this large volume is then virtually all reabsorbed. Very little is yet known of how these fluid movements
are driven and almost nothing of how they are controlled.
The absorption of the products of digestion in insects is
thought to be largely driven by uptake of water from the gut
lumen (Treherne, 1967). This so concentrates soluble materials
in the lumen that both their passive and active uptake is
greatly accelerated. Nothing is known of whether this fluid
transport is regulated and, if so, how.
Work on *Apis* and *Anisotarsus* could be said to have been
pioneering in awakening interest in how insects control their
water balance. Strangely the role of hormones in water relations in Hymenoptera and Coleoptera has not been pursued; it
now should be.
The control of cuticular water permeability known in the
cockroach is so far the only such case known. It is of obvious
interest to discover whether such control is a feature of the
physiology of other insects.
Possibly the most important areas requiring investigation
concern the control mechanisms regulating the excretory system.
In many cases, hormones are known to exist which activate the

Malpighian tubules. In fewer cases hormones have been discovered which affect reabsorption by the hindgut. What is now needed is some knowledge of the stimuli and sense organs which trigger the release of these hormones, how (or indeed whether) the strength of the relevant stimuli is related to the resulting concentration of hormone in circulation, how osmoregulatory hormones are removed from circulation, how activities of different parts of the excretory system are coordinated; does an imposed change involve one hormone or several?

As a final point, the regulatory activity of the insect hindgut is of critical importance to insect survival yet little is known of how this regulatory activity is achieved. Of all the areas of which we are still ignorant in the field of osmotic and ionic regulation in insects this seems to be the one where more research is the most needed.

REFERENCES

Altmann, G. (1956). Die Regulation des Wasserhaushaltes der Honigbiene. *Insectes soc.* 3, 33-40.

Aston, R.J. (1975). The role of adenosine 3',5'-cyclic monophosphate in relation to the diuretic hormone of *Rhodnius prolixus*. *J. Insect Physiol.* 21, 1873-1877.

Berridge, M.J. (1966). The physiology of excretion in the cotton stainer, *Dysdercus fasciatus* Signoret. IV. Hormonal control of excretion. *J. exp. Biol.* 44, 553-566.

Berridge, M.J. (1968). Urine formation by the Malpighian tubules of *Calliphora erythrocephala*. I. Cations. *J. exp. Biol* 48, 159-174.

Cazal, M. and Girardie, A. (1968). Controle humoral de l'équilibre hydrique chez *Locusta migratoria migratorioides*. *J. Insect Physiol.* 14, 655-668.

Dores, R.M., Dallmann, S.H. and Herman, W.S. (1979). The regulation of post-eclosion and post-feeding diuresis in the monarch butterfly, *Danaus plexippus*. *J. Insect Physiol.* 25, 895-901.

Edwards, J.S. (1964). Diuretic function of the labial glands in the adult giant silk moths, *Hyalophora cecropia*. *Nature, Lond.* 203, 668-669.

Florkin, M. and Jeuniaux, C. (1964). Hemolymph:composition. pp.109-152 in Vol.3 of "The Physiology of Insecta", (M. Rockstein, ed.), Academic Press, New York.

Gee, J.D. (1976). Active transport of sodium by the Malpighian tubules of the tsetse fly, *Glossina morsitans*. *J. exp. Biol. 64*, 357-368.

Jungreis, A.M. (1979). Physiology of moulting in insects. pp.109-184. In "Advances in Insect Physiology" (J.E. Treherne, M.J. Berridge & V.B. Wigglesworth, eds). Academic Press Inc., London.

Kafatos, F.C. and Williams, C.M. (1964). Enzymatic mechanism for the escape of certain moths from their cocoons. *Science, N.Y. 146*, 538-540.

Knowles, G. (1976). The action of the excretory apparatus of *Calliphora vomitoria* in handling injected sugar solution. *J. exp. Biol. 64*, 131-140.

Maddrell, S.H.P. (1962). A diuretic hormone in *Rhodnius prolixus* Stål. *Nature, Lond. 194*, 605-606.

Maddrell, S.H.P. (1963). Excretion in the blood-sucking bug, *Rhodnius prolixus* Stål. I. The control of diuresis. *J. exp. Biol. 40*, 247-256.

Maddrell, S.H.P. (1966). The site of release of the diuretic hormone in *Rhodnius* - a new neurohaemal organ in insects. *J. exp. Biol. 45*, 499-508.

Maddrell, S.H.P. and Gardiner, B.O.C. (1974). The passive permeability of insect Malpighian tubules to organic solutes. *J. exp. Biol. 60*, 641-652.

Maddrell, S.H.P. and Gardiner, B.O.C. (1980). The retention of amino acids in the haemolymph during diuresis in *Rhodnius prolixus*. *J. exp. Biol.* (in press).

Maddrell, S.H.P., Gardiner, B.O.C., Pilcher, D.E.M. and Reynolds, S.E. (1974). Active transport by insect Malpighian tubules of acidic dyes and acylamides. *J. exp. Biol. 61*, 357-377.

Maddrell, S.H.P. and Phillips, J.E. (1975). Secretion of hypo-osmotic fluid by the lower Malpighian tubules of *Rhodnius prolixus*. *J. exp. Biol. 62*, 671-683.

Maddrell, S.H.P. and Phillips, J.E. (1978). Induction of sulphate transport and hormonal control of fluid secretion by Malpighian tubules of larvae of the mosquito, *Aedes taeniorhynchus*. *J. exp. Biol.* 75, 133-145.

Mills, R.R. (1967). Hormonal control of excretion in the American cockroach. I. Release of a diuretic hormone from the terminal abdominal ganglion. *J. exp. Biol.* 46, 35-41.

Mordue, W. (1969). Hormonal control of Malpighian tubules and rectal function in the desert locust *Schistocerca gregaria*. *J. Insect Physiol.* 15, 273-285.

Nicolson, S.W. (1976). The hormonal control of diuresis in the Cabbage white butterfly, *Pieris brassicae*. *J. exp. Biol.* 65, 565-575.

Nijhout, H.F. and Carrow, G.M. (1978). Diuresis after a bloodmeal in female *Anopheles freeborni*. *J. Insect Physiol.* 24, 293-298.

Nuñez, J.A. (1956). Untersuchungen über die Regelung des Wasserhaushaltes bei *Anisotarsus cupripennis* Germ.. *Z. vergl. Physiol.* 38, 341-354.

Phillips, J.E. (1964). Rectal absorption in the desert locust, *Schistocerca gregaria* Forskål. III. The nature of the excretory process. *J. exp. Biol.* 41, 69-80.

Pilcher, D.E.M. (1970). Hormonal control of the Malpighian tubules of the stick insect, *Carausius morosus*. *J. exp. Biol.* 52, 653-665.

Ramsay, J.A. (1954). Active transport of water by the Malpighian tubules of the stick insect, *Dixippus morosus* (Orthoptera, Phasmidae). *J. exp. Biol.* 31, 104-113.

Ryerse, J.S. (1978). Developmental changes in Malpighian tubule fluid transport. *J. Insect Physiol.* 24, 315-319.

Schwartz, L.M. and Reynolds, S.E. (1979). Fluid transport in *Calliphora* Malpighian tubules: a diuretic hormone from the thoracic ganglion and abdominal nerves. *J. Insect Physiol.* 25, 847-854.

Spring, J.H. and Phillips, J.E. (1980a). Studies on locust rectum: I. Stimulants of electrogenic ion transport. *J. exp. Biol.* (in press)

Spring, J.H. & Phillips, J.E. (1980b). Studies on locust
    rectum: II. Identification of specific ion transport pro-
    cesses regulated by corpora cardiaca and cyclic-AMP.
    J. exp. Biol. (in press)

Treherne, J.E. (1967). Gut absorption. A. Rev. Ent. 12,
    45-58.

Treherne, J.E. and Willmer, P.G. (1975). Hormonal control of
    integumentary water-loss: evidence for a novel neuroendo-
    crine system in an insect (Periplaneta americana). J. exp.
    Biol. 63, 143-159.

Wigglesworth, V.B. (1931). The physiology of excretion in a
    blood-sucking insect, Rhodnius prolixus (Hemiptera,
    Reduviidae). I. Composition of the urine. J. exp. Biol.
    8, 411-427.

THE FAT BODY AS A PROTEIN FACTORY

Gerard R. Wyatt

Department of Biology
Queen's University
Kingston, Ontario

I. INTRODUCTION

For the study of the regulation of differentiated cell
function, the fat body of insects is an organ or exceptional
interest. As has long been known (Wigglesworth, 1939, The
Principles of Insect Physiology, p. 238), the fat body cells
are responsible for a wide range of roles. These include the
metabolism of carbohydrates, lipids and nitrogenous compounds,
the synthesis and regulation of blood sugar, storage of glycogen, fat and protein, and synthesis of the major blood
proteins - a diversity that may be unequalled in any other
metazoan cell. The fat body cell can switch its activity
pattern in response to nutritional, hormonal and developmental
signals, to provide the successive needs of the growing, metamorphosing, migrating and reproducing insect. Thus, the fat
body cell plays not one, but an orderly succession of roles.
As Wigglesworth has pointed out, "fat body" is a misnomer.
Had this fascinating organ not been branded with such a discouraging name before its many potentialities were recognized,
it would doubtless have been better appreciated by biologists.
In a review of the biochemistry of insect fat body, Kilby
(1963) emphasized its conduct of intermediary metabolism. At
that time, its role as the source of plasma proteins had only
recently been demonstrated by analysis of the products released when silkworm fat body was incubated *in vitro*
(Shigematsu, 1958), and its role in protein storage, although
inferred from histological studies, had not been examined biochemically. Ten years later, an extensive review on protein
and nucleic acid metabolism in insect fat body was possible

(Price, 1973). The rapid increase in knowledge in this area
depended on the application of new radioisotope, electrophoretic and immunochemical techniques, and on improved understanding of insect endocrinology and cell biology. More
recently, there have appeared a stimulating review on patterns
of gene activity during insect development, emphasizing the
changing role of the fat body (Thomson, 1975), and reviews on
the insect plasma proteins (Wyatt and Pan, 1978) and the
endocrine regulation of fat body development and function
(Keeley, 1978). This essay aims to complement those of Locke,
Steele and Engelmann in the present volume by considering the
conclusions, problems and opportunities that arise from the
biochemical study of the synthesis and storage of specific
proteins in the insect fat body. Many of the older references,
available in reviews, are omitted.

II. STORAGE PROTEINS AND PROTEIN STORAGE

    Since the late nineteenth century, it has been repeatedly
observed that prepupal fat body cells contain abundant dense
cytoplasmic bodies variously described as albuminoid spheres,
proteinaceous globules and so on (reviews: Wigglesworth,
1972, The Principles of Insect Physiology, 7th Ed., pp. 443-
445; Price, 1973; Thomson, 1975). While the origin and fate
of these was obscure, their appearance just before metamorphosis and disappearance during the growth of the adult organs
suggested a role as a protein reserve. More recently, studies
with the electron microscope have revealed in *Calpodes* several
types of cytoplasmic inclusions, which appeared to participate
in the digestion of intracellular organelles, and also to incorporate protein from the hemolymph (Locke and Collins,
1968). The hemolymph protein concentration rose steeply
during the last larval instar and then declined sharply in the
prepupal stage just when granules were forming in the fat
body. Peroxidase, injected as a tracer, was shown to be taken
up. That insect fat body can selectively take up hemolymph
proteins has been shown in a number of species by immunochemical, electrophoretic and radiolabelling experiments.
    A specific hemolymph protein which fitted a storage role
was first discovered in *Calliphora* (Munn and Greville, 1969).
In extracts of mature larvae, abundant particles were first
observed with the electron microscope and then purified in the
centrifuge and characterized as a high molecular weight protein which was named calliphorin (Munn *et al.*, 1971). At the
end of the larval feeding stage, calliphorin makes up some 75%
of the hemolymph protein. The hemolymph of one individual at

this stage (weighing 120 mg) contains about 7 mg of calliphorin, but this falls by the time of pupariation to 3 mg, and in the newly emerged fly, after metamorphosis, to 0.03 mg (Kinnear and Thomson, 1975).

Calliphorin has a native molecular weight of 530,000 and subunits of 87,000, indicating hexameric structure. It has exceptionally high contents of tyrosine and phenylalanine, which may provide for tanning of the adult cuticle. Similar proteins have now been characterized from other Diptera: the blowfly, *Lucilia cuprina* (lucilin; Thomson *et al.*, 1976), and *Drosophila melanogaster* (larval serum proteins, or LSP 1 and 2; Wolfe *et al.*, 1977; Roberts *et al.*, 1977; Akam *et al.*, 1978). In addition to similar size and composition, these proteins show immunological cross-reactions.

A relationship between fat body granules and specific hemolymph proteins has been established in the silkmoth, *Hyalophora cecropia* (Tojo *et al.*, 1978). Protein granules, isolated by centrifugation from pupal fat body, were shown to consist chiefly of two proteins, migrating close together in electrophoresis (Fig. 1), which were purified and characterized. The native and subunit molecular weights were close to those of calliphorin, but there was no immunochemical cross-reaction. During the feeding period of the last larval instar, these proteins are synthesized by the fat body and secreted into the hemolymph, where they accumulate temporarily (Fig. 1); then during the prepupal period after the cessation of larval feeding they are taken back into the fat body and deposited in dense, partially crystalline granules. Two similar proteins, one of which is restricted to the female sex, have been characterized in the silkworm, *Bombyx mori* (Tojo *et al.*, 1980a). The accumulation of protein granules in prepupal fat body has also been observed in certain Coleoptera and Hymenoptera. Thus, the production of a family of proteins capable of condensing into dense storage granules is probably a general feature of holometabolous insects. The apparent value of secretion followed by resorption is to increase the efficiency of use of a limited volume of fat body cells by temporal specialization: the cytoplasm is dedicated to biosynthesis while nutrition is available, and to storage during the non-feeding pupal stage.

The storage proteins are synthesized, in the life cycle of each species, only during a limited period of the last larval instar. Regulation by changing endocrine balance seems possible, but the available evidence does not present a consistent picture. In *Calliphora*, the synthesis of calliphorin and other hemolymph proteins is inhibited by ecdysterone added to cultured larval fat body, while juvenile hormone (JH) had no effect (Pau *et al.*, 1979). In *Bombyx*, on the other hand,

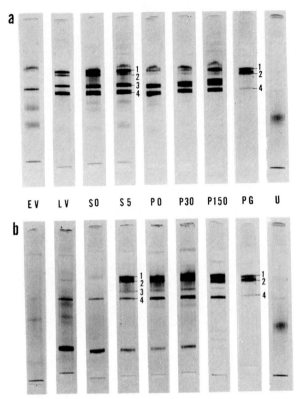

Fig. 1. Electrophoretic patterns of hemolymph and fat body proteins from female Hyalophora cecropia of different stages. Gels were run in 4.5% polyacrylamide and stained with Coomassie blue. a, Hemolymph; b, extract of fat body. EV, early fifth instar larva; LV, late fifth instar; SO, larva on the day of spinning; S5, 5 days after spinning; PO, freshly molted pupa; P30, 30-day pupa; P150, 150-day pupa. Also shown are proteins dissolved from isolated protein granules (PG) and urate granules (U). Protein bands: 1 and 2, storage proteins; 3, vitellogenin plus a co-migrating protein; 4, unidentified. (From Tojo et al., 1978, with permission.)

the synthesis of storage proteins is repressed by JH (Tojo et al., 1980b). As a step toward the study of the mechanisms of regulation, messenger RNAs for Drosophila and Calliphora storage proteins have been isolated and translated in cell-free systems (Sekeris et al., 1977; Kemp et al., 1978). The resorption of proteins and deposition in granules, both in Calpodes and in Drosophila, are stimulated by ecdysterone, although not entirely dependent on this hormone (Collins,

1974; Butterworth *et al.*, 1979). The regulation of the fat
body's reversed treatment of the same protein presents a
challenge.

Can any similar proteins and processes be discerned among
hemimetabolous insects? In cockroaches, a larval-specific
protein has been identified, the titre of which becomes elevated before each molt, especially the metamorphic molt, and
declines to low levels in the adult (Kunkel and Lawler, 1974).
This protein is reported to share physical properties with
calliphorin, and an evolutionary relationship has been suggested (Duhamel and Kunkel, 1978). In *Locusta*, some crystalline dense granules are present in the fat body of the newly
molted adult (Lauverjat, 1977), and a protein that resembles
calliphorin is abundant in the hemolymph of the mature larval
stage (B. Loughton, personal communication). We may here be
seeing the antecedents of the process which the Holometabola
have developed so highly.

Another question is the nature of protein granules found
in some adult insects. In the viviparous cockroach, *Diploptera punctata* (Stay and Clark, 1971), and in the Colorado
beetle (DeLoof and Lagasse, 1970), the adult female fat body
contains protein granules which are abundant during gestation
or diapause and become depleted during vitellogenesis. The
stored protein may provide amino acids for the synthesis of
vitellogenins. In *Locusta*, dense bodies and vesicular bodies
appear in the fat body cells after the first gonotrophic cycle
(Couble *et al.*, 1979). Adult fat body of *Calliphora* (Thomsen
and Thomsen, 1974; 1978) and *Aedes aegypti* (Behan and
Hagedorn, 1978) also contains dense protein granules. Some of
these granules, however, are undoubtedly formed from retired
intracellular organelles, and a relationship with a specific
protein has not yet been demonstrated in any adult insect.

The production and deposition of proteins specifically for
amino acid storage is a feature which insects share with seed
plants but not with vertebrate animals. It involves a remarkable switchover of fat body function from specific synthesis
and secretion to resorption and intracellular deposition, the
subcellular and molecular bases of which will be fascinating
to unravel.

III.   HEMOGLOBINS

In chironomid larvae are found a set of unique hemoglobins
with high affinity for oxygen, appropriate for the lake-bottom
habitat of these insects. The only other insects known to
possess hemoglobin are certain parasitic maggots and aquatic

bugs, where it is localized in specialized cells associated
with the tracheal system. In *Chironomus*, hemoglobins are produced in the fat body (Bergtrom *et al.*, 1976; Schin *et al.*,
1977) and secreted into the hemolymph plasma. They occur as
monomers (about 16,000 daltons) and sometimes as dimeric
forms, but do not exhibit the functional subunit interactions
characteristic of the hemoglobins of vertebrates. A *Chironomus* hemoglobin that has been purified has only about 25% of
its amino acid sequence corresponding to that of lamprey hemoglobin, or 20% to whale myoglobin, yet the tertiary structure
is closely similar to that of whale myoglobin. The similarities between insect and vertebrate hemoglobins strongly
suggest evolutionary homology, and the appearance of this
protein in a few isolated insect groups is difficult to explain. It appears to represent the expression of a group of
genes that have been preserved unexpressed through much of
insect evolution.

Multiple forms of hemoglobin are found in each *Chironomus*
species, differing in sequence and representing multiple gene
loci. The occurrence and production of these forms is stage-
specific: thus, in *Chironomus thummi*, five hemoglobins are
distinguished by electrophoresis of stage III hemolymph and
three additional ones in stage IV (Schin *et al.*, 1979). In
mature larvae, hemoglobin is said to represent some 90% of the
total hemolymph protein, but in metamorphosis
synthesis is terminated and the hemoglobin disappears through
absorption into the intestine and other tissues (Travis and
Schin, 1976). Since the hemoglobins are larval-specific proteins that build up to high levels just before metamorphosis
and then disappear, Thomson (1975) has suggested that they
constitute a protein reserve, replacing the storage proteins
found in other holometabolous insects.

Thus, the *Chironomus* hemoglobins are a set of protein products of the fat body, that are produced at specific stages
according to a developmental program. Recent evidence indicates that hemoglobin synthesis is stimulated by JH and
inhibited by ecdysone (H. Laufer, personal communication).
This can explain hemoglobin synthesis in the larva, ceasing at
each molt and before pupation. The basis for the activation
of new hemoglobin genes in the final larval instar, however,
is not yet clear.

IV. VITELLOGENINS

A. *Structure and Evolution*

The vitellogenins comprise another group of proteins to which the fat body, usually only in the female sex, devotes its resources at particular times in the life cycle. Discovered in saturniid silkmoths as female-specific hemolymph antigens which were taken up into the ovaries (Telfer, 1954), this family of proteins was later shown to be produced in the fat body, and was given the name *vitellogenin* to signify precursor of yolk (Pan *et al.*, 1969). The term was later applied to the corresponding proteins in oviparous vertebrates, which are synthesized in the liver, transported in the blood and cleaved in the ovary to produce the major yolk proteins, phosvitin and lipovitellin. In insects, the protein deposited in the yolk is called *vitellin*, and may differ from vitellogenin in the amount of bound lipid, though the apoproteins are generally unaltered (Chino *et al.*, 1977; Chinzei *et al.*, 1980a). Because their hormonally controlled synthesis in massive amounts presents excellent opportunities for the analysis of gene regulation, the vitellogenins have recently become favored subjects for research, which is summarized in several reviews (insects: Hagedorn and Kunkel, 1979; Engelmann, 1979; vertebrates: Tata and Smith, 1979).

The insect vitellogenins and vitellins that have been characterized are glycolipoproteins with 1-14% of carbohydrate and 6-12% of lipid. There may be a little protein-bound phosphorus, but highly phorphorylated proteins like phosvitin have not been found in insects, presumably because the insect embryo does not need a reserve of phosphate for the construction of bone.

The molecular weights of the insect vitellogenins, the polypeptides that are released upon denaturation, and the primary products of synthesis, show patterns (Table 1) that suggest evolutionary change. The species studied in most detail is *Locusta migratoria*. Its vitellogenin releases, in sodium dodecyl sulfate polyacrylamide gel electrophoresis, a set of polypeptides ranging from 126,000 down to 54,000 daltons, but pulse-labelling (confirmed by translation of the mRNA) shows that the primary products of translation are two subunits of over 200,000 daltons. Within the fat body cell, before secretion, these are "processed" by enzymic cleavage at sensitive sites. Although nicked, the molecule is held together by secondary forces until denatured, when the cleavage products are released. Dimerization and addition of carbohydrate and lipid make up the observed molecule of 550,000

TABLE 1. The Polypeptides of Some Representative
          Insect Vitellogenins

Data are for proteins which have been at least partially
purified, and for which the sizes of the primary translation
products have been determined. Molecular weights of denaturation products are from SDS-polyacrylamide gel electrophoresis. Primary polypeptides were identified by pulse-
labelling, usually for 1-30 min, in Leucophaea maderae for
5 h.

Order and Species	Molecular weights x 10^{-3}			References[a]
	Native protein	Denaturation products	Primary polypeptides	
Dictyoptera				
Leucophaea maderae	560	118,96,87,57	260,179?	1,2
Orthoptera				
Locusta migratoria	550	126,117,112, 104,96,64, 57,54	235,225	3,4
Lepidoptera				
Hyalophora cecropia	510	180,47	220	5,6
Coleoptera				
Tenebrio molitor	460	160,150,145, 104,56,41	204	6
Diptera				
Aedes aegypti	350	175,165	175,165	6
Drosophila melanogaster	220	46,45,44	46,45,44	6,7,8
Calliphora eryth- rocephala	225	50,47	ca. 50	9

[a]References: 1, Dejmal & Brookes (1972); 2, Koeppe & Ofengand
(1976; 3, Chen et al. (1978); 4, Chen (1980); 5, Pan & Wallace
(1974); 6, Harnish (1979); 7, Bownes & Hames (1977); 8, Warren
& Mahowald (1979); 9, Fourney (1979).

daltons.

Other non-dipterous insects (Table 1, plus less complete data for other species) form a group showing a similar pattern (Harnish, 1979). The intracellular cleavage may yield only two polypeptides, one large and one small (as in *Hyalophora cecropia*), but in every species examined, the smallest fragment is close to 50,000 daltons. In *Manduca sexta* (Mundall and Law, 1979), the native molecular weight is 260,000, indicating monomeric structure, and, after treatment of the protein with trypsin, the smaller of the two polypeptides (180,000 and 50,000) remains undigested. This suggests two domains in the protein, the smaller occupying a protected interior location.

The vitellogenins of Diptera do not fit the pattern just described, and seem to fall into two further groups. In the mosquito, *Aedes aegypti*, the native molecule is 350,000 daltons (or 270,000; Hagedorn and Judson, 1972), and is a dimer of subunits of about 170,000; with adequate precautions against proteolysis in preparation, no small polypeptide appears. In *Drosophila melanogaster*, on the other hand, there is no *large* polypeptide: the subunits of about 45,000 daltons correspond to the primary products of synthesis (except for short signal sequences), as shown by both pulse labelling in intact tissue and translation of isolated mRNA. The vitellogenins of other *Drosophila* species (Srdic *et al.*, 1978) and *Calliphora erythrocephala* are also built of 45,000-50,000 dalton subunits, the number differing with the species. The native molecular sizes of these higher dipteran vitellogenins have been difficult to determine, because of streaking and dissociation during electrophoresis, and their relation to the subunits is not yet clear.

These observations may be interpreted by a unifying hypothesis (Harnish *et al.*, 1979; Harnish, 1979). The ancestral insect vitellogenin gene was similar to those now expressed in most insect orders. The polypeptide product, in the range of 200,000-250,000 daltons, consists of two domains, of about 180,000 and 50,000 daltons. These are divided by post-translational cleavage, and the larger product is sometimes further split. In most species, the native vitellogenin consists of two such units. In a second group, typified by the mosquitos (representing lower Diptera; Hymenoptera may also be included), the vitellogenin gene is derived from the DNA coding for the large domain of the ancestral type, that coding for the small domain having been lost or rendered inactive. In the third group, typified by *Drosophila* (higher Diptera), the genes are derived from the DNA for the small domain of the primitive type, the large domain having been lost. Within each of these groups, duplication, resulting in different

numbers of active genes, and mutational modification, producing changes in size and sequence, have also occurred. This
model of insect vitellogenin gene evolution gains plausibility
from the recent evidence from vertebrate systems that the
coding portions of split genes may represent different domains
in the resultant proteins (Gilbert, 1978; Sakano et al., 1979).

B. Control of Vitellogenin Synthesis by Juvenile Hormone

Vitellogenin synthesis in the fat body of many insects is
dependent on stimulation by juvenile hormone, although in some
it is influenced by ecdysterone or by developmental factors
other than direct hormonal action. Since the control of
vitellogenin synthesis is discussed by Engelmann in this
volume, I shall merely summarize some recent findings on
Locusta migratoria, a species selected in my own laboratory
for study of the control of protein synthesis by JH (Chen et
al., 1976).

In adult female Locusta, vitellogenin usually first
appears in the hemolymph about the eighth day after eclosion,
rises to a maximum, and then fluctuates with successive gonotrophic cycles (Gellissen and Emmerich, 1978; Chinzei et
al., 1980b).   Capability of the fat body to produce vitellogenin, assayed by incubation in vitro with ^{3}H-leucine and
measurement of labelled immunospecific protein in the medium,
appears about the same time (Chen et al., 1979). If the
corpora allata, the source of JH, are eliminated either surgically or by treatment with the specific cytotoxic agent,
6-methoxy-7-ethoxy-2,2-dimethyl chromene ("Precocene III";
Bowers, 1977), no vitellogenin is made. Synthesis can then be
induced by JH or the more stable synthetic analog, ZR-515.
That the hormone can act directly on the fat body has been
demonstrated by induction of synthesis by ZR-515 added to
tissue cultured in vitro (Abu-Hakima and Wyatt, 1980). In
most experiments so far, however, the hormone analog has been
applied in vivo, and the synthetic capacities of the fat body
then measured after explantation. In fully stimulated female
fat body, some 60% of the export protein synthesis, or 15% of
the total protein synthesis, is vitellogenin; the fat body of
one individual can make about 35 mg of this protein per day.
Male fat body does not normally produce vitellogenin, and we
have been unable to induce detectable synthesis in males under
a variety of hormonal regimes.

In preparation for vitellogenesis, the female fat body
undergoes impressive adaptation, changing from a tissue largely devoted to storage, in the fresh adult, to one specialized
for protein synthesis and export (Lauverjat, 1977; Couble et

al., 1979). Lipid and glycogen decrease, while cytoplasm containing rough endoplasmic reticulum and Golgi vesicles increases. After a cycle of vitellogenesis, much of the rough endoplasmic reticulum becomes packed into tight layers which may be temporarily inactive, conserved for the next gonotrophic cycle. The cell nuclei, which were initially compressed between the fat droplets, become rounded, enlarged and much increased in basophilic content.

The nuclear changes suggest an increase in DNA, which has been confirmed by biochemical analysis (Chen *et al.*, 1979; Irvine, 1979). No mitosis is observed, but, instead, the fat body cells become polyploid, as shown by microcytophotometric scanning of Feulgen-stained preparations (Chen *et al.*, 1977; Nair *et al.*, 1980). Female adult fat body cells, which are predominantly tetraploid on the day of eclosion, become octaploid at the initiation of vitellogenin synthesis and may develop even higher ploidy. Polyploidy develops in male fat body also, but to a lower average level than in the female. DNA replication is prevented when the corpora allata are destroyed and is then rapidly induced in fat body of both sexes by ZR-515. Its relationship to capacity for vitellogenin synthesis is not known. It may represent an increase in genome copies and total transcriptional capacity, rather than an effect on specific genes.

The kinetics of stimulation of vitellogenin synthesis after hormone treatment are of interest (Fig. 2). After a first administration of ZR-515, synthesis rises only slowly for the first 48 hours, then increases steeply to a peak at 72 hours and thereafter declines gradually. If a second dose is applied after 2 weeks, when the primary response has fallen almost to zero, a secondary stimulation is obtained that is much more rapid than the first, lacking the conspicuous lag phase. In considering possible mechanisms for this cellular memory effect, it is important to know whether production of vitellogenin mRNA is accelerated, or whether translation may merely be more efficient due to the retention of a population of ribosomes.

Locust fat body RNA has been analyzed by electrophoresis under denaturing conditions (Fig. 3). The 26S rRNA, like that of other insects, is nicked and splits into two fragments which migrate close to the 18S rRNA, leaving clear the high molecular weight region of the gel. In RNA from mature females a sharp band is visible at about 32S, or 6800 nucleotides, which is lacking from non-vitellogenic females and from males. This is nearly the same size as chicken vitellogenin mRNA (Deeley *et al.*, 1977a), and has been identified as the locust vitellogenin message. It can be estimated quantitatively by densitometric scanning, and in fully stimulated fe-

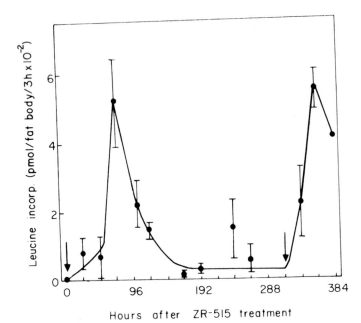

Fig. 2. Time course of primary and secondary induction of vitellogenin synthesis in Locusta migratoria. ZR-515 (250 μg) was applied topically to allatectomized females at the times marked by arrows, and the activity of the fat body in vitellogenin synthesis was assayed at the times shown. Each point shows the mean and SEM from six animals. (From Chen et al., 1979, with permission.)

male fat body it makes up 1.5% of the total RNA, an exceptional proportion for a single species of mRNA (Chinzei et al., 1980b).

After primary stimulation of precocene-treated locusts with ZR-515, vitellogenin mRNA is first detectable by this technique after 48 hours, and accumulates rapidly only after a lag of two more days. Total (chiefly ribosomal) RNA builds up about six-fold during several days. In secondary stimulation, on the other hand, production of vitellogenin mRNA takes off almost immediately, with greatly reduced lag, but there is very little synthesis of rRNA. This result shows enhanced sensitivity of the vitellogenin genes, but diminished transcription of ribosomal RNA, when fat body is stimulated after a previous exposure to the hormone. The accelerated secondary stimulation of specific mRNA production parallels similar findings for certain steroid-controlled systems, including estrogen-dependent vitellogenin synthesis in frogs and

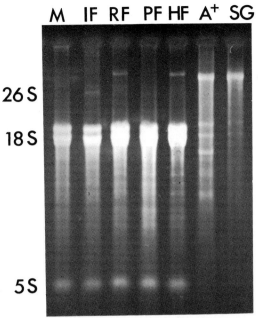

M IF RF PF HF A⁺ SG

26 S

18 S

5S

mRNA$_{VG}$

Fig. 3.   Electrophoretic patterns of Locusta fat body RNA,
showing vitellogenin mRNA.   Total fat body RNA was denatured in methyl mercuric hydroxide and electrophoresed in
agarose gel, then stained with ethidium bromide and photographed by fluorescence. M, male; IF, immature adult female;
RF, reproductive female; PF, precocene-treated female; HF,
precocene-treated female, treated with the JH analog, ZR-515;
A⁺, polyadenylated fraction from mature female RNA; SG,
sucrose gradient 30S fraction from polyadenylated RNA.
(Chinzei and Wyatt, unpublished.)

chickens (Deeley et al., 1977b; Baker and Shapiro, 1978).
     To trace the fate of the hormone in the target cell, we
have used ^{3}H-JH to look for receptors (Roberts and Wyatt,
1980).   Fat body cytosol contains a protein which specifically
binds the hormone and is separable chromatographically from a
JH-binding protein in the hemolymph (Fig. 4).   Preliminary
measurements indicate a K_D of about 5 x 10^{-9} M and a sedimen-
tation constant of 12S - significantly larger than several
steroid hormone receptors of vertebrate cells.   This protein
is present in both female and male fat body, but the level is
higher in the female, especially in the vitellogenic stage.
Its characteristics are consistent with those of a cytosol
hormone receptor.
     Thus, although JH is not a steroid, what we have learned

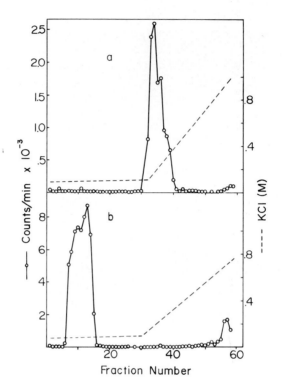

Fig. 4. *Separation of JH-binding proteins from Locusta hemolymph and fat body. Hemolymph and fat body cytosol from mature female locusts were chromatographed on columns of DEAE-cellulose, eluted with a gradient of KCl. Each fraction was analyzed for specific binding of ^{3}H-JH 1 by a competitive binding assay. a, Hemolymph; b, cytosol. When hemolymph and cytosol were mixed and chromatographed in the same manner, the expected components were resolved. (Roberts and Wyatt, unpub.)*

about its induction of vitellogenin synthesis in *Locusta* fat body suggests that, like several steroidal hormones, it is transported to the nucleus in company with a receptor protein and there stimulates transcriptional activity in the chromatin, resulting in the synthesis of DNA, mRNA, rRNA and protein. Analysis of the causal relationships among these synthetic activities requires fresh experimental approaches, which will be discussed at the end of this essay.

V.   LIPOPROTEINS AND JUVENILE HORMONE BINDING PROTEINS

     Although the lipid reserves of the fat body are chiefly
triglycerides, lipids are released and transported in the hemolymph to sites of utilization chiefly as diglycerides, carried on a distinctive class of lipoprotein. Discovered in
silkmoths, this process appears to be general (though not necessarily universal) among the insects (reviews: Gilbert and
Chino, 1974; Gilbert et al., 1977), and contrasts with the
transport of lipids in vertebrates. Release of diglycerides
from fat body depends upon acceptance by the carrier protein,
and uptake by the protein depends upon energy-utilizing processes in the fat body. The protein can be loaded and unload-
ed reversibly, forming a shuttle between donor and acceptor
sites - a further distinction from the vertebrates, in which
serum lipoproteins are synthesized de novo for each passage.
Release of diglyceride from the fat body is controlled by an
adipokinetic neurohormone (Steele, this volume).
     The diglyceride-carrying lipoproteins, now called lipopro-
tein I, have been purified and characterized from several insects. They have molecular weights in the range of 600,000-
800,000 and contain 30-45% of lipid, including phospholipids
and neutral lipids, the most abundant being diglyceride. The
subunits reported are, for Manduca, 285,000 and 81,000 (Pattnaik et al., 1979) and, for Locusta, only 85,000 (Gellissen
and Emmerich, 1980) - a difference which it may be premature
to assign to evolutionary change or to experimental technique.
     Lipoprotein I is present and functional in both the larval
and adult stages. In adult female Locusta, the hemolymph
titre rises during the first three days after eclosion and
then remains essentially constant, in contrast to vitellogenin, the titre of which fluctuates with the cycles of ovarian
development (Fig. 5). The rate of synthesis of lipoprotein I
in the fat body shows only small variations during adult life,
and is unaffected by JH (Gellissen and Wyatt, unpublished).
     JH, a lipoidal molecule, can be bound with low affinity by
hemolymph lipoproteins, but this probably has little biological significance. A class of hemolymph JH-binding proteins
which are not lipoproteins, but possess high-affinity, stereospecific sites, serve to protect the hormone from degradation
by general esterases (Ferkovich et al., 1976; Kramer et al.,
1976; Peterson et al., 1978). From Manduca sexta, a 28,000-
dalton JH-binding protein has been purified, and is produced
in the fat body (Nowock et al., 1975). Locusta has a JH-
binding protein of apparently larger molecular size (Peter et
al., 1979), the separation of which from the fat body cytosol
JH receptor is shown in Fig. 4.

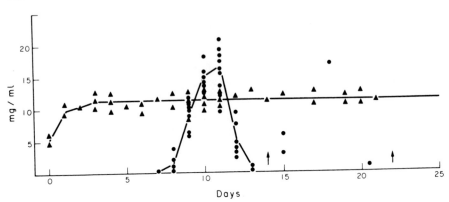

*Fig. 5. Changes in hemolymph titre of vitellogenin (●)
and lipoprotein I (▲) in Locusta migratoria, measured by
rocket immunoelectrophoresis. Each point represents the
analysis of a hemolymph sample from 5 animals. Arrows indicate times of oviposition. (From Gellissen and Emmerich,
1978, with permission.)*

VI.   THE FAT BODY IN DEFENSE

Although insects do not possess the complex genetic and
cellular equipment necessary for the production of immunoglo-
bulins, a primitive immunity system does exist, for insects
sublethally infected with bacteria can rapidly develop greatly
increased resistance to a subsequent challenge. In diapausing
silkmoth pupae, a group of proteins appear in the hemolymph
during the acquisition of immunity that collectively exercise
antibacterial activity (Faye et al., 1975). Injected radioactive bacteria were found phagocytosed in hemocytes that were
associated with fat body (Faye, 1978). When fat body from
immunized pupae is incubated in vitro, the immunity proteins
are synthesized and released into the medium (Faye and Wyatt,
1980), but some uncertainty remains whether they are products
of the fat body cells themselves or of the adsorbed hemocytes.
After wounding of the integument of diapausing pupae, fat
body protein synthesis is greatly enhanced (Stevenson and
Wyatt, 1962), but how the wound stimulus is transmitted to the
fat body, and the nature and significance of the proteins that
are made, have not been established.

VII. PERSPECTIVES

A. *The Varying Pattern of Gene Expression in the Fat Body*

The examples given have illustrated the changing patterns of gene expression in the fat body during the ontogeny of insects, as reflected in the proteins that are secreted into the hemolymph. During larval development, hemolymph protein rises to a peak concentration at each molt, and specific molting proteins may occur. In the last larval instar, hemolymph protein content commonly rises even higher, and some new species appear: storage proteins, and (in *Chironomus*) new hemoglobins. In the pharate pupa, storage proteins are resorbed into the fat body. Close to the larval-pupal ecdysis, in silkmoths, vitellogenin synthesis begins. During metamorphosis, storage proteins are digested, much of the fat body is destroyed through cell lysis, and that which survives (or arises newly from undifferentiated cells) emerges with new competence in the adult. In the adult female, the main synthetic duty of the fat body, timed in correlation with reproductive cycles, is to produce the precursors of yolk. Some proteins, such as the lipoproteins involved in fat transport, are needed and produced at all stages of the life cycle.

Some, at least, of these changes are regulated by the balance of developmental hormones. The enhanced synthesis of some proteins and decrease in others at each molt is probably due to ecdysone. The new proteins of the pre-metamorphic instar may be attributed to the declining titre of JH. The adult fat body, with its fresh competence developed under the influence of ecdysone in the absence of JH, can respond to JH (or to ecdysone) to produce new proteins needed for reproduction.

How complete is this summary of the ontogeny of major protein export by the fat body? It must be far from complete, for electrophoretic analysis of hemolymph and fat body extracts show major components about which we know little (for example, band 4 and the fast-migrating fat body band in Fig. 1). *Bombyx mori* hemolymph contains proteins, especially abundant in the late fifth instar, which give subunits in the 30,000-dalton range (Fujie *et al.*, 1979), but nothing is known of their function. Completion of the physical and physiological characterization of the major insect plasma proteins should be high among the priorities of insect biochemistry. But are all of these proteins made in the fat body? Probably so, since we have as yet no evidence for any major insect plasma protein being produced in any other organ.

Stage- and sex-specific gene programming is well illustra-

ted by the vitellogenins. Usually, vitellogenins are produced
only in the adult female, though the female is often the homo-
gametic sex and carries no unique genes. There are exceptions
to the usual stage-specificity: in silkmoths, vitellogenin
synthesis begins early in metamorphosis. There are also exceptions to sex-specificity: in *Rhodnius*, males normally produce vitellogenin (Chalaye, 1979), and in *Diploptera* they can
be induced to do so under adequate JH stimulation (Mundall and
Tobe, 1979). But in most insects, it is only in the adult
female that the vitellogenin gene is equipped to respond to
hormonal stimulation. This differentiation of the sexes
should provide an opportunity for analysis of the molecular
basis for hormonal responsiveness of a gene.

Protein synthesis in the fat body can also be regulated by
non-hormonal signals. The polysome population in *Bombyx*
larval fat body declines during starvation and is rapidly re-
built upon re-feeding, through a control mechanism that
apparently does not depend directly on the intracellular
supply of amino acids (Bosquet, 1979). Little is known about
such mechanisms.

B. *The Future*

Further advances in understanding must come from application to insect systems of the rapidly changing contemporary
technology of cell and molecular biology.

Fat body, constructed of thin cellular layers which normally exchange nutrients and products with the bathing hemolymph, is designed for easy maintenance in appropriate media
in vitro, and analysis of its activities in culture is essential to permit precise control of conditions and freedom from
interactions with other organs. A refinement will be the culture of dissociated fat body cells; whether cell lines can
ever arise from fat body, with its limited mitotic capacity,
however, is doubtful.

For the assay and isolation of gene products, immunochemical techniques, already invaluable, will become more widely
applicable through the production of monoclonal antibodies in
hybridomas (Melchers *et al.*, 1978). This technique, in which
lymphocytes from an immunized animal are fused with myeloma
cells to create immunoglobulin-secreting cell clones, can
yield pure antibodies without the need for purification of the
antigen. This will make possible the discrimination of closely related proteins such as the *Chironomus* hemoglobins.

Studies of specific nucleic acid sequences have become
possible through the cloning of recombinant DNA. Where individual mRNA species can be isolated in pure form, the specific

complementary DNAs can be inserted into plasmid or bacterio-
phage vectors for cloning. Some mRNAs, like that for *Locusta*
vitellogenin, can be purified by virtue of their distinctive
size. Others may be isolated by immunoprecipitation of polysomes that are engaged in making a specific antigen. Alternatively, it may be more efficient to clone from cDNA prepared
against the total mRNA of the tissue, and to select from among
the clones by means of sequence-enriched probes (Gordon *et
al.*, 1978).

Cloned cDNA can provide probes for the quantitative assay
of specific mRNA and DNA sequences, for the identification of
gene loci in polytene chromosomes, and for the selection of
clones from libraries of genomic DNA. Analysis of the structures of cloned genes, and the binding of proteins and possibly RNAs to regulatory sequences, will lead to understanding
of the mechanisms that control gene expression and the process
of development.

ACKNOWLEDGEMENTS

It is a pleasure to thank Dr. Bradley White for stimulating interactions that contributed importantly to ideas here
expressed, and several colleagues for permission to cite unpublished findings. Work in my own laboratory has been
supported by grants from NSERC Canada and the US NIH.

REFERENCES

Abu-Hakima, R., and Wyatt, G.R. (1980). Vitellogenin synthe-
     sis induced in locust fat body by juvenile hormone analog
     added *in vitro*. In preparation.
Akam, M.E., Roberts, D.B., and Wolfe, J. (1978). Characteri-
     zation and genetic mapping of larval serum protein 2 in
     Drosophila melanogaster. *Biochem. Genetics* 16, 101-120.
Baker, H.J., and Shapiro, D.J. (1978). Rapid accumulation of
     vitellogenin messenger RNA during secondary estrogen sti-
     mulation of *Xenopus laevis*. *J. Biol. Chem.* 253, 4521-
     4524.
Behan, M., and Hagedorn, H.H. (1978). Ultrastructural changes
     in the fat body of adult female *Aedes aegypti* in relation-
     ship to vitellogenin synthesis. *Cell Tiss. Res.* 186,
     499-506.
Bergtrom, G., Laufer, H., and Rogers, R. (1976). Fat body: a
     site of hemoglobin synthesis in *Chironomus thummi* (Dip-
     tera). *J. Cell Biol.* 69, 264-274.

Bosquet, G. (1979). Occurrence of an active regulatory mechanism of protein synthesis during starvation and refeeding in *Bombyx mori* larvae. *Biochimie* 61, 165-170.

Bownes, M.E., and Hames, B.C. (1977). Accumulation and degradation of three major yolk proteins in *Drosophila melanogaster*. *J. Exp. Zool.* 200, 149-156.

Butterworth, F.M., Tysell, B., and Waclawski, I. (1979). The effect of 20-hydroxyecdysone and protein on granule formation in the *in vitro* cultured fat body of *Drosophila*. *J. Insect Physiol.* 25, 855-860.

Chalaye, D. (1979). Etude immunochimique des protéines hémolymphatiques et ovocytaires de *Rhodnius prolixus*. *Can. J. Zool.* 57, 329-336.

Chen, T.T. (1980). Vitellogenin in locusts (*Locusta migratoria*): translation of vitellogenin mRNA in *Xenopus* oocytes and analysis of the polypeptide products. *Arch. Biochem. Biophys.* (in press).

Chen, T.T., Couble, P., De Lucca, F.L., and Wyatt, G.R. (1976). Juvenile hormone control of vitellogenin synthesis in *Locusta migratoria*. *In* "The Juvenile Hormones" (L.I. Gilbert, ed.), pp. 505-529. Plenum Press, New York.

Chen, T.T., Couble, P., Nair, K.K., and Wyatt, G.R. (1977). Juvenile hormone-induced DNA synthesis in the adult locust fat body. *Can. Fed. Biol. Sci. Proc.* 20, 181.

Chen, T.T., Strahlendorf, P.W., and Wyatt, G.R. (1978). Vitellin and vitellogenin from locusts (*Locusta migratoria*). Properties and post-translational modification in the fat body. *J. Biol. Chem.* 253, 5325-5331.

Chen, T.T., Couble, P., Abu-Hakima, R., and Wyatt, G.R. (1979). Juvenile hormone-controlled vitellogenin synthesis in *Locusta migratoria* fat body. Hormonal induction *in vivo*. *Devel. Biol.* 69, 59-72.

Chino, H., Yamagata, M., and Sato, S. (1977). Further characterization of lepidopteran vitellogenin from hemolymph and mature eggs. *Insect Biochem.* 7, 125-131.

Chinzei, Y., Chino, H., and Wyatt, G.R. (1980a). Purification and properties of vitellogenin and vitellin from *Locusta migratoria*. *Insect Biochem.* (in press).

Chinzei, Y., White, B.N., and Wyatt, G.R. (1980b). Vitellogenin mRNA from *Locusta migratoria*: accumulation during primary and secondary induction by juvenile hormone. In preparation.

Collins, J.V. (1974). Hormonal control of protein sequestration in the fat body of *Calpodes ethlius*. *Can. J. Zool.* 52, 639-642.

Couble, P., Chen, T.T. and Wyatt, G.R. (1979). Juvenile hormone-controlled vitellogenin synthesis in *Locusta migratoria* fat body: cytological development. *J. Insect Physiol.* 25, 327-337.

Dejmal, R.K., and Brookes, V.J. (1972). Insect lipovitellin.
    Chemical and physical characteristics of yolk protein
    from the ovaries of Leucophaea maderae. J. Biol. Chem.
    247, 869-874.
De Loof, A., and Lagasse, A. (1970). Juvenile hormone and the
    ultrastructural properties of the fat body of the adult
    Colorado beetle Leptinotarsa decemlineata. Z. Zellforsch.
    106, 439-450.
Deeley, R.G., Gordon, J.I., Burns, A.T.H., Mullinix, K.P.,
    Bina-Stein, M., and Goldberger, R.F. (1977a). J. Biol.
    Chem. 252, 8310-8319.
Deeley, R.G., Udell, D.S., Burns, A.T.H., Gordon, J.I., and
    Goldberger, R.F. (1977b). Kinetics of avian vitellogenin
    messenger RNA induction. Comparison between primary and
    secondary response to estrogen. J. Biol. Chem. 252,
    7913-7915.
Duhamel, R.C., and Kunkel, J.G. (1978). A molting rhythm for
    serum proteins of the cockroach, Blatta orientalis.
    Comp. Biochem. Physiol. 60B, 333-338.
Engelmann, F. (1979). Insect vitellogenin: identification,
    biosynthesis and role in vitellogenesis. Adv. Insect
    Physiol. 14, 49-108.
Faye, I. (1978). Insect immunity: early fate of bacteria
    injected in saturniid pupae. J. Invertebr. Pathol. 31,
    19-26.
Faye, I., and Wyatt, G.R. (1980). Insect immunity: the syn-
    thesis of antibacterial proteins in isolated fat body
    from cecropia silkmoth pupae. Experientia (in press).
Faye, I., Pye, A., Rasmuson, T., Boman, H.G., and Boman, I.A.
    (1975). Insect immunity. II. Simultaneous induction of
    antibacterial activity and selective synthesis of some
    hemolymph proteins in diapausing pupae of Hyalophora
    cecropia and Samia cynthia. Infect. Immun. 12, 1426-1438.
Ferkovich, S.M., Silhacek, D.L., and Rutter, R.R. (1975).
    Juvenile hormone binding proteins in the hemolymph of the
    Indian meal moth. Insect Biochem. 5, 141-150.
Fourney, R.M. (1979). "Identification and partial characteri-
    zation of the yolk proteins of the blowfly, Calliphora
    erythrocephala." M.Sc. Thesis, Queen's University,
    Kingston, Ontario.
Fujie, J., Izumi, S., and Tomino, S. (1979). Biosynthesis of
    major hemolymph proteins (30K proteins) in the silkworm,
    Bombyx mori. Japan Zool. Soc., 50th Annual Meeting,
    Tokyo. Abstract.
Gellissen, G., and Emmerich, H. (1978). Changes in the titre
    of vitellogenin and of diglyceride carrier lipoprotein in
    the blood of adult Locusta migratoria. Insect Biochem.
    8, 403-412.

Gellissen, G., and Emmerich, H. (1980). Purification and properties of a diglyceride-binding lipoprotein (LP I) of the adult male *Locusta migratoria*. *J. Comp. Physiol. B* (in press).

Gilbert, L.I., and Chino, H. (1974). Transport of lipids in insects. *J. Lipid Res.* 15, 439-456.

Gilbert, L.I., Goodman, W., and Bollenbacher, W.E. (1977). Biochemistry of regulatory lipids and sterols in insects. *In* "Biochemistry of Lipids II" (T.W. Goodwin, ed.), *Int. Rev. Biochem.* 14, 1-50, Univ. Park Press, Baltimore, MD.

Gilbert, W. (1978). Why genes in pieces? *Nature* 271, 501.

Gordon, J.I., Burns, A.T.H., Christmann, J.L., and Deeley, R.G. (1978). Cloning of a double-stranded cDNA that codes for a portion of chicken preproalbumin. A general method for isolating a specific DNA sequence from partially purified mRNA. *J. Biol. Chem.* 253, 8629-8639.

Hagedorn, H.H., and Judson, C.L. (1972). Purification and site of synthesis of *Aedes aegypti* yolk proteins. *J. Exp. Zool.* 182, 367-378.

Hagedorn, H.H., and Kunkel, J.G. (1979). Vitellogenin and vitellin in insects. *Annu. Rev. Entomol.* 24, 475-505.

Harnish, D.G. (1979). "Evolution of the insect egg yolk protein, vitellin." M.Sc. Thesis, Queen's University, Kingston, Ontario.

Harnish, D.G., Fourney, R., Chinzei, Y., Flynn, T.G., White, B.N., and Wyatt, G.R. (1979). The structure and evolution of insect vitellins. *21st Int. Congr. Biochem., Toronto, Canada*. Abstracts, p. 227.

Irvine, D.J. (1979). "The development of polyploidy in the fat body of *Locusta migratoria*." M.Sc. Thesis, Queen's University, Kingston, Ontario.

Keeley, L.L. (1978). Endocrine regulation of fat body development and function. *Annu. Rev. Entomol.* 23, 329-352.

Kemp, D.J., Thomson, J.A., Peacock, W.J., and Higgins, T.J.V. (1978). Messenger RNA for the insect storage protein calliphorin: *in vitro* translation and chromosomal hybridization analyses of a 20S poly(A)-RNA fraction. *Biochem. Genetics* 16, 355-371.

Kilby, B.A. (1963). The biochemistry of insect fat body. *Adv. Insect Physiol.* 1, 111-174.

Kinnear, J.F., and Thomson, J.A. (1975). Nature, origin and fate of major hemolymph proteins in *Calliphora*. *Insect Biochem.* 5, 531-552.

Kunkel, J.G., and Lawler, D.M. (1974). Larval-specific serum protein in the order Dictyoptera - I. Immunologic characterization in larval *Blattella germanica* and cross-reaction throughout the order. *Comp. Biochem. Physiol.* 47B, 697-710.

Koeppe, J., and Ofengand, J. (1976). Juvenile hormone-induced biosynthesis of vitellogenin in *Leucophaea maderae*. *Arch. Biochem. Biophys.* 173, 100-113.

Kramer, K.J., Dunn, P.E., Peterson, R.C., and Law, J.H. (1976). Interaction of juvenile hormone with binding proteins in insect hemolymph. *In* "The Juvenile Hormones" (L.I. Gilbert, ed.), pp. 327-341. Plenum Press, New York.

Lauverjat, S. (1977). L'évolution post-imaginale du tissu adipeux femelle de *Locusta migratoria* et son contrôle endocrine. *Gen. Comp. Endocrinol.* 33, 13-34.

Locke, M., and Collins, J.C. (1968). Protein uptake into multivesicular bodies and storage granules in the fat body of an insect. *J. Cell Biol.* 36, 453-483.

Melchers, F., Potter, M., and Warner, N. (ed.) (1978). Lymphocyte hybridomas. *Curr. Top. Microbiol. Immunol.*, vol. 81.

Mundall, B.C., and Law, J.H. (1979). Physical and chemical characterization of vitellogenin from the hemolymph and eggs of the tobacco hornworm, *Manduca sexta*. *Comp. Biochem. Physiol.* 63B, 459-468.

Mundall, B.C., and Tobe, S.S. (1979). Induction of vitellogenin and growth of implanted oocytes in male cockroaches. *Nature* 282, 97-98.

Munn, E.A., and Greville, G.D. (1969). The soluble proteins of developing *Calliphora erythrocephala*, particularly calliphorin, and similar proteins in other insects. *J. Insect Physiol.* 15, 1935-1950.

Munn, E.A., Feinstein, and Greville, G.D. (1971). The isolation and properties of the protein calliphorin. *Biochem. J.* 124, 367-374.

Nair, K.K., Chen, T.T., and Wyatt, G.R. (1980). Juvenile hormone-stimulated polyploidy in adult locust fat body. Submitted for publication.

Nowock, J., Goodman, W., Bollenbacher, W.E., and Gilbert, L.I. (1975). Synthesis of juvenile hormone binding proteins by the fat body of *Manduca sexta*. *Gen. Comp. Endocrinol.* 27, 230-239.

Pan, M.L., and Wallace, R.A. (1974). Cecropia vitellogenin: isolation and characterization. *Am. Zool.* 14, 1239-1242.

Pan, M.L., Bell, W.J., and Telfer, W.H. (1969). Vitellogenin blood protein synthesis by insect fat body. *Science* 165, 393-394.

Pattnaik, N.M., Mundall, E.C., Trambusti, B.G., Law, J.H., and Kezdy, F.J. (1979). Isolation and characterization of a larval lipoprotein from the hemolymph of *Manduca sexta*. *Comp. Biochem. Physiol.* 63B, 469-476.

Peter, M.G., Gunawan, S., Gellissen, G., and Emmerich, H.
    (1979). Differences in hydrolysis and binding of homo-
    logous juvenile hormones in *Locusta migratoria* hemolymph.
    Z. Naturforsch. 34c, 588-598.
Peterson, R.C., Reich, M.F., Dunn, P.E., Law, J.H., and Kat-
    zenellenbogen, J.A. (1978). Binding specificity of the
    juvenile hormone carrier protein from the hemolymph of
    the tobacco hornworm *Manduca sexta*. *Biochemistry* 16,
    2305-2311.
Price, G.M. (1973). Protein and nucleic acid metabolism in
    insect fat body. *Biol. Rev.* 48, 333-375.
Roberts, D.B., Wolfe, J., and Akam, M.E. (1977). The develop-
    mental profiles of two major hemolymph proteins from
    Drosophila melanogaster. *J. Insect. Physiol.* 23, 871-878.
Roberts, P.E., and Wyatt, G.R. (1980). Juvenile hormone re-
    ceptor protein from fat body of *Locusta migratoria*. In
    preparation.
Sakano, H., Rogers, J.H., Huppi, K., Brack, C., and Traunecker,
    A. (1979). Domains and the hinge region of an immuno-
    globulin heavy chain are encoded in separate DNA segments.
    Nature 277, 627-633.
Srdic, Z., Beck, H., and Gloor, H. (1978). Yolk protein dif-
    ferences between species of *Drosophila*. *Experientia* 34,
    1572-1574.
Schin, H., Laufer, H., and Carr, E. (1977). Cytochemical and
    electrophoretic studies of hemoglobin synthesis in the
    fat body of a midge, *Chironomus thummi*. *J. Insect
    Physiol.* 23, 1233-1242.
Schin, H., Laufer, H., and Clark, R.M. (1979). Temporal spec-
    ifity of hemoglobin synthesis in the fat body of *Chirono-
    mus thummi* during development. *J. Exp. Zool.* 210, 265-
    275.
Sekeris, C.E., Perassi, R., Arnemann, J., Ullrich, A., and
    Scheller, K. (1977). Translation of mRNA from *Calliphora
    vicina* and *Drosophila melanogaster* larvae into calli-
    phorin and calliphorin-like proteins of *Drosophila*.
    Insect Biochem. 7, 5-9.
Shigematsu, H. (1958). Synthesis of blood proteins by the fat
    body in the silkworm, *Bombyx mori*. *Nature* 182, 880-882.
Stay, B., and Clark, J.K. (1971). Fluctuation of protein
    granules in the fat body of the viviparous cockroach,
    Diploptera punctata, during the reproductive cycle. *J.
    Insect Physiol.* 17, 1747-1762.
Stevenson, E., and Wyatt, G.R. (1962). The metabolism of
    silkmoth tissues. 1. Incorporation of leucine into pro-
    tein. *Arch. Biochem. Biophys.* 99, 65-71.
Tata, J.R., and Smith, D.F. (1979). Vitellogenesis: a versa-
    tile model for hormonal regulation of gene expression.
    Recent Progr. Hormone Res. 35, 47-95.

Telfer, W.H. (1954). Immunological studies of insect metamorphosis. II. The role of a sex-limited blood protein in
egg formation by the cecropia silkworm. *J. Gen. Physiol.*
37, 539-558.

Thomsen, E., and Thomson, M. (1974). Fine structure of the
fat body of the female of *Calliphora erythrocephala* during the first egg-maturation cycle. *Cell Tiss. Res. 152*,
193-217.

Thomsen, E., and Thomson, M. (1978). Production of specific-
protein secretion granules by fat body cells of the blowfly, *Calliphora erythrocephala*. *Cell Tiss. Res. 193*,
25-33.

Thompson, J.A. (1980). Major patterns of gene activity during
development in holometabolous insects. *Adv. Insect*
Physiol. 11, 321-368.

Thompson, J.A., Radok, K.R., Shaw, D.C., Whitten, M.J., Foster,
G.G., and Birt, L.M. (1976). Genetics of lucilin, a
storage protein from the sheep blowfly, *Lucilia cuprina*
(Calliphoridae). *Biochem. Genetics 14*, 145-149.

Tojo, S., Betchaku, T., Ziccardi, V.J., and Wyatt, G.R. (1978).
Fat body protein granules and storage proteins in the
silkmoth, *Hyalophora cecropia*. *J. Cell Biol. 78*, 823-838.

Tojo, S., Nagata, M. and Kobayashi, M. (1980a). Storage
proteins in the silkworm, *Bombyx mori*. *J. Insect Physiol.*
(in press).

Tojo, S., Kiguchi, K., and Shigeru, K. (1980b). Hormonal regulation of the synthesis and uptake of storage proteins in
the silkworm, *Bombyx mori*. In preparation.

Travis, J.L., and Schin, K. (1976). Evidence for hemoglobin
uptake by oocytes of *Chironomus thumi*. *J. Insect*
Physiol. 22, 1601-1608.

Warren, T.G., Brennan, M.D., and Mahowald, A.P. (1979). Two
processing steps in maturation of vitellogenin polypeptides in *Drosophila melanogaster*. *Proc. Natl. Acad. Sci.*
USA 76, 28-48-2852.

Wolfe, J., Akam, M.E., and Roberts, D.B. (1977). Biochemical
and immunological studies on larval serum protein 1, the
major hemolymph protein of *Drosophila melanogaster* third-
instar larvae. *Eur. J. Biochem. 79*, 47-53.

Wigglesworth, V.B. (1939). "The Principles of Insect Physiology." Methuen, London.

Wigglesworth, V.B. (1972). "The Principles of Insect Physiology." 7th edition. Chapman and Hall, London.

Wyatt, G.R. and Pan, M.L. (1978). Insect plasma proteins.
Ann. Rev. Biochem. 47, 779-817.

THE CELL BIOLOGY OF FAT BODY DEVELOPMENT

Michael Locke

The Cell Science Laboratories
Department of Zoology
The University of Western Ontario
London, Ontario

"An important tissue bathed by the haemolymph is the fat body, the main organ of intermediary metabolism."
Wigglesworth, 1974b.

I. INTRODUCTION

The fat body hangs in its bathing medium, the hemolymph, growing and dividing like a child's guide to cell biology. Its cells are electrically coupled with their neighbours but take most of their instructions from the molecules around them, which they receive, metabolize and store. The fat body continues to carry out its activities while we watch, single cells or sheets are readily prepared for tissue culture and microscopy, allowing most important organelles to be resolved as they change in the day to day life of the cell (Wigglesworth, 1967a, d). Insects are epithelial organisms in the sense that most of their organization can be related to the problems of coordination within sheets and cylinders of cells. The remaining tissues (pace the CNS) are organized like tissue cultures, independent but sensitive to and communicating through their bathing media, preadapted to life in cultures of our devising in which we can try to observe and interpret their chemical dialogues.

Although it would seem to be a relatively easy task to copy the composition of the hemolymph in which the fat body lives, we have scarcely begun to do so. We have failed to realize the complexity of its life history and have given no

thought to the subtlety of the chemical environment needed for
the control of its development. The timetable for the
activities of fat body cells is like the contents page of a
cell biology textbook; fat body cells not only do the things
expected of cells, as though they are on display, they also
do them in a precise order. Their tidy sequences of
organelle formation and loss contrast with the dynamic state
of activity in the liver cells with which they are often
functionally compared. Function, and preparation for that
function, are sequential in fat body but concurrent in the
liver. Only in its embryonic maturation can we find in liver
the sequential changes that recur repeatedly in insects. The
fat body is like a cultured tissue synchronously developing
and displaying in precise sequence a gamut of cell processes.

   This essay describes the kinds of things that fat body
cells do and how we may experiment to determine what makes
them do them. It is necessarily eclectic and leans heavily
upon work on the fat body of Lepidoptera, particularly
Calpodes.

II. THE POST EMBRYONIC DEVELOPMENT OF THE FAT BODY

   In each larval stadium the fat body begins with intermoult activities, the synthesis and mobilization of reserves,
and then passes to moulting, involving growth and cell
division. This pattern becomes more complicated in the
stadium prior to pupation when the intermoult syntheses are
more extensive and prolonged. There are then separate phases
of cell preparation before both intermoult and molt. The
preparations are of totally different kinds. Intermoult
preparations ready the cells for the synthesis and accumulation of reserves. Pupal moult (metamorphic) preparations are
for organelle lysis and the storage of reserves, occupations
that continue into the pupa until the rather drastic
rearrangement occurs to make the adult fat body (Fig. 1).
Within each of these phases there is a closely coordinated
sequence of activities, some of which are so transient that
we should have difficulty studying them if the cells were not
so conveniently precise in their timing.

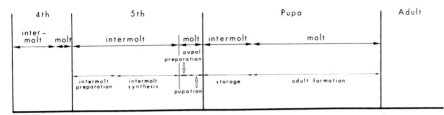

FIGURE 1. The timetable for fat body development. Each
stadium has a phase devoted to intermolt syntheses followed
by activities related to molting to the next stage. In the
last larval stadium (5th) the intermolt is more extensive
and both intermolt and molt are preceded by phases of cell
preparation.

A. Tissue Morphogenesis

Larval fat body cells within their basal lamina form
longitudinal ribbons arranged loosely around the gut and more
tightly below the integument. The ribbons increase in area
by cell division but their number and arrangement change
little during larval life until the premetamorphic stadium.
The fat body is then among the first tissues to change its
activities. By the time that the epidermis alters its
commitment to make pupal rather than larval cuticle, the fat
body assumes a new form. The single layers of cells making
the ribbons have become double, creating a space between them
that is occupied by hemolymph filtered through the basal
lamina. The doubling of the layer increases the amount of
fat body available for the massive premetamorphic syntheses
to follow, without altering the area and arrangement of the
ribbons. The fat body changes form once more at the end of
the stadium after the time that the epidermis realizes its
commitment to make pupal cuticle. The constituent cells
separate but are restrained by the basal lamina, like sacks
of oranges piled between the other organs. The cells remain
like this until the late pupa, when they aggregate in lobes
around tracheae in the adult form.

Fat body development thus involves the arrangement of
cells into four consecutive tissue patterns, single layered
ribbons, double layered ribbons, separate cells and lobes
attached to tracheae. The fat body knows how to make these
changes and makes each of them at the right time in response
to hormonal cues (Fig. 2).

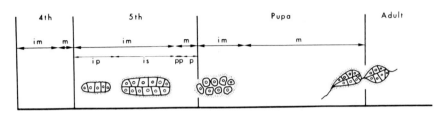

FIGURE 2.   The sequences of tissue morphogenesis.   The
early stadia have the fat body in ribbons one cell thick.
These become two cells thick for the 5th instar phase of
intermolt syntheses (is).   The cells separate for pupation (p)
and reform as lobes attached to tracheae in the adult
(im: intermolt, m: molt, ip: intermolt preparation, pp:
pupal preparation).

B. Junctions, Communication and Electrical Coupling

   The fat body is held together by very fine desmosomes
between cells and by hemidesmosomes attaching the basal
lamina.   There are also gap junctions which are presumed to
be the cause of the electrical coupling between cells when
they are in ribbons.   Junctions (and coupling) are lost with
cell separation and reform in the adult.   The coupling may
account for the considerable degree of synchrony of almost
all fat body activities.   Among the few events not exactly
synchronized are mitosis, amitosis and endomitosis leading to
polyploidy.

C. DNA Synthesis, Mitosis, Amitosis, Endomitosis and
   Polyploidy

   Polyploid cells are often assumed not to be able to
divide.   However, Wigglesworth (1967d) showed that Rhodnius
fat body cells begin larval life as tetraploids and replicate
with a constant ploidy at each molt except after starvation
when ploidy increases by nuclear fusion.   Lepidopteran fat
body is probably similar to Rhodnius in being tetraploid
through most of its larval life but it differs in that the
endomitosis of the 5th stage produces polyploid nuclei and
large cells for the elevated intermolt syntheses and for
pupation.   Even some of these large polyploid cells may later
divide, since they keep their centrioles.

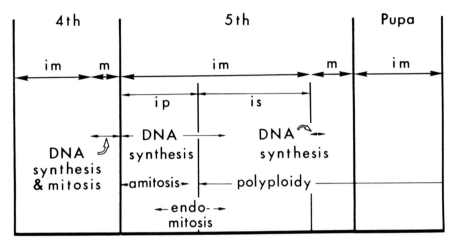

FIGURE 3. DNA synthesis, cell division and ploidy. DNA
synthesis and mitosis occur at each molt as the ribbons of
fat body grow in area. In the last stadium before
metamorphosis intermolt preparation (ip) involves amitosis to
form the double layered sheets followed by endomitosis which
leaves the cells polyploid for intermolt syntheses (is).

DNA synthesis and cell division occur regularly at each
moult in *Calpodes* so that each new stadium is furnished with
more fat body cells. For example, prior to the 4th – 5th
ecdysis fat body nuclei incorporate H^3 thymidine and the
frequency of mitoses can be counted after colchicine arrest
(Locke, 1970a). In the 5th stadium this pattern of cell
multiplication prior to ecdysis changes (Fig. 3). DNA
replication begins early in the stadium and is followed, not
by mitosis but by amitotic division, followed by endomitosis
and polyploidy. The extent of the ploidy is currently being
investigated in collaboration with K.K. Nair. DNA synthesis
in the 5th stadium extends throughout the phase of preparation for the intermolt and slightly beyond. It is first
correlated with amitotic division in the plane of the ribbons,
increasing their area as the larva grows. With the restoration of the area, the amitotic divisions shift to a plane at
right angles to the ribbon to create the double layered
structure. DNA synthesis continues as the fat body becomes
double layered but is now correlated with endomitosis and
polyploidy. Each cell becomes much larger. It may be that

such large cells are easier to manipulate in the later stages
of tissue morphogenesis, particularly in relation to their
role as storage cells. Although the polyploidy may function
in gene amplification there is no evidence that this is
selective, since the female heterochromatin which is
presumably inactive in transcription, also replicates. There
is a further round of DNA replication during preparation for
the pupal molt, but no mitosis. Thus metamorphosis in the
fat body involves amitosis and endomitosis leading to
polyploidy, and this begins after the 4th to 5th ecdysis,
long before all outward signs of metamorphic change in other
tissues. The epidermis, for example, does not become
committed to pupal cuticle formation, let alone pupal cuticle
synthesis, until the time when the fat body becomes polyploid.

The fat body is thus a remarkable tissue in its program
for growth, featuring mitosis, amitosis and endomitosis in
sequence.

D. *The Accumulation of Lipid and Glycogen Reserves and Their*
   Mobilization

"*It is generally agreed that the main function of the fat*
body of insects is the storage of those reserve substances
which require rapid mobilization during molting and
metamorphosis." *Wigglesworth, 1942b.*

With feeding in each stadium the fat body stores lipid and
glycogen (Wigglesworth, 1947a) and manufactures hemolymph
proteins (Price, 1973), which it may use at molting for
constructing the next stage. This simple pattern changes in
the 5th or premetamorphic stadium when the extent of reserve
accumulation greatly increases. Although the fat body in the
5th stage accumulates some reserves as soon as feeding begins,
there is almost no addition to this store until after the
phase of cell preparation and the formation of the two
layered ribbons. There is then a sudden elevation of the
rates of synthesis until the beginning of overt pupation
when some reserves are used to make the pupa (Fig. 4).
However, most remain in or are retrieved by the fat body,
which becomes the main pupal store of the materials needed
for adult development. In late pupal life the fat body is
once again depleted of reserves.

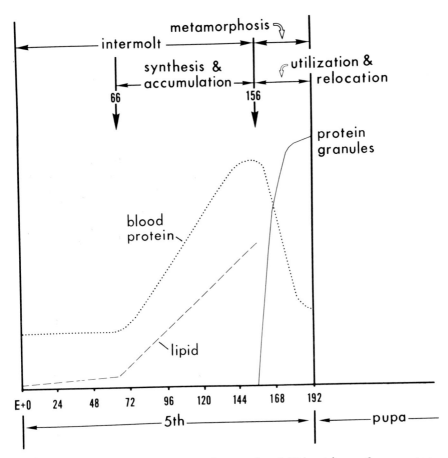

FIGURE 4. *The accumulation and mobilization of reserves. In the premetamorphic stadium, preparation for the intermolt fits the cells for the massive synthesis and accumulation of lipid (. . . . .), glycogen and hemolymph protein (- - - - -). These syntheses are turned on suddenly at 66h, the time when the prothoracic glands are activated by the brain. They are turned off at the end of the intermolt. At this time the hemolymph proteins are retrieved to accumulate as fat body protein storage granules (_____).*

E. *Nucleoli, the RER, Golgi Complexes and Hemolymph Protein Synthesis*

   "All these ideas fit in well with the view, which has been current among biologists for many years, that ribonucleic acid produced in the nucleolus and discharged into the cytoplasm..is intimately concerned with the synthesis of proteins." Wigglesworth, 1957d.

   The increased synthetic activity taking place in the latter part of the 5th intermolt (Fig. 4) requires extensive cell preparation. The first obvious signs are enlargement of the nucleoli and RNA synthesis. In the fat body (as in the epidermis at this time, Locke and Huie, 1980), the nucleoli become multilobed coincident with an elevation in RNA synthesis (Figs. 5 and 6). However, in the fat body the appearance is complicated by the increase in ploidy. The lobed nucleoli are arranged in clusters which increase in number with the increase in ploidy. In most diploid cells

   FIGURE 5. The fat body nucleoli at the beginning of the intermolt. Bismuth stained (Locke and Huie, 1977) whole mount shows few lobes per nucleus.

   FIGURE 6. The nucleoli later in intermolt preparation. There are numerous clusters of lobed nucleoli resulting both from enlargement for RNA synthesis and from polyploidy.

   FIGURE 7. The origin of Golgi Complexes in the FB. Bismuth staining of the GC beads during the phase of intermolt preparation shows smooth faces of distended RER with single rings of beads through which transition vesicles move to form saccules of the GC.

   FIGURE 8. From the time that the hemolymph proteins increase in concentration (Fig. 4) the fat body GC secretory vesicles enlarge and have a characteristic crystalline structure.

   FIGURE 9. A multivesicular body at the time of the switch to form storage granules. During the intermolt the MVBs are much smaller than this one which is destined to become a protein storage granule (cf Fig. 11).

   FIGURE 10. An early stage protein storage granule when membrane is still being digested and the central crystal has yet to form (cf Fig. 11).

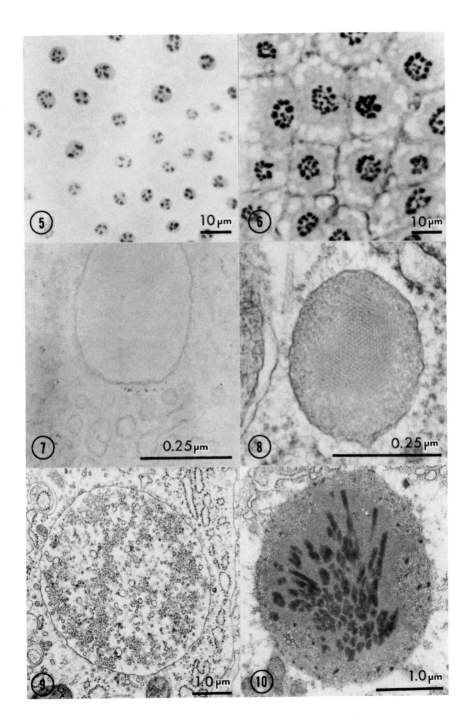

the nucleolus disappears during mitosis. There is no such
loss of nucleoli in fat body during amitosis and endomitosis.
Replication for polyploidy presumably does not require the
cessation of activities unrelated to division as happens at
mitosis.

When the nucleolar lobes are largest they have numerous
particles at their periphery that are believed to be
ribosomal precursor particles since they pass through the
nuclear pores to the cytoplasm. At this time ribosomes and
ER membranes increase and together form RER. Some Golgi
complexes (GCs) remain from the 4th stage but others now
arise. Staining for the GC beads (Locke and Huie, 1976)
shows that the first sign of these new GCs is the formation
of one or a few bead rings on a face of RER lacking ribosomes
(Fig. 7). The saccules and other GC components are presumably
made from the membranes of the transition vesicles that are
borne through the bead rings. The beads play midwife to
baby GCs.

All these preparations take place early in the 5th stadium
during the phase of intermolt preparation (Fig. 1). Initially
the cells have simple nucleoli and little RER. After preparation they are multinucleolate with much RER and many GCs.
They are now ready to be turned on. Quite suddenly lipid and
glycogen accumulate at a faster rate (Fig. 4) and the GCs form
secretory vesicles (Fig. 8) which exocytose at the surface as
the hemolymph protein level rises (Locke and Collins, 1968).
During the period of intermolt synthesis the hemolymph protein
concentration increases from about 2 to 14% and constitutes
the major protein reserve (Collins, 1969).

In the epidermis, pupal preparation repeats intermolt
preparation with a second round of nucleolar activity and
ribosome formation. At both times, the epidermal cells have
recently divided and depleted their cytoplasmic components by
dilution. The fat body nuclei, on the other hand, have
replicated without later division and have already enlarged
their cytoplasm. There is no marked second phase of
nucleolar activity at the beginning of pupal preparation.
Pupal preparation in the fat body takes a different form
from that in the epidermis, a form appropriate for its role
as the chief store of material for adult development.

F. *Pupal Preparation: The Uptake of Specific Proteins for
Storage and Reutilization*

Shortly before the fat body changes from being a two
layered ribbon to a collection of rounded and almost separate
cells, it suddenly increases its rate of pinocytosis of
hemolymph proteins. Some pinocytosis occurs throughout the
stadium, the vesicles carrying their contents to make the

perinuclear multivesicular bodies (MVBs). This process now
becomes exaggerated with the formation of protein storage
vacuoles (Figs. 9 and 10) rather than MVBs (Locke and Collins,
1968) (Fig. 11). During the intermolt, the protein synthesized by the fat body accumulates to make the hemolymph as
much as 14% protein. This massive reserve, about 5% of the
wet weight of the larva, is transferred to the fat body in
about 12hrs.

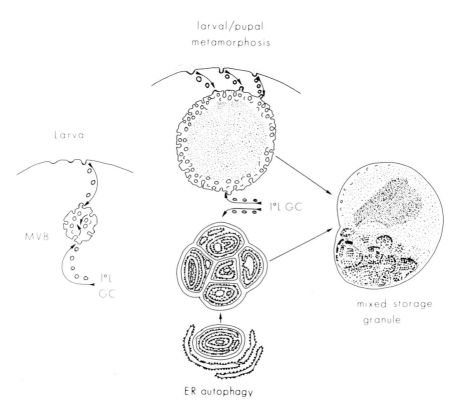

*FIGURE 11. At the end of the intermolt in the 5th stadium
there is a switch from hemolymph protein synthesis to hemolymph protein storage (Fig. 4). Sequestration increases and
MVBs become protein storage granules. These heterophagic
vacuoles fuse with autophagic vacuoles containing RER to make
stores of protein and RNA that are used up during adult
development.*

The protein storage vacuoles at first contain much
membrane in the form of fragments of peripheral microvesicles
blebbed inwards from their surfaces. 1° lysosomes also fuse
with them and the vacuoles come to contain lytic enzymes,
perhaps primarily involved in the digestion of membrane,
since such massive pinocytosis almost certainly involves a
complete turnover of the cell surface (Locke, 1980). As the
membrane fragments disappear, the protein vacuole condenses
to form a storage granule with a crystalline core.

Although foreign proteins such as horseradish peroxidase
can be sequestered, much of the pinocytosis is probably
specific. ^{14}C labelled hemolymph proteins are pinocytosed
preferentially (Collins, 1975a). Antigenically distinct
proteins from the hemolymph appear in the fat body during
the formation of the storage granules (Chippendale and Kilby,
1969; Collins and Downe, 1970; Collins, 1974). We may expect
that a main component of the hemolymph and the granules will
be storage protein, the larval equivalent of vitellogenin, as
has been described for *Manduca*, where it has been called
Manducin (Law, 1980 this volume). A characteristic of these
proteins is their large size. The pericardial cells take up
many hemolymph components in *Calpodes* but the main storage
protein is too large to pass through the sieve pores ($\sim$10nm)
between the pericardial cell doublets (Wrightnour, 1970). In
a similar way the storage protein is probably excluded from
the Malpighian tubules since colloidal gold particles fail to
penetrate the basal lamina.

Protein storage granules are thus a special category of
secondary lysosome (that is a 1° lysosome fused with a vesicle
of sequestered protein), in which there is initially only
digestion of part of the contents – the invaginated membranes.
Most protein granules also fuse with autophagic vacuoles containing RER (Fig. 11, see section III *C* below). Their nucleic
acid component is digested slowly and is presumably used for
the growth of tissues early in the pupal period. The remaining protein is digested much later, at the time of adult
emergence, and perhaps requires a new generation of 1°
lysosomes to bring lytic enzymes with different capabilities.
The way that these phagic/storage vacuoles can hydrolyse
ribosomes and membranes while allowing proteins to crystallize
out for later utilization is a problem for future cell
biologists.

III. THE LIFE HISTORY OF CERTAIN ORGANELLES DURING FAT BODY
     DEVELOPMENT

Much of the development described above (Section II) has

the characteristics of synchronously growing embryonic or tissue cultured cells; fat body cells do things in unison. The comparison is even more apt when the life history of individual organelles such as peroxisomes and mitochondria are considered and compared with those in vertebrate liver.

In rat liver the half lives of peroxisomes and mitochondria are about 3½ days and 5-10 days respectively. There are about 1200 mitochondria per cell and far fewer peroxisomes, so that on average only 2-3 of these organelles are lost and replaced in a cell each hour. The number per cell and their life spans are similar in fat body, but all or most of them arise and are destroyed within a few hours. Such synchrony makes the fat body very favourable for observing transient events rarely seen in vertebrate cells.

A. *The Formation of Peroxisomes*

4th stage peroxisomes which remain at the beginning of the 5th stadium are soon lost. A new generation then arises from diverticula of the RER which detach as vesicles, and enlarge progressively until the end of intermoult preparation when they are fully formed (Fig. 12). They contain urate oxidase and catalase, which at least initially come from the RER cisternae where they originate, before the GCs are involved with the export of cisternal proteins. Thus, preparation for the intermolt involves the synchronous occupation of fat body cells by a new population of 5th stage peroxisomes (Locke and McMahon, 1971).

Peroxisomes are lacking in pupal fat body since they are lost once more at the end of the 5th stadium (III *C*). As the fat body prepares for its adult functions at the end of the pupal stage, the process of peroxisome formation is repeated and a new adult population arises from the RER (Larsen, 1976). It would be especially interesting to know if they have the same complement of oxidases as the larval peroxisomes.

B. *Mitochondrial Replication and Division*

"Comparatively little is known about the morphological changes in the mitochondria during different phases in the activity of a given cell." Wigglesworth, 1967a.

The cell division in the fat body at the end of the 4th stadium dilutes the number of mitochondria, leaving fewer per cell by the beginning of the 5th stage. This dilution would be exaggerated in the ensuing growth for polyploidy if it were not for a round of mitochondrial division (Fig. 13). The mitochondria divide early in the phase of intermolt preparation (Tychsen, 1978). After functioning in the

intermolt, most of these mitochondria are destroyed prior to
pupation (III *C*). The surviving mitochondria undergo another
round of replication resulting in a sixfold increase in the
newly emerged adult. From 20-30hrs after ecdysis, mitochondrial profiles show division figures (Fig. 14), a large crista
dissects the inner compartment and is followed by the outer
membrane with the formation of two daughter mitochondria
(Larsen, 1970).

Larval fat body mitochondria are sausage shaped, tending
to become more oval prior to division and during starvation
as Wigglesworth found in *Rhodnius* (1967a). Adult mitochondria
are spherical or oval. The change in form suggests a kind of
mitochondrial differentiation. We may ask whether these
differences reflect changed functions and enzyme compositions
and whether they are the result of their lineage or of the
larval or adult environment. Do they result from the proliferation of a stem line set aside to survive pupal destruction
or is their form caused solely by the adult cytoplasm around
them? It would be especially interesting to know whether the
shift from larva to adult involves the selective loss by
autophagy of a population of larval type mitochondria.

FIGURE 12. A mature fat body peroxisome.

*FIGURE 13. Mitochondria dividing during intermolt
preparation.*

*FIGURE 14. Mitochondrial division in the new adult
(Larsen, 1970).*

*FIGURE 15. Isolation of a peroxisome, the first step in
autophagy during preparation for pupation.*

*FIGURE 16. Isolation of a mitochondrion, the first step
in their autophagy which occurs after the loss of the
peroxisomes (cf Fig. 18) and prior to protein sequestration
(Fig. 11).*

*FIGURE 17. Isolation of RER, the first step in RER
autophagy which occurs at the end of protein sequestration in
preparation for pupation (cf Figs. 11 and 18). (Photograph
courtesy of R. Dean).*

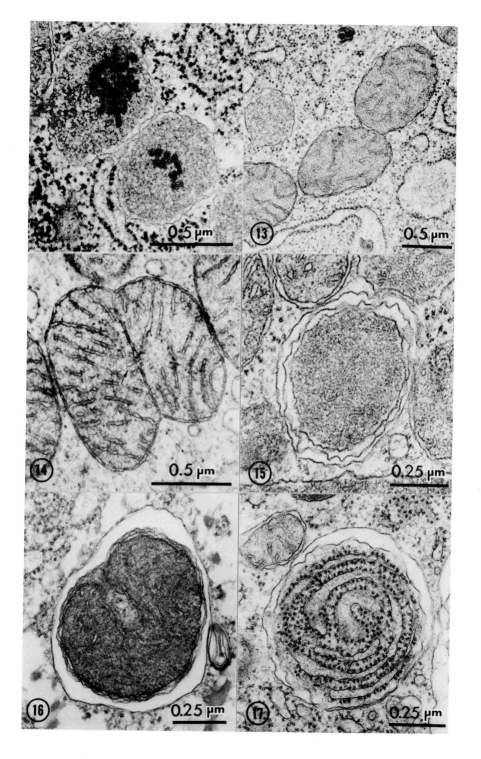

C. *Autophagy, the Controlled Destruction of Cell Components*

The switch in function from active larval synthesis in the intermolt to storage and reutilization of reserves in the pupa requires extensive cell remodelling and in particular, the loss of organelles. The problem facing a cell that is intent upon destroying part of itself is how to restrict the digestive environment to the particular organelles that are scheduled for destruction. The answer, from studies on metamorphosing fat body and other tissues of *Calpodes*, is that components to be digested are first isolated from the cytoplasm (Locke and Collins, 1965; Locke and McMahon, 1971) and only then do 1° lysosomes fuse with the new, topologically external compartments, to digest their contents (Locke and Sykes, 1975). Fat body acid hydrolase activity increases 15 fold at this time (Collins, 1979). This two step principle is shown in Fig. 18.

In the fat body the first indication that an organelle is to be destroyed is the presence of a tiny vesicle closely apposed to its surface. As more vesicles fuse with it, the isolating envelope seems to creep over the surface until investment is complete. The close apposition between the envelope and its prey suggests that there may be a special kind of adhesion between their surfaces. This would be required to explain the specificity of destruction. The contents of auotphagic vacuoles (AVs) are not a random sample of the cytoplasmic constituents of the cell. Although most cell components may be destroyed, they are isolated separately and in a particular order, first peroxisomes, then mitochondria. This is followed by protein sequestration (II *F*) after which there is a second phase of autophagy when the RER is isolated. The RER is cut off in envelopes making fragments of about the same size as mitochondria, suggesting that there is a mechanism for making a vacuole of about that size independently of the shape and surface of the RER. These mixed vacuoles are not digested quickly like the AVs containing mitochondria. They remain as storage granules (Fig. 11).

The general mechanism of autophagy outlined in Fig. 18 serves to remove and digest almost all cell components not needed in the pupa. The net result is a fat body cell containing little but storage vacuoles (II *F*), lipid and glycogen (II *D*). As these stores are depleted to make the adult the cells are repopulated with organelles appropriate for adult syntheses (III *A, B*).

Isolation

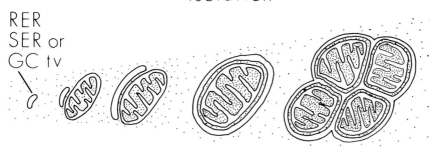

Digestion

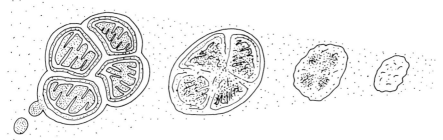

FIGURE 18. *Autophagy in the fat body is in two steps, first isolation then digestion. Autophagy in preparation for pupation is organelle specific, beginning with peroxisomes, then mitochondria and finishing with RER (After Locke, 1980).*

D. *Urate Storage Granules and the Giant Vacuoles*

"*The significance of watery vacuoles, which are generally present in fat body cells (Wigglesworth, 1942b, 1947a) is not known (Wigglesworth, 1967a).*"

Although Wigglesworth observed large watery vacuoles in the fat body of *Aedes* and *Rhodnius* after feeding and saw urate-like crystals appearing within them after fixation, these structures have received little attention and have yet to be correlated with studies upon nitrogen metabolism.

Studies on *Calpodes* (H. McDermid, personal communication)
show that they are easily overlooked by light microscopy,
resembling lipid droplets in non osmicated tissue.   The
vacuoles do not contain urate.   They increase in size during
each stadium (Fig. 19) until ecdysis when they disappear in
as little as six hours.   They are infrequent or absent from
the 5th stadium, which may be correlated with the change in
nitrogen metabolism related to the synthesis and storage of
proteins.   Urate granules (Tojo *et al.*, 1978; Fig. 20) which
have a very different morphology from the watery vacuoles,
appear just prior to the sequestration of protein for storage
after the peroxisomes have been destroyed.   The relation between vacuoles, urate storage granules and changes in nitrogen
metabolism from larva to pupa make an interesting problem for
the future.

IV. THE CONTROL OF DEVELOPMENT

The development of the fat body can be viewed as a
succession of intrinsically controlled sequences triggered or
influenced by previous exposure to three interwoven groups of
external factors.   (1) The general background influence is
nutritional.   (2) Against this can be set the results of the
interaction between prolonged exposure to hormones, particularly juvenile hormone (JH) and molting hormone (MH).   (3)
Superimposed upon this are hemolymph borne pulses of JH, MH
and perhaps other hormones (see Steele, this volume).

*FIGURE 19.   The watery vacuoles are the major part of
the fat body in early stages.   Mid 4th stage Calpodes fat
body.   LM section courtesy of H. McDermid.*

*FIGURE 20.   Urate granules appear for the first time after
the switch from intermolt syntheses to preparation for
pupation.   They appear just as the peroxisomes containing
urate oxidase are lost.*

*FIGURE 21.   The formation of giant mitochondria by fusion.
Fat body from 5th instar larvae starved for 24hrs.*

*FIGURE 22.   The induction of division in the giant
mitochondria.   Four hours after feeding the mitochondria have
divided to become normal in size and shape.*

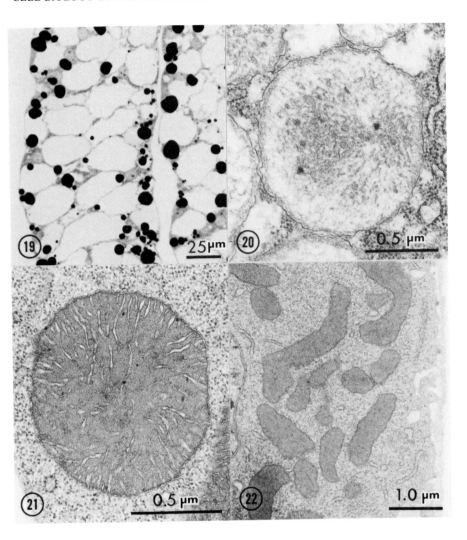

At the moment our knowledge of control is fragmentary. We know that mitochondrial fusion and division can be influenced by nutrition. Autophagy, and probably protein sequestration are triggered by ecdysteroids but intrinsically controlled thereafter. Several major switches in development correlate temporally with hemolymph ecdysteroid pulses.

The fat body in its turn may influence the development of other tissues (Dutkowski and Oberlander, 1973, 1974).

A. *The Nutritional Control of Mitochondrial Fusion and Division*

"The extensive changes in form which the mitochondria of the fat body undergo are closely correlated with the state of nutrition."
"The mitochondria in the fat body cells of Rhodnius are exceedingly pleomorphic. During starvation the normal filamentous forms are gradually reduced to rounded granules or short rods." "Other shperical inclusions... are clearly cytolysomes derived from the breakdown of mitochondria."
"If the insect is fed... the granules become elongated to form rods and filaments... which break up into chains of granules... to form more filaments." Wigglesworth, 1967a.

In Lepidoptera as in *Rhodnius*, starvation results in autophagy of mitochondria by the same mechanism as that seen at metamorphosis (Fig. 18). Starvation also results in mitochondrial fusion, so that each cell comes to contain only a very few giant mitochondria (Fig. 21). These divide to become normal sized mitochondria within four hours of feeding (Fig. 22). It is thus clear that nutrition can influence the death of mitochondria and their size. It is less certain that it influences their birth and death in normal mitochondrial growth, DNA replication and division (III *B, C*). Mitochondrial autophagy is clearly induced by MH at metamorphosis (Dean, 1978). The integration of mitochondrial division with other kinds of cell preparation at the beginning of the 5th intermolt and in the new adult, suggest that increases in number may also be part of a hormonally controlled sequence. We should be able to discover how nutrition influences mitochondria and whether this influence is comparable to the control of the phases of mitochondrial division (III *B*) and mitochondrial destruction (III *C*) that occur so precisely in normal fat body development. The temporal separation of mitochondrial division from destruction and the separation of both events from nuclear replication and cell division gives us a unique opportunity for studying the factors controlling mitochondrial life history.

B. *The Hormonal Stimulation of Autophagy*

The autophagy of 5th stage peroxisomes and mitochondria in the fat body is the first overt metamorphic event occurring as the hemolymph level of MH approaches it prepupal peak (Peak 3, Fig. 23). Fat body isolated in culture before this time does not undergo autophagy unless MH is added to the medium (Dean, 1978). Once MH has induced the beginning of autophagy however, the sequence proceeds independently of

external hormone. Thus, although the initiation is induced
by MH, the autophagic sequence itself is intrinsically
controlled. We have yet to determine whether the previous
history of the cell (with respect to JH exposure for example)
and the presence of organelles of a particular age to be
invested, are important for the induction of autophagy.

C. Hormones and Protein Sequestration

The switch from hemolymph protein synthesis to hemolymph
protein storage (Fig. 11) is a second overt metamorphic
activity. It begins just after the peak level of MH in the
hemolymph (Peak 3, Fig. 23) and *in vivo* depends upon the
presence of active prothoracic glands and of MH when kept in
a culture medium (Collins, 1969, 1974, 1975b; Butterworth *et
al.*, 1979). The role of the MH in protein sequestration is
more complicated than in the induction of autophagy since
external protein is required. Since the protein uptake is
fairly specific, the hormone may be involved in the induction
of membrane receptors which require the presence of the
storage proteins for pinocytosis and the completion of the
uptake sequence. The time needed for new protein receptors to
form could also explain why the uptake does not begin until
after other MH induced events such as autophagy. However, it
may also be that the GC can only be involved sequentially in
such diverse activities as the formation of isolation
envelopes and the 1° lysosomes needed for organelle digestion
and later for hemolymph protein condensation.

D. General Correlations with Hemolymph Ecdysteroids

*"Within a few hours after feeding the nucleolus begins to
enlarge and soon RNA begins to accumulate in the cytoplasm"
Wigglesworth, 1957d, on "the action of growth hormones."*

The changes in haemolymph ecdysteroid titre in *Calpodes*
are shown in Fig. 23. In the 5th stadium there are three
main peaks and at least one in the pupa (Dean *et al.*, 1980).
Each of these peaks precedes major changes in fat body development.
The first, or intermolt peak, precedes DNA synthesis,
amitosis and endomitosis which are concurrent with nucleolar
activity, RNA synthesis and the formation of cytoplasmic
organelles - mitochondria, peroxisomes, RER and GCs. 5th
stage *Rhodnius* are very like *Calpodes* in that nucleolar
activity (Wigglesworth, 1957d) and RNA synthesis (Locke, 1970)
are stimulated by a blood meal. It is especially interesting
that Colin Steel (personal communication) has found that

these events are correlated with an elevated level of
hemolymph ecdysteroid.

The second or epidermal commitment peak precedes the
decline of RNA synthesis. With a full complement of
organelles and a two layered structure, the synthesis of
glycogen, lipid and hemolymph protein are turned on. The GCs
become active, secretory vesicles form and move to the plasma
membrane for exocytosis.

The third or prepupal peak coincides with the switch from
larval synthesis to autophagy and storage after which the
ribbons separate into single cells.

The very marked pupal peak precedes the rearrangement of
the fat body into lobes attached to tracheae.

There is thus good circumstantial evidence that hemolymph
ecdysteroids may have a role in controlling several steps in
fat body development. There is also experimental confirmation
that MH acts directly upon the fat body to initiate two
activities - autophagy and protein sequestration (Dean, 1978;
Collins, 1969, 1975). In *Calliphora* also, MH induces lysosomal activity (Pelt-Verkuil, 1979; Pelt-Verkuil *et al.*, 1979).

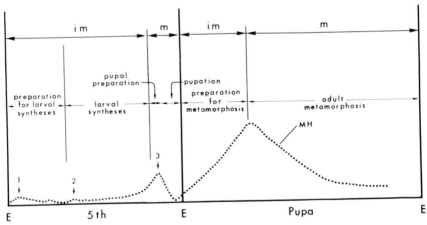

*FIGURE 23. Hemolymph ecdysteroids and the fat body. Each
peak precedes major changes in fat body development (After
Dean et al., 1980). Peak 1 marks the beginning of preparations for intermolt syntheses. Peak 2 (epidermal commitment)
occurs after the switch from single to double layered ribbons
at the time when preparation is complete and intermolt
syntheses are suddenly elevated. Peak 3 (prepupal) coincides
with the cessation of intermolt syntheses and the beginning of
pupal preparation. The main pupal peak corresponds with
changes related to adult formation.*

V. DISCUSSION AND PROMISES FOR THE FUTURE

A. *The Complexity of Development*

The complex sequential nature of fat body development (and of other apparently simple insect tissues) shows why early attempts at culture never resulted in spectacular growth or sustained high levels of syntheses. The apparent independence of cells suspended in hemolymph is an illusion. Both metabolically (see Steele, this volume) and developmentally they are dependent upon a succession of hormonal cues, all of which we must duplicate in the appropriate time sequence if we wish to mimic natural growth. The first need outlined in this essay, is to determine the nature of all of the separate steps in development. When this has been accomplished it will be possible to find the cues initiating each step and how the steps may relate to one another.

B. *The Role of Hemolymph Proteins*

All insect tissues seem to pinocytose proteins from the hemolymph, at least during phases of growth. The fat body is distinguished by the magnitude and specificity of its sequestration. The hemolymph contains many different proteins, not all of which are detectable in the fat body. Presumably, some are synthesized by other tissues. The fat body differs from other tissues in the greater magnitude of its protein synthesis. It is clearly possible and desirable to construct a balance sheet for all of the hemolymph proteins at all stages. We need to know how their concentrations change, where they are synthesized and what their destination may be. If specific receptors come and go in the plasma membranes of different cell types, then very intricate kinds of communication between tissues become possible. Even common growth hormones could be given tissue specificity by protein carriers and receptors. Such studies may even yield clues to the communication in the epidermis that gives rise to gradients.

ACKNOWLEDGMENTS

I am grateful to Mr. P. Huie for technical assistance and to Dr. R. Dean for reading the manuscript. The work was supported by a grant from the Natural Science Engineering Research Council of Canada.

REFERENCES

Butterworth, F.M., Tysell, B. and Waclawski, I. (1979). The
    effect of 20-Hydroxyecdysone and protein on granule
    formation in the *in vitro* cultured fat body of *Drosophila*.
    J. Insect Physiol. *25*, 855-860.
Chippendale, G.M. and Kilby, B.A. (1969). Relationship between
    proteins of the hemolymph and fat body during development
    of *Pieris brassicae*. *J. Insect Physiol*. *15*, 905-926.
Collins, J.V. (1969). The hormonal control of fat body
    development in *Calpodes ethlius* (Lepidoptera, Hesperiidae).
    J. Insect Physiol. *15*, 341-352.
Collins, J.V. (1974). Hormonal control of protein sequestra-
    tion in the fat body of *Calpodes ethlius* Stoll. *Can. J.
    Zool*. *52*, 639-642
Collins, J.V. (1975a). Secretion and uptake of ^{14}C proteins
    by fat body of *Calpodes ethlius* Stoll. (Lepidoptera,
    Hesperiidae). *Differentiation 3*, 143-148.
Collins, J.V. (1975b). Soluble acid phosphatases of the
    hemolymph and fat body of *Calpodes ethlius* (Stoll) and
    the control of protein storage by fat body. *Can. J. Zool*.
    53, 480-489.
Collins, J.V. (1979). Acid hydrolase activity and the control
    of autophagy and heterophagy in larval fat body of
    Calpodes ethlius Stoll (Lepidoptera). *Comp. Biochem.
    Physiol*. *62B*, 317-324.
Collins, J.V. and Downe, A.E.R. (1970). Selective accumula-
    tion of haemolymph proteins by the fat body of *Galleria
    mellonella*. *J. Insect Physiol*. *16*, 1697-1708.
Dean, R.L. (1978). The induction of autophagy in isolated
    insect fat body by β-ecdysone. *J. Insect Physiol*. *24*,
    439-447.
Dean, R.L., Bollenbacher, W.E., Locke, M., Smith, S.L. and
    Gilbert, L.I. (1980). Haemolymph ecdysteroid levels and
    cellular events in the intermoult/moult sequence of
    Calpodes ethlius. *J. Insect Physiol*. (in press).
Dutkowski, A.B. and Oberlander, H. (1973). The influence of
    larval fat body on wing disk development *in vitro*. *J.
    Insect Physiol*. *19*, 2155-2162.
Dutkowski, A.B. and Oberlander, H. (1974). Interactions
    between beta-ecdysone and fat body during wing disk
    development *in vitro*. *J. Insect Physiol*. *20*, 743-749.
Larsen, W.J. (1970). Genesis of mitochondria in the fat body
    of an insect. *J. Cell Biol*. *47*, 373-383.
Larsen, W.J. (1976). Cell remodeling in the fat body of an
    insect. *Tissue and Cell 8*, 73-92.

Locke, M. (1970a). The molt/intermolt cycle in the epidermis and other tissues of an insect *Calpodes ethlius* (Lepidoptera, Hesperiidae). *Tissue and Cell 2*, 197-223.

Locke, M. (1980). Cytological and morphological changes during insect metamorphosis. *In* "Metamorphosis" (E. Frieden and L.I. Gilbert, eds.). Plenum Press, New York (in press).

Locke, M. and Collins, J.V. (1965). The structure and formation of protein granules in the fat body of an insect. *J. Cell Biol. 26*, 857-885.

Locke, M. and Collins, J.V. (1968). Protein uptake into Multivesicular bodies and storage granules in the fat body of an insect. *J. Cell Biol. 36*, 453-483.

Locke, M. and Huie, P. (1976). The beads in the Golgi complex/endoplasmic reticulum region. *J. Cell Biol. 70*, 384-394.

Locke, M. and Huie, P. (1977). Bismuth staining for light and electron microscopy. *Tissue and Cell 9*, 347-371.

Locke, M. and Huie, P. (1980). The nucleolus during epidermal development in an insect. *Tissue and Cell 12*, 175-194.

Locke, M. and McMahon, J.T. (1971). The origin and fate of microbodies in the fat body of an insect. *J. Cell Biol. 48*, 61-78.

Locke, M. and Sykes, A.K. (1975). The role of the Golgi complex in the isolation and digestion of organelles. *Tissue and Cell 7*, 143-158.

Pelt-Verkuil, E. van. (1979). Hormone mediated induction of acid phosphatase activity in *Calliphora* fat body. *J. Insect Physiol. 25*, 965-973.

Pelt-Verkuil, E. van, Rongen, E. van and de Priester, W. (1979). Normal and experimentally induced lysosomal activity in the larval fat body of *Calliphora erythrocephala* Meigen. *Cell Tissue Res. 203*, 443-455.

Price, G.M. (1973). Protein and nucleic acid metabolism in insect fat body. *Biol. Rev. 48*, 333-375.

Tojo, S., Betchaku, T., Ziccardi, V.J. and Wyatt, G.R. (1978). Fat body protein granules and storage proteins in the silkmoth, *Hyalophora cecropia*. *J. Cell Biol. 78*, 823-838.

Tychsen, C.M. (1978). Mitochondrial generation in the fat body cells of *Calpodes ethlius* (Stoll) (Lepidoptera: Hesperiidae). M.Sc. Thesis, University of Western Ontario, 175 pp.

Wigglesworth, V.B. (1942b). The storage of protein fat, glycogen and uric acid in the fat body and other tissues of mosquito larvae. *J. Exp. Biol. 19*, 56-77.

Wigglesworth, V.B. (1947a). The epicuticle in an insect, *Rhodnius prolixus* (Hemiptera). *Proc. Roy. Soc. B. 134*, 163-181.

Wigglesworth, V.B. (1957d). The action of growth hormones in insects. *Symp. Soc. Exp. Biol. 11*, 204-227.

Wigglesworth, V.B. (1967b). Cytological changes in the
     fat body of *Rhodnius* during starvation, feeding and
     oxygen want. *J. Cell Sci. 2*, 243–256.
Wigglesworth, V.B. (1967e). Polyploidy and Nuclear Fusion in
     the fat body of *Rhodnius* (Hemiptera). *J. Cell Sci. 2*,
     603–616.
Wigglesworth, V.B. (1974b). Insecta. *Encyclopaedia Britannica
     15th Edn.*, 608–622.
Wrightnour, V.E. (1970). The pericardial cells of an insect,
     Calpodes ethlius Stoll, Lepidoptera, Hesperiidae. Ph.D.
     Thesis, Case Western Reserve University, Clevland, Ohio,
     178 pp.

HORMONAL MODULATION OF CARBOHYDRATE AND LIPID
METABOLISM IN FAT BODY

J.E. Steele

Department of Zoology
University of Western Ontario
London, Canada

I. INTRODUCTION

The fat body of the insect plays a role in carbohydrate
and lipid metabolism comparable to that of liver and adipose
tissue in mammals. One of the first studies showing the importance of the fat body in intermediary metabolism was undertaken by Wigglesworth (1942b) on the fat body of the mosquito.
In retrospect we can see that the fluctuations he described in
the concentration of reserve substances were indicative of
hormone action. Since then, a number of hormones have been
found to alter the level of glycogen and lipid in fat body.
Two such hormones are trehalagon[1] and adipokinetic hormone
(AKH), both of which occur in the corpora cardiaca (CC). Each
of these hormones influence physiological mechanisms through a
direct action on pathways associated with energy metabolism.
In the following essay the relationship of these hormones to
lipid and carbohydrate reserves in the fat body will be exam-

[1]It is proposed that 'trehalagon' (i.e. trehalose mobilizing) be the term used to describe the active principle in
the corpora cardiaca which elevates the level of trehalose in
haemolymph. The similarity in name to the mammalian hormone
glucagon is intended because the mode of action and specificity of both hormones have much in common. The terms hyperglycaemic and hypertrehalosemic, although adequately describing the result of trehalagon action, do not reflect its
function in mobilizing trehalose from glycogen stored in the
fat body.

253

ined. It will be seen that both hormones have certain effects
in common and each plays a regulatory role in the metabolism
of lipid and carbohydrate. These particular hormones have
been chosen because they appear related and have the fat body
as their primary site of action. It is important to remember,
however, that their physiological significance extends beyond
the fat body and that change in fat body metabolism subtends
physiological mechanisms elsewhere.

II. THE ORIGIN AND NATURE OF THE HORMONES

A. *Trehalagon*

The distinguishing feature of this hormone is the hypertrehalosemic effect it produces in certain insects. Relatively little is known of its chemical nature. The loss of
activity which occurs when incubated with trypsin (Natalizi
et al, 1970) or chymotrypsin (Steele, unpublished results)
suggests it is a peptide. In the locust the hypertrehalosemic
activity associated with the glandular lobe of the CC is due
to the adipokinetic hormone (Jones *et al*, 1977). Thus in this
species at least, there is proof that a peptide is the cause
of the hypertrehalosemia. Gel permeation studies on *Peri-*
planeta CC using Bio-Gel P2 as the chromatographic medium indicated a molecular weight for trehalagon in the range of
1200-1500 daltons (Holverda *et al*, 1977). This agrees well
with the finding that the K_d of the active substance on a Bio-
Gel P10 column, although at the end of the range for that
particular gel, is consistent with a molecular weight of
approximately 1500 (Natalizi and Frontali, 1966; Steele, unpublished observations).

B. *Adipokinetic Hormone (AKH)*

A hormone modulating the release of diacylglycerol from
insect fat body was first described in locusts by Mayer and
Candy (1969). Because lipid is important as a metabolic substrate for flight in locusts the hormone has excited much
interest and numerous studies by those interested in hormonal
control of metabolism in insects. The active material is a
heat stable peptide. Its structure has now been elucidated
and shown to be a blocked decapeptide having the amino acid
sequence: < Glu-Leu-Asn-Phe-Thr-Pro-Asn-Trp-Gly-Thr-NH$_2$ (Stone
et al, 1976). The structure has been confirmed by synthesis
and the synthetic product shown to have the same potency on a
molar basis as the natural product (Broomfield and Hardy, 1977).

III.   REGULATION OF CARBOHYDRATE METABOLISM

The periodic shedding of the cuticle and its replacement
in the course of development has probably received more intensive study than any other aspect of insect life. These
events are of considerable importance in carbohydrate metabolism because chitin is the major component of the cuticle.
Just as fat body glycogen represents a pool of carbohydrate to
be utilized for chitin synthesis so may the chitin be regarded
as a reserve for glycogen synthesis. In this exchange the
sugars in the blood are the vehicle by which it occurs. The
carbohydrate reserves of the fat body are not restricted to a
role in cuticle formation but are also a major source of
energy for flight and other purposes. It is clear that the
'ebb and flow' of metabolites in such a complex system requires a sophisticated set of controls. The fact that hormones profoundly influence carbohydrate metabolism is therefore hardly surprising.

A.   *Hormonal Modulation of Haemolymph Trehalose*

The hypertrehalosemic effect of the CC has been demonstrated in a number of species and reflects events occurring
in the fat body. This response, however, is not universal.
Locusta does not respond to the CC (Chalaye, 1969) although
Goldsworthy (1969) has claimed an effect between the third and
sixth day of adult life. The reason is not that the CC lacks
trehalagon since CC extract is active when injected into
Periplaneta (Mordue and Goldsworthy, 1969). Furthermore,
extirpation of the CC in *Locusta* causes a significant decline
in blood trehalose (Cazal, 1971). Possibly, trehalagon is
only effective when the level of haemolymph trehalose is low,
otherwise feedback control of trehalose synthesis negates the
action of the hormone. Like *Locusta* the CC of *Carausius* do
not induce hypertrehalosemia in the donor species but are
active when tested in *Periplaneta* (Gäde, 1979). An earlier
report (Dutrieu and Gordoux, 1967) claimed a hypertrehalosemic effect for the CC of *Carausius* but the concentration of
extract used was not physiological.
The hypertrehalosemic effect caused by the CC in headless
cockroaches clearly shows it is independent of any factor from
the remaining cephalic endocrine organs (Hanaoka and Takahashi,
1976). Until recently the hypertrehalosemic response was
assumed to be due entirely to the presence of trehalagon in
the CC. That view is no longer tenable since AKH has also
been shown to induce hypertrehalosemia (Jones *et al*, 1977).

B. Glycogen Regulation in the Fat Body

Most of the additional trehalose appearing in the haemolymph of the cockroach following injection of CC extract
originates from glycogen in the fat body (Steele, 1963;
Hanaoka and Takahashi, 1976). In those insects where the CC
do not raise the level of circulating trehalose the level of
glycogen would not be expected to change. In *Locusta*, however,
fat body glycogen declines (Goldsworthy, 1969) and phosphorylase activity increases (Goldsworthy, 1970). It seems that
the reserve of glycogen in the fat body is either too low to
support a significant rise in the level of haemolymph trehalose or else it is channelled into other uses. On the other
hand glycogen in *Phormia* fat body is unaffected by the CC unless the flies have first been starved for 24 h. Presumably
this reduces the concentration of trehalose in the blood and
diminishes feedback inhibition of trehalose synthetase
(Friedman, 1967). *In vitro* studies have confirmed the fat
body as a principal target for trehalagon. The CC significantly increase total trehalose released from *Phormia* fat
body (Friedman, 1967). Other studies show that although the
initial rate of trehalose release in *Leucophaea* fat body is
increased by the CC the subsequent rate is reduced so that
total trehalose released does not differ from that of control
tissues (Wiens and Gilbert, 1967). This suggests that trehalose synthesis is regulated by feedback control.

C. Trehalose Synthesis

1. *Regulation of Trehalose Synthesis.* The major effect of
trehalagon appears to be directed toward the degradation of
glycogen and concomitant synthesis of trehalose. Glycogen
synthesis, however, must also be considered since both pathways share common substrates. It will be useful to describe
trehalose biosynthesis, first without any reference to trehalagon, and then to review the effects of the hormone on the
pathway.

The biosynthetic pathway for trehalose and glycogen is
depicted in Fig. 1. It can be seen that UDP-glucose and
glucose-6-PO_4 occupy key positions in the synthesis of both
glycogen and trehalose such that one mechanism cannot predominate without affecting the other. The relative rates of
glycogen and trehalose synthesis depend on the concentration
of intermediates and kinetic properties of the enzymes. Our
basic understanding of the mechanism is based on a single
paper describing these processes in silkmoth fat body (Murphy
and Wyatt, 1965). Although other authors have produced
additional important information none has made such a detailed

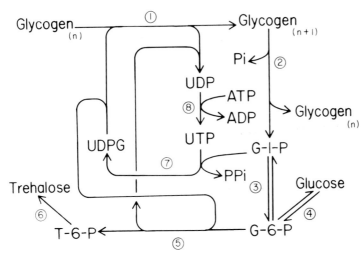

FIGURE 1. Glycogen and trehalose biosynthetic pathways in fat body. The circled numbers represent the following enzymes: 1, glycogen synthetase; 2, phosphorylase; 3, phosphoglucomulase; 4, hexokinase,; 5, trehalose-6-phosphate synthetase; 6, trehalose-6-phosphatase; 7, UDP-glucose pyrophosphorylase; 8, nucleoside diphosphokinase.

study on a single system. The trehalose-6-PO_4 synthetase reaction is controlled by a number of factors, including the concentration of glucose-6-PO_4, intracellular Mg^{2+} and trehalose. Trehalose inhibits trehalose-6-PO_4 synthetase by feedback control. It is therefore of paramount importance in determining whether glucose-6-PO_4 arising from dietary glucose is converted into trehalose or into glycogen. In the absence of any feedback control of trehalose-6-PO_4 synthetase, glucose-6-PO_4 is preferentially converted into trehalose because the K_m for UDPG, the glycosyl donor, is lower for the trehalose-6-PO_4 synthetase (0.3 mM) than it is for glycogen synthetase (1.6 mM). As the synthesis of trehalose proceeds, the trehalose-6-PO_4 synthetase reaction is subjected to feedback inhibition. This has two important consequences; the concentration of both glucose-6-PO_4 and UDPG will tend to rise. The increase in concentration of glucose-6-PO_4 activates glycogen synthesis because it is an activator of the reaction (K_a = 0.6 mM). At the same time the rise in UDPG concentration permits the rate of the reaction to increase. Other studies also attest to the importance of trehalose in feedback control of trehalose-6-PO_4 synthetase. In *Phormia* fat body the

synthesis of trehalose *in vitro* is completely blocked by trehalose in the medium as low as 10% of that normally present in
haemolymph (Friedman, 1967). What is the explanation for this
anomaly? Murphy and Wyatt (1965) have shown that Mg^{2+} at
concentrations normally present in the cell are potent activators of trehalose-6-PO_4 synthetase. Thus the resultant of
Mg^{2+} and trehalose level in the cell probably determines the
activity of the enzyme. During larval-pupal transformation in
the silkmoth the intracellular Mg^{2+} concentration in fat body
decreases and trehalose in the haemolymph is reduced (Jungreis
et al, 1974). At the same time the intracellular concentration of trehalose also declines but not nearly so precipitous-
ly as that in haemolymph (Jungreis and Wyatt, 1972). The
intracellular level of trehalose is maintained at a higher
concentration because of reduced permeability of the fat body
cell membrane to trehalose (Jungreis and Wyatt, 1972). Reducing the permeability at the onset of diapause prevents
undue loss of trehalose to the haemolymph with the consequence
that feedback inhibition of the synthetase is maintained.
Reduction of the Mg^{2+} concentration similarly reduces the
activity of the enzyme. In this way glycogen is redirected
from trehalose to glycerol synthesis.

Although nearly two decades have passed since the hypertrehalosemic effect of trehalagon was first described,
virtually nothing is known of its effect on the intermediary
metabolism of glycogen apart from the activation of phosphorylase. Recently we have shown that treatment of
Periplaneta fat body *in vitro* with highly purified CC extracts
doubles the concentration of glucose-6-PO_4 in the tissue
(Coulthart and Steele, unpublished observations). Because
glucose-6-PO_4 is the substrate for trehalose-6-PO_4 synthetase
the increase can explain the rise in trehalose synthesis. It
follows that the rate of glucose-1-PO_4 synthesis must also
increase since it is an intermediate in the synthesis of glu-
cose-6-PO_4 from glycogen (Fig. 1). This, of course, has the
effect of stimulating trehalose synthesis since it is the
obligatory glycosyl donor for the formation of UDPG. It is
more difficult to explain how trehalagon stimulates trehalose
synthesis in those insects which must be starved first (e.g.
Phormia) (Friedman, 1967). Possibly, normal levels of blood
trehalose strongly inhibit the trehalose-6-PO_4 synthetase
reaction. Only when they decrease, as occurs following
starvation (Duve, 1978), is inhibition relieved and the hormone able to express its effect. Although cardiacectomy
reduces the activity of the trehalose synthesizing pathway by
30% (Chen and Friedman, 1977) the reason is unrelated to the
hypertrehalosemic effect of the CC since the activity of
glycogen synthetase is reduced by the same amount.

2. *Activation of Glycogen Phosphorylase.* Soon after the discovery of trehalagon its site of action was identified as the rate-limiting enzyme glycogen phosphorylase. Regulation of phosphorylase activity is a complex process requiring the participation of additional enzymes. Until recently a limiting factor in efforts to provide a detailed understanding of the mode of action of trehalagon has been the lack of information on phosphorylase and its associated enzymes. This obstacle has now been largely overcome. A generalized model illustrating the activation of fat body phosphorylase is included in Fig. 2.

The first evidence that fat body phosphorylase occurs as interconvertible active and inactive (i.e. *a* and *b*) forms was obtained by Stevenson and Wyatt (1964) who showed that activity was increased by 5'-AMP. We now know that phosphorylase *b* (inactive) is converted to the active *a* form by the action of a kinase (Wiens and Gilbert, 1967; Yanagawa and Horie, 1978; Ashida and Wyatt, 1979). The two latter studies are of particular importance because they show that phosphorylase kinase is activated by ATP and Mg^{2+}. Ca^{2+} further enhances this activation (Ashida and Wyatt, 1979). The requirement for ATP and Mg^{2+} strongly suggests that activation is mediated by phosphorylation of the enzyme protein.

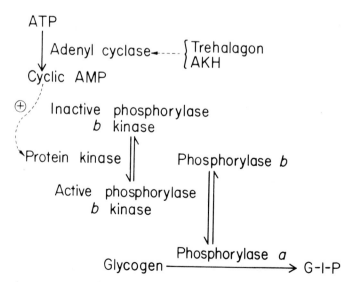

FIGURE 2. *Scheme illustrating the control of phosphory-*
lase activity by trehalagon and AKH.

When cockroach fat body is treated with CC extract
in vitro, total phosphorylase in the *a* form increases by as
much as 150% (Steele, 1963). Wiens and Gilbert (1967) using
Leucophaea measured both forms of the enzyme and showed that
the CC increased the phosphorylase *a/b* ratio. Although
Locusta does not exhibit a hypertrehalosemic response to the
hormone, there is an increase in the phosphorylase *a/b* ratio.
Not all insects respond in this manner. Fat body phosphorylase in *Hyalophora cecropia* is insensitive to conspecific CC
extracts as well as those prepared from *Periplaneta* CC (Wiens
and Gilbert, 1967).

   3. Role of Cyclic Nucleotides. The possibility that
various hormones acting on fat body utilize a second messenger
for expression of their effects has prompted several investigators to enquire whether fat body contains enzymes for the
synthesis and degradation of cyclic nucleotides. Adenyl
cyclase has been described from fat body of various insects,
including *Bombyx mori* (Morishima, 1978, 1979), *Hyalophora
cecropia* (Filburn and Wyatt, 1976) and *Periplaneta* (Hanaoka
and Takahashi, 1977), clearly demonstrating that this tissue
has the capacity to synthesize adenosine-3',5'-cyclic monophosphate (cyclic AMP). Morishima (1979) has shown that
adenyl cyclase in silkworm pupal fat body is regulated by a
Ca^{2+}-dependent regulator protein whose activity is determined
by Ca^{2+} concentrations in the range of those normally occurr-
in cells. This finding will undoubtedly have far-reaching
implications.
   The level of cyclic AMP in fat body is greatly augmented
by the CC (Gäde and Holwerda, 1976; Gäde and Beenakkers, 1977;
Gäde, 1977; Hanaoka and Takahashi, 1977). Since the CC may
contain more than one factor capable of stimulating adenyl
cyclase it is not possible to ascribe the increase in cyclic
AMP to a particular factor. A current model depicts cyclic
AMP as an activator of a protein kinase whose function is to
phosphorylate an enzyme. This alters the activity of the
enzyme which in turn modulates a physiological process. Recently it has been shown that *Periplaneta* fat body contains at
least two cyclic AMP-dependent protein kinases (Takahashi and
Hanaoka, 1977) thus confirming the presence of a key element
in the model. A possible means by which cyclic AMP mediates
the effect of trehalagon on fat body phosphorylase is shown in
Fig. 2. Treatment of fat body with cyclic AMP or its dibutyryl derivative causes a marked conversion of phosphorylase
b to *a* (Steele, 1964; Ziegler *et al*, 1979). CC extract increases three-fold the activity of adenyl cyclase in
Periplaneta fat body and as might be anticipated there is a
rise in the concentration of cyclic AMP (Hanaoka and Takahashi,
1977). The activation of phosphorylase by trehalagon or

cyclic nucleotide has been observed in intact fat body only.
When partially purified phosphorylase kinase is used, no
activation by cyclic AMP can be shown (Ashida and Wyatt, 1979).
Although the evidence is suggestive, a direct role for cyclic
AMP in the activation of fat body phosphorylase remains cir-
cumstantial.

   4. Synthesis of Glycogen from Trehalose. A few hours
after cockroaches have been injected with CC extract the high
levels of blood trehalose begin to decrease as the sugar is
reconverted into glycogen (Steele, 1963). The trehalose is
first hydrolyzed to free the constituent glycosyl residues
which are then phosphorylated by the fat body. The increase
in glucose-6-PO_4 synthesis is probably an important step in
the reconversion of trehalose into glycogen since it is an inhibitor of phosphorylase (Applebaum and Schlesinger, 1973).
Glycogen synthetase in *Periplaneta* is activated by glucose-1-
PO_4 but not by glucose-6-PO_4 (Vardanis, 1963). Under circumstances where trehalose-6-PO_4 synthetase is inhibited
because of high levels of trehalose the equilibrium between
glucose-6-PO_4 and glucose-1-PO_4 probably favours the latter.
This, however, cannot entirely explain the intense glycogen
synthesis which follows the action of the extract. Very likely it is related to the sharp decrease in the phosphorylase
a/b ratio (White and Steele, unpublished results). These
studies suggest that activation of the enzyme responsible for
the conversion of phosphorylase *a* to *b* (phosphorylase phosphatase?) occurs during the changeover from trehalose to
glycogen synthesis.

   5. Ca^2-Dependant Action of Trehalagon. The stimulatory
effect of purified CC extract on trehalose efflux from cockroach fat body *in vitro* is absolutely dependent on Ca^{2+} in the
bathing medium (Fig. 3). The $[Ca^{2+}]$ used was less than that
in haemolymph. This suggests that the phenomenon may also
occur *in vivo* where it acts as a second messenger. The enzymatic activation of fat body phosphorylase kinase is greatly
enhanced by Ca^{2+} but unaffected by cyclic AMP (Ashida and
Wyatt, 1979). It seems likely, therefore, that Ca^{2+} may play
an indirect but pivotal role in the activation of phosphorylase and trehalose synthesis.

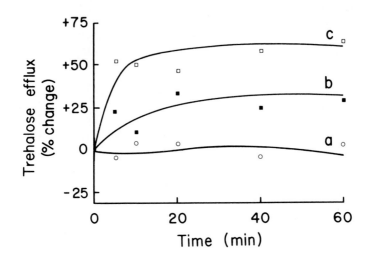

FIGURE 3. An experiment showing that Ca^{2+} is required for trehalagon stimulation of trehalose efflux from Periplaneta fat body in vitro. The effect is concentration dependent with respect to Ca^{2+}. Each fat body was divided into halves. One half was incubated with trehalagon and the other used as a control. CC extract (0.1 pair ml^{-1}) was the source of trehalagon. The concentration of Ca^{2+} in the Ringer was a, Ca^{2+}-free; b, 0.1 mM Ca^{2+}; c, 1 mM Ca^{2+}.

IV. REGULATION OF LIPID METABOLISM

A. *Lipid Level in Haemolymph*

The adipokinetic effect of the CC was first demonstrated by Mayer and Candy (1969) in *Schistocerca* and later by Downer (1972) in *Locusta* and in both species by Goldsworthy *et al* (1972). Lipid levels in the blood are increased by as much as five-fold. The onset of flight is also characterized by an increase in haemolymph diglyceride. Thus the increase in diglyceride caused by AKH is probably an adaptation for flight. The potent adipokinetic effect of the locust CC is not found when the glands are assayed in *Periplaneta,* but interestingly, extracts prepared from *Periplaneta* have a strong adipokinetic effect in *Locusta* (Goldsworthy *et al*, 1972). A possible reason for this effect is that the concentration and kinetic properties of enzymes in fat body differs between species. A recent study has shown that factors capable of elevating the level of diglyceride are not restricted to the CC. Dallman and Herman, (1978) have described an adipokinetic effect of the brain and thoracic nervous system of the Monarch butterfly in addition to that of the CC. This agrees well with the finding by Goldsworthy *et al* (1977) that removal of the medial neurosecretory cells lowers slightly the level of blood lipid in resting locusts. The procedure did not prevent the rise in lipid which normally accompanies the initiation of flight. One may conclude from this that the factor present in the neurosecretory cells is not identical to that in the CC.

B. *Lipolysis in Fat Body*

There is a remarkable dearth of information on the effect of AKH on fat body. This is most surprising in view of the numerous studies appearing in recent years describing its effect on lipid levels in haemolymph and the regulation of flight muscle metabolism. That fat body is inferred to be the primary target for AKH is based on the observation that CC extract promotes the release of diglyceride from fat body into haemolymph *in vitro* (Mayer and Candy, 1969; Beenakkers, 1969; Spencer and Candy, 1976). The fat body is presumably the origin of diglyceride since it is the only tissue with sufficient triglyceride for its synthesis. The steps by which the stored triglyceride is converted to diglyceride for release to the haemolymph are unknown. Diglyceride may arise by mono-acyl cleavage of stored triglyceride or by resynthesis from monoacylglycerol produced by the action of triacylglycerol lipase on the triglyceride. Evidence can be found to support both points of view. Regardless of which pathway is used by the fat body to synthesize diglyceride it seems likely that the increase in haemolymph diglyceride must be preceded by an increase in lipase activity. This notion is prompted by studies on mammalian adipose tissue in which glucagon and epinephrine have been shown to activate lipase. Despite this, attempts to show activation of fat body lipase by the CC have been unsuccessful (Spender and Candy, 1976).

In spite of the fact that activation of fat body lipase by AKH (or any other hormone, for that matter) remains to be demonstrated, it has been assumed that the increase in lipolytic activity is caused by a rise in the titre of cyclic AMP. This is a reasonable view since dibutyryl cyclic AMP raises the level of blood lipid *in vivo* (Gäde and Holwerda, 1976) and increases diglyceride output from locust fat body *in vitro* (Spencer and Candy, 1976). That cyclic AMP is probably a normal mediator of AKH-induced glyceride release is in agreement with the finding that the concentration of nucleotide increases when locust fat body is treated with CC extract or

purified AK   either *in vivo* (Gäde and Holwerda, 1976; Gäde
and Beenakkers, 1977) or *in vitro* (Spencer and Candy, 1976).
These authors suggest that a rise in cyclic AMP is responsible
for the activation of a lipase. The active factor in the CC
is thought to activate adenyl cyclase thus increasing the synthesis of cyclic AMP. This is followed by an increase in protein kinase activity. (See Section I.C.3 in which these enzymes and their relationship to the CC have been discussed).

Locust fat body is unable to respond to AKH by increasing
the output of diglyceride unless Ca^{2+} is present in the bathing medium. When all Ca^{2+} in the medium has been chelated
with EGTA, production of diglyceride by the fat body ceases,
even though hormone may be present. (Spencer and Candy, 1976).
These results are particularly interesting because a similar
relationship has been established for trehalagon (Fig. 3).
The reason for the Ca^{2+} requirement has yet to be determined.

C. *Oxidation of Lipid*

Experiments using *Leucophaea* have shown that the CC increase the rate of lipid oxidation relative to that of carbohydrate. These conclusions were arrived at by measuring the
$^{14}CO_2$ released by fat body *in vitro* from $1-^{14}C$-acetate or
$1-^{14}C$-palmitate and $U-^{14}C$-glucose added to the incubation
medium. Fatty acids were oxidized about 30% faster in the
presence of hormone and accompanied by a reduction in the rate
of oxidation of glucose (Wiens and Gilbert, 1967a). These are
important observations because they suggest that energy required for hormone-stimulated trehalose synthesis is obtained
from lipid. This view is supported by *in vivo* studies showing
that enhancement of lipid oxidation is coincident with the
period of rapid trehalose synthesis (Coulthart and Steele, unpublished observations.

When cockroaches are starved, the concentration of acetoacetate in the blood rises as much as six-fold (Shah and
Bailey, 1976). A similar phenomenon has been observed in
locusts (Hill *et al*, 1972). The level of acetoacetate in
haemolymph is thought to indicate the state of lipid utilization in the insect. Although precise details concerning the
synthesis of acetoacetate in insects remain to be described we
may infer by analogy with mammals that the rise occurs because the supply of acetyl CoA originating from fatty acids
exceeds the demand by the citric acid cycle. Similar results
are obtained when intact locusts are injected with CC extracts
(Hill *et al*, 1972). This suggests that the increase in acetoacetate has a common cause, possibly an over supply of free
fatty acids leading to a rise in acetyl CoA. Lipid is the
preferred source of energy during starvation after carbohydrate

reserves have become depleted and is partly or completely
hydrolyzed under the influence of the CC (Mayer and Candy,
1969); both are situations in which free fatty acids might be
expected to accumulate. Although the stimulation of lipid
hydrolysis by the CC undoubtedly occurs for different reasons
in locusts and cockroaches an increase in the intracellular
fat body pool of free fatty acids may occur in both instances.

V. ARE TREHALAGON AND AKH SYNONYMOUS?

A close relationship exists between carbohydrate and lipid
metabolism in insects as in higher organisms. This is apparent
when one recalls that catabolism of both utilizes the citric
acid cycle as a common pathway. Thus it is germane to ask
whether trehalagon and AKH are identical, the different effects
reflecting variation in the enzyme properties of the fat body
in the different insect groups. The problem would be solved
quickly if the structure of the active factors in the CC of
two or three species were known. At the present time that of
AKH alone has been described. The appreciable hypertrehalosemic activity displayed by locust AKH when assayed in cockroaches (Jones et al, 1977) suggests that both hypertrehalosemic and hyperlipaemic responses are caused by a single
factor. Additional evidence for this view is the recent finding that the CC of Carausius cause neither hypertrehalosemia
nor hyperlipaemia in that species but do in Periplaneta and
Locusta respectively. A study by Holwerda et al (1977) in
which gel permeation and electrofocusing techniques failed to
separate the two activities from locust CC leads to the same
conclusion. It should not, however, be inferred that the
structure of the factor is identical in each species. The CC
extracts quantitatively most active in eliciting the hyperlipaemic or hypertrehalosemic response are those prepared from
glands taken from the same species used for the assay
(Goldsworthy et al, 1972). This suggests some variation in the
structure of the factor between species.

Holwerda et al (1977) have presented data purporting to
show that cockroach CC contain separate factors having hypertrehalosemic and hyperlipaemic activity. Their data also
suggest a structural relationship between the two substances.
It is true that initial chromatography on polyacrylamide gels
results in two peaks; a rapidly moving one with hypertrehalosemic activity and a slower peak with hyperlipaemic activity.
When the faster moving material is rechromatographed much of
the hypertrehalosemic activity is replaced by slower moving
material having the hyperlipaemic effect. A possible explanation for these observations is that trehalagon is structurally

modified during purification to yield a product having adipokinetic activity. This is especially interesting since a
similar mechanism occurring *in vivo* might be of great physiological significance. In this context it is worth recalling
that hormone induced trehalose synthesis in fat body is accompanied by an increase in lipolytic activity.

VI. PROBLEMS FOR THE FUTURE

     There is an urgent need to pursue trehalagon and AKH re-
search on two fronts. First, we need to know how the structure of trehalagon and AKH differ between species, and whether
hypertrehalosemic and hyperlipaemic factors from a single
species are identical. Second, more information describing
the effect of the hormones on lipid and carbohydrate metabolism is essential. A better understanding of the role played
by these hormones will be arrived at if their effects are
studied in diverse insect groups. The importance of this is
exemplified by the finding that *Carausius* CC cause neither hypertrehalosemia nor hyperlipaemia in that species yet the former effect is produced in *Periplaneta* and the latter in *Locusta*
(Gäde, 1979). These interesting observations suggest the
possibility that certain effects of trehalagon and AKH which
appear to be species or group specific are really special uses
which the organism has found for the hormone. It is possible
that additional functions common to all, or most insects, may
exist which arose earlier in the course of evolution.

ACKNOWLEDGEMENTS

     The author wishes to thank Michael Locke and Gordon
McDougall for reading the manuscript and suggesting numerous
improvements to the text. The technical assistance of Terry
Paul in the work associated with Figure 3 is also appreciated.

REFERENCES

Applebaum, S.W., and Schlesinger, H.M. (1973). Regulation of locust fat body phosphorylase. *Biochem. J. 135*, 37-41.

Ashida, M., and Wyatt, G.R. (1979). Properties and activation of phosphorylase kinase from silkmouth fat body. *Insect Biochem. 9*, 403-409.

Broomfield, C.E., and Hardy, P.M. (1977). The synthesis of locust adipokinetic hormone. *Tetrahedron Letters, No. 25*, 2201-2204.

Cazal, M. (1971). Action des corpora cardiáca sur la tréhalosé et la glycĕmie de *Locusta migratoria L. C. r. hebd. Séanc. Acad. Sci., Paris, Ser. D. 272*, 2596-2599.

Chalaye, D. (1969). La tréhalosémie et son contrôle neuro-endocrine chez le Criquet migrateur *Locusta migratoria migratoriodes*. 2. Role de corpora cardiaca et des organes perisympathiques. *C. r. hebd. Séanc. Acad. Sci., Paris, Sér. D. 268*, 3111-3114.

Chen, A.C., and Friedman, S. (1977) Hormonal regulation of trehalose metabolism in the blowfly *Phormia regina* Meig.: effects of cardiacectomy and allatectomy at the subcellular level. *Comp. Biochem. Physiol. 58(b)*, 339-344.

Dallman, S.H., and Herman, W.S. (1978). Hormonal regulation of hemolymph lipid concentration in the monarch butterfly, *Danaus plexippus. Gen. Comp. Endocr. 36*, 142-150.

Downer, R.G.H. (1972). Interspecificity of lipid regulating factors from insect corpus cardiacum. *Can. J. Zool. 50*, 63-65.

Dutrieu, J., and Gourdeaux, L. (1967). Le contrôle neuro-endocrinien de la trehalosémie de *Caransius morosus. C. r. hebd. Séanc. Acad. Sci., Paris, Sér. D. 265*, 1067-1070.

Duve, H. (1978). The presence of a hypoglucemic and hypo-trehalocemic hormone in the neurosecretory system of the blowfly *Calliphora erythrocephala. Gen. Comp. Endocr. 36*, 102-110.

Filburn, C.R., and Wyatt, G.R. (1976). Adenylate and guany-
late cyclases of cecropia silkmoth fat body. *J. Insect
Physiol. 22,* 1635-1640.

Friedman, S. (1967). The control of trehalose synthesis in
the blowfly, *Phormia regina Meig. J. Insect Physiol. 13,*
397-405.

Gäde, G. (1977). Effect of corpus cardiacum extract on cyclic
AMP concentration in the fat body of *Periplaneta americana.
Zool. Jb. Physiol. 81,* 245-249.

Gäde, G. (1979). Adipokinetic and hyperglycaemic factor(s)
in the corpora cardiaca/corpora allata complex of the
stick, *Caransius morosus* I. Initial characteristics.
Physiological Entomolgy 4, 131-134.

Gäde, G., and Beenakkers, A.M.T. (1977). Adipokinetic
hormone-induced lipid mobilization and cyclic AMP accumulation in the fat body of *Locusta migratoria* during development. *Gen. Comp. Endocr. 32,* 481-487.

Gäde, G., and Holwerda, D.A. (1976). Involvement of adenosine 3',5'-cyclic monophosphate in lipid mobilization in
Locusta migratoria. Insect Biochem. 6, 535-540.

Goldsworthy, G.J. (1969). Hyperglycaemic factors from the
corpus cardiacum of *Locusta migratoria. J. Insect Physiol.
15,* 2131-2140.

Goldsworthy, G.J. (1970). The action of hyperglycaemic
factors from the corpus cardiacum of *Locusta migratoria*
on glycogen phosphorylase. *Gen. Comp. Endocr. 14,* 78-85.

Goldsworthy, G.J., Lee, S.S., and Jutsam, A.R. (1977).
Cerebral neurosecretory cells and flight in the locust.
J. Insect. Physiol. 23, 717-721.

Goldsworthy, G.J., Mordue, W., and Guthkelch, J. (1972).
Studies on insect adipokinetic hormones. *Gen. Comp.
Endocr. 18,* 545-551.

Hanaoka, K., and Takahashi, S.Y. (1976). Effect of a hyperglycaemic factor on haemolymph trehalose and fat body
carbohydrates in the American cockroach. *Insect Biochem.
6,* 621-625.

Hanaoka, K., and Takahashi, S.Y. (1977). Adenylate cyclase system and the hyperglycemic factor in the cockroach, Periplaneta americana. Insect Biochem. 7, *95-99*.

Hill, L., Izatt, M.E.G., Horne, J.A., and Bailey, E. (1972). Factors affecting concentrations of acetoacetate and D-3-hydroxybutyrate in haemolymph and tissues of the adult desert locust. J. Insect Physiol. *18*, 1265-1285.

Holwerda, D.A., van Doorn, J., and Beenakkers, A.M.T. (1977). Characterization of the adipokinetic and hyperglycaemic substances from the locust corpus cardiacum. Insect Biochem. *7*, 151-157.

Holwerda, D.A., Weeda, A., and van Doorn, J.M. (1977). Separation of the hyperglycaemic and adipokinetic factors from the cockroach corpus cardiacum. Insect Biochem. *7*, 477-481.

Jones, J., Stone, J.V., and Mordue, W. (1977). The hyperglycaemic activity of locust adipokinetic hormone. Physiological Entomology *2*, 185-187.

Jungreis, A.M., Jatlow, P., Wyatt, G.R (1974). Regulation of trehalose synthesis in the silkmoth Hyalophora cecropia: the role of magnesium in the fat body. J. Exp. Zool. *187*, 41-46.

Jungreis, A.M., and Wyatt, G.R. (1972). Sugar release and penetration in insect fat body: relations to regulation of haemolymph trehalose in developing stages of Hyalophora cecropia. Biol. Bull. *143*, 367-391.

Mayer, R.J., and Candy, D.J. (1969). Control of haemolymph lipid concentration during locust flight: an adipokinetic hormone from the corpora cardiaca. J. Insect. Physiol. *15*, 611-620.

Mordue, W., and Goldsworthy, G.J. (1969). The physiological effects of corpus cardiacum extracts in locusts. Gen. Comp. Endocr. *12*, 360-369.

Morishima, I. (1978). Adenylate cyclase in silkworm. Properties of the enzyme in pupal fat body. J. Biochem. (Tokyo) *84*, 1495-1500.

Morishima, I. (1979). Adenylate cyclase in silkworm: Regulation by calcium and a calcium-binding protein. Agric. Biol. Chem. *43*, 1127-1131.

Murphy, T.A., and Wyatt, G.R. (1965). The enzymes of glycogen and trehalose synthesis in silkmoth fat body. *J. Biol.
Chem. 240,* 1500-1508.

Natalizi, G.M., and Frontali, N. (1966). Purification of
insect hyperglycaemic and heart accelerating hormones. *J.
Insect Physiol. 12,* 1279-1287.

Natalizi, G.M., Pansa, M.C., d'Agello, V., Casaglia, O.,
Bettini, S., and Frontali, N. (1970). Physiologically
active factors from corpora cardiaca of *Periplaneta
americana. J. Insect Physiol. 16,* 1827-1836.

Shah, J., and Bailey, E. (1976). Enzymes of ketogenesis in
the fat body and the thoracic muscle of the adult
cockroach. *Insect Biochem. 6,* 251-254.

Spencer, I.M., and Candy, D.J. (1976). Hormonal control of
diacyl glycerol mobilization from fat body of the desert
locust, *Schistocerca gregaria. Insect Biochem. 6,* 289-296.

Steele, J.E. (1963). The site of action of insect hyperglycaemic hormone. *Gen. Comp. Endocr. 3,* 46-52.

Steele, J.E. (1964). The activation of phosphorylase in an
insect by adenosine, 3',5'-phosphate and other agents. *Am.
Zool. 4,* 328.

Stevenson, E., and Wyatt, G.R. (1964). Glycogen phosphorylase
and its activation in silkmoth fat body. *Archs. Biochem.
Biophys. 108,* 420-429.

Stone, J.V., Mordue, W., Batley, K.E., and Morris, H.R.
(1976). Structure of locust adipokinetic hormone, a neurohormone that regulates lipid utilisation during flight.
Nature, Lond. 263, 207-214.

Takahashi, S.Y., and Hanaoka, K. (1977). Multiple protein
kinases in the American cockroach, *Periplaneta americana.
Insect. Biochem. 7,* 133-139.

Vardanis, A. (1963). Glycogen synthesis in the insect fat
body. *Biochim. Biophys. Acta. 73,* 565-573.

Wiens, A.W., and Gilbert, L.I. (1967a). Regulation of carbohydrate mobilization and utilization in *Leucophaea
maderae. J. Insect Physiol. 13,* 779-794.

Wiens, A.W., and Gilbert, L.I.   (1967b).   The phosphorylase
    system of the silkmoth, *Hyalophora cecropia*.   *Comp.
    Biochem. Physiol.* *21*, 145-159.

Wigglesworth, V.B.   (1942).   The storage of protein, fat,
    glycogen and uric acid in the fat body and other tissues
    of mosquito larvae.   *J. Exp. Biol.* *19*, 56-77.

Yanagawa, H.-A., and Horie, Y.   (1978).   Activating enzyme of
    phosphorylase *b* in the fat body of the silkworm, *Bombyx
    mori*.   *Insect Biochem.* *8*, 155-158.

Zeigler, R., Ashida, M., Fallon, A.M., Wimer, L.T., Wyatt, S.S.,
    and Wyatt, G.R.   (1979).   Regulation of glycogen phos-
    phorylase in fat body of cecropia silkmoth pupae.   *J.
    Comp. Physiol.* *131*, 321-332.

HEMOLYMPH AS A DYNAMIC TISSUE

Arthur M. Jungreis

Department of Zoology
University of Tennessee
Knoxville, Tennessee

I. PROLOGUE

The concept of homeostasis as currently conceived arose from Claude Bernard's early recognition that systemic responses were of three static non-overlapping types: arrested, temperature dependent and temperature independent (Bernard, 1878). Although these concepts were overly simplistic, they aided in the construction of numerous experimental paradigms that led to an increased understanding of organismal or systemic regulation. The explicit concept of homeostasis as an example of *constancy* was proposed some 50 years after Bernard by W.B. Cannon (1929). It is necessary to review Cannon's definition of homeostasis, for much of todays thinking about regulation in insects continues to reflect Cannon's original conceptualization:

"The constant conditions which are maintained in the body might be termed *equilibria*. That word, however, has come to have fairly exact meaning as applied to relatively simple physico-chemical states, in closed systems, where known forces are balanced. The coordinated physiological processes which maintain most of the steady states in the organism are so complex and so peculiar to living being that I have suggested a special designation for these states, *homeostasis*. The word does not imply something set and immobile, a stagnation. It means a condition--a condition which may vary, but which is relatively constant."

273

As employed by Cannon, homeostasis presumably explains why
basal levels (be they concentrations, quantities, functions)
change only gradually in response to accelerated changes in
input (e.g. feeding) or output (e.g. excretion). This implies
that during homeostasis changes in input are normally accompanied by corresponding and equal changes in output or storage.
Thus, the content of a system is said to be *constant*.

Cannon's concept of constancy was soon accepted universally. Unfortunately, the discovery, as early as 1942, that
so called constant quantities of metabolites present in
(mammalian) blood (e.g., glucose) are in fact being rapidly
exchanged (Schoenheimer, 1942) neither dislodged nor superseded Cannon's implicit *static* concept of systemic content. The
dynamic nature of Cannon's constancy has now been recognized
and a more expansive definition of homeostasis proposed:

"homeostasis does not necessarily imply a lack of
change, because the steady states to which the
regulatory mechanisms are directed may shift with
time. But throughout the change they remain under
more or less close control (emphasis added)."
("Symposia of the Society for Experimental Biology",
Volume XVIII)

Although investigators now recognize the dynamic nature of
constancy, much of the literature dealing with insect
hemolymph continues to view homeostatic regulation as static
(=passive) rather than dynamic (=active).

II   INTRODUCTION

Hemolymph or blood is that fluid which bathes the tissues
of insects. The view of Mellanby (1939), who stated that:

"the function of the hemolymph is to serve as a
reserve...which can be drawn upon as needed....
So long as there is sufficient hemolymph to
circulate, metabolism is not affected...,"

is generalized in the current literature. This interpretation
of the role of hemolymph is derived directly from Cannon's
concept of homeostasis as a non-dynamic constancy. Support
for this interpretation of hemolymph function seemingly came
from (e.g.) histochemical observations in the mosquito,
Aedes aegypti, during selective feeding where little change

in hemolymph content was noted despite the rapid exchange, accumulation and deposition of (e.g.) fatty acids and glycogen from gut to blood and from blood to fat body tissue (Wigglesworth, 1942b). In interpolating the general thinking of so many insect physiologists on the subject of hemolymph function, Wigglesworth summarized their interpretations and conclusions thusly:

> "The circulating haemolymph is the common pool from which all the tissues can help themselves. Any deficiancy or excess within this pool is corrected in the short term by the release of material from storage or by synthesis, on the one hand, and by excretion, breakdown or consignment to reserve on the other." (Wigglesworth, V.B., 1970, "Insect Hormones", p. 108).

In this paper, the dynamic in contrast to the static nature of insect hemolymph will be demonstrated. The turnover in hemolymph of trehalose, amino acids and ecdysone are examined in the context that hemolymph is not a reservoir or "sink" that serves as an extra-cellular reserve for the cells and tissues. The conclusion is drawn that despite the presence of open circulatory systems, insect hemolymph compares favorably with mammalian blood as a dynamic tissue.

III. TREHALOSE

The subject of carbohydrate regulation in insects has been covered extensively in a number of recent reviews (Chippendale, 1978; Friedman, 1978; Jungreis, 1978; Steele, 1978). Although these authors deal with questions of hormonal control of synthesis, release and metabolism of carbohydrates, the role of sugar in hemolymph is glossed over. This absence of attention to sugar in hemolymph is not altogether surprising, since hemolymph is viewed as a sink from which trehalose can be mobilized during periods of high energy demand (flight) or moulting (cuticle formation). This sink concept arises in part from the belief that open circulatory systems are too inefficient to rapidly transport materials from their sites of synthesis to their target tissues, especially during periods of enhanced utilization.

The literature is filled with observations, which by inference assign a sink role to sugars in general, and trehalose in particular. Locust (Hansen, 1964), horse bot fly,

Gastrophilus intestinalis (Levenbook, 1950), and bumble bee, *Bombus* (cited in Wyatt, 1967) fed on diets rich in levan have fructose in hemolymph. Transfer to diets deficient in fructose causes its disappearance. In *Manduca sexta*, hemolymph trehalose levels change with diet (Dahlman, 1975). Thus, hemolymph is a *site for* the *storage* of readily metabolizable sugars such as fructose and trehalose.

In a representative Lepidopteran, the commercial silkworm, *Bombyx mori*, low levels of glucose (an <u>active</u> component in blood) in the presence of much trehalose (a *passive* component in blood) during larval and pupal development might result from high rates of glucose but not trehalose utilization--except during moulting (Duchateau-Bosson, et al., 1963). If *B. mori* are either starved (Horie, 1960) or undernourished for one week (Bricteaux-Gregoire, et al., 1965), hemolymph trehalose is *spared* at the expense of fat body glycogen (a source of glucose). Only after glycogen reserves are severely depleted does one see a decline in hemolymph trehalose. When oak silkmoths, *Antheraea pernyi*, are injected with glucose, hemolymph trehalose doubles over a four hour period at the expense of the added glucose. Thereafter, trehalose remains at an elevated level for prolonged periods (Egorova and Smolin, 1962).

The rapid disappearance of glucose from hemolymph is coupled with the quantitative appearance of trehalose following administration of labeled glycose to larvae of the cecropia silkworm, *Hyalophora cecropia* (Wyatt, 1967; Jungreis, 1978). Little metabolism of the labeled trehalose in hemolymph occurs even after prolonged periods. During diapause pupal development, when *H. cecropia* fat body produces and releases little trehalose (Jungreis and Wyatt, 1972; Jungreis, 1978), hemolymph trehalose declines very slowly over a period of weeks. These observations all appear to support the view that trehalose is a *passive* component of hemolymph. If this view is correct, then rates of trehalose exchange between hemolymph and fat body, the site of trehalose synthesis, should be proportional to the rates of hemolymph trehalose turnover. Further, rates of trehalose utilization should be less than the rates of carbohydrate utilization except during those periods that require massive quantities of sugars: flight and moulting.

The contribution of hemolymph trehalose to whole body carbohydrate metabolism can be calculated from three facts: size of the trehalose pool (Table 1), rate of respiration (Table 2) and the contribution of carbohydrates to the

	A body weight (g)	B hemolymph trehalose (µmoles/ml)	C total hemolymph trehalose (µmoles/animal)	D fat body trehalose (µmoles/g)	E fat body weight (g/animal)	F total fat body trehalose (µmoles/animal)
mature feeding fifth instar larva	9.20 ±0.09 (50)	30.1 ±1.2 (5)	105.4 ±4.2	37.7 ±4.6 (4)	0.52 ±0.05 (9)	23.1 ±2.8
non-diapause pupa	4.87 ±0.06 (50)	52.2 ±1.1 (4)	76.0 ±1.6	231.3 ±7.0 (4)	0.69 ±0.07 (4)	159.6 ±4.8

Table 1. Quantities of trehalose in fat body and hemolymph of representative larval and pupal horn-worms, *Manduca sexta*, reared at 25°C on synthetic diet. Values for hemolymph volume and fat body weight/animal are taken from Williams-Boyce and Jungreis (unpublished). Pupal body weights were obtained from the identical animals that had been weighed at the larval stage in development. Tissue weights and blood volumes were obtained from a second group of animals and normalized to values characteristic of 9.2 gram larvae and 4.87 gram pupae. Following chromatographic separation from other sugars, trehalose was measured with Mokrasch's (1954) anthrone reagent in hemolymph and fat body collected from yet third and fourth groups of larvae and pupae, respectively. All tissue weights have been corrected for adhering hemolymph, and all fat body trehalose concentrations have been corrected for adhering hemolymph and endogenous glucose. n = number of independent observations or determinations.

	No. of animals	OXYGEN CONSUMPTION* (µliters/ gram-hr)	(µmoles/ animal-hr)	R.Q.*+	UTILIZATION carbohydrate (%)	$\underline{G}$ trehalose (µmoles/ animal-hr)	$\underline{G/C}$** (%/hr)
mature feeding fifth instar larvae	150	476.0 ±48.0 (3)	123.2 ±7.2 (3)	0.89 ±0.01 (3)	63.0	10.3	9.7
non-diapause pupa	20	150.9 ±3.7 (3)	32.8 ±0.8 (3)	0.76 ±0.00 (3)	20.0	2.7	3.6

Table 2. Percentages of total hemolymph trehalose metabolized per hour by tobacco hornworms, *Manduca sexta*, during the larval and pupal stages in development. Respiratory measurements for pupae were made in a 600 ml capacity cylindrical lucite chamber with sampling ports (Triple J Valve Respirometer Chamber, manufactured by Warren E. Collins, Inc., 220 Wood Road, Braintree, Mass. 02184). Approximately 80 grams of animals representing 20 individuals (average weight 3.87 grams; weights were normalized to 4.87 grams for purposes of comparison with data in Table 1) were monitored for a 60 minute period. The chamber was then flushed out with compressed air, resealed, and measured for two additional one hour periods. Proper mixing in the chamber was insured by passing 50 ml of air across the chamber 20 times prior to sampling. A 50 ml sample was collected with a glass syringe lubricated with ethylene glycol, and following

Table 2 Legend – Continued

collection, the syringe was sealed with a "t" valve. Oxygen
and carbon dioxide content were measured before and after the
periods of respiration on a MicroScholander Gas Analyser
(Scholander, 1947). Readings were made at $22.5^{\circ}C$, but rates
of oxygen consumption were adjusted to $25^{\circ}C$ by applying a Q_{10}
correction of 2.25 for the range $22.5 - 25^{\circ}C$ (recalculated
from data in Arceneaux, 1979). Respiratory measurements for
larvae were carried out at $25^{\circ}C$ on 150 fifth instar larvae
(average weight 4.86 grams; weights were again normalized
to 9.2 grams for purposes of comparison with data in Table 1).
Animals were manually placed in a 900 ml capacity flat bottle
with sampling ports on both ends. The rate at which dry gas
(compressed air passing through drierite columns) passed
through the chamber was 138.4 ml/minute at STP. The chamber
was flushed for 10 minutes, whereupon the exhausted gases were
passed into a 50 liter capacity polyethylene bag (Minnesota
Mining and Manufacturing Company, Scotch Pak$^{trade mark}$).
Following 20 minute collection periods, the bag was stoppered,
the gas contents mixed, and two 50 ml samples taken for
analysis on a MicroScholander Gas Analyser.
n = number of independent determinations
*uliters/g-hr were converted to μmoles/animal-hr by multiplying
the oxygen consumption per gram times the body weight (c.f.
Table 1) and then dividing by 22.4×10^6 (= μliters/mole).
*+
    Respiratory quotients are defined as volume of carbon dioxide
released divided by the volume of oxygen consumed. A respiratory quotient (R.Q.) of 0.70 is assigned to metabolism that
is exclusively lipid, while a respiratory quotient of 1.00 is
assigned to metabolism that is exclusively carbohydrate.
**
    Twelve moles of oxygen are required to metabolize 1 mole of
trehalose ($C_{12}H_{22}O_{11}$) to carbon dioxide. Oxygen consumption
per animals was therefore divided by 12 to obtain the moles of
trehalose that could be metabolized. This value was then
multiplied by the percentage of oxygen consumption that is
associated with carbohydrate metabolism to obtain a measure of
trehalose utilization.

respiratory rate (Table 2). In diet reared tobacco hornworms, *Manduca sexta,* a maximum of 9.7% and 3.6% of the total hemolymph trehalose in larvae and pupae, respectively, is metabolized per hour (Table 2). These values are only slightly higher than those measured by injecting hornworms with ^{14}C trehalose and studying its disappearance (Jungreis, unpublished). Since the respiratory rates in these hornworms compare favorably with basal metabolic rates in homeotherms, the primary reason hemolymph trehalose appears to turnover so slowly is the large size of the trehalose pool. However, if hemolymph were simply a sink, then rates of exchange between fat body and hemolymph should be small. Further, effective rates of exchange should decline if the quantity of trehalose in fat body increases, and when the respiratory rate (a measure of carbohydrate utilization) decreases (assuming an invariant respiratory quotient).

The time required to exchange 50% of the fat body trehalose has been determined (Figures 1,2, Table 3; Arceneaux, 1979). *Instead of decreasing* with increasing intracellular pool size (38 versus 231 μmoles/g in larval versus pupal fat body, Table 1), *rates of exchange between fat body and hemolymph increased* between the larval (34.4%) and pupal (231%) stages in development (Table 3). Further, when these rates of exchange are expressed as functions of hemolymph trehalose, *increases* that far exceed the measured 25% decline in hemolymph trehalose pool sizes (105 versus 76 μmoles, in larvae and pupae, respectively; Table 1) are found in pupae (304.5%) relative to larvae (32.6%).

The conclusion drawn from these studies is that the content of hemolymph is dynamically exchanging with the tissues. In addition, seemingly low rates of component turnover should not be used as evidence for static constancy of hemolymph.

IV.   AMINO ACIDS

Lists of amino acids in tissues and hemolymph from a wide range of insect orders exemplified by numerous species at selected stages in development have been published (see citations in Buck, 1953; Wyatt, 1961; Florkin & Jeuniaux, 1974; Neville, 1975). In general, these studies have been primarily taxonomic rather than physiological or biochemical in outlook, in that they describe the distribution of amino acids at a single fixed point in time. Even when examined in the context

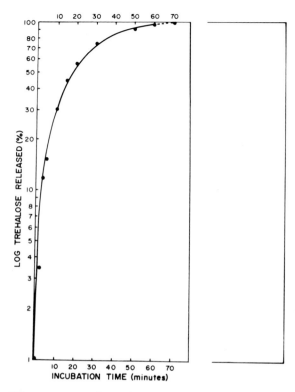

Figure 1. Time course for the release of intra-cellular trehalose from fat body of tobacco hornworms, *Manduca sexta,*
incubated *in vitro* at 25°C. Unanesthetized, unchilled, fifth
instar larvae were bled and the fat body removed and blotted
on glassine type paper. Equal contributions (0.2-3.0 grams)
from two larvae were pooled and incubated in medium similar
to Grace's medium (lacking vitamins and sugars except 20 mM
glucose-(U)-^{14}C (0.5 uCi/mmole)). Tissue was incubated in
the presence of ^{14}C-glucose for only two minutes, whereupon
it was transferred serially four times into 1 ml volumes of
medium lacking isotope. The appearance of label in the medium
was monitored by collecting 2 microliter aliquots at either 2,
3,5 or 10 minute intervals. Aliquots were chromatographed on
Gelman ITLC Type SA thin layer plates and ^{14}C glucose separated from ^{14}C-trehalose following procedures outlined in
Jungreis (1976). The quantity of ^{14}C-trehalose released
approached an asymptote after 70 minutes, and this quantity
was defined as maximal (=100%) release. Quantities of trehalose released at various sampling times are expressed as
percentages of maximal (=100%) release, and are graphed as
log functions.

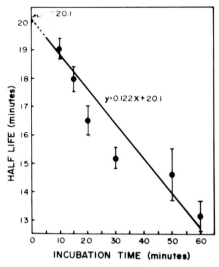

Figure 2. Determination of the time required for the exchange of 50% of the total fat cell trehalose. The half life of intra-cellular trehalose was determined from the following equation at elapsed times between 10 and 60 minutes (see Figure 1):

$$f = (0.5)^{T_e/T_{0.5}}$$

Refactoring:

$$T_{0.5} = -0.301 \ T_e (\log f)^{-1},$$

where f = fraction of labeled trehalose remaining in fat body (1.0 at T_0, 0.0 at T_{70}); $T_{0.5}$ = time in minutes required to exchange 50% of the intra-cellular trehalose; and T_e = elapsed time in minutes. Influxes and effluxes of trehalose into and out of fat cells are exponentially related. The rate functions vary inversely with one another. I therefore determined the $T_{0.5}$ at each time point between 10 through 60 minutes, and extrapolated the least squares relationship back to a theoretical $T_{0.5}$ at T = 0 minutes.

of changes during development or as functions of diet, only concentrations of amino acids are recorded without reference to quantity (i.e., has the contribution of the blood volume to the unit body weight changed?) or metabolic flux (=turnover).

Why have studies of amino acids in insects not moved past the 1950's? The answer is all too clear. While the static nature of hemolymph sugar is often implicit in the many reports appearing on this subject in the literature, that for amino acids is explicit with panache. In an otherwise excellent volume on insect physiology, Patton (1963) writes:

"...the values (of amino acids) for the blood of immature stages have been selected, the reason being that these values are more likely to remain constant than those of adult blood...."

	$T_{0.5}$ (min)	fat body trehalose exchanged (%/hr)	total trehalose (umoles/animal) fat body	hemolymph	fat body trehalose exchanged (µmoles/animal-hr)	fat body trehalose exchanged as a function of hemolymph trehalose (%/hr)
mature feeding fifth instar larva	20.1	149	23.1	105.4	34.4	32.6
non-diapause pupa	20.7	145	159.6	76.0	231.4	304.5

Table 3. Exchange of trehalose at 25°C between fat body and hemolymph in synthetic diet reared tobacco hornworms, *Manduca sexta*, during the larval and pupal stages in development. Larval values are taken from Figure 2. Pupal values were calculated from data in Arceneaux (1979).

hormone source	experimental organism	$T_{0.5}$ (min)	turnover (%/hr)	citation
human ACTH	*Homo sapiens*	19.8	152	Besser, et al., 1971
ovine LH	white faced ewes	43	70	Akbar, et al., 1974
ovine FSH	white faced ewes	102	29	Akbar, et al., 1974
ovine prolactin	white faced ewes	23	130	Akbar, et al., 1974
ovine LH	*Rattus norvegicus*	5	600	Ascoli and Puett, 1976
equine LH	pony mares	286	10	Ginther, et al., 1974
testosterone	sheep	3.8	789	Lipset, 1978
dihydrotestosterone	sheep	6.6	455	Lipset, 1978
Hyalophora cecropis C18-JH	*Manduca sexta*	20**	150	Slade and Zibitt, 1972
M. sexta ecdysial gland	*Manduca sexta*	210-340*	18-29	Figures 5,6

Table 4. Half lives and turnover times (%/hr) for protein and steroid hormones in blood.
*normalized to equivalent turnovers at 37°C by assuming a Q_{10} of 2.5 between 25-37°C.
**determined in feeding larvae at 25°C.

> One characteristic of amino acidemia in the
> blood of insects is its constancy...free amino
> acids found in the blood in the largest quantities
> are not those amino acids essential to the nutrition
> of the insect. From this it can be suggested that
> the high amino acid concentration in the blood of
> insects represents the storage of nitrogenous
> materials that can be drawn upon, according to the
> needs of the tissues...or it may indicate that an
> excess of amino acids are produced from the diet
> and that the amino acids are stored in blood until
> they can be eliminated...." (Patton, 1963, "Introductory
> Insect Physiology")

This view was independently championed by Wyatt (1968), who
concludes after discussing papers by Boyd and Mitchell (1966)
with *Drosophila*, and Chen and Levenbook (1966) with *Phormia*,
dealing with amino acid incorporation into hemolymph protein:

> "Since the blood free amino acids clearly cannot be
> intermediates (in protein synthesis), some form of
> direct transformation of blood proteins into tissue
> proteins is suggested. The data seem only to rule
> out *hemolymph* (Wyatt's italics) free amino acids as
> intermediates and do not oppose degradation to free
> amino acids which remain within the tissues and are
> rapidly used in resynthesis."

These forceful statements would certainly cause one to conclude that hemolymph amino acids are not in free exchange with
those in the tissues, a conclusion reached in an independent
study by Dinamarca and Levenbook (1966). Again, the primary
conclusion drawn is that *amino acids in hemolymph are in
excess,* and isolated from the metabolically more active intracellular amino acid pools. Is it any wonder then that as careful a worker as Wigglesworth would in discussing hemolymph
amino acids include examples that demonstrate the passive
nature and putative storage functions of hemolymph?

> "There seems to be no exact regulation of the amino
> acid patterns: the hemolymph of the aphid *Megoura*
> contains the same amino acids as honey dew and in
> similar concentrations (Ehrhardt, 1962). If *Rhodnius*
> is fed on horse serum with added alanine, alanine
> appears in the haemolymph within a few minutes and
> in the urine in half an hour, but the high level in
> the haemolymph persists for weeks (Harrington, 1961).
> (Cited from Wigglesworth, V.B., 1965, "The Principles

of Insect Physiology", 6th Edition, p. 384).

The half lives of selected amino acids were determined in hemolymph during feeding stages and throughout the larval-pupal transformation (LPT) in the tobacco hornworm, *Manduca sexta*. Throughout this period, the concentrations of glutamine, lysine, proline and histidine were maintained at stable levels of 20, 2.5, 8 and 22 mM, respectively. Examined in the context that amino acids are stored in hemolymph, and further that they fail to exchange with cellular pools, one might conclude that these amino acids are maintained statically. However, tremendous changes in blood volume and body weight occur during this period (Jungreis and Tojo, 1973; Jungreis, 1978; Williams-Boyce and Jungreis, unpublished). Therefore, these representative amino acids must be regulated in hemolymph.

The half lives of glutamine, lysine and proline were relatively short (2-5 hours) during feeding, despite their high concentrations in hemolymph (Fig. 3). During the LPT, when increases in tissue degradation and new protein synthesis are said to occur preliminary to the pupal stage in development, half lives either remained about the same (glutamine and proline) or increased four fold (lysine)(Fig. 3). While histidine is present in hemolymph at the same concentration as is glutamine, it has an extremely long half life (as high as 170 hours), which is the same during both feeding and non-feeding stages. The half lives of the amino acids do not change in parallel fashions during the developmental period studied, and one must conclude that they are regulated independently from one another. When turnovers are calculated, an average of 10% (except for histidine at 2%) of the total hemolymph amino acid pool turns over hourly (Figure 4).

Percent turnovers decline between feeding and pupal stages in development, a reflection of the drop in respiratory rate between larval and pupal stages in development (476 and 151 ul/g-hr, respectively; Table 2).

Two conclusions can be drawn from these observations. Firstly, amino acids in hemolymph are regulated. Although some amino acids such as histidine appear to be *stored* in hemolymph (a role in lipid transport?), most are dynamically maintained. Secondly, rapid exchange of amino acids must occur between those present in hemolymph and those localized intra-cellularly.

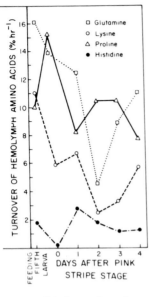

Figure 3. Half lives of glutamine, lysine, proline and histidine in diet reared *Manduca sexta* preceding and during the larval-pupal transformation. Fifteen animals were injected with a single ^{14}C or ^{3}H labeled amino acid (0.1 uCi) in the absence of unlabeled carrier. After 3, 6 or 9 hours, hemolymph was collected from five animals, phenylthiourea added to retard melanization, and spun at 9000 x g for 2 minutes. Supernatants were decanted and frozen at -25°C. Blood was deproteinated by addition of 0.1 volume of 30% sulfosalicylic acid (final concentration 3%). Following centrifugation, supernatant fractions were chromatographed on Gelman ITLC type SA thin layer plates with n-butanol:glacial acetic acid:water (4:1:1,v:v:v) or propanol:water (7:3,v:v), the specific amino acid localized and the radioactivity determined by liquid spectroscopy on a Beckman Model 8100 Liquid Scintillation counter. The pattern of amino acid disappearance was fitted to a curvo-linear equation of the type $Y = aX^{b}$, and the half life determined. Although the concentrations of unlabeled amino acids in hemolymph were known from independent measurements, half lives can be determined without regard for this information.

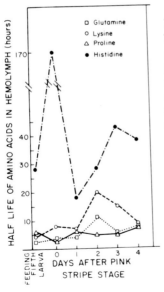

Figure 4, *In vivo* turnover times of hemolymph amino acids in *Manduca sexta* during feeding and pharate pupal stages in development. Turnover times were calculated from the estimated half lives (Figure 3) with the acid of the following equation:

$$\% \text{ turnover} = 100\% \times (1/T_{0.5})(1/2)$$

where $T_{0.5}$ = half life.

V.   ECDYSONE

Changes in hormone titers have always been used as indicators of metabolism, neurosecretory activity or as temporal
markers of processes such as moulting (Wigglesworth, V.B.,
1970, "Insect Hormones"; Morgan and Poole, 1977; Riddiford and
Truman, 1978; Jungreis, 1979). In the context of thinking
about hemolymph during normal development, appearance or
change in the titer of a hormone reflects its requirement by
the tissues. This view is held despite the observation that
(e.g.) in fifth instar *M. sexta*, C18-JH has a half life of
only 20 minutes (Slade and Zibitt, 1972). What seems important is that hormones be present continuously to promote their
effects (Riddiford, 1978). In this section, an attempt is
made to illustrate three principles: the half life of ecydsone
is relatively short; blood titers are not accurate indicators
of hormone availability; and that organisms with open and
closed circulatory systems may be equally effective in responding to hormones.

The titers of ecydsone in hemolymph and whole bodies of
tobacco hornworms, *M. sexta*, were measured throughout the
pupal-adult transformation (Fig. 5,6). Hemolymph titers
averaged only 0.1% of the total quantity of ecdysone stored in
fat body and other tissues at comparable stages. When maximal
half lives for ecdysone were indirectly estimated from the
quantities of stored hormone, values of 3.3 to 5.6 hours were
obtained (Figure 5). Interestingly, increases in hemolymph
titers appear to inferentially reflect decreases in degradation or metabolism (longer half lives) rather than increases
in hormone release or synthesis (compare half lives of Fig. 5
with titers in Fig. 6). When half lives and hourly percent
hormone turnovers are compared in mammals and insects (Table
4), the presence of a closed circulatory system does not
appear to confer an advantage, since hormone receptors in target tissues should be equally responsive *per se* to hormones
(subject to evolved tissue or species specific temperature
optima).

In summary, changes in target tissue receptors activity
or numbers are of greater significance than changes in blood
titer, since hormones are turned over rapidly.

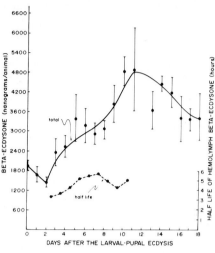

Figure 5. Total ecdysone and calculated half lives of hemolymph ecdysone in *Manduca sexta* during the pupal-adult transformation. Hornworms were reared at 25°C on synthetic diet according to procedures outlined in Ely and Jungreis (1977). Animals were staged as a function of days after the larval-pupal ecdysis (Day 0) without regard to sex or other morphologic features. On each day in development, 3-6 animals were weighed, the proboscis nicked and blood collected into microcentrifuge tubes and weighed. The remainder of the animal was then minced with scissors, and sonicated in four volumes of 20% methanol. Sonicates were centrifuged at 9000 x g and the supernatant fractions decanted and frozen at -25°C. The quantities of ecdysone present in hemolymph and in the tissues (total body) were quantitated by radioimmune assay using antiserum prepared by Tim Kingan (Dept. of Biochem. and Biophys., Oregon State Univ., Corvallis, Oregon). This anti-serum had an equal specificity for the alpha- and beta- anomers of ecdysone. Ecdysone was determined following procedures outlined in McCarthy and Skinner (1977) with one major modification: free ecdysone was separated from bound by centrifugation following addition of 0.6% Norit T-70 Dextran Coated charcoal. The distribution of body ecdysone was apportioned between hemolymph and tissues. Individual animal weights were normalized to the stage specific body weight, using figures reported in Williams-Boyce (1977). At each stage in development, weight specific normalized hemolymph volumes (calculated by isotope dilution) were also employed (Jungreis, unpublished). At days 2 thru 11 in development, hemolymph ecdysone per animal was subtracted from the total, and increases in total body ecdysone recorded. The minimal half life of hemolymph ecdysone was then calculated from the following equation:

$$E_{hemolymph} \times V_{hemolymph} = E_{increase} (1/2)^{(24/T_{0.5})}$$

where $E_{hemolymph}$ = concentration of ecdysone in hemolymph; $V_{hemolymph}$ = volume of stage specific hemolymph per normalized animal weight unit; $E_{increase}$ = increase in body ecdysone assuming that 100% of ecdysone turned over was stored in the tissues in an immunologically active form; $T_{0.5}$ = half life of hemolymph ecdysone.

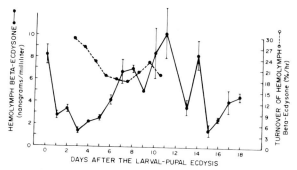

Figure 6. Hemolymph ecdysone and turnover in *Manduca sexta* during the pupal-adult transformation. Ecdysone was determined following procedures described in the legend for Fig. 5. Turnover rates were calculated from the half lives of ecdysone in hemolymph as per the legend in Fig. 4

VI.   EPILOGUE

Hemolymph as a tissue is found to be dynamic and not static. The capacity for delivery in the open circulatory systems of insects compares favorably with the closed circulatory systems of homeotherms. Turnover times for compounds are rapid with relatively brief half lives. For many components, hemolymph is an extra-cellular extension of the intra-cellular fluid compartment. Armed with this information, we are in a position to examine the effects of hormones and metabolite fluxes in more sophisticated ways. The myth is exploded that homeostasis in heterotherms is inherently inferior to that in homeotherms. Insect physiologists will increasingly abandon studies on the taxonomy of physiology in exchange for more informative, expansive and rigorous studies dealing with fluxes, cellular receptors and enzymatic regulation. The knowledge that hemolymph functions as an extension of intra-cellular environments should facilitate new insights into intra-cellular regulation and its hormonal and metabolic control.

Acknowledgment

Supported in part by National Institutes of Health Grant # AI-12779.

VII.   REFERENCES

Akbar, A.M., Nett, T.M., and Niswender, G.D. (1974).
      Netabolic clearance and secretion rates of gonado-
      tropins at different stages of the estrous cycle in
      ewes. Endocrinology 94, 1318-1324.

Arceneaux, M.L. (1979). Trehalose in tobacco hornworms,
      Manduca sexta: Regulation during diapause and non-
      diapause pupal development. M.S. Thesis, Univ. of
      Tenn. Knoxville, TN 71 pages.

Ascoli, M., and Puett, D. (1976). Biotransformations of
      pituitary luteinizing hormone in serum and urine.
      II. Evidence for reduced potency following urinary
      excretion. Endocrinology 99, 1237-1243.

Bernard, C. (1978). Lecons sur les phenomenes de la vie
      communs aux animaux et aux vegetaux. tom I. pp. 67,
      111-114, 123-124. Paris: Balliere.

Besser, G.M., Orth, D.N., Nicholson, W.E., Bynny, R.L., Abe,
      K. and Woodham, J.P. (1971). Dissociation and the
      disappearance of bioactive and radio-immunoreactive
      ACTH from plasma in man. J. Clin. Endocr. 32,
      595-603.

Boyd, J.B., and Mitchell, H.K. (1966). Turnover of the
      hemolymph proteins in Drosophila melanogaster.
      Arch. Biochem. Biophys. 117, 310-319.

Bricteus-Gregoire, S., Jeuniaux, Ch., and Florkin, M. (1965).
      Biochimie du ver a soie. XXX Biosynthese de tre-
      halose et de glycogene a partir de glucose-1-
      phosphate. Comp. Biochem. Physiol. 16, 333-340.

Buck, J.B. (1953). Physical properties and chemical composi-
      tion of insect blood. In "Insect Physiology"
      (Roeder, K.D. Editor) pp. 147-190. New York:
      John Wiley and Sons.

Cannon, W.B. (1929). Organization for physiological homeo-
      stasis. Physiol. Rev. 9, 399-431.

Chen, P.S., and Levenbook, L. (1966). Studies on the hemo-
    lymph proteins in the blowfly, Phormia regina. II.
    Synthesis and breakdown as revealed by isotopic
    labelling. J. Insect Physiol. 12, 1611-1627.

Chippendale, G.M. (1978). The functions of carbohydrates in
    insect life processes. In "Biochemistry of Insects"
    (Rockstein, M. Ed.) pp. 1-55. New York: Academic
    Press.

Dahlman, D.L. (1975). Trehalose and glucose levels in hemo-
    lymph of diet reared, tobacco leaf reared and
    parisitized tobacco hornworm larvae. Comp. Biochem.
    Physiol. 50A, 165-167.

Dinamarca, M.L. and Levenbook, L. (1966). Oxidation,
    utilization and incorporation into protein of
    alanine and lysine during metamorphosis of the blow-
    fly, Phormia regina. Arch. Biochem. Biophys. 117,
    110-119.

Duchateau-Bosson, G., Jeuniaux, Ch., and Florkin, M. (1963).
    Contributions a la biochemie du ver a sole. IIVII
    Trehalose, trehalase et mue. Arch. int. Physiol.
    Biochem. 71, 566-576

Egorova, T.A., and Smolin, A.N. (1962). Trehalose in
    Antheraea pernyi at different developmental stages.
    Biokhimiya 27, 476-479.

Ely, M.J., and Jungreis, A.M. (1977). Effects of X-irradiation
    on egg hatch-ability, larval and pupal survival in
    the tobacco hornworm, Manduca sexta. J. Insect
    Physiol. 23, 95-101.

Florkin, M. and Jeuniaux, Ch. (1974). Hemolymph: Composition.
    In "The Physiology of Insecta", 2nd Edition
    (Rockstein, M. Ed.) pp. 255-307, New York: Academic
    Press.

Friedman, S. (1978) Trehalose regulation, one aspect of
    metabolic homeostasis. Ann. Rev. Entomol. 23, 389-
    407.

Ginther, O.J., Pineda, M.H., Wentworth, B.C. and Nuti, L.
    (1974). Rate of disappearance of exogenous LH from
    the blood in mares. J. Animal Sci. 39, 397-403.

Hansen, O. (1964). Effect of diet on the amount and composi-
    tion of locust blood carbohydrates. Biochem. J.
    92, 333-337.

Horie, Y. (1960). Blood trehalose and fat body glycogen in the silkworm, Bombyx mori. Nature, Lond. 188, 583-584.

Jungreis, A.M. (1976). Changes in fat body hexokinase activity during the larval-pupal transformation of the silkmoth Hyalophora cecropia. Comp. Biochem. Physiol. 53B, 201-204.

Jungreis, A.M. (1978). Insect dormancy, In "Mechanisms of Dormancy and Developmental Arrest". (Clutter, M.E. Editor) pp. 47-112, New York: Academic Press.

Jungreis, A.M. (1979). Physiology of moulting. Adv. Insect Physiol. 14, 109-183.

Jungreis, A.M., and Tojo, S. (1973). Potassium and uric acid content in tissues of the silkmoth Hyalophora cecropia. Amer. J. Physiol. 224, 21-26.

Jungreis, A.M., and Wyatt, G.R. (1972). Sugar release and penetration in insect fat body: Relations to regulation of haemolymph trehalose in developing stages of Hyalophora cecropia. Biol. Bull. 143, 367-391.

Levenbook, L. (1950). The composition of horse bot fly (Gastrophilus intestinalis) larva blood. Biochem. J. 47, 336-346.

Lipset, M.B. (1978). Steroid hormones, In "Reproductive Endocrinology, Physiology, Pathophysiology and Clinical Management" (Yen, S.S.C., and Jaffe, R.B. Editors) pp. 80-92. Philadelphia: W.B. Saunders.

McCarthy, J.F., and Skinner, D.M. (1977). Pro-ecdysial changes in serum ecdysone titers, gastrolith formation, and limb regeneration following molt induction by limb autotomy and/or eyestalk removal in the land crab, Cecarcinus lateralis. Gen. Comp. Endocrinol. 33, 278-292.

Morgan, E.D., and Poole, C.F. (1977). Chemical control of insect moulting. Comp. Biochem. Physiol. 57B, 99-110.

Neville, A.C. (1975) "Biology of the Arthropod Cuticle", Zoophysiology and Ecology 4/5, Springer-Verlag: New York, 448 pages.

Patton, R.L. (1963) "Introductory Insect Physiology", p. 48,
     Philadelphia: W.B. Saunders.

Riddiford, L.M. (1978). Ecdysone-induced change in cellular
     committment of the epidermis of the tobacco horn-
     worm, Manduca sexta, at the initiation of meta-
     morphosis. Gen. Comp. Endo. 34, 438-446.

Riddiford, L.M., and Truman, J.W. (1978). Biochemistry of
     insect hormones and insect growth regulators. In,
     "Biochemistry of Insects", (Rockstein, M. Ed.)
     pp. 307-357. New York: Academic Press.

Scholander, P.F. (1947). Analyzer for accurate estimation of
     respiratory gases in one half cubic centimeter
     samples. J. Biol. Chem. 167, 235-250.

Schoenheimer, R. (1942). "The Dynamic State of Body Constitu-
     ents". Cambridge: Harvard University Press.

Slade, M., and Zibitt, C.H. (1972). Metabolism of Cecropia
     juvenile hormone in insects and mammals. In.
     "Insect Juvenile Hormones". (Menn, J.J., and
     Beroza, M. Editors) pp. 155-177, New York:
     Academic Press.

Steele, J.E. (1978). Hormonal control of metabolism in insects.
     Adv. Insect Physiol. 12, 239-323.

Wigglesworth, V.B. (1942b). The storage of protein, fat,
     glycogen and uric acid in the fat body and other
     tissues of mosquito larvae. J. Exp. Biol. 19, 56-77.

Wigglesworth, V.B. (1965). "The Principles of Insect Physi-
     ology", 6th Edition (revised) London: Methuen. 741
     pp.

Wigglesworth, V.B. (1970). "Insect Hormones". Edinburgh:
     Oliver and Boyd, 159 pp.

Williams-Boyce, P.K., (1977). Regulation of fat body urate
     accumulation in the development of the tobacco
     hornworm, Manduca sexta. M.S. Thesis Knoxville,
     University of Tennessee 106 pp.

Wyatt, G.R. (1961). The biochemistry of insect hemolymph.
    Am. Rev. Entom. 6, 75-102.

Wyatt, G.R. (1967). The biochemistry of sugars and poly-
    saccharides in insects. Adv. Insect Physiol. 4,
    287-360.

Wyatt, G.R. (1968). Biochemistry of insect metamorphosis.
    In. "Metamorphosis" (Etkin, W., and Gilbert, L.I.
    Editors) pp. 143-219, New York: Appleton-Crofts.

LIPID-PROTEIN INTERACTIONS IN INSECTS[1]

John H. Law

Department of Biochemistry
The University of Chicago
Chicago, Illinois

I. INTRODUCTION

A. Hydrophobic compounds in a hydrophilic environment

In the course of testing several compounds for juvenile hormone activity, Wigglesworth (1969a, 1969b, 1973a) pointed out the apparent importance of hydrophobic-hydrophilic balance essential for hormonal activity, and speculated on the interactions of juvenile hormone with membrane lipoproteins, transport proteins, and cellular proteins. Today, we know much more about how hydrophobic substances behave in a hydrophilic environment, and especially how lipophilic compounds interact with proteins. We know, for example, that a balance between the hydrophobic and hydrophilic character of juvenile hormone is important in the interaction with transport proteins (Peterson et al., 1977). It seems likely that Sir Vincent recognized years ago that the interaction of lipids and proteins was a phenomenon of fundamental importance, not only in the action of the amphiphilic (or amphipathic; compounds that have both hydrophobic and hydrophilic character, and thus are able to accommodate admirably to the lipid-water interface) hormones, but in all aspects of insect biochemistry. This essay will attempt to convince the reader that

[1] Work from the author's laboratory, summarized in this paper, was supported by grants from the National Science Foundation and from the Institute of General Medical Services, U.S. Public Health Service.

295

a detailed understanding of these phenomena will be a major area
of the future insect biochemistry.

B. *Types of lipid-protein interaction in biological systems*

In most cases, we know something of the lipids involved in
lipid-protein interactions, but the key proteins have most often not
been isolated and characterized. We will want to understand not
only how small regulatory molecules are bound to proteins, and how
these ligand-protein complexes control, among other things, gene
expression; but we will want to understand receptor-pheromone
complexes, enzyme-substrate complexes, and the formation of stable
macromolecular complexes that contain lipid molecules and proteins.
These sorts of associations are usually either quite specific or quite
non-specific. In mammals, the former are represented by enzyme-
lipid substrate complexes (Brockerhoff and Jensen, 1974), by carrier
proteins for steroids and vitamins in the blood (Westphal, 1971), and
by receptor interactions with regulatory steroids (Jensen and De
Sombre, 1972), etc., while the latter type are best represented by
the serum lipoproteins (Morrisett *et al.*, 1977). Both classes of
proteins can be found in insects, either in tissue or in hemolymph,
and while these have not been extensively studied, recent progress
has indicated both interesting similarities to and differences from
the mammalian systems. Part of our task in the future will be to
explore the similarities and exploit the differences, for our understanding of these will be important to our basic comprehension of
how the insect functions, how it differs from the mammal, and
possibly how we can use this information in controlling insect
behavior, development, or viability.

It should be emphasized that lipid-protein interactions constitute
only a small part of the functions of proteins and peptides. In the
insect biology of the future, these molecules will be seen to play
exceedingly important roles, and extensive investigations into structure and function will need to be undertaken. For these studies,
new methods will be required, a few of which are now being
developed.

C. *Methodology*

New rapid technology for the separation and structure determination of proteins will be needed for future investigations. At present,
high performance liquid chromatography (HPLC) methods are being
developed in our laboratory for rapid separation of proteins from
the hemolymph of the tobacco hornworm, *Manduca sexta*, using a
gel permeation HPLC column. The separation is accomplished in
only 25 minutes, and the effluent can be collected with a fraction

collector. The column can be scaled up for larger loads.

For structural studies, new techniques that will give amino acid sequences on very small samples are under development (Hunkapiller and Hood, 1980) and the use of DNA technology, cloning techniques, and rapid DNA sequencing techniques may allow assignment of protein and peptide sequence indirectly. Immunological techniques and the availability of monoclonal antibodies will doubtless prove valuable. We can expect that new methodology will keep pace with the advancing exploration of insect proteins, so that projects that seem difficult or impossible today will become routine in the future.

II. JUVENILE HORMONE-PROTEIN INTERACTIONS

A. Amphiphilic Character of Juvenile Hormone

As recognized many years ago by C.M. Williams (1956), juvenile hormone I behaves as a lipid in terms of extractibility into organic solvents. It turns out that the famous "golden oil" is perhaps not so lipophilic as originally imagined (Kramer et al., 1974; Giese et al., 1977), but it certainly retains a hydrophobic character which is a prominent feature of some of its interactions with proteins (Peterson et al., 1977; Goodman et al., 1978). The hydrophobic character of juvenile hormone also imparts the unfortunate tendency to adsorb tightly to glassware, plastic, and other surfaces that the investigator wishes to employ when probing its biochemistry and biological properties. Thus, inert surfaces such as Teflon or polyethylene glycol-treated glassware must be employed if one wishes to keep juvenile hormone in aqueous solution (Akamatsu et al., 1975; Giese et al., 1977).

B. Specific Interactions of Juvenile Hormones

Juvenile hormones form at least two different types of specific interactions with proteins in insects. In Lepidoptera (Kramer et al., 1974; Ferkovich et al., 1975; Goodman and Gilbert, 1974; Kramer and Childs, 1977), Diptera (Klages and Emmerich, 1979), and in some locusts (Hartmann, 1978) juvenile hormones are transported in the hemolymph by highly specific carrier proteins. The best studied of these has been isolated from *Manduca sexta* larvae (Kramer et al., 1976; Goodman et al., 1978). This protein has a molecular weight of 28,000 and consists of a single polypeptide chain with a single binding site for juvenile hormone (dissociation constant, 3×10^{-7} M). It is specific for the geometrical shape of the hormone chain (Peterson et al., 1977; Goodman et al., 1978) and binds only the natural optical isomer (Schooley et al., 1978). It is of some interest to compare the relative affinities of the geometrical isomers for this binding protein with the biological activities found earlier by Wigglesworth (1973a) (Table I). Considering the differences in the systems, the agreement is surprisingly good.

Juvenile hormones also form a specific association with receptor proteins in cells. Following the demonstration of high affinity receptor proteins for ecdysteroids in insect cell cytoplasm (Maroy et al., 1978; Yund et al., 1978), Ernest Chang, working both in our laboratory and in that of J.D. O'Connor, demonstrated the presence of a specific, high affinity binding protein for juvenile hormones in cytoplasm of *Drosophila* Kc cells, and Chang and Thomas Coudron in our laboratory have partially purified and characterized this molecule. It has a molecular weight of about 80,000 and a dissociation constant for juvenile hormone I of 1×10^{-8} M (Chang et al., 1980). It can be expected that JH binding proteins will also be found in nuclei (Riddiford and Mitsui, 1978), and thus the juvenile hormones fall into the pattern familiar from studies with steroid hormones in terms of their entry into target cells (Jensen and De Sombre, 1972). Dissection of the details of the hormone-protein interactions will be essential to our understanding of the mode of action of both juvenile hormone and ecdysone. It may also provide new insights into practical means of manipulating insect development in economically useful ways.

Another type of specific interaction between juvenile hormones and proteins can be found in esterolytic enzymes that destroy juvenile

TABLE I. *Comparison of Biological Activity and Carrier Protein Affinity for Isomers of Juvenile Hormone I*

Isomer	Relative Biological Activity[a]	Relative Affinity[b]
trans, trans, cis (natural)	100	100
trans, trans, trans	28	64
trans, cis, cis	7.3	12
cis, trans, cis	3.3	8
trans, cis, trans	1.7	27
cis, trans, trans	1.5	3
cis, cis, trans	.28	1
cis, cis, cis	.22	2

[a]Wigglesworth, 1973a (Rhodnius)
[b]Goodman et al., 1978 (Manduca)

hormones. Hemolymph esterases have been extensively demonstrated but relatively rarely studied in detail.   Whitmore *et al.* (1972) reported appearance of esterases in response to juvenile hormone administration to pupae of *Hyalophora gloveri*.   Weirich and Wren (1973) and Weirich *et al.* (1973) showed that esterases of larval *Manduca* hemolymph could hydrolyze juvenile hormones and were rather specific for the native hormone structure.   We were able to separate larval *Manduca* hemolymph esterases by gel permeation chromatography and to show that two broad classes, which we termed general and JH-specific esterases, were present (Sanburg *et al.*, 1975).   It could also be shown that general esterases were unable to hydrolyze juvenile hormone bound to its carrier protein, while JH-specific esterases hydrolyzed either free or bound hormones (Sanburg *et al.*, 1975;   Hammock *et al.*, 1975).   In addition to a difference in molecular size and substrate specificity, these classes showed differential susceptibility to the organophosphate esterase inhibitor, diisopropylphosphorofluoridate (DFP);   the specific esterases were much more slowly inhibited.   The same difference has been found in a number of other species.   Differential DFP inhibition allowed rapid assay of the two types of esterases during different life stages of the insect.   In *Manduca*, specific esterases appear in the fifth larval instar prior to metamorphosis.   Vince and Gilbert (1977), studying *Manduca*, and Sparks *et al.* (1979) and Sparks and Hammock (1979), using *Trichoplusia ni*, have shown that there are two major peaks of specific esterase activity in the last larval instar, and that these are temporally coordinated with the disappearance of juvenile hormone from the hemolymph.   Thus it seems likely that the specific JH esterases play a role in the determination of JH titers.

C. *Non-Specific Interactions of Juvenile Hormones*

Juvenile hormones also form non-specific associations with lipo-proteins in several insect species (Whitmore and Gilbert, 1972; Trautmann, 1972;   Emmerich and Hartmann, 1973;   Bassi *et al.*, 1977;   Kramer and deKort, 1978).   These interactions are generally considered to be low in specificity and affinity, although a recent study (Hartmann, 1978) suggests that a high affinity protein may be a minor component of the lipoprotein fraction, and that once things are sorted out, high affinity JH carrier proteins may be more prevalent than previously supposed.   The study by Hartmann with the grasshopper *Gomphocerus rufus* is of particular interest, for it shows that antibodies raised to the carrier protein, when injected into the adult female, can interfere with juvenile hormone function. This is compelling evidence for an essential role for specific hormone carriers in hemolymph.

III. NON-LIGAND SPECIFIC INTERACTIONS

A. *Types of Non-Ligand Specific Lipid-Protein Interactions in Insect Hemolymph*

In addition to the ligand specific interactions in hemolymph, there are several examples of non-specific interactions between lipids and proteins.   The best studied examples are the high density lipoproteins (diglyceride carrier lipoproteins), vitellogenins, and the hemolymph storage proteins.   We have recently isolated and chracterized examples of all three of these proteins from larval *M. sexta* hemolymph (Pattnaik *et al.*, 1979;   Mundall and Law, 1979; Kramer *et al.*, 1980), so that we can now compare lipid–protein interactions in each of these types of macromolecular complexes.

B. *Lipoprotein and Vitellogenin*

Non-ligand specific lipid-protein interactions in mammalian serum fall into two types — lipid binding to proteins, as in the fatty acid-albumin complexes, and the true lipoproteins, which are high molecular weight particles composed of triacylglycerols, sterol esters, phospholipids, and proteins (Morrisett *et al.*, 1975;   Morrisett *et al.*, 1977).   While lipid-to-protein ratios vary, the human lipoproteins fall into classes of restricted molecular weight range, and the composition can be satisfactorily harmonized with a uniform general structure (Shen *et al.*, 1977).   These authors show that all mammalian lipoproteins may be organized by the physical properties of their component parts, with a non-polar lipid "core" covered by a monolayer of phospholipid and cholesterol and with polypeptide chains lying between the phospholipid head groups (Figure 1).

A most interesting feature of the polypeptides is that they seem to have a repeating structure composed of units 22 amino acids in length (Fitch, 1977;   McLachlan, 1977).   These segments are thought to have a helical configuration, in which hydrophobic residues fall at every 3rd or 4th position, thus imparting a hydrophobic face to the helix along the helical axis (Segrest *et al.*, 1974;   Fukushima *et al.*, 1979).   This amphiphilic helix also contains hydrophilic residues flanking the hydrophobic portion, so that the regions are clearly delineated (Figure 2).   It is proposed that the hydrophobic portion of the helix associates with the alkyl chains of the phospholipids in the monolayer coating of the lipoprotein particle, as "logs float on water" (McLachlan, 1977).

Serum albumin also has large helical hydrophobic domains to which fatty acids, lysolecithin, and other hydrophobic ligands can be bound (Brown, 1977).   Unlike the apolipoproteins, however, the hydrophobic portions associate with themselves to form a ligand

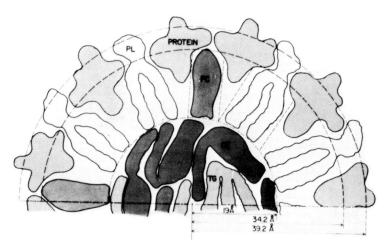

FIGURE 1. A model for the structure of human lipoprotein HDL₃. Symbols are PL, phospholipid, FC, free cholesterol, CE, cholesterol ester, TG, triglyceride. From Edelstein et al., 1979, with permission of the publisher.

binding pocket (Figure 3).   The interactions are more specific than those found in lipoproteins and the ultimate lipid-to-protein ratio in serum albumin is much lower than in lipoproteins.

In contrast to mammalian serum, larval *Manduca* hemolymph has only one major lipoprotein, a high density type (HDL).   This particle appears to be virtually identical to the diglyceride carrier protein of other insects (Chino *et al.*, 1969;   Peled and Tietz, 1975; Thomas, 1979).   Insect HDL is distinguished from mammalian serum lipoproteins by its relatively high content of diglycerides and paucity of triglycerides.   Diglycerides are significantly more polar than triglycerides and it is difficult to envision them in the non-polar core of a lipoprotein particle.   Thus the structure of the insect HDL must differ from that of mammalian HDL in important respects. We have probed the structure of the particle by using proteolytic enzymes and iodination, and we have concluded that the smaller of the two apoproteins has restricted access to the aqueous environment, *i.e.* it is neither hydrolyzed by trypsin nor iodinated, while the larger apoprotein is modified by either technique (Pattnaik *et al.*, 1979; Mundall *et al.*, 1980).   This further emphasizes the unique structure of the insect lipoproteins.

Manduca vitellogenin, isolated from the egg or adult female hemolymph, is similar to vitellogenins of other insects (Hagedorn and Kunkel, 1979), and represents a very low density lipoprotein particle.   Like insect HDL, the complex contains two apoproteins,

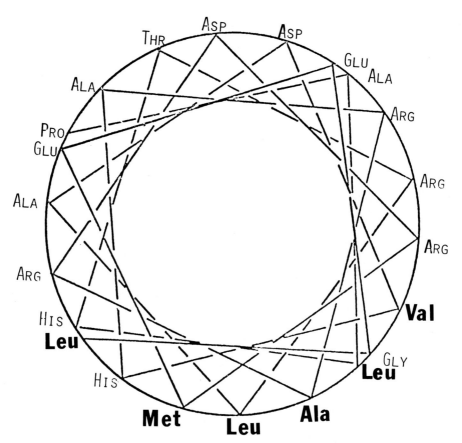

FIGURE 2. A portion of human apolipoprotein A-I, residues
147-168 (Baker et al., 1975), shown on a helical wheel. This
representation indicates the distribution of residues as one looks
down the axis of an α helix. Hydrophobic residues are shown in
bold face letters.

a large one and a small one. The apovitellogenins have an amino
acid composition similar to apoproteins of insect HDL, but there is
no immunological cross-reactivity between HDL and vitellogenin.
The composition of the vitellogenin does not fit the human serum
pattern (Shen et al., 1977) and it is clear that study of the
organization of vitellogenin will yield new information about lipoproteins. We do not yet know if the apoproteins of insect HDL and
vitellogenin contain repetitive hydrophobic sequences, but it would
not be surprising to find them, for insect structural proteins are
frequently highly repetitive in sequence (Lucas et al., 1962; Regier
et al., 1978).

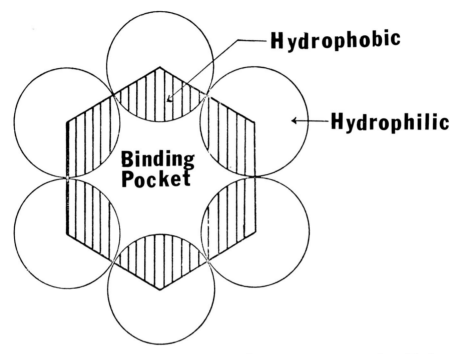

FIGURE 3. Schematic diagram of bovine serum albumin. Circles represent helical wheels such as the one shown in detail in Fig. 2. Six amphiphilic helices associate to form a lipophilic binding pocket. Redrawn from Brown (1978).

C. Hemolymph Storage Proteins

A final example of lipid-protein interactions is found in the hemolymph storage proteins (Thomson, 1975; Wyatt and Pan, 1978). These are large glycoproteins that have 1-2% lipid associated with them. They have been isolated, so far, from Diptera and Lepidoptera, where they are accumulated in the larva and apparently utilized for construction of the adult proteins. We recently reported the characterization of the Manduca storage protein, which we have called manducin (Kramer et al., 1980). The protein has a molecular weight of about 5×10^5 and consists of six polypeptide chains. In common with other storage proteins, the content of aromatic amino acids is unusually high (20%). Manducin accounts for 80% of the total hemolymph proteins at the end of the last larval instar. Associated with manducin are a variety of lipids, constituting 2% of the weight. The spectrum of lipids is quite similar to that found in HDL or vitellogenin, but clearly the amount is much too small to provide the organizing framework for a lipoprotein particle. Furthermore, manducin differs by having 6 very similar or identical subunits, rather than 2 dissimilar ones, as in the case of HDL and vitellogenin, and there is no immunological cross-reactivity between manducin and HDL or vitellogenin. Perhaps manducin has albumin-like hydrophobic domains that function as lipid binding regions. Further investigations may help us to understand the biological role of lipid binding domains as well as to provide us with a rationale for association of lipids with storage proteins.

It is generally accepted that storage proteins are accumulated during the larval feeding stages of holometabolous insects and utilized for the extensive protein and exoskeleton synthesis that accompanies metamorphosis (Thomson, 1975). A thorough investigation of the mechanism by which these proteins are taken up into the pupal fat body and processed for utilization of the amino acid components is in order. Whether the carbohydrate and lipid portions of the protein play any role in these events is not yet clear. However, the uptake of lipoprotein by cells is an important biological phenomenon in mammals (Goldstein and Brown, 1977) and will doubtless prove at least equally interesting in insects.

IV. CONCLUDING REMARKS

It is my hope that the reader has not missed my conviction that protein structure and function will be fundamental to insect science of the future, as well as to research on other invertebrates (Cohen, 1979). A recent review of insect proteins (Agosin, 1978) conveys the fact that our present knowledge is really very meager. While nucleic acids are the archivists and scribes of biology, proteins are the builders and doers, and we cannot understand biological processes without understanding the workings. We will need to recruit scientists trained in unraveling structure-function relationships in proteins in order to solve these problems. Sir Vincent Wigglesworth has provided much rich background in his papers and especially in Principles of Insect Physiology that will help us in this task.

ACKNOWLEDGMENT

I thank my colleague, F.J. Kézdy, for helpful discussions in the course of preparing this paper.

REFERENCES

Agosin, M. (1978). Functional role of proteins. *In* "Insect Biochemistry" (M. Rockstein, ed.), pp.93-144. Academic Press, New
York.

Akamatsu, Y., Dunn, P.E., Kézdy, F.J., Kramer, K.J., Law, J.H.,
Reibstein, D., and Sandburg, L.L. (1975). Biochemical aspects
of juvenile hormone action in insects. *In* "Control Mechanisms
in Development" (R.H. Meints and E. Davies, eds.), pp. 123-149.
Plenum Press, New York.

Baker, H.N., Gotto, A.M., and Jackson, R.L. (1975). The primary
sequence of human plasma high density apolipoprotein glutamine
I (apo A-I). II. The amino acid sequence and alignment of
cyanogen bromide fragments IV, III, and I. *J. Biol. Chem. 250,*
2725-2738.

Bassi, S.D., Goodman, W., Altenhofen, C., and Gilbert, L.I. (1977).
The binding of exogenous juvenile hormone by the haemolymph
of *Oncopeltus fasciatus. Insect Biochem. 7,* 309-312.

Brockerhoff, H., and Jensen, R.G. (1974). "Lipolytic Enzymes."
Academic Press, New York.

Brown, J.R. (1978). Structure and function of serum albumin. *Proc.
FEBS 50, Coll. B9,* 1-10.

Chang, E.S., Coudron, T.A., Bruce, M.J., Sage, B.A., O'Connor, J.D.,
and Law, J.H. (1980). in preparation.

Chino, H., Murakami, S., and Harashima, K. (1969). Diglyceride-
carrying lipoproteins in insect hemolymph. Isolation, purification
and properties. *Biochim. Biophys. Acta 176,* 1-26.

Cohen, S.S. (1979). Comparative biochemistry and drug design for
infectious disease. *Science 205,* 964-971.

Edelstein, C., Kézdy, F.J., Scanu, A.M., and Shen, B.W. (1979).
Apolipoproteins and the structural organization of plasma lipo-
proteins: human plasma high density lipoprotein-3. *J. Lipid
Res. 20,* 143-153.

Emmerich, H., and Hartmann, R. (1973). A carrier lipoprotein for
juvenile hormone in the haemolymph of *Locusta migratoria. J.
Insect Physiol. 19,* 1663-1675.

Ferkovich, S.M., Silhacek, D.C., and Rutter, R.R. (1975). Juvenile
hormone binding proteins in the hemolymph of the Indian meal
moth. *Insect Biochem. 5,* 141-150.

Fitch, W.M. (1977). Phylogenies constrained by crossover process
as illustrated by human hemoglobins and a thirteen-cycle,
eleven-amino-acid repeat in human apolipoprotein A-I. *Genetics
86,* 623-644.

Fukushima, D., Kupferberg, J.P., Yokoyama, S., Kroon, D.J., Kaiser,
E.T., and Kézdy, F.J. (1979). A synthetic amphiphilic helical
docosapeptide with the surface properties of plasma apolipoprotein A-I. *J. Am. Chem. Soc. 101,* 3703-3704.

Giese, C., Spindler, K.D., and Emmerich, H. (1977). The solubility of insect juvenile hormone in aqueous solutions and its adsorption by glassware and plastics. *Z. Naturforsch.* *32c*, 158-160.

Goldstein, J.L., and Brown, M.S. (1977). The low-density lipoprotein pathway and its relation to atherosclerosis. *Ann. Rev. Biochem.* *46*, 897-930.

Goodman, W., and Gilbert, L.I. (1974). Hemolymph protein binding of juvenile hormone in *Manduca sexta*. *Am. Zool.* *14*, 1289.

Goodman, W., Schooley, D.A., and Gilbert, L.I. (1978). Specificity of the juvenile hormone binding protein: the geometrical isomers of juvenile hormone I. *Proc. Natl. Acad. Sci. USA* *75*, 185-189.

Hagedorn, H.H., and Kunkel, J.G. (1979). Vitellogenin and vitellin in insects. *Ann. Rev. Entomol.* *24*, 475-575.

Hammock, B., Nowock, J., Goodman, W., Stamoudis, J., and Gilbert, L.I. (1975). The influence of hemolymph-binding protein on juvenile hormone stability and distribution in *Manduca sexta* fat body and imaginal discs *in vitro*. *Molec. Cell. Endocr.* *3*, 167-184.

Hartmann, R. (1978). The juvenile hormone-carrier in the hemolymph of the acridine grasshopper *Gomphocerus rufus* L.: blocking of the juvenile hormone's action by means of repeated injections of an antibody to the carrier. *Wilhelm Roux's Arch. Dev. Biol.* *184*, 301-324.

Hunkapiller, M.W., and Hood, L.E. (1980). New protein sequenator with increased sensitivity. *Science* *207*, 523-525 (1980).

Jackson, R.L., Morrisett, J.D., and Gotto, A.M. (1976). Lipoprotein structure and metabolism. *Physiol. Rev.* *56*, 259-314.

Jensen, E.J., and De Sombre, E.R. (1972). Mechanism of action of the female sex hormones. *Ann. Rev. Biochem.* *41*, 203-230.

Klages, G., and Emmerich, H. (1979). Juvenile hormone binding proteins in the haemolymph of third instar larvae of *Drosophila hydei*. *Insect Biochem.* *9*, 23-30.

Kramer, K.J., Sanburg, L.L., Kézdy, F.J., and Law, J.H. (1974). The juvenile hormone binding protein in the hemolymph of *Manduca sexta* Johannson (*Lepidoptera: Sphingidae*). *Proc. Natl. Acad. Sci. USA* *71*, 493-497.

Kramer, K.J., and Childs, C.N. (1977). Interaction of juvenile hormone with carrier proteins and hydrolases from insect hemolymph. *Insect Biochem.* *7*, 397-403.

Kramer, S..J., and de Kort, C.A.D. (1978). Juvenile hormone carrier lipoproteins in the haemolymph of the Colorado potato beetle, *Leptinotarsa decemlineata*. *Insect Biochem.* *8*, 87-92.

Kramer, S.J., Mundall, E.C., and Law, J.H. (1980). Purification and properties of manducin, an amino acid storage protein of the haemolymph of larval and pupal *Manduca sexta*. *Insect Biochem.*, in press.

Lucas, F., Shaw, J.T.B., and Smith, S.G. (1957). The amino acid sequence in a fraction of the fibroin of *Bombyx mori*. *Biochem. J.* *66*, 468-479.

Maroy, R., Dennis, R., Beckers, B., Sage, B.A., and O'Connor, J.D. (1978). Demonstration of an ecdysteroid receptor in a cultured cell line of *Drosophila melanogaster. Proc. Natl. Acad. Sci. USA 75*, 6035-6038.

McLachlan, A.D. (1977). Repeated helical pattern in apolipoprotein-A-I. *Nature, Lond. 267*, 465-466.

Morrisett, J.D., Jackson, R.L., and Gotto, A.M. (1975). Lipoproteins: structure and function. *Ann. Rev. Biochem. 44*, 183-207.

Morrisett, J.D., Jackson, R.L., and Gotto, A.M. (1977). Lipid-protein interactions in the plasma lipoproteins. *Biochim. Biophys. Acta 472*, 93-133.

Mundall, E.C., and Law, J.H. (1979). Physical and chemical characterization of vitellogenin from the hemolymph and eggs of the tobacco hornworm, *Manduca sexta. Comp. Biochem. Physiol. 63B*, 459-468.

Mundall, E.C., Pattnaik, N.M., Trambusti, B.G., Hromnak, G., Kézdy, F.J., and Law, J.H. (1980). Structural studies on an insect high density lipoprotein. *Ann. N.Y. Acad. Sci.*, in press.

Pattnaik, N.M., Mundall, E.C., Trambusti, B.G., Law, J.H., and Kézdy, F.J. (1979). Isolation and characterization of a larval lipoprotein from the hemolymph of *Manduca sexta. Comp. Biochem. Physiol. 63B*, 469-476.

Peled, Y., and Tietz, A. (1975). Isolation and properties of a lipoprotein from the haemolymph of the locust, *Locusta migratoria. Insect Biochem. 5*, 61-72.

Peterson, R.C., Reich, M.F., Dunn, P.E., Law, J.H., and Katzenellenbogen, J.A. (1977). Binding specificity of the juvenile hormone carrier protein from the hemolymph of the tobacco hornworm, *Manduca sexta* Johannson (Lepidoptera: Sphingidae). *Biochemistry 16*, 2305-2311.

Regier, J.C., Kafatos, F.C., Kramer, K.J., Heinrikson, R.L., and Keim, P.S. (1978). Silkmoth chorion proteins. Their diversity, amino acid composition, and the NH_2-terminal sequence of one component. *J. Biol. Chem. 253*, 1305-1314.

Riddiford, L.M., and Mitsui, T. (1978). Loss of cellular receptors for juvenile hormone during the change in commitment of the epidermis of the tobacco hornworm, *Manduca sexta* (1978). *In* "Comparative Endocrinology" (P.J. Gaillard and H.H. Boer, eds.), p.519. Elsevier/North Holland, Amsterdam.

Sanburg, L.L., Kramer, K.J., Kézdy, F.J., and Law, J.H. (1975). Juvenile hormone-specific esterases in the haemolymph of the tobacco hornworm, *Manduca sexta. J. Insect Physiol. 21*, 873-887.

Schooley, D.A., Bergot, B.J., Goodman, W., and Gilbert, L.I. (1978). Synthesis of both optical isomers of insect juvenile hormone III, and their affinity for the juvenile hormone-specific binding proteins of *Manduca sexta. Biochem. Biophys. Res. Commun. 81*, 743-749.

Segrest, J.P., Jackson, R.L., Morrisett, J.D., and Gotto, A.M. (1974). A molecular theory of lipid-protein interactions in the plasma lipoproteins. *FEBS Letters* 38, 247-253.

Shen, B.W., Scanu, A.M., and Kezdy, F.J. (1977). Structure of human serum lipoproteins inferred from compositional analysis. *Proc. Natl. Acad. Sci. USA* 74, 837-841.

Sparks, T.C., and Hammock, B.D. (1979). Induction and regulation of juvenile hormone esterases during the last larval instar of the cabbage looper, *Trichoplusia ni*. *J. Insect Physiol.* 25, 551-560.

Sparks, T.C., Willis, W.S., Shorey, H.H., and Hammock, B.D. (1979). Haemolymph juvenile hormone esterase activity in synchronous last instar larvae of the cabbage looper, *Trichoplusia ni*. *J. Insect Physiol.* 25, 125-132.

Thomas, K.K. (1979). Isolation and partial characterization of the haemolymph lipoproteins of the wax moth, *Galleria mellonella*. *Insect Biochem.* 9, 211-219.

Thomson, J.A. (1975). Major patterns of gene activity during development in holometabolous insects. *Adv. Insect Physiol.* 11, 321-398.

Trautmann, K.H. (1972). *In vitro* Studium der Trägerproteine von ^{3}H-markierten juvenilhormonwirksamen Verbindungen in der Hämolymphe von *Tenebrio molitor* L. Larven. *Z. Naturforsch.* 27b, 263-273.

Vince, R.K., and Gilbert, L.I. (1977). Juvenile hormone esterase activity in precisely timed last instar larvae and pharate pupae of *Manduca sexta*. *Insect Biochem.* 7, 115-120.

Weirich, G., and Wren, J. (1973). The substrate specificity of juvenile hormone esterase from *Manduca sexta* haemolymph. *Life Sci.* 13, 213-226.

Weirich, G., Wren, J., and Siddall, J.B. (1973). Developmental changes of the juvenile hormone esterase activity in haemolymph of the tobacco hornworm, *Manduca sexta*. *Insect Biochem.* 3, 397-407.

Westphal, J. (1971). "Steroid-Protein Interactions." Springer-Verlag, Berlin.

Wigglesworth, V.B. (1969a). Chemical structure and juvenile hormone activity. *Nature, Lond.* 221, 190-191.

Wigglesworth, V.B. (1969b). Chemical structure and juvenile hormone activity: comparative tests on *Rhodnius prolixus*. *J. Insect Physiol.* 15, 73-94.

Wigglesworth, V.B. (1973a). Assays on *Rhodnius* for juvenile hormone activity. *J. Insect Physiol.* 19, 205-221.

Williams, C.M. (1956). The juvenile hormone of insects. *Nature, Lond.* 178, 212-213.

Whitmore, E., and Gilbert, L.I. (1972). Haemolymph lipoprotein transport of juvenile hormone. *J. Insect Physiol.* 18, 1153-1167.

Whitmore, D., Whitmore, E., and Gilbert, L.I. (1972). Juvenile hormone induction of esterases: a mechanism for the regulation of juvenile hormone titer. *Proc. Natl. Acad. Sci. USA* 69,

1592-1595.
Wyatt, G.R., and Pan, M.L. (1978).   Insect plasma proteins.   *Ann. Rev. Biochem. 47*, 779-817.
Yund, N.A., King, D.S., and Fristrom, J.W. (1978).   Ecdysteroid receptors in imaginal discs of *Drosophila melanogaster*.   *Proc. Natl. Acad. Sci. USA 75*, 6039-6043.

ENDOCRINE CONTROL OF VITELLOGENIN SYNTHESIS[1]

Franz Engelmann

Department of Biology
University of California
Los Angeles, California

I. INTRODUCTION

Vitellogenesis, a phase of accelerated egg growth leading to the production of fully grown eggs, involves the massive accumulation of protein and lipid yolk, often within a short period of time. This sequestration of reserves for use in the ensuing embryogenesis is frequently triggered by specific events such as periodic food intake, mating, or changes in photoperiod. In the majority of species studied to date the endocrine gland mediating these stimuli is the corpus allatum which in turn may be under the control of the brain (cf. Engelmann, 1979). Juvenile hormone (JH) is then produced and liberated according to 'demands'. With the pioneering work of Wigglesworth (1936d) on *Rhodnius prolixus* the experimental and conceptual groundwork was laid for the wealth of research efforts in many laboratories. In *Rhodnius* it is the periodic food intake which triggers an activation of the single corpus allatum to produce JH, and vitellogenesis follows. During this early phase of research no information was available on the details of how vitellogenesis, the phase of rapid yolk accumulation, is actually controlled. It is, however, remarkable that as early as 1943 Wigglesworth identified hemoglobin in the *Rhodnius* eggs, a component of the yolk which must have been

[1]*The research reported here was supported in part by a Biomedical Science Support Grant, grants from NSF (GB 14965) and National Institutes of Health (AI 12878). This support is gratefully acknowledged.*

311

derived from the blood meal. Viewed in retrospect this observation appears to have led the way to the formulation of
present concepts regarding the mode of accumulation of reserves
in the oocytes by pinocytosis of extraovarian proteins.

II. THE VITELLOGENINS AND VITELLINS

Vitellogenins are defined as a class of proteins which are
precursors of the major yolk proteins, the vitellins (Pan et
al., 1969). It was first recognized by Telfer (1954) that in
Hyalophora one of the female hemolymph proteins is immunologically identical to the predominant egg protein. He drew the
conclusion that yolk proteins are derived from extraovarian
sources and taken up intact by the growing oocytes against a
concentration gradient. Practically identical findings were
subsequently reported for many species of insects of different
orders (cf. Wyatt and Pan, 1978; Engelmann, 1979). It is now
generally agreed that in the majority of insects most of the
yolk proteins are not produced by the ovaries themselves.
However, some of the egg proteins, notably the chorion proteins,
are made by the follicular epithelium of the oocyte follicles.
It ia also reported for *Drosophila* that mRNA extracted from
fat bodies and ovaries could be translated *in vitro*, yielding
vitellogenins indistinguishable from each other; this allowed
the speculation that vitellogenin is normally made by both
fat bodies and ovaries in this species (Bownes, 1979; Bownes
and Hames, 1978). The relative contributions of each to the
mature egg are not known in this case.

Convincing documentation for vitellogenin synthesis in
extraovarian tissues was provided for *Periplaneta* (Pan et al.,
1969) by an *in vitro* culture of female fat bodies and subsequent immunoprecipitation of released radiolabeled vitellogenin.
Similar conclusions were drawn from results obtained in
Leucophaea (Brookes, 1969; Engelmann, 1969), *Hyalophora* (Pan
et al., 1969), as well as other species. Fat body cells of
vitellogenic females contain the cytoarchitecture characteristic of cells engaged in massive protein synthesis, namely, a
well developed rough endoplasmic reticulum (rER). Vitellogenin
could be identified within the cisternae of fat body rER of
Locusta in electron micrographs (Chen et al., 1976; Couble et
al., 1979), and immunologically in *Leucophaea* (Engelmann, 1974;
Engelmann and Barajas, 1975). Taken together, these reports
unquestionably show that vitellogenin is produced by fat body
cells of the females and exported into the hemolymph from where
it is taken up by the growing oocytes. The export of

vitellogenin from the fat bodies follows the same mode as has been shown for other exportable proteins, i.e., the nascent polypeptides are secreted into the cisternae where they may be processed and later released into the circulation.

III. THE HORMONAL CONTROL PATTERNS

Following the immunological identification of vitellogenin in the hemolymph of *Hyalophora*, 12 years elapsed before it was shown that the corpora allata control its synthesis in another species. In *Leucophaea*, the removal of the corpora allata eliminated vitellogenin from the hemolymph and their reimplantation was followed by reappearance of vitellogenin as identified by immunoelectrophoresis (Engelmann and Penney, 1966). Juvenile hormone (JH) applied to allatectomized females had the same effect as reimplantation of active corpora allata (Engelmann, 1969) (Fig. 1). The relative ease by which vitellogenins can be

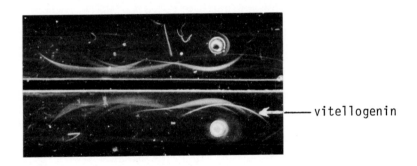

———— vitellogenin

Fig. 1. Identification of vitellogenin in the hemolymph of Leucophaea after JH application (lower trace). Hemolymph of an allatectomized female (upper trace) serves as a control.

reliably identified facilitated the research efforts and it was shown that identical endocrine control mechanisms are operative in many species of several orders of insects (cf. Engelmann, 1979). A graded response of vitellogenin synthesis to increasing doses of JH occurs in *Leucophaea*

(Engelmann, 1971a), *Danaus* (Pan and Wyatt, 1976), *Nauphoeta* (Bühlmann, 1976), and *Locusta* (Chen et al., 1976); the same presumably holds for other species as well.

JH has been the one hormone most often identified as the key agent that controls vitellogenin synthesis and thus vitellogenesis. On the other hand, for *Hyalophora*, the species for which vitellogenin was first identified, no endocrine control of its synthesis is known (Pan, 1977); the same holds for some additional moth species.

In contrast to this, it has been shown that ecdysone, another developmental hormone, can induce vitellogenin synthesis in *Aedes aegypti* (Spielman et al., 1971; Hagedorn, 1974) and *Drosophila* (Handler and Postlethwait, 1978). In *Leucophaea*, however, ecdysone inhibits vitellogenin synthesis (Engelmann, 1971b), and in species such as houseflies and beetles (Robbins et al., 1968), or *Rhodnius* (Garcia et al., 1979) vitellogenesis is curtailed after application of this hormone. It remains to be seen how these results can be reconciled with the well established role of JH in vitellogenin induction (cf. Engelmann, 1979) and whether both JH and ecdysone may have similar modes of action but are operative in different species. The mere extractability of ecdysone from ovaries and other tissues in adult insects or its effects upon injections at relatively high doses does not allow the postulation of a normal role *in vivo*, identical to that of JH.

IV. THE VITELLOGENIN POLYRIBOSOMES

While the overall effects of JH on vitellogenin biosynthesis is clear and fairly well documented for at least 15 species (cf. Engelmann, 1979) many of the details are less well understood. One may justifiably conjecture that one of the main roles of JH is the induced transcription of the coded information for vitellogenin. In *Leucophaea* the messenger for vitellogenin is contained in a class of polysomes of about 40 ribosones; nascent vitellogenin could be identified in such polyribosomes from fat bodies of vitellogenic females, but not in non-vitellogenic females or males (Engelmann, 1977). The rather unusual polysome profile obtained from vitellogenic females, with a very prominent population of the large polysomes in the lower portion of the sucrose gradient, reflects the fact that about 90% of the protein synthesized by these fat bodies is vitellogenin. The RNAs of these vitellogenin polysomes were fractionated on oligo dT cellulose (Engelmann, 1978) and the poly (A) containing fractions translated *in vitro*. A product precipitable by anti-vitellogenin was obtained (Engelmann, unpublished) which was primarily composed of the three vitellogenin subunits. Further analysis will have to show whether these subunits are identical and whether they occur in exactly the same ratios as in the native vitellogenin of the ER and the hemolymph. There is good reason to assume that once the specific vitellogenin messenger has been isolated, the procedures established for many other systems will yield translation products identical to the authentic vitellogenin.

V. THE JUVENILE HORMONE CYTOSOL RECEPTOR

Steroid and peptide hormones are known to be translocated via membrane, cytoplasmic, and/or nuclear receptors to the site of action. It is not known whether the sesquiterpenoid JHs, a different class of chemicals, act in a similar fashion. It is only logical to assume a search for such JH receptors, particularly since the research on ecdysone receptors is well under way. The available technology can readily be adopted for such investigations on JH receptors, provided that the same principles operate for ecdysone and JH.

If such receptors are part of the normal response system to JH, the fat bodies of the adult insects are the most likely tissues where they could be identified. Fat bodies of vitellogenic females of *Leucophaea* were homogenized in the presence of inhibitors of esterases (p-hydroxy mercuribenzoate) and proteases (Trasylol). Following two centrifugations at 12,000 g and one at 150,000 g the supernate (cytosol) was used to test for the presence of compounds with affinity for radiolabeled JH. In such preparations two compounds saturable with JH, a criterion for specific hormone binding molecules, were identified. Scatchard analysis revealed dissociation constants of approximately 2 to 5 x 10^{-9}M and 3 to 8 x 10^{-8}M (Fig. 2). These molecules lost their binding properties for JH upon heating to 65°C for 3 to 5 minutes. Fat bodies of non-vitellogenic females contained binding compounds of similar characteristics, indicating that the production of these molecules is not under the control of JH. Cold JH effectively competed with the binding of radiolabeled JH-III to these macromolecules, and at 100-fold excess the binding of labeled JH was down to about 20% or less of the original value (Fig. 3).

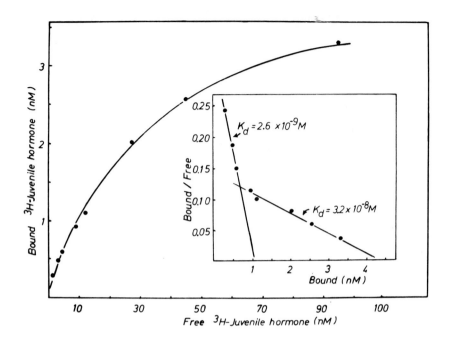

Fig. 2. Affinity of ^{3}H-juvenile hormone to compounds of the fat body cytosol from vitellogenic females of Leucophaea. The cytosol was incubated with various concentrations of ^{3}H-JH with or without unlabeled JH at 100-fold excess at 5°C for 90 minutes. The unbound hormone was then removed by incubation with dextran coated charcoal for 90 sec. The charcoal was spun down and the radioactivity of the supernate determined by scintillation counting. The cytosol had been stabilized prior to incubation by the addition of γ-globulin (2mg/ml). The inset shows the Scatchard analysis revealing two binding compounds. The compound with the higher affinity for JH is considered to be the cytosol receptor.

In an attempt to identify the specific JH cytosol receptor in the fat bodies one certainly cannot neglect the possibility of contamination with the presumed hemolymph JH carrier molecules. JH carrier proteins are made by the fat bodies. In order to identify this latter molecule, hemolymph of vitellogenic females was used for a binding analysis similar to that employed for fat body cytosol. A compound with a K_d of between 5 and 8 x 10^{-8}M was identified,

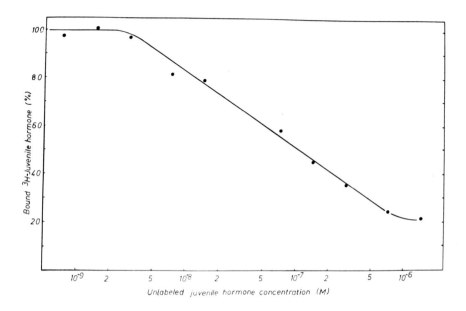

Fig. 3. Suppression of ³H-juvenile hormone binding to cytosol receptors by the addition of unlabeled hormone. Aliquots of the cytosol were incubated with ³H-JH (6.7 x 10⁻⁹M in the presence of various concentrations of unlabeled hormone. Bound JH was determined as described for Fig. 2.

i.e., it had characteristics similar to one of the cytosol binding molecules. Further analysis will have to verify the identity of these compounds. This may be the hemolymph JH carrier protein described for other species.

As is seen, the fat bodies contain two compounds with very high affinity for JH. These molecules are heat labile and presumably are proteins. Can we postulate that one of them, the one with the highest affinity, is the cytosol receptor for JH which is functional in translocating the hormonal message to the nucleus? It's characteristics speak for this.

VI. PROLIFERATION OF ERGASTOPLASMIC MEMBRANES STIMULATED BY JUVENILE HORMONE

The transduction of the hormonal message resulting in the making of the specific vitellogenin mRNA is an all-or-none event and is certainly the essential step for induction of the vitellogenins. The production of these molecules at a high rate is very likely accompanied by the stepped up efficiency of additional supporting systems. For example, electron microscopy revealed that concomitant with vitellogenin production an extensive ER develops in the fat body cells. Since vitellogenin production occurs on rER and since it is secreted into the cisternae just like other exportable proteins (Engelmann, 1974; Engelmann and Barajas, 1975; Chen et al., 1976), a rich supply of membranes could facilitate an enhanced translation rate. The question can then be asked whether proliferation of ER is also stimulated by JH and thus is part of the JH controlled rate of vitellogenin production.

Microsomal membranes from vitellogenic or JH treated females of *Leucophaea* incorporated ^{14}C-choline *in vivo* or ^{32}P *in vitro* at a higher rate than those from the controls. Following a one time topical application of 40 µg JH-III a peak of ^{14}C-choline incorporation five times higher than in the controls was reached on the third day (Fig. 4) (della-Cioppa and Engelmann, 1980). In this context an apparent novel effect of JH was observed: uptake of ^{32}P by the fat body cells *in vitro* was approximately two-fold higher in hormone treated females than in control animals, thus denoting an apparent increase in the permeability of the plasmamembranes to inorganic phosphorus. This was not observed in parallel *in vivo* experiments and therefore was perhaps an artifact of the *in vitro* conditions (della-Cioppa and Engelmann, 1980). The incorporation of both ^{14}C-choline and ^{32}P into ergastoplasmic membranes was between 3.5 and five-fold higher compared to controls in either *in vivo* or *in vitro* experiments. We can therefore interpret the enhanced incorporation of the phospholipid precursors into ER lipids as denoting a JH enhanced proliferation of the ER in the fat body cells.

The resulting increase in available membranes for polyribosome attachment could facilitate a more efficient and accelerated translation of the vitellogenin messenger. At this time it is not known whether vitellogenin polysomes settle only on the newly made ER or whether preexisting sER can be transformed into well stacked and organized rER when

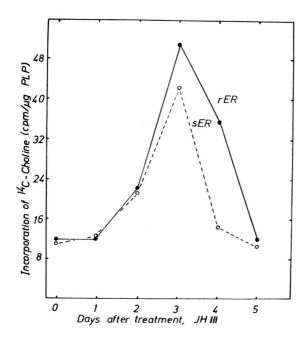

Fig. 4. Increased incorporation of ^{14}C-choline into phospholipids of microsomal membranes of fat bodies of Leucophaea following topical application of 40 μg of JH-III. The animals were injected with 2.0 μCi ^{14}C-choline four hours prior to harvesting of the microsomes. Each point represents the pool of the microsomal phospholipids of 3 - 5 animals.

vitellogenin polysomes become available. The fact that the peak in membrane proliferation coincides and does not precede the peak of vitellogenin production (Engelmann, 1971b) speaks for the latter alternative.

VII. THE MAKING OF A MATURE EGG

It is the complexity of vitellogenesis, the multiple processes that must be intercalated towards the production of the mature egg, that truly excites the researcher's imagination. While we have, for many years, focused our attention on the control of endocrine glands, and then on the controlled synthesis of vitellogenin, the identifiable

final product, it is obvious that the making of a mature
egg involves innumerable mechanisms which must be integrated. We can but speculate on most of the details.

The question of how the hormones involved reach the
target tissues such as fat bodies and ovaries, is not yet
answered. We assume that the hemolymph contains carrier
proteins for JH which serve as vehicle and may also protect
this molecule from enzymatic degradation as it is known for
certain immature insect species (Kramer et al., 1974, 1976).
The mode of translocation of the hormonal message to the
site of transcription of the vitellogenin mRNA is not understood, except that we have begun to identify a cytosol JH
receptor in the fat body cells. Nuclear JH receptors may
be postulated as well. We may ask whether the production
of such receptors is under the control of JH. Vitellogenin
mRNAs have been isolated from several species of insects and
translated in cell free *in vitro* systems. For *Drosophila*
such translation products have been characterized and found
to be nearly identical to the native vitellogenin polypeptides (Postlethwait and Kaschnitz, 1978; Warren et al.,
1979). JH appears to stimulate the production of new endoplasmic reticulum in *Leucophaea* which in turn facilitates
the translation of more vitellogenin molecules than otherwise would be possible (della-Cioppa and Engelmann, 1980).
Virtually nothing is known on posttranslational modifications of the nascent vitellogenin polypeptides; glycosylation and lipidation probably occur within the cisternae of
the ER. The export of the mature vitellogenin from the fat
body cells appears to be under control of the JH molecule.
This is suggested by the observation that fat bodies of
pregnant *Leucophaea* contain large amounts of vitellogenin
at a time when the corpora allata are inactive and vitellogenin is no longer produced or is detectable in the hemolymph (Engelmann, 1971a). Lastly, vitellogenin uptake by
the growing oocytes is under control of JH as evidenced by
a number of observations (cf. Engelmann, 1979).

As this brief summary of the suggested molecular events
illustrates, JH is the key molecule which controls the production of vitellogenin and the making of the mature egg.
Its effect is pleiotropic. The realization emerges that JH
does more than just influence transcriptional events. The
latter action, nonetheless, is the all-or-none phenomenon,
whereas other actions are manifested in the enhancement of
on-going events. The hormone-induced production of an easily identifiable specific end product lends itself well for
an analysis of the details of a complex machinery that ultimately leads to the production of mature eggs. A great num-

ber of questions remain to be answered before we can have a clear understanding of the processes involved. Promising progress has been made recently in several areas of research. It is particularly noteworthy that several laboratories familiar with *Drosophila* biology have begun to use this species for an analysis of vitellogenin control (Bownes and Hames, 1978; Bownes, 1979; Postlethwait and Kaschnitz, 1978; Warren et al., 1979). Through the joint and competitive efforts of many laboratories we will undoubtedly gain insight into the fascinating story of how a hormone activates a specific protein synthesis machinery.

REFERENCES

Bownes, M. (1979). Three genes for yolk proteins in *Drosophila melanogaster*. *FFBS Lett. 100*, 95-98.

Bownes, M., and Hames, B. D. (1978). Analysis of the yolk proteins in *Drosophila melanogaster*. *FEBS Lett. 96*, 327-330.

Brookes, V. J. (1969). The induction of yolk protein synthesis in the fat body of an insect, *Leucophaea maderae* by an analog of the juvenile hormone. *Develop. Biol. 20*, 549-571.

Bühlmann, G. (1976). Haemolymph vitellogenin, juvenile hormone, and oocyte growth in the adult cockroach *Nauphoeta cinerea* during first pre-oviposition period. *J. Insect Physiol. 22*, 1101-1110.

Chen, T. T., Couble, P., De Lucca, F. L., and Wyatt, G R. (1976). Juvenile hormone control of vitellogenin synthesis in *Locusta migratoria*. *In* "The Juvenile Hormones" (L. I. Gilbert, ed.), pp. 505-529. Plenum press, New York and London.

Couble, P., Chen, T. T., and Wyatt, G. R. (1979). Juvenile hormone-controlled vitellogenin synthesis in *Locusta migratoria* fat body: Cytological development. *J. Insect Physiol. 25*, 327-337.

della-Cioppa, G., and Engelmann, F. (1980). Juvenile hormone-stimulated proliferation of endoplasmic reticulum in the fat body cells of a vitellogenic insect, *Leucophaea maderae* (Blattaria). *In press.*

Engelmann, F. (1969). Female specific protein: Biosynthesis controlled by corpus allatum in *Leucophaea maderae*. *Science* (Wash.) *165*, 407-409.

Engelmann, F. (1971a). Juvenile hormone-controlled synthesis of female-specific protein in the cockroach *Leucophaea maderae*. *Archs. Biochem. Biophys.* *145*, 439-447.

Engelmann, F. (1971b). Endocrine control of insect reproduction, a possible basis for insect control. *Acta Phytopathol. Acad. Sci. Hung. 6*, 221-217.

Engelmann, F. (1974). Juvenile hormone induction of the insect yolk protein precursor. *Amer. Zool. 14*, 1195-1206.

Engelmann, F. (1977). Undegraded vitellogenin polysomes from female insect fat bodies. *Biochem. Biophys. Res. Comm. 78*, 641-647.

Engelmann, F. (1978). Synthesis of vitellogenin after long-term ovariectomy in a cockroach. *Insect Biochem. 8*, 149-154.

Engelmann, F. (1979). Insect vitellogenin: Identification, biosynthesis, and role in vitellogenesis. *Adv. Insect Physiol. 14*, 49-108.

Engelmann, F., and Barajas, L. (1975). Ribosome-membrane association in fat body tissue from reproductively active females of *Leucophaea maderae*. *Exptl. Cell Res. 92*, 102-110.

Engelmann, F., and Penney, D. (1966). Studies on the endocrine control of metabolism in *Leucophaea maderae* (Blattaria). I. The hemolymph proteins during egg maturation. *Gen. Comp. Endocrinol. 7*, 314-325.

Garcia, M. L. M., Mello, R. P., and Garcia, E.S. (1979). Ecdysone, juvenile hormone and oogenesis in *Rhodnius prolixus*. *J. Insect Physiol. 25*, 695-700.

Hagedorn, H. H. (1974). The control of vitellogenesis in the mosquito, *Aedes aegypti*. *Amer. Zool. 14*, 1207-1217.

Handler, A. M., and Postlethwait, J. H. (1978). Regulation of vitellogenin synthesis in *Drosophila* by ecdysone and juvenile hormone. *J. Exptl. Zool. 206*, 247-254.

Herman, W. S., and Baker, J. F. (1976). Ecdysterone antagonism, mimicry, and synergism of juvenile hormone action on the monarch butterfly reproductive tract. *J. Insect Physiol. 22*, 643-648.

Kramer, K. J., Sandburg, L. L., Kezdy, F. J., and Law, J. H. (1974). The juvenile hormone binding protein in the hemolymph of *Manduca sexta* Johannson (Lepidoptera: Sphingidae). *Proc. Nat. Acad. Sci. USA 71*, 493-497.

Kramer, K. J., Dunn, P. E., Peterson, R. L., and Law, J. H. (1976). Interaction of juvenile hormone with binding proteins in insect hemolymph. *In* "The Juvenile Hormones." (L. I. Gilbert, ed.), pp. 327-341. Plenum Press, New York and London.

Pan, M. L. (1977). Juvenile hormone and vitellogenin synthesis in the *cecropia* silkworm. *Biol. Bull. Woods Hole 153*, 336-345.

Pan, M. L., Bell, W. J., and Telfer, W. H. (1969). Vitellogenic blood protein synthesis by insects fat body. *Science* (Wash.) *165*, 393-394.

Pan, M. L., and Wyatt, G. R. (1976). Control of vitellogenin synthesis in the monarch butterfly by juvenile hormone. *Develop. Biol. 54*, 127-134.

Pappas, C., and Fraenkel, G. (1978). Hormonal aspects of oogenesis in the flies *Phormia regina* and *Sarcophaga bullata*. *J. Insect Physiol. 24*, 75-80.

Postlethwait, J. R., and Kaschnitz, R. (1978). The synthesis of *Drosophila melanogaster* vitellogenins *in vivo*, in culture, and in a cell free translation system. *FEBS Lett. 95*, 247-251.

Robbins, W. E., Kaplanis, J. N., Thompson, M. J., Shortino, T. J., Cohen, C. F., and Joyner, S. C. (1968). Ecdysones and analogs: Effects on development and reproduction in insects. *Science* (Wash.) *161*. 1158-1159.

Spielman, A., Gwadz, R. W., and Anderson, W. A. (1971). Ecdysone-initiated ovarian development in mosquitoes. *J. Insect Physiol. 17*, 1807-1814.

Telfer, W. H. (1954). Immunological studies of insect metamorphosis. II. The role of a sex-limited blood protein in egg formation by the *cecropia* silkworm. *J. Gen. Physiol. 37*, 539-558.

Warren, T. G., Brennan, M. D., and Mahowald, A. P. (1979). Two processing steps in maturation of vitellogenin polypeptides in *Drosophila melanogaster. Proc. Nat. Acad. Sci. USA 76*, 2848-2852.

Wigglesworth, V. B. (1936d), The function of the corpus allatum in the growth and reproduction of *Rhodnius prolixus* (Hemiptera). *Quart. J. Micr. Sci. 79*, 91-121.

Wigglesworth, V. B. (1943). The fate of hemoglobin in *Rhodnius prolixus* (Hemiptera) and other blood-sucking arthropods. *Proc. Roy. Soc. B, 131*, 313-339.

Wyatt, G. R., and Pan, M. L. (1978). Insect plasma proteins. *Ann. Rev. Biochem. 47*, 779-817.

THE PHYSIOLOGY OF REPRODUCTION IN *RHODNIUS* AND
OTHER INSECTS: SOME QUESTIONS[1]

K.G. Davey

Department of Biology
York University
Downsview, Ontario, Canada

I. INTRODUCTION

Although he was visualised by a distinguished American literary figure as having "the Sperm Club in to tea" (Updike, 1955), apart from critical early discoveries on the control of vitellogenesis and accessory glands by the corpus allatum (Wigglesworth, 1936d, 1963b, 1964b), Wigglesworth has rarely turned his attention to the wider aspects of the physiology of insect reproduction. As a consequence, with the conspicuous exception of endocrinological aspects, the general field of reproductive physiology remains in a relatively undeveloped, not to say rudimentary state.

This relative neglect of the field is particularly regrettable, for reproductive mechanisms play a crucial role in the relationship between insects and man. As Wigglesworth (1951b) has pointed out, insects have an enormous reproductive potential, and their numbers are only held in check by huge mortalities. When natural controls are removed, as in the simplified ecology which obtains in an agricultural monoculture, insect populations may increase in an explosive way. Knowledge of the reproductive physiology of insects may enable man to interfere with this great potential for damage.

[1]*Supported by a grant from the Natural Sciences and Engineering Research Council of Canada.*

This essay will not attempt to document our ignorance. It will, in a highly selective way, examine some aspects of the general field and focus on a series of questions which might be worth attacking in the future. In some few cases, these questions can be stated in a precise way. In others, the undeveloped state of the field will permit only vague and ill defined questions to be formulated. In approaching the field I have chosen to emphasize the physiology of *Rhodnius*. In doing so I am conscious of the remarkable diversity of reproductive mechanisms among insects and the consequent dangers of generalising too readily, but space limitations require selectivity.

II. SPERMATOGENESIS

The processes culminating in the appearance of fully functional spermatozoa in insects have not been extensively studied, yet they are probably at least as complex as the comparable processes in the female. While spermatozoa are usually present in the seminal vesicles of males by the time of eclosion to the adult, spermatogenesis may continue throughout a sometimes prolonged adult life in some species. For example, the testis of *Rhodnius* continues to produce spermatozoa during an adult life span which, in the laboratory, exceeds six months (Dumser, 1974).

A. *Early Events*

For those insects which have been examined, the spermatogonia arise from stem cells located in the apex of each seminiferous tubule; each division of a stem cell results in a spermatogonium and another stem cell. The initial spermatogonium becomes enclosed in a cyst or follicle composed of a single layer of mesodermal cells. All subsequent events within the testis occur in the cyst, and all cells within a cyst behave synchronously (Dumser, 1980a). In *Rhodnius*, as in other insects, the number of mitotic divisions which a spermatogonium undertakes before meiosis begins is fixed and characteristic of the species (Dumser and Davey, 1974). While the course of this "sequential auto-differentiation" (Dumser, 1980a) is independent of hormonal influences in that the presence or absence of morphogenetic hormones such as ecdysone or JH does not alter the number of required divisions, the rate at which these divisions occur is, to some extent, dependent on these hormones. Thus, there is a basal rate of mitosis in the *Rhodnius* testis and this basal rate is approximately doubled by ecdysone. The ecdysone-stimulated mitosis, but not the basal rate, is inhibited by juvenile hormone (Dumser and Davey, 1975a,b). The precise mechanism by which these hormones exert these effects is unknown. Recent studies on cultures of testes of *Locusta migratoria* demonstrate that ecdysterone stimulates the movement from G_1 into S and from G_2 into M, thus confirming that ecdysterone acts on the rate of division rather than by recruiting more cells from a non-dividing pool into a dividing pool (Dumser, 1980b).

The system outlined above is potentially important in more general terms. The possible effects of ecdysone and juvenile hormone on cell division of other target cells has been a preoccupation of insect endocrinologists (Wigglesworth, 1963c). The recognition that ecdysterone may sometimes act, not so much as a switch, permitting cell division to occur, but as a volume control, increasing the rate of an ongoing process, may be quite liberating in terms of hypotheses. Moreover, the availability of a system which behaves in an approximately normal way *in vitro* affords an opportunity to confront certain questions in a very direct way. What is the site of ecdysterone action in this system? Does JH act at the same site? Is there a classical antagonism between the two hormones in this case?

B. *Spermiogenesis*

The timing of the appearance of mature spermatozoa in the *Rhodnius* testis is further regulated by autolysis of the most differentiated component of the testis: until events associated with the final moult begin, some of the most differentiated elements, whether these be spermatids, spermatocytes or spermatogonia, undergo autolysis (Dumser and Davey, 1974). A similar phenomenon occurs in most species that have been studied (Dumser, 1980a).

Because autolysis is abolished or decreased during the penultimate instar, it is probable that autolysis is under the control of the morphogenetic hormones. Some clue as to how this is achieved may emerge from studies on a blood-borne factor which halts autolysis *in vitro* of the spermatids in the testes of giant silk moths. This "macromolecular factor" (MF) is thought to be excluded from the testis except in the presence of ecdysterone (Kambysellis and Williams, 1971a,b). The origin of MF appears

to be the haemocytes (Landureau and Szollosi, 1974). While
there are attractive possibilities presented by such a
model, it is still inadequately described. How does MF
act to maintain spermatids? Does MF affect other stages
in spermatogenesis? Does MF play a role in cell division?
Does JH alter the permeability of the testis to MF? Is
the production of MF regulated by JH or ecdysterone?

III. OOGENESIS

A. *Nurse Cells*

Egg formation is complicated in insects by the existence
in some species of nurse cells or trophocytes. These are
sister cells of the oogonia which follow a different developmental path, contributing primarily RNA, and eventually
the whole of their substance, to the oocyte. The formation
and functioning of the oocyte-trophocyte complex has been
examined in an elegant review by Telfer (1975). Much of
our knowledge of the relationships between oocytes and
trophocytes is derived from studies on the polytrophic
ovariole, particularly those of King and his colleagues
in *Drosophila*. Oogonial stem cells divide to produce a
cystoblast, which leaves the apex of the germarium, and
an oogonium, which remains at the apex as a stem cell.
Subsequent divisions of the cystoblast are incomplete,
so that the 16 cystocytes which result are connected by
cytoplasmic bridges (ring canals). The cystocytes are
packaged in a single follicle, and one of the cystocytes,
the oocyte, grows at the expense of its sister cells, the
trophocytes, which pass material to the oocyte through
the cytoplasmic bridges (Brown and King, 1964; Koch and
King, 1966, 1969; Koch *et al*, 1967; Telfer, 1975).

We know very much less about the development of the
telotrophic ovariole. In the adult of *Rhodnius*, the trophocytes are located towards the apex of the ovariole, while
the oocytes are grouped below them. Each oocyte is connected
to a central trophic core by a cytoplasmic extension, the
trophic cord. The trophocytes arise from mitotically active
cells at the apex of the ovariole and enlarge as they move
downwards toward the trophic core area. At this stage,
cytoplasmic continuity between the trophic core and the
maturing trophocyte is established (Case, 1970; Huebner
and Anderson, 1972).

While the interrelationships between oocyte and trophocyte are clear insofar as they exist in the adult, we know
less about how they arise. From the work of Case (1970)
we know that the germ cells in the female of *Rhodnius* undergo
a differentiative division on the sixth day after ecdysis
to the fifth instar, during which the presumptive oocytes,
but not the trophocytes, expel a feulgen-positive body.
Similar observations have been made for *Oncopeltus* by Wick
and Bonhag (1955). Shortly thereafter, the trophocytes
move to the apex of the ovariole and the trophic core appears. The oocytes do not undergo further divisions in
the ovary. While Case (1970) interpreted the feulgen bodies
as polar bodies resulting from the first meiotic division,
it is unlikely that the first meiotic division was completed
at this time, for that would imply that the trophocytes
were meiocytes. It is perhaps more likely that the feulgen
bodies may represent the expulsion of DNA coding for ribosomal material, since most, if not all, of the ribosomal material of the oocyte is to be manufactured by the trophocytes.
Similar bodies have been noted in a few polytrophic and
panoistic species (Telfer, 1975).

Electron microscope studies on the fifth instar ovary
of *Rhodnius* demonstrate that the developing trophic core
is a tangled mass, resembling a neuropile, suggesting that
it arises as a result of incomplete cytokineses in the
trophocytes. However, it is not at all clear what the
relationship of the dividing trophic primordium is to the
trophic core (Huebner and Anderson, 1972). Are all of
the trophocytes connected to the trophic core by cytoplasmic
bridges, or do these arise by fusion during differentiation
of trophocytes? How is movement out of the trophocytes
and down the trophic core into a particular oocyte effected?
It has been suggested that electrical polarity is responsible
for some of the movement in the polytrophic follicle of
Hyalophora (Telfer, 1975), but we have no information which
points in a similar direction for telotrophic ovarioles.
The trophic core and trophic cords of *Rhodnius* are rich
in microtubules, the organisation of which can be destroyed
by vinblastine sulphate (Huebner and Anderson, 1970).
By analogy with axoplasmic translocation, it may be that
intact microtubules are essential to the functioning of
the trophic cords, and this material may prove to be a
useful model for studying such transport.

There are signs that the development of some telotrophic
ovarioles may be more readily related to that of polytro
phic ovarioles. Thus, Buning (1978) suggests that in the

development of the telotrophic ovariole of the beetle *Bruchid-ius* the oocyte-trophocyte syncytium arises as a result first of incomplete cytokineses during development of the germ tissue followed by fusion of trophocytes.

B. *Coordination within the Ovariole*

While we know something of the hormonal control of events within the ovary, it is clear that in *Rhodnius* at least the situation is complicated by a degree of intra-ovariolar coordination which is entirely mysterious. This coordination is perhaps best exemplified by the fact that only one oocyte is in vitellogenesis in any one ovariole at any one time. The penultimate oocyte in an ovariole never enters vitellogenesis until its elder sister, the terminal oocyte has completed vitellogenesis and its chorion has begun to form (Pratt and Davey, 1972a). What is the message which the terminal oocyte sends back to its sisters, and how is it carried? The fact that the trophic cord of the terminal oocyte remains intact perhaps until chorion formation begins (Pratt and Davey, 1972a) offers a potential pathway for communication among the oocytes via the trophic core. It is to be emphasized that in *Rhodnius* this coordination lies within the ovariole. Synchrony among ovarioles, while reasonably good, is far from perfect, so that the penultimate oocyte of one ovariole may enter vitellogenesis while that of a neighbouring ovariole remains inhibited by the presence of a vitellogenic follicle in its ovariole.

IV.VITELLOGENESIS

A. *Uptake of Vitellogenin*

During the process of vitellogenesis, yolk proteins are deposited in the oocyte. Wigglesworth (1936d) discovered more than 40 years ago that this process was governed by the corpus allatum in *Rhodnius*, and it is now clear that JH regulates vitellogenesis in a wide variety of, although by no means all, insects. In most insects, JH intervenes in the process of vitellogenesis at more than one level. Thus, it is well known that juvenile hormone regulates the synthesis by the fat body of vitellogenin which is

eventually incorporated into the growing oocyte. This
function of juvenile hormone will be dealt with elsewhere
in this volume.

The vitellogenin from the haemolymph passes into the
follicle via spaces between the follicle cells (Telfer,
1961), and, in *Rhodnius* at least, the appearance and size
of these spaces is regulated by JH (Pratt and Davey, 1972a;
Davey and Huebner, 1974). Thus, JH regulates not only
the synthesis of the vitellogenin but the mechanism by
which the extra-ovarian proteins enter the follicle. It
is worth noting that the first clear demonstration of the
uptake by oocytes of proteins from the haemolymph was made
in *Rhodnius* by Wigglesworth (1943).

The spaces between the follicle cells in *Rhodnius* are
very large, occupying as much as 30% of the total surface
area of a follicle, and they arise as a result of a decrease
in volume of the cells (Abu-Hakima and Davey, 1977a).
This decrease in volume occurs in response to JH, develops
rapidly, is reversible, and is independent of macromolecular
synthesis (Abu-Hakima and Davey, 1977a,b). All of this
suggests that JH acts at the membrane of the follicle cell,
a suggestion that is further supported by the observation
that the action of JH is inhibited by ouabain, a specific
inhibitor of $Na^+ K^+$ ATPase (Abu-Hakima and Davey, 1979).
The nature and directness of the action of JH on the follicle
cells has yet to be determined. Does the hormone bind
directly to the enzyme, altering its conformation and increasing its activity? Does the hormone act to uncover additional
active enzyme sites, much as insulin acts on the ATPase
of frog epithelium (Grinstein and Erlu, 1974)? Is the
enzyme both the receptor and effector molecule?

B. JH and Early Events

JH has another, quite different, effect upon follicle
cells in *Rhodnius*, an effect which is exerted earlier in
their development. Only a few follicles in allatectomised
females enter vitellogenesis, and entry of these follicles
into vitellogenesis is markedly delayed. There is thus
a tendency for the terminal follicles to accumulate in
a size range which immediately precedes vitellogenesis,
implying that a JH-dependent process occurs at this stage.
This process has been called "activation" (Pratt and Davey,
1972a). A clearer demonstration of the effect of JH on
the previtellogenic follicle is provided by the observation

that follicle cells from vitellogenic follicles taken from allatectomised females will not respond to JH *in vitro* (Abu-Hakima and Davey, 1975). In other words, follicle cells must differentiate in the presence of JH in order, at a later stage in their development, to be able to respond to JH. It is perhaps significant that the Na$^+$ K$^+$ ATPase activity of homogenates prepared from previtellogenic follicles fails to respond to added JH (Ilenchuk, personal communication). Does "activation" consist of the synthesis of an appropriate form of the ATPase, thus rendering the follicle cell competent to respond to JH?

While JH may not be universally required for vitellogenic growth of the follicle, there is some evidence which suggests that the corpus allatum is essential for earlier pre-vitellogenic growth in all insects. Thus in many Diptera, such as tsetse flies (Ejezie and Davey, 1979) and mosquitoes (Gwadz and Spielmann, 1973), allatectomy does not inhibit vitellogenesis, but the corpora allata appear to be required for earlier growth. The nature of this effect, or indeed its site, remain undescribed. While the parallel with the process of activation in *Rhodnius* is obvious, it should be used with caution since, in *Glossina austeni* at least, prominent spaces do not appear in the follicular epithelium during vitellogenesis, and the bulk of the yolk protein is synthesized within the ovary (Huebner *et al*, 1975).

C. *Follicle Cell Products*

Even in those insects in which the follicular epithelium acts as a gate, controlling access of the haemolymph proteins to the oocyte surface, the follicle cells have other roles to play in the process of vitellogenesis. In *Rhodnius*, as in other insects, the follicle cells show ultrastructural signs of synthetic activity and exocytosis (Huebner and Anderson, 1970), and there is no doubt that in some insects, such as *Glossina austeni*, the follicle cells make substantial contributions to the yolk (Huebner, Tobe and Davey, 1975).

In *Hyalophora cecropia*, the haemolymph proteins are concentrated in the interfollicular cell spaces to a level 2.5 - 4.5 times that in the blood and a factor is present in the spaces which is selective for vitellogenin (Anderson and Telfer, 1970). While this factor is held to be a product of the follicle cells, attempts to demonstrate its secretion *in vitro* have not yet been convincing. A follicle cell product stimulates pinocytosis in naked oocytes *in vitro*, but part of the process by which vitellogenin is selectively concentrated in the oocyte appears to reside at the oocyte surface (Anderson, 1971). In *Periplaneta*, the synthesis of a histidine-rich follicle cell product which eventually appears in the oocyte is JH-dependent (Bell and Sams, 1974). While the story suggested by the work on *H. cecropia* is seductive, there are many unanswered questions concerning both the mechanism of protein concentration in the spaces in the follicular epithelium and the selectivity of the pinocytotic process.

D. Loss of JH Sensitivity

While the follicle cells clearly serve many functions, at least three of which are potentially controlled by JH, their ultimate failure to respond to JH is at least as interesting a phenomenon. Thus, in *Rhodnius*, as the follicle approaches 1.6 mm in length, a size at which the chorion is secreted, the follicle cells fail to respond to JH in that spaces between them disappear. This may be a consequence of an alteration of the cytoskeleton, but there is no evidence that the epithelium decreases in height at this time (Abu-Hakima and Davey, 1977a). Have the receptors for JH disappeared or become masked? Is the follicle cell at this stage in fact responding to JH by pumping out fluid? If so, how is the effect of this tendency to decrease the volume masked so as to cause the spaces to disappear?

V. COPULATION AND SEMEN TRANSFER

A. Semen Transport

In *Rhodnius*, the spermatozoa are transported from the bursa copulatrix to the spermathecae by contractions of the common oviduct set up by the product of the opaque accessory gland of the male (Davey, 1958). This work is now more than 20 years old and deserves some reinvestigation, particularly in view of its potential importance in pest control. For example, the active material in the accessory glands of cockroaches has been tentatively identified as an indolalkyl amine (Davey, 1960), a conclusion that was

equally tentatively supported by Colhoun (1963). The precise
identity of the active factor is a necessary first step
in the further exploration of this phenomenon.

B. *Activation of Spermatozoa*

In many insects, the transfer of semen to the female
results in an "activation" of the spermatozoa, usually
signalled by an increase in frequency of beating of the
flagellum. In *Periplaneta*, the increase in tail beat frequency is followed closely by changes in the membrane in
the acrosomal region, and these changes appear to require
a period of residence in the female tract (Hughes and Davey,
1969). On the other hand, the changes in activity in the
spermatozoa of Lepidoptera result instantaneously from
the mixing of the spermatozoa with other elements of the
seminal fluid (Shepherd, 1974). Shepherd (1975) has isolated
an activator which is a peptide of molecular weight near
3000 and which appears to act at hormonal concentrations.
What is the mode of action of this material? It appears
not to act via the cyclic nucleotides (Shepherd, 1975).

About other aspects of the physiology of insect spermatozoa we are even more in the dark. What is the identity
of the spermathecal secretions which maintain the activity
of spermatozoa? Are spermatozoa from the male capable
of fertilizing an egg, or is some period of residence in
the female ("capacitation") required? Cockroaches, in
which active spermatozoa can be obtained from both the
male and the female (Hughes and Davey, 1969) and in which
spermatozoa can be observed to enter the micropyle (Dewitz,
1886), would appear to constitute an interesting model.
How does the spermatozoon find the micropyle, which is
frequently of a diameter not much larger than the spermatozoon itself?

C. *Nutritive Role of Semen Transfer*

Of course, spermatozoa are not the only materials
transferred during the mating process, and it is no surprise that various accessory secretions of the male find
their way into the female (Leopold, 1976). Various authors (references in Leopold, 1976) have speculated on
a possible nutritive role for spermatophores and other
accessory secretions. More recently, however, Friedel
and Gillot (1977) have demonstrated that soluble proteins

from the accessory glands of the males of *Melanoplus sanguinipes* are transferred from the spermatophore to the haemolymph of the female, and that some of this material is accumulated unchanged by developing oocytes. Because this species normally transfers several spermatophores during a single copulation, this nutritive transfer from the male to the next generation is thought to be significant.

IV. THE CONSEQUENCES OF COPULATION

A. *The Nature of the Stimulus*

Copulation in insects sets in train a variety of physiological and behavioural responses in the female. These responses, usually mediated via the hormonal system, vary greatly from insect to insect. In *Rhodnius*, mated females produce more eggs, begin to lay them sooner after feeding, and lay them more rapidly than virgin females (Buxton, 1930; Davey, 1965; Pratt and Davey, 1972b). Past work from our laboratory has suggested that the following system might operate. A mated female produces a hormone, released from mated spermathecae (Davey, 1965). Mated females release a neurosecretory myotropin from the pars intercerebralis (Davey, 1967), the release of which leads to oviposition. Failure to release the hormone leads to retention of the eggs in the ovary and the release of an antigonadotropin which antagonises the action of JH on the follicle cells (Pratt and Davey, 1972b; Huebner and Davey, 1973; Liu and Davey, 1974). This tidy and internally consistent model, however, is no longer sufficient to explain all of the accumulating facts.

What is the precise relationship between the spermathecal factor and the increase in egg production and oviposition rate? Recent experiments by R.P. Ruegg in this laboratory have confirmed that transplantation of mated spermathecae into virgin females will increase both the total egg production and the rate of oviposition of the recipient to the mated level. However, in a related species *Triatoma infestans*, Mundall and Engelmann (1977) have reported that severing the ventral nerve cord within 12 hours of mating prevents the stimulation of vitellogenesis which normally follows mating. Such experiments are difficult to interpret, if only because it is not known whether the interruption of descending signals is of functional significance. It is worth nothing that the abdominal neurosecretory structures

which produce the antigonadotropin are conspicuously innervated (Davey, 1978), and preliminary nerve section experiments
suggest that these structures may be under nervous inhibition
in mated females. Nevertheless, it is possible that there
is more than one route by which information concerning
matedness is communicated to the brain. The existence
of at least two different mating stimuli is illustrated
by recent work on the mating behaviour of fireflies (Zorn
and Carlson, 1978). Mating in *Photuris versicolor* induces
two sorts of changes in behaviour of females. Firstly,
mated females no longer respond to the triple flashes of
conspecific males. Females mated to sterile males also
exhibit this response. Secondly, during the 3 days following
mating, the females develop the ability to respond to the
double flashes of heterospecific males on which they prey;
they become "femmes fatales". The development of femme
fatale behaviour does not occur when females are mated
to sterile males; transfer of viable spermatozoa to the
spermathecae appears to be essential.

B. *Rate of Oviposition*

    Evidence that egg production and oviposition rate can
be uncoupled in *Rhodnius* is provided by the effects of
various mimics of JH on egg production in *Rhodnius*. While
farnesyl methyl ether appears to stimulate egg production
in a virgin female by virtue of its effect on the neurosecretory cells of the pars intercerebralis and hence on oviposition (Pratt and Davey, 1972b) C18 JH or ZR-515 increase
egg production without affecting oviposition rate (Ruegg
and Davey, 1979). Moreover, the effects of C18 JH and
ZR-515 are discontinuous with respect to dose, suggesting
an indirect effect on egg production. The interpretation
of these varied effects of analogues of JH is difficult
in the face of our ignorance of the structure of JH in
Heteroptera.

    The myotropic hormone, which recent experiments by
F.L. Kriger have demonstrated to emanate from 5 large
neurosecretory cells on either side of the pars intercerebralis, may be released at rather precise times during
the cycle of egg production. Thus, monitoring of the contraction rates of the ovarian muscles through windows in the
abdomens of otherwise intact insects reveals two peaks
of activity in mated females, one immediately following
feeding, and another on the fifth or sixth day after feeding,
when oviposition is normally rising to a peak. In virgin

females the second peak is absent, as it is in females
lacking their neurosecretory cells.

C. *The Control of the Allatum*

The allatum in *Rhodnius* is clearly under inhibitory
central control as it is in many other insects. Thus,
denervating the allatum in *Rhodnius* leads to a very marked
increase in egg production, even in mated females, thereby
paralleling the results obtained by Mundall and Engelmann
(1977) in *Triatoma*. It is not the intention here to discuss
the area of endocrine homeostasis in the reproductive system,
for that is the subject of another review in this volume,
but it is important only to establish that the allatum
is under nervous control at least.

D. *Central Integration*

All of these facts - the central restraint placed on
the allatum, the discontinuous release of the myotropin,
the indirect effect of JH and its analogues, and the suggestion that the abdominal neurosecretory organs which release
antigonadotropin receive at least an inhibitory innervation
- argue powerfully for an unexpected degree of central
integration of information.

It is clear, for example that matedness alone is not
a sufficient stimulus for the second release of the myotropic
hormone, for that occurs in mated females when mature eggs
are present in the ovary. How then is the brain made aware
that mature eggs are present in the ovary? Is this a potential function for ecdysone, which has been shown to have
effects on egg production when fed to adult *Rhodnius* (Garcia
et al, 1979), and which in turn is known to be produced
by the ovaries of other insects (Hagedorn et al, 1975;
Lagueux et al, 1977), and in one species at least by the
follicle cells themselves (Goltzene et al, 1978). The
situation in *Rhodnius* is similar to that in *Glossina austeni*
in which ovulation is under neurosecretory control (Ejezie
and Davey, 1974) and in which both matedness and the presence
of a mature egg in the ovary are required for ovulation/par-
turition (Ejezie and Davey, 1977). It is worth noting
that injections of ecdysone lead to abortion in *Glossina*
(Denlinger, 1975), and that ecdysone has been postulated
to act as a signal to the neurosecretory system in larval
Rhodnius (Steel, 1975).

If the allatum is under nervous control, what role
is there for the antigonadotropin? Once more, the difference
between matedness and virginity is only expressed after
the first wave of eggs has been made, resulting in an accumulation of mature eggs in the pedicels of unmated females
(Pratt and Davey, 1972b). A release of antigonadotropin
as a result of the stretching of the ovaries has been invoked
to explain the abrupt inhibition of vitellogenesis in the
virgin female (Pratt and Davey, 1972b; Davey, 1978), but
the fact that the abdominal neurosecretory organs are innervated suggests a possible role for central control of the
organs. While circumstantial evidence suggests that the
corpus allatum may remain at least partially active in
virgin females (Pratt and Davey, 1972b), direct evidence
concerning the relative roles of JH and antigonadotropin
will have to await reliable methods for the assay of these
two hormones in the haemolymph.

If there are many unanswered questions about the integrated control of function in the female system, our knowledge
of analogous phenomena in the male is even more rudimentary.
In *Rhodnius*, it has been known for many years that the
corpus allatum governs the growth of the accessory glands,
such that glands in males allatectomised early in adult
life do not develop fully (Wigglesworth, 1936d). In Lepidoptera, the male accessory glands store huge quantities of
JH (Dahm *et al*, 1976). In *Rhodnius*, the accessory glands
produce the spermatophore (Davey, 1959), and this structure
probably represents a substantial amount of protein. Presumably the rate of synthesis of the secretion is under the
control of JH, and the rate of synthesis will be higher
in a recently or newly emerged male than in one which has
not mated. This implies the possibility of a control over
the allatum which may be as complex as that in the female.
But, like much else in this essay, this is only conjecture;
the system awaits exploitation.

REFERENCES

Abu-Hakima, R., and Davey, K.G. (1975). Two actions of
     juvenile hormone on the follicle cells of *Rhodnius
     prolixus*. *Can. J. Zool.* *53*, 1187-1188.

Abu-Hakima, R., and Davey, K.G. (1977a). The action of juvenile hormone on the follicle cells of *Rhodnius prolixus*: the importance of volume changes. *J. Exp. Biol. 69*, 33-44.

Abu-Hakima, R., and Davey, K.G. (1977b). Effects of hormones and inhibitors of macromolecular synthesis on the follicle cells of *Rhodnius*. *J. Insect Physiol. 23*, 913-917.

Abu-Hakima, R., and Davey, K.G. (1979). A possible relationship between ouabain-sensitive ($Na^+ - K^+$) dependent ATPase and the effect of juvenile hormone on the follicle cells of *Rhodnius prolixus*. *Insect Biochem. 9*, 195-198.

Anderson, L.M., and Telfer, W.H. (1970). Extracellular concentrating of proteins in the cecropia moth follicle. *J. Cell. Physiol. 65*, 37-54.

Anderson, L.M. (1971). Protein synthesis and uptake by isolated cecropia oocytes. *J. Cell. Sci. 8*, 735-750.

Bell, W.J., and Sams, G.R. (1974). Factors promoting vitellogenic competence and yolk deposition in the cockroach ovary: the post-ecdysial female. *J. Insect Physiol. 20*, 2475-2485.

Brown, E.H. and King, R.G. (1964). Studies on the events resulting in the formation of an egg chamber in *Drosophila melanogaster*. *Growth. 28*, 41-91.

Buxton, P.A. (1930). The biology of a blood-sucking bug, *Rhodnius prolixus*. *Trans. Roy. Ent. Soc. Lond. 78 (Pt. II)*, 227-236.

Buning, J. (1978). Development of telotrophic-meroistic ovarioles of polyphage beetles with special reference to the formation of nutritive cords. *J. Morph. 156*, 237-256.

Case, D.C. (1970), "Postembryonic Development of the Ovary of *Rhodnius prolixus*." M.Sc. Thesis, McGill University, Montreal, Canada.

Colhoun, E.H. (1963). Synthesis of 5-hydroxytryptamine in the american cockroach. *Experientia. 19*, 1-4.

Dahm, K.H., Bhaskaran, G., Peter, M.G., Shirk, P.D., Seshan, K.R., and Roller, H. (1976). On the identity of juvenile hormone in insects. In "The Juvenile Hormones" (L.I. Gilbert, ed.). Plenum Press, New York, U.S.A. pp. 19-47.

Davey, K.G. (1958). The migration of spermatozoa in the female tract of Rhodnius prolixus. J. Exp. Biol. 35. 694-701.

Davey, K.G. (1959). Spermatophore production in Rhodnius prolixus. Quart. J. Micr. Sci. 100, 221-230.

Davey, K.G. (1960). A pharmacologically active agent in the reproductive system of insects. Can. J. Zool. 38, 39-45.

Davey, K.G. (1965). Copulation and egg production in Rhodnius prolixus: the role of the spermathecae. J. Exp. Biol. 42, 373-378.

Davey, K.G. (1967). Some consequences of copulation in Rhodnius prolixus. J. Insect Physiol. 13, 1629-1636.

Davey, K.G. (1978). Hormonal stimulation and inhibition in the ovary of an insect, Rhodnius prolixus. In "Comparative Endocrinology" (P.J. Gaillard and H.H. Boer, eds.). pp. 13-16: Elsevier/North Holland Biomedical Press, Amsterdam.

Davey, K.G., and Huebner, E. (1974). The response of the follicle cells of Rhodnius prolixus to juvenile hormone and antigonadotropin in vitro. Can. J. Zool. 52, 1407-1412.

Denlinger, D. (1975). Insect hormone as tsetse abortifacients. Nature. 253, 347-348.

Dewitz, J. (1886). Ueber der Setzmussigkeit in der Ortsveranderung der Spermatozooen und in der Vereinigung derselben mit dem Ei. Archiv. ges. Physiol. 1886, 358-392.

Dumser, J.B. (1974). "Control of Spermatogenesis in Rhodnius prolixus." Ph.D. Thesis, McGill University, Montreal, Canada.

Dumser, J.B. (1980a). The regulation of spermatogenesis in insects. Ann. Rev. Ent. 25, 341-369.

Dumser, J.B. (1980b). *In vitro* effects of ecdysterone on the spermatogonial cell cycle in *Locusta*. *Int. J. Invert. Reprod. in the press*.

Dumser, J.B., and Davey, K.G. (1974). Endocrinological and other factors influencing testis development in *Rhodnius prolixus*. *Can. J. Zool. 52*, 1011-1022.

Dumser, J.B., and Davey, K.G. (1975a). The *Rhodnius* testis: hormones, differentiation of the germ cells, and duration of the moulting cycle. *Can. J. Zool. 53*, 1673-1681.

Dumser, J.B., and Davey, K.G. (1975b). The *Rhodnius* testis: hormonal effects on germ cell division. *Can. J. Zool. 52*, 1682-1689.

Ejezie, G.C., and Davey, K.G. (1974). Changes in the neuro-secretory cells, corpus cardiacum, and corpus allatum during pregnancy in *Glossina austeni* Newst. *Bull. Ent. Res. 64*, 247-256.

Ejezie, G.C., and Davey, K.G. (1976). Some effects of allatectomy in the female tsetse, *Glossina austeni*. *J. Insect. Physiol. 22*, 1743-1749.

Ejezie, G.C., and Davey, K.G. (1977). Some effects of mating in female tsetse, *Glossina austeni*. *J. Exp. Zool. 22*, 303-310.

Friedel, T., and Gillot, C. (1977). Contribution of male-produced proteins to vitellogenesis in *Melanoplus sanguinipes*. *J. Insect Physiol. 23*, 145-152.

Garcia, M.L.M., Mello, R.P., and Garcia, E.S. (1979). Ecdysone, juvenile hormone and oogenesis in *Rhodnius prolixus*. *J. Insect Physiol. 25*, 695-700.

Goltzene, F., Lagueux, M., Charlet, M., and Hoffmann, J.A. (1978). The follicle cell epithelium of maturing ovaries of *Locusta migratoria*: a new biosynthetic tissue for ecdysone. *Hoppe-Seyler's Z. Physiol. Chem. 359*, 1427-1434.

Grinstein, S., and Erlu, D. (1974). Insulin unmasks latent sodium pump sites in frog muscle. *Nature. 251*, 57-58.

Gwadz, R.W., and Spielman, A. (1973). Corpus allatum control of ovarian development in *Aedes aegypti*. *J. Insect Physiol*. *19*, 1441-1448.

Hagedorn, H.H., O'Connor, J.D., Fuchs, M.S., Sage, B., Schlaeger, D.A., and Bohm, M.K. (1975). The ovary as a source of α-ecdysone in an adult mosquito. *Proc. Nat. Acad. Sci. U.S.A.* *72*, 3255-3259.

Huebner, E., and Anderson, E. (1970). The effects of vinblastine sulfate on the microtubular organization of the ovary of *Rhodnius prolixus*. *J. Cell Biol*. *46*, 191-198.

Huebner, E., and Anderson, E. (1972). A cytological study of the ovary of *Rhodnius prolixus*. II. Ooctye differentiation. *J. Morph.37*, 385-416.

Huebner, E., and Anderson, E. (1973). A cytological study of the ovary of *Rhodnius prolixus*. III. Cytoarchitecture and development of the trophic chamber. *J. Morph*. *138*, 1-40.

Huebner, E., and Davey, K.G. (1973). An antigonadotropin from the ovaries of the insect *Rhodnius prolixus*. *Can. J. Zool*. *51*, 113-120.

Huebner, E., Tobe, S.S., and Davey, K.G. (1975). Structural and functional dynamics of oogenesis in *Glossina austeni*: vitellogenesis with special reference to the follicular epithelium. *Tissue and Cell*. 7, 535-558.

Hughes, M., and Davey, K.G. (1969). The activity of spermatozoa of *Periplaneta*. *J. Insect Physiol*. *15*, 1607-1616.

Kambysellis, M.P., and Williams, C.M. (1971a). *In vitro* development of insect tissues. I. A macromolecular factor prerequisite for insect spermatogenesis. *Biol. Bull*. *141*, 527-540.

Kambysellis, M.P. and Williams, C.M. (1971b). *In vitro* development of insect tissues. II. The role of ecdy sone in the spermatogenesis of silkworms. *Biol. Bull*. *141*, 541-552.

Koch, E.A., and King, R.C. (1966). The origin and early differentiation of the egg chamber of *Drosophila melanogaster*. *J. Morph*. *119*, 283-304.

Koch, E.A., and King, R.C. (1969). Further studies on the ring canal system of the ovarian cystocytes of *Drosophila melanogaster*. *Z. Zellforsch. mikrosk. Anat.* *102*, 129-152.

Koch, E.A., Smith, P.A., and King, R.C. (1967). The division and differentiation of *Drosophila* cystocytes. *J. Morph.* *124*, 143-166.

Lagueux, M., Hirn, M., and Hoffman, J.A. (1977). Ecdysone during ovarian development in *Locust migratoria*. *J. Insect Physiol.* *23*, 109-119.

Landureau, J.-C. and Szollosi, A. (1974). Demonstration par la methode de culture *in vitro* der role des hemocytes dans la spermatogenese d'un insecte. *C. R. Acad. Sci. Ser. D.* *278*, 359-62.

Leopold, R.A. (1976). The role of male accessory glands in insect reproduction. *Ann. Rev. Ent.* *21*, 199-221.

Liu, T.P., and Davey, K.G. (1974). Partial characterization of a proposed antigonadotropin from the ovaries of the insect *Rhodnius prolixus*. *Gen. Comp. Endocrinol.* *24*, 405-408.

Mundall, E., and Engelmann, F. (1977). Endocrine control of vitellogenin synthesis and vitellogenesis in *Triatoma infestans*. *J. Insect Physiol.* *23*, 825-836.

Pratt, G.E., and Davey, K.G. (1972a). The corpus allatum and oogenesis in *Rhodnius prolixus*. I. The effects of allatectomy. *J. Exp. Biol.* *56*, 201-214.

Pratt, G.E., and Davey, K.G. (1972b). The corpus allatum and oogenesis in *Rhodnius prolixus*. III. The effect of mating. *J. Exp. Biol.* *56*, 223-237.

Ruegg, R.P., and Davey, K.G. (1979), The effect of C18 juvenile hormone and Altosid in the efficiency of egg production in *Rhodnius prolixus*. *Internat. J. Invert. Reprod.* *1*, 3-8.

Shepherd, J.G. (1974). Sperm activation in saturniid moths: some aspects of the mechanism of activation. *J. Insect Physiol.* *20*, 2321-2328.

Shepherd, J.G. (1975). A polypeptide sperm activator from male saturniid moths. *J. Insect Physiol.* *21*, 9-22.

Steel, C.G.H. (1975). A neuroendocrine feedback mechanism in the insect moulting cycle. *Nature.* *253*, 267-269.

Telfer, W.H. (1975). Development and physiology of the oocyte nurse cell syncytium. *Adv. Insect Physiol.* *11*, 223-319.

Telfer, W.H. (1961). The route of entry and localisation of blood proteins in the oocytes of saturniid moths. *J. Biophys. Biochem. Cytol.* *9*, 747-759.

Updike, J. (1955). V.B. Nimble, V.B. Quick. *New Yorker* April 2, 1955, 36.

Wick, J.R., and Bonhag, P.F. (1955). Postembryonic development of the ovaries of *Oncopeltus fasciatus* (Dallas). *J. Morph.* *96*, 31-60.

Wigglesworth, V.B. (1936d). The function of the corpus allatum in the growth and reproduction of *Rhodnius prolixus* (hemiptera). *Quart. J. Micr. Sci.* *79*, 91-121.

Wigglesworth, V.B. (1943). The fate of haemoglobin in *Rhodnius prolixus* (Hemiptera) and other blood-sucking arthropods. *Proc. Roy. Soc. B.* *131*. 313-339.

Wigglesworth, V.B. (1951b). Insects and human affairs. *Essex Farmer's Journal.* *30*. 25.

Wigglesworth, V.B. (1963b). The juvenile hormone effect of farnesol and some related compounds: quantitative experiments. *J. Ins. Physiol.* *9*, 105-119.

Wigglesworth, V.B. (1964b). The hormonal regulation of growth and reproduction in insects. *Advances in Insect Physiology.* *2*, 247-336.

Zorn, L.P., and Carlson, A.D. (1978). Effect of mating on response of female *Photuris* firefly. *Anim. Behav.* *26*, 843-847.

REGULATION OF THE CORPORA ALLATA IN ADULT FEMALE INSECTS

Stephen S. Tobe

Department of Zoology
University of Toronto
Toronto, Ontario, Canada

"The experiments described earlier in this paper show, among other things, that the corpus allatum of the adult ... may vary in its activities .... That raises the question of control and determination of the normal function of the corpus allatum. It may be that the normal secretory function is ensured only when the integrity of the central nervous system − corpus allatum complex is unbroken and that the timing of the activities of the corpus allatum is controlled by the brain." (Wigglesworth, 1948a).

"One must conclude that the normal regulation (of the corpus allatum) is dependent on its connexion with the central nervous system and that the signal to the corpus allatum to change its secretory activity comes from the brain." (Wigglesworth, 1952d).

These two quotations, from two of the classic papers in insect endocrinology, have provided our laboratory with some of the paradigms used in our studies on the regulation of juvenile hormone biosynthesis by the corpus allatum. In this essay, I will examine some of the evidence for the regulation of corpus allatum activity and the mechanism of regulation. I will also examine some of the future experimental directions which may provide unequivocal data on the regulatory mechanisms of insect endocrine systems.

I. THE CORPUS ALLATUM (CA) AND JUVENILE HORMONE (JH) BIOSYNTHESIS

The corpus allatum (CA) is the defined site of synthesis of juvenile hormone (JH) in those insects studied   (for example, *Hyalophora cecropia* - Röller and Dahm, 1970; *Schistocerca gregaria* - Pratt and Tobe, 1974; *Manduca sexta* - Judy *et al.*, 1973; Reibstein and Law, 1973; *Periplaneta americana* - Müller *et al.*, 1975; Pratt *et al.*, 1975a, b; *Diploptera punctata* - Tobe and Stay, 1977; *Nauphoeta cinerea* - Lanzrein *et al.*, 1975; *Leptinotarsa decemlineata* - Kramer, 1978a; *Tenebrio molitor* - Weaver *et al.*, 1980). The majority of these insects synthesize C_{16}JH as adults (methyl 10R, 11-epoxy-3,7,11-trimethyl-2E,6E-dodecadienoate), although   at least in *Manduca*, *Hyalophora* and *Heliothis*, the CA synthesize the higher homologues of C_{16}JH, i.e. C_{17}JH and C_{18}JH.

A. *Female Reproduction and JH Biosynthesis*

With the possible exception of some Lepidoptera, the CA are necessary for female reproduction. In the absence of CA, oocyte growth and maturation ceases (see Engelmann, 1970 for review). This cessation can occur at either the previtellogenic or vitellogenic stage of oocyte growth, depending upon the species, with the most common blockage occurring at the beginning of the vitellogenic stage. However, to date it has not been possible to demonstrate that JH is responsible for the pinocytotic uptake of vitellogenin. It can only be demonstrated that the CA are required for vitellogenesis. Wigglesworth (1936d) was one of the first workers to realize the importance of the CA in female reproduction but despite the long interval since his observation, the precise mode of action of the hormone remains uncertain. JH is probably necessary for both the synthesis of the yolk protein precursor vitellogenin and its subsequent uptake by the developing oocytes (see Engelmann, this volume). In the absence of CA, complete oocyte maturation and oviposition will occur when females of the viviparous cockroach *Diploptera punctata* are treated with the JH analogue ZR512 (Tobe and Stay, 1979). The analogue is thus a functional mimic of the authentic hormone and since the replacement therapy corrects the hormonal deficiency after allatectomy, this shows that JH is indeed a major regulator of oocyte growth and maturation in *Diploptera*.

1. *Synthesis of Vitellogenin by Males.* The synthesis
and release of vitellogenin from the fat body and the uptake
of vitellogenin by developing oocytes may be processes which
are regulated by different titres of JH; recently we demonstrated that males of *D. punctata* will synthesize vitellogenin when JH titres are effectively raised either by implantation of female CA or by application of ZR512 (Mundall *et al.*,
1979). Vitellogenin is incorporated into implanted oocytes
only in the presence of these exogenous sources of JH. The
threshold titre of JH necessary for induction of vitellogenin
synthesis may be lower than that required for uptake of
vitellogenin by the oocytes (see also Lanzrein *et al.*, 1978).
Vitellogenin occurs in male *Rhodnius* (Chalaye, 1979) which
explains Wigglesworth's (1936d) observation that oocyte maturation in decapitated female *Rhodnius* could be supported by
parabiosis to intact male *Rhodnius.*

B. *Assays for JH Biosynthesis*

It is only in the past five years that it has been
possible to study the regulation of JH synthesis. Prior to
1974, there were no reliable methods for determining the
activity of the CA although transplantation bioassay, hormone
replacement therapy, and CA volume were all used as indicators
of CA activity. However the limitations of these methods
have long been appreciated -- as Wigglesworth (1948a) noted,
"From the standpoint of experimental method, it is obvious
that the transplantation of corpus allatum alone may give a
misleading impression of its function." More recently, we
have demonstrated that at least in *Schistocerca gregaria*,
there is no correlation between CA volume and JH synthesis
(Tobe and Pratt, 1975a); also in *D. punctata*, the use of CA
volume as an indicator of JH synthesis may not be reliable
under experimental conditions (Szibbo, in preparation).

1. *The Radiochemical Assay.* In 1973 and 1974, work at
the University of Sussex led to the development of a simple
and rapid radiochemical assay for JH synthesis *in vitro*
(Pratt and Tobe, 1974; Tobe and Pratt, 1974a). This assay
utilized the fact that in the presence of radiolabelled
methyl-methionine, the molar incorporation ratio for
methionine and farnesenic acid was approximately 1:1 -- in
other words, equimolar quantities of the methyl moiety of
methionine and farnesenic acid were incorporated into C_{16}JH.
Methionine thus is the major source of the methyl group in
the esterification of farnesenic acid (Tobe and Pratt, 1974a;
1976). Accordingly, by following the incorporation of the
radiolabelled methyl moiety of methionine into C_{16}JH, the

precise rate of synthesis of C_{16}JH can be measured. Under
normal circumstances, using ^{14}C-methyl methionine, the sensitivity of this assay is approximately 10^{-13} mol (0.1 pmol)
although this can be extended by almost two orders of magnitude (10^{-15} mol or 1 fmol)with the use of high specific radioactivity ^{3}H-methyl methionine (Hamnett and Pratt, 1978). Using this method, identification of the higher homologues in
the presence of C_{16}JH can be performed, to a ratio of $1:10^{-5}$.
At these levels of sensitivity, measurement of JH synthesis
by individual pairs of CA over short-term incubation periods
can be performed routinely.

For each species investigated, it is important that the
basic parameters for JH synthesis be defined, including
identification of biosynthesized hormone, linearity of JH
synthesis during the incubation period, the relationship
between JH synthesis and release, as well as the influence of
substrate concentrations, pH, incubation media and oxygenation
(see Tobe and Pratt, 1974a; Weaver *et al.*, 1980).

II. THE REGULATION OF JH TITRE BY CA ACTIVITY

A. *Synthesis vs. Breakdown in Control*

In those insects for which reliable data is available
(for example *Diatrea*) (Bergot *et al.*, 1976), the haemolymph
JH titres undergo striking changes during larval life. JH
titres must reflect the net difference between JH biosynthesis
and JH catabolism but their relative contributions to regulation remains uncertain. In no animal has a detailed and
accurate study of both biosynthesis and catabolism been coupled with determinations of JH titre. A major mechanism for
regulation of JH titres in larval insects has been suggested
to be the catabolism of JH in the haemolymph by esterases
(Akamatsu *et al.*, 1975). These authors have suggested that
changes in JH biosynthesis would contribute little to changes
in haemolymph titre. On the other hand, we have suggested
that changes in biosynthesis are a major contributor to
changes in titre (see Stay and Tobe, 1978; Tobe and Stay,
1980). A similar conclusion has been reached by Kramer and
de Kort (1976); de Kort *et al.* (1978) and Kramer (1978a, b).
Several lines of evidence support this view:
   i. large changes in rates of JH biosynthesis occur during
      oocyte maturation (Tobe and Pratt, 1975b; Tobe and Stay,
      1977; Weaver and Pratt, 1977);
  ii. implantation of supernumerary CA or unilateral allatect-
      omy exert profound effects on rates of oocyte maturation
      (Stay and Tobe, 1977, 1978; Tobe and Stay, 1980);

iii. implantation of supernumerary CA and denervation of CA alters both the time of spermatophore release and oviposition, two probable JH-dependent events (Stay and Tobe, 1978; Tobe and Stay, 1980);

iv. rates of JH synthesis by host CA can be altered dramatically by implantation of supernumerary CA, by unilateral allatectomy or by application of a JH analogue (Stay and Tobe, 1978; Tobe and Stay, 1979, 1980). This suggests that changes in JH titre are monitored by the insect and biosynthesis modified accordingly;

v. male CA with different rates of JH biosynthesis support different degrees of oocyte development when implanted into allatectomized females (Szibbo, Mundall, unpublished);

vi. inhibition of JH biosynthesis by precocene results in suppression of JH-dependent events (Brooks *et al.*, 1979; Masner *et al.*, 1979).

In view of the rapid and profound changes in JH synthesis during oocyte maturation, exclusive regulation of JH titre by JH esterases and/or JH binding proteins (Gilbert *et al.*, 1978) would seem unlikely, particularly in the light of the existence of feedback loops which appear to regulate the CA themselves (Hodkova, 1977; Stay and Tobe, 1978; Tobe and Stay, 1979, 1980; Schooneveld *et al.*, 1979).

B. *Binding Proteins and CA Activity*

The role of JH binding protein in regulation of JH titres is not clear (Gilbert *et al.*, 1978) although the protein can protect JH from degradation, at least at specific times during larval life of Lepidoptera (Sanburg *et al.*, 1975; Gilbert *et al.*, 1978). The question of the responsiveness of the CA or those portions of the CNS which regulate the CA response to the hormone-binding protein complex remains to be resolved. The complex may not be detected by the JH regulatory centres and thus may play no role in the regulation of JH biosynthesis or JH titres. The relatively high affinity but low capacity of JH-binding proteins for JH (Kramer *et al.*, 1974; Gilbert *et al.*, 1978) may indicate a protective but non-regulatory function. However, the existence of high affinity JH-binding proteins in orders other than the Lepidoptera remain to be demonstrated conclusively.

C. *The Relationship Between CA Activity and Oocyte Growth*

Although the roles of JH esterases and JH binding protein in regulation of JH titres cannot be completely defined, there is no doubt that CA are precisely regulated. In *Diploptera*, this regulation is particularly striking and precise, as shown in Fig. 1. At 27°C rearing temperature, the oocytes usually enter vitellogenesis 3-4 days after adult emergence. All oocytes grow at the same rate. Chorion formation is complete by day 7 and oviposition occurs on day 7.9 (Stay and Coop, 1973). The insect is 'pregnant' from the time of oothecal retraction and gestation usually lasts about 63 days (Stay and Coop, 1973). These precise and predictable events make it an ideal species with which to study CA regulation.

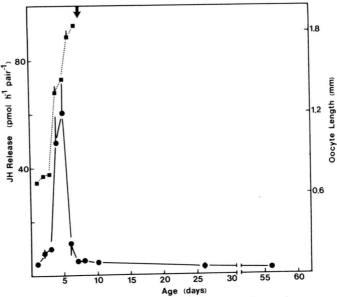

Fig. 1. JH release ● and basal oocyte length ■ as a function of age in D. punctata. The arrow indicates the time of oviposition. (Redrawn from Tobe and Stay, 1977).

Fig. 1 shows that the CA of *D. punctata* undergo changes of up to 10-fold in rate of JH synthesis during the reproductive cycle that correlate closely with oocyte growth (as determined by the lengths of the oocytes) as shown in Fig. 2. The CA are necessary for oocyte growth (see Tobe and Stay, 1979) and vitellogenin synthesis (Mundall *et al.*, 1979) in this species.

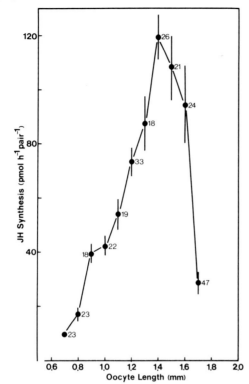

Fig. 2.   JH synthesis (mean ± S.E.M.) as a function of basal oocyte length in D. punctata.   Oocytes enter vitellogenesis at 0.8 mm and complete chorionation at 1.6-1.7 mm. Numerical values show sample sizes for each point.   Data for oocyte lengths were grouped to the nearest 0.1 mm.

III. THE REGULATION OF JH BIOSYNTHESIS

A. Regulation of Biosynthesis as the Major Mechanism of Control

If biosynthesis and release of sesquiterpenoids is regulated by means similar to steroid biosynthesis in vertebrates, it may occur at several levels. One of the most obvious mechanisms is storage of hormone after biosynthesis within the endocrine gland, with release occurring in response to specific signals. However, regulation at the level of release does not occur in *Schistocerca* (Tobe and Pratt, 1974b), *Periplaneta* (Pratt *et al.*, 1975a), *Diploptera* (Tobe and Stay, 1977; Feyereisen, Friedel and Tobe, in preparation); biosynthesized JH can be detected in the incubation medium within 5-10 min of the addition of the radiolabelled methyl donor,

methionine. Release of JH is proportional to biosynthesis
and to intraglandular content. Thus release is unregulated
and hormone probably enters the medium directly by diffusion.

Because JH is released from the CA as soon as it is synthesized, regulation of synthesis must be the major mechanism
controlling the quantity entering the haemolymph. Accordingly,
the activity and/or concentration of critical enzymes in the
biosynthetic pathway probably regulate JH biosynthesis. Rate
limitation in the JH biosynthetic pathway occurs prior to the
final two steps in JH biosynthesis, namely the methylation and
epoxidation of the farnesyl precursor (Pratt and Tobe, 1974;
Tobe and Pratt, 1974a, 1976). The addition of farnesenic acid,
an exogenous precursor of C_{16}JH biosynthesis, to media containing CA stimulates significantly the rate of JH biosynthesis (Tobe and Pratt, 1974a, 1976) and although saturation
of the methyl farnesoate monooxygenase (the enzyme responsible
for epoxidation) has been observed in farnesenic acid-stimu-
lated CA of *Periplaneta* (Pratt *et al.*, 1975b), rate limitation
does not occur at this step. There is no saturation of the
monooxygenase in *Schistocerca* or *Diploptera* (Tobe and Pratt,
1974a, 1976; Feyereisen, Friedel and Tobe, in preparation).

B. *End Product Inhibition*

Inhibition of JH biosynthesis by JH itself has been
suggested as a possible regulatory mechanism as in the conversion of ecdysone to 20-hydroxyecdysone by ecdysone 20-mono-
oxygenase (Feyereisen and Durst, 1978). Although the enzyme
responsible for the terminal step in 20-hydroxyecdysone biosynthesis belongs to the same class as that responsible for
the terminal step in JH biosynthesis, end product inhibition
does not occur in JH biosynthesis. The evidence for the
absence of end product inhibition can be summarized as follows:

i. JH synthesis by *Diploptera* CA continues at a linear rate
   in vitro for at least 24 hr (Stay and Tobe, 1977;
   Feyereisen, Friedel and Tobe, in preparation), in spite
   of the accumulation of JH in the incubation medium;

ii. rates of JH synthesis by CA of *Periplaneta* are virtually
    unaffected by the presence of 10^{-3}M C_{16}JH (Pratt and
    Finney, 1977);

iii. in the presence of 20-30 μM farnesenic acid, rate
     limitation at the final two steps in JH biosynthesis is
     not observed in the CA of *Schistocerca* (Tobe and Pratt,
     1974a, 1976) and *Diploptera* (Feyereisen, Friedel and
     Tobe, in preparation).

This is not to say that JH titres have no effect on JH biosynthesis, but rather that JH titres have no *direct* influence

on the biosynthetic capability of the CA, suggesting that the CA are regulated by factors which originate outside themselves.

C. Feedback Loops and the Regulation of the CA

Regulators of JH synthesis which originate outside the CA may be divided into two groups: the *allatotropic* factors (*allatotropins*) which stimulate or enhance JH biosynthesis, and the *allatostatic* factors (*allatostatins*) which inhibit or reduce JH biosynthesis. Although these elusive factors have been sought for several years, there is little direct evidence for their existence. Much information on these substances has been obtained indirectly, by investigations of regulatory feedback loops.

1. Feedback Control in Larval Growth.
The regulation of CA by feedback loops has been known for at least 30 years. For example, Wigglesworth (1948a) observed that when CA of young adults were implanted in larval *Rhodnius*, a partial premature metamorphosis ensued. He hypothesized that "the effect might be due to the gland (CA) from the maturing insect acting upon the gland (CA) of the young host and weakening its capacity to secrete the juvenile hormone." In fact, much of the evidence presented by Wigglesworth (1948a) strongly suggests the existence of feedback loops which regulate the CA, both implanted and host. He concluded, "it is clear that the functional activity of the corpus allatum is not determined wholly by humoral means; nor is this determination wholly autonomous." "One must conclude that the normal regulation is dependent upon its connexion with the central nervous system and that the signal to the corpus allatum to change its secretory activity comes from the brain." (Wigglesworth, 1952d). The consequences of these feedback loops were realized clearly by Wigglesworth (1948a). As quoted earlier, "From the standpoint of experimental method, it is obvious that the transplantation of the corpus allatum alone may give a misleading impression of its function."

The existence of feedback loops regulating the CA has been confirmed in *Diploptera*, utilizing our direct radiochemical assay for JH synthesis. These feedback loops operate by both humoral and direct nervous means, although the nervous pathways may take precedence over the humoral factors (Tobe and Stay, 1980; see also Hodkova, 1977). The feedback loops involved in CA regulation may be complex, but a picture summarized for *Diploptera* is beginning to emerge.

2. The Importance of Intact Nervous Connection to the CNS.
The integrity of the nerves which innervate the CA and in particular, the *nervi corporis allati* I (NCA I) is necessary

to 'restrain' the activity of the CA of cockroaches
(*Leucophaea maderae* - Scharrer, 1952; Engelmann, 1957;
Periplaneta americana - Fraser and Pipa, 1977; *Diploptera
punctata* - Engelmann, 1959; Stay and Tobe, 1977; Tobe and
Stay, 1980). In *L. maderae* and *D. punctata*, denervation of
CA of pregnant or virgin females results in activation of the
CA (Engelmann, 1957, 1959; Stay and Tobe, 1977). Engelmann's
earlier work utilized oocyte growth as the assay for CA activity and his conclusion on *Diploptera* have been confirmed
using our radiochemical assay. Wigglesworth (1936d) observed
a hypertrophy of CA in larval *Rhodnius* after brain removal,
again suggesting an inhibition of the CA. Denervation of CA
in virgin *Diploptera* mimics mating, causing an abrupt increase
in JH synthesis. This activation is extremely rapid, becoming
apparent within 4 hours of the operation (Stay and Tobe, in
preparation). It is also striking that denervated CA of
virgin females go through a normal cycle of JH synthesis in
association with oocyte growth (Stay and Tobe, 1977). Innervation of the CA is not necessary for either the increase in
JH synthesis at the beginning of the gonotrophic cycle or for
the decline at the end. On the basis of these experiments,
it can be concluded that JH synthesis is normally inhibited by
neural elements which innervate the CA. The nature of this
inhibition remains completely undefined, but it may be mediated neurohormonally (Scharrer, 1964). Potential mechanisms
include:
  i. a direct neurohormonal inhibition of JH synthesis.
 ii. Neurohormonal or neural blocks to release of a stimula-
     tory neurohormone.

   3. *Denervation of CA in the Presence of Elevated JH Titres.*
JH synthesis by innervated CA of normal female and by denervated CA of virgin and mated *Diploptera* show similar patterns
of decline at the completion of oocyte maturation showing that
neural inhibition is not the cause of this natural decline.
(Stay and Tobe, 1977; Tobe and Stay, 1980). However, innervation does permit modulation of JH synthesis in response to
changing JH titres. When supernumerary CA are transplanted
into female *Diploptera* in which the host CA have been denervated, JH synthesis by both pairs of CA is similar and both
resemble that in control animals or in animals with a single
pair of denervated CA, except for two differences: 1. Oviposition and spermatophore release occur significantly earlier
in those animals with two pairs of CA and oocyte growth is
also faster. These data suggest that the effective JH titre
is elevated in the experimental animals. 2. Although rates
of synthesis of JH are similar for both pairs, the peak rates
are lower than the control values (though not significantly).

In the presence of elevated JH titres, a humoral regulator may exert a slight modulatory effect on the CA. This downward modulation in JH synthesis could be mediated by an inhibitory factor or by the absence of a stimulatory factor (Tobe and Stay, 1980).

4. *Innervation of CA in the Presence of Elevated JH Titres.* When a pair of supernumerary CA is transplanted into female *Diploptera* in which the host CA remain innervated, a very different pattern of JH synthesis is observed. JH synthesis by the innervated host CA is suppressed significantly by the presence of the implanted CA although oocyte growth is similar to control animals or to animals with denervated CA (Tobe and Stay, 1980). Thus intact nervous connections between the CA and the CNS are necessary for suppression of JH synthesis, as suggested by Wigglesworth (1948a, 1952d). The CNS of *Diploptera* may be able to monitor JH titres in the haemolymph and compare them to a 'set point' -- when JH titres exceed this set point, JH synthesis is suppressed, either by an inhibitory substance or by a lack of stimulatory substances. From this hypothesis, it can be predicted that when JH titres are below the set point, the CA are stimulated, either by a stimulatory substance or by the lifting of an inhibitory signal or both.

5. *Denervation and Innervation in the Presence of Lowered JH Titres.* Unilateral allatectomy may reduce the rate of oocyte growth and prolong the time to oviposition and spermatophore release (Stay and Tobe, 1978; Tobe and Stay, 1980), when compared to normal animals. Thus JH titres have probably been lowered in unilaterally allatectomized animals. However, one CA is capable of synthesizing JH at rates approaching those of two CA (Tobe and Stay, 1980; Schooneveld *et al.*, 1979) suggesting that when JH titres are below the set point, a negative feedback loop operates via the CNS to stimulate JH biosynthesis.

Innervated single CA synthesize JH at rates similar to a pair of CA, although there is a time lag of 24-48 hours for peak rates of JH synthesis by single CA (Tobe and Stay, 1980). Denervation of the single CA in unilateral allatectomized animals results in a pattern of JH synthesis similar to that in their innervated counterparts. This suggests that any inhibitory signals which suppress JH synthesis have been removed when JH titres are below the set point. But is JH synthesis stimulated under these circumstances? Such a possibility appears likely because:

i. rates of JH synthesis per CA must double in unilateral allatectomized animals i.e. one CA must make as much JH as a pair of normal CA;

ii. denervation of CA in normal animals may cause a slight
    stimulation in JH synthesis (Stay and Tobe, 1977; Tobe
    and Stay, 1980).
Although JH synthesis may be normally suppressed, complete
removal of the inhibitory signals (by denervation) does not
result in a statistically significant stimulation (and certainly not a doubling). Thus the increase in the rate of JH
synthesis in animals with one CA is a result both of lifting
inhibitory signals and direct stimulation.

   6. Elevation of JH Titres With JH Analogue. We have
investigated further the effect of apparent elevated JH titres
on JH synthesis through the topical application of the JH
analogue ZR512 (Tobe and Stay, 1979). This analogue supports
complete oocyte maturation, spermatophore release and oviposition in allatectomized animals and is a complete mimic
of $C_{16}JH$.

   a. Evidence for negative and positive feedback loops.
High doses of ZR512 suppress the cycle of JH synthesis in a
dose-dependent fashion whereas lower doses (2.5 µg per
animal) actually stimulate JH synthesis (Tobe and Stay, 1979).
The most significant stimulation of JH synthesis occurs 4 days
after emergence, when rates of JH synthesis increase rapidly
(Tobe and Stay, 1979). Thus positive, as well as negative
feedback loops, may regulate JH synthesis during the gonotrophic cycle. Positive feedback would increase the rate of
synthesis, with increasing titres of JH stimulating more
synthesis until the set point. Deviations from the set point
would then modulate synthesis by negative feedback until the
JH monitoring centre(s) become unresponsive.

D. The Ovary as a Regulator of JH Synthesis

   From the foregoing discussion, it is clear that both
allatotropic and allatostatic factors regulate JH synthesis.
The CNS is the mediator of these stimulatory and inhibitory
responses, but not necessarily the primary source of these
factors. Wigglesworth (1936d) observed that female *Rhodnius*
will mature oocytes in the absence of the brain, but with the
CA intact. Nonetheless, signals from the CNS are probably
responsible for the *normal* functioning of the CA in the adult
female.

   1. The Effect of Ovariectomy on JH Synthesis. Target
organs, such as the ovary, are logical sources of regulatory
signals. JH has been implicated clearly in uptake of vitellogenin by developing oocytes (see Davey, this volume) and in

the previtellogenic growth of oocytes of some species (see, for example, Gwadz and Spielman, 1973; Tobe and Pratt, 1975b; Weaver and Pratt, 1977). But can signals from the ovary influence JH synthesis? Certainly in *Diploptera*, the presence of the ovary is required for the normal cycle of synthesis (Stay and Tobe, 1978; in preparation). Ovariectomy of adults causes a rapid decline in JH synthesis whereas ovariectomy of last instar nymphs abolishes the normal cycle and suppresses JH synthesis in adults (Stay and Tobe, 1978). The ovary thus plays a permissive role in the regulation of JH synthesis in adults. But these results may also indicate that the ovary is the source of a trophic factor which stimulates JH synthesis. Recent experiments suggest that the latter interpretation may in fact be correct. Implantation of ovaries into ovariectomized females showing low rates of JH synthesis (8 days old; see Fig. 1) evokes a rapid increase in JH synthesis and maturation of oocytes in the implanted ovary (Tobe and Stay, in preparation). Clearly the ovary exerts a stimulatory effect on the CA; this is reminiscent of the trophic effect which vertebrate ovaries exert on the hypothalamic-hypophyseal system.

Although the ovary is in part responsible for the increase in JH synthesis associated with oocyte growth, the situation is more complex because this stimulation is also observed in CA implanted into males (Stay *et al.*, 1980). CA from newly emerged (day 0) females implanted into males show an apparently normal increase in JH synthesis, with a peak on days 5-6. However, JH synthesis does not decrease to the low levels associated with the completion of the gonotrophic cycle in normal females (Stay *et al.*, 1980). But a large decline in JH synthesis at the end of the cycle *is* observed if ovaries are implanted into the males at the same time as female CA. This decline is associated with the completion of maturation of oocytes in the implanted ovary (Stay *et al.*, 1980) (see Fig. 3).

2. Ecdysteroids as Regulators of JH Synthesis. The large decline in JH synthesis in the presence of the ovary at the end of the gonotrophic cycle provides strong evidence for a regulatory role for the ovary in suppressing JH synthesis. This suppression must act via a humoral pathway because the implanted ovaries are not innervated, but the identity of the compounds is unknown. However, one of these allatostatic agents may be an ecdysteroid. The ovary of *Diploptera* contains ecdysteroids (Stay, in preparation), particularly during the later stages of oocyte maturation, in common with other cockroach species (Nijhout and Koeppe, 1978; Bullière *et al.*, 1979). In *Blaberus*, ecdysteroids can be detected in the haemolymph and reach maximal levels just before oviposition

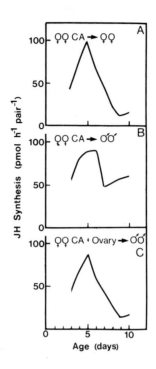

Fig. 3. Diagrammatic representation of effect of 'environment' on JH synthesis. A) 0 day female CA implanted into 0 day females; B) 0 day female CA implanted into 0 day males; C) 0 day female CA plus ovary implanted into 0 day males. (Data from Stay and Tobe, 1977, Stay et al., 1980 and Tobe and Stay, 1980.)

(Bullière *et al.*, 1979). Injection of ecdysterone into male *Diploptera* containing female CA inhibits JH synthesis by these CA in a dose-dependent fashion and mimics the effect of the implanted ovary (Stay *et al.*, 1980). This effect of ecdysterone is indirect because there is no inhibition of JH synthesis *in vitro* by 1 x 10^{-5}M ecdysterone (Friedel, Feyereisen, Mundall and Tobe, in preparation). Whether ecdysteroids operate to shut down JH synthesis in females at the end of the gonotrophic cycle remains to be determined. However, injections of ecdysterone into females suppress JH synthesis and oocyte growth (Friedel, Feyereisen, Mundall and Tobe, in preparation). Ecdysterone therefore may be a natural regulator of JH synthesis *in vivo* in female *Diploptera* and may be responsible in part for the decline in JH synthesis at the end

of the gonotrophic cycle. This provides a hitherto undescribed function for ecdysteroids in adult females.

IV. ALLATOTROPINS AND ALLATOSTATINS

Taking all the evidence presented above into consideration,
the following scheme for regulation of JH synthesis during the
gonotrophic cycle in female *Diploptera* is proposed:
  i. JH synthesis is stimulated by a trophic factor from the
     ovary;
 ii. positive feedback causes a rapid increase in JH synth-
     esis, possibly by stimulating release of an allatotropin
     from the CNS;
iii. negative feedback maintains JH synthesis at a high rate
     during the period of most active vitellogenesis;
 iv. cessation of trophic signals from the ovary as oocytes
     approach maturity cause a decline in JH synthesis;
  v. release of ecdysteroids from the ovary further suppresses
     JH synthesis, possibly by acting through the CNS, i.e.
     by preventing allatotropin release or by stimulating
     release of allatostatins;
 vi. re-establishment of 'neural' inhibition, operating via
     the NCA I and in combination with the absence of the
     ovarian trophic factor, results in the continued
     suppression of JH synthesis during gestation.
The existence of both allatotropins and allatostatins originating in the CNS remains uncertain. The occurrence of allatotropins in the brain of larval *Galleria mellonella* has been
proposed (Granger and Sehnal, 1974; Sehnal and Granger, 1975)
although Pipa (1977) has suggested these experiments demonstrate a prothoracotropin rather than an allatotropin. However, the evidence presented in this essay strongly suggest
that such regulatory substances do exist; the precise regulation of the CA both during the gonotrophic cycle of *Diploptera*
and under conditions of altered JH titre is perhaps the most
telling evidence in favour of their existence. The difficulty
in establishing an assay system for these substances remains
the major problem with their isolation and identification.
Simple incubations of brains with CA *in vitro* may not be an
appropriate experimental approach for the following reasons:
  i. the duration of exposure required for responses of the
     CA is unknown;
 ii. the absence of responses by the CA does not necessarily
     indicate that the regulatory substances are absent;
iii. other tissues may mediate the responses of the CA to
     the regulators *in vivo*;
 iv. the ability of denervated CA to respond to regulators

may be altered;
v. the time required for responses to regulators may exceed
   the time over which JH synthesis is linear.
The ratio of *de novo* JH synthesis to JH synthesis in the presence of exogenous precursors such as farnesenic acid (the
fractional endocrine activity ratio, FEAR -- see Tobe and
Pratt, 1976) may reveal the precise times and rate limiting
steps for allatostatic and allatotrophic activities
(Feyereisen, Friedel and Tobe, in preparation) and may provide
an assay system for these substances.

V. REGULATION OF THE CA IN RELATION TO REPRODUCTIVE MODE

The CA of *Diploptera* are precisely regulated during adult
life, a degree of regulation that no doubt reflects the mode
of reproduction of this animal -- viviparity -- probably
because the presence of JH at inappropriate times disrupts the
reproductive process (Stay, personal communication). It is of
interest to examine the precision of CA regulation in other
insect species showing different reproductive modes.

A. *Oviparity, Ovoviviparity and Viviparity*

In the cockroaches (Dictyoptera), a complete range of
reproductive modes can be seen, from oviparity to ovoviviparity to viviparity. Although CA regulation has been studied
in few insect species, it is fortuitous that representatives
of each of these reproductive modes have been utilized.

1. Oviparity. In *Periplaneta americana*, an oviparous
species, CA undergo cyclic changes in JH synthesis, with the
number of peaks corresponding to the number of batches of
oocytes formed (Weaver *et al.*, 1975; Weaver and Pratt, 1977).
Nonetheless, it is difficult to show a functional correspondence between CA activity and the maturation of any given
batch of oocytes, in part because both basal and penultimate
oocytes are vitellogenic at the same time and in part because
batches of oocytes are continuously produced. However, the
basal oocytes grow in synchrony in this species and accordingly, discrete cycles of JH synthesis can be observed (Weaver
and Pratt, 1977). CA show a difference in activity (between
minimum and maximum JH synthesis) of 3-6 fold during each
cycle.

2. Ovoviviparity. *Nauphoeta cinerea* is an ovoviviparous
cockroach in which basal oocytes grow synchronously.

Developing embryos are retained in the brood sac until gestation is complete and during this period, no additional oocytes
are matured. The CA of *Nauphoeta* show a cycle of JH synthesis
associated with the gonotrophic cycle, with maximal rate of JH
synthesis occurring during this period of rapid ovarian growth
(Lanzrein *et al.*, 1978). This correspondence is more obvious
in this species because only one batch of oocytes is matured
for each pregnancy cycle. The CA show at least 10-fold differences in activity during the gonotrophic cycle (Lanzrein
et al., 1978).

   3. Viviparity. Diploptera punctata, a viviparous cockroach, also matures oocytes synchronously. The developing
embryos are incubated in the brood sac and the next wave of
oocytes become vitellogenic just before parturition (Roth and
Stay, 1961). The CA of *Diploptera* show a cycle of activity
precisely correlated with oocyte growth and maturation (see
Fig. 1). The middle period of vitellogenic growth (oocyte
lengths - 1.3-1.5 mm) is associated with the highest rates of
JH synthesis (Fig. 2) and the CA show 10-fold differences in
activity during the gonotrophic cycle.

B. *CA Regulation, Synchrony of Oocyte Growth and Continuity of Oocyte Production*

   In both *Nauphoeta* and *Diploptera*, there is a close correspondence between oocyte growth and JH synthesis, although only
for *Diploptera* has oocyte size been plotted as a function of
JH synthesis (Fig. 2). The relationship for *Periplaneta*
remains to be determined (Weaver and Pratt, 1977). Nonetheless all three species show synchronous oocyte growth and the
principal difference between their reproductive modes is
simply that *P. americana* produces batches of oocytes
continuously whereas in *N. cinerea* and *D. punctata*, each wave
of oocyte maturation is followed by a prolonged period of
ovarian 'quiescence'. The CA of all three species may be
regulated by similar mechanisms and thus the model proposed
above for the regulation of the CA of *D. punctata* may be
applicable to other cockroach species.
   It is instructive to look outside the Dictyoptera at other
reproductive strategies and mechanisms for regulation of CA in
order to appreciate the relationship between reproductive mode
and mechanisms for CA regulation. *Schistocerca gregaria* shows
some similarity to *P. americana* in that oocyte production is
both synchronous and continuous. However, CA regulation in
Schistocerca occurs in a very different fashion -- in this
species, the CA are not restrained by inhibitory signals from
the CNS. Rather, the CA may be regulated simply by the

presence or absence of an allatotropin which reaches the CA
by the nervous tracts (Tobe *et al.*, 1977). Although
Schistocerca CA show some cyclic activity associated with the
gonotrophic cycles, the relationship is imprecise (Tobe and
Pratt, 1975b) and certainly less precise than that seen in
cockroaches. Thus the CA of *Schistocerca* may not be regulated
precisely and this lack of precision may stem simply from the
mechanism of regulation -- endocrine glands regulated simply
by the presence or absence of trophic factors cannot exhibit
the precision of regulation shown by glands which are controlled by additional mechanisms (for example, neural inhibition and inhibition and stimulation by ovarian factors).
Although the regulation of CA by the presence or absence of an
allatotropin is simple, it is nonetheless effective, and permits control by negative feedback loops. No doubt this mechanism operates *in part* to regulate the CA of cockroaches.
However, the brief period of high CA activity followed by
periods of inactivity observed in the ovoviviparous and viviparous cockroaches probably requires a more complex regulatory
mechanism and for this reason, 'restraining' signals and more
complex trophic regulators may be necessary. But for
Schistocerca, a simple on-off signal may be sufficient and
correlates well with the continuous but synchronous production
of oocytes.

In *Tenebrio molitor*, oocytes develop asynchronously and
continuously and the regulation of CA activity in these
animals may be even less precise than in *Schistocerca*
(Weaver *et al.*, 1980). This is hardly surprising because the
continuous production of oocytes would require the continued
presence of JH. Accordingly, once the CA have been activated,
they may remain in this state for the duration of the reproductive period. No regulatory mechanisms would be necessary,
except under conditions of stress.

It appears that the degree of regulation of the CA can be
associated with at least two aspects of the reproductive mode:
  i. degree of synchrony in oocyte growth and maturation;
 ii. the interval between successive gonotrophic cycles.
Thus insects which exhibit a high degree of synchrony in
oocyte maturation also show cyclic changes in JH synthesis
which correlate with oocyte growth and maturation. Presumably,
the cyclic appearance (and disappearance) of JH would tend to
synchronize oocyte development. However, the ovulation of
oocytes as they complete maturation and the immediate entry of
the former penultimate oocytes into vitellogenesis (Tobe,
1977) would tend to mask declines in JH synthesis associated
with the completion of the gonotrophic cycle. Accordingly,
in those insects which reproduce continuously but synchronously (i.e. the interval between successive gonotrophic cycles
is short), the cyclical changes in JH synthesis are not as

clear-cut as in those insects which show periods of ovarian 'quiescence'.

Studies on the regulation of the CA in adult insects are revealing surprising similarities between insects with similar reproductive modes and equally surprising, are beginning to reveal the remarkable similarity between regulation of endocrine glands in insects and in vertebrates. The feedback loops which operate between the hypothalamus, anterior pituitary and ovary may have an exact counterpart in insects. Future research may provide the data necessary for the development of novel regulators of reproductive processes in insects in the same fashion as such information has already been utilized in vertebrates.

REFERENCES

Akamatsu, Y., Dunn, P., Kezdy, F., Kramer, K., Law, J. H., Reibstein, D., and Sanburg, L. (1975). *In* "Control Mechanisms in Development" (R. Meintz and E. Davies, eds.), pp. 123-149, Plenum, New York.

Bergot, J. B., Schooley, D. A., Chippendale, G. M., and Yin, C.-M. (1976). Juvenile hormone titer determinations in the southwestern corn borer, *Diatraea grandiosella*, by electron capture-gas chromatography. *Life Sci. 18*, 811-820.

Brooks, G. T., Pratt, G. E., and Jennings, R. C. (1979). The action of precocene in milkweed bugs (*Oncopeltus fasciatus*) and locusts (*Locusta migratoria*). *Nature 281*, 570-572.

Bullière, D., Bullière, F., and de Reggi, M. (1979). Ecdysteroid titres during ovarian and embryonic development in *Blaberus craniifer*. *Whilhelm Roux's Arch. Devl. Biol. 186*, 103-114.

Chalaye, D. (1979). Étude immunochimique des protéines hémolymphatiques et ovocytaires de *Rhodnius prolixus* (Stål.). *Can. J. Zool. 57*, 329-336.

Engelmann, F. (1957). Die Steuerung der Ovarfunkton bei der ovoviviparen Schabe *Leucophaea maderae* (Fabr.). *J. Insect Physiol. 1*, 257-278.

Engelmann, F. (1959). The control of reproduction in *Diploptera punctata* (Blattaria). *Biol. Bull. 116*, 406-419.

Engelmann, F. (1970). "The Physiology of Insect Reproduction" Pergamon Press, Oxford.

Feyereisen, R., and Durst, F. (1978). Ecdysterone biosynthesis: A microsomal cytochrome-*P*-450-linked ecdysone 20-monooxygenase from tissues of the African migratory locust. *Eur. J. Biochem. 88*, 37-47.

Fraser, J., and Pipa, R. (1977). Corpus allatum regulation during the metamorphosis of *Periplaneta americana*: Axon pathways. *J. Insect Physiol. 23*, 975-984.

Gilbert, L. I., Goodman, W., and Granger, N. (1978). Regulation of juvenile hormone titer in Lepidoptera. *In* "Comparative Endocrinology" (P. J. Gaillard and H. H. Boer, eds.), pp. 471-486, Elsevier, North-Holland.

Granger, N. A., and Sehnal, F. (1974). Regulation of larval corpora allata in *Galleria mellonella*. *Nature 251*, 415-417.

Gwadz, R. W., and Spielman, A. (1973). Corpus allatum control of ovarian development in *Aedes aegypti*. *J. Insect Physiol. 19*, 1441-1448.

Hamnett, A. F., and Pratt, G. E. (1978). Use of automated capillary column radio gas chromatography in the identification of insect juvenile hormones. *J. Chromat. 158*, 387-399.

Hodkova, M. (1977). Function of the neuroendocrine complex in diapausing *Pyrrhocoris apterus* females. *J. Insect Physiol. 23*, 23-28.

Judy, K. J., Schooley, D. A., Dunham, L. L., Hall, M. S., Bergot, B. J., and Siddall, J. B. (1973). Isolation, structure, and absolute configuration of a new natural insect juvenile hormone from *Manduca sexta*. *Proc. Nat. Acad. Sci. 70*, 1509-1513.

de Kort, C. A. D., Kramer, S. J., and Wieten, M. (1978). Regulation of juvenile titres in the adult colorado beetle: Interaction with carboxylesterases and carrier proteins. *In* "Comparative Endocrinology" (P. J. Gaillard and H. H. Boer, eds.), pp. 507-510, Elsevier, North-Holland.

Kramer, K. J., Sanburg, L. L., Kezdy, F. J., and Law, J. H. (1974). The juvenile hormone binding protein in the hemolymph of *Manduca sexta* Johannson (Lepidoptera: Sphingidae). *Proc. Nat. Acad. Sci. 71*, 493-497.

Kramer, S. J., and de Kort, C. A. D. (1976). Some properties of hemolymph esterases from *Leptinotarsa decemlineata* Say. *Life Sci. 19*, 211-218.

Kramer, S. J. (1978a). Age-dependent changes in corpus allatum activity *in vitro* in the adult Colorado potato beetle, *Leptinotarsa decemlineata*. *J. Insect Physiol. 24*, 461-464.

Kramer, S. J. (1978b). Regulation of the activity of JH-specific esterases in the Colorado potato beetle, *Leptinotarsa decemlineata*. *J. Insect Physiol. 24*, 743-747.

Lanzrein, B., Hashimoto, M., Parmakovich, V., Nakanishi, K., Wilhelm, R., and Lüscher, M. (1975). Identification and quantification of juvenile hormones from different developmental stages of the cockroach *Nauphoeta cinerea*. *Life Sci. 16*, 1271-1284.

Lanzrein, B., Gentinetta, V., Fehr, R., and Lüscher, M. (1978). Correlation betwen haemolymph juvenile hormone titre, corpus allatum volume, and corpus allatum *in vivo* and *in vitro* activity during oocyte maturation in a cockroach (*Nauphoeta cinerea*). *Gen. Comp. Endocrinol. 36*, 339-345.

Masner, P., Bowers, W. S. Kälin, M., and Mühle, T. (1979). Effect of precocene II on the endocrine regulation of development and reproduction in the bug, *Oncopeltus fasciatus*. *Gen. Comp. Endocrinol. 37*, 156-166.

Müller, P. J., Masner, P., Trautmann, K. H., Suchy, M., and Wipf, H.-K. (1975). The isolation and identification of juvenile hormone from cockroach corpora allata *in vitro*. *Life Sci. 15*, 915-921.

Mundall, E. C., Tobe, S. S., and Stay, B. (1979). Induction of vitellogenin and growth of implanted oocytes in male cockroaches. *Nature 282*, 97-98.

Nijhout, M. M., and Koeppe, J. K. (1978). Ovarian-produced steroid in *Leucophaea maderae*. *Am. Zool. 18*, 626.

Pipa, R. L. (1977). Do the brains of wax moth larvae secrete an allatotropic hormone? *J. Insect Physiol. 23*, 103-107.

Pratt, G. E., and Finney, J. R. (1977). Chemical inhibitors of juvenile hormone biosynthesis *in vitro*. *In* "Crop Protection Agents" (N. R. McFarlane, ed.), pp. 113-132, Academic Press, London.

Pratt, G. E., and Tobe, S. S. (1974). Juvenile hormone radiobiosynthesised by corpora allata of adult female locusts *in vitro*. *Life Sci. 14*, 575-586.

Pratt, G. E., Tobe, S. S., Weaver, R. J., and Finney, J. R. (1975a). Spontaneous synthesis and release of C_{16} juvenile hormone by isolated corpora allata of female locust *Schistocerca gregaria* and female cockroach *Periplaneta americana*. *Gen. Comp. Endocrinol. 26*, 478-484.

Pratt, G. E., Tobe, S. S., and Weaver, R. J. (1975b). Relative oxygenase activities in juvenile hormone biosynthesis of corpora allata of an African locust (*Schistocerca gregaria*) and American cockroach (*Periplaneta americana*). *Experientia 31*, 120-122.

Reibstein, D., and Law, J. H. (1973). Enzymatic synthesis of insect juvenile hormone. *Biochem. Biophy. Res. Comm. 55*, 266-272.

Röller, H., and Dahm, K. H. (1970). The identity of juvenile hormone produced by corpora allata *in vitro*. *Naturwiss. 57*, 454-455.

Roth, L. M., and Stay, B. (1961). Oocyte development in *Diploptera punctata* (Eschscholtz) (Blattaria). *J. Insect Physiol. 7*, 186-202.

Sanburg, L. L., Kramer, K. J., Kezdy, F. J., Law, J. H., and Oberlander, H. (1975). Role of juvenile hormone esterases and carrier proteins in insect development. *Nature 253*, 266-272.

Scharrer, B. (1952). Neurosecretion. XI. The effects of nerve section on the intercerebralis-cardiacum-allatum system of the insect *Leucophaea maderae*. *Biol. Bull. 102*, 261-272.

Scharrer, B. (1964). Histophysiological studies on the corpus allatum of *Leucophaea maderae*. IV. Ultrastructure during normal activity cycle. *Z. Zellforsch. 62*, 125-148.

Schooneveld, H., Kramer, S. J., Privee, H., and van Huis, A. (1979). Evidence of controlled corpus allatum activity in the adult Colorado beetle. *J. Insect Physiol. 25*, 449-453.

Sehnal, F., and Granger, N. A. (1975). Control of corpora allata function in larvae of *Galleria mellonella*. *Biol. Bull. 148*, 106-116.

Stay, B., and Coop, A. (1973). Developmental stages and chemical composition in embryos of the cockroach, *Diploptera punctata*, with observation on the effect of diet. *J. Insect Physiol. 19*, 147-171.

Stay, B., and Tobe, S. S. (1977). Control of juvenile hormone biosynthesis during the reproductive cycle of a viviparous cockroach. I. Activation and inhibition. *Gen. Comp. Endocrinol. 33*, 531-540.

Stay, B., and Tobe, S. S. (1978). Control of juvenile hormone biosynthesis during the reproductive cycle of a viviparous cockroach. II. Effects of unilateral allatectomy, implantation of supernumerary corpora allata, and ovariectomy. *Gen. Comp. Endocrinol. 34*, 276-286.

Stay, B., Friedel, T., Tobe, S. S., and Mundall, E. C. (1980). Feedback control of juvenile hormone synthesis in cockroaches: Possible role for ecdysterone. *Science 207*, 898-900.

Tobe, S. S. (1977). Inhibition of growth in developing oocytes of the desert locust. *Experientia 33*, 343-345.

Tobe, S. S., and Pratt, G. E. (1974a). The influence of substrate concentrations on the rate of insect juvenile hormone biosynthesis by corpora allata of the desert locust *in vitro*. *Biochem. J. 144*, 107-113.

Tobe, S. S., and Pratt, G. E. (1974b). Dependence of juvenile hormone release from corpus allatum on intraglandular content. *Nature 252*, 474-476.

Tobe, S. S., and Pratt, G. E. (1975a). The synthetic activity and glandular volume of the corpus allatum during ovarian maturation in the desert locust *Schistocerca gregaria*.

Life Sci. *17*, 417-422.

Tobe, S. S., and Pratt, G. E. (1975b). Corpus allatum activity *in vitro* during ovarian maturation in the desert locust *Schistocerca gregaria.* *J. Exp. Biol. 62*, 611-627.

Tobe, S. S., and Pratt, G. E. (1976). Farnesenic acid stimulation of juvenile hormone biosynthesis as an experimental probe in corpus allatum physiology. *In* "The Juvenile Hormones" (L. I. Gilbert, ed.), pp. 147-163, Plenum Press, New York.

Tobe, S. S., and Stay, B. (1977). Corpus allatum activity *in vitro* during the reproductive cycle of the viviparous cockroach, *Diploptera punctata* (Eschscholtz). *Gen. Comp. Endocrinol. 31*, 138-147.

Tobe, S. S., and Stay, B. (1979). Modulation of juvenile hormone synthesis by an analogue in the cockroach. *Nature 281*, 481-482.

Tobe, S. S., and Stay, B. (1980). Control of juvenile hormone biosynthesis during the reproductive cycle of a viviparous cockroach. III. Effects of denervation and age on compensation with unilateral allatectomy and supernumerary corpora allata. *Gen. Comp. Endocrinol. 40*, 89-98.

Tobe, S. S., Chapman, C. S., and Pratt, G. E. (1977). Decay in juvenile hormone biosynthesis by insect corpus allatum after nerve transection. *Nature 268*, 728-730.

Weaver, R. J., and Pratt, G. E. (1977). The effect of enforced virginity and subsequent mating on the activity of the corpus allatum of *Periplaneta americana* measured *in vitro*, as related to changes in the rate of ovarian maturation. *Physiol. Entomol. 2*, 59-76.

Weaver, R. J., Pratt, G. E., Hamnett, A. F., and Jennings, R. C. (1980). The influence of incubation conditions on the rates of juvenile hormone biosynthesis by corpora allata isolated from adult females of the beetle *Tenebrio molitor.* *Insect Biochem.* (in press).

Wigglesworth, V. B. (1936d). The function of the corpus allatum in the growth and reproduction of *Rhodnius prolixus* (Hemiptera). *Quart. J. Micr. Sci. 79*, 91-121.

Wigglesworth, V. B. (1948a). The functions of the corpus allatum in *Rhodnius prolixus* (Hemiptera). *J. Exp. Biol. 25*, 1-14.

Wigglesworth, V. B. (1952d). Hormone balance and the control of metamorphosis in *Rhodnius prolixus* (Hemiptera). *J. Exp. Biol. 29*, 620-631.

GROWTH IN INSECTS

Carroll M. Williams[1]

The Biological Laboratories
Harvard University
Cambridge, Massachusetts

I. THE CENTRAL DOGMA

Insects grow by molting. This sentiment constitutes the Central Dogma of Entomology. In one way or another it has found its way into virtually all accounts of insect development. For example, in the most consequential publication on insect physiology (Wigglesworth, 1939) we read the following:

> Since the cuticle is incapable of growth and,
> in the more rigid parts such as the head capsule
> or appendages, is incapable even of being stretched,
> it must be shed from time to time as the insect
> grows, and a new and larger cuticle laid down.

Thirty-three years later the same statement appears unchanged in the latest (seventh) edition of that famous text (Wigglesworth, 1972).

A further version of the dogma is encountered in the foremost English account of insect morphology (Snodgrass, 1935):

> The nonelastic nature of the arthropod cuticula
> gives the body wall but little tensibility.
> When the cuticula is once formed, therefore,
> the integument can ordinarily increase in
> extent only in so far as the wrinkles and folds
> of the cuticula may be straightened out.

---

[1]The previously unpublished work reported in this essay was carried out with the support of Harvard University and grants from the National Institutes of Health, the National Science Foundation, and the Rockefeller Foundation.

The ubiquity of the dogma is further illustrated by the following quotation from the most influential treatise on applied entomology (Metcalf, Flint, and Metcalf, 1962):

> An insect does not grow by regular, gradual, imperceptible degrees like a child, just as its sclerotized exoskeleton will not expand like the mammalian skin to permit this. Therefore growth inside this inexpansible shell cannot be regular and continuous. In order to make any considerable increase in size, the shell must be split off....At this point there is a considerable expansion in the size of the insect before its new exo- cuticle becomes sclerotized or set to the definitive size of the next instar.... Subsequently there is a relatively long period during which the insect is feeding and accumulating reserve materials within its body, but without any noticeable increase in size. This is followed by another molt and period of constancy in size, and so on.

The latest version of the dogma strikes closer to home (Williams, 1979):

> Under normal conditions the larva (caterpillar) postpones metamorphosis until it attains a certain critical size. To accommodate this growth the external (cuticular) part of the insect skin is molted from time to time after a new and larger cuticle has been secreted.

II. SALTATORY GROWTH OF CRUSTACEANS

Growth by molting having received such a good press, it may be foolhardy to question whether it is so. One thing we can say immediately is that it will not be easy to grow by molting. Consider, for example, that feeding ceases at the outset of molting and is resumed only after the molt is concluded. Consequently, molting routinely involves an overall loss rather than gain in dry weight --- a state-of-affairs hardly propitious for growth. Moreover, throughout the body as a whole the new cuticle must necessarily form internal to the old one. Therefore the entire operation seems more suited for turning a large insect into a smaller one rather than the reverse.

Notwithstanding these complications, it is a documented fact that countless arthropods make use of molting as the sole vehicle for increasing their size. A case in point is the decapod Crustacea, as exemplified by the following quotation from Teissier (1960):

> In a crustacean endowed with a rigid integument, like a brachyuran, the linear dimensions are constant in the interval between two molts, but they increase abruptly at ecdysis to remain again unchanged until the next molt. Growth in size is therefore essentially discontinuous; the same animal in the course of its life exhibits only a finite number of distinct dimensions, at most equal to the number of stages which it traverses.

To achieve saltatory growth of this sort, special maneuvers are obviously necessary. In the case of Crustacea an essential happening is the rapid uptake of water to distend the gut and increase the blood volume during and immediately after ecdysis. The added volume of fluid, acting as an internal "space occupier", combines with muscular contractions to raise hemolymph pressure or turgor. The net effect is to stretch and unfurl the new cuticle which is then soft and flexible. That accomplished, the size of the various bodily parts is stabilized until the next molt by the deposition and mineralization of new endocuticle to produce the typically dense and inelastic integument seen, for example, in crabs and lobsters. During the period between molts, space for the enlarging muscles and other internal organs is made available by a progressive decline in body water by about one-third (Drach, 1939) --- an obvious necessity if internal growth is to continue during the intermolt.

III. SALTATORY GROWTH OF INSECTS

Can insects emulate the Crustacea in undertaking this sort of stepwise increase in size? They can indeed --- and never more so than during and immediately after adult eclosion. Then during a brief period when the new cuticle is soft and flexible, one routinely witnesses an often spectacular increase in size in terms of the unfurling of the

wings and the unfolding and stretching of the integument
throughout the body as a whole. Here again, a key happening
is the active uptake of a space occupier --- in this case
usually air --- into the gut, crop, and tracheal sacs. In
the Lepidoptera another internal space occupier is the rectal
sac distended by the voluminous meconium which is ordinarily
voided only after the wings have been fully spread.
Following the eclosion of adult insects, specific and often
extensive zones of cuticle undergo rapid sclerotization --- a
change which in adult Diptera and Lepidoptera is known to be
triggered by the polypeptide hormone, bursicon (see Riddiford
and Truman, 1978, for summary).

Growth by molting is by no means limited to freshly
eclosed adults. It is also evident in at least certain parts
of virtually all larval insects --- in particular, those
regions that become heavily sclerotized. Such hardened
regions can ordinarily expand in size only by molting, the
old cuticle being shed and replaced by a new and larger one.
The epidermis of the molting insect proves to be the prime
mover in bringing about this enlargement. After detachment
of the epidermis from the overlying cuticle, its growth and

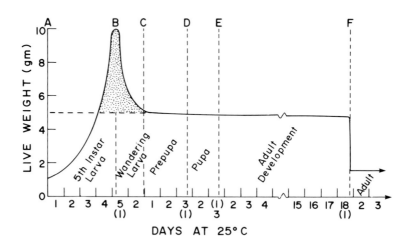

*Fig. 1. The live weight of the final (fifth) instar of the
tobacco hornworm during growth and metamorphosis at 25°C.
A, signals the time of ecdysis to the fifth larval instar;
B, the termination of the phagoperiod and initiation of the
wandering stage; C, the apolysis of the epidermis signaling
the initiation of the prepupal period; D, pupal ecdysis; E,
the apolysis of the epidermis signaling initiation of adult
development; F, eclosion of the adult moth. Stippled area
corresponds to transient mass cast away.*

resulting increase in surface area promote the formation of the numerous folds and plications that are so conspicuous in histological sections of molting integument. The new cuticle deposited upon these corrugations thereby acquires additional distensibility that is brought into play during and immediately after ecdysis. Sclerotization of the newly formed cuticle then stabilizes the stepwise increase in size.

Saltatory growth has been particularly emphasized in studies of the head capsule of caterpillars --- a heavily sclerotized object that is replaced at each larval molt. In the first of such studies the lepidopterist, Harrison Dyar (1890), achieved lasting fame by discovering that the width of the head capsule increased at each molt by a ratio (usually about 1.4) that was generally constant for a given species --- an empirical relationship that came to be known as "Dyar's rule" or "Dyar's law".

IV. NON-SALTATORY GROWTH OF INSECTS

Up to this point we have considered those aspects of insect development which are in full accord with the dogma that insects grow by molting. I now direct attention to additional findings that document the shortcomings, if not downright error, of this generalization. We shall see that, in more ways than one, the growth of insects can and often does have little to do with molting.

A case in point is illustrated in Figure 1 where the steeply rising curve depicts the growth of the tobacco hornworm, *Manduca sexta* during its five days of feeding in the final (fifth) larval instar. It can be seen that the the caterpillar's live weight increases from one to ten grams without any trace of molting. Simultaneously, its average length increases from 42 to 79 millimeters. This is by no means the maximal size that *Manduca* can attain without molting. For example, by adding juvenile hormone to the hornworm diet, one can prolong the fifth instar and cause the formation of giant caterpillars up to twice-normal size (Safranek, 1974).

It seemed most unlikely that this enormous increase in size and surface area could be accommodated by the stretching of the preexisting cuticle, as has generally been supposed. Bjerke and Williams (1980) therefore carried out a detailed study in which the chitosan recovered from the entire cuticle of hornworm larvae was measured at successive stages throughout the fourth and fifth larval instars.

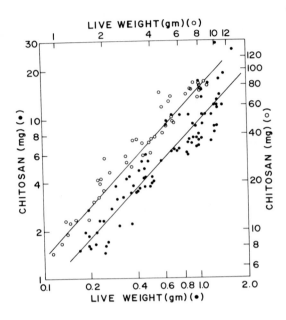

Fig. 2. *Chitosan content of the integument of the tobacco hornworms during the fourth* (closed circles) *and fifth* (open circles) *larval instars plotted on a double log grid as a function of the live weights of the animals in question.* (After Bjerke and Williams, 1980).

In Figure 2 our findings have been plotted on a double logarithmic grid as a function of the live weight of the corresponding larvae. The pair of straight lines fitted by the method of least squares to the two sets of data have slopes differing only trivially from unity. This implies that throughout the two instars the deposition of the parental compound, chitin, proceeds at the same relative rate as does the growth of the larva as a whole. These findings are in full accord with those obtained in Locke's (1970) detailed cytological study of integumentary growth in caterpillars. We concur with his conclusion (page 203) that:

> The intermolt period, far from being a time of rest between molts, is quantitatively the period of most active cuticle deposition.

During the intermolt of the fifth instar of the tobacco hornworm the 10-fold increase in mass would correspond to an increase in the area of the integument by approximately $10^{2/3}$

which is equivalent to a 4.6-fold increase. Whereas the
necessary increase in the size of the cuticle is brought
about by *de novo* growth, the question arises as to how the
underlying epidermis will meet this challenge if, as is
commonly supposed, its cells can undergo growth and mitotic
divisions only when they lose their attachments to the
overlying cuticle at the outset of a molt.

Here again, the dogma of growth by molting proves
deceptive. In point of fact, Locke (1970) found that, in the
larval epidermis of the lepidopteran, *Calpodes ethlius* DNA
replication as well as mitotic divisions take place during
the middle and later stages of the intermolt and are
suspended during and immediately after the molt itself.
Kindred findings have been reported for several other insects
(see Zacharuk, 1976, for review). Consequently, there is no
reason to deny the epidermis the ability to grow and expand
in surface area along with the overlying cuticle.

V. GROWTH OF SCLEROTIZED CUTICLE

For these several reasons we came to view the dogma of
growth by molting as relevant only to those integumentary
regions that are heavily sclerotized. Then we went on to
think the unthinkable: that sclerotized cuticle itself might
also be able to grow without molting.

To test this proposition we selected for study the head
capsule of the tobacco hornworm (Bjerke and Williams, 1980).
Figure 3 documents the surprising fact that at successive
stages in the fifth larval instar the chitosan recovered from
individual head capsules increases progressively, thereby
signaling a corresponding deposition of the parental
compound, chitin. The straight line fitted to the double log
plot in Figure 3 has a slope of 0.5, implying that chitin
deposition in the head capsule proceeds at a rate of about
half that recorded for the cuticle as a whole. Meanwhile, in
conformity with Dyar's law, the head capsules showed
insignificant increase in width. Evidently, the increase in
chitin content is attributable to increase in the *thickness*
of the head capsule, presumably by appositional growth.
Only later did we associate these findings with those
observed by Neville nearly twenty years ago --- namely, the
deposition of daily growth layers in the sclerotized cuticles
of adult locusts as well as many other insects (see Neville,
1967, for review). Thus in retrospect, the growth in
thickness of the sclerotized cuticle of *Manduca* might have
been anticipated had we not been under the spell of the dogma
of growth by molting.

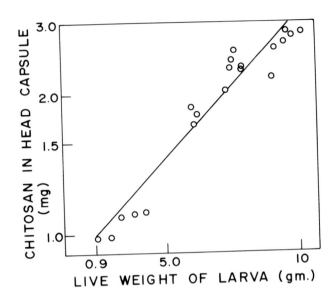

*Fig. 3. Chitosan content of the head capsules of fifth
instar tobacco hornworms plotted on a double log grid as
a function of the live weights of the animals in question.*
(After Bjerke and Williams, 1980).

VI. GROWTH OF IMAGINAL DISCS

Up to this point we have considered integumentary growth
as well as some aspects of the growth of the insect as a
whole. We now turn attention to the growth of internal
organs.

The increase in size of the viscera during the period
between molts is self-evident in dissections performed at the
outset and conclusion of any instar. Far more interesting is
the growth of imaginal discs during larval life. Indeed, it
has often been supposed that growth of the discs takes place
only at metamorphosis and is inhibited by juvenile hormone
during larval life.

Many years ago, in the course of a study of the action of
juvenile hormone, I investigated the growth of the wing discs
of the Cecropia silkworm. To this end, the four wing discs
were excised from individual larvae at precise stages in the
fourth and fifth instars and treated as follows: They were
trimmed free of their peripodal sacs, briefly rinsed in

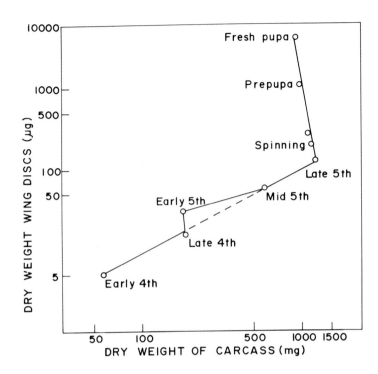

Fig. 4. The dry weights attained by an average wing disc (or wing) of the Cecropia silkworm are plotted on a double log grid as a function of the dry weight of the carcasses of the animals in question.

distilled water, placed on tared pieces of foil, dried to constant weight at 105°C, and weighed on a microtorsion balance reading directly to 5 μg. Fourth instar larvae were handled in homogeneous groups of four the sixteen discs being pooled. Individual larvae were studied during the fifth instar, the four discs again being pooled. The average weight of a single disc was computed at each stage. Meanwhile, the blood, gut, and silkglands were removed from the donor larvae. The residual carcasses were rinsed in distilled water, reduced to dryness, and weighed on an ordinary analytical balance.

In Figure 4 the dry weight of an average wing disc at each stage has been plotted on a double log grid as a function of the dry weight of the carcass. A partially hatched theoretical line has been drawn through four of the points with a slope of one. The goodness of fit implies that the growth of the wing discs is isometric with that of the animal as a whole. It will be noted that a discontinuity occurs during the molt from fourth to fifth instar. During this two-day interval the molting larva, and the carcass thereof, actually lose weight whereas the wing discs continue to grow. It is of interest that, after fmeding is resumed, the carcass "catches up" to reestablish the isometric relationship.

A new and steeper linear relationship takes over in the late fifth instar after the cessation of feeding. Spinning begins and the residual carcass once again starts to lose weight. Meanwhile the wing discs undergo a spurt of growth. They are everted in the prepupa and finally externalized at pupal ecdysis.

When similar measurements were carried out on the gonads, the isometric growth of ovaries as well as testes was evident. The one striking difference was that pupation constituted a less potent growth stimulus for the gonads than for the wings. The weight of the pupal gonads, in point of fact, corresponded almost exactly to that which one would anticipate in a hypothetical sixth instar Cecropia silkworm having a live weight of 40 grams which corresponds to a dry carcass of approximately 4 grams. Thus insofar as the gonads are concerned, pupation and the onset of pupal diapause seems equivalent to a supernumerary larval instar. By contrast, pupation is a far more effective growth stimulus in the case of the wings.

VII. SIZE AND METAMORPHOSIS

Attention is once again directed to Figure 1 where the live weight of the tobacco hornworm is plotted during five successive stages in metamorphosis beginning with ecdysis to the final (fifth) larval instar and continuing until eclosion of the full-fledged moth. We have already noted the spectacular growth of the hornworm from 1 to 10 grams during 5 or 6 days of feeding. A remarkable change in behavior then ensues. The larva stops feeding, purges its gut, and begins a two-day "wandering period" when it would dig into the soil if allowed to do so. Meanwhile, the "wandering larva" jettisons half its weight, mainly in the form of a viscous fluid expelled from its anus. Then at the time indicated as "C" in Figure 1, the epidermis detaches and retracts from the overlying larval cuticle --- an event that signals the termination of the final larval instar and the initiation of the prepupal stage.

It is of considerable interest that, as shown in Figure 1, sufficient fluid is ejected to reduce the live weight to 5 grams --- a plateau which then persists for some three weeks until the pharate adult is fully formed and ready to emerge. As F. Nijhout (1975) has shown, 5 grams is for *Manduca sexta* a critical weight which, when first attained on the fourth day of the fifth instar, sets in motion the entire chain of events that culminates in the onset of metamorphosis. Manifestly, the picture here presented is one of swift increase in mass followed by an equally swift decline to the 5 grams that seems to have such special physiological significance for *Manduca*.

Nijhout (1975) inquired as to how an insect might be able to assess its own size or mass. He came to the conclusion that the simplest if not only way in which an individual can monitor its own size is by some sort of allometry --- by detecting, for example, a critical rate of firing of stretch receptors which grow more slowly than the animal as a whole and are therefore progressively stretched as the insect grows to a critical size.

Subsequently, in studies carried out on the milkweed bug, *Oncopeltus fasciatus*, Nijhout (1979) and, independently, Blakely and Goodner (1979) have found support for the proposed model in that larvae of subcritical weight were induced to molt when their abdomens were distended by saline injection in the absence of further food intake or growth. Experiments of this sort have proved to be exceedingly difficult, if not impossible, to carry out on hornworms where, as we have seen, the critical enlargement from 1 to 5 grams is brought about, not by stretching or distension, but by the growth of all components of the integument --- a process manifestly impossible to mimic by any injection procedure.

VIII. NUMBER OF MOLTS

The tobacco hornworm ordinarily undergoes four larval molts while traversing five larval instars prior to the two metamorphic molts depicted in Figure 1. Throughout all these molts the insect is in an essentially helpless condition being incapable of either feeding or locomotion. Since these and even greater physiological hazzards are encountered by virtually all molting insects, one might expect evolutionary pressures for economizing on the number of larval molts.

This prospect is examined in Table 1 in terms of the number of larval molts typical of the various Orders of insects. The primitive condition as encountered in the Apterygota is to have many molts, not only before, but especially after attaining the adult condition. Adult Collembola are reported to molt up to 50 times with little or no additional growth (Wallace and Mackerras, 1970). In the Pterygote insects molting is suppressed in adults, the sole exception being the mayflies (Ephemeroptera) where, as is well known, a molt from subimago to imago takes place soon after emergence.

The inability of adult insects to molt does not terminate their ability to grow. We have seen that, without molting, sclerotized cuticle can grow in thickness while unsclerotized cuticle can continue to grow in all dimensions. The most spectacular example of adult growth is encountered in the physogastric queen termites where the huge proliferation of ovaries and fat body is accommodated by the enormous growth of unsclerotized abdominal cuticle. The original contiguous terga and sterna come to resemble isolated islands of sclerotized cuticle afloat on a sea of intersegmental membrane.

Table 1 reveals that among the hemimetabolous Orders there is a clear-cut tendency to reduce the number of larval molts and, consequently, the number of larval instars. The holometabolous Orders also economize on the number of larval molts, though in this case they must add an additional metamorphic molt to accommodate the pupa. It is of interest that the Coleoptera --- the largest of all Orders in terms of species ---typically undergo only two larval molts corresponding to three larval instars. The beetles nevertheless include the largest of all insects in terms of mass or bulk. The largest insects in terms of mass are probably the mature larvae of the tropical American beetles, *Megasoma elephas* and *Dynastes hercules*, both members of the Family Scarabaeidae (Britton, 1970). The Lepidoptera also contain many giants. The largest in terms of mass is probably the mature larva of the wild silkworm, *Antheraea mylitta* where female larvae weigh up to 65 grams (nearly 3 ounces) and are therefore larger than many birds and mammals. Despite that fact, the larva attains this huge bulk while undergoing only the four molts commonly encountered in Lepidoptera. These findings once again illustrate the extent to which growth can proceed without molting.

Table I. Number of Larval Molts Typical of Various Orders of Insects[a]

Order	Common name	Number of larval molts
Collembola	*Spring-tails*	4 to 5 (up to 50 as adults)
Thysanura	*Silver-fish*	9 to 13 (dozens as adults)
Ephemeroptera	*Mayflies*	27 to 44
Plecoptera	*Stoneflies*	21 to 32
Odonata	*Dragonflies*	9 to 14
Blattodea	*Roaches*	5 to 11
Isoptera	*Termites*	4 to 10
Mantodea	*Mantids*	4 to 8
Dermaptera	*Earwigs*	3 to 5
Orthoptera	*Grasshoppers, etc.*	4 to 9
Embioptera	*Embiids*	3
Psocoptera	*Booklice*	5
Anoplura	*Lice*	2
Hemiptera	*True bugs*	2 to 6
Neuroptera	*Lacewigs, etc.*	2
Coleoptera	*Beetles*	2
Mecoptera	*Scorpionflies*	3
Siphonaptera	*Fleas*	2
Diptera	*Flies*	2 to 3
Trichoptera	*Caddisflies*	5 to 6
Lepidoptera	*Butterflies and moths*	2 to 10 (usually 4 or 5)
Hymenoptera	*Bees, wasps, ants, etc.*	2 to 4

[a]*Data derived mainly from Waterhouse (1970) and Joly (1977).*

IX. CONCLUSIONS

Where does all this leave the dogma of insect growth by molting? Obviously, it leaves it in something of a shambles. A much better generalization would be "insect development by molting" for that would bring metamorphosis into the picture. Though much and perhaps most insect growth occurs without molting, it is difficult to conceive of metamorphosis taking place that way. Presumably this is a theme meriting further analysis the next time we join in saluting our distinguished mentor.

REFERENCES

Bjerke, J.S. and Williams, C.M. In preparation (1980).

Blakely, N. and Goodner, S.R., Size-dependent timing of metamorphosis in milkweed bugs (Oncopeltus) and its life history implications. Biol. Bull., 55: 499-510 (1979).

Britton, E.B., Coleoptera. In "The Insects of Australia" (D.F. Waterhouse, ed.), p. 496, Melbourne Univ. Press (1970).

Drach, P., Mue et cycle d'intermue chez les Crustaces Decapodes. Ann. inst. oceanog. (Paris), 19: 103-391 (1939).

Dyar, H.G., The number of molts of lepidopterous larvae. Psyche 5, 420-423 (1890).

Joly, P., Le developpment postembryonnaire des insectes. In "Traite de Zoologie" (P.P. Grasse, ed.), 8, Fasc. V-A, p. 411 (1977).

Locke, M., The molt/intermolt cycle in the epidermis and other tissues of an insect Calpodes ethlius (Lepidoptera, Hesperiidae). Tissue & Cell, 2, 197-223 (1970).

Metcalf, C.L., Flint, W.P., and Metcalf, R.L., Destructive and Useful Insects, 4th edition, p. 165. McGraw-Hill, N.Y. (1962).

Neville, A.C., Chitin orientation in cuticle and its control. Advances Insect Physiol., 4, 213-280 (1967).

Nijhout, H.F., A threshold size for metamorphosis in the tobacco hornworm, Manduca sexta (L.) Biol. Bull., 149, 214-225 (1975).

Nijhout, H.F., Stretch-induced moulting in Oncopeltus fasciatus. J. Insect Physiol. 25, 277-281 (1979).

Riddiford, L.M. and Truman, J.W., Biochemistry of insect hormones and insect growth regulators. In "Biochemistry of Insects" (M. Rockstein, ed.), Academic Press, N.Y., p. 339 (1978).

Safranek, L.L. Hormonal Control of Pigmentation in the Tobacco Hornworm, Manduca sexta. Honor s Thesis, Harvard University (1974).

Snodgrass, R.E., Principles of Insect Morphology, 1st edition, p. 64, McGraw-Hill, N.Y. (1935).

Teissier, G. Relative growth. In "The physiology of Crustacea" (T.H. Waterman, ed.), 1, p. 541, Academic Press, N.Y. (1960).

Wallace, M.M.H. and Mackerras, I.M., The entognathous hexapods. In "The Insects of Australia" (D.F. Waterhouse, ed.), p. 207, Melbourne Univ. Press (1970).

Waterhouse, D.F. (ed.), The Insects of Australia. Melbourne Univ. Press (1970).

Wigglesworth, V.B., The Principles of Insect Physiology, 1st edition, p. 24, Methuen, London (1939).

Wigglesworth, V.B., The Principles of Insect Physiology, 7th edition, p. 29, Chapman and Hall, London (1972).

Williams, C.M., How basic studies of insects have helped man. In "The Biological Revolution" (G. Weissmann, ed.), p.67, Plenum Press, N.Y. (1979).

Zacharuk, R.Y., Structural changes of the cuticle associated with moulting. In "The Insect Integument" (H.P. Hepburn, ed.), p. 304, Elsevier, N.Y. (1976).

ECLOSION HORMONE: ITS ROLE
IN COORDINATING ECDYSIAL
EVENTS IN INSECTS[1]

James W. Truman

Department of Zoology
University of Washington
Seattle, Washington

I. INTRODUCTION

The most characteristic feature of arthropods is their
exoskeleton. This covering provides form and support as well
as protection from physical damage and dessication. Because
of the relative rigidity of the exoskeleton, the periodic
production of a new cuticle and the casting off of the old one
is a prerequisite for growth and metamorphosis. The physiological and endocrine events underlying the production of a
new cuticle (or molting) has served as a major focus for
insect physiologists over the past 45 years. These studies
were pioneered by the seminal experiments of Wigglesworth
(1934b, 1936d) and they have culminated in our present day
appreciation of the roles of the prothoracicotropic hormone
(PTTH), ecdysone, and juvenile hormone in the initiation and
direction of the molting process (e.g. Gilbert, 1974;
Riddiford and Truman, 1978).

Although the initiation of molting has received extensive
attention, the end of the process, the shedding or ecdysis of
the cuticle, has been comparatively neglected. Reynolds
(1980) has comprehensively reviewed the physiological and
behavioral aspects of ecdysis and readers are referred there

[1]*Supported by grants from NSF (PC M77-24878) and from NIH
(R01 NS13079 and K04 NS 00193)*

for a detailed treatment of this event. This paper will be
confined primarily to 2 ecdysial events, adult eclosion and
pupal ecdysis in Lepidoptera, although examples from other
groups will be brought in to clarify specific points. It will
focus on the hormone that triggers ecdysis, and the central
role of this hormone in coordinating the physiological and
behavioral events that occur at ecdysis.

In the giant silkmoths and the tobacco hornworm, *Manduca
sexta*, adult eclosion occurs at the end of an 18 to 21 day
developmental program. The end product of this metamorphosis
is a well-muscled and partially hardened pharate adult moth.
In moths, as in many other insects, the eclosion of adult
shows temporal gating. The behavior is confined to precise
daily gates, the time of which is determined by an interaction
of the insect's circadian clock with the environmental photoperiod (Pittendrigh and Skopik, 1970). Thus, animals that
complete development after the closing of a gate then wait
inside the old cuticle until the opening of the gate on the
following day.

The pharate adult moth is a relatively robust animal that
must escape from a rigid shell of pupal cuticle. The ecdysial
seams are split by flexing movements of the wing bases. The
legs than push off the cuticle covering the head and ventral
thorax while peristaltic contractions of the abdomen propel
the animal out of the old skin. Unlike other stages, the
successful emergence of the well muscled moth is relatively
independent of the integrity of the pupal cuticle.

In contrast to adult eclosion, pupal ecdysis in *Manduca
sexta* culminates a brief 60 hour process that transforms the
wandering larva into the pupa. As with the preceding larval
ecdyses in this insect (Truman, 1972a) pupal ecdysis is not
gated. Its time of onset occurs at a fixed time after the
appearance of various developmental markers (Truman *et al.*,
1980b) and the event itself is independent of photoperiod
cues. The time of pupal ecdysis appears to be a function only
of the time of PTTH release (Truman, 1972a; Truman and
Riddiford, 1974) and the ambient temperature.

From the standpoint of a behavioral program, pupal ecdysis is relatively simple. The ecdysis movements consist of
waves of contraction that begin at the end of the abdomen and
move anteriorly. These movements pull the old larval cuticle
back over the surface of the animal. As the cuticle is moved
back, the appendages are drawn out of the larval skin and

pulled down by the old cuticle into the approximate positions
that they occupy in the fully tanned and hardened pupa.

Coordination of the ecdysial event with the state of
cuticle breakdown and molting fluid resorption is critical for
the pupal ecdysis. If the old endocuticle is not sufficiently
digested at ecdysis, the ecdysial sutures do not rupture and
the insect becomes trapped inside the cuticle. This happens
when ecdysis behavior is experimentally triggered before the
completion of endocuticle digestion (Truman *et al.*, 1980b).
Since the integrity of the old cuticle is essential for withdrawal of the appendages, a mistake in the other direction is
equally disastrous. If molting fluid resorption has
progressed too far and the drying cuticle tears during
shedding, then the appendages of the pupa remain encased
within the old skin. It is not known what accounts for the
precise coordination between the digestion of the old cuticle
and the onset of ecdysial behavior.

II. THE HORMONAL REGULATION OF ECDYSIS

The existence of an ecdysis stimulating hormone was first
demonstrated for adult eclosion in the giant silkmoths (Truman
and Riddiford, 1970; Truman, 1971). Removal of the brain from
developing moths drastically interfered with the subsequent
ecdysis of these animals. The emergence behavior of debrained
moths was badly organized and the event itself was no longer
gated. Gating and the proper organization of the behavior
were restored by implantation of a brain into the abdomen of
these animals. These and related experiments led to the
conclusion that the moth brain contains a photoreceptor and
clock that controls the time of ecdysis (Truman, 1972b) and
that the clock acts through the release of an eclosion stimulating factor. This factor was present in the brain and
corpora cardiaca (CC) (Truman, 1973a) and it appeared in the
blood just prior to the onset of the eclosion behavior
(Reynolds *et al.*, 1979). This hormone has been named the
eclosion hormone and has been characterized as an acidic peptide (pI = 4.8) of apparent molecular weight of 8500 daltons
(Reynolds and Truman, 1980; Mumby, Truman and Reynolds, in
preparation).

When the above experimental approach was applied to
larval ecdysis, anomalous results were obtained. Removal of
the brain by neck ligation of larvae 36 hours before ecdysis
had no effect on the subsequent timing of that behavior

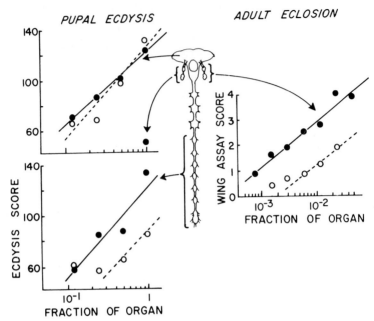

FIGURE 1.   Eclosion hormone activity extracted from the
brain, corpora cardiaca-corpora allata complex, and abdominal
nervous system before and after (left) pupal ecdysis or
(right) adult eclosion of Manduca sexta. Hormone titers were
measured by the pupal ecdysis assay or the isolated wing assay.
Closed circles are tissues before ecdysis; open circles after
ecdysis. (Data from Truman, 1978a, and Taghert et al., 1980)

(Truman, 1972a). Also, subjection of larval and prepupal
brains and CC to adult eclosion hormone bioassays showed only
trace amounts of activity (Truman, 1973a). The significance
of these data has been revealed by recent studies of pupal
ecdysis in Manduca sexta (Truman et al., 1980b; Taghert et al.,
1980). Prepupae proved to be sensitive to eclosion hormone in
that they showed precocious ecdysis behavior in response to
injection of hormone preparations. Interestingly, prepupae
were sensitive to hormone dosages that were 10 fold lower than
those required to provoke eclosion behavior in the smaller
pharate adult stage. Also, hormonal activity appeared in the
blood of prepupae about 30 minutes before the onset of ecdysis
behavior. The source of this activity was the prepupal CNS
which contained a substance which was identical to the adult
hormone in apparent molecular weight, charge, and spectrum of
biological activities (Taghert et al., 1980). Thus, eclosion

hormone appears to be involved in triggering pupal ecdysis as well as adult eclosion. Preliminary evidence also implicates it in the control of larval ecdysis (Copenhaver and Truman, unpublished).

Figure 1 summarizes an important difference between the eclosion hormone systems in the prepupa and the pharate adult. In the latter stage, the timing of eclosion is controlled by the brain. Large stores of hormone were found in the pharate adult CC and these were depleted at the time of eclosion (Truman, 1973a, 1978a). In the prepupa, eclosion hormone was present in the brain and the ventral chain of ganglia (Taghert *et al.*, 1980). Interestingly the cephalic hormone was found only in the brain, none was detected in the CC. As seen in Fig. 1 during ecdysis the store of hormone in the pupal brain remained unchanged whereas the activity in the ventral nerve cord showed a 50 to 75% depletion. A release of that magnitude is required to account for the hormone titers found in the blood at ecdysis. Thus, the hormone that triggers pupal ecdysis appears to come from thoracic and abdominal centers rather than from the head. Indeed, debrained prepupae subsequently show normal blood titers of hormone at the time of ecdysis (Taghert *et al.*, 1980).

Thus, in the moth there are 2 endocrine centers that make eclosion hormone: one in the brain and the other distributed through the chain of segmental ganglia. The former is used during the gated adult eclosion whereas the latter is used for nongated, developmentally-triggered ecdyses. Whether the choice of a particular endocrine center depends solely on the association of the ecdysis with a circadian clock awaits the examination of more examples.

The greater sensitivity afforded by the pupal ecdysis assay has allowed a reexamination of other insect groups for eclosion hormone activity. A preliminary screening has revealed activity in both orthopterans and hemipterans (Truman and Taghert, unpublished). Moreover, in both crickets (Carlson, 1977) and locusts (Miller & Mills, 1976) preliminary data have been reported which implicate a hormonal factor in the triggering of ecdysial behavior. Consequently, it appears likely that eclosion hormone may be used throughout the insects to release ecdysial behaviors and associated physiological events.

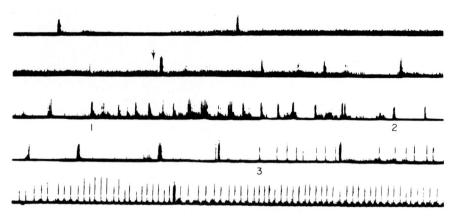

FIGURE 2.   An integrated record of the spontaneous motor activity from an isolated abdominal nervous system of Hyalophora cecropia.   Each line represents successive one hour periods of continuous recording.   The sustained bursts showed the patterning characteristic of rotary movements; the brief bursts showed that of peristaltic movements.   Arrow: addition of eclosion hormone to the bath; 1, start of the pre-eclosion active phase; 2, start of quiet period; 3, eclosion phase. (From Truman, 1978b).

III.   ECLOSION HORMONE ACTION ON THE INSECT NERVOUS SYSTEM

The most obvious action of the eclosion hormone is the stimulation of ecdysial behaviors.   In insects that have to withdraw long appendages from the old cuticle, these behaviors may be extremely complex.   For example, in crickets (Carlson, 1977) ecdysial behavior is divisible into 4 phases, each of which is made up of numerous distinct motor programs. Some sequences of programs appear to be prepatterned into the CNS whereas in other cases the duration of a particular program or the recruitment of new ones depends on sensory input during the progression of the behavior.

The best understanding of the relationship of the eclosion hormone to these ecdysial motor programs comes from studies of adult eclosion in the silkmoth, *Hyalophora cecropia*.   In this species the eclosion hormone triggers a sequence of 3 major behaviors: 1) the pre-eclosion behavior begins about 15 minutes after hormone exposure and consists of a 30 minute period of frequent rotary movements of the abdomen followed by a 30 minute quiet period, 2) eclosion behavior

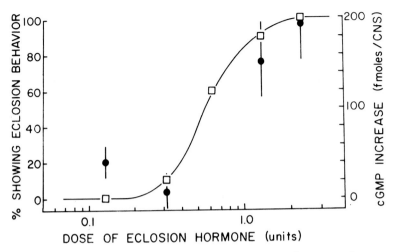

Figure 3. The responses of isolated abdomens of H. cecropia to various doses of eclosion hormone. Squares: per cent showing eclosion behavior after injection; circles: average increase (± s.e.) in CNS cyclicGMP at 10 minutes after injection. (Data from Truman et al., 1980a).

includes the abdominal peristaltic contractions and the wing and leg movements that free the moth from the pupal cuticle, and 3) wing inflation behavior involves a program of abdominal and wing postures which result in expansion of the wings. Studies on isolated nervous system preparations showed that at least the first 2 behaviors are prepatterned into the CNS (Truman, 1978b). As seen in Fig. 2, addition of hormone to the isolated abdominal nervous system resulted in a 3 part motor response. The first phase consisted of frequent bursts that had a rotary patterning, the second phase was a quiet period, and the resumed activity during the third phase showed peristaltic bursts. Manifestly, the spontaneous motor output released by the eclosion hormone showed the proper motor patterning and temporal organization of the respective behaviors. The hormone appears to act as a trigger in releasing these programs. A brief, 5 minute pulse of hormone applied to the CNS was sufficient to release the long program of spontaneous motor activity (Truman, 1978b).

The sequential arrangement of the 3 major behaviors appears due to latency differences among the respective motor programs (Truman, 1978b; unpublished). This conclusion is based largely on the result that following various experimental manipulations each of the programs can be relased in isolation. Importantly, in these cases, each program still shows its characteristic onset latency relative to the time of application of hormone.

The release of behavior by the eclosion hormone appears mediated through an increase in cyclic nucleotides in the target cells (Truman *et al.*, 1980a). Application of exogenous cyclicGMP to *H. cecropia* preparations triggered the pre-eclosion and eclosion behaviors under both *in vivo* and *in vitro* conditions. CyclicAMP was also effective but required doses that were 10 to 100 times higher. Injection of *H. cecropia* with purified eclosion hormone preparations resulted in a rapid increase in cyclicGMP in the abdominal CNS. CyclicAMP levels were not altered. As seen in Fig. 3, the cyclicGMP increase was dose dependent and showed a similar threshold to the behavioral response. Thus, cyclicGMP appears to play an early role in the response of the nervous system to the hormone.

Besides releasing the behaviors involved in ecdysis, the eclosion hormone also activates sets of behavioral programs that are characteristic of the new stage. This "behavioral switching" (Reynolds, 1980) is best seen in the behavior of pharate adult moths from which the pupal cuticle has been peeled away just prior to eclosion. Even though these animals have completed development, such "peeled" moths failed to show many of the behaviors that are characteristic of the adult (Blest, 1960; Truman, 1971, 1976). These behavioral deficits then abruptly vanished at the time of the eclosion gate. The switching on of sets of behaviors at ecdysis is not unique to moth eclosion. At pupal ecdysis in *Manduca sexta*, certain pupa-specific behaviors and reflexes abruptly appear at ecdysis (Levine and Truman, unpublished). Likewise in a cricket, adult singing behavior becomes activated at the time of ecdysis (Bentley and Hoy, 1970). In at least the moth examples, the switching on of the behaviors is due to eclosion hormone (Truman, 1971, 1976; Levine, unpublished).

The inhibition of many of the adult behaviors in the pharate adult appears to be transient, being imposed during the last days or hours of adult development (Blest, 1960; Truman, 1976; Kammer and Kinnamon, 1977). Blest hypothesized that this transient inhibition might function to prevent premature ecdysis at the time when the old cuticle was sufficiently digested to allow its rupture. This would seem especially useful in the case of a gated ecdysis in which the insect may have to wait a number of hours after the completion of development for the opening of the next gate.

IV. ECLOSION HORMONE AND MUSCLE DEGENERATION

In many instances ecdysis is followed by the breakdown of
some of the muscles that were used for the behavior
(Finlayson, 1975). This muscle loss is most evident when the
ecdysis marks the transition from one morphological stage to
another such as after adult eclosion in Lepidoptera
(Finlayson, 1956) and Diptera (Cottrell, 1962b), after pupal
ecdysis (Finlayson, 1975) and after hatching in some insects
(Bernays, 1972). In the case of repetitive larval ecdyses,
the ecdysial musculature usually persists between successive
molts (Reynolds, 1980). A notable exception, however, is the
blood-sucking bug, *Rhodnius*, in which the ventral segmental
muscles undergo involution after each ecdysis and then must
regrow during the next molt (Wigglesworth, 1956i).

Endocrine regulation of post-ecdysial muscle degeneration
is best understood in the saturniid moths. The abdomen of the
pharate adult is lined with longitudinal bands of muscle, the
intersegmental muscles (ISM). These muscles are used during
eclosion but within a few hours they begin to break down and
by 48 hours they are gone (Finlayson, 1956; Lockshin and
Williams, 1965a). Lockshin and Williams (1965b) originally
demonstrated that enhanced activity of the motorneurons that
supplied the ISM retarded or prevented degeneration. Later,
it was found that isolation of the abdomen of pharate adult
Antheraea polyphemus prevented muscle breakdown, but if
isolation was delayed until the time of eclosion, the muscles
degenerated on schedule (Lockshin, 1969). These findings
indicated that muscle death was triggered by a signal from the
anterior end of the animal that was given just prior to the
time of ecdysis. When extracts that contained the eclosion
hormone were injected into isolated abdomens from pharate
adults, prompt degeneration of the muscles then followed
(Truman, 1970). Thus, it was concluded that the hormone was
the normal trigger for muscle degeneration and, based on the
finding of Lockshin and Williams (1965b), that this came about
through an alteration in the physiology of the motorneurons
that supplied the muscles.

This hypothesis has recently been tested in this laboratory by L. M. Schwartz (unpublished). In brief, he found that
isolated *A. polyphemus* abdomens whose muscles were denervated
by removal of the abdominal CNS showed retention of the ISM,
but injection of these abdomens with eclosion hormone caused
prompt muscle degeneration. When denervations were carried
out earlier at the outset of adult development, the ISM showed

only slight degeneration at the end of the 3 weeks of metamorphosis. Importantly, these chronically denervated muscles
still showed a complete sensitivity to the hormone. Thus, in
A. polyphemus the post-ecdysial breakdown of the ISM appears
due to a direct action of the eclosion hormone on the muscle
itself.

Considering the extent of postecdysial muscle death in
insects, it is tempting to speculate that the eclosion
hormone is the trigger in all cases. However, in the moth,
Manduca sexta, another mechanism may be operating (Schwartz
and Truman, unpublished). Isolation of abdomens of this
species prior to hormone release does not prevent ISM degeneration. Breakdown occurs on schedule or is even accelerated
depending on the time of isolation. The nature of the cue
regulating degeneration in *Manduca* is not clear at this time
but the data are not compatible with the eclosion hormone
serving as a trigger for the event.

V. ECLOSION HORMONE AND BURSICON SECRETION

In experiments on the blowfly, Cottrell (1962a) and
Fraenkel and Hsiao (1962) separately reported that postecdysial cuticular tanning is regulated by a tanning hormone that
later became known as bursicon (Fraenkel and Hsiao, 1965). In
Manduca bursicon secretion appears to be dependent on the
prior secretion of eclosion hormone. This dependence is evident both at adult eclosion (Truman, 1973b) and also during
pupal ecdysis (Reynolds, Taghert, and Truman, in preparation).

At adult eclosion in *Manduca*, bursicon is released from
the abdominal nerve cord (Truman, 1973b) and appears in the
blood as a large pulse shortly after the moth settles at a
wing-inflation site (Reynolds, Taghert, and Truman, 1979). As
in the case of the fly, this secretion of bursicon requires
the proper sensory cues. *Manduca* normally pupate in the soil
and hormone release can be delayed for a number of hours by
forcing the newly emerged moths to dig (Truman, 1973b). Bursicon secretion occurs once the animals are freed from con-
finement. However, when pharate adults were removed from
their pupal cuticles and placed in a situation that provided
the proper stimuli for bursicon release, secretion did not
occur until after the insects had been exposed to the eclosion
hormone (Truman, 1973b). Thus at adult eclosion, the neuroendocrine reflex responsible for bursicon secretion appears
to be activated by the eclosion hormone.

The relationship among eclosion hormone, bursicon, and
sensory input at pupal ecdysis (Reynolds, Taghert, and Truman,
in preparation) is more complex than at adult eclosion. Examination of bursicon titers in the blood of ecdysing animals
showed a small release of hormone at the outset of the ecdysial behavior followed by a larger surge at the time of the
rupturing of the ecdysial seam along the back of the thorax.
This second release of bursicon, but not the first, could be
suppressed by peeling a ring of larval cuticle from around
the first abdominal segment so that the insects could shed the
abdominal cuticle but the thoracic cuticle remained intact.
As in the adult, the manual removal of the larval cuticle
prior to ecdysis did not result in early bursicon secretion,
but eclosion hormone injection which evoked early ecdysial behavior also resulted in precocious bursicon release. Thus, at
pupal ecdysis, the inital peak of bursicon appears to be a
programmed release that is a direct response to the eclosion
hormone. The second release depends on both the proper sensory input and a prior exposure to the eclosion hormone.

VI.   INDUCTION OF CUTICLE PLASTICITY BY THE ECLOSION HORMONE

In pharate adults of *Manduca sexta*, the wing cuticle
becomes plastic about 2 hours before the animal subsequently
ecloses. This increase in cuticle plasticity was shown by
Reynolds (1977) to be due to the eclosion hormone. Based on
this finding, he then developed a sensitive isolated wing
assay that was sensitive down to 10^{-3} CC equivalents of
eclosion hormone. The physiological significance of this
action in the pharate adult is unclear since bursicon, which
is released at the outset of wing-inflation behavior, also has
a transient but pronounced effect on cuticle plasticity
(Reynolds, 1977). An increase in cuticle plasticity by the
eclosion hormone would seem more useful at pupal ecdysis
during which time some of the disc derived structures begin
expansion as soon as they are drawn out of the cuticle. We
have not yet tested this hypothesis.

VII.   ECLOSION HORMONE AND THE DERMAL GLAND ACTIVITY

During hydrolysis of the old larval cuticle, the breakdown products apparently diffuse through the forming pupal
cuticle and are pinocytotically taken up by the epidermal

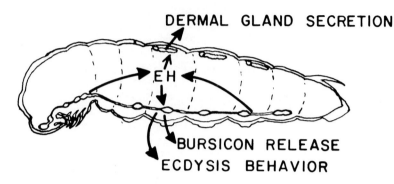

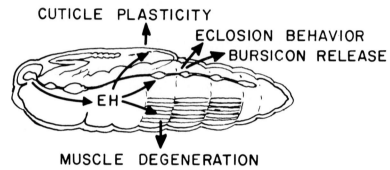

Figure 4. Summary of the origin and known effects of the eclosion hormone that triggers (upper) pupal ecdysis and (lower) adult eclosion.

cells (Jungries, 1979). A few hours later, after ecdysis, the pupal cuticle has become impervious to water. This water-proofing of the cuticle is due in part to the cement layer at the surface (Wigglesworth, 1947a). In lepidopteran larvae, this cement is apparently produced by large segmentally arranged glands, the Verson's glands. These glands enlarge during the molt and discharge their products during ecdysis (Way, 1950). In *Manduca*, the discharge of these glands is precisely timed to coincide with the rupturing of the dorsal ecdysial seam in the larval cuticle. As a result, the old skin, as it moves over the animal, spreads the secretory product over the entire surface of the new pupa.

The eclosion hormone appears involved in the control over the discharge of the Verson's glands. The stimulation of early ecdysial behavior by the hormone also results in precocious secretion by the glands. In cases in which the larval cuticle could not be shed because it was not sufficiently

digested, the gland products were nevertheless discharged
into the exuvial space (Truman, unpublished). The exact
mechanism of secretion has not been worked out for these
glands but a few clues exist. In *Calpodes* just before ecdysis, cytoplasmic fingers of the secretory cell withdraw from
the lumen of the saccule cell and thereby open up a channel
out which the secretion may pass. (Lai-Fook, 1973). When
Manduca prepupae are severely bled prior to ecdysis they still
shed the old cuticle but the amount of Verson's gland discharge is markedly reduced (Truman, unpublished). Since in
some insects, the peak of blood pressure occurs at the time of
splitting of the old skin (Slama, 1976), this pressure likely
serves as the primary force for the discharge of the glands.
The eclosion hormone is indirectly responsible for this in its
role as the trigger for the ecdysis motor program. In
addition, the eclosion hormone may induce the cellular changes
within the gland that allow secretion but there is not yet
evidence to support this possibility.

VIII. CONCLUSIONS

     There are numerous questions that remain as to the role
of the eclosion hormone. The most obvious one is how widespread is the hormone among the arthropods? As stated above,
eclosion hormone activity is found in insect orders besides
the Lepidoptera but the chemical similarity of the hormones
from other orders with the moth hormone has yet to be
explored. Also, as seen in Fig. 4, the eclosion hormone is
produced in 2 endocrine centers. Only a series of comparative
studies will reveal whether the choice of release site depends
solely on the circadian involvement in the release or whether
other factors are also important.

     As seen in Fig. 4, in its action of coordinating the
events of ecdysis, the hormone acts on various target tissues
including the CNS, muscles, and epidermis in the adult. The
dermal glands may also be targets in earlier stages. Future
studies will likely reveal other target tissues for this
peptide.

     Numerous questions exist on the behavioral level. Where
are the target cells in the CNS and how do these cells relate
to the neurons that are programmed for the various ecdysial
behaviors? As the life history of the animal progresses,
different motor programs are used for larval ecdysis, pupal

ecdysis and adult eclosion. Do the target cells change with
the alteration in motor programs or do they stay constant and
only their connections change?

The mode of action of the hormone also presents
interesting questions. CyclicGMP appears to be involved with
the action of the hormone on the CNS (Truman, Mumby, and
Welch, 1980), the intersegmental muscles (Schwartz, unpublished) and the wing epidermis (Truman, unpublished). Is this
cyclic nucleotide involved in the action of the hormone at all
stages and in all tissues? What are the connections between
the cGMP increase and the physiological response?

REFERENCES

Bentley, D. R., and Hoy, R. R. (1970). Postembryonic
    development of adult motor patterns in crickets: a neural
    analysis. *Science 170*, 1409-1411.
Bernays, E. A. (1972). The muscles of newly hatched
    Schistocerca gregaria larvae, and the possible functions
    in hatching, digging, and ecdysial movements. *J. Zool.
    Lond. 166*, 141-158.
Blest, A. D. (1960). The evolution, ontogeny, and quantita-
    tive control of settling movements of some new world
    saturniid moths, with some comments on distance communi-
    cation by honey bees. *Behaviour 16*, 188-253.
Carlson, J. R. (1977). The imaginal ecdysis of the cricket
    Teleogryllus oceanicus, I. Temporal structure and
    organization into motor programs. *J. Comp. Physiol. 115*,
    299-317.
Cottrell, C. B. (1962a). The imaginal ecdysis of blowflies.
    Detection of the blood-borne darkening factor and
    determination of some of its properties. *J. Exp. Biol.
    39*, 413-430.
Cottrell, C. B. (1962b). The imaginal ecdysis of blowflies.
    Observations on the hydrostatic mechanisms involved in
    digging and expansion. *J. Exp. Biol. 39*, 431-448.
Finlayson, L. H. (1956). Normal and induced degeneration of
    the abdominal muscles during metamorphosis in the
    Lepidoptera. *Quart. J. Micro. Sci. 97*, 215-233.
Finlayson, L. H. (1975). Development and degeneration. *In*
    "Insect Muscle" (P.N.R. Usherwood, ed). pp. 75-149.
    Academic Press, London.
Fraenkel, G. and Hsaio, C. (1962). Hormonal and nervous
    control of tanning in the fly. *Science 138*, 27-29.
Fraenkel, G., and Hsaio, C. (1965). Bursicon, a hormone
    which mediates tanning of the cuticle in the adult fly

and other insects. *J. Insect Physiol.* *11*, 513-556.

Gilbert, L. I. (1974). Endocrine action during insect growth. *Recent Prog. Hormone Res. 30*, 347-390.

Jungreis, A. M. (1979). Physiology of moulting in insects. *Adv. Insect Physiol. 14*, 109-183.

Kammer, A. E. and Kinnamon, S. C. (1977). Patterned muscle activity during eclosion in the hawkmoth, *Manduca sexta*. *J. Comp. Physiol. 114*, 313-326.

Lai-Fook, J. (1973). The fine structure of Verson's glands in molting larvae of *Calpodes ethlius* (Hesperiidae, Lepidoptera). *Can. J. Zool. 51*, 1201-1210.

Lockshin, R. A. (1969). Programmed cell death. Activation of lysis by a mechanism involving the synthesis of a protein. *J. Insect Physiol. 15*, 1505-1516.

Lockshin, R. A., and Williams, C. M. (1965a). Programmed cell death. I. Cytology of degeneration in the intersegmental muscles of the pernyi silkmoth. *J. Insect Physiol. 11*, 123-133.

Lockshin, R. A., and Williams, C. M. (1965b). Programmed cell death. III. Neural control of the breakdown of the intersegmental muscles of silkmoths. *J. Insect Physiol. 11*, 601-610.

Miller, P. L., and Mills, P. S. (1976). Some aspects of the development of breathing in the locust. *In* "Perspectives in Experimental Biology." Vol. I. "Zoology" (P. Spencer-Davies, ed.). pp. 199-208. Pergamon Press, Oxford.

Pittendrigh, C. S., and Skopik, S. D. (1970). Circadian systems. V. The driving oscillation and the temporal sequence of development. *Proc. Nat. Acad. Sci. (Wash.) 65*, 500-507.

Reynolds, S. E. (1977). Control of cuticle extensibility in the wings of adult *Manduca* at the time of eclosion: effects of eclosion hormone and bursicon. *J. Exp. Biol. 70*, 27-39.

Reynolds, S. E. (1980). Integration of behaviour and physiology in ecdysis. *Adv. Insect Physiol. 15*, in press.

Reynolds, S. E. and Truman, J. W. (1980). Eclosion Hormone. *In* "Insect Neurohormones." (T. A. Miller, ed.). Springer-Verlag, New York. In press.

Reynolds, S. E., Taghert, P. H., and Truman, J. W. (1979). Eclosion hormone and bursicon titres and the onset of hormonal responsiveness during the last day of adult development in *Manduca sexta* (L). *J. Exp. Biol. 78*, 77-86.

Riddiford, L. M. and Truman, J. W. (1978). Biochemistry of insect hormones and insect growth regulators. *In* "Insect Biochemistry" (M. Rockstein, ed.), pp. 307-357. Academic Press, New York.

Sláma, K. (1976). Insect haemolymph pressure and its determination. *Acta Ent. Bohemoslav. 73*, 65-75.

Taghert, P. H., Truman, J. W., and Reynolds, S. E. (1980). Physiology of pupal ecdysis in the tobacco hornworm, *Manduca sexta*. II. Chemistry, distribution, and release of eclosion hormone at pupal ecdysis. Submitted.

Truman, J. W. (1970). The eclosion hormone: its release by the brain and its action on the central nervous system of silkmoths. *Amer. Zool. 10*, 511–512.

Truman, J. W. (1971). Physiology of insect ecdysis. I. The eclosion behaviour of saturniid moths and its hormonal release. *J. Exp. Biol. 54*, 805–814.

Truman, J. W. (1972a). Physiology of insect rhythms. I. Circadian organization of the endocrine events underlying the moulting cycle of larval tobacco hornworms. *J. Exp. Biol. 57*, 805–820.

Truman, J. W. (1972b). Physiology of insect rhythms. II. The silkmoth brain as the location of the biological clock controlling eclosion. *J. Comp. Physiol. 81*, 99–114.

Truman, J. W. (1973a). Physiology of insect ecdysis. II. The assay and occurrence of the eclosion hormone in the Chinese Oak Silkmoth, *Antheraea pernyi*. *Biol. Bull. 144*, 200–211.

Truman, J. W. (1973b). Physiology of insect ecdysis. III. The relationship between the hormonal control of eclosion and of tanning in the tobacco hornworm, *Manduca sexta*. *J. Exp. Biol. 58*, 821–829.

Truman, J. W. (1976). Development and hormonal release of adule behavior patterns in silkmoths. *J. Comp. Physiol. 107*, 39–48.

Truman, J. W. (1978a). Rhythmic control over endocrine activity in insects. *In* "Comparative Endocrinology" (P. J. Gaillard and H. H. Boer, eds.), pp. 123–148. Elsevier/North Holland, Amsterdam.

Truman, J. W. (1978b). Hormonal release of stereotyped motor programmes from the isolated nervous system of the Cecropia silkmoth. *J. Exp. Biol. 74*, 151–173.

Truman, J. W., and Riddiford, L. M. (1970). Neuroendocrine control of ecdysis in silkmoths. *Science 167*, 1624–1626.

Truman, J. W., and Riddiford, L. M. (1974). Physiology of insect rhythms. III. The temporal organization of the endocrine events underlying pupation of the tobacco hornworm. *J. Exp. Biol. 60*, 371–382.

Truman, J. W., Mumby, S. M., and Welch, S. K. (1980a). Involvement of cyclicGMP in the release of stereotyped behaviour patterns in moths by a peptide hormone. *J. Exp. Biol.*, in press.

Truman, J. W., Taghert, P. H., and Reynolds, S. E. (1980b). Physiology of pupal ecdysis in the tobacco hornworm, *Manduca sexta*. I. Evidence for control by eclosion hormone. Submitted.

Way, M. J.   (1950).   The structure and development of the
    larval cuticle of *Diataraxia oleracea* (Lepidoptera).
    Quart. J. Micr. Sci. 91, 145–182.
Wigglesworth, V. B.   (1934b).   The physiology of ecdysis in
    Rhodnius prolixus (Hemiptera). II. Factors controlling
    moulting and metamorphosis.   *Quart. J. Micr. Sci. 77*,
    191–222.
Wigglesworth, V. B.   (1936d).   The function of the corpus
    allatum in the growth and reproduction of *Rhodnius
    prolixus* (Hemiptera).   *Quart. J. Micr. Sci. 79*, 91–121.
Wigglesworth, V. B.   (1947a).   The epicuticle in an insect,
    Rhodnius prolixus (Hemiptera).   *Proc. Roy. Soc. B. 134*,
    163–181.
Wigglesworth, V. B.   (1956i).   Formation and involution of
    striated muscle fibres during the growth and moulting
    cycle of *Rhodnius prolixus* (Hemiptera).   *Quart. J. Micr.
    Sci. 97*, 465–480.

THE HORMONAL CONTROL OF MORPHOGENESIS
OF A LEPIDOPTERAN EPIDERMAL CELL[1]

Lynn M. Riddiford

Department of Zoology
University of Washington
Seattle, Washington

INTRODUCTION

Sir Vincent Wigglesworth has been an inspiring leader in many aspects of insect physiology as evidenced by a perusal of his long list of publications. But nowhere has his influence been more monumental than in the endocrine regulation of growth, molting, and metamorphosis in insects. His initial studies on the hemipteran *Rhodnius prolixus* (Wigglesworth, 1934b, 1936d, 1940b) showed the necessity of two hormones, the "moulting hormone" and an inhibitory or "juvenile hormone," for the control of molting and metamorphosis and ushered in the science of insect endocrinology. Similarly, his detailed studies of the insect epidermal cell through a molting cycle (beginning with Wigglesworth, 1933d and continuing to the present) have served as a model and inspiration to workers ever since.

In my tribute to this pioneer in the field, I will confine my discussion to the hormonal control of molting and metamorphosis in a lepidopteran epidermal cell, particularly what we have learned about the action of these two hormones in directing its morphogenesis from study of the tissue *in vitro*.

[1] *Unpublished studies cited herein are supported by NSF, NIH, and the Rockefeller Foundation.*

403

ENDOCRINE CONTROL OF MOLTING AND METAMORPHOSIS IN LEPIDOPTERA

As in all insects, ecdysone release from the prothoracic glands initiates the molting process in Lepidoptera. Ecdysone is then converted to 20-hydroxyecdysone (20HE) by the peripheral tissues, most notably the fat body, and this latter hormone directs the epidermis to produce a new cuticle. Since most of the general body epidermal cells make successively several larval cuticles, then a pupal cuticle, and finally an adult cuticle, juvenile hormone (JH) from the corpora allata regulates the progressive read-out of this information. Consequently, during the onset of larval molts (including the one in embryonic life which produces the first instar larval cuticle), the JH titer is high (Gilbert and Schneiderman, 1961; Schooley, personal communication; see Riddiford, 1980, for review) so that the typical flexible larval cuticle is produced. Heteromorphosis may be seen among the different larval instars (Williams, 1961) in some species; whether this is controlled by the JH titer as first suggested by Wigglesworth (1952d) for similar features in *Rhodnius* or by an inherent sequential program within the epidermal cells activated by ecdysone (Willis, 1974) is not yet clear.

Metamorphosis in the Lepidoptera entails a change in body form which is effected by utilization of imaginal anlage and discs for completely new structures such as the adult eyes, wings, and genitalia as well as by a reprogramming of the general body epidermis. Therefore, during the final larval instar, a complex series of endocrine events occur. As reviewed in Riddiford (1980), the JH titer is high at ecdysis, falling during feeding to a very low or undetectable level by the end of that period, then rising transiently during the prepupal period. When the JH titer falls below some threshold level, a small amount of ecdysone is released to initiate metamorphosis. Thus one observes the cessation of feeding and the onset of prepupal behaviors. Also, at this time the epidermal cells are reprogrammed for the production of pupal cuticle. A second longer and larger release of ecdysone occurs sometime later to cause formation of the pupa. During this prepupal period the JH titer transiently rises and falls again by the time of pupal ecdysis.

After pupal ecdysis the JH titer remains undetectable, and ecdysone is again released, first causing the cellular changes in both the general body epidermis and in the imaginal discs that allow subsequent adult differentiation, then as the titer increases causing the formation of the adult cuticle.

LARVAL MOLTING

From the tobacco hornworm, *Manduca sexta*, we have utilized two types of epidermis to study the hormonal control of larval cuticle deposition. The first is the crochet epidermis which makes the biordinal rows of hooked setae or crochets on the abdominal prolegs and which dies at metamorphosis. Since this epidermis is detached from the overlying cuticle during the intermolt period, it can be readily explanted and caused to molt *in vitro* (Fain and Riddiford, 1977). Immediately after ecdysis to a given instar, this epidermis was not competent to respond to 20HE by molting, but gradually regained this ability during the first day. Moreover, when excised from larvae with JH in the hemolymph, additional JH in the culture medium was unnecessary for production of a new set of larval crochets, provided the 20HE was given immediately after explantation. By contrast, when exposed to hormone-free conditions, the competence for a larval molt in the absence of added JH gradually declined. Restoration of molting competence occurred during exposure to JH in an intermolt larva when the tissue was explanted from a penultimate instar larva but not when taken from a final instar larva. The latter was programmed to die once JH was withdrawn.

Thus here we have a uniquely larval tissue which is absolutely dependent on JH for its being, but which does not require the presence of the hormone at the time that 20HE initiates the molt. Obviously, the critical cellular processes that JH promotes and maintains are sufficiently long-lived so that they do not decay during the extremely short exposure to 20HE (3 hrs) necessary to initiate the molt. What these processes are is not known, but possibly they are directed toward proteins concerned with maintenance of the cells in a state of readiness to respond to ecdysteroids by molting. If so, when JH is withdrawn, these proteins would not be re-synthesized to balance degradation, so gradually the molting response would be lost. Re-exposure to JH would again allow the synthesis of these proteins provided that the dissolution of the cells had not been initiated by the playing-out of the normal 5th instar program prior to the JH decline.

The fourth instar dorsal abdominal epidermis is similar to
the crochet epidermis in that it will form a new larval cuticle (complete with bristles) in the absence of JH *in vitro*
when exposed to 20HE immediately upon explantation (Kiguchi,
unpublished). This production requires exposure to 5µg/ml
20HE for 6-12 hrs (Riddiford, unpublished), similar to the
longer time required *in vivo* as compared to the crochet epidermis (Truman *et al.*, 1974). *In vivo* the competence to
respond by a larval molt to exogenous 20HE declined dramatically with the fall of endogenous JH, although a pupal molt
could not be immediately elicited (Fain and Riddiford, 1976).
Larval molting can also be evoked in final instar abdominal
epidermis either *in vivo* (Truman *et al.*, 1974; Nijhout, 1975)
or *in vitro* (Mitsui and Riddiford, 1978; Riddiford *et al.*,
1980a; Kiguchi and Riddiford, in preparation) when JH is
present. In contrast to the crochet epidermis, in the absence of JH, it responds to high concentrations of 20HE with a
pupal molt (Riddiford et al., 1980; Kiguchi and Riddiford,
in preparation). However, it retains its competence for a
larval molt if re-exposed to JH before and during exposure
to 20HE (Mitsui and Riddiford, 1978) (see below). Thus, the
presence of JH and/or its effects is necessary for larval
molting and for preventing expression of the pupal program
similar to the role of JH in the larval development of
Rhodnius originally proposed by Wigglesworth (1934b, 1936d,
1940b).

In *Manduca* the presence of JH is not only important for
a new larval cuticle but also for its color. When the hormone is absent about 18 hrs after prothoracicotropic hormone
(PTTH) and ecdysone release initiating the molt to the final
instar, the newly formed cuticle melanizes at ecdysis 30 hrs
later (Truman et al., 1973). Beginning about 10 hrs after
ecdysis, the epidermis acquires a pink pigment and loses its
blue color [due to insecticyanin (Cherbas, 1973)]. This pink
pigment is comprised primarily of dihydroxanthommatin with a
small amount of a second ommochrome (Hori and Riddiford, in
preparation). When JH is present at the critical time in the
molting process, neither melanization nor the subsequent
accumulation of dihydroxanthommatin occurs. Studies on the
black mutant (Safranek and Riddiford, 1975) have indicated
that one of the actions of JH at this critical time is to
prevent the later activation (and/or synthesis) of the enzyme
converting 3-hydroxykynurenine to xanthommatin, since the
former compound accumulates in the epidermis of JH-treated
animals during the 5th instar (Hori and Riddiford, unpublished).
The presence of JH at this time also must prevent the deposition of phenoloxidases in the newly forming epicuticle

(Locke and Krishnan, 1971) so that later melanization is impossible. Whether it has additional effects on tyrosine
and/or tryptophan metabolism of the epidermal cell in its role
in larval pigmentation is under investigation.

INTERMOLT CUTICLE DEPOSITION

Within the Lepidoptera the cellular events concerned with
intermolt cuticle deposition during growth are best known in
Calpodes ethlius (Condoulis and Locke, 1966; Locke, 1970;
Dean *et al.*, 1980). To accommodate the large increase in volume during the final larval instar, both cuticular unfolding
and stretching accompanied by intussusception of proteins
(Condoulis and Locke, 1966) are necessary. In *Manduca* each
epidermal cell secretes a vertical column of chitin microfibrils (5μ diameter) during the first 2 days of feeding
(Wolfgang and Riddiford, unpublished). Then during subsequent
growth these bundles stretch more than the surrounding cuticle
due to their orientation. We do not know yet what contribution, if any, intussusception makes during this stretching.

Lamellate endocuticle deposition has been thought to require some neuroendocrine control (Condoulis and Locke, 1966;
Wielgus and Gilbert, 1978). *In vitro Manduca* day 1 final instar epidermis continues to deposit endocuticle (consisting
of both chitin and protein) for 4 days so that the thickness
of the cuticle keeps pace with that produced *in situ* (Mitsui
et al., 1980). Under our culture conditions of defined
Grace's medium at pH 6.6 with a constant perfusion of $95\%O_2-5\%$
CO_2, no nutritive sources such as fat body or neuroendocrine
factors were necessary for this deposition. Lamellae are
deposited regularly *in vitro* and, cytologically, the new endocuticle appears similar, although not as densely staining as
that formed *in situ* (Riddiford *et al*, 1980a; Wolfgang and
Riddiford, unpublished). Presumably, the stretching which
occurs *in situ* is partly responsible for this difference.
Whether the protein composition of the two cuticles is identical has not been determined, but some differences are to be
expected from the results of Willis and Hollowell (1976) on
pupal and adult cuticle deposited *in vitro*. Such differences
could also produce the staining difference observed.

THE CHANGE IN EPIDERMAL CELL COMMITMENT

Endocrine Regulation

During larval life the abdominal epidermis is committed
to a larval program of differentiation. It may undergo cell
division first prior to production of a new larval cuticle
(Sehnal and Novak, 1969), but the daughter cells retain (or
regain) this larvally-committed state as long as JH is present
whenever they are exposed to ecdysteroids. By contrast, when
exposed to ecdysteroids in the presence of little or no JH,
this epidermis becomes committed to pupal differentiation and
can no longer produce larval cuticle when subsequently exposed
to a molting concentration of 20HE in the presence of JH
(Truman et al., 1974; Riddiford, 1976, 1978; Riddiford et al.,
1980a).

As summarized above, in Lepidoptera the onset of metamorphosis is signaled by a dramatic decline in JH followed by
two releases of ecdysone. Contributing to this fall in JH
toward the end of the feeding period is the appearance of a
"JH-specific" esterase (reviewed in Riddiford, 1980). Hwang-
Hsu et al. (1979) concluded from the type of cuticle formed
by *Galleria mellonella* epidermal cells in response to injected
20HE that reprogramming of these cells occurs during the JH
esterase-induced fall of JH prior to the increase in ecdysone.
Certainly this increase in JH-esterase activity in both the
hemolymph and in the tissues is critical for eliminating JH
and, consequently, those cellular processes dependent on JH
so that the tissues can metamorphose. But their experiments
did not directly test the commitment of the cells at the time
since to do so would have required that the cells molt in the
presence of JH. The results of Sehnal and Schneiderman (1973)
with both implants of active corpora allata and applications
of JH mimics suggest that up to 128 hr after ecdysis, the time
of the first ecdysteroid peak (Hwang-Hsu et al., 1979), the
addition of JH permits continued larval differentiation of the
abdominal and thoracic epidermis of *Galleria*. These findings
support the idea that ecdysteroid action as well as the fall
of JH is necessary for epidermal reprogramming.

In *Manduca* the reprogramming of the abdominal epidermal
cells clearly occurs only in response to ecdysteroids after
the fall of JH based on the following evidence: 1) The cells
of day 2 larvae in which JH-esterase activity is high and the
JH titer is low to undetectable (Riddiford, 1980) remain larvally-committed (Riddiford, 1978). 2) Even when these cells

are exposed to hormone-free Grace's medium for 3 days, they can still produce a larval cuticle *in vitro* when exposed to 20HE in the presence of JH (Mitsui and Riddiford, 1978). 3) These day 2 cells become committed to pupal differentiation on a regional basis over the 24 hr exposure to ecdysteroids either *in vivo* or *in vitro* as long as JH is absent (Truman *et al.*, 1974; Riddiford, 1978). 4) Epidermis from larvae allatectomized 12 hrs after PTTH and ecdysone release to initiate the molt to the 5th larval instar (Kiguchi and Riddiford, 1978) retains its larval commitment in spite of the absence of endogenous JH until the release of ecdysone signaling the cessation of feeding in the 5th instar (Kiguchi and Riddiford, in preparation).

The virtual absence of JH (or at least concentrations < 10 pg/ml JHI in the medium) is necessary for all of the abdominal epidermal cells of *Manduca* to become pupally-committed in response to low concentrations of 20HE (Riddiford, 1976). By contrast, in *Pieris brassicae* (Mauchamp *et al.*, 1979), the JHI level increases slightly to about 1 ng/ml during the first release of ecdysone suggesting that JH may be necessary for the pupal reprogramming of at least some tissues in this species. Whether it is necessary for the pupal reprogramming of the abdominal epidermis remains to be tested by additional studies, preferably *in vitro*.

Cellular Changes

During the change in cellular commitment the epidermal cells detach from the overlying cuticle in response to the low level of ecdysteroid in the absence of JH (Riddiford and Curtis, 1978). But the plasma membrane plaques are still present and endocuticle continues to be deposited (Riddiford and Curtis, 1978; Wielgus and Gilbert, 1978; Riddiford *et al.*, 1980a; Wolfgang and Riddiford, unpublished). When the ecdysone subsides, the epidermis reattaches and by the following day the cells have changed from their columnar state during the feeding stage to cuboidal (Riddiford and Curtis, 1978). At this time fewer microvilli appear to be present (Wolfgang and Riddiford, unpublished). Thus as in *Rhodnius* (Wigglesworth, 1955f), epidermal detachment and accompanying macromolecular events in response to ecdysteroids are not necessarily antecedent to a molt.

The exposure to ecdysteroids in the absence of JH also causes the migration of the insecticyanin granules (Cherbas, 1973) from the apical region of the cell to the basal region and thence into the hemolymph. This begins first in the abdominal epidermis overlying the dorsal vessel just before the onset of wandering and proceeds over the remainder of the animal during the next few days. As wandering starts, the epidermal cells overlying the dorsal vessel begin synthesizing dihydroxanthommatin in response to the previous hormonal conditions (Truman and Riddiford, 1974; Hori and Riddiford, unpublished). Similar, more extensive epidermal ommochrome synthesis is initiated by ecdysteroids at this time in *Cerura vinula* (see review of these studies in Linzen, 1974). These effects of ecdysteroid on the epidermal cell in the absence of JH are similar to those described above in the regulation of larval pigmentation.

In *Manduca* abdominal epidermis two synchronous bursts of DNA synthesis are seen, one on day 2 and a second one 24 hrs later on day 3 (Wielgus *et al.*, 1979). These lead to a transient increase in octaploidy in 25% of the cells on day 3 (Dyer *et al.*, 1980). The meaning of this DNA synthesis and its relationship to later pupal differentiation of the epidermis is unclear. This synthesis is not initiated by the first release of ecdysone since the first burst occurs on day 2 before ecdysone is released (Wielgus *et al.*, 1979) and the second occurs irrespective of whether or not the epidermis is exposed to 20HE *in vitro* (Dyer *et al.*, 1980). In fact, the circumstantial evidence to date suggests that this DNA synthesis may be a response to the declining JH titer on day 2 and may be synchronized by some sort of neuroendocrine signal. This DNA synthesis, at least that occurring during the first release of ecdysone, is not necessary for the epidermal cells to become pupally committed since its inhibition by cytosine arabinoside does not affect the epidermal cell response to 20HE (Dyer *et al.*, 1980). However, those cells which underwent DNA synthesis at this time in the presence of the thymidine analog bromodeoxyuridine could not later express the pupally differentiated state (Dyer *et al.*, 1980). Importantly, they did not lose the capacity for laval differentiation; thus the genes already turned on were unaffected by the incorporation of this analog but new ones could not be expressed, as seen in other developing systems (Harding *et al.*, 1978).

In contrast to DNA synthesis, both concurrent mRNA and protein synthesis are critical for the ecdysteroid-induced change to pupal commitment (Riddiford et al., 1980b). When total cellular RNA from epidermis before, during, and after the ecdysteroid-induced change of commitment was translated in a wheat germ cell-free system, many mRNA's were seen to disappear and only a few new ones appeared (Chen and Riddiford, 1980). Of interest is the finding that the majority of changes were seen in mRNA's for relatively low molecular weight acidic proteins, especially the new ones that appeared in response to ecdysone release. Some of these might be nuclear regulatory proteins, but no evidence for or against this hypothesis is presently available. Some of the mRNA's that are no longer translatable are undoubtedly for larval cuticular proteins since endocuticle deposition ceases by the onset of wandering. Most or all the RNA's for pupal cuticular proteins seem not to be present at this time as the translation products at the onset of pupal cuticle synthesis (Riddiford, unpublished) or just before pupal ecdysis (Chen and Riddiford, 1980) show a whole new spectrum of protein bands compared to those from either cells exposed to ecdysteroids undergoing the change to pupal commitment or cells from wandering stage (pupally committed) larvae.

When the proteins being synthesized by the cells at the various times are analyzed (Kiely and Riddiford, unpublished), somewhat similar conclusions can be drawn. Many more proteins are turned off than on, and quantitative changes are more prevalent than qualitative ones. These studies have shown that there are also changes in proteins above 40,000 molecular weight whose RNA's were poorly translated in the wheat germ system. The spectrum of changes in both proteins and mRNA's during the ecdysone-induced change of commitment are manifold and only by careful detective work and a modicum of good fortune are we ever going to be able to say which newly synthesized RNA's and proteins are critical for the change of commitment. But we hope to be able to identify that class of pupal commitment-specific molecules and learn something about their regulation by both ecdysteroids and JH.

PUPAL CUTICLE FORMATION

Before pupal cuticle production is initiated in pupally committed cells by the second release of ecdysone, many cellular events must occur in preparation for the molt just as Wigglesworth (1933d; 1976, Insects and the Life of Man, Ch. 13) so aptly described in *Rhodnius*. In the Lepidoptera these events have been best studied in *Calpodes* (Locke, 1970, 1974; Dean *et al.*, 1980). Here I shall confine my discussion to the DNA synthesis and mitoses which occur at this time. Although in *Calpodes* (Dean *et al.*, 1980), and to some extent in *Manduca* (Dyer *et al.*, 1980) epidermis, mitosis begins during or shortly after the first ecdysone release, the major increase in cell number is not seen in either *Manduca* (Wielgus *et al.*, 1979) or *Galleria* (Sehnal and Novak, 1969) until the beginning of the second rise of ecdysone. In *Manduca* late on the day of wandering the dorsal abdominal nuclei, which usually range in diameter from 4μm to 10μm, all transiently expand in a wave that moves from anterior to posterior down the abdomen (Dyer *et al.*, 1980). At this time they do not change their ploidy, but this expansion is likely the initial response to the rise in ecdysone and the preparatory event for the wave of mitosis which occurs on the following day. It is noteworthy that this expansion and the following mitoses are initiated by a level of ecdysteroid no higher than that found during the change of commitment. The pupally committed cell can respond quickly to this low level of hormone and begin the necessary preparations for the molt whereas the larvally committed cell cannot. Evidently, the initial priming by ecdysteroids in the absence of JH prepares the cell for this rapid response to hormone in a manner similar to that seen in primary and secondary responses to hormones in vertebrate systems such as the chick oviduct (Schimke *et al.*, 1975).

These preparatory events occur in different regions of the epidermis at different times. Consequently, different regions of an abdominal segment are seen to require varying durations of exposure to the prothoracic glands *in vivo* (Truman *et al.*, 1974) or to similar concentrations of 20HE *in vitro* (Mitsui and Riddiford, 1976). Since duration of exposure rather than concentration of 20HE used was more important to the formation of cuticle, cells apparently have different lag periods in their response to ecdysteroids; whether this be due to a differing number of initial receptors for the hormone or to differing read-out times is not known. The set of cell divisions necessary for gin trap formation occurs early in the night of day 6 (Abbott and Riddiford, unpublished) whereas the formation of the rosettes of cells which subsequently produce the intrasegmental pocks occurs later that night (Roseland and Riddiford, 1980). These events are quite well-correlated with the times at which these abdominal regions no longer require additional ecdysone from the prothoracic glands (Truman *et al.*, 1974).

The ability to culture the insect epidermis in a defined culture medium makes it possible to learn more about both the hormonally-mediated events and the cellular processes involved in a molt. Most importantly, it allows one to define those processes which are intrinsic to the epidermal cell and those which depend on substances from the hemolymph other than simple nutrients such as sugars, amino acids, and various cofactors. In the case of pupal cuticle formation by *Manduca* epidermis *in vitro*, the surface features and histological appearance of the cuticle are similar to that formed *in vivo* (Mitsui and Riddiford, 1976). Preliminary electrophoretic analysis showed that many (although not all) of the SDS-soluble cuticular proteins had similar properties (Chen, Kiguchi, and Riddiford, unpublished). Although initially tanning of the newly formed pupal cuticle required 12 to 20 days *in vitro* (Mitsui, Riddiford, 1976) as compared to at most 24 hrs *in vivo*, recent studies have indicated that the larval epidermis before the change of commitment contains the necessary substance(s) to effect the beginning of tanning by the 5th day *in vitro* (after 3 days exposure to 5μg/ml 20 HE) and its completion by the 7th day (Riddiford *et al.*, 1980a; Kiguchi and Riddiford, in preparation). Although the identity of this substance(s) is not yet known, it appears to be lost from the epidermal cells during the change in commitment; then it or derivatives thereof are taken up by these cells at the time of tanning, possibly in response to the fall of ecdysteroids about 24 hrs prior to pupal ecdysis.

Since the surface features of the newly formed cuticle *in vitro* were characteristic of the region from which the epidermis was explanted (Mitsui and Riddiford, 1976), the analysis of an ecdysteroid-induced morphogenetic differentiation of a spaced cuticular pattern was possible. Exposure of the dorsal intrasegmental epidermis from wandering stage larvae to 5μg/ml 20HE for 3 days caused first an increase in cell density similar to that seen *in vivo*, then a differentiation of sets of rosettes of apparently polyploid cells which in turn formed the pocks (regularly spaced round depressions) in the pupal cuticle (Roseland and Riddiford, 1980). Analysis of the spacings among centrally located pocks and among those located at the edges suggested that the pock pattern arises by the differential accumulation of a cell-produced morphogen in certain cells to a threshold level that causes them to become pock-forming cells. This postulated mechanism is consistent with Wigglesworth's (1940a) hypothesis that the spacing of sensory hairs in *Rhodnius* was due to a depletion of the morphogen from the surrounding cells by the developing hair so no others could differentiate.

ADULT CUTICLE FORMATION

Many studies have been concerned with the pupal-adult
transformation of Lepidoptera and its hormonal control (see
reviews by Doane, 1972, and Willis, 1974). As is well known,
JH prevents adult development while allowing the reformation
of the pupa (Williams, 1961). As in the larval-pupal transformation, JH must be present at the onset of the rise of the
ecdysteroid titer (i.e., at the time of adult commitment) to
have this effect. Although many recent studies have been
concerned with both the cytological and biochemical (see reviews by Willis, 1974; Sridhara et al., 1978) aspects of
epidermal cell development in the presence and absence of JH,
little analysis of the initial cellular events relating to the
reprogramming of the cells for adult differentiation has
appeared. Presumably now that wing fragments can be caused to
produce either adult or pupal cuticle in vitro (Willis and
Hollowell, 1976), such an analysis is possible.

Some lepidopteran larval epidermis can form adult cuticle
without forming pupal cuticle (Nayar, 1954) whereas that of
other species cannot (Kato, 1973). The reason for this difference is unclear, but could be related to the type of coupling
that exists among the three different programs within the
genome in the different species. Normally, in vivo there is
some JH present during the prepupal period although the timing
of the prepupal JH rise in relation to cuticle deposition
appears to be different in different species (Mauchamp et al.,
1979; Riddiford, 1980). Manduca abdominal epidermis does not
require JH at the time of the pupal molt (Mitsui and Riddiford, 1976; Kiguchi and Riddiford, 1978). But when exposed
to a very low level of ecdysteroid over 15-20 days in the
absence of JH (in a neck-ligated wandering stage larva), then
to a spontaneous molting surge of endogenous ecdysone, a few
regions produce an adult cuticle with scales while the surrounding cells make pupal cuticle (Kirchner, Bellamy, and
Riddiford, unpublished). Similarly, Ephestia larval wing
discs may produce adult cuticle directly in vitro in response
to certain continuous low levels of 20HE (Nardi and Willis,
1979). Somehow low levels of ecdysteroids in the absence of
JH can eventually activate the adult program without the
expression of the preceding program. Consequently, each of
the sequential states of the polymorphic epidermal cell is
expressed independently of the others and depends only on the
hormonal signals.

HOW IMAGINAL DISCS DIFFER

Throughout the above discussion I have considered only how
the general body epidermis makes sequentially a larval, pupal,
and adult cuticle. Imaginal discs are epidermal derivatives
which make no cuticle until the onset of metamorphosis,
i.e., in the pupa. Therefore, it is of interest to compare
their response to the same hormonal signals as the abdominal
epidermis.

During larval life the wing imaginal discs of Lepidoptera
appear to grow continuously at a low rate, then at the onset
of metamorphosis show an abrupt increase in growth rate culminating in the formation of the pupal wing. By contrast, the
genital disc remains relatively small until the initiation of
adult development when it undergoes both extensive growth and
differentiation resulting in the formation of the external
genitalia. Consequently, the two seem to respond somewhat
differently to the hormonal milieu of metamorphosis.

In the case of the wing disc, JH can prevent metamorphosis
only until a critical cell number is attained (Kurushima and
Ohtaki, 1975). This usually occurs in the first days after
ecdysis to the final instar well before the release of ecdysone for metamorphosis. *In vitro* wing imaginal discs are
insensitive to the molting action of 20HE until the critical
event has occurred (Kurushima and Ohtaki, 1975; Oberlander and
Silhacek, 1976). Likely the fall of JH after the onset of
feeding in the final instar (Riddiford, 1980), coupled with the
small rise of ecdysteroid noted in *Manduca* and *Calpodes*
(Wielgus *et al.*, 1979; Dean *et al.*, 1980), is responsible for
these critical mitoses. Although nothing is known about the
cellular events occurring at this time, it is clear that after
this time JH can no longer prevent their metamorphosis. Consequently, supernumerary larvae with uneverted tanned pupal
wing discs are often obtained when exogenous JH is supplied
prior to ecdysone release but after this critical period
(Sehnal and Schneiderman, 1973; Oberlander and Silhacek, 1976;
Riddiford, 1980). Pupal commitment of the wing disc then
occurs prior to that of the abdominal epidermis, but it is not
acted upon until the small release of ecdysone in the absence
of JH initiates metamorphosis, a time when increased RNA and
protein synthesis in the discs occurs (Kurushima and Ohtaki,
1975; Lafont *et al.*, 1977).
  In some lepidopteran species but not in others the absence
of the corpora allata during the pupal molt allows precocious
adult differentiation of certain areas of the wing and genital

discs and of the eye anlage (Williams, 1961; Kiguchi and Riddiford, 1978). JH application at the time of the second release of ecdysone for pupation prevents this effect in *Manduca* indicating that one function of the prepupal rise in JH at this time (Riddiford, 1980) is to regulate the metamorphosis of the imaginal discs. In other species such as *Galleria* or *Pieris* where precocious metamorphosis is not observed, the prepupal rise in JH appears somewhat later (Hsiao and Hsiao, 1977; Mauchamp *et al.*, 1979) and presumably has another role.

CONCLUSIONS

Although we may now know much more about the insect epidermal cell and the hormonal control of its polymorphic differentiation than when Wigglesworth published his initial observations 46 years ago (see also Wigglesworth, 1976b), we still are a long way from understanding its genetic and molecular basis. How are the three programs of differentiation organized in the genome? How does JH regulate the activation of a particular program by 20HE? What are the essential differences between a larvally committed and a pupally committed cell? Why under normal conditions can a cell once it has progressed from one state to the next usually not go backwards? These and many other questions remain to be answered. Hopefully, the tremendous explosion of technology that has allowed the probing of eukaryotic gene structure and regulation in the past few years will provide new insights into the nature of the insect epidermal cell and the hormonal control of its morphogenesis.

ACKNOWLEDGMENTS

This paper was written at Stanford University while the author was supported by a fellowship from the Guggenheim Foundation.

REFERENCES

Chen, A. C., and Riddiford, L. M. (1980). The involvement of messenger RNA in the cellular commitment of *Manduca* epidermis. Submitted for publication.

Cherbas, P. T. (1973). Biochemical studies of insecticyanin. Ph.D. Thesis, Harvard University, Cambridge.

Condoulis, W. V., and Locke, M. (1966). The deposition of endocuticle in an insect, *Calpodes ethlius* Stoll. (Lepidoptera, Hesperiidae). *J. Insect Physiol. 12,* 311-323.

Dean, R. L., Bollenbacher, W. E., Locke, M., Gilbert, L. I., and Smith, S. L. (1980). Haemolymph ecdysteroid levels and cellular events in the intermoult/moult sequence of *Calpodes ethlius. J. Insect Physiol.* (in press).

Dyer, K. A., Thornhill, W., and Riddiford, L. M. (1980). DNA synthesis during the change to pupal commitment of *Manduca sexta* epidermis. Submitted for publication.

Fain, M. J., and Riddiford, L. M. (1976). Reassessment of the critical periods for prothoracicotropic hormone and juvenile hormone secretion in the larval molt of the tobacco hornworm *Manduca sexta. Gen. Comp. Endocrinol. 30,* 131-141.

Fain, M. J., Riddiford, L. M. (1977). Requirements for molting of the crochet epidermis of the tobacco hornworm larva *in vivo* and *in vitro. Wilh. Roux Arch. 181,* 285-307.

Gilbert, L. I., and Schneiderman, H. A. (1961). The content of juvenile hormone and lipid in Lepidoptera: sexual differences and developmental changes. *Gen. Comp. Endocrinol. 1,* 453-472.

Harding, J. D., Przybyla, A. E., MacDonald, R. J., Pictet, R. L., and Rutter, W. J. (1978). Effects of dexamethasone and 5-bromodeoxyuridine on the synthesis of amylase mRNA during pancreatic development *in vitro. J. Biol. Chem. 253,* 7531-7537.

Hsiao, T. H., and Hsiao, C. (1977). Simultaneous determination of molting and juvenile hormone titers of the greater wax moth. *J. Insect Physiol. 23,* 89-93.

Hwang-Hsu, K., Reddy, G., Kumaran, A. K., Bollenbacher, W. E., and Gilbert, L. I. (1979). Correlations between juvenile hormone esterase activity, ecdysone titre and cellular reprogramming in *Galleria mellonella. J. Insect Physiol. 25,* 105-111.

Kato, Y. (1973). Can larval epidermis omit the secretion of a pupal cuticle in a saturniid moth, *Samia cynthia ricini? J. Insect Phsyiol. 19,* 495-504.

Kiguchi, K., and Riddiford, L. M. (1978). A role of juvenile
    hormone in the pupal development of the tobacco hornworm,
    Manduca sexta. *J. Insect Physiol. 24*, 673-680.
Kurushima, M., and Ohtaki, T. (1975). Relation between cell
    number and pupal development of wing disks in *Bombyx mori*.
    J. Insect Phsyiol. 21, 1705-1712.
Lafont, R., Mauchamp, B., Blais, C., and Pennetier, J. L.
    (1977). Ecdysones and imaginal disk development during
    the last larval instar of *Pieris brassicae*. *J. Insect
    Physiol. 23*, 277-283.
Linzen, B. (1974). The tryptophan → ommochrome pathway in
    insects. *Adv. Insect Physiol. 10*, 117-246.
Locke, M. (1970). The molt/intermolt cycle in the epidermis
    and other tissues of an insect *Calpodes ethlius* (Lepi-
    doptera, Hesperiidae). *Tiss. Cell 2*, 197-223.
Locke, M., and Krishnan, N. (1971). The distribution of
    phenoloxidases and polyphenols during cuticle formation.
    Tiss. Cell 3, 103-126.
Mauchamp, B., Lafont, R., and Jourdain, D. (1979). Mass
    fragmentographic analysis of juvenile hormone I levels
    during the last larval instar of *Pieris brassicae*.
    J. Insect Physiol. 25, 545-550.
Mitsui, T., and Riddiford, L. M. (1976). Pupal cuticle for-
    mation by *Manduca sexta* epidermis *in vitro*: patterns of
    ecdysone sensitivity. *Develop. Biol. 54*, 172-186.
Mitsui, T., and Riddiford, L. M. (1978) Hormonal require-
    ments for the larval-pupal transformation of the epidermis
    of *Manduca sexta in vitro*. *Develop. Biol. 62*, 193-205.
Mitsui, T., Nobusawa, C., Fukami, J., Collins, J., and
    Riddiford, L. M. (1980). Inhibition of chitin synthesis
    by diflubenzuron in *Manduca* larvae. *J. Pesticide Sci.*,
    in press.
Nardi, J. B., and Willis, J. H. (1979). Control of cuticle
    formation of wing imaginal discs *in vitro*. *Develop.
    Biol. 68*, 381-395.
Nayar, K. K. (1954). Metamorphosis in the integument of
    caterpillars with omission of the pupal stage. *Proc. Roy.
    Ent. Soc. London, Ser. A 29*, 129-134.
Nijhout, H. F. (1975). Dynamics of juvenile hormone action
    in larvae of the tobacco hornworm, *Manduca sexta (L)*.
    Biol. Bull. 149, 568-579.
Oberlander, H., and Silhacek, D. L. (1976). Action of juve-
    nile hormone on imaginal discs of the Indian meal moth.
    In "The Juvenile Hormones" (L. I. Gilbert, ed.), pp. 220-
    233. Plenum Press, New York.
Riddiford, L. M. (1976). Hormonal control of insect epidermal
    cell commitment *in vitro*. *Nature 259*, 115-117.

Riddiford, L. M. (1978). Ecdysone-induced change in cellular commitment of the epidermis of the tobacco hornworm, *Manduca sexta*, at the initiation of metamorphosis. *Gen. Comp. Endocrinol. 34*, 438-446.

Riddiford, L. M., and Curtis, A. T. (1978). Hormonal control of epidermal detachment during the final feeding stage of the tobacco hornworm larva. *J. Insect Physiol. 24*, 561-568.

Riddiford, L. M. (1980). Interaction of ecdysteroids and juvenile hormone in the regulation of larval growth and metamorphosis of the tobacco hornworm. In "Progress in Ecdysone Research" (J. A. Hoffmann, ed.), Elsevier, Amsterdam, in press.

Riddiford, L. M., Kiguchi, K., Roseland, C. R., Chen, A. C., and Wolfgang, W. J. (1980a). Cuticle formation and sclerotization *in vitro* by the epidermis of the tobacco hornworm, *Manduca sexta*. In "Invertebrate Systems in Vitro" (E. Kurstak, K. Maramorosch, and A. Dubendorfer, eds.), pp. 103-115. Elsevier / North Holland, Amsterdam.

Riddiford, L. M., Chen, A. C., Graves, B. J., and Curtis, A. T. (1980b). RNA and protein synthesis during the change to pupal commitment of *Manduca sexta* epidermis. Submitted for publication.

Roseland, C. R., and Riddiford, L. M. (1980). Analysis of a cuticular spacing pattern after metamorphosis *in vitro* of larval integument. In "Invertebrate Systems *In Vitro*" (E. Kurstak, K. Maramorosch, and A. Dubendorfer, eds.), pp. 117-123. Elsevier / North Holland, Amsterdam.

Safranek, L., and Riddiford, L. M. (1975). The biology of the black larval mutant of the tobacco hornworm, *Manduca sexta*. *J. Insect Physiol. 21*, 1931-1938.

Schimke, R. T., McKnight, G. S., Shapiro, D. J., Sullivan, D., and Palacios, R. (1975). Hormonal regulation of ovalbumin synthesis in the chick oviduct. *Rec. Prog. Horm. Res. 31*, 175-211.

Sehnal, F., and Novak, V.J.A. (1969). Morphogenesis of the pupal integument in the wax moth (*Galleria mellonella*) and its analysis by means of juvenile hormone. *Acta. Ent. Bohemoslov. 66*, 137-145.

Sehnal, F., and Schneiderman, H. A. (1973). Action of the corpora allata and of juvenilizing substances on the larval-pupal transformation of *Galleria mellonella L.* (Lepidoptera). *Acta Ent. Bohemoslov. 70*, 289-302.

Sridhara, S., Nowock, J., and Gilbert, L. I. (1978). Biochemical endocrinology of insect growth and development. In *Intern. Rev. Biochem.*, "Biochemistry and Mode of Action of Hormones II," vol. 20 (H.V. Rickenberg, ed.), pp. 133-188. University Park Press, Baltimore.

Truman, J. W., and Riddiford, L. M. (1974). Physiology of insect rhythms. III. The temporal organization of the endocrine events underlying pupation of the tobacco hornworm. *J. Exp. Biol.* 60, 371-382.

Truman, J. W., Riddiford, L. M., and Safranek, L. (1973). Hormonal control of cuticle coloration in the tobacco hornworm, *Manduca sexta*: basis of an ultrasensitive bioassay for juvenile hormone. *J. Insect Physiol.* 19, 195-203.

Truman, J. W., Riddiford, L. M., and Safranek, L. (1974). Temporal patterns of response to ecdysone and juvenile hormone in the epidermis of the tobacco hornworm, *Manduca sexta*. *Develop. Biol.* 39, 247-262.

Wielgus, J. J., and Gilbert, L. I. (1978). Epidermal cell development and control of cuticle deposition during the last larval instar of *Manduca sexta*. *J. Insect Physiol.* 24, 629-637.

Wielgus, J. J., Bollenbacher, W. E., and Gilbert, L. I. (1979). Correlations between epidermal DNA synthesis and haemolymph ecdysteroid titre during the last larval instar of the tobacco hornworm, *Manduca sexta*. *J. Insect Physiol.* 25, 9-16.

Wigglesworth, V. B. (1933d). The physiology of the cuticle and of ecdysis in *Rhodnius prolixus* (Triatomidae, Hemiptera); with special reference to the function of the oenocytes and of the dermal glands. *Quart. J. Micr. Sci.* 76, 269-318.

Wigglesworth, V. B. (1934b). The physiology of ecdysis in *Rhodnius prolixus* (Hemiptera) II. Factors controlling moulting and "metamorphosis". *Quart. J. Micr. Sci.* 77, 191-222.

Wigglesworth, V. B. (1936d). The functions of the corpus allatum in the growth and reproduction of *Rhodnius prolixus* (Hemiptera). *Quart. J. Micr. Sci.* 79, 91-121.

Wigglesworth, V. B. (1940a). Local and general factors in the development of "pattern" in *Rhodnius prolixus* (Hemiptera). *J. Exp. Biol.* 17, 180-200.

Wigglesworth, V. B. (1940b). The determination of characters at metamorphosis in *Rhodnius prolixus* (Hemiptera). *J. Exp. Biol.* 17, 201-222.

Wigglesworth, V. B. (1952d). Hormone balance and the control of metamorphosis in *Rhodnius prolixus* (Hemiptera). *J. Exp. Biol.* 29, 620-631.

Wigglesworth, V. B. (1955f). The role of the haemocytes in the growth and moulting of an insect, *Rhodnius prolixus* (Hemiptera). *J. Exp. Biol.* 32, 649-663.

Wigglesworth, V.B. (1976b). Juvenile hormone and pattern formation. *In* "Insect Development", *Symp. Roy. Ent. Soc. Lond. 8*, 186-202.

Williams, C. M. (1961). The juvenile hormone. II. Its role in the endocrine control of molting, pupation, and adult development in the cecropia silkworm. *Biol. Bull. 116*, 323-338.

Willis, J. H. (1974). Morphogenetic action of insect hormones. *Ann. Rev. Entomol. 19*, 97-115.

Willis, J. H., and Hollowell, M. P. (1976). The interaction of juvenile hormone and ecdysone: antagonistic, synergistic, or permissive? *In* "The Juvenile Hormones" (L. I. Gilbert, ed.), pp. 270-287. Plenum Press, New York.

MORPHOGENESIS IN TISSUE CULTURE:
CONTROL BY ECDYSTEROIDS

Herbert Oberlander

Insect Attractants, Behavior and Basic Biology
Research Laboratory, Agricultural Research,
Science and Education Administration, USDA
Gainesville, Florida

I. INTRODUCTION

Investigations of both insect endocrinology and insect tissue culture were initiated more than a half-century ago (Goldschmidt, 1915; Kopec, 1922), although the two interests did not intersect in a meaningful way until the 1960s. This productive union of tissue culture and endocrinology resulted from significant advances made in both fields. In the area of insect tissue culture the development of a culture medium sufficient to maintain continuous cell lines was developed by Grace (1962). During the same period the structures of ecdysone and 20-hydroxyecdysone were elucidated and proven by synthesis (see review by Morgan and Poole, 1977). Most importantly, ecdysteriods were found in high concentrations in certain plants (e.g. Nakanishi et al., 1966), and were made generally available. Thus, the conditions were ready for the utilization of tissue culture techniques to solve problems in insect endocrinology. To borrow the words of Sir V. B. Wigglesworth's introduction to the 1939 edition of *The Principles of Insect Physiology,* I believe that tissue culture provides..."an ideal medium in which to study all the problems of physiology, but if this medium is to be used to best advantage, the principles and peculiarities" must be appreciated.

I will consider four morphogenetic systems that have been studied *in vitro*: tracheole migration, cellular elongation, imaginal disc evagination, and cuticle deposition. In each of these cases experimental analysis of morphogenesis was significantly aided by the utilization of tissue culture techniques.

Three of the case studies utilized organ cultures (tracheole migration, cuticle deposition and evagination), and one study (cellular elongation) involved established cell lines. The variety of systems examined here will permit a broad view of the mode of action of the ecdysteroids on the subcellular basis of morphogenesis. Much of this work was directly or indirectly stimulated by the research of Sir V. B. Wigglesworth.

II. TRACHEOLE MIGRATION

Wigglesworth (1954b, 1959e) showed that *Rhodnius* tracheoles move to adjacent oxygen-deficient areas of the epidermis by means of attachment to contractile projections from the epidermal cells. Such movement can exceed one mm. During studies in my laboratory on the effects of ecdysone on *Galleria mellonella* wing discs *in vitro* we noted that tracheoles migrate from the base of the wing disc into the lacunae following hormone treatment (Oberlander and Fulco, 1967; Oberlander, 1969). Stimulated by Wigglesworth's observations on the mode of tracheole movement we investigated the subcellular basis of tracheole migration into the wing disc lacunae. We learned that microtubules were present in large numbers in the tracheoles, and were oriented with their long axis parallel to the long axis of the tracheole. Moreover, both vinblastin and colchicine disrupted the microtubules and prevented ecdysone-induced tracheole migration (Hasskarl et al., 1973) (Table 1).

TABLE I*. Inhibition *in vitro* of α-Ecdysone (3 μg/ml) Induced Tracheole Migration in Wing Discs

Treatment	Number of discs	Percentage of discs with tracheole migration
Colchicine 10^{-5} M	50	10
Control	50	75
Vinblastin 10^{-8} M	50	0
Control	50	84

*Hasskarl et al., 1973.

Thus, one explanation for the movement of the tracheoles into lepidopteran wing discs is that the microtubules "stiffen",

and the tracheoles then uncoil following the path of least
resistance into the established lacunae. However, we could
not ascertain from these early tissue culture studies whether
the tracheoles were in fact actively moving in response to
stimulation by ecdysone, or whether they were being drawn to
the metabolically active wing disc cells by some other means.

Additional information on the mechanism of movement of
the tracheoles required direct observation of the intact wing
discs at various stages. To accomplish this Mitzenmacher
(1972) and Stephens, investigated tracheole migration in *G.
mellonella* wing discs with a Zeiss-Nomarski® differential
interference-contrast microscope. A wing disc immediately
after dissection from last instar larvae on the seventh day
of the stadium (tracheole migration initiated) is shown in
Figure 1. Fifth day wing discs were cultured *in vitro* in
chemically defined Grace's medium and 3 µg/ml of ecdysone and
photographed after 36 h. The tracheoles appear to uncoil as
they progress through the lacunae, but projections from the
adjacent wing disc cells were not noted (Fig. 2).

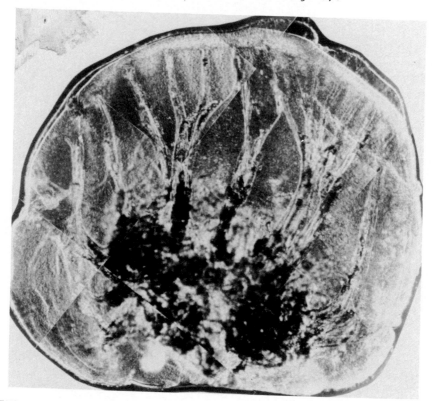

FIGURE 1.   *Tracheole migration in wing disc of last instar
larva* (G. mellonella) *(Mitzenmacher, 1972).*

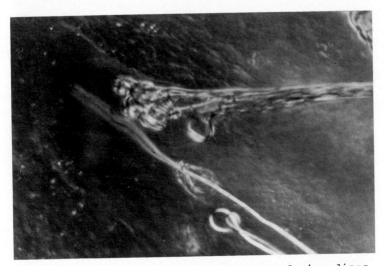

FIGURE 2.   Extended tracheoles in lacunae of wing discs
            cultured in vitro with ecdysone (Mitzenmacher, 1972).

    If the tracheole migration in lepidopteran wing discs is
the result of a "mechanical uncoiling" of the tracheoles it
should be possible to cause uncoiling of the tracheoles
independent of the epidermis. Mitzenmacher accomplished this
by treating isolated tracheole masses from wing discs of
fifth day last instar larvae, and incubating them in calcium-
free medium (with 0.1 mm EDTA). In such experiments the
tracheoles projected out from the mass within 20 sec (Fig. 3).
In Locke's early studies of tracheoles he also recognized a
role for mechanical uncoiling in tracheole migration (Locke,
personal communication).

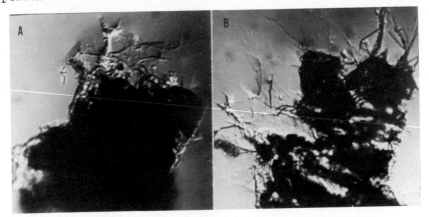

FIGURE 3.   Extension of tracheoles from isolated masses
            incubated in vitro in calcium-free medium, A - zero time,
            B - 20 seconds (Mitzenmacher, 1972).

Wigglesworth (1977a) observed that tracheole movement in *Rhodnius* could be related to the presence of oriented microtubules in the tracheoles, but he noted that the "Microtubules function as tendons rather than as muscles." This may also be the case for the wing disc tracheoles. However, the evidence at this time points to the tracheoles themselves as the source of ecdysone-induced motility in developing lepidopteran wing discs.

The action of ecdysone on the wing disc tracheoles required protein synthesis as demonstrated by inhibition of tracheole migration *in vitro* by cycloheximide. However, there was no apparent effect on the amount of microtubular protein present in the cells (Hasskarl, Stephens and Oberlander, unpublished observations). Thus, while it is clear that ecdysteroid-induced tracheole migration in wing discs depends on the presence of oriented microtubules, the mechanism of hormone action in this system requires further elucidation.

III. CELLULAR ELONGATION

Tracheole migration in imaginal discs *in vitro* provided an opportunity to investigate cellular morphogenesis within an organized tissue. It would be advantageous as well to study changes in form in cells grown as continuous lines. This became possible with the development of the first stable insect cell lines (Grace, 1962). Early efforts to demonstrate ecdysone-induced biochemical or morphological changes with Grace's Antheraea cells were not clearcut (Judy, 1969; Mitsuhashi and Grace, 1970; Reinecke and Robbins, 1971). However, in 1972 Courgeon reported that ecdysone induced a series of morphological changes in a diploid cell line derived three years earlier from *Drosophila melanogaster*.

Courgeon (1972, 1975) found that as little as 0.5 - 5.0 X 10^{-8} M 20-hydroxyecdysone induced cells from a variety of established *Drosophila* cell lines either to flatten or become spindle-shaped. The changes in cell shape usually occurred within 24 h of hormone application, and were followed by cellular aggregation. Peak sensitivity to hormone was observed during the third through seventh month after cloning from the parent cell population.

Cherbas et al. (1977) and Berger et al. (1978) have confirmed and extended Courgeon's observations on the effects of 20-hydroxyecdysone on clones from *Drosophila* KC cell lines. Both groups noted a 5-fold increase in cell length to a maximum of 40-50 µm. The KC-H cells (Cherbas et al., 1977) required 10^{-8} M 20-hydroxyecdysone, while the related KC cells were treated with 10^{-5} M 20-hydroxyecdysone (Berger et al., 1978). The presence of long-thin processes following treatment with hormone were suggestive of neurone-like cells, and indeed the cells had acquired acetylcholinesterase activity (Cherbas et al., 1977).

The lack of morphological effects of hormone in lepidopteran cell lines continued to be a puzzle until Marks and Holman (1979) reported that 20-hydroxyecdysone induced cellular elongation in an established *Manduca sexta* cell line derived from embryos. In this study the number of days required to induce elongation of the cells was recorded. At a treatment dose of 2 X 10^{-8} M 20-hydroxyecdysone, cellular elongation took eight days, but at 1 X 10^{-6} M hormone it took only two days. Thus, the response of the *Manduca* CH II cells to hormone was not as rapid or sensitive as was the response of *Drosophila* HC cells. However, the CH II cell line had several morphological cell types present that may have reduced the overall response to hormone.

In 1978 Marks provided our laboratory with CH I cells that were established from *Manduca sexta* embryos at the same time as the CH II cells (Eide et al., 1975). The cells were in the 187th passage at the time we received them. Our initial experiments with CH I cells confirmed Marks' observations on the morphological effects of 20-hydroxyecdysone (Lynn et al., 1980). We established a new bioassay that depended upon the percentage of elongated cells in 10 predetermined areas of the culture flask (0.93 mm^2 total area). Six clones were isolated and investigated. In three of the clones, many cells were spindle-shaped before the addition of hormone, while the other three clones consisted primarily of round cells. In all clones, however, the cells responded to 20-hydroxyecdysone by elongating. The minimum elongation response scored as positive for the spindle-shaped cells was 100 μm, while it was set at 70 μm for the round cells (Lynn et al., 1980). An example of this pronounced response is seen in Figure 4. Maximal response in the CH-I-GV1 clone (50% elongation) was achieved two days after treatment with 2 X 10^{-6} M 20-hydroxyecdysone, while the threshold response was 2 X 10^{-8} M. Thus, Marks' conclusions from his work with mixed parent population were supported by our studies of cloned populations from a related cell line.

The mechanism of hormone-induced elongation in the *Drosophila* KC cells and in the *Manduca* CHI-GV1 cells has been addressed by Berger (1979) and Lynn et al. (1980), respectively. Berger has taken a biochemical approach and found an apparent increase in both tubulin and actin following treatment of the KC cells with 20-hydroxyecdysone. Furthermore, Berger et al. (1979) found that both colchicine and cytochalasin B inhibited hormone-induced elongation. Our studies of the *Manduca* CHI-GV1 cells support the hypothesis that elongation of the

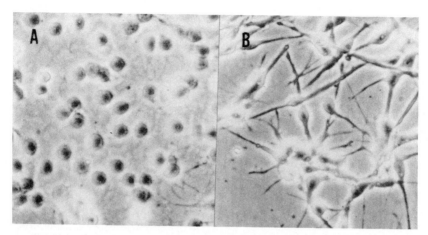

FIGURE 4. Elongation of cells of a Manduca sexta clone (CHI-
GVI), A - control, B - 5 days with 1 µg/ml 20-hydroxy-
ecdysone.

cells incubated with 20-hydroxyecdysone depends upon the
integrity of the microtubules. In our experiments both
vinblastin and colcemid inhibited the response to hormone
(Lynn et al., 1980). An example from the data is shown in
Table 2.

TABLE II*. Colcemid and Cellular Elongation

Treatment	Elongated cells %
Control (no hormone or colcemid)	10
1.0 µg/ml 20-hydroxyecdysone (3 days)	47
1.0 µg/ml 20-hydroxyecdysone (3 days) + 1.0 µg/ml colcemid (2 h)	12

*Lynn et al., 1980.

Manifestly, cellular elongation in established lines provides an excellent system for examining the cellular and
molecular basis of hormone-induced morphogenesis. We are at
the threshold of elucidating mechanisms involved in cellular
elongation in vitro.

V. EVAGINATION OF IMAGINAL DISCS

The investigations of tracheoles and cell lines discussed
in the previous two sections of this chapter demonstrate how
changes in the movement and shape of individual cells may be
examined *in vitro*. The role that movement and the alteration
of the shape of cells may play in morphogenesis becomes
pertinent to our consideration of hormone-induced evagination
of imaginal discs. The study of the evagination of the flat
imaginal discs into the tubuler leg or elongated wing structures began more than a half-century ago. Frew (1928) cultured leg imaginal discs obtained from blowfly larvae in larval haemolymph and did not observe any changes though the
tissue remained healthy for several days. However, when leg
discs from mature larvae were cultured in pupal haemolymph,
"The discs evaginated in the culture and grew into definite
segmented limbs." Frew concluded, "Evagination, therefore,
depends in part at least on changes in the composition of the
body fluids." We now know that the level of ecdysteroids in
the "body fluids" is the key to evagination.

The search for the mechanism of ecdysteroid-induced
evagination has been taken up in recent years in the laboratories of Fristrom and Mandaron. Mandaron (1970) demonstrated
unequivocally that evagination of *Drosophila* imaginal discs
occurred *in vitro* only in the presence of ecdysteriods. These
results were in accord with those of Oberlander and Fulco
(1967), who showed that ecdysteroids stimulated evagination of
lepidopteran wing discs cultured *in vitro*. This research has
now focused on the possible role of microtubules and microfilaments in evagination. Mandaron and Sengel (1973),
Hasskarl et al. (1973) and Fristrom and Fristrom (1975)
demonstrated that cytochalasin B, an inhibitor of microfilament function, prevented ecdysteroid-induced evagination of
imaginal discs. In their study of the effects of cytochalasin
B on the ultrastructure of imaginal discs, Fristrom and
Fristrom (1975) found that the filaments associated with the
basal surface were disorganized. However, effects of the
inhibitor on the cell membrane were also evident. Because the
basal filaments are transient structures observed during
evagination these authors concluded that microfilament
integrity was essential for evagination. Inhibitors of microtubule function, colcemid, colchicine and vinblastin, do not
prevent ecdysteroid-induced evagination at non-toxic doses
(Fristrom, 1972; Hasskarl et al., 1973; Fristrom and Fristrom,
1975).

The identification of microfilaments as essential
structures for evagination did little to explain how evagination occurred. Subsequent studies by Fristrom (1976) and

Fristrom et al. (1977) emphasized the primary role of cell
rearrangement with a secondary role for changes in cell shape;
but Mandaron et al. (1977) concluded the reverse. A role for
changes in cell shape in the evagination process had been
suggested by a number of scientists (Poodry and Schneiderman,
1970; Fristrom, 1972; Mandaron, 1973). Mandaron's (Mandaron
et al., 1977) time-lapse cinematographic and scanning
electron microscopic analysis led him to conclude that the
cell movement during evagination was very limited, but that
"Changes in cell shape and cell flattening represent the
essential mechanism of disc evagination." Fristrom (1976)
also observed that cell flattening occurred during evagination, but concluded that this was insufficient to account
for evagination. Figure 5 shows how a cylinder (such as a leg
disc) could elongate by either changes in cell shape or by

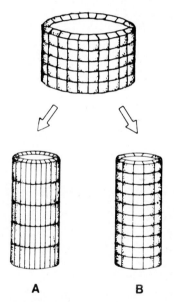

A   **B**

*FIGURE 5. Diagram of ways to change the shape of a cylindri-
cal piece of tissue with a given number of cells, A -
change in cell shape, B - cell arrangement (Fristrom, 1976).*

cellular rearrangement. If cellular rearrangement is
responsible for evagination only small movements of the cells
are required, but the result would be a reduced number of
cells in the circumference of the cylinder. Just such a
reduction in circumferential cell number was observed in leg
discs after evagination (Table 3). Also, during evagination
the total number of cells in the leg disc did not increase

significantly. The manner in which the cells rearrange
themselves in response to ecdysteroid is at this time a matter
of speculation, although a hypothetical scheme has been proposed (Fristrom, 1976).

TABLE III*. Changes in Cell Distribution in the
Basitarsus During the Final Stages of
Evagination

Degree of evagination	Mean cell number ($\pm$ SD)		
	Height	Circumference	Total
Partial (n = 3)	13 $\pm$ 2.6	69 $\pm$ 6.0	888 $\pm$ 101
Intermediate (n = 5)	20 $\pm$ 2.3	45 $\pm$ 6.6	884 $\pm$ 74
Full (n = 5)	30 $\pm$ 1.2	31 $\pm$ 4.8	921 $\pm$ 130

*Fristrom, 1976.

The unraveling of the cellular interactions during
evagination provides a most interesting system for exploring
relative significance of changes in cell shape and cell movement in ecdysteroid-induced morphogenesis.

VI. CHITIN SYNTHESIS AND CUTICLE DEPOSITION

In insects, changes in body form are fixed by the cuticle
which is both skin and skeleton to insects. Wigglesworth
(1959) summarized this view as follows: "The outward form of
the insect is fixed by the form of its external skeleton or
cuticle. This cuticle is the product of a single layer of
epidermal cells. Thus in the ultimate analysis it is the
functional activity of the epidermal cell which is mainly
responsible for the growth and form of the insect. The
control of growth resolves itself into the control of the
enzyme systems contained within this cell." In the 20 years
since this statement appeared there have been numerous efforts
to probe the control of the epidermal cell's enzyme systems.
However, surprisingly few studies of the hormonal control of
the biosynthesis of the cuticle's unique constituent, chitin,

have been undertaken. Recently, therefore, the action of ecdysteroids on chitin synthesis in cultured tissues has been investigated in several laboratories.

Ecdysteroid-induced cuticle production in cultured tissues has been reported for imaginal discs, embryos, and epidermis from Diptera, Lepidoptera and Orthoptera (reviewed in Oberlander, 1980). In addition, the quality of the cuticle produced *in vitro* has been examined with the electron microscope for imaginal discs (Mandaron, 1976; Dutkowski et al., 1977) and integument (Landureau, 1976).

In our investigations of morphogenesis in *Plodia interpunctella*, we found that a 24-h pulse of ecdysteroid produced the most complete cuticle in wing discs cultured *in vitro* (Fig. 6). It was evident that this imaginal disc *in vitro* system would be suitable for an exploration of the

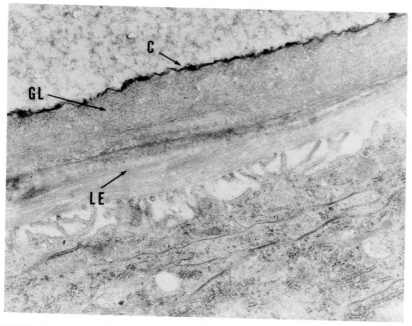

FIGURE 6. *Cuticle produced by wing disc of* G. mellonella *cultured for 72 h following a 24-h treatment with 20-hydroxyecdysone, C - cuticulin, GL - granular layer, LE - lamellate endocuticle (Dutkowski et al., 1977).*

hormonal control of chitin synthesis. Determining the role of ecdysteroids in controlling the induction of chitin synthesis is central to our understanding the impact of hormones on the form of the cuticular exoskeleton. The feasibility of this *in vitro* approach was established by Sowa and Marks (1975)

and Vardanis (1976) who demonstrated that the small amount of
chitin produced in organ culture (by orthopteran tissues)
could be studied by acceptable biochemical methods.

An analysis of *P. interpunctella* imaginal discs *in vivo*
has shown that chitin synthesis is not pronounced until the
prepupal stage, when a 60-fold increase in incorporation of
radiolabeled ^{14}C-N-acetylglucosamine was noted. However,
wing discs cultured *in vitro* respond to 20-hydroxyecdysone by
synthesizing chitin even when the tissue was obtained from
larvae early in the stadium. The ability (competence) to
respond to ecdysteroids increases steadily during the last larval stadium and is maximal with wing discs taken from mature
feeding, wandering or spinning larvae (Ferkovich et al., 1979).

Our experiments showed that while exposure to hormone (≥ 2
$\times 10^{-7}$ M 20-hydroxyecdysone) for 16-24 h was an effective
stimulus, there was a lag period and chitin synthesis did not
begin until ≈8 h after the conclusion of the hormone treatment
(Ferkovich et al., 1979). Moreover, studies with various
inhibitors indicated that synthesis of RNA and protein was
required during the hormone treatment period. Once exposure
to ecdysteroid was complete, inhibition of protein but not RNA
synthesis blocked the initiation of chitin synthesis
(Oberlander et al., 1980). The nature of the critical proteins
(for example, enzymes in the chitin biosynthetic pathway)
synthesized in response to 20-hydroxyecdysone remains to be
determined. The use of tissue culture techniques will
certainly continue to be important in defining the biochemical
actions of ecdysteroids that result in the production of
chitin.

VII. CONCLUSIONS

Wigglesworth (1959) has succinctly stated the area of
concern of the insect endocrinologist: "In some animals the
form of the body is strikingly influenced by disturbances in
hormone secretion; and thus the whole field of hormones and
morphogenesis fall within our theme." The four examples discussed in this essay, tracheole migration, cellular elongation,
evagination and chitin synthesis, demonstrate that hormone-
induced morphogenesis can be effectively studied *in vitro* from
the ultrastructural and biochemical view points. In fact
there may be a common basis for all four of these morphogenetic
processes. Whether microfilaments and/or microtubules play a
role in cuticle deposition (if not chitin synthesis) needs to
be explored. Our preliminary experiments with colcemid and
vinblastin suggest that ecdysteroids do not stimulate cuticle
formation in cultured wing discs when the microtubular system
is disrupted.

It should be evident that the combination of tissue culture, ultrastructural and biochemical techniques provides a significant approach that can scarcely be ignored by those interested in hormone-induced morphogenesis. I am confident that the student of insect biology has seen only the beginning of the utilization of this integrated approach for the elucidation of morphogenesis in insects.

ACKNOWLEDGMENT

Figures 1-3 were provided courtesy of D. Mitzenmacher and R. E. Stephens. Table 3 and Figure 5 are reprinted with the permission of Academic Press and D. Fristrom. Figure 6 is reprinted courtesy of Springer-Verlag. I wish to thank D. Lynn and D. L. Silhacek for useful discussions during the preparation of this manuscript.

Mention of a commercial or proprietary product in this chapter does not constitute an endorsement of that product by the U. S. Department of Agriculture.

REFERENCES

Berger, E., Ringler, R., Alahiotis, S., and Frank, M. (1978)
    Ecdysone-induced changes in morphology and protein
    synthesis in *Drosophila* cell cultures. *Develop. Biol.*
    62, 498-511.
Berger, E. (1979) Morphogenesis in embryonic *Drosophila*
    cell lines exposed to β-ecdysone. *In Vitro* *15*, 211.
Cherbas, P., Cherbas, L., and Williams, C. M. (1977)
    Induction of acetylcholinesterase activity by β-ecdysone
    in a *Drosophila* cell line. *Science 197*, 275-277.
Courgeon, A. M. (1972) Action of insect hormones at the
    cellular level. *Exptl. Cell. Res. 74*, 327-336.
Courgeon, A. M. (1975) Action of insect hormones at the
    cellular level II. *Exptl. Cell. Res. 94*, 283-291.
Dutkowski, A. B., Oberlander, H., and Leach, C. E. (1977)
    Ultrastructure of cuticle deposited in *Plodia inter-*
    punctella wing discs after various β-ecdysone treatments
    in vitro. *Wilhelm Roux's Archives 183*, 155-164.
Eide, P. E., Caldwell, J., and Marks, E. P. (1975) Estab-
    lishment of the cell lines from embryonic tissue of the
    tobacco hornworm, *Manduca sexta*. *In Vitro 6*, 395-399.
Ferkovich, S. F., Oberlander, H., Leach, C. E., and Van
    Essen, F. (1979) Hormonal control of chitin bio-
    synthesis in imaginal discs. *In* Proc. Inter. Conf. on
    Invertebrate Tissue Culture: Developments and
    Applications. Rigi, Switzerland. In press.
Frew, J. G. H. (1928) A technique for the cultivation of
    insect tissues. *J. Exp. Biol. 65*, 1-11.
Fristrom, D. (1976) The mechanism of evagination of
    imaginal discs of *Drosophila melanogaster*, III.
    Develop. Biol. 54, 163-171.
Fristrom, D., and Fristrom, J. W. (1975) The mechanism of
    evagination of imaginal discs of *Drosophila melanogaster*
    I. *Develop. Biol. 43*, 1-23.
Fristrom, J. W. (1972) The biochemistry of imaginal disk
    development. *In* "The Biology of Imaginal Disks"
    (H. Ursprung and N. Nothiger, eds.). pp 109-154,
    Springer-Verlag, Berlin and New York.
Fristrom, J. W., Fristrom, D. K., Fekete, E., and Kuniyuki,
    A. H. (1977) The mechanism of evagination of imaginal
    discs of *Drosophila melanogaster*. *Am. Zool. 17*, 671-684.
Goldschmidt, R. (1915) Some experiments on spermatogenesis
    in vitro. *Proc. Nat'l. Acad. Sci. (USA) 1*, 220-222.
Grace, T. D. C. (1962) Establishment of four strains of
    cells from insect tissues grown *in vitro*. *Nature 195*,
    788-789.

Hasskarl, E., Oberlander, H., and Stephens, R. E. (1973) Microtubules and tracheole migration in wing disks of *Galleria mellonella*. *Develop. Biol. 33*, 334-343.

Judy, K. J. (1969). Cellular response to ecdysterone *in vitro*. *Science 165*, 1374-1375.

Kopec, S. (1922) Studies on the necessity of the brain for the inception of insect metamorphosis. *Biol. Bull. Woods Hole 42*, 323-342.

Landureau, J. C. (1976) Insect cell tissue culture as a tool for developmental biology. *In* "Invertebrate Tissue Culture, (E. Kurstak and K. Maramorosch, eds.). pp 101-130, Academic Press, New York.

Lynn, D. E., Oberlander, H., and Leach, C. E. (1980) Effects of colcemid, vinblastine, cytochalasin B and cytochalasin D on the morphological response of *Manduca sexta* CH-I-GVI cells to 20-hydroxyecdysone. (In preparation)

Mandaron, P. (1970). Development *in vitro* des disques imaginaux de la drosophile, aspects morphologiques et histologiques. *Develop. Biol. 22*, 298-320.

Mandaron, P. (1973) Effects of α-ecdysone, β-ecdysone and inokosterone on the *in vitro* evagination of *Drosophila* leg discs and the subsequent differentiation of imaginal integumentary structures. *Develop. Biol. 31*, 101-103.

Mandaron, P. (1976) Ultrastructure desdisques de patte de drosophile cultives *in vitro*. *Wilhelm Roux' Archives 179*, 185-196.

Mandaron, P., and Sengel, P. (1973) Effect of cytochalasin B on the evagination *in vitro* of leg imaginal discs. *Develop. Biol. 32*, 301-207.

Mandaron, P., Guillermet, C., and Sengel, P. (1977) *In vitro* development of *Drosophila* imaginal discs: Hormonal control and mechanism of evagination. *Am. Zool. 17*, 661-670.

Marks, E. P., and Holman, G. M. (1979) Ecdysone action on insect cell lines. *In Vitro 15*, 300-307.

Mitsuhashi, U., and Grace, J. D. C. (1970) The effects of insect hormones on the multiplication rates of cultured insect cells *in vitro*. *Appl. Entomol. Zool. 5*, 182-188.

Mitzenmacher, D. (1972) Tracheole migration in *Galleria mellonella* wing disks. M.S. Thesis, Brandeis University, Waltham, Massachusetts.

Morgan, E. D., and Poole, C. F. (1977) Chemical control of insect moulting. *Comp. Biochem. Physiol. 57B*, 99-109.

Nakanishi, K., Koreeda, M., Sasuki, S., Chang, M. L., Hsu, H. Y. (1966) The structure of ponasterone A, an insect hormone from the leaves of *Podocarpus nakaii*. *Chem. Comm. 24*, 915-917.

Oberlander, H. (1969) Effects of ecdysone, ecdysterone and inokosterone on the *in vitro* initiation of metamorphosis of wing disks of *Galleria mellonella*. *J. Insect Physiol.* *15*, 297-304.

Oberlander, H. (1980) Tissue culture methods. *In* "Techniques in the Study of Arthropod Cuticle" (T. A. Miller, ed.). Springer-Verlag, New York, Berlin. (In press)

Oberlander, H., and Fulco, L. (1967) Growth and partial metamorphosis of imaginal disks of the greater wax moth, *Galleria mellonella, in vitro*. *Nature 216*, 1140-1141.

Oberlander, H., Ferkovich, S., Leach, E., and Van Essen, F. (1980) Inhibition of chitin biosynthesis in cultured imaginal discs: Effects of alpha-amanitin, actinomycin D, cycloheximide and puromycin. *Wilhelm Roux' Archives* (In press).

Poodry, C. A., and Schneiderman, H. A. (1970) The ultrastructure of the developing leg of *Drosophila melanogaster*. *Wilhelm Roux' Archives 166*, 1-44.

Reinecke, J. P., and Robbins, J. D. (1971) Reaction of an insect cell line to ecdysterone. *Exptl. Cell. Res. 64*, 335-338.

Sowa, B. A., and Marks, E. P. (1975) An *in vitro* system for the quantitative measurement of chitin synthesis in the cockroach: Inhibition by TH 6040 and polyoxin D. *Insect Biochem 5*, 855-859.

Vardanis, A. (1976) An *in vitro* assay system for chitin synthesis in insect tissue. *Life Sci. 19*, 1949-1956.

Wigglesworth, V. B. (1939) *The Principles of Insect Physiology*. Methuen, London.

Wigglesworth, V. B. (1959) *The Control of Growth and Form*. Cornell University Press, Ithaca.

HORMONAL CONTROL OF RNA SYNTHESIS IN WING EPIDERMIS[1]

S. Sridhara

Department of Biochemistry
University of Mississippi Medical Center
Jackson, Mississippi

Karen S. Katula[2]

Lawrence I. Gilbert

Department of Biological Sciences
Northwestern University
Evanston, Illinois

I. INTRODUCTION

Although Professor Wigglesworth's major contributions to the problem of the control of insect growth and development are usually thought to be in the areas of endocrine gland physiology and gland-gland interactions, his cytological studies (Wigglesworth, 1957d; 1963c) on the effects of molting hormone on the epidermal cells of *Rhodnius* set the stage for the currently accepted concept of steroid hormone action at the level of transcription. He noted that within a few hours of the administration of molting hormone, the epidermal cells were "activated," a condition characterized by enlarged nucleoli, increased cytoplasmic RNA and a profound increase in mitochondrial quantity. In essence, "activation" is the means by which the epidermis prepares for the subsequent synthesis of cuticular proteins. Whether or not the epidermis

[1]Supported by grants AM-02818 (L.I.G.) and GM 26549 (S.S.) from the National Institutes of Health and PCM 7903276 (S.S.) from the National Science Foundation.

[2]Present address: Department of Biochemistry and Biophysics, Oregon State University, Corvallis, Oregon.

439

was concomitantly exposed to juvenile hormone made no apparent difference, i.e., the basic cytological picture of "activation" remained the same. As will be seen in the present essay, the use of the most modern techniques of cell biology, including the *in vitro* translation of poly A$^+$ RNA, has not added a great deal to these observations on the mechanism of action of molting hormone (20-hydroxyecdysone; ecdysterone) or juvenile hormone.

In a sense, the cuticle *is* the insect, and growth of the organism depends on the temporally precise shedding of the partially digested old cuticle and the synthesis and secretion of a new and larger version. Since the cuticle is comprised primarily of chitin and protein, the synthesis of cuticular proteins by the epidermal cells, which themselves are targets of molting hormone and juvenile hormone (see Oberlander, Riddiford, this volume), has been postulated many times to be a good model system for examining the control of transcriptional events. The wing epidermis of saturniid moth pupae and pharate adults has been utilized in the present studies.

Sufficient circumstantial evidence exists to suggest that the primary effect of 20-hydroxyecdysone (see Williams, this volume) is on the nucleus leading to the stimulation of the synthesis of a diversity of mRNA sequences. The existence of specific cytoplasmic receptors for 20-hydroxyecdysone (and juvenile hormone as well) was predicted on the basis of the following two observations. First, salivary gland cell nuclei do not exhibit specific puffing when incubated with molting hormone *in vitro* although whole cells respond quite well (Berendes and Boyd, 1969). Second, the injection of molting hormone into the cytoplasm of these cells results in the stimulation of a normal puffing pattern but is ineffective when injected directly into the nucleus (Brady *et al.*, 1974). Recent data on *Drosophila* imaginal discs (Yund *et al.*, 1978) and cell cultures (Maroy *et al.*, 1978) have proven the existence of steroid hormone receptors for 20-hydroxyecdysone and cytosol receptors have apparently been demonstrated for juvenile hormone as well (O'Connor, personal communication). Now that the technical hurdle of demonstrating receptors for the major insect growth hormones apparently has been solved, one should be able to study the binding of these hormone-receptor complexes to specific chromatin sites as has been done with the vertebrate steroid hormones. It is, of course, this interaction which elicits the effects representing hormone action. Although such studies are desirable, they have yet to find their way into the entomological literature. Therefore, at this time we must be satisfied with reporting data pertaining to the synthesis of specific RNAs after hormone administration.

A. *Imaginal Discs*

During larval-pupal-adult metamorphosis, the imaginal discs grow and differentiate, finally giving rise to most of the adult structures (eyes, wings, legs, antennae, genitalia, etc.). Since this developmental process is dependent upon 20-hydroxyecdysone, it is expected that the hormone would have considerable effects on RNA synthesis. The ability to isolate these discs in large quantities from *Drosophila* larvae, as well as the capacity of 20-hydroxyecdysone to elicit development *in vitro* (Fristrom, 1972), suggested strongly that this was *the* model system for understanding the effects of molting hormone, ans possibly juvenile hormone, on RNA synthesis at the molecular level. Although the data resulting from such studies indicate that new RNA synthesis occurs in imaginal discs as a consequence of molting hormone treatment, the characterization and function of the newly synthesized RNA have eluded analysis. As expected, the effects are much more pronounced on rRNA synthesis than on mRNA synthesis (Scheller *et al.*, 1978; Fristrom, 1980), and in the few cases where mRNA induction has been investigated, their function has yet to be identified (Bonner and Pardue, 1976; Fristrom, 1980). Notwithstanding the above, the imaginal disc system has attracted very competent investigators and remains a prime candidate for elucidating insect hormone action at the molecular level.

B. *Epidermis*

Current hypotheses on the effects of insect hormones on RNA synthesis originated from the work of Karlson and his colleagues (Clever, Sekeris, etc.) on the effects of molting hormone on chromosomal puffing in dipteran salivary glands and on the induction of the enzyme DOPA (dihydroxy phenylalanine) decarboxylase in the epidermal cells of the blowfly, *Calliphora*. Indeed, the latter system remains the only well-documented case of hormonal regulation of mRNA in insects. This enzyme, i.e. DOPA decarboxylase, is required for the production of dopamine, which is employed for tanning of the cuticle after N-acetylation. This cuticular tanning occurs during the larval-pupal metamorphosis of Diptera when the soft larval cuticle is transformed into the hard, dark puparium. The enzyme content of the epidermis is very low during larval growth and increases just before metamorphosis as the

ecdysteroid titer climbs to its zenith. Furthermore, deprivation of the hormone by ligation prevents enzyme induction
while administration of 20-hydroxyecdysone to these "isolated"
abdomens induces the appearance of the enzyme. Based on these
observations, considerable research has been carried out on
this system showing that the induction of enzyme activity is
a consequence of increased *de novo* synthesis of new enzyme
molecules which in turn is dependent on RNA synthesis. A
comparison of the amount of enzyme present, the ability of
isolated mRNA to direct *in vitro* translation into DOPA decarboxylase, and the capacity of epidermal cell polysomes to
direct the formation of the enzyme *in vitro* when derived from
animals experiencing an endogenous increase in molting hormone titer, all demonstrate that the mRNA for this enzyme is
induced by 20-hydroxyecdysone (Fragoulis and Sekeris, 1975;
Fragouli-Fournogeraki *et al.*, 1978). Recent studies with the
Drosophila DOPA decarboxylase, cloning of the DOPA decarboxylase gene, etc. will surely result in sophisticated genetic
and molecular biological analyses of the action of 20-
hydroxyecdysone at the level of the genome.

II. CONTROL OF TRANSCRIPTION IN WING EPIDERMIS

A. *Cuticular Proteins*

The wing epidermis of silkmoth pupae *(Hyalophora cecropia,
Antheraea polyphemus, Antheraea pernyi)* has also been considered an excellent model system for studying hormonal control of transcription in general, and specific gene expression
in particular. The diapausing pupa is characterized by a very
low level of metabolism and the virtual absence of cell division and growth. Transfer of these saturniid pupae from low
temperature to room temperature results in the initiation of
adult development as a consequence of a rise in titer of
molting hormone. The following will summarize our investigation of RNA synthesis in the wing epidermis as a consequence
of molting hormone action as well as the effects of juvenile
hormone.
The wing epidermis responds to the insect hormones by
synthesizing and secreting specific proteins, some of which
may be characteristic of a particular developmental stage.
Normally, the pupal wing epidermis will never encounter juvenile hormone (JH), but if the hormone is applied experimentally in the presence of 20-hydroxyecdysone (20-Ec), the epidermis will respond by secreting a second pupal cuticle.
Thus, depending on the hormonal milieu, the pupal epidermis

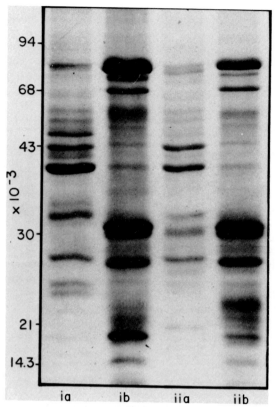

Figure 1. SDS gel electrophoresis of adult and pupal
wing cuticular proteins extracted from A. polyphemus. Proteins were extracted by homogenization with either 8M urea
(i) or 6M guanidine hydrochloride (ii) and dialyzed overnight
against 2% SDS before subjecting them to electrophoresis.
Numbers represent molecular weight standards. The stain was
Coomassie blue. Series (a) derived from adult scales; series
(b) derived from untanned, second pupal cuticle (see text for
details).

has the capacity to secrete a second pupal cuticle or complete its normal program of development and differentiation
and secrete adult cuticle, produce scales, etc. The thin,
translucent, adult wings replete with colored scales differ
dramatically from those of the pupa which are covered by
thick, highly tanned pupal cuticle and it is reasonable to
assume that such differences are in part the result of differences in the protein content of the two cuticle types.

To determine the validity of this assumption, a series of *A. polyphemus* pupae were injected with either 20-Ec to elicit synchronous adult development or with 20-Ec and enough JH I to ensure the production of a second pupal cuticle by the wing epidermis. Adult scales were extracted to represent adult wing cuticle since previous studies demonstrated that scales and cuticle yield essentially the same protein composition (unpublished information), while untanned second pupal wing cuticle derived from pupae injected with 20-Ec + JH represented pupal wing cuticle. The latter was chosen over normal pupal wing cuticle because it was reasoned that the proteins of untanned cuticle would be more completely extracted than those of the highly sclerotized normal pupal cuticle. The two cuticle types were extracted with different solvents and analyzed by sodium dodecyl sulfate (SDS) acrylamide electrophoresis (Fig. 1). It can be concluded from many such analyses that adult and pupal cuticle each contain at least 20-25 polypeptides, among which about 10 are unique to each stage and these cover a range of 10,000 to 90,000 daltons. Further, the pupal cuticle is characterized by one major polypeptide of about 80,000 daltons and a larger population of low molecular weight polypeptides (< 25,000) than is found in adult cuticle. These differences are amplified by analyses in two dimensions (Fig. 2). Despite the limitations of the amounts of protein that could be loaded and shifts in the pH gradient of the isoelectric focusing gel, it is clear that differences exist between the two samples. The pupal cuticle yields a preponderance of proteins in the low molecular weight range not seen among the proteins of the scale extract. Four polypeptides appear identical on the basis of pI values and molecular weights (marked as a, b and by arrows in Fig. 2). Having established the firm possibility of differences in cuticular proteins in pupae and adults, we next explored the possible mechanisms involved in establishing these stage-specific differences.

B. *Synthesis of Protein and Total RNA*

Regardless of whether the epidermal cells will synthesize pupal or adult cuticle, the initial response to the administration of molting hormone is an increased rate of incorporation of [^{3}H] uridine into RNA during the first 24 hr (Wyatt, 1968; 1972). To examine other aspects of the hormonal control of RNA synthesis in wing epidermis, i.e., alterations in mRNA population and RNA polymerase activity, it was first necessary to establish the developmental patterns of rates of synthesis of RNA and protein in tissue exposed to 20-Ec or 20-Ec + JH.

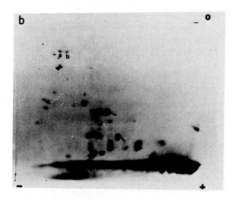

FIGURE 2. Two dimensional electrophoretic analysis of adult and pupal wing cuticular proteins. Proteins were extracted by homogenization of adult scales (a) and untanned, second pupal cuticle (b) in 1.0 M Tris pH 7.5 and 0.5 M KCl using a teflon-glass homogenizer. The homogenate was centrifuged, and the protein in the supernatant precipitated with ten times its volume of 80% acetone. The solution was centrifuged after standing on ice for 10 min and the pellet taken up in isoelectric focusing sample buffer. This was added to the pellet from the first centrifugation, warmed to 37°C and the undissolved material removed. The samples were focused on 4% polyacrylamide gels containing 2% ampholines for 16 hr at 350 V and 1 hr at 800 V. The focusing gel was subjected to electrophoresis in the second dimension on 12.5% polyacrylamide gels for 5-6 hr at 25mA and the gels stained with Coomassie blue.

The former lays down adult cuticle while in the latter case,
a second pupal cuticle is produced. Both species of macro-
molecule begin to increase rapidly in the wing epidermis
within a few hr of hormone treatment (Fig. 3). By the sixth
day of hormone administration, the 20-Ec + JH treated animals
have already deposited a second pupal cuticle, but their wing
epidermal RNA content is similar to that of the 20-Ec treated
pupae; however, the protein content of the 20-Ec + JH wings
is slightly greater than that of wings exposed to molting hormone alone. These studies show no profound difference between the 20-Ec and 20-Ec + JH wing epidermis.

To examine further whether JH application affects either
RNA or protein synthesis in the wing, biosynthetic studies
were conducted which accounted for both pool size and the
kinetics of precursor incorporation. The results demonstrated
once again the absence of any dramatic differences between

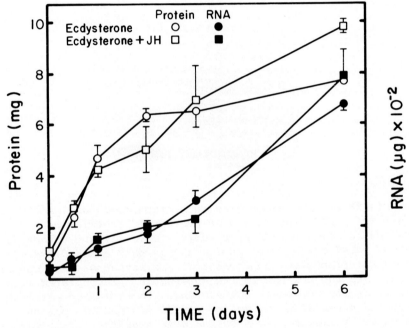

FIGURE 3. *A comparison of protein and RNA content in
wing epidermis of* A. polyphemus *pupae treated with 20-
hydroxyecdysone (ecdysterone) (circles) or 20-hydroxyecdysone
plus juvenile hormone (squares). RNA (filled) and protein
(open) were determined at various periods after hormone
treatment. Values are expressed as amounts in the total
wing tissue of one animal.*

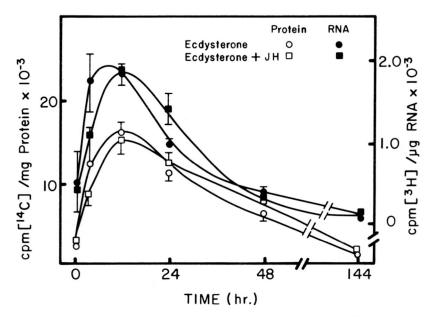

FIGURE 4. The kinetics of incorporation of [^{14}C] leucine
(open) and [^{3}H] uridine (filled) into the acid insoluble material of A. polyphemus wing epidermis. Wing epidermis was removed from insects at the times indicated after the administration of hormone (20-hydroxyecdysone [ecdysterone]; 20-
hydroxyecdysone [ecdysterone] + juvenile hormone) and incubated in Grace's medium with the appropriate labelled precursor. The amount of label present in the acid precipitable
material was determined by standard procedures.

epidermal cells already engaged in the synthesis of a second
pupal cuticle and those destined to synthesize adult cuticle
(Fig. 4). This similarity in patterns of RNA and protein
synthesis between epidermis exposed to different hormonal
regimens does not necessarily mean that identical molecular
events are occurring within the cells. In fact, although the
wings of 20-Ec + JH treated animals grow, they do not increase
in surface area to the same extent as those of 20-Ec treated
insects. In the latter case, much of the synthetic activity
is growth related, while in the former instance, a greater
proportion of the RNA and protein synthesis is probably related to cuticular synthesis. The rapid increase in the rate
of protein synthesis following hormone treatment is almost
coincident with the increased rate of RNA synthesis. The
absence of a significant lag period between these events

suggests that this early increase in protein synthesis is probably independent of the hormone-elicited RNA synthesis.

C. Synthesis of mRNA

The next step was to probe mRNA synthesis in the expectation of uncovering differences in response to the two hormone
regimens. Since mRNA comprises only about 2% of the total
cellular RNA, one could not discern subtle differences in the
mRNA population by the use of techniques such as those employed above. Rather, one must isolate mRNA from wing epidermis at various developmental stages and compare individual
species by translational techniques and/or hybridization.
This is now possible since most eucaryotic mRNAs possess
poly A tails and sensitive procedures are available to isolate and quantify these poly A^+ mRNAs. Preliminary data on
quantification of total wing epidermal mRNA at different periods following hormone treatment are presented in Table I.
These data reveal no gross differences between the mRNA content of wing tissue undergoing normal development and epidermis synthesizing a second pupal cuticle, although there may

TABLE I.   Poly A Containing RNA in A. polyphemus *Wing*
            Epidermis Following Hormone Treatment

Treatment of pupae	Time after treatment (hr)	% Recovery of Poly A	% Poly A containing mRNA	Poly A containing RNA (µg/wing pair)
--	0	90.0	1.63	0.51
20-Ec	24	85.7	1.24	1.7
	48	98.1	1.47	2.5
	72	96.4	2.10	3.8
	144	111.4	1.03	8.9
20-Ec + JH	24	109.1	1.67	2.4
	48	106.5	2.54	3.1
	72	110.2	1.56	4.2
	144	94.8	1.77	14.2

One to three mg of total RNA was fractionated on oligo-
dT cellulose. Total RNA before fractionation and bound RNA
were hybridized to [^{3}H]poly(U) in order to measure the recovery and percent poly A.

be a significant increase in the poly A RNA of the latter after 72 hr. A more detailed and comprehensive analysis has been conducted with epidermal RNA extracted from wings during normal adult development. These data, derived from binding studies with oligo (dT), indicate that the mRNA as a percent of total RNA increases slightly faster than other RNA species during adult development, i.e., 1.8% in pupae to about 3% by day 6-10 of adult development.

These mRNA populations have been analyzed by *in vitro* translation utilizing the wheat germ cell free system and employing either [^{35}S] methionine or [^{3}H] leucine as the labelled precursor. The products were analyzed by both one-dimensional and two-dimensional electrophoresis followed by fluorography. Figure 5 clearly demonstrates the presence of mRNAs

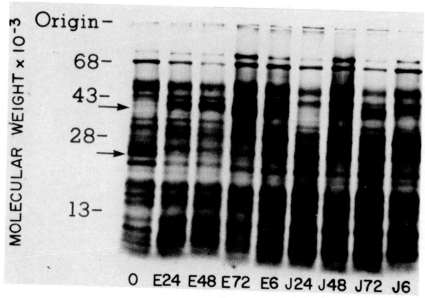

FIGURE 5. *Fluorogram after SDS polyacrylamide gel electrophoretic analysis of the in vitro translation products of poly A+ mRNA extracted from A. polyphemus wing epidermis. Translation of extracted mRNAs was carried out in a cell-free wheat germ system containing 5 μCi [^{35}S] methionine. Equal acid insoluble counts were loaded on each channel for electrophoresis. After the run, the gels were washed with acid and subjected to fluorography. 0, pupa; E 24, 48, 72 and 6 corresponds to 24 hr, 48 hr, 72 hr and 6 days after 20-hydroxyecdysone administration; J 24, 48, 72 and 6 corresponds to 24 hr, 48 hr, 72 hr and 6 days after administration of 20-hydroxyecdysone + juvenile hormone. Numbers along ordinate represent molecular weight markers.*

in wing epidermis that code for polypeptides in the range of 13,000 to 70,000 daltons. Upon longer exposure, some products of higher molecular weight can be observed. A comparison of the various mRNA populations in Figure 5 indicates that the quantity of two mRNAs coding for polypeptides in the 40,000 dalton range (top arrow) increases considerably in 20-Ec treated pupae, but is reduced in epidermis from 20-Ec + JH treated pupae. In the 24 hr and 48 hr 20-Ec + JH samples, these particular mRNAs are nearly undetectable as is the case with pupae, while at 72 hr and 6 days they appear at reduced levels. In contrast, the quantity of an mRNA coding for a protein of approximately 29,000 daltons found in pupal wing epidermis (bottom arrow) is reduced in epidermis from animals receiving either of the hormonal regimens. The lower molecular weight (29,000) component could represent an mRNA typical of diapausing pupae that is no longer transcribed after the initiation of development. Transcription of the mRNAs of the higher molecular weight components (40,000) may be stimulated by molting hormone but inhibited by JH. Their reduced but significant level in 20-Ec + JH animals at 3 and 6 days may be due to the failure of some pupae to respond to JH by 6 days.

There is evidence for the existence of some mRNAs in eucaryotes that lack poly A sequences at the 3' end (Greenberg, 1976; Ruderman and Pardue, 1977; Miller, 1978) and a controversy exists as to whether these mRNAs and poly A^+ mRNAs are similar or different. These poly A^- RNAs would be lost during oligo (dT) fractionation and it is possible that such sequences may contain mRNAs of biological significance. We tested this possibility by translating and analyzing replicate poly A^+ mRNA samples from 72 hr wing epidermis as well as the corresponding total RNA. The data demonstrated that replicate samples yield virtually identical *in vitro* translation products, indicating a high degree of reproducibility and very few qualitative differences between the translation products of Poly A^+ mRNAs and the corresponding total RNA. Although there appear to be more *in vitro* translation products of higher molecular weight in tht total RNA sample, the overall data indicate that essentially all of the mRNA sequences in silkmoth wing epidermal cells are polyadenylated.

In the above studies [35S] methionine was the labelled precursor, but if the epidermal products are poor in methionine, some important polypeptides could have been overlooked. To examine this possibility, the same mRNA populations translated previously (Fig. 5) were translated *in vitro* once again with [3H] leucine as the labelled precursor. Although slight differences were evident, e.g. more high molecular weight translation products seen with methionine, the composite data

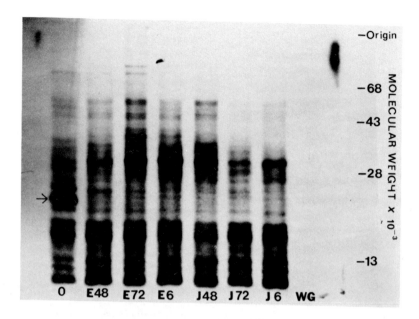

FIGURE 6. Same as Figure 5 except that the labelled amino acid was [³H] leucine. WG = wheat germ alone with no mRNA.

revealed no profound disparity (Fig. 6), and since [³⁵S] is a more suitable label than [³H] leucine for fluorography, the former was used in most subsequent studies.

During the course of these studies, it was frequently observed that some extracts of mRNA from pupal (0 hr) wing epidermis were not translated in the wheat germ system. Only two of six independent extracts were translated to any degree, and even these were only 10% as efficient as mRNA from animals receiving 20-Ec from 1-15 days previously. This observation is similar to those demonstrating the inefficiency of mRNAs isolated from dormant *Artemia* embryos (Amaldi *et al.*, 1977) and sea urchin embryos (Rudensy and Infante, 1979). The pupal mRNA inefficiency is not due to the presence of low molecular weight inhibitory components as is the case for *Artemia* since size determinations show no differences between pupal wing mRNA and mRNA from later developmental stages, and the addition of increasing amounts of pupal mRNA to mRNA preparations from later stages does not reduce the efficiency of translation of the latter. These results indicate that the translational inefficiency is intrinsic to the pupal mRNA. The possibility existed that the proper "cap" structure was absent from the pupal mRNA and that this is required for the proper

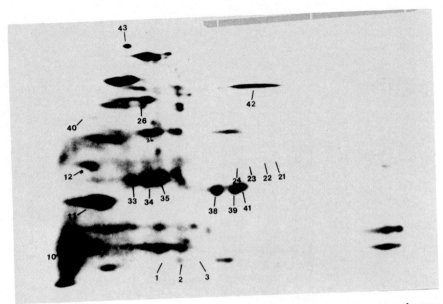

FIGURE 7. Fluorogram after two-dimensional electrophoretic analysis of the in vitro translation products of poly A$^+$ mRNA extracted from pupal (0 hr) wing epidermis. Translation was as for Figure 5 using [^{35}S] methionine.

initiation of translation. This was ruled out by translating pupal wing mRNA in the presence of increasing amounts of S-adenosyl methionine (Paterson and Rosenberg, 1979) with no improvement. In any event, it appears that the mRNAs present in the wing epidermis of chilled pupae are inefficient as messengers. Perhaps a maturation process is required during the first hours of 20-Ec treatment in which the mRNAs are attached to ribosomes to form polysomes and translation begins. This hypothesis is supported by sucrose gradient analyses (Cohen and Gilbert, unpublished observations) and by electron microscopic observations (Greenstein, 1972) in which a rapid formation of polysomes is noted within a few hours of adult development.

To further analyze the mRNA populations in wing epidermis subjected to the two hormonal environments, the *in vitro* translation products were subjected to two-dimensional electrophoresis in which the products were first separated according to charge differences by isoelectric focusing and then separated according to size by SDS electrophoresis (Fig. 7). This detailed analysis revealed both qualitative and quantitative changes in the mRNA population following 20-Ec

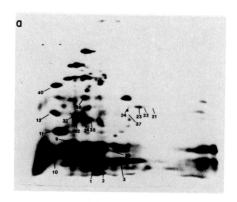

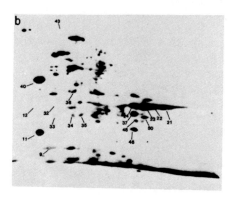

FIGURE 8. Fluorograms after two-dimensional electrophoretic analysis of the in vitro translation products of poly A+ mRNA extracted from hormone treated wing epidermis. Conditions as in Figure 7. Poly A+ RNA was extracted 24 hr after administration to pupae of: (a) 20-hydroxyecdysone plus juvenile hormone; (b) 20-hydroxyecdysone.

administration (Fig. 8). The major changes occurred during the first 24 hr; over the next five days only a few quantitative alterations were observed. The 20-Ec + JH wing epidermis did exhibit quantitative change in its mRNA population but, surprisingly, no unique mRNAs were observed in epidermis from these animals. Among the changes that occur during the first 24 hr after 20-Ec injection (compare Figures 7 and 8) is the appearance of a group of mRNAs coding for approximately four polypeptides of similar molecular weight (spots 21-24). Their synthesis appears to be coordinated as their intensities increase or decrease together. It is possible that the mRNAs coding for these polypeptides are coding for subunits of a single protein. Another hormone induced polypeptide is spot 40, which is virtually absent when pupal mRNA is translated; it is about 40,000 daltons, incorporates more methionine than leucine and has a pI of 5.5. Although these are criteria for actin, there is no direct evidence that spot 40 represents actin.

In addition to the above increases, a number of decreases in mRNA activity were also observed. Two peptides (38, 39) are of particular interest since they appear to be unique to pupal wing epidermis (Fig. 7) and may correspond to the unique band seen in one-dimensional gels (Figures 5 and 6). Apparently, the genes for these products are not transcribed once development is initiated. Spots 33-36 also seem to be more intense in pupal epidermis relative to surrounding spots. JH application appears to stimulate the transcription of mRNAs for certain relatively low molecular weight polypeptides and some notable differences are observed between these patterns and those from epidermis undergoing adult development (Figures 5 and 8). As can be readily seen, spots 21-24 are present in E 24, but essentially absent in J 24. Similarly, spots 9 and 32-36 are more intense in J 24 than E 24. The most interesting fluorograms for comparison are those derived from 0 hr (pupal) epidermis 6 days after 20-Ec treatment, 6 days after treatment with 20-Ec + JH and 10 days after receiving 20-Ec since they represent: uncommitted epidermis (Fig. 9a); epidermis committed to synthesize adult cuticular proteins (Fig. 9b); epidermis synthesizing pupal cuticular proteins (Fig. 9c); and epidermis depositing adult cuticle (Fig. 9d). For example, the increase in the intensity of spots in the middle and high molecular weight range, when mRNA is used that had been exposed to 20-Ec 10 days previously, may represent mRNAs coding for adult cuticular proteins. These data provide compelling evidence that new mRNAs do appear in wing epidermis at times when it is secreting either a second pupal or adult cuticle, but the gross morphological differences in the type of cuticle secreted probably cannot be explained on the basis of these subtle alterations in mRNA content. On the other hand, our inability to detect a preponderance of pupal and adult mRNAs after the appropriate treatment may be due to technical deficiencies rather than to their absence *in vivo*. For example, since the wheat germ system does not translate mRNAs for high molecular weight proteins very well and only sustains a few rounds of initiation, it may be very inefficient in translating the mRNAs for adult cuticular proteins. In addition, the translation of some cuticular proteins may

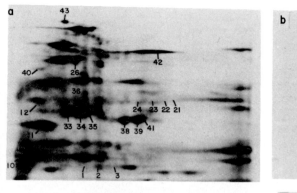
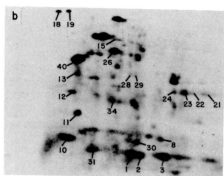
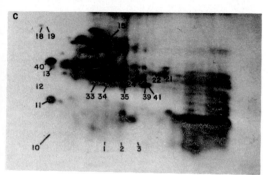
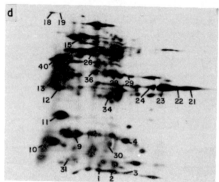

FIGURE 9. Fluorograms after two-dimensional electrophoretic analysis of the in vitro translation products of poly A⁺ mRNA extracted from wing epidermis. Conditions as in Figure 7. a = pupal; b = six days after 20-hydroxyecdysone; c = six days after 20-hydroxyecdysone + juvenile hormone; d = ten days after 20-hydroxyecdysone.

require specific initiation factors, tRNAs, membrane association, etc.

In the final analysis, the complex process of transcription must be clarified in order to define in molecular terms how the expression of specific genes, or groups of genes, essential for each stage of development is controlled by the interaction of the 20-hydroxyecdysone-receptor complex (and/ or JH-receptor complex) with chromatin in the nucleus. Since this process must involve the recognition of specific DNA sequences by DNA dependent RNA polymerase, followed by the initiation of nucleotide chains, elongation, termination and release of the RNA chains, it is reasonable to assume that the enzyme responsible for initiation this process in involved in regulation.

D. RNA Polymerases

In those systems where protein synthesis is stimulated by hormones, a rapid increase in RNA synthesis precedes the synthesis of new proteins as a result of a time dependent increase in RNA polymerase activity (Roeder, 1976). Since the injection of 20-Ec into silkmoth pupae leads to an increased rate of RNA synthesis, polysome formation and an increase in the RNA content of the wing epidermis, we have investigated the RNA polymerases of this tissue. It should be noted that transcription is mediated by multiple forms of RNA polymerase in eucaryotes. Three distinct classes can be distinguished on the basis of differences in chromatographic properties, salt and cationic requirements, α-amanitin sensitivity, nuclear topography and structure (Chambon, 1975; Roeder, 1976). Nucleolar RNA polymerase I (A) is insensitive to α-amanitin and transcribes genes coding for ribosomal RNA. The class II (B) enzyme is highly sensitive to α-amanitin and mediates the synthesis of heterogeneous DNA-like (Hn) RNA, while RNA polymerase III (C) is responsible for the transcription of 5S RNA and tRNA. Each class in turn is comprised of a diversity of forms with similar enzymatic properties, but having slightly different subunit compositions.

To examine putative alterations in wing epidermis polymerase activity during development and its possible control by 20-Ec, *Antheraea pernyi* pupae were utilized and the developmental pattern of macromolecular changes in relation to the hormonal milieu was first determined (Nowock *et al.*, 1978). Total wing DNA begins to increase between day 2 and 3 of pharate adult life and levels off at day 11, while total RNA increases in three phases with maxima at days 2, 7 and 9 (Fig. 10). RNA polymerase activity develops in a bimodal fashion related to the hormonal status of the animals. Within the first day of transfer of pupae to conditions that elicit adult development, both RNA polymerase I and II activity increases. However, this is a transient increase that also occurs in debrained animals, dissipates rapidly and is probably a consequence of the low but significant ecdysteroid titer in chilled pupae of this species. As expected, the developmental pattern of total wing RNA is in good agreement with the alteration in α-amanitin resistant RNA polymerase activity which, for the most part, reflects stable rRNA production (rRNA + tRNA). When these results are expressed per unit DNA instead of per wing pair, one notes two major phases of enhanced RNA polymerase activity. The initiation of adult development is characterized by increased α-amanitin resistant and sensitive polymerase activity. The subsequent dramatic increase in hemolymph ecdysteroid titer which peaks at day 4

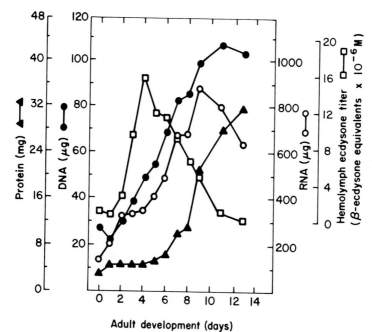

Adult development (days)

FIGURE 10. *Adult wing development in* A. *pernyi: corre-lative data. Wings of pupae (day 0) and developing adults were analyzed. Three independent determinations were performed in duplicate for each time point. All data except for the ecdysteroid titer are normalized to represent values of a set of wings of one animal. From Nowock* et al., *1978.*

of adult development correlates well with the second increase in the activity of both classes of RNA polymerase. A point that remains unclear for this and other eucaryotic systems is whether the observed increase in RNA polymerase activity is due to synthesis of new enzyme molecules, activation of inactive precursor molecules, covalent modification, etc. This problem was investigated using isolated nuclei from the wing epidermis of A. *polyphemus* and solubilized enzymes.

Within 4 hr of injection of 20-Ec, there was an increase in nuclear polymerase I and II activity. By 26 hr post-injection, the nuclear activity increased to approximately three to four times the pupal (0 hr) value for enzyme I and at least two-fold for enzyme II (Fig. 11). Since the controls also exhibited the initial increase, the increased transcriptional rate at 4 hr is probably hormone independent and may reflect injury induced by injection or temperature stress resulting from the transfer of pupae from 5°C to 25°C. Notwithstanding this possibility, the RNA polymerase activity of hormone stimulated wing epidermal nuclei is much higher than

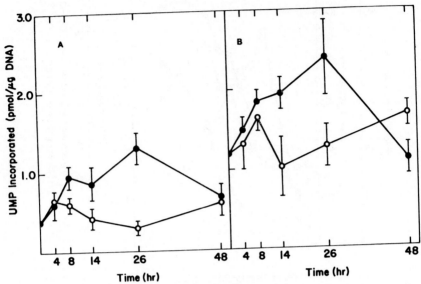

FIGURE 11.   Time course of nuclear RNA polymerase activity following injection of 20-hydroxyecdysone (●) or water
(o) into A. polyphemus pupae.   At the times indicated, nuclei
were isolated from wing epidermis and assayed for RNA polymerase activity.   (a), nuclei assayed at 35 mM ammonium sulfate
with α-amanitin; activity represents enzyme I (or I + III).
(b), nuclei assayed at 300 mM ammonium sulfate without α-
amanitin; activity represents RNA polymerase II.

controls and continues at a high rate for a longer period of
time. The apparent decrease at later time periods, e.g. 48
hr in hormone treated animals, is due in part to the increasing DNA content of the wing epidermis (cf. Fig. 10).
       To determine if this increase in nuclear RNA polymerase
activity is due to changing enzyme activity or to the template, the enzymes were solubilized by sonication in high
salt, fractionated on DEAE-cellulose, and RNA polymerase I and
III separated from enzyme II. When assayed separately following injection of 20-Ec, enzyme II activity increased by 4 hr
while polymerase I activity rose at about 14 hr post-injection.
By 26 hr the level of polymerase I had increased more than 9-
fold over the pupal value (0 hr), while the level of polymerase II increased over 8-fold. In contrast, the level of nuclear transcriptional activity at 26 hr was only twice that
seen at 0 hr. However, if the total solubilized enzyme activity is expressed per μg DNA as was done for nuclear activity,

TABLE II. Effects of Inhibitors and 20-Hydroxyecdysone
(20-Ec) on Solubilized Polymerase Activity
from Wing Epidermis

Treatment of Pupae	Time after treatment (hr)	Total UMP incorporated (pmol)	
		Polymerase I	Polymerase II
--	0	62.5	154.0
20-Ec	4	54.5	307.8
20-Ec	14	196.7	888.2
20-Ec	26	558.7	1,197.4
Water	26	92.0	200.1
Puromycin + 20-Ec	26	42.4	112.8
Actinomycin + 20-Ec	26	133.0	224.0
20-Ec	144	963.5	1,802.0

this discrepancy is minimized. The close agreement between
nuclear activity and solubilized enzyme activity indicates
that between 0 hr and 26 hr post-injection, there is a real
increase in the amount of solubilized RNA polymerase I and II
per unit DNA. Since most of the polymerases are "bound" to
chromatin, these data suggest that the increased transcriptional activity resulting from molting hormone action is due
to an increase in the template engaged polymerases.

If transcriptional rates are indeed a function of the number of active polymerase molecules, the level of solubilized
polymerases at 144 hr after the injection of molting hormone
should be reduced since the rates of RNA synthesis and nuclear
transcriptional activity are much less at this time than at
26 hr (Fig. 4). Surprisingly, the level of solubilized polymerases I and II from wing epidermis continues to increase
beyond 26 hr post-injection (Table II). One possible explanation for these observations is that the chromatin structure is
changed so that the binding of RNA polymerase is altered. A
minimum cellular concentration of RNA polymerases may be
needed for optimal transcriptional activity and as the number
and/or volume of epidermal cells increase, so does the number
of polymerase molecules. In fact, during the initial stages
of wing differentiation, there is substantial cell growth and
an increase in cell number; at this time the tissue content of
polymerase molecules increases. If new polymerase molecules
or subunits are synthesized, then the increase would depend on
new protein synthesis and perhaps RNA synthesis as well. This
was explored by injecting inhibitors of protein or RNA synthesis, puromycin and actinomycin D, into pupae at levels which
showed no gross detrimental effects and determining the effects

on the solubilized polymerase activity of wing epidermis.
Table II reveals that puromycin reduced the levels of both
classes of polymerase activity to those of the 0 hr (pupal)
controls. Actinomycin D was also effective, but not to the
same degree as puromycin. These results suggest strongly that
the increase is a consequence of the actual synthesis of new
enzyme molecules or protein regulatory molecules.

III. CONCLUSIONS

The data derived from our studies of *Antheraea* wing epidermis indicate that transcriptional activity, and the activity of those enzymes involved in transcription, undergoes
changes as a consequence of the action of 20-Ec. However, a
complex developmental program such as imaginal wing differentiation is probably not controlled completely by a single effector molecule such as 20-Ec although the hormone is certainly needed for the program to proceed. Only further
studies can determine if the 20-hydroxyecdysone-receptor complex acts to define the specificity of the RNA polymerases or
the accessibility of the enzymes to specific regions of the
genome. An analysis of wing epidermal transcriptional products, particularly those of polymerase II, during early periods of hormone action should also aid our understanding of
the interactions between molting hormone, RNA polymerase and
chromatin, and perhaps lead to more quantitative definitions
of gene sets, switching "on" and "off" of genes, etc. This
approach is actually a logical extension of the cytological
observations of Professor Wigglesworth on epidermal cell "activation" in *Rhodnius* (see INTRODUCTION), and if it is ultimately successful, he will be indirectly responsible for
the solution of one more important biological problem.

ACKNOWLEDGMENTS

Thanks are due to Thelma Carter and Rick Swanson for technical assistance and to Nancy Grousnick and Romie Brown for
secretarial assistance.

REFERENCES

Amaldi, P.P., Felicitti, L. and Camponi, N. (1977). Flow of informational RNA from cytoplasmic poly(A)-containing particles to polyribosomes in *Artemia salina* cysts at early stages of development. *Dev. Biol. 59,* 49-61.

Berendes, H.D. and Boyd, J.B. (1969). Structural and functional properties of polytene nuclei isolated from salivary glands of *Drosophila hydei. J. Cell. Biol. 41,* 591-599.

Bonner, J.J. and Pardue, M.L. (1976). Ecdysone-stimulated RNA synthesis in imaginal discs of *Drosophila melanogaster.* Assay by *in situ* hybridization. *Chromosoma 58,* 87-99.

Brady, T., Berendes, H.D. and Kuijpers, A.M.C. (1974). Gene activation following microinjection of β-ecdysone into nuclei and cytoplasm of larval salivary gland cells of *Drosophila. Mol. Cell. Endocrinol. 1,* 249-257.

Chambon, P. (1975). Eucaryotic nuclear RNA polymerases. *Ann. Rev. Biochem. 46,* 613-638.

Fragoulis, E.G. and Sekeris, C.E. (1975). Translation of mRNA for 3,4-dihydroxy phenylalanine decarboxylase isolated from epidermis tissue of *Calliphora vicina* R.-D. in a heterologous system. *Eur. J. Biochem. 51,* 305-316.

Fragouli-Fournogeraki, M.E., Fragoulis, E.G. and Sekeris, C.E. (1978). Protein synthesis by polysomes from the epidermis of blowfly larvae: dependence of formation of DOPA-decarboxylase on developmental stage. *Insect Biochem. 8,* 435-441.

Fristrom, J.W. (1972). The biochemistry of imaginal disk development. in "The Biology of Imaginal Discs" (H. Ursprung and R. Nöthiger, eds.), pp. 109-154. Springer-Verlag, Berlin.

Fristrom, J.W. (1980). Imaginal discs as a model system for the study of metamorphosis. in "Metamorphosis" 2nd Edition (L.I. Gilbert and E. Frieden, eds.). Plenum Press, New York (in press).

Greenberg, J.R. 1976). Isolation of L-cell messenger RNA which lacks poly(adenylate). *Biochemistry 15,* 3516-3522.

Greenstein, M.E. (1972). The ultrastructure of developing wings in the giant silkmoth, *Hyalophora cecropia* I. Generalized epidermal cells. *J. Morph. 136,* 1-22.

Maroy, P., Dennis, R., Beckers, C., Sage, B. and O'Connor, J.D. (1978). Demonstration of an ecdysteroid receptor in cultured cell line of *Drosophila melanogaster. Proc. Natl. Acad. Sci. USA 75,* 6035-6038.

Miller, L. (1978). Relative amounts of newly synthesized poly(A)$^+$ and poly(A)$^-$ messenger RNA during development of *Xenopus laevis*. *Dev. Biol. 64,* 118-129.

Nowock, J., Sridhara, S. and Gilbert, L.I. (1978). Ecdysone-initiated developmental changes in wing epidermis RNA polymerase activity during the adult development of the oak silkmoth, *Antheraea pernyi*. *Mol. Cell. Endocrinol. 11,* 325-341.

Paterson, B.M. and Rosenberg, M. (1979). Efficient translation of prokaryotic mRNAs in a eucaryotic cell-free system requires addition of a cap structure. *Nature 279,* 692-696.

Roeder, R.G. (1976). Eucaryotic nuclear RNA polymerases. in "RNA Polymerase" (R. Losick and M. Chamberlin, eds.), pp. 285-329. Cold Spring Harbor Laboratory, New York.

Ruderman, J.V. and Pardue, M.L. (1977). Cell-free translation analysis of messenger RNA in echinoderm and amphibian early development. *Dev. Biol. 60,* 48-68.

Rudensy, L.M. and Infante, A.A. (1979). Translational efficiency of cytoplasmic nonpolysomal messenger ribonucleic acid from sea urchin embryos. *Biochemistry 18,* 3056-3063.

Scheller, K., Karlson, P. and Bodenstein, D. (1978). Effects of ecdysterone and juvenile hormone analogue methoprene on protein, RNA and DNA synthesis in wing discs of *Calliphora vicina*. *Z. Naturforschg. 33c,* 253-260.

Wigglesworth, V.B. (1957d). The action of growth hormones in insects. *Symp. Soc. Exp. Biol. 11,* 204-227.

Wigglesworth, V.B. (1963c). The action of moulting hormone and juvenile hormone at the cellular level in *Rhodnius prolixus*. *J. Exp. Biol. 40,* 231-245.

Wyatt, G.R. (1968). Biochemistry of insect metamorphosis. in "Metamorphosis" (W. Etkin and L.I. Gilbert, eds.), pp. 143-184. Appleton-Century-Crofts, New York.

Wyatt, G.R. (1972). Insect hormones. in "Biochemical Action of Hormones" Vol. II (G. Litwack, ed.), pp. 385-490. Academic Press, New York.

Yund, M.A., King, D.S. and Fristrom, J.W. (1978). Ecdysteroid receptors in imaginal discs of *Drosophila melanogaster*. *Proc. Natl. Acad. Sci. USA 75,* 6039-6043.

HORMONE ACTION - A SEARCH FOR
TRANSDUCING MECHANISMS

Michael J. Berridge

A.R.C. Unit of Invertebrate Chemistry & Physiology
Department of Zoology
University of Cambridge
Cambridge, U.K.

I. INTRODUCTION

Much of the early success in insect physiology was derived from studies on insect hormones particularly those responsible for metamorphosis. Sir Vincent made a major contribution both to the discovery of these morphogenic hormones (juvenile hormone and ecdysterone) and to elucidating how they act to control moulting and morphogenesis (Wigglesworth, 1966b, 1970). After the discovery of these morphogenic hormones, other hormones were described which can be loosely classified as homeostatic hormones in that they regulate the second to second activity of all somatic cells. A classic example is the diuretic hormone of *Rhodnius* which is released immediately following a blood meal to activate the Malpighian tubules (Maddrell, 1962, 1964, 1966). The total number of such chemical agents is likely to be very large and many remain to be described especially in relation to the nervous system. The vertebrate nervous system, for example, has a large battery of signal molecules and new transmitters are being discovered all the time. The identification of classical hormones such as vasopressin and vasoactive intestinal peptide (VIP) in the CNS has raised interesting questions concerning not only their mode of action but also the evolutionary development of such transmitters. Although the insect nervous system has not been studied quite so extensively as its vertebrate counterpart, there is every likelihood that it will also be found to possess a plethora of signal molecules some of which may resemble typical hormones. Such a

possibility is supported by the morphology of the neurosecretory cell which secretes the *Rhodnius* diuretic hormone
(Maddrell, 1966). In addition to sending out an axon to the
neurohaemal organ, the neurosecretory cell also has a collater-
al which disappears into the ganglion where it presumably
innervates other nerve cells using the diuretic hormone as a
neurotransmitter. Faced with such a multiplicity of hormones
and neurotransmitters, the cell biologist is confronted with a
formidable task in trying to unravel how each of these chemical
signals might act. In the following discussion, attention is
focussed on some recent developments concerning the action of
homeostatic hormones.

The first question to consider is whether or not each of
these external signals communicates with its target cell
through its own discrete pathway. Since each agonist was known
to act on a specific receptor, the existence of separate second
messenger pathways was a distinct possibility. Fortunately,
however, the whole problem is greatly simplified by the fact
that this wide range of different receptors may be connected to
relatively few transducing elements responsible for transforming external signals into relatively few internal signals
recognizable by the intracellular effector systems (Fig. 1).
The principle of connecting a large number of different
receptors to a much smaller number of transducers is not unique
to eucaryotic cells but has also been developed by procaryotes
as part of their chemotactic response to a range of nutrients
(Springer *et al* 1979). There are a large number of chemoreceptors which are connected to one of the three available
transducing mechanisms responsible for adjusting the direction
of rotation of the bacterial flagellum. In eucaryotes, the
nature and number of transducing elements have not been fully
described and most of the information has been gathered on
vertebrate cells. In the years ahead, it will be fascinating
to find out how the transducing elements in insects compare
with those which are being uncovered in vertebrate cells. It
is important to appreciate, therefore, that the following
description of transducing mechanisms is based primarily from
studies performed on vertebrate tissues. One of the aims of
this article will be to describe the characteristics of each
transducing mechanism which could be used subsequently as
diagnostic features to identify and characterize the transducers which are associated with different receptors.

Such an approach may be particularly important for trying to
unravel how transmitters act within the CNS. As mentioned earlier,
many conventional hormones are turning up in the nervous system.
It will be fascinating to find out whether or not they act in the
same way at their different target sites. Studies on conventional
hormones could thus provide important clues to the more difficult problem of how transmitters act within the nervous system.

II. SOME GENERAL PROPERTIES OF TRANSDUCING MECHANISMS

The complexity of the chemical communication system operating between cells is compounded by the fact that many external
signals can have more than one receptor (e.g. agonist 2 in
Fig. 1). A classical example is the cholinergic system where

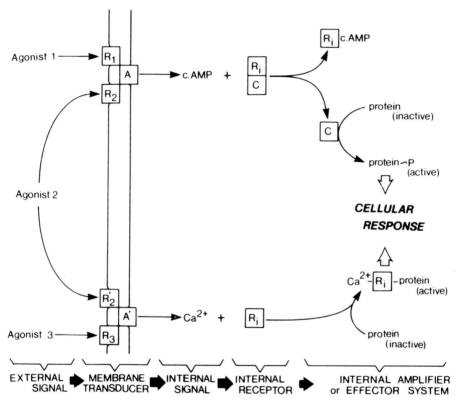

FIGURE 1. A summary of the two important pathways for passing
information into cells. Some agonists (1 & 3) use either one
or other pathway, whereas certain agonists (2) have access to
both pathways by being able to interact with two types of
receptor (R2 and R'2) which can be distinguished using specific
agonists or antagonists. These receptors act on two separate
amplifiers (A, A') to generate either cyclic AMP or calcium.
These second messengers act within the cell by binding to
specific receptors (Ri). See text for further details.

there are nicotinic and muscarinic receptors. A similar separation of receptor types has been recognised for the adrenergic system (α and β), histamine (H_1 and H_2), dopamine (D_1 and D_2) and serotonin (D & M). Even polypeptide hormones such as vasopressin are capable of acting through either pathway. Earlier studies on its antidiuretic effect on toad bladder clearly revealed an action through cyclic AMP (Orloff and Handler, 1967). However, recent studies on liver have shown that vasopressin can stimulate glycogenolysis using calcium as a second messenger independently of cyclic AMP (Assimacopoulos-Jeannet et al 1977; Keppens et al 1977; van de Werve et al 1977). In all these examples, therefore, receptors differ not only in the way they bind to specific agonists or antagonists but also in the nature of the information they transmit to the cell. For example, noradrenaline can bind to α-adrenergic receptors to give an increase in calcium entry (e.g. receptor R_2 in Fig. 1) whereas binding to β-adrenergic receptors results in an increase in the synthesis of cyclic AMP (receptor R_2 in Fig. 1). One of the remarkable features to emerge over the last few years is that these two second messenger pathways for passing information into the cell are widely used by many other agonists. In addition to the α-adrenergic receptor, the cholinergic (muscarinic), histaminergic (H_1), dopaminergic (D_2), serotonergic (D), and one type of vasopressin response all seem to act in some way through calcium. On the other hand, the β-adrenergic, histaminergic (H_2), dopaminergic (D_1), and many other hormones act through cyclic AMP. Calcium and cyclic AMP thus represent two very important lines of communication into the cell and the transducing mechanisms responsible for the generation and action of these two second messengers will be described in greater detail.

One way of summarizing these transducing mechanisms is to trace the flow of information from the external receptor to the final effector system (Fig. 1). These two second messenger systems reveal some remarkable similarities. The sequence begins when the external agonists bind to an external receptor (Fig. 1, R_1-R_3) which is then connected to an amplifier which together with the receptor may be considered as a membrane transducer acting to generate the second messenger. There is a corresponding internal transducing mechanism poised to respond to such an elevation in the intracellular level of cyclic AMP or calcium (Fig. 1). In both cases, there are specific internal receptors (R_i) which bind to these second messengers but there are important differences in the way they initiate the final cellular response. In the case of cyclic AMP, the unoccupied receptor binds tightly to the catalytic subunit of protein kinase (C in Fig. 1) thus inhibiting its activity. When cyclic AMP binds to the receptor, however, this inhibition

is removed and the free catalytic subunit is able to phosphorylate key rate-limiting proteins such as phosphorylase b kinase
or lipase thus enhancing their activity to give a characteristic response. Calcium also acts through a specific receptor
but the latter plays a direct role in the final response in
that the calcium-receptor complex binds directly to some component of the effector system (Fig. 1).

III. THE CYCLIC AMP SIGNALLING SYSTEM

A. *Formation of Cyclic AMP*

The membrane transducer which generates cyclic AMP in
response to a wide range of different hormones or neurotransmitters is composed of discrete subunits which interact with
each other in order to transform information which is transmitted across the bilayer. A receptor subunit, unique for each
external signal, sits on the outside of the membrane. Adenylate cyclase, which functions as an amplifier, lies on the
inside of the membrane where it can draw upon the cellular pool
of ATP to produce cyclic AMP. These two peripheral subunits
are linked by an additional subunit(s), often referred to as
the nucleotide regulatory components (N), which serves to convey information from the receptor to the adenylate cyclase.
This role of N as a transmembrane coupling agent is critically
dependent upon GTP and it is this GTP requirement which might
serve to characterise this type of transducing mechanism. The
transmission of information across this membrane transducer
begins when the agonists bind to the surface receptor (Fig. 2).
In the unstimulated condition the N-subunit binds strongly to
GDP but when the agonist occupies the receptor it induces a
conformational change in N such that it loses its affinity for
GDP and develops a strong affinity for GTP. When GTP binds to
the new site it induces a conformational change in adenylate
cyclase such that it begins to form cyclic AMP. The agonist
acting from the outside with GTP acting from within constitutes
a distinct on-reaction (Cassell and Selinger, 1978).
One of the intriguing aspects of this sequence of events is
that the receptor is sensitive to GTP in that its affinity for
the agonist is markedly reduced when the nucelotide binds to N
during the on-reaction (Maguire *et al* 1977). As GTP binds to
N it not only serves to activate AC but it also dissociates
the receptor which is then free to react with another agonist.
This reversal of the agonist-receptor interaction is the first
part of the off-reaction. The second part is to reverse the
activation of adenylate cyclase by the GTP-N complex. This
active arrangement of the N-AC subunits has a finite life span

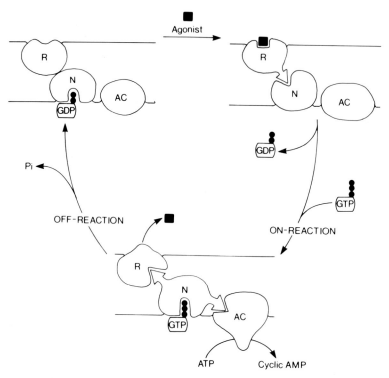

FIGURE 2. *A summary of the subunit interactions responsible for generating a cyclic AMP signal. R, receptor for external agonist; N, GTP-binding protein which links R to adenylate cyclase (AC). See text for further details.*

and is terminated by a GTPase, which seems to be associated with the N subunit, which hydrolyses GTP to GDP thus inactivating the complex (Fig 2). Cholera toxin, which is capable of activating most adenylate cyclase systems, acts by inhibiting the GTPase through an ADP ribosylation reaction which effectively blocks the off-reaction. This action of cholera toxin may thus constitute a diagnostic feature for recognizing this type of transducing mechanism.

B. *The Intracellular Action of Cyclic AMP*

Once the external signal has been transduced, the next step is to translate this change in the intracellular level of cyclic AMP into a change in cellular activity by stimulating a protein kinase. The cyclic AMP-dependent protein kinase is

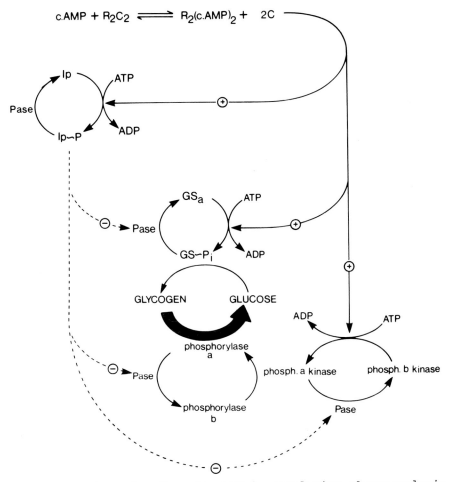

$$c.AMP + R_2C_2 \rightleftharpoons R_2(c.AMP)_2 + 2C$$

FIGURE 3.   The role of cyclic AMP in regulating glycogenolysis
in skeletal muscle (Taken from Nimmo and Cohen, 1977).   R,
regulatory subunit; C, catalytic subunit of protein kinase;
1P, inhibitor protein; Pase, phosphatase enzyme; GS, glycogen
synthetase which is converted from an active (a) to an inactive form (GS-P_i) when it is phosphorylated by C.

a complex composed of two regulatory subunits (R), which function as receptors for cyclic AMP, and two catalytic subunits
(C), which transfer phosphate groups from ATP to serine or
threonine residues of their protein substrates (Fig. 1).   As
mentioned earlier, the inactive holoenzyme is activated when
cyclic AMP levels rise within the cell and can release the
catalytic subunits by binding to the R subunits (Figs. 1 & 3).
The free catalytic subunit then phosphorylates various rate-

limiting proteins. The complexity of the integrated control
networks within the cell is illustrated by some of the main
processes responsible for regulating glycogen metabolism in
muscle (Fig. 3)(Nimmo and Cohen, 1977). Cyclic AMP increases
the formation of glucose not only by stimulating the breakdown
of glycogen but also by inhibiting glycogen synthesis and both
effects are mediated through a phosphorylation reaction as
shown in Fig. 3. In the case of glycogenolysis, there is an
enzyme cascade beginning with the phosphorylation of phosphorylase b kinase which is then responsible for activating phosphorylase through another phosphorylation reaction. All these
phosphorylation reactions are reversed by phosphatases. One
of the intriguing aspects of this control network is that
activity of these phosphatases is regulated by an inhibitory
protein which, in turn, is controlled by cyclic AMP. The
cyclic AMP-dependent protein kinase can also phosphorylate and
thus activate this inhibitor which is then capable of dampening
the activity of the phosphatase which normally reverse the
various phosphorylation reactions induced by the catalytic
subunit (Fig. 3). By stimulating this inhibitory action, the
effect of cyclic AMP is greatly potentiated and thus represents
an elegant form of amplification for this internal transducer.
Similar phosphorylation-dephosphorylation reactions are central
to the action of cyclic AMP on many other effector systems.

IV. THE CALCIUM SIGNALLING SYSTEM

     The transducing mechanism responsible for generating a
calcium signal is complicated by the existence of internal
reservoirs and hence the necessity for studying the mechanisms
which release internal calcium in addition to the mechanisms
which gate calcium across the plasma membrane.

A. *Entry of External Calcium*

     In the case of agonist-dependent calcium gating, the prob-
lem is to determine how the occupation of certain receptors is
translated into an increase in membrane permeability to calcium. A characteristic feature of this receptor mechanism
appears to be an increase in the hydrolysis of phosphatidylinositol (Michell, 1975; Michell *et al* 1975). The relationship between receptor occupation, phosphatidylinositol (PI)
hydrolysis and calcium gating has been examined in the insect
salivary gland (Fain and Berridge, 1979a,b; Berridge and Fain,
1979a,b). Specific techniques for continuously monitoring PI
hydrolysis and calcium gating during the action of 5-hydroxy-

tryptamine (5-HT), revealed that these two parameters were very closely related. More direct evidence for the role of PI has come from experiments where the membrane content of this phospholipid was reduced resulting in a severe reduction in the 5-HT-dependent increase in calcium gating. This receptor desensitization was readily reversed if the cells were allowed to resynthesize PI when provided with inositol. There is thus growing evidence that the membrane transducer responsible for generating a calcium signal somehow involves the hydrolysis of PI which may thus emerge as a diagnostic feature for this type of transducing mechanism. Just how PI hydrolysis functions to regulate calcium gating has not been established and much more work remains to be done before this transducing mechanism can be understood in the sort of detail which is now available for the cyclic AMP system described earlier.

B. Release of Internal Calcium

The transducing mechanisms responsible for releasing calcium from internal reservoirs are even more mysterious. The system which has been studied most extensively is the sarcoplasmic reticulum of skeletal muscle where triads and diads are thought to represent the coupling sites for excitation-contraction coupling. The problem is to explain how the excitation which spreads into the T-tubules is capable of triggering an explosive release of calcium from the neighbouring sarcoplasmic reticulum. One of the suggestions is that the electrical signal in the outer membrane is transmitted to the inner membranes through some form of mechanical deformation transmitted through the "tube feet" which seem to connect the two membrane systems. Such a transducing mechanism may not be unique to muscle since structural features closely resembling the triadic junction of muscle have now been described in nerve cells (Henkart et al 1976) and in fibroblasts (Henkart and Nelson, 1979). It remains to be seen therefore, whether the mechanism found in muscle represents a highly specialized version of a rather general transducing mechanism of linking excitation in external membranes to the release of internal calcium.

Another possibility is that the coupling between the surface and internal membrane system is mediated chemically. Calcium itself could function as the chemical signal because a phenomenon of calcium-induced calcium release has been described in certain muscle cells (Endo et al 1970; Fabiato and Fabiato, 1975). This mechanism may not be restricted to muscle because a similar phenomenon occurs in medaka eggs where a local increase of calcium at the point of fertilization spreads as a wave towards the opposite pole by means of a regenerative

release of stored calcium (Gilkey *et al* 1978). The possible
involvement of cyclic AMP in the regulation of internal calcium
has been suggested for a number of systems but much of the evidence is indirect and there is no detailed biochemical information on how this nucleotide might act. An understanding of how
the calcium which is stored within internal reservoirs is regulated represents a challenging problem for the future.

C. *The Intracellular Mode of Action of Calcium*

Until recently our understanding of how calcium acted within the cell was restricted to the process of muscle contraction.
The role of troponin C as an internal transducer is well-
established and we now have detailed models concerning its mode
of action at the molecular level. The muscle proteins may be
considered as an enormous amplifier whose activity is triggered
by a small change in the concentration of calcium which is
detected by troponin C. Binding of calcium to troponin C
induces a subtle shift in the tropomyosin chains which then
allows myosin to interact with actin to initiate contraction.
Troponin C thus functions as the internal receptor (R_i) in the
sequence of events shown in Fig. 1. Studies on molluscan
muscle has uncovered another form of control based on the
calcium-sensitive myosin light chains. Here again calcium
acts to remove a restraint on the myosin thus allowing it to
interact with actin.

In addition to its role in excitation-contraction coupling,
calcium had long been recognised as a second messenger in many
other cellular processes even though the nature of the internal
transducing mechanism was still obscure. While there were
clear indications as to the nature of the amplifier or effector
system, what was missing was information as to the nature of
the internal calcium receptor. Over the last few years, however, there has been a gradual realization that a single calcium binding protein, originally described as an activator of
cyclic nucleotide phosphodiesterase, may function as this calcium receptor (Wolff and Brostom, 1979). There is considerable
debate concerning what this protein should be called. So far,
it has gone under the label of activator protein and calcium-
dependent regulator (CDR) but the terminaology which appears to
be gaining general acceptance is *calmodulin*. Calmodulin is
found throughout the animal kingdom and its central importance
can be judged from the wide range of processes which are controlled through this calcium receptor protein (Table 1).

Calmodulin has a molecular weight of 18,000 which is very
similar to troponin C with which it shares many similarities.
The amino acid composition is very similar, one notable difference is that calmodulin contains a trimethyllysine residue not

TABLE I. The Pleiotropic Action of Calmodulin

Functions controlled by calmodulin	Effect
1. Activation of adenylate cyclase	Increased levels of cyclic AMP
2. Activation of cyclic GMP phosphodiesterase	Decreased levels of cyclic GMP
3. Activation of phosphorylase kinase	Glycogen breakdown
4. Activation of myosin light chain kinase	Musle contraction
5. Dissassembly of microtubules	Mitosis
6. Activation of chloride transport	Intestinal secretion
7. Stimulation of membrane fusion	Exocytosis
8. Activation of membrane calcium ATPase	Increased calcium pumping across plasma membrane and sarcoplasmic reticulum

present in troponin C. However, sequence studies have shown
many similarities suggesting that they are homologous proteins
which have evolved from a common precursor (Perry et al 1979).
The close structural similarities extend to some functional
similarities in that calmodulin can replace troponin C in
muscle contraction but the latter cannot activate phosphodiesterase. In nature there is probably little overlap of
function which is often avoided through an interesting distribution of these calcium-binding proteins. For example, in
skeletal muscle where contraction is primarily controlled
through troponin C, there is very little calmodulin. The
opposite applies to smooth muscle which presents a good
example to illustrate how calmodulin mediates one of its many
functions by regulating contraction (Fig. 4). As noted previously, this calcium receptor participates directly in the
activation of the myosin light chain kinase which represents
the first step in the stimulation of contraction. Calmodulin
may also regulate certain forms of motlity in non-muscle cells
and has already been postulated to play a role in mitosis
(Dedman et al 1979).

V. SECOND MESSENGER INTERACTIONS

It is important to realize that the two signalling systems described in the last two sections are not separate private lines of communication but that they interact at many different levels. A good example of interactions taking place at the receptor level is found in the mammalian salivary gland where the activation of α-adrenergic or cholinergic receptors can markedly impair the generation of cyclic AMP via the β-receptors (Harper and Brooker, 1977; Oron *et al* 1978a,b). This inhibitory

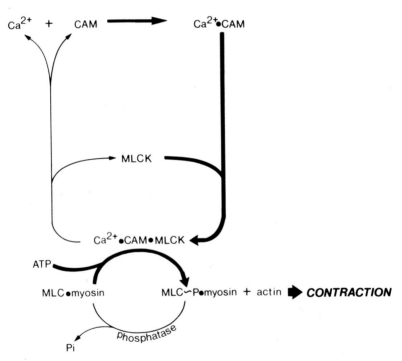

FIGURE 4. The role of calmodulin (CAM) in mediating the onset of contraction in smooth muscle. The thick lines represent the flow of information during contraction whereas the thinner lines trace the reversal processes which cause relaxation when calcium is withdrawn. The Ca^{2+}-calmodulin complex activates the myosin light chain kinase (MLCK) which is responsible for phosphorylating the myosin light chains (MLC) which are attached to myosin. When these light chains are phosphorylated (MLC-P), they allow myosin to interact with actin to initiate contraction.

effect, which seems to be directed against adenylate cyclase, need not involve calcium because the non-specific refractoriness induced by acetylcholine is independent of external calcium. In some other systems, calcium working through calmodulin causes a marked stimulation of adenylate cyclase (Table 1) (Wolff and Brostrom, 1979). Indeed, calmodulin seems to play a pivotal role in cyclic nucleotide-calcium interactions because it also mediates the stimulatory effect of calcium on phosphodiesterase (Table 1). All these second messenger pathways of control must not be considered as separate entities but rather as part of an integrated network much of whose complexity and subtlety remains to be discovered.

VI. CONCLUSION

Many hormones and neurotransmitters induce profound changes in cellular activity without entering the cell.

A limited number of transducing mechanisms are responsible for transforming all forms of sensory information into relatively few internal signals. The detection of these external signals is carried out on the cell surface by specific receptors which are then connected to an internal signalling system responsible for carrying information to the specific effector systems within the cell. During this flow of information, the original signal from the external receptors is transduced into a form which can be recognised by the effector systems. In vertebrates, the two major transducing mechanisms which have been uncovered so far are centred around the second messengers cyclic AMP and calcium. This essay summarizes the enormous advances which have been made during the last few years in uncovering the major components of these two signalling systems. Many diverse external signals use one or other of these two lines of communication and in many cases certain agonists can gain access to both.

Most forms of cellular control are explicable on the basis of using these two signalling systems organized as part of an integrated network. However, there are still some missing links especially with regard to how the ebb and flow of calcium across internal reservoirs is controlled. It is quite likely, therefore, that there may be other transducing mechanisms awaiting discovery. So far, studies on insect material have not featured significantly in this search for internal signalling systems. In the years ahead it will be fascinating to see what sorts of transducing mechanisms are present in the invertebrates and how they compare with those found in vertebrates. Such comparisons will provide valuable insights into the evolutionary development of this internal signalling system.

REFERENCES

Assimacopoulos-Jeannet, F.D, Blackmore, P.F. and Exton, J.H.
    (1977). Studies on α-adrenergic activation of hepatic
    glucose output. Studies on role of calcium in α-adrenergic
    activation of phosphorylase. *J. Biol. Chem. 252*, 2662.

Berridge, M.J. and Fain, J.N. (1979a). Inhibition of phospha-
    tidylinositol synthesis and the inactivation of calcium
    entry after prolonged exposure of the blowfly salivary
    gland to 5-hydroxytryptamine. *Biochem. J. 178*, 59.

Berridge, M.J. and Fain, J.N. (1979b). Phosphatidylinositol
    metabolism and calcium gating. *Medicinal Chemistry XI*,
    117.

Cassel, D. and Selinger, Z. (1978). Mechanism of adenylate
    cyclase activation through the β-adrenergic receptor:
    catecholamine-induced displacement of bound GDP by GTP.
    Proc. Natl. Acad. Sci. U.S.A. 75, 4155.

Dedman, J.R., Brinkley, B.R. and Means, A.R. (1979). Regula-
    tion of microfilaments and microtubules by calcium and
    cyclic AMP. *Adv. Cyclic Nucleotide Res. 11*, 131.

Endo, M., Tanaka, M. and Ogawa, Y. (1970). Calcium induced
    release of calcium from the sarcoplasmic reticulum of
    skinned skeletal muscle fibres. *Nature, Lond. 228*, 34.

Fabiato, A. and Fabiato, F. (1975). Contractions induced by a
    calcium-triggered release of calcium from the sarcoplasmic
    reticulum of single skinned cardiac cells. *J. Physiol. 249*,
    469.

Fain, J.N. and Berridge, M.J. (1979a). Relationship between
    hormonal activation of phosphatidylinositol hydrolysis,
    fluid secretion and calcium flux in the blowfly salivary
    gland. *Biochem. J. 178*, 45.

Fain, J.N. & Berridge, M.J. (1979b). Relationship between
    phosphatidylinositol synthesis and recovery of 5-hydroxy-
    tryptamine-responsive Ca^{2+} flux in blowfly salivary glands.
    Biochem. J. 180, 655.

Gilkey, J.C., Jaffe, L.F., Ridgway, L.B. and Reynolds, G.T.
    (1978). A free calcium wave traverses the activating egg
    of the medaka, *Oryzias latipes. J. Cell Biol. 76*, 448.

Henkart, M., Landis, D.M.D. and Reese, T.S. (1976). Similarity of junctions between plasma membranes and endoplasmic reticulum in muscle and neurons. *J. Cell Biol. 70*, 338.

Henkart, M.P. and Nelson, P.G. (1979). Evidence for an intra-cellular calcium store releasable by surface stimuli in fibroblasts (L cells). *J. Gen. Physiol. 73*, 655.

Keppens, S., Vandenheede, J.R. and De Wulf, H. (1977). On the role of calcium as second messenger in liver for the hor-monally induced activation of glycogen phosphorylase. *Biochem. Biophys. Acta 496*, 448.

Maddrell, S.H.P. (1962). A diuretic hormone in *Rhodnius prolixus* Stål. *Nature, Lond. 194*, 605.

Maddrell, S.H.P. (1964). Excretion in the blood-sucking bug, *Rhodnius prolixus* Stål. III. The control of the release of the diuretic hormone. *J. exp. Biol. 41*, 459.

Maddrell, S.H.P. (1966). The site of release of the diuretic hormone in *Rhodnius* - a new neurohaemal system in insects. *J. exp. Biol. 45*, 499.

Maguire, M.E., Ross, E.M. and Gilman, A.G. (1977). β-Adrener-gic receptor: ligand binding properties and the interaction with adenylyl cyclase. *Adv. Cyclic Nucleotide Res. 8*, 1.

Michell, R.H. (1975). Inositol phospholipids and cell surface receptor function. *Biochem. Biophys. Acta 415*, 81.

Michell, R.H., Jafferji, S.S. and Jones, L.M. (1977). The possible involvement of phosphatidylinositol breakdown in the mechanism of stimulus-response coupling at receptors which control cell-surface calcium gates. *Adv. Exp. Biol. Med. 83*, 447.

Nimmo, H.G. and Cohen, P. (1977). Hormonal control of protein phosphorylation. *Adv. Cyclic Nucleotide Res. 8*, 145.

Orloff, J. and Handler, J.S. (1967). The role of adenosine 3',5'-phosphate in the action of antidiuretic hormone. *Am. J. Medicine 42*, 757.

Perry, S.V., Grand, R.J.A., Nairn, A.C., Vanaman, T.C. and Wall, C.M. (1979). Calcium-binding proteins and the regulation of contractile activity. *Biochem. Soc. Trans. 7*, 619.

Springer, M.S., Goy, M.F. and Adler, J. (1979). Protein methyl-
     ation in behavioural control mechanisms and in signal
     transduction. *Nature, Lond.* *280*, 279.

van de Werve, G., Hue, L. and Hers, H-G. (1977). Hormonal and
     ionic control of the glycogenolytic cascade in rat liver.
     Biochem. J. *162*, 135.

Wolff, D.J. and Brostrom, C.O. (1979). Properties and functions
     of the calcium-dependent regulator protein. *Adv. Cyclic
     Nucleotide Res.* *11*, 27.

Wigglesworth, V.B. (1966). Hormones controlling growth and
     development in insects. *Aspects of Insect Biochemistry*,
     T.W. Goodwin (ed), Academic Press: London & New York, 79-
     82.

Wigglesworth, V.B. (1970). *Insect Hormones.* Edinburgh:
     Oliver & Boyd

POSITIONAL INFORMATION AS A REGULATOR OF GROWTH IN
THE IMAGINAL WING DISC OF *DROSOPHILA MELANOGASTER*[3]

Christine Duranceau[1]
Susanne L. Glenn
Howard A. Schneiderman[2]

Developmental Biology Center
and
Department of Developmental and Cell Biology
University of California, Irvine
Irvine, California

INTRODUCTION

Most studies of the factors regulating insect
growth have focused on hormones, (Wigglesworth, 1970,
Insect Hormones; Doane, 1973; Gilbert *et al.*, 1977;
Riddiford and Truman, 1978). Evidence that factors
other than hormones regulate insect growth comes from
studies of the regeneration of the abdominal epidermis
of bugs and of the imaginal disc epidermis of flies.
For example, in *Rhodnius*, wounding the abdominal epidermis stimulates localized cell division, which comes
to an end when the cell density normal for the species
is restored in the epidermis (Wigglesworth, 1937a,
1959, The Control of Growth and Form). In *Drosophila*,
a fragment of an imaginal disc cultured in an adult

[1]*Present address: School of Medicine, Yale
University, New Haven, Connecticut*
[2]*Present address: Research and Development, Monsanto
Company, St. Louis, Missouri*
[3]*Original work described in this paper was supported
in part by Grants No. AI 10527 and HD 06082, awarded
by the National Institutes of Health, DHEW.*

abdomen ceases to grow when it reaches a certain size
(Hadorn and Garcia-Bellido, 1964; Ursprung and Hadorn,
1962; Tobler, 1966). Yet, if this cultured fragment
is again cut into fragments, some growth is renewed
in the fragments, and if the tissue is dissociated
into many fragments that are then mixed together and
reaggregated, extensive growth occurs (Tobler, 1966;
see review by Gehring and Nöthiger, 1973). Clearly,
factors besides hormones regulate growth of epidermal
cells.

Sir Vincent Wigglesworth drew explicit attention to
these nonhormonal factors in several papers, notably
in the Messenger Lectures on the "control of growth
and form," presented at Cornell University (Wigglesworth,
1959, The Control of Growth and Form) and in a stimulating
paper on "homeostasis and insect growth" presented
to the Society of Experimental Biology (Wigglesworth,
1964c). These papers revealed that, unlike most investigators who focused on either the developmental hormones
of insects or on the epidermis, which is the most
conspicuous target tissue of the hormones, Sir Vincent
attended to both with equal fervor. It is our belief
that this intimacy with both insect growth hormones
and with the insect epidermal cells themselves, is
in part responsible for Sir Vincent's special insights
into what he has aptly called "life in the two-dimensional
world of insect epidermal cells" (Wigglesworth, 1964c).

In his 1964 paper, Sir Vincent expressed the view that
growth and pattern are closely coupled (Wigglesworth,
1964). He argued that the nonhormonal factors regulating
growth are the same factors that regulate pattern
and form. He asserted that the capacity for localized
growth in normal development is as much an element
of body pattern as is a localized capacity for forming
a pigmented cuticle or a particular type of bristle.
He also suggested (Wigglesworth, 1959, The Control of
Growth and Form; 1965) that the pattern and form of
an organ were regulated by local homeostatic responses
involving direct physical contact and continuity between
one epidermal cell and the next. If these ideas are
correct, then in order to understand the control of
growth it is necessary to understand the phenomena
of pattern formation and regulation (a term we use
to denote developmental responses to surgical intervention). Recent advances in understanding the mechanism
of pattern formation have made it possible to test

the validity of Sir Vincent's idea that the same factors control both spatial patterns of differentiation and growth within a tissue. They also permit the assessment of his suggestion that this control depends on communication between epidermal cells.

One advance has been the realization that a useful distinction can be drawn between the process whereby cells initially acquire differences according to their physical position in a developing tissue (positional information) and their subsequent activities (interpretation) carried out in response to this positional information (Wolpert, 1969; Wolpert, 1971). The principal reasons for making this distinction are that many mutations seem to alter the local response to positional information rather than alter the positional information system itself (see Bryant, 1974; Postlethwait and Schneiderman, 1973; Schneiderman, 1979) and that positional information is apparently the same in different imaginal discs but utilized differently (Postlethwait and Schneiderman, 1971).

A second advance in understanding pattern formation is the polar coordinate model of pattern regulation in epimorphic fields proposed by French, Bryant and Bryant (1976). This model accounts for the regulative responses of whole tissues such as imaginal discs in terms of the behavior of interacting cells. In this model, it is proposed that when cells are juxtaposed with other cells that are not their normal neighbors and therefore are of different positional values, they are stimulated to divide, and the new cells acquire the positional values missing between the confronted cells. The model predicts that during normal development, growth will occur until the pattern is complete, and that during culture of an imaginal disc fragment, growth will occur until either regeneration or duplication is complete. It also predicts that small fragments of discs will duplicate and then cease to grow, whereas reaggregated fragments will grow until intercalation of missing positional values is complete. These predictions are in accord with experimental findings (French, Bryant and Bryant, 1976).

We have conducted experiments to analyze the relationship between the regulation of growth and of pattern formation in imaginal wing discs of *Drosophila*. We have analyzed the growth of wing disc fragments and mixtures of fragments during various periods of culture.

We have also ascertained the developmental capacities
of these fragments and mixtures after various periods
of culture by analyzing the range of structures they
produce after metamorphosis.

MATERIALS AND METHODS

     Drosophila melanogaster were raised at 26°C on
cornmeal-sugar-yeast agar medium using standard culture
techniques. Imaginal wing discs were removed from
mature third instar larvae of the Oregon-RC strain of
Drosophila melanogaster aged 110 ± 4 hrs after oviposition.
The discs were cut into fragments in buffered Ringer's
solution (Schubiger, 1971), using tungsten needles.
Cuts were made along the lines indicated in Figure 1,
most of which coincide with natural folds in the disc.
Fragments were mixed by folding together with tungsten
needles until they formed a coherent mass, as described
by Haynie and Bryant (1976).

     Growth was determined by measuring the volume of the
tissue before and after culture *in vivo* with a calibrated
micropipette which also served as an injection needle.
The pipette was of traditional design (Ephrussi and
Beadle, 1936; Ursprung, 1967). The volume of the micropipette from the tip to the constriction was calculated
from measurements made with an ocular micrometer (Fig. 2).
The accuracy of this method of estimating the volume
of the micropipette was checked by weighing the volume of
mercury taken up in the pipette and also by measuring
spectrophotometrically the amount of a fluorescent dye
taken up in the pipette. The different methods of
volume measurement agreed within ± five percent. Pipette
volumes from tip to constriction were usually between
7 and 11 nanoliters. The tissue was taken up into the
capillary to the constriction, and the length of capillary
not occupied by the tissue was measured (Fig. 2). The
volume of the tissue was then calculated. The smallest
tissue volume that could conveniently be measured was
about 0.5 nanoliters and the largest was about 10 nanoliters. The reproducibility of the method was checked
by making successive volume measurements of the same
disc or disc fragment. These agreed within ± 10 percent.
When a disc was cut into two or three fragments, the
initial volume of the disc was equal to the combined
volumes of the fragments within ± 10 percent.

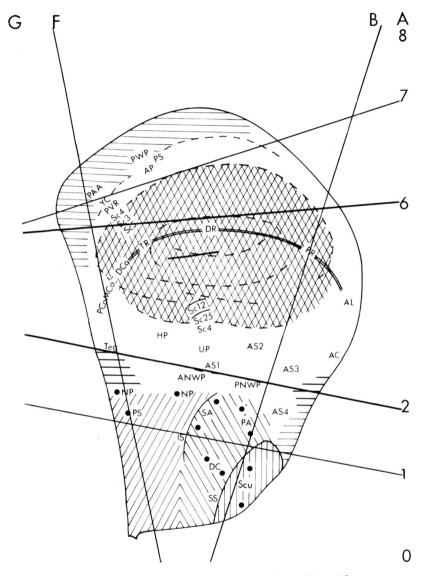

Fig. 1. Fate map of the imaginal wing disc (from
Bryant, 1975). The location of cuts used to generate
the fragments used in this study are shown. The guidelines
for the cuts were natural folds in the wing disc (see
Bryant, 1975). Transverse cuts 1, 2, 6 and 7 generated
fragments 01, 02, 68, and 78, respectively. Longitudinal
cuts B and F generated fragments AB and FG, respectively.
For the abbreviations of cuticular structures, see Table 1.

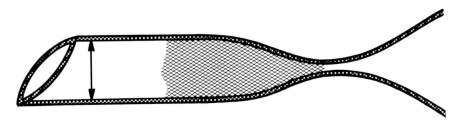

Fig. 2. Diagram of micropipette used for measurements of tissue volume and for injection. Method of calculating volume is described in the text.

To ascertain the extent to which tissue volume reflects cell number, we measured the number of cells
within a given volume of tissue by dissociating the
tissue in a maceration fluid and then counting the number
of cells. The maceration fluid was composed of acetic
acid, glycerol and water in a 1:1:6 ratio (H. Bode,
personal communication). The tissue was kept in maceration
fluid for five days and then transferred to a measured
drop of macerating fluid (0.02 ml) in a hemocytometer.
The tissue was then disrupted within the drop by mechanical
stirring with tungsten needles until cell clumps had
disappeared and an evenly distributed population of
cells was produced. The number of cells within the drop
was estimated from the number of cells counted in a 100 nl
volume in the hemacytometer.

After the tissue volume was measured, the tissue was
transplanted into fertilized female adult hosts (3-4 days
after eclosion) and cultured *in vivo* by the method of
Bodenstein (1939). After 7, 14, 21, or 28 days of culture,
the tissues were removed, their volumes were measured,
and they were transplanted by the method of Ephrussi
and Beadle (1936) into mature third instar larvae which
had been aged 110 $\pm$ 4 hrs at 26° C after oviposition.
After the larvae had metamorphosed, the implants were
removed, dehydrated in absolute alcohol, dissected
and mounted in Euparal between cover slips.

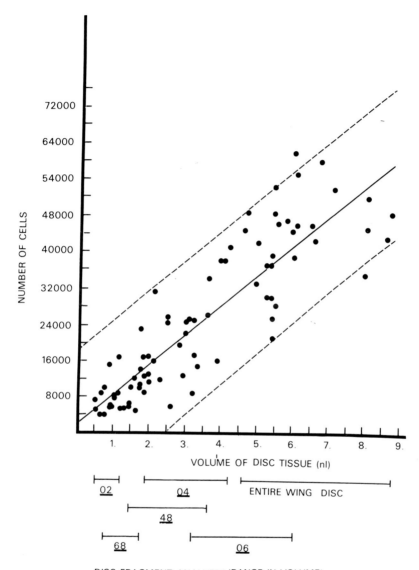

Fig. 3. *Number of cells in fragments of mature imaginal wing discs of different volumes. The line was derived by a regression analysis of the data. The dotted lines indicate 95% confidence levels. The fragments measured were 02, 04, 48, 68, 06, and entire wing discs.*

We checked for the presence in the implant of any of
the 36 cuticular structures of the wing identified
by Bryant (1975) which are listed in Table 1. When
part of a structure was detected in an implant, it
was recorded as present; for instance, one bracted bristle
indicated the presence of the proximal costa.

RESULTS

Correlation Between Tissue Volume and Cell Number

The volume of intact wing discs or fragments of discs
was measured, and then the numbers of cells within
these tissues were determined by the dissociation
method described in the Methods section. The results
in Figure 3 show that in the mature wing disc, there is
an approximately linear relationship between tissue
volume and cell number.

We next determined whether changes in tissue volume
after culture *in vivo* were associated with changes
in cell number. *O2* fragments of wing discs were measured
and were then injected into adult females for 7 or
14 days of culture. The number of cells in the *O2* fragment
prior to injection was estimated by measuring the
number of cells in the *O2* fragment from the contralateral
wing disc. After culture, the volumes of the implants
were measured, the tissue was dissociated and the cell
numbers counted. After seven days of culture, the fragments had increased in volume 2.20 ± 0.39-fold ($\pm$ =
standard error), and the number of cells had increased
2.31 ± 0.39-fold. After 14 days of culture, the fragments
had increased in volume 2.22 ± 0.25-fold, and the number of
cells had increased 1.98 ± 0.27-fold. These results
show that in wing disc fragments cultured *in vivo*,
there is a simple relationship between tissue volume
and cell number. Hence the changes in volume of imaginal
wing disc tissue reported in the rest of this paper
are to be interpreted as the result of changes in
cell number.

Growth of Intact Wing Discs and Fragments of Wing Discs

In the following experiments, we examined the effects
of different periods of culture *in vivo* on the growth

TABLE 1. Abbreviations for Structures in Metamorphosed Implants from the Wing Disc[a]

Abbr.	Structure	Abbr.	Structure
PAA,	Prealar apophysis	PR,	Posterior row of hairs
PWP,	Pleural wing process	Sc12,	Group of 12 sensilla campaniformia between first and second septa
AP,	Axillar pouch		
PS,	Pleural sclerite	Sc25,	Group of 25 sensilla campaniformia on the proximal dorsal distal radius
YC,	Yellow club		
PVR,	Proximal ventral radius	Sc4,	Group of four sensilla campaniformia on the proximal dorsal distal radius
Sc4,	Group of four sensilla campaniformia on the proximal ventral radius	HP,	Humeral plate
		UP,	Unnamed plate
Sc3,	Group of three sensilla campaniformia on the proximal ventral radius	AS1,	First axillary sclerite
		AS2,	Second axillary sclerite
		AS3,	Third axillary sclerite
Sc5,	Group of five sensilla campaniformia on the proximal ventral radius	AS4,	Fourth axillary sclerite
		SA(2),	Supraalar bristles
		PA(2),	Postalar bristles
Pco,	Proximal costa, bearing bracted bristles	DC(2),	Dorsocentral bristles
		Scu(2),	Scutellar bristles
Mco,	Medial costa	Scutum,	Central region of notum
Dco,	Distal costa	AL,	Alar lobe
TR,	Triple bristle row (anterior wing margin)	AC,	Axillary cord
		Pleura,	Mesopleura, pteropleura, postpleura
Teg,	Tegula	Wing,	Dorsal and ventral wing surfaces
NP(2),	Notopleural bristles		
PS(1),	Presutural bristle		
DR,	Double bristle row (distal wing margin)		

[a]We have used the terminology and abbreviations of Bryant (1975).

of intact discs and on the inventory of structures
they formed. Intact wing discs were removed from
mature third instar larvae and their volumes measured.
They were then cultured for either 7, 14, 21, or 28
days, and after their volumes had been remeasured,
they were implanted into third instar larvae for metamorphosis. Table 2A shows that the wing discs neither
grew nor shrank significantly during 28 days of culture.
It also shows that the average number of cuticular
structures formed was not affected significantly by
the 28 days of culture. After seven days of culture,
an average of 30.7 ± 2.25 structures (75 percent of
possible structures) formed, whereas after 28 days
an average of 27.1±2.27 (60 percent of possible structures)
were formed. Table 2B shows that the diversity of
structures formed was not markedly affected by the
different periods of culture.

Table 3 records the effects of various periods of
culture on the growth of individual disc fragments

TABLE 2A. *Growth and Metamorphosis of Entire Imaginal Wing*
          Discs Cultured In Vivo *for Different Periods*

Days in culture	*7*	*14*	*21*	*28*
Number of implants measured	*47*	*56*	*50*	*45*
Average growth (final volume/ initial volume) ± standard error	*0.96 ±0.03*	*1.03 ±0.05*	*0.94 ±0.05*	*0.82 ±0.05*
Number of implants metamorphosed	*15*	*11*	*8*	*7*
Average number of structures per implant ± standard error	*30.7 ±2.25*	*28.4 ±2.83*	*24.6 ±4.74*	*27.1 ±2.27*

TABLE 2B. *Metamorphosis of Entire Imaginal Wing Discs Cultured In Vivo for Different Periods*

Days in culture	7	14	21	28
Number of implants metamorphosed	15	11	8	7
Structure	Percent of implants where marker is completely or partially present			
PAA	80	73	63	86
PWP	93	82	75	86
AP	53	45	63	43
PS	93	91	75	86
YC	73	82	63	71
PVR	93	64	75	86
Sc4	33	36		14
Sc3	53	18	13	14
Sc5	40			14
Pco	80	64	38	86
Mco	93	82	50	86
Dco	93	91	75	86
TR	100	73	75	43
Teg	87	55	63	86
NP (2)	73	82	75	57
PS (1)	73	64	75	57
DR	73	73	75	43
PR	80	73	63	71
Sc12	67	55	63	43
Sc25	80	64	25	86
Sc4	60	64	38	86
HP	67	64	25	86
UP	53	36	25	71
AS1	87	91	75	100
AS2	87	91	75	100
AS3	87	82	75	86
AS4	87	64	63	71
SA (2)	67	73	63	57
PA (2)	73	73	63	57
DC (2)	73	82	63	57
Scu (2)	73	82	38	43
Scutum	73	82	75	71
AL	87	64	50	71
AC	53	36	38	43
Pleura	100	100	100	100
Wing blade	100	100	100	100

TABLE 3. *Growth and Metamorphosis of 02 and of 68 Fragments of Wing Discs Cultured In Vivo for Different Periods*

02 Fragment

Days in culture	0	7	14	21	28
Number of implants measured	--	47	56	50	45
Growth (final volume/ initial volume) ± standard error	1.00	1.86±0.12	2.27±0.15	1.85±0.10	1.61±0.11
Number of implants metamorphosed	16	15	13	15	11
Average number of structures per implant ± standard error	10.4±0.75	21.4±1.60	18.0±3.61	18.7±3.87	11.6±3.32

TABLE 3 (continued)

68 Fragment

Days in culture	0	7	14	21	28
Number of implants measured	--	46	40	45	40
Growth (final volume/ initial volume) ± standard error	1.00	1.88±0.12	2.59±0.18	2.35±0.17	2.59±0.23
Number of implants metamorphosed	14	15	14	17	8
Average number of structures per implant ± standard error (duplicated and regenerated)	6.9±0.69	10.8±1.37	11.1±0.96	9.9±1.31	13.4±3.82
Average number of structures from the 68 region of the fate map that were produced by the 68 fragment ± standard error	6.8±0.67	9.7±1.27	9.5±0.94	7.5±0.99	8.1±1.20

and on the inventory of structures formed by these
fragments. The *02* fragment includes the presumptive
notum and some dorsal hinge structures, whereas the *68*
fragment includes presumptive ventral hinge structures,
pleura and wing blade (Bryant, 1975). The results
in Table 3 show that after seven days in culture both
types of fragment had increased in volume 1.9-fold. After
14 days, the *02* fragment and the *68* fragments had
increased in volume 2.3 and 2.6-fold, respectively.
Between 14 and 28 days, the average volume of the
02 fragment decreased significantly to 1.6 times the
initial volume, whereas the average volume of the
68 fragment had not changed.

Table 4 indicates the numbers and kinds of structures
formed after metamorphosis of these fragments. The
number of structures per implant was counted. We scored
only structures in which we could decide whether a
duplication had occurred. For example, the *68* fragment
produces wing blade when immediately metamorphosed,
but when wing blade is formed by a cultured *68* implant,
the original may be fused with the duplicate wing
blade, and as a consequence, we cannot determine whether
a duplication of wing blade had occurred. Hence, the
wing blade, pleura, and scutum were not included in
our calculations.

When the *02* and *68* fragments were immediately metamorphosed without culture in adults, the structures
produced by each fragment were similar to those reported
by Bryant (1975). However, the total number of structures
produced by each fragment was modified by a period of
culture *in vivo*. In the case of the *02* fragment, the
average number of structures formed (original + duplicate)
increased from 10.4 ± 0.75 after no culture to 21.4
± 1.60 after seven days of culture. This doubling of
the average number of structures reflects the duplication

of this fragment (Bryant, 1975). The average number
of structures formed by the duplicated *02* fragment
did not change significantly until after 28 days of culture
when it decreased to 11.6 $\pm$ 3.32 structures per implant
(P<.05). Thus, after seven days of culture, on the
average 75% of the structures appeared in each implant
and 42% of the structures were duplicated. After 28
days of culture, on the average 45% of the structures
appeared in each implant and 20% of the structures
were duplicated. Apparently, the *02* fragment undergoes
an initial duplication during the first seven days,
and it continues to produce the same kinds of structures
at similar frequencies for two more weeks. However,
some time after 21 days of culture, both the original
and duplicate halves lose the capacity to form some
structures. Although there was a decrease in the number of
structures formed in each implant, there was no decrease in
the variety of structures formed; 14 different structures
were detected in 7-day cultures, and the same 14 structures
were detected in 28-day cultures.

During the first seven days of culture, the *68* fragments behaved like *02* fragments and underwent duplication.
However, after 21 or 28 days of culture, these fragments
regenerated many structures belonging to other parts
of the disc that were never detected in implants metamorphosed without prior culture. The longer the culture
period, the greater the variety of structures regenerated
and the greater the proportion of implants showing
regeneration (Table 4). After 28 days, 38 percent
of the *68* fragments had regenerated. Figure 4 shows the
sequence of appearance of structures in these fragments.
In two cases, almost all of the wing disc derivatives
were produced. At the same time, there was no significant
reduction in the frequency of structures that the
fate map would lead us to expect from *68* fragments. After
seven days of culture, on the average 67% of the structures

TABLE 4. *Structures Formed by* O_2 *and by* 68 *Fragments After Culture* In Vivo *for Different Periods and Subsequent Metamorphosis*

	O_2									
Days in culture:	0		7		14		21		28	
No. of implants metamorphosed:	16		15		13		15		11	
	P	D	P	D	P	D	P	D	P	D
Structure	Percent of implants where marker									
PAA										
PWP										
AP										
PS										
YC										
PVR										
Sc4										
Sc3										
Sc5										
Pco										
Mco										
Dco										
TR										
Teg			67^a	27	46^a	23^a	20^a	07^a	18^a	09^a
NP (2)	81		100	80	83	62	87	60	64	56
PS (1)	63		87	73	92	67	87	67	45	27
DR										
PR										
Sc12										
Sc25										
Sc4										
HP										
UP										
AS1	38		40		38	15	53	40	36	
AS2	06		40	33	54	15	60	27	36	
AS3	63		60		69	31	47	40	36	18
AS4	81		80	33	85	69	60	31	56	27
SA (2)	81		100	87	77	62	87	67	82	45
PA (2)	100		87	80	85	46	93	53	45	27
DC (2)	75		100	47	92	54	93	53	73	09
Scu (2)	88	06	93	67	77	46	93	53	45	27
Scutum	100		100		100		100		100	
AL										
AC	31		40		08		07		09	
Pleura	100		100		100		100		100	
Wing										

[^{a}denotes structures that regenerated and were not normally produced by the fragment when it was metamorphosed immediately. P denotes the percent of implants in which the structure was present after metamorphosis; D denotes the percent of implants in which the structure was duplicated after metamorphosis]

68									
0		7		14		21		28	
14		15		14		17		8	
P	D	P	D	P	D	P	D	P	D

is completely or partially present

P	D	P	D	P	D	P	D	P	D
57		80	40	79	50	65	47	63	38
93	07	87	80	100	71	88	29	100	50
86	07	87	33	79	50	59	24	63	13
93		87	87	100	71	88	41	100	63
79		73	40	93	36	76	41	63	25
79	07	73	47	79	43	71	47	75	50
43		40	20	07		12		50	13
50		53	13	43	14	24		25	
36		27	13	29		24			
						06		13[a]	
		20[a]						13[a]	13[a]
		07[a]		14[a]		18[a]		25[a]	13[a]
				14[a]		06[a]		38[a]	13[a]
				07[a]				13[a]	
				14[a]		29[a]	06[a]	13[a]	13[a]
				14[a]		18[a]		13[a]	13[a]
		47[a]		43[a]		24[a]		25[a]	
		13[a]		07[a]		12[a]			
								13[a]	
								13[a]	
								13[a]	
								25[a]	
								13[a]	13[a]
								25[a]	13[a]
								25[a]	13[a]
								38[a]	
								25[a]	
				14[a]		12[a]		38[a]	
		27[a]		14[a]		24[a]			
36						06			
100		100		100		100		100	
100		100		100		100		100	

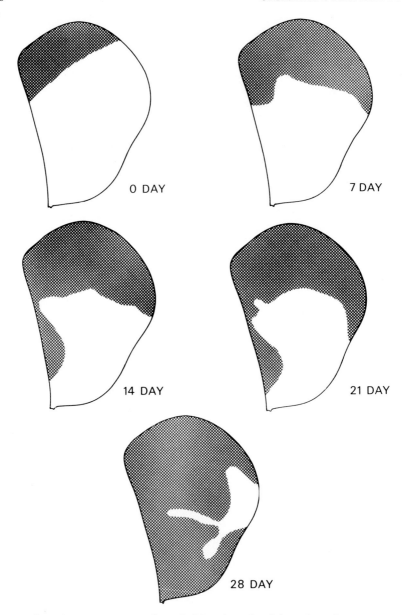

Fig. 4. *Regeneration following duplication in*
68 *fragments of imaginal discs. The figure indicates
the sequence in which various wing structures appeared
in* 68 *fragments that had been cultured in* vivo *for
various periods. The crosshatched areas denote the
appearance of the structures from that area of the
fate map (Fig. 1) in at least one implant.*

found in the 68 region of the fate map appeared in
each implant and 41% of those structures were duplicated.
After 28 days of culture, there was no significant
decrease in the frequency of appearance of these 68 structures in the implants (60%); however, the frequency
of duplications decreased to 28% ($P < 0.05$). Therefore,
during the first seven days of culture, the 68 fragment
undergoes duplication, but after 21 days of culture,
it appears to lose some duplicated structures. Along with
the loss of 68 duplicated structures, there is a regeneration of structures not normally produced by the 68
fragment. In one case, after 28 days of culture,
not only were the structures of the 68 fragment duplicated,
but even some of the regenerated structures had duplicated.

Figure 4 also shows that even after 28 days of culture,
some structures, such as certain sclerites, did not
appear to regenerate in any of the fourteen 68 implants
we analyzed. We are not prepared to attribute significance
to this apparent failure to regenerate certain structures
because in our experience the structures missing in these
28-day cultures are hard to identify in large implants that
contain exensive areas of smooth cuticle.

Growth of Grafts Composed of Different Fragments

We next examined the results of mixing two fragments
from either the same side or from opposite sides of
the wing disc. The fragments selected were the 01
and 78 fragments. In each experiment, the two fragments
were mixed together with tungsten needles and the volume of
the combination measured. The tissue was then cultured
in an adult host for 7, 14, or 21 days, the volume
of the implant was remeasured, and the implant was
transferred to a larval host for metamorphosis.

The growth of the different combinations of fragments
is recorded in Table 5. After seven days, the $01 + 01$
combination and the $78 + 78$ combination had about
doubled in size, whereas the $01 + 78$ combination had
grown significantly more than the other combinations
($P < 0.05$) almost tripling in size. After 14 days of
culture, the $01 + 01$ and $78 + 78$ combinations had
not changed significantly from about double their original
size ($P < 0.45$ and $P < 0.1$), whereas the $01 + 78$ combination
had increased significantly ($P < 0.05$) to four times

TABLE 5. *Growth and Metamorphosis of* 01 + 01, 78 + 78, *and* 01 + 78 *Combinations Cultured* In Vivo *for Different Periods*

Combination:		01 + 01		
Days in culture:	0	7	14	21
Number of implants measured:	--	58	47	52
Growth $\pm$ standard error (final volume/ initial volume):	--	1.82 $\pm$0.08	1.81 $\pm$0.11	2.19 $\pm$0.13
Number of implants metamorphosed:	15	14	10	10
Structure			Percent of implants	
Notum	100	100	100	100
Scu	47	50	60	30
HP				
AS				
Dorsal radius				
Teg				
Costa				
TR				
DR				
PR				
AL				
AC				
Wing				
Ventral hinge				

[a]denotes structures that regenerated and were not normally produced by the combination when it was metamorphosed immediately.

	78 + 78				01 + 78		
0	7	14	21	0	7	14	21
--	64	56	52	--	46	56	54
--	2.28 ±0.12	2.60 ±0.16	1.99 ±0.13	--	2.93 ±0.27	4.10 ±0.51	3.58 ±0.30
11	14	10	9	14	14	14	11

where marker is completely or partially present

	7	14	21	0	7	14	21
	14[a]	30[a]	22[a]	93	93	93	82
				71	71	22	18
							09[a]
			11[a]		29[a]	36[a]	18[a]
		10[a]			07[a]	22[a]	18[a]
		20[a]			14[a]	14[a]	36[a]
		10[a]	22[a]		22[a]	14[a]	36[a]
						07[a]	18[a]
			11[a]		14[a]	07[a]	27[a]
	14[a]		22[a]		14[a]	14[a]	18[a]
	07[a]		22[a]		07[a]	22[a]	
	29[a]	20[a]	33[a]	07	22[a]	29[a]	36
100	71	90	89	100	86	86	64
82	93	80	89	93	64	57	55

their original size. After 21 days the *01 + 01* and
78 + 78 combinations were still double their original
size, whereas the *01 + 78* combination was 3.6 times its
original size.

The inventory of structures produced by various
combinations of *01* and *78* fragments is also recorded
in Table 5. The *01 + 01* combination produced similar
ranges of structures after all the periods of culture.
In contrast, the *78 + 78* combination gradually regenerated structures normally formed by other parts of
the wing disc. After seven days of culture, a few
structures had regenerated in some of the implants,
but after 21 days of culture, 50% of the *78* fragments
had regenerated at least one structure. In a few cases,
most of the derivatives of the disc had been regenerated
within a single implant. The *01 + 78* combination rapidly
regenerated missing structures, and after seven days of
culture, almost all of the structures normally formed
by the wing disc appeared in the metamorphosed implants.

We also examined the results of other combinations
involving identical sides, opposite sides and adjacent
sides of the wing disc, using an experimental procedure
similar to that described above. A 14-day culture
was used because in the previous series of experiments
(Table 5), this had proven long enough to permit the
detection of significant differences in the growth
of implants. The results in Tables 6 and 7 indicate
that *78 + 78, 01 + 01, AB + AB, FG + FG,* and *78 + AB*
combinations approximately doubled in size, whereas
78 + FG, 01 + 78, and *AB + FG* increased in size three-
to six-fold. After 14 days of culture, the average
volume of the *01 + 78* combination is significantly
less than the average volume of a whole wing disc
($P < 0.01$), while the average volume of *AB + FG* combination is greater than the average volume of a whole
wing disc ($P < 0.05$) (Table 6).

The combinations showing the greatest frequency of
regeneration as judged from the structures present
after metamorphosis (Table 7) were *78 + FG, 01 + 78,*
and *AB + FG.* The *78 + 78* combination as mentioned in
the previous section slowly regenerated, but only after
21 days of culture did a single implant regenerate the
full range of structures found in a whole disc. Those
combinations that usually duplicated and only rarely
regenerated structures were the *AB + AB, 78 + AB,*

TABLE 6. *Average Volumes of Fragments and of Combinations of Fragments of Imaginal Wing Discs Cultured* In Vivo *for 14 Days*

	Number of implants measured	Initial volume $\pm$ standard deviation (nanoliters)	Number of implants measured	Volume after 14 days of culture $\pm$ standard deviation (nanoliters)
Whole disc	198	7.25±1.97	56	7.02±2.03
02	189	2.40±0.87	50	5.15±2.48
68	180	2.04±0.79	43	4.70±2.11
01 + 78	158	1.48±0.41	58	5.47±4.78
78 + 78	173	1.51±0.56	56	3.68±2.22
01 + 01	160	1.52±0.38	49	2.66±1.37
AB + AB	36	2.05±0.53	36	4.76±2.78
AB + 78	27	1.54±0.37	27	3.88±1.82
FG + 78	27	1.65±0.61	27	5.12±3.12
FG + FG	36	2.07±0.86	36	4.26±2.00
AB + FG	33	1.85±0.75	33	11.47±10.54

TABLE 7. *Growth and Metamorphosis of Combinations of Wing Disc Fragments Cultured* In Vivo *for 14 Days*

Combination:	78 + 78		AB + AB		FG + FG		01 + 01	
Days in culture:	0	14	0	14	0	14	0	14
Number of implants measured:	64		36		36		47	
Growth ± standard error (final volume/ initial volume):	2.32±0.12		2.32±0.19		2.32±0.23		1.81±0.11	
Number of implants metamorphosed:	11	19	13	14	15	18	15	10
Percent of implants that regenerated:	47		7		22		0	

Structure	Percent of implants where marker is							
Notum		32[a]	84	43	100	78	100	100
Scu		05[a]	84	79			47	50
HP					40			
AS			84	79		17[a]		
Dorsal radius		11[a]		07[a]		06[a]		
Teg		16[a]			47	44		
Costa		05[a]			47	11		
TR						06[a]		
DR		11[a]		07[a]		11[a]		
PR				07[a]		06[a]		
AL			31	21		06[a]		
AC		16[a]	08	14		06[a]		
Wing	100	79	92	86	33	50		
Ventral hinge	82	79			07	11		

[a]denotes structures that regenerated and were not normally produced by the combination when it was metamorphosed immediately.

78 + AB		78 + FG		01 + 78		AB + FG	
0	14	0	14	0	14	0	14
27		27		56		33	
2.54 ± 0.20		3.39 ± 0.39		4.10 ± 0.51		6.10 ± 0.87	
14	11	13	15	14	14	13	10
9		47		43		80	

completely or partially present

78 + AB		78 + FG		01 + 78		AB + FG	
0	14	0	14	0	14	0	14
29	36	85	100	93	93	61	90
21	18		07[a]	71	21	23	40
		15				15	10
57	18	08	47		36[a]	61	90
	09[a]	08	07		21[a]	08	60
		46	40		14[a]	46	70
		23	67		14[a]	31	60
			47[a]		07[a]		60[a]
	09[a]		27[a]		07[a]		80[a]
	09[a]				14[a]		50[a]
	09[a]				21[a]	08	40
14	18		33[a]	07	28	08	10
93	100	100	67	100	86	92	100
71	36	92	60	93	57	38	50

The growth of 78 + FG, 01 + 78, and AB + FG combinations is significantly different from 78 + 78, AB + AB, FG + FG, 01 + 01, and 78 + AB combinations with P values less than .05, .02, and .01, respectively.

and $01 + 01$. On rare occasions, the $FG + FG$ combinations
regenerated structures normally not found in the FG
fragment. In general, there seems to be a correlation
between the frequency of regeneration and the growth of
the implants. Table 6 records the actual volumes of
the tissues before and after 14 days of culture. A
larger variability in the volumes of the tissues after
culture was observed in combinations of opposite sides
of the disc than in the combinations of identical
sides of the disc.

DISCUSSION

*Interaction Between Different Regions of the Wing
Imaginal Disc*

     The results show that tissues from different regions
of the wing imaginal disc influence each other's growth.
The greatest stimulation of growth occurred when tissues
from opposite sides of a disc were juxtaposed and
the least occurred when tissues from adjacent or identical
sides were juxtaposed. Evidently positional information
is important in regulating growth. Cells interact
differently according to their positions within a
developing tissue. The results also emphasize that it is
not the process of fragmentation and the accompanying
injury that determines the extent of cell division
when an imaginal disc is fragmented and then regenerates.
It is rather the juxtaposition of cells with nonadjacent
positional values that stimulates cell division.

     It is of special interest that the cell interactions
that control growth within an imaginal disc appear
to be the same as those that control the spatial pattern
of differentiation within the disc. The differences in the
growth of combinations of tissue from different regions
of the wing disc are, in general, as predicted by
the polar coordinate model of epimorphic pattern regulation
proposed by French, Bryant and Bryant (1976). This model
explains the pattern regulation and growth that occur
after wounding and grafting in terms of the specific
interactions among cells from different positions that
have been juxtaposed.

According to the model, the position of a cell in a developing system like an imaginal disc is specified in terms of polar coordinates (Fig. 5). Each cell is assumed to have information with respect to its position on the circumference of a circle (0-12) and its position on a radius (A-E). Positions 0 and 12 are identical, so that the circular sequence is continuous. In the wing disc, the outer circle is the disc boundary and the center is the presumptive distal tip of the wing. The behavior of cells within a developmental system like a wing imaginal disc is defined by two rules for interaction (Fig. 6): (1) *The shortest intercalation rule.* When cells with normally non-adjacent positional values in either the circular or radial sequence are juxtaposed either in a graft or as the result of wound healing, growth is stimulated at the graft junction ntil cells with the intermediate positional values are

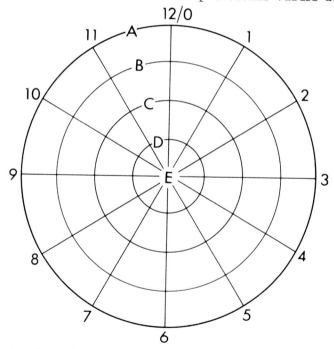

Fig. 5. The concept of a polar coordinate model of a positional information field. Each cell is assumed to have information with respect to its position around the circle (0-12) and its position in the radius (A-E). Positions 12 and 0 are identical, creating a continuous circular sequence. In the wing disc the outer circle represents the disc boundary and the center is the presumptive distal tip of the wing.

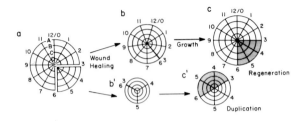

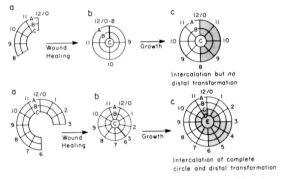

Fig. 6. *Rules proposed by polar coordinate model for the behavior of cells in a developing system like an imaginal disc. (a)* Shortest *intercalation rule. When cells with normally non-adjacent positional values in either the circular or radial sequence are juxtaposed, growth occurs at the graft junction until cells with the missing values are intercalated. In the example illustrated, in both a three-quarter fragment and a one-quarter fragment, the cut edges heal by the fusion of position 3 and position 6. According to the shortest intercalation rule, both fragments intercalate the missing values, 4 and 5. For the three-quarter fragment it means regeneration, whereas for the one-quarter fragment it means duplication. The regenerated or duplicated tissue is stippled. (b) Complete circle rule for distal transformation. Only fragments that possess (or can regenerate) the complete sequence of circular values (0-12) are able to regenerate missing distal positional values. In the examples illustrated, the (8, 9, 10, 11, 12) fragment with the central (DE) part removed is unable to regenerate missing distal positional values. However, the (6, 7, 8, 9, 10, 11, 12, 1, 2, 3) fragment with the central (DE) part removed is able to regenerate a complete sequence of circular values and is therefore able to regenerate missing distal positional values.*

intercalated and the positional information discontinuity
is eliminated; then growth ceases. In the case of
the circular sequence, the discontinuity is resolved
along the shorter of the two arcs separating the two positions. (2) *The complete circle rule.* Whenever a complete
circle of positional values is either exposed at an
amputation surface or generated by intercalation,
growth occurs within the circle to generate all of the more
distal positional values, a phenomenon usually called
distal transformation.

A key feature of the polar coordinate model is that
the regulative behavior of an imaginal disc fragment
is not a function of the independent behavior of the
free cut edges but is the result of the interaction between
the cut edges of fragments after they fuse during wound
healing.

The polar coordinate model predicts that if the
circular, positional values are equally spaced around
the disc, then the larger the discontinuity in the
circular positional values at a wound healing site, the
larger the amount of growth and intercalary regeneration
that should occur. The model also predicts that when
identical sides of the disc are mixed together, there
will be little stimulation of growth between cells
with small differences in their positional values, and as
a consequence, little intercalary regeneration will
occur. These predictions are in accordance with our
experimental observations.

When disc fragments were grafted together or cultured
individually and their growth measured at specific
time intervals, we observed that they usually reached
their maximum size--about their initial size--by 14
days. After 14 days, there was no significant difference
in the amount of growth between *02* and *68* fragments,
and any combination of two identical sides except
for the *01 + 01* mixtures, which grew significantly less.
When the implants were metamorphosed, it was found that
individual fragments and combinations of two fragments
from the same side of the disc had duplicated, except
for the *68* fragment and the *78 + 78* combination which
first duplicated and then regenerated, a matter that will
be discussed later.

01 + 78 combinations increased in size four-fold after 14 days of culture, whereas *AB + FG* combinations increased in size six-fold in the same period. When these implants were metamorphosed, it was found that these combinations of fragments from opposite sides of the disc showed intercalary regeneration more frequently than did other grafts. In the case of the *01 + 78* combinations, our results were similar to the results of *02 + 68* combinations analyzed by Haynie and Bryant (1976). Therefore, there is a direct correlation between the frequency of intercalary regeneration and the amount of growth: extensive growth is a reflection of intercalary regeneration.

The polar coordinate model predicts that when opposite sides of the disc are mixed, a large amount of intercalary growth will occur. Cells from opposite sides of the disc have a large difference in positional values and when juxtaposed, will interact to replace the missing values following the shortest intercalation rule. In this way, a complete external circle will be restored, and following the complete circle rule, the distal values will be regenerated. As a result, most of the values of the wing disc should be produced.

When adjacent sides of the disc were grafted, some combinations (such as *AB + 78*) showed no regeneration and a doubling in size, whereas other combinations (such as *FG + 78*) showed regeneration and much more than a doubling in size. This is to be expected if the positional values in the wing disc are arranged so that some combinations of adjacent sides contain more than half the circular sequence of values and are able to regenerate, whereas other combinations of adjacent sides contain less than half of the circular sequence of values and therefore only duplicate. Figure 7 shows a disposition of circular sequence values that is consistent with our results. (The assignment of a total of 12 positional values in the circular sequence arbitrary; we could have just as easily assigned 50.) The axes 3-9 and 12-6 were determined from the data on cultured fragments of the wing disc which show the levels where reversal from duplication to regeneration occurs both in the horizontal and vertical direction (Bryant, 1975). With the circular sequence values shown in the figure, the *78 + AB* would contain 12, 2, 3, and 4, which should only duplicate, since less

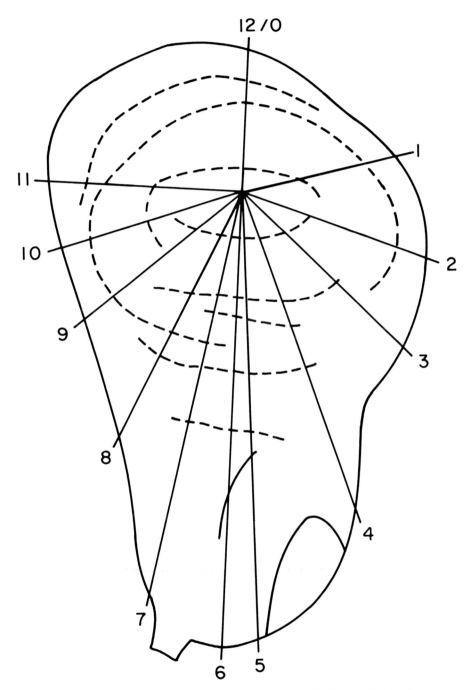

Fig. 7. *Proposed arrangement of radial positional values within a mature imaginal wing disc.*

than half the circular sequence of values are present, whereas the *78 + FG* would contain 7, 8, 9, 10, 11, and 12/0 which should either regenerate or duplicate, since half the circular sequence of values are present.

The proposed arrangement of positional values within the disc (Fig. 7) can also explain the difference in growth between the *01 + 78* combination and the *AB + FG* combination. The number of positional values present within the *01 + 78* combination (12 + 5, 6, 7) is much less than in the *AB + FG* combination (7, 8, 9, 10, 11 + 1, 2, 3, 4), however, the average amount of tissue in the original combinations is approximately the same (Table 7). Therefore, the probability that a group of cells will be juxtaposed to a group of cells of disparate values is greater in the *AB + FG* combination than in the *01 + 78* combination. Hence, more growth should occur in the *AB + FG* combination.

Whole Wing Discs

Our results indicate that intact mature wing discs do not significantly change in volume during culture in adult females. This is consistent with the polar coordinate model, since entire mature wing discs contain all the positional values, and intercalation would be expected only if the disc were injured, thus juxtaposing cells with non-adjacent positional values. Previous results indicate that in most cases, it is necessary to cut or otherwise damage a mature disc to stimulate growth. When intact mature eye-antenna discs (Schlapfer, 1963; Ginter and Kuzin, 1969) or wing discs (Ginter and Kuzin, 1969; Bryant, 1975) were cultured in adults for seven days, they were reported to decrease in size.

In our experiments, whole wing discs did not lose the ability to form any structures after prolonged culture: The number of metamorphosed structures per implant was similar after 7 or 28 days of culture. Ursprung (1962) noticed in the genital disc that with culture times greater than seven days, there was no loss of ability to form cuticular structures but a loss of ability to form soft parts. It is possible that there was a loss of the presumptive muscular elements in the wing disc after prolonged culture, but this was not investigated.

Growth of Parts of Discs and of Combinations

Although intact mature wing discs did not grow when cultured in adult females, *02* or *68* fragments doubled in size during the first 14 days of culture. In the case of the *02* fragment the volume of the implant decreased between 14 and 28 days of culture whereas in the case of the *68* fragment the average volume reached a maximum after 14 days and remained the same between 14 and 28 days.

It had been shown previously that parts of imaginal discs grew asymptotically to a maximum in fertilized females (Ursprung, 1962; Hadorn and Garcia-Bellido, 1964; Tobler, 1966). When half a genital disc was cultured in female adults, the fragment doubled in size during the first eight days but growth slowed thereafter (Ursprung, 1962). Similarly, both lateral and medial half leg discs approximately doubled in size during the first eight days of culture, but did not increase in size during the next eight days (Tobler, 1966). Haltere fragments double in size during the first 11 days of culture but had decreased in size by the 29th day of culture (Van der Meer and Ouweneel, 1974).

When we compare the sizes of the combinations of fragments cultured for 14 days (Table 7), we find a larger variability in the size of combinations *AB + FG* and *01 + 78* than we find in combinations of identical fragments. Two experiments were done with *78 + 78* combination and a comparison of the results from the two sets of data (2.60 ± 1.60 and 2.32 ± 0.98, final volume/initial volume ± standard deviation) indicates the reproducibility of the growth of the combinations as well as the amount of variability in each sample. The larger standard deviation seen in the growth of combinations from opposite sides of the disc (Table 7) indicates that the location of the cuts varied slightly from disc to disc and that the mixing process was not uniform. Thus, when opposite sides were mixed, complete circular sequences of positional values were formed in some mixtures by intercalary regeneration and, as predicted by the model, distal regeneration and extensive growth occurred. However, when a complete circle was not regenerated, distal regeneration and extensive growth did not occur. When identical sides were mixed, a complete

circle was not produced since each side is known to only
duplicate. All combinations of identical sides only
showed duplications and approximately doubled in volume
with little variability from combination to combination.

If a whole disc were to be dissociated and then
reaggregated one would anticipate a tremendous amount
of growth because of the greater amount of mixing
and chance for cells of opposite sides to interact.
When such an experiment was conducted (Tobler, 1966),
the largest amount of growth occurred in the dissociated
and reaggregated whole leg discs, the fragments showing
a five-fold increase in size after 16 days of culture
as compared to doubling in size for half leg disc
fragments.

*Regeneration Following Duplication: An Exceptional Result
not Explained by the Polar Coordinate Model*

After culture *in vivo* for two weeks or more, certain
wing disc fragments that normally only duplicate,
first duplicated but then regenerated structures belonging
to other parts of the disc which were never detected in
implants metamorphosed without prior culture. Presumptive
notum *(02* and *01 + 01* fragments) only duplicated after
one to four weeks of culture *in vivo.* After four
weeks of culture the fragments had shrunk and produced
fewer duplicate structures than after two weeks of
culture. Presumptive ventral wing blade *(68* and *78 + 78*
fragments) also duplicated after one week of *in vivo*
culture, but then began to regenerate. The presumptive
ventral wing blade fragments reached their maximum
average size after two weeks and remained at that average
size throughout four weeks of culture, unlike the
presumptive notum fragments. Regeneration in the ventral
wing blade fragments was clearly evident after two
weeks and by four weeks all but a few structures of the
wing disc were detected in at least one implant. One-half
of the presumptive ventral wing blade fragments showed
measureable regeneration, and about one-fourth of them
regenerated almost a complete range of wing structures.
Regeneration followed a characteristic pattern: certain
structures regenerated first and others last. Further,
the appearance of regenerated structures was often
paralleled by the disappearance of one copy of duplicated
structures. Regeneration after an initial duplication

of the fragments has also been observed in the genital
disc in which one-quarter of the disc will regenerate
the whole disc in progressive stages, duplication
first, then regeneration (Lüond, 1961; Bryant and
Hsei, 1977).

The phenomenon of regeneration following duplication
is not readily explained in terms of the polar coordinate
model. For the wing disc the model predicts that
the ventral wing blade fragment should only duplicate.
Perhaps the regeneration process involves a loss of
duplicated or single copies by cell death (as occurs
in the presumptive notum fragment) and the subsequent
orderly regeneration of single copies and of new structures
by some unknown mechanism (which does not occur in
the presumptive notum fragment). Alternatively the
process might involve a change in positional values of
cells destined to form duplicate copies into positional
values of new structures. However, apart from these
anomalous results that occur after prolonged culture,
the polar coordinate model appears to account for almost
all of the growth regulation and pattern regulation
that has been observed in imaginal wing discs.

SUMMARY

In this chapter we have analyzed some of the factors
that regulate growth and pattern formation in insect epidermal cells, a problem to which Sir Vincent Wigglesworth
has contributed original insights and discoveries.
Surgical experiments were described demonstrating that
positional information plays an important role in regulating both growth and pattern formation in the imaginal
wing discs of Drosophila, and that this regulation
involves extensive intercellular communication between
the cells of the disc. Evidence was also presented
that the polar coordinate model of pattern regulation
(French et al., 1976) can account for most features
of both growth and pattern regulation in imaginal
discs except for the regeneration that occurs after
prolonged culture.

The experiments we have described confirm the
validity of Sir Vincent's idea (1964c) that the regulation
of pattern formation and growth are closely coupled

in imaginal discs and other sheets of epidermal cells. Our
results also confirm Sir Vincent's suggestion (1959, The
Control of Growth and Form; 1964c) that the extent to which
specific regions grow and the pattern of cytodifferentia-
tion in imaginal discs and other epidermal sheets are both
controlled by local homeostatic responses involving contact
and continuity between one epidermal cell and the next.
Finally, our evidence also extends and refines Sir
Vincent's proposal (1937a, 1964c) that during the regulation that occurs after wounding, cells continue to divide
until the cell density normal for the species is restored.
The results we have reported and the polar coordinate model
of pattern regulation (French *et al.*, 1976) indicate that
positional information is another important factor in regulating cell division. After wounding, the juxtaposition
of cells with non-adjacent positional values stimulates
cells to divide until missing positional values have been
intercalated.

The results emphasize that growth and pattern formation in the "two-dimensional world in which insect epidermal cells live" depends upon intercellular communication.
To discover the nature of the intercellular signals by
which those cells "consult" one another during development,
is one of the major challenges of developmental biology.

ACKNOWLEDGMENTS

We are indebted to our colleagues in the Developmental
Biology Center, especially Professors Peter Bryant and
Susan Bryant with whom it has been a pleasure to work and
from whom we have learned much. We thank the following
who provided useful comments on the typescript: Dr.
Peter Bryant, Dr. Lewis Held, Ms. Brooke Kirby, Mr.
Eugene Levinson, and Dr. Presley Martin. We also thank
Ms. Marjorie Boyette for her technical assistance and
Ms. Virginia Berger, Ms. Betty Hermann, and Ms. Sharley
Torri for their helpful assistance on the typescript.

REFERENCES

Bodenstein, D. (1939). Investigations on the problem
      of metamorphosis. V. Some factors determining
      the facet number in the *Drosophila* mutant *Bar.*
      Genetics 24, 494-508.

Bryant, P. J. (1974). Determination and pattern formation in the imaginal discs of Drosophila. Curr. Topics Develop. Biol. 8, 41-80.

Bryant, P. J. (1975). Pattern formation in the imaginal wing disc of Drosophila melanogaster: Fate map, regeneration and duplication. J. Exp. Zool. 193, 49-78.

Bryant, P. J., Hsei, B. (1977). Pattern formation in asymmetrical and symmetrical imaginal discs of Drosophila melanogaster. Am. Zool. 17, 595-611.

Doane, W. W. (1973). Role of hormones in insect development. In "Developmental Systems: Insects" (S. J. Counce and C. H. Waddington, eds.), Vol. 2, pp. 291-497. Academic Press, New York.

Ephrussi, B., Beadle, G. W. (1936). A technique of transplantation for Drosophila. Am. Nat. 70, 218-225.

French, V., Bryant, P. J., Bryant, S. V. (1976). A theory of pattern regulation in epimorphic fields. Science 193, 969-981.

Gehring, W., Nöthiger, R. (1973). The imaginal disc of Drosophila. In "Developmental Systems: Insects" (S. J. Counce and C. H. Waddington, eds.), Vol. 2, pp. 212-290. Academic Press, New York.

Gilbert, L. I., Goodman, W., Bollenbacher, W. E. (1977). Biochemistry of regulatory lipids and sterols in insects. In "Biochemistry of Lipids II" (T. W. Goodwin, ed.), Vol. 14. University Park Press, Baltimore.

Ginter, E. K., Kuzin, B. A. (1969). Growth of the imaginal discs of Drosophila in the adult host. Drosoph. Inform. Serv. 44, 74.

Hadorn, E., Garcia-Bellido, A. (1964). Zur proliferation von Drosophila-Zellkulturen im Adultmilieu. Rev. Suisse Zool. 71, 576-582.

Haynie, J. L., Bryant, P. J. (1976). Intercalary regeneration in imaginal wing disk of Drosophila melanogaster. Nature 259, 659-662 (1976)

Lüönd, H. (1961). Untersuchungen zur Mustergliederung in fragmentierten Primordien des mannlichen Geschlechtapparates von Drosophila seguyi. Develop. Biol. 3, 615-656.

Postlethwait, J. H., Schneiderman, H. A. (1971). Pattern formation and determination in the antenna of the homoeotic mutant Antennapedia of Drosophila melanogaster. Develop. Biol. 25, 606-640.

Postlethwait, J. H., Schneiderman, H. A. (1973). Developmental genetics of Drosophila imaginal discs. Annu. Rev. Genet. 7, 381-433.

Riddiford, L. M., Truman, J. W. (1978). Biochemistry
    of insect hormones and insect growth regulators.
    In "Biochemistry of Insects" (M. Rockstein, ed.),
    pp. 307-357. Academic Press, New York.
Schlapfer, T. (1963). Der Einfluss des adulten Wirtsmi-
    lieus auf die Entwicklung von larvalen Augenantennen-
    Imaginalscheiben von *Drosophila melanogaster.*
    Wilhelm Roux' Arch. 154, 378-404.
Schneiderman, H. A. (1979). Pattern formation and
    determination in insects. *In* "Mechanisms of
    Cell Change" (J. D. Ebert and T. S. Okada, eds.),
    pp. 243-272. John Wiley and Sons, New York.
Schubiger, G. (1971). Regeneration, duplication and
    transdetermination in fragments of the leg disc
    of *Drosophila melanogaster. Develop. Biol. 26*,
    277-295.
Tobler, H. (1966). Zellspezifische Determination und
    Beziehung zwischen Proliferation und Transdeter-
    mination in Bein und Flugelprimordien von *Drosophila
    melanogaster. J. Embryol. Exp. Morphol. 16*, 609-633.
Ursprung, H. (1967). *In vivo* culture of *Drosophila*
    imaginal discs. *In* "Methods in Developmental
    Biology" (F. H. Wilt and N. K. Wessels, eds.),
    pp. 485-492. Crowell, New York.
Ursprung, H., Hadorn, E. (1962). Weitere Untersuchungen
    uber Musterbildung in Kombinaten aus teilweise dis-
    soziierten Flugel-Imaginalscheiben von *Drosophila
    melanogaster. Develop. Biol. 4*, 40-66.
Van der Meer, J. M., Ouweneel, W. J. (1974). Differen-
    tiation capacities of the dorsal metathoracic
    (haltere) disc of *Drosophila melanogaster.*
    II. Regeneration and duplication. *Wilhelm Roux'
    Arch. 174*, 361-373.
Wigglesworth, V. B. (1937a). Wound healing in an insect
    (*Rhodnius prolixus* Hemiptera). *J. Exp. Biol. 14*,
    364-381.
Wigglesworth, V. B. (1959). "The Control of Growth and
    Form," 140 pp. Cornell University Press, New York.
Wigglesworth, V. B. (1964c). Homeostasis in insect
    growth. *Symp. Soc. Exp. Biol. 18*, 265-281.
Wigglesworth, V. B. (1970). "Insect Hormones." W. H.
    Freeman and Company, San Fransisco.
Wolpert, L. (1969). Positional information and the
    spatial pattern of cellular differentiation.
    J. Theoret. Biol. 25, 1-47.
Wolpert, L. (1971). Positional information and pattern
    formation. *Curr. Topics Develop. Biol 6*, 183-224.

PHYSICAL AND PATTERN CONTINUITY
IN THE INSECT EPIDERMIS[1]

Peter J. Bryant
Jack R. Girton
Presley Martin

Developmental Biology Center
University of California, Irvine
Irvine, California

A. *Introduction*

The insect epidermis produces patterns of cell differentiation of astonishing complexity and reproducibility, which have attracted investigators of pattern formation for decades. The patterns produced by *Drosophila* imaginal discs are no exception to this statement, and in addition these patterns offer the opportunity for genetic analysis using mutational modifications and for cell-lineage analysis using induced mitotic recombination to mark developing clones of cells. In this article, we consider some recent progress in the genetic analysis of pattern formation in the *Drosophila* epidermis, in the context of the developmental properties of the insect epidermis in general. We will argue that many of the developmental properties of the insect epidermis can be related to two very fundamental properties: its ability to restore physical continuity through wound healing, and its ability to restore pattern continuity through intercalation. We will consider the extent to which mutant phenotypes reflect the outcome of these two activities of the epidermis.

B. *Physical Continuity of the Insect Epidermis Restored by Wound Healing*

When the insect epidermis is accidentally damaged or experimentally cut, it demonstrates an impressive ability to restore its physical continuity by wound healing. One of the

[1]*The authors' research is funded by Grants HD06082 and HD07029 from the National Institutes of Health, and PF-1440 and PF-1599 from the American Cancer Society*

first studies of this process was by Wigglesworth (1937) who
used the abdominal epidermis of *Rhodnius* to show that wound
healing involved first, enlargement (activation) of the cells
surrounding the wound; second, migration of these cells over
the wound site to restore physical continuity of the epithelium, together with accumulation of haematocytes under the
wound; third, mitosis in the zone which was depleted of cells
by the migration, or in the case of burns, in the cells immediately adjacent to the damage. Wigglesworth found that the
mitosis ceased when the normal epithelial continuity and cell
density had been restored.

Other studies have also documented the strong tendency of
insect epithelia to reestablish their physical continuity following damage, even if this involves extensive tissue distortion. In Lepidoptera, the epithelial cells of a flat piece of
integument implanted into a host larva will grow around the
attached cuticle to form a hollow sphere with the cuticle on
the inside (see Kühn, 1971). Wigglesworth (1936) found that
if a cylindrical piece of integument (epithelium plus cuticle)
was implanted into the abdomen of a host insect, the epithelial cells would spread from the cut ends along the outer surface of the cuticle until they united with the cells spreading
from the opposite end. Locke (1966) found that when a teflon
barrier was placed in an integumentary wound in *Rhodnius,* the
epithelial cells would grow inward and restore continuity
around the barrier. With *Drosophila* imaginal discs, Reinhardt
et al. (1977) and Reinhardt & Bryant (1980) showed that a variety of fragments would undergo wound healing to reestablish
a topologically spherical epithelial vesicle. Studies of the
metamorphosed derivatives of imaginal disc fragments (Loosli,
1959; Poodry *et al.,* 1971) also demonstrated the tendency of
the fragments to round up and differentiate cuticular structures on the inside, even when only a small number of cells
was present. Of course, all of these examples are relatively
trivial when compared to the amazing ability of the entire
metamorphosing insect to maintain physical continuity of its
body surface even while its constituent larval cells are
replaced by the proliferating imaginal cells (see Poodry &
Schneiderman, 1970; Roseland & Schneiderman, 1979).

C. *Pattern Continuity of the Insect Epidermis Restored
by Growth*

After physical continuity is established in the insect
epidermis, subsequent growth often occurs to bring about
continuity in the pattern of structures produced in the
overlying cuticle. By continuity, we refer to a situation

in which each cell, or pattern element, is adjacent to its
normal nearest neighbors, whether or not the overall pattern
is normal. Thus, a mirror-image duplication of a partial pattern shows continuity, even though it is globally abnormal.
Winfree (1979) and Lewis (1980) have recently elaborated on
the idea of continuity and shown that it represents a general
form of some of the postulates used in a recent, more specific, model of pattern formation in both insects and amphibians,
called the polar coordinate model (French et al, 1976; Bryant
et al, 1980).

The idea of pattern continuity can be most clearly understood by reference to some experiments on the cockroach leg
by Bohn (1970, 1971) and Bullière (1971). When a distal leg
fragment is grafted onto a proximal stump, a mismatch in the
proximal-distal amputation levels of the donor and host creates a discontinuity in the proximal-distal dimension of the
pattern and produces a leg which is longer or shorter than
normal. If this operation is done in a larval stage (so that
subsequent growth can occur), provided that the discontinuity
is within one leg segment, subsequent growth reestablishes
pattern continuity by intercalating those pattern elements
that would normally separate the two amputation levels. In
the shortened leg, the intercalary regenerate has normal
polarity and reconstitutes a normal pattern, whereas in the
lengthened combination the intercalary regenerate has reversed
proximal-distal polarity. This illustrates two points of importance. First, in these systems pattern continuity is
restored by addition of new pattern elements during growth, a
mechanism referred to as epimorphosis. In some other pattern-
forming systems, continuity is reestablished by altering the
fate of some of the constituent cells, a process called mor-
phallaxis (Morgan, 1901). Second, the results illustrate
that continuity can be achieved by the addition of supernumerary pattern elements in abnormal polarity, giving a final
result which is globally abnormal, but in which each cell (or
pattern element) is adjacent only to a mirror image of itself
or to its normal nearest neighbors. We have illustrated the
continuity principle using the proximal-distal axis, but the
experiments of French (1978) show that similar phenomena can
be demonstrated in the transverse, or circumferential, direction in the cockroach leg.

Recent studies have shown that intercalary regeneration
can also occur in Drosophila imaginal discs (Haynie & Bryant,
1976; Strub, 1979; Duranceau et al, 1980). Furthermore, as
has been shown elsewhere (Bryant, 1978) much of the pattern
regulation which occurs in cultured imaginal disc fragments
can be understood as a result of intercalation between dif-

ferent parts of the presumptive pattern which are confronted
during wound healing. It is important to point out that with
imaginal discs, as well as with cockroach legs and amphibian
limbs, if intercalation occurs in the (presumptive) circumferential direction it adds the shorter of the two arcs of presumptive pattern which separate the two confronted parts.
This is known as the "shortest intercalation rule" (French *et
al*, 1976). One of its consequences is that pattern continuity
is restored in some imaginal disc fragments by regeneration,
whereas in others it is restored by pattern duplication.

D. *Pattern Formation Studied Genetically*

We have been developing a genetic approach to the problem of pattern formation. We are studying various mutations
which cause distinct abnormalities, in order to determine
whether their phenotypes are consistent with known properties
of the insect epidermis. We hope, in this way, to find mutational effects on patterns which will provide clues to the
underlying mechanisms of pattern formation.

We are interested, first of all, in whether mutational
alterations of the pattern conform to the two continuity principles mentioned earlier. Of course, our attention is drawn
towards mutations which cause pattern deficiencies or duplications, since these provide interesting tests of the pattern
continuity argument. Since we now know that supernumerary
structures (eg, pattern duplications) can arise in response
to the removal of a sufficiently large part of an imaginal
disc (Bryant, 1975), we are interested in whether some
pattern-duplicating mutants work by causing degeneration in
the disc. Those which cause pattern duplications without
involving degeneration are also important as possible cases
of a direct effect of a genetic alteration on pattern formation.

E. *Degeneration Caused by Cell-Lethal Mutations*

Cell lethals are mutations which prevent the appearance of
a small patch of mutant tissue (usually a somatic cell clone)
in an otherwise nonmutant individual. They are thought, and
in some cases have been shown, to operate by causing the death
of cells which carry them in the homo- or hemizygous state.
We are interested in using mutations of this class as "genetic
scalpels" for inducing cell death in or removing clones or
patches of cells from imaginal discs. The high penetrance of
these mutations allows the analysis of the restoration of

physical and pattern continuity in the epidermis at a level of resolution which is not attainable with conventional techniques. Furthermore, temperature-sensitive alleles of such lethals can readily be obtained (Russell, 1974; Arking, 1975; Simpson & Schneiderman, 1975; Jurgens & Gateff, 1979) and these allow the investigator to study the effects of cell death induced at different developmental stages.

Some cell lethals affect only certain regions of some imaginal discs, so they are called position-specific cell lethals. Under these circumstances they do not necessarily lead to the death of the organism, but instead produce pattern abnormalities. Examples include *vestigial, scalloped, Beadex, cut* and *apterous-Xasta* which produce wing deficiencies (Fristrom, 1968, 1969; James & Bryant, 1980) and the mutations *Bar* and *eyeless*, which produce eye deficiencies (Fristrom, 1969). These mutations are interesting in that the cell death affects only particular cells, and must reflect an underlying difference in the cells of the imaginal disc, which may be of importance in normal development. James & Bryant (1980) have suggested that the cell death in *vestigial* wing discs may be an extension or expansion of a pattern of low-level cell death seen in normal wing discs. This normal cell death may be related to the regulation of cell number in different parts of the presumptive wing blade region. Clark & Russell (1977) showed that *l(1)ts726,* a temperature-sensitive cell-lethal allele of the *suppressor-of-forked* locus which has been used in several pattern regulation experiments discussed below, induces localized patches of cell death in several imaginal discs. Unlike the wing mutations mentioned previously, cell death in this mutant is not restricted to a particular location within any of the imaginal discs. Patches of death could appear anywhere in the discs studied although certain regions (eg., the lower eye-forming region of the eye-antenna disc and the upper half of the leg disc) showed a high frequency of death patches.

F. *Physical Continuity Maintained Despite Degeneration*

Given the importance of understanding the effects of cell lethals, surprisingly little histological analysis has been done on these mutants. The first comparative study was by Fristrom (1968, 1969) who found that the pattern of cell degeneration followed a similar course in several lethals affecting the wing disc. In *vestigal,* degeneration involved shrinkage, condensation and fragmentation of cells followed by phagocytosis of the cellular remains by neighboring cells. D. O'Brochta (unpublished) has since shown that large numbers

of cells and cell fragments in *vestigial* wing discs are physically extruded from the basal surface of the disc epithelium
(Figure 1). Some of these fragments are extruded in an apparently healthy state, whereas others are condensed before they
are extruded. A study of the cell death induced by *1(1)ts726*
showed several differences from this situation including apical, rather than basal extrusion of the remains of degenerating cells (Clark & Russell, 1977). These studies suggest that
much could be learned from a careful ultrastructural examination of the effects of cell lethals. In any case, in both of
these mutants the extrusion of the degenerating cells or fragments illustrates the ability of the epithelium to maintain
its physical continuity in the face of extensive cell loss.
In all of the mutants so far mentioned, the absence of gaps in
the adult cuticle further suggests that physical continuity of
the epithelium is either retained or restored during the larval and pupal stages.

G. *Pattern Continuity Restored by Duplication*

The wings formed in the *vestigial* mutant are lacking parts
of the pattern and therefore represent an example of a pattern
discontinuity. The reason for this seems to be that degeneration of the presumptive wing margin in the wing disc occurs
throughout the third larval instar, so that there is no opportunity for compensatory growth to replace the missing structures (James & Bryant, 1980). In fact, degeneration continues
to occur when the wing discs are given extra time for growth
by culturing them *in vivo* (D. O'Brochta, personal communication).

Some animals of the *vestigial* and *scalloped* stocks are
entirely lacking a wing, and in its place is a mirror-image
duplicate of the remainder of the wing-disc derivatives,
mainly the dorsal part of the half thorax (James & Bryant,
1980). In these cases, pattern continuity is restored, as
each pattern element is next to its normal nearest neighbor
even though the overall pattern is abnormal. We interpret
these abnormalities as resulting from unusually extensive
cell death in the wing disc, the remaining viable piece being
so small that it is unable to regenerate but can only duplicate. Such behavior is exactly as expected by analogy with
the behavior during growth of fragments of wild-type wing
discs (Bryant, 1975).

Pattern duplication is also one of the abnormalities produced by temperature-sensitive cell-lethal mutants (Russell,
1974; Arking, 1975; Simpson & Schneiderman, 1975; Jurgens &

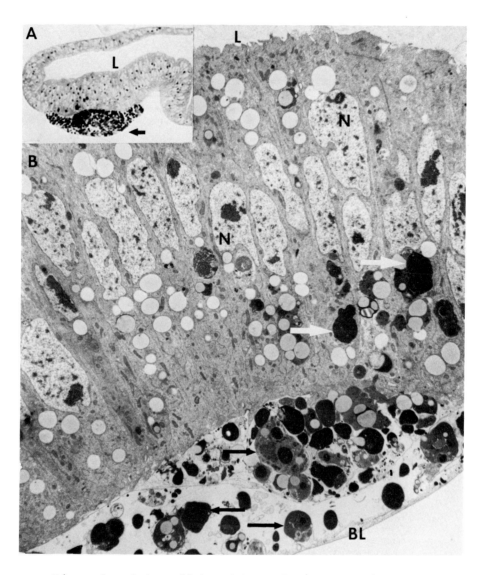

Figure 1. (a) A light micrograph of a toludine-blue stained section of the wind pouch area of a late third instar vestigial wing disc showing the darkly staining basally extruded vacuoles (arrow). (b) An electron micrograph through the same area of a similar disc showing condensed vacuoles within the disc epithelium (white arrows) and extruded vacuoles located basally (black arrows). The latter are confined by the basal lamella (BL) (X1140). L = lumen of the disc, N = nucleus. (Courtesy of D. O'Brochta.)

Gateff, 1979). The most extensively studied such mutation is
1(1)ts726, isolated by Russell (1974), which was mentioned
previously. A 48-hour, 29°C treatment given to *1(1)ts726* larvae at any time between mid-first instar and pupariation often
results in pattern abnormalities such as duplications associated with deficiencies and triplications (Russell *et al*, 1977;
Postlethwait, 1978; Girton, 1980). Such treatments have been
shown to induce cell death (Clark & Russell, 1977) and it
is assumed that the abnormalities occur in response to this
death.

Abnormalities in *1(1)ts726* animals are a function of the
the developmental stage at which the 29°C treatment is given
(Figure 2). Leg and head duplications associated with deficiencies result from treatments initiated between first and
second instar, whereas leg triplications result from treatments initiated in the first 12-16 hours of the third instar
and tergite deficiencies and missing bristles result from
treatments initiated in the late third instar (Russell *et al*,
1977; Postlethwait, 1978; Girton, 1980).

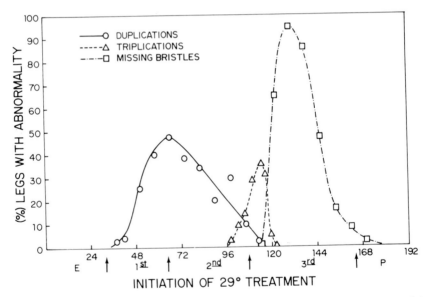

*Figure 2. The effects of 48-hour 29°C treatments applied
at different stages in the development of 1(1)ts726 leg discs.
Time points refer to the time of initiation of the 29° treatment. Data from Russell et al (1977) and Girton (unpublished).*

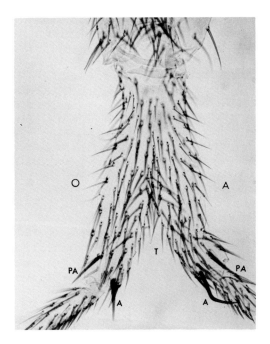

*Figure 3. A pattern duplication in the mesothoracic leg
induced by 1(1)ts726, showing the mirror-image symmetry of
the orthodromic (O) and antidromic (A) patterns. T = tibia,
A = apical bristle, PA = preapical bristle.*

The development of *1(1)ts726*-induced leg duplications (Figure
3) has been studied in two clonal analyses (Girton & Russell,
1980 a, b) and the results indicate that duplicate development
is similar in many respects to normal leg development. Duplicates are initiated by a small number (7 - 21) of cells within
12 hours of the end of the 29° treatment. Within the next 12
hours, this population of cells becomes subdivided into anterior and posterior compartments and shortly thereafter the duplicates begin to grow. These results suggest that certain
portions of the genetic mechanisms directing normal development may be used to direct the development of pattern duplications.

H. Pattern Continuity Restored by Triplication

The leg triplications induced by *1(1)ts726* (Figure 4)
each consist of a complete set of structures with normal symmetry (labeled orthodromic) and two partial sets of structures; one with reversed symmetry (labeled antidromic) and

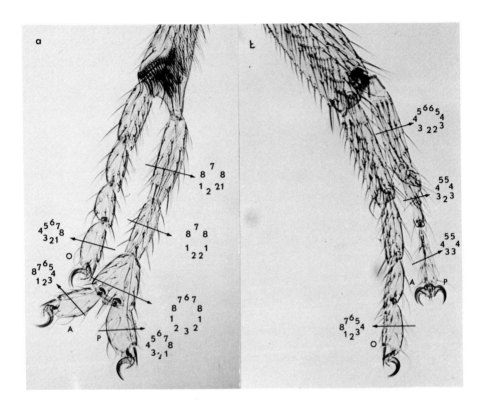

Figure 4. (a) Diverging and (b) Converging pattern triplications in the tarsus of the leg induced by l(1)ts726, showing the complete set of structures (orthodromic = O) and the
two partial sets (antidromic = A, paradromic = P) in the symmetrical outgrowths. The numbers refer to the bristle rows
(Hannah-Alava, 1958) which are present at various proximal-
distal levels.

one with normal symmetry (labeled paradromic; terminology from
Jurgens & Gateff, 1979). In some cases, the anti- and paradromic parts <u>diverge</u> distally; that is, the number of bristle
rows increases towards the distal tip, and at the point where
two complete sets of bristle rows are present, physical
branching occurs (Figure 4a). In other cases, the anti- and
paradromic parts <u>converge</u> distally; there are fewer bristle
rows toward the distal end, and usually the structure tapers

away to nothing before the normal distal tip is reached (Figure 4b). In both convergent and divergent types, the bristle rows are added or lost at the line of symmetry rather than elsewhere. In every case, pattern continuity is absolutely maintained in all parts of these complex appendages.

The patterns seen in *l(1)ts726*—induced triplications are in precise agreement with Bateson's rules of symmetry (Bateson, 1894) which were derived from a study of supernumerary appendages and other pattern abnormalities found in nature. Bateson found that triple extremities were one of the most common of the abnormalities and noted that the three distal patterns were always in a certain relationship to one another. The appendage next to the one in the normal position was always a mirror-image of it, and the one farther from the normal was always a mirror-image of the nearer. Bateson constructed a mechanical model to illustrate this principle, which also demonstrated that the symmetry relationships applied to longitudinal planes of symmetry at various directions in the appendage (Figure 5). These are exactly the symmetry relationships of the ortho-, anti- and paradromic elements of the outgrowths and normal parts of the triplications produced by temperature-sensitive cell-lethal mutations in *Drosophila* imaginal discs.

The similarities between the experimental results and the natural abnormalities suggest that many of the latter might be explained as the results of accidental damage to the appendages earlier in the life of the animal, but whatever the cause of these abnormalities, they illustrate an important point about pattern continuity. That is, that when multiple patterns are present on an appendage with a normal base, in order to satisfy pattern continuity they must be present in odd numbers, and the number of patterns showing the asymmetry of the base must be one more than the number with reversed asymmetry. These rules are followed by the experimentally induced supernumerary regenerates in both amphibians and insects (French *et al*, 1976) as well as by the triplications caused by cell-lethal mutations. In order for a simple duplication of structure to be consistent with pattern continuity, both orthodromic and antidromic halves of the pattern must extend to the edge of the field, as is the case with duplications caused by surgical manipulations or by cell-lethal mutations.

Figure 5. *Bateson's 1894 mechanical model which illustrates the relations of symmetry in supernumerary limbs found in nature. Each limb is attached at its base to a cogwheel which meshes with that of the adjacent limb. The central limb R (orthodromic) is fixed to the baseplate, whereas the two supernumerary limbs SL & SR (anti- and paradromic) are carried on the wooden sector which is free to rotate about the central axis of the orthodromic limb. As it rotates, the supernumerary limbs rotate in opposite directions, always maintaining planes of symmetry between ortho- and antidromic (R & SL) and anti- and paradromic (SL & SR) limbs. From Bateson, 1894.*

I. A Mutation Which May Cause Pattern Duplication Directly

We have recently been studying a mutation which appears
to produce pattern discontinuities directly, the resolution
of these discontinuities leading to pattern duplication. This
mutation, $l(3)C43^{hsl}$ (3 - 49.0, hereafter referred to as *C43*),
is a temperature-sensitive larval—lethal mutation which produces a variety of defects in both larval and imaginal tissues
(Martin *et al*, 1977). Early analysis of this mutant established that all the defects result from a single mutation, and
that the effects on disc development are disc-autonomous. We
will be concerned here with three aspects of the mutant phenotype: overgrowth of disc tissue, cell death and pattern duplication.

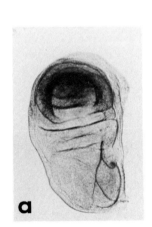

*Figure 6. Overgrowth of wing disc produced by the C43
mutation. (a) Wing disc from a mature C43 larva raised at
the permissive temperature of 20°C. Size and morphology are
normal. (b) Wing disc from a mature C43 larvae raised at
the restrictive temperature of 25°C. 160 X.*

The most distinctive effect of the *C43* mutation is an extensive overgrowth of the wing disc, and to a lesser extent, of the haltere disc (Figure 6). Thus, a normal late third-instar wing disc contains 50-60,000 cells, while a late third-instar *C43* wing disc averages from 150-250,000 cells, and even reached 600,000 in one case. As can be seen in Figure 6b, the *C43* wing discs are not only much larger than normal, but they also have an abnormal pattern of folds, which suggests a disorganized pattern of growth. The overgrowth of disc tissue is not found in any of the other discs, and somewhat surprisingly, the eye disc is very small. It has recently been shown that the small size of the eye disc results from cell death (P. Martin, in preparation). Thus, the effect of this *C43* allele on disc development is quite complex - the wing and haltere discs become enlarged, the eye disc degenerates and other discs develop normally. As would be expected, the abnormalities in the larval development of the discs are correlated with pattern defects in the adult disc derivatives.

Pattern duplication in *C43* homozygotes can be produced either by continuous culture of the larvae at restrictive temperature or by a brief (24-hour) exposure to restrictive temperature at an appropriate larval stage. Several types of pattern duplication result from these treatments. One type is "multiplication of units" (Schubiger, 1971) which affects certain bristles of the legs and thorax. In particular, the number of sexcomb teeth on the male foreleg can be increased greatly and on the thorax local multiplication of macrochaetes and microchaetes is observed. This type of duplication is produced by a number of other mutations including a variety of temperature-sensitive cell lethals (Russell, 1974; Arking, 1975; Simpson and Schneiderman, 1975), ey^D and shi^{ts} (Poodry & Schneiderman, 1976). It has been suggested that all of these mutations produce these local multiplications in response to small amounts of cell death in the discs (Simpson & Schneiderman, 1975). We have not examined this possibility directly in *C43*, but such a mechanism seem reasonable once cell death is known to occur.

A second type of duplication affects the antenna and may also be related to cell death. Antennal duplications occur frequently and are always associated with large eye deficiencies. In addition, other mutations causing cell death and eye reduction produce similar antennal duplications (see Bryant, 1978).

The final type of duplications to be considered are those affecting the wing disc, which differ in several ways from those associated with cell death. Two examples of wing duplications produced by a 24 hour exposure to restrictive temperature are shown in Figure 7. Strictly speaking, these are not duplications at all but multiplications of particular regions of the wing, the region affected depending on the time of exposure to the restrictive temperature (Martin et al, 1977). Early exposure affects anterior, proximal margin elements, while later exposure affects distal and posterior margin regions. A feature common to all of the affected wings is that the number of copies of the pattern present, e.g. the number of costal or triple row regions, is always odd, as expected from the continuity argument presented earlier. Most commonly, either three or five copies of a region are present. In some cases there appears to be an even number of patterns, e.g. Figure 7b, but in each of these cases one of the apparent copies actually consists of two very closely spaced partial patterns which are symmetrical with one another.

Several types of circumstantial evidence indicate that the extra growth of the wing disc and the pattern duplications of the wing in C43 are not produced by cell death. First, there are no deficiencies associated with the duplications in the wing, but the extra copies occur in addition to a complete wing. Second, extra growth of disc tissue as it occurs in C43 is not seen in any other cell-lethal mutant. Third, C43 wing disc tissue can be cultured in vivo for extended periods of time without any evidence of gross degeneration. However, since cell death causes pattern duplications in other mutants, and may be responsible for the other duplications produced by C43, we have examined more carefully the relationship between cell death, overgrowth and pattern duplication in the C43 wing. Homozygous C43 larvae were grown to early third instar at permissive temperature and then shifted to restrictive temperature. At various intervals after the shift, larvae were dissected and the discs examined for morphological abnormalities and stained with trypan blue to reveal cell death.

The results of the experiment clearly showed that the abnormal pattern of growth is evident very shortly after the shift to restrictive temperature and that the growth abnormalities precede detectable cell death. Furthermore, we were surprised to find that the same sequence of events occurred in both the wing disc and the eye disc. By 12 hours after the

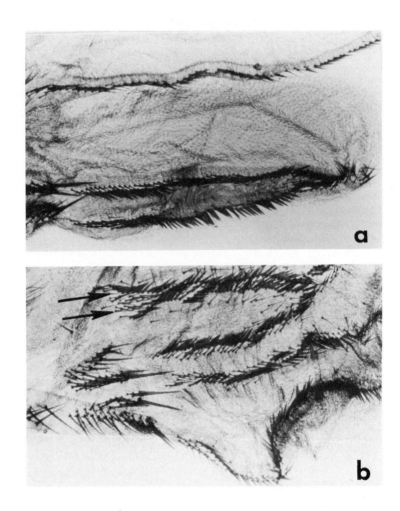

*Figure 7. Wing margin duplications produced by C43.
Homozygous C43 larvae were exposed to restrictive temperature
(27°C) for 24 hours beginning 96 hours after egg laying. (a)
Wing containing three triple row regions characteristic of
the anterior margin. (b) Wing containing five triple row
regions. Note that two very closely spaced triple rows are
present at the top (arrows).*

shift, abnormal folds of tissue were present in both the eye and wing discs (Figure 8a) but no cell death was evident at this time. At 24 and 36 hours after the shift, the growth abnormality was more evident and patches of cell death were revealed by trypan blue staining (Figure 8b). In the wing disc, cell death occurred in small patches which were peripheral to the area in which the abnormal growth was occurring. In contrast, cell death in the eye was more extensive and occurred in the same areas as the abnormal folds. Ultimately, the wing disc becomes greatly enlarged and the eye disc degenerates.

Several conclusions can be drawn from these observations. The first is that the difference between the effect of the mutant on the eye and wing discs is quantitative rather than qualitative. Both discs go through the same sequence of extra growth followed by the appearance of cell death. However, the death is much more extensive in the eye than in the wing, so that it overwhelms any extra growth that may occur. Second,

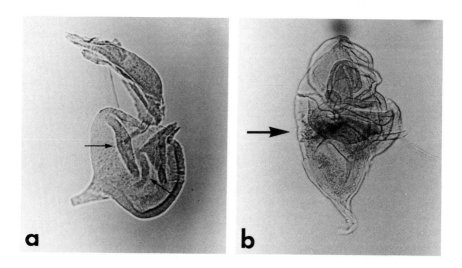

a   b

Figure 8. Growth of C43 eye and wing discs after shift to restrictive temperature. Homozygous C43 larvae were grown at 20°C for 5 days and then shifted to 27°C. (a) Eye disc 12 hours after shift to restrictive temperature. Several abnormal folds are present (arrows). 260 X. (b) Wing disc 36 hours after shift to restrictive temperature. Overgrowth and abnormal folding pattern are evident. A band of dead cells, stained with trypan blue, extends across the middle of the disc (arrow). 160 X.

the abnormal growth precedes cell death so that the latter
cannot be the cause of the growth effects. Finally, in the
wing disc the areas of cell death are physically removed from
the area showing the most extensive growth, again indicating
that the growth is not a secondary effect of cell death. Thus
the mutation appears to produce the growth abnormalities
directly, and then either as an independent effect or as an
effect secondary to the growth abnormality, it causes cell
death.

According to the pattern continuity argument, extra growth
in a mutant imaginal disc could come about if the mutation
were to somehow create unusual discontinuities in the pattern,
for example by adding presumptive pattern elements in ectopic
locations. The differentiation of *C43* wing discs that have
been grown continuously at restrictive temperature suggests
a possible basis for such an abnormal discontinuity pattern.
In addition to structures normally derived from the wing,
enlarged *C43* wing discs also produce a large amount of atypical cuticle (Martin *et al*, 1977), which is devoid of bristles
or hairs, is highly folded, and often forms closed spheres.
This material is clearly not a normal derivative of the wing
disc. The cells which produce this material may do so because
they have positional values which do not correspond to any
normal structures. The presence of these cells with "foreign"
positional values would yield a positional-value discontinuity
that would in turn stimulate extra growth. Pattern duplications could then arise in either of two ways. First, they
could arise directly as a result of intercalation between the
normal tissue and the tissue carrying abnormal positional
values. This appears to occur in the discs grown continuously
at restrictive temperature since some regions of the disc are
produced in great excess. However, discs which receive a
short exposure of restrictive temperature do not produce this
atypical cuticle. Thus, after the discs are returned to permissive temperature, the cells with abnormal positional values
might reacquire normal positional values. The reintegration
of the abnormal tissue into the normal pattern may then lead
to pattern duplications.

J. Duplications Caused by a Mutation Affecting Leg and Antennal Segmentation

In the final mutant that we will consider, *1(3)1215*
(1215; 3 - 50.6), defects in the process of segmentation in
the leg and antenna imaginal discs seem to lead to pattern
duplications in these appendages. *1215* is a recessive lethal
mutation isolated by Shearn *et al* (1971) which causes death at

the stage of pharate adult or very young adult. The legs of
1215 adults are much shorter than normal (Figure 9a) and are
essentially non-functional. While all of the leg segments
are present, each is shorter and has fewer bristles than normal. In the tibia of these animals (Figure 9b), proximal
pattern elements are replaced by duplicated distal pattern
elements with reversed proximal-distal polarity. This is a
uniform feature of the *1215* phenotype and occurs in the pro-,
meso- and metathoracic legs. Duplications of this type do
not occur in any other leg segments, although pattern deficiencies and bristles with reversed polarity are found in
other locations.

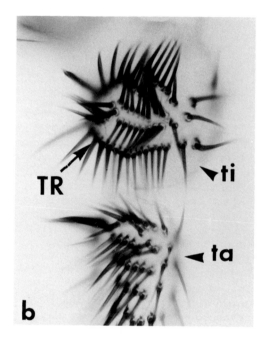

Figure 9. *1215 leg disc abnormalities. (a) Comparison
of the gross morphology of a normal (left) and 1215 (right)
foreleg. 40 X. (b) 1215 foreleg showing reversed polarity
duplication of the transverse rows of the tibia. The most
proximal bristles of the tarsus also show reversed polarity.
ta, tarsus; ti, tibia; TR, transverse row. 160 X.*

The other major effect of the *1215* mutation is on segmentation. The joints between leg segments are abnormally
formed and the tarsus, instead of being divided into segments,
is completely unsegmented. The *1215* antennae are similarly
affected, with all joints being either abnormal or absent.
In addition, the second antennal segment has a reduced number of bristles.

Several characteristics of the *1215* mutation suggest that
its primary effect is on the process of segmentation:

1. Both of the segmented discs, the leg and antenna,
develop abnormally in *1215* homozygotes.

2. All of the remaining discs, which are not segmented,
develop normally.

3. Each segment of the leg is abnormal.

4. All of the joints of the legs and antennae are either
abnormal or completely absent.

The regulative behavior of both cockroach legs (Bohn,
1970, 1971; Bullière, 1971) and *Drosophila* leg discs (Strub,
1979), suggest that the leg contains two types of developmental fields, the whole leg field and the segment field. The
results also show that each segment field is homologous to
each of the others such that grafts made between homologous
levels of two different segments will not stimulate intercalation. Therefore, during normal development the leg primordium
must become subdivided into homologous segment fields. The
process of segmentation is shown schematically in Figure 10,
which also shows how a defect in this process could lead to
the duplications characteristic of the *1215* tibia. The initial
defect produced by *1215* is postulated to be the appearance of
a band of developmentally inactive tissue in the region of
segment boundary formation. Regulative growth in response to
this inactivation then produces the duplications. A similar
interpretation of the defects in ey^D and shi^{ts} legs was proposed by Poodry & Schneiderman (1976). This model explains
the location and orientation of the tibial duplications and
deficiencies, and the abnormality of *1215* joints. The model
also predicts that the region of the tibial duplication with
reversed polarity arises by regulative growth from the tibial
elements with normal polarity. We are currently checking this
prediction by clonal analysis of growth in the *1215* legs.

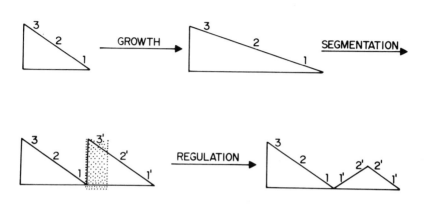

*Figure 10. Model to account for 1215 tibial duplica
tion. The leg initially consists of a single segment gradient. After growth, the disc divides into two segments with
homologous segment gradients. In 1215 legs, inactivation of
cells at the segment boundary (shaded area) leads to abnormal
joint formation, proximal segment deficiencies, and after
regulation, reversed polarity duplications of distal pattern
elements.*

K. Conclusions

We have illustrated some of the ways in which genetic
mutations are contributing to our understanding of pattern
formation in *Drosophila* and of the developmental properties
of the insect epidermis. It seems clear that one of the common mutant phenotypes, pattern duplication, can arise by several different mechanisms but in each case, pattern continuity
is ultimately restored. We have ignored several important
approaches to the problem of pattern formation which are being
taken in other laboratories, such as the use of mutations
which alter mitotic rates, and the use of homoeotic mutations.
Evidently, we are only beginning to understand the many ways

in which genetics can help to solve developmental questions,
and we can look forward to rapid progress in identifying those
activities of cells which enable them to interact with each
other in generating the mysterious properties shown by the
tissues of developing organisms.

REFERENCES

Arking, R. (1975). Temperature-sensitive cell lethal mutants
of *Drosophila:* Isolation and characterization. *Genetics*
80, 519-537.

Bateson, W. (1894). "Materials for the Study of Variation."
Macmillan, London

Bohn, H. (1970). Interkalare Regeneration und segmentale
Gradienten bei den Extremitäten von *Leucophaea*-Larven
(Blattaria). I. Femur und Tibia. *Wilhelm Roux Arch.*
165, 303-341.

Bohn, H. (1971). Interkalare Regeneration und segmentale
Gradienten bei den Extremitäten von *Leucophaea*-Larven
(Blattaria). III. Die Herkunft des interkalaren Regen-
erates. *Wilhelm Roux Arch.* *167*, 209-221.

Bryant, P. J. (1975). Pattern formation in the imaginal
wing disc of *Drosophila melanogaster:* fate map, regeneration and duplication. *J. Exp. Zool.* *193*, 49-77.

Bryant, P. J. (1978). Pattern formation in imaginal discs.
In "The Genetics and Biology of Drosophila" (T. R. F.
Wright & M. Ashburner, eds.). Vol. 2c, 229-335. Aca-
demic Press, New York.

Bryant, S. V., French, V. and Bryant, P. J. (1980). Distal
regeneration and symmetry. Submitted for publication.

Bullière, D. (1971). Utilisation de la régénération inter-
calaire pour l'étude de la détermination cellulaire au
cours de la morphogenèse chez *Blabera craniifer* (Insecte
Dictyoptere). *Develop. Biol.* *25*, 672-709.

Clark, W. C. and Russell, M. A. (1977). The correlation of
lysosomal activity and adult phenotype in a cell-lethal
mutant of *Drosophila*. *Develop. Biol.* *57*, 160-173.

Duranceau, C., Glenn, S. and Schneiderman, H. A. (1980). Positional information as a regulator of growth in the imaginal discs of *Drosophila melanogaster*. This volume, pp _____.

French, V. (1978). Intercalary regeneration around the circumference of the cockroach leg. *J. Embryol. Exp. Morphol. 47*, 53-84.

French, V., Bryant, P. J. and Bryant, S. V. (1976). Pattern regulation in epimorphic fields. *Science 193*, 969-981.

Fristrom, D. (1968). Cellular degeneration in wing development in the mutant *vestigial* of *Drosophila melanogaster*. *J. Cell. Biol. 39*, 488-491.

Fristrom, D. (1969). Cellular degeneration in the production of some mutant phenotypes in *Drosophila melanogaster*. *Molec. Gen. Genetics 103*, 363-379.

Girton, J. R. (1980). Pattern formation in a temperature-sensitive cell-lethal mutant of *Drosophila*: pattern triplications induced by late larval heat treatments. In preparation.

Girton, J. R. and Russell, M. A. (1980a). A clonal analysis of pattern duplication in a temperature-sensitive cell-lethal mutant of *Drosophila melanogaster*. *Develop. Biol*. In press.

Girton, J. R. and Russell, M. A. (1980b). An analysis of compartmentalization in pattern duplications induced by a cell-lethal mutation in *Drosophila*. In preparation.

Hannah-Alava, A. (1958). Morphology and chaetotaxy of the legs of *Drosophila melanogaster*. *J. Morphol. 103*, 281-310.

Haynie, J. L. and Bryant, P. J. (1976). Intercalary regeneration in imaginal wing disk of *Drosophila melanogaster*. *Nature, Lond. 259*, 759-762.

James, A. A. and Bryant, P. J. (1980). Mutations causing pattern deficiencies and duplications in the imaginal wing disc of *Drosophila melanogaster*. *Develop. Biol*. In press.

Jurgens, C. and Gateff, E.. (1979). Pattern specification in imaginal discs of *Drosophila melanogaster:* developmental analysis of a temperature-sensitive mutant producing duplicated legs. *Wilhem Roux's Arch.* 186, 1-25.

Kühn, A. (1971). "Lectures on Developmental Physiology." Springer, New York.

Lewis, J. (1980). Simpler rules for epimorphic regenera tions: the polar coordinate model without polar coordinates. *J. Theoret. Biol.* (In press)

Locke, M. (1966). Cell interactions in the repair of wounds in an insect *(Rhodnius prolixus)*. *J. Insect Physiol.* 12, 389-395.

Loosli, R. (1959). Vergleich von Entwicklungspotenzen in Normalen, Transplantierten und Mutierten Halteren - Imaginalscheiben von *Drosophila melanogaster*. *Develop. Biol.* 1, 24-64.

Martin, P., Martin, A. and Shearn, A. (1977). Studies of $l(3)c43^{hs1}$, a polyphasic, temperature-sensitive mutant of *Drosophila melanogaster* with a variety of imaginal disc defects. *Develop. Biol.* 55, 213-232.

Morgan, T. H. (1901). "Regeneration." Macmillan, New York.

Poodry, C. A. and Schneiderman, H. A. (1970). The ultrastructure of the developing leg of *Drosophila melanogaster*. *Wilhelm Roux's Arch* 166, 1-44.

Poodry, C. A. and Schneiderman, H. A. (1976). Pattern formation in *Drosophila melanogaster:* the effects of mutations on polarity in the developing leg. *Wilhelm Roux's Arch.* 180, 175-188.

Poodry, C. A., Bryant, P. J. and Schneiderman, H. A. (1971). The mechanism of pattern reconstruction by dissociated imaginal discs of *Drosophila melanogaster*. *Develop. Biol.* 26, 464-477.

Postlethwait, J. H. (1978). Development of cuticular patterns in the legs of a cell lethal mutant of *Drosophila melanogaster*. *Wilhelm Roux's Arch.* 185, 37-57.

Reinhardt, C. A. and Bryant, P. J. (1980). Wound healing in the imaginal discs of *Drosophila*. II. Transmission electron microscopy of normal and healing wing discs. Submitted for publication.

Reinhardt, C. A., Hodgkin, N. M. and Bryant, P. J. (1977). Wound healing in the imaginal discs of *Drosophila*. I. Scanning electron microscopy of normal and healing wing discs. *Develop. Biol. 60,* 238-257.

Roseland, C. R. and Schneiderman, H. A. (1979). Regulation and metamorphosis of the abdominal histoblasts of *Drosophila melanogaster*. *Wilhelm Roux's Archives 186,* 235-265.

Russell, M. A. (1974). Pattern formation in the imaginal discs of a temperature-sensitive cell-lethal mutant of *Drosophila melanogaster*. *Develop. Biol. 40,* 24-39.

Russell, M. A., Girton, J. R. and Morgan, K. (1977). Pattern formation in a ts-cell-lethal mutant of *Drosophila:* the range of phenotypes induced by larval heat treatments, *Wilhelm Roux's Arch. 183,* 41-59.

Schubiger, G. (1971). Regeneration, duplication and transdetermination in fragments of the leg disc of *Drosophila melanogaster*. *Develop. Biol. 26,* 277-295.

Shearn, A., Rice, T., Garen, A. and Gehring, W. (1971). Imaginal disc abnormalities in lethal mutants of *Drosophila*. *Proc. Natl. Acad. Sci. U.S.A. 68,* 2594-2598.

Simpson, P. and Schneiderman, H. A. (1975). Isolation of temperature sensitive mutations blocking clone development in *Drosophila melanogaster,* and the effects of a temperature sensitive cell lethal mutation on pattern formation in imaginal discs, *Wilhelm Roux's Arch. 178,* 247-275.

Strub, S. (1979). Leg regeneration in insects: an experimental analysis in *Drosophila* and a new interpretation. *Develop. Biol. 69,* 31-45.

Wigglesworth, V. B. (1936). The function of the corpus allatum in the growth and reproduction of *Rhodnius prolixus* (Hemiptera). *Quart. J. Microsc. Sci. 79,* 91-121.

Wigglesworth, V. B.   (1937).   Wound healing in an insect
    (*Rhodnius prolixus* Hemiptera).   *J. Exp. Biol. 14,*
    364-381.

Winfree, A.   (1979).   "The Geometry of Biological Time (Bio-
    mathematics, Vol. 8)."   Springer, New York.

THE GENETICS OF PATTERN FORMATION

Michael A. Russell
Pliny H. Hayes

Department of Genetics
University of Alberta
Edmonton, Alberta

The development of an insect, like that of any other
multicellular eukaryote, is characterised by the emergence of
a spatially ordered array of differentiated cells. Since
each cell carries in general the same set of genes, functional
differentiation must be ascribed to differential gene expression. Not only is the set of genes that functions in a
particular cell subject to genetic control, but the spatial
order exhibited by a set of such cells is similarly constrained, for mutants can modify the spatial pattern that develops,
with no diminution in the repertoire of differentiated
functions expressed. Such mutants may be called pattern
mutants, and are by definition regulatory, since they alter
the pattern of cells which display activity for other genes.
They may be used to elucidate the genetic control of the
process of pattern formation.

The power of mutant analysis depends critically on the
success of the first step--the isolation of a representative
set of mutants blocked specifically in the process of interest.
Unfortunately there are no elegant selective methods for the
isolation of pattern mutants and some genes of interest may
mutate, perhaps exclusively, to lethal alleles. This means
that the mutants presently available may not be representative of all the loci involved. In addition, because pattern
formation involves cellular interactions which depend upon
the proper operation of a large number of elementary cellular
functions, we must expect many pattern mutants to define genes
whose wild-type activities are necessary factors, but not
controlling variables, in the pattern formation process. Such
mutants will have fortuitous pleiotropic effects on pattern
formation, but will not define the loci of primary interest,

543

whose wild-type functions are regulatory. This means that
the mutants presently available probably include a great many
that are not blocked specifically in the process of interest.
An important task therefore, is to extend the analysis of
these mutants so as to classify the loci identified into
those with intrinsic as opposed to fortuitous effects.

To specify a biological pattern genetic information is
necessary. The set of genes involved may be thought of as a
set of instructions like a computer program designed to
accomplish a particular task. A mutant is similar to a missing or defective instruction which causes premature termination of the program's execution (a lethal) or an incorrect
answer at the end (a pattern defect). A mutant would thus be
expected to reduce the information content of a pattern,
leading to one of two kinds of phenotype: increased disorder;
or transformation to a simpler pattern. Special interest
attaches to mutants of the second kind because of the precision with which such transformations can be characterised.
Our task is to deduce the informational roles of the genes
involved and the logic of the program from the variety of
defects pattern mutants cause.

I. THE BIOLOGICAL SYSTEM: PATTERN MUTANTS IN *DROSOPHILA*

In *Drosophila melanogaster* most pattern mutants have been
identified by their effects on the distribution of pattern
elements--trichomes, chaetae, sensillae and so on--in the
imaginal exoskeleton. To understand the significance of a
transformation, it is important to know quite a lot about the
development of the wild-type pattern.

In *Drosophila* the imaginal exoskeleton is a product of
pattern formation in two systems: the embryo and the imaginal
discs. Pattern formation in the embryonic system gives rise
to the segmented larva, which includes the undifferentiated
anlagen of the adult ectoderm, the segmentally derived
imaginal discs. Each disc consists of a single layer of
epidermal cells continuous with the hypoderm and derived from
it at an early stage. The discs differentiate at metamorphosis into the parts of the adult exoskeleton appropriate to
their segmental origins.

Experiments using two quite different methodological
approaches have shed light on the developmental mechanisms
involved. The first approach uses surgical or similar means
to study the development of different parts of the system in
isolation or grafted together in combinations. The second

uses genetic labelling to evaluate the developmental potential *in situ* of the clones derived from single cells at particular stages of development.

   1. Concepts Derived from Surgical Intervention. Isolation
experiments done on the embryonic system suggest that until
the blastoderm stage the embryo behaves with respect to the
pattern of segments as a single regulative field, i.e., as a
unit in which a pattern of segmentation is specified by a
mechanism involving communication between the parts. Thus,
in many insect systems including *Drosophila*, the segments
which differentiate from a particular region can be changed
by any kind of experimental intervention that interferes with
interactions between the parts (Sander, 1971; Schubiger *et al.*,
1977). The system changes from a regulative to a mosaic
state at the blastoderm stage.
   It is also at or shortly after this stage that cells
determined for particular imaginal fates are first detected
(Illmensee, 1978), and experiments that monitor pattern formation in isolated disc fragments suggest that each disc may
behave thereafter as an independent regulative field. The
pattern elements formed are position specific, and detailed
fate maps of many discs have been made by compiling results
from a series of defined fragments (see Nöthiger, 1972 for a
review). This observation alone would suggest that each disc
is a mosaic system, but it is found that the developmental
potential of a fragment can be changed if it is cultured in
intimate contact with a fragment from a different part of the
disc. The interaction generates pattern elements normally
formed at positions intermediate between the cut edges of the
two fragments, and this implies that the disc as a whole is a
regulative field (Haynie and Bryant, 1976). The phenomenon
is analogous to the regeneration of intercalary elements
observed in cockroach legs when different segmental levels
are juxtaposed by grafting (reviewed in Lawrence, 1972).
   Wolpert (1969) theorised that a regulative field might
be a system in which position is defined with respect to the
same set of spatial coordinates which might be specified, for
example, by gradients in the concentration of one or more
morphogens. Communication between the parts would be involved
in the establishment and maintenance of such a gradient field.
Pattern formation would be a process comprising two conceptually distinct steps: the *specification* of positional values
throughout the system, and the *interpretation* of positional
information at particular points. Different cells in a field
would independently assess their local positional values, and
differentiate accordingly, and they might also participate

cooperatively in the establishment of the global system of
positional information. Individual mutants might be defective in one step but not the other.

   2. Concepts from Clonal Analysis. Clonal analysis makes
use of mutants which affect the appearance of pattern elements
like bristles and hairs without affecting their arrangement.
Exposure to X-rays of larvae heterozygous for such mutants
induces genetic recombination in somatic cells, resulting in
the segregation of cells homozygous for the mutant alleles at
the next division. Thus the clonal descendents of a cell
labeled at a particular time in development can be recognised
in the adult exoskeleton. Clones are progressively restricted
in size when induced at later stages of development, but this
problem has been ameliorated by the introduction of the
"*Minute* technique" (Morata and Ripoll, 1975). This method
exploits the fact that cells heterozygous for a dominant
Minute mutation divide more slowly than their wild-type
counterparts. The genotype is set up so that the segregation
of a recessive marker is coincident with the removal of a
Minute factor. Such clones grow faster than the heterozygous
Minute background cells in which they are induced and consequently even late clones populate large areas of cuticle.
   This technique has been used to detect *in situ* the
occurence of heritable restriction in the developmental
competence of individual cells. Preblastoderm nuclei have
been shown to be totipotent (Illmensee, 1978). However when
cellular blastoderm stage embryos are irradiated, it is found
that clones never cross between segments or even between anterior and posterior regions of certain segments (Steiner,
1976). The regions bounded by these lines of clonal restrictions have been called compartments (Garcia-Bellido *et al.*,
1973). A sequence of further compartmentalisation events
also occurs in certain discs at characteristic stages of
larval development. In the wing disc, each event involves
the binary subdivision of one or more of the pre-existing
compartments; this observation led Garcia-Bellido to suggest
that the cells of the two new compartments are distinguished
from each other by the state (ON/OFF) of a particular gene
called a selector gene (Garcia-Bellido, 1975a).
   Support for this idea comes also from several mutants
that transform one compartment into another. Thus, a mutant
called *engrailed* causes an incomplete and variable transformation of the posterior compartment of the wing into a
mirror image copy of the anterior (Garcia-Bellido and
Santamaria, 1972). Mutants at the *bithorax* locus transform
anterior metathorax into anterior mesothorax, and *postbithorax*
mutants transform posterior metathorax into posterior mesothorax (Lewis, 1963). The domains within which the effects

of these mutants are expressed, are delineated by precisely
the same boundaries as are revealed by clonal analysis.
Lawrence and Morata (1976) were able to show that clones homozygous for *engrailed* defined the anterio-posterior compartment
boundary when they approached it from the anterior compartment,
but crossed the compartment boundary when they originated from
the posterior. This behaviour is explicable if the *engrailed*
gene is switched on in the posterior compartment and remains
off in the anterior compartment and if the distinction between
anterior and posterior is contingent only upon the state of
this locus. Such are the properties that define a selector
gene.

II. THE MUTANTS

We are now in a position to consider in more detail,
examples of mutants that cause simple pattern transformations.
Our treatment is not intended to be comprehensive and more
systematic reviews of related topics may be found elsewhere
(Garcia-Bellido, 1975b; Ouweneel, 1976; Shearn, 1978;
Tokunaga, 1978). Instead we have tried to illustrate the
ideas that seem to us to be important with the aid of suitable examples.

A. *Mutants That Cause Mirror Image Duplications*

Many loci yield mutants that cause mirror image duplications. The importance of these phenotypes stems from the fact
that no way has been found to explain them without recourse
to models involving gradients which might provide the physical
basis for positional information. These mutants and their
phenocopies therefore represent one of the few available
experimental approaches to the theory of positional information. The logic that connects experimental observation with
theory is, however, indirect and subtle.

1. Bicaudal. This mutant, isolated and originally described by Bull (1966) behaves genetically as a recessive
maternally influenced embryonic pattern mutant. Eggs from
homozygous mutant females differentiate into embryos in which
the normal anterior pattern is replaced by a mirror image
copy of the posterior. Thus, the mutant affects organisation
specifically with respect to the anterio-posterior embryonic
axis. All embryonic structures except the pole cells are
affected. The phenotype is variable with respect to the
point along the AP axis at which polarity reversal takes place,

and the number of posterior segments that form anterior to
this point. This has been carefully documented by Nüsslein-
Volhard (1977, 1979) who points out that the pattern posterior
to the point of polarity reversal is also affected. Although
the segments in this region are in normal sequence and orientation, a particular segment appears at a position more anterior than in the wild-type. The phenotype may be explained by
assuming that an anterio-posterior gradient controls the
sequence of segments in the embryo. On the basis of its
behaviour as inferred from the observed phenotypes, Nüsslein-
Volhard suggests that the physical basis for the hypothetical
gradient might be a reaction-diffusion system (Turing, 1952)
such as that modelled mathematically by Gierer and Meinhardt
(1972). Given certain kinetic constraints such systems are
capable of assuming a bipolar form that would account at
least for the symmetrical patterns. In relation to this
hypothesis it is significant that *bicaudal* is a maternal
effect mutant. The phenotype is completely uninfluenced by
the genetic contribution of the male, showing that the locus
must function during oogenesis. Since the genotype of the
blastoderm cells would be involved in *interpretation* of
positional information, *bicaudal* is thought of as a mutant
that influences the *specification* of positional values. We
have no evidence, however, that the effect of *bicaudal* is
inherent in the wild-type function of the locus. The mutant
might merely interfere indirectly with the expression of
maternal information, not with the information itself.

   2. Dorsal. Nüsslein-Volhard *et al.*, (1980) have also
described another maternal-effect mutant called *dorsal*. In
homozygous condition *dorsal* causes the replacement of ventral
embryonic structures with a mirror image copy of dorsal ones.
As a heterozygote the effect is less extreme; the most ventral structures disappear, and more dorsal ones are shifted
ventrally. Thus the effects of *dorsal* parallel those of
bicaudal except that the embryonic organisation is modified
specifically with respect to the dorso-ventral axis.
   The existence of these two mutants might thus be taken
to imply that position on the blastoderm is specified on a
2-dimentional rectangular coordinate system provided by
orthogonally oriented gradients in two morphogens. Although
this interpretation may be sufficient, it has not been
directly tested. Such a test would necessitate the identification, assay and experimental manipulation of the hypothetical morphogens. Until this difficult task is accomplished
a question must remain as to what extent the interpretation
is a necessary one. Nevertheless it is hard to see how the

continuous variation in the patterns produced can be explained without invoking the concept of continuous gradients specifying positional information.

   3. Cell Lethals. Another class of mutants thought to influence the specification of positional values includes those which cause limited amounts of cell death in imaginal discs. These often cause mirror-image duplications about a line of symmetry that varies freely in position from disc to disc. A starting point for an explanation is the behaviour of surgical disc fragments cultured *in vivo* under conditions that permit cell proliferation. Regardless of where in relation to the fate map the cut is made, one of the two fragments produced generally regenerates, while the other duplicates a mirror image copy of the fate map elements it contains. The patterns formed by such fragments consist of two parts, the partial pattern formed *in situ* corresponding to the fate map, and a new partial pattern formed by epimorphosis in a regeneration blastema initially consisting of a few cells at the cut edge. Disc fragments fold up in culture bringing into juxtaposition cells that were far apart in the original disc. As in other systems, when epidermal cells from different sites are brought close together, this is thought to stimulate cell division creating a regeneration blastema. French *et al.* (1976) found that they could account for regeneration and duplication by assuming that positional values are assigned in the regeneration blastema by transformations operating on the confronted positional values of cells at the cut edge. They assumed that position in the disc epithelium is specified on a 2-dimentional coordinate system by means of an angular and a radial variable. A positional information model of some kind is evidently necessary to explain the continuously graded correlation of regenerative potential with the site of the cut, but as we shall see, it is not the case that this specific model is the only one that will suffice. J. Fristrom (1970) first suggested that pattern duplication mutants might generate duplicating disc fragments *in situ* by causing localised cell death. This idea was vindicated by isolating temperature sensitive cell-lethal mutants and testing them for effects on pattern formation (Russell 1974). One such mutant, subsequently studied in detail is *l(1)ts726* (Clark and Russell, 1975; Russell *et al.*, 1977). Pattern duplications could be induced by subjecting larvae to a 48 hour treatment at the non-permissive temperature. The factor causing this morphological phenotype was mapped cytologically and genetically to a position indistinguishable from that responsible for the temperature-sensitive lethality. Temperature-sensitive cell-lethals at several other loci (Arking, 1975; Simpson and Schneiderman 1975) have similar effects. This persuades us

that these mutants cause pattern duplications by the method
suggested by Fristrom and that other pattern duplication
mutants not yet identified as cell lethals, might work in a
similar way.

There is of course no reason to suppose that the effects
of these mutants are intrinsic. The wild-type functions of
loci that can mutate to cell-lethals must include all sorts
of housekeeping functions that are merely invariant precon-
ditions for the normal process of pattern formation.
Nevertheless these mutants should help us understand similar
ones with unknown effects, and they have also been useful as
tools to supplement the surgical methods.

   *a. Functional significance of compartments in pattern
formation.* The patterns generated by disc fragments are not
easy to account for, unless we invoke gradients of positional
information as controlling variables. Clonal analysis, on
the other hand, implicates heritable determinative decisions
which restrict the developmental potential of a cell lineage
to a progressively smaller segment of the pattern as a whole.
The two concepts are not inherently contradictory, but the
observation that compartmental boundaries are not respected
during regeneration calls into question the connection of
both concepts with pattern formation. It is possible to
make either of two extreme and contradictory inferences.
Perhaps compartment boundaries do not really represent heritable commitments to particular developmental pathways, and
thus have no functional significance in pattern formation.
Alternatively, regeneration might be misleading because it
involves processes different from those that occur in normal
development. We have attempted to investigate this by
monitoring the fates of clones labeled at different stages
during a regeneration experiment (Girton and Russell 1980a,b).
Mesothoracic leg duplications were induced by heat treatment
of larvae homozygous for a ts cell lethal. At the time of
heat treatment, this disc comprises an anterior and a posterior compartment derived from cell populations clonally
distinct since the blastoderm stage. Clones originating from
the anterior compartment of the original pattern were able
to populate both anterior and posterior parts of the duplicate
if induced before 12 hours after the end of the heat treatment. In contrast, clones induced at 24 hours or more after
heat treatment defined a new compartment boundary within the
duplicate pattern which separated the same subsets of anterior
and posterior markers as the normal A/P boundary. Formation
of such a boundary would not be anticipated if compartments
had no function in the establishment of the pattern. This
parallel with normal development is consistent with the idea
that the duplicate pattern develops by a precise reiteration

of the normal sequence of events. Since the symmetry and
variation in the extent of the duplicate patterns are explicable only in terms of a positional information model, we
draw the conclusion that the compartment boundary forms at a
site determined by positional values in the regeneration
blastema. Consequently we feel that the formation of a compartment boundary might be a necessary step in the interpretation of positional information. We must conclude that
after compartment formation at blastoderm, the positional
system persists, permitting the assignment of spatial values
in a regeneration blastema in the event that the disc is disrupted by injury or experimental intervention.

   4. Engrailed. We have already alluded to *engrailed* in
connection with the theory of selector genes. As explained,
this mutant transforms the posterior compartment of the wing
into a mirror image copy of the anterior compartment.
Although compartment specificity, and the behaviour of anterior and posterior clones at the A/P boundary are neatly
explained if it is a selector gene, there is no reason on
the basis of this model to expect mirror image symmetry. An
important feature of the *engrailed* wing pattern is the invariant position of the line of symmetry. It coincides, in
fact, with the normal position of the compartment boundary.
This is true even of small *engrailed* clones separated from
the boundary by large numbers of wild-type cells. Such
clones typically differentiate the pattern found in a position
symmetrical to that of the clone about the A/P boundary. This
rules out the possibility that *engrailed* might be a compartment specific cell-lethal, or that it might act by affecting
the spatial distribution of a morphogen. Autonomous differentiation of the mutant pattern in a small clone suggests
rather, that *engrailed* affects the interpretation of positional values. This supports our earlier inference that compartments might be involved in the interpretation of positional
values.
   How could a defect in interpretation lead to a symmetrical
pattern? Bateson (1971) developed an approach that we can
usefully apply to *engrailed*. He argued that a *3-dimentional*
system of coordinates is necessary to specify position in a
curved epithelial surface such as that of an appendage. Let
us assume for example, that positional information in imaginal
discs is embodied in concentration gradients of three morphogens specifying, respectively, an anterio-posterior, a dorso-
ventral, and a proximo-distal axis. The gradients might be
established by diffusion between fixed high and low points
via neighbouring cells in the epithelial surface, and the
fate of a cell would be determined by the local relative concentration, unique at each point in the system, of the three

morphogens. According to Bateson symmetry implies loss of
information. A positional field of this kind would degenerate
into a bilaterally symmetrical one, were the cells unable to
distinguish values in one of the three gradients. Thus, the
engrailed mutant might be defective in the interpretation
specifically of an anterio-posterior coordinate of positional
information. If so, the fact that the line of symmetry is the
compartment boundary assumes new significance, for it suggests
that compartment boundaries might be formed at symmetries
inherent in the positional system. If we superimpose the
symmetries generated by deleting each coordinate in turn,
we get a geometry remarkably like that of the pattern of compartments in the wing disc. That the geometry of compartmentalisation can be derived from a hypothetical system of
positional information provides an unexpected source of
support for its validity. Further support comes from the
phenotypes of two other pattern mutants.

    5. Polycomb. Polycomb is a dominant homeotic which was
originally described as a mutant transforming second and
third legs into first legs. In addition, however, *Polycomb*
mutants partially transform ventral wing into a mirror image
copy of the dorsal pattern (S. Y. Tiong, unpublished observations). As with *engrailed*, the line of symmetry is invariant
and coincides with the dorso-ventral compartment boundary,
which follows the wing margin. *Polycomb* can therefore be
interpreted in a similar way to *engrailed*--as a mutant
defective in interpretation specifically of the dorso-ventral
coordinate. It will be interesting to see if the analogy
with *engrailed* extends to the behaviour of clones at the
dorso-ventral compartment boundary.

    6. Wingless. Another mutant, *wingless* (Sharma and Chopra,
1976) causes mirror image duplication of the wing disc
pattern specifically with respect to the proximo-distal
axis. It has been suggested that *wingless* acts like *engrailed*,
causing duplications about the proximo-distal compartment
boundary (Morata and Lawrence, 1977), and, clonal analysis
indicates that the duplicate results from transformation
rather than regeneration. However in *wingless* the site of
the line of symmetry is somewhat variable in position (Deàk,
1978) and clones induced during larval development differentiate non-autonomously, suggesting perhaps that *wingless* interferes with the specification of the proximo-distal coordinate
rather than its interpretation.

B. *General Conclusions*

As we have seen, the concepts of positional information and compartmentalisation are both indispensible in an attempt to explain the origin of the pattern mutant phenotypes discussed. The construction of any positional-information model involves a piece of circular logic. First we must invent a system of positional values capable of specifying the normal pattern. Next we must deduce the modified distribution of positional values present in the mutant or experimental situation. Finally we must attempt to infer rules of cellular or gradient behaviour, capable of accounting for the transformation of the wild-type system into that of the mutant. Until the physical or chemical variables underlying such hypothetical positional values can be measured, such models can never be subjected to direct experimental test. As experimentalists we can describe our results in terms of any coordinate system we wish to impose: but which one do the cells use? Under the circumstances, the only grounds for confidence in the validity of a particular model are (1) biological plausibility of the system and the rules governing its transformations, and (2) the range of experimental and mutant situations it is capable of explaining.

A specific model for positional information in imaginal discs that has gained wide acceptance is the polar-coordinate system (French, 1976; French *et al.*, 1976). This model requires that position be specified by an angular measure continuous across all intervals, for which no physical analogue has yet been devised. In addition, the cellular behaviour necessary to account for the regeneration results are complex, and the model fails to explain the geometry of compartmentalisation, or the effects of mutants like *engrailed*. On the other hand, the three coordinate model we have presented as an explanation for these effects has also been shown to be capable of explaining disc regeneration and duplication behaviour on the basis of a single simple intercalation rule (Russell, in preparation). It seems significant to us that the rule governing assignment of positional values in a regeneration blastema is much less complex in the 3-dimentional coordinate system. All that is required is that new cells be assigned gradient values intermediate between those of the cells juxtaposed when the cut edge folds. Such a property is entirely consistent with the way cells might behave if morphogen gradients were to be set up in the course of normal development; no new properties need be invented to account for regeneration. Consequently we feel that as a way of integrating the available evidence this model deserves serious consideration.

Although the mutants we discussed all appeared superficially to act in quite different ways, it appears that a common positional system might be the basis for their common phenotypic effects. It might even be suggested that a homologous positional system exists in the embryo, and that *bicaudal* and *dorsal* act not by creating bipolar gradient forms, but by eliminating particular coordinates.

C. Mutants Which Cause Intersegmental Transformations

The second class of transformations we wish to discuss is that caused by homeotic mutants where the pattern of a particular disc is transformed into that normally formed by another disc.

Wolpert suggested that as the pattern formation process is evolutionarily ancient, it is to be expected that positional information systems might be universal. In *Drosophila*, evidence consistent with this idea comes from experiments in which intercalary regeneration in a specific fragment of the wing disc is stimulated by specific fragments of other discs (Wilcox and Smith, 1977; Bryant *et al.*, 1978). Thus, position within discs may be specified on homologous sets of spatial coordinates. A corollary is the requirement that cells in the various discs be capable of responding to homologous positional values by differentiating in different ways. As developmental fields are in general not larger than a millimeter in diameter (Wolpert, 1971), the appropriate differentiation of different discs cannot be ascribed to continued reading of the primary embryonic field. Rather, the positional information in the field must somehow be translated into a heritably stable form. Wolpert and Lewis (1975) have argued that response to transient fields must take the form of position-specific activation of genes which promote their own transcription thereafter. Such genes would thus provide for the clonal transmission of developmental decisions taken at an earlier stage as well as the means of effecting those decisions by activation of other downstream genes. The homeotic mutants appear to be defective in the interpretation of the primary embryonic field. It seems reasonable therefore, to think of them as mutants in the class of genes proposed by Wolpert and Lewis, defective either in site-specific activation, in feedback, or in executive functions. The transformations seen in homeotics are thus of interest, as they may provide insight into the genetic logic by which the positional information of the embryonic field is translated into determined states.

There are two important characteristics associated with
each homeotic (1) the patterns which are transformed (the
mutant's *domain*), and (2) the patterns to which the domains
are transformed (which we shall call the mutant's *range*).
The interpretation of these characteristics depends in turn
upon the genetic properties of the mutation as defined by
dosage studies. Mutations are considered "neomorphs" if
the addition of extra doses of the wild-type allele has no
alleviating effect on the mutant phenotype. Neomorphic
homeotics may be considered to cause transformations by the
improper activation of a control gene in a location in
which it is normally silent. Thus, the *range* of a neomorphic
allele defines the domain of the *wild-type* allele at that
locus. "Amorphic" and "hypomorphic" mutations affect the
phenotype by a loss in function of a gene. A mutation is considered to be amorphic if it causes the same degree of
phenotypic aberrancy as a deletion of the locus. Hypomorphic
mutations are similar, but retain some residual wild-type
activity. In contrast to neomorphs, it is the *domain* of an
amorphic allele which defines the domain of the wild-type
allele at that locus.

As a general rule, eukaryotes do not exhibit the cluster-
ing of genes of related function so commonly seen in prokaryotes. Two exceptions exist among the homeotics, however,
in the "Bithorax Complex" and the "Antennapedia Complex".
Whether these gene complexes reflect coordinate control as
in prokaryotes, or evolution by gene duplication, or both,
are considerations to be borne in mind in the following
discussion.

1. The Bithorax Complex. Extensively studied by E. B.
Lewis (1978), the Bithorax Complex consists of at least ten
tightly linked loci. The proximal loci are defined by both
hypomorphs and neomorphs, and are thought to control the
development of the metathorax and the first abdominal segment. The more distal loci, defined only by neomorphs as yet,
control the development of the rest of the abdominal and
genital segments (Lewis, 1978). We shall restrict our discussion to the proximal region which is well characterised.

a. The bx *and* pbx *loci.* The development of the metathorax requires the action of the wild-type alleles of the
bithorax (*bx*) and *postbithorax* (*pbx*) loci. Mutants at these
loci are hypomorphs, and transform the anterior (*bx*) and
posterior (*pbx*) compartments of the metathorax--haltere and
third leg--to their mesothoracic homologues--wing and second
leg. The continued presence of the wild-type alleles of
these loci is required from blastoderm to late third instar
to prevent the transformations, the transformations are

cell-autonomous, and the domains of the mutants correspond
exactly to the compartment boundaries defined by clonal
analysis (Garcia-Bellido, 1975a). These are features expected
of autocatalytic genes controlling the development of the
anterior and posterior compartments of the metathorax. Two
neomorphic mutations exist whose phenotypes are entirely
consistent with the above interpretation. The *Contrabithorax*
(*Cbx*) mutant causes a variable transformation of the mesothorax to metathorax, presumably by an abnormal derepression
in the mesothorax of control genes for the metathorax. The
fact that this neomorph maps between the two hypomorphs
supports the idea that this genetic region controls the
development of the metathorax and in addition, that the
proximity of *bx* and *pbx* is a reflection of coordinate control.
A second neomorph, *Haltere mimic* (*Hm*), transforms the anterior
compartment of the wing to haltere, presumably by derepression
of the *bx* locus; the posterior compartment of the wing is
reduced in size, but remains wing tissue (Hayes *et al.*, in
preparation). Accompanying this neomorphic effect is a loss
in function of the *pbx* locus. Both effects are readily
understood, as *Hm* is associated with a chromosomal rearrangement with a breakpoint in the Bithorax Complex. A class of
amorphic mutations also exists with effects on both the *bx*
and *pbx* loci, the *Ultrabithorax* (*Ubx*) mutants. These behave
as deletions or inactivations of both loci, and *Ubx* point
mutations also map between *bx* and *pbx*, again suggesting
coordinate control.

   b. Mutant interactions. In a sense, the existence of
separate loci for the two metathoracic compartments is surprising. Disc regeneration experiments and the mutant transformations themselves strongly suggest that the positional
information within the haltere and wing discs is homologous.
One might therefore expect a single control gene for "Metathorax" to distinguish the two discs, with the remaining
determinative decisions within the discs being identically
encoded. Thus, by homology with the mesothorax, "Metathorax"[ON] engrailed[OFF] might define the anterior metathorax and
"Metathorax"[ON] engrailed[ON] the posterior metathorax. This
combinatorial scheme is implicit in the selector gene model
of Garcia-Bellido (see above), and it has been claimed that
engrailed controls posterior development in just such a
fashion (Garcia-Bellido and Santamaria, 1972). If indeed
engrailed controls the anterior-posterior nature of the
metathorax, it must do so by differential activation of *bx*
and *pbx*. Let us examine the evidence. The morphology of
the haltere is unchanged in engrailed mutants. The arguments
for the action of *engrailed* in the metathorax are not based
on morphology, however, but on the phenotypes of the *en bx*

and *en pbx* double mutants. In the *en bx* combination the
anterior haltere is transformed to wing while the posterior
haltere remains haltere. This is, in fact, the phenotype
of the *bx* mutant alone: had engrailed transformed the posterior haltere into a second anterior compartment, both
"anterior" compartments would have been transformed to wing
by the *bx* mutation. In the *en pbx* combination the posterior
haltere is transformed to anterior wing. That the wing
tissue is anterior rather than posterior as in the *pbx* mutant
alone has been interpreted as indicating that engrailed controls the ability to make posterior haltere (Garcia-Bellido
and Santamaria, 1972). However, the appearance of any wing
tissue in *en pbx* halteres indicates the continued existence
of a posterior compartment in the absence of engrailed product, for *pbx* only transforms the posterior haltere to wing.
The fact that the wing tissue is anterior merely confirms
the inability of *en* mutants to make posterior wing. Thus
the *bx* and *pbx* loci are seen to control haltere development
independent of the state of the *en* locus.

A further demonstration of this independence is seen in
the *Hm en* combination. *Hm* derepresses the *bx* gene in the
anterior compartment of the wing, creating a hybrid anterior-
haltere::posterior-wing. *en* mutants create a mirror image
anterior-wing::anterior-wing. In the *Hm en* combination one
still observes a hybrid appendage, but it is now anterior-
haltere::*anterior*-wing (Hayes *et al.*, in preparation). The
extent of the wing to haltere transformation is unaffected
by the addition of a second "anterior" compartment, indicating again that the *bx* locus responds directly to positional
information rather than to the state of the *en* locus.

The *bx* and *pbx* locus thus respond directly to the positional information in the imaginal disc. That they also
respond directly to the primary field has been shown by
Tiong *et al.* (1977), who used a ts cell lethal to study the
properties of the *bx* and *pbx* loci during regeneration *in situ*.
Flies of the genotype $bx^- pbx^+$ have third legs whose anterior
compartments are transformed to mesothorax while their posterior compartments remain unaffected, as expected. When
discs of this genotype were caused to duplicate it was observed that in the duplicate both anterior and posterior
compartments were sometimes transformed to mesothorax,
implying a failure to activate the pbx^+ locus when the duplicate posterior compartment was formed. As the duplicate
posterior is *never* transformed in $bx^+ pbx^+$ flies, the results
imply that activation of the pbx^+ locus during regeneration
requires the presence of the bx^+ allele. This would not be
the case if the memory of the metathoracic commitment resided
at a locus other than *bx* or *pbx*.

The determination to segment depends upon position within the primary embryonic field while the determination to anterior or posterior compartment depends on position within a secondary field. In the selector gene model these decisions are assumed to be independent, the determined state being combinatorially defined by the states of individual loci. We have seen, however, that in the metathorax the decisions to segment and to anterior or posterior compartment are not separately encoded. The primary and secondary fields cooperate in the activation of a single locus which summarises their conjoint state. The fact that the clonal boundaries between the anterior and posterior compartments of the thoracic segments are established at the same time as the boundaries between these segments is consistent with the existence of these summary genes. Additionally, the various control mutants and the interaction between the *bx* and *pbx* loci during regeneration strongly suggest some form of coordinate control and functional interaction among the loci of the proximal Bithorax Complex. For further discussion, see Hayes *et al.* (1979).

2. *The Antennapedia Complex.* The Antennapedia Complex is the site of several neomorphic, hypomorphic and amorphic mutations whose transformations suggest the existence of control genes for the pro- and mesothoraces. Recent studies by Kaufman, Denell, and co-workers have revealed much about the interrelationships of these mutations (Denell, 1973; Duncan and Kaufman, 1975; Kaufman *et al.*, 1980; Lewis *et al.*, 1980a,b; Denell *et al.*, 1980; Wakimoto and Kaufman, 1980).

A useful feature of neomorphic mutations is that by selection for revertants of neomorphs one can obtain amorphs and deletions of the gene of interest. This strategy was used with *Nasobemia* (*Antp*^{NS}), a homozygous viable neomorph in the Antennapedia Complex, to saturate the region with mutations. Complementation tests revealed that the neomorphs and point revertants of *Nasobemia* can be variously ascribed to two neighbouring lethal complementation groups while a third homeotic locus, *proboscipedia* (*pb*) lies very closely proximal.

a. *The proboscipedia locus.* The *pb* locus is unique among homeotics in that the phenotypes of hypomorphic and amorphic mutations differ qualitatively rather than quantitatively. Amorphs transform the proboscis, a derivative of the labial disc, to leg structures while hypomorphs transform it to antennal structures (Kaufman, 1978). In addition, *pb* mutants cause abnormalities of the maxillary palps,

derivatives of the antennal disc, which have been interpreted
as transformations to antenna. The significance of alternative transformations of mutations at a single locus is not
clear.

   b. *The Scr and Antp lethal complementation groups.* Male
D. melanogaster have sets of characteristically modified
bristles called sex combs on their prothoracic legs. The
deficiencies used by Lewis *et al.* (1980a,b) to isolate
lethals are associated with a dominant reduction in the
number of sex comb teeth. Five of the lethals also showed
this effect. They fall into a single complementation group
which defines the *Sex combs reduced* locus (*Scr*). An analysis
of homozygous lethal embryos reveals that the lethality is
associated with a transformation of the prothorax to mesothorax, and the rare surviving flies have sex comb teeth
severely reduced in number or absent altogether, while mesothoracic markers are present. The Scr^+ locus thus appears
to be a control gene for the prothorax, and the dominant
sex combs reduced phenotype is an indication that it is
haplo-insufficient. The neomorph *Multiple sex combs* (*Msc*)
appears to be a mutation in the control region of this
prothoracic control gene, for it transforms the second and
third legs to first legs. Interestingly, it also has an
amorphic effect on the *Scr* gene in its wild-type domain, the
prothorax: it causes a reduction in the number of sex
comb teeth on the first legs, and its recessive lethality is
not complemented by *Scr* mutants. The combination of neo- and
amorphic effects implies that control of the *Scr* gene has
been modified such that it is now expressed in the meso- and
metathoraces *instead of* in the prothorax. The association
of a neomorphic effect in one region with an amorphic effect
in another is also seen in some mutants at the neighbouring
Antp lethal complementation group.
   Nasobemia ($Antp^{Ns}$) transforms the antenna and head to
second leg and thorax. It thus appears to derepress a mesothoracic control gene which has been called *Antp* in the eye-
antennal disc. Supporting this contention is the fact that
revertants of *Nasobemia*, presumed amorphs at *Antp*, are
lethals which cause an embryonic transformation of mesothorax
to prothorax, in homozygous condition.
   Antennapedia mutants (*Antp*) combine the effects of *Nasobemia* and its revertants. They transform the antenna to
second leg, but are recessive lethals which fail to complement
Nasobemia revertants and are associated with a meso- to
prothoracic embryonic transformation. They are thus analogous
to *Msc*, as the mesothoracic gene is now being expressed in the
antenna *instead of* the mesothorax. The only difference is
that *Antp* is not haplo-insufficient.

A different and interesting combination of effects is seen in the *Extra sex comb* (*Antp^{Scx}*) mutant. It transforms the second and third legs to first legs like *Msc*, but there is no reduction in the number of sex comb teeth on the first leg; instead, its recessive lethality is associated with the *Antp* locus and a transformation of meso- to prothorax in embryos. It thus appears to combine a neomorphic effect on the *Scr* locus with a concomitant amorphic effect on *Antp*.

Because of the wealth of different lesions, certain patterns emerge. First, we see an interesting relationship between amorphic phenotypes: amorphs at the *Scr* locus transform prothorax to mesothorax, while amorphs at the neighbouring *Antp* locus reciprocally transform mesothorax to prothorax. Wakimoto and Kaufman (1980) have suggested that such a pattern is consistent with mutual repression: the *Scr* gene would control development of the prothorax and repress the *Antp* gene; in the mesothorax the *Antp$^+$* gene would control development and repress *Scr*. There thus may be a functional interaction between these loci. Second, in *Antp^{Scx}* we see a mutation affecting the control of both loci, suggesting strongly a common structural control component as well. In these respects, the Antennapedia Complex mirrors the Bithorax Complex--proximity appears to reflect structural and functional integration.

REFERENCES

Arking, R. (1975). Temperature sensitive cell lethal mutants of *Drosophila*, isolation and characterisation. *Genetics* *80*, 519-537.

Bateson, G. (1971). A re-examination of "Bateson's Rule". *J. Genet. 60*, 230-240.

Bryant, P. J., Adler, P. N., Duranceau, C., Fain, M. J., Glenn, S., Hsei, B., James, A. A., Littlefield, C. L., Reinhardt, C. A., Strub, S., and Schneiderman, H. A. (1978). Regulative interactions between cells from different imaginal discs of *Drosophila melanogaster*. *Science 201*, 928-930.

Bull, A. (1966). *Bicaudal*, a genetic factor which affects polarity of the embryo in *Drosophila melanogaster*. *J. Exp. Zool. 161*, 211-241.

Clark, W. C., and Russell, M. A. (1977). The correlation of lysosomal activity and adult phenotype in a cell lethal mutant of *Drosophila*. *Develop. Biol. 57*, 160-173.

Deàk, I. (1978). Thoracic duplications in the mutant *wingless* of *Drosophila* and their effect on muscles and nerves. *Develop. Biol. 66*, 422-441.

Denell, R. E. (1973). Homoeosis in *Drosophila*. I. Complementation studies with revertants of *Nasobemia*. *Genetics* *75*, 279-297.

Denell, R. C., Hummels, K. R., Wakimoto, B. T., and Kaufman, T. C. (1980). Developmental studies of lethality associated with the Antennapedia Gene Complex in *Drosophila melanogaster*. *Develop. Biol.*, submitted.

Duncan, I. W., and Kaufman, T. C. (1975). Cytogenetic analysis of chromosome 3 in *Drosophila melanogaster*: Mapping of the proximal portion of the right arm. *Genetics 80*, 733-752.

French, V. (1976). Leg regeneration in the cockroach, *Blatella germanica*. II. Regeneration from a non-congruent tibial graft/host junction. *J. Embryol. exp. Morph. 35*, 267-301.

French, V., Bryant, P. J., and Bryant, S. V. (1976). Pattern regulation in epimorphic fields. *Science 193*, 969-981.

Fristrom, J. W. (1970). The developmental biology of *Drosophila*. *Ann. Rev. Genet. 4*, 325-346.

Garcia-Bellido, A. (1975a). Genetic control of wing disc development in *Drosophila*. *In* "Cell Patterning" *Ciba Found. Symp. 29*, pp. 161-182, Elsevier, Amsterdam.

Garcia-Bellido, A. (1975b). Genetic control of imaginal disc morphogenesis in *Drosophila*. *In* "Developmental Biology" ICN-UCLA Symposia (D. McMahon and C. F. Fox, eds.), Benjamin, London.

Garcia-Bellido, A., and Santamaria, P. (1972). Developmental analysis of the wing disc in the mutant *engrailed* of *Drosophila melanogaster*. *Genetics 72*, 87-104.

Garcia-Bellido, A., Ripoll, P., and Morata, G. (1973). Developmental compartmentalisation of the wing disc of *Drosophila*. *Nature New Biology 245*, 251-253.

Gierer, A., and Meinhardt, H. (1972). A theory of biological pattern formation. *Kybernetik 12*, 30-39.

Girton, J. R., Russell, M. A. (1980a). A clonal analysis of pattern duplication in a temperature sensitive lethal mutant of *Drosophila melanogaster*. *Develop. Biol.*, in press.

Girton, J. R., and Russell, M. A. (1980b). An analysis of compartmentalisation in pattern duplications induced by a cell-lethal mutation in *Drosophila*. In preparation.

Hayes, P. H., Girton, J. R., and Russell, M. A. (1979). Positional information and the Bithorax Complex. *J. Theor. Biol. 79*, 1-17.

Haynie, J. L., and Bryant, P. J. (1976). Intercalary regeneration in imaginal wing disc of *Drosophila melanogaster*. *Nature 259*, 659-662.

Illmensee, K. (1978). Drosophila chimeras and the problem of determination. *In* "Genetic Mosaics and Cell Differentiation" (W. J. Gehring, ed.), pp. 52-69. Springer-Verlag, Berlin.

Kaufman, T. C. (1978). Cytogenetic analysis of chromosome 3 in *Drosophila melanogaster*: isolation and characterization of four new alleles of the *proboscipedia* (*pb*) locus. *Genetics 90*, 579-596.

Kaufman, T. C., Lewis, R. A., and Wakimoto, B. T. (1980). Cytogenetic analysis of chromosome 3 in *Drosophila melanogaster*: the homoeotic gene complex in polytene chromosome interval 84A-B. *Genetics*, in press.

Lawrence, P. A. (1972). The development of spatial patterns in the integument of insects. *In* "Developmental Systems --Insects", Vol. *1* (S. Counce and C. H. Waddington, eds.), Academic Press, New York.

Lawrence, P. A., and Morata, G. (1976). Compartments in the wing of *Drosophila*: a study of the engrailed gene. *Develop. Biol. 50*, 321-337.

Lewis, E. B. (1963). Genes and developmental pathways. *Amer. Zool. 3*, 33-56.

Lewis, E. B. (1978). A gene complex controlling segmentation in *Drosophila. Nature 276*, 565-570.

Lewis, R. A., Kaufman, T. C., Denell, R. E., and Tallerico, P. (1980a). Genetic analysis of the Antennapedia Gene Complex (ANT-C) and adjacent chromosomal regions of *Drosophila melanogaster*. I. Polytene chromosome segments 84B-D. *Genetics*, in press.

Lewis, R. A., Wakimoto, B. T., Denell, R. E., and Kaufman, T. C. (1980b). Genetic analysis of the Antennapedia Gene Complex (ANT-C) and adjacent chromosomal regions of *Drosophila melanogaster*. II. Polytene chromosome segments 84A-84B1,2. *Genetics*, in press.

Morata, G., and Lawrence, P. A. (1977). Homoeotic genes, compartments and cell determination in *Drosophila. Nature 265*, 211-216.

Morata, G., and Ripoll, P. (1975). Minutes: mutants of *Drosophila* autonomously affecting cell division rate. *Develop. Biol. 42*, 211-221.

Nöthinger, R. (1972). The larval development of imaginal discs. *In* "The Biology of Imaginal Discs" (H. Ursprung and R. Nöthinger, eds.), pp. 1-34. Springer-Verlag, Berlin.

Nüsslein-Volhard, C. (1977). Genetic analysis of pattern formation in the embryo of *Drosophila melanogaster*-- characterisation of the maternal-effect mutant *bicaudal. Wilhelm Roux Archiv. 183*, 249-268.

Nüsslein-Volhard, C. (1979). Maternal effect mutations that alter the spatial coordinates of the embryo of *Drosophila melanogaster*. *In* "Determinants of Spatial Organisation" (Subtelny, S. and Konigsberg, I. R., eds.) *Symp. Soc. Develop. Biol. 37*, 185-211. Academic Press, New York.

Nüsslein-Volhard, C., Lohs-Schardin, M., Sander, K., and Cremer, C. (1980). A dorso-ventral shift of embryonic primordia in a new maternal-effect mutant of *Drosophila*. *Nature 283*, 474-476.

Ouweneel, W. J. (1976). Developmental genetics of homeosis. *Adv. Genet. 18*, 179-248.

Russell, M. A. (1974). Pattern formation in the imaginal discs of a temperature sensitive cell lethal mutant of *Drosophila melanogaster*. *Develop. Biol. 40*, 24-39.

Russell, M. A., Girton, J. R., and Morgan, K. (1977). Pattern formation in a ts cell lethal mutant of *Drosophila*: the range of phenotypes induced by larval heat treatments. *Wilhelm Roux Archiv. 183*, 41-59.

Sander, K. (1971). Pattern formation in longitudinal halves of leaf hopper eggs (Homoptera) and some remarks on the definition of "Embryonic regulation". *Wilhelm Roux Archiv. 167*, 336-352.

Schubiger, G., Moseley, R. C., and Wood, W. J. (1977). Interaction of different egg parts in determination of various body regions in *Drosophila melanogaster*. *Proc. Natl. Acad. Sci. U.S. 74*, 2050-2053.

Sharma, R., and Chopra, V. I. (1976). Effect of *wingless* (*wg*) mutation on wing and haltere development in *Drosophila melanogaster*. *Develop. Biol. 48*, 461-465.

Shearn, A. (1978). Mutational dissection of imaginal disc development. *In* "The Genetics and Biology of *Drosophila*", Vol. 2c (M. Ashburner and T. R. F. Wright, eds.). Academic Press, London.

Simpson, P., and Schneiderman, H. A. (1975). Isolation of temperature sensitive mutations blocking clone development in *D. melanogaster*, and the effects of a temperature sensitive cell lethal mutation on pattern formation in imaginal discs. *Wilhelm Roux Archiv. 178*, 247-275.

Steiner, E. (1976). Establishment of compartments in the developing leg imaginal discs of *Drosophila melanogaster*. *Wilhelm Roux Archiv. 180*, 9-30.

Tiong, S. Y., Girton, J. R., Hayes, P. H., and Russell, M. A. (1977). Effect of regeneration on compartment specificity of the bithorax mutant of *Drosophila melanogaster*. *Nature 268*, 435-437.

Tokunaga, C. (1978). Genetic mosaic studies of pattern
    formation in *Drosophila melanogaster*, with special
    reference to the prepattern hypothesis. *In* "Genetic
    Mosaics and Cell Determination" (W. J. Gehring, ed.),
    pp. 157-204. Springer-Verlag, Berlin.
Turing, A. (1952). The chemical basis of morphogenesis.
    Phil. Trans. Roy. Soc. B 237, 37-72.
Wakimoto, B. T., and Kaufman, T. C. (1980). Analysis of
    larval segmentation in lethal genotypes associated with
    the Antennapedia Gene Complex (ANT-C). *Develop. Biol.*,
    submitted.
Wilcox, M., and Smith, R. J. (1977). Regenerative interactions
    between *Drosophila* imaginal discs of different types.
    Develop. Biol. 60, 287-297.
Wolpert, L. (1969). Positional information and the spatial
    pattern of cellular differentiation. *J. Theoret. Biol.*
    25, 1-47.
Wolpert, L. (1971). Positional information and pattern
    formation. *Curr. Topics Develop. Biol. 6*, 183-224.
Wolpert, L., and Lewis, J. H. (1975). Towards a theory of
    development. *Fedn. Proc. Fedn. Am. Socs. exp. Biol.*
    34, 14-20.

CELL COMMUNICATION
AND PATTERN FORMATION
IN INSECTS

Stanley Caveney

Department of Zoology
University of Western Ontario
London, Ontario, Canada

I. INTRODUCTION

*"The cuticle has a 'pattern', since it varies in structure
and in coloration in different regions. The individual cells
in each region are 'determined' for the formation of different elements in this pattern. Certain elements in the pattern,
however, are capable of regeneration ... the cells retain
potencies which are normally suppressed." Wigglesworth, 1940a.*

The harmoney of proportion so characteristic of biological
structure is the direct consequence of spatial coordination
during growth. Yet precisely how cells interact during
development to generate spatial order remains a mystery. In
a pioneering study done 40 years ago, Wigglesworth (1940a)
showed that the uniform spacing of sensory bristles on the
larval cuticle of *Rhodnius* is determined by short-range interactions between the underlying epidermal cells that generate
the pattern. Existing bristles create radial zones of ex-
clusion around themselves that prevent new bristles from
forming in their proximity. Consequently, new bristles develop at points furthest away from bristles already established in the segment. Wigglesworth's data also led him to suggest that the number of cells intervening between established
bristles, rather than the absolute distance, was important in
determining where new bristles would form. In presenting a
model (discussed later) that explained the arrangement of
structures that show a regularity of spacing, Wigglesworth's

565

paper is a milestone in the development of our understanding of the concept of cell patterning.

Another aspect of the bristle pattern is its polarity. Bristles, as well as scales and hairs, are not only evenly spaced, but their orientation is under tissue control. Whereas spacing patterns result from local cellular interactions within the epidermis, polarity is the consequence of a wider-range order within the segment. Locke (1959) transplanted or rotated squares of larval integument in *Rhodnius* and noted the effect on the transverse ripple pattern in the adult. His analysis led him to propose that the orientation of the cuticle could be explained by the existence of a gradient of a cellular property that varied in the anteroposterior direction of a segment. The gradient slope defines cell polarity and the gradient contour level at which a cell finds itself in the gradient gives "positional information" (Wolpert, 1971) to the cell. This positional value may influence the type of cuticle the cell secretes (Stumpf, 1968).

Cell polarity and cell patterning both depend on cellular interactions in the epidermis during postembryonic development. The striking ability of the insect epidermis to replace missing pattern elements (intercalary regeneration) or to delete supernumerary ones (pattern relaxation) underscores the need for cell communication. When regions of the epidermis are killed by burning, or squares of integument are rotated or transposed, the normal pattern reappears through ensuing moults.

How does a cell perceive its position in the epidermis? When are the "positional signals" transmitted? The purpose of this essay is to consider briefly two plausible mechanisms that could explain the basics of cell patterning and pattern regeneration in the post-embryonic epidermis, and to consider when such mechanisms might operate. In support of the two mechanisms, I shall draw on evidence obtained from many insect species, but shall give specific examples from work done on metamorphosis in the beetle *Tenebrio molitor*. The adult cuticle in this beetle is highly patterned (Fig. 1).

The two mechanisms are (i) diffusional transfer, and (ii) contact-mediated transfer, of pattern information. These two mechanisms, in my opinion, do not represent alternatives, but rather two components of the complex way in which growing cells continually interact during development to generate the complex spatial patterns. A major goal for the future would be to identify the morphogens involved and to characterize their modes of transmission.

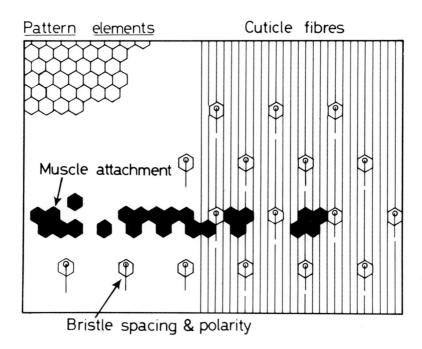

FIGURE 1. Pattern elements in the adult cuticle of the beetle Tenbrio. The epidermal cells produce a sculptured polygonal pattern in the epicuticle (upper left) and polarized fibres in the endocuticle (right). On this backdrop, a spaced pattern of bristles with characteristic polarity, and regions of muscle-attachment tendinous cells appear (black).

II. DIFFUSION-MEDIATED TRANSFER OF PATTERN INFORMATION

In models based on this mechanism, the cell-cell interaction depends on the passage of morphogenetically-active molecules between the cytoplasms of interconnected cells. Several authors (reviewed in Lawrence, 1970; 1973) have proposed that the segmental gradient is based on the transmission of a diffusible factor. Stumpf (1968), for example, suggested that a diffusible "morphogen" was maintained at two extreme levels at the anterior and posterior margins of the segment, and its concentration varied monotonically in the epidermal cells between these two levels. In its extreme form, this model suggests that disturbances in the gradient profile are smoothed out by morphogen diffusion. Transplanted epidermal cells have their positional values reset *in situ* according to the new morphogen concentrations.

Crick (1970) elaborated on this model. He concluded that, provided the diffusion constant for the morphogen was low (i.e. its MW $\leq$ 500), and a special mechanism existed to facilitate morphogen transfer between the cells, a concentration gradient could be set up over a millimetre within several hours. Hence diffusion is a feasible mechanism whereby a gradient could be set up in the insect segment. But subsequent analysis of computer-simulations based on this simple "source-sink" model proved it to be inadequate (Lawrence, Crick and Munro, 1972). Rather, a "homeostatic" diffusion gradient model in which cells try to retain their original concentration after transposition, gave better agreement with grafting experiments. According to this model, a cell's positional value may only be reset at certain times of development, and preliminary data suggested that this could be during cell division.

A diffusion-based signalling system would operate best if a special membrane channel existed at regions of cell contact. This would provide direct cytoplasmic continuity between the cells, allowing a precise gradient profile to be set up in the tissue. (A signalling mechanism that requires an extracellular step would be subject to random morphogen dilution in the body fluids). In insects, a specialized membrane junction - the B-type gap junction - may serve this function. The gap junction is present in most, if not all, non-excitable tissues. Research on insect epithelia show this junction to be permeable to inorganic ions and organic molecules up to MW 1400 and its permeability sensitive to cytosolic Ca^{++} levels (Rose and Loewenstein, 1976; Rose *et al.*, 1977). A channel of this rather general nature would be an economical way of transmitting the varied signals involved in setting up patterns at different times in development.

In the epidermis, the permeability of the junctional channels fluctuates prior to metamorphosis (Caveney, 1978), possibly in response to blood β-ecdysone levels (Caveney and Blennerhassett, 1980). If the junctional channels are involved in signal transmission, their presence, opening and closure would control the range over which a morphogen source influences spatial patterning. It is frustrating that a direct involvement of these low-resistance channels in development remains to be shown.

A tenet of the segmental gradient concept is that the intersegmental region is the site of a gradient discontinuity, these cells separating the bottom of one gradient from the top of that in the next segment (Locke, 1959). Each body segment behaves as an autonomous developmental field that does not interact with adjacent segments. Yet ionic coupling (Warner and Lawrence, 1973; Caveney, 1974) and gap junctions (Lawrence and Green, 1975) are continuous across the segment boundary. At first glance, this would appear to be a serious blow to a signalling mechanism dependent on diffusion for signal transmission. However, only a transient closure of the boundary junctions during the moult cycle may be required at the time when the gradient is set up. Furthermore, certain models for patterning (Meinhardt and Gierer, 1974) generate periodic structure with continuous coupling between adjacent developmental fields. Slight changes in cell shape at the segment boundary may suffice to reinforce its barrier function (Sheridan, 1973).

Diffusion could also occur across the extracellular space. Bhaskaran and Röller (1980) have confirmed the finding of Piepho and Hintze-Podufal (1971) that the posterior margin of the segment in *Galleria* is the source of a diffusible morphogen that influences both scale pattern and polarity. The insertion of a nucleopore filter (pore size 0.03 μm) between implanted posterior margin and overlying host epidermis failed to prevent the induction of scale pattern and polarity changes in the host epidermis.

Diffusion is an attractive candidate for the transmission of positional signals. This is especially true for very short-range interactions between cells, as diffusion is rapid over short distances but slow over long distances.

III. SPACING PATTERNS - A CASE FOR DIFFUSION

The non-random array of bristles (Wigglesworth, 1940a), scales (Nardi and Kafatos, 1976a), and other "organules" (reviewed in Lawrence, 1973) on the cuticle are examples of "spacing patterns" (Wolpert, 1971). The distance between these structures is typically 20 to 200 micrometres (about 2 to 20 cell diameters). Several models have been proposed that would generate the two-dimensional spacing patterns of the bristle-type in the developing epidermis. All depend on the spread of inhibitors and/or activators over several cell diameters in the plane of the epidermis. Wigglesworth (1940a) originally suggested that existant bristles may deplete the surrounding epidermis of a diffusible activator of bristle formation produced by the epidermal cells. Only epidermal cells remote from existing bristles differentiate into new bristles as the insect grows resulting in a non-random spacing pattern. In principle, the same result could be obtained by the spread of a bristle inhibitor from existing bristles. An elegant "lateral inhibition" model (Meinhardt and Gierer, 1974) generates bristle spacing patterns due to short-range activation of bristle-forming sites and long-range inhibition of other sites. In this model, the diffusible activator stimulates both its own production and that of a diffusible inhibitor which in turn inhibits activator production. The activator diffuses slowly, the inhibitor rapidly, away from the source. The steady state results in a sharp activator peak and broad inhibitor peak centered around the same point. The spacing of the peaks depends on the activator range. Given realistic diffusion constants for molecules in the MW range 300-500, stable inhibitory fields of the range appropriate to bristle-type patterns could be set in less than an hour (see Crick, 1970).

The generally radial nature of the inhibitory field implies a diffusion process. But is the diffusion through the extracellular space, or directly from cell interior to cell interior? I favour the cell-to-cell route.

The insect epidermis is typically a near-hexagonal array of isodiametric cells. Electrophysiologically, it is an "isodiffusion network" of interconnected cells (Caveney, 1974), that does not distort radial spread away from a point source in the epidermis (at least of ions). Wigglesworth (1940a) showed that it was not the absolute separation between existing bristles that determined where new bristles would appear during development. Rather it was the *effective* distance, as measured by the number of cells intervening between existing bristles, that was important. The number of new bristles that appeared in a moult cycle depended on the number of cells between existing bristles at the start of the moult cycle. If the body wall was stretched to stimulate excessive cell proliferation - to maintain a constant cell density - more than normal extra bristles subsequently appeared to keep the bristle: epidermal cell ratio constant.

This compensatory ability of the epidermis can be studied in another way. When transposed or rotated epidermis is examined after the subsequent moult, the cell density in the graft area is generally higher than that in the surrounding host tissue (Locke, 1959; Lawrence, Crick and Munro, 1972; Nardi and Kafatos, 1976a,b; Nübler-Jung, 1977). What effect does this have on bristle density? Does the number of cells intervening between bristles remain constant irrespective of cell density?

The ventral integument in the adult abdomen of *Tenebrio* is covered with spaced pit glands (Wigglesworth, 1948b). Each gland has a single bristle at its anterior margin. The unspecialized epidermal cells between the pit glands produce a polygonally sculptured epicuticle, each polygon reflecting the extent of the cell that secreted it (Fig. 2A). Consequently, epidermal cell and bristle densities may be obtained from cuticle preparations. Since the sites at which adult bristles appear in the epidermis are determined immediately after epidermal proliferation in the prepupa, squares of early prepupal integument were rotated or transposed. The animals were allowed to pass through metamorphosis, and the cell and bristle density in the central graft area compared with that in the contralateral host region. Figure 2B shows that a 25% increase in cell density results in a 72% increase in bristle density. It follows that as cell density increases so the number of cells intervening between bristles decreases. According to the data in Fig. 2B, the radius of influence of each bristle drops from 32 μm (equivalent to 64 epidermal cells per bristle) to 24.5 μm (47 cells per bristle) as cell density climbs from 20,000 cells/mm^2 to 25,000 cells/mm^2. This does not agree with a model in which the cells act as repeater stations to maintain a constant ratio of bristle density to cell density. (If the cell number per bristle remains constant as cell density increases, the radius of influence of each bristle would only drop to 28.5 μm.)

A better fit is obtained if a diffusion mechanism is considered, in which the major barrier to diffusion is the junctional channels connecting the cell interiors. I modelled this with an electrical analogue. A hexagonally packed monolayer of cells is assigned a specific junctional resistance to ion flow and a negligible cytoplasmic resistance (Caveney and Blennerhassett, 1980). The membrane potential of the source cell is raised to some fixed level above that of its neighbours. Since the cells are ionically coupled, this potential change will have an electrotonic effect on the surrounding cells. The effect is calculated for different cell densities. The important finding was that by arbitrarily setting a threshold of influence equal to the electrotonic effect at 32 μm from the source cell at a density of 20,000 cells/mm^2, this threshold is seen at 19 μm away from the source cell at a density of 30,000 cells/mm^2. By increasing the contribution of the cytoplasm to the total resistance to ion flow in epidermis, the best fit with the experimental data was obtained when the junctional component comprised 80% of the total intercellular pathway resistance at 20,000 cells/mm^2 (Fig. 2B). This rather simple model is satisfying as it explains the non-proportional increase in bristle density as cell density rises, and emphasizes the membrane junction as the major barrier to diffusion. As there is no reason to presume that cell density should affect diffusion distance if the inhibitor spread extracellularly (although a closed

extracellular route using the lateral intercellular spaces
between the cells might be an exception) an intercellular
transmission route is an attractive possibility.

   If the epidermis consisted of anisometric cells, or cells
with anisometric junctions, the bristles would be spaced
further apart in one dimension than in another; butterfly
wing spots would be oval rather than round (see Nijhout,
1978). Since electrical fields are quite widespread in
developing systems (Jaffe and Nuccitelli, 1977), the possibility of ionized morphogen electrophoresis in the epidermal
plane cannot be excluded.

   *FIGURE 2(A). Micrograph of the cuticle surface of the
adult beetle. The polygon of cuticle secreted by each
epidermal cell is clearly visible, as are the dispersed pit
gland apertures (p) and their associated bristles (b). The
bristles point towards the posterior margin of the segment.
Scale bar: 20 μm.*

   *FIGURE 2(B). Effect of increased cell density in the
prepupa on bristle density in the adult integument. The
normal cell density in the adult sternite is about 20,000
cells/mm². When pieces of integument are transposed in the
late larva, cell density in the grafted area increases to
over 25,000 cells/mm². Under these conditions, bristle
density jumps from 308 to 530 bristles/mm² (means ± S.D. are
shown). Dashed line: predicted increase in bristle density
if bristle density:cell density remains constant as cell
density increases. Solid line: relationship predicted by
an electrical model in which the range of influence of a
bristle site is influenced by the resistance of the
intercellular pathway. The specific junctional resistance of
a hexagonal array of cells was set at 0.21 Ω cm² and
cytoplasmic resistivity set at 65 Ω cm (Caveney and
Blennerhassett, 1980). As the cell density increases, the
proportional contribution of the resistance of the membrane
junctions to total pathway resistance rises, while that of
the cytoplasm drops.*

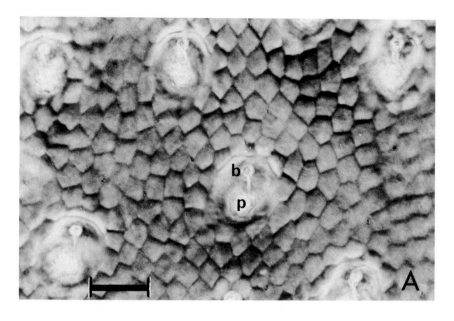

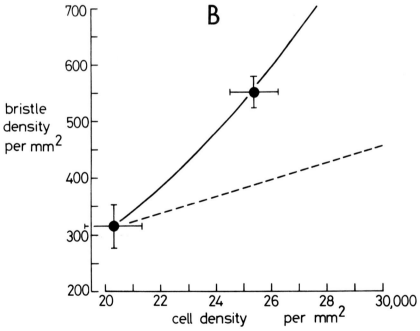

FIGURES 2(A) and (B).

IV. CONTACT-MEDIATED TRANSFER OF PATTERN INFORMATION

Morphogenetic information in the insect epidermis appears to be encoded in fixed cell surface properties (Nardi and Kafatos, 1976a,b; Nübler-Jung, 1977,1979). According to these authors, pattern information is communicated through membrane interactions between nearby cells, and no physical transfer of molecules may be involved. The epidermal gradient is visualized as a gradient in differential adhesiveness between cells of different axial regions in the segment or appendage. This concept explains features of epidermal transposition experiments not predicted by existing diffusion models, namely the final shape and increased cell density in the graft area.

Impetus for models of this type came when a trilogy of short papers (Bohn, 1974; Lawrence, 1974; Nübler-Jung, 1974) revealed that cell migration and cell sorting may be an integral component of pattern regulation in the epidermis. Grafts rotated through 90° "de-rotated" to regain continuity with host cells of the appropriate gradient levels. This cell sorting suggests differential surface affinities along the segment axis.

The most rigorous analysis of the consequences of selective cell adhesion in the epidermis appears in Nardi and Kafatos (1976b). Grafting experiments in the pupal wing of *Manduca* showed that scale polarity could be altered by using transposition of epidermis along the proximo-distal axis of the wing, or by graft rotation (Nardi and Kafatos, 1976a). The results implied a morphogenetic gradient along the wing axis. However, grafts showed an extreme non-equivalence. Epidermal squares transposed distally formed "rosettes" in which scales on the graft pointed outwards, but squares transposed proximally displayed relatively normal scale orientation. Grafts rotated through 90° in either a clockwise or anticlockwise direction showed similar asymmetry in their effect on scale polarity. Their experimental findings could be suitably explained by a model in which cellular adhesiveness is greatest in proximal wing regions, the gradient in adhesiveness decaying non-linearly towards the wing tip. The adhesiveness differential between host and graft tissue will determine the extent of cell rearrangement in the graft tissue, and consequently the polarity of the scales. Nardi and Kafatos noted that by grafting in the early pupa, only scale polarity could be altered. Pattern elements such as scale morphology and colors were fixed by this time.

Nübler-Jung's (1977,1979) work on the abdominal segment of *Dysdercus* reinforce the relevance of cell affinity

relationships in our attempt to understand cell patterning in
the segment. In her view, intercalary regeneration of missing
pattern elements, and the observed de-rotation of certain
grafts, result from a mismatch of cell adhesive properties
at a graft-host boundary. Within the segment, the juxtaposition of two cell regions with different adhesive
strengths would lead, through cell division, to the intercalation of the missing cell adhesion states. Pattern regulation in this model is epimorphic, i.e. it requires cell
division. Polarity changes however, may not require cell
division. They result when cells sort out to maximize their
adhesive relations (Nardi and Kafatos, 1976a).

Differential adhesion may also serve to stabilize the
boundaries between adjacent segments (and compartments in
general) during normal development. The segment boundary is
a straight line because the cells on either side of it have
stronger affinities to cells in their own segment than to
each other (Nübler-Jung, 1979).

V. MUSCLE PATTERNING IN THE SEGMENT

Clearly, surface properties play an important role in
cell patterning in the epidermis. Can the segmental
gradient be used to govern the overall, three-dimensional
form, of the insect segment? That is, can tissues that interact with the epidermis - such as muscles and tracheae -
utilize epidermal positional information? At metamorphosis,
the spatial relationship between these tissues may change
dramatically. Wolpert's (1977) thesis that the spatial
control of the interactions between tissues can be accounted
for by three processes - cell movement, cell contact and
gradients of positional information - can be tested on the
development of muscle patterning in the segment.

In the beetle pupa, certain muscles migrate relative to
the overlying epidermis at metamorphosis - a process we have
termed "myokinetic movement" (Williams and Caveney, 1980a).
As a result, the attachment sites of the adult muscles are
considerably displaced when compared to the attachment sites
of the larval muscles from which they are derived. Does
the epidermal gradient govern the position at which new
muscle attachments form? To answer this question, we preformed grafts on the larva that have predictable results
in terms of the disruptions they produce in the topography of
the gradient (Williams and Caveney, 1980b). The area chosen
was that into which a muscle migrated during metamorphosis.
Changes in the attachment site(s) of the muscle were compared
with distortions in the adult cuticle pattern that result

from such grafts (Caveney, 1973). An anterior-posterior exchange of two adjacent rectangles, for example, generates a valley and a peak in the segmental gradient (Fig. 3A). In a contour map, these are seen as two whorls (Fig. 3B). Furthermore, three horizontal levels of certain contour values are created where normally only one exists. A muscle, migrating posteriorly into the graft area and seeking its prospective attachment site, no longer has a single site, but three potential sites to choose from. The various muscle patterns that resulted from this grafting experiment could be adequately explained by this model. The most common result seen was an anterior displacement of the muscle insertion (Fig. 3C) although attachment at more than one level, and muscle fibres spanning between two nearby insertion points was commonly seen (Fig. 3D). Grafts involving 90° or 180° rotation of epidermal squares resulted in distortions in the muscle pattern also compatible with the gradient model (Williams and Caveney, 1980b). The determination of muscle insertion sites is regulative. The adult muscle pattern was most perturbed when grafts were performed late in the prepupal stage; grafts done earlier resulted in a less pronounced disruption in the muscle pattern. Relaxation in graft-induced changes in the topography of the epidermal gradient is known to occur at this time (Caveney, 1973).

FIGURE 3. Gradient control of muscle distribution in the segment. (A) Schematic of the gradient concept with arbitrarily chosen boundary contour values 0 and 12. Contour 6 (thick line) is a prospective site of muscle attachment. An anterior ⟷ posterior exchange (A⟷P) of adjacent integument squares generates a valley and a peak in the gradient. (B) Top view of the contour map in (A) after some relaxation of the contour pattern. Note the whorls corresponding to the anterior valley and the posterior peak which are separated by a region of reversed gradient slope. Level 6 now appears at three axial levels in the segment. (C) Adult cuticle pattern resulting from an A⟷P exchange. The orientation and polarity of the cuticle fibres is shown and the region of reversed slope is marked by the arrowheads pointing anteriorly. Level 6 is shown as a thick dashed line. In this experiment, muscle attached to the most anterior level 6 only (black dots). (D) Polarized light micrograph of a segment whole mount after an A⟷P exchange. In this case, muscle attached to all three levels of contour 6 generated by the graft. The left-hand side of the segment is the operated side, the right-hand side of the segment serves as a control. (After Williams and Caveney, 1980b).

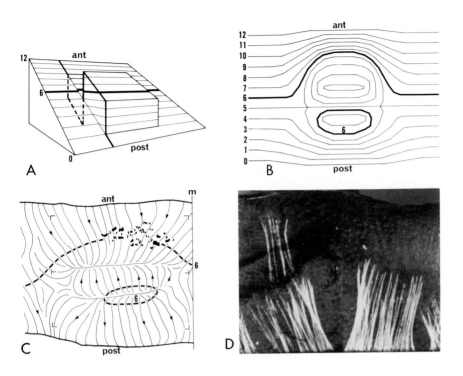

FIGURE 3.

In order to position muscles correctly in the segment, the
muscle and epidermis must communicate with each other. The
site of muscle attachment in the adult could well be determined by differential adhesiveness between the developing
muscle and different regions of the segmental epidermis.
Myoblasts in the degenerating larval muscles may extend processes at random until they establish contact with prospective
tendinous epidermal cells. In addition, graded changes in
epidermal surface adhesiveness may guide myoblast migration
to these sites. (In principle, myoblasts could use the epidermal basal lamina to seek prospective attachment sites.
Since the pupal basal lamina is loose and poorly differentiated, and is thought to be a haemocyte secretion (Wigglesworth, 1979), its regional specificity in the segment must
be suspect).
    The epidermis thus provides a spatial map to aid muscle

relocation. But the process is not entirely one-sided; the firm attachment of mature muscle to the integument involves specialized epidermal "tendon" cells. How a myoblast-epidermal cell interaction triggers epidermal specialization is a problem for the future. It may be a rare example of induction in insects.

VI. WHEN ARE POSITIONAL SIGNALS TRANSMITTED THROUGH THE EPIDERMIS

Future success in biochemically identifying the morpho-genetic factors involved in spatial patterning will depend on a precise knowledge of when these factors are present in the segment. The signalling of information controlling linear and spacing patterns (and the ability of cells to respond to these signals) is probably periodic. A safe assumption would be that specific signals are transmitted once in each moult cycle, although the signals controlling different pattern elements may appear at different times. In order to control the extent of epidermal proliferation during the moult cycle (Lawrence, Crick and Munro, 1972) the slope of the segmental gradient would have to be set up before proliferation; but, in Hemiptera, the bristle-type spacing mechanism operates when proliferation is complete (Wigglesworth, 1940a) or nearing completion (Lawrence, 1966, 1973).

The situation may be similar in holometabolous insects. Signalling within the epidermis, or our ability to detect it, appears to be restricted to the early metamorphic period. In *Galleria,* the regional pattern elements on the abdomen are fixed by the prepupal stage (Stumpf, 1968). In the wing of *Manduca,* the colour pattern and scale morphology is fixed before pupation (Nardi and Kafatos, 1976a); scale polarity along is influenced by pupal graft transpositions in the early pupa. The colour patterns on the wings of other lepidoptera are largely determined by pupation, although some pattern elements are not fixed until 2 days after pupation (reviewed in Nijhout, 1978). In the abdomen of *Galleria* an unidentified diffusible morphogen, produced by the posterior margin of the segment, apparently to regulate scale morphol-ogy and polarity, is produced during the prepupal stage. The epidermis loses its sensitivity to this factor soon after pupation (Bhaskaran and Röller, 1980). When abdominal epi-dermis is rotated during segment metamorphosis in *Tenebrio,* the disturbed contours of the epidermal gradient are seen in the adult as distorted cuticle fibre orientation and bristle polarity (Caveney, 1973). By varying the time of graft

rotation from late-larval to early-pupal, it can be shown
that pattern regulation is limited to a 48-hr period ending
about 72 hr before pupation. This period coincides with the
pre-metamorphic phase of epidermal proliferation in this
insect. I suggested that the ability of tissue to change its
polarity may depend on cell division (Caveney, 1973). However, Nardi and Kafatos (1976a) suggest that pattern regulation in the pupal wing of *Manduca* may not require proliferative cell divisions. They argue that changes in scale
polarity after graft transposition occur without detectable
proliferative divisions in the wing (wound-induced divisions
along the graft margin and differentiative divisions of
scale cells do occur, however). The replacement of missing
pattern elements (intercalary regeneration - see Bryant in
this volume) depends on cell division.

Pattern relaxation at metamorphosis also appears to be
restricted to periods when the epidermis is detached from
both the cuticle and the supportive basal lamina (Nardi and
Kafatos, 1976b; Williams and Caveney, 1980). This supports
the idea expressed earlier that pattern relaxation requires
cell motility to allow the cells to sort out according to
their adhesive properties.

Metamorphosis is a particularly dramatic example of cell
patterning. The information available suggests that the
adult pattern is specified in the prepupa, and the covert
pattern interpreted in the pupa. The pupal epidermis serves
as a mould bearing a positional map that is used by other
tissues. Whatever the mechanisms involved in setting up this
map, "a plausible and parsimonious interpretation of grafting
results is that by the pupal stage the ... gradient is in
fact a gradient of cellular adhesiveness, rather than a
gradient of diffusible morphogen" (Nardi and Kafatos, 1976b).
Diffusible morphogens, if involved in both the segmental
gradient and spacing patterns, would, in this interpretation,
cease to exist after the prepupal stage.

Within the pupal epidermis, an adhesiveness gradient
would serve to maintain compartment boundaries and to
"fine tune" the orientation of structures such as bristles
and scales during their differentiation. More importantly,
it could control the distribution of many internal tissues.
I have already mentioned the evidence favouring epidermal
involvement in the relocation of the developing adult muscles
in *Tenebrio*. The epidermis, however, is also capable of
directing the migrating tracheal cells by tugging at them
with cytoplasmic processes as long as 125 μm (Wigglesworth,
1959g); in the pupal wing, new tracheae may be attracted up
vacant wing lacunae (Whitten, 1962) by gradients of epidermal
cell-tracheal cell surface adhesiveness. Sensory neurons in

the pupal wing and elsewhere on the body surface might utilize the epidermal surface in their centripetal migration to the CNS (Nardi and Kafatos, 1976b), although it is equally likely that pioneer axons already present in the undifferentiated epidermis may be used instead for this purpose (see Edwards (1977) and in this volume).

VII. CONCLUSIONS

Much has been learnt about the control of cell patterning in the insect segment and appendage since Wigglesworth's (1940a) pioneering paper. Yet our knowledge is derived mainly from experimental surgery and our designation of a cell's position in a developing field remains an arbitrarily chosen numerical analogue. We need basic details as to when the primary segmental field is set up, when it is reaffirmed during development, the route through which positional signals pass in the epidermis, the biochemistry of the illusive molecules involved, and how the segmental gradient is expressed on the cell surface. This is a formidable challenge for the future! The two model mechanisms presented here use features of cellular interaction currently under intense investigation; in conjunction they may be able to generate the spatial order of the segment. But on conception of how cells communicate positional information may be far removed from reality.

REFERENCES

Bhaskaran, G. and Röller, H. (1980). Segmental gradients specifying polarity and pattern in the waxmoth, *Galleria mellonella:* The posterior margin as a source of a diffusible morphogen. *Devl. Biol.* (in press).

Bohn, H. (1974). Pattern reconstitution in abdominal segment of *Leucophaea maderae* (Blaffaria). *Nature (Lond.) 248,* 608-609.

Caveney, S. (1973). Stability of polarity in the epidermis of a beetle, *Tenebrio molitor* L. *Devl. Biol. 30,* 321-335.

Caveney, S. (1974). Intercellular communication in a positional field: Movement of small ions between insect epidermal cells. *Devl. Biol. 40,* 311-322.

Caveney, S. (1978). Intercellular communication in insect development is hormonally controlled. *Science 199,* 192-195.

Caveney, S. and Blennerhassett, M.G. (1980). Elevation of ionic conductance between insect epidermal cells by β-ecdysone *in vitro*. *J. Insect Physiol.* (in press).

Crick, F.H.C. (1970). Diffusion in embryogenesis. *Nature (Lond.) 225*, 420-422.

Edwards, J.S. (1977). Pathfinding by arthropod sensory nerves. *In* "Identified Neurons and Behaviour of Arthropods" (G. Hoyle, ed.), pp. 483-493, Plenum, New York.

Jaffe, L.F. and Nuccitelli, R. (1977). Electrical controls of development. *Ann. Rev. Biophys. Bioeng. 6*, 445-476.

Lawrence, P.A. (1966). Development and determination of hairs and bristles in the milkweed bug, *Oncopeltus fasciatus* (Lygaeidae, Hemiptera). *J. Cell Sci. 1*, 475-498.

Lawrence, P.A. (1970). Polarity and patterns in the post-embryonic development of insects. *Adv. Insect Physiol. 7*, 197-266.

Lawrence, P.A. (1973). The development of spatial patterns in the integument of insects. *In* "Developmental Systems - Insects" (S.J. Counce and C.H. Waddington, eds.), Vol. 2, pp. 157-209, Academic Press, New York.

Lawrence, P.A. (1974). Cell movement during pattern regulation in *Oncopeltus*. *Nature (Lond.) 248*, 609-610.

Lawrence, P.A., Crick, F.H.C. and Munro, M. (1972). A gradient of positional information in an insect, *Rhodnius*. *J. Cell Sci. 11*, 815-853.

Lawrence, P.A. and Green, S.M. (1975). The anatomy of a compartment border. The intersegmental boundary in *Oncopeltus*. *J. Cell Biol. 65*, 373-382.

Locke, M. (1959). The cuticular pattern in an insect, *Rhodnius prolixus* Stal. *J. Exp. Biol. 36*, 459-477.

Meinhardt, H. and Gierer, A. (1974). Applications of a theory of biological pattern formation based on lateral inhibition. *J. Cell Sci. 15*, 321-346.

Nardi, J.B. and Kafatos, F.C. (1976a). Polarity and gradients in lepidopteran wing epidermis. I. Changes in graft polarity, form, and cell density accompanying transpositions and reorientations. *J. Embryol. Exp. Biol. 36*, 469-487.

Nardi, J.B. and Kafatos, F.C. (1976b). Polarity and gradients in lepidopteran wing epidermis. II. The differential adhesiveness model: gradient of a non-diffusible cell surface parameter. *J. Embryol. Exp. Biol. 36*, 489-512.

Nijhout, H.F. (1978). Wing pattern formation in lepidotera: A model. *J. Exp. Zool. 206*, 119-136.

Nübler-Jung, K. (1974). Cell migration during pattern reconstitution in the insect segment (*Dysdercus intermedius* Dist., Heteroptera). *Nature (Lond.) 248*, 610-611.

Nübler-Jung, K. (1977). Pattern stability in the insect
    segment. I. Pattern reconstitution by intercalary
    regeneration and cell sorting in *Dysdercus intermedius*
    Dist. *Wilhelm Roux Arch. 183,* 17-40.
Nübler-Jung, K. (1979). Pattern stability in the insect
    segment. II. The intersegmental region. *Wilhelm Roux
    Arch. 186,* 211-233.
Piepho, H. and Hintze-Podufal, C. (1971). Zur Polarität des
    Insekten segments. *Biol. Zbl. 90,* 419-431.
Rose, B. and Loewenstein, W.R. (1976). Permeability of a cell
    junction and the local cytoplasmic free ionized calcium
    concentration: A study with aequarin. *J. Membrane Biol.
    28,* 87-119.
Rose, B., Simpson, I. and Loewenstein, W.R. (1977). Calcium
    ion produces graded changes in permeability of membrane
    channels in cell junction. *Nature (Lond.) 267,* 625-627.
Sheridan, J.D. (1973). Functional evaluation of low resistance
    junctions: Influence of cell shape and size. *Amer. Zool.
    13,* 1119-1128.
Stumpf, H.F. (1968). Further studies on gradient-dependent
    diversification in the pupal cuticle of *Galleria
    mellonella. J. Exp. Biol. 49,* 49-60.
Warner, A.E., and Lawrence, P.A. (1973). Electrical coupling
    across developmental boundaries in insect epidermis.
    Nature (Lond.) 245, 47-49.
Wigglesworth, V.B. (1940a). Local and general factors in the
    development of "pattern" in *Rhodnius prolixus* (Hemiptera).
    J. Exp. Biol. 17, 180-200.
Wigglesworth, V.B. (1948b). The structure and deposition of
    the cuticle in the adult mealworm, *Tenebrio molitor* L.
    (Coleoptera). *Quart. J. microsc. Sci. 89,* 197-217.
Wigglesworth, V.B. (1979). Secretory activities of plasmato-
    cytes and oenocytoids during the moulting cycle in an
    insect (*Rhodnius*). *Tissue and Cell 11,* 69-78.
Williams, G.J.A. and Caveney, S. (1980a). Changing muscle
    patterns in a segmental epidermal field. *J. Embryol.
    Exp. Morph.* (in press).
Williams, G.J.A. and Caveney, S. (1980b). A gradient of
    morphogenetic information involved in muscle patterning.
    J. Embryol. Exp. Biol. (in press).
Wolpert, L. (1971). Positional information and pattern
    formation. *Curr. Top. Devl. Biol. 6,* 183-224.
Wolpert, L. (1977). The development of pattern and form in
    animals. *In* "Carolina Biology Readers" (J.J. Head, ed.),
    Vol. 51, pp. 1-16, Carolina Biological Supply Company.
    Burlington, North Carolina.

PHEROMONES AND THEIR CHEMISTRY

Wendell L. Roelofs

Department of Entomology
New York State Agricultural Experiment Station
Geneva, New York

"Although it is not the purpose of physiology to furnish directly the means of controlling insect pests, yet the rational application of measures of control - whether these be insecticides of one sort or another, or artificial interferences with the insect's environment - is often dependent on a knowledge of the physiology of the insect in question."
Wigglesworth 1939. *The Principles of Insect Physiology*, preface.

I. INTRODUCTION

The wisdom of the above statement has been particularly evident in research associated with insect pheromones. The lure of utilizing insect pheromones as behavior-modifying chemicals for the manipulation of insect pest populations has drawn many researchers and considerable financial support to this area. In the past two decades there has been a flurry of pheromone-related activities, which were spurred on by agencies interested in new methods of insect control, as well as by the development of instruments and techniques needed in working with minute quantities of communicative chemicals. Great advances were made in defining the chemistry of pheromones in various insect Orders, and research expanded to include associated studies of neurophysiology, biochemistry, ethology, and so forth. However, as Wigglesworth predicted, the application of pheromones in insect control was not always rational because of a huge lack of knowledge about the physiology and behavior of the insect in question. By 1972 many pheromone structures had been identified, but Kennedy (1972) pointed out that "the expertise and pertinacity of the organic chemist only showed up the emptiness on the behavioral side". He stated that the one thing that "sex attractants" have not been shown to do is attract. It became obvious that an understanding of pheromone systems and their manipulation for insect control were dependent on in-depth physiological and behavioral studies of the insects in conjunction with the chemical analyses.

The present essay will concentrate on several specific areas of research that involve in-depth studies of insects related to the practical use of pheromones for insect control. There will be no attempt to review the hundreds of identified chemicals used by insects as sex, aggregation, alarm, or trail pheromones, since this has been done many times in the past decade (for example see Brand *et al.*, 1979; Ritter, 1979; Roelofs, 1978a; Henrick, 1977; Shorey and McKelvey, 1977; Roelofs and Cardé, 1977; Shorey, 1976; Baker and Evans, 1975; Mayer and McLaughlin, 1975; Birch, 1974; MacConnell and

Silverstein, 1973; Jacobson, 1972; Law and Regnier, 1971; Beroza, 1971; and Eiter, 1970). It is hoped that the discussion of several select topics will help to convey the enthusiasm present in insect pheromone research today, and that it will show some of the many interesting, unanswered questions to be tackled in the future.

II. THE NATURE OF A SEX PHEROMONE

A. *Definition*

Throughout the past decade efforts in the field of chemical communication have made it painfully clear that it is extremely difficult to describe accurately the chemical signals used by any particular set of individuals in their own unique environments and physiological states. General classifications have been made, however, to categorize some of the types of chemical interactions between individuals. The chemical signals, or semiochemicals (Law and Regnier, 1971), used for intraspecific communication are called pheromones (Karlson and Butenandt, 1959; Karlson and Lüscher, 1959). This broad heading was divided into two categories by Wilson (1963).

He proposed that "primers" be used for pheromones that do not elicit a direct behavioral response, but rather induce long-term changes in the physiology of the receiving animal. The most researched insect primer pheromones are those that are agents of caste determination in social insects, such as the "queen substance", 9-oxodec-(*E*)-2-enoic acid, which suppresses the ovarian development of honey bee workers and their proclivity to construct queen cells.

The second category was named "releasers" for pheromones that trigger an almost immediate behavioral response in the receiving animal. Shorey (1976) further defined "releasers" to be pheromones that "stimulate specific chemosensory organs to relay action-potential-coded messages via their sensory neurons to the central nervous system. There the messages modify (increase or reduce) the likelihood that messages will leave the central nervous system via specific motor neurons, causing the animal to respond in a correspondingly specific way." Releaser pheromones include those involved in mating, alarm, recruitment, aggregation, flight, food exchange, territorial display, raiding, building initiation, marking, and so forth. This chapter will discuss specifically those involved in the mating process.

According to the original definition and modifications of it (Kalmus, 1965; Shorey, 1976), a pheromone is a chemical mixture that is released to the exterior by an organism and that induces a response by another individual of the same species. The pheromone could be a mixture of chemicals that are (a) produced *de novo*, (b) metabolic products of ingested substances or of symbionts such as intestinal bacteria, or (c) acquired intact from materials in the environment. It could be argued that chemicals produced by host material and released by some action of the insect also are part of the pheromone mixture (Silverstein, 1977). An example of that would be the tree-produced chemical, α-cubebene as a component of the smaller European elm bark beetle pheromone (Pearce *et al.*, 1975). One of the major problems, particularly in efforts to decode pheromones for insect control, is the identification of all compounds used in any particular pheromone system.

Another major problem discussed at length by Kennedy (1978) in defining pheromones is that usually the insects' behavior is classified indirectly by teleological, blanket terms for the behavioral effects of chemicals. This discounts the fact that the observed behavior results from an integration of multiple inputs and should be classified directly by locomotor reactions to odors (Kennedy, 1977a; 1978). This problem also is critical in efforts to use pheromones for insect control.

B. *The Chemical Composition of a Pheromone*

Generally, the major pheromone components are pooled from a number of insects for identification. This could involve extracts from a million female moths, such as in the outstanding pioneering work on the first insect pheromone identified by Butenandt and coworkers (1959). In a 30-year effort they identified (E,Z)-10,12-hexadecadien-1-ol (I)

as the pheromone for the domestic silkworm, *Bombyx mori*. Research on the cotton boll weevil, *Anthonomus grandis*, involved over 4 million weevils and 54.7 kg of fecal material before 4 pheromone components (II–V) were identified. However, the development of highly-sensitive instruments and microtechniques have made it possible to identify some pheromones with only hundreds of individuals instead of thousands.

Tissue extraction is not always the best method for obtaining the pheromone, however, because closely related analogs of the pheromone components are frequently present in these extracts and, in some cases, pheromone components are not stored in detectable quantities. The presence of additional related compounds complicates the study because it is difficult to determine if any of them function in the pheromone system, and, in some cases, their presence negatively affects the behavioral repertoire of responses to the pheromone.

These problems can often be circumvented by collection of the pheromone after its emission from the insect. A variety of techniques have been used for this purpose, such as cryogenic traps or absorption traps (see reviews Brand *et al.*, 1979; Roelofs, 1978). A notable example involving collection of air-borne pheromone components on a solid-phase absorbent, Porapak Q, is in that of the identification of three active components of the smaller European elm bark beetle (VI–VIII) (Pearce *et al.*, 1975). In this study

batches of 4000–7000 virgin females were aerated continuously for 7 days, after which the trapped volatiles were found to contain the two beetle-produced components (VI, VII) and the host-produced component (VIII).

Regardless of the collection method, the active chemical must be isolated and identified. With many lepidopteran species, the electroantennogram technique (Schneider, 1974) can be used to detect the major pheromone components in fractionated extract or effluvium (Roelofs, 1977, 1979). It also can be used as a specialized analytical instrument for predicting the chain length, functional group, and the position and configuration of double bonds for the major pheromone component of many lepidopterous species. The first pheromone structure determined by this method was (*E,E*)-8,10-dodecadien-1-ol (IX) for the codling moth (*Cydia pomonella*) (Roelofs *et al.*, 1971b).

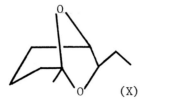

(IX)

Chemicals can be detected and monitored by various methods, but it is essential that a suitable bioassay be used to determine which ones function as pheromone components. The development of a suitable bioassay (Young and Silverstein, 1975; Kennedy, 1977b; Cardé, 1979) for each species is a critical, but sometimes neglected, part of research programs. A number of incorrect pheromone identifications in the literature can be traced to inadequate biological testing of the isolated materials. Many bioassays utilize a certain "key" response to assess activity, but ultimately the complete pheromone blend can only be tested by an assay system that allows the insect to undergo the entire repertoire of behavioral responses (discussed later in this chapter).

The development of both chemical and biological expertise made it possible to characterize components of pheromone systems more precisely. Although many pheromones have been found to contain mixtures of isomers, analogs, homologs, and a variety of other related and unrelated compounds, the isomers possessing similar physical properties appear to be the ones used in precise ratios for mate recognition signals. The identification of these isomeric ratios and how they are produced and regulated by the insect is central to an understanding of pheromones and how they can be used in insect control.

1. *Geometric Isomers.* It has become very common, particularly with lepidopteran pheromones, to find that a particular narrow range of *Z*- and *E*-isomer mixtures is a critical part of the pheromone system. Better GLC systems, e.g. splitless injection capillary systems (Klun and Maini, 1979) and liquid-crystal columns (Lester, 1978) have made it possible to determine the natural isomer ratio on small quantities of material and to maintain good quality control over samples used in biological testing. One example of many that have been found (see reviews listed above) is with the closely-related leafroller moths that utilize precise blends of *Z*- and *E*-11-tetradecenyl acetate (Z11-14:Ac/E11-14:Ac) (Table I). In most cases, additional components also are used along with the isomer mixture.

In some insects the exact ratio of geometric isomer does not appear to be as critical. For example, in *Dendroctonus* beetles, *exo*-brevicomin (X) is one of the main pheromone components in some species (Silverstein *et al.*, 1968), although they also produce the apparently inactive *endo*-isomer (XI). The cotton boll weevil pheromone in-

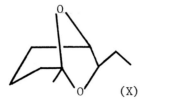

(X)

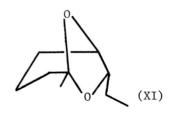

(XI)

TABLE I. Leafroller Moth Pheromone Blends Utilizing Specific Blends of Geometric Isomers [a]

Species	Z11-14:Ac	E11-14:Ac	References	
Choristoneura rosaceana	97%	3%	Hill & Roelofs	1978
Argyrotaenia velutinana	92	8	Roelofs et al.	1975
Adoxophyes sp.	90	10	Tamaki et al.	1979
Archips mortuanus	90	10	Cardé et al.	1977b
Archips argyrospilus	60	40	Cardé et al.	1977b
Archips podana	50	50	Persoons et al.	1974
Archips semiferanus	33	67	Miller et al.	1976
Sparganothis directana	24	76	Bjostad et al.	1980
Archips cerasivoranus	15	85	Cardé et al.	1977b
Platynota stultana	12	88	Hill & Roelofs	1975

[a] Additional components are used in most cases.

volves a pair of geometric isomers (II, III), but a precise component ratio was not found to be critical for activity. The San Jose scale pheromone was found to be composed of 3 isomers (XII–XIV), two of which are geometric isomers, but each one was independently active and not influenced by the presence of the others (Gieselmann et al., 1979).

(XII) (XIII) (XIV)

2. Positional Isomers. A number of species have been found to use positional isomers in specific ratios. An example of this would be with the summerfruit tortrix moth, Adoxophyes orana and the smaller tea tortrix moth, Adoxophyes sp. The pheromone of the former was found to be a 90:10 mixture of Z9- and Z11-14:Ac's (Meijer et al., 1972; Tamaki et al., 1971b), whereas, the latter was found to use a 70:30 mixture (Tamaki et al., 1971a). The 70:30 mixture was not competitive with virgin females of the smaller tea tortrix moth, and so a reinvestigation of the pheromone gland was undertaken (Tamaki et al., 1979). Analysis of ca. 100,000 female glands revealed that they contained ca. 10 related acetates, and that the pheromone consisted of a 63:31:4:2 mixture of Z9-14:Ac, Z11-14:Ac, E11-14:Ac, and an interesting new pheromone component, 10-methyldodecyl acetate.

3. Optical Isomers. The importance of geometric and positional isomers became evident in the early 1970's, but the role of enantiomers was generally overlooked until the middle of the decade. Studies with the alarm pheromone of several species of Atta ants, showed that the naturally-occurring (S)-(+)-4-methyl-3-heptanone was about 100 times more active than the (-) enantiomer (Riley et al., 1974a). These data indicated that chirality could be important in pheromone perception.

Research in subsequent years confirmed the fact that pheromone behavioral responses could be as specific to optical isomers or mixtures thereof as they are to geometric and positional isomers. Much of the progress in determining the role of optical isomers came as a result of an intensive assault by K. Mori on the synthesis of all possible optical isomers of many pheromone components. A sample of these syntheses includes the optical isomers of the following: (a) *exo*-brevicomin (X) (Mori, 1974a), frontalin (Mori, 1975a), *trans*-verbenol (Mori, 1976a) and seudenol (Mori *et al.*, 1978a) for *Dendroctonus* beetles; (b) ipsenol (Mori, 1975b), ipsdienol (Mori, 1976b, 1979), and *cis*-verbenol (Mori *et al.*, 1976a) for *Ips* beetles; (c) disparlure for gypsy moths (Mori *et al.*, 1976b); (d) (Z)-14-methylhexadec-8-en-1-ol (Mori, 1974b) and the corresponding aldehyde (Mori *et al.*, 1978b) for dermestid beetles; (e) sulcatol for ambrosia beetles (Mori, 1975c); (f) 4-methylheptan-3-ol (I) for elm bark beetles (Mori, 1977); (g) grandisol (IV) for the cotton boll weevil (Mori, 1978); (h) *erythro*-3,7-dimethylpentadec-2-yl acetates and propionates for pine sawflies (Mori and Tamada, 1979); and (i) 3,11-dimethyl-2-nonacosanone for the German cockroach (Mori *et al.*, 1978c).

The availability of synthetic optical isomers allowed researchers to match the optical rotation of the natural product against that of the synthetic, and also allowed researchers to conduct biological assays with the enantiomers and various mixtures thereof. A pheromone component of the elm bark beetle was found to be (1S, 1R, 4S, 5R) (-)α-multistriatin (VII) by synthesizing the 4 diastereomers and comparing the specific rotations with that of the natural material (Pearce *et al.*, 1976). There are 4 possible geometric and optical isomers of each of the 2 pheromone components of the California red scale, *Aonidiella aurantii*, but synthesis (Anderson *et al.*, 1980) and bioassays of all possible isomers (Gieselmann *et al.*, 1980) showed that only one isomer of each component (XV-3S,6R and XVI-3Z,6R) was active.

(XV)

(XVI)

The exact isomeric blend emitted by the insect could not be obtained by the above techniques, but some enantiomeric pheromone blends have been determined by NMR spectrometry involving chiral derivatives and chiral lanthanide shift reagents (Plummer *et al.*, 1976; Stewart *et al.*, 1977).

The data show that in some cases the enantiomer blend is important, and, in others, one of the enantiomers is either inactive or antagonistic to the behavioral responses mediated by the active enantiomer. For example in ambrosia beetles, the species *Gnathotrichus sulcatus* produces a 65:35 mixture of S-(+)- and R-(-)-6-methyl-5-hepten-2-ol (sulcatol) as its aggregating pheromone (Bryne *et al.*, 1974), and optimally responds to a 50:50 mixture (Borden *et al.*, 1976). Another species, G. *retusus* produces the S-(+) enantiomer and its responses to this isomer are decreased by the presence of the R-(-) enantiomer.

The use of only one pheromone component enantiomer has been found for a number of insect species. Monitoring traps for gypsy moth were inefficient for years until the enantiomers of disparlure (*cis*-7,8-epoxy-2-methyloctadecane) (XVII) were synthesized and tested. Some field tests showed that the presence of 2% or more of (-)-disparlure greatly decreased trap catches to (+)-isomer (Vite *et al.*, 1976; Miller *et al.l*, 1977; Carde *et al.*, 1977; Plimmer *et al.*, 1977). Efforts to prove the structure of the Japanese beetle pheromone, (Z)-5-(l-decenyl)dihydro-2(3H)-furanone (XVIII), were frustrated for a long time until the enantiomers were synthesized (Tumlinson et al., 1977). It was found that males were very responsive to the pure R,Z-isomer, but the S,Z-isomer was antagonistic to these responses even in very small amounts. Other examples of the importance of optical isomers will be discussed later in this chapter.

(XVII)   (XVIII)

III. BEHAVIORAL ASSAYS

It is very important in pheromone chemistry research to know if a particular identified chemical is involved in the insects' communication system. This was accomplished at first by demonstrating activity in a key response bioassay or by indirect means, such as trap catch. These studies are sufficient for determining the main pheromone components and for providing lures that can be used in practical programs involving traps. Further in-depth behavioral studies must be conducted, however, to define the communicative role of all the pheromone components and ultimately to understand the whole behavioral sequence involved.

Kennedy (1978) has emphasized that the behavioral sequence depends on central nervous integration of multiple inputs and outputs, and not just on chemical stimuli. The pheromone also could have many indirect effects, such as triggering the insect's reaction to another stimulus (e. g. visual or accoustic). Attraction can result from the interaction between non-orienting odor cues and orienting cues from outside the insect (allothetic sensory information) or from information stored in their own nervous systems (idiothetic sensory information). Arrestment can occur at any point in the behavioral sequence and can result from interaction between ortho- and klinokinetic reactions to the odor.

It is extremely difficult to develop an assay system that includes all of these inputs and permits a simulation of the insects' behavioral repertoire in natural field conditions, but several assays have been developed to conduct more quantitative behavioral analyses. A wind tunnel equipped with a moving floor (see Kennedy, 1977a; Miller and Roelofs, 1978) has been used to show that insects flying to an upwind pheromone source are guided by odor-regulated, optomotor anemotaxis. It also was shown that the regulation of airspeed according to the wind speed (orthokinetic component) was a reaction to the optomotor input from the apparent movement of the ground pattern. In another assay system an ingenious servosphere, developed by Kramer (1975), is used to study chemo-orientation mechanisms involved in pheromone responses of walking insects (Kramer, 1975; Bell and Kramer, 1979). The motorized sphere acts like a 2-dimensional treadmill and allows the insect to run freely for long distances in any direction. The intensity, direction, and pattern of chemical stimuli can be regulated while the insect is moving freely in 2-dimensional space.

A. *The Behavioral-Response Sequence*

The type of behavioral analysis needed to verify that a particular chemical functions as a pheromone component depends on the species involved and on the behavioral response mediated by that chemical (either alone or in mixture). The behavioral response involved can depend on a particular sequence of precopulatory behaviors. For example, with the western pine beetle, the females initiate an attack by finding a suitable host tree and boring through the outer bark into the phloem tissue. The components *exo*-brevicomin and myrcene are released in this process and "attract" predominantly male beetles to the host tree. The males then release frontalin, and the combination of pheromone components aggregate beetles in a 1:1 ratio throughout the mass attack (see Wood, 1972).

In some cases, the pheromone component can be present in the emitted pheromone blend, but have no observable behavioral effect until late in the precopulatory behavioral sequence. In field tests with the redbanded leafroller moth, the geometric isomer pheromone components, Z11- and E11-14:Ac in a 95:5 ratio mediated long-distance, upwind flight of the male moths to within about 1 m of the odor source. A third pheromone component, dodecyl acetate, released simultaneously from the odor source, greatly increased the incidence of males landing near the source, but appeared to have no effect on the long-distance behavioral sequence (Baker et al., 1976). Addition of the 3rd component to traps emitting the natural ratio of the other two pheromone components can increase trap catch by 5- to 10-fold. If only trap catch were used as an assay, the 3rd component would be labelled an "attractant synergist", but it is obvious that it increases trap catch only because it causes more males to land in the trap.

It is difficult to label any individual component because the behavioral effect depends on the context. With the 3-component system of the redbanded leafroller moth, discussed above, an individual component can act as an excitant, synergist or inhibitor depending on its ratio to the other components or the release rate used (Baker et al., 1976). This makes it critical to assess pheromone blends at the natural component ratios and rates of emission.

A general classification system (Roelofs and Cardé, 1977) has been proposed for lepidopteran pheromone components because of the importance of using chemicals involved in the long-distance component of the attraction process in "mating disruption" programs. In these programs, the air in large-field or forest areas is permeated with these chemicals to "disrupt" the attraction process by habituation, adaptation or confusion. *Primary pheromone components* are those involved in long-distance (over 1 m) positive anemotaxis, and also can be involved in mediating reactions, such as landing, wing fanning, hair pencilling, and other courtship responses. *Secondary pheromone components* are those that are not essential for the long-distance attraction process, but are involved only in the close-range responses. These behavioral classes also have been labelled as *early* (long-range) and *late* (close-range) behaviors in the male response sequence (Baker and Cardé, 1979). Although the distinctions are important for insect control programs, it is difficult in many cases to separate single components from the blend. One study involving an in-depth analysis of pheromone-mediated behaviors involving a 4-component blend will be presented as an example of research designed to describe behavioral roles to individual components.

B. *Analysis of Pheromone-Mediated Behaviors in Oriental Fruit Moth Males.*

1. *Courtship Behavior.* The Oriental fruit moth, *Grapholitha molesta*, which is a pest of peaches and apples, is a good species to use for an example because the mating communication system not only is involved in long-distance attraction of the males, but also

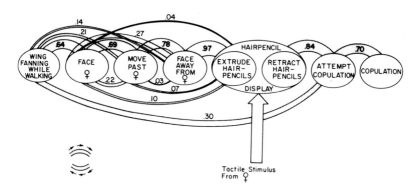

Fig. 1. Sequence of courtship behavior observed with male Oriental fruit moths. Decimal numbers of corresponding thicknesses of bonds are the conditional probabilities of a particular transition occurring between two behaviors. From Baker and Cardé, 1979a.

in a unique courtship behavior (Fig. 1). After the male moth lands close to a calling Oriental fruit moth female, he will successfully mate with her (within 1.5 seconds) only they undergo a relatively stereotyped sequence of behaviors (Baker and Cardé, 1979). The landed male first walks while wing fanning towards the female, pauses briefly in front of her (visual stimulus probably important) and then continues on to face away from her on the upwind side. At this point, the male carries out an elaborate display of abdominal-tip hairpencil organs directed toward the female's antennae. The display consists of multiple extrusions and retractions of the white hairpencils and the claspers accompanied by 45 and 90 cm/sec, respectively, puffs of wind generated by the wing-fanning male. The female responds to the stimuli at the hairpencil chemicals (pheromone) and the wind by walking the 1 or 2 cm to the male and touching his abdomen with her head and antennae. The tactile stimulus causes the male to whirl around and attempt copulation. This chemical dialogue is somewhat unique because there have been only a few reports (Grant and Brady, 1975; Grant, 1976) on lepidopteran courtship behavior in which male hairpencil pheromone evokes a female movement to the males. The most dramatic account of hairpencil usage in the Lepidoptera is with the queen butterfly (see Pliske and Eisner, 1969). In this case the males have well-developed eversible scent brushes that are fanned out during courtship to distribute the pheromone (Meinwald et al., 1969) to aerially induce female quiescence.

2. *The Female-Produced Pheromone Blend.* In the present example, the problem is to determine which female-produced chemicals are involved in mediating the sequence of male behavioral responses leading up to the hairpencil display. The most abundant pheromone component, (Z)-8-dodecenyl acetate (Z8-12:Ac), was reported first (Roelofs et al., 1969), but later field tests showed that the geometric isomer, E8-12:Ac (Beroza et al., 1973), the corresponding alcohol, Z8-12:OH (Cardé et al., 1975), and the saturated alcohol, 12:OH (Roelofs et al., 1973) were all effective in increasing trap catch if used within certain dosage ratios. Finally, it was shown (Cardé et al., 1979) that all four compounds are emitted by the Oriental fruit moth females.

Early studies (Cardé et al., 1975) in the field indicated that the two acetate isomers were involved in the long-distance attraction process if used in an approximate 100:7 Z/E ratio and released at a rate of about 1-30 ng/h [a calling Oriental fruit moth female releases the acetate at a rate of about 4 ng/h (Baker and Cardé, 1979b)]. It appeared in the first study that 12:OH was a *secondary pheromone compound* and caused an increase in landing, wing fanning while walking and hairpencil display. However, further definitive behavioral observations (Baker and Cardé, 1979b) utilizing all 4 pheromone components showed that the unsaturated alcohol, Z8-12:OH, was much more important for these behavioral effects than the saturated alcohol. The saturated alcohol, 12:OH, was found to influence behavioral response only in a subtle way in increasing hairpencil display, and then only when the unsaturated alcohol, Z8-12:OH, was present in suboptimal levels.

A sustained-flight wind tunnel assay was used to quantify changes in the males' response behaviors of walking while wing fanning prior to flight, initiating flight, hovering flight, upwind flight, landing, post-flight walking while wing fanning, and hairpencil display to a series of different chemical combinations and concentrations. Field observations were made to record male Oriental fruit moth responses to the various blends. In this assay the observed behaviors were upwind flight, flying to within 10 cm of the arena's edge, landing, wing fanning while walking, hairpencil display, duration of wing fanning, and closest approach to the odor source. The results showed that the 2 acetate isomers could elicit preflight wing fanning and upwind flight, as well as landing and wing fanning while walking after landing, when used in ratios (5-7% E-isomer) close to that used by the female. The addition of as little as 0.1% Z8-12:OH, however, effected significant behavioral increases in all of those responses. It appears that the blend of these 3 components functions as a unit that affects the whole sequence of male behavioral responses. Thus, the Z8-12:OH strictly would not be a *secondary pheromone component* even though its presence is not obligatory for the long-distance attraction process to occur, but is obligatory for the occurrence of hairpencil displays.

Quantitative behavioral analyses as seen in this example are based on the mean response of many responding insects. The actual pheromone used by any individual insect in the field could vary slightly in composition or concentration. It is important to know the extent of this variation in different geographic areas for population monitoring and to know how easily the pheromone blend can be altered under artificial pressures, such as mass trapping or mating disruption programs.

IV. VARIABILITY OF PHEROMONE BLENDS AMONG POPULATIONS

As discussed above, a pheromone generally is isolated from a group of individuals and is assayed by determining the mean behavioral responses or trap catch from many replicates or a population of insects. The pheromone emitted and perceived may vary from population to population, and it could have narrower variances in some populations than others. Although these possibilities exist, such variations have has been observed for only a few species. For most species studied, trap catch generally has been maximum to the same synthetic pheromone in all countries tested. Some of the exceptions will be discussed.

A. *Ips pini*

Pheromone variation has been indicated in a number of beetle species (Lanier and Burkholder, 1974), but the best documented account is that of *Ips pini*. This pine engraver beetle attacks pines and spruces throughout most of North America, and has been known by a variety of names. The eastern and western populations are morphologically distinguishable, but they apparently are on the ends of a gradient that has intermediate types in the northern Rocky Mountains. Lanier *et al.* (1972) found this to be true also in the beetles' responses to aggregation pheromone in laboratory tests. New York and California populations strongly preferred their own pheromone, whereas,

Idaho populations gave intermediate responses. Ipsdienol (Vité et al., 1972) was reported to be a major component of the aggregation pheromone, but further definition of the pheromone system required analyses for the possible optical isomers. Surprisingly, *I. pini* beetles in California (Birch et al., 1980) and Idaho (Lanier et al., 1980) both produce only (-)-ipsdienol (XIX), whereas, the *I. pini* beetles in New York produce a

(XIX)

35:65 ratio of (-)- to (+)-isomer (Lanier et al., 1980). The New York beetles respond to the (+)-isomer alone, but are most responsive in the field to a 50:50 mixture. The California beetles respond only to the (-)-isomer and the response is almost eliminated by the presence of 5% or more of the (+)-isomer. The beetles in Idaho also respond best to the (-)-isomer, but give intermediate responses to the 50:50 mixture. Thus, the New York and California populations are specific for their own pheromones, but were not considered to be separate species (Lanier and Burkholder, 1974) because the pheromone and morphological differences of the extreme end populations appear to intergrade in between. Electrophysiological studies (Mustaparta, 1980) have shown that beetles from both the eastern and western populations have receptors that distinguish between the two enantiomers, but that the receptor fields in these populations do not differ. Since there appears to be no synergistic or inhibitory interactions at the receptor level to account for the opposite effects of the (+)-isomer with the 2 populations, it was concluded that the different behavioral effects observed with various isomer mixtures are a result of specificity in the central nervous system.

B. Fruittree Leafroller Moth

The fruittree leafroller moth populations in New York and British Columbia appear to differ in the males' response specificity to the Z/E mixture of 11-tetradecenyl acetate pheromone components (Roelofs et al., 1974). Females in both populations produce approximately a 60:40 ratio, but males in British Columbia are attracted to lures containing these components in a 90:10 to 40:60 ration. The eastern population is captured only in traps containing ratios between 70:30 and 60:40. It was suggested that males in the eastern population were much more specific to the female-produced ratio because of the presence of several other sympatric leafroller species that utilize Z/E ratios of 90:10 and 95:5.

C. Dendroctonus frontalis

A number of geographically isolated pest populations of *D frontalis* have been found to differ significantly in their production of volatile pheromone components and in their host preferences (Vité et al., 1974). Beetles from loblolly pine in Virginia and in Texas produce the same volatiles and readily interbreed. Beetles from *Pinus leiophylla* in central Mexico produce a different blend of volatiles and do not interbreed with the beetles from Texas. Beetles from *Pinus oocarpa* from Honduras produce a pattern of volatiles different from the other populations, but do interbreed with the beetles from Texas. The data indicate that the pest populations in central Mexico and Texas have different mating communication systems and should be classified as different species.

D. *Larch bud moth*

The pheromone of the larch bud moth, *Zeiraphera diniana*, was found to be E11-14:Ac (Roelofs *et al.*, 1971a). As research progressed on this insect towards the usage of the pheromone for insect control, it was discovered that some populations used E9-12:Ac, instead of E11-14:Ac. Further investigation revealed that the population on larch, *Larix decidua*, used E11-14:Ac, but populations on cembran pine, *Pinus cembra* (Baltensweiler *et al.*, 1979), and on spruce, *Picea excelsa* (Vrkoč *et al.*, 1979) use E9-12:Ac. It was found that the two populations can interbreed in the laboratory and produce a hybrid that responds to both compounds (Priesner, 1979). The specific mating signals of these two populations support a separate species status for both.

E. *European corn borer—Genetic Control*

Pheromone studies with the European corn borer, *Ostrinia nubilalis*, revealed that there are two distinct population types. One type, which is found in central Europe and throughout most of North America east of the Rocky Mountains, uses a 97:3 blend of Z11-14:Ac/E11-14:Ac (Klun and Robinson, 1971; Klun and cooperators, 1975). The other population type, which is found in Italy and New York, uses the opposite blend (4:96) of Z- and E-isomers (Kochansky *et al.*, 1975). This agricultural pest was brought to North America with shipments of broomcorn imported from central Europe and Italy in the early 1900's. In addition to the pheromone differences, there appear to be disparate biological characteristics, such as in food plant specificity, number of yearly generations, and diel rhythm of mating. Electrophoretic analyses (Cardé *et al.*, 1978) also showed that there was genetic divergence between the two population types. These data suggest that the two populations most likely are two sibling species and are not an example of a large variation in the pheromone blend within a species.

An interesting study (Klun and Maini, 1979) with hybrids of the two population types showed that the Z/E ratio is controlled by simple Mendelian inheritance involving a single pair of alleles. It was found that the genes controlling the isomer ratio are not sex-linked because females of F_1 progenies from both reciprocal crosses produced an average 35:65 Z/E ratio. Females of the F_2 population from these crosses were found to produce the 3:97/35:65/97:3 Z/E blends in a 1:2:1 occurrence ratio. Further support for pheromonal control by a pair of alleles at one locus was that progeny from F_1 backcrossed with each parent population exhibited the 35:65 blend and original parent blend in a 1:1 occurrence ratio.

In contrast to the above findings, a study on the inheritance of male pheromone production in the sulphur butterflies, *Colios eurytheme* and *C. philodice*, has shown that the X-chromosome carries most of the genes controlling production of the main component, 13-methyl heptacosane (Grula and Taylor, 1979).

V. VARIABILITY OF PHEROMONE BLENDS AMONG INDIVIDUALS

Pheromones can be species specific communication signals that are inherited as blocks of co-adapted gene complexes (as discussed above), but there is evidence that some pheromone systems also have enough intraspecific variations to make possible individual recognition. In the latter case, loci affecting intraspecific pheromone variation would be distributed throughout the genome and inherited independently. Thus, with *Drosophila melanogaster* (Averhoff and Richardson, 1976), genetic variation was expressed in female pheromones that stimulate the males to court and in male pheromones that stimulate the female to accept. Pheromones of the courting male involve a volatile component associated with loci on the second and/or third chromosomes, and a nonvolatile component associated with the X and/or fourth chromosome. It was postulated that individuals are less responsive to pheromones to which they are constantly exposed, such as those produced by themselves and by similar genotypes. This negatively assortative mating pattern based upon variation in pheromonal signals would be a counterforce to inbreeding during population bottlenecks.

Evidence for intraspecific variation in pheromones also was found with halictine bees (Barrows et al., 1975). It was suggested that such variation was important in the maintenance of genetic polymorphism. Perception of individual differences was found in responses of males to previously non-receptive females and in responses of guard bees at nest entrances to their nest-mates.

Pheromone polymorphism within a population could be less evident in cases where the mating communication system is species specific. For example, with most moth species a narrow-range sex pheromone blend appears to be important for mate location. Analyses of the pheromone component ratio of individual female redbanded leafroller moths collected from a wild population showed that all females produced a Z11-/E11-14:Ac mixture within a narrow range of 4-15%E-isomer (the mean was 9.1 + 1.8% E-isomer) (Miller and Roelofs, 1980).

Specificity can be effected by the emitting insects, the receiving insects, or both. It is more difficult, however, to obtain quantitative data on the range of behavioral responses in the receiving insect. Male moths usually can be captured in traps by a wider range of component ratios than that produced by the female moths, but the lowest moth activation threshold still could be coincident with the mixture produced by the female moths. This was demonstrated in a capture-marking-recapture test with wild Oriental fruit moth males (Cardé et al., 1976). Males were attracted to blends of 3,8 or 11% E8-12:Ac in Z8-12:Ac and marked with a color-coded fluorescent dye coded by color for each blend. The marked males were recaptured in succeeding nights in sticky traps baited with one of the same 3 component blends. If there were disparate phenotypes attuned optimally to the different mixtures, then males should preferentially have been marked and recaptured by that mixture. The test revealed that males were marked mainly by the natural 8% E-isomer blend, and that males marked by the other two blends were trapped back mainly by the natural blend.

The range of component ratios to which the Oriental fruit moth responds apparently is governed by the central nervous system and depends upon a variety of inputs affecting several behavioral thresholds. With the natural pheromone blend there are upper and lower concentration thresholds that determine the boundaries of the "active space" for upwind flight (Baker and Roelofs, 1980). These same thresholds also could be involved in determining the range of component ratios to which a male responds in the field. A narrow range of ratios can be involved in the males' response when the isomers are released at the females' natural emission rate, but the response range can be much broader when higher release rates are used (Roelofs, 1978b). Since there apparently is an upper concentration threshold level that causes termination of the males' upwind flight, the overall range of component ratios that can be used to trap males can be narrow or broad depending on all the factors that affect the level of this central nervous system threshold.

VI. CONCLUSIONS

The use of pheromones to control insect pests depends on a knowledge of the insects as predicted by Wigglesworth, but it also has become obvious that the accumulation of some knowledge of this communication system invariablty leads to additional unanswered questions. The availability of synthetic pheromone components leads to problems in how to formulate them for economical usage in insect control programs. The use of pheromones in monitoring traps leads to problems in relating trap catch to population densities. Some knowledge of the pheromone components and behavioral responses of a certain insect leads to questions of additional minor pheromone components and how quantitative and qualitative changes in the pheromone blend can affect the responding insects. Some knowledge of the pheromone blend opens the way for further projects on physiological aspects of its release, its biosynthesis and the genetics controlling these enzymic reactions. Studies of the receiving insect lead to research on the specificity and relative sensitivities of antennal receptor cells, on how these receptors converge in the deutocerebrum and transmit their input to the central olfactory neurons (see Boeckh and Boeckh, 1979), and on the factors affecting nervous system thresholds that determine how the signal is perceived and translated into action. These studies not only are important for the application of pheromones in insect control, but they also provide knowledge and insights of value to many areas of science.

REFERENCES

Anderson, R. J., Adams, K. G., Chinn, H. R., and Henrick, C. A. (1980). Synthesis of the optical isomers of 3-methyl-6-isopropenyl-9-decen-1-yl acetate, a component of the California red scale pheromone. *J. Org. Chem.*, In Press.

Averhoff, W. W., and Richardson, R. H. (1974). Pheromonal control of mating patterns in *Drosophila melanogaster*. *Behav. Genet. 4*, 207-225.

Baker, T. C., and Cardé, R. T. (1979a). Courtship behavior of the Oriental fruit moth (*Grapholitha molesta*): Experimental analysis and consideration of the role of sexual selection in the evolution of courtship pheromones in the lepidoptera. *Ann. Entomol. Soc. Amer. 72*, 173-188.

Baker, T. C., and Cardé, R. T. (1979b). Analysis of pheromone-mediated behaviors in male *Grapholitha molesta*, the Oriental fruit moth (Lepidoptera: Tortricidae). *Environ. Entomol. 8*, 956-968.

Baker, T. C., and Roelofs, W. L. (1980). Factors affecting sex pheromone communication distance in the Oriental fruit moth, *Grapholitha molesta*. *Environ. Entomol. 9*, In Press.

Baker, T. C., Cardé, R. T., and Roelofs, W. L. (1976). Behavioral responses of male *Argyrotaenia velutinana* (Lepidoptera: Tortricidae) to components of its sex pheromone. *J. Chem. Ecol. 2*, 333-352.

Baker, R., and Evans, D. A. (1975). Biological chemistry. Part (i). Insect chemistry. *Ann. Rept. Prog. Chem. Sect. B. Org. Chem. 72*, 347-365.

Baltensweiler, W., Priesner, E., Arn, H., and Delucchi, V. (1978). Unterschiedliche Sexuallockstoffe bei Lärchen - und Arvenform des Grauen Lärchenwicklers (*Zeiraphera diniana* Gn., Lep. Tortricidae). *Mitt. Schweiz. Ent. Ges. 5I*, 133-142.

Barrows, E. M., Bell, W. J., and Michener, C. D. (1975). Individual odor differences and their social functions in insects. *Proc. Nat. Acad. Sci. USA 72*, 2824-2828.

Bell, W. J., and Kramer, E. (1979). Sex pheromone stimulated orientation responses by the American cockroach on a servosphere apparatus. *J. Chem. Ecol.*, In Press.

Beroza, M. (1971). Insect sex attractants. *Amer. Sci. 59*, 320-325.

Beroza, M., Muschik, G. M., and Gentry, C. R. (1973). Small proportion of opposite geometric isomer increases potency of synthetic pheromone in Oriental fruit moth. *Nature 244*, 149-150.

Birch, M. C. (ed.) (1974). "Pheromones". American Elsevier, New York.

Birch, M. C., Light, D. M., Wood, D. L., Browne, L. E., Silverstein, R. M., Bergot, B. J., Ohloff, G., West, J. R., and Young, J. C. (1980). Pheromonal attraction and allomonal interruption of *Ips pini* in California by the two enantiomers of ipsdienol. *J. Chem. Ecol. 6*, In Press.

Bjostad, L. B., Taschenberg, E. F., and Roelofs, W. L. (1980). Sex pheromone of the chokecherry leafroller moth, *Sparganothis directana. J. Chem. Ecol. 6*, In Press.

Boeckh, J., and Boeckh, V. (1977). Threshold and odor specificity of pheromone-sensitive neurons in the deutocerebrum of *Antheraea pernyi* and *A. polyphemus* (Saturnidae). *J. Comp. Physiol. 132*, 235-242.

Borden, J. H., Chong, L., McLean, J. A., Slessor, K. N., and Mori, K. (1976). *Gnathotrichus sulcatus*; synergistic response to enantiomers of the aggregation pheromone sulcatol. *Science 192*, 894-896.

Brand, J. M., Young, J. C., and Silverstein, R. M. (1979). Insect pheromones: A critical review of recent advances in their chemistry, biology, and application. *Fortschritte d. Chem. org. Naturst. 37*, 1-190.

Butenandt, A., Beckmann, R., Stamm, D., and Hecker, E. (1959). Über den Sexuallockstoff des Seidenspinners *Bombyx mori.* Reindarstellung und Konstitution. *Z. Naturforsch. B14*, 283-284.

Byrne, K., Swigar, A., Silverstein, R. M., Borden, J. H., and Stokkink, E. (1974). Sulcatol: population aggregation pheromone in *Gnathotrichus sulcatus* (Coleoptera: Scolytidae). *J. Insect Physiol. 20*, 1895-1900.

Cardé, R. T. (1979). Behavioral responses of moths to female-produced pheromones and the utilization of attractant-baited traps for population monitoring. *In* "Movement of Highly Mobile Insects: Concepts and Methodology in Research" (R. Rabb and G. Kennedy, eds.), pp. 286-315. North Carolina Univ., Raleigh, North Carolina.

Cardé, R. T., Baker, T. C., and Roelofs, W. L. (1975). Ethological function of components of a chemical sex attractant system in the Oriental fruit moth, *Grapholitha molesta. J. Chem. Ecol. 1*, 475-491.

Cardé, R. T., Baker, T. C., and Roelofs, W. L. (1976). Sex attractant responses of male Oriental fruit moths to a range of component ratios: pheromone polymorphism. *Experientia 32*, 1406-1407.

Cardé, R. T., Doane, C. C., Baker, T. C., Iwaki, S., and Marumo, S. (1977a). Attractancy of optically active pheromone for male gypsy moths. *Environ. Entomol. 6*, 768-772.

Cardé, R. T., Hill, A. S., Carde, A. M., and Roelofs, W. L. (1977b). Sex attractant specificity as a reproductive isolating mechanism among the sibling species *Archips argyrospilus* and *mortuanus* and other sympatric tortricine moths. *J. Chem. Ecol. 3*, 71-84.

Cardé, R. T., Roelofs, W. L., Harrison, R. G., Vawter, A. T., Brussard, P. F., Mutuura, A., and Munroe, E. (1978). European corn borer: pheromone polymorphism or sibling species. *Science 199*, 555-556.

Cardé, A. M., Baker, T. C., and Cardé, R. T. (1979). Identification of a four-component sex pheromone of the female Oriental fruit moth, *Grapholitha molesta* (Lepidoptera: Tortricidae). *J. Chem. Ecol. 5*, 423-427.

Eiter, K. (1970). Insektensexuallockstoffe. *Fortschr. d. Chem. org. Naturst. 28*, 204-255.

Gieselmann, M. J., Rice, R. E., Jones, R. A., and Roelofs, W. L. (1979). Sex pheromone of the San Jose scale. *J. Chem. Ecol. 5*, 891-900.

Gieselmann, M. J., Henrick, C. A., Anderson, R. J., Moreno, D. S., and Roelofs, W. L. (1980). Responses of male California red scale to sex pheromone isomers. *J. Insect Physiol.*, In Press.

Grant, G. G. (1976). Courtship behavior of a phycitid moth, *Vitula edmundsae. Ann. Entomol. Soc. Amer. 69*, 445-449.

Grant, G. G., and Brady, U. E. (1975). Courtship behavior of phycitid moths. I. Comparison of *Plodia interpunctella* and *Cadra cautella* and role of male scent glands. *Can. J. Zool. 53*, 813-826.

Grula, J. W., and Taylor, O. R. (1979). The inheritance of pheromone production in the sulphur butterflies *Colias eurytheme* and *C. philodice. Heredity 42*, 359-371.

Henrick, C. A. (1977). The synthesis of insect sex pheromones. *Tetrahedron 33*, 1845-1889.

Hill, A., and Roelofs, W. (1975). Sex pheromone components of the omnivorous leafroller moth, *Platynota stultana. J. Chem. Ecol. 1*, 91-99.

Hill, A. S., and Roelofs, W. L. (1978). Sex pheromone components of the obliquebanded leafroller moth, *Choristoneura rosaceana. J. Chem. Ecol. 5*, 3-11.

Kalmus, H. (1965). Possibilities and constraints of chemical telecommunication. *Proc. Int. Congr. Endocrinol., 2nd, 1964*, 188-192.

Karlson, P., and Butenandt, A. (1959). Pheromones (ectohormones) in insects. *Ann. Rev. Entomol. 4*, 39.

Karlson, P., and Lüscher, M. (1959). "Pheromones": A new term for a class of biologically active substances. *Nature 183*, 55.

Kennedy, J. S. (1972). The emergence of behavior. *J. Aust. Entomol. Soc. 11*, 168-176.

Kennedy, J. S. (1977a). Olfactory responses to distant plants and other odor sources. *In* "Chemical Control of Insect Behavior: Theory and Application" (H. Shorey and J. McKelvey, eds.), pp. 67-91. J. Wiley and Sons, New York.

Kennedy, J. S. (1977b). Behaviorally discriminating assays of attractants and repellents. *In* "Chemical Control of Insect Behavior: Theory and Application" (H. Shorey and J. McKelvey, eds.), pp. 215-229. J. Wiley and Sons, New York.

Kennedy, J. S. (1978). The concepts of olfactory "arrestment" and "attraction". *Physiol. Entomol. 3*, 91-98.

Klun, J. A., and Cooperators. (1975). Insect sex pheromones: intraspecific pheromonal variability of *Ostrinia nubilalis* in North America and Europe. *Environ. Entomol. 4*, 891-894.

Klun, J. A., and Maini, S. (1979). Genetic basis of an insect chemical communication system: the European corn borer. *Environ. Entomol. 8*, 423-426.

Klun, J. A., and Robinson, J. F. (1971). European corn borer moth: sex attractant and sex attraction inhibitors. *Ann. Entomol. Soc. Am. 64*, 1083-1086.

Kochansky, J., Carde, R. T., Liebherr, J., and Roelofs, W. L. (1975). Sex pheromones of the European corn borer in New York. *J. Chem. Ecol. 1*, 225-231.

Kramer, E. (1975). Orientation of the male silkmoth to the sex attractant Bombykol. *In* "Olfaction and Taste, V" (D. Denton and J. Coghlan, eds.), pp. 329-335. Academic Press, New York.

Jacobson, M. (1972), "Insect Sex Pheromones." Academic Press, New York.

Lanier, G. N., and Burkholder, W. E. (1974). Pheromones in speciation of Coleoptera. *In* "Pheromones" (M. Birch, ed.), pp. 161-189. American Elsevier, New York.

Lanier, G. N., Birch, M. C., Schmitz, R. F., and Furniss, M. M. (1972). Pheromones of *Ips pini* (Coleopter: Scolytidae): variation in response among three populations. *Can. Entomol. 104*, 1917-1923.

Lanier, G. N., Claesson, A., Stewart, T. E., Piston, J. J., and Silverstein, R. M. (1980). *Ips pini*: the basis for interpopulational differences in pheromone biology. *J. Chem. Ecol. 6*, In Press.

Law, J. H., and Regnier, F. E. (1971). Pheromones. *Ann. Rev. Biochem. 40*, 533-548.

Lester, R. (1978). Smectic liquid crystal for the gas-liquid chromatographic separation of lepidopterous sex pheromones and related isomeric olefins. *J. Chromatography 156*, 55-62.

MacConnell, J. G., and Silverstein, R. M. (1973). Recent results in insect pheromone chemistry. *Angew. Chem. Int. Ed. Engl. 12*, 644-654.

Mayer, M. S., and McLaughlin, J. R. (1975), "An annotated compendium of insect sex pheromones." Florida Agric. Expt. Sta. Monograph Series, No. 6, Gainesville, Florida.

Meijer, G. M., Ritter, F. J., Persoons, C., Minks, A., and Voerman, S. (1972). Sex pheromones of summer fruit tortrix moth *Adoxophyes orona*: two synergistic isomers. *Science 175*, 1469-1470.

Meinwald, J., Meinwald, Y., and Mazzocchi, P. (1969). Sex pheromone of the queen butterfly: chemistry. *Science 164*, 1174-1175.

Miller, J. R., and Roelofs, W. L. (1978). Sustained-flight tunnel for measuring insect responses to wind-borne sex pheromones. *J. Chem. Ecol. 4*, 187-198.

Miller, J. R., and Roelofs, W. L. (1980). Individual variation in sex pheromone component ratios in two populations of the redbanded leafroller moth, *Argyrotaenia velutinana*. *Environ. Entomol. 9*, In Press.

Miller, J. R., Baker, T. C., Cardé, R. T., and Roelofs, W. L. (1976). Reinvestigation of oak leaf roller sex pheromone components and the hypothesis that they vary with diet. *Science 192*, 140-143.

Miller, J. R., Mori, K., and Roelofs, W. L. (1977). Gypsy moth field trapping and electroantennogram studies with pheromone enantiomers. *J. Insect Physiol. 23*, 1447-1453.

Mori, K. (1974a). Synthesis of *exo*-brevicomin, the pheromone of western pine beetle, to obtain optically active forms of known absolute configuration. *Tetrahedron 30*, 4223-4227.

Mori, K. (1974b). Absolute configurations of (-)-14-methylhexadec-8-*cis*-en-1-ol and methyl(-)-14-methylhexadec-8-*cis*-enoate, the sex pheromone of female dermestid beetle. *Tetrahedron 30*, 3817-3820.

Mori, K. (1975a). Synthesis of optically active forms of frontalin. *Tetrahedron 31*, 1381-1384.

Mori, K. (1975b). Synthesis and absolute configuration of (-)-ipsenol (2-methyl-6-methylene-7-octen-4-ol), the pheromone of *Ips paraconfusus* Lanier. *Tetrahedron Letters*, 2187-2190.

Mori, K. (1975c). Synthesis of optically active forms of frontalin, the pheromone of *Dendroctonus* bark beetles. *Tetrahedron 31*, 1381-1384.

Mori, K. (1976a). Synthesis of optically pure (+)-*trans*-verbenol and its antipode, the pheromone of *Dendroctonus* bark beetles. *Agr. Biol. Chem. 40*, 415-418.

Mori, K. (1976b). Absolute configuration of (+)-ipsdienol, the pheromone of *Ips paraconfusus* Lanier, as determined by the synthesis of its (R)-(-)-isomer. *Tetrahedron Letters*, 1609-1612.

Mori, K. (1977). Absolute configuration of (-)-4-methylheptan-3-ol, a pheromone of the smaller European elm bark beetle, as determined by the synthesis of its (3R,4R)-(+)- and (3S,4R)-(+)-isomers. *Tetrahedron 33*, 289-294.

Mori, K. (1978). Synthesis of both enantiomers of grandisol, the boll weevil pheromone. *Tetrahedron 34*, 915-920.

Mori, K., and Tamada, S. (1979). Stereocontrolled synthesis of all of the four possible stereoisomers of *erythro*-3,7-dimethylpentadec-2-yl acetate and propionate, the sex pheromone of the pine sawflies. *Tetrahedron 35*, 1279-1284.

Mori, K., Mizumachi, N., and Matsui, M. (1976a). Synthesis of optically pure (1S,4S,5S)-2-pinen-4-ol (*cis*-verbenol) and its antipode, the pheromone of *Ips* bark beetles. *Agr. Biol. Chem. 40*, 1611-1615.

Mori, K., Takigawa, T., and Matsui, M. (1976b). Stereoselective synthesis of optically active disparlure, the pheromone of the gypsy moth (*Porthetria dispar* L.). *Tetrahedron Letters*, 3953-3956.

Mori, K., Tamada, S., Uchida, M., Mizumachi, N., Tachibana, Y., and Matsui, M. (1978a). Synthesis of optically active forms of seudenol, the pheromone of Douglas fir beetle. *Tetrahedron 34*, 1901-1905.

Mori, K., Suguro, T., and Uchida, M. (1978b). Synthesis of optically active forms of (Z)-14-methylhexadec-8-enal. *Tetrahedron 34*, 3119-3123.

Mori, K., Suguro, T., and Masuda, S. (1978c). Stereocontrolled synthesis of all the four possible stereoisomers of 3,11-dimethyl-2-nonacosanone, the female sex pheromone of the German cockroach. *Tetrahedron Letters*, 3447-3450.

Mori, K., Takigawa, T., and Matsuo, T. (1979). Synthesis of optically active forms of ipsdienol and ipsenol. *Tetrahedron 35*, 933-940.

Mustaparta, H., Angst, M. E., and Lanier, G. N. (1980). Receptor discrimination of enantiomers of the aggregation pheromone, Ipsdienol, in two species of *Ips. J. Chem. Ecol. 6*, In Press.

Pearce, G. T., Gore, W. E., Silverstein, R. M., Peacock, J. W., Cuthbert, R., Lanier, G. N., and Simeone, J. B. (1975). Chemical attractants for the smaller European elm bark beetle, *Scolytus multistriatus* (Coleoptera: Scolytidae). *J. Chem. Ecol.1*, 115-124.

Pearce, G. T., Gore, W. E., and Silverstein, R. M. (1976). Synthesis and absolute configuration of multistriatin. *J. Org. Chem. 41*, 2797-2803.

Persoons, C. J., Minks, A. K., Voerman, S., Roelofs, W. L., and Ritter, F. J. (1974). Sex pheromones of the moth, *Archips podana*: isolation, identification and field evaluation of two synergistic geometrical isomers. *J. Insect Physiol. 20*, 1181-1188.

Plimmer, J. R., Schwalbe, C. P., Paszek, E. C., Bierl, B. A., Webb, R. E., Marumo, S., and Iwaki, S. (1977). Contrasting effectiveness of (+) and (-) enantiomers of disparlure for trapping native populations of gypsy moth in Massachusetts. *Environ. Entomol. 6*, 518-522.

Pliske, T. E., and Eisner, T. (1969). Sex pheromones of the queen butterfly: biology. *Science 164*, 1170-1172.

Plummer, E. L., Stewart, T. E., Byrne, K., Pearce, G. T., and Silverstein, R. M. (1976). Determination of the enantiomorphic composition of several insect pheromone alcohols. *J. Chem. Ecol. 2*, 307-311.

Priesner, E. (1979). Specificity studies on pheromone receptors of noctuid and tortricid lepidoptera. *In* "Chemical Ecology: Odour Communication in Animals" (F. Ritter, ed.), pp. 57-71. Elsevier/North-Holland Biomedical Press, Amsterdam.

Riley, R. G., Silverstein, R. M., and Moser, J. C.(1974). Biological responses of *Atta texana* to its alarm pheromone and the enantiomer of the pheromone. *Science 183*, 760-762.

Ritter, F. J. (ed.) (1979), "Chemical Ecology: Odour Communication in Animals." Elsevier/North-Holland Biomedical Press, Amsterdam, New York, Oxford.

Roelofs, W. L. (1977), "The Scope and Limitations of the Electroantennogram Technique in Identifying Pheromone Components." *In* Crop Protection Agents - Their Biological Evaluation" (N. McFarlane, ed), pp. 147-165. Academic Press, New York.

Roelofs, W. L. (1978a). Chemical control of insects by pheromones. *In* "Biochemistry of Insects" (M. Rockstein, ed.), pp. 419-464. Academic Press, New York.

Roelofs, W. L. (1978b). Threshold hypothesis for pheromone perception. *J. Chem. Ecol. 4*, 685-699.

Roelofs, W. L. (1979). Electroantennograms. *Chemtech 9*, 222-227.

Roelofs, W. L., and Cardé, R. T. (1977). Responses of Lepidoptera to synthetic sex pheromone chemicals and their analogues. *Ann. Rev. Entomol. 22*, 377-405.

Roelofs, W. L., Comeau, A., and Selle, R. (1969). Sex pheromone of the Oriental fruit moth. *Nature 224*, 723.

Roelofs, W. L., Cardé, R. T., Benz, G., and von Salis, G. (1971a). Sex attractant of the larch bud moth found by electroantennogram method. *Experientia 27*, 1438.

Roelofs, W., Comeau, A., Hill, A., and Milicevic, G. (1971b). Sex attractant of the codling moth characterization with electroantennogram technique. *Science 174*, 297-299.

Roelofs, W. L., Cardé, R. T., and Tette, J. (1973). Oriental fruit moth attractant synergists. *Environ. Entomol. 2*, 252-254.

Roelofs, W. L., Hill, A., Cardé, R. T., Tette, J., Madsen, H., and Vakenti, J. (1974). Sex pheromones of the fruittree leafroller moth, *Archips argyrospilus. Environ. Entomol. 3*, 747-751.

Roelofs, W., Hill, A., and Cardé, R. (1975). Sex pheromone compounds of the redbanded leafroller moth, *Argyrotaenia velutinana. J. Chem. Ecol. 1*, 83-89.

Schneider, D. (1974). The sex-attractant receptor of moths. *Sci. Amer. 231*, 28-35.

Shorey, H. H. (1976), "Animal Communication by Pheromones." Academic Press, New York.

Shorey, H. H., and McKelvey, J. J. (eds.) (1977), "Chemical Control of Insect Behavior: Theory and Application." J. Wiley and Sons, New York.

Silverstein, R. M. (1977). Complexity, diversity, and specificity of behavior-modifying chemicals: examples mainly from Coleoptera and Hymenoptera. *In* "Chemical Control of Insect Behavior: Theory and Application" (H. Shorey and J. McKelvey, eds.), pp. 231-251. J. Wiley and Sons, New York.

Silverstein, R. M., Brownlee, R. G., Bellas, T. E., Wood, D. L., and Browne, L. E. (1968). Brevicomin: principal sex attractant in the frass of the female western pine beetle. *Science 159*, 889-891.

Stewart, T. E., Plummer, E. L., McCandless, L. L., West, J. R., and Silverstein, R. M. (1977). Determination of enantiomer composition of several bicyclic ketal insect pheromone components. *J. Chem. Ecol. 3*, 27-43.

Tamaki, Y., Noguchi, H., Yushima, T., and Hirano, C. (1971a). Two sex pheromones of the smaller tea tortrix: isolation, identification, and synthesis. *Appl. Entomol. Zool. 6* 139-141.

Tamaki, Y., Noguchi, H., Yushima, T., Hirano, C., Honma, K., and Sugawara, H. (1971b). Sex pheromone of the summerfruit tortrix: isolation and identification. *Kontyu 39*, 338-340.

Tamaki, Y., Noguchi, H., Sugie, H., and Sato, R. (1979). Minor components of the female sex-attractant pheromone of the smaller tea tortrix moth (Lepidoptera: Tortricidae): isolation and identification. *Appl. Ent. Zool. 14*, 101-113.

Tumlinson, J. H., Klein, M. G., Doolittle, R. E., Ladd, T. L., and Proveaux, A. T. (1977). Identification of the female Japanese beetle sex pheromone: inhibition of male response by an enantiomer. *Science 197*, 789-792.

Vité, J. P., Bakk, A., and Renwick, J. A. A. (1972). Pheromones in *Ips* (Coleoptera: Scolytidae): occurrence and production. *Can. Entomol. 104*, 1967-1975.

Vité, J. P., Islas, S. F., Renwick, J. A. A., Hughes, P. R., and Kliefoth, R. A. (1974). Biochemical and biological variation of southern pine beetle populations in North and Central America. *Z. ang. Ent. 75*, 422-435.

Vité, J. P., Klimetzek, D., Loskant, G., Hedden, R., and Mori, K. (1976). Chirality of insect pheromones: response interruption by inactive antipodes. *Naturwiss. 63*, 582-583.

Vrkoč, J., Skuhravy, V., and Baltensweiler, W. (1979). Freilanduntersuchungen zur Sexuallockstoff-Reaktion der Fichtenform des grauen Lärchenwicklers, *Zeiraphera diniana* Gn. (Lep., Tortricidae). *Anz. Schadlingskde., Pflanzenschutz, Umweltschutz 52*, 129-130.

Wigglesworth, V. B. (1939), "The Principles of Insect Physiology." Methuen, London.

Wilson, E. O., and Bossert, W. H. (1963). Chemical communication among animals. *Recent Progr. Horm. Res. 19*, 673-716.

Wood, D. (1972). Selection and colonization of ponderosa pine by bark beetles. *In* "Insect/Plant Relationships," pp. 101-117, Symp. Roy. Entomol. Soc. Lond. (6). Blackwell Scientific Publications, Oxford.

Young, J. C., and Silverstein, R. M. (1975). Biological and chemical methodology in the study of insect communication. *In* "Methods in Olfactory Research " (D. Moulton, A. Turk, and J. Johnson, eds.), pp. 75-161. Academic Press, New York.

INSECT ANTIFEEDANTS[1]
FROM PLANTS

Koji Nakanishi

Department of Chemistry
Columbia University
New York, N.Y.

I. INTRODUCTION

In recent years we have been searching for various bioactive compounds from tropical plant sources guided by simple
and quick bioassays which can be carried out in a chemical
laboratory by chemists. The crude extracts are also submitted
to 10-20 different pharmacological assays carried out elsewhere, and if the activity is significant the particular
activity is also pursued in the isolation; however, this
latter process necessarily takes a much longer time because
each fraction has to be sent out until the activity can be
correlated with a specific spectroscopic property.

It is not surprising to expect that tropical flora, in
contrast to their temperate zone counterparts, have developed
a more efficient and varied defense mechanism because of the
far more severe conditions for survival. They have indeed
turned out to provide a rich and intriguing source for isolating natural products which exhibit interesting properties
such as plant or insect growth regulatory, cytotoxic, antimicrobial, molluscicidal (snail-killing) and other activities.

The current studies on insect antifeedants being carried
out in New York were initiated at the International Centre of
Insect Physiology and Ecology (ICIPE), Nairobi, Kenya,where I
was a Research Director from 1969 (when ICIPE started) to 1977

[1]*supported by NIH Grant AI-10187*

603

and Dr. Isao Kubo[2] was a Senior Research Scientist for the
years 1975/1976. The plants currently under investigation
originated mostly from East Africa and Mexico, and a few from
South America.

II. COLLECTION OF PLANTS AND BIOASSAY

   Plants are collected on the basis of information gathered
from literature survey and on local knowledge on insect resistant species.
   In our laboratory in the Chemistry Department we maintain
colonies of the Southern army-worm *(Spodoptera eridania)*, the
spruce bud-worm *(Choristoneura fumigerana)* and the Mexican
bean bettle *(Epilachna varivestes)* for antifeedant studies.
The first two are maintained on artificial diet whereas the
bettle is fed with pole beans. The simplest bioassay system
is schematically depicted in Fig. 1. In certain cases the
crude extract is mixed with the artificial diet but the

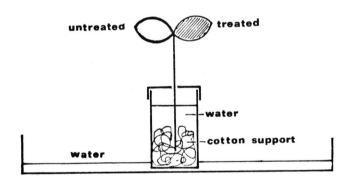

   *FIGURE 1. The vial with the leaf is put in a petri dish
which contains water to keep the larvae from escaping. The
larvae are placed at the branching point of the leaves, and
the treated and untreated leaves are scored at appropriate
time intervals.*

feeding of the insect is considerably affected by the shape of

[2]*present address: Division Entomology & Parasitology
                    University of California,Berkeley,CA.*

the diet. Alternatively, in the assay employing natural
leaves, e.g., spruce and Lima beans, we have noticed variations depending on the freshness of the leaf. Hence, unless
the antifeedant is extremely potent, complications arising
from securing reproducible results have been encountered.

Probably a more revealing assay is the one based on electrophysiology. Namely, initial studies carried out at ICIPE
(Ma, 1977) on the monophagous (and therefore sensitive) African army-worm *(S.exempta)* turned out to be very promising
since the activity could be followed time-wise by impulse/
second readings recorded as oscillographs. In the case of the
potent warburganal (see Fig.2)he found that contact of the
medial sensilla with a filter paper impregnated with the compound led to a drastic drop in the readings in a few minutes;
the sense of taste recovered in ten minutes but two more
contacts resulted in irreversible damage in the electrophysiology readings. This in practiceleads to an interesting case;
when the varacious larvae are left on corn-leaves treated with
warburganal for 1 hour and then transferred to untreated
leaves, they will not eat and starve. The electrophysiological assay is being continued at our place by Dr. Camilla Zack
who has built a unit and has started working with *S. eridania*.
Preliminary studies have revealed that there are probably
multiple mechanisms for antifeeding activities (Zack,1980).

In addition to antifeedant assays, we are also looking for
antiecdysones (if any - with *Bombyx mori* or silk worm), heli-
cocides (Nakanishi and Kubo,1977) (with *Biomphalaria pfeifferei*
- a snail which is a host for schistosomes, parasitic nematodes
responsible for the wide-spread occurrence of shistosomiasis)
and plant growth regulators.

The crude plant extract which is obtained by immersion of
the air-dried material in 40% aqueous MeOH is then extracted
with the following four solvents and each extract is processed separately:

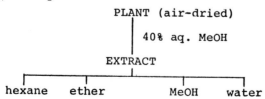

a) Each extract bioassayed separately.

b) Isolation is based on bioassay.

c) Pure compound assayed for other
   activities; also submitted to
   Ames test.

If any of the assays give a positive response, the extraction is followed through and the pure principle is
structurally determined with the minimum possible quantity.
The remainder of the sample is submitted to more extensive
antifeedant and other assays and are also sent out for wider
screening such as antibiotic activities.

We have found that compounds isolated on the basis of
insect antifeedant activity almost invariably exhibit other
activities. A typical case was the leaf extract of the East
African *Croton macrostachys*. The antifeedant principle was
isolated according to bioassays with *S. exempta* and the
structure was fully determined to be the 1-benzylate of 1,2,3,
4-diepoxy-5,6-diacetoxycyclohexane (unpublished). To our
surprise we then found that the same compound had been isolated from the same tree by the late Kupchan and NCI by
following tumor-inhibiting antileukemic activities. There are
several other cases. Hence we now regard the "antifeedant"
assays as a quick means of isolating bioactive compounds from
plants in general. Compounds isolated as weak antifeedants
have been shown to be potent antibiotics occasionally.

III.ANTIFEEDANTS

Studies on antifeedants from plants have been carried out
extensively by Munakata and co-workers (1970). We have also
reviewed our studies in this area (Nakanishi,1977; Kubo and
Nakanishi,1977; Kubo and Nakanishi,1979). Several compounds
which we have isolated are shown in Figs. 2 and 3. Brief
comments are given for some selected compounds *Azadirachtin*
(Zanno,et al.1975; Nakanishi,1975).

This is a well-documented insect antifeedant (Gill and
Lewis,1971; Ruscoe,1972; Morgan and Thornton,1973) which is
contained in the leaves and berries of *Azadirachta indica*
(Indian neem tree) and *Melia azedarach* (China-berry tree).
Extensive structural studies were carried out by Morgan and
co-workers (Butterworth, et al.1972) but the noncrystalline
compound was too difficult to deal with in the days preceding
^{13}C-NMR. We were able to isolate 800 mg from 300 g of the
large fruit seeds of fresh berries collected from trees near
Mombasa. However, the yield is usually much lower, and it may
well be due to seasonal variation. It is one of the most
potent antifeedants against the African desert locust
Schistocerca gregaria, the limiting concentration to cause
100% inhibition of feeding being 40 µg/liter or when impregnated onto filter paper 1 nanogram/cm^2 (Morgan and Thornton,
1973). There is great interest in this tree, or the anti-

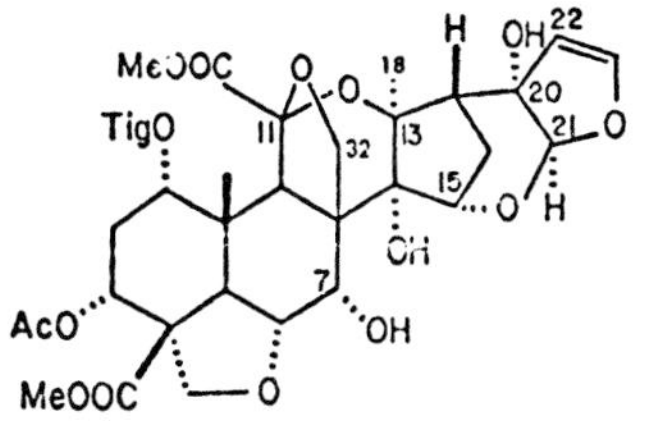

azadirachtin

J. Am.Chem.Soc., 97, 1975(1975)

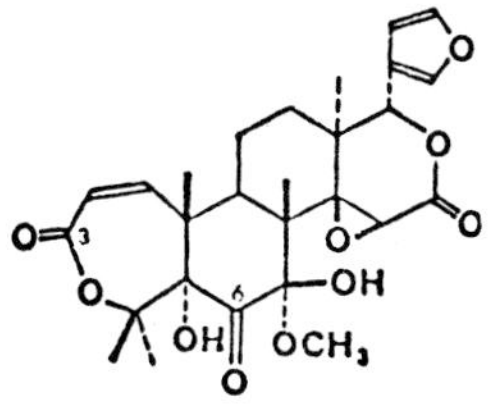

harrisonin

Heterocycles, 5, 485(1976)

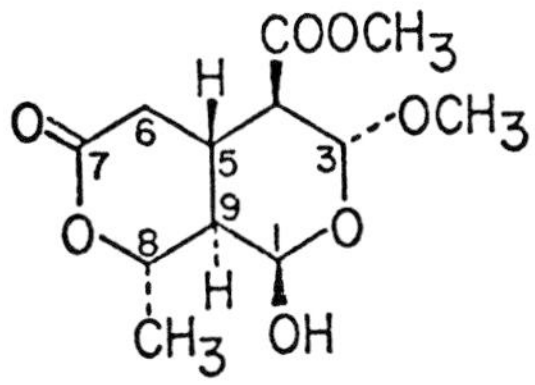

xylomolin

J. Am.Chem.Soc., 98, 6704(1976)
J. Am.Chem.Soc., 100, 7079(1978)

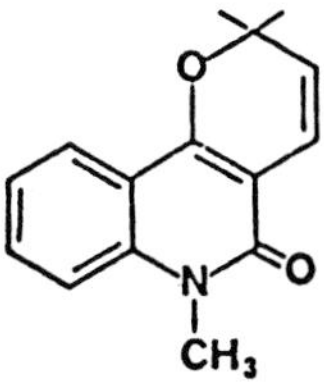

N-methylflindersine

Heterocycles, 7, 969(1977)

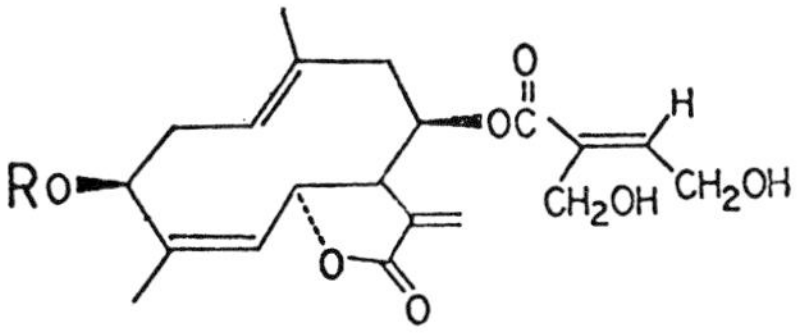

schkurin-I   R = Ac

II   R = $-C-C-C\overset{Me}{\underset{Me}{}}$

HETEROCYCLES, 11, 471(1978)

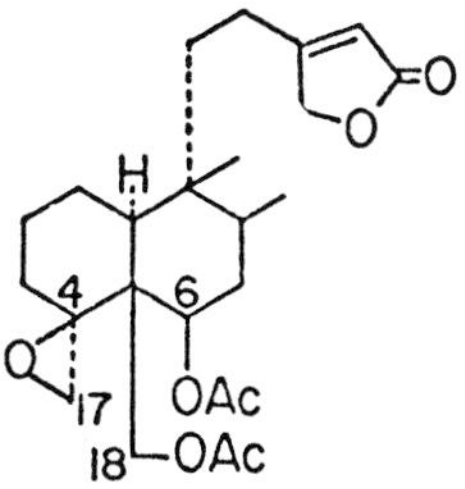

ajugarin-I
-II (6-OH)
-III (4,17-diol)

J.C.S.CHEM.COMM.,
949 (1976)

FIGURE 2.   Some Antifeedants isolated from East African Plants.

Warburgia ugandensis (Canellaceae)

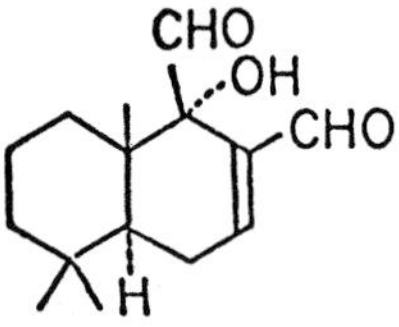

warburganal
Chem. Comm. 1013(1976)

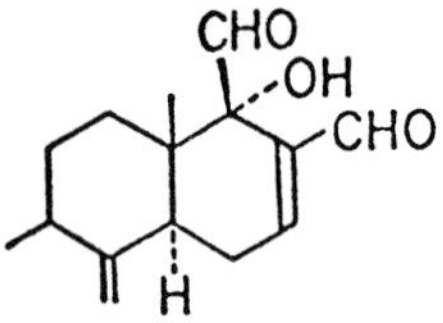

muzigadial
Tet. Let., 4553(1977)

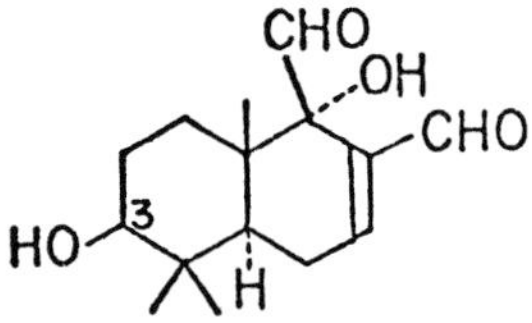

3-OH warburganal

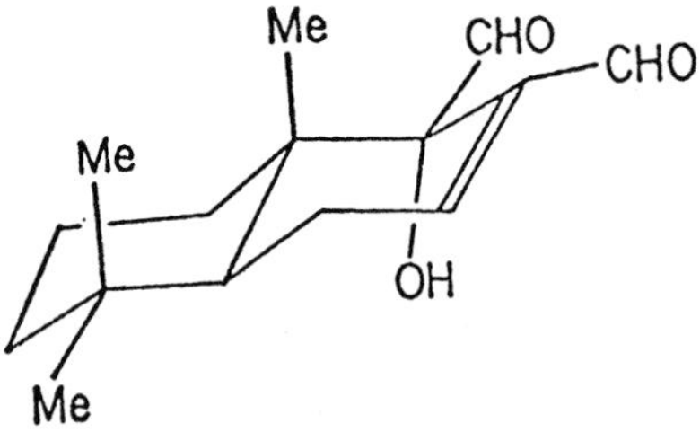

Biological Activity of Warburganal - I

Insect antifeedant "choice test"

Spodoptera exempta (oligophagous)   0.1 ppm
S. littoralis (polyphagous)   10   ppm

Schistocerca gregaria (polyphagous) and
Locusta migratoria (gramnivorous)
    85-90% inhibition at 0.01% dry weight
    of fiber disc containing 5% sucrose
    [Dr.E.A. Bernays, COPR, London]

weakly or nonactive against

S. eridania   Epilachna varivestis
Schistocerca vaga   Manduca sexta

Antimicrobial

Saccharomyces cerevisiae   12.5 µg/ml
Candida utilis   3.1
Sclerotinia libertiana   50
Mucor mucedo   100

Molluscicidal

Biompharis glabratus   5 ppm - 2 hrs
B. pfeifferi   5 ppm - 2 hrs
Lymnaca natalensis   10 ppm - 2 hrs

Cytotoxicity

KB test   0.01 µg/ml

Acute toxicity

subcutaneous injection in mice, LD_{50} 20.4 mg/kg

FIGURE 3. Activities of Warburganal.

feedant(s), for potential use as a means of controlling pest
insects. The structure is too complex to be synthesized on a
practical basis but studies are ongoing at various places to
cultivate the tree, isolate other active principles, etc.
In fact the Frist International Neem Conference will be held
in June, 1980 in West Germany to discuss future approaches.
      Warburganal (Kubo, et al.1976,1977).   This sesquiterpene
is one of the strongest against the African army-worm (see
above) and besides exhibits a broad spectrum of activity. Its
synthesis has also been completed by at least three groups
(Tanis and Nakanishi,1979; Nakata, et al.1979; Ohsuka and
Matsukawa,1979). The bark of the tree is a favorite spice
used by East Africans; it has a pleasant hot taste which is
also true for warburganal. The too broad activity may
severely restrict its use as a practical antifeedant.

IV. SUMMARY

     The tropical flora offer a rich source of bioactive com-
pounds. Although natural products chemist have indeed been
studying plants extensively it is only recent that the
isolation is being followed on a more purpose oriented and
systematic manner. The natural products thus isolated will
serve to suggest entirely new types of active compounds, an
aspect which has been so fruitful in microbial antibiotics;
another case, exemplified by *azadirachtin*, is the cultivation
of the plant itself to let nature take care of the synthesis.
As far as I am aware of, no commercial antifeedant is known;
obviously numerous untested difficulties have to be overcome
even if a potentially useful compound was discovered. However, the antifeedant may well provide an additional means
for the integrated control of insects. One advantage is that
they are frequently extracted from plants which have been used
over the years in folk medicine and hence are less likely to
be toxic to animals.

ACKNOWLEDGMENTS

     The systematic studies carried out in our laboratory was
led by Professor Isao Kubo who was here for the years 1977 -
1979 before going to Berkeley.
     I am grateful to my other colleagues who are quoted in the
references and to the entire ICIPE organization.

REFERENCES

Butterworth, J.H., and Morgan, E.D. (1968). Isolation of a
    substance that suppresses feeding in locusts. *Chem.Commun.*
    23 - 24.
Butterworth, J.H., and Morgan, E.D. (1971). *J. Insect Physiol.*
    17, 969.
Butterworth, J.H., Morgan, E.D., and Percy, G.R. (1972). The
    structure of azadirachtin; the functional groups.
    J. Chem. Soc. Perkin Trans.I, 2445 - 2450.
Gill, G.S., and Lewis, C.T. (1971). Systemic action of an
    insect feeding deterrent. *Nature 232*, 402 - 403.
Kubo, I., Lee, Y.-W., Pettei, M.J., Pilkiewicz, F., and Naka-
    nishi, K. (1976). Potent army worm antifeedants from the
    East African *Warburgia* Plants. *Chem.Commun.*, 1013 - 1014.
Kubo, I., Miura, I., Pettei, M.J., Lee, Y.-W., Pilkiewicz, F.,
    and Nakanishi, K. (1977). Muzigadial and warburganal,
    potent antifungal, antiyeast, and African army worm anti-
    feedant agents. *Tetrahedron Lett.*, 4553 - 4556.
Kubo, I., and Nakanishi, K. (1977). Insect antifeedants and
    repellents from African plants. In "Host plant resistance
    to pests", Am. Chem. Soc. Symposium Series, 62, (P.A.
    Hedin, ed.) pp 165 - 178.
Kubo, I., and Nakanishi, K. (1979). Some terpenoid insect
    antifeedants from tropical plants. In "Advances in pesti-
    cide Science" Part 2, (H. Geissbuhler,ed.), pp. 284 - 294.
    Pergamon Press, Oxford.
Kupchan, S.M., Hemingway, R.J., and Smith, R.M. (1969). Tumor
    inhibitors.XLV crotepoxide, a novel cyclohexane diepoxide
    tumor inhibitor from *Croton macrostachys. J. Org. Chem.*
    34, 3898 - 3902.
Ma, W.-C. (1977). Alterations of chemoreceptor function in
    army worm larvae *(Spodoptera exempta)* by a plant-derived
    sesquiterpenoid and by sulfhydryl reagents. *Physiol*
    Entomol. 2, 199 - 207.
Ma, W.-C., and Kubo, I. (1977). Phagostimulants for Spodopt-
    era exempta: Identification of adenosine from Zea and mays.
    Entomol. Exp. Appl. 22, 107 - 112.
Morgan, E.D., and Thornton, M.D. (1973). Azadirachtin in the
    fruit of *Melia azadarach. Phytochem. 12*, 391 - 392.
Munakata, K. (1970). Insect antifeedants in plants. In
    "Control of Insect Behavior by Natural Products" (D.L.
    Wood,ed.) pp. 179 - 187. Academic Press, New York, N.Y.
Nakanishi,K. (1975). In "Recent Advances in Phytochemistry"
    (V.C. Runeckles, ed.), *9*, 283.

Nakanishi, K. (1977). Insect growth regulators from plants. *Pontificiae Academiae Scientiarvm Scripta Varia 41*, 185-198.

Nakanishi, K., and Kubo, I. (1977). Studies on warburganal, muzigadial and related compounds. *Israel J. Chem. 16*, 28 - 31.

Nakata, T., Akita, H., Naito, T., and Oishi, T. (1979). A total synthesis of (±)-warburganal. *J.Am. Chem. Soc. 101*, 4400 - 4401.

Ohsuka, A., and Matsukawa, A. (1979). Synthesis of (±)warburganal and (±) isotadeonal. *Chem. Lett.*, 635 - 636.

Ruscoe, C.N.E. (1972). Growth disruption effects of an insect antifeedant. *Nature (London), New Biol. 236*, 159 - 160.

Tanis, S.P., and Nakanishi, K. (1979). Stereospecific total synthesis of (±)-warburganal and related compounds. *J. Am. Chem. Soc. 101*, 4398 - 4400.

Zack, C. (1980). Unpublished.

Zanno, P.R., Miura, I., Nakanishi, K., and Elder, D.L. (1975). Structure of the insect phagorepellent azadirachtin. Application of PRFT/CWD carbon-13 nuclear magnetic resonance. *J. Am. Chem. Soc. 97, 1975 - 1977.*

CHEMISTRY OF PLANT/INSECT INTERACTIONS

William S. Bowers

Department of Entomology
New York State Agricultural Experiment Station
Cornell University
Geneva, New York

I. INTRODUCTION

The coevolution of plants and insects has generated an incredibly complex variety of chemical interactions. Plants produce chemicals as a means of defense against insect predation. These compounds may be toxic, repellant, serve as antifeedants or induce subtle perturbations of insect growth, development, reproduction, diapause and behavior. The latter group of chemicals are becoming increasingly known as "insect growth regulators". The pioneering research of Professor Wigglesworth in insect endocrinology provided the basis for the current interest over insect hormones, not only in the academic view of them as exciting regulators of insect metamorphosis and reproduction, but also to many agricultural scientists as potential insect control agents (Wigglesworth, 1934, 1935). The researches of Williams, who prepared the first juvenile hormone extract from an insect (1956) and who later in collaboration with Slama found the first plant-derived chemical with juvenile hormone activity in 1965, established the possibility that plants might employ hormone analogs to interrupt important aspects of insect development and reproduction. The discovery in plants of insect molting hormones (ecdysones) by Nakanishi et al. (1966), powerfully reinforced this concept.

More recently, additional compounds with extremely high juvenile hormone activity have been identified from the sweet basil plant (Bowers and Nishida, 1980). Compounds with anti-juvenile hormone activity called "precocenes" were isolated from the Ageratum plant (Bowers, 1976; Bowers et al., 1976). The precocenes destroy the gland (corpus allatum) which produces the juvenile hormone. This action prevents the secretion of the juvenile hormones and results in precocious metamorphosis, sterilization and induction of diapause in sensitive species.

Plants have also been found to provide chemicals of communicative significance to insects either directly or as precursors of chemical messengers called pheromones. While it is clear that certain of the pheromones are directly derived from plants, the chemical origin of other pheromones has been shown to be produced in total by the insect. A large gray area exists in which the biogenesis of chemicals employed by insects for communication is unknown, including both alarm pheromones and sex pheromones. Certain plants have been shown to contain compounds which are identical to various insect pheromones and/or compounds which, although not related chemically to certain pheromones, are able to mimic their precise biological effect upon the insect, arousing the suspicion that plants are perhaps using pheromonal components to confuse or otherwise interrupt insect communication.

For their part insects have also learned to take advantage of the chemical qualities of plants by keying in upon specific plant chemicals for the location of shelter, food and ovipositional sites. A few highly specialized insects produce unique chemicals which influence the growth of plants such as gall formation by certain Hymenoptera, who secrete chemicals that stimulate plant tissues to proliferate in highly specific ways (Grummer, 1955). Insects are known to sequester substances from plants which are used in defense. These are called allomones. Certain chemical emanations from plants are used by insect parasites to locate the plants upon which their prey feeds. Such chemical messages are known as kairomones (Brown et al., 1970).

The large number of insect plant chemical interactions known and suspect is far too broad a subject to be considered in this brief treatise. Fortunately other contributors will deal in depth with kairomones, pheromones and antifeedants. The present account will detail, albeit briefly, subjects in which the author has been involved, including plant-derived synergists, hormones, anti-hormones and pheromones.

II. INSECTICIDAL CONSTITUENTS OF PLANTS

Insects are conspicuous consumers of plants. When those plants are important sources of food and fiber to humans, methods of preventing insect attack become a serious human preoccupation. Perhaps some of the earliest interest in the chemistry of plants followed the perception that certain plants resisted insect attack and moreover could be demonstrated to contain substances poisonous to insects. There is little question that the earliest insecticides were plant-derived toxicants. An outstanding example of a natural plant insecticide is the extract derived from the dried flowers of Chrysanthemum cinerariaefolium, a member of the plant family Compositae. The powder of the flowers has been used as an insecticide since ancient times. The original home of the pyrethrum flower is believed to be the Middle East. In the 19th Century these plants were introduced into Europe, the United States, and then Japan, Africa and South America. Today approximately 30,000 tons of natural pyrethrum extract is produced for a world-wide export market. The largest producer is Kenya, followed by Tanzania and Japan. Several related toxic compounds are present in the crude pyrethrum extract; the most toxic one is called pyrethrin I (Fig. 1). Although the pyrethrins are very useful as insecticides, their toxicity is greatly enhanced by co-formulation with compounds called insecticide synergists. These are compounds which are not intrinsically toxic by themselves, but which increase the toxicity of other compounds, usually by interferring with the poison detoxifying enzymes in the target insect. It was discovered by Eagelson in 1942 that sesame oil markedly increased the effective insecticidal action of pyrethrins. It was demonstrated that the sesame oil contained several synergistic compounds including sesamin (Haller et al., 1942), and sesamolin (Beroza, 1954) (Fig. 1). The discovery that the combination of two plant-derived components (one from pyrethrum flower and the other from sesame oil) made a more effective insecticide seemed simply to be a fortuitous coincidence. However, Doskotch and El-Feraly in 1969 found that the natural pyrethrum extract also contained sesamin. The effect of such a combination of toxin and synergist clearly supports the idea that plants have evolved highly complex and effective chemical defense mechanisms against insect attack. It is also possible that such synergists have dual roles in plant protection. I found that the natural synergists sesamin and sesamolin, and certain synthetic synergists including piperonyl butoxide and sesoxane possessed juvenile hormone activity. Combining chemical structural features of the synergists and the natural hormones resulted in juvenile hormone mimics (Fig. 1) with hormonal activity far exceeding that of the natural hormones (Bowers, 1968, 1969), and led to the birth of a new class of insect growth regulators. Subsequently, Fales et al. (1970), found that several of these *hybrid* hormonal compounds which had been "optimized" for juvenile hormone activity possessed significant synergism for pyrethrum against houseflies.

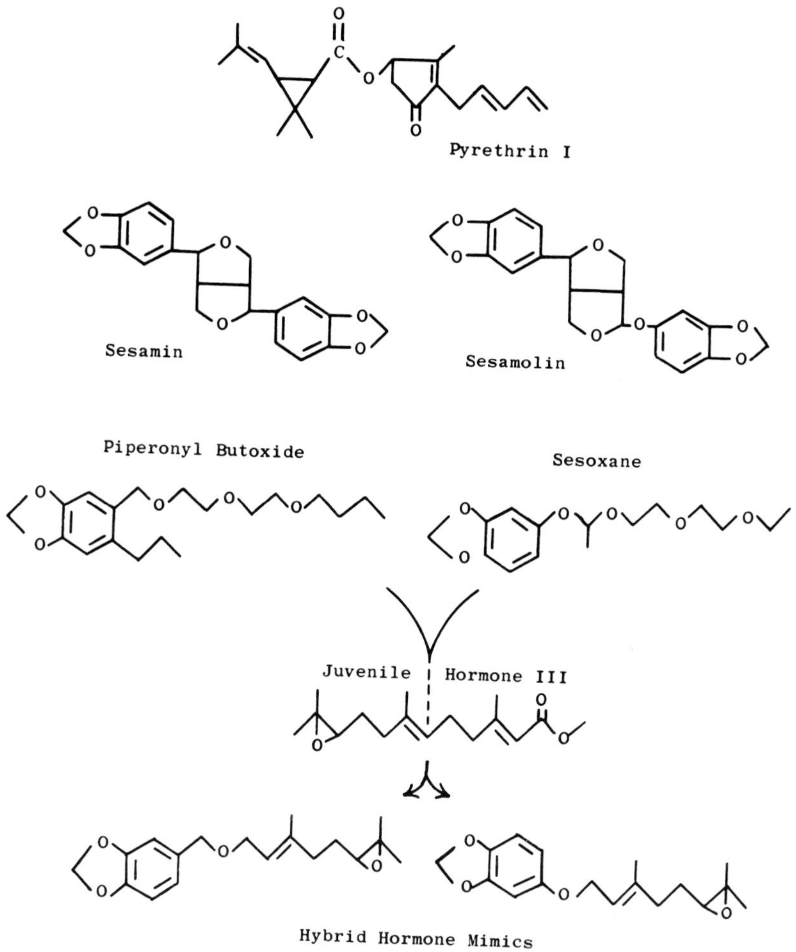

Pyrethrin I

Sesamin

Sesamolin

Piperonyl Butoxide

Sesoxane

Juvenile Hormone III

Hybrid Hormone Mimics

FIGURE 1. A natural insecticide (pyrethrin) and synergists (sesamin, sesamolin) provided the basis for the development of synthetic synergists and juvenile hormone-active growth regulators.

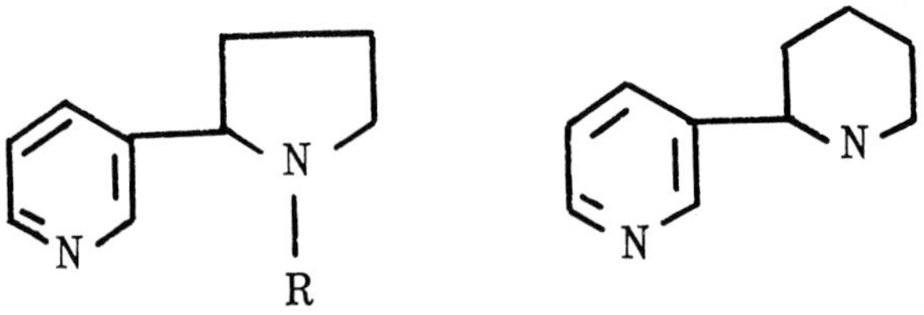

R = CH$_3$, Nicotine   Anabasine

R = H, Nornicotine

FIGURE 2. Principal insecticidal alkaloids of Nicotiana.

Long before chemists isolated and identified the principle toxic component in the tobacco plant, farmers were using powdered tobacco leaves or water extracts of the plant to control insects. As long ago as 1690 reference has been made to the use of tobacco as an insecticide in Europe. At that time tobacco was a trade item between the American Colonies and Europe (Schmeltz, 1971). Nicotine, as we now know it, is toxic to insects by contact, fumigation, or by feeding. Nicotine (Fig. 2) is well known now as a physiologically active substance, and as a major component of tobacco smoke is considered a significant health hazard. That this compound does not at present enjoy widespread use as an insecticide is understandable. The nicotine alkaloid occurs in a wide variety of plants not being restricted to the tobacco plant, *Nicotiana tabacum*. In the tobacco plant levels of nicotine up to 6% are common, while in a related species *Nicotiana rustica* higher levels of nicotine (up to 18%) are found and in the past were used for the extraction of nicotine for insecticidal preparations. Other unrelated plants containing significant amounts of nicotine are *Asclepias syriaca* (milkweed), *Atropa belladonna* (deadly nightshade), *Equisetum arvense* (horse tails), and *Lycopodium clavatum* (club moth). Thus, nicotine is found widely in plants and doubtless serves as a mechanism of defense against insect attack. Related compounds such as nornicotine, and anabasine (Fig. 2) are also found in a variety of plants and have been used for insecticidal purposes.

Other naturally-occurring insecticides in plants are the rotenoids. For centuries plants in the genus *Derris* of the family Leguminosae have been used to kill the fish in rivers and ponds (chemical fishing) or to make poison spears or arrow points as an aid in hunting. Natives in the far eastern tropics, as well as in South America, tropical Africa and elsewhere, all commonly used extracts of these plants as a source of poison. Oxley in 1848 suggested the use of "tuba root" against leaf-eating caterpillars. Fukami and Nakajima (1971) mentioned that the Chinese had a long history of preparing an insecticide from the root of *Derris*. The active ingredient isolated from *Derris chinensis* was called "roten" by the natives in Formosa. Because it was shown to be a ketone it was assigned the name "rotenone" (Fig. 3). Approximately ten chemically related "rotenoids" from higher plants are known. A rotenone insecticide was of value in the control of leaf chewing insects and caterpillars because it did not leave a toxic residue. Rotenone has a very low degree of toxicity to vertebrates and is rapidly degraded to non-toxic substances. Thus, for many purposes, it was an ideal insecticide. The complicated structure, dependency upon natural sources, and the excessive cost of commercial synthesis, ruled out rotenone as a competitor to the more modern synthetic insecticides. However, rotenone serves as a reminder that compounds with significant toxicity to insects, without a special vertebrate toxicity, are to be found in natural

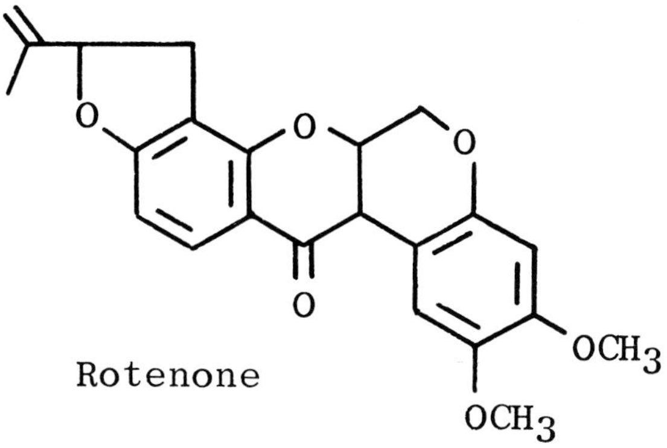

FIGURE 3. Rotenone.

sources. Unhappily, significant chemical investigation of rotenone has not been carried to the point of developing simpler, more cost-effective analogs.

While the aforementioned plant-derived insecticides were probably the most important and widely used in commercial practice, only analogs of the pyrethrins have survived the test of time and economics. It should be emphasized that the new pyrethroids are perhaps among the most effective insecticides ever known, and will doubtless play an ever-increasing and important role in the future protection of plants and the public health from insect predators and disease vectors. Dozens of other compounds with insecticidal potential have been identified in plants in the past. Cottage industries in many countries developed and revolved about the collection or cultivation of plants useful for their insecticidal components. The increased effectiveness and cost competition of synthetic insecticides has eliminated nearly all of these industries from the marketplace. At the same time it should be recognized that many of the natural insecticides from plants are also quite toxic to vertebrates, and would never pass the stringent requirements currently imposed for environmental protection.

III. CHEMICAL COMMUNICATION BETWEEN INSECTS AND PLANTS

Plants and insects possess a very complex variety of chemicals of communicative significance. Insects use specific plant chemicals as recognition signals for shelter, food and oviposition. In turn, plants produce a variety of chemicals important in influencing insect behavior including insect growth regulators, repellants, feeding deterrents and toxicants. The attractive fragrances produced by flowers for the promotion of plant pollination by insects is so widespread and well recognized as to deserve little additional comment.

Many plant chemicals are sequestered by insects and used for purposes of communication or defense. The concentration of toxic cardenolides from milkweed (*Asclepiadaceae*) by the Monarch butterflies for defensive purposes is well established (Roeske *et al.*, 1975). Sex and aggregation pheromones secreted by various insects have been found to contain plant-contributed components and precursors. In the western pine beetle, *Dendroctonus brevicomis*, a multi-component pheromone complex has been identified as a sex and aggregation mixture containing three compounds, one produced by the female, one produced by the male, and a third component contributed by the pine tree itself (Fig. 4). The pine tree-derived material is the well-known myrcene. Dozens of other examples of plant-derived poisons and their immediate

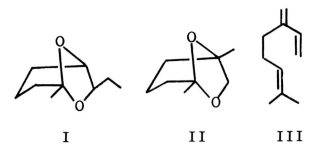

I   II   III

FIGURE 4. Multicomponent pheromone mixture of the western pine beetle, Dendroctonus brevicomis. The female and male produce compounds I and II respectively, while
the host tree produces compound III.

precursors used by insects for defensive purposes might be mentioned. Rothschild
(1972) has tabulated 43 examples from six orders of invertebrates known to sequester
and store plant toxins.

A. *Aphid Alarm Pheromone*

Another important group of chemicals employed in insect communication are the
alarm pheromones which have been rather well studied in social insects, particularly
ants, termites and bees. Less well studied are the alarm pheromones of aphids, which
are best characterized as presocial insects displaying only a primitive sociality.
Nevertheless, aphids exist in aggregations and are usually composed of a
parthenogenetic female surrounded by her female offspring. When attacked by a
predator or a parasite, aphids respond by secreting droplets of fluid from specialized
organs on the tip of the abdomen called cornicles. This fluid contains many sticky
materials which are probably repugnant and irritating to a variety of predators. The most
interesting component of this secretion, however, is the alarm pheromone which
signals to other aphids in the aggregation the presence of danger. These aphids respond by moving quickly away from the source of pheromone or jumping off of the plant.
Since the pheromone is produced only in seriously distressful situations it might be
regarded as a signal equivalent to a dying gasp. This alarm response of aphids was first
noticed by Dahl (1971) in the pea aphid, *Acyrthosiphon pisum*. We were able to isolate
and identify the active substance in this and several related aphids as *trans-β-*
farnesene (Fig. 5) (Bowers et al., 1972). Farnesenes are very common sesquiterpene
hydrocarbons found in a variety of plants and animals. The closely related *trans,trans-*
α-farnesene (Fig. 5) has been identified from Dufour's gland in ants and probably
serves as an alarm pheromone (Cavill et al., 1967). *α*-Farnesene has also been
reported as the only sesquiterpene present in the coating of "Granny Smith" apples by
Huelin and Murray in 1966. Wearing and Hutchins (1972) have identified *α*-farnesene
in apple coatings as a naturally occurring oviposition stimulant for the codling moth,
Laspeyresia pomonella. Sutherland and Hutchins (1972) found that the larvae of the
codling moth similarly were attracted to two farnesene isomers, *trans,trans-α*-
farnesene and *cis,trans-α*-farnesene. Clearly the farnesenes have been selected by a
variety of insects including aphids, ants and moths to serve as chemical cues for alarm,
oviposition, and attraction to food. More complex interactions occur between ants and
Myrmecophilous aphids, which are cared for and protected by ants. When these aphids
are free-living, they respond readily to their alarm pheromones by dispersal; however,

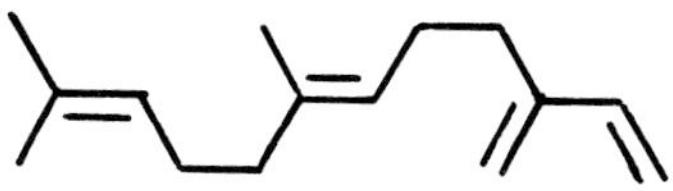

(E) - β - Farnesene 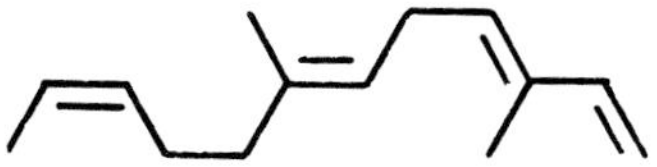   (E, E) - α - Farnesene

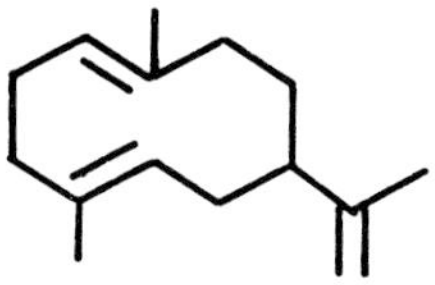

Germacrene A

FIGURE 5. Alarm pheromones of aphids and ants.

when they are tended by ants we have found (Nault et al., 1976) that the aphids tend to lose their instinctive dispersal when exposed to the alarm pheromone and instead simply waggle their bodies. In such situations it was clearly seen that the protecting ants rush to the source of the alarm pheromone and attack any predators disturbing the aphids. Synthetic trans-β-farnesene could be shown to readily provoke rapid attack by aphidicolus ants confirming that the ants were indeed responding to the alarm pheromone itself and not some other component of the cornicle secretion.

We found that the macrocyclic plant-derived sesquiterpene "germacrene A" was the principal alarm pheromone (Fig. 5) of several forage crop aphids including the sweet clover aphid, Therioaphis riehmi and the spotted alfalfa aphid, Therioaphis maculata (Bowers et al., 1977). This sesquiterpene is much less common in plants than the farnesenes, being found in Douglas fir needles and also in a gorgonian coral, Eunicea mammesa by Weinheimer et al., 1970.

B. American Cockroach Sex Pheromone

One of the most difficult problems in the structural determination of pheromones has been the long-standing problem of the structure of the American cockroach, Periplaneta americana, sex pheromone. Early attempts at structural elucidation were complicated by reports (Jacobson et al., 1963) of an incorrect structure for this attractant. Following its retraction by Jacobson and Beroza (1965) we (Bowers and Bodenstein, 1971) found that several compounds in plants would mimic the sex pheromone activity including (+)-bornyl acetate, α- and β-santalol, and an unidentified $C_{15}H_{24}$ hydrocarbon. Later, in more detailed studies of structure-biological activity, we (Nishino et al., 1977a) found that the related trans verbenyl acetate was also highly active (Fig. 6).

Tahara et al. (1975) correctly determined the nature of the unknown $C_{15}H_{24}$ hydrocarbon, which we had found in these plants, as germacrene D. Nishino et al. (1977b) authenticated germacrene D as a male specific pheromone mimic through electroantennogram studies. The very difficult isolation and identification of the natural sex pheromone of the American cockroach was finally accomplished by the elegant work of Persoons et al. (1976), who identified the structure as a highly oxygenated derivative of germacrene D and called it periplanone B (Fig. 6). The reason for the activity of other plant-derived compounds such as (+)-bornyl acetate and (+)-trans-verbenyl acetate which mimic completely the natural sex pheromone is unknown. This may be

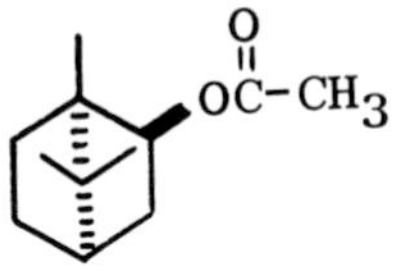

FIGURE 6. Sex pheromone mimics of the American cockroach, (I) bornyl acetate, (II) verbenyl acetate, and (III) germacrene D. The natural pheromone (IV) periplanone B.

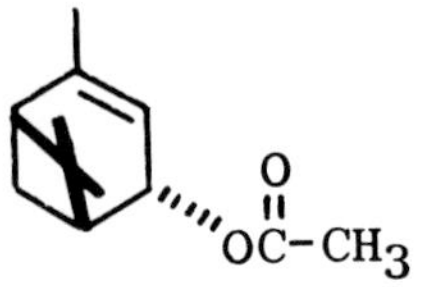

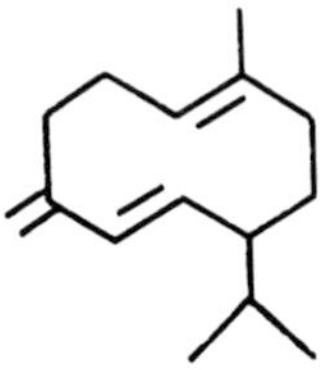

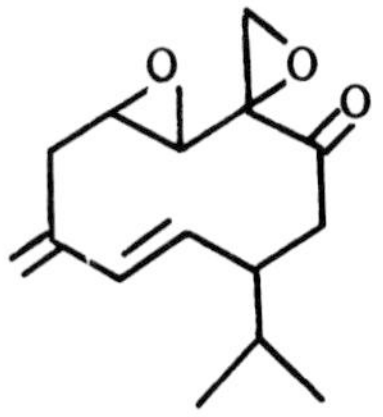

the first discovery of pheromone mimics which bear absolutely no chemical relationship with the natural pheromone, yet produce the exact behavioral response and even show the same electrophysiology. Whether the fortuitous discovery of such pheromone mimics presages similar discoveries for other pheromones such as sex, alarm or even kairomone-type pheromones provides interesting food for thought. Certainly the idea of developing pheromone analogs or mimics should receive attention in the future.

IV. INSECT HORMONES AND PLANT CHEMISTRY

A. Juvenile Hormones

Three natural juvenile hormones have been shown to occur in insects. We were fortunate to synthesize one of them now called juvenile hormone III (Bowers et al., 1965) prior to its identification from natural sources by Judy et al. in 1973. Roller et al. identified juvenile hormone I in 1967 and Meyer et al. identified juvenile hormone II in 1968. Hundreds of optimized analogs have been prepared and tested as candidates for insect control. The discovery by Schmialek (1961) that farnesol had juvenile hormone activity was the stimulus to the preparation of a large variety of acyclic juvenile hormone analogs. When I discovered that certain insecticide synergists possessed juvenile hormone activity a new generation of aromatic juvenile hormone analogs was soon forthcoming (Bowers, 1968, 1969).

During a sabbatical leave with Professor Williams at Harvard, Karel Slama discovered that his favorite experimental animal, the bug Pyrrhocoris apterus, consistently molted into intermediate forms in culture in the Harvard Laboratories, giving every evidence of having been exposed to a juvenile hormone. This perplexing situation led to the discovery by Slama and Williams in 1965 that when the developing insects were exposed to paper made from the balsam fir tree (an indigenous pulp wood of North

America), they acted just as though they had been treated with juvenile hormone. Ether extracts of the paper could be shown to induce juvenilization confirming that an organosoluble factor was responsible and apparently mimicked the juvenile hormone; the active substance was termed the "paper factor". Following this lead, we (Bowers *et al.*, 1966) isolated and identified the compound responsible for the activity and named it "juvabione" (Fig. 7). Its relationship with the known juvenile hormones is obvious, although it contains a monocyclic ring structure. Subsequently, Cerny *et al.* (1967) reported a related but somewhat less-active analog of juvabione, "dehydrojuvabione," from a Czechoslovakian fir tree.

Barton and MacDonald (1972) revealed that an extract of the western red cedar tree, *Thuja plicata*, exhibited juvenile hormone activity when applied to the abdomens of *Tenebrio* pupae in the assay described by Bowers in 1968. Isolation and identification of the active compound revealed thujic acid (Fig. 7) as the active component. Since this last work, little attention seems to have been paid to searching for additional juvenile hormone analogs in plants. Recently, we have identified several active compounds from plants including a new methylenedioxy analog from *Macropiper excelsum* (Nishida and Bowers, 1980) and two extremely active compounds from the herb, sweet basil, *Ocimum basilicum* (Bowers and Nishida, 1980) (Fig. 7). The latter two compounds are active against certain Hemiptera in the picogram range making them perhaps the most active juvenile hormone compounds discovered. Whether their presence in plants is evidence of a protective mechanism against predatory insects is extremely difficult to answer, but will serve as food for thoughtful investigators of the future concerned with plant-insect endocrinological interactions.

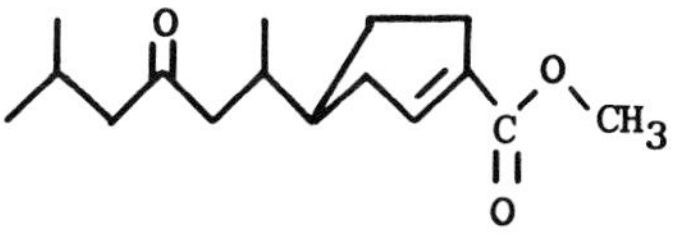

Juvabione

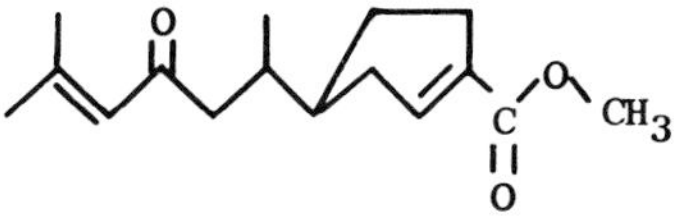

Dehydro Juvabione

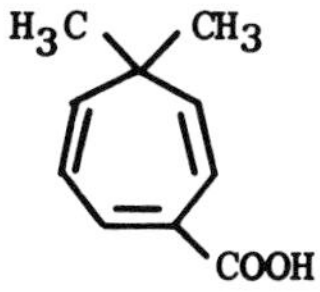

Thujic Acid

Macropiper Juvenile
Hormone Mimic

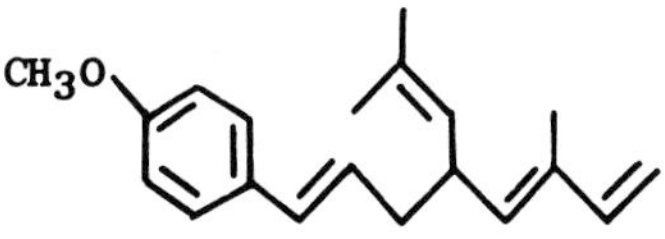

I

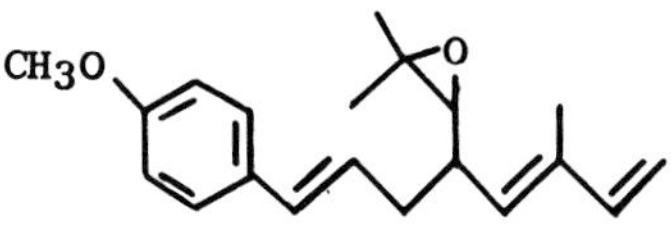

II

Juvocimenes

FIGURE 7. Plant derived juvenile hormone-active chemicals.

B. *Anti-Juvenile Hormones*

Although a juvenile hormone analog has been developed and registered for the control of flood water mosquito larvae and manure breeding flies (Henrick *et al.*, 1973), juvenile hormones or analogs of them have failed as generally useful methods for the control of plant-destroying insects. Unhappily the juvenile hormones are effective in deranging insect development only after the principal feeding stages have done their damage. Therefore, the juvenile hormones can only be used against those insects which are of economic importance in the adult stages.

Taking a somewhat different view I reasoned that since the juvenile hormones are important to the immature stages to control their development, and to the adult stages to assist in reproduction, the most useful approach to controlling insects through their endocrine system would be to interfere with the production of the juvenile hormone. We began searching for compounds in plants which might interfere with the synthesis, transport or action of the juvenile hormone. Ideally, a method of preventing the action of a juvenile hormone would result in the untimely early metamorphosis from the feeding stages to a tiny precocious adult. An adult lacking juvenile hormone would be sterilized since the juvenile hormone functions as a gonadotropic hormone in the adult female.

1. *Biological Activities.* I was fortunate to discover in the common bedding plant *Ageratum houstonianum* two compounds that on contact with certain insects induced their precocious metamorphosis into tiny sterile adults. This action prevents the continued feeding by the immature stages and eliminates further reproductive potential by the ensuing diminutive adults. In addition, normal adult reproducing females treated with these compounds become permanently sterilized (Fig. 8).

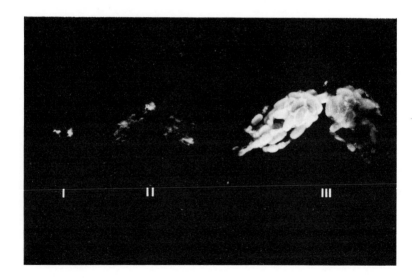

FIGURE 8. Effect of precocene II on ovarian development of milkweed bugs. Ovaries of: 5th stage precocious adult (I), precocene sterilized normal adult (II), and developed ovaries of normal adult (III).

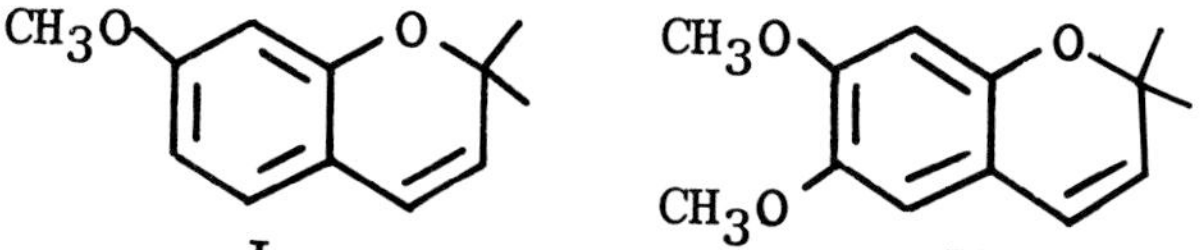

FIGURE 9. Anti-juvenile hormonal compounds from Ageratum and an optimized analog.

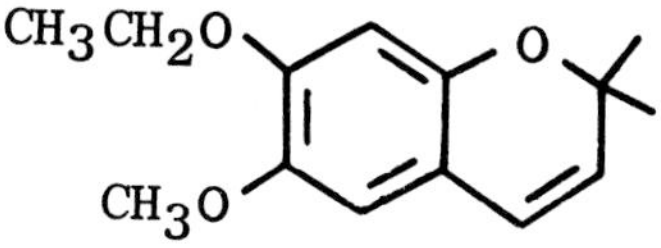

Certain species which normally diapause as adult insects were found to enter diapause soon after exposure to the plant-derived agents. The action of these compounds duplicated in every way the effects of surgical ablation of the insect corpus allatum, giving indisputable evidence that they were indeed anti-juvenile hormonal agents. This view was strengthened by the discovery that each effect of the anti-juvenile hormones could be reversed by treatment with juvenile hormone III. In view of their action we called the active compounds "precocene I and II" (Fig. 9) (Bowers, 1976, Bowers et al., 1976).

It was clear at the outset that the precocenes were most effective against hemimetabolous insects including several species of Hemiptera such as the milkweed bug, Oncopeltus fasciatus, the cotton stainer, Dysdercus cingulatus, the lesser milkweed bug, Lygaeus kalmii, and the leaf-footed bug, Leptoglossus phyllopus. Attempts to induce precocious maturation in several holometabola by feeding precocenes to the immatures were unsuccessful. These included larvae of the corn earworm, Heliothis zea, the wax moth, Galleria mellonella, and the mealworm, Tenebrio molitor. We were successful in sterilizing certain holometabolous adult insects by topical or contact treatment such as the Mexican bean beetle, Epilachna varivestis, and the plum curculio, Conotrachelus nenuphar. Many other adult holometabola were found to be refractory to treatment with the natural precocenes. Pener and Orshan (1977) and Nemec et al. (1978) demonstrated that precocene II would induce precocious metamorphosis in the African migratory locust, Locusta migratoria, identical with that produced by surgical allatectomy. Mackauer et al. (1978) found that treatment of young apterous viviparous pea aphids with precocene II produced alate offspring when reared under conditions that should have produced exclusively apterous offspring. Moreover they were able to show that this effect was reversible if the aphids were subsequently treated with juvenile hormone I. This study revealed a new order of insects sensitive to the precocenes and proves that the juvenile hormone is important in regulating apterae in aphids. Quite unexpectedly the precocenes have been shown to be active in Arthropods other than insects. Following Leahy's (1977) report of the sterilization of the soft tick, Argas persicus, with precocene II, Pound and Oliver (1979) were able to restore full ovarian development in precocene (II) sterilized Ornithodoros parkeri (Fig. 10) by their subsequent treatment with the insect juvenile hormone III. The conclusions to be drawn from these reports are as astonishing as unexpected; i.e., ticks must regulate their ovarian development with a hormone similar to, or identical with, the insect gonadotropic hormone(s) and must possess an (as yet undiscovered) endocrine gland equivalent to the insect corpus allatum. This is the first evidence of a role for a juvenile/gonadotropic hormone in ticks. The precocenes emerge here as important tools in investigating the control of physiological events by the juvenile hormone in insects and other animals where a surgical allatectomy is difficult or impossible.

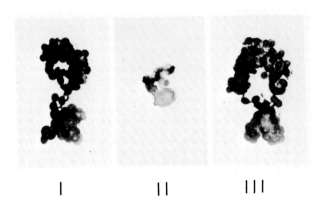

I   II   III

FIGURE 10. Reproductive systems of female ticks Ornithodoros parkeri. (I) From control tick treated with solvent only showing mature eggs in the uterus. (II) From a precocene treated tick, showing undeveloped eggs in the ovary and no eggs in the uterus. (III) From a precocene treated tick subsequently treated with JH III. The reproductive system shows mature eggs in the uterus, oviducts and ovary. (Photographs courtesy of Professor J. H. Oliver, Georgia Southern College).

Cupp et al. (1977) demonstrated the inhibition of pupation in the yellow fever mosquito, Aedes aegypti, on exposure of the larvae to precocene II, and Tarrant and Cupp (1978) showed that precocene II was highly effective against the immature stages of Rhodnius prolixus, an important vector of South American trypanosomiasis (Chagas' disease). In Rhodnius, treatment of the immature stages resulted in precocious metamorphosis from all nymphal stages into diminutive sterile adults. In addition, they found that precocious adults were produced following the treatment of eggs with precocene II. The resulting precocious adults were unable to feed and these researchers suggest that precocene derived adultoids would be unable to transmit disease.

2. Structure-Biological Activity Relationships. Optimization of the action of the precocenes through the synthesis of analogs has resulted in a variety of compounds more active than the two natural precocenes (Bowers, 1977). Structural elements important to activity are the unsubstituted chromene ring, and substitution with a small alkoxy group at the 7 position. It was clear from the outset that a substituent in the 6 position is not necessary to activity; however, substitution with a small alkoxy group in the 6 position increases activity for certain insects. One of the more active analogs against a variety of insects is the 7-ethoxy analog (Fig. 9) of precocene II. Several di-chromenes were also found to be active but at a reduced level.

3. Mode of Action. One of the most exciting aspects about the precocenes is their ability to somehow prevent the production of juvenile hormone. The mode of action is

therefore of critical importance if one is considering either the utilitarian possibilities of developing anti-juvenile hormones for insect control agents, or the use of the precocenes as physiological probes to understand insect metamorphosis development, reproduction, diapause or behavior. The earliest evidence for the mode of action was our observation (Bowers and Martinez-Pardo, 1977) that the corpus allatum of sterilized female milkweed bugs was very small compared with that of reproducing controls. It was observed that precocene treatment of newly emerged milkweed bug females prevented the corpora allata from increasing in size at all, whereas the corpora allata of control insects increased rapidly during post-imaginal development, reaching its maximum size in approximately 9 days. If reproducing females with fully developed corpora allata were treated with precocene there was a rapid diminuition in size of the corpus allatum and ovarian development came to a halt. Such insects were permanently sterilized. Treatment of sterilized insects with juvenile hormone III resulted in rapid ovarian development and successful reproduction, demonstrating that precocene had no direct effect upon the ovary. There seemed little doubt that precocene interfered somehow with the development and functionalization of the corpus allatum. Masner et al. (1979) showed that the corpora allata of treated insects remained inactivated even when transplanted into untreated insects, emphasizing the irreversibility of changes induced by precocene treatment. We (Unnithan et al., 1977) found that the corpora allata of treated insects contained disintegrating nuclei, degenerating mitochondria, lysosome-like bodies and autophagic vacuoles. Liechty and Sedlak (1978) found that the ultrastructure of cells in the corpora allata of precocene-treated milkweed bugs contained vast accumulations of vesicles usually seen only in immature glands. In Locusta, Schooneveld (1979) found that irreversible regression of the corpora allata in fourth instar nymphs occurs very rapidly after application of precocene. Degenerative changes could be observed in cells of the corpus allatum as early as 90 minutes after treatment, and cells began to collapse within 2 hours. Unnithan et al. (1980) shows total distruction of the cells of the corpus allatum in the desert locust, Schistocerca gregaria following precocene treatment. The corpora allata become invaded by connective tissue and no normal allatal cells remain. The glandular residue is essentially a scar. An effect of precocene on the neurosecretory A cells in the pars intercerebralis of the milkweed bug was reported by Unnithan et al. (1977). They found a significant diminuition in the stainable material of the A cells and moreover demonstrated that treatment with juvenile hormone III restored the stainable material in these cells. These results suggested a possible involvement of the neurosecretory cells in the brain with the action of precocene. At this juncture it was important to determine whether precocene was affecting the cells in the corpus allatum directly or whether its action was mediated somehow through the neurosecretory cells of the brain. The importance in the timing of precocene treatment for the destruction of the corpus allatum in the milkweed bug was highlighted in the work of Unnithan and Nair (1979) who demonstrated that precocene would destroy the corpora allata only in those stages during which the gland was actively secreting juvenile hormone. Treatment of fourth stage nymphs of the milkweed bug with precocene resulted in either precocious adults with inactive corpora allata, or in normal development through the fifth instar to adults which were sterile and whose corpora allata had been inactivated. If, on the other hand, precocene treatment was performed on the last nymphal stage during which the corpora allata are normally inactive, reproductively competent adults ensued. These data revealed that the precocenes result in the destruction of corpus allatum cells only in glands which are secreting juvenile hormone. Since the corpora allata are known to be controlled by the brain it was necessary to determine whether precocene was acting via an effect on the brain, or directly upon the corpus allatum. Pratt and Bowers (1977) found that precocene II inhibited juvenile hormone biosynthesis in vitro, but the level of precocene required left a residue of uncertainty on the specificity of action. In the milkweed bug, we have found that when the nerve connections between the brain and the corpus allatum were severed surgically, treatment with precocene inevitably resulted in sterilization and destruction of the gland itself. Moreover, transplantation of these glands into last instar milkweed bug nymphs did not produce supernumerary molting (Bowers and Aldrich, 1980). This was irrefutable evidence that precocene was acting directly upon the cells of the corpus allatum and that its cytotoxic effect was not the result of mediation by the brain or other tissue. Muller et al. (1979) found that corpora allata of the milkweed bug cultured with precocene II *in vitro* were destroyed, since subsequent implantation into last instar milkweed bug nymphs did not result in supernumerary molting.

In metabolism tests on 11 species of insects using carbon-14 radiosynthesized precocene II, the 3,4-diol was identified as an early and very important metabolite (Ohta et al., 1977). The rapid appearance of the diol suggested that the double bond had undergone epoxidation by mixed function oxidase enzymes followed by rapid hydration. We wondered whether the intermediate epoxide might in fact be an activation product. Attempts to isolate the epoxide from insects was at first believed successful. Although this identification appears doubtful on re-examination (Soderlund et al., 1980), the intermediacy of the epoxide and its role as an activated intermediate appeared very likely. Accordingly, every effort was made to synthesize epoxy precocene. We were finally able to prepare the elusive compound by base closure of the bromohydrin (Soderlund et al., 1980) under strictly anhydrous conditions. All other synthetic attempts including the use of organic peracids or photo-chemical catalysis resulted in the preparation of half-esters and/or the 3,4-diol. Subsequently, Jennings and Ottridge (1979) successfully prepared precocene I epoxide by the same procedure. The very lability of the epoxide suggested its mode of action, since we found that the epoxide reacts with any nucleophile instantaneously. This implies that while most of the precocene is rapidly epoxidized, hydrated, conjugated and eliminated from the insect body, a small aliquot reaches the corpus allatum, is epoxidized (perhaps by the same enzyme which epoxidizes juvenile hormone) and then instantaneously reacts with important cellular components through the formation of covalent alkylation (Fig. 11).

ACTIVATION—METABOLISM OF PRECOCENE II

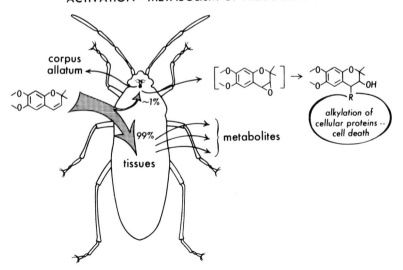

FIGURE 11. Presumptive mode of action of the precocenes.

The products of alkylation then cause cellular disintegration and collapse. Important elements of any future study of the metabolism and mode of action of the precocenes will of necessity involve the identification of the precocene-alkylated cellular products. We believe this mode of action fully explains the unique cytotoxicity of the precocenes in the insect corpus allatum. Brooks *et al.* (1979) showed that the methylenedioxy analog of precocene inhibits epoxidation and prevents the activity of precocene. This lends strong support to the theory of epoxidative bioactivation of the precocenes.

C. *Molting Hormones (Ecdysones)*

The insect molting hormones (ecdysones) are produced from endocrine glands usually located in the prothoracic region of immature insects. These hormones regulate processes which lead to ecdysis. Growth and development, as well as metamorphosis, depend upon these critical hormones. Frankel (1935) demonstrated that ligation of a blowfly larva at an appropriate time would allow pupation in the anterior portion only, and that the posterior half of the larva could be induced to pupate when blood from a new pupa was injected into this portion of the larva. This provided clear evidence that a hormone was present in the blood derived from some anterior aspect of the maggot, which induced pupation. Wigglesworth identified the source of one hormone necessary to pupation as coming from the brain in 1940. Fukuda in 1940 (a, b) found that the molting hormones were produced in the prothoracic gland of silkworm larvae. Williams (1946, 1947, 1950), in a series of experiments, demonstrated that the brain produced a hormone which acted upon the prothoracic gland, which in turn produced the actual molting hormone. Becker and Plagge (1938, 1939) prepared the first active extracts of the molting hormones and developed the biological assay utilizing ligated *Calliphora* larvae. In 1954 Butenandt and Karlson were able to isolate 25 milligrams of the pure crystalline hormone from one-half ton of silkworm pupae. They named this compound ecdysone (Greek, ecdysis = molt). Later, in 1956, Karlson isolated 2.5 milligrams of a second more polar hormone which he called β-ecdysone to distinguish it from the earlier isolated hormone now called α-ecdysone. Final proof of structure for ecdysone was developed in the work of Huber and Hoppe (1965) who proved that ecdysone was indeed a steroid and assigned the structure $2\beta,3\beta,-14\alpha,22R,25$-pentahydroxy-5$\beta$-cholest-7-en-6-one. The chemistry of the second rarer natural ecdysone referred to as β-ecdysone was properly identified by Horn *et al.* (1966) from crayfish. It differs from α-ecdysone in having a 20-hydroxy substituent. It was originally called crustecdysone. However, Hocks and Wiechert (1966) proved that crustecdysone and β-ecdysone were identical.

A third ecdysone was identified by Thompson *et al.* (1967) as 20,26-dihydroxyecdysone. Its biological activity in the housefly test is somewhat less than that of β-ecdysone. The first two ecdysones isolated from insects are shown in Fig. 12.

1. *Phytoecdysones.* Following the structural determination of the natural ecdysones Nakanishi *et al.* (1966) found compounds in plants with ecdysone activity. The discovery of ecdysones in plants paralleled our isolation and identification of compounds with insect juvenile hormone activity from plants (Bowers *et al.*, 1966). The first phytoecdysone isolated by Nakanishi from *Podocarpus nakaii* was called ponasterone A. It was shown to differ from insect hormones by lacking a C-25 hydroxyl group. However, it possessed the same C-20C-22diol function of β-ecdysone (Fig. 12). A very large number of additional phytoecdysones have been discovered and reviewed in detail far beyond the context of this summary (Horn, 1971).

In view of the widespread occurrence of phytoecdysones in a large variety of unrelated plant families one must consider the very real possibility that the phytoec-

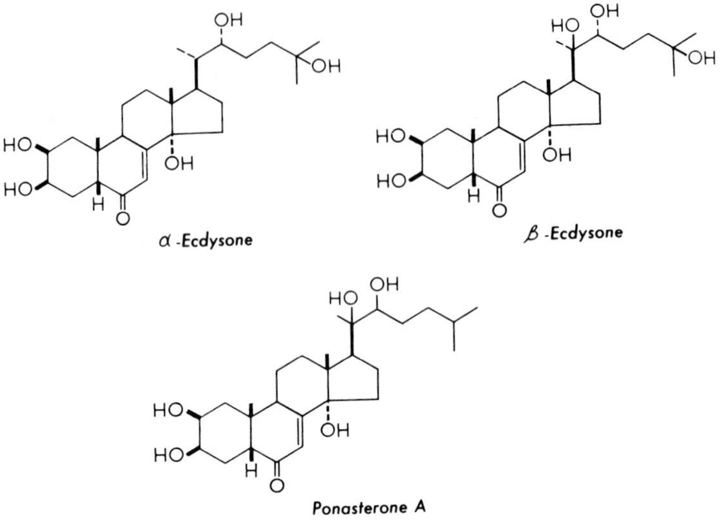

FIGURE 12. Insect ecdysones and a plant derived ecdysone-active steroid.

dysones are in fact being employed by plants to protect them from predation by insects. Certainly the phytoecdysones can interfere with insect development. Nakanishi (1969) reported the successful use of phytoecdysones in the control of mosquito larvae dipped in an aqueous solution containing 10 ppm of ponasterone A. A 0.5% methanolic solution of ponasterone A was toxic to the rice stem borer, *Chilo suppressalis*. Feeding cabbage worms on leaves sprayed with a 0.5% solution of ponasterone A resulted in 25% mortality. Feeding or injecting the phytoecdysones will induce extra molting which can result in the premature death of a variety of insects.

The highly polar steroidal nature of the phytoecdysones severely limits their movement through the insect cuticle. Thus, they are less effective by contact than less polar compounds such as the juvenile hormones. The complex structure of ecdysones seriously limits their availability by synthesis, and the possibility of isolating ecdysones from plants in commercial quantities is unrealistic. No commercial utility for the phytoecdysones as insect control agents is anticipated. Svoboda *et al.* (1972) prepared a number of azasteroids which inhibited insect molting and metamorphosis, perhaps by interferring with ecdysone biosynthesis, which indicates that a much more effective approach to the use of our fundamental knowledge of the mode of action of ecdysones in controlling insects would be to search for methods of interferring with ecdysone production or utilization. In short, the discovery of antiecdysones would offer an insect-specific approach to insect control since molting is an arthropod-related process lacking an equivalent in higher animals.

V. SUMMARY

Zoologists and botanists have long recognized that insect predation upon plants is highly specific and that this specificity is in large part dependent upon the defensive screen of chemicals produced by the plant. It seems safe to say that all plants have a variety of chemical methods of defense against attack by not only insects but also plant pathogens, nematodes, etc. Since all plants are not equally preyed upon by all insects, successful attack of a particular plant species by an insect must depend upon the avoidance of the chemical screen or the development of resistance to the chemical's action upon the insect. Certain insects are able to attack only those portions of a plant which do not contain a defensive chemical, whereas other insects develop metabolic machinery able to rapidly inactivate or destroy the poison. These insects can then successfully prey upon a plant which otherwise is able to overcome the attacks of less persistent and biochemically flexible insects. Early researchers examined plants for compounds which could clearly be classified as direct toxicants, since they killed insects rapidly. Although a number of toxicants were discovered in this way the basis for the resistance of most plants to most insects remained a complete mystery. Now, thanks to the basic researches of such notables as Professor Wigglesworth, we are able to percieve a much wider spectrum of interaction between insects and plants. He unravelled for us much of the intricacies of the insect endocrine system which we now know is often the target of subtle plant chemical defenses which disrupt insect growth, development, reproduction, diapause, behavior and communication. The development of hormone and pheromone mimics as well as antihormones depended upon his groundwork. While the efforts of Professor Wigglesworth might not have been perceived as being in direct support of economic entomology a few years ago, the current intensive research on insect growth and behavior regulators is clearly a result of his imaginative and pioneering spirit.

VI. REFERENCES

Barton, G. M., and MacDonald, B. F. (1972). Juvenile hormone-like activity of Thujic acid, an extractive of western red cedar. *Bi-monthly Research Notes: Environment Canada 28*, 22-23.

Becker, E., and Plagge, E. (1939). Uber das die pupariumbildung auslosende hormon der fliegen. *Biol. Zentr. 59*, 326-341.

Beroza, M. (1954). Pyrethrum synergists in sesame oil. Sesamolin, a potent synergist. *J. Amer. Oil. Chem. Soc. 31*, 302-305.

Bowers, W. S. (1968). Juvenile hormone activity of natural and synthetic synergists. *Science 161*, 895-897.

Bowers, W. S. (1969). Juvenile hormone activity of aromatic terpenoid ethers. *Science 164*, 323-325.

Bowers, W. S. (1976). Discovery of insect antiallatotropins. *In* "The Juvenile Hormones" (L. I. Gilbert, ed.), pp. 394-408. Plenum Press, New York.

Bowers, W. S. (1977). Anti-juvenile hormones from plants: Chemistry and biological activity. *In* "Natural Products and the Protection of Plants" (G. B. Marini-Bettolo, ed.), *Proc. Pontifical Acad. of Sci.*, Vatican City, Italy.

Bowers, W. S., and Aldrich, J. (1980). *In vivo* inactivation of denervated corpora allata by precocene II in the bug *Oncopeltus fasciatus. Experientia.* (In press).

Bowers, W. S., and Bodenstein, W. G. (1971). Sex pheromone mimics of the American cockroach. *Nature 232*, 259-261.

Bowers, W. S., and Martinez-Pardo, R. (1977). Antiallototropins:: Inhibition of corpus allatum development. *Science 197*, 1369-1371.

Bowers, W. S., and Nishida, R. (1980). Juvocimenes: Potent juvenile hormone mimics from sweet basil. *Science.* (Submitted).

Bowers, W. S., Thompson, M., and Uebel, E. C. (1965). Juvenile and gonadotropic hormone activity of 10,11-epoxyfarnesenic acid methyl ester. *Life Sci. 4*, 2323-2331.

Bowers, W. S., Fales, H. M., Thompson, M. J., and Uebel, E. C. (1966). Juvenile hormone:: Identification of an active compound from balsam fir. *Science 154*, 1020-1022.

Bowers, W. S., Nault, L. R., Webb, R. E., and Dutky, S. R. (1972). Aphid alarm pheromone: Isolation, identification and synthesis. *Science 177*, 1121-1122.

Bowers, W. S., Ohta, T., Cleere, J. S., and Marsella, P. A. (1976). Antiallatotropins: Inhibition of corpus allatum development. *Science 197*, 1369-1371.

Bowers, W. S., Nishino, C., Montgomery, M. E., Nault, L. R., and Nielson, M. W. (1977). Sesquiterpene progenitor, germacrene A: An alarm pheromone in aphids. *Science 196*, 680-681.

Brooks,G. T., Pratt, G. E., and Jennings,R. C. (1979). The actions of precocenes in milkweed bugs and locusts. *Nature 281*, 570-572.

Brown, W. L., Eisner, T., and Whittaker, R. H. (1970). Allomones and kairomones: Transpecific chemical messengers. *Bioscience 20*, 21-22.

Butenandt, A., and Karlson, P. (1954). Uber die isolierung eines metamorphosehormons der insecten in kristalliesierter form. *Z. Naturforsch. 9b*, 389-391.

Cavill, G. W. K., Williams, P. J., and Whitfield, F. B. (1967). α -Farnesene, Dufour's gland secretion in the ant *Aphaenogaster longiceps* (F. Sm.). *Tetrahedron Lett.*, 2201-2205.

Cerny, V., Dolys, L., Labler, L., Sorm, F., and Slama, K. (1967). Dehydrojuvabione, a new compound with juvenile hormone activity from balsam fir. *Coll. Czech. Chem. Commun. 32*, 3926-3933.

Cupp, E. W., Lok, J. B., and Bowers, W. S. (1977). The developmental effects of 6,7-dimethoxy-2,2-dimethyl chromene on the pre-imaginal stages of *Aedes aegypti*. *Ent. Exp. Appl. 22*, 23-28.

Dahl, M. L. (1971). On an alarm substance in aphids. *Dtsch. Entomol. Z.18*, 121-127.

Doskotch, R. W., and El-Feraly, F. S. (1969). Isolation and characterization of (+)-sesamin and β-cyclopyrethrosin from pyrethrum flowers. *Can. J. Chem. 47*, 1139-1142.

Eagelson, C. (1942). Sesame oil as a synergist for pyrethrum insecticides. *Soap and Sanit. Chem. 18*, 125-127.

Fales, J. H., Bodenstein, O. F., and Bowers, W. S. (1970). Seven juvenile hormone analogs as synergists for pyrethrins against house flies. *J. Econ. Entomol. 63*, 1379-1380.

Fraenkel, G. (1935). A hormone causing pupation in the blowfly, *Calliphora erythrocephala*. *Proc. Roy. Soc. (Lond.) 118*, 1-12.

Fukami, H., and Nakajima, M. (1971). Rotenone and the rotenoids. *In* "Naturally Occurring Insecticides" (Jacobson and Crosby, eds.), pp. 71-95. Marcel Dekker, Inc., New York.

Fukuda, S. (1940a). Induction of pupation in silkworm by transplanting the prothoracic gland. *Proc. Imp. Acad. (Tokyo) 16*, 414-416.

Fukuda, S. (1940b). Hormonal control of molting and pupation in the silkworm. *Proc. Imp. Acad. (Tokyo) 17*, 417-420.

Grummer, G. (1955). "Die Gengenseitige Beeinflussung Hoherer Pflanzen Allelopathie." Fisher, Jena.

Haller, H. L., McGovran, E. R., Goodhue, L. D., and Sullivan, W. N. (1942). The synergistic action of sesamin with pyrethrum insecticides. *J. Org. Chem. 7*, 183-184.

Henrick, C. A., Staal, G. B., and Siddall, J. B. (1973). Alkyl 3,7,11-trimethyl-2,4-dodecadienoates, a new class of potent insect growth regulators with juvenile hormone activity. *J. Agric. Food Chem. 21*, 354-359.

Hocks, P., and Wiechert, R. (1966). 20-Hydroxyecdysone, isoliert aus insekten. *Tetrahedron Lett.*, 2989-2993.

Horn, D. H. S. (1971). The Ecdysones. *In* "Naturally Occurring Insecticides" (Jacobson and Crosby, eds.), pp. 333-459. Marcel Dekker, Inc., New York.

Horn, D. H. S., Middleton, E. J., Wunderlich, J. A., and Hampshire, F. (1966). Identity of the moulting hormones of insects and crustaceons. *Chem. Commun.*, 339-341.

Huber, R., and Hoppe, W. (1965). Zur Chemie des Ecdysons, VII. Die Kristall-und Molekulstrukturanalyse des Insektenverpuppungshormons. Ecdysen mit der automatisierten faltmolekulmethode. *Chem. Ber. 98*, 2403-2424.

Huelin, F. E., and Murray, K. E. (1966). α-Farnesene in the natural coating of apples. *Nature 210*, 1260-1261.

Jacobson, M., Beroza, M., and Yamamoto, R. T. (1963). Isolation and identification of the sex attractant of the American cockroach. *Science 139*, 48-49.

Jacobson, M., and Beroza, M. (1965). American cockroach sex attractant. *Science 147*, 748-749.

Jennings, R. C., and Ottridge, A. P. (1979). The synthesis of precocene I epoxide. *J. C. S. Chem. Commun.*, 920-921.

Judy, K. J., Schooley, D. A., Dunham, L. L., Hall, M. S., Bergot, B. J., and Siddall, J. B. (1973). Isolation, structure and absolute configuration of a new natural insect juvenile hormone from *Manduca sexta. Proc. Natl. Acad. Sci. U.S.A. 70*, 1509-1513.

Karlson, P. (1956). Biochemical studies on insect hormones. *Vitamins and Hormones 14*, 227-266.

Leahy, M. G. (1977). Paper presented at the 1977 meeting of the Entomological Society of America and personal communication.

Liechty, L., and Sedlak, B. J. (1978). The ultrastructure of precocene-induced effects on the corpora allata of the adult milkweed bug, *Oncopeltus fasciatus. Gen. and Comp. Endocrinol. 36*, 433-436.

Mackauer, M., Nair, K. K., and Unnithan, G. C. (1979). Effect of precocene II on alate production in the pea aphid, *Acyrthosiphon pisum. Can. Jour. Zool. 57*, 856-859.

Masner, P., Bowers, W. S., Kalin, M., and Muhle, T. (1979). Effect of precocene II on the endocrine regulation of development and reproduction in the bug *Oncopeltus fasciatus. Gen. and Comp. Endocrinol. 37*, 156-166.

Meyer, A. S., Schneiderman, H. A., Hanzman, E., and Ko, J. H. (1968). The two juvenile hormones from the cecropia silk moth. *Proc. Natl. Acad. Sci. U.S.A. 60*, 853-860.

Muller, P. J., Masner, P., Kalin, M., and Bowers, W. S. (1979). *In vitro* inactivation of corpora allata of the bug *Oncopeltus fasciatus* by precocene II. *Experientia 35*, 704-705.

Nakanishi, K. (1969). *In* "Insect Plant Interactions." *Proc. Natl. Acad. Sci.*, 50. Washington, DC.

Nakanishi, K., Koreeda, M., Sasaki, S., Chang, M. L., and Hsu, H. Y. (1966). Insect hormones: The structure of ponasterone A, an insect moulting hormone from the leaves of *Podocarpus nakaii* Hay. *Chem. Commun.*, 915-917.

Nault, L. R., Montgomery, M. E., and Bowers, W. S. (1976). Ant-aphid association: Role of aphid alarm pheromone. *Science 142*, 1347-1351.

Nemec, V., Chen, T. T., and Wyatt, G. R. (1978). Precocious adult locust, *Locusta migratoria*, induced by precocene. *Acta. Entomol. Bohemoslovaca 75*, 285-286.

Nishida, R., and Bowers, W. S. (1980). A juvenile hormone mimic from *Macropiper excelsum.* (Submitted).

Nishino, C., Tobin, T. R., and Bowers, W. S. (1977a). Sex pheromone mimics of the American cockroach in monoterpenoids. *Appl. Ent. Zool. 12*, 287-290.

Nishino, C., Tobin, T. R., and Bowers, W. S. (1977b). Electro-antennogram responses of the American cockroach to germacrene D sex pheromone mimic. *J. Insect Physiol. 23*, 415-419.

Ohta, T., Kuhr, R. J., and Bowers, W. S. (1977). Radiosynthesis and metabolism of the insect anti-juvenile hormone, Precocene II. *Agric. Food Chem. 25*, 478-481.

Pener, M. P., and Orshan, L. (1977). Morphogenetic effect of precocene 2, an anti-juvenile hormone, in the African migratory locust, Locusta migratoria. Israel J. Zool. 26, 262-263.

Persoons, C. J., Verwiel, P. E. J., Ritter, F. J., Talman, E., Nooijen, P. J. F., and Nooijen, W. J. (1976). Sex pheromones of the American cockroach, Periplaneta americana: A tentative structure of periplanone B. Tetrahedron Lett., 2055-2058.

Plagge, E., and Becker, E. (1938). Wirkung arteigener und artfremder verpuppungshormone in extracten. Naturwissenschaften 26, 430-431.

Pound, J. M., and Oliver, J. M. (1979). Juvenile hormone: Evidence of its role in the reproduction of ticks. Science 206, 355-357.

Pratt, G. E., and Bowers, W. S. (1977). Precocene II inhibits juvenile hormone biosynthesis by cockroach corpora allata in vitro. Nature 265, 548-550.

Roeske, C. N., Seiber, J. N., Brown, L. P., and Moffitt, C. M. (1975). Milkweed cardenolides and their comparative processing by Monarch butterflies. In "Biochemical Interaction Between Plants and Insects" (Wallace and Mansell, eds.), pp. 93-167. Plenum Press, New York.

Roller, H., Dahm, K. H., Sweeley, C. C., and Trost, B. M. (1967). Die struktur des juvenilhormons. Angew. Chem. 79, 190-191.

Rothschild, M. (1972). Some observations on the relationship between plants, toxic insects, and birds. In "Phytochemical Ecology" (J. B. Harborne, ed.). Academic Press, New York.

Schmeltz, I. (1971). Nicotine and other tobacco alkaloids. In "Naturally Occurring Insecticides" (Jacobson and Crosby, eds.), pp. 99-136. Marcel Dekker, Inc., New York.

Schmialek, P. (1961). Die identifizierung zwier im tenebriokot und in hefe vorkommender substanzen mit juvenilhormonwirkung. Zeitschrift fur Naturforschung 16, 461-464.

Schooneveld, H. (1979). Precocene-induced collapse and resorption of corpora allata in nymphs of Locusta migratoria. Experientia 35, 363-364.

Slama, K., and Williams, C. M. (1965). Juvenile hormone activity for the bug Pyrrhocoris apterus. Proc. Natl. Acad. Sci. U.S.A. 54, 411-414.

Soderlund, D. M., Messeguer, A., and Bowers, W. S. Precocene II metabolism in insects: Synthesis of potential metabolites for identification of initial in vitro biotransformation products. (Submitted to Journal of Ag. Food Chem.).

Sutherland, O. R. W., and Hutchins, R. F. N. (1973). Attraction of newly hatched codling moth larvae, (Laspeyresia pomonelal) to synthetic stereo-isomers of farnesene. J. Insect Physiol. 19, 723-727.

Svoboda, J. A., Thompson, M. J., and Robbins, W. E. (1972). Azasteroids: Potent inhibitors of insect molting and metamorphosis. Lipids 7, 553-556.

Tahara, S., Yoshida, M., Mizutani, J., Kitamura, C., and Takahashi, S.s (1975). A sex stimulant to the male American cockroach in Compositae plants. Agri. Biol. Chem. 39, 1517-1518.

Tarrant, C. A., and Cupp, E. W. (1978). Morphogenetic effects of precocene II on the immature stages of Rhodinus prolixus. Trans. Royal Soc. Trop. Med. Hygiene 72, 666-668.

Thompson, M. J., Kaplanis, J. N., Robbins, W. E., and Yamamoto, R. T. (1967). 20,26-Dihydroxyecdysone, a new steroid with molting hormone activity from the tobacco hornworm, Manduca sexta. Chem. Commun. 13, 650-653.

Unnithan, G. C., Nair, K. K., and Bowers, W. S. (1977). Precocene-induced degeneration of the corpus allatum of adult females of the bug Oncopeltus fasciatus. J. Insect Physiol. 23, 1081-1094.

Unnithan, G. C., Nair, K. K., and Kooman, C. J. (1977). Effects of precocene II and juvenile hormone III on the activity of neurosecretory A-cells in *Oncopeltus fasciatus. Experientia 34*, 411-412.

Unnithan, G. C., and Nair, K. K. (1979). The influence of corpus allatum activity on the susceptibility of *Oncopeltus fasciatus* to precocene. *Ann. Ent. Soc. Amer. 72*, 38-40.

Unnithan, G. C., Nair, K. K., and Syed, A. (1980). Precocene-induced metamorphosis in the desert locust, *Schistocerca gregaria. Experientia 36*, 135-136.

Wearing, C. H., and Hutchins, R. F. N. (1973). α-Farnesene, a naturally occurring oviposition stimulant for the codling moth, *Laspeyresia pomonella. J. Insect Physiol. 19*, 1251-1256.

Weinheimer, A. J., Youngblood, W. W., Washechec, P. H., Karns, T. K. B., and Ciereszko, L. S. (1970). Isolation of the elusive (-)-germacrene A fromn the gorgonian, *Eunicea mammosa.* Chemistry of coelenterales XVIII. *Tetrahendron Lett.,* 497-500.

Wigglesworth, V. B. (1934). The physiology of ecdysis in *Rhodnius prolixus* (Hemiptera). II. Fac;tors controlling molting and metamorphosis. *Quart. J. Micr. Sci. 77*, 191-222.

Wigglesworth, V. B. (1935). Functions of the corpus allatum of insects. *Nature 136*, 338.

Wigglesworth, V. B. (1940). The determination of characters at metamorphosis in *Rhodnius prolixus. J. Exptl. Biol. 17*, 201-222.

Williams, C. M. (1946). Physiology of insect diapause. The role of the brain in the production and termination of pupal dormancy in the giant silkworm, *Platysamia cecropia. Biol. Bull. 90*, 234-243.

Williams, C. M. (1947). Physiology of insect diapause. Interaction between the pupal brain and prothoracic glands in the metamorphosis of the giant silkworm. *Biol Bull. 43*, 89-98.

Williams, C. M. (1950). The metamorphosis of insects. *Sci. Amer. 182*, 24-28.

Williams, C. M. (1956). The juvenile hormone of insects. *Nature 178*, 212-213.

NEURAL MECHANISMS

Graham Hoyle

Department of Biology
University of Oregon
Eugene, Oregon

I. PROLOGUE: THE GENERAL AND THE SPECIAL IN PHYSIOLOGY

The future must necessarily be seen in light of the present, and all prophecies must be based upon what the past has shown to be possible in principle. We shall start, therefore, by looking at the historical events, review the present, and then try to predict the way ahead.

Sir Vincent B. Wigglesworth made two very significant statements for students of neural mechanisms in insects. One was that insects offer good models for studies of general fundamental physiological processes (Wigglesworth, 1948 e). The other, was to define behavior in The Principles of Insect Physiology as being a branch of physiology. There was, perhaps, a great deal of wishful thinking in both. Persons addicted to the frog regard their findings as general "by definition". The frog is a vertebrate, and so close to man - at any rate closer than any insect. On the other hand, the principle of there being a "general" physiology has been more powerfully accepted on behalf of a specialized cephalopod mollusc - the squid, or rather its giant axons, than for any other piece of tissue.

[1] Research reported in this chapter was supported by Research Grant BNS 75-00463 from the National Science Foundation to Dr. Hoyle.

The truth is that general physiology is an abstraction for the convenience, and to some extent the self- and cross-glorification, of its practitioners. No one doubts that there are general features in physiological events in diverse animals from various phyla, but this is largely an act of faith and only to a small extent supported by actual observation and experiment. William Harvey (1628) did a very much better job in the context of generality than did Hodgkin, Huxley & Katz when he expounded on his view of the circulation of blood, as a general principle of physiology. He had taken the trouble to examine over 40 different species, including various worms, insects, crustaceans, fish, and mammals, including man, before he felt that he had established a general principle. He set a sterling example, that has never since been equalled, of how to set about doing general physiology properly.

The truth is that as a result of adaptive radiation and evolution a very great deal of diversity exists. It follows by the simplest rules of logic that a general principle of physiology can be deduced only by use of the comparative method, as exemplified by William Harvey and his study of circulation. Had circulation existed only in higher mammals it would not have generality, but be an attribute of specifically mammalian physiology. Of course it may be that many scientists, especially physiologists, do not use the term general in its strict sense. They are not concerned with the evolutionary imperative; what some of them mean by general is that it occurs in some mammals. For others, perhaps the majority, what is implied by general is any major cellular process. However, close inspection of the latter premise indicates that it is not true either. Cellular events occurring in slime molds or the slow-type muscle fibers of an arthropod are major processes but not quite acceptable to the high priests of general physiology for recognition. Heilbrunn (1943) complained a long time ago that what was called general physiology was usually "dilute mammalian physiology", and that it thrived on a diet of "simplified physical chemistry". Anyone who has ever researched on an aspect of insect physiology that is not exclusive to insects, such as ecdysis of Holometabola, will understand what Heilbrunn was getting at.

There is a very special kind of frustration about working over a period of many years with insects as if they are indeed objects well-suited to the study of general physiology: lack of acceptance. Mammalian-oriented "general" physiologists long ago made a pact with the frog. Then they accepted the squid giant axon (but no other part of the squid) and eventually the sea hare Aplysia - or rather the giant nerve cells of its abdominal ganglion. But they continue to be

stuffy about insects. The chances are rather strong that they will
regard insects as "nasties" that are somehow outside the realm of
their serious consideration. As long as this attitude persists,
researchers who select insects as subjects on which to initiate their
attack on a general problem in physiology will be forced to look
enviously at their colleagues in eukaryote genetics in the matter of
acceptance of their work by "mainstream" scientists.

However, insects are economically important to man, not only
as destroyers but also as producers. There have been occasions,
in history, when some insect producers have been valued more
highly than the humans tending them. Their economic importance
has endowed insect research with an unique flavor that has
engendered support of this research with public finance on a fairly
generous scale. Therefore, work on insects need not be justified
on the basis of the use of parts as "simple models of more complex
systems", even if the use of insects were more acceptable to the
community of general physiologists.

In the area of our direct concern, that of neural mechanisms,
researchers have one enormous advantage. Whilst a few enjoy
working on insects for their own sakes, and some wish to understand
their neural mechanisms in order to kill them more efficiently, in
recent years many have been recruited because insects have
interesting, complex behavior that seems amenable to electrophysiological analysis. This relatively new breed of scientist, now
termed a neuroethologist (Hoyle, 1970; Burrows, 1977), is a person
trying to understand those properties of individual nerve cells and
of the circuits within which they act, that generate the motor output
causing behavior in general. Neuroethology is not, at this time, a
fashionable word. Although offerred as a subject choice for
meetings of the American Society for Neuroscience, its sessions
are the least often chosen and the worst attended. Its practitioners
prefer to be called students of neuronal circuits, pattern generation,
motor control, or just invertebrate neurobiologists: i.e. the most
completely non-commital descriptive denomination they could
possibly adopt. Neuroethologist is not yet a label to be proud of,
though I predict that will change. The detailed study of behavior,
and of its neural bases in particular, was given a tremendous
impetus by the european researchers who came to call themselves
ethologists. When Konrad Lorenz, Nikko Tinbergen and Karl von
Frisch shared the 1973 Nobel prize for physiology and medicine
they not only attracted a great deal of attention to the study of animal
behavior, they gave the subject a much-needed aura of scientific
respectability. But they indirectly did a great deal for the subject

that concerns us. Karl had worked exclusively on insects, and
Nikko about equally on insects and birds. The great generalizations,
and principles, even though they were made principally by Konrad,
who had not himself worked with insects, were intended to apply to
all animals. Insects were widely used to provide illustrative
examples, and considered together with birds and mammals on an
entirely equal footing.

The ethological principles were explicitly stated at first, and
although ethologists have since come to prefer much looser
definitions, or none at all, the basic tenets, including the concepts
of drive, reaction specific energy, releaser, displacement activity,
appetitive behavior, fixed action pattern and consummatory act,
are clearly all here to stay. Behind all of these ran a strong
undercurrent of implied common neurophysiological mechanisms.
This was most clearly apparent in Lorenz's (in)famous (toilet)
hydraulic model, expounded at the 4th symposium of the Society
for Experimental Biology held in 1949, on Physiological Mechanisms
in Animal Behavior (1950). This happened to be when I myself
came into the field, with a desire to become a neurobiologist but
having a zoological as well as hard-science background and having
acquired from G. P. Wells a fondness for comparative physiology.
I was looking for problems to try to solve and hoping for a field to
develop. The one covered by the symposium provided an obvious
happy hunting ground: there seemed plenty to occupy one in
attempting to substitute real neuronal mechanisms for the water in
the model.

II. TAKING STOCK OF PROGRESS

Historical Background

No insect neurobiologist had expounded at the 1949 Cambridge
meeting. Indeed only one scientist in the world seriously counted
in insect neurobiology at the time: Kenneth Roeder. He was a true
pioneer, and can definitely be regarded as the founding father of
insect neuroethology. Roeder had started working on basic insect
neurophysiology just before the 2nd world war and as a contribution
to the rapidly developing field of pesticides had examined the site
of action of DDT. His first pure work was on the actions of cations
on cockroach nerve cord (Roeder, 1948). He was also drawn

towards ethology, to which he made a notable series of contributions
from 1955 on, using the praying mantis and cockroach before
settling down to a major study on moths (Roeder, 1965).

Another pioneer, Vince Dethier, had been initially interested in
the chemical factors determining food selection by insects. In turn
this work led him to develop a powerful insight into the neural
control of a fixed action pattern - blowfly feeding (Dethier, 1969).
This was accomplished without benefit of the present-day mainstays:
electrical recording of motor output and of central nervous system
activity. Meanwhile, John Pringle showed that motor output in the
cockroach is readily recordable, simple, and can be understood
and measured quantitatively. He used his recording skills to obtain
valuable information about motor output in flight (Pringle, 1939)
and automatic control of stability in the yawing plane in flight in
Diptera (Pringle, 1948).

Intracellular recording was introduced to insects by José del
Castillo, Xenia Machne and myself, (in insect muscle) in 1952
(del Castillo et al, 1953). In 1954 I placed intracellular electrodes
into motor neuron cell bodies expecting to see action potentials.
Yet all I obtained were 4-5 mV squiggles, which I thought
represented spikes aborted by severe damage. This belief was
strengthened when Susumu Hagiwara and Akira Watanabe published
intracellular records from motor neurons of the cicada (Hagiwara
& Watanabe, 1956), that were large, overshooting action potentials.
Their work might have been expected to have led to intensive
research on insect neural mechanisms. But although many starts
were made, for example - by the late Donald Maynard, Sherman
Ripley, Ed Rowe and Joan Kendig, their experiences, like my own,
were disappointing. Peggy Ellis and I made an early attempt to
link neurophysiology with behavior in locusts (Ellis & Hoyle, 1954).
We started with the assumption, borrowed from the ethologists,
that much of the fixed behavioral repertoire in locusts would be
centrally-programmed, not generated by reflexes. We argued that
the expression of a given behavior would be markedly affected by
the blood's ionic composition, which, in locusts, fluctuates wildly
in relation to diet (Hoyle, 1954). However, there was plenty to do
at the neuromuscular level, and much of the rest of the animal
kingdom was waiting to be explored. I did spend a lot of time from
1955 through 1970 recording extracellularly from free-walking
locusts and cockroaches using fine implanted trailing wire leads two
feet long. But the results were highly varied and complex and most
of the several miles of paper still await detailed analysis. One
significant finding was that antagonistic muscles often co-contract
(Hoyle, 1964; 1970).

In the late 1950's Franz Huber (1959) initiated what was destined
to be a lifetime's work on the neuroethology of cricket singing.
Huber found that he could cause stridulation and locomotion with
local brain stimulation (Huber, 1959). A very significant figure
emerged in the USA, a student of T. H. Bullock, Donald Wilson,
who showed (Wilson, 1961) that normal co-ordinated flight patterns
occur in locusts even after extensive disruption of the sensory
feed-back elements (Wilson, 1961). These experiments were
extremely influential because they added direct physiological fuel
to a controversial fire started by the ethologists that helped to
destroy the traditional notion of complex behavior as being
generated by chains of reflexes. Wilson's finding gave direct
experimental support to the Lorenz/Tinbergen idea of genetically-
determined fixed action patterns that are simply "released" by a
suitable, brief stimulus, or as "displacement activities", or can
occur spontaneously. The notion of such pre-programmed
behaviors was appealing to neuroethologists, partly because it
suggested that such behaviors would be repeated precisely and
therefore could be the subjects for cellular-level analysis and
therefore in-depth understanding.

We had a brief incursion into analyzing motor output during
cricket singing (Ewing & Hoyle, 1965) in a period that brought a
number of young scientists into the field, including Wolfram Kutsch,
Keir Pearson and David Bentley. Bentley not only successfully
analyzed cricket calling song production (1969a, b), he went on to do
a brilliant analysis of genetic involvement in determing the overall
pattern generation (1971). This work stands alone (unfortunately):
it has not yet led to the hoped for initiation of combined genetic and
neurophysiological analysis. Adrian Horridge began to turn his
attention to insects, coming up in 1961 (Horridge, 1962) with his
celebrated headless learning preparation, before turning the
attention of his large research group in Canberra to a massive
attack on the insect visual system. Follow-up on his learning
preparation has been largely from our laboratory (Hoyle, 1965;
Tosney & Hoyle, 1977; Woollacott & Hoyle, 1977; Hoyle, 1979 &
1980; Woollacott & Hoyle, in preparation) although many others,
especially Ed Eisenstein, have explored behaviorial aspects of the
learning.

Norbert Elsner, in Germany, developed the trailing-lead
electromyographic method to an extraordinary pitch of perfection
and usefulness (Elsner, 1968; 1974a, b). He implanted as many as
30 fine, insulated steel wires into as many muscles of mature male
grasshoppers Gomphocerippus and Stenobothrus. Each wired

insect still gave its complex stereotyped fixed action pattern of courtship behavior when in the presence of a female. Elsner was enabled to record with great precision the underlying motor patterns and to show that they are very precisely determined, down to the level of single impulses in a train. The work has been extended to include sensory studies, so that it now encompasses the entire spectrum of acoustic communication (Elsner & Popov, 1978). Most recently the interneurons involved have become the objects of intracellular study (Wohlers & Huber, 1978).

With various visitors to our laboratory, attempts were made to return to recording from neurons and we eventually succeeded in obtaining records intracellularly from the single excitatory motorneuron innervating the anterior adductor of the coxa (Hoyle, 1970), with the electrode either in the principal neurite or in the soma. It had by now become obvious to all would-be neuro-ethologists that progress in neuron identification and recording was imperative. David Bentley inspired us with the records he obtained intracellularly from motorneurons of a male cricket that sang continually for several hours following a discrete brain lesion (Bentley, 1969a), and the mapping of mesothoracic flight motor-neurons (Bentley, 1969b). The records did not show full-blown spikes, but they were convincing enough and the potentials initiating them were tantalizing indicators of neural patterns in process of generation. To go along with the intracellular recording it was clearly desirable to have a suitable dye that could be injected into the neuron penetrated, if for no other reason than to let the investigator know precisely where the recordings had been made. Melvin Cohen and Jon Jacklet with help from David Young, re-constructed a three-dimensional view of the larger neurons in the third thoracic ganglion of the cockroach (Cohen & Jacklet, 1967), and Betty Moberly and I proceeded to do the same for the locust, but these drawings were of no value in the absence of individual neuron identification. They were tantalyzing, though, because many of the neurons looked eminently suitable targets for intracellular electrodes. The following year a very important development occurred: Stretton & Kravitz (1968) introduced a really useful intracellular dye, Procyon yellow, which glows a bright yellow in ultraviolet light. We soon found that it fills major branches of insect nerves in about an hour so we immediately dropped other projects and started attacking the locust metathoracic ganglion with glass capillary microelectrodes filled with Procyon dyes. I had the good fortune to enjoy the presence in the lab of an extraordinarily gifted experimentalist, Malcolm Burrows. Those disappointing

squiggles from motorneuron cell bodies were quickly found to be
the genuine thing for most locust motorneurons. Between us we
succeeded in locating, identifying and filling 26 of the motorneurons,
and located a few of the interneurons (Hoyle & Burrows, 1973a,b;
Burrows & Hoyle, 1973). Each identified nerve cell, when filled
again and again in different specimens, turned out to have
essentially the same cell-body location, pathway through the
ganglion and branching pattern, permitting construction of a neuron
map that quickly proved its usefulness as a guide in planned
experiments, with two, then three, electrodes, aimed at understanding interactions between the neurons. A basis for the ultimate
objectives of neuroethology was beginning to be realizable.

Some Surprises: Neurons with Unexpected Properties

   1. Dorsal unpaired median (DUM) Neurons. Ronald Pitman (1969)
first penetrated the large neurons that occur in the mid-line on the
dorsal surface of several ganglia of several species of insects. He
found the cell body to show large, overshooting action potentials
with large undershoots, a rather slow time-course and low repetition
rate. The cells are unpaired, but the principal neurite makes a T
branch. We (Hoyle et al, 1974) traced the two arms of the largest
of these cells in the locust metathoracic ganglion into the left and
right main leg nerves respectively. There they end blindly, in the
extensor tibiae muscle (Hoyle et al, 1974; Hoyle, 1980), hence the
neuron is the dorsal, unpaired, median neuron innervating the
extensor tibiae (DUMETi) whose location is shown in Figure 1.
   Ernst Florey and I (unpublished) found these cells to release a
biogenic amine, and in 1975 I obtained strong evidence for its being
octopamine (Hoyle, 1975). This was later confirmed by direct
analysis of isolated, pre-identified DUMETi somata by Evans &
O'Shea (1978). Octopamine does many things to locust legs,
including inhibiting a slow intrinsic rhythmicity (Hoyle, 1975),
facilitating the first few slow excitatory junctional potentials in a
train and promoting relatively rapid relaxation (O'Shea & Evans,
1979).
   It also has biochemical actions that may be functionally more
significant, such as stimulation of oxidative metabolism (Candy,
1978) and adenylcyclase activity (Nathanson & Greengard, 1973).
Octopamine therefore begins to look like a possible general-purpose
preparer for action: an insect equivalent of adrenaline.

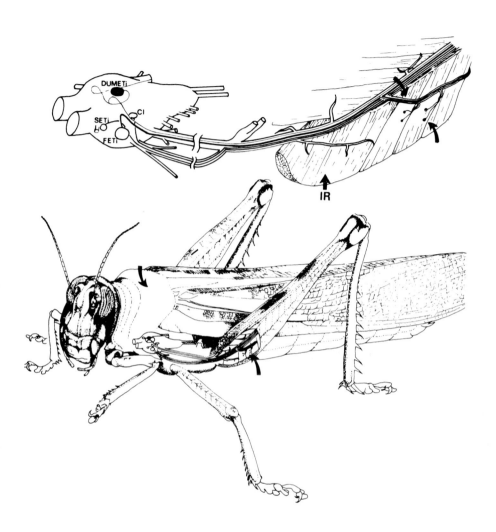

FIGURE 1. Below: location of the locust identified octopaminergic
dorsal unpaired median neuron that innervates the extensor tibiae
muscle (DUMETi). The lower arrow indicated position where
neurosecretory-type release sites were located. The upper arrow
indicates position of similar release sites for another such neuron,
that innervates the dorsal longitudinal flight muscle. Above: higher
scale drawing to show site of muscle fibers showing intrinsic
rhythm (IR) in relation to known release sites (arrow) for octopamine.
Other neurons innervating the jumping muscle are shown.
From Hoyle, Colquhoun & Williams, 1980.

2. Non-Spiking Interneurons. Keir Pearson, who had made notable contributions by recording electromyograms from cockroaches during walking (Pearson, 1972) and by discovering common peripheral inhibitory neurons in the cockroach (Pearson & Bergman, 1969), now began using intracellular electrodes on ganglia. Pearson, Fourtner & Wong (1973) found interneurons that did not show any spike-like activity, hence they termed them non-spiking interneurons (NSIs). These did show a lot of synaptic input plus slow oscillatory membrane potential fluctuations. The latter occurred whenever the cockroach would walk, but not otherwise, and they were of two classes: one in which the depolarizing phase coincided with bursts of action potentials in coxal levator muscles (Type I), and another in which the polarizing phase coincided with levator bursts (Type II). The authors were able to obtain bursts of action potentials in coxal levator motorneurons at times when these were not discharging, by passing depolarizing current into Type I NSIs. This work was done not by penetrating the neuron soma, which in the case of these interneurons is small and relatively distant, but from the principal neurite. Pearson later fully established the new cell type when he filled examples with cobalt (Pearson & Fourtner, 1975).

Pearson showed Burrows and myself how to recognize NSIs in locusts and since then Burrows & Siegler (1978), Siegler & Burrows (1979) and Wilson (1979) have studied the properties of locust NSIs intensively. Actions on follower motorneurons include co-excitation, co-inhibition and reciprocity. Some of the actions greatly outlast the period of stimulation of the NSI. Excitation of a follower is achieved by depolarization for some NSIs, but by hyperpolarization for others.

Pearson (1977) has proposed that some NSIs in cockroaches may embody within themselves the basic oscillatoriness of walking, and therefore be the long-sought ultimate "oscillators", or generators of the walking pattern predicted by Donald Wilson (1967). The arguments advanced for this attractive idea are, however, not yet compelling. Burrows (1979) is somewhat mystical about the roles of NSIs in locusts, suggesting only that "graded interactions between these local interneurons are an essential element in the generation of motor patterns". This clearly leaves the initiation, and possibly also the "master-minding", to unspecified neurons.

Sensory Neurons - The Other End of The System

It was my personal choice (following Sherrington) to start with motor output and attempt to work inwards. It has been the choice of many others to start with a particular set of sense organs. The problem with the latter approach has been that most of its proponents are still spending their whole lives getting no farther inwards than the sensory element itself. This is particularly true of most groups working on visual systems. Some are quite ready to work on esoteric questions involving behavior and to suggest black box "explanations", but they draw the line at recording.

An exception has been provided by Hugh Fraser-Rowell, who has taken input from a large interneuron of the eye in the lobular giant movement detector (O'Shea & Williams, 1974) and traced its pathway to actions on motorneurons. First it synapses with the contralateral decending giant movement detector interneuron (Rowell, 1971). This passes posteriorly to the metathoracic ganglion, where it makes 10 known synaptic connections onto identified neurons, of exactly the same kinds on left and right homologous pairs. These are excitatory onto the fast extensor tibiae, the two flexor inhibitor pairs, and the common inhibitor. Inhibitory inputs are made onto the anterior adductor of the coxa. This combination of inputs strongly suggests a major role in visual elicitation of a jump reflex.

As a result of the work on identified neurons involved in jumping (Hoyle & Burrows, 1973b; Burrows & Horridge, 1974; Heitler & Burrows, 1977; Pearson, in preparation), the neuronal circuitry associated with the locust jump has now been almost completely elucidated.

Another area where knowledge of sensory inputs has been combined with identified motor and interneuron studies, under conditions permitting at least simulated natural movements, is flight. This has been due to a model series of investigations by Malcolm Burrows (1973a, 1975a,b, 1977) and was closely coupled to morphological studies both on the principal receptor (Tyrer & Altman, 1974) and the motorneurons themselves (Burrows, 1973b, 1977; Tyrer & Altman, 1974).

Relevance of Morphological Studies

The morphological work had very little direct relevance to the working out of the neuronal circuitry, synaptic activities and patterning of output. Nevertheless it has played an important psychological role, not only in this research but on the whole of recent progress in neuroethology. The traditional distinction between anatomists and physiologists happily disappeared, the same people doing both electrophysiology and morphology. To know that one was dealing with an identifiable entity that always looked the same, or very nearly so, not only in different specimens of the same species, but also in different species, genera and families, provided a satisfying link to mainstream and evolutionary zoology for the physiologist. It gave confidence that the nervous system is relatively simple, or at least orderly, dispelling the despair that was expressed not long ago (Hughes, 1953; Horridge, 1968) about ever being able to understand the anatomical underpinning of integrative function in insects.

Perhaps equally important in this connection was the sheer beauty of neurons as seen after individual filling by whatever method. We were intensely thrilled by the first Procyon yellow fills of motorneurons, that now seem very crude.

Procyon dyes were soon replaced by cobalt sulphide, introduced by Bob Pitman, C. D. Tweedle & Mel Cohen in 1972. Cobalt enabled us to see many more of the finer branches, and to dispense with the tedious, time-consuming, expensive serial sectioning and reconstruction that were needed with Procyon. Cobalt was found to be picked up and rapidly transported inwards from a cut end of a neuron (Tyrer & Altman, 1974). This provided an important step forward, because it showed the investigator where to probe for as yet unidentified motorneurons and inter-segmental interneurons. A motor nerve branch could be dipped into cobalt for a few hours, and the ganglion "developed" with sulphide, to locate the cell bodies and branches of all the axons travelling in it.

Michael O'Shea and J. L. D. Williams, exploring with a cobalt-filled electrode in the locust eye, located and filled a large, complex interneuron which they termed the lobular giant movement detector that clearly integrates inputs from the whole eye (O'Shea & Williams, 1974). The sheer beauty of their fill was breathtaking and soon it was used on a poster to advertise the graduate neuro-biology training program at Berkeley. The latest in the series of

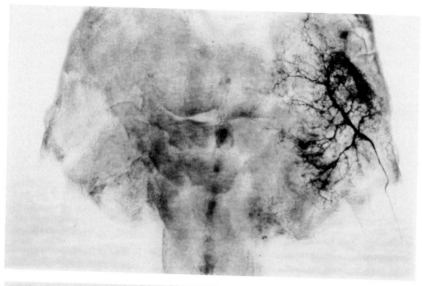

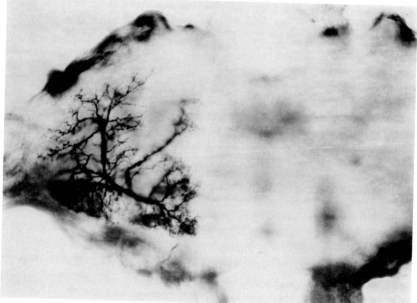

FIGURE 2.   Neurons of S.gregaria filled with cobalt and subjected
to intensification. Above: the metathoracic anterior adductor of
the coxa (AAdC).   Below: a mesothoracic non-spiking interneuron.
Micrographs courtesy of Dr. John Wilson.

dyes is Lucifer yellow (Stewart, 1978), which provides a yellow fluorescence similar to that of Procyon yellow, though about a hundred times brighter. With Lucifer, fine branches are readily seen and photographed after even a short filling time and it is not poisonous in low concentration.

A method has also been developed for the deposition of silver grains around cobalt sulphide particles in a process of intensification resembling photographic development (Bacon & Altman, 1977). The images provided after intensification revealed that dendritic branching patterns are actually more extensive and complex than had previously been suspected. But of greater significance was the realization that now a very low concentration of cobalt could be used in electrodes. The concentrations used earlier had killed the neurons quickly, so investigators had used one electrode for recording and a different one for filling. This was alright for easily penetrated large cell bodies, but for tiny ones that might not readily be found again this was not feasible. Using small quantities of cobalt, followed by intensification and rapid follow-up for electron microscopic study, good fixation has been obtained (Phillips, 1979). The cobalt/silver grains can easily be detected in ultrathin sections, permitting positive identification of all parts of the injected neuron, including its synapses onto other neurons. Examples of intensified cobalt direct fills are shown in Figure 2, and of synapse identification in Figure 3.

III. STRATEGIES FOR THE FUTURE

The techniques now available are so powerful that they permit, in principle, the in-depth understanding of the entire nervous system of a large insect such as the locust. We are already supplied with superb tools, in the form of ultrafine intracellular electrodes, dyes for individual neurons, insulated wire electrode leads that do not prevent the intact insect from behaving in a normal manner, and fabulous laboratory computers to carry out data analysis and control of experiments. It remains to be seen to what extent it will be possible to work with the smaller neurons, especially those in the brain. But at this time no neuron need be regarded as totally out of reach. The limitations lie only with the skill, resolve and patience of investigators.

In the future there will be problems of funding and basic organization. The competitive, individualistic, laissez faire, lore of

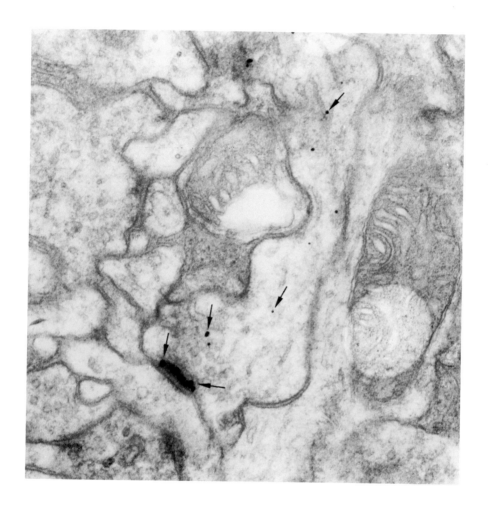

FIGURE 3. Identified synapse in locust ganglion. This is an out-going synapse of a dendritic branch of the metathoracic fast extensor tibiae FETi). A small amount of cobalt was iontophoresed into the soma from an intracellular electrode, prepared for electron microscopy and intensified with silver. Grains of cobalt/silver arrowed.

Micrograph courtesy of Dr. Christine Phillips. x 50,000

the western world, strongly dependent on the Universities and
utulizing the drives of personal ambition and wish for a sense of
immortality have proven to be excellent for the initiation of new
pathways. But they have not yet been asked to cope with problems
comparable to those which now face us in comparative neurobiology
and neuroethology. That is, the systematic application of techniques
that are highly demanding of personal skill and dedication for many
hours per day over a time span to be measured in at least tens of
years. There are no forseeable short-cuts, or break-throughs of
the kind science has come to expect. Certainly there will be
surprises. New kinds of neurons will be found, previously unknown
types of cellular and synaptic process will be uncovered and new
circuit principles encountered. But the process will be essentially
one of fact-gathering and sifting on a massive scale.

At this time we are not adjusted psychologically to this kind of
approach. Some in the field already act as if bored because the
sheer amount of information and the increasing rate of its aquisition
make it difficult to keep it all in mind; the hoped-for expectation of
quick solutions is receding rapidly. It is unlikely that the general
principles of neural mechanisms that have doubtless been exploited
during the course of the evolution of nervous systems will emerge
either abruptly or soon. As I pointed out in the Prologue the
principles can only be guessed at, rather than deduced, until we
have gleaned a great deal of information about many different kinds
of nervous systems, including those of insects. This may not be
intellectually satisfying, but it can be entertaining.

This is not meant to be a message of despair. Those who truly
find biological processes fascinating will not be dismayed by the
realization that many generations to come will be able to enjoy the
pleasures of tinkering in the laboratory and gradually pushing back
the frontiers.

What, then is a realistic estimate of future progress, assuming
no drastic change in the manner in which we pursue science?
It has taken a decade for the half dozen western scientists fully
involved in it to locate and identify the first 100 or so neurons in
the locust, a number that includes the larger, and therefore easier
to penetrate, motorneurons. There are an estimated 100,000
neurons altogether, in the entire central nervous system, as many
as 2/3 of which are small interneurons concerned with reduction of
the voluminous input from single sense organs. Fortunately for
progress in neuroethology it is not necessary to work with all of
these to understand the nervous system. Quite possibly most can
be ignored.

I suggest that the best ploy will be to continue to work from the sure footing in the motor system, gradually penetrating deeper. There are now about 40 people in Europe, the U.S. and Canada working on the locust nervous system who have the facilities, aptitude and inclination for intracellular recording and an equal number work on the cricket, cockroach, moths and flies. Together they now produce about 300 relevant papers per year and the number can only increase greatly in the future!

I give here some personal suggestions on where newcomers to the growing field may devote their energies, in order of priority.

Recommendations for Future Development

1. Intracellular Recording in Intact Preparations. No matter how well we know the details of connectivity and synaptic interaction from studies on simplified preparation, and possibly on isolated ganglia, we shall not be able to possess a full grasp of neuro-ethological principles until we know the cellular neuronal events that occur in the intact insect. Additional factors are undoubtedly brought into play in the whole organism, interacting with its environment. There are areas of importance to understanding behavior, such as variations in mood, drive and appetite, that are reflections of events that are necessarily only present in the whole animal. Most of these actions are in the class generally termed "modulatory". Both the sites of origin of these, and the mechanisms by which they influence behavior, are major targets for study.

Although the basic elements for the production of complex co-ordinated behavior are likely to be present in simplified prep-arations, it is also desirable to know how they are modulated by specific inputs, especially in the control of orientation, posture and locomotion. Behavior is undoubtedly initiated and terminated, as well as modified, by major inputs, especially from the head. A headless locust can walk, fly or jump because the basic neural program generators are located within the thoracic ganglia, but it is extremely unlikely to do so. The kinds of activation and control mechanism descending from the head need to be extensively examined. David Bentley (1977) has found descending interneurons in the cricket that when excited by a train of stimuli at moderate frequencies called forth normal calling song patterns. The stimuli did not contain any timing cues. The chirp rate, but not the pattern, was affected by frequency, and at higher frequencies the overall

pattern produced was different, equivalent to that used in aggression
song. Comparable interneurons have been extensively studied in
crustaceans (Larimer, 1976), where different ones elicit a wide
range of behaviors. A major significant feature of the cricket
results, was that such a marked change in character of the behavior
was produced by simply increasing the frequency of the single
channel. A major question was answered by this experiment. There
may have been two separate pathways, one for each kind of song
exclusively. Ewing & Hoyle (1965) opted for the simpler possibility
actually found by Bentley. Much more work on the motor effects
of stimulating descending interneurons is needed in insects. A
promising start has been made in this direction by Roddan
Williamson and Martin Burns at the University of Glasgow (Figure 4).

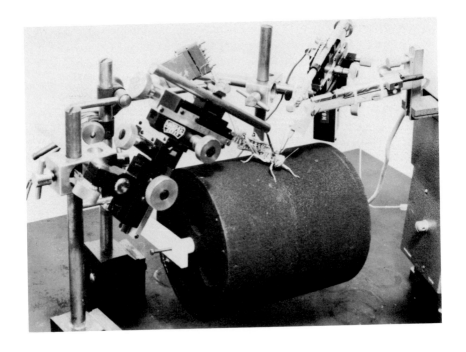

FIGURE 4. Assembly for studying behavioral actions of interneurons in neck connectives of locust.
Courtesy of R. Williamson and M. D. Burns.

Whilst I do not wish to underestimate the problems associated with working intracellularly with essentially intact insects, I have done sufficient development in this field (Figure 5) to assure myself that it is feasible. The insect is opened up from the dorsal surface after cutting off the wings, and held by clips that are clamped onto the wing bases. The ganglia to be studied are exposed and firmly supported on a wax-covered platform to which they are adhered by both pins and suction.

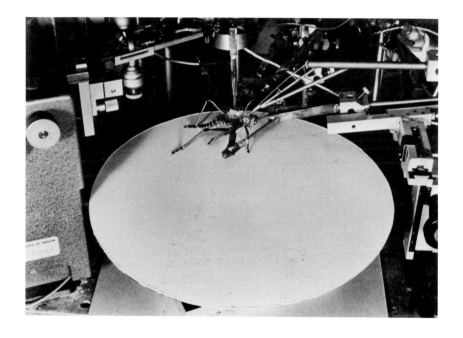

FIGURE 5. Assembly for study of intracellular activity in identified neurons of locusts and grasshoppers during walking. Author's laboratory.

The insect's feet are allowed to touch a ball-bearing-pivoted 10"
horizontal disc. Grasshoppers and locusts walk normally on the
disc after being set up for recording (Figure 6). The connectives
can be stripped and small segments stimulated, as in the Bentley
cricket experiments. One small neuron bundle has been found that
promoted forwards walking in the resting animal when stimulated
repetitively, and another that promoted properly-co-ordinated
backwards walking. Microelectrodes were inserted into nerve cells
directly across the sheath. We have used this preparation so far
principally to study the natural discharge patterns occurring in the
octopaminergic dorsal unpaired median neuron that innervates the
metathoracic extensor tibiae DUMETi (Hoyle & Dagan, 1978,
Figure 7). However, motorneuron cell bodies at the periphery can
be penetrated readily, medial ones after passing the tip of the
electrode through the neuropile. This operation must do some
damage to the neuropile, but normal walking usually continues.
The dorsal approach is the normal one for many non-spiking interneurons.

FIGURE 6. Intracellular recording during walking. Continuous
sequence from 16 mm movie made in author's laboratory.

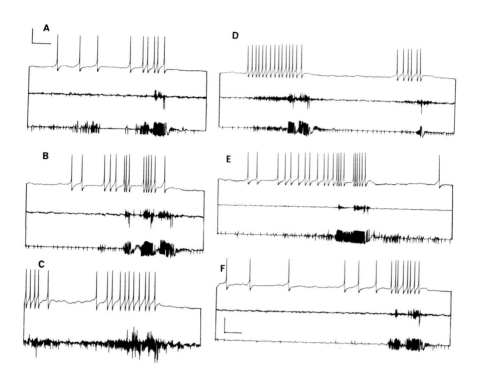

FIGURE 7. A-F Intracellular recording from an identified
neuron, DUMETi - upper traces, during spontaneous activity.
Electromyographs from antagonist leg muscles on lower traces.
From Hoyle & Dagan, 1978.

As the major priority with the whole animal preparation, I
suggest long-term intracellular recording from non-spiking interneurons combined with depolarization and hyperpolarization, all
correlated with intense observation of behavior. The long-range
intent of this work would be to try to decipher the roles of specific
non-spiking interneurons in determining behavior. Perhaps I should
caution the reader though, since a grant application I made to do
just this was squashed on the grounds that such work "will probably
prove unfeasible". Anyone for the challenge! ?

2. Studies Correlated with Genetics. Geneticists have so far regrettably avoided studying the large orthopterans favored by electrophysiologists, hoping that Drosophila would eventually come under their electrodes. To a very limited extent it has (e. g. Ikeda & Kaplan, 1974; Siddiqi & Benzer, 1976) but it will never be possible to study individual neurons in Drosophila to the extent that this has already been done with locusts. Locusts and grasshoppers can develop parthenogenetically and isogenic strains are relatively easy to produce (Goodman, 1979). It should be possible to make, detect, select and clone behavioral mutants of locusts. There are several laboratories anxious to examine any that may be produced for possible neuronal abnormalities.

3. Development. The potential for the study of developmental questions using locusts has fortunately already been realized and started to be grasped. Corey Goodman, Michael O'Shea, Richard McCaman and Nicholas Spitzer (1979), following a lead by C. M. Bate (1976) found that they could recognize DUMETi in 10-day embryos, from the moment of its formation, fill it with Lucifer yellow dye, follow its subsequent development and correlate anatomical stages with pharmacology. They were thus able to resolve questions about the effects on morphology of axons reaching the target organs, and the timing of production of the transmitter substance (which I had earlier recognized to be probably octopamine – Hoyle, 1975).

4. Learning. If there is any area of fundamental research in which there truly seems a possibility of insects making a significant - even Nobel prize-worthy-first, it must be in the cellular mechanisms underlying positive (i. e. as opposed to habituation) learning, memory and memory address. At this time no vertebrate preparation is known to be yielding data at the cellular level on these questions simply because it is not known which cells to investigate. Many insects are good learners. Bees can not only memorize geographical landmarks, directions and distances, they can also communicate the latter two to their hive mates by means of their famous waggle dance (von Frisch, 1967).

The rather simple modifiable behaviors of tonic posture, and movement of a single joint, to a specific temporary position, are easily entrainable in operant conditioning by coupling them either to positive or negative reinforcement (Hoyle, 1979; 1980). Both are achieved, in major part, for some joints, by changes in output of but a single motorneuron and the change may be within that neuron.

The cellular nature of the change is under investigation in our laboratory. Preliminary studies have shown that there is a resistance change, the basis of which may be no more complex than altered potassium ion conductance. Tests with different joints and different movement requirements, perhaps even patterns and sequences, for reinforcement, should be made. It would be desirable to follow up all successes with cellular studies, starting at the level of the motorneurons involved, then trying to find associated interneurons and examining the changes that occur in them.

It should be well worth while trying to obtain classical conditioning in neurons accessible to intracellular recording.

5. Hormone Actions in Behavior. Hormones, in addition to promoting the structural changes of metamorphosis and molting, affect the nervous system in discrete ways to produce behaviors that are markedly different from those constituting the normal repertoire.

Molting behavior, which is hormonally initiated, provides perhaps the longest (1 - 3 hours) of all complex fixed action patterns comprising a series of precisely-timed subroutines. These can now be studied in locusts using intracellular techniques after installing the insect, close to molting, in a decompression chamber that causes adequate expansion of the body wall (Carlson, 1980). Stretch is needed in combination with the hormonal influence, to initiate the behavior.

The $1\frac{1}{2}$ hour pre-molting (eclosion) behavior of moths is brought about by a peptide hormone that has been isolated. The latter initiates appropriate motor activity when applied to an isolated nervous system, permitting intracellular study of underlying events (Truman, Mumby & Welch, 1979). Jim Truman and his collaborators have recently suggested a possible mechanism determining the relative delays in timing of the different subroutines. A subroutine starts when the cGMP level in key neurons, driven upwards by the presence of the peptide hormone, rises above a threshold. The times to rise above threshold are characteristically different for each subroutine.

These are important new developments that hopefully will be fully explored in the near future. Several complex behaviors occur in insects only after sexual maturation, either spontaneously, or in the presence of a potential mate. These are characteristic, and markedly different, for each sex, and it is likely that hormonal effects are of major significance in controlling them. Since such behaviors are widespread among all animals, insects may provide useful models in addition to their intrinsic interest. One such behavior is digging, by the abdomen in female locusts, that is controlled by the last abdominal ganglion. Merely to sever the nerve cord above the ganglion elicits continuous digging movements after maturation (Thompson, 1979).

6. Pheromone Actions in Behavior. Many behaviors are initiated and maintained by the presence of minute amounts of a specific chemical (pheromone) released by other members of the species. Examination of the cellular neuronal mechanisms by which these are brought about in suitably large insects is feasible and should be of wide interest.

7. Basic Biophysics, Biochemistry and Receptor Pharmacology. The biophysical properties and biochemistry of both motorneurons and interneurons of insect nervous systems are as yet very inadequately known. The membrane characteristics of motorneurons change drastically between the axon and the cell body, from spiking to non-spiking. Precisely where the change occurs may be guessed at, but is known only for the locust metathoracic fast extensor tibiae (Gwilliam & Burrows, 1980). The differences in underlying ionic conductances are only just beginning to be studied (Goodman & Heitler, 1979). To study these adequately requires local voltage clamping and control of the immediate extracellular environment. In view of the inability to see the neurons before dye-filling this will be a supremely difficult task. Furthermore, the close packing and the presence of glial cells must be expected to interfere with attempts to control the cellular environment. The attempt needs to be made, in spite of the difficulties, and the same is also true for all types of interneurons, but especially for the non-spikers. Do the latter have weak gradedly responsive electrically excited conductance changes, permitting some propagation, or are they conducting only electrotonically?
      The specific nature of synaptic transmitters onto motorneurons and most interneurons of insects is totally unknown, although it is now fairly well established that inputs onto interneurons from sensory nerves are cholinergic. There is no reason why standard identification techniques for transmitters should not be widely applied in insects: it is again a matter of overcoming the mental resistance engendered by working with small, not directly-visualizable units. It is particularly important to identify the

substances released by non-spiking interneurons, since their
discrete application will be required to help work out their
functional roles.

As I mentioned earlier, I think it quite likely that new types of
interneurons, releasing hitherto unsuspected transmitter
substances, will be located. These may well have novel actions,
including indirect ones of slow time-course, such as the build-up
of cGMP as proposed by Jim Truman for eclosion hormone in moths.

Epilogue: Summary of Prospects

There is a very great deal to be done, but this is nice to know
for anyone who enjoys the hands-on process of obtaining the
information. The portents for success with insects on all fronts
outlined are very good indeed. As the fragments come in they will
more and more fit together until eventually a complete picture is
sure to emerge. This should be the first overview for any kind of
articulated terrestrial animal, and it should provide insights as to
how nervous systems in general function, and how they have evolved:
a very satisfying prospect. There should in this field be "rich veins
of gold awaiting the real specialist who cares to utilize the insect as
a medium for the advancement of physiology" (p. 445, Wigglesworth,
1948 e).

REFERENCES

Bacon, J. P., and Altman, J. S. (1977). A silver intensification
    method for cobalt-filled neurones in wholemount preparations.
    Brain Res. 138, 359-363.
Bate, C. M. (1976). Embryogenesis of an insect nervous system.
    I. A map of the thoracic and abdominal neuroblasts in Locusta
    migratoria. J. Embryol. Exp. Morph. 35, 107-123.
Bentley, D. R. (1969a). Intracellular activity in cricket neurons
    during generation of song patterns. Z. vergl. Physiol. 62, 267-
    283.
Bentley, D. R. (1969b). Intracellular activity in cricket neurons
    during the generation of behavior patterns. J. Insect Physiol.
    15, 677-699.
Bentley, D. R. (1971). Genetic control of an insect neuronal network.
    Science. 174, 1139-1141.

Bentley, D. R. (1977). Control of cricket song patterns by descending interneurons. J. comp. Physiol. 116, 19-38.

Burrows, M. (1973a). The role of delayed excitation in the co-ordination of some metathoracic flight motoneurones of a locust. J. comp. Physiol. 83, 135-164.

Burrows, M. (1973b). The morphology of an elevator and a depressor motoneuron of the hindwing of a locust. J. comp. Physiol. 83, 165-178.

Burrows, M. (1975a). Monosynaptic connexions between wing stretch receptors and flight motor neurons of the locust. J. Exp. Biol. 62, 189-219.

Burrows, M. (1975b). Co-ordinating interneurones of the locust which convey two patterns of motor commands: their connexions with flight motoneurones. J. Exp. Biol. 63, 713-734.

Burrows, M. (1977). In: "Identified neurons and behavior of arthropods" (G. Hoyle, ed.), pp. 339-356. Plenum Press, New York and London.

Burrows, M. (1979). Graded synaptic interactions between local premotor interneurons of the locust. J. Neurophysiol. 42, 1108-1123.

Burrows, M., and Horridge, G. A. (1974). The organization of inputs to motoneurons of the locust metathoracic leg. Phil. Trans. Roy. Soc. Lond. B. 269, 49-94.

Burrows, M., and Hoyle, G. (1973). Neural mechanisms under-lying behavior in the locust Schistocerca gregaria. III. Topography of limb motor neurons in the metathoracic ganglion. J. Neurobiol. 4, 167-186.

Burrows, M., and Siegler, M.V.S. (1978). Graded synaptic transmission between local interneurones and motor neurones in the metathoracic ganglion of the locust. J. Physiol. 285, 231-255.

Candy, D. J. (1978). The regulation of locust flight muscle metabolism by octopamine and other compounds. Insect Biochem. 8, 177-181.

Carlson, J. (1980). A method for controlling body wall turgor during electrophysiological recording from central neurons in ecdysing insects. J. Neurobiol. 11, 219-226.

del Castilo, J., Hoyle, G., and Machne, X. (1953). Neuromuscular transmission in a locust. J. Physiol. 121, 539-547.

Cohen, M. J., and Jacklet, J. W. (1967). The functional organization of motor neurons in an insect ganglion. Phil. Trans. Roy. Soc. Lond. B. 252, 561-572.

Dethier, V.G. (1969). Feeding behavior of the blowfly. Adv.Study Behav. 2, 111-266.

Ellis, P.E., and Hoyle, G. (1954). A physiological interpretation of the marching of hoppers of the African migratory locust. J.Exp.Biol. 31, 271-279.

Elsner, N. (1968). Die neuromuskularen Grundlagen des Werbeverhaltens der roten Kenlenheuschrecke Gomphocerippus rufus (L.). Z.vergl.Physiol. 60, 308-350.

Elsner, N. (1974a). Neuroethology of sound production in gomphocerine grasshoppers (Orthoptera: Acrididae) I. Song patterns and stridulatory movements. J.comp.Physiol. 88, 67-102.

Elsner, N. (1974b). Neural economy: Bifunctional muscles and common central pattern elements in leg and wing stridulation of the grasshopper Stenobothrus rubicundus Germ. (Orthoptera: Acrididae) J.comp.Physiol. 89, 227-236.

Elsner, N., and Popov, A.V. (1978). Neuroethology of acoustic communication. Adv.Insect Physiol. 13, 229-355.

Evans, P.D., and O'Shea, M. (1978). The identification of an octopaminergic neurone and the modulation of a myogenic rhythm in the locust. J.Exp.Biol. 73, 235-260.

Ewing, A., and Hoyle, G. (1965). Neuronal mechanisms underlying control of sound production in a cricket: Acheta domesticus. J.Exp.Biol. 43, 139-153.

Frisch, K. von. (1967). "The Dance Language and Orientation of Bees". Harvard University Press, Cambridge, Mass.

Goodman, C.S., and Heitler, W.J. (1979). Electrical properties of insect neurones with spiking and non-spiking somata: normal, axotomized, and colchicine-treated neurones. J.Exp.Biol. 83, 95-122.

Goodman, C.S., O'Shea, M., McCaman, R., and Spitzer, N.C. (1979). Embryonic development of identified neurons: Temporal pattern of morphological and Biochemical differentiation. Science. 204, 1219-1222.

Gwilliam, F., and Burrows, M. (1980). J.Exp.Biol.

Hagiwara, S., and Watanabe, A. (1956). Discharges in motoneurons of cicada. J.Cell.comp.Physiol. 47, 415-428.

Harvey, W. (1628). "Exercitatio anatomica de motu cordis et sanguinis in animalibus".

Heilbrunn, L.V. (1943). "An outline of general physiology". 2nd Edn. Saunders, Philadelphia and London.

Heitler, M., and Burrows, M. (1977). The locust jump. I. The motor programme. J. Exp. Biol. 66, 203-220.

Horridge, G. A. (1962). Learning of leg position by the ventral nerve cord in headless insects. Proc. Roy. Soc. Lond. B. 157, 33-52.

Horridge, G. A. (1968). "Interneurons". Freeman, London and San Francisco.

Hoyle, G. (1954). Changes in the blood potassium concentration of the African migratory locust (Locusta migratoria migratoriodes R. and F.) during food deprivation, and the effect on neuromuscular activity. J. Exp. Biol. 31, 260-270.

Hoyle, G. (1964). In: "Neural Theory and Modelling" (R. F. Reiss, ed.), pp. 346-376. Stanford University Press.

Hoyle, G. (1965). In: "The Physiology of the Insect Central Nervous System" (J. E. Treherne and J. W. L. Beament, eds.). pp. 203-232. Academic Press, London and New York.

Hoyle, G. (1970). Cellular mechanisms underlying behavior - neuroethology. Adv. Insect Physiol. 7, 349-444.

Hoyle, G. (1975). Evidence that insect dorsal unpaired median (DUM) neurons are octopaminergic. J. Exp. Zool. 193, 425-431.

Hoyle, G. (1979). Mechanisms of simple motor learning. Trends in Neuroscience. 2, 153-155.

Hoyle, G. (1980). Learning, using natural reinforcements, in insect preparations that permit cellular neuronal analysis. J. Neurobiol. 11,

Hoyle, G., and Burrows, M. (1973a). Neural mechanisms underlying behavior in the locust Schistocerca gregaria. I. Physiology of identified motoneurons in the metathoracic ganglion. J. Neurobiol. 4, 3-41.

Hoyle, G., and Burrows, M. (1973b). Neural mechanisms underlying behavior in the locust Schistocerca gregaria. II. Integrative activity in metathoracic neurons. J. Neurobiol. 4, 43-67.

Hoyle, G., and Dagan, D. (1978). Physiological characteristics and reflex activation of DUM (Octopaminergic) neurons of locust metathoracic ganglion. J. Neurobiol. 9, 59-79.

Hoyle, G., Dagan, D., Moberly, B., and Colquhoun, W. (1974). Dorsal unpaired median insect neurons make neurosecretory endings on skeletal muscle. J. Exp. Zool. 187, 159-165.

Huber, F. (1959). Auslosung von Bewegungsmustern durch elektrische Reizung des oberschlundganglions bei Orthopteren (Saltatoria: Gryllidae, Acridiidae). Zool. Anz. (Suppl. 23) 248-269.

Hughes, G. M. (1953). Differential effects of direct current on insect ganglia. J. Exp. Biol. 29, 387-402.

Ikeda, K., and Kaplan, W. D. (1974). Neurophysiological genetics in Drosophila melanogaster. Am. Zool. 14, 1055-1066.

Larimer, J. L. (1976). Command interneurons and locomotor behavior in crustaceans. In: "Neural Control of Locomotion" (R. Herman, S. Grillner, P. S. G. Stein and D. G. Stuart, eds.) pp. 293-326. Plenum Press, New York and London.

Lorenz, K. Z. (1950). The comparative method in studying innate behaviour patterns. Symp. Soc. Exp. Biol. 4, 221-268.

Nathanson, J. A., and Greengard, P. (1973). Octopamine-sensitive adenylate cyclase: evidence for a biological role of octopamine in nervous tissue. Science. 180, 308-310.

O'Shea, M., and Evans, P. D. (1979). Potentiation of neuro-muscular transmission by an octopaminergic neurone in the locust. J. Exp. Biol. 79, 169-190.

O'Shea, M., and Williams, J. L. D. (1974). The anatomy and output connection of a locust visual interneurone; the lobular giant movement detector (LGMD) neurone. J. Comp. Physiol. 91, 257-266.

Pearson, K. G. (1972). Central programming and reflex control of walking in the cockroach. J. Exp. Biol. 56, 173-193.

Pearson, K. G. (1977). Interneurons in the ventral nerve cord of insects. In: "Identified Neurons and Behavior of Arthropods" (G. Hoyle, ed.), pp. 329-338. Plenum Press, New York and London.

Pearson, K. G., and Bergman, S. J. (1969). Common inhibitory motor neurons in insects. J. Exp. Biol. 50, 445-471.

Pearson, K. G., and Fourtner, C. R. (1975). Nonspiking inter-neurons in walking system of the cockroach. J. Neurophysiol. 38, 33-52.

Pearson, K. G., Fourtner, C. R., and Wong, R. K. (1973). Nervous control of walking in the cockroach. Adv. Behav. Biol. 7, 495-514.

Phillips, C. E. (1979). Synaptic ultrastructure of single physiologically identified neurons using cobalt. Abst. #1706. 9th Mtg. Soc. Neurosci.

Pitman, R. M. (1969). Electrical activity in insect nerve cell bodies. Ph. D. Thesis, University of Southampton.

Pitman, R. M., Tweedle, C. D., and Cohen, M. J. (1972). Branching of central neurons. Intracellular cobalt injection for light and electron microscopy. Science. 176, 412-414.

Pringle, J. W. S. (1939). The motor mechanism of the insect leg. J. Exp. Biol. 16, 220-231.

Pringle, J. W. S. (1948). The gyroscopic mechanism of the halteres of Diptera. Phil. Trans. Roy. Soc. Lond. B. 233, 347-384.

Roeder, K. D. (1948). The effect of potassium and calcium on the nervous system of the cockroach. J. Cell. comp. Physiol. 31, 327-338.

Roeder, K. D. (1965). Moths and ultrasound. Am. Sci. 212, 93-102.

Rowell, C. H. F. (1971). The orthopteran descending movement detector (DCMD) neurones: a characterization and review. Z. vergl. Physiol. 73, 167-194.

Siddiqi, O., and Benzer, S. (1976). Neurophysiological defects in temperature-sensitive paralytic mutants of Drosophila melanogaster. Proc. Nat. Acad. Sci. 9, 3253-3257.

Siegler, M. V. S., and Burrows, M. (1979). The morphology of local non-spiking interneurones in the metathoracic ganglion of the locust. J. Comp. Neurol. 183, 121-148.

Stewart, W. W. (1978). Functional connections between cells as revealed by dye-coupling with a highly fluorescent naphthalimide tracer. Cell. 14, 741-759.

Stretton, A. O. W., and Kravitz, E. E. (1968). Neuronal geometry; determination with a technique of intracellular dye injection. Science. 162, 132-134.

Thompson, K. J. (1979). Locust oviposition: a system for the study of pattern generation. Abst. #872. 9th Mtg. Soc. Neurosci.

Tosney, T., and Hoyle, G. (1977). Computer-controlled learning in a simple system. Proc. Roy. Soc. Lond. B. 195, 365-393.

Truman, J. W., Mumby, S. M., and Welch, S. K. (1979). Peptide hormone release of stereotyped motor programs in an insect: role of cyclic GMP. Abst. #1835. 9th Mtg. Soc. Neurosci.

Tyrer, N. M., and Altman, J. S. (1974). Motor and sensory flight neurones in a locust demonstrated using cobalt chloride. J. Comp. Neurol. 157, 117-138.

Wilson, D. M. (1961). The central nervous control of flight in a locust. J. Exp. Biol. 38, 471-490.

Wilson, D. M. (1967). An approach to the problem of control of rhythmic behavior. In: "Invertebrate Nervous Systems" (C. A. G. Wiersma, ed.), pp. 219-229. The University of Chicago Press, Chicago and London.

Wilson, J. A. (1979). There are unique, identifiable local non-spiking interneurons. Abst. #879. 9th Mtg. Soc. Neurosci.

Wohlers, D., and Huber, F. (1978). Intracellular recording and staining of cricket auditory interneurons (Gryllus campestris L., Gryllus bimaculatus DeGreer). J. Comp. Physiol. 127, 11-28.

Woollacott, M., and Hoyle, G. (1977). Neural events underlying learning in insects: changes in pacemaker. Proc. Roy. Soc. Lond. B. 195, 395-415.

NEURONAL GUIDANCE AND PATHFINDING IN THE DEVELOPING SENSORY NERVOUS SYSTEM OF INSECTS

John S. Edwards[1]

Department of Zoology
University of Washington
Seattle, Washington

I. INTRODUCTION

To address the future in science is at once simple and impossible. The predictable can only be the filling in of expected details in existing models, but the evolution of science comes from the unpredictable, the new observations that force the abandonment of old hypotheses, and the opening of new ideas. There remain nonetheless many fascinating and important details to be filled in the great tapestry woven by Sir Vincent Wigglesworth when insect physiology became a discipline, and the development and organisation of the nervous system remains a major part of the great design where progress toward completion of the pattern will yield the new and unexpected.

The major item on the agenda of developmental neurobiology of insects now is to establish the lineage and life histories of peripheral and central neurons, and to explore their capacities for specificity and plasticity in making connections during development and regeneration. As descriptive knowledge of the behavior of neurons accumulates it becomes possible to ask questions about the mechanisms that underly the extraordinary properties of growing neurons, properties that enable them to make appropriate cellular contacts before they

[1]*My work discussed in this essay was supported by NIH grant NB07778.*

contribute information to the functional unity of the
organism, and to make at least some sorts of adjustment in the
light of experience.

Here I will consider the brief past and the bustling
present as pointers to the future of a central theme in insect
developmental neurobiology--the pathfinding behavior of
sensory neurons. Comprehensive reviews document earlier
(Nüesch 1968; Edwards 1969; Young 1973; Bate 1978) and current
(Edwards and Palka 1976; Bate 1978; Palka 1979a; Anderson,
Edwards and Palka 1980) contributions to the burgeoning
subject of developmental neurobiology. Much of this essay is
based on material reviewed in these works and I will generally
restrict citations to most recent studies. Palka (1979a) has
recently assessed the applicability of current theories of
pattern formation to the development of the insect nervous
system. My objective here is to consider the natural history
of the developing neuron.

II. THE PROBLEM OF NEURONAL PATHFINDING

A. *Beginnings*

Thirty years after the publication of his first paper, and
now nearly thirty years ago, Wigglesworth (1953) described the
origin of sensory neurons in the integument of *Rhodnius*. This
work, together with that of Henke and Rönsch (1951), Krumins
(1952) and Nüesch (1952), finally established the peripheral
origin of sensory cells and concluded a long history of
indecision as to their source. It was the last major milestone to be passed in understanding the basic design of the
insect body. The demonstration that sensilla are added to the
integument at each molt by differentiation of epidermal cells
means that with each successive instar new axons must find
their way to the central ganglia. Among the earliest events
in the cell cluster that generates the sensillum is the
appearance of an axonal process from the cell that will become
the sensory neuron. The axon grows across the inner surface
of the epidermis, between it and the basal lamina, until it
encounters an axon from a sensillum formed earlier in development. It proceeds along the surface of the axon, or its glial
sheath, uniting with others to form a bundle that passes
through the basal lamina and subsequently to the central
nervous system, where it makes synaptic connection within the
neuropile.

Just how this feat of pathfinding is achieved raises a fundamental question of morphogenesis: how does directed growth occur? Clues were afforded by observations first presented by Wigglesworth (1953, 1965g) that axons from sensilla regenerating in a wound site where preexisting axons were not to be found, would wander about as if lost, but if they should make contact with their own axon they would sometimes follow their own surface to form a ring bundle, rather like the caterpillars of Fabre which endlessly followed the silken thread, or perhaps the pheromone, they had laid down on the lip of a glass. Neurons recognise other neurons and seem to aggregate as if selective adhesion of their cell surfaces holds them more strongly than the epidermal cell surface they first traversed. Selective adhesion, contact guidance, mechanical guidance – there is no shortage of models implicit in these descriptive terms to account for the mechanics of the observed behavior. It is for the future to sort out the specific mechanisms; meanwhile it remains to determine the rules for congregation. For example it is established that the midline can be crossed, while segmental boundaries are seldom traversed (Bate 1978), but it is an open question whether compartment boundaries can set limits. Nor is it known whether neurons serving similar modalities aggregate preferentially.

B. Embryonic Origin of Sensory Nerves

The postembryonic growth of sensory nerves clearly depends on the fasciculating behavior of axons in the periphery with pre-existing nerves but how are the very first connections set up between periphery and center? It is surprising that despite the many detailed studies of central nervous system development dating back to the later decades of the 19th century, the sensory system has escaped attention until recent years. So far our knowledge is restricted to orthopterans, but the findings to be summarised below will probably prove to be general.

The first cellular connections between the embryonic epidermis and rudiments of the central nervous system occur at about the half-way point in embryogenesis in locusts (Bate 1976) and in crickets (Edwards 1977). The embryo has just completed the return movements of katatrepsis that complete blastokinesis and the epidermis is still extending upward from the ventral surface of the embryo, to be completed with the attainment of dorsal closure. Segmentation has been established but the lobes that will extend to become the appendages of the homologous segmental series bear little indication of their future form. In the cricket axon-like processes appear within the short cercal rudiments after about half of the time required to complete embryonic development has elapsed. These structures, termed pioneer fibres (Bate 1976), extend from cell bodies that lie against the lumen surface of the apical epidermis and extend through the appendage to the nearest ganglion rudiment. In the locust leg they grow along the basal lamina of the epidermis, their growth cones reaching thoracic ganglion primordia about 15 hours after growth is initiated. The processes are axon-like in their circular outline and microtubular contents. They lie in contact with the surface of the basal lamina at first, but soon become enveloped by neurilemmal glial cells whose source is not yet known. The cell bodies of these pioneer fibres lack any dendritic processes that might give the cells a sensory function. It seems likely that the pioneer fibres are ephemeral structures serving a morphogenetic function and dying thereafter, rather like the radial glial cells of the monkey cerebral cortex (Rakic 1971). We have not seen the death of these cells, and it may be difficult to determine their fate with certainty because they are joined by a population of cells early in embryogenesis that occupy comparable positions under the epidermis and which become bipolar putative mechanoreceptors.

C. The Origin of Pioneer Fibres

The source of the peripheral pioneer fibre cell bodies is an important question, with profound implications for theories of neurogenesis. Precursor cells have been seen to emerge from specific sites in embryonic legs of locusts where individual cells from the embryonic epithelium, that had not previously been distinguishable, enlarge and take up positions on the luminal surface of the epithelium. Keshishian (1979) who observed these cells directly with interference optics and injected them with fluorescent dye, found that the precursor cell divides after leaving the epithelium to give the characteristic pairs of cells seen in locusts. These cells then form monopolar outgrowths that become the pioneer fibres. They produce the centrally directed processes shortly before the embryonic appendages begin to elongate, and as limb morphogenesis proceeds, the pioneer fibres are spun out so that a pathway is set up between the now distant tip of the appendage and the ganglion. This process, referred to as

"passive stretching" by Ross Harrison (1935) is most
dramatically seen in the migration of the lateral line nerve
from head to tail in developing fish.

The ultimate source of the pioneer fibre cell bodies
remains to be determined. Their lineage may originate as
part of the patterning process of the appendage, but it is
also possible that precursor cells migrate to the site of
presumptive limb rudiment areas from the ventral band of
embryonic neurectoderm before limb differentiation begins.
In that case the first cell processes to reach ganglia from
the periphery would be clonally related to the central
targets and the mechanisms of cell recognition in the primor-
dial neuropile could then be based on the similarity of cell
surface characteristics. These are questions for the future.

D. *Some Characteristics of Pioneer Fibres*

Pioneer fibre cells are characteristically monopolar.
They do not become bipolar or acquire a form that might
suggest a sensory function. Their processes are axon-like
in their circular profile and microtubule disposition but
they are not necessarily neuronal in function, and may be
purely morphogenetic and evanescent.

The pioneer fibres occupy very precisely determined sites
in the embryonic appendages. In the cricket cercus they
occupy the mid-dorsal and mid-ventral lines and are at first
closely in contact with the basal lamina along these axes
(Edwards and Chen 1979). No specialization of the epidermal
cells or the basal lamina is evident from ultrastructural
studies. For now it is proposed that the mid-dorsal and
mid-ventral epidermal cells impart a special quality to their
basal laminae that provides for differential adhesion. The
cerci have a pronounced circumferential polarity, as
evidenced by the capacity of rotated grafts to restore normal
axial relationships (Palka and Schubiger 1975). Further, the
conformation of mechanosensory sensilla along the dorsal and
ventral midlines of the functional cercus implies that these
axes are in some way uniquely labelled. It is proposed, and
it remains for the future to test the hypothesis that the
basal lamina underlying the dorsal and ventral midlines
carries materials on its surface that are differentially
adhesive to the pioneer fibres and their accompanying glia.

The pattern of increase in numbers of cells that fasciculate with the pioneer fibres deserves some attention in relation to the development of the integument. We have found that
even while the cercus is undergoing its rapid elongation and
before the embryonic cuticle is secreted, new axon-like
processes are added. Studies with methylene blue injection
show a growing population of bipolar cells, all or most of
which underly the epidermis. The dendrites of these luminal
cells contain microtubular arrays characteristic of scolopi-
dia. These sensilla may perhaps serve as proprioceptors to
monitor developmental changes of form. Development of the
epidermal sensilla only begins after the apolysis of the
embryonic cuticle formed on completion of epidermal continuity
at dorsal closure. Axons from these sensilla follow the pathway set up by the pioneer fibres, their associated neurilemma
cells and the axons that are added from luminal cells, and in
doing so reach the terminal abdominal ganglion. Most of the
functional axons are added to the cercal nerve during the last
15% of embryonic development. At this time the dorsal and
ventral bundles detach from the basal lamina, to lie free in
the hemocoel of the cercus.

III. SENSORY DEVELOPMENT AT METAMORPHOSIS

The pattern of embryonic sensory development in the
orthopteran egg finds a striking parallel in the metamorphosis
of the tobacco hornworm *Manduca sexta* (Sanes and Hildebrand
1975; 1976) where during passage from the larva to the adult a
massive antenna develops as a product of the imaginal disk,
elongating dramatically as the pupal stadium is entered. The
cuticle of the pupal antenna, like the cuticle of the embryo
formed after dorsal closure, lacks sensilla and yet a pair of
bundles of axon-like processes traverse the lumen from cell
bodies at the apex to the developing brain. They form the
axis with which the enormous number of axons from adult
olfactory sensilla fasciculate during adult development and,
following them proximally, find their way to the olfactory
lobe of the brain. Most, if not all, imaginal disks have
neural connections with the central nervous system that are
probably established during embryogenesis (Bate, 1978) and
these connections evidently provide the guide path for the
adult sensory neurons at metamorphosis. In the visual system
of Holometabola where the larva frequently has only rudimentary structures, it is the stemmatal nerve that provides for
the access of neurons from the differentiating compound eye

to the optic lobes: the metamorphosis of the monarch butterfly *Danaus plexippus* brain (Nordlander and Edwards 1969) is one of the many examples that demonstrate the continuity between larval and adult sensory projections.

The importance of the continued link between periphery and center throughout development is to maintain a pathway. The possibility that the connecting cells have some further organising role that depends on contact with the central nervous system, perhaps trophic in nature, was disproven by observations on *in vitro* cultured imaginal disks that were induced to metamorphose by hormonal manipulation (Edwards, Milner and Chen, 1978). Despite their isolation from the body, sensillar differentiation proceeded and sensory nerve bundles were formed in appropriate positions.

IV. DEVELOPMENT OF THE VISUAL SYSTEM: AN EXERCISE IN TIME AND SPACE

The development of retinotopic projections in the compound eye requires great accuracy in the preservation of spatial relationships, but retinula axons do not select particular lamina cartridges, as Anderson (1978), and Macagno (1978) showed by ablation and transposition of retinal tissue. It is rather the precise temporal sequence in which retinal axons follow pre-existing pathways to waiting lamina neurons that generates successive cartridges in the growth zone of the eye (Meinertzhagen 1975).

V. GENERALISATIONS SO FAR

Two generalisations emerge from the foregoing examples of embryonic and postembryonic development. First, that pioneer connections between periphery and center arise so early in development that distances to be traversed by cell processes are short, and the geometry is simple. Separations between pioneer fibre cell bodies and central targets are probably never more than 100 - 200 μm and are thus within the range through which diffusion gradients might act as morphogenetic growth-directing agents (Crick 1971). Insect epidermal cells respond to deprivation of their tracheal supply by forming neurite-like processes that may extend as far as 200 μm from the cell and function as grappling hooks in the capture and redirection of fine tracheoles, which

in turn drag tracheal branches (Wigglesworth 1959g; 1977a).
Their activity provides the basis for a simple model of
pioneer fibre growth if it is allowed that the target
ganglion is the source of a diffusing substance which, acting
in concert with a preformed pathway, guides pioneer fibres to
their destination.

The second generalisation is that the development of the
sensory system in both Hemimetabola and Holometabola from
embryogenesis throughout postembryonic development is based
on continuity of sensory projections.

VI.   ARE PIONEER FIBRES NECESSARY?

The developmental observations sketched above suggest that
pioneer fibres play a role in neurogenesis, but are they
necessary? Can neurons find the way without their aid? We
have addressed this question by inflicting lesions with a
laser microbeam to the tips of embryonic cerci in the cricket
Acheta domesticus just before the pioneer fibres differentiate
and begin their journey down the cercus to the ganglion. We
find that when the pioneer fibre cells are removed before they
spin out their processes, the functional fibres that differentiate later fail to form the normal dorsal and ventral midline
bundles. Instead they show variably distributed fascicles
(Edwards, Berns and Chen, 1979). The lesion itself is
localised and does not appear to be the direct cause of the
altered bundling, for lesions inflicted after the pioneer
tracts are formed, when the pioneer fibres (but not the glial
sheaths) are destroyed, do not alter the normal fasciculation
of the functional fibres: the glia alone, or the products of
degenerating pioneer fibres, are sufficient to serve as
aggregation foci.

These observations perhaps find a parallel in the role
assigned to glia during neurogenesis in vertebrates. Rakic
(1974) has proposed that ephemeral glial cells, the radial
glia, provide the scaffold on which neurons migrate during
development of the monkey cortex, and glia have been
similarly implicated in the development of the cerebellum in
mice (Sidman 1974). The possibility remains that comparable
cells may play a role in the guidance of neurons in the
insect. In *Daphnia*, glial cells may serve to order the
growth of axons in the developing eye (LoPresti, Macagno and
Levinthal, 1973).

VII.   SENSORY REGENERATION

A seeming paradox arises when the regeneration of sensory axons during postembryonic life is considered. Cercal sensory nerves that regenerate *in situ* re-establish central connections even though continuity has been disrupted throughout the greater part of postembryonic life by extirpation of the cercus at hatching as well as subsequent regenerates (Edwards and Palka, 1971). No cercal sensory fibres were present to guide the successful regenerate neurons.

Axons from transplanted sensilla can find their way to central ganglia (e.g Edwards and Sahota 1967; Anderson and Bacon 1979). The explanation of pathfinding successes in such cases evidently lies in the ability of regenerate fibres to fasciculate with the nearest nerves in the vicinity of the graft site. Anderson and Bacon's (1979) work with wind-sensitive hairs on the head of the locust has special significance in this context, for they showed that the characteristic projection patterns of particular sensilla within the tritocerebrum, suboesophageal ganglion and prothoracic ganglion were maintained, even though the integument in which they originated was interchanged by grafting before sensilla differentiated. Neither displacement nor entry to central ganglia by abnormal routes affected their behavior within the neuropile. Some further aspects of sensory axon growth within the ganglion will now be considered.

VIII.   PATHFINDING WITHIN THE CENTRAL NERVOUS SYSTEM

A.   *Pathfinding in the Neuropile*

Having found their way into the ganglion, afferent fibres are faced with a new set of challenges, culminating in synapse formation. It is one thing to find the ganglion, and perhaps to enter it along pathways established during early embryogenesis, but it is another to locate a specific site on a target cell. The spatial and temporal organisation of afferent nerves may be important in placing the neurons in appropriate positions as they enter the ganglion. Sensory nerves are somatotopically organised (Edwards and Palka 1974; Zill *et al.* 1979) and this must influence the path of individual neurons. Murphey (1979) has shown that

successively added sensilla from a particular mechanosensory
population of receptors, the clavate hairs of the cricket
cercus, have projections within the neuropile that reflect
both spatial position and time of origin.

There is no reason to expect that a single mechanism
suffices for the guidance of axons from the periphery to the
center; indeed it seems likely that a sequence of factors
should dominate as the growing neuron approaches its target.
The succession of sensory modalities used by predatory wasps
of the genus *Philanthus* as they approach their honeybee prey
(Tinbergen 1935) may be an apt analogy for the afferent
neuron.

B. *Genetic Approaches*

Genetic manipulation is now opening up new and incisive
ways to attack the difficult questions of how neurons find
their way through the neuropile. Homeotic mutants in which
one structure is substituted for another, and ingeniously
devised homeotic mosaics, provide means for assessing the
response of growing sensory axons to a changed mileu. In the
antennapedia mutant, for example, parts of the antenna become
leg-like and yet the projections of sensilla conform principally to that of the antenna (Stocker *et al.* 1976), as if
members of the homologous limb series are interchangeable.
But the behavior of the fly in response to stimulation of the
transformed limb show that some connections must have been
formed that are the equivalent of normal leg sensilla (Stocker
1977). In bithorax mutants the characteristic dipteran
haltere-bearing metathoracic segment bears a wing and this
system provides for a comparison of the projection of wing and
haltere mechanoreceptors (Palka 1979b). Palka, Lawrence and
Hart (1979) recognised three different projection patterns in
sensory axons from the metathoracic wing and emphasised the
need to recognise that each sensillar neuron carries a
developmental program, a set of instructions concerning its
behavior in the neuropile as well as the capacity to respond
to cues in the milieu,the central neuronal and glial surfaces
over which they grow. Ghysen's (1978) analysis of similar
experiments emphasises the role of guidepaths. One reserva-
tion concerning the interpretation of homeotic mutants is the
possible pleiotropic effect of the homeotic gene on the neuropile, which may also be modified. The generation of mosaic
flies in which only the integument undergoes transformation
(Palka, Lawrence and Hart 1979) circumvents this complication.
A further refinement in the use of bithorax mutants is

achieved by removing the anterior wing genetically or surgically (Schubiger and Palka 1979). The postsynaptic sites left vacant by absence of the wing do not have the effect of deflecting afferent axons from the haltere path. The extraordinary progress since studies began recently with genetic manipulations as a tool in developmental neurobiology (Palka 1980) make it a safe prediction that the near future will bring great refinement to concepts of how neurons find their way.

C. Life Histories of Identified Central Neurons

New anatomical and physiological techniques also make the assault on the neuropile productive. Observations of large individually identifiable neurons in grasshopper embryos by means of interference optics and microelectrode impalement have enabled Goodman and Spitzer (1979) to reconstruct the life histories of central neurons from birth to maturation. The paths of their outgrowths are highly stereotyped and the gridwork they establish provides a scaffolding for subsequent neurons to elaborate the open meshwork into which sensory neurons finally project.

The grasshopper neurons follow patterns of development and regression in which numerous initial fine neurites and supernumerary peripheral neurites disappear as the cell assumes its definitive form. The best known of the identified cells is the unique dorsal unpaired median excitor tibiae motor neuron (DUMETi). The first product of the cell body is a median neurite whose distal end produces multiple branches as the growth cone extends in a generally anterior direction with excursions that are often as much as 20 microns in the wrong direction. At this time the neuropile framework is essentially an orthogonal grid composed of two longitudinal fibre tracts, two commissures in each segment, and lateral fibre tracts extending to the periphery. When the growing process of DUMETi reaches the anterior commissure within the embryonic ganglion, the neurite bifurcates and symmetrical divergent branches, each with numerous fine evanescent branches grow laterally toward the periphery. Beyond the margin of the developing ganglion the neuron branches multiply, simultaneously sending neurites to several 'wrong' muscles as well as to the correct extensor tibiae muscle. After the correct target is reached other branches recede, and thereafter central branches begin to proliferate within the neuropile. Neurochemical and physiological maturation of the cells follows a correlated program. An echo of this developmental pattern is

seen in regenerating motor neurons. Cut motor neurons in a
cockroach leg reestablish correct connections after initial
outgrowths branch to several different muscles (Denburg,
Seecof and Horridge 1977). The trial and error program may
seem to contrast with the apparent determinacy of sensory
development but this difference may simply reflect the
relative ease in distinguishing right and wrong targets of
motor neurons as opposed to neuropile sites, as well as
experimental design, since most studies of sensory neuron
growth limit observations to end points only.

Close scrutiny of the form of particular cells, for
example the mesothoracic wing stretch receptors of locusts
(Altman and Tyrer 1977a,b) reveals variation in the pathway
of the sensory neurons through the neuropile even though the
patterns of termination are uniform, and Goodman's (1978)
survey of ocellar neuron form in the brain of locusts
emphasises variability, but does imply that the number of
variant pathways taken by the growing neurons is limited: the
advancing cell process is not a free agent.

D. *Similarities Between Central and Peripheral Neurogenesis*

The early neuronal scaffolding of the central nervous
system, the template for central neuronal development is
built, at least in part, of temporary fibres that exercise a
guidance function for a brief period of embryogenesis before
disappearing (Spitzer, Bate and Goodman, 1979). These early
pathways seem to be the central counterpart of the peripheral
guide fibres described above. A further parallel is to be
seen in the morphogenesis of central ganglia, which originate
in close proximity, separating and moving apart after
connectives have been established at close range, just as
first connections between periphery and center are established
before the appendages elongate.

IX. SIMILARITIES BETWEEN INSECT AND VERTEBRATE NEURAL
     DEVELOPMENT

Based on their extensive studies of amphibian spinal cord
development and regeneration, Singer, Nordlander and Egar
(1979) have recently epitomised concepts of neuronal
guidance mechanisms as a 'blueprint' in which trace pathways,

envisioned as mechanical-chemical itineraries expressed by germinal neuroepithelium, are followed by neurites according to their individual affinities. It is becoming clear that neurogenesis in insects may be seen in similar terms.

X. THE FUTURE

The rule book for the growing neuron is beginning to make sense. Ways must now be found to determine just what mechanical and chemical cues are read by the advancing neurite. Cell surface phenomena, the role of surface glyco-proteins, and cell contacts will provide sufficient challenges to the insect developmental neurobiologist for the foreseeable future. And that may only be a beginning for the full understanding of neuronal specificity.

ACKNOWLEDGMENTS

I thank my colleagues Drs. Hilary Anderson and John Palka for their comments and Ms. Margaret Dawson for timely assistance with the manuscript.

REFERENCES

Anderson, H. (1978). Postembryonic development of the visual system of the locust *Schistocerca gregaria*. II. An experi-mental investigation of the formation of the retina-lamina projection. *J. Embryol. exp. Morph. 46*, 147-170.

Altman, J. S., and Tyrer, N. M. (1977). The locust wing stretch receptors II. Variation, alternative pathways and 'mistakes' in the central arborizations. *J. comp. Neurol. 172*, 431-440.

Anderson, M., and Bacon, J. (1979). Developmental determina-tion of neuronal projection patterns from wind-sensitive hairs in the locust, *Schistocerca gregaria. Develop. Biol. 72*, 364-373.

Anderson, H., Edwards, J. S. and Palka, J. (1980). Developmen-tal neurobiology of invertebrates. *In* "Annual Reviews of Neuroscience" In press.

Bate, C. M. (1976). Pioneer neurones in an insect embryo. *Nature 260*, 54-56.

Bate, M. (1978). Development of sensory systems in arthropods. *In* "Handbook of Sensory Physiology IX: Development of Sensory Systems (M. Jacobson, ed.), pp. 1-53. Springer Verlag.

Crick, F.H.C. (1971). The scale of pattern formation. *Symp. Soc. Exptl. Biol. 25*, 429-438.

Denburg, J. F., Seecof, R. L., and Horridge, G. A. (1977). The path and rate of growth of regenerating motor neurons in the cockroach. *Brain Research 125*, 213-226.

Edwards, J. S. (1969). Postembryonic development and regeneration of the insect nervous system. *In* "Advances in Insect Physiology" 6 (J.W.L. Beament, J. E. Treherne and V. B. Wigglesworth, eds), pp. 97-137. Academic Press, New York.

Edwards, J. S. (1977). Pathfinding by arthropod sensory nerves. *In* "Identified Neurons and Behavior of Arthropods" (G. Hoyle, ed.), pp. 483-493. Plenum Press, New York and London.

Edwards, J. S., Berns, M. W. and Chen, S. W. (1979). Laser lesions of embryonic cricket cerci disrupt guidepath role of pioneer fibres. *Soc. Neuroscience Abstracts, 5*, 158.

Edwards, J. S. and Chen, S. W. (1979). Embryonic development of an insect sensory system, the abdominal cerci of *Acheta domesticus. Wilhelm Roux' Arch. Devel. Biol. 186*, 151-178.

Edwards, J. S., Milner, M. and Chen, S.-W. (1978). Integument and sensory nerve differentiation of *Drosophila* leg and imaginal disk *in vitro. Wilhelm Roux' Arch. Devel. Biol. 185*, 59-77.

Edwards, J. S. and Palka, J. (1971). Neural regeneration: delayed formation of central contacts by insect sensory cells. *Science* (Washington D.C.) *172*, 591-594.

Edwards, J. S., and Palka, J. (1974). The cerci and abdominal giant fibres of the house cricket *Acheta domesticus*. I. Anatomy and physiology of normal adults. *Proc. Roy. Soc. Lond. B. 185*, 83-103.

Edwards, J. S. and Palka, J. (1976). Neural generation and regeneration in insects. *In* "Simpler Networks and Behavior" (J. C. Fentress, ed.), pp. 167-185. Sinauer Associates, Sunderland, Mass.

Ghysen, A. (1978). Sensory neurones recognize defined pathways in *Drosophila* central nervous system. *Nature 274*, 869-872.

Goodman, C. S. (1978). Isogenic locusts: Genetic variability in the morphology of identified neurons. *J. comp. Neurol. 182*, 681-705.

Goodman, C. S. and Spitzer, N. C. (1979). Embryonic development of identified neurones: differentiation from neuroblast to neurone. *Nature 280*, 208-214.

Harrison, R. G. (1935). The origin and development of the nervous system studied by the methods of experimental embryology. *Proc. Roy. Soc. Lond. B. 118*, 155-196.

Henke, K. and Rönsch, G. (1951). Über Bildungsgleichheiten in der Entwicklung epidermaler Organe und die Entstehung des Nervensystems in Flügel der Insekter. *Naturwiss 14*, 335-336.

Keshishian, H. (1979). Origin and differentiation of pioneer neurons in the embryonic grasshopper. *Soc. Neuroscience Abstracts 5*, 166.

Krumins, R. (1952). Die Borstenentwicklung bei der Wachsmotte *Galleria mellonella* L. *Biol. Zbl. 71*, 183-210.

LoPresti, V., Macagno, E. and Levinthal, C. (1973). Structure and development of neuronal connections in isogenic organisms: cellular interactions in the development of the optic lamina of *Daphnia*. *Proc. Nat. Acad. Sci. USA. 70*, 433-437.

Meinertzhagen, I. A. (1975). The development of neuronal connection patterns in the visual system of insects. *In* "Cell Patterning." Ciba Symposium *29*, 265-288.

Murphey, R. K. (1979). The development of distinct terminal arborizations in the cricket nervous system is correlated with birthday and position in a receptor array. *Soc. Neuroscience Abstracts 5*, 256.

Nordlander, R. H. and Edwards, J. S. (1969). Postembryonic brain development in the monarch butterfly, *Danaus plexippus plexippus* L. II. The optic lobes. *Wilhelm Roux' Archiv für Entwicklungs.163*, 197-220.

Nüesch, H. (1952). Über den Einfluss der Nerven auf die Muskelentwicklung bei *Telea polyphemus* (Lepid). *Rev. Suisse Zool. 59*, 294-301.

Nüesch, H. (1968). The role of the nervous system in insect morphogenesis and regeneration. *Ann. Rev. Entomol. 13*, 27-44.

Palka, J. (1979a). Theories of pattern formation in insect neural development. *Advances in Insect Physiol. 14* (Treherne, J. E., Berridge, M. J. and Wigglesworth, V. B., eds), pp. 251-344. Academic Press.

Palka, J. (1979b). Mutants and mosaics, tools in insect developmental neurobiology. *Symp. Soc. Neurosci. 4*, 209-227.

Palka, J., Lawrence, P. A., and Hart, H. S. (1979). Neural projection patterns from homeotic tissue of *Drosophila* studied in *bithorax* mutants and mosaics. *Develop. Biol. 69*, 549-575.

Palka, J., and Schubiger, M. (1975). Central connections of receptors on rotated and exchanged cerci of crickets. *Proc. Nat. Acad. Sci. USA 72*, 966-969.

Rakic, P. (1971). Neuron-glia relationships during granule cell migration in developing cerebral cortex. A golgi and electron micrographic study in *Macacus rhesus*. *J. comp. Nuerol. 141*, 283-312.

Rakic, P. (1974). Neurons in rhesus monkey visual cortex: systematic relation between time of origin and eventual disposition. *Science 183*, 425-427.

Sanes, J., and Hildebrand, J. G. (1975). Nerves in the antennae of pupal *Manduca sexta* Johannsen (Lepidoptera: Sphingidae). *Wilhelm Roux' Arch. Entw. Mech. Org. 178*, 71-78.

Sanes, J. R., and Hildebrand, J. (1976). Origin and morphogenesis of sensory neurons in an insect antenna. *Develop. Biol. 51*, 300-319.

Schubiger, M., and Palka, J. (1979). The haltere-like projection of segmentally translocated wing receptors in *Drosophila* homeotic mutants. *Soc. Neuroscience Abst. 5*, 178.

Sidman, R. L. (1974). Contact interaction among developing mammalian brain cells. *In* "The Cell Surface in Development" (A. A. Moscona, ed.), pp. 221-253. Wiley, New York.

Singer, M., Nordlander, R. H. and Egar, M. (1979). Axonal guidance during embryogenesis and regeneration in the spinal course of the newt: the Blueprint Hypothesis of neuronal pathway patterning. *J. comp. Neurol. 185*, 1-22.

Spitzer, N. C., Bate, C. M., and Goodman, C. S. (1979). Physiological development and segmental differences of neurons from an identified precursor during grasshopper embryogenesis. *Soc. Neuroscience Abstracts 5*, 181.

Stocker, R. F. (1977). Gustatory stimulation of a homeotic mutant appendage, *Antennapedia*, in *Drosophila melanogaster*. *J. comp. Physiol. 115*, 351-361.

Stocker, R. F., Edwards, J. S., Palka, J., and Schubiger, G. (1976). Projection of sensory neurons from a homeotic mutant appendage, *Antennapedia*, in *Drosophila melanogaster*. *Develop. Biol. 52*, 210-220.

Tinbergen, H. (1935). Über die Orientierung des Bienenwolfes. II. Die Bienenjagd. *Z. vergl. Physiol. 21*, 699-716.

Wigglesworth, V. B. (1953). The origin of sensory neurons in an insect *Rhodnius prolixus* (Hemiptera). *J. exp. Biol. 94*, 93-112.

Wigglesworth, V. B. (1959g). The role of epidermal cells in the "migration" of tracheoles in *Rhodnius prolixus* (Hemiptera). *J. exp. Biol. 36*, 632-640.

Wigglesworth, V. B. (1965g). Cell associations and organo-
    genesis in the nervous system of insects. *In*
    "Organogenesis" (R. L. DeHaan and H. Ursprung, eds),
    pp. 199-217. Holt, Rinehart and Winston.
Wigglesworth, V. B. (1977a). Structural changes in the
    epidermal cells of *Rhodnius* during tracheole capture.
    J. Cell Sci. 26, 161-174.
Young, D. (1973). "Developmental Neurobiology of Arthropods."
    London Cambridge University Press.
Zill, S. N., Underwood, N. A., and Rowley, J. C. (1979).
    An orderly projection of afferents in insect peripheral
    nerves. *Soc. Neuroscience Abstracts 5*, 266.

PHEROMONE COMMUNICATION IN MOTHS
SENSORY PHYSIOLOGY AND BEHAVIOUR

Rudolf Alexander Steinbrecht
Dietrich Schneider

Max-Planck-Institut für Verhaltensphysiologie
Seewiesen

I. THE OLD CHALLENGE

The impressive capability of male moths to find their female partners over distances of several hundreds of meters has been already described by 18th century naturalists such as Réaumur, Lesser, and Rösel von Rosenhof (cf. Forel, 1910). Although most of these early observers assume an odourous signal to be involved, experimental evidence was not obtained until 1879 when Fabre observed that male Peacock moths, *Saturnia pyri,* paid no attention to a female put under a glass bell jar, but assembled on a paper where she had been sitting a short time earlier. Fabre concluded correctly that the male moths oriented towards the female scent. However, he still believed that this cue could guide the moths only over a short range, for large distance attraction he postulated unknown radiations emanating from the luring female.

Olfaction in insects, as apparent from Forel's book (1910), was a controversal subject at this time. Unlike insect vision, even the identification of the sense organs involved remained ambiguous. Amputation of the antennae was recognized quite early to abolish many behaviour reactions to odours, but still – the antenna being a multimodal receptor organ – the question remained which of the various sensillum types contained the olfactory receptors. Selective elimination of sensilla was possible only in exceptional cases (Dethier, 1941; Wigglesworth, 1941c; Bolwig, 1946).

Sex attraction in moths remained a largely unexplored field until Butenandt et al. (1959) succeeded to isolate the

effective agent from the female lure glands of *Bombyx mori*.
This was a heroic enterprise in those pre-gas chromatography
days, involving in the final isolation step the death of half
a million female silk moths to obtain 12 mg of a pure crystalline nitro-azo-ester of the sex attractant. The compound was
identified and synthetized as (E)10-,(Z)12-Hexadekadien-1-ol,
and given the name *bombykol* (Butenandt et al., 1959, 1962).
During these endeavours, Schneider (1957) introduced the electroantennogram technique and performed the first electrophysiological experiments on olfaction in insects with *Bombyx*. At
the same time the term *pheromone* was coined by Karlson and
Lüscher (1959) to designate the chemical messengers that serve
in intra-specific communication.

In retrospect we might ask why the study of moth pheromone
communication became such a flourishing field of sensory
physiology during the following twenty years. Among the reasons are:

(1) Pheromone messages of insects, compared with other
natural odours such as food flavours are relatively pure mixtures, containing only a few chemically defined and physiologically characterized components.

(2) The olfactory receptors are readily accessible in
morphologically well defined units, the sensilla. This generally favours micro-electrode recording from single receptor
cells in insects much more than e.g. in vertebrates.

(3) Compared to the situation with mammals, behavioural
reactions to pheromone stimuli in insects are rather stereotyped and can be easily standardized in simple bioassays; this
is especially true for *Bombyx*.

(4) Pheromone receptors are well suited for the study of
principal questions of olfaction since they are found on the
male antenna in very large numbers with extreme sensitivity
and identical response specificity.

It should not be forgotten, however, that factors other
than those favouring basic research of the physiology of olfaction nourished the boom in insect pheromone research to an
even greater extent. The urgent need of insect pest control
measures which are more specific and less harmful than the
general use of insecticides soon brought up the idea of using
pheromones in insect pest control.

It is therefore not surprising that the majority of moth
pheromones have now been identified in species of economic
importance (Tamaki, 1977; Roelofs, this volume). Numerous
attempts have been made to control pest insects either by
mass trapping the males with pheromone-baited traps or by dis-
rupting the orientation of the males to their mates with artificial pheromone dispensers throughout the habitat. Neither

of the two strategies turned out to be a panacea against pest insects, but it is now common practice to use pheromone traps for monitoring population density, to guide and time insecticide use and other measures of integrated pest control (cf. Ritter, 1979, pp. 249 ff). In special cases even the suppression of population density below the noxious level, *insectostasis,* may be achieved using pheromones alone (mass trapping of storage pests: Levinson and Levinson, 1979; communication disruption in cotton pests: Brooks et al., 1979).

It is clear that a fruitful symbiosis between applied and basic research on pheromone biology should be established, as pointed out by Wigglesworth (1971b) when he stated: .... "scientific research depends on asking the right questions; and some of the most pregnant questions arise from the field of practice", and also: "Cut off the continuing supply of new basic scientific knowledge and the applied sciences quickly run out of steam".

II. THE SILKMOTH PHEROMONE SYSTEM

Research in pheromone communication is multidisciplinary and has to be carried out at all levels, from the 'behaviour' of single molecules to that of cells, organs, whole animals, and even populations. As an example, we will now consider the sex attraction system in *Bombyx mori* (Fig. 1; see also Schneider, 1974).

The calling female evaporates pheromone from the *sacculi laterales.* These consist of a modified and enlarged intersegmental membrane and are everted by hemolymph pressure (Fig. 1a, b). With the onset of pheromone production in the pharate adult, lipid droplets (LD) appear which absorb UV light at the same wavelength as bombykol, and the apical cell membrane (AM) forms a fluted border (Fig. 1c). There is, however, no secretory duct, and the only structural candidates for the passage of pheromone molecules to the surface are *epicuticular filaments* (EF) in the outer cuticle (Fig. 1d) (Steinbrecht, 1964b).

Recently the aldehyde *bombykal* ((E)10-,(Z)12-hexadekadien-1-al) was discovered as a second pheromone component in the gland besides bombykol (Fig. 1e) (Kaissling et al., 1978; Kasang et al., 1978).

The male antenna (length 6 mm) has a large outline area due to side branches of the flagellum and carries 17 000 long *sensilla trichodea* in a regular and dense array (Fig. 1f-h). These structures filter out a large proportion of pheromone molecules from the passing air stream (Kaissling, 1971). Moreover, the dimensions of the sensory hairs (length 100 μm, mean diameter 2 μm) are such that adsorption of odour molecules by convective diffusion preferentially occurs on the hair surface. *Pores* (P) and *pore tubules* (PT) in the hair wall are supposed

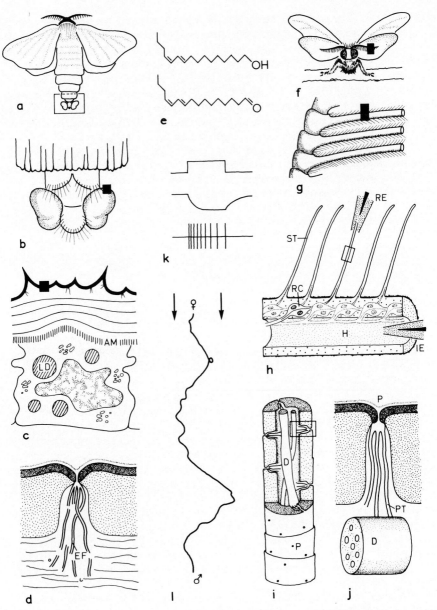

Figure 1. Pheromone communication in Bombyx mori. a-d, the female sender (frames indicate subsequent enlargements); e, the pheromone components bombykol (above) and bombykal (below); f-j, the male receiver; k, receptor reactions: time course of stimulation (above), receptor potential (middle) and nerve impulses (below); l, path of a male moth within the odour plume of a luring female (arrows: wind direction). See text also.

to be the routes along which the stimulus molecules diffuse to reach the receptor dendrites (D) in the hair lumen (Fig. 1i). Some of the pore tubules directly end in contact with the dendritic membrane (Fig. 1j) (Steinbrecht, 1973).

Each of the s. trichodea (ST) on the male antenna comprises two receptor cells (RC). One is stimulated maximally by *bombykol* and much less by its stereosomers, the key compound of the other one is *bombykal* (Kaissling, 1977; Kaissling et al., 1978). Thus, the specificity of the reaction cannot be explained by different specificities of the stimulus conduction (adsorption and diffusion of odour molecules), but is given by the receptor molecules in the receptor membrane, which interact with the stimulus molecules, possibly in similar ways as in other processes of molecular recognition (for references see Kaissling and Thorson, 1980).

In the electrophysiological experiment (Fig. 1h, recording electrode (RE) slipped over a hair with cut tip, indifferent electrode (IE) in the hemolymph (H)), signal-receptor interaction is indicated by a depolarization of the receptor membrane; the amplitude of this receptor potential increases with stimulus strength and correlates with the frequency of nerve impulses propagated to the brain (Fig. 1k). In *Bombyx*, and presumably in other moths as well, a single pheromone molecule may elicit a nerve impulse, but several hundred receptor cells have to be activated to overcome the noise of spontaneously firing receptor cells and trigger the behavioural reaction (Kaissling and Priesner, 1970).

In the male silk moth, stimulation with bombykol induces wing fluttering and - provided an air stream is present - an anemotactic upwind march. The flightless moth approaches and eventually reaches the luring female zigzagging within the odour plume like a sailing boat crossing against the wind (Fig. 1l) (Kramer, 1975).

III. FOCAL POINTS OF CURRENT RESEARCH

Here we do not intend to give a complete review of present knowledge, nor should the reader expect a diorama of speculation. We try to meet the challenge of this book by pointing out areas of ignorance in such a way as to stimulate further experiments in these fields. This necessitates the delineation of the circumference of such white areas, the description of possible starting points for new ventures, and of less developed topics. This selection is necessarily subjective and so are the citations, where we preferentially refer to review or key articles.

A. *Production and Release of Female Sex Pheromones*

The number of identified female moth pheromone compounds
has rapidly increased with the availability of modern gas
chromatography and mass spectrometry techniques, and the list
is growing steadily. The compounds are in the majority mono-
or dienic fatty alcohols, aldehydes, or acetates of a chain
length of C10-C21 (Tamaki, 1977; Roelofs, this volume). Very
little is known about the biosynthesis of these sex pheromones
(Inoue and Hamamura, 1972; Kasang et al., 1974), but the pathways of biosynthesis need not be very spectacular and might be
split off the fatty acid metabolism (Levinson, 1972; Mitlin
and Hedin, 1974). Epidermal cells in general have the ability
to synthetize similar compounds during epicuticle formation,
and the evolution of pheromones from metabolites of cuticular
waxes has been hypothetized (Levinson, 1979).

The ultrastructure of the female pheromone gland has been
studied in several species (reviewed by Percy and Weatherston,
1974; see also Percy, 1979), and the findings first obtained
in *Bombyx* (Steinbrecht, 1964b) appear to be generally valid.
However, the lack of specificity of lipid cytochemistry does
not yet allow the precise location of a pheromone or its precursors. The hypothesis, that the final liberation of the active pheromone compound is achieved outside the cells in the
gland cuticle (possibly by esterase splitting of an inactive
ester precursor), which was based on indirect evidence
(Steinbrecht, 1964a,b) has since been neither proven nor rejected. The involvement of epicuticular filaments in the transport of the pheromone to the gland surface is extensively discussed by Percy (1979).

With respect to the great number of species under study,
and the long list of identified pheromone compounds, there is
amazingly little quantitative information about pheromone release rates, as influenced by age, copulation, and external
environmental constraints (see Roelofs and Cardé, 1977). Another pertinent question concerns the composition of multi-
component pheromones (see section D) and wether they remain
constant over long periods, or change, e.g. after copulation.
The answer might very well be different for different species
(see Kuwahara and Casidy, 1973; Roelofs, 1979). It is noteworthy, that environmental and physiological factors governing the calling behaviour of the female (e.g. temperature,
light intensity, wind speed, circadian rhythms) often influence male responsiveness as well, thus synchronizing the pheromone communication system of a given species and providing
additional cues for reproductive isolation between species
(Shorey, 1974; Roelofs and Cardé, 1977).

B. Functional Morphology of Receptors

The fine structure of the pheromone receptors of male moths closely follows the general scheme of insect olfactory receptors, which are fairly well studied (reviewed by Altner and Prillinger, 1980). In particular, the discovery of pores and pore tubules in the wall of the cuticular setae has helped to understand, how desiccation of the receptor may have been prevented without impeding the access for stimulating molecules. A thin wall is no longer taken as a prerequisite for an olfactory hair; in fact, the s. trichodea of moths which comprise the pheromone receptors are quite thick-walled and rigid. The longest hairs are found on the antennae of male hawk moths (500 μm), but also in other species these sensilla are always predominant in size and number.

Two types of stimulus conducting structures are known from insect olfactory receptors: (i) spoke channels filled with dense secretion and (ii) pores with pore tubules (Altner and Prillinger, 1980). Of these only type ii is found with pheromone sensilla of moths. This may be of functional significance for the class of stimuli perceived and/or the requirements of a highly effective stimulus transport. It is important to note that the pore tubules strongly resemble epicuticular filaments in other types of cuticle (compare Figs. 1d and j) which are suggested as lipid transport routes (cf. Locke and Krishnan, 1971). The pores are filled with an electron lucid material continuous with the outer epicuticle of the hair surface, which is insoluble in lipid solvents and possibly represents stabilized lipid in the sense of Wigglesworth (1970b; Steinbrecht and Kasang, 1972; cf. Filshie, 1970, and this volume). However, more evidence about the physical and chemical nature of these structures is urgently needed.

Likewise, many features of the remarkably complex internal fine structure of pheromone sensilla still lack an interpretation in functional terms. Morphometric data which may now be derived more reliably from cryofixed receptors (Steinbrecht, 1980) submitted to computer models of receptor circuitry (Kaissling and Thorson, 1980) may give more insight into the functional adaptations of these sensilla. A general hypothesis on the functional organization of insect sensilla, derived mainly from mechanoreceptors, but possibly applicable to pheromone receptors as well, has been established by Thurm (1970; see also Thurm and Küppers, this volume).

C. *Primary Receptor Processes and Receptor Cell Specificity*

Once a stimulus molecule has reached the receptor membrane by adsorption and diffusion, four consecutive steps are postulated as the minimum of primary receptor processes to occur (Kaissling, 1974):

(1) *binding* of the stimulus molecule to a receptor molecule on the receptor membrane;

(2) *activation* of the receptor molecule, e.g. a conformational change, induced by the binding;

(3) *increase of membrane conductance* due to receptor activation resulting in the receptor potential, and

(4) *inactivation* of the stimulus.

In the electrophysiological experiment, the first reaction observable upon very weak stimulation is an *elementary receptor potential,* a small negative potential ("*bump*") preceding each nerve impulse or the first in a group of two or three impulses. According to Kaissling and Thorson (1980) this receptor potential might reflect a membrane conductance change produced by opening of an ion channel due to the impact of a single stimulus molecule. With increasing stimulus intensity the elementary potentials sum up to form a fluctuating receptor potential.

At present there is little possibility for direct experimental analysis of these individual steps of stimulus receptor interaction, but it should be born in mind, that each of these steps may have its own chemical specificity, as was inferred from the evaluation of different response parameters upon stimulation of *Bombyx* antennae with various bombykol analogues (Kaissling, 1977).

The *chemical specificity* of a pheromone receptor cell is usually described by its key compound(s) (the stimulus with maximal efficacy) and the dose-response relationships to systematically altered derivatives (response spectrum). There are structural modifications, such as changes in chain length, in the position and geometrical configuration of double bonds, and in the position and type of functional groups which gradually reduce the efficacy (Priesner et al., 1977; Priesner, 1979a,b).

Kafka and Neuwirth (1975) made a first attempt to simulate the interaction between stimulant molecules and receptor sites by physico-chemical models, employing electroantennogram data of several moth species.

On the other hand a great number of response spectra, reported meanwhile, has permitted the detailed comparison of receptor specificities between species and the definition of structure-response relationships characteristic of higher taxonomic groups of moths. With the exception of interspecific

hybrids response spectra of pheromone receptor cells in moths
are generally consistent with the notion of a single type of
receptor molecule in each cell type (for reviews see Priesner,
1979a,b, 1980).

D. Multi-Component Pheromone Messages

The earlier concept of sex attractants to be species-spe-
cific single compounds had to be abandoned with the finding of
multi-component pheromones in practically all moth species
studied in detail and also in other insect groups (Silverstein
and Young, 1976). However, whereas chemical identification of
pheromone components is in rapid progress, information about
production and release rates of multi-component pheromones is
scanty. Electrophysiological work has started to elucidate the
encoding of such messages into the activity pattern of a
corresponding set of specialist receptors. However, the deco-
ding of these receptor patterns in the brain is still largely
unknown. Finally, more detailed information is needed about
the behavioural effects of the different components. Such
effects need not be restricted to a given species, but may
pertain to related and sympatric species, as observed with
inter-specific attraction inhibitors.

As a consequence of the discovery of multi-chemical messages, the term pheromone is now often used with different
meanings. At present, a *pheromone* should be defined as the
mixture of all those compounds which are emitted by the conspecific partner and act together in eliciting a defined behaviour reaction. A single chemical compound of such a multi-
chemical mixture would then be a *pheromone component*.

It has now become evident that the reproductive isolation
of closely related species is achieved not as much by the
change of the primary pheromone components, but rather by
shifted ratios of the same components or the admixture of additional secondary components (cf. Roelofs and Cardé, 1977;
Roelofs, this volume). Present electrophysiological evidence
indicates that the female pheromone components are usually
matched by a corresponding set of specialist receptor cells in
the male. Thus, the attractive blend of the female may be encoded in a specific activity pattern of the pertaining receptors, well distinguished by the brain from a pattern produced
by the signal of a closely related species which uses the same
compounds at a different ratio (cf. Kaissling, 1979; Priesner,
1979a,b, 1980).

E. Central Processing of Receptor Messages

Neuroethology, in our case the central processing of the sensory input eventually leading into motor output which becomes manifest in behavioural reactions, is one of the largest unexplored areas in pheromone biology. Only recently have some morphological and physiological findings on interneurons in the deutocerebrum of moths been reported.

The deutocerebrum of male *Antheraea pernyi, A. polyphemus* (Boeckh and Boeckh, 1979), and *Manduca sexta* (Hildebrand et al., 1980) has a large macroglomerular complex near the entrance of the antennal nerve, which is not seen in the female. Interneurons which arborize extensively within this macroglomerulus have been identified morphologically. The convergence factor between peripheral receptor cells and deutocerebral neurons is at least 100:1. Comparable work on *Bombyx* is in progress (R. Olberg and M. Koontz, Seewiesen, unpubl.).

Hildebrand et al. (1980) discriminated by intracellular recording a high number of *local interneurons,* which – after $CoCl_2$ injections – showed multiglomerular arborization, but no extensions to higher brain centres, and comparatively few *output interneurons* with uniglomerular dendritic arborization leading to the mushroom bodies and other protocerebral regions.

In *Antheraea* (Boeckh and Boeckh, 1979) – and even more so in *Bombyx* (R. Olberg, unpubl.) – the central neurons always have a lower threshold to pheromone stimulation than the peripheral pheromone receptors on the antenna. This feature can be readily explained by the high degree of spatial convergence, since central neurons connected to hundreds or thousands of receptors receive some input even when few sensory cells are excited by a very weak stimulus. This phenomenon eventually leads to the extreme sensitivity of behavioural reactions which surpasses that of single receptors by a factor of 100 at least (Kaissling and Priesner, 1970).

'Odour quality convergence' was observed by Boeckh and Boeckh (1979) in *Antheraea*, where the receptor cells responded to only one of the two pheromone components, respectively, whereas the deutocerebral neurons showed some degree of response also to the other component. In *Bombyx,* on the other hand, most central neurons were found to discriminate qualitatively between bombykol and bombykal. Inhibitory as well as excitatory responses were observed. Some neurons, however, were excited only when both compounds were presented. Most central neurons sensitive to pheromone were multimodal, in that they also responded to odourless air puffs (R. Olberg, unpubl.); thus, information about wind direction could be processed via this mechanosensitive input.

Interneurons have been observed in the thoracic ganglia of the ventral nerve cord in *Bombyx*, the activity of which

could be switched on and off by pheromone stimulation of the
antennae. Furthermore, these units also responded to wind and/
or visual stimuli (R. Olberg, unpubl.). These neurons are
quite close to the motor output of the system and give hope to
understand the neural control of the moth's behaviour.

F. Behavioural Responses to Pheromone Stimuli

The increasing complexity of chemical signals urgently
calls for behaviourally more discriminating assays (Kennedy,
1977b). Compared to the progress in pheromone chemistry and
sensory physiology, it is surprising to note the paucity of
detailed studies of moth behaviour. Standardized bioassays,
such as laboratory activity tests or trap catches, usually
allow few inferences about the underlying behavioural mechanisms. Only in the recent past the tendency changed towards
a more detailed analysis of behavioural sequences as documented in the reviews by Roelofs and Cardé (1977) and Cardé
(1979). Cardé (1979) lists a sequence of behavioural responses
which should be observed:

(1) the latency and proportion of wing fanning,
(2) the duration of pre-flight walking while wing fanning
(3) the duration of up-wind flight and its path, the number of turns, deviations from the odour plume, tack angle etc.,
(4) landing or flight arrest close to the pheromone source,
(5) courtship behaviour, which in itself may comprise a
complex sequence of male (walking while wing fanning, display
of hairpencils, dissemination of a male sex pheromone), and
female (arrest of calling, aquiescence, walking towards male)
behaviour responses. These may be induced not only by chemical,
but also by mechanical and visual stimuli (Baker and Cardé,
1979a).

It is an exciting question which one of these behavioural
steps is controlled by which pheromone component, singly or in
a certain mixture, or even antagonistically. There are promising approaches in a few species: In the redbanded leafroller,
Argyrotaenia velutinana, the appropriate combination of two
pheromone components evokes upwind flight, while landing near
the source requires a third component (Baker et al., 1976).
However, in the Oriental fruit moth, Grapholitha molesta,
three pheromone components appear to act as a unit during the
early as well as the later steps of the response chain. Such
conclusions are based on detailed observations in the field
and wind-tunnel arrangements (Baker and Cardé, 1979b). Although based upon the study of a few species so far, the discrimination and specific measurement of distinct steps in the
whole sequence of male behaviour responses to pheromones has

provided a more realistic idea about the insect's behaviour in the field.

G. Far-Distance Orientation

Within the sequence of male pheromone responses, the far-distance approach towards the female has received most attention since Fabre's days, and communication distances of up to 11 km have been estimated based on returning of marked moth individuals released at varying distances from a luring female (Mell, 1922; see Priesner, 1973, for further references and critique).

Bossert and Wilson (1963) treated theoretically the constraints of pheromone communication as induced by the release rate of the sender, the threshold sensitivity of the receiver, and the decrease of odour concentration caused mainly by turbulences of the conveying wind. They defined as the *active space* of a chemical signal the space in which the pheromone concentration is above the threshold of the receiver. Possibly only in some groups of moths with high pheromone production and release rates in the female, and enlarged antennae in the male sex (e.g. in the family Saturniidae, Bombycidae, Lymantriidae, Lasiocampidae) this active space may exceed 1000 m. In most other families (e.g. Noctuidae, Tortricidae) the active spaces are probably limited to 100 m or less.

The orientation mechanisms that could guide an insect to a distant odour source have been extensively discussed by Kennedy (1977a). *Chemotropotaxis* is generally excluded, because an odour gradient steep enough can exist only very close to the source. Other mechanisms relying entirely on chemical cues would be *chemoklinotaxis* (if the moth steers back into the pheromone plume, once it has emerged at the margin) or *chemoklinokinesis* (if random turns bring it eventually back into the scent). So far no conclusive evidence has been established that one of these mechanisms could guide the flying moth, and it is now accepted that additional cues are necessary, such as an *odour-modulated visual* or *anemotactic orientation*.

The latter case has been clearly demonstrated for the flightless *Bombyx mori* (Schwinck, 1954). With a refined experimental setup, Kramer (1975) showed that the silk moth walks upwind in a zigzag course also when the air stream contains a homogenous concentration of Bombykol. Angles of $30-50°$ are held to the wind direction (*anemomenotaxis*) with spontaneous turns from one side of the windline to the other (e.g. $+50°$ to $-50°$). Lowering the bombykol concentration consistently induced an extra change of sign of the anemomenotactic angle. Such a change would bring the animal back into the plume, once it overshot the margin. Eventually these reactions lead the male moth to its mate (Fig. 11).

Information about wind direction is easily obtained by mechanosensory input in a walking animal, but how can it be achieved by an air born insect? Kennedy and Marsh (1974) gave quantitative experimental evidence that a male *Plodia*, flying in a wind-tunnel towards a calling female is guided upwind anemotactically by optomotoric reactions to the ground pattern. Loss of the olfactory signal changed the anemomenotactic angle from into-wind to across-wind with left-right reversals at lengthening intervals. Thus, upwind progress is stopped until wind-oriented zigzag casting with increasing amplitude has eventually led the animal back into the odour plume. We are, however, far from understanding how the animal evaluates these various input signals during its maneuvres.

IV. CONCLUDING REMARKS

It is almost inevitable, that in an essay on pheromone communication in moths, emphasis is put on female sex pheromones. Male courtship pheromones, on the other hand, are widely distributed in most lepidopteran groups, including butterflies, and differ largely from the female pheromones by their chemical composition, biosynthesis, and dissemination mechanisms (reviews by Birch, 1974; Schneider, 1979).

Although the era of pheromone physiology started with work on Lepidoptera about twenty years ago, pheromone research is now equally flourishing on other insect orders, such as the Coleoptera, where the concept of multi-component pheromones was first advanced (cf. Silverstein, 1977; Borden, 1977), and the Hymenoptera, which - in the social species - possibly use the most complex chemical language among insects (cf. Silverstein, 1977; Blum, 1977, 1979). Promising fields have also been opened up with Diptera (cf. Fletcher, 1977), cockroaches (cf. Persoons and Ritter, 1979) and termites (cf. Moore, 1974), and further expansion onto new groups is to be expected. On the other hand, as shown by the silkmoth paradigm, research on the traditional experimental animals continues to be of great importance, through applying new experimental techniques to new questions. However, we refrain from too much 'crystal-gazing' about the future developments of insect pheromone biology, concurring with Sir Vincent, who - in his George Bidder Lecture (Wigglesworth, 1971b) - has appropriately emphasized the non-predictability of science.

ACKNOWLEDGMENTS

We are indebted to Ernst Priesner for useful comments and constructive criticism.

REFERENCES

Altner, H., and Prillinger, L. (1980). Ultrastructure of invertebrate chemo-, thermo-, and hygroreceptors and its functional significance. *Int. Rev. Cytol. 67*, in press.

Baker, T.C., and Cardé, R.T. (1979a). Courtship behavior of the Oriental fruit moth *(Grapholitha molesta)*: experimental analysis and consideration of the role of sexual selection in the evolution of courtship pheromones in the Lepidoptera. *Ann. Ent. Soc. Amer. 72*, 173-188.

Baker, T.C., and Cardé, R.T. (1979b). Analysis of pheromone-mediated behaviors in male *Grapholitha molesta*, the Oriental fruit moth (Lepidoptera: Tortricidae). *Environmental Entomology 8*, 956-968.

Baker, T.C., Cardé, R.T., and Roelofs, W.L. (1976). Behavioral responses of male *Argyrotaenia velutinana* (Lepidoptera: Tortricidae) to components of its sex pheromone. *J. Chem. Ecol. 2*, 333-352.

Birch, M.C. (1974). Aphrodisiac pheromones in insects. *In* "Pheromones" (M.C. Birch, ed.), pp. 115-134. North-Holland Publ. Comp., Amsterdam.

Blum, M.S. (1977). Behavioral responses of Hymenoptera to pheromones, allomones, and kairomones. *In* "Chemical Control of Insect Behavior" (H.H. Shorey and J.J. McKelvey, jr., eds.), pp. 149-167. John Wiley & Sons, New York.

Blum, M.S. (1979). Hymenopterous pheromones: optimizing the specificity and accurity of the signal. *In* "Chemical Ecology: Odour Communication in Animals" (F.J. Ritter, ed.), pp. 201-211. Elsevier/North-Holland Biomed. Press, Amsterdam.

Boeckh, J., and Boeckh, V. (1979). Threshold and odor specificity of pheromone-sensitive neurons in the deutocerebrum of *Antheraea pernyi* and *A. polyphemus* (Saturnidae) *J. comp. Physiol. 132*, 235-242.

Bolwig, N. (1946). Senses and sense organs of the anterior end of the house fly larvae. *Vidensk. Medd. Dansk Naturhist. Foren. 109*, 81-217.

Borden, J.H. (1977). Behavioral responses of Coleoptera to pheromones, allomones, and kairomones. *In* "Chemical Control of Insect Behavior" (H.H. Shorey and J.J. McKelvey, jr., eds.), pp. 169-198. John Wiley & Sons, New York.

Bossert, W.H., and Wilson, E.O. (1963). The analysis of olfactory communication among animals. *J. Theoret. Biol. 5*, 443-469.

Brooks, T.W., Doane, C.C., and Staten, R.T. (1979). Experience with the first commercial pheromone communication disruptive for suppression of an agricultural pest. *In* "Chemical Ecology: Odour Communication in Animals" (F.J. Ritter, ed.), pp. 375-388. Elsevier/North-Holland Biomed. Press, Amsterdam.

Butenandt, A., Beckmann, R., Stamm, D., and Hecker, E. (1959). Über den Sexuallockstoff des Seidenspinners *Bombyx mori*. Reindarstellung und Konstitution. *Z. Naturforsch. 14b*, 283-284.

Butenandt, A., Hecker, E., Hopp, M., and Koch, W. (1962). Über den Sexuallockstoff des Seidenspinners IV. Die Synthese des Bombykols und der cis-trans-isomeren Hexadecadien -(10.12)-ole-(1). *Liebigs Ann. Chem. 658*, 39-64.

Cardé, R.T. (1979). Behavioral responses of moths to female-produced pheromones and the utilization of attractant-baited traps for population monitoring. *In* "Movement of Highly Mobile Insects: Concepts and Methodology in Research" (R.L. Raab and G.G. Kennedy, eds.), pp. 286-315. North Carolina State Univ. Press.

Dethier, V.G. (1941). The function of the antennal receptors in lepidopterous larvae. *Biol. Bull. 80*, 403-414.

Fabre, J.H. (1879). "Souvenirs Entomologiques", I.-X. Sér.. Ch. Delagrave, Paris.

Filshie, B.K. (1970). The resistance of epicuticular components of an insect to extraction with lipid solvents. *Tissue & Cell 2*, 181-190.

Filshie, B.K. (1980). Insect cuticle through the electron microscope - distinguishing fact from artefact. *In* "Insect Biology in the Future" (M. Locke and D.S. Smith, eds.), pp.   . Academic Press, New York.

Fletcher, B.S. (1977). Behavioral responses of Diptera to pheromones, allomones and kairomones. *In* "Chemical Control of Insect Behavior" (H.H. Shorey and J.J. McKelvey, jr., eds.), pp. 129-148. John Wiley & Sons, New York.

Forel, A. (1910). "Das Sinnesleben der Insekten". E. Reinhardt, München.

Hildebrand, J.G., Matsumoto, S.G., Camazine, S.M., Tolbert, L.P., Blank, S., Ferguson, H., and Ecker, V. (1980). Organization and physiology of antennal centers in the brain of the moth *Manduca sexta*. *In* "Insect Neurobiology and Pesticide Action (Neurotox 79)" (F.E. Rickett, ed.), pp. 375-382. Soc. Chem. Industry, London.

Inoue, S., and Hamamura, Y. (1972). The biosynthesis of "bombykol", sex pheromone of *Bombyx mori*. *Proc. Japan Acad. 48*, 323-326.

Kafka, W.A., and Neuwirth, J. (1975). A model of pheromone molecule-acceptor interaction. *Z. Naturforsch. 30c*, 278-282.

Kaissling, K.-E. (1971) Insect olfaction. *In* "Handbook of Sensory Physiology Vol. IV/1" (L.M. Beidler, ed.), pp. 351-431. Springer, Berlin.

Kaissling, K.-E. (1974). Sensory transduction in insect olfactory receptors. In "Biochemistry of Sensory Functions" (L. Jaenicke, ed.), pp. 243-273. Springer, Berlin.

Kaissling, K.-E. (1977). Structure of odour molecules and multiple activities of receptor cells. In "Olfaction and Taste VI". (J. Le Magnen and P. Mac Leod, eds.), pp. 9-16. Information Retrieval, London.

Kaissling, K.-E. (1979). Recognition of pheromones by moths, especially in Saturniids and *Bombyx mori*. In "Chemical Ecology: Odour Communication in Animals" (F.J. Ritter, ed.), pp. 43-56. Elsevier/North-Holland Biomed. Press, Amsterdam.

Kaissling, K.-E., and Priesner, E. (1970). Die Riechschwelle des Seidenspinners. *Naturwissenschaften 57*, 23-28.

Kaissling, K.-E., and Thorson, J. (1980). Insect olfactory sensilla: structural, chemical and electrical aspects of the functional organization. In "Insect Neurotransmitter, Hormone, and Pheromone Receptors" (D.B. Satelle, L.M. Hall, J.G. Hildebrand, eds.), Elsevier/North-Holland Biomed. Press, Amsterdam (in press).

Kaissling, K.-E., Kasang, G., Bestmann, H.J., Stransky, W., and Vostrowsky, O. (1978). A new pheromone of the silkworm moth *Bombyx mori*. Sensory pathway and behavioral effect. *Naturwissenschaften 65*, 382-384.

Karlson, P., and Lüscher, M. (1959). "Pheromones": a new term for a class of biologically active substances. *Nature 183*, 55-56.

Kasang, G., Schneider, D., and Beroza, M. (1974). Biosynthesis of the sex pheromone disparlure by olefin-epoxide conversion. *Naturwissenschaften 61*, 130-131.

Kasang, G., Kaissling, K.-E., Vostrowsky, O., Bestmann, H.J. (1978). Bombykal, eine zweite Pheromonkomponente des Seidenspinners *Bombyx mori* L. *Angewandte Chemie 90*, 74-75.

Kennedy, J.S. (1977a). Olfactory responses to distant plants and other odor sources. In "Chemical Control of Insect Behavior" (H.H. Shorey and J.J. McKelvey, jr., eds.), pp. 67-91. John Wiley & Sons, New York.

Kennedy, J.S. (1977b). Behaviorally discriminating assays of attractants and repellents. *Ibidem*, pp. 215-229.

Kennedy, J.S., and Marsh, D. (1974). Pheromone-regulated anemotaxis in flying moths. *Science 184*, 999-1001.

Kramer, E. (1975). Orientation of the male silkmoth to the sex attractant bombykol. In "Olfaction and Taste V" (D. Denton and J.D. Coghlan, eds.), pp. 329-335. Academic Press, New York.

Kuwahara, Y., and Casidy, J.E. (1973). Quantitative analysis of the sex pheromone of several phycitid moths by electron-capture gas chromatography. *Agr. Biol. Chem. 37*, 681-684.

Levinson, H.Z. (1972). Zur Evolution und Biosynthese der terpenoiden Pheromone und Hormone. *Naturwissenschaften 59*, 477-484.

Levinson, H.Z. (1979). Reflections on pheromones and hormones in evolution. *Acta endocrin. 91, Suppl. 1*, 423-426.

Levinson, H.Z., and Levinson, A.R. (1979). Trapping of storage insects by sex and food attractants as a tool of integrated control. *In* "Chemical Ecology: Odour Communication in Animals" (F.J. Ritter, ed.), pp. 327-341. Elsevier/North-Holland Biomed. Press, Amsterdam.

Locke, M., and Krishnan, N. (1971). The distribution of phenoloxidases and polyphenols during cuticle formation. *Tissue & Cell 3*, 103-126.

Mell, R. (1922). "Biologie und Systematik der südchinesischen Sphingiden." Friedländer, Berlin.

Mitlin, N., and Hedin, P.A. (1974). Biosynthesis of grandlure, the pheromone of the boll weevil, *Anthonomus grandis*, from acetate, mevalonate, and glucose. *J. Insect Physiol. 20*, 1825-1831.

Moore, B.P. (1974). Pheromones in the termite societies. *In* "Pheromones" (M. Birch, ed.), pp. 250-266. North-Holland Publ. Comp., Amsterdam.

Percy, J. (1979). Development and ultrastructure of sex-pheromone gland cells in females of the cabbage looper moth, *Trichoplusia ni* (Hübner) (Lepidoptera: Noctuidae). *Can. J. Zool. 57*, 220-236.

Percy, J.E., and Weatherston, J. (1974). Gland structure and pheromone production in insects. *In* "Pheromones" (M.C. Birch, ed.), pp. 11-34. North-Holland Publ. Comp., Amsterdam.

Persoons, C.J., and Ritter, F.J. (1979). Pheromones of cockroaches. *In* "Chemical Ecology: Odour Communication in Animals" (F.J. Ritter, ed.), pp. 225-236. Elsevier/North-Holland Biomed. Press, Amsterdam.

Priesner, E. (1973). Artspezifität und Funktion einiger Insektenpheromone. *Fortschr. Zool. 22*, 49-135.

Priesner, E. (1979a). Specificity studies on pheromone receptors of noctuid and tortricid Lepidoptera. *In* "Chemical Ecology: Odour Communication in Animals" (F.J. Ritter, ed.), pp. 57-71. Elsevier/North-Holland Biomed. Press, Amsterdam.

Priesner, E. (1979b). Progress in the analysis of pheromone receptor systems. *Ann. Zool. Ecol. anim. 11*, in press.

Priesner, E. (1980). Sensory encoding of pheromone signals and related stimuli in male moths. *In* "Insect Neurobiology and Pesticide Action (Neurotox 79)" (F.E. Rickett, ed.), pp. 359-366. Soc. Chem. Industry, London.

Priesner, E., Bestmann, H.-J., Vostrowsky, O., and Rösel, P. (1977). Sensory efficacy of alkyl-branched pheromone analogues in noctuid and tortricid Lepidoptera. *Z. Naturforsch. 32c,* 979-991.

Ritter, F.J. (1979). "Chemical Ecology: Odour Communication in Animals". Elsevier/North-Holland Biomed. Press, Amsterdam.

Roelofs, W. (1979). Production and perception of lepidopterous pheromone blends. *Ibidem,* pp. 159-168.

Roelofs, W.L. (1980). Pheromones and their chemistry. *In* "Insect Biology in the Future"(M. Locke and D.S. Smith, eds.), pp.   . Academic Press, New York.

Roelofs, W.L., and Cardé, R.T. (1977). Responses of Lepidoptera to synthetic sex pheromone chemicals and their analogues. *Ann. Rev. Entomol. 22,* 377-405.

Schneider, D. (1957). Elektrophysiologische Untersuchungen von Chemo- und Mechanorezeptoren der Antenne des Seidenspinners *Bombyx mori* L. *Z. vergl. Physiol. 40,* 8-41.

Schneider, D. (1974) The sex-attractant receptor of moths. *Scientific American 231(1),* 28-35.

Schneider, D. (1979). Pheromone von Insekten: Produktion - Reception - Inaktivierung. *Nova acta Leopoldina N.F. 51,* 191-213.

Schwinck, I. (1954). Experimentelle Untersuchungen über Geruchssinn und Strömungswahrnehmung in der Orientierung bei Nachtschmetterlingen. *Z. vergl. Physiol. 37,* 19-56.

Shorey, H.H. (1974). Environmental and physiological control of insect sex pheromone behavior. *In* "Pheromones" (M.C. Birch, ed.), pp. 62-80. North-Holland Publ. Comp., Amsterdam.

Silverstein, R.M. (1977). Complexity, diversity and specificity of behavior-modifying chemicals: examples mainly from Coleoptera and Hymenoptera. *In* "Chemical Control of Insect Behavior" (H.H. Shorey and J.J. McKelvey, jr., eds.), pp. 231-251. John Wiley & Sons, New York.

Silverstein, R.M., and Young, J.C. (1976). Insects generally use multicomponent pheromones. *In* "Pest Management with Insect Sex Attractants and Other Behavior-Controlling Chemicals" (M. Beroza, ed.), pp. 1-29, Am. Chem. Soc., Washington. D.C.

Steinbrecht, R.A. (1964a) Die Abhängigkeit der Lockwirkung des Sexualduftorgans weiblicher Seidenspinner (*Bombyx mori*) von Alter und Kopulation. *Z. vergl. Physiol. 48,* 341-356.

Steinbrecht, R.A. (1964b). Feinstruktur und Histochemie der Sexualduftdrüse des Seidenspinners *Bombyx mori* L. *Z. Zellforsch. mikr. Anat. 64,* 227-261.

Steinbrecht, R.A. (1973). Der Feinbau olfaktorischer Sensillen des Seidenspinners (Insecta, Lepidoptera). Rezeptorfortsätze und reizleitender Apparat. *Z. Zellforsch. mikr. Anat.* *139*, 533-565.

Steinbrecht, R.A. (1980). Cryofixation without cryoprotectants. Freeze substitution and freeze etching of an insect olfactory receptor. *Tissue & Cell 12*, 73-100.

Steinbrecht, R.A.,and Kasang, G. (1972). Capture and conveyance of odour molecules in an insect olfactory receptor. *In* "Olfaction and Taste IV" (D. Schneider, ed.), pp. 193-199. Wiss. Verlagsges., Stuttgart.

Tamaki, Y. (1977). Complexity, diversity, and specificity of behavior-modifying chemicals in Lepidoptera and Diptera. *In* "Chemical Control of Insect Behavior" (H.H. Shorey and J.J. McKelvey, jr., eds.), pp. 253-285. John Wiley & Sons, New York.

Thurm, U. (1970). Untersuchungen zur funktionellen Organisation sensorischer Zellverbände. *Verh. Dtsch. Zool. Ges. 64*, 79-88.

Thurm, U., and Küppers, J. (1980). Epithelial physiology of insect sensilla. *In* "Insect Biology in the Future" (M. Locke and D.S. Smith, eds.), pp.   , Academic Press, New York.

Wigglesworth, V.B. (1941c). The sensory physiology of the human louse *Pediculus humanus corporis* De Geer (Anoplura). *Parasitology 33*, 67-109.

Wigglesworth, V.B. (1970b). Structural lipids in the insect cuticle and the function of the oenocytes. *Tissue & Cell 2*, 155-179.

Wigglesworth, V.B. (1971b). Experimental biology, pure and applied. *J. Exp. Biol. 55*, 1-12.

THE COMPOUND EYE

Adrian Horridge
David Blest

Department of Neurobiology
Australian National University
Canberra, Australia

Those who predict the course of events have traditionally been given high status, whether as magician, military tactician or investment analyst, but no word exists to distinguish the scientific prophet. That should warn us that his predictions have not, on the whole, proved effectual. Whatever his qualifications, to make them he must be granted immunity from the consequences, for their outcome is likely to be laughter and consignment to the waste paper basket before the ink is dry.

Having thus absolved ourselves from any charge of seriousness, we can pretend that for the compound eye a recent turn in the course of events has made the short-term future of research quite obvious. If we prove to be right, we can, like all prophets, claim that our fairy-story was really meant to be profound.

The study of compound eyes is a synthesis of half a dozen different kinds of research: optics, retinal anatomy and electrophysiology together elucidate the properties of receptors. There are new types of eyes still to be described. Visual behaviour and model-building combine to tell us how information from the eyes is actually used. Little is understood in that area. At a molecular level, analysis of transduction mechanisms requires the techniques of biochemistry and physical chemistry. Work on that topic has hardly started. In Canberra, our vision group has been mainly concerned with compound eye optics and information processing, with emphasis on comparative studies to display the great evolutionary diversity of arthropod visual systems.

A curious gap in this otherwise orderly fabric of research has sprung from an unvoiced assumption: it has always been

taken for granted that the rhabdoms of compound eyes are
stable structures – that despite the dramatic photomechanical
changes which occur during light and dark adaptation, the
total area and arrangement of membrane containing photopigment
to trap photons remains the same.

We now know that this is not always true; some spiders
engage in the almost total destruction of the rhabdoms of
their ocelli at dawn, and re-synthesise them at dusk (Blest,
1978). More startlingly, so do some insects and crustaceans.
Nässel and Waterman (1979) have shown the same pattern of
turnover in compound eyes of a grapsid crab, and we have confirmed it in our local *Leptograpsus* (Blest, Stowe and Price,
1980). Furthermore, we now show (Fig. 3) that the same waxing
and waning of the rhabdoms in relation to the daily cycle can
be demonstrated in the locust. This brings what at first
seemed a rather obscure phenomenon right into the area of
physiological optics which has been most studied and debated.
Before discussing its implications we should ask the obvious
question: why were these cyclical events overlooked before?
A short answer is that eyes were not fixed outside working
hours!

Vertebrate photoreceptors are now well-known to shed and
renew their transductive membrane (Young and Droz, 1968).
However, photoreceptor membrane turnover was first demonstrated for rhabdoms by White (1967) and Eguchi and Waterman (1967).
Unfortunately, the former author used white-eyed mutant
larval mosquitos for his work, and both groups employed highly
artificial laboratory cycles of light and darkness. As a result, their findings were regarded largely in terms of a
pathology of rhabdom 'damaged' by excessively bright light.
Worse, no-one related the changes that they described to the
light-microscope observations made by earlier workers, notably Debaisieux (1944) on the large changes in the eyes of the
phyllopod crustacean *Artemia salina* (reproduced in Bullock
and Horridge, fig. 19.1, 1965). Similar volume increases in
rhabdoms were noted by Sato (1950) and Sato *et al* (1957) for
adult mosquito eyes under fairly natural conditions, but
their ultrastructural cause was not pursued by later workers
until Brammer and Clarin (1976). Now that we have a 'dictionary' of turnover strategies which helps us to interpret what
we see under the electron microscope (Blest, 1980), it is
remarkable how much can be inferred from published micrographs in the anatomical papers of the last decade. For
example, figure 5 in Walcott and Horridge (1971) shows the
microvilli in the eye of a megalopteran, each with a pale tip
which we now know must be destined to drop off during the
disposal phase of turnover (Williams and Blest, 1980); Meyer-
Rochow and Horridge (1975) show that in the Christmas beetle

in the light-adapted state 'large accumulations of regularly arranged endoplasmic reticulum appear in the retinula cell cytoplasm in the rhabdom region'. Accumulations of this kind are typical of arthropods with fast and massive rhabdom turnover.

I.HOW RHABDOM CROSS-SECTION AFFECTS EYE PERFORMANCE

The anatomy of the ommatidium of a representative insect, the locust, is shown in Fig. 1.

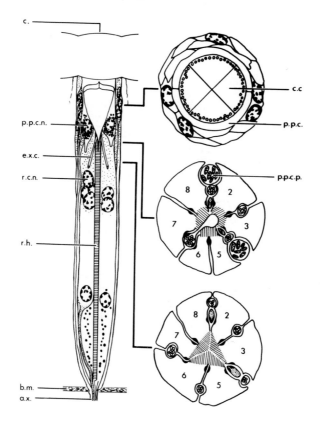

FIGURE 1. Summary of the critical region of the locust ommatidium. ax axons; bm basement membrane, c convex corneal surface, cc crystalline cone; exc extension of the cone, ppc primary pigment cell, ppcp processes of ditto: ppcn nuclei of ditto: rcn retinula cell nuclei: rh rhabdom. The cells are numbered according to Wilson & al. 1978.

Effectively, the tip of the rhabdom catches light that is focussed upon it by the lens. Therefore it acts as does a silver halide grain in a photographic film (Fig. 2b). The angular field size and sensitivity of the grain (and also of the tip of the rhabdom) can be calculated from the dimensions of the optical system. In particular, the field is the angle subtended by the rhabdom tip in the outside world. This is the angle projected through the posterior nodal point of the lens ($\Delta\sigma$, in Fig. 2a), increased by a small angle because the lens contributes some diffraction (Fig. 2b).

The field of the rhabdom tip, measured in the outside world, is defined as the relation (in angular co-ordinates) of the sensitivity of the rhabdom to a point source of constant intensity plotted as a function of the direction of the point source with respect to the optical axis. Sensitivity, in this context, is defined as the reciprocal of the intensity computed to be required to give a chosen, constant amplitude of response. Thus, sensitivity to a point source at each angle, ϕ, is the reciprocal of the attenuated intensity caused by moving the point source off-axis. Therefore, the field can be depicted graphically in terms of the attenuation of light as a function of angle off-axis, and described as a surface with a peak which resembles a Gaussian function.

The cross section of the rhabdom which captures light is also taken as a Gaussian function, of full angular width $\Delta\sigma = d/f$ radians at the 50% level of effective absorption subtended at the posterior nodal point. A point source of light of the kind used for measuring the fields produces on the tip of the rhabdom a patch of light which is not of uniform intensity (the Airy disc). The distribution of intensity across the Airy disc closely resembles a Gaussian distribution with an angular width of $\Delta\sigma$ radians at the 50% level of intensity subtended at the nodal point (Fig. 2b). The field of width $\Delta\rho$ radians is the convolution of these two Gaussian functions and is given by the approximation

$$\Delta\rho^2 = \Delta\alpha^2 + \Delta\sigma^2 \quad\dots\dots\dots\dots\dots\dots\dots\dots\dots\dots \quad (1)$$

where the angle $\Delta\rho$ can be measured outside the eye because the other angles are subtended at the nodal point.

The width of the field of the silver halide grain or rhabdom is therefore always a little larger than its geometrical angle subtended through the posterior nodal point. If diffraction is discounted the most important parameter of the eye, the width of the field, is proportional to the rhabdom diameter.

The sensitivity (S) of the grain or rhabdom to extended sources which fill the field is proportional to the integral

of all the light in the field multiplied by the area of the
lens which gathers the light. As the integral within a
Gaussian field is proportional to the square of the field
width $\Delta\rho$, we have:-

$$S = K \; \Delta\rho^2 \; D^2 \qquad \dots\dots\dots\dots\dots\dots\dots\dots\dots\dots\dots \quad (2)$$

where D is the aperture of the lens. When the diffraction
component is negligible compared to the size of the rhabdom or
grain, this reduces to the well-known formula for a camera,

$$S \; = \; K \; d^2 \; D^2/f^2 = K \; d^2/F^2 \qquad \dots\dots\dots\dots\dots\dots\dots \quad (3)$$

where d is the diameter of the halide grain or rhabdom, f is
the focal length (distance from posterior nodal point to
focal plane), and F is the focal ratio (F/D). Thus, the capture cross-sectional area of the rhabdom d^2 exerts its full
effect on the sensitivity to extended sources.

Field width and sensitivity to diffuse sources are two of
the basic parameters of the eye. Because both depend on rhabdom diameter, its cyclical changes necessarily affect vision,
as is evident if Figs. 2c and 2d are compared. Night vision is
accompanied by a new set of functional relationships, generated in part by changes in rhabdom diameter. The field width
will increase roughly in proportion to the increase in diameter and sensitivity will increase in proportion to the area of
the rhabdom tip. The eye becomes better at seeing in dim light,
but loses resolution because the large rhabdom tip smooths out
the highest spatial frequencies that are passed during the day.
These conclusions are implicit in the more detailed treatment given by Horridge (1978), where it is stressed that in
real compound eyes there must always be a compromise between
sensitivity and resolution, the point of balance being determined by natural selection as a lifestyle evolves. In fact,
other mechanisms are involved in the modulation of sensitivity of which movement of screening pigment is an example.
Compounded with rhabdom growth and diminition, they mean that
the analysis of the eye mechanisms of even a single species is
both difficult and demanding; we are a long way from achieving
a satisfactory natural history of the compound eye. Let us
consider, briefly, some of the problems which have barely
been touched upon, and to which we do not have satisfactory
answers.

II. PREDICTING FIELD SIZES FROM ANATOMY

Returning to the theory of field sizes summarized in figure 2 and looking back on the interaction of theory and experiment over the past few years, we can now see that:-

1. Fields were first measured about 1961 (Burkhardt, 1962).
2. About 1965 intracellular recordings of retinula cells of locust were made to measure the fields with reference to the anomalously high resolution described by Burtt and Catton (1962) and to estimate field size for calculations of photon flux (Scholes 1966).
3. In the early description of the anatomy of locust retinula (Horridge, 1966), the palisade around the rhabdom appeared in the dark-adapted but not in the light-adapted state (Horridge & Barnard, 1965). We did not notice the change in diameter of the rhabdom, and the animals were reared in continuous light.
4. We found an increase in angular sensitivity from average $\Delta\rho_{LA} = 3.4°$ to $\Delta\rho_{DA} = 6.6°$ upon dark adaptation (Tunstall and Horridge, 1967) but errors arose from using animals cultured in continuous light and from mechanical damage. Better values were obtained by Wilson (1975). We inferred that the widening of the field in the dark-adapted state was due to rays at greater angles to the axis being conducted down the rhabdom as a light guide. This was attributed to the smaller refractive index of the palisade around the rhabdom as compared to the mass of mitochondria which it replaced. This idea may still apply in some eyes, e.g. Cockroach, but cannot now be the explanation in the locust.
5. Improvements followed in techniques for measuring the fields of insect photoreceptors. a) About 1969 - avoided mechanical damage, by making a small hole in cornea.

FIGURE 2. Summary of the interaction between the size of the rhabdom tip and the aperture of the lens in determining the field size.
   a. The rhabdom subtends an angle d/f at the nodal point.
   b. A distant point source is focused to an Airy disc of width $\Delta a = \lambda/D$ subtended at the nodal point.
   c. As the point source moves through an angle ϕ the Airy disc moves across the rhabdom tip.
   d. When the rhabdom is wider, the field is correspondingly wider than in (b).

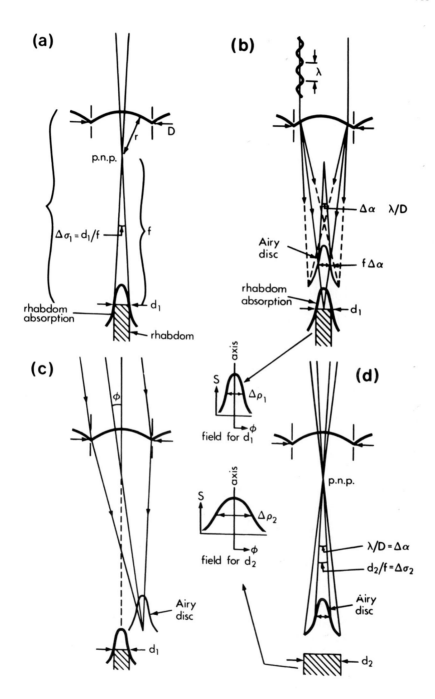

FIGURE   2.

b)   About 1970 - used whole respiring animal instead of isolated head. c)   About 1972 - checked optics by the pseudopupil.
d)   About 1977 - recorded from known ommatidia that are identified by the pseudopupil with measurements of optically relevant anatomy of the same ommatidia. e)   Where possible, identified the cell by number, because between 1970 and 1979 it
became obvious that every retinula cell can be identified
within the ommatidium.

6.   We discovered, in the dragonfly, that the stop in the
optical system caused by the principal pigment cells around
the narrowest part of the cone decreases in diameter in the
light and opens in the dark (Horridge, 1969b), providing an
alternative mechanism for the change in field size. Fields
were still not calculated from anatomy. Dark-adaptation was
done during the day but whether this was significant still
has to be tested for dragonflies.

7.   About 1976 by a circuitous route we revived the theory
of Kuiper (1962) that the field of the receptor is the result
of the convolution in angular coordinates of the point spread
function with the subtense of the effective capture cross
section of the rhabdom. This was clarified by Colin Pask and
Allan Snyder, who produced the convenient formula in equ (1).

8.   From careful recordings in the dronefly *Eristalis*
(Horridge, Mimura and Hardie 1976) and in the blowfly (Hardie,
1978) we found that the geometrical diameter of the rhabdom
tip gives a good prediction of the field size. The field of
retinula cell 7 is less than that in cells 1-6 because the
rhabdomere tip of cell 7 is smaller in diameter. Uncertainty
due to shrinkage during fixation is greater than that due to
measurement of fields.

9.   As a sideline we proved experimentally that if the
properties of rhabdoms as light guides alone are considered,
their field width would be very large (unpublished work,
Horridge and Marcelja). Therefore the angle at which rays
strike the rhabdom (the field of the rhabdom as a light guide)
need not be considered in the calculation of the fields of
retinula cells.

10.   Finally we had experimental proof that for mantids and
dragonflies, and therefore also probably for locust because
they have similar eyes, the field sizes are predicted quite
well by the formula in equ (1). Therefore the eyes are focused.
The anatomical measurements were made on animals fixed under
the same conditions as the fields were measured electrophysiologically (Horridge and Duelli 1979; Rossel 1979; Horridge
1980).

11.   It was found that at the centre of the foveas the
Airy disc and the rhabdom agree in size, so that $\Delta\alpha = \Delta\sigma$;
therefore resolution and sensitivity are optimized together

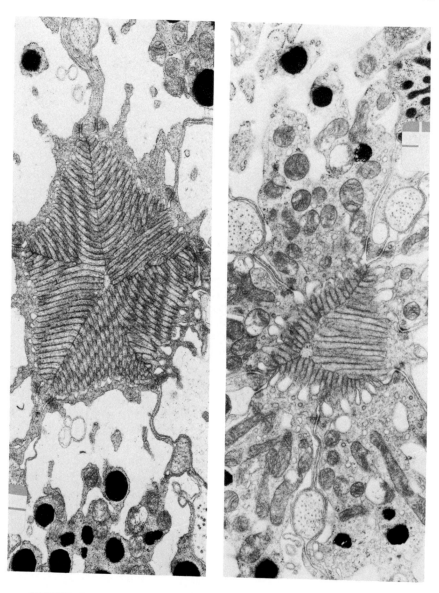

FIGURE 3. Transverse sections through the tip of the rhabdom of the locust Valanga at the fovea. One eye was removed during the day for fixation, the cavity sealed with vacuum grease and the animal maintained on a normal daily cycle of illumination until the second eye was fixed at midnight.
Left: At midnight, dark adapted.
Right: In mid-afternoon, light adapted.
Both X 16,500.

in the fovea. In peripheral parts of the mantid eye the field
sizes are dominated by the rhabdom diameter (Rossel 1979;
Horridge 1980).

12.   During 1979 a diurnal rhythm volume in a variety of
insects and crustaceans with compound eyes came to the fore
(Williams and Blest, 1980 on tipulid flies; Waterman and
Eguchi, 1979; Blest, 1980 and Blest, Stowe and Price, 1980
on shore crabs). When locust eyes were examined we immediately
found that the rhabdom tips are of greater diameter at night
than during the day (Fig. 3). This means that time of day and
the check of the anatomical measurements become essential,
and all earlier work must be re-examined with this new
phenomenon in mind.

The diurnal changes in rhabdom diameter provide a new
opportunity to check the formula $\Delta\rho^2 = \Delta\alpha^2 + \Delta\sigma^2$ from equ
(1), and therefore the theory on which it is based. The
diurnal rhythm implies that the dark-adapted state must be
examined after nightfall and in animals reared in the natural
light cycle. As electrophysiology of visual cells is almost
always done during the day in a darkened room it is likely
that many previous results relate to an abnormal situation.
The sensitivity of night eyes to a strong flash of light
which modulates turnover, means that only low light levels
can be shown to night eyes.

III. THE FUNCTIONAL SIGNIFICANCE OF RHABDOM DIAMETER

Rhabdoms differ in size in different insects, and in different parts of the eye, during the day. Recent work already
quoted has shown that the field width can be predicted by the
anatomy of the optical part of the ommatidium. We considered
eyes where the cone abuts on the rhabdom tip, so that events
after that point no longer influence the field. To give the
theory summarized in equ (1) a fair test we worked with eyes
with strong foveas which provided a wide range of field widths
in a single eye. A major finding was that larger facets have
narrower rhabdoms behind them (Horridge and Duelli 1979). This
relation is explained by the match in size between the Airy
disc and the rhabdom diameter as follows.

A point source on axis causes a patch of light in the
focal plane called the circle of confusion or Airy disc (Fig.
2b). The angular width of the Airy disc is given by $\Delta\alpha = \lambda/D$
radians subtended at the posterior nodal point. λ is the wavelength of light and D is the facet diameter. This solid angle
$\Delta\alpha$ is the diffraction component of the field.

The solid angle subtended by the rhabdom is d/f where d

is the rhabdom tip diameter and f is the focal length (Fig. 2a and d). This solid angle $\Delta\sigma$ is the anatomical component of the field.

If the Airy disc exactly fits the rhabdom (Fig. 2b) then no light from the point source on axis is lost, but conversely no area of the rhabdom tip is wasted. Then $\lambda/D = d/f$. In the mantid *Tenodera* (Rossel 1979) the mantid *Ciulfina* and the dragonfly *Austrogomphus* (Horridge 1980) we have found that this is the situation at the centre of the fovea. In the mantids the rhabdom outside the fovea is larger so that $\Delta\sigma > \Delta\alpha$ and fields are dominated by rhabdom diameter, as seen from the equation $\Delta\rho^2 = \Delta\alpha^2 + \Delta\sigma^2$ when $\Delta\sigma > \Delta\alpha$ and as shown in Fig. 2d.

In the dragonfly *Austrogomphus* we found the interesting situation that over the whole eye the rhabdom diameter is matched exactly to the facet size so that $\Delta\sigma = \Delta\alpha$ everywhere. Therefore $d/f = \lambda/D$ and $d^2D^2/f^2 = \lambda^2$, which is a constant, and the sensitivity towards diffuse sources is the same for all parts of the eye. The point is that this analysis can be done from the anatomy and checked electrophysiologically.

The consequence of the cycle of changes in rhabdom tip diameter is that a new set of functional relations takes over at night. The enlarged rhabdoms at night inevitably increase the field width approximately in proportion to rhabdom tip diameter, and sensitivity in proportion to rhabdom tip area. The eye becomes better at seeing in dim light but loses resolution because the larger rhabdom tip smooths out the highest spatial frequencies that are passed during the day.

Many locusts are active at night, as shown by recent work in tracking them with radar and by captures at night, especially in ecological situations of low humidity and high day temperatures (Clark 1969; Farrow 1974). The diurnal changes in the eye (Fig. 3) show that locusts actually have an adaptation to night vision. When we look into the situation we find that some other insects that are normally studied during the day, such as Mantids, are also active at night, and the question is immediately raised whether they too have a diurnal rhythm of rhabdom size.

This type of work will probably lead to the conclusion that arthropods that are active at night as well as by day have larger rhabdoms at night. If they take the route followed by some spiders, day insects will have breakdown of receptors (not enlargement) at night while nocturnal insects will have breakdown during the day. If this turns out to be general, then what about those which are active only in bright sunlight, such as our common small blue butterfly *Zizina*, or

those that are active only at one light intensity, such as
the dragonfly *Zyxomma* which flies for less than an hour during the short tropical twilight (Horridge 1978).

IV. RELATED TOPICS ON RETINAL FUNCTION

If the eye is adapted as an organ of vision its most important characteristic is that the brain behind it should have
as much information as possible about the visual scene. In
terms of physical measurements this means that there must be a
maximum number of sampling points, each of minimum width, each
as sensitive and as rapidly responsive as possible. This gives
four very significant parameters for every receptor. Apart
from speed of response, all are related directly to the size
of the rhabdom.

Over the past five years a group working on the compound
eye at Canberra have tackled several aspects of how compound
eyes have become adapted to seeing. The first step was to
analyse the compromise that has to be made in a compound eye
between the number of facets and the resolution of each.

Compound eyes differ fundamentally from lens eyes in several important ways. First the more sampling stations they
have, the more separate lenses there have to be, but there is
a limit to the minimum size of the lenses as set by diffraction because the minimum field width with a rhabdom of negligible size is closely related to the lens resolving power which
depends on the aperture. More sampling stations means smaller
apertures and poorer resolving power. Therefore a compromise
has to be struck in any compound eye between number of facets
and the resolving power of each. The advance made recently
was to show exactly how this compromise should theoretically
depend on the ambient intensity at which the eye normally
functions (Snyder, Stavenga and Laughlin 1978). It turns out
that in dim light animals the facets must be larger than
otherwise because they have to catch more light to overcome
photon noise. So facets can be large for two reasons, for
resolution, as a consequence of diffraction theory, and for
sensitivity as a consequence of facet area because photons
are in short supply.

This theory made a great number of assumptions and new
facts have since come to light, but the function of a good
theory is to point towards new experiments. Let us work
through the steps that will lead towards better theories.

The position of the lens is not at all clear in many of
the commonest arthropods. The external curvature of the cornea

is often insufficient to provide enough power. A very small refractive index gradient in the cornea or crystalline cone is theoretically sufficient to make a lens, but can hardly be measured experimentally. A large area of investigation is how the different focal lengths are caused in eyes with foveas (as in mantids) or gradients (as in flies) involving different cone lengths.

2. The question of whether apposition eyes are focused or not still remains open except that more and more examples are being found (Rossel 1979; Horridge 1980) where the acceptance angle is predicted by equ (1), which implies that a distant point source is focused on the rhabdom tip.

3. An important way in which compound eyes differ from lens eyes is that the fields of individual receptors can vary in size and can overlap. The diversity of mechanisms controlling the fields has not been fully explored.

4. The compound eye can be considered as the classical parallel processing device, and the theory that the number of visual axes and the width of each field together inform the brain with the best possible picture of the surrounding world rests on this assumption (Snyder, Stavenga and Laughlin 1978). Nevertheless, it is still a matter of faith, and experiments have not yet been designed to test it.

5. In most sophisticated behavioural or physiological experiments it is assumed that moving striped patterns are an adequate model of the world perceived by the compound eye. This is convenient, because successive processing stages can be analysed in terms of the spatial frequency transfer functions between them. As a method of approach it is biased, because it takes the reality of parallel processing for granted, and begs the question of whether compound eye and optic lobe together may not be designed to use form vision for the discrimination of different classes of objects such as prey or mates.

6. The significance of much anatomical detail is obscure. Why, for example, do so many nocturnal insects have rhabdoms with baroque cross sectional profiles? The shape of the cone and in particular the function of its long, tapering neck has never been satisfactorily explained. Recent electron microscopy has repeatedly shown that there must be a refractive index gradient across the transverse section, with a dense thread down the middle leading straight to the rhabdom (Horridge and Duelli 1979). It looks as though there is a kind of impedance matching device between free space optics in the cone and mode optics in the rhabdom as a light guide. Whatever the true situation may be it will certainly influence field size and the other properties which relate to it.

V. THE CELL BIOLOGY OF CHANGES IN RHABDOM SIZE

The massive cyclical synthesis and degradation of microvillar membrane present exaggerated versions of problems
common to all highly differentiated cells. For example, nothing is understood about processes which ensure that while
plasma membrane is turned over the overall morphology of cells
varies only within narrowly prescribed limits. This question
may relate to how the morphological polarities of cells are
determined in the first place. Also, we know almost nothing
about why plasma membranes turn over at all, and why some
phototransductive membranes apparently need to turn over faster than others.
Arthropod eyes such as those described by Blest (spider:
1978), Nässel and Waterman (crab: 1979), Blest, Stowe and
Price (crab: 1980), Williams and Blest (tipulid fly: 1980),
Horridge, Duniec and Marcelja (locust: 1980) are outstanding
material for the study of these problems because the synthesis
of membrane and its degradation occur separately at dusk and
at dawn respectively. Other arthropod eyes may be less amenable to analysis because the mass effects at dawn and dusk are
relatively trivial (S.J. Stowe, unpublished data from the crab
Mictyris), because at dawn re-synthesis rapidly succeeds
breakdown (Chamberlain and Barlow 1979, for *Limulus*), or because at least under the particular experimental conditions
employed synthesis and breakdown are concurrent and stages of
illumination merely adjust the relative rates at which they
proceed (Eguchi and Waterman 1967; White 1967a, 1968; White
and Lord 1975; Krauhs, Mahler and Moore 1978). We regard this
latter category of results with mild suspician, because the
experiments which yielded them did not take account of possible circadian effects, and until very recently workers did
not realise that synthesis and degradation can be very rapid
indeed when they are triggered at the 'correct times' of day
(Blest 1978, 1980; Blest, Kao and Powell 1979).

SYNTHESIS OF RHABDOMERE MEMBRANE

Synthesis of plasma membranes has mostly been studied in
particular vertebrate cells which can be stimulated to amplify
membrane quickly. Classical examples are the nasal salt-glands
of ducklings (Levine, Higgins and Barrnet 1972), lactating
mammary gland (Franke, *et al* 1976) and rat deciduoma (Yunghans,
et al). These preparations show that the major components of
plasma membrane are synthesised by endoplasmic reticulum and

passed to the Golgi by membrane flow to allow the insertion or addition of further components. Saccules or vesicles from the *trans* face of the Golgi then carry pre-formed membrane to the cell surface where it fuses with the existing plasma membrane, a mode of addition which has been termed 'patching'. It is also possible that some membrane proteins proceed from the endoplasmic reticulum to the cell surface freely in the cytosol and are inserted directly (cf. review by Morre 1977). There is evidence that vertebrate photopigment proteins (Opsins) are synthesised in the endoplasmic reticulum, then terminally glycosylated in the Golgi, and finally transported in the membranes of Golgi-derived saccules ('schleppersomes') to the forming basal discs of the receptor outer segments (Papermaster *et al* 1978). In this respect, vertebrate opsins seem to behave like many other membrane proteins.

How does synthesis of arthropod rhabdomeral membrane relate to the broader vertebrate picture outlined above?

Firstly, 'fast' in the invertebrate photoreceptor can be very fast indeed. Full amplification of membrane in the salt glands of salt-stressed ducklings and during the development of rat deciduona requires periods of the order of days. A grapsid crab retinula cell multiplies the area of microvillar membrane in its rhabdom by some 20 times during normal night adaptation (Nässel and Waterman 1979). Unpublished observations by S.J. Stowe imply that widening of a given longitudinal region of the fused rhabdom of *Leptograpsus* from 2 to 5μm may take place within 30 mins. The geometry of the microvillus lengthening which underlies widening of the rhabdom is complex and will not be described here. We already know, however, that no single geometry of assembly is common to rhabdomeres of all species. In crayfish, Itaya (1976) suggested that whorls of membrane which he called 'ellipsoid bodies' lying at the bases of and often attached to the microvilli represent newly synthesised microvillar membrane which is about to be added to the rhabdom by membrane flow. He traced continuities between the ellipsoid bodies and smooth endoplasmic reticulum, and considered that the former might serve as a 'store' of microvillar membrane. In a number of species with mass synthesis of microvillar membrane at dusk, we find that membrane apparently derived from smooth endoplasmic reticulum is characteristic of the synthetic phase, but it is of very varied configuration. In *Leptograpsus* receptors ellipsoid bodies are only present during the synthetic phase and only numerous and highly developed during the most active part of it (Stowe, in preparation). The continuities with other organelles noted by Itaya (1976) are confirmed in *Leptograpsus*, and it seems that a model of microvillus growth based on the flow and re-organisation of preassembled membrane will probably prove to be correct.

We must also confront the problem posed by the thermodynamic instability of narrow tubes of fluid membrane. How might
irregular whorls of membrane with a relatively high radius of
curvature become re-organised to form tubules with a uniform
small one? Theoretically, the intrinsic curvature of biological membranes could be altered by the phosphorylation of their
membrane proteins, or by alterations of charge-distribution
(Kirkpatrick 1979). Radical changes in shape are imposed upon
erythrocyte ghosts by phosphorylation of the submembrane cytoskeletal protein spectrin (Birchmeier and Singer 1977; Sheetz
and Singer 1977), but there is no reason to suppose that such
mechanisms could result by themselves in the production of
arrays of identical tubules from geometrically heterogeneous
precursors. A more promising approach is to consider whether
the actin model proposed by Tilney (1979) for the assembly of
vertebrate intestinal brush-border microvilli is consonant
with what we know of the structure of rhabdomeral microvilli,
which are both smaller and perform quite different functions.

The microvilli of brush borders contain axial actin filaments which are attached by a terminal density to the microvillus tip. At the base, the actin filaments enter an extensive network of similar filaments derived from adjacent microvilli, and are also associated with filaments of myosin in a
complex known as the 'terminal web'. It is supposed that the
myosin component effects movements, shortening and lengthening,
of the microvilli. The axial actin filaments are linked to the
walls of the microvilli by side arms, described as α-actinin-
like, but possibly of different composition. Under certain
experimental conditions, microvilli can be made to disassemble
and re-grow. Observations of regrowth suggest that the initial
assembly site for each microvillus is a terminal density, and
that the first events are the polymerisation of F-actin from
this site, and the addition of side arms to stitch the forming
membrane into place as a tube.

Saibil (1978) has provided strong circumstantial evidence
for the existence of a major actin component in rhabdomeral
microvilli from squid, and has noted that transverse sections
show not only axial densities, but profiles which could be
interpreted as the side arms (H. Saibil, personal communication).

Numerous electron micrographs of rhabdomeral microvilli
show an axial density (e.g. Horridge 1969; Chi and Carlson
1979; Williams and Blest 1980), usually poorly defined. As
osmium fixation destroys actin, and is prolonged when invertebrate eyes are being post-fixed for electron microscopy, it
is reasonable to suggest that this is the remains of an axial
array of actin filaments. There is nothing resembling the
terminal web at the bases of the microvilli, and, as the

latter are non-motile, the absence of a myosin component is to
be expected. If the rhabdomeral microvillus proves to have an
intrinsic cytoskeleton analogous to that of the brush border,
microvilli of both kinds could, in principle, be assembled in
similar ways. Certainly a stitching mechanism of assembly
seems to be required if sheets of membrane are to be re-organised in the manner observed. A cytoskeleton in the microvillus
would also clarify membrane shedding during turnover.

Meanwhile, some of the problems posed by our present state
of ignorance need to be stated, for they indicate the directions in which future research on the assembly of rhabdom must
go. Currently, there are major difficulties in reconciling
observations made by different techniques on the turnover
process. We are suggesting here that microvillus growth is
achieved by the flow and stitching of previously assembled
membrane. Yet, all labelling experiments using ^{3}H-leucine show
that this marker is incorporated diffusely over rhabdoms soon
after injection (e.g. Perrelet 1972; Hafner and Bok 1977). In
the case of vertebrates, Basinger, Bok and Hall (1976) have
shown that ^{3}H-leucine is predominantly incorporated into outer
segment rhodopsin, so that it can effectively be regarded as
a rhodopsin label as it is in mosquito retinae (Stein, Brammer
and Ostroy 1979). However, Wehner and Goldsmith (1975) and
Goldsmith and Wehner (1977) find almost no lateral diffusion
of visual pigment in crayfish rhabdoms: we suppose either
that the high cholesterol content of microvillus membranes so
increases their viscosity as to prevent it, or that a submembrane cytoskeleton exerts a direct or indirect anchoring
effect on the intrinsic membrane proteins. The simplest explanation of these dissonant facts would be that the phospholipid and cholesterol components of the membrane are assembled
first (although if stitching were to take place, some intrinsic membrane proteins would also need to be present), and opsin
or rhodopsin sites added later. This is not, however, in agreement with the present belief that vertebrate opsins are
inserted into endoplasmic membranes when they are formed, and
transported in saccules, for vesicles or saccules are never
seen *within* microvilli.

The resolution of these paradoxes is important in at least
two ways. The answer will help to clarify our current ideas
about the assembly of plasma membrane; we also predict that it
will reveal a 'new' strategy of adaptation. If membrane proteins can be inserted into preformed membrane, it follows that
the photon capture efficiency of a rhabdom could be increased
by boosting the density of rhodopsin sites in its membrane,
irrespective of the synthesis of new lipid. This concept has
never been tested, and like our speculations about the role
of a cytoskeleton in the assembly of microvilli is at variance

with the hypothesis that the opsin/phospholipid/cholesterol ratio is critical for the architectural stability of microvilli and is therefore held constant (Hamdorf 1979, p. 188). There is little to suggest that rhodopsin densities are thus manipulated in insects such as blowfly which we believe to have slow turnover (Blest and Maples 1979), except in vitamin A-deficient flies (Harris *et al* 1977). However, adjustment of opsin or rhodopsin density may be a feature of rapid, massive turnover and constitute an explanation for it:

Turnover of vertebrate photoreceptor membrane has been discussed in terms of a need to repair damage to unsaturated phospholipids by singlet oxygen generated by illumination of rhodopsin (cf. Crouch 1980). We doubt that this hypothesis can be used as a unifying explanation for the enormous range of turnover rates implied by our qualitative observations. However it is attractive to suggest that gradual addition of opsin sites to membrane after it has been formed at night would leave the retina with no alternative but to destroy membrane at dawn in order to remove them.

Another way of looking at the patterns of turnover of invertebrate receptors emphasises the geometry of membrane addition. In the retinae of vertebrates, membrane is added to a stack whose length may alter, but whose diameter remains constant (Young and Droz 1968); because the cross sectional area of the stack remains the same, the receptor is exempt from significant distortion of its optics during turnover. We have shown that the opposite is true for rhabdoms, and we also know that while many rhabdoms grow and shrink daily, others adjust their turnover rates so that their cross sectional areas do not change. It is plausible that separation of synthesis and breakdown in time and fitting the two processes to the 24 hour cycle of illumination has been imposed by natural selection as a fringe benefit which helps to extend the range of illuminances over which the eyes can work.

Finally, the deployment of intracellular compartments during synthesis poses further problems. Most of the glycosylation of vertebrate rhodopsin takes place in the Golgi (Bok, Basinger and Hall 1974) but we find that in arthropod eyes the Golgi is poorly-developed and apparently not directly involved in synthesis. This may mean that the sugar chains are completed at an earlier stage or that arthropod opsins do not possess them in full.

VII. THE DEGRADATION OF RHABDOMERE MEMBRANE

All plasma membrane turns over, but the impression received from the multiplicity of mechanisms in photoreceptors is
that transductive membrane requires faster turnover than most.
The first question is whether the membrane lost from microvilli is degraded or returned unaltered. Degradation is not,
in principle implied by shedding during turnover. There is
much circumstantial evidence that synaptic membrane is largely
re-cycled through local systems without being degraded (Holtzman 1977; Holtzman, Schacher, Evans and Teichberg 1977; Fried
and Blaustein 1978; Schaeffer and Raviola 1978), and it has
been pointed out that re-cycling of synaptic vesicles is so
rapid and on so large a scale that degradation and re-synthesis of their components would be grossly uneconomical.
      The position for most arthropod receptors is unequivocal.
In some species membrane is shed to extracellular space, from
which it is retrieved either by glial cells (Blest and Maples
1979), or after collapse to a mixed vesicular and micellar
detritus by the receptors which engulf it by means of pseudo-
podia (Williams and Blest 1980). In most species membrane is
shed from the bases of the microvilli by pinocytosis into the
receptors themselves. The resulting coated vesicles are incorporated into multivesicular bodies which then degrade to
multilamellar bodies and are either lysed at that stage or
after a further degradation to amorphous residual bodies
(Eguchi and Waterman 1967, 1976; Blest, Kao and Powell 1978;
Blest 1978). Fusion with primary lysosomes and the appearance
of acid phosphatases have been demonstrated for several such
sequences of degradation (Eguchi and Waterman 1976; Blest,
Price and Maples 1979; Blest, Stowe and Price 1980). We doubt
that any components are merely shunted back to the rhabdoms
unaltered after being shed.
      An interesting feature of these lysosomal systems in
arthropod photoreceptors is the diversity of compartments used
to convey hydrolytic enzymes to the membrane-derived secondary
lysosomes. Zinkler (1974) compared the major constituents of
rhabdomeral membranes from several orders of insects, finding
few significant differences between them. Thus, in all such
photoreceptors, the lysosomal systems concerned with membrane
degradation can be assumed to be concerned with biochemically
similar tasks. In the photoreceptors of the spider, *Dinopis*,
acid phosphatases are supplied to late-stage secondary lysosomes by a specialised system derived from endoplasmic reticulum which resembles the hypertrophied GERL found in some
vertebrate tissues, although it is not topographically related to the Golgi (Blest, Powell and Kao 1978; Blest, Price and

Maples 1979). The Golgi is not a source of hydrolases to any significant extent. Contrastingly, the degradation of membrane in photoreceptors of the crab *Leptograpsus* is initiated by primary lysosomes derived from the *trans* face of the Golgi, and there is no system identifiable as GERL in this context (Blest, Stowe and Price 1980). A second wave of primary lysosomal activity supplies acid phosphatases from smooth endoplasmic reticulum to secondary lysosomes at a more advanced stage of degradation.

The origin of isolation membranes and primary lysosomes in arthropods has been a subject of controversy, particularly the extent to which they are the product of the Golgi compartments *sensu strictu* (cf. Locke and Sykes 1975; Blest, Kao and Powell 1978). It is encouraging to find in so well-defined a context that both the Golgi *and* the endoplasmic reticulum can be responsible for the genesis of these primary lysosomal systems, and that in cells performing the same task in different species one system may be developed at the expense of another. Not only does this allow all parties to the controversy to be right, but it emphasises the evolutionary lability and interdependence of the mechanisms involved.

In different species, very different amounts of transductive membrane are turned over although meaningful quantification is difficult to achieve for geometrical reasons. Where much shed membrane has to be degraded, the lysosomal systems are correspondingly highly evolved. Where the amounts are trivial, either because membrane shedding is extracellular so that the receptors themselves are not responsible for breakdown, or because it is slow, as it appears to be in diurnal Diptera with open rhabdoms, primary lysosomal systems are poorly developed (Blest and Maples 1979). It is possible that differences of this kind underlie some of the differences in the ease with which it is possible to record intracellularly from photoreceptors. Flies with open rhabdoms such as *Lucilia* and *Calliphora*, with feeble lysosomal systems in the receptors are easy material for intracellular recordings, and cells can be held for many hours. Reliable intracellular recordings are difficult to obtain from crabs; their receptors are replete with primary lysosomes (Blest, Stowe and Price 1980). In blowfly retinae, it is already known that the major lysosomal systems are contained in the glia. Substantial injury to the receptors causes the transfer of latent acid phosphatases (and therefore by implication other latent hydrolases) from the glial cells into the axons, and their concurrent activation (Griffiths 1979). The process of transfer and activation is extremely rapid and can be shown to be well-advanced some three minutes after injury. The possible rapid effects of small axonal injuries and their relationship to the lysosomal

equipments of the receptors have not been considered by neuro-
physiologists, and it is possible that 'difficult' receptors
are those in which less-than-perfect electrode penetrations
easily activate intrinsic primary lysosomes. Certainly something is needed to explain the reputation some preparations
acquire for being 'difficult to work with' and others 'easy'.

VIII. VERTEBRATE AND ARTHROPOD PHOTORECEPTOR TURNOVER

Continual reference has been made to well-known vertebrate
preparations in order to emphasise that the problems are of
the same kinds. We can expect arthropod preparations to complement the results obtained by workers on vertebrate retina.
Arthropod eyes are less susceptible to direct biochemical
investigation because of their architectural complexity, and
the difficulty of separating receptors from their glial investiture. Nevertheless, they synthesise and destroy membrane
faster than vertebrate preparations, and are amenable to the
techniques of ultrastructural cytochemistry. The chain of
events which co-ordinate the synthesis of phospholipids,
cholesterol, opsin, other membrane proteins, and a cytoskeletal component which is capable of making these components
into small stable tubes offers a particularly challenging
problem of morphogenesis. The removal of membrane either by
pinocytosis or by extracellular shedding presents another
problem, where the behaviour of cytoskeletal components is
likely to be a key factor, if we can extrapolate, once again,
from recent studies of erythrocyte membranes (Hardy, Bensch
and Schrier 1979; Tokuyasu, Schekman and Singer 1979).
    In one respect, however, invertebrate photoreceptors
behave in more complex ways than their vertebrate counterparts.
A receptor which makes new membrane in a burst at dusk, and
internalises and degrades it some twelve hours later is manipulating two interdependent cycles, for at one point in the
cycle it is synthesising transductive membrane while at the
other it is manufacturing the enzymes with which to degrade it.
The control of these two phases of the daily cycle has barely
been explored. Vertebrate rods are known to synthesise membrane components cyclically (Besharse, Hollyfield and Rayborn
1977). Hollyfield and Basinger (1978) comment.....'It is
possible that this cyclic pattern of outer segment assembly
results from a cyclic pattern in transcription and/or translation. Certainly, one of the major goals of vision scientists
working in this area is a complete description of the molecular events which regulate and initiate these cyclic phenomena.' Many arthropods maintain two cycles, dependent in part

on immediate states of illumination, but also upon underlying
circadian rhythms whose existence can be inferred from indirect evidence (Blest 1978, 1980). However these rhythms may
prove to be controlled at the molecular level, their existence makes these cells amongst the most active and complex
known to us.

IX. SENSES OTHER THAN VISION

The system discovered in some arthropods which replaces
the visual transducer daily is timed in such a way that the
sensory organelles are out of action at a time of day or
night, as the case may be, when they are least needed.

As for vision, so perhaps for other senses, but the story
for vision is recent and apparently no-one has yet examined
the others. For example, the bottle cicada, *Schistosoma*,
sings only at about dusk. Therefore the ear and possibly even
the song generator could well be in less than perfect condition at other times of day. Although a number have been working
on the auditory system of this animal in Neurobiology in
Canberra, none have examined the physiology or anatomy of the
sensory cells with reference to the time of day. Similarly if
you work on the olfactory sense or the visual pigments in
moths but go home every day at 5 o'clock, you might be missing
something. And there is no reason to stop at sense organs. Any
aspect of the physiology is likely to be tied in to the day-
night cycle but would be missed by the 9 to 5 fraternity.

X. DISCUSSION

The significance of the finding of the diurnal cycle of
rhabdom replacement has *simply not sunk in*. We now have to
think of the electrophysiology, the function, the adaptive
radiation and the ecology of diurnal changes in the rhabdom,
with much of the work repeated at the proper time *of the
night*, and many new experiments are suggested.

As an example of old facts now explained, let us mention
Gribakin's (1969) demonstration that upon shining coloured
lights into bee eyes there was a peculiar blistering in some
of the rhabdomeres but not in others. The phenomenon was used
to determine the cellular identity of cells of differing known
spectral sensitivities, but with doubtful success (Menzel and
Blakers 1976). Now we can see that the rhabdom blistering is
probably the early stages of light-initiated rhabdom breakdown.

As an example of work to be done at the proper time of
night, there has been a great deal of work on comparisons of
the physiology and anatomy of light-adapted and dark-adapted
eyes, mostly done from 9-5 in the day. Work on bumps (photon
captures) in locust retinula cells (Lillywhite 1978), will
have to be re-examined. The calculation of photon flux and
therefore of the capture efficiency towards photons depended
on the simultaneous measurement of the field, so no error was
caused by rhabdom size. However some workers say that the
preparations give better bumps in the middle of the night.
This raises questions such as whether brand-new rhabdom membrane is different from old rhabdom membrane in measurements
of bump amplitude, membrane noise, membrane resistance and so
on. As side issues it is easy to see that deep-sea crustacea
and arctic and antarctic species have special situations that
will have to be investigated. Do they adopt continuous turnover, a circadian rhythm or patchy turnover in cells that are
out of phase? Further, no-one can say what light does to the
receptor that it must be turned over, although free radical
damage has been suggested. In conclusion the compound eye
lends itself to many tributories of science, and now another,
the cyclical turnover of receptor membrane, adds another
branch.

REFERENCES

Basinger, S., Bok, D. and Hall, M. (1976). Rhodospin in the
    rod outer segment plasma membrane. *J. Cell Biol. 69,*
    29-42.
Besharse, J.C., Hollyfield, J.G. and Rayborn, M.E. (1977).
    Turnover of rod photoreceptor outer segments. II. Membrane
    addition and loss in relationship to light. *J. Cell Biol.*
    75, 507-527.
Birchmeier, W. and Singer, S.J. (1977). On the mechanism of
    ATP-induced shape changes in human erythrocyte membranes.
    II. The role of ATP. *J. Cell Biol. 73,* 647-657.
Blest, A.D. (1978). The rapid synthesis and destruction of
    photoreceptor membrane by a dinopid spider: a daily cycle.
    Proc. R. Soc. Lond. B. (in press).
Blest, A.D. (1980). Photoreceptor membrane turnover in arthro-
    pods: comparative studies of breakdown processes and their
    implications. *In* "The Effects of Constant Light on Visual
    Processes" (T.P. Williams and B.N. Baker, eds.), pp. 217-
    246. Plenum Press, New York.
Blest, A.D., Kao, L. and Powell, K. (1978). Photoreceptor
    membrane breakdown in the spider *Dinopis*: the fate of
    rhabdomere products. *Cell Tissue Res. 195,* 425-444.
Blest, A.D. and Maples, J. (1979). Exocytotic shedding and
    glial uptake of photoreceptor membrane by a salticid
    spider. *Proc. R. Soc. Lond. B. 204,* 105-112.
Blest, A.D., Powell, K. and Kao, L. (1978). Photoreceptor
    membrane breakdown in the spider *Dinopis*: GERL differen-
    tiation in the receptors. *Cell Tissue Res. 195,* 277-297.
Blest, A.D., Price, G.D. and Maples, J. (1979). Photoreceptor
    membrane breakdown in the spider *Dinopis*: localisation of
    acid phosphatases. *Cell Tissue Res. 199,* 455-472.
Blest, A.D., Stowe, S. and Price, G.D. (1980). The sources of
    acid hydrolases for photoreceptor membrane degradation in
    a grapsid crab. *Cell Tissue Res.* (in press).
Bok, D., Basinger, S. and Hall, M.O. (1974). Autoradiographic
    and radiobiochemical studies on the incorporation of
    $[6-^3H]$ glucosamine into frog rhodopsin. *Exp. Eye Res. 18,*
    225-240.
Brammer, J.D. and Clarin, B. (1976). Changes in volume of the
    rhabdom in the compound eye of *Aedes aegypti* L. *J. exp.*
    Zool. 195, 33-39,
Bullock, T.H. and Horridge, G.A. (1965). Structure and Func-
    tion in the Nervous Systems of Invertebrates. I. & II.
    W.H. Freeman & Co. San Francisco and London.
Burtt, E.T. and Catton, W.T. (1962). Resolving power in the
    compound eye. *Symp. Soc. Exp. Biol. 16,* 72-85.

Chamberlain, S.C. and Barlow, R.B. (1979). Light and efferent
activity control rhabdom turnover in *Limulus* photoreceptors. *Science 206*, 361-363.

Chi, C. and Carlson, S. (1979). Ordered membrane particles in
rhabdomeric microvilli of the housefly (*Musca domestica*
L.). *J. Morph. 161*, 309-322.

Clark, D.P. (1969). Night flights of the Australian plague
locust *Chortiocetes terminifera* in relation to storms.
Austral. Journ. Zool. 17, 329-352.

Crouch, R.K. (1980). *In vitro* effects of light on the regener-
ation of rhodopsin. *In* "The Effects of Constant Light on
Visual Processes" (T.P. Williams and B.N. Baker, eds.).
Plenum Press, New York.

Debaisieux, P. (1944). Les yeux de crustacés: structure,
developpement, réactions à l'éclairement. *Cellule 50*,
9-122.

Eguchi, E. and Waterman, T.H. (1967). Changes in retinal fine
structure induced in the crab *Libinia* by light and dark
adaptation. *Z. Zellforschung 79*, 209-229.

Eguchi, E. and Waterman, T.H. (1976). Freeze-etch and histochemical evidence for cycling in crayfish photoreceptor
membranes. *Cell Tissue Res. 169*, 419-434.

Farrow, R.A. (1974). A modified light trap for obtaining
large samples of night-flying locusts and grasshoppers.
J. Austral. Entomol. Soc. 13, 357-380.

Franke, W.W., Luder, M.R., Kartenbeck, J., Zerban, H. and
Keenan, T.W. (1976). Involvement of vesicle coat material
in casein secretion and surface regeneration. *J. Cell
Biol. 69*, 173-195.

Fried,R.C. and Blaustein, M.P. (1978). Retrieval and recycling
of synaptic vesicle membrane in pinched-off nerve terminals (synaptosomes). *J. Cell Biol. 78*, 685-700.

Goldsmith, T.H. and Wehner, R. (1977). Restrictions on rota-
tional and translational diffusion of pigment in the
membranes of a rhabdomeric photoreceptor. *J. gen. Physiol.
70*, 453-490.

Gribakin, F.G. (1969). Cellular basis of colour vision in the
honey bee. *Nature (Lond.) 233*, 639-641.

Griffiths, G.W. (1979). Transport of glial cell acid phosphatase by endoplasmic reticulum into damaged axons. *J. Cell
Sci. 36*, 361-389.

Hafner, G. and Bok, D. (1977). The distribution of ^{3}H-leucine
labelled protein in the retinula cells of the crayfish
retina. *J. comp. Neurol. 174*, 397-416.

Hamdorf, K. (1979). The physiology of invertebrate visual
pigments. *In* "Handbook of Senory Physiology VII/6A"
(H. Autrum, ed.), pp. 145-224. Springer-Verlag, Berlin-
Heidelberg-New York.

Hardie, R. (1978). Ph.D. Thesis. Australian National
    University, Canberra, Australia.
Hardy, B., Bensch, K.G. and Schrier, S.L. (1979). Spectrin
    rearrangement early in erythrocyte ghost endocytosis.
    J. Cell Biol. 82, 654-663.
Harris, W.A., Ready, D.F., Lipson, E.D., Hudspeth, A.J. and
    Stark, W.S. (1977). Vitamin A deprivation and *Drosophila*
    photopigments. *Nature 266*, 648-650.
Hollyfield, J.G. and Basinger, S.F. (1978). Cyclic metabolism
    of photoreceptor cells. *Invest. Ophtal. vis. Sci. 17*,
    87-89.
Holtzman, E. (1977). The origin and fate of secretory pack-
    ages, especially synaptic vesicles. *Neuroscience 2*,
    327-355.
Holtzmann, E., Schacher, S., Evans, J. and Teichberg, S.
    (1977). Origin and fate of the membrane of secretion
    granules and synaptic vesicles: membrane circulation
    in neurons, gland cells and retinal photoreceptors.
    Cell Surface Reviews, 4: The synthesis, assembly and
    turnover of cell surface components, 165-246.
Horridge, G.A. (1966). The retina of the locust. *In* "The
    Functional Organisation of the Compound Eye" (C.G.
    Bernhard, ed.), pp. 513-541. Oxford, Pergamon Press.
Horridge, G.A. (1969a). The eye of *Dytiscus* (Coleoptera).
    Tissue and Cell 1, 425-442.
Horridge, G.A. (1969b). Unit studies on the retina of dragon-
    flies. *Z. vergl. Physiol. 62*, 1-37.
Horridge, G.A. (1978). The separation of visual axes in
    apposition compound eyes. *Phil Trans. Roy. Soc. Lond.
    B. 285*, 1-59.
Horridge, G.A. (1980). Apposition eyes of large diurnal
    insects as organs adapted to seeing. *Proc. Roy. Soc.
    Lond. B.* (in press).
Horridge, G.A. and Barnard, P.B.T. (1965). Movement of
    palisade in locust retinula cells when illuminated.
    Quart. J. micr. Sci. 106, 131-135.
Horridge, G.A. and Duelli, P. (1979). Anatomy of the regional
    differences in the eye of the mantis *Ciulfina*. *J. exp.
    Biol. 80*, 165-190.
Horridge, G.A., Mimura, K. and Hardie, R. (1976). Fly photo-
    receptors III. Angular sensitivity as a function of wave-
    length and the limits of resolution. *Proc. Roy. Soc. Lond.
    B. 194*, 151-177.
Itaya, S.K. (1976). Rhabdom changes in the shrimp
    Palaemonetes. Cell Tissue Res. 169, 419-434.
Kirkpatrick, F.H. (1979). New models of cellular control: Mem-
    brane cytoskeletons, membrane curvature potential, and
    possible interactions. *Biosystems 11*, 93-101.

Krauhs, J.M., Mahler, H.R. and Moore, W.J. (1978). Protein
    turnover in photoreceptor cells of isolated *Limulus*
    lateral eyes. *J. Neurochem. 30,* 625-632.
Kuiper, J.W. (1962). The optics of the compound eye. *Symp.
    Soc. Exp. Biol. 16,* 58-71.
Levine, A.M., Higgins, J.A. and Barrnet, R.J. (1972). Bio-
    genesis of plasma membranes in salt glands of salt
    stressed ducklings. *J. Cell Sci. 11,* 855-873.
Lillywhite, P.G. (1977). Single photon signals and trans-
    duction in an insect eye. *J. comp. Physiol. 122,* 189-200.
Locke, M. and Sykes, A.K. (1975). The role of the Golgi
    complex in the isolation and digestion of organelles.
    Tissue and Cell 7, 143-158.
Menzel, R. and Blakers, M. (1976). Colour receptors in the
    bee eye - morphology and spectral sensitivity. *J. comp.
    Physiol. 108,* 11-33.
Meyer-Rochow, V.B. and Horridge, G.A. (1975). The eye of
    Anoplognathus (Coleoptera, Scarabaeidae). *Proc. Roy.
    Soc. Lond. B. 188,* 1-39.
Morré, D.J. (1977). The Golgi apparatus and membrane bio-
    genesis. *Cell Surface Reviews 4,* The synthesis, assembly
    and turnover of cell surface components, 165-246.
Nässel, D.R. and Waterman, T.H. (1979). Massive diurnally
    modulated photoreceptor membrane turnover in crab light
    and dark adaptation. *J. comp. Physiol. 131,* 205-216.
Papermaster, D.S., Schneider, B.G., Zorn, M.A. and
    Kraehenbuhl, J.P. (1978). Immunocytochemical localisation
    of opsin in outer segments and Golgi zones of frog
    photoreceptor cells. *J. Cell Biol. 77,* 196-210.
Perrelet, A. (1972). Protein synthesis in the visual cells of
    the honeybee drone as studied with electron microscope
    autoradiography. *J. Cell Biol. 55,* 595-605.
Rossel, S. (1979). Regional differences in photoreceptor
    performance in the eye of the praying mantis. *J. comp.
    Physiol. 131,* 95-112.
Saibil, H. (1978). Actin in squid retinal photoreceptors.
    J. Physiol. 281, 17P.
Sato, S. (1950). Compound eyes of *Culex pipiens* var. *pallens*
    Coquillett. *Sci. Rep. Tohoku Univ. Ser. 4, 18,* 330-341.
Sato, S., Kato, M. and Toriumi, M. (1957). Structural changes
    of the compound eye of *Culex pipiens* var. *pallens*
    Coquillet in the process of dark adaption. *Sci. Rep. Res.
    Insts. Tohoku Univ. 23,* 91-99.
Schaeffer, S.F. and Raviola, E. (1978). Membrane recycling in
    the cone cell endings of the turtle retina. *J. Cell Biol.
    79,* 802-825.

Scholes, J.H. (1965). Discontinuity of the excitation process
    in locust visual cells. *Cold. Spr. Harb. Symp. Quant.
    Biol. 30*, 517-527.
Sheetz, M.P. and Singer, S.J. (1977). On the mechanism of ATP-
    induced shape changes in human erythrocyte membranes. I.
    The role of the spectrin complex. *J. Cell Biol. 73*,
    638-646.
Snyder, A.W., Stavenga, D.G. and Laughlin, S.B. (1977).
    Spatial information capacity of compound eyes. *J. comp.
    Physiol. 116*, 183-207.
Stein, R.J., Brammer, J.D. and Ostroy, S.E. (1979). Renewal
    of opsin in the photoreceptor cells of the mosquito.
    J. gen. Physiol. 74, 565-582.
Tilney, L.G. (1979). Actin, motility and membranes. *In*
    "Membrane Transduction Mechanisms" (R.A. Cone and J.E.
    Dowling, eds.), pp. 163-186. Raven Press, New York.
Tokuyasu, K.T., Schekman, R. and Singer, S.J. (1979). Domains
    of receptor mobility and endocytosis in the membranes of
    neonatal human erythrocytes and reticulocytes are
    deficient in spectrin. *J. Cell Biol. 80*, 481-486.
Tunstall, J. and Horridge, G.A. (1967). Electrophysiological
    investigations of the optics of the locust retina.
    Z. vergl. Physiol. 55, 167-182.
Walcott, B. and Horridge, G.A. (1971). The compound eye of
    Archichauliodes (Megaloptera). *Proc. Roy. Soc. Lond. B.
    179*, 65-72.
Wehner, R. and Goldsmith, T.H. (1975). Restrictions on trans-
    lational diffusion of metarhodopsin in the membranes of
    rhabdomeric photoreceptors. *Biol. Bull. 149*, 450.
Williams, D.S. and Blest, A.D. (1980). Extracellular shedding
    of photoreceptor membrane in the open rhabdom of a
    tipulid fly. *Cell Tissue Res.* (in press).
Wilson, M., Garrard, P. and McGinness, S. (1978). The unit
    structure of the locust compound eye. *Cell Tissue Res.
    195*, 205-226.
Wilson, M. (1975). Angular sensitivity of light and dark
    adapted locust retinula cells. *J. comp. Physiol. 97*,
    323-328.
White, R.H. (1967). The effect of light deprivation upon the
    ultrastructure of the larval mosquito eye. II. The
    rhabdom. *J. exp. Zool. 166*, 405-425.
White, R.H. (1968). The effect of light and light deprivation
    upon the ultrastructure of the larval mosquito eye. III.
    Multivesicular bodies and protein uptake. *J. exp. Zool.
    169*, 261-278.
White, R.H. and Lord, E. (1975). Diminution and enlargement
    of the mosquito rhabdom in light and darkness. *J. gen.
    Physiol. 65*, 583-598.

Young, R.W. and Droz, B. (1968). The renewal of protein in retinal rods and cones. *J. Cell Biol. 39*, 169–184.

Yunghans, W.N., Morre, D.J., Karin, N.J. and Werderitsh, D.A. (1979). Observations on the origins of plasma membrane in rat deciduoma. *Cell Tissue Res. 200*, 35–44.

Zinkler, D. (1974). Zum lipidmuster der photoreceptoren von insekten. *Verh. Dtsch. Zool. Ges. 67*, 28–32.

EPITHELIAL PHYSIOLOGY OF INSECT SENSILLA

Ulrich Thurm
Josef Küppers

Department of Zoology
University of Münster
Münster, FR Germany

I. PROBLEMS

The specifically sensitive structure of epidermal sensory
cells of insects is part of a modified cilium. These outer segments of the receptor cells retain the basic distribution of
functional elements which is characteristic of cilia: the organelles of energy supply accumulate beneath the base of the
cilium; the cilium itself remains an arrangement only of micro-
tubular- and membrane-bound structures (cf. Thurm, 1965 a,
1968, 1969). From the usual location of mitochondria in the vicinity of energy consuming membranes, and from the expected
identity of excitable membrane areas with areas for restoring
ion pump activity (suggested by the organization of axons), the
membrane of the inner segment of ciliated dendrites - rather
than that of the cilium itself - had been considered to be the
site of initiation and control of the receptor current. This
idea was supported by estimates which suggested that energizing
the receptor current by a pump mechanism located within the ciliary outer segment (e.g. of vertebrate rod-photoreceptors)
would be impeded by the limitation of ATP diffusion through the
ciliary neck (cf. Thurm, 1969, 1974 b). These considerations
called for an intracellular signal transmission to connect the
primary stimulus transduction in the modified cilium with the
membrane conductance change expected to take place basally of
the cilium. It was considered that conformational changes within the connecting microtubules (Thurm, 1968, Atema, 1973) or
mechanical microtubule properties (Moran and Varela, 1971)
might provide the missing signal transmission.

Two findings made on campaniform mechanoreceptors of flies
changed the line of reflection abruptly and considerably ten
years ago: (i) a large area of the apical membranes surrounding the outer receptor segment has a special particle covering
and a configuration characteristic of certain ion-secreting
membranes (Fig. 2) (Smith, 1969; Thurm, 1970) e.g. those of
the silkworm midgut which transport monovalent cations actively and electrogenically out of the cell ("K-transport",Harvey
and Nedergaard, 1964; Anderson and Harvey, 1966; Wood et al.,
1969; see also Harvey, this volume); (ii) there is a locally
high positive electrical potential (up to 100 mV) at the outside of sensilla (Thurm, 1970) which is acutely dependent upon
oxidative metabolism in the same way as the potential of the
electrogenically transporting epithelium in the silkworm midgut (Haskell et al., 1965). These discoveries resulted in a
re-evaluation of the ultrastructure of sensilla, with more attention being paid to non-neural cells than before and especially realizing that - according to the distribution of junctional
complexes - sensilla maintain an epithelial organization (Thurm,
1970). The long known fact was brought to mind that most types
of sensory cells are epithelial cells. The findings demanded
of us to open our receptor physiologist's minds to the knowledge of ion transporting epithelia which has accumulated. For
the problem of primary signal transmission within the receptor
cell epithelial physiology offered a simple solution but it
needed to accept a spatial distribution for receptor circuit
elements which has previously been unconventional in neurophysiology (with exception of the vertebrate cochlea: Davis, 1965;
for comparison with vertebrate photoreceptors see Thurm, 1974 b).

Recognizing the epithelial organization of sensilla sets
off the fact that the region of the receptor cell which receives the adequate stimulus is located outside the haemolymph
space of the body. In terrestrial insects it would face the air
if not shielded by the cuticular layer. This layer is a passive
structure and can only influence the spatial distribution of
the gradient of the water potential (Wigglesworth, 1941 a,
1945 c, 1948 f, 1957 a, 1958 a; Neville, 1975). It might be expected therefore that water and ions surrounding the critical
receptor region are supplied and their concentrations regulated
by the epithelium.

We shall survey here the main results obtained so far in
following up these facts and problems.

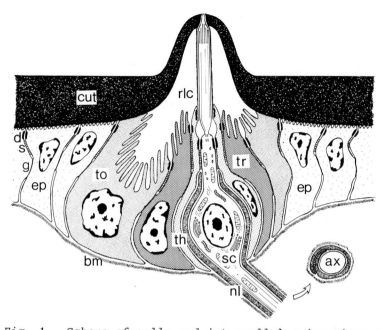

Fig. 1.   Scheme of cells and intercellular junctions of an insect sensillum; the outer segment characterized as that of a mechanoreceptor (drawing by Th. Keil).
ax: axon; bm: basement membrane; cut: cuticle; d: desmosome; ep: epidermis; g: gap junction; hl: haemolymph; nl: neurilemma cell; rlc: receptor lymph cavity; s: septate junction; sc: sensory cell; th: thecogen cell; to: tormogen cell; tr: trichogen cell.

II. EPITHELIAL ORGANIZATION OF INSECT SENSILLA

A. The Cells

In insect sensilla three, more rarely two, specialized non-neural epithelial cells surround one or several sensory neurons in rings. These non-neural epithelial cells are defined according to their morphogenetic function of secreting certain parts of the cuticular apparatus: the innermost thin ring of the thecogen cell (the last of these cells discovered and named: Schmidt and Gnatzy, 1971; Steinbrecht and Müller, 1976), further the trichogen and the tormogen cell (Fig. 1). In an example where only two of these cells are found in the fully developed state, Keil (1978) proved that the trichogen cell is lost during

the final stage of morphogenesis. A glial sheath cell regularly protrudes into this complex of epithelial cells but it does
not reach the borderline of the epithelial junctional complex.

B. The Junctional Complex

The intercellular membrane junctions have been a recognition mark to discern the epithelial arrangement of sensillum
cells (Thurm, 1970, 1972) in spite of the complicated cellular
configurations. The complex of septate junctions and desmosomes
(maculae adhaerentes) forms an apical belt between all cells of
a sensillum in the same way as between unspecialized epidermal
cells (Fig. 1). Thus the epidermal layer of interconnected
cells is continuous throughout the sensillum - a finding which
corresponds to the epidermal origin of the cells forming a sensillum (Henke and Rönsch, 1951; Lawrence, 1966). As judged from
morphological inspection, the junctional complex closes systematically all those often highly folded intercellular clefts
traversing the epithelial layer.

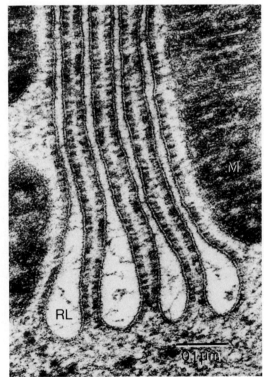

Fig. 2
Apical membrane of a tor-
mogen cell (campaniform
mechanoreceptor of Calli-
phora prepared by freeze
substitution; electron
micrograph by W. Völker).
M: mitochondrion; RL: re-
ceptor lymph space.

At the site of the sensillum the apical membranes of the corresponding cells separate from the cuticle and form a sub-cuticular space which is morphologically delimited by the bor-derline of the junctional complex from the haemolymph space: the receptor lymph cavity (Nicklaus et al., 1967). The ciliary segment of sensory cells partially surrounded by the thecogen cell protrudes into this cavity.

Gap junctions, which are known to establish low resistance intercellular pathways, have been found consistantly between all the non-neural cells of sensilla just as they are found be-tween epidermal cells (Fig. 1) (Keil, 1978; Keil and Thurm, 1979; Thurm et al., in prep. a) but they have never been found to connect a sensory cell to another epithelial cell. Thus a sensory cell is surrounded by an epithelial compartment of elec-trically interconnected cells (see Küppers and Thurm, 1979, Fig. 1).

The glial sheath cells (perineural cells), wrapping inner segment, soma and axon of the sensory cell, form a further plas-matic compartment separated from the epithelial one. It delimits a perineural space around all proximal parts of the sensory cell. This space is separated from the haemolymph space by sep-tate junctions closing the inter-sheath cell clefts (Keil and Thurm, 1979, Thurm et al., in prep. a; cf. Lane and Treherne, 1972).

C. The "Tightness" of the Epithelium

The electrophysiology of epithelial cells is crucially af-fected by the height of the transepithelial resistance of the paracellular pathway (i.e. of the intercellular clefts travers-ing the epithelium). The relation of this resistance to the pa-rallel resistance of the cells (the cellular pathway) decides whether the clefts constitute an appreciable shunt for electri-cal transport activities of the cells. For the sensory epithe-lium of cockroach antennae we found a specific transepithelial resistance of about 3,000 Ω cm² (determined as the difference of the resistance of epithelium plus cuticle minus the resist-ance of the isolated cuticle: Thurm et al., in prep. a; Thurm, 1974 a). This value is in the range of specific resistances of continuous cell membranes. In a comparative study Frömter and Diamond (1972) demonstrated that the transepithelial resistance of epithelia in which the transepithelial clefts contribute low resistance shunts ("leaky" junctions) ranges between 6 and 113 Ω cm². The value found for the insect epithelium, in con-trast, is close to the resistance range of 365 to 2,000 Ω cm² of the second group of epithelia in which no significant para-cellular shunts exist ("tight" epithelia). From these results

we conclude that in insect sensilla the prevailing amount of
transepithelial current flows across the cell membranes. Such
currents therefore contribute to membrane voltages according
to Ohm's law, independently of the location of their sources.

In a study on the location and the nature of the current
and diffusion barriers within the transepithelial clefts, we
found that the diffusion of extracellular ionic lanthanum
(5-10 mM/l) in the living state of the epithelium is strongly
slowed down within the septate junctions (Fig. 3) (Keil and
Thurm, 1979; Thurm et al., in prep. a; cf. Keil, 1979).Although
La^{3+} invades these junctions, it does not pass them within
60 min if applied from the haemolymph side only. Also the peri-

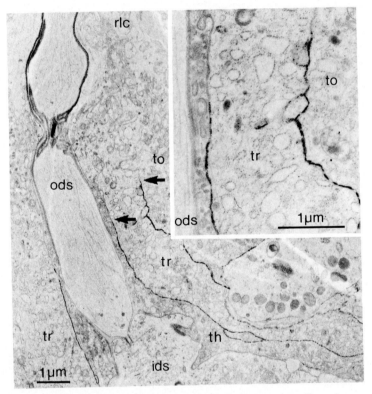

Fig. 3. Quasistationary distribution of La^{3+} within the
intercellular clefts of a tibial hair sensillum of Acheta after
40 min invasion (in vitro) from the haemolymph side (preparation and electron micrograph by Th. Keil). Arrow heads: most
apical location of La-deposit within septate junction;
ids: inner dendritic segment; ods: outer dendritic segment;
rlc: receptor lymph space; th: thecogen cell; to: tormogen cell;
tr: trichogen cell.

neural space around the afferent axons proves to be closed towards the haemolymph space (cf. Lane and Treherne, 1972), with
exception - at least in several mechanoreceptors of flies and
crickets - that these spaces are interconnected via the cleft
between epithelial and perineural cells.

Since the physiological importance of membrane junctions is
comparable to that of cell membranes, their neglect in schematic representations of sensory epithelia is equivalent to incomplete membrane representations.

D. The "Cable" Properties

The spatial distribution of voltages within the plane of an
insect sensory epithelium can be understood only by considering
the network of resistances constituted by the epidermis as a
whole (see Thurm and Wessel, 1979, Fig. 1). From a point-like
transepithelial electrical source, voltage and current spread
in the plane of the epithelium according to the ratio of resistance within this plane to those traversing the epithelium.
The network can be considered as a two-dimensional cable. The
spread of voltage and current in this case is described by a
Bessel-function. This theoretical expectation has been confirmed for sensilla of caterpillars of the waxmoth $Galleria$ (Erler
and Thurm, in prep.; Thurm, 1974 a). The long radial spread of
voltage (radial length $\lambda_{1/2}$ for voltage decay to half the source
value: several 100 µm) found in these larval objects, which
have a cuticle of little density, is, however, contrasted by
$\lambda_{1/2}$ in the range of 10 µm in the integument of the imaginal
type (measured at the haltere of $Calliphora$). The imaginal-type
cuticle obviously functions as an isolator where it surrounds
a sensillum: there is a ring of special contact between epithelial cells and cuticle which is tight for the diffusion of La^{3+};
that diffusion is unimpeded, in contrast, in the cleft beneath
the unspecialized cuticle outside this ring of contact (Thurm
et al., in prep. a). Experiments indicate that by this arrangement of resistances the area of epithelium to which a cell of
a sensillum has electrical access is approximately as small as
the membrane area of the sensillum itself. Therefore the load
resistance connected to the local electrical sources of a sensillum is high enough to allow appreciable local voltage (see
below; for details see Thurm and Wessel, 1979). Coating the
cuticular surface around a sensillum by an electrolyte-deter-
gent mixture which shunts the isolation of the cuticle, nearly
abolishes the local voltage at the site of the sensillum as
well as the transepithelial receptor potential.

III. EPITHELIAL ION TRANSPORT IN INSECT SENSILLA

A. *Metabolism-dependent Transepithelial Voltage*

The local increase of transepithelial voltage (TEV) of 20 to 100 mV discovered in campaniform mechanoreceptors of the fly as mentioned above, has been found to be a universal property of insect sensilla, from apterygotes to hemi- and holometabola (Fig. 4) (Thurm and Wessel, 1979). Its occurrence is independent of the modality of stimuli for which a sensillum is specialized; some probability of finding higher voltages in mechano- than in chemoreceptors exists. The sensillum-bound voltage source is easily characterized by its acute oxygen dependence, which is not paralleled by any voltage change across the sensilla-free epidermis. This dependence on oxidative metabolism (Küppers and Thurm, 1979) is one piece of evidence for its origin by active transport and can be used to distinguish an active component form possible diffusion and Donnan potentials. Large differences between the voltage amplitude of different types of sensilla (e.g. 20 versus 80 mV) occur often within one and the same specimen, inversely correlated with the distance between neighbouring sensilla (cf. voltage spread around sensilla, above).

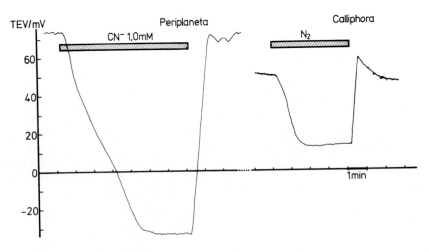

Fig. 4.   *Time course of transepithelial voltage at a cercal mechanosensitive thread hair of* Periplaneta *and a labellar gustatory hair of* Calliphora *enclosing a period of blocked oxidative metabolism.*

B. Evidence for Active Ion Transport

If the TEV is clamped to zero, sensilla supply a short-circuit current (SCC) as long as their metabolism is active. The same result has been obtained when identical solutions were applied on both sides of a sensory epithelium (cockroach antenna: Küppers and Thurm, 1979). The SCC has the same acute dependence on oxidative metabolism as the TEV. Although the access to the receptor lymph cavity was hindered in this experiment by the cuticle, considering the quantitative circumstances these results demonstrate clearly that the basis of the electric source involves active ion transport.

C. The Site of Ion Transport

For campaniform sensilla of the fly's haltere the measured SCC of 0.3 nA per sensillum is a lower limit of its activity.

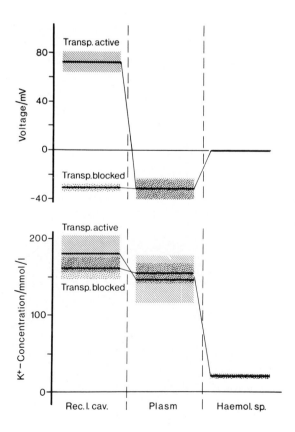

Fig. 5
Electrical potential (reference within the haemolymph space; upper diagram) and K^+ activity (calibrated by standard concentrations; lower diagram) within the receptor lymph cavity, the cytoplasmic compartment of tormogen and trichogen cells, and the haemolymph space of cercal thread hairs of Periplaneta *during active transport and during transport blocked by blockage of oxidative metabolism (1 mM/l CN^-). Mean values and standard deviation (hatched or stippled zones, respectively) of six sensilla. Haemolymph space perfused by ringer solution (Pichon, 1970).*

Only in relating this current to the highly folded apical membrane of the tormogen cell one arrives at a current density (10 $\mu A/cm^2$) which is not much higher than any other known density of active transport currents (Thurm, 1974 a). It has been possible recently to measure the transepithelial potential profile for the large tormogen-trichogen cell compartment of cercal thread hairs of *Periplaneta* (Fig. 5) (Küppers, in prep.). A particularly high voltage step (about 100 mV) indeed is found across the apical cytomembrane. Solely this step exhibits the acute metabolism-dependence, thus indicating the location of transport activity within this membrane. Similar results have been obtained by Wood et al. (1969) in the K^+-transporting silkworm midgut.

The special apical membrane is studded by roughly 5,000 particles per μm^2 on its cytoplasmic side and is associated with a high concentration of mitochondria (Fig. 2). Many comparative observations suggest the particle coat to be functionally correlated with the special transport activity. In ultrastructural studies of several sensilla the membrane particles have not been found. Since these structures proved to be more labile than the membrane proper, and since the metabolism-dependent voltage component has been found in all types of insect sensillum tested so far, the statement of their absence needs to be confirmed by reliable quick-freezing preparatory methods.

During the periodic morphogenetic phases of hemimetabolous insects the apical membrane areas of tormogen and trichogen cells become extremely reduced and model the sculpture of the cuticular parts which they secrete (e.g. Schmidt and Gnatzy, 1971; Gnatzy and Schmidt, 1972; Gnatzy, 1978). This periodic morphogenetic function of this membrane induced some doubt whether also in hemimetabolous insects this membrane region can be the site of intensive ion transport. Thurm and Gnatzy studied cercal mechano- and chemoreceptors of *Gryllus* to see whether a metabolism-dependent voltage component might be consistent with morphogenetic activity (Thurm, 1974 a; Gnatzy, 1978; Gnatzy and Thurm, in prep.). A strong decay of absolute and metabolism-dependent TEV began with apolysis and nearly reached zero 2 days before ecdysis. Thus, the TEV indeed reflects the conspicuous change in the structural and functional state of these membranes.

D. *The Type of Ion Transport*

The ultrastructural analogy between the apical tormogen membrane and the apical membrane of silkworm midgut cells was the first indication that active transport within sensilla might be of the type of the electrogenic K^+-outward-transport intensively studied in the midgut by Harvey, Zerahn and coworkers (references see chapter I). Thus the apical tormogen-trichogen membrane is suggested to transport monovalent cations, preferably K^+, from the plasm into the receptor lymph cavity. The electrogenic nature of this transport type easily explains the steep and synchronous change in TEV and SCC which occurs during the switching on of metabolism and transport after a period of anoxia (Fig. 4 and Thurm, 1974 a, Fig. 2 and 6; see also Küppers and Thurm, 1979, Fig. 5); ΔTEV of 58 mV within 10 s at cercal receptors of *Acheta*. A transport-flux dependent (rheogenic) voltage-increase needs, as a minimum, only that number of ions transported which is necessary to charge the membrane capacity. Synchronous measurements of K^+ activity and TEV within the receptor lymph cavity of cockroach cercal hairs during this switching phase indeed reveal that the voltage increase occurs without a simultaneous significant change in K^+ activity (Fig. 5; Küppers, recent unpublished measurements), although this activity principally depends on the transport and the TEV also depends on the K^+ gradient (see below).

Also characteristic features of transport are similar in sensilla, as studied in the perfused cockroach antenna, and in the silkworm midgut (Küppers and Thurm, in prep.; Thurm, 1974 a; Harvey et al., 1968; Nedergaard and Harvey, 1968; Zerahn, 1971). The transport cannot be influenced by the inhibitor of the Na-K-transport, Ouabain or by the inhibitor of carboanhydrase, acetazolamide. The transport is independent of the kind of anions present basally or apically of the epithelium. The transport is strongly reduced by K^+ deprivation at the basal side of the epithelium, whereas it works well with only KCl on both sides. Only NH_4^+ can substitute for K^+ in the normal state of the cockroach epithelium. If Ca^{2+} and Mg^{2+} are removed from the basal side, however, the transport is unspecifically sustained by all alkali-ions from Li^+ to Rb^+ at the basal side.

From these various results we conclude that in both systems the same type of transport mechanism works which has been specified to perform a purely electrogenic cation-outward-flux. Measurements of the ionic composition of the receptor lymph suggest that K^+ is preferably transported (see below).

E. *The Transport-Current Circuit*

In contrast to several other K^+-transporting epithelia, in sensilla the luminal space into which ions are transported is a closed and small cavity. Nevertheless the transport appears to work continuously in the stationary state of the system, whether the receptor cells are stimulated or resting. Several pieces of evidence suggest this continuous activity:

1. If oxidative metabolism is blocked abruptly by anoxia,
the free running TEV decays with a time source very similar to
that of the SCC (within about 1 min in the fly) (cf. Thurm,
1974 a, Fig. 2 and 6).

2. According to the load conductance of the epithelium
accessible within a sensillum (around 10^{-7} Ω^{-1}) and the electrochemical K^+ gradient a continuous discharging K^+ current of
some nA will result and must be compensated by a continuous
loading current during the stationary normal TEV. In this state
the distribution of K^+ across the apical tormogen membrane is
far from equilibrium (Fig. 5). In thread hair sensilla of the
cockroach a membrane voltage of 100 mV (outside positive) contrasts with an insignificantly small K^+ gradient across this
membrane (cytoplasm $\cong$ 170 mM/receptor lymph $\cong$ 180 mM; Küppers,
in prep.). K^+ activities of receptor lymph and haemolymph are
compared for two other systematic groups in Fig. 6. For the
fly a transepithelial equilibrium potential for K^+ of -65 mV
contrasts with a TEV of +50 to +100 mV during transport activity (with reference to haemolymph) (Küppers, 1974). Kaissling
and Thorson (1980) found the K^+ concentrations to be not much
higher than the activities.

3. If NH_4^+ is substituted for K^+ at the haemolymph side,
the K^+ activity within the receptor lymph decays during transport activity (Küppers, in prep.).

These results indicate that during transport activity a dynamic equilibrium exists between an active K^+-outward-transport
flux and a passive downhill flux. In the inactive state (blocked
metabolism) K^+ activity within the receptor lymph is stable at
about the value of the active state (Fig. 5; Küppers, in prep.)
as is to be expected from the small concentration gradient and
the fading voltage across the apical membrane. Consistent with
this transport-current circuit is the monotonous strong temperature dependence of the TEV in the active state of the transport and its very small, non-monotonous dependence during anoxia
(Thurm, 1974 a and in prep.). A quantitative analysis of this
current circuit is hampered by the fact that anoxia and temperature not only change transport activity but also strongly affect passive membrane conductance (Thurm, 1974 a; Gödde, 1978;
Küppers and Thurm, 1979).

For Cl^- the transepithelial equilibrium potential has been
found to be -25 mV in campaniform receptors of the fly (78 and
28 mM/l in haemo- and receptor lymph, respectively; Küppers,
1974). In spite of the difference of this E_{Cl} to a TEV of
> +50 mV, Cl^- may be passively distributed since a higher con-
centration of impermeable organic ions within the receptor lymph
is conceivable (see Kaissling and Thorson, 1980). Although the
activity of Na^+ in the receptor lymph (concentration 25 mM/l
in silkmoth antennal hairs; Kaissling and Thorson, 1980) appears

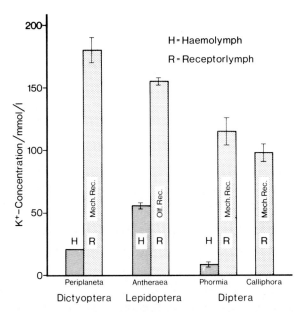

Fig. 6
K$^+$ activity (calibrat-
ed by standard concen-
trations) within re-
ceptor lymph of three
types of sensilla of
three groups of in-
sects as compared to
corresponding values
of haemolymph (cercal
thread hairs of Peri-
planeta, *antennal ol-*
factory hairs of An-
theraea *measured in*
collaboration with
K.E. Kaissling, and
campaniform mechano-
receptors of flies).
Mean values and stan-
dard errors of the
mean; mean value of
haemolymph of Periplaneta *according to Pichon (1970).*

to be much lower than of K$^+$, it is probably higher than follows
from purely passive distribution. The same is to be expected
for Ca^{++} and, perhaps, H$^+$ which otherwise would have acitivities
about 3-4 and 2 decades, respectively, lower than within the
cytoplasm. However, data are lacking for these ions so far.

F. Effect of Ion Transport on Water Potential Distribution

Control of the water potential gradient across the apical
membranes may be one of the functions of epithelial ion transport at sensilla. This is suggested especially by the structural
and functional analogies which exist between the tormogen (and,
eventually, trichogen) cell of sensilla, on the one hand, and
the cells of the posterior rectum of Lepismatidae, on the other
(see Küppers and Thurm, this volume). The latter are devoted to
stabilizing a non-equilibrium state between the high water potential of the animal and the lower of the atmospheric environment. The electroosmotic ion-water coupling found to occur in
that epithelium which is energized apparently by electrogenic
K$^+$ transport encourages us to test the transport-current circuit
of sensilla for a similar electroosmotic function. However, in
contrast to the very low water potential of the subcuticular

space of the posterior rectum which causes a net uptake of water
from the atmosphere,in sensilla the main component of the huge
difference in water potential between atmosphere and cytoplasm
apparently lies across the epicuticle, according to our experimental experience and measurements at isolated lymphatic fluid
by Kaissling and Thorson (1980).

An electroosmotic force might allow some evaporation of the
receptor lymph while the regular high water potential within the
receptor terminal and the sheath cells is maintained. Polyan-
ionic material found within the receptor lymph cavity (Gnatzy
and Weber, 1978; Keil, 1979) should guarantee the fluidity of
the lymph also at a lowered water potential. If polyanions are
fixed within the cavity the effective water potential would be
lower than that of the isolated fluid.

By coupling between water and ions in the receptor pores an
outward-directed water potential gradient will reduce the in-
ward-directed driving force of the receptor current. The significance of this effect for sensitivity of the receptor is proportional to the pressure gradient and to the number of water
molecules passing the channels together with one ion (the coupling ratio, see Küppers and Thurm, this volume).

At a receptor membrane with the pores permanently open, this
effect might sufficiently modulate the driving force for the receptor current to produce the current response of a water receptor (i.e. a gustatory receptor measuring the water concentration of a stimulating solution) and of hygroreceptors if the
coupling ratio is especially high (10 - 100 H_2O/e_o). Rees has
proposed a similar principle (1970, 1972) and reported some evidence but assumed the improbable contrary direction of the water
gradient.

Epithelial transport in sensilla can be controlled by serotonin and by (so far unspecified) extracts of neurosecretory organs as studied on the cockroach antenna (Küppers and Thurm,
1975). The hormone sensitivity which appears to be mediated by
cAMP relates this transport to that of organs of water transport
(Malpighian tubules and salivary glands: Berridge, 1971; Maddrell et al., 1971) which exhibit a comparable humoral control.
It also relates to effects which probably are due to increases
in hydrostatic pressure in the receptor lymph cavity: the opening of gustatory hairs of locusts controlled by the feeding
state of the animal (Bernays and Chapman, 1972) and the secretion of fluid through the cuticular wall of sensilla observed
in various insects following states of strong excitation of the
animals (Küppers and Thurm, 1975).

IV. THE RECEPTOR CURRENT CIRCUIT IN INSECT SENSILLA

Only selected problems can be touched upon in the following brief survey. The circuit diagram used will be schematic since quantitative data have not been determined for single circuit elements. Estimations on the basis of morphological data are hampered by the fact that the applicability of mean specific membrane parameters is uncertain for highly specialized membrane regions.

A. *The Conducting Pathways*

The electron microscopic results suggest the existence of two parallel pathways traversing the epithelium via the sensory (S-channel) and the non-neural cells (T-channel), respectively. These channels are connected apically by the receptor lymph and basally by the haemolymph, via the basolateral cell membranes. Their separation within the epithelium is strongly suggested by the absence of gap junctions between sensory and the surrounding epithelial cell; whereas the existence of gap junctions between all surrounding cells und the unspecialized epithelial cells suggests their consideration as a single non-neural pathway. The high specific resistance of the epithelium being in the range of that of membranes (see II C) suggests interpreting the properties of the pathways as those of the membranes engaged. I.e., a transepithelial electrical measurement is comparable to an intracellular measurement as there is no significant extracellular shunt between the electrodes. With appropriate electrode positions and a voltage clamp device, most transepithelial receptor current can be recorded. It will be shown that the biologically relevant component of the receptor current indeed takes the transepithelial pathway.

B. *The Basic Configuration of the Receptor Current Circuit*

Results on the receptor current circuit have been obtained for campaniform mechanoreceptors of the fly's haltere (Thurm, 1970, 1972, 1974 a; Thurm and Gödde, in prep.), hair mechanoreceptors of the head of the locust and olfactory hairs of a bug (Bernard and Guillet, 1972) and of silkmoths (Kaissling and Thorson, 1980) and for bristle mechanoreceptors of the fly's thorax (Gödde, 1978; Thurm et al., in prep. b; morphology: Keil, 1978). For the latter large sensillum it has been possible to obtain direct electrical access to the receptor lymph cavity by three different methods, reducing resistances which may lie in

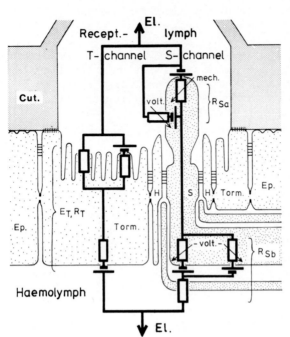

Fig. 7
*Equivalent circuit of
a mechanosensitive
sensillum; cable pro-
perties of epithelium
and axon neglected.
Cut.: cuticle, El.:
electrodes; Ep.: un-
specialized epidermal
cell; H.: thecogen
cell; S.: sensory cell;
Torm.: tormogen and
trichogen cell; mech.:
mechanically controlled
resistance; E_T, R_T:
effective electromotive
force and resistance,
resp., of the T-chan-
nel; R_{Sa}, R_{Sb}: effective apical and basal
resistances, resp., of
the S-channel.*

series to the epithelium to a negligible amount and measuring
transepithelially through the area of a single sensillum by voltage or current clamp. The following statements therefore refer
mainly to data upon this sensillum but the conclusions represented by Fig. 7 are compatible also with the particular results
on other sensilla.

1. A variable conductance which is controlled by the adequate stimulus is accessible transepithelially. The extent of
its increase (up to $1.2 \cdot 10^{-8}$ S; Fig. 8) is adequate to induce
nervous impulses within the sensory cell due to an inward current which is driven by the voltage sources present (see 3.).
We interpret the conductance change to occur within the sensory
cell (g_S) and the current to be the receptor current as is suggested also by the correlation of its time course to that of
spike frequency (Fig.9). The current is measured by transepithelial voltage clamp at the regular TEV to amount to about 10^{-9} A
during maximal phasic responses (ΔI_{sat}). The stimulus-controlled
conductance is open for alkali and alkali earth cations with
little specifity (as studied in the fly mechanoreceptor: Kastrup,
Vohwinkel, and Thurm, to be published). Thus the inward receptor current should be carried mainly by K^+ according to the
ionic composition of the receptor lymph (see III E).

2. The variable conductance g_S controlled by the adequate

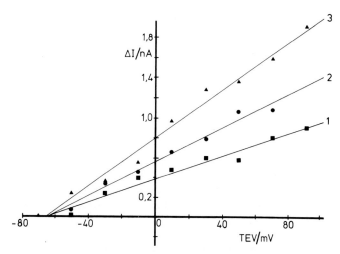

Fig. 8. Phasic peak amplitudes of transepithelial current responses (ΔI) to three different stimulus intensities (Stim. 1-3) as a function of clamped transepithelial voltage (TEV). Bristle mechanoreceptors at the metathorax of Calliphora; *bending stimuli. (Measurements by B. Vohwinkel) Endogenous TEV at +20 mV. Each point is the mean of six records. Linear regression lines.*

stimulus lies in series to an electromotive force (E_S) of about −60 mV: the current via this conductance becomes zero on clamping the TEV to this voltage (equilibrium potential) (Fig. 8). The receptor current (measured by voltage clamp) is driven by the difference between the transepithelial net emf (E_T, caused by the associated ion transport, see III B) and E_S: ($E_T − E_S$)Δg = ΔI; for the bristle mechanoreceptor (representative values): (25 mV + 60 mV) · 1.2 · 10^{-8} S = 10^{-9} A for saturated responses. The main component of E_S probably is located across the basal membrane of the receptor cell (K^+ equilibrium potential) since the concentration gradients of Na^+ and K^+ across the apical membrane must be small, due to the ionic composition of the receptor lymph (see III E, Fig. 5 and 6), compared to that of usual cytoplasm. Nevertheless, some evidence suggests that a smaller inwardly directed emf (or 2 different parallel emfs) exists across the apical receptor membrane (cf. Thurm, 1974 a; Kastrup, personal communication). The receptor potential amplitude depends on the activity of oxidative metabolism, as does the ion transport of the T-channel (see III B). In contrast, the stimulus-induced conductance and the equilibrium potential depend less acutely on metabolism. Therefore the receptor potential amplitude can be reconstituted during blocked transport by an exogenous current source (Thurm, 1970, 1972, 1974 a). This indicates that the transport source of the non-neural cells is enclosed in the receptor current circuit. The relation between transport activity and receptor potential, however, is complicated by increases in R_T which are caused by blocking the metabolism (Thurm, 1974 a; Küppers and Thurm, 1979) as well as by lowering the temperature (Gödde, 1978).

3. The transepithelial voltage response of the sensillum, called the receptor potential (e.g. Morita, 1959; Wolbarsht, 1960), can be predicted from above parameters of sources and current response if the resistance of the T-channel R_T (measured as total transepithelial resistance of the sensillum in its un-stimulated state) is included into the pathway of outward flow of the receptor current according to the basic scheme of the equivalent circuit of Fig. 7. For this circuit the voltage change caused by an increase in conductance of the S-channel is described by:

$$\Delta U = \frac{\Delta I \cdot R_T (E_T - E_S)}{\Delta I \cdot R_T + E_T - E_S} \quad \text{(since } \Delta g_S = \Delta I / (E_T - E_S), \text{ see above)}$$

For the representative values of saturating responses used above and R_T = 6 MΩ, as correspondingly found, the equation yields ΔU = 5.6 mV. This corresponds to measured values of about 6 mV. Thus, this equivalent circuit seems to describe the functional structure of a sensillum adequately at the present level of analysis.

The maximal receptor potential amplitude in most sensilla studied amounts to less than 30 % of the voltage difference $E_T - E_S$. This can be attributed to the fact that during maximal stimulation, R_S still remains considerably larger than R_T as found in all sensilla studied by voltage or current clamp of their responses (4 different mechanoreceptors) or by changes in total resistance (Kaissling and Thorson, 1980, for an olfactory receptor). Correspondingly the receptor current is found to be proportional to the voltage response (within the limits of ex-perimental accuracy) for all amplitudes of stimuli (Fig. 9) (Gödde, 1978; Kaissling and Thorson, 1980; Thurm et al., in prep. b). The factor of proportionality is found in our measure-ments to be equal to R_T. This corresponds to the possibility of reducing above equation to $\Delta U \cong \Delta I \cdot R_T$ as far as $\Delta I \cdot R_T$ is considered to be small with respect to $E_T - E_S$.

4. The finding $R_S > R_T$ for all intensities of stimuli is paralleled by the ratio between the membrane area of the sen-sory cell on the one hand and the much larger area of the non-neural cells on the other. Within the pathway via the sensory cell (S-channel), apparently it is the basal membrane region in series with the resistance of the perineural shielding (com-

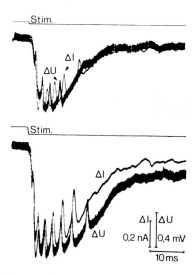

Fig. 9
*Superimposed records of correspond-
ing transepithelial voltage (ΔU)
and current (ΔI) responses to mechanical stimuli (Stim.) of two different intensities; equal calibration
as indicated for responses to both
stimulus intensities. TEV = 40 mV
for both modes of record. Superimposed ΔU and ΔI recorded for consecutive stimuli of equal intensity.
Different time courses of adaptation
of ΔU and ΔI during stronger stimulus probably due to the difference
in membrane voltage which occurs
necessarily between free running
(ΔU) and clamped voltage (ΔI) (see
Gödde, 1978, for effect of TEV on
adaptation). Records by B. Vohwinkel
from a bristle mechanoreceptor at the metathorax of Calliphora.
Nervous impulses as usual superimposed on the receptor current
and voltage.*

prised as R_{Sb}) which limits the conductance during strong stimuli. This is suggested by the large range of stimulus controlled
conductance changes (to be ascribed to R_{Sa}) spanning about four
decades as determined indirectly from differently adapted stimulus-response curves of hair plate mechanoreceptors (Thurm,
1965 b). From that study a strongly non-linear relation between
the voltage response ΔU and the stimulus controlled conductance
g_{Sa} can be deduced. This contrasts to the practically linear
relation found between ΔU and g_S (the conductance of g_{Sa} and
g_{Sb} in series). This points to $g_{Sa} > g_{Sb}$ during strong stimuli.

Also the resistance of the apical cuticular sheath and of
the apical part of the thecogen cell, both surrounding the outer
receptor segment in mechano- and gustatory receptors, must be
subsumed to g_{Sb}. These structures apparently do not contribute
an electrically significant shielding of the receptor terminal
(cf. Barth, 1971); otherwise the electrical phenomena of sensilla should be different from those observerd and could not
be described by the equivalent circuit of Fig. 7. This conclusion agrees with the plain access of La- and ruthenium-red ions
from the receptor lymph to the total apical receptor membrane
(Keil, 1979; Thurm et al., in prep. a).

C. *The Coupling of the Spike Generator to the Receptor Current*

From the polarity of transepithelially recorded nerve impulses, which is inverse with respect to the depolarizing receptor potential, and from the ratio of the amplitudes of these types of response (Fig. 9) it has long been concluded that the pacemaker of spikes is located basally of a high resistance which is extracellular with respect to the sensory cell (e.g. Morita and Yamashita, 1959; Wolbarsht, 1960; Thurm, 1963). This resistance and diffusion barrier indicated also by a local effect of apically applied Tetrodotoxin (Wolbarsht and Hanson, 1965; Erler and Thurm, 1978 and submitted), is identified by the electrical measurements and tracer results (see II) to be the apical cell membranes of a sensillum, its system of septate junctions, and the surrounding cuticle. The pacemaker zone is accessible to transepithelial current in a way consistent with such a location basally of the epithelial borderline: inward current (depolarizing the basal neural membrane) increases a spike frequency elicited by an adequate stimulus (Fig. 10) (Wolbarsht, 1958; Guillet and Bernard, 1972; Maes, 1977; Erler and Thurm, 1978 and submitted).

The transepithelial access to the pacemaker zone is gated by the stimulus controlled conductance; in several or most types of sensilla transepithelial current elicits impulses only during adequate stimulation of the receptor (Erler and Thurm, 1978; Thurm and Gödde, in prep.; cf. Maes, 1977). The resting conductance is so low and the sensitivity of the pacemaker membrane so high (Maes, 1977) as to make it conceivable that the opening of a single apical membrane pore of an elementary conductance of some 10 pS (as known from postsynaptic membranes, see Neher and Stevens, 1977) may elicit a spike (cf. Kaissling and Thorson, 1980).

For these sensilla the receptor current to pacemaker coupling is adequately described by the equivalent circuit of Fig. 7 (ignoring time-dependent processes). This circuit predicts a multiplicative interaction between the TEV and the conductance of the S-channel g_S: $(TEV - E_S) \cdot \Delta g_S = \Delta I$. Since the impulse frequency F is roughly proportional to the amplitude ΔU of transepithelial receptor potentials (comparing equal times after an increase of the stimulus) (e.g. Wolbarsht, 1960; Thurm, 1962) and $\Delta U \propto \Delta I$ as reported above (IV B 3) latter equation can be written $(TEV - E_S) \cdot \Delta g_S \propto \Delta F$ or $\Delta F / \Delta TEV \propto g_S$; i.e. the effect of increasing the spike frequency due to an increase in the outside positive TEV is amplified by intensification of the stimulus which augments g_S. Vice versa, an increase in postive TEV should amplify the frequency response to a given stimulus. Since at a given $(TEV - E_S)$ the conductance g_S is proportional to F as mentioned before, $\Delta F / \Delta TEV \propto F$ should be found. This propor-

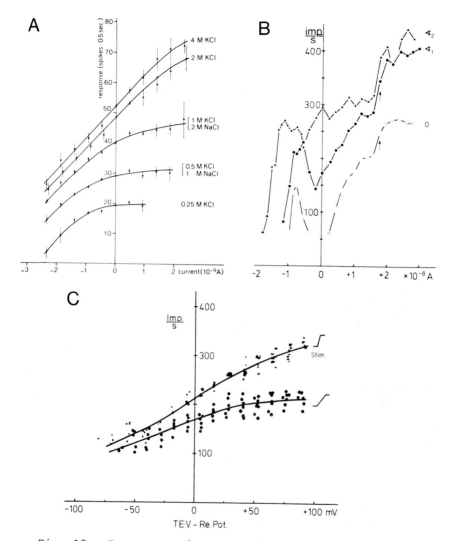

Fig. 10. *Frequency of nervous impulses as a function of transepithelial current (A, B) or voltage (C) and intensity of adequate stimuli. A: labellar salt receptor of* Calliphora, *stimuli as indicated (from Maes, 1977); B: tibial hair mechanoreceptor of* Acheta, *two different bending stimuli (⚥ 1, ⚥ 2) and without stimulus (0) (from Erler and Thurm, submitted); C: phasic campaniform mechanoreceptor at the haltere of* Calliphora, *compressional stimuli of two different speeds of increase, apical electrode with low resistance to the receptor lymph space (Thurm and Gödde, in prep.). Relative portions of the injected current passing the receptor cell are probably small and different in A and B.*

tionality indeed describes the data reported by Maes (1977) for
gustatory receptors of the fly fairly well (around zero transepithelial current) and is found (with some complications, see
below) also for mechanoreceptors of the fly (Erler and Thurm,
1978; Thurm and Gödde, in prep.).

Two effects complicate the dependence of spike frequency on
the TEV (Erler and Thurm, 1978 and submitted):

i) Not only the basal membrane region of the sensory cell
is electrically excitable and generates spikes but in many sensilla also the apical region (outer segment)(e.g. Morita and
Yamashita, 1959; Thurm, 1963; Wolbarsht and Hanson, 1965; Guillet and Bernard, 1972). Since the effect of a transepithelial
current is opposite at the apical receptor membrane to that at
the basal the dependence of the spike frequency on the TEV becomes complicated as far as the apical spike generation interferes with the basal pacemaker zone.At stronger depolarizations
of the epithelium a reversal of the TEV-dependence of spike frequency occurs as the apical membrane of the sensory cell becomes
the pacemaker zone itself (Fig. 10 B).

ii) Besides the latter electrically controlled conductance
of the apical receptor membrane which has been shown to be Na-
dependent, a Na^+-independent stationary conductance of this membrane is "open" during absence of adequate stimuli in some mechanoreceptors (cf. Guillet and Bernard, 1972). The voltage dependence of this conductance probably is the cause for a non-
linear (rectifying) dependence of spike frequency on the TEV in
the absence of an adequate stimulus. The rectifying property becomes still stronger as additional conductance is evoked by the
adequate stimulus; until, at stronger stimuli, the high spike
frequency can become fully independent of an increase of the
positive TEV, whereas a negativation of the TEV diminishes the
spike frequency (Fig. 10 B). Similar but weaker rectifying properties of the outer segment conductance may be rather ubiquitous in insect sensilla (cf. Fig. 10 C) and are partially time-
dependent (cf. Fig. 9).

The reduction in TEV which occurs during a moulting period
(see III D) may diminish the over-all sensitivity of a sensillum. The above variations and non-linearity in spike generation
and considerable differences in other electrical parameters of
the particular sensilla indicate that general predictions on
corresponding changes in sensitivity are impossible at present
(cf. Wigglesworth, 1953 b; Moran et al., 1976; Gnatzy and Tautz,
1977).

V. CONCLUSIONS

Consideration of the epithelial organization of insect sensilla provides a unifying concept for many functional and structural findings and problems. It makes a quantitative prediction of the electrical behaviour of these sensory elements possible. Since the general aspects of epithelial organization of sensilla are not unique, sensilla may be models for more complex sensory organs.

The receptor current traversing the sensory cell in a transepithelial direction connects the stimulus-receiving apical receptor region, which probably contains the current modulator (exposed to the receptor lymph), to the basal receptor region, which supplies energy metabolism and, probably, ion transport and a voltage source (surrounded by the perineural or haemolymph). In this latter region the receptor current elicits nervous impulses.

The epithelial organization of insect sensilla joins the sensory cell(s) and the surrounding specialized epithelial cells in a functional unit. The non-neural cells and, eventually, other sensory cells of the same sensillum constitute the pathway which closes the receptor current circuit outside the particular receptor cell. In this path an electrogenic ion transport performed by non-neural cells is enclosed. This ion transport contributes to the sensory function of a sensillum:

a) It determines the ionic composition of the receptor lymph by elevating its K^+ concentration. This leads probably to similar compositions of the receptor current (predominantly K^+) as it enters and as it leaves the sensory cell. Thus a change of cation concentrations within the cell during the current flow should be reduced.

b) The outside positive transepithelial voltage generated by this transport is an energetic contribution of non-neural cells to the receptor function. It produces an intensification of the receptor current by about 1.3 to 2.3 times (varying with the transepithelial resistance and voltage of sensilla) as compared to the alternative of an assumed epithelial receptor-surrounding of negligible resistance and no voltage contribution. This increase in current intensity can be found to be reflected in an increased sensitivity of the spike response of the sensory cell; in detail this effect is subject, as mentioned above, to the properties of the special sensory cell considered.

c) The outside positive TEV generated by the non-neural cells opens up the possibility that some water potential gradient may be sustained across the apical membranes of a sensillum.

ACKNOWLEDGMENTS

This work has been supported by grants of the Deutsche Forschungsgemeinschaft. Its achievement is due to the co-operation
with Dr. G. Erler, Dr. Th. Keil, J. Gödde, H. Kastrup, and B.
Vohwinkel to whom we address our appreciation. We are indebted
to Mrs. I. Beständig for typing the manuscript, to Miss I. Bunse
for careful technical assistance and for drawing of figures,
and to H. Meschede and J. Weil for building of mechanical and
electronic equipment.

REFERENCES

Anderson, E., and Harvey, W.R. (1966). Active transport by the Cecropia midgut. II. Fine structure of the midgut epithelium. *J. Cell. Biol. 31*, 107-134.

Atema, J. (1973). Microtubule theory of sensory transduction. *J. theor. Biol. 38*, 181-190.

Barth, F.G. (1971). Der sensorische Apparat der Spaltsinnesorgane (*Cupiennius salei* Keys., *Araneae*). *Z. Zellforsch. 112*, 212-246.

Bernard, J., and Guillet, J.C. (1972). Changes in the receptor potential under polarizing currents in two insect receptors. *J. Insect Physiol. 18*, 2173-2187.

Bernays, E.A., and Chapman, R.F. (1972). The control of changes in peripheral sensilla associated with feeding in *Locusta migratoria* (L.). *J. Exp. Biol. 57*, 755-763.

Berridge, M.J., and Prince, W.T. (1971). The electrical response of isolated salivary glands during stimulation with 5-hydroxytryptamine and cyclic AMP. *Phil. Trans. Roy. Soc. Lond. B. 262*, 111-120.

Davis, H. (1965). A model for transducer action in the cochlea. *Cold Spring Harbor Symp. Quant. Biol. 30*, 181-189.

Erler, G., and Thurm, U. (1977). Eine vereinfachte Methode zur Ableitung von Rezeptorpotentialen und Nervenimpulsen epidermaler Mechanorezeptoren von Insekten. *Z. Naturforsch. 32 c*, 1029-1030.

Erler, G., and Thurm, U. (1978). Die Impulsantwort epithelialer Rezeptoren in Abhängigkeit von der transepithelialen Potentialdifferenz. *Verh. Dtsch. Zool. Ges. 71*, 279.

Erler, G., and Thurm, U. Dendritic impulse initiation in an epithelial sensory neuron. (submitted).

Erler, G., and Thurm, U. Cable properties and transepithelial voltage (TEV) of an insect integument: Measurements on caterpillars of the waxmoth *Galleria*. (in preparation).

Frömter, E., and Diamond, J. (1972). Route of passive ion permeation in epithelia. *Nature New Biology 235*, 9-13.

Gnatzy, W. (1978). Development of the filiform hairs on the cerci of *Gryllus bimaculatus* Deg. (Saltatoria, Gryllidae). *Cell Tiss. Res. 187,* 1-24.

Gnatzy, W., and Schmidt, K. (1972). Die Feinstruktur der Sinneshaare auf den Cerci von *Gryllus bimaculatus* Deg. (Saltatoria, Gryllidae). IV. Die Häutung der kurzen Borstenhaare. *Z. Zellforsch. 126,* 223-239.

Gnatzy, W., and Tautz, J. (1977). Sensitivity of an insect mechanoreceptor during moulting. *Physiological Entomology 2,* 279-288.

Gnatzy, W., and Weber, K.M. (1978). Tormogen cell and receptorlymph space in insect olfactory sensilla. Fine structure and histochemical properties in *Calliphora. Cell Tiss. Res. 189,* 549-554.

Guillet, J.C., and Bernard, J. (1972). Shape and amplitude of the spikes induced by natural or electrical stimulation in insect receptors. *J. Insect Physiol. 18,* 2155-2171.

Gödde, J. (1978). Abhängigkeit der Adaptation eines Mechanorezeptors von mechanischen, elektrischen und Temperaturbedingungen. Diplomarbeit, Fachbereich Biologie, Universität Münster.

Harvey, W.R., and Nedergaard, S. (1964). Sodium independent active transport of potassium in the isolated midgut of the Cecropia silkworm. *Proc. Nat. Acad. Sci. US 51,* 757-765.

Harvey, W.R., Haskell, J.A., and Nedergaard, S. (1968). Active transport by the Cecropia midgut. III. Midgut potential generated directly by active K-transport. *J. Exp. Biol. 48,* 1-12.

Haskell, J.A., Clemons, R.D., and Harvey, W.R. (1965). Active transport by the Cecropia midgut. I. Inhibitors, stimulants, and potassium-transport. *J. cell.comp. Physiol. 65,* 45-56.

Henke, K., and Rönsch, G. (1951). Über Bildungsgleichheiten in der Entwicklung epidermaler Organe und die Entstehung des Nervensystems im Flügel der Insekten. *Naturwissenschaften 38,* 335-336.

Kaissling, K.E., and Thorson, J. (1980). Insect olfactory sensilla: Structural, chemical, and electrical aspects of the functional organization. *In* "Insect Neurotransmitter, Hormone, and Pheromone Receptors" (Hall, L.M., Hildebrand, J.G., and Satelle, D.B., eds. Elsevier, Amsterdam).

Keil, Th. (1978). Die Makrochaeten auf dem Thorax von *Calliphora vicina* Robineau-Desvoidy (Calliphoridae, Diptera). Feinstruktur und Morphogenese eines epidermalen Insekten-Mechanorezeptors. *Zoomorphologie 90,* 151-180.

Keil, Th. (1979). Rutheniumrot-Färbung sensorischer Einheiten der Insekten-Epidermis. *Europ. J. of Cell Biol. 19,* 78-82.

Keil, Th., and Thurm, U. (1979). Die Verteilung von Membrankontakten und Diffusionsbarrieren in epidermalen Sinnesorganen von Insekten. *Verh. Dtsch. Zool. Ges. 72,* 285.

Küppers, J. (1974). Measurements of ionic milieu of the receptor terminal in mechanoreceptive sensilla of insects. *In* "Mechanoreception" (J. Schwartzkopff, ed.) pp. 387-397. Abh. Rhein. Westf. Akad. Wiss. Opladen.

Küppers, J., and Thurm, U. (1975). Humorale Steuerung eines Ionentransportes an epithelialen Rezeptoren von Insekten. *Verh. Dtsch. Zool. Ges. 67,* 46-50.

Küppers, J., and Thurm, U. (1979). Active ion transport by a sensory epithelium. I. Transepithelial short circuit current, potential difference, and their dependence on metabolism. *J. Comp. Physiol. 134,* 131-136.

Küppers, J., and Thurm, U. (1980). Water transport by electroosmosis (this volume)

Lane, N.J., and Treherne, J.E. (1972). Studies on perineural junctional complexes and the sites of uptake of microperoxidase and lanthanum in the cockroach central nervous system. *Tissue & Cell 4,* 427-436.

Lawrence, P.A. (1966). Development and determination of hairs and bristles in the milkweed bug, *Oncopeltus fasciatus* (Lygaeidae, Hemiptera). *J. Cell Sci. 1,* 475-498.

Maddrell, S.H.P., Pilcher, D.E.M., and Gardiner, B.O.C. (1971) Pharmacology of the Malpighian tubules of *Rhodnius* and *Carausius*: The structure-activity relationship of tryptamine analogues and the role of cyclic AMP. *J. Exp. Biol. 54,* 779-804.

Maes, F.W. (1977). Simultaneous chemical and electrical stimulation of labellar taste hairs of the blowfly *Calliphora vicina. J. Insect Physiol. 23,* 453-460.

Moran, D.T., and Varela, F.G. (1971). Microtubules and sensory transduction. *Proc. Nat. Acad. Sci. US 68,* 757-760.

Moran, D.T., Rowley III, J.C., Zill, S.N., and Varela, F.G. (1976). The mechanism of sensory transduction in a mechanoreceptor. *J. Cell Biol. 71,* 832-847.

Morita, H. (1959). Initiation of spike potentials in contact chemosensory hairs of insects. II. D. C. stimulation and generator potential of labellar chemoreceptor of *Calliphora. J. cell. comp. Physiol. 54,* 189-204.

Morita, H., and Yamashita, S. (1959). The back-firing of impulses in a labellar chemosensory hair of the fly. *Mem. Fac. Sci. Kyushu Univ. E 3,* 81-87.

Nedergaard, S., and Harvey, W.R. (1968). Active transport by the Cecropia midgut IV. Specifity of the transport mechanism for potassium. *J. Exp. Biol. 48,* 13-24.

Neher, E., and Stevens, C.F. (1977). Conductance fluctuations and ionic pores in membranes. *Ann. Rev. Biophys. Bioeng. 6,* 345-381.

Neville, A.C. (1975). Biology of arthropod cuticle. *Zoophysiology and Ecology 4/5*. Springer-Verlag, Berlin.

Nicklaus, R., Lundquist, P.-G., Wersäll, J. (1967). Elektronenmikroskopie am sensorischen Apparat der Fadenhaare auf den Cerci der Schabe *Periplaneta americana*. *Z. Vergl. Physiol.* 56, 412-415.

Pichon, Y. (1970). Ionic content of haemolymph in the cockroach *Periplaneta americana*. *J. Exp. Biol.* 53, 195-209.

Rees, C.J.C. (1970). The primary process of reception in the Type 3 ('water') receptor cell of the fly, *Phormia terranovae*. *Poc. Roy. Soc. Lond.* B 174, 469-490.

Rees, C.J.C. (1972). Responses of some sensory cells probably associated with the detection of water. *In* Olfaction and Taste IV. (D. Schneider, ed.) pp. 88-94. Wissensch. Verlagsgesellschaft, Stuttgart.

Schmidt, K., and Gnatzy, W. (1971). Die Feinstruktur der Sinneshaare auf den Cerci von *Gryllus bimaculatus* Deg. (Saltatoria, Gryllidae) II. Die Häutung der Faden- und Keulenhaare. *Z. Zellforsch.* 122, 210-226.

Smith, D.S. (1969). The fine structure of haltere sensilla in the blowfly, *Calliphora erythrocephala* (Meig.), with scanning electron microscopic observations on the haltere surface. *Tissue & Cell 1*, 443-484.

Steinbrecht, R.A., and Müller, B. (1976). Fine structure of the antennal receptors of the bed bug *Cimex lectularius* L. *Tissue & Cell 8*, 615-636.

Thurm, U. (1962). Die Beziehungen zwischen Reiz, Rezeptorpotential und Nervenimpulsen bei einzelnen mechanorezeptorischen Zellen von Bienen. Dissertation, Naturwissenschaftliche Fakultät, Universität Würzburg.

Thurm, U. (1965a). An insect mechanoreceptor. I. Fine structure and adequate stimulus. *Cold Spring Harbor Symp. Quant. Biol.* 30, 75-82.

Thurm, U. (1965b). An insect mechanoreceptor. II. Receptor potentials. *Cold Spring Harbor Symp. Quant. Biol.* 30, 83-94.

Thurm, U. (1968). Steps in the transducer process of mechanoreceptors. *Symp. zool. Soc. Lond.* 23, 199-216.

Thurm, U. (1969). General organization of sensory receptors. *In* Processing of Optical Data by Organisms and by Machines (W. Reichardt, ed.) pp. 45-68. Academic Press, London.

Thurm, U. (1970). Untersuchungen zur funktionellen Organisation sensorischer Zellgruppen. *Verh. Dtsch. Zool. Ges.* 64, 79-88.

Thurm, U. (1972). The generation of receptor potentials in epithelial receptors. *In* Olfaction and Taste IV (D. Schneider, ed.) pp. 95-101. Wissenschaftliche Verlagsgesellschaft, Stuttgart.

Thurm, U. (1974a). Basics of the generation of receptor potentials in epidermal mechanoreceptors of insects. *In* "Mechanoreception" (J. Schwartzkopff, ed.) pp. 355-385. Abh. Rhein. Westf. Akad. Wiss., Opladen.

Thurm, U. (1974b). Mechanisms of electrical membrane responses in sensory receptors, illustrated by mechanoreceptors. 25. Mosb. Colloq. d. Ges. f. Biol. Chemie.

Thurm, U., and Gödde, J. Effects of transepithelial voltage on sensitivity of epidermal mechanoreceptors in a fly (in preparation).

Thurm, U., and Wessel, G. (1979). Metabolism-dependent transepithelial potential differences at epidermal receptors of arthropods. I. Comparative data. *J. Comp. Physiol.* *134*, 119-130.

Thurm, U., Keil, Th., and Küppers, J. The epithelial nature of insect sensilla. (in preparation a).

Thurm, U., Gödde, J., Kastrup, H., and Vohwinkel, B. The receptor current circuit of an insect mechanoreceptor. (in preparation b).

Wigglesworth, V.B. (1941a). Permeability of insect cuticle. *Nature* *147*, 116.

Wigglesworth, V.B. (1945c) Transpiration through the cuticle of insects. *J. Exp. Biol.* *21*, 97-114.

Wigglesworth, V.B. (1948f). The insect cuticle. *Biol. Rev.* *23*, 408-451.

Wigglesworth, V.B. (1953b) The origin of sensory neurones in an insect, *Rhodnius prolixus* (Hemiptera). *Quart. J. Micr. Sci.* *94*, 93-112.

Wigglesworth, V.B. (1957a). The physiology of insect cuticle. *Ann. Rev. Ent.* *2*, 37-54.

Wigglesworth, V.B. (1958a). Abrasion of the insect cuticle by aqueous suspensions of small particles. *Nature* *181*, 779-780.

Wolbarsht, M.L. (1958). Electrical activity in the chemoreceptors of the blowfly. II. Responses to electrical stimulation. *J. Gen. Physiol.* *42*, 413-428.

Wolbarsht, M.L. (1960). Electrical characteristics of insect mechanoreceptors. *J. Gen. Physiol.* *44*, 105-122.

Wolbarsht, M.L., and Hanson, F. (1965). Electrical activity in the chemoreceptors of the blowfly. III. Dendritic action potentials. *J. Gen. Physiol.* *48*, 673-683.

Wood, J.L., Farrand, P.S., and Harvey, W.R. (1969). Active transport of potassium by the Cecropia midgut. VI. Microelectrode potential profile. *J. Exp. Biol.* *50*, 169-178.

Zerahn, K. (1971). Active transport of the alkali metals by the isolated mid-gut of *Hyalophora cecropia*. *Phil. Trans. Roy. Soc. Lond. B.* *262*, 315-321.

FUNCTIONAL ORGANISATION OF
ARTHROPOD NEUROGLIA

Nancy J. Lane
John Treherne

A.R.C. Unit of Invertebrate Chemistry & Physiology
Department of Zoology
University of Cambridge
Cambridge, U.K.

I. INTRODUCTION

Since their discovery, by Virchow in 1846, glial cells
have been shown to be conspicuous components of most invertebrate and all vertebrate nervous systems. Despite their promi-
nence, the full functional role of neuroglia is far from clear
(cf. Kuffler and Nicholls, 1976). Possible functions attributed to neuroglia, apart from their supportive role, include
metabolic interactions with neurones, transmitter synthesis
and inactivation, and homeostatic control of the chemical
composition of the brain microenvironment. In this article we
review the current state of knowledge of neuroglia in the
largest of the animal groups, which exhibits relatively wide
differences in the structural and functional organization of
the glial elements. This topic is particularly appropriate
for the theme of this volume, for Sir Vincent Wigglesworth
carried out pioneer work both on the structure of arthropod
glial cells (Wigglesworth, 1959f) and on the possible involvement of insect neuroglia in the nutrition of central nervous
tissues (Wigglesworth, 1960g). Since Wigglesworth's research,
many further developments have taken place. We shall consider
some of the more recently determined structural attributes of
arthropod glia cells as well as their interactions with each
other and with the nerve cells they ensheath. The main data
currently available as to their physiological significance will
be correlated with these morphological features.

II. GENERAL ORGANISATION OF THE NEUROGLIA

A. *Categories of glial cells*

The glial cells in arthropod tissues can be subdivided into a variety of categories, chiefly dependent on their location within the nervous tissue; different names have often been applied to them in the various systems (see Radojcic and Pentreath, 1979). Perhaps the most interesting distinction physiologically is that between the peripheral, epithelial, glial cells and the inner, more centrally-situated, astrocyte-like neuroglia. The former are modified to form an outer peri-neurial layer ensheathing the nervous system while the latter underlie the sheath and are directly involved in enveloping the nerve cells proper. Since the insect nervous system lacks an intrinsic circulatory system, unlike the crustacea (Abbott, 1971) and certain arachnids (Lane, Harrison and Bowerman, 1980), its perineurial cells must be traversed by any substance that enters the CNS. Hence these outer glial cells are likely to be specialized for this functional role. It was Wigglesworth (1959f) who, having distinguished these different categories of glial cells, had the insight to perceive that the sheath around the nerve and inner glial cells was not connective tissue but in fact a variation on a glial theme (cf. Scharrer, 1939). There are a number of distinctions between these peripheral, so-called perineurial, glial cells and the underlying ones which have gradually emerged over the intervening years since their classification.

1. *Outer Epithelial Glia: the Perineurium*

a. *Ensheathing neural lamella.* The peripheral glial cells are modified to form a complete cellular layer that totally encompasses the glial-neuronal mass. These perineurial cells are themselves surrounded by an acellular layer of connective tissue commonly termed the nerual lamella. This neural lamella contains collagen-like and elastic fibrils lying in a muco-polysaccharide matrix (Ashhurst and Costin, 1971) and is of variable depth; it occurs ubiquitously throughout the arthropods, as indeed would be expected given its basal laminar characteristics (Fig. 1).

b. *Complex interdigitations of lateral cell borders.* One of the most striking features of the arthropod perineurial glial layer is the complex degree of interdigitation that occurs between adjacent lateral cell borders. The numerous interdigitations produce extremely attenuated cell processes since the total depth of the perineurium, although variable, is on the whole thin (Fig. 1). These processes frequently run back and forth parallel to the outer surface and exhibit a variety of intercellular junctions; each group of arthropods possess different numbers and kinds of these junctional modifications (Fig. 1), although the glial cells of all of them are coupled by gap junctions (Fig. 2).

2. *Inner astrocytic glial cells*. The underlying glial cells consist of equally attenuated cell processes. These, however, emerge from the glial perikaryon and may be oriented in any direction rather than being mainly restricted to lateral extensions, as happens in the perineurium. These inner glial processes wrap closely around the nerve cells, and different arthropod nervous systems possess varying proportions of a number of possible arrangements (Fig. 1).

B. *Features of Glial Cell Distribution and Arrangements*

1. *Trophospongial processes*. In the ganglion, the peripheral nerve cell bodies are free of synaptic contacts and tend to be ensheathed very intimately by a number of glial layers, which may derived from one or more glial cells (Fig. 1). These glia may send processes into the peripheral cytoplasm of the very large nerve cell bodies; such invaginations are termed 'canals of Holmgren' or 'trophospongia', which we shall return to later.

2. *Glial lacunar system*. As is typical of invertebrates, arthropod ganglia are characterised by an outer layer of nerve cell bodies and a central neuropile of axons and synaptic contacts. Between these two in insects may lie an area, originally recognised as distinctive by Wigglesworth (1960g) who termed it the 'glial lacunar system'. This is a vacuolated region with lacunae where the glial processes run around the central neuropile and in which lie tracheoles. We will consider this region again shortly for it seems that it may play a peculiar role in the nutrition of the CNS.

3. *Mode of ensheathing axons*. The inner glial cells which encompass the axons in the ganglionic neuropile or the interganglionic connectives, do so in one of a variety of ways. In some cases, particularly with smaller axons, several may be ensheathed by the one glial cell (either separately or as a mass) or several glial cells may surround one axon (Fig. 1). In the case of the larger or giant axons, an extensive cell process may be spirally wound round each axon; this resembles the myelin sheath arrangement before the cytoplasm is squeezed

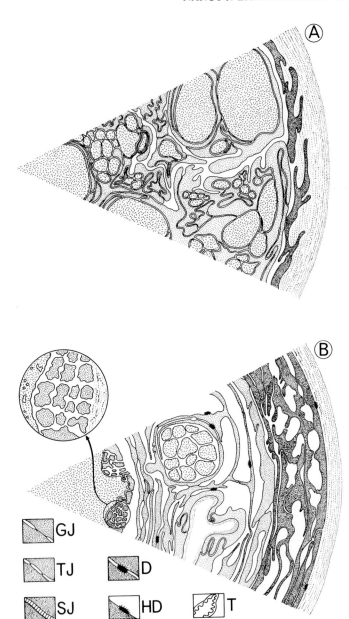

FIGURE 1.   Diagram of the glial cells in the CNS of arthropods: A, Limulus; B, the crayfish; C, insects; and D, certain
arachnids.   To the right lies the neural lamella (NL), under
which is found the peripheral glial layer, the perineurium (PN).

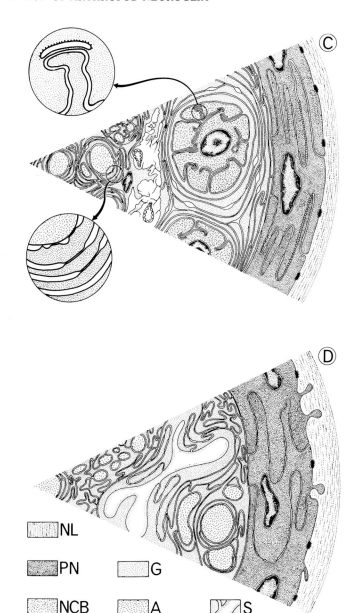

Beneath that the axons (A) are ensheathed by inner glial cells
(G) in a variety of ways. Blood sinuses (S) occur in B and
D, and tracheoles (T) in the glial lacunar system of C. Glial
cells are associated by gap junctions(GJ), desmosomes (D), in
the PN of C and D, by tight junctions (TJ), and in C by septate junctions (SJ). Hemidesmosomes (HD) also occur. Circular
inserts are: B, transglial channels; C, sub-surface cisternae
of glia trophospingia and axo-glial junctions.

out by membrane compaction, and is referred to as the mesaxon.
Myelination as such does not occur in the arthropod ganglia as
it does in vertebrates, although the glial processes may be
remarkably thin. The inner glial cells are also associated
with one another by a variety of junctional types, but these
and their physiological impact we shall consider later.

4. *Extracellular space between glial processes.* In some
arthropods the glial processes are packed together with little
intervening extracellular space between them. In the insects,
for example, there are occasionally slight distensions (Fig.
1), which contain mucopolysaccharides (Ashhurst and Costin,
1971), but generally the insect system has very restricted
extracellular space apart from the glial lacunar system. The
ticks (Binnington and Lane, 1980), the crustaceans (Abbott,
1977) and the more primitive horseshoe crab, *Limulus* (Harrison
and Lane, 1980), may possess much larger interglial dilatations
(Fig. 1). These contain a flocculent extracellular material,
which sometimes possesses wispy, collagen-like fibrils (Fig.
3). The physiological significance of these potential reservoirs will be assessed later.

C. *Glial Cell Inclusions*

1. *Microtubules.* Glial cells in the insects frequently
possess numerous microtubules which may in some cases be associated with desmosomal contacts (Ashhurst, 1970). The preponderance of these microtubules in massive arrays, aligned parallel to the longitudinal axis of the nerve cord's interganglionic connectives or nerves, in such insects as the adult moth
Manduca sexta (Lane, 1972) and the bug *Rhodnius* (Lane,
Leslie and Swales, 1975), suggests that they play a part in
maintaining the structural integrity and shape of these
structures. Arthropod glia in general seem not to possess the
filaments that are so prominent in the glial cells of annelids
and molluscs (see Radojcic and Pentreath, 1979).

2. *Gliosomes.* The cytoplasm of inner, but not perineurial,
glia often exhibits electron opaque, membrane-bound granules,
or gliosomes (Scharrer, 1939). These appear to be lysosomal in
nature (Lane, 1968a, 1968b) in that they possess hydrolytic
activity and may contain dense lamellae and other lysosome-like
inclusions.

3. *Glycogen and lipid deposits.* Glia in many arthropods
also have glycogen and lipid deposits (Wigglesworth, 1960g;
Smith, 1967). Such nutrients may have reached these cells from
the fat body which lies in intimate contact with the CNS (Lane,

1974), even forming a complete sheath around the ventral nerve cord in *Carausius* (Maddrell and Treherne, 1966). These reserves may also be enhanced after feeding in such groups as the ticks (Binnington and Lane, 1979) or may be depleted under conditions of starvation, as Wigglesworth observed (1960g), and then restored with feeding, first in glia and then nerve cells. This strongly suggests an involvement of the glia in the regulation of neuronal nutrition, with the possibility of precursors to lipid and glycogen moving from the one to the other (Smith, 1967). In the horseshoe crab, *Limulus*, it has

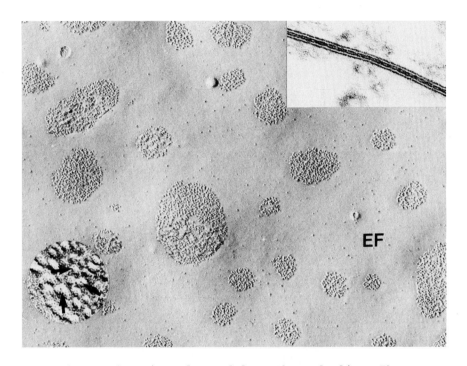

FIGURE 2. *Gap junctions from adult arthropod glia. These are characterized in thin section (insert) by a reduced intercellular space of 2-4 nm. In freeze-fracture replicas they appear, in representatives from all the groups of arthropods considered here - Limulus, ticks, spiders, scorpions, crustaceans and insects, both holo- and heterometabolous, as macular plaques or clusters of E face (or outer membrane leaflet, EF) particles. These possess complementary P face (or inner membrane leaflet, PF) pits and the plaques exhibit a range of diameters. The small central channels (in circular insert) in the particles represent the pores through which ions and molecules are thought to be exchanged between the coupled cells. X32,700; insert, X147,900; circular insert, X144,500.*

been suggested that the neuroglia containing glycogen which
occur in the haemocoelic spaces, are the equivalent of reserve
cells, possibly modulating the glucose level in the brain
(Fahrenbach, 1976).

D. Glial Membrane Modifications

Crustacean neuroglia display an unusual feature which has
not been reported in the glia of the other arthropods thus far
investigated. This is the existence of trans-glial channels
and tubular lattice systems (Figs. 1B and 3) which are present
as very simple transcellular pores or more complex anastomosing
channels lying across the glial cytoplasm. These may have a
role as a short-circuit during ion exchange; the extracellular
pathway to the axon surface from the exterior is extremely
lengthy unless the ions can take a 'short-cut' across these
channels. They are patent to exogenous tracers (Holtzman,
Freeman and Kashner, 1970; Shivers, 1976; Lane, Swales and
Abbott, 1977), suggesting ions could pass rapidly across them
to the glia-neuronal intercellular spaces. They also contain
cholinesterase (Holtzman et al 1970) and hence could be sites
of neurotransmitter destruction. Other glial membranous modifications, such as junctions, are dealt with in the succeeding
sections.

E. Oxygen Supply to Glial Cells and Neurones

The arthropods have a wide range of solutions to the problems of acquiring appropriate levels of oxygen for the CNS.
For the essential oxygen supply to the nerve and glial cells,
aquatic arthropods (such as Limulus and the crayfish), have a
blood supply either directly surrounding the CNS, and entirely
accessible to the nerve cells, or their CNS is vascularized so
that blood channels are distributed throughout the nervous
tissue (Fig. 1A,B). Extensive tracheation is to be found within the CNS in terrestrial groups, such as insects (Fig. 1C),
and the ticks. Both of these have a CNS that is avascular;
that of the ticks, however, is totally enveloped by a blood
vessel which has direct access to the nervous tissues
(Binnington and Lane, 1980). In insects, all the nutritive
exchanges between ganglia and haemolymph must take place
through the outer glial perineurium. The arachnids tend to
have book lungs with little in the way of tracheae, but, at
least in the case of scorpions, their CNS has a blood vascular
system (Fig. 1D) (Lane, Harrison and Bowerman, 1980).

III. GLIAL-GLIAL INTERACTIONS

A. *Intercellular Junctions*

1. Gap junctions. Glial cells associate with one another by a variety of intercellular junctions, each of which plays a particular role in glial activity. One of the most striking and certainly the most ubiquitous is the gap junction which is found between glial cells at all levels of the arthropod nervous system and between all types of glial cell (Fig. 1). Thus these junctions occur not only between the peripheral, perineurial, glial cells, but they also couple the outer perineurial cells with the underlying, axon-enveloping, glial cells.

Gap junctions are low resistance sites of cell-to-cell coupling, where the exchange of ions and small molecules between cells occurs (Bennett, 1977; Loewenstein *et al* 1978). In profile in thin-section they have a characteristic reduced intercellular cleft of about 2-4 nm (Fig. 2). Although they were originally considered to be occluding tight junctions (see Refs. in Lane and Skaer, 1980), improved staining techniques makes it possible to distinguish the gap from the tight junctions which are quite different structures (see Section III.A. 5). They are thought to mediate trophic and/or information exchange between glial cells, so that the glia can act in synchrony.

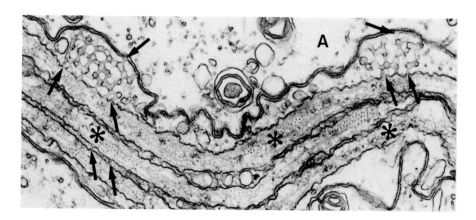

FIGURE 3. *Tubular lattice systems and trans-glial channels from the inner glial cells of the crayfish, lying next to an axon (A). These are continuous from one side of the glial cell membrane to the other (at arrows) and are patent to tracers. Note the extracellular collagen-containing matrix (*) between glial cells. X38,300.*

In freeze-fracture, gap junctions appear as clusters of intramembranous particles arranged in macular plaques (Fig. 2). These particles measure about 13 nm and fracture onto the E face (the extracellular or outer membrane half), making them subtly different from those of vertebrate gap junctions, the component particlts of which measure 6-10 nm and fracture onto the P face (the cytoplasmic or inner membrane half). These peculiar arthropod features have made it possible to analyze certain aspects of junctional development more accurately than is possible in vertebrates (Lane, 1978; Lane and Swales, 1978a, b, 1979, 1980; Lane and Skaer, 1980). In metamorphosing lepidopterans, the gap junctions undergo a dispersal of their component particles (Lane and Swales, 1980), as the junctions disappear with glial cell dissociation. The glial cells are then reoriented during the pupal development and, through their redistribution, may play a role in nerve cord shortening (Pipa and Woolever, 1964).

2. *Desmosomes*. Glial cells are also linked by desmosomes, both at the periphery, where they more frequently occur as hemi-desmosomes between the outer perineurial layer and the acellular neural lamella (see Fig. 1), and in the interior. These junctions possess a structure that reflects their function as they have dense fibrils and associated microtubules at either side of a cleft containing dense cross-striations (Fig. 1). They act to maintain the physical integrity of the nervous system by holding inner glial cytoplasmic folds together and to strengthen the intimate spatial associations between glia and neurones. They are more commonly found between the inner glial cells in certain groups, for example, the muscids and moths, than they are in others such as the cockroach, locust and stick insect (Lane, Skaer and Swales, 1977).

3. *Scalariform-like junctions*. Another interesting structural modification found between glial cells is that observed between the adjacent processes that envelop the nerve cell bodies in insect ganglia (Fig. 8b in Lane, 1968a; Figs. 5 & 6 in Lane and Treherne, 1970; Fig. 1.15A in Lane, 1974). These, referred to as scalariform-like junctions (Lane and Skaer, 1980), frequently are associated with cisternae of endoplasmic reticulum that lie in the glial cytoplasm in very intimate contact with the junctional membrane; the cisternal face next to the membrane is smooth, and that facing away is ribosome-studded. These demonstrate some features in common with the perikaryal sub-surface cisternae by the trophospongial invaginations (Smith, 1967) and may by implication also be involved in the exchange of molecules. Given the suggestion that the glial cells have a role in cation regulation by storing and pumping ions at the appropriate time, and given that the scalariform junctions

observed in other insect tissues are thought to be involved in transport by ion pumping (Lane, 1979b), it seems possible that the glial scalariform-like junctions play some part in glial-mediated homeostasis.

4. Septate junctions. Peripheral glial cells in insects are commonly associated by septate junctions while inner glial cells and the outer glial cells of other arthropods, usually are not. These very characteristic, ladder-like, junctions exhibit a number of septae or cross-striations (Fig. 1C) in thin-sections and their adjacent membranes are separated by a 15-20 nm cleft. In freeze-cleaved preparations they have a characteristic appearance of undulating rows of separate 8-10 nm PF particles with complementary EF grooves; it is possible, although this is still a matter of controversy (see Noirot-Timothee *et al* 1978), that the intercellular septae insert into the membranes via these intramembranous P face particles (see Lane and Skaer, 1980). In any case, they are quite distinct from the other junctional modifications that occur between glial cells and probably provide a means of maintaining spatial relationships in the insect perineurium, where desmosomes, on the whole, are lacking. In some invertebrate systems (Lord and DiBona, 1976; Noirot-Timothee *et al* 1978) it is thought that these junctions may play a part in maintaining homeostasis by forming a permeability barrier and restricting the entry of exogenous substances. Although they may well act to slow down the entry of molecules, their absence in the perineurium of certain arthropods which have distinct blood-brain barriers (see Lane and Skaer, 1980; Lane and Chandler, 1980) suggests that they do not perform the function of sealing observed in the CNS. This appears to be the responsibility of tight junctions.

5. Occluding or tight junctions. One of the most physio-logically important junctional modifications which the CNS of arthropods has been found to possess is the tight or occluding junction (*zonula occludens*) which excludes tracers (Lane and Treherne, 1970, 1971, 1972; Lane, 1972; Lane, Skaer and Swales, 1977). The presence of these junctions in the outer, perineur-ial glial cells, as points of punctate membrane appositions in thin-sections, is now established (Fig. 4B) in insects (Lane, 1972; Lane *et al* 1977; Lane and Swales, 1979), and spiders (Lane and Chandler, 1980), and they are quite distinct from the gap junctions whose intercellular space is reduced but not obliterated by points of membrane fusion. In freeze-fracture, the tight junctions of insects are extremely simple (Fig. 4A) (Lane, Skaer and Swales, 1977; Lane and Swales, 1978a, 1979; Lane, 1978; Lane and Skaer, 1980), being unbranching linear P face ridges and E face grooves. In the arachnids, how-ever, the situation is more complex. The perineurium of the

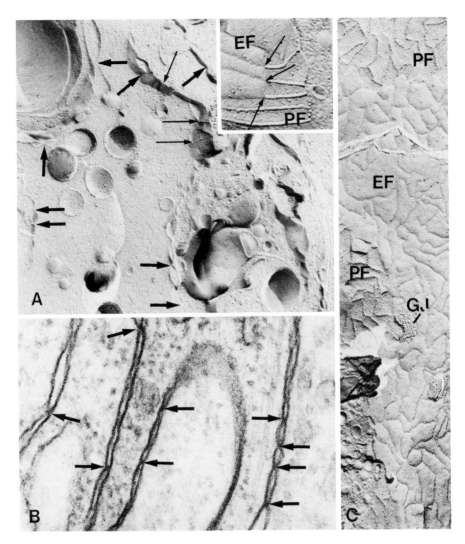

FIGURE 4. Tight junctional complexes in the peripheral glial (perineurial) cell sheath in arthropod nervous systems. A. Freeze-fracture replica showing P face (PF) ridges (arrows) and complementary E face (EF) grooves in occluding junctions in the insect eye. Large arrows indicate cross fractures through punctate appositions or points of fusion of adjacent cell membranes. X34,500. B. Thin-section of the punctate membrane appositions (arrows) between adjacent lateral cell borders in a hatchling insect, X84,500; C. Freeze-fracture replica from an arachnid adult exhibiting its more complex arrays of tight junctional PF ridges and EF grooves. GJ, intercalated gap junction. X26,300; Insert, X54,300.

spider (Fig. 4C) (Lane and Chandler, 1980) and the scorpion (Lane, Harrison and Bowerman, 1980) are much more extensively supplied with tight junctional membrane fusions; this is reflected in the freeze-cleave data which show that spider perineirium possesses circumferential regions of intramembranous P ridges and complementary EF grooves in the form of complex networks (Fig.4C) (Lane and Chandler, 1980), very like the vertebrate tight junctions (Claude and Goodenough, 1973). These arachnid junctional complexes, which have EF gap junctions intercalated between the tight junctional grooves (see Fig. 4, C), also appear to prevent the entry of tracer substances into the underlying CNS (Lane and Chandler, 1980; Lane, Harrison and Bowerman, 1980). Tight junctions therefore appear to form the morphological basis of both the insect and arachnid blood-brain barriers.

This occluding type of intercellular junction is not present in all arthropod perineurial cells; they are absent between the glial cells of the marine horseshoe crab, *Limulus*, (Harrison and Lane, 1980) as well as between the adjacent glial membranes of the terrestrial tick (Binnington and Lane, 1980). In the crustacea, they are only present as very infrequent fasciar junctions in the midst of numerous gap junctions (Lane, Swales and Abbott, 1977).

B. *Permeability of the Blood-Brain Interface*

1. 'Open' systems. The available physiological evidence can be correlated with the ultrastructural organization of the peripheral neuroglia which constitute the blood-brain interface of arthropod nervous systems. The rapid electrophysiological responses of the axons in *Limulus* leg nerves to alterations in external sodium and potassium concentrations, indicate a relatively free intercellular access of these water-soluble cations from the bathing medium to the fluid bathing the axon surfaces in intact preparations (Willmer and Harrison, 1979). This finding is corroborated by the intercellular accessibility of extraneously applied extracellular tracer substances to both peripheral and central nervous systems (Harrison and Lane, 1980). A relatively leaky blood-brain interface in the central nervous system of the tick, *Boophilus microplus*, is also indicated by the unrestricted intercellular penetration of ionic lanthanum from the medium (Binnington and Lane, 1980).

2. Poorly developed barrier systems. In crayfish central nervous connectives no zonular tight junctions occur in the perineurial clefts, only fasciar or punctate ones, and gap junctions; the former appear to be too infrequent and non-

circumferential to exclude water-soluble ions or molecules
(Lane and Abbott, 1975; Lane, Swales and Abbott, 1977).
Nevertheless, the complex electrical responses (measured with
the sucrose-gap and with intracellular and extracellularly-
located microelectrodes) indicate that a transient potential
difference is established across the outer perineurial glial
layer in response to alterations in external potassium concentration (Abbott, Moreton and Pichon, 1975). This suggests
that there is some degree of restriction to intercellular
diffusion of potassium in the perineurial clefts. The perineurial component of potassium depolarization is absent in
peripheral nerves where perineurial tight and gap junctions
are also missing (Lane and Abbott, 1975) and the extracellular
fluid is readily accessible to exogenous tracers (Lane, Swales
and Abbott, 1977).

There is thus, in the crustacea, a correlation between the
presence of sparsely distributed perineurial junctions with a
reduced cleft and a degree of restriction to intercellular
diffusion sufficient to induce a transient perineurial potential on exposure of central nervous connectives to high-potas-
sium saline (Abbott *et al* 1975).

3. *'Closed' blood-brain barriers*

a. *Central nervous system*. Exposure of insect central
nervous connectives to elevated external potassium concentrations induce large and sustained perineurial potential changes
(Treherne *et al* 1970; Pichon and Treherne, 1970). These can
be correlated with the perineurial tight junctions that are
far more extensive than those of crustaceans. These, by restricting the inward diffusion along the perineurial clefts, are
held to limit potassium depolarization to the outwardly-
directed perineurial membranes (Treherne *et al* 1970). The
severe restriction to penetration through the perineurial
clefts of insects is also indicated by the very slow effects
of sodium-deficient saline on the sodium-dependent action
potentials (Schofield and Treherne, 1978), by the inability of
lithium ions to gain access to the axonal surfaces (Schofield
and Treherne, 1978) and the lack of penetration of exogenous
tracer substances to the underlying extracellular spaces in the
central nervous system (Lane and Treherne, 1970, 1971, 1972;
Lane, 1972).

b. *Peripheral nervous system*. The peripheral nervous
system is very much less highly organized than the central
nervous system in that the peripheral nerves, apart from the
larger and medium-sized ones in insects, have a much less
developed peripheral glial system. In the nerves of some groups,
the peripheral glia are not really perineurial because they do

not ensheath the whole of the underlying nervous tissue and are not associated by junctions; only small clusters of inner glial-ensheathed axons, separated by large areas of neural lamella-like connective tissue matrix, are apparent. Although their minute diameter makes the smallest peripheral nerves difficult to impale for electrophysiological recordings, tracer uptake studies on such insect nerves (Lane and Treherne, 1972) show that exogenous substances are allowed access into the nerve interior without restriction, as is also the case for even the largest peripheral nerves of *Limulus* (Harrison and Lane, 1980), the tick (Binnington and Lane, 1980) and the crayfish (Lane, Swales and Abbott, 1977).

C. *Cation Movements in Neuroglia*

1. Role of perineurial glia. Despite the peripheral restriction to intercellular access of water-soluble ions and molecules through perineurial neuroglia of the insect central nervous system, relatively rapid radio-cation exchanges can, nevertheless, occur across the blood-brain interface of insects (Treherne, 1962; Tucker and Pichon, 1972). In the case of radio-sodium, ion efflux from isolated cockroach connectives is reduced by externally-applied ouabain (Treherne, 1966) and by potassium-deficient saline (Treherne, 1961). This suggests that sodium efflux across the blood-brain interface involves some active extrusion, by linked Na/K pumps, most probably via the outwardly-directed membranes of the perineurial cells. The available electrophysiological evidence also indicates that an inwardly-directed accumulation of sodium ions occurs at the outer perineurial membranes, by a mechanism which will also accept lithium ions (Treherne and Schofield, 1978, 1979).

2. Role of inner neuroglia. The sodium uptake by insect perineurial neuroglia appears to be associated with regulatory processes in the deeper glial elements. This interaction is indicated by the very substantial changes in sodium content, of cockroach connectives, which occur when the perineurial neuroglia are exposed to sodium-deficient saline, without a reduction in extracellular sodium concentration - as indicated by action potential amplitude (Schofield and Treherne, 1975, 1978). Since there is no indication of changes in extracellular or axonal concentrations of sodium it follows that the large changes in tissue sodium must have occurred in the neuroglia in response to alteration in external sodium level. This is also indicated by the substantial uptake of lithium by cockroach central nervous tissues (Bennett *et al* 1975) which occurs in the absence of extracellular accumulation of this cation (Schofield and Treherne, 1978).

3. *Explanatory model.* According to the model illustrated
in Fig. 5 the superficial, perineurial, glia are linked, via
gap junctions, to the underlying glial elements to form an
intracellular sodium reservoir. The sodium within the perineurial cytoplasm is thus controlled by the inwardly- and outwardly-directed ion pumps on the perineurial membranes and is
in equilibrium with that contained in the underlying glial
elements. As discussed later, this postulated glial sodium
store appears to be involved in the maintenance of adequate
extracellular sodium levels during fluctuation in external
sodium concentration.

IV.   GLIAL-NEURONAL INTERACTIONS

A. *Structural Interrelationships*

1. *Trophospongial exchanges.* There are several situations
in arthropods in which glial cells make particularly intimate
associations with neurones. One of these, as detailed by
Wigglesworth (1959f, 1960g), is in the characteristic involu-
tions of the plasmalemma of the larger nerve cell bodies by
glial invaginations - the trophospongia (Fig. 1). This
increases the area of apposition between the two cells and
hence these processes could play a trophic role providing
nutrients for the very extensive volume of perikaryal cytoplasm
possessed by these large neurones. The directional transfer of
glucose has, for example, also been postulated for the trophospongial infoldings of leech glial cells (Wolfe and Nicholls,
1967). Interesting membranous modifications in insects which
could be involved in this exchange are the areas within the
nerve cell body that lie in direct contact with the trophospongial glial process (Smith, 1967) (Fig. 1, top circular
insert in C); these are referred to as the 'confronting' or
'sub-surface' cisternae and are saccules of endoplasmic reticulum with the rough side facing away, and a smooth side facing
to, the apposed plasma membranes (Fig. 1). Although there is
little direct evidence to support the contention that these
arthropod neuronal sub-surface cisternae represent the sites of
exchange of metabolites, or transfer of them from glial cells
to neurones, the circumstantial evidence seems fairly compelling. Junctional modifications between axons and glia are
sometimes also observed; these will be described later.

2. *Glial lacunar system and its role.* The glial lacunar
system also seems involved in the nourishment of the CNS as a
pool of nutrients; when insects are starved, glycogen stores, in
the glial cells and neurones are depleted and the lacunar

system develops even more extensive spaces (Wigglesworth, 1960g), while the effect on the overall ganglionic volume is negligible. This glial area may thus also be a provision for maintaining unchanged the outward form of the ganglion; it may expand or shrink according to the state of nutrition. Nothing is as yet understood about this peculiar neuronal-glial interaction but it is an area for potentially fruitful study.

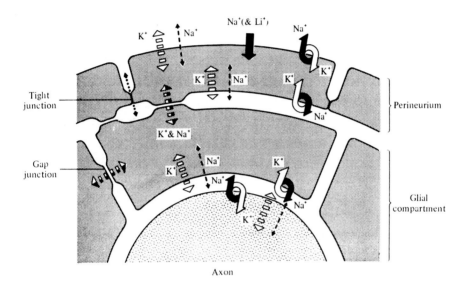

FIGURE 5. Model for regulation of extracellular sodium concentration in the cockroach nerve cord. Intercellular passage of sodium between the extracellular fluid and the bathing medium (dotted arrow) is limited by tight junctions at the inner ends of the clefts between the perineurial cells. Passage by a transcellular route, through the perineurial and glial cells, involves diffusion across the cell membranes (broken arrows) and conventional Na/K pumps extruding sodium from the cells (linked arrows). Entry of sodium (and lithium) at the outer perineurial membranes could be carrier-mediated (single solid arrow) or be by diffusion down an electrochemical gradient. The presence of both inward and outward transfer of sodium provides dynamic control of its extracellular concentration. [The neural lamella over the perineurium is not incorporated in the model since it is relatively leaky to small water soluble ions and molecules (cf. Treherne, 1974)].

B. *Ionic Homeostasis*

1. Effects of restricted extracellular environment. The
absence of cerebrospinal fluid and the close packing of the
glial and neuronal elements creates fluid environments of
central neurones which consist largely of very narrow, inter-
connecting, extracellular clefts. The restricted volume of
this neuronal microenvironment imposes some constraints which
affect electrical signalling within the nervous system. This
is seen in the effects of the transient accumulation of potassium ions (resulting from the outward current of the action
potential) in inducing the depolarizing negative after-potential (Narahashi and Yamasaki, 1960) and of the local ultrastructural organization of the mesaxon clefts in affecting its
rate of decay in cockroach giant axons (Smith and Treherne,
1963). Relatively small fluctuations in extracellular potassium concentration associated with nervous activity could also
have profound effects on neuronal resting potential and consequently, on axonal and synaptic excitability (cf. Erulkar and
Weight, 1979).
     The necessity for effective extracellular cation regulation
imposed by the restricted intercellular environment, delimited
by the neuroglia, is most extreme in the avascular insect
central nervous system, in which the fluid bathing the axon
surfaces is isolated from the blood by the occluded perineurial
clefts. In such a system the net passive efflux of potassium
ions from adjacent cells into the intercellular clefts of 20 nm
in width could, in the absence of effective homeostatic control,
result in a rate of increase in potassium concentration at the
axon surfaces of as much as 1 mM sec^{-1} (Treherne *et al* 1970).

2. Crustaceans - spatial buffering. A primitive form of
extracellular ionic homeostasis has been recognized in the
relatively leaky central nervous systems of decapod crustaceans.
This is shown by the asymmetrical movements of potassium and
sodium ions between the external medium and the axon surfaces.
In crayfish connectives, for example, entry of potassium ions
is approximately ten times slower than efflux from the extra-
axonal fluid (Abbott, Pichon and Lane, 1977). This asymmetry
seems not to be imposed by active Na/K transport via the glial
elements for it is not abolished by the sodium transport inhibitors, ethacrynic acid or strophanthidin. It is concluded
that purely passive processes are involved, resulting from the
ion-selective behaviour of the mucopolysaccharide matrix, which
lies between the glial and neuronal elements, and/or from
"spatial buffering" by linked glial processes (Abbott, 1979).
As originally proposed by Kuffler (1967) neuroglia contribute
to this "spatial buffering" by removing potassium ions from
local regions of high concentration, and distributing it by

movement through the glial cytoplasm to regions of lower extra-cellular potassium concentration.

   3. Insects - glial-mediated homeostasis. Extracellular ionic homeostasis appears to be achieved by very different mechanisms in insect central nervous tissues. In cockroach connectives, unlike those of the crayfish, the net movements of sodium between the axon surfaces and the external medium are affected by a metabolic inhibitor, DNP, and by ethacrynic acid (Schofield and Treherne, 1975). Furthermore, a glial involvement in extracellular potassium homeostasis has been demonstrated using ion-selective microelectrodes in the drone retina (Coles and Tsacopoulous, 1979). In this preparation stimulation resulted in a loss of about 25% of the intracellu-lar potassium from the photoreceptor cells which was accompan-ied by a rapid, transient, rise in extracellular potassium activity. Subsequently, the extracellular potassium activity declined to a *lower* level than before stimulation and was accompanied by a substantial increase in the potassium activity measured within the neuroglia. The potassium regulation by the neuroglia in this insect preparation is unlikely to be achieved by local "passive buffering", as has been postulated in the crustacea CNS (Abbott, 1979) and also in vertebrate brain (Trachtenberg and Pollen, 1970; Gardner-Medwin, 1977), for photostimulation of the drone retina involves the activation of more than a thousand photoreceptor cells which would thus induce a uniform release of potassium ions into the extra-cellular system (Coles and Tsacopoulos, 1979).

   The available evidence, for insects, thus indicates a glial involvement in the regulation of potassium and sodium concentrations in the fluid bathing the neuronal surfaces. This regulation can be accounted for by a model (Fig. 5) in which the sodium within the perineurial cells is in equilibrium with that contained in the underlying neuroglia (via gap junctions). This neuroglial sodium fraction is largely main-tained by a balance between sodium uptake at the outer peri-neurial membranes and its extrusion into the extracellular clefts and into the blood by linked Na/K pumps, as shown in Fig. 5. The glial sodium fraction is postulated to function as a reservoir that contributes to the maintenance of stable extracellular cation levels during the massive fluctuation in blood sodium concentration that can occur, for example, in the cockroach (Lettau *et al* 1977). The sodium contained within this intracellular reservoir is pumped into the extracellular fluid bathing the axon surfaces by conventional linked Na/K pumps situated on the glial membranes. This would explain the inability of lithium to gain access to the extra-axonal fluid (Schofield and Treherne, 1975, 1978), for this cation is known not to be transported by conventional sodium pumps in other

excitable cells (cf. Keynes and Swan, 1959; Baker, 1965). It
also accounts for glial regulation of extracellular potassium
for the extrusion of sodium would be associated with an uptake
of potassium into the glial cytoplasm (Coles and Tsacopoulos,
1979).

C. Metabolic Interactions of Glia with Neurones

1. *Significance of the intracellular glial pathway.* The
coupling of the perineurium with the underlying neuroglia by
gap junctions provides a direct intracellular pathway which
links the blood-brain interface with glial elements adjacent to
neuronal membranes deep within the central nervous system of
arthropods. This can be seen, for example, in the relatively
rapid axonal responses to alterations in external sodium concentration revealed when the sodium reservoir, in insects, is
depleted, by prolonged exposure of connectives to sodium-
deficient saline (Schofield and Treherne, 1975, 1978). As
would be expected from glial-mediated transport, these rapid
responses are slowed by metabolic and sodium-transport inhibitors and, in addition, are not mimiced by lithium-substituted
saline.

2. *Transfer of nutrients.* The importance of the intracellular, glial, pathway in the transfer of nutrient substances
to central neurones was demonstrated by Wigglesworth (1960g) in
his histochemical observations of a sequential deposition of
glycogen, first in the perineurium, then in the glial cytoplasm
and finally, as mentioned earlier, in the region of the glial
trophospongium of the nerve cell bodies. As emphasised by
Kuffler and Nicholls (1966), Wigglesworth's observations constitute one of the first pieces of experimental evidence for the
metabolic interaction of neuroglia with the neurones - a concept
which has more recently been confirmed by the demonstrated
ability of neuroglia to absorb amino acids, to synthesise proteins using them and to transfer these proteins to the axoplasm
of squid giant axons (cf. Gainer, 1978).
There is circumstantial evidence that such protein synthesis and transfer occurs in crustacean neuroglia and could
include enzymes responsible for transmitter synthesis. This
was suggested by the observation that the activity of glutamic
acid decarboxylase was maintained in the large, non-cholinergic,
axons of crayfish leg nerves when these axons were separated
from their cell bodies (Sarne, Neal and Gainer, 1976; Sarne,
Schrier and Gainer, 1976). It has also been suggested that
crustacean motor axons receive trophic inputs from adjacent
glial cells during transplantation experiments (Bittner and
Mann, 1976).

3. *Axo-glial junctions*. As for the morphological site of
transfer of substances between glia and neurones, only a few
reports have thus far appeared in the literature pertaining to
arthropod axo-glial junctions. One of the most convincing is
that found between axons and ensheathing glial cells in the
crayfish (Peracchia, 1974). Here arrays of intramembranous
particles and complementary pits lie in regular arrays on the
apposing membrane faces of both axons and glial cells; it has
been suggested that they could represent sites of trophic or
metabolic exchange, areas of cell-to-cell adhesion, or structures involved in the mechanism of excitation (Perrachia, 1974).
In thin-sections, close associations between axons and glia
are encountered which could be the morphological counterpart
of these freeze-fracture particle plaques. Similarly, in
insect CNS, particle arrays of several sorts have been observed
which together with thin-section images of intimate axo-glial
associations (see Fig. 1C) (Lane *et al* 1977; Lane and Swales,
1978a,b; Lane, 1978), suggest the possibility that these could
represent sites of metabolic exchange. Rather comparable
observations of possible axo-glial junctions have also recently
been made on the tick CNS (Binnington and Lane, 1980). These
arthropod junctions show some similarities to the axo-glial
structures observed in the paranodal area of vertebrate myeli-
nated axons (Schnapp and Mugniani, 1975). Here it has been
suggested that, in addition to adhesion, these junctions may
serve as sites of communication between the axons and myelina-
ting glial cells, since these cells must both establish non-
random contact and be able to signal maintenance, or dissolution, of the structural relationship. Further studies on the
arthropod axo-glial junctions are required to establish which,
if any, of these functional possibilities may pertain.

There is some evidence to suggest continuity between the
smooth ER of satellite glial cells and extracellular sites
beside photoreceptor cell axons in dipteran retina (Griffiths,
1979). The satellite glia are thought to play a destructive
role, using acid hydrolases, with respect to the photoreceptor
cell axons, thereby supporting the general concept of a
destructive class of glial cells (Bittner and Mann, 1976).
Recent studies on photoreceptor cells with freeze-fracture
reveal a number of particle arrays which could be the morphological correlates of sites of glial-axonal exchange (Lane,
unpublished observations).

D. *Glial Inactivation of Transmitters*

Evidence derived from arthropod preparations suggests that
neuroglia may be involved in the inactivation of transmitter
compounds for which there is no evidence of extracellular

breakdown. This is deduced from observations on insects
(Salpeter and Faeder, 1971) and crustaceans (Orkand and Kravitz,
1971; Evans, 1974) that the inhibitory transmitter (GABA) and
the putative excitatory transmitter (glutamate) are, apparently,
selectively taken up by neuroglia at neuromuscular junctions
and in the central nervous system.

E. Electrical Signalling between Nerve and Glial Cells

The available evidence indicates that electrical signalling
can occur between neurones and glial cells: in the leech CNS,
it is suggested by graded glial depolarizations (induced by
potassium released into the narrow intercellular clefts during
neuronal excitation) (Kuffler, 1967) and in squid glia by
cholinergic transmission (which induces sustained hyperpolarization of the glial membranes following excitation of the giant
axon) (cf. Villegas, 1978). The discovery of the latter system
provides an explanation for the extensive acetylcholinesterase
activity, demonstrated histochemically on the glial membranes
in cockroach ganglia (Smith and Treherne, 1965).

F. Glial Cells in the Developing CNS

The role of the glial cell in nerve cell development, both
in cell death and in neuronal orientation, has been little
studied in arthropods, although glial transformations from
playing a supportive to a destructive role, have been observed
(Bittner and Mann, 1976; Griffiths, 1979). A glial involvement
in neuronal distribution during the migratory phase of development, by contact guidance via membranous modifications, has
been postulated for embryonic and pupal insect CNS (Lane, 1979a).
Moreover, during pupal metamorphosis in insects, the axonal rearrangements are always closely associated with glial separation
and reorientation wherein junctional complexes are broken down,
rearranged and ultimately reformed (Lane and Swales, 1978b,
1980). Glial involvement in the rearrangements during nerve
cord shortening has also been suggested (Pupa and Woolever,
1965) but exactly how the glial cells and axons exchange information before and after their separation is not yet clear.

V. PROSPECTS FOR THE FUTURE

A. Summary

For many years neuroglia have been rather mysterious entities to which a variety of physiological functions have been
attributed. We now have some evidence for the involvement of

neuroglia in both short and long-term ionic homeostasis, in metabolic interactions with neurones and in transmitter synthesis and inactivation.

B. *Problems*

However, the problems that still face us are manifold; these include such matters as the fact that the evidence for the trophic role of the glial cells is mainly circumstantial. More unequivocal data regarding the transfer of radioactively labelled compounds from glia to nerve cells would be helpful, but in this regard the limits of resolution of the autoradiographic technique restrict our interpretation. The study of the intracellular transport of fluorescent substances via gap or axo-glial junctions has not been possible due to the attenuated nature of the glial cell processes. Biochemical analyses on arthropod glia concerning their synthetic, storage and pumping capacities are rendered well nigh impossible by the paucity of material and the improbability of obtaining purified preparations. Furthermore, the electrical characterization of arthropod neuroglia present formidable technical problems due to the generally small size of the glial elements.

C. *Techniques for the Future*

It seems most likely that future research will provide unequivocal evidence for some glial functions by using the more sophisticated technology which can be reasonably expected to be developed. These will no doubt include microprobe x-ray analyses of frozen hydrated tissue, an increasing array of chemically-selective microelectrodes, immunochemical methodology and cell culturing techniques whereby interactions between co-cultured glial and nerve cells may be monitored in a variety of ways including the exchange of radioactively labelled compounds. Better methods for visualizing intracellular tracers at the fine structural level may also be available in the near future. New freeze-fracture methods involving the rapid freezing of non-cryoprotected material, deep-etching, complementary replicas and rotary shadowing will be more routine procedures within the next few years as well. This research should provide a more complete understanding of the role of neuroglia, which has so far been largely ignored in studies on complex neural functioning.

ACKNOWLEDGEMENTS

We would like to thank Mr John Rodford for preparing the diagrams in Figure 1. We are very grateful to Mr William Lee for his photographic assistance and to Mrs Margaret Clements for her patient and expert preparation of the typescript.

REFERENCES

Abbott, N.J. (1971). The organization of the cerebral ganglia in the shore crab, *Carcinus maenas*. II. The relation of intracerebral blood vessels to other brain elements. *Z. Zellforsch. 120,* 401-419.

Abbott, N.J. (1979). Primitive forms of brain homeostasis. *Trends in Neurosciences 2,* 91-93.

Abbott, N.J., Moreton, R.B. and Pichon, Y. (1975). Electrophysiological analysis of potassium and sodium movements in crustacea nervous system. *J. exp. Biol. 63,* 85-115.

Abbott, N.J., Pichon, Y. and Lane, N.J. (1977). Primitive forms of potassium homeostasis: observations on crustacean central nervous system with implications for vertebrate brain. *Exp. Eye Res., Suppl., 25,* 259-271.

Ashhurst, D.E. (1970). An insect desmosome. *J. Cell Biol. 46,* 421-425.

Ashhurst, D.E. and Costin, N.M. (1971). Insect mucosubstances. II. The mucosubstance of the central nervous system. *Histochem. J. 3,* 297-310.

Baker, P.F. (1965). Phosphorus metabolism of intact crab nerve and its relation to the active transport of ions. *J. Physiol., Lond. 180,* 383-423.

Bennett, M.V.L. (1977). Electrical transmission: a functional analysis and comparison to chemical transmission. Ch. 11 in "Handbook of Physiology", Vol.I, Amer. Physiol. Soc., Bethesda, Md.

Bennett, R.R., Buchan, P.B. and Treherne, J.E. (1975). Sodium and lithium movements and axonal function in cockroach nerve cords. *J. exp. Biol. 62,* 231-341.

Binnington, K.C. and Lane, N.J. (1980). Perineurial and glial
cells of the tick nervous system: a tracer and freeze-
fracture study. *J.Neurocytol.*, in press.

Bittner, G.D. and Mann, D.W. (1976). Differential survival
of isolated portions of crayfish axons. *Cell Tiss. Res.*
169, 301-311.

Claude, P. and Goodenough, D.A. (1973). Fracture faces of
zonulae occludentes from 'tight' and 'leaky' epithelia.
J. Cell Biol. 58, 390-400.

Coles, J.A. and Tsacopoulos, M. (1979). Potassium activity in
photoreceptors, glial cells and extracellular space in
the drone retina: changes during photostimulation.
J. Physiol. 290, 525-549.

Erulkar, S.D. and Weight, F.F. (1979). Ionic environment and
the modulation of transmitter release. *Trends in Neurosciences 2*, 298-301.

Evans, P.D. (1974). An autoradiographical study of the
localization of the uptake of glutamate by the peripheral
nerves of the crab, *Carcinus maenas (L.)*. *J. Cell Sci.*
14, 351-367.

Fahrenbach, W.H. (1976). The brain of the horseshoe crab
(Limulus polyphemus). 1. Neuroglia. *Tissue and Cell 8*,
395-410.

Gainer, H. (1978). Intercellular transfer of proteins from
glial cells to axons. *Trends in Neurosciences 1*, 93-96.

Gardner-Medwin, A.R. (1977). The migration of potassium
produced by electric current through brain tissue.
J. Physiol. 269, 32-33P.

Griffiths, G.W. (1979). Transport of glial cell acid phosphatase by endoplasmic reticulum into damaged axons.
J. Cell Sci. 36, 361-389.

Harrison, J.B. and Lane, N.J. (1980). Lack of restriction
at the blood-brain interface in *Limulus*, despite
novel junctional structures. *J. Neurocytol.* (Submitted)

Holtzman, E., Freeman, A.R. and Kashner, L.A. (1970). A cyto-
chemical and electron microscope study of channels in the
Schwann cells surrounding lobster giant axons. *J. Cell
Biol. 44*, 438-445.

Keynes, R.D. and Swan, R.C. (1959). The permeability of frog
    muscle fibres to lithium ions. *J. Physiol. Lond. 147,*
    626-638.

Kuffler, S.W. (1967). Neuroglial cells: physiological proper-
    ties and a potassium mediated effect of neuronal activity
    on the glial membrane potential. *Proc. Roy. Soc. Lond. B.
    168,* 1-21.

Kuffler, S.W. and Nicholls, J.G. (1966). The physiology of
    neuroglial cells. *Ergeb. Physiol. 57,* 1-90.

Kuffler, S.W. and Nicholls, J.G. (1976). "From Neurone to
    Brain". Sinauer, Sunderland, Massachusetts.

Lane, N.J. (1968a). The thoracic ganglia of the grasshopper,
    Melanoplus differentialis: Fine structure of the peri-
    neurium and neuroglia with special reference to the
    intracellular distribution of phosphatases. *Z. Zell-
    forsch. 86,* 293-312.

Lane, N.J. (1968b). Lipochondria, neutral red granules and
    lysosomes: synonymous terms? *In* "Cell Structure and its
    Interpretation". Essays presented to J.R. Baker (S.M.
    McGee-Russell & K.F.A. Ross, eds.), Ch.15, pp.169-182.
    Edward Arnold (Publ.) Ltd., London.

Lane, N.J. (1972). Fine structure of a lepidopteran nervous
    system and its accessibility to peroxidase and lanthanum.
    Z. Zellforsch. 131, 205-222.

Lane, N.J. (1974). The organization of the insect nervous
    system. *In* "Insect Neurobiology" (J.E. Treherne, ed.)
    Frontiers of Biology 35, pp.1071. Elsevier/North-Holland,
    Amsterdam & New York.

Lane, N.J. (1978). Intercellular junctions and cell contacts
    in invertebrates. *In* "Electron Microscopy 1978. Vol. 3.
    State of the Art" Symposia (J.M. Sturgess, ed.). Proc.
    9th International Congress on Electron Microscopy, pp.
    673-691. The Imperial Press Ltd., Canada.

Lane, N.J. (1979a). Intramembranous particles in the form of
    ridges, bracelets or assemblies in arthropod tissues.
    Tissue and Cell 11, 1-18.

Lane, N.J. (1979b). Freeze-fracture and tracer studies on the
    intercellular junctions of insect rectal tissues. *Tissue
    and Cell 11,* 481-506.

Lane, N.J. and Abbott, N.J. (1975). The organization of the
    nervous system in the crayfish *Procambarus clarkii*, with
    emphasis on the blood-brain interface. *Cell Tiss. Res.*
    156, 173-187.

Lane, N.J. and Chandler, H.J. (1980). Definitive evidence for
    the existence of tight junctions in invertebrates. *J.*
    Cell Biol., (submitted).

Lane, N.J., Harrison, J.B. and Bowerman, R. (1980). A
    vertebrate-like blood-brain barrier, with intracerebral
    blood vessels and occluding junctions, in the scorpion
    (Arachnida; Scorpionidea). In preparation.

Lane, N.J., Leslie, R.A. and Swales, L.S. (1975). Insect
    peripheral nerves: accessibility of neurohaemal regions
    to lanthanum. *J. Cell Sci.* *18*, 179-197.

Lane, N.J. and Skaer, H. le B. (1980). Intercellular junct-
    ions in insect tissues. *Adv. Insect Physiol.*, in press.

Lane, N.J., Skaer, H. le B. and Swales, L.S. (1977). Inter-
    cellular junctions in the central nervous system of
    insects. *J. Cell Sci.* *26*, 175-199.

Lane, N.J. and Swales, L.S. (1978a). Changes in the blood-
    brain barrier of the central nervous system in the blow-
    fly during development, with special reference to the
    formation and disaggregation of gap and tight junctions.
    I. Larval development. *Devel. Biol.* *62*, 389-414.

Lane, N.J. and Swales, L.S. (1978b). Changes in the blood-
    brain barrier of the central nervous system in the blowfly
    during development with special reference to the forma-
    tion and disaggregation of gap and tight junctions. II.
    Pupal development and adult flies. *Devel. Biol.* *62*, 415-431.

Lane, N.J. and Swales, L.S. (1979). Intercellular junctions
    and the development of the blood-brain barrier in *Manduca*
    sexta. *Brain Res.* *169*, 227-245.

Lane, N.J. and Swales, L.S. (1980). Dispersal of gap junction-
    al particles, not internalization, during the *in vivo*
    disappearance of gap junctions. *Cell 19*, 579-586.

Lane, N.J., Swales, L.S. and Abbott, N.J. (1977). Lanthanum pene-
    tration in crayfish nervous system; observations on intact
    and desheathed preparations. *J. Cell Sci.* *23*, 315-324.

Lane, N.J. and Treherne, J.E. (1970). Uptake of peroxidase by the cockroach central nervous system. *Tissue and Cell 2*, 413-425.

Lane, N.J. and Treherne, J.E. (1971). The distribution of the neural fat body sheath and the accessibility of the extra-neural space in the stick insect, *Carausius morosus*. *Tissue and Cell 3*, 589-603.

Lane, N.J. and Treherne, J.E. (1972). Studies on perineurial junctional complexes and the sites of uptake of micro-peroxidase and lanthanum in the cockroach central nervous system. *Tissue and Cell 4*, 427-436.

Lane, N.J. and Treherne, J.E. (1973). The ultrastructural organization of peripheral nerves in two insect species (*Periplaneta americana* and *Schistocerca gregaria*). *Tissue and Cell 5*, 703-714.

Lettau, J., Foster, W.A., Harker, J.E. and Treherne, J.E. (1977). Diel changes in potassium activity in the haemo-lymph of the cockroach, *Leucophaea maderae*. *J. exp. Biol. 71*, 171-186.

Loewenstein, W.R., Kanno, Y. and Socolar, S.J. (1978). The cell-to-cell channel. *Fed. Proc. 37*, 2645-2650.

Lord, B.A.P. and diBona, D.R. (1976). Role of the septate junction in the regulation of paracellular transepithelial flow. *J. Cell Biol. 71*, 967-972.

Maddrell, S.H.P. and Treherne, J.E. (1966). A neural fat-body sheath in a phytophagous insect (*Carausius morosus*). *Nature, Lond. 211*, 215-216.

Narahashi, T. and Yamasaki, T. (1960). Mechanism of after-potential production in the giant fibres of the cockroach. *J. Physiol. 151*, 75-88.

Noirot-Timothée, C., Smith, D.S., Cayer, M.L. and Noirot, C. (1978). Septate junctions in insects: comparison between intercellular and intramembranous structures. *Tissue and Cell 10*, 125-136.

Orkand, P. and Kravitz, E.A. (1971). Localization of the sites of γ-amino-butyric acid (GABA) uptake in lobster nerve-muscle preparations. *J. Cell Biol. 49*, 75-89.

Peracchia, C. (1974). Excitable membrane ultrastructure. I. Freeze-fracture of crayfish axons. *J. Cell Biol. 61*, 107-122.

Pichon, Y. and Treherne, J.E. (1970). Extraneuronal potentials and potassium depolarization in cockroach giant axons. *J. exp. Biol. 53*, 485-493.

Pipa, R.L. and Woolever, P.S. (1964). Insect neurometamorphosis. I. Histological changes during ventral nerve cord shortening in *Galleria mellonella L.* (Lepidoptera). *Z. Zellforsch. 63*, 405-417.

Radojcic, T. and Pentreath, V.W. (1979). Invertebrate glia. *Progress in Neurobiology 12*, 115-179.

Salpeter, M.M. and Faeder, I.R. (1971). The role of sheath cells in glutamate uptake by insect nerve muscle preparation. *Prog. Brain Res. 34*, 103-114.

Sarne, Y., Neale, E.A. and Gainer, H. (1976). Protein metabolism in transected peripheral nerves of the crayfish. *Brain Res. 110*, 73-89.

Sarne, Y., Schrier, B.S. and Gainer, H. (1976). Evidence for the local synthesis of a transmitter enzyme (glutamic acid decarboxylase) in crayfish peripheral nerve. *Brain Res. 110*, 91-98.

Scharrer, B.C.J. (1939). The differentiation between neuroglia and connective tissue sheath in the cockroach (*Periplaneta americana*). *J. comp. Neurol. 70*, 77-88.

Schnapp, B. and Mugnaini, E. (1975). The myelin sheath: electron microscopic studies with thin sections and freeze-fracture. *In* "Golgi Centennial Symp. Proc." (M. Santini, ed.) pp.209-233. Raven Press, New York.

Schofield, P.K. and Treherne, J.E. (1975). Sodium transport and lithium movements across the insect blood-brain barrier. *Nature, Lond. 225*, 723-725.

Schofield, P.K. and Treherne, J.E. (1978). Kinetics of sodium and lithium movements across the blood-brain barrier of an insect. *J. exp. Biol. 74*, 239-251.

Shivers, R.R. (1976). Trans-glial channel-facilitated translocation of tracer protein across ventral nerve root sheaths of crayfish. *Brain Res. 108*, 47-58.

Smith, D.S. (1967). The trophic role of glial cells in insect ganglia. *In* "Insects and Physiology" (J.W.L. Beament & J.E. Treherne, eds.) pp.187-198. Oliver and Boyd, London.

Smith, D.S. and Treherne, J.E. (1963). Functional aspects of the organization of the insect nervous system. *Adv. Insect Physiol.* *1*, 401-484.

Smith, D.S. and Treherne, J.E. (1965). The electron microscopic localization of cholinesterase activity in the central nervous system of an insect, *Periplaneta americana L. J. Cell Biol. 26*, 445-465.

Trachtenberg, M.C. and Pollen, D.A. (1970). Neuroglia: biophysical properties and physiological function. *Science N.Y. 167*, 1248-1252.

Treherne, J.E. (1961). The movements of sodium ions in the isolated nerve cord of the cockroach, *Periplaneta americana. J. exp. Biol. 38*, 629-636.

Treherne, J.E. (1962). The distribution and exchange of some ions and molecules in the central nervous system of *Periplaneta americana. J. exp. Biol. 39*, 193-217.

Treherne, J.E. (1966). The effect of ouabain on the efflux of sodium ions in the nerve cords of two insect species *(Periplaneta americana* and *Carausius morosus). J. exp. Biol. 44*, 355-362.

Treherne, J.E. (1974). The environment and function of insect nerve cells. *In* "Insect Neurobiology" (J.E. Treherne, ed.), pp.187-244. Elsevier/North-Holland, Amsterdam.

Treherne, J.E., Lane, N.J., Moreton, R.B. and Pichon, Y. (1970). A quantitative study of potassium movements in the central nervous system of *Periplaneta americana. J. exp. Biol. 53*, 109-136.

Treherne, J.E. and Pichon, Y. (1972). The insect blood-brain barrier. *Adv. Insect Physiol. 9*, 257-313.

Treherne, J.E. and Schofield, J.E. (1978). A model for extracellular sodium regulation in the central nervous system of an insect. *J. exp. Biol. 77*, 251-254.

Treherne, J.E. and Schofield, P.K. (1979). Ionic homeostasis of the brain microenvironment in insects. *Trends in Neurosciences 2*, 227-230.

Tucker, L.E. and Pichon, Y. (1972). Sodium efflux from the
   central nervous connectives of the cockroach. *J. exp.
   Biol. 56,* 441-457.

Villegas, J. (1978). Cholinergic systems in axon-Schwann cell
   interactions. *Trends in Neurosciences 1,* 66-68.

Wigglesworth, V.B. (1959f). The histology of the nervous
   system of an insect *Rhodnius prolixus* (Hemiptera). II.
   The central ganglia. *Quart. J. Micr. Sci. 100,* 299-313.

Wigglesworth, V.B. (1960g). The nutrition of the central
   nervous system in the cockroach *Periplaneta americana L.
   J. exp. Biol. 37,* 500-512.

Willmer, P.G. and Harrison, J.B. (1979). Cation accessibility
   of the peripheral nervous system in *Limulus polyphemus* -
   an electrophysiological study. *J. exp. Biol. 82,* 373-376.

Wolfe, D.E. and Nicholls, J.G. (1967). Uptake of radioactive
   glucose and its conversion to glycogen by neurons and
   glial cells in the leech central nervous system.
   J. neurophysiol. 30, 1593-1609.

THE PAST AND FUTURE OF INSECT MUSCLES

David S. Smith

University of Miami and
Papanicolaou Cancer Research Institute
Miami, Florida

I. PREAMBLE

Despite its title, this essay does not have any direct bearing on the origin of flight in insects or on the muscular specializations that must have accompanied the adaptation of various flaps and appendages, relatively rapidly, to become the wings of powered flight. The title came to mind as I remembered an incident in the Cambridge Zoology department tearoom, when the general plaudits greeting G. S. Carter's "One Hundred Years of Evolution" were interrupted by M.G.M. Pryor's "Wouldn't have thought you'd get much evolution in a hundred years, George." Coincidentally however, a century is a useful round figure for considering the evolution of concepts of muscle structure and function-- a process in which work on insect material has always played, and continues to play an important part.

II. EARLY STUDIES ON MUSCLE CELLS

No student of insect anatomy/physiology, or indeed of anatomical illustration techniques in general, should be unfamiliar with the work of Lyonet and Straus-Durckheim, who respectively dissected the larva of *Cossus* (1762) and the adult of *Melolontha* (1828). Examples from these works are shown in Figs. 1 & 2, with reference to musculature. The still earlier observations of Malpighi, Swammerdam and others started

Previously unpublished work described in this essay was supported by N.I.H. Grant NS-10447

797

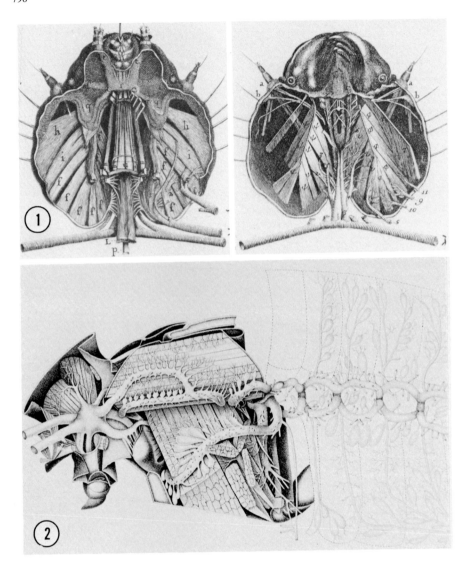

FIGURE 1. *Two stages in the dissection of the head capsule of the goat moth* Cossus *(from Lyonet, 1762).*

FIGURE 2. *A figure from Straus-Durckheim's work (1828) on the anatomy of the beetle* Melolontha, *showing the disposition of muscles and tracheal structures in the thorax.*

the exploration of the 'insides' of the insect body, but were generally concerned with other tissues and organs, several later investigated by Wigglesworth and others, including contributors to this volume. The above works, beautiful as they are, take us well beyond the century stipulated, but they laid the groundwork for the future discipline of cellular organization and function.

The perhaps disproportionate interest (as judged by the number of published works) in muscle *versus* other equally worthy cell systems, in the latter half of the nineteenth century, may in part be ascribed to practicality. While teasing apart a piece of liver or kidney must generally have resulted in a terrible mess (and a whole mount of, say, an insect ganglion would have been comparably discouraging) the same approach to a fascicle of muscle fibers yielded describable and even repeatable results. Von Siebold (1848) noted that some insect flight muscles were especially readily teased into coherent striated fibrils, and for these the term 'fibrillar' has persisted as a mildly confusing term until the present. Retzius (1890), before embarking on a vast range of anatomical studies ranging from invertebrate spermatozoa to the gross morphology of the brains of noted mathematicians and musicians described and accurately figured single striated myofibrils from muscle of a beetle *Oryctes*, and spherical 'sarcosomes', identical with the bodies seen in Altmann's (1890) sections of insect flight muscle and recognized on a structural basis, in the early days of electron microscopy, as the mitochondria of the muscle cell.

In short, these studies on teased preparations and on the sections provided by the first (and sometimes very effective) microtomes showed that striated muscles of insects and other animals comprise aligned arrays of striated myofibrils, which Kölliker (1888) surmised might reflect a degree of order beyond the resolving power of the light microscope. It is probable that some of the above anatomists, who were not hard core insect people, may have arrived at the use of this material *via* distressing experiences with small vertebrates where the slip of a scalpel may obscure progress in a pool of rapidly congealing blood and, if that disaster is avoided, muscle fascicles are found to be stuck together by connective tissue. This is a far cry from the insect with its innocuous hemolymph and readily accessible muscle cells, which in some instances fall apart under a needle or cover slip to reveal myofibrils from which mitochondria detach as readily as peas from a pod.

But there is much more to a muscle cell than fibrils and mitochondria, and flashes of potentially important information are found in the early descriptions, the significance of which was recognized only decades later. For example, when Sir

Vincent was two years old, a pupil of Golgi, Emilio Veratti noted (1902) an ordered system of silver-stained threads in the cytoplasm of insect and other muscles, comprising a very regular arrangement of transverse elements in precise register with the striations together with longitudinal components; an observation interpreted much later in terms of the physical basis of excitation-contraction coupling *via* membrane mediated events. It is unfortunate that, so far as I know, Veratti and Wigglesworth never met, though Sir Vincent grew up to publish over 150 papers during Veratti's lifetime. I believe that they would have found much in common, notably in superlative use of the light microscope and special preparative techniques and they might, between them, have recognized the functional significance of Veratti's work in reconciling fiber diameter with the onserved speed of onset of contraction following stimulation. Such a meeting might, also, have made this contributor's task easier, since apart from an intriguing paper on the waxing and waning of the contractile system of *Rhodnius* intersegmental muscle in concert with the feeding/ molt cycle (Wigglesworth, 1956h), striated muscle has not been one of Sir Vincent's demonstrably favorite tissues-- perhaps because it seemed too similar to that of conventional laboratory animals.

III.   RECENT STUDIES

   A.   *General*

   From the functional standpoint, the contractile fibrils of striated muscles are best considered in terms of the accompany- ing membranes involved in control of cyclic length changes, but it is descriptively convenient to consider them separately. Recent work on 'primitive contractile systems', which figures conspicuously in any cell biological journal over the past few years, has shown that Carnoy was correct (though for all the wrong reasons) in proposing, a century ago, that almost all animal cells possess the property of contractility and that muscle is peculiar mainly in its degree of structural order.

   At first sight, Ogden Nash's brief but perceptive comment that "In the World of mules/There are no rules" could well be taken to apply to muscle structure in invertebrates other than arthropods. In these phyla we find, for example, both smooth and transversely striated muscle in coelenterates (Chapman *et al.*, 1962) and a sharp demarcation between the smooth 'catch' muscle and the rapidly contracting striated portion of the molluscan adductor (Hanson and Lowy, 1960; Millman and Bennett, 1976). In somatic muscles of *Ascaris*, the mountain is brought

to Mahomet (the cns) *via* extensions of the fiber membrane
(del Castillo and Morales, 1969); clearly an awkward device
in terms of more neurones and synapses, appendages and other
evolutionary *desiderata*. In the pharyngeal muscle of this
nematode (Reger, 1966) a peculiar unstriated muscle performs
a comparable mechanical role to muscle in some annelids
(*Syllis spongiphila*, del Castillo *et al.*, 1972; Smith *et al.*,
1973) which contrives a 'striated' pattern in the contractile
system but in which only a single Z-band is included in a
40 μm 'sarcomere'. Other variations include the obliquely
striated fibers of the body wall of the bloodworm *Glycera* and
other annelids (Rosenbluth, 1968). In place of Nash's
epigram, we should perhaps more productively liken consideration of these contractile systems to watching a complex card
game where one knows a couple of basic rules, and the nuances
are derivable, if one watches long enough. In arthropods,
the game is evidently much simpler and one problem seems to
be that of distinguishing between functionally important
variation *vis-à-vis* vertebrate fibers, and evolutionary gloss.

B. *Contractile System*

In insects, visceral muscles, the functional counterparts
of which in the vertebrate body are smooth, are striated in
common with the skeletal cells, and display a 12-membered
actin orbital around each myosin filament, though imperfect
preservation and/or sectioning may suggest a less regular
situation. Flight muscles on the other hand, regardless of
contraction frequency and excitation-contraction characteristics opted in their evolution for a 6-actin orbital in the
configuration that is found in an assortment of crustacean
muscles including the lobster tail fast flexor (Hayes *et al.*,
1971) and the slowly contracting cells of the heart (Smith
and Anderson, 1972) of this animal and, with reference to the
last section, in the muscles responsible for the rapid and
flickering progress of the chaetognath *Sagitta* (Halvarson and
Afzelius, 1969; Duvert *et al.*, 1980). Even this degree of
diversity, together with the variability in insect muscle
sarcomere length, is in marked contrast to the precisely
standardized sarcomere and trigonal actin disposition of
skeletal myofibrils of vertebrates (Huxley, 1957).

The myosin filament is a complex structure, incorporating
a large number of individual myosin molecules into an
aggregate that not only contributes to defining the sarcomere
length but to the disposition and number of actin filaments
that satisfy its cross-bridging capacity. That the pattern
of aggregation of a particular molecular 'species' of myosin

determines the accompanying actin complement is suggested by
recent work (Hayashi *et al.*, 1977) showing that rabbit psoas
myosin, when reconstituted into a filament *in vitro* provides
the framework on which G-actin polymerization results in the
formation of bipolar assemblies including ca. 6-membered
actin orbitals as in the intact muscle (Fig. 3).

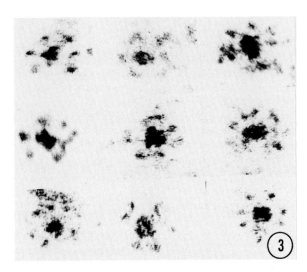

FIGURE 3. *Cross-sections of* in vitro-*assembled actin-myosin
    complexes in which G-actin was polymerized on reconstit-
    uted myosin filaments, both proteins being isolated from
    rabbit skeletal muscle. (From Hayashi et al., 1977)*

In comparable preparations of lobster claw myosin, which *in
vivo* displays a 12-actin ring, preliminary results (Hayashi
et al., 1980) show that this myosin reassembles in a manner
that dictates polymerization of up to 12 actin filaments in
each assembly. Such studies offer a valuable biochemical/
fine structural handle in quest of a solution to a striking
aspect of myofibrillar diversity.

    Wray (1977) pointed out that while much is known about
the enzymatic properties of the cross-bridging 'heads' of the
myosin molecules aligned within the filament, very little is
known of the disposition of the myosin rods within the
filament 'backbone'. Electron micrographs of cross-sectioned
myosin filaments show that these are quite variable: some
are apparently solid and polygonal in profile, while others,
notably some arthropod myosin filaments are conspicuously
tubular in appearance. Wray considered this point and *inter
alia* suggested a model for some insect flight muscles in which

possibly twelve myosin rods are disposed in ring format at
any sectional level.

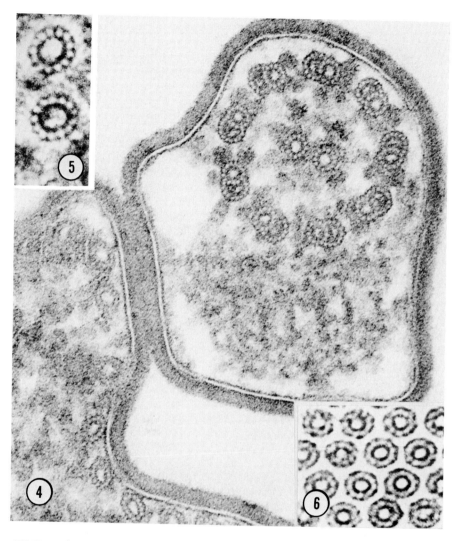

FIGURE 4. Flagellum and cell body surface of a trypanosome
    (T. rhodesiense) fixed in presence of tannic acid. The
    protofilaments of axonemal and subpellicular microtubules
    are seen in negative contrast x 350,000.
FIGURE 5. Similarly prepared microtubules in central glia of
    a cockroach (Periplaneta). Note the 13 negatively stained
    protofilaments (subunits) within each x 600,000.
FIGURE 6. Tannic acid 'stained' microtubular structures in
    venom-secreting cells of a stingray x 430,000.

The similarity of such a structure to the disposition of tubulin protofilaments in cytoplasmic microtubules is clear. The introduction of glutaraldehyde as a primary fixative in place of osmium tetroxide, twenty years ago, preserved a range of microtubules beyond those earlier recognized in cilia and flagella and opened up new insights into how cells divide, maintain and change their shape, and translocate structures and molecules (refs. in Soifer, 1975). More recently, the addition of tannic acid to the fixative (Mizuhira and Futa-esaku, 1971) revealed the constituent subunits or protofila-ments of cytoplasmic and axonemal microtubules in negative contrast. An example of this effect is shown in Fig. 4, in a trypanosome, while Fig. 5 illustrates the ring of thirteen protofilaments in microtubules of central glia of *Periplaneta* where they presumably act as cytoskeletal supports.

If the mordanting action of tannic acid displays the sub-structure of tubulin polymers, may not the same trick work for other similarly constructed protein complexes? It seems to do so in the case of some unusual 'microtubules' in venom cells of the stingray (Smith *et al.*, 1980) which are probably assemblies of protein(s) other than tubulin (Fig. 6). We are attempting to extend this approach to the myosin filament and preliminary results are encouraging. A transverse section of tannic acid/glutaraldehyde fixed flight muscle of a dragon-fly (*Celithemis*) is illustrated in Fig. 7. The superficial similarity of the myosin filaments to tubulin structures is evident, and it appears that some component of the filament, presumably the rods of the myosin molecules, is revealed as a ring, in negative contrast. We hope to resolve this 'ring' in current high resolution studies. This approach, on a comparative basis, may make direct analysis of the structural diversity of the myosin filament more accessible.

Before we leave the contractile system, it is worth look-ing briefly at another fine structural approach that may help to unravel details of myofilament organization-- though this is a much longer shot! Freeze-etch and -fracture replication is now a standard technique for studying the fabric of cell-ular membranes and has led to the most satisfactory and dynamic picture of lipoprotein membranes and their functional and structural diversity. It is not generally realised, however, that the fracture plane may yield useful information as it passes through non-membranous regions. In arthropod cuticle, for example, details are revealed during splitting (which takes place much as a wedge splits a log, without the predictability of lipid bilayer separation) that are not seen in conventional thin sections (Filshie and Smith, 1980).

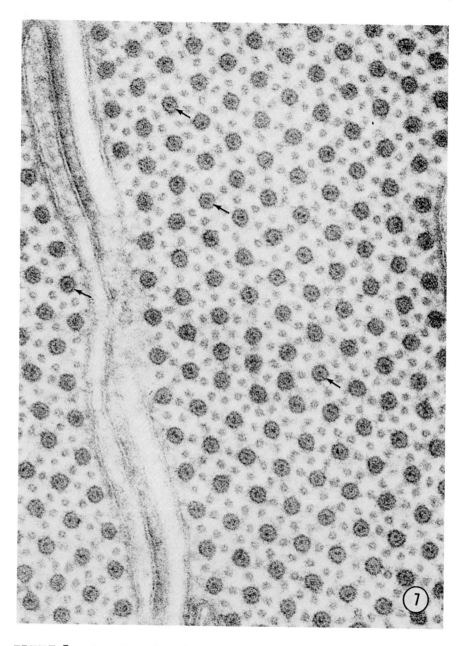

FIGURE 7. *Tannic acid/glutaraldehyde fixed flight muscle of a dragonfly (Celithemis). Each myosin filament includes an unstained ring (arrows) in a position similar to that of the circlet of tubulin protofilaments in the microtubules shown in Figs. 4 & 5   x 180,000.*

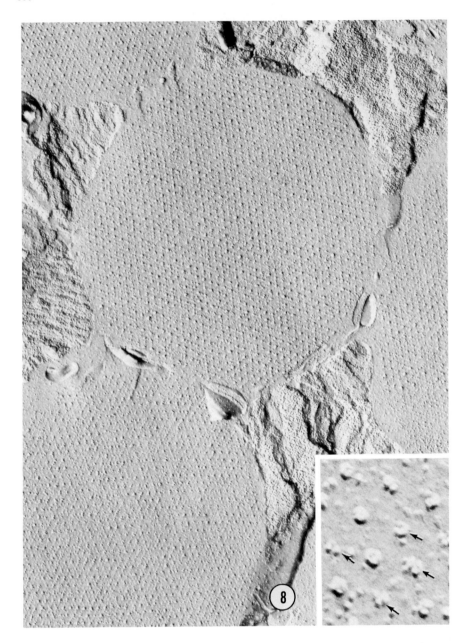

FIGURE 8. Replica of freeze-fractured flight muscle of the honey bee Apis. Note the regular hexagonal arrays of myosin in the cross-fractured myofibrils and evidence of substructure in these filaments at higher magnification (inset: arrows)   x 35,000;   inset x 160,000

Replicas of insect muscle have told us a good deal about the
fine structure of the plasma membrane and other membrane
systems of the fiber (see Figs. 10, 11) and it is possible
that well oriented replicas may contain useful information on
the contractile material. Figure 8 represents a cross-
-fracture of *Apis* flight muscle: cryofracture has preserved
the hexagonal arrangement of myosin filaments in the A-bands,
but less adequately the actin orbitals. While it is possible
that loss in resolution resulting from deposition of the
carbon and metal of the replica on the cleaved surface may
often obscure useful detail across the cleavage plane in a
myofibril, some evidence of the composite nature of the myosin
filaments is apparent (Fig. 8, inset) and future technical
advances may reveal, more precisely, structural details exposed by this technique.

C. Membrane Systems of the Fiber

1. General and Historical. Despite the variation in
disposition of myofilaments in striated muscles and in their
separation into myofibrils, these muscle cells, in vertebrates
and invertebrates, have much in common in the way their membranes are distributed. Skeletal muscle cells are typically
in synaptic contact with one or more motor nerve terminals,
while other muscles may be equipped to receive transmitter
molecules arriving *via* the circulatory system or may be
electrotonically coupled, ultimately to chemically excitable
cells, *via* gap-junctional 'nexus' intercellular contacts. As
might be expected, the 'taxonomy' of muscles and their control
mechanisms do not conform to any single tabulation, any more
than there can be a unique or final scheme for classifying a
family of Lepidoptera. The recognition of new 'taxonomic'
parameters are part and parcel of comparative cell biology as
much as of insect systematics and much of the excitement of
each lies in the recognition of significant similarities
underlying apparent differences.

Veratti's work, at the turn of the century, has already
been mentioned. It is now well known that the silver-stained
threads he saw in the sarcoplasm represent the invaginated
transverse (T-) tubules, confluent with the surface plasma
membrane, along which an excitatory signal initiated at the
depolarized surface is distributed rapidly and regularly to
the interior of the cell. The longitudinal threads proved to
represent an intracellular membrane-limited compartment, the
sarcoplasmic reticulum (SR). Where these two sets of membranes are closely juxtaposed, they form either a two-membered
dyad or a three-membered triad, respectively in arthropod or

vertebrate skeletal fibers (Figs. 9 & 10). What happens at
these points of apposition remains an important question in
muscle biochemistry and physiology, though some possibilities
are discussed by Franzini-Armstrong (1975). In brief, the
signal coupled with surface excitation (as yet not completely
characterized) enters the fiber along the ranks of parallel
T-tubules initiating, by a still obscure mechanism, sudden
release of free calcium ions from the adjacent SR cisternae
at the dyad or triad by a signal acting across the intermembrane gap. The raised calcium level permits actin-myosin
interaction resulting in contraction; rapid calcium sequestration by the SR depletes the calcium level in the *milieu* of
the fibrils and the cycle is completed by relaxation.

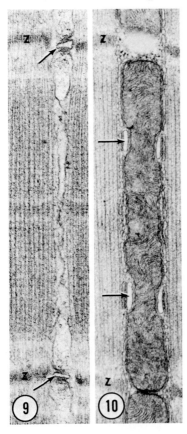

FIGURES 9 & 10. *Illustrating the*
placing of triads and dyads,
respectively in frog sartorius and
dragonfly flight muscle. In the
former, the triads are centered on
the Z-levels, where each T-tubule
(arrows) is flanked by a pair of
SR cisternae. In the dragonfly
muscle, two dyads (arrows) adjoin
each sarcomere surface (Fig. 10):
these are placed approximately mid-
way between the Z-level and the
center of the sarcomere. The
rectangular profiles of the T-
tubules are conspicuous, and each
lies in a trough indenting the
surface of the large mitochondria
which are placed in register with
the sarcomere divisions.
Fig. 9, x 38,000 Fig. 10, x 34,000.

The development of the SR compartment and of the rapid T-
-tubule triggering device must have gone hand in hand with the
evolution of large diameter fibers and their grouping into
massive anatomical muscles, as impressive, to scale in the
insect body, as any in a mammal. Most skeletal fibers respond

synchronously to the motor excitation train and there may be a very approximate relationship between the rapidity of the length change cycle and the volume of the SR. More impressive than such variation, however, is the precision with which the T-tubules traverse the fibrils at a level characteristic of a particular muscle. Beyond these generalities, the descriptive taxonomy of membrane topography becomes either tedious or intriguing, depending on one's point of view. In vertebrate cells, the T-tubules lie in the sarcoplasm either at the Z- or A/I junction levels (refs. in Smith, 1972), while in most synchronous insect fibers the preferred level is mid-way between the Z level and the H-zone in the center of the sarcomere (Figs. 9 & 10). In many vertebrate fibers the SR of the triad is morphologically distinct as the dilated 'terminal cisternae' (Peachey, 1965) as in the frog sartorius (Fig. 9) while in insect cells the SR, while comparably close to the T-tubule, is less obviously zoned along the sarcomere. If we take the maximum diffusion path of calcium released from the SR as the distance between the SR at the dyad or triad and the point within the fibril furthest from the former (whether the fibril is cylindrical or lamellar but with a diameter or width of 1 µm) this path for a 3 µm sarcomere (within the range of many arthropod and vertebrate muscles) is $ca.1.6$ µm and $ca.$ 0.9 µm respectively for the Z-level and mid Z-H examples. In the case of the vertebrate A-I junction muscles (refs. in Smith, 1966) the corresponding distance is $ca.$ 1µm. These distances are all maximal and any differences are probably of no physiological significance since while calcium release may take place initially from the junctional SR next to the T-tubule, it is likely that in muscles where terminal cisternae are not well differentiated (as in insect fibers), release and uptake may take place more generally along the SR surface, thus further reducing the calcium diffusion path.

Altogether, we cannot make any obvious functional sense of the variation in dyad/triad configuration or of the varying levels at which the T-tubules enter the fiber. Some variation even at the fine structural level may be evolutionary 'gloss' of no readily perceptible functional significance. As we go down the scale from gross morphology to subcellular design, the greater becomes the obvious conformity between structure and function-- a measure of the evolutionary levels involved in arriving at, for example, an efficient water-conserving rectal epithelium *versus* the determination of wing pigmentation in two seasonal forms of a butterfly species. If we are too rigidly attuned to a quest for structural and functional links at all levels of enquiry, we may overlook some precepts of cellular evolution. In the first flush of tannic acid

preparation of microtubules, Fujiwara and Tilney (1975) posed
the question "Why has God created thirteen protofilaments?"
and made some suggestions in terms of strain and mechanically
useful instability. Later work, however, showed that He
created nothing so circumscribed and that tubulin polymers of
from 12 to 15 are present in a variety of cell types (Burton
et al., 1975). Following the same general line of thought, in
a different direction, it may be noted that insect structural
colors have been achieved by a variety of macromolecular
devices in cuticular design (Neville, 1975).

But, returning to muscle, what of the 'odd and curious'
fibers-- the pharyngeal muscles of some syllid worms with
their gigantic sarcomeres or the asynchronous flight muscles
of some insect Orders that can achieve oscillatory length-
-change frequencies of up to 1KHz? At the fine structural
level, these are interpretable in the same terms as the more
conventional fibers. The extended sarcomeres of the former
are penetrated by numerous tubular membrane invaginations that
make dyad contacts with small SR cisternae, and while these
dyads lack the precise placing of their counterparts in other
cells they are evidently adequately distributed to mediate
the slow length changes of this muscle. The asynchronous
('fibrillar') flight muscles are remarkable for a similar
paucity of SR, again reduced to small sacs in dyad configuration (Smith, 1961) but here, once the muscle is activated, it
contracts at a frequency determined by mechanical parameters
rather than by that of motor excitation (Pringle, 1965).

2. Membranes of the Dyad and Triad. As suggested above,
perhaps the most controversial region of striated muscle cells,
at present, is the *ca.*8-10 nm 'gap' between the incurrent T-
-tubules and the membrane surface of the calcium-sequestering
SR. This is clearly a junction in the physiological sense,
but its structure does not conform to any of the types of
intermembrane junction described in other cell types. Specifically, it is not a gap-junction , as found in electrotonic
synapses or the nexus regions of vertebrate smooth and cardiac
muscle and many epithelia, with their characteristic intimate
membrane association and arrays of intercalated particles seen
in freeze-fracture replicas (Staehelin, 1974; Larsen, 1977).
This region is considered later, as it appears in an insect
flight muscle.

This volume contains a number of instances where general
questions may be well, or even ideally approached through use
of insect material, and the distribution of membranes in
striated muscle is a case in point. The direct flight muscles

of dragonflies are cylindrical cells possessing radially arranged lamellar fibrils alternating with what may well be the
most massive mitochondria in the Animal Kingdom, together with
a precisely arranged system of T-tubules and SR. There is
nothing unique about these features individually; some muscles
in vertebrates have lamellar rather than cylindrical fibrils,
other insect fibers have a comparable total mitochondrial
volume and the internal membranes are placed in the standard
insect position (Fig. 10). But anyone who has dissected a
frog sartorius, rabbit psoas or even a bat cricothyroid (Revel,
1962) could not fail to be delighted by the ten-second bisect-
ion of the dragonfly thorax that displays the flight muscles
and their apodemal insertions to perfection. Here is anatomy
in a delectable form and, as mentioned before, it is likely
that the seventeenth and eighteenth century pioneers were
similarly encouraged on opening their first few insects, in
finding a clearly organized microcosm of a body, complete with
well defined muscles, nerves and brain, gut and all manner of
fascinating tubules.

   3. Membranes in Dragonfly Muscle. In this muscle, the
T-tubules engage in dyads with the SR which elsewhere forms a

FIGURE 11. *Replica of surface plasma membrane of dragonfly*
    flight muscle (Celithemis). Arrow shows the fiber long
    axis and arrowheads the mouths of the flattened T-tubules
    (cf. Figs. 10-16) x 36,000.

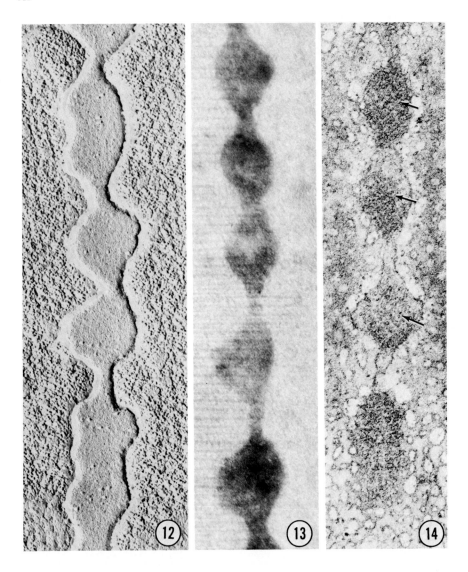

FIGURE 12. A portion of a T-tubule in dragonfly flight muscle
    seen in a freeze-fracture replica. Note the beaded con-
    tour of the tubule   x 85,000.
FIGURE 13. Thin section in similar plane in which the T-
    -tubule has been infiltrated with an electron-opaque
    marker; otherwise unstained   x 85,000.
FIGURE 14. A T-tubule in same plane, after conventional pre-
    paration. Note the processes occupying the dyad junction
    (arrows) opposite dilatations of the tubule, further ill-
    ustrated in Figs. 15 & 16   x 85,000.

fenestrated sheet closely applied to the myofibrillar surface
(Smith and Aldrich, 1971; Smith, 1972). The tubules arise as
open mouthed invaginations, two rows per sarcomere of the
underlying myofibrils, and are readily seen in replicas of the
plasma membrane (Fig. 11), while in vertebrate muscle their
origin is generally onscured by surface caveolae (Smith et al.
1975). Each tubule, in dragonfly muscle, is flattened parallel with the long axis of the fiber, with a larger cross-
-sectional area than their vertebrate counterparts. These
features, together with their straight radial path (compared
with the kinked course of tubules winding between cylindrical
fibrils) offer an ideal geometry for studying the detailed
organization of the T-tubule and its dyad regions.

The triad junction has been extensively studied in skeletal cells of vertebrates. For example, Revel (1962) and
Peachey (1965) described 'foot processes' or pleats extending
from the SR membrane surface towards the T-tubule membrane
respectively in bat cricothyroid and frog sartorius muscle,
and more recently Franzini-Armstrong (1975) described an
orthogonal array of junctional 'feet' stemming from the SR in
frog and fish skeletal fibers, but because of the limited
areas of apposition between the two membranes in this material
had to resort to image reinforcement to make the point clear.
Further details of the triad junction have been added by
Kelly and Kuda (1979) but the question of the relationship
membranes and the feet/processes/dimples has not been fully
answered. Further studies have been published on muscle
membranes and the vertebrate triad, fixed in presence of
tannic acid which, in addition to its value with respect to
tubular protein assembly resolution, provides a very clear
image of the unstained lipid bilayer of biological membranes
(Saito et al., 1978; Somlyo, 1979). The latter study included
a model of the triad junction invoking physical continuity
between the T- and SR membranes via 'sharing' of a lipid monolayer across the triad gap-- a situation which, if true,
would provide a novel basis for considering possible mechanisms of transmembrane linkage in excitation-contraction
coupling.

The architecture of dragonfly flight muscle provides a
more complete picture. Three aspects of the T-tubules are
illustrated in Figs. 12-14. The first shows the characteristically beaded appearance of the tubule, in a replica, as
it traverses the surface of one of the giant mitochondria
(Smith, 1972). In Fig. 13, the continuity of the tubule lumen
with the extracellular space surrounding the fiber is demonstrated by the entry of lanthanum as a marker, while Fig. 14

includes, within its *ca.* 50nm thickness, the surface of a
tubule and compact arrays of dyad processes arising from the
flanking SR cisterna, which is fenestrated except in the dyad
regions. At this magnification these junctional structures
are not individually resolved, but their discontinuous grouping primarily opposite the dilated portions of the tubule is
evident. At higher magnification (Fig. 15) their orthogonal
arrangement (as in vertebrate muscles) and the inset suggests
that each process is square in profile. The spacing of the
processes is *ca.* 20-22nm, and counts on fields such as that
in Fig. 15 show a packing density of *ca.* 1000/μm^2, a figure
similar to that arrived at in fish skeletal muscle (Franzini-
Armstrong, 1975). The complementary aspect of the dyad, in a
section prepared with tannic acid, is illustrated in Fig. 16.

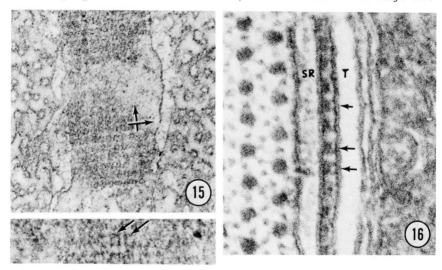

FIGURE 15. *A field similar to the last, at higher magnific-*
   ation. Note the orthogonal disposition of processes
   (axes arrowed) arising from the SR membrane. Their indiv-
   idually square contour in en face view is suggested in the
   inset. Their appearance in transverse section is shown
   in the next figure x 110,000; inset x 180,000.
FIGURE 16. *A transversely sectioned dyad in dragonfly flight*
   muscle after tannic acid fixation. The plane of this
   section is normal to that in Fig. 15. Note the regular
   arrangement of processes stemming from the SR membrane
   and bridging the gap to the T-tubule surface. Each
   process includes an opaque 'base piece' and, probably,
   four projections (cf. Fig. 15), but the alignment of the
   latter in this field shows them as apparent 'pairs'
   x 240,000.

Here the plane of section passes transversely through the dyad as seen at low magnification in Fig. 10. The micrograph shows a regular sequence of complex processes extending from the SR membrane, not merely into the gap but extending all the way across the intermembrane space. In this plane, each process appears to comprise a dense basal structure and a pair of projections. Most gaps examined in such sections are 'noisy' with little or no suggestion of repeating pattern and the regularity seen in Fig. 16 is thought to result from the fortuitous alignment of processes, each including four prongs. The rows of processes are about 20nm apart (center-to-center) (cf. Fig. 15); the section is very thin (ca. 50-60nm) so about three rows are aligned in Fig. 16, one behind the other. To some readers, a familiar analogy might be the alignment of four-legged stools, upended and placed by a meticulous bar tender along a linear counter.

The above results, albeit preliminary, do not accord with the proposal of sharing of integral lipid membrane moieties across the triad (or in this case the dyad) gap and show new structural features of the junctional region. This work continues in an attempt to define more completely the macromolecular details of the junction towards a better understanding of the functional coupling. The primary purpose of this section in the present context, however, has been to illustrate the claim that, at the fine structural level as at other levels, selection of insect material has its advantages. What the 4-pronged feet represent remains to be seen, though their superficial resemblance to some channel molecules (e.g. Potter and Smith, 1977) comes to mind. Why are they grouped primarily opposite the dilated regions of the T-tubule and is their distribution in fibers less amenable to study also discontinuous but overlooked? Why are the tubules in dragonfly muscle considerably larger than in frog sartorius? What are the cable conduction properties of a flattened, periodically dilated tubule? These are all questions posed by insect material, but of relevance to considerations of muscle function in general.

REFERENCES

Altmann, R. (1890). Die Elementarorganismen und ihre Beziehungen zu den Zellen. Viet Co., Leipzig.

Burton, P. R., Hinkley, R. E. and Pierson, G. B. (1975). Tannic acid-stained microtubules with 12, 13 and 15 protofilaments. J. Cell Biol. 65, 227-233.

Chapman, D. M., Pantin, C. F. A. and Robson, E. A. (1962).
    Muscle in coelenterates. *Rev. Canad. Biol. 21*, 267-278.
Del Castillo, J. and Morales, T. (1969). Electrophysiological
    experiments in *Ascaris lumbricoides*. *In* "Experiments in
    Physiology and Biochemistry" *2*, 209-273. Academic Press,
    London.
Del Castillo, J., Anderson, M. and Smith, D. S. (1972). Pro-
    ventriculus of a marine annelid: Muscle preparation with
    the longest recorded sarcomere. *Proc. natn. Acad. Sci.*
    69, 1669-1672.
Duvert, M., Gros, D. and Salat, C. (1980). Ultrastructural
    studies on the junctional complex in the musculature of
    the arrow-worm (*Sagitta setosa;* Chaetognatha). *Tissue &*
    Cell, 12, 1-11.
Filshie, B. K. and Smith, D. S. (1980). A proposed solution
    to a fine-structural puzzle: The organization of gill
    cuticle in a crayfish (*Panulirus*). *Tissue & Cell, 12*,
    209-226.
Franzini-Armstrong, C. (1975). Membrane particles and trans-
    mission at the triad. *Fed. Proc. 34*, 1382-1389.
Fujiwara, K. and Tilney, L. G. (1975). Substructural analysis
    of the microtubule and its polymorphic forms. *Ann. N. Y.*
    Acad. Sci. 253, 27-50.
Halvarson, M. and Afzelius, B. A. (1969). Filament organizat-
    ion in the body muscles of the arrow-worm. *J. Ultrastruct.*
    Res. 26,289-295.
Hanson, J. and Lowy, J. (1960). Structure and function of the
    contractile apparatus in the muscles of invertebrate
    animals. *In* "The Structure and Function of Muscle" (G.H.
    Bourne, ed.), Vol. 1, 265-335. Academic Press, New York.
Hayashi, T., Silver, R. B., Ip, W., Cayer, M. L. and Smith,
    D. S. (1977). Actin-myosin interaction. Self-assembly
    into a bipolar "contractile unit" *J. molec. Biol. 111*,
    159-171.
Hayashi, T., Hinssen, H. and Smith, D. S. (1980). Comparative
    actin-myosin self-assembly studies. *In* 2nd. Int. Congr.
    on Cell Biol., Berlin. (In press).
Hayes, D., Huang, M. and Zobel, C. R. (1971). Electron micro-
    scope observations on thick filaments in striated muscle
    from the lobster, *Homarus americanus*. *J. Ultrastruct.*
    Res. 37, 17-30.
Huxley, H. E. (1957). The double array of filaments in
    cross-striated muscle. *J. biophys. biochem. Cytol. 3*,
    631-648.
Kelly, D. E. and Kuda, A. M. (1979). Subunits of the triadic
    junction in fast skeletal muscle as revealed by freeze-
    -fracture. *J. Ultrastruct. Res. 68*, 220-233.

Larsen, W. J. (1977). Structural diversity of gap junctions. A review. *Tissue & Cell, 9,* 373-394.

Lyonet, P. (1762). "Traité Anatomique de la Chenille qui ronge le Bois de Saule." The Hague.

Millman, B. M. and Bennett, P. M. (1976). Structure of cross--striated adductor muscle of the scallop. *J. molec. Biol. 103,* 439-467.

Mizuhira, V. and Futaesaku, Y. (1971). On the new approach of tannic acid and digitonin to the biological fixatives. *In* 29th Ann. Proc. E. M. S. A., Boston. Claitor, Baton Rouge, La.

Neville, C. (1975). Biology of the Arthropod Cuticle. Springer, Berlin, Heidelberg & New York.

Peachey, L. D. (1965). The sarcoplasmic reticulum and transverse tubules of the frog's sartorius. *J. Cell Biol. 25,* 209-232.

Pringle, J. W. S. (1965). Locomotion: Flight. *In* "The Physiology of Insecta" (M. Rockstein, ed.), Vol. 2, 283-329. Academic Press, New York.

Reger, J. F. (1966). The fine structure of fibrillar components and plasma membrane contacts in esophageal myoepithelium of *Ascaris lumbricoides* (var. suum). *J. Ultrastruct. Res. 14,* 602-617.

Revel, J. P. (1962). The sarcoplasmic reticulum of the bat cricothyroid muscle. *J. Cell Biol. 12,* 571-588.

Retzius, G. (1890). Muskelfibrille und Sarcoplasma. *Biol. Untersuch., 1* (N.F.). 51-88.

Rosenbluth, J. (1968). Obliquely striated muscle. IV. Sarcoplasmic reticulum, contractile apparatus, and endomysium of the body muscle of a polychaete, *Glycera,* in relation to its speed. *J. Cell Biol. 36,* 245-259.

Saito, A., Wang, C-T., and Fleischer, S. (1978). Membrane asymmetry and enhanced ultrastructural detail of sarcoplasmic reticulum revealed with use of tannic acid. *J. Cell Biol. 79,* 601-616.

Siebold, C. T. (1848). Vergleichende Anatomie der wirbellosen Tiere. p.562.

Smith, D. S. (1961). The structure of fibrillar flight muscle: A study made with special reference to the membrane systems of the fiber. *J. biophys. biochem. Cytol. 10,* suppl. 123-158.

Smith, D. S. (1966). The organization and function of the sarcoplasmic reticulum and T-system of muscle cells. *Progr. Biophys. Molec. Biol. 16,* 107-142.

Smith, D. S. (1972). Muscle. Academic Press, New York and London.

Smith, D. S. and Aldrich, H. C. (1971). Membrane systems of freeze-etched striated muscle. *Tissue & Cell, 3,* 261-281.

Smith, D. S. and Anderson, M. E. (1972). The disposition of membrane systems in cardiac muscle of a lobster, *Homarus americanus*. *Tissue & Cell, 4,* 629–645.

Smith, D. S., del Castillo, J. and Anderson, M. (1973). Fine structure and innervation of an annelid muscle with the longest recorded sarcomere. *Tissue & Cell, 5,* 281–302.

Smith, D. S., Baerwald, R. J. and Hart, M. A. (1975). The distribution of orthogonal assemblies and other intercalated particles in frog sartorius and rabbit sacrospinalis muscle. *Tissue & Cell, 7,* 369–382.

Smith, D. S., Cayer, M. L. and Russell, F. E. (1980). Tannic acid staining of 'microtubules' in venom-secreting cells of the stingray. *Toxicon,* (In press).

Soifer, D. (1975). The biology of cytoplasmic microtubules. (D. Soifer, ed.). *Ann. N. Y. Acad. Sci. 253.*

Somlyo, A. V. (1979). Bridging structures spanning the junctional gap at the triad of skeletal muscle. *J. Cell Biol. 80,* 743–750.

Staehelin, L. A. (1974). Structure and function of intercellular junctions. *Int. Rev. Cytol. 39,* 191–283.

Straus-Durckheim, H. (1828). Considérations générales sur l'anatomie comparée des Animaux Articulés... Paris and Strasbourg.

Veratti, E. (1902). Richerche sulle fine struttura della fibra muscolare striata. *Mem. ist. lomb., Classe sc. mat. e nat. 19,* 87–133. (Translation: *J. biophys. biochem. Cytol. 10,* suppl. 3–59.

Wigglesworth, V. B. (1956h). Formation and involution of striated muscle fibres during the growth and moulting cycles of *Rhodnius prolixus* (Hemiptera). *Quart. J. micr. Sci. 97,* 465–480.

Wray, J. S. (1979). Structure of the backbone in myosin filaments of muscle. *Nature, Lond. 277,* 37–40.

PACEMAKER NEURONES AND RHYTHMIC BEHAVIOR

P. L. Miller

Department of Zoology
Oxford

A. INTRODUCTION

For Wigglesworth (1939) the physiological analysis of insect behaviour consisted of "... the analysis of movements of the whole organism into a series of reflexes or observed correlations between stimulus and response". He was keenly aware that responses to standard stimuli vary greatly with the condition of the insect and with the time since the last stimulus, and stated that "... in practice the analysis of behaviour along these lines does not go very far..." without the introduction of "... psychological terminology". It is this psychological terminology which is now beginning to yield to physico-chemical explanations and to an understanding of mechanisms at the cell level ... but it is yielding rather slowly.

Rhythmic activity characterises a great deal of the behaviour of arthropods, perhaps in part because they possess a hard exoskeleton and their many dicondylic joints are controlled by pairs of antagonistic muscles (Miller, 1974). Repetitive activity is also a feature of several 'physiological' systems such as heartbeat, breathing, gut movement and moulting. Much is known about the neural basis of a few rhythmic activities whose pattern-generating neurones lie outside the CNS, for example in the crustacean stomatogastric (Selverston, 1977) or cardiac (Hartline, 1979) ganglia, but those controlled from within the CNS are less well understood since the relevant neurones are often inaccessible.

In this chapter I will describe what is known of one type of cellular oscillator, and juxtapose this to a review of a few types of rhythmic behaviour. The adoption of a viewpoint from which mechanisms and phenomena can simultaneously be

viewed may help to indicate common features of interest. But
convergent behaviour may conceal divergent mechanisms. For
example,gastropod, crayfish and leech hearts all produce
rhythmic contractions, but the first is myogenic and the
others neurogenic. Moreover motor patterns for heartbeat are
formed in the cardiac ganglion of the crayfish, but in the
CNS of the leech (Stent et al, 1979). However at the membrane
level they may perhaps depend on similar ionic mechanisms -
just as the same bricks can be used to construct many
different types of building.

All rhythmic forms of insect behaviour which have been
examined depend at least in part on central pattern generators.
Peripheral input may initiate, control, adjust the frequency
of, orientate, and terminate the repetitive activity, but it
never seems to be essential for its patterning. This is
built into the design of the engine. Many central pattern
generators depend on pacemakers. One type of pacemaker
neurone produces regular brief oscillations of potential each
of which generates a single spike, and it fires in long
trains of spikes. Another type generates a similar pacemaker
potential, but this is followed by a plateau of depolarisation before it repolarises. A burst of spikes may appear
on the depolarisation plateau, and repetitive bursts characterise the activity of this type. Both types of pacemaker,
sometimes called fast and slow, may be able to generate
oscillations of potential without spikes. It is important to
distinguish these two from a third type of cell which has no
pacemaking capacity, but in response to a short stimulus such
as an EPSP produces a depolarization plateau and a burst of
spikes. This has been termed a driver potential (Tazaki and
Cooke, 1979a). The possible contributions of burst-forming
pacemakers and of driver potentials to the generation of
motor output has received rather little attention in
arthropods.

Bursts of impulses can be produced not only by bursting
pacemakers, as described above, but also by the interaction
of pools of neurones which may include some fast but no
bursting pacemakers. Bursts result from excitatory or
inhibitory couplings between cells. The interneurones
responsible for the swimming motor programme in leeches are
linked by inhibitory synapses (Stent et al, 1978), and the
same may be true for the interneurones which produce locomotory patterns in some insects (Pearson, 1977, 1979;
Burrows, 1980).

In practice it may be difficult to distinguish single-cell
from multi-cell burst production, but one test is to isolate
neurones. The soma of a burst-producing neurone in Aplysia
continued to burst after its isolation (Alving, 1968), but
this has not been observed so far in arthropods. Single-cell

bursters may interact with each other in a net: for example
three such cells cooperate to produce the pyloric rhythm in
the crayfish stomatogastric ganglion (Selverston, 1977).
Moreover in the same ganglion some neurones of the gastric
pool which can normally generate bursts only by mutual interaction may nevertheless be capable of acting as endogenous
bursters under exceptional conditions. This has also been
found to be the case for some of the follower neurones of the
pyloric system (Russell and Hartline, 1978). Moreover in the
crab heart-ganglion, large follower cells can produce driver
potentials (plateaux) in response to brief stimuli (Tazaki
and Cooke, 1979a). Thus many neurones may be capable of
burst generation and of pacemaker activity under certain
conditions. It may not therefore be easy to distinguish
between pacemaker and non-pacemaker, burster and non-burster
and single-cell or multi-cell burst production. The only
valid criterion is to establish the cell's natural contribution to activity in vivo.

Only a few insect pacemaking systems have been identified.
Myogenic examples are found in the muscles of tubular systems
such as the heart, gut and Malpighian tubules. They also
occur in asynchronous flight muscle and in a small region of
the extensor tibiae muscle of the hindleg of the locust
(Hoyle, 1978). Neurogenic pacemakers are probably common
among interneurones. (In Aplysia ganglia, 76% of all neurones
may be spontaneously active; Koester and Kandel, 1977). They
have also tentatively been identified in a few insect motor
neurones such as that supplying the locust anterior coxal
adductor and those to some spiracle muscles. In these,
'pacemaker' activity consists of tonic trains of impulses.
It is difficult to distinguish continual firing due to auto-
activity from that which results from a sustained depolarisation imposed by other cells. In the first example however
antidromic stimulation and perfusion of the neuropile with
magnesium-rich, calcium-zero Ringer which abolishes all reflex
activity and makes the firing of the 'pacemaker' neurone
steadier, strongly suggest that it is autoactive (Woollacott and Hoyle, 1977).

Insect motor neurones are not known to cooperate in the
generation of rhythmic patterns, although cases of this have
been described in other arthropods such as in the crustacean
swimmeret system whose motor neurones are electrically
coupled and constitute a part of the oscillator (Heitler,
1978). In insects, patterned rhythmic activity seems to
arise exclusively in interneurones. Technical problems in
recording from interneurones have caused an understanding of
insect pattern generators to lag behind what is known in some
other invertebrates. This is one reason why it may be useful
to look closely at other invertebrate examples to see if

their outputs share properties with those in insects, and to
ask if common principles of pattern generation can be distinguished. We can start by looking briefly at some of the best
known rhythmically active cells - those found in gastropod
ganglia.

B. SINGLE-CELL BURSTING PACEMAKERS

Two mechanisms for producing rhythmic activity in cells
have been distinguished (Tsien et al, 1979) (Fig. 1). The
first operates at the membrane level and depends on inter-
related potential fluctuations and delayed conductance
changes which alone may be adequate to explain sustained
oscillatory activity (Meech, 1979). The second links biochemical intracellular oscillations to events at the membrane
and suggests that they are fundamental to the maintenance of
the electrical rhythm (Rapp and Berridge, 1977).

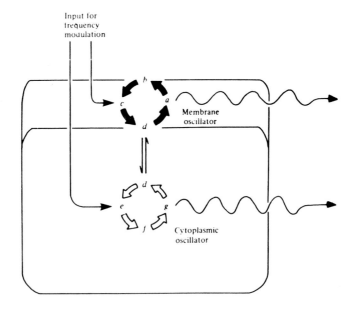

FIGURE 1. A diagram of the location of two types of cellular
oscillator. a-d represent the components of a membrane
oscillator, and d-g, those of a cytoplasmic biochemical
oscillator. The two types are linked by sharing a common
component, d. (From Berridge and Rapp, 1979.)

Some of the most intensively studied single-cell bursters are those from the ganglia of Aplysia and Helix (Arvanitaki and Chalazonitis, 1968; Chalazonitis, 1968). They may be neuro-secretory cells but the significance of their burst production is not known (Kandel, 1976, 1979). Other well studied examples include leech-heart interneurones (Calabrese, 1979; Stent et al., 1979), pyloric neurones in crayfish and crab stomatogastric ganglia (Selverston, 1977; Hermann, 1979) and neurones in the crustacean cardiac ganglion (Tazaki and Cooke, 1979b). Many other types of cell, including verte-brate heart pacemakers, (Noble, 1979) produce rhythmic slow depolarisations and hyperpolarisations, and they may depend on similar ionic mechanisms (Rapp and Berridge, 1977; Berridge and Rapp, 1979; Rapp, 1979; Meech, 1979; Berridge, 1979). It is not the intention here to go into details of the hypotheses and evidence which account for slow oscilla-tions in neurones, but only to indicate briefly a possible ionic mechanism.

In outline the ionic hypothesis is as follows: a steady, slow, inward current carried by sodium and calcium ions depolarises the pacemaker membrane; a decay of outward potassium current also contributes to depolarisation. The accumulation of calcium inside the cell gradually increases potassium conductance. The consequent slow outward potassium current hyperpolarises the cell. Time- and voltage-dependent mechanisms may also contribute to the rise in potassium conductance. As calcium is removed from the cytosol, potassium conductance falls again and the slow inward sodium and calcium current is renewed: once more the cell starts to depolarise and the next slow cycle is initiated. This type of mechanism seems to be common in many types of oscillator.

If the depolarising wave reaches threshold, a burst of spikes is produced, each spike being dependent on fast calcium, sodium and potassium channels which are independent of the slow channels described above. According to Thompson and Smith (1976) each spike may be followed by a brief de-polarising after-potential which helps to sustain the burst. Spikes often tend to wax and wane in frequency during a burst, giving it a 'parabolic' shape. Thus in summary the burst of spikes in this type of pacemaker is dependent on cyclical changes of potassium conductance.

Treatment of an Aplysia ganglion with tetrodotoxin abolishes the spikes but slow waves persist in pacemaker cells. A similar finding has been made in vertebrate heart (McDonald and Sachs,1975). Spikes are not therefore an essential part of the mechanism. Gorman and Thomas (1978) have demonstrated in Aplysia pacemakers that a large rise in intracellular calcium occurs during the burst, but a small and definite one can still be measured in non-spiking cells during the slow

depolarisation. Injection of calcium causes pacemakers to
hyperpolarise more than normal and reduces the burst frequency,
whereas injection of calcium-chelating agents may reduce the
hyperpolarising wave and make the cells more excitable (Meech,
1974, 1979). Calcium levels therefore seem to play a key role
by controlling potassium conductance: normally their gradual
elevation promotes the hyperpolarisation which terminates the
burst. Strumwasser (1973) claimed that Aplysia pacemakers
continued to oscillate in the absence of calcium, a result
which can be explained either if time- and voltage-dependent
changes in potassium conductance are alone adequate to hyperpolarise the cell, or if residual amounts of calcium remained
in his preparations.

In its simplest form therefore the hypothesis depends on a
changing cytosol calcium level which affects the membrane
potential by controlling potassium conductance. The rate of
calcium removal from the cytosol would provide a means of
regulating the frequency of oscillations. Such a mechanism
could be self-sustaining, or it could be driven by underlying
biochemical oscillations. Rapp and Berridge (1977) have
suggested that a negative feedback loop formed by the interaction of calcium with cyclic nucleotides could form such an
intracellular oscillator. Intracellular calcium interacts
with a binding protein, calmodulin, which then may act on
several systems in the cell. One may be to activate a
plasma-membrane calcium pump, and another to activate adenylate cyclase which synthesises cAMP. cAMP promotes the
sequestration of calcium within intracellular compartments.
Thus the entry of calcium into the cell promotes its own
removal. Theoretical calculations and experimental evidence
have been combined to support the suggestion that such a
Ca-cAMP loop could produce sinusoidal oscillations in intracellular calcium levels with periods ranging from 100 ms to
5 minutes, provided that the enzyme was allosteric and capable
of cooperative interaction. Adenylate cyclase is thought to
have such properties. Experiments in which calcium and cAMP
levels were altered in cells have provided supporting evidence
for the hypothesis. Thus, in summary, calcium and cAMP levels
may oscillate 180° out of phase in a cell and thereby provide
the driving force for the membrane potential oscillations
which underlie burst production. Other metabolic or biochemical intracellular oscillating systems dependent on
mitochondria, or on glycolysis, are also known and could in
some cells provide a comparable engine for rhythmic activity.

Rapp and Berridge have suggested that the calcium-cAMP
mechanism, with some modifications, could account for sustained oscillations in many types of cell including vertebrate
heart pacemakers. Some pyloric neurones in the crab stomatogastric ganglion have been shown to be capable of endogenous

burst production, and there is good evidence that the ionic
mechanism is the same as that described here (Hermann, 1979).
Whether an underlying biochemical oscillator is also involved
in the crab is unknown.

We can now look at a few selected examples of oscillatory
neural activities mainly in insects to see what information
is available about their genesis and whether they show
features like those elsewhere.

C. SOME NON-LOCOMOTORY LEG RHYTHMS

Repetitive contractions and relaxations are features of
the activity of one or more leg muscles in several species
when locomotion is not occurring. Mention has already been
made of the locust myogenic rhythm which arises in a small
group of fibres in the extensor tibiae muscle of the hindleg
(the jumping muscle). It is normally over-ridden by resistance reflexes in the intact insect, but is readily visible
in a leg whose nerve supply has been cut (Hoyle, 1974, 1978).
All other leg rhythms which have been described depend on
repetitive motor bursts which may arise endogenously either in
interneurones or in motor neurones. Examples can be found in
stick insects (Carausius and Extatasoma) which tend to make
side-to-side rocking movements generated by alternating bursts
in antagonistic muscles at the femoro-tibial joint. Deaffer-
entation shows that the rhythm can be produced endogenously,
although its frequency in Carausius is then reduced. Pro-
prioceptive mechanisms evidently accelerate the endogenous
rhythm and maintain it close to the resonant frequency of
the system (Pflüger, 1977; Bässler and Pflüger, 1979).

Two types of tarsal twitching have been observed in stick
insects (Carausius): one occurs at 80-120 min^{-1} (wagging)
and the other at 8-22 min^{-1} (waving). Both depend on repetitive activity of the retractor unguis, but their origin is
not understood (Walther, 1969). The retractor unguis is also
responsible for tarsal twitching in wasps and bees, an activity which can readily be observed when a foot is held off the
ground. By recording electromyograms from Paravespula
vulgaris and Bombus spp., combined with intracellular records
from muscle fibres, some features of this activity have been
examined (Miller, unpubl.). Bursts can be recorded at all
times in quiescent insects, even in queen wasps aroused from
winter hibernation, and they normally take place at a stable
frequency of 2-5 Hz (Fig. 2A,B). The bursts occur independently in each leg, and are not related to other rhythmic
activity such as ventilation. Each burst normally consists of
2-10 spikes usually at a declining frequency. They continue

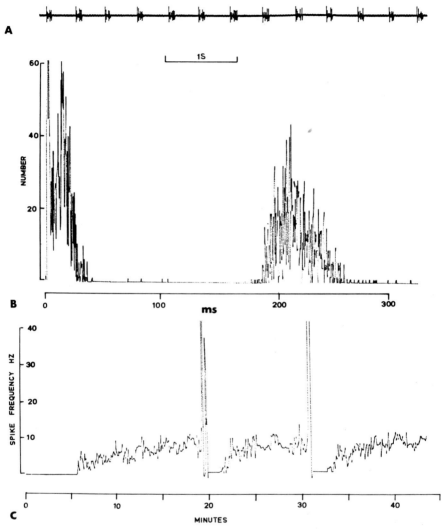

FIGURE 2. Activity recorded from the retractor unguis muscle
of the leg of a quiescent queen wasp, _Paravespula vulgaris_.
A, electromyograms of regular bursts of motor impulses.
B, a non-sequential histogram based on 256 sweeps: each
sweep, triggered by the start of a burst, includes two bursts
which are shown to occur at very regular intervals. C, a
pulse-density histogram measured after a period of struggling.
Activity commences after 5 min and is subsequently interrupted after 19 and 31 min by brief struggles which are
followed by 2-min silent intervals. The frequency then
gradually climbs back to the previous value.

unchanged when the foot is in the air or on the ground, but
are replaced by tonic firing if the leg is forcibly extended.
They cease during other types of activity of the leg and are
resumed about 1 minute after such activity ceases, but it may
take a further 2-3 minutes before the resting frequency is
restored (Fig. 2C). Bursts continue unchanged when the leg
is removed and recordings are made from the proximal nerve
stump.

These features suggest that there is a separate burst-
forming endogenous oscillator for a retractor unguis motor
neurone of each leg which is persistently active in quiescent
insects but which is suppressed both during spontaneous leg
movements and by proprioception during forcible leg extension.
The fine structure of the retractor unguis of a wasp has been
examined recently by Weaving and Cullen (1978); they have
drawn attention to the unusually rich amount of sarcoplasmic
reticulum and to the paucity of mitochondria in this muscle,
features which it is not easy to relate to the activity
described.

The functions of these various types of leg rhythm are in
some cases uncertain. Rocking by stick insects may have
cryptic value. Tarsal twitching in the beetle Sisyphus was
held to represent a general stimulatory or arousal mechanism
(see Wigglesworth, 1972, p.310). Myogenic activity in locust
legs may possibly serve a circulatory function (Hoyle, 1978).
Lateral swaying movements in locusts and other species
probably allow for visual scanning.

D. TWITCHING IN THE ISOLATED LEGS OF OPILIONES

A clearer functional role may be ascribed to the twitching
of autotomised legs of Opiliones (harvestmen) and of some
pholcid spiders (Smeringopus, Crossopriza). It is believed
to attract the attention of predators while the harvestman
or spider escapes notice. The discarded legs twitch violently
and rapidly at the femoro-patellar and tibio-metatarsal joints
(Miller, 1977). Flexions at each joint are brought about by
short bursts of motor impulses in a single 'fast' motor
axon to each flexor muscle. Extensions result from elastic
mechanisms. Recording from the nerve and the muscle simultaneously has confirmed that the activity is neurogenic
(Fig. 3A). Autotomy breaks the leg at the trochantero-
femoral joint in Opiliones and it is suggested that the injury
current produced in severed axons excites a pacemaking system
which generates reiterated bursts of impulses. The characteristic bursting activity can be initiated in any of the following ways:

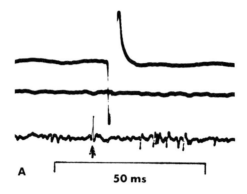

FIGURE 3. Electrical records from isolated harvestmen legs. A, upper trace, electromyogram from the metatarsal flexor; middle trace, electromyogram from the tibial flexor; lower trace, record from the main nerve trunk in the femur, all in Oligolophus spinosus. A single distally propagating motor spike (arrow) precedes the potential in the metatarsal flexor by 6 ms. Every muscle potential recorded was similarly preceded by a motor spike indicating the neurogenic origin of the activity. A burst of sensory spikes follows each muscle twitch. B, electromyogram from the tibial flexor muscle of Oligolophus agrestis. A small drop of Ringer solution (Rathmayer, 1965) containing 50 mM/l. potassium was placed outside the femur. At the arrow, a tiny pin prick was made through the femoral cuticle at the midpoint, and bursting started after 2-3 s.

1. By autotomy.
2. By injury of the leg nerve proximal to the trochanter: this usually produces bursting which is slower and longer-lasting than normal.
3. By stretching the nerve in the femur.
4. By keeping the animal in 5% oxygen in nitrogen.
5. By electrical stimulation with DC pulses across the femur.
6. By injection of extremely small amounts of Ringer (Rathmayer, 1965) containing 50 mM/l potassium into the femur (Fig. 3B). The injection of small amounts elsewhere, and of normal Ringer into the femur are without effect.

All except the first two treatments are fully reversible and can be repeated on the same leg a number of times. These different treatments may all excite bursting by depolarising a pacemaker system. Permanent injury is not an essential requirement. Moreover bursting in the fast motor nerve can coincide with centrally generated activity in the slow axon to the same muscle; the joint can then be observed to make slow movements with twitches superimposed on them.

By whatever means it is evoked, bursting activity shows the following features:
1. Bursting in the two motor axons of the same leg is independent. It is also independent of bursting in other legs.
2. Sensory loops are not involved. The joints can be fixed, removed, or mechanically driven at various requencies all without effect on the motor bursts.
3. Bursting typically starts at a high frequency (15 Hz) and gradually falls to a plateau of 1-3 Hz. It may continue for only a few seconds, or be maintained for many minutes or an hour.
4. As the number of spikes in a burst declines during a burst sequence, so the interburst interval shortens and the burst frequency therefore accelerates (Fig. 4).
5. Burst duration shows only a slight fall as the spike frequency declines.
6. Bursts are sometimes 'parabolic' in shape. They may be exact replicas of each other for long periods.
7. In both motor axons bursts arise in the proximal region of the femur.

No other part is capable of burst generation.

Some of these features resemble the characteristics of bursting cells in Aplysia. For example in both the bursts occur for long periods at very regular frequencies, show little variation of burst structure, are largely independent of activity elsewhere, may have a parabolic shape, respond similarly to hypoxia, and show a linear relationship between spike frequency (or number of spikes/burst) and the duration of the subsequent interburst interval. In Aplysia pacemakers

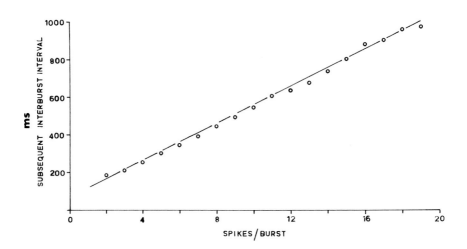

FIGURE 4. The number of spikes per burst plotted against the
duration of the subsequent interburst, from an actively
twitching isolated leg of Oligolophus agrestis. The data
were taken from late in a bursting sequence when there was a
slow increase in burst frequency and a decline in the number
of spikes in each burst.

the degree of hyperpolarization and the duration of the interburst are both related to the size of the preceding burst:
more spikes may cause a greater entry of calcium into the
cell and thus an increased potassium conductance with
consequently greater hyperpolarization. A decreased sodium
conductance and an increased rate of electrogenic sodium pump
activity could also be contributory mechanisms. The initial
decline in bursting frequency after autotomy of a harvestman's
leg is possibly accounted for by accommodation, like that
described in Aplysia bursting cells when injected with a
steady depolarising current (Arvanitaki and Chalazonitis,
1968).
     Where does bursting activity arise? No unusual neural
structures have been observed in sections of the femur
examined by electron microscopy. However Foelix (1975)
described synapses in the tibiae of Opiliones which he suggested might occur between sensory and interneurones, the latter
representing expressways to the CNS for priority sensory
information; but twitching is not dependent on such activity.
Alternatively, interneurones might synapse with motor neurones

in the femur, in a similar way to those reported in the legs of Drosophila (King, 1977). Bursting activity could then arise in the peripheral parts of the interneurones, which would in turn drive the motor neurones. More simply, bursts might be generated by the motor axons themselves, but this cannot be resolved without more experiments.

Neither autotomy nor the injection of potassium-rich Ringer evokes bursting in the legs of other species of pholcid spiders whose legs do not twitch when discarded. Unpatterned and brief injury discharges are all that can be recorded from them. Twitching in autotomised legs is therefore an unusual property shown only in Opiliones and some pholcid species. It must depend on a neural burst-forming pacemaker with some properties like those known in Aplysia: it resides near the middle of the femur either in the fast motor axon or in some other neuron, and it may be excited by sustained depolarisation.

Arvanitaki (1939) showed that squid axon kept in calcium-free Ringer spontaneously developed local subthreshold depolarising membrane oscillations, each lasting for about 5-10 ms; periodically these built up to threshold and each then initiated a spike. After a few spikes the oscillations waned but then waxed again. In this way successive bursts of impulses were generated. Spontaneous oscillations with or without spikes have also been seen in crab nerve at frequencies as low as 2 Hz (Hodgkin, 1948). Bursts in squid axon differ from those produced by the legs of Opiliones in that their duration was more variable, their component spikes occurred at fixed intervals, and the interburst was not related to the length of the preceding burst. The shape and form of bursts in Opiliones therefore resemble more closely those from Aplysia pacemakers rather than those in squid axons. However the differences may not be of great significance.

Since calcium plays important roles in pacemaker cells, it was decided to alter calcium levels in the legs of Opiliones. Only preliminary experiments have so far been attempted. Injections of very small amounts of calcium-rich Ringer (containing 64 mM/l, i.e. 16 times normal concentration) into the femur were found to curtail and sometimes to abolish all bursting in legs when they were subsequently autotomised. The injections of similar amounts of calcium-rich Ringer into the tibia, and into parts of the body were without effect. Reduced calcium levels have not yet been applied. The multiplicity of functions served by calcium makes interpretations of the result difficult. Not only does calcium affect the conductance of other ions, but it may also carry inward current itself, and act at several sites within the cell as a secondary messenger. However the result is probably due to hyperpolarisation of the pacemaker, in

agreement with what is known in squid axon where a five times
increase of external concentration is equivalent to hyperpolarising the membrane by 10-15 mV (Frankenhaeuser and
Hodgkin, 1957; cf. Tazaki and Cooke, 1979b). As already
mentioned the injection of calcium into Aplysia pacemakers
also causes increased hyperpolarization and a slower rate of
bursting.

In insect axons inward current during a spike is carried
by sodium ions. However sodium and calcium ions both contribute to the inward current of spikes which occur in the
somata of certain dorsal unpaired median neurones in locust
ganglia (Goodman and Heitler, 1979). This agrees with what
is known of soma spikes in Aplysia (Kuno and Llinas, 1970).
If the pacemaker responsible for twitching in the legs of
Opiliones proves to be comparable to that in some Aplysia
neurones, its spikes may also be partly dependent on inward
calcium current. However, little is known of the ionic basis
of spikes in arachnids. In conclusion it can be said that
while the form of the bursts in isolated legs of Opiliones
resembles that produced by Aplysia pacemakers, nothing is yet
known of the generating mechanism.

E. SLOW RHYTHMS

Many behaviour patterns in insects are organised into
sequences of bouts. When each bout in a sequence is more or
less the same in form, the sequence may be described as
homogeneous (Hinde and Stephenson, 1969). Bouts and interbouts may remain unchanged in duration throughout a sequence,
or they may alter in a stereotyped manner, or again they may
each be affected by various environmental influences. When
successive bouts are formed from different acts, but in a
predictable order, the sequence is termed heterogeneous.
Patterns such as locomotion, grooming, feeding, stridulation,
moulting and even breathing are sometimes expressed as one
or the other type of sequence, and they provide examples of
long-term rhythms. Such rhythms could be due to an underlying
slow oscillator, similar in principle to those which drive
faster rhythms, or they could result simply from feedback,
either from the periphery, or from pools of active neurones.

Running in flies and ventilation in cockroaches will be
taken as examples of homogeneous sequences, and moulting in
locusts to represent a heterogeneous sequence. Outlines of
the behaviour are given below as a first stage in the analysis
of their neural basis.

1. Homogeneous sequences: fly-running

    A repetitive activity appearing as a series of short stereo-
typed bouts, may be thought of as being gated by a central or
a peripheral mechanism which permits its periodic expression.
Some insects show such a gated pattern in their running
activity: short runs alternate with brief halts. This
behaviour has been examined in a phorid fly, Megaselia
scalaris, by means of filming at 64 and 500 frames s^{-1}
(Miller, 1979). These flies always exhibit a stop-go pattern
of running, sometimes making about 4-5 stops each second,
during which they are motionless. Each stop lasts about 100
ms, and runs have a similar duration (Fig. 5). Running in
these small flies can occur at up to 0.2 m s^{-1}, and they can
step at 57 Hz. The durations of runs and stops vary with
temperature, degree of crowding, presence of food, and other
factors. Large movements in the visual field may initiate

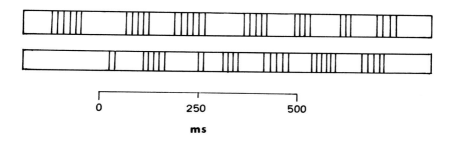

FIGURE 5. Records, based on ciné film at 64 frames s^{-1}, of
running activity in the phorid fly, Megaselia scalaris.
Groups of vertical bars represent bouts of running, with
intervening stops. Two runs are shown. (Based on Miller,
1979.)

panic-running in which runs are greatly extended. Blinded
flies, or flies with antennae removed, continue to exhibit
a stop-go pattern of locomotion.
    The occurrence of stop-go patterns under all conditions
tested suggests that it may arise endogenously even though
it can be strongly affected by sensory input, and temporarily
over-ridden when panic-running occurs. The function of stop-
go running may be to allow improved visual or chemosensory
discrimination. Grooming is divided into bouts of comparable

duration in this species, and it too may have a similar basis.
It is interesting to note that when quiescent or restrained,
phorid flies make strong continual pumping movements with the
abdomen at about 1-2 Hz, but this activity ceases during and
for several seconds after running. Thus rhythmic activities
of one sort or another pervade the behaviour of these flies
for much of the time.

2. Homogeneous sequences: cockroach ventilation

A second example of a homogeneous sequence in which both
central and peripheral mechanisms can influence the rhythm
is provided by cockroach ventilation. Undisturbed resting
adults of Periplaneta americana have been shown to release
CO_2 in a series of bursts, although oxygen consumption
continues steadily throughout the cycle (Wilkins, 1960). The
pattern is like that described in saturniid pupae and shown to
be dependent on spiracle activity (Schneiderman, 1960).
Kestler (1971) has demonstrated that each burst of CO_2 in the
cockroach is accompanied by a phase of abdominal ventilation.
During the interburst the spiracles initially are tightly
constricted, but later commence to make small fluttering movements. These allow air to be sucked into the tracheal system
as a result of negative pressure brought about by oxygen
uptake and the storage of much CO_2 as bicarbonate. By
examining the cycle at different temperatures, Kestler has
shown that the period (from the start of one ventilatory bout
to the next) is dependent on the metabolic rate, and is
probably controlled by tracheal CO_2 levels. Thus elevated
CO_2 initiates ventilation which persists until tracheal CO_2
again falls below a critical level. However in Byrsotria, a
Cuban genus, Myers and Retzlaff (1963) had already described
patterns of periodic ventilation in the intact insect, and
similar patterns of motor activity in isolated nerve cords.
They thought that both the ventilatory strokes and the
patterning of periodic ventilation depended on endogenous
mechanisms. Similar periodic patterns of ventilation have
been recorded using electromyograms from nymphs of Blaberus
craniifer which were relatively unrestrained and allowed to
bury themselves (Miller, 1966; unpubl.). Bouts of ventilation
occur in this species at more or less regular intervals with
a period of 15-30 min at $22^{\circ}C$. Each bout consists of 10-30
pumping strokes and occupies about a fifth of the whole cycle.
Moreover similar patterns of motor activity can be recorded
from the isolated nerve cord, the pattern then normally being
more regular than in the intact insect (Fig. 6). Thus it
seems that in intact insects the slow cycle of intermittent
ventilation is timed largely by exogenous factors (CO_2
concentration principally), but an endogenous mechanism can be

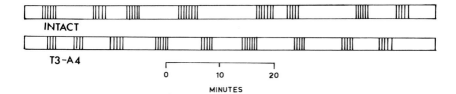

FIGURE 6. The top trace is based on electromyograms from an abdominal dorso-ventral muscle of a last-instar nymph of Blaberus craniifer. Vertical bars represent periods of ventilation, with intervening non-ventilatory pauses. The lower trace is based on electrical records from a lateral abdominal nerve of an isolated preparation consisting of the metathoracic and first four abdominal ganglia. Bouts of 'ventilatory' activity continue to appear with silent intervals between bouts.

shown to exist at least in the isolated cord of blaberids.

If CO_2 levels alone were to control ventilation, it is possible that the system would find a stable level at which pumping strokes occurred singly or in very small groups at regular short intervals. On reaching threshold one or two strokes would be excited and they would be adequate to reduce the tracheal CO_2 level again to below threshold. However the presence of an endogenous oscillator may permit ventilation to have a higher triggering threshold: once this threshold was reached a bout a ventilation would follow partly at least as a result of an oscillation of the slow pacemaker. Thus the rate of CO_2 production would determine the length of the interburst, while the duration of the ventilatory bout would arise in part endogenously. The system would act as a relaxation oscillator.

The adaptive value of this activity may be to allow a prolonged interval to occur between bouts of ventilation, when oxygen delivery can both be by diffusion and by suction of air through slightly fluttering spiracle valves (diffusive-convective flow) - an activity which the careful measurements by Kestler (1971, 1978a,b) have shown to lead to improved water conservation. Thus in summary the central oscillator may be used in the intact insect to produce a bout of ventilation normally triggered by mounting CO_2 levels.

Both the stop-go pattern of running in flies and inter-

mittent ventilation in cockroaches may therefore depend partly
on endogenous pacemakers, although both are strongly
influenced by peripheral factors. Each can be over-ridden by
strong input so that the repetitive activity is no longer
gated. Examples of cellular oscillators altered by various
forms of input are numerous and they range from the vertebrate
heart to Aplysia pacemakers. The latter may have their period
shortened by EPSPs and extended by IPSPs (Kandel, 1976), and
similar effects have been described in the pyloric system of
the crayfish stomatogastric ganglion (Ayers and Selverston,
1979).

3. Heterogeneous sequences: Insect moulting

    Some of the most thoroughly analysed heterogeneous
sequences are those occurring in the stridulatory or courtship behaviour of crickets and grasshoppers (Elsner and Hirth,
1978; Elsner and Popov, 1978). Kutsch (1969) suggested that
the calling song of crickets was produced by two superimposed
oscillators which acted at 3-4 Hz for the chirp interval, and
at 30 Hz for the pulses. Similar interactions among hier-
archies of oscillators are envisaged as underlying the complex
stridulatory movements of gomphocerine grasshoppers (Elsner,
1974). In Gomphocerippus rufus the courtship sequence can
still be organised correctly in the absence of the metathoracic ganglion which normally contributes stridulatory bouts to
the performance (Loher and Huber, 1966). High-order
oscillators may therefore exist in the anterior parts of the
nervous system. Similarly in moulting a variety of
oscillators seems to interact to produce long sequences of
activity, but these are organised mainly from the metathorax.
    Moulting behaviour consists of complex sequences of inter-
locking programmes of motor activity which first prepare the
insect, then extricate it from the old cuticle, and finally
expand the new cuticle. Moulting may temporarily inactivate
many sense organs (Gnatzy and Tautz, 1977), and central programming is then probably important (Carlson, 1977; Truman,
1978, 1979). In the locust each programme is dominated by a
fairly simple temporal pattern to which various pools of
motor neurones are coupled in complex spatial arrays. The
various programmes which appear at different times during the
moult each represent heterogeneous sequences of activities
(Hughes, 1978, 1980).
    One programme which has been examined in some detail
commences just after the locust has extricated itself from
the old cuticle when it hangs upside down by the abdominal
brustia from its own exuvium. The programme continues with
small changes during wing expansion and folding, and for some

time afterwards. This, the expansional motor programme, is largely executed by abdominal muscles, although many other muscles participate for short periods. The programme consists of a) a brief phase of fast abdominal pumping, b) strong muscular expansion, followed by c) a long maintained tonic compression with all spiracles closed, which occupies most of the cycle (Fig. 7). Once initiated, the sequence can be

Expansional motor programme ; compression strokes

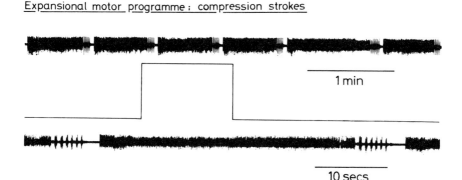

FIGURE 7. Electromyograms from a dorso-ventral abdominal expiratory muscle (L176) of a moulting Schistocerca gregaria, during the expansional motor programme (stage 4). In each cycle, about six short pumping strokes are followed by a deep expansion and then by a long tonic compression. (From Hughes, 1980.)

recorded from the motor nerves of an isolated nervous system, and even from a separate metathoracic ganglion. A similar independence of ganglia generating eclosion activity in moth pupae has been reported by Truman (1979).

The period of the sequence varies systematically at different times, for example accelerating just after wing folding. The phase occupied by abdominal pumping strokes can be extended by perfusion with CO_2/air mixtures until it occupies the whole of the phase of tonic compression, the period of the sequence meanwhile being largely unaffected. Alternatively pumping strokes can be reduced or abolished in decapitated insects, the sequence then comprising an alternation of deep expansions and long compressions. The

abdominal pumping phase therefore shows much greater lability
than the other components of the sequence and its absence
does not affect them. As in the cockroach, ventilation seems
to be gated facultatively by central processes.

The programme gradually breaks down 1-2 hours after the
moult. As it does so the deep compressions first disappear
and are replaced by irregular slow ventilation (Fig. 8).
Groups of fast pumping strokes occur with a similar but
gradually lengthening periodicity. Next, the deep
expansions cease but the slow rhythm persists for some time

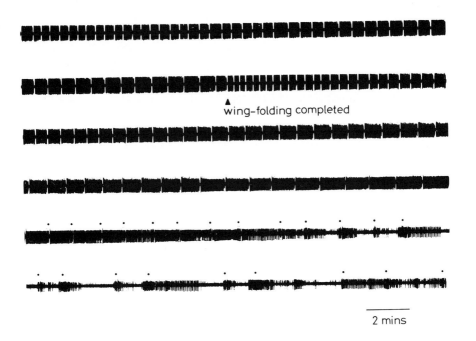

wing-folding completed

2 mins

FIGURE 8. Electromyograms, similar to those in Fig. 7, taken
over an extended time, from stage 5 (during wing expansion)
until 1.2 h after the start of stage 6. They show the
gradual decay of the expansional motor programme. Dots
indicate bouts of fast ventilation which persist after the
tonic compressions have disppeared. (From Hughes, 1980.)

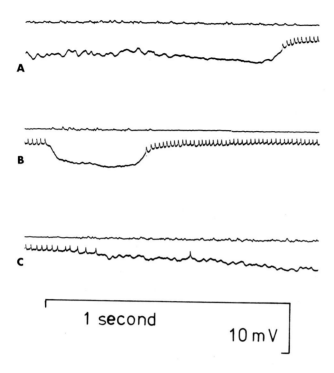

FIGURE 9. Intracellular records from an inspiratory motor neurone in the first abdominal ganglion of <u>Schistocerca gregaria</u> (lower records), together with electromyogram records from an expiratory muscle (upper records) during the expansional motor programme (cf Fig. 7). A, towards the end of the tonic compression the separate IPSPs cease to be distinguishable but the neurone becomes more hyperpolarised, possibly as a result of activity of a different inhibitory source. B, part of the last pumping cycle is shown and the ensuing deep expansion when the unit fires tonically. C, towards the end of the deep expansion the unit fires more slowly and stops as it is gradually hyperpolarised by a barrage of IPSPs. (Elliott, unpubl.)

after, expressed as regular changes in pumping frequency. Elliott (pers. com.) has noted that whereas pumping strokes start nearly synchronously in all segments, the tonic compression spreads anteriorly or posteriorly as a meta-chronal wave. By recording intracellularly from abdominal motor neurones he has been able to examine the underlying bursts of EPSPs and IPSPs derived at least in part from interneurones, which time the activity (Fig.9) Groups of PSPs which coordinate pumping strokes differ in size and frequency from those which initiate the tonic compressions. They may therefore represent the activity of different groups of interneurones. Thus a slow oscillator which times the sequence may interact at the motor neurones with a fast ventilatory oscillator to control the output. This is a speculative interpretation and further intracellular recordings are needed.

The expansional motor programme is therefore delineated centrally by interneurones which formulate the activity and distribute it to appropriate segmental ganglia up and down the cord. Much of the formulation seems to occur in the metathoracic ganglion, where ventilation may also be organized. Sensory input may trigger, trim and terminate the programme. Two superimposed orders of oscillatory processes can be identified. One is responsible for the rapid pumping strokes and the other for the repetition of the sequence. In other moulting programmes three or more oscillators may cooperate to organize respectively acts, bouts and programmes (cf. Carlson, 1977; Hughes, 1980), but these wait more detailed description.

F.   CONCLUSIONS

Endogenous oscillators with periods of less than 1 s are responsible for motor bursting in certain muscles in the legs of inactive stick insects, wasps, bees and harvestmen. In the last example the activity arises outside the CNS and may be generated by motor axons, but in the others the rhythms arise centrally. The bursts may be generated in nets or in single cells.

Slow oscillators, whose periods are relatively long, may act in a variety of behaviour patterns to gate repetitive activity: examples may be found in phorid running behaviour, in cockroach ventilation and in locust moulting, all of which are executed in a series of bouts. The evidence suggests that these oscillators are not dependent on feedback from the periphery. Nor do they seem to depend on central feed-

back from motor neurones since bouts and interbouts can vary
independently. It may therefore be suggested that neural
pacemakers, separate from the motor neurones and from the
generators of the fast rhythms, time these events.

Much of the activity considered here is still at a descriptive stage. Accurate descriptions of behaviour should
suggest models of mechanisms, and such models help with the
analysis. However the CNS can formulate activity in numerous
ways, and any model will have probably only a brief existence.

In only a few insect rhythmic systems, such as cockroach
walking (Pearson, 1977) and cicada singing (Simmons, 1977),
have some of the underlying oscillatory neurones been
identified, and in both these examples they are non-spiking.
But the number of such cells in each system is not known,
nor is the basis of their oscillatory activity understood.
Even in non-rhythmic systems where a circuit can be followed
through from input to output, the variety of parallel inputs
makes predictions of output very difficult (Kien, 1979).

There is no shortage of ideas - but only of adequate
techniques and competent neurobiologists. To record from
some of the numerous (Pearson, 1977), small and sometimes
anaxonic intraganglionic interneurones which formulate
behaviour, and to identify the·functional nets responsible
for particular acts are formidable tasks. Some interneurones
may be shared between different outputs; others may be
specific to one. Overlapping pools of interneurones may
specify particular outputs and "transfer information to each
other and to motor neurones in a continuously graded manner"
(Burrows, 1979), but there is no certainty that the same
pools will produce the same acts on different occasions
(Burrows, 1980). Will single-cell recording, the most powerful tool available, ever allow us to see an adequate number
of relevant events at one time, or will an approach which
looks simultaneously at specified groups of neurones be
necessary (cf. Pickard, 1979)? Is it better to look down
from a particular behaviour pattern at relevant neurones, or
to gaze up from identified neurones to a variety of
behavioural outputs? Insect tend to do a few things most of
the time and a large variety of things rarely. One neurone
may be involved at different times in many outputs. Will
the first approach, downwards, give an oversimplified picture
of the capacity of neurones, and will the second, upwards,
produce a bewildering assortment of neural properties
(Bullock, 1979), which cannot be accounted for in behavioural
terms?

ACKNOWLEDGMENT

I am grateful to John Iles and Chris Elliott for helpful comments.

REFERENCES

Alving, B.O. (1968). Spontaneous activity in isolated somata of Aplysia neurons. J. gen. Physiol. 51, 29–45.

Arvanitaki, A. (1939). Recherches sur la réponse oscillatoire locale de l'axone géant isolé de "Sepia". Arch. Int. Physiol. 49, 209–256.

Arvanitaki, A. and Chalazonitis, N. (1968). Electrical properties and temporal organization in oscillatory neurons (Aplysia). In Symposium on Neurobiology of Invertebrates (1967). (Ed. J. Salanki), Plenum, New York. 169–199.

Ayers, J.L. and Selverston, A.I. (1979). Monosynaptic entrainment of an endogenous pacemaker network: a cellular mechanism for von Holst's magnet effect. J. comp. Physiol. 129, 5–17.

Bässler, U. and Pflüger, H.-J. (1979). The control system of the femur-tibia-joint of the phasmid Extatasoma tiaratum and the control of rocking. A contribution to the evolution of behaviour. J. comp. Physiol. 132, 209–215.

Berridge, M.J. (1979). Modulation of nervous activity by cyclic nucleotides and calcium. In The Neurosciences. Fourth Study Program. (Eds. F.O. Schmitt and F.G. Worden). The MIT Press, Cambridge, Mass., and London. 873–889.

Berridge, M.J. and Rapp, P.E. (1979). A comparative survey of the function, mechanism and control of cellular oscillations. J. exp. Biol. 81, 217–279.

Bullock, T.H. (1979). Evolving concepts of local integrative operations in neurons. The Neurosciences. Fourth Study Program. (Eds. F.O. Schmitt and F.G. Worden). The MIT Press, Cambridge, Mass., and London. 43–49.

Burrows, M. (1979). Graded synaptic interactions between local pre-motor interneurons of the locust. J. Neurophysiol. 42, 1108–1123.

Burrows, M. (1980). The control of sets of motoneurons by local interneurons in the locust. J. Physiol. Lond. 298, 213–233..

Calabrese, R.L. (1979). The roles of endogenous membrane properties and synaptic interactions in generating heartbeat rhythm of the leech, Hirudo medicinalis. J. exp. Biol. 82, 163-176.

Carlson, J.R. (1977). The imaginal ecdysis of the cricket (Teleogryllus oceanicus). I and II. J. comp. Physiol. 115, 299-317; 319-336.

Chalazonitis, N. (1968). Synaptic properties of oscillatory neurons (Aplysia and Helix). In Symposium on Neurobiology of Invertebrates (1967). (Ed. J. Salanki). Plenum Press, New York. 201-226.

Elsner, N. (1974). Neuroethology of sound production in gomphocerine grasshoppers. J. comp. Physiol. 88, 67-102.

Elsner, N. and Hirth, C. (1978). Short- and long-term control of motor coordination in a stridulating grasshopper. Naturwiss. 65, 160.

Elsner, N. and Popov, A.V. (1978). Neuroethology of acoustic communication. Adv. Insect Physiol. 13, 229-355.

Foelix, R.F. (1975). Occurrence of synapses in peripheral sensory nerves in arachnids. Nature, Lond. 254, 146-148.

Frankenhaeuser, B. and Hodgkin, A.L. (1957). The action of calcium on the electrical properties of squid axons. J. Physiol. 137, 218-244.

Gnatzy, W. and Tautz, J. (1977). Sensitivity of an insect mechanoreceptor during moulting. Physiol. Ent. 2, 279-288.

Goodman, C.S. and Heitler, W.J. (1979). Electrical properties of insect neurons with spiking and non-spiking somata: normal, axotomized and colchicine-treated neurons. J. exp. Biol. 83, 95-121.

Gorman, A.L.F. and Thomas, M.V. (1978). Changes in the intracellular concentration of free calcium ions in a pacemaker neurone, measured with the metallochromic indicator dye arsenazo III. J. Physiol. Lond. 275, 357-376.

Hartline, D.K. (1979). Integrative neurophysiology of the lobster cardiac ganglion. Amer. Zool. 19, 53-65.

Heitler, W.J. (1978). Coupled motoneurons are part of the crayfish swimmeret central oscillator. Nature, Lond. 275, 231-234.

Hermann, A. (1979). Generation of a fixed motor pattern. I and II. J. comp. Physiol. 130, 221-228; 229-239.

Hinde, R.A. and Stevenson, J.G. (1969). Sequences of behaviour. Adv. Study Behav. 2, 276-296.

Hodgkin, A.L. (1948). The local electrical changes associated with repetitive action in non-medullated axon. J. Physiol. 107, 165-181.

Hoyle, G. (1974). A function for neurons (DUM) neurosecretory on skeletal muscle of insects. J. exp. Zool. 189, 401–406.

Hoyle, G. (1978). Intrinsic rhythm and basic tonus in insect skeletal muscle. J. exp. Biol. 73, 173-203.

Hughes, T.D. (1978). Physiological studies of ecdysis in locusts. D.Phil. Thesis, Oxford.

Hughes, T.D. (1980). The imaginal ecdysis of the desert locust, Schistocerca gregaria. III. Motor activity underlying the expansional and post-expansional behaviour. Physiol. Ent. 5 (in press).

Kandel, E.R. (1976). Cellular Basis of Behaviour. Freeman, San Francisco.

Kandel, E.R. (1979). Behavioral Biology of Aplysia. Freeman, San Francisco.

Kestler, P. (1971). Die diskontinuierliche Ventilation bei Periplaneta americana L. und anderen Insekten. Dissertation, Wurzburg, 1971.

Kestler, P. (1978a). Atembewegungen und Gasaustausch bei der Ruheatmung adulter terristrischer Insekten. Verh. Dtsch. Zool. Ges. 1978, 269.

Kestler, P. (1978b). Gas balance of external respiration by electronic weighing in water saturated air. Deutsche Physiol. Ges. Abstr. 49th Meeting, R36 (113).

Kien, J. (1979). Variability of locust motoneuron responses to sensory stimulation: a possible substrate for motor flexibility. J. comp. Physiol. 134, 55-68.

King, D.G. (1977). An interneuron in Drosophila synapses within a peripheral nerve onto the dorsal longitudinal muscle motor neurone. Neurosc. Abstr. 3, 180.

Koester, J. and Kandel, E.R. (1977). Further identification of neurons in the abdominal ganglia of Aplysia using behavioural criteria. Brain Res. 121, 1-20.

Kuno, M. and Llinas, R. (1970). Calcium ions as inward current carriers in molluscan neurons. Comp. Biochem. Physiol. 35, 857-866.

Kutsch, W. (1969). Neuromuscular activity in three cricket species during various behavioural patterns. Z. vergl. Physiol. 63, 335-379.

Loher, W. and Huber, F. (1966). Nervous and endocrine control of sexual behaviour in a grasshopper (Gomphocerus rufus L. Acridinae). Symp. Soc. Exptl. Biol. 20, 381-400.

McDonald, T.F. and Sachs, H.G. (1975). Electrical activity in embryonic heart cell aggregates. Pacemaker oscillations. Pflügers Arch. 354, 165-176.

Meech, R.W. (1974). Prolonged action potentials in Aplysia neurons injected with EGTA. Comp. Biochem. Physiol. 48A, 387-395.

Meech, R.W. (1979). Membrane potential oscillations in molluscan "burster" neurones. J. exp. Biol. 81, 93-112.

Miller, P.L. (1966). The regulation of breathing in insects. Adv. Insect Physiol. 3, 279-354.

Miller, P.L. (1974). Rhythmic activities and the insect nervous system. In Experimental Analysis of Insect Behaviour (Ed. L. Barton Browne). Springer, Berlin. 114-138.

Miller, P.L. (1977). Neurogenic pacemakers in the legs of Opiliones. Physiol. Ent. 2, 213-224.

Miller, P.L. (1979). A possible sensory function for the stop-go patterns of running in phorid flies. Physiol. Ent. 4, 361-370.

Myers, T.B. and Retzlaff, E. (1963). Localization and action of the respiratory centre of the Cuban burrowing cockroach. J. Insect Physiol. 9, 607-614.

Noble, D. (1979). The Initiation of the Heartbeat. 2nd ed. Clarendon Press, Oxford.

Pearson, K.G. (1977). Interneurons in the ventral nerve cord of insects. In Identified Neurons and Behavior of Arthropods. (Ed. G. Hoyle). Plenum, New York and London. 329-337.

Pearson, K.G. (1979). Local neurons and local interactions in the nervous systems of invertebrates. In The Neurosciences. Fourth Study Program. (Eds. F.O. Schmitt and F.G. Worden). The MIT Press, Cambridge, Mass., and London. 145-157.

Pickard, R.S. (1979). Printed circuit microelectrodes. Trends in Neurosciences. 2, 259.

Pflüger, H.-J. (1977). The control of rocking movements of the phasmid Carausius morosus. J. comp. Physiol. 120, 181-202.

Rapp, P.E. (1979). An atlas of cellular oscillators. J. exp. Biol. 81, 281-306.

Rapp, P.E. and Berridge, M.J. (1977). Oscillations in calcium-cyclic AMP control loops form the basis of pacemaker activity and other high frequency biological rhythms. J. Theor. Biol. 66, 497-525.

Rathmayer, W. (1965). Neuro-muscular transmission in a spider and the effect of calcium. Comp. Biochem. Physiol. 14, 673-687.

Russell, D.F. and Hartline, D.K. (1978). Bursting neural networks: a re-examination. Science, 200, 453-456.

Simmons, P.J. (1977). Neural generation of singing in a cicada. Nature Lond. 270, 243-245.

Schneiderman, H.A. (1960). Discontinuous respiration in insects. Role of the spiracles. Biol. Bull. Wood's Hole, 119, 494-528.

Selverston, A.I. (1977). Mechanisms for the production of
     rhythmic behavior in crustaceans. In Identified Neurons
     and Behavior in Arthropods. (Ed. G. Hoyle) Plenum,
     New York and London. 209-225.
Stent, G.S., Kristan, W.B., Friesen, W.O., Ort, C.A., Poon,
     M. and Calabrese, R.L. (1978) Neuronal generation of
     the leech swimming movement. Science 200, 1348-1356.
Stent, G.S., Thompson, W.J.and Calabrese, R.L. (1979).
     (1979) Neural control of heartbeat in the leech and in
     some other invertebrates. Physiol. Rev. 59, 101-136.
Strumwasser, F. (1973). Neural and humoral factors in the
     temporal organization of behavior. Physiologist 16,
     9-42.
Tazaki, K. and Cooke, I.M. (1979a). Isolation and characteri-
     zation of slow depolarizing responses of cardiac ganglion
     neurons in the crab, Portunus sanguinolentus.
     J. Neurophysiol. 42, 1000-1021.
Tazaki, K. and Cooke, I.M. (1979b). Ionic bases of slow
     depolarizing responses of cardiac ganglion neurons
     in the crab, Portunus sanguinolentus. J. Neurophysiol.
     42, 1022-1047.
Thompson, S.H. and Smith, S.J. (1976) Depolarizing after-
     potentials and burst production in molluscan pacemaker
     neurons. J. Neurophysiol. 39, 153-161.
Truman, J.W. (1978). Hormonal release of stereotyped motor
     programmes from the isolated nervous system of the
     cecropia moth. J. exp. Biol. 74, 151-173.
Truman, J.W. (1979). Interaction between abdominal ganglia
     during the performance of hormonally triggered
     behavioural programmes in moths. J. exp. Biol.
     82, 239-253.
Tsien, R.W., Kass, R.S. and Weingart, R. (1979). Cellular and
     subcellular mechanisms of cardiac pacemaker oscillations.
     J. exp. Biol. 81, 205-215.
Walther, C. (1969) Zum Verhalten des Krallenbeugersystems bei
     der Stabheuschrecke Carausius morosus Br. Z. vergl. Physiol.
     62, 421-460.
Weaving, J.N. and Cullen, M.J. (1978). Unusual high volume of
     sarcoplasmic reticulum in a wasp leg muscle.
     Experientia 34, 796-797.
Wigglesworth, V.B. (1939). The Principles of Insect Physiology.
     Methuen, London. 1st ed.
Wigglesworth, V.B. (1972). The Principles of Insect Physiology.
     Methuen, London. 7th ed.
Wilkins, M.B. (1960). A temperature-dependent endogenous rhythm
     in the rate of carbon dioxide output of Periplaneta
     americana. Nature Lond. 185, 481-482.
Woollacott, M. and Hoyle, G. (1977). Neural elements underlying
     learning in insects: changes in pacemaker. Proc. Roy. Soc.
     B. 195, 395-415.

CHEMISTRY, DEFENSE, AND SURVIVAL:
CASE STUDIES AND SELECTED TOPICS

Thomas Eisner

Section of Neurobiology and Behavior
Division of Biological Sciences
Cornell University
Ithaca, New York

One of the major subdisciplines of biology to make its
mark in the last two decades is chemical ecology, the field
dealing with the chemically mediated environmental interactions of organisms. Insect biologists were early drawn into
this field, in part no doubt because of the special suita-
bility of insects for work in the area. Insects are abundant, diversely specialized, observable in nature, managea-
ble in the laboratory, and above all, chemically oriented in
many of their basic activities. But chemical ecology was
appealing on other grounds as well. By the mid-1950's when
the field was emergent, insect biologists were ready to
think of the environmental interactions of insects in chemical terms. Great technical innovation had taken place in
chemistry itself, particularly in the area of organic analytical procedures. Where previously large amounts of
starting material had been required for elucidation of chemical structure, minute samples were now proving sufficient,
and improved procedures had been developed for isolating
active components from complex mixtures. The prospects of
actual identification of natural products from insects had
vastly increased. And there was also the indirect but
decided influence of insect endocrinology. The whole concept
of biological regulation through chemical agents had been
brought into focus by the study of hormones. And the concept
was clearly applicable to regulatory chemicals operating at
the level of the environment beyond the systemic boundaries
of the insect. The growing knowledge of hormones inevitably
helped set in motion the study of the environmental counterparts of hormones. The those of us whose interest in the
chemical ecology of insects dates back to the days when
this field was in its formative stages, the efforts of insect
endocrinologists, and in particular the far-reaching and

847

elegant studies by V. B. Wigglesworth of hormonal regulation, were an inspiration.

Chemical ecology is nowadays a flourishing interdisciplinary field, fostered by a contingent of specialists, including behaviorists, ecologists, physiologists, neurobiologists, biochemists, and chemists. My purpose here is to discuss some topics pertaining to an aspect of chemical ecology that is receiving considerable attention these days: the defensive chemistry of insects. Insects are threatened by predators in every environment and at each stage of their life cycle. The chemical defenses that they have evolved to counter the threat are many and varied, and constitute a primary key to their survival. Dozens of papers per year are currently being written on the chemical weaponry of insects, and one major book dealing with the topic has recently appeared (Bettini, 1978). But this subject is neither factually nor conceptually exhausted. It is still full of exploratory possibilities and — as might hopefully be apparent from the somewhat personal narrative that follows — still the source of considerable excitement to the explorer.

I. PULSED EMISSION OF A DEFENSIVE SPRAY

One of the most spectacular of animal defenses is the spray mechanism of bombardier beetles. These insects have a pair of large glands situated posteriorly in the body which open, like barrels on a gun emplacement, on the abdominal tip. When disturbed, as when one of their appendages is seized, they revolve the abdominal tip and discharge an accurately aimed jet of fluid toward the site of disturbance (Fig. 1). The ejections are visible and are accompanied by distinctly audible detonations. Predators are deterred by the fluid (Eisner, 1958; Eisner and Dean, 1976; Dean, 1979, 1980a, 1980b), which contains a mixture of highly repellent p-benzoquinones (Schildknecht, 1957).

Quinones are not stored as such in the glands, but are synthesized at the moment of ejection by oxidation of hydroquinones (Schildknecht and Holoubek, 1961). It is these hydroquinones that are stored in the glands, together with hydrogen peroxide, the oxidizing agent. Each gland consists of two compartments. The inner and larger compartment contains the hydroquinones and hydrogen peroxide, while the smaller outer compartment — the so-called reaction chamber — through which the contents of the inner compartment must pass when they are ejected, contains a mixture of catalases and peroxidases (Schildknecht et al., 1968). When the

FIGURE 1. Bombardier beetle (Stenaptinus insignis) *ejecting spray toward its left front leg, which is being pinched with forceps. For photographic purposes the beetle has been fastened to a wire hook attached to its back with wax.*

contents of the inner compartment enter the reaction chamber (which takes place presumably because of muscular compression of the inner chamber) there occurs essentially an explosion: the catalases promote the decomposition of hydrogen peroxide, while the peroxidases force the oxidation of hydroquinones to quinones. The gaseous oxygen also provides the propellant, causing the reacting mixture to "pop" out. Thermodynamic calculations predicted that the formation of the spray should be accompanied by liberation of considerable heat. This was verified empirically: the spray is ejected with a heat content of 0.2 calorie/mg, at a temperature of 100°C (Aneshansley *et al.*, 1969).

We recently showed that the spray is not emitted continuously during a discharge, but is pulsed in the form of short squirts. The first indication of this came from acoustical recordings of the ejections, which showed the sound itself to be pulsed, with a pulse repetition rate of from 400 to 1000 pulses/sec. By causing beetles to discharge upon a piezoelectric crystal, and recording both the electric output of the crystal and the sound of the ejections, we noted that the output of the crystal is also periodic, and concordant in phase with the periodicity of the sound (Fig. 2).

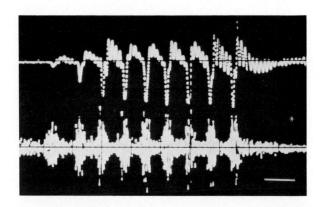

*FIGURE 2. Bombardier beetle (S. insignis) discharge:
simultaneous recording of sound (lower trace) and of electric
output of a piezoelectric crystal (upper trace) upon which the
beetle directed the discharge. (reference bar = 2 msec).*

This could only mean that the individual sound pulses are the
concomitants of actual squirts (Aneshansley and Eisner, unpublished). A definitive demonstration of the discontinuous nature of the emission was provided by a film taken at over 2500
frames/sec, in collaboration with Dr. Harold Edgerton of the
Massachsetts Institute of Technology.

We do not know for certain why the beetles' ejections are
pulsed. One hypothesis, for which we have as yet no proof, is
that pulsed emission is a consequence of pulsation of the explosive process itself, brought about by pulsed delivery of
chemical precursors into the reaction chamber. Such intermittent addition of cold precursor could have a cooling effect on
the reaction chamber, which might otherwise overheat during
the course of the discharge, to the detriment of the enzymes
within. We are currently attempting to record temperature in
the reaction chamber during spray ejections.

II. TIME COURSE OF A PREDATOR-PREY INTERACTION

Although it had been established from observations of
predator-prey encounters in the laboratory that many glandular
and other chemical defenses of insects are indeed effective,
virtually no efforts had been made to quantify some of the
parameters pertaining to these interactions. We recently set
out to determine how quickly a bombardier beetle responds to

an ant's bite, and how quickly the ant releases its hold after being sprayed. To obtain the first measurement we built an artificial ant consisting of a metal hook that could be made to snap audibly onto a bombardier's leg and induce the beetle to discharge. The interval between the two sounds — the sound of the "bite" and that of the subsequent discharge — could be measured from acoustic tape recordings. The results showed that the beetle responds with varying delay, depending where it is bitten (Fig. 3). If the stimulus is applied to a hindleg, the beetle responds relatively quickly, since it needs only to revolve the abdominal tip over a relatively small arc in order to aim the spray. If the stimulus is applied more anteriorly, to a mid- or foreleg, aiming takes longer and the delay is accordingly lengthened (Aneshansley and Eisner, unpublished). Response times of bombardiers recently measured by a different technique also proved variable (Dean, 1979). Minimal response times, as determined by both us and Dean (1979), were in the order of 0.05 sec, in line with the evasive response latencies reported for a variety of animals (references in Dean, 1979).

The response time of ants to the beetle's spray was determined from visual recordings made with television cameras. Beetle-ant encounters were staged within range of a sensitive microphone that picked up the discharge sounds. The sounds were relayed to an oscilloscope where they became visibly displayed on the screen. Two television cameras monitored the events: one aimed at the oscilloscope screen and the other

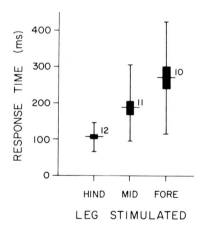

FIGURE 3. *Time interval between pinching of legs and discharge in bombardier beetles (S. insignis). (Horizontal lines, vertical bars, and vertical lines give means, standard error of means, and ranges respectively; numbers give sample sizes.)*

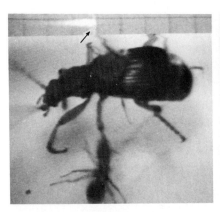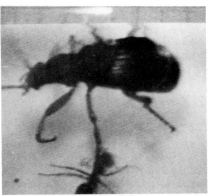

FIGURE 4. Response time of ant (Formica exsectoides) *to impact of bombardier beetle's spray* (S. insignis). *The moment of spray is given by the acoustical signal (arrow) on the oscilloscope screen at left. On the frame at right, 0.05 sec later, the ant has already released its hold on the beetle's leg.*

at the ant itself. The two images were recorded side by side on the same videotape and could be analyzed concurrently by tape playback (Fig. 4). The time delay between sound signal and the first visible sign of ant detachment from the beetle was somewhat variable ($\bar{x}$ = 0.17 $\pm$ 0.14; N = 28). Minimal delays were again in the order of 0.05 sec. It follows that an entire beetle-ant encounter, from ant bite, to beetle discharge, to ant release, can transpire quickly — in 0.1 sec when latencies are minimal, and in no more than 1 sec when they are maximal.

While observing staged encounters between bombardier beetles and the ant *Formica exsectoides* we noticed that occasional ants persist in their hold on the beetle and by so doing elicit a succession of discharges that eventually kills the ants. Whether such persistence occurs also in nature and is to be viewed as sacrificial altruism that evolved in the context of eusociality (Wilson, 1971), remains to be seen.

III.   FLUIDICS AND THE AIMING OF A JET OF SPRAY

The term bombardier is traditionally applied to species of several genera, including *Brachinus* and *Stenaptinus*, of the carabid subfamily Carabinae. Recent work has shown that beetles of two other carabid subfamilies, the Paussinae and Metriinae, also discharge hot quinones (Eisner *et al.*, 1979 and unpublished; Roach *et al.*, 1979). Moreover, they produce these by oxidation of hydroquinones, in two-chambered glands that are apparently comparable functionally to those of *Brachinus* and their carabine relatives (Eisner and Alsop, unpublished). While we initially suggested that the Paussinae and Metriinae might have evolved their bombarding ability independently from the Carabinae (Aneshansley *et al.*, 1969), we now favor the view that bombardiers as a group are of monophyletic origin (Eisner *et al.*, 1977). Whichever alternative may eventually prove true, it is clear that some bombardiers have evolved specializations that are uniquely their own. One such specialization is the aiming mechanism of the Paussinae. These beetles are characterized by the possession of two flanges, diagnostic for the group, which flare out from the outer margins of the elytra just in front of the two gland openings (Fig. 5A-C). No function had hitherto been demonstrated for these flanges, which we have now shown to serve as launching guides for anteriorly directed discharges.

The Paussinae do not aim their spray by revolving the abdominal tip, nor do they discharge simultaneously from both glands as do carabine bombardiers. The glands open separately at some distance from the abdominal tip, and the beetles discharge from one gland or the other, depending from which side they are attacked. They are able to deflect the abdominal tip downward only slightly, which they do, for example, when discharging toward a stimulated hindleg (Fig. 6). But if a stimulus is applied to an antenna or foreleg, they resort to a different strategy. They then press the abdominal tip upward against the elytra, with the result that the gland openings become precisely aligned with their corresponding flanges (Fig. 5A). Jets of fluid discharged under such conditions inevitably emerge along the outer margins of the flanges which are grooved and curved (Fig. 5B,C). As we were able to show through high speed cinematography, the jets actually follow the curvature of the flanges, and by so doing are deflected from a trajectory that is initially misdirected away from the beetle to one directed accurately forward in parallel to the body (Figs. 5D,6). Although the phenomenon of jet deflection by curved surfaces is well known in fluidics technology (Reba,

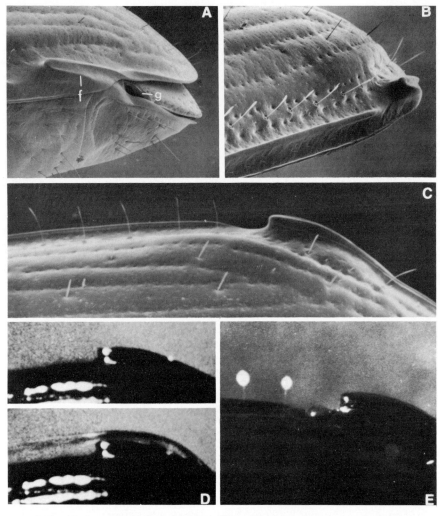

FIGURE 5. Ozaenine bombardier beetle (A-C,E, Goniotropis nicaraguensis; D, Ozaena magna). A. Abdominal tip, showing left gland opening (g), lined up with corresponding elytral flange (f), in the arrangement that prevails during a forwardly directed discharge. B. Lateral view of posterior portion of an elytron, showing the curved and grooved flange, and the row of hairs aligned along the direction of emergence of the spray from the flange. C. Dorsal view of posterior portion of an elytron showing flange and hairs. D. Frames from motion picture (400 frames/sec) showing flange before (top) and during (bottom) a forwardly ejected discharge. Note how stream of fluid follows the curvature of the flange. E. Droplets of spray retained by elytral hairs after a discharge.

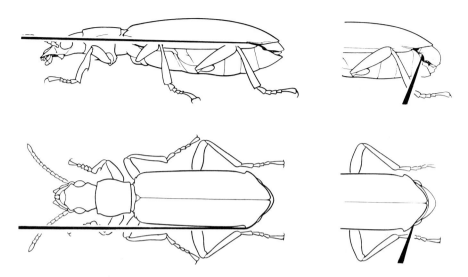

*FIGURE 6. Anteriorly (left) and posteriorly (right) directed discharges of an ozaenine bombardier beetle (*Goniotropis nicaraguensis*). The anteriorly directed discharges follow the curvature of the small flanges that project outward from the margins of the elytra near the gland openings.*

1966), it has not to my knowledge been previously demonstrated for a biological system.

In some paussine species (for example the ozaenine *Goniotropis nicaraguensis*), there is a row of spatulate hairs on each elytron lined up precisely along the direction of emergence of the spray from the flanges (Fig. 5B,C). As we were again able to show by still and motion pictures, these hairs are hit and left wetted by droplets of secretion whenever forward-directed discharges occur (Fig. 5E). The beetles routinely wipe the droplets away with the legs after an ejection, which enables them to use the wetted legs defensively for direct administration of quinone to an enemy. Defensive application of secretion by use of legs has been demonstrated in other insects and arachnids (Eisner *et al.*, 1971, 1974a; Tschinkel 1975; Remold 1962).

IV.   COORDINATED DEFENSE IN A SOCIAL INSECT

Defense in social insects typically occurs through collec-
tive action. Alarm signals alert individuals to a state of
emergency, and group recruitment brings them together at the
site of trouble for concerted use of their stings, bites, or
other weaponry. Social defensive strategies have been studied thoroughly in ants, bees, and other Hymenoptera (Wilson
1971; Hölldobler 1977), and more recently also in termites
(Wilson 1971, Prestwich 1979). Most peculiar among termites
are the so-called nasutitermites, a successful group of species comprising the largest subfamily of the Termitinae,
whose soldiers are characterized by a large protruding snout,
or nasus, on the front of the head (Fig. 7A). Nasute soldiers
are essentially mobile spray guns. When disturbed, they eject
an odorous and sticky jet of fluid from the nasus, produced by
a gland that occupies much of their cranial cavity. We recently undertook a detailed study of the highly integrated defensive behavior of *Nasutitermes exitiosus* (Eisner *et al.*,
1976; Kriston *et al.*, 1977), an Australian species whose principal potential enemies, as perhaps those of any termite, are
ants.
Both soldiers and workers of *N. exitiosus* take part in the
defensive actions. The soldiers eject their spray in response
to direct contact stimulation and aim their discharges accurately by pointing the snout toward sites stimulated (Fig. 7B).
The secretion acts on ants both chemically and mechanically.
The chemical action, essentially an irritation, is apparently
induced by simpler terpenoids such as α-pinene and β-pinene
which the secretion is known to contain (Moore 1968). Applied
topically to cockroaches, these compounds induce scratch reflexes, and it seems likely that they are responsible for the
pronounced cleansing activities that ants invariably undertake
upon being sprayed by soldiers. The mechanical action, a
consequence of the extremely viscous and tacky nature of the
fluid, manifests itself in ants by hindrance of movement,
secondary encrustment with debris, and spiracular occlusion.
The substances that account for the viscosity are complex
novel isoprenoids called trinervitenes, only recently identified and found in a variety of nasutitermite species (Prestwich 1976a, 1976b). The workers of *N. exitiosus* contribute to
defense by biting. They are able to crush smaller ants outright, or to drag down larger ants by clinging to them with
the mandibles, thereby rendering them more susceptible to being sprayed by soldiers. None of the ants, spiders, and centipedes that were presented to *N. exitiosus* in our laboratory
tests survived the encounters.

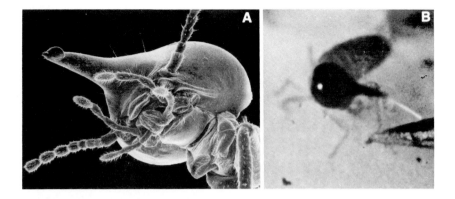

FIGURE 7. Nasutitermes exitiosus *soldier.* <u>A</u>. *Head in ventrolateral view.* <u>B</u>. *Individual discharging an aimed jet of spray toward a leg being pinched with forceps. (from Eisner et al., 1976).*

In line with what had already been learned from other nasutitermites (Ernst 1959; Maschwitz and Mühlenberg, 1972; Nutting *et al.*, 1974), we found the secretion of *N. exitiosus* to be a potent alarm pheromone. When a soldier ejected its spray, other soldiers became attracted to the target and positioned themselves neatly in a circle around it (Fig. 8<u>E</u>). In order to study such alarm behavior in detail, we confronted termites with artificial ants, consisting of mechanical dummies that could be positioned and mobilized at will and made to attack termites in Petri-dish arenas. One such device was a small ferromagnetic bar set into rotation by the twirling action of a magnet placed beneath it under the arena. Ant attacks upon a column of termites marching in an arena were staged simply by moving the arena relative to the underlying magnet in such fashion as to draw the rotating bar toward the flank of the column. Such bars were treated like real ants. No sooner had one been encountered and sprayed by a soldier than it was encircled by other soldiers that converged upon the site (Fig. 8<u>A-D</u>). The new arrivals did not themselves add spray to target unless individually prompted to do so by direct contact with the rotating bar. The recruits were evidently programmed to be merely poised for action, and to discharge only if the continuing liveliness of the enemy demanded it.

A diversity of experiments with rotating bars and other mechanical devices were videotaped, and various parameters of the interactions were quantified by tape analysis. It was

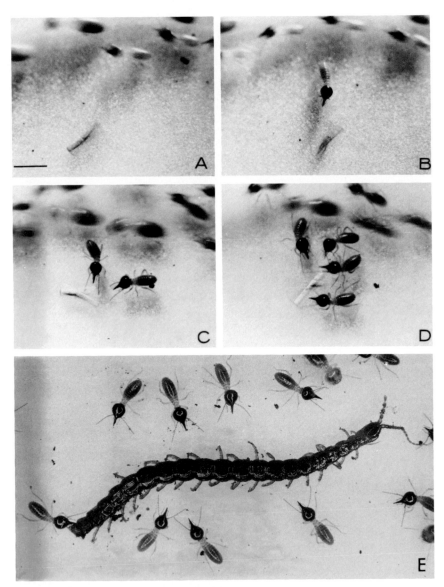

FIGURE 8. A-D. Stages in the defensive response of termites to an "ant" (a twirling metallic bar) that is approaching the column of termites marching in the background. Initial inspection by a single soldier (B) leads to spraying and
eventual attraction of other soldiers to the "enemy."
E. Centipede, partially immobilized by repeated sprayings, encircled by surveillant soldiers that were attracted by the
secretion. (from Eisner et al., 1976).

found that the alarming effect is restricted, or largely restricted, to the soldiers. These are attracted to secretion
even when they are marching in trail and the trail pheromone
provides a conflicting chemical cue. Attractiveness is highly effective within a radius of 3 cm. Soldiers drawn to a
sprayed target remain longer in surveillance if the target is
in motion than when it is still. They gauge target "liveliness" by direct contact, as well as by detection of the air
motion engendered in the immediate vicinity of the target by
its movements. An air movement as slight as 0.6 mm/sec
proved effective. Conventional acoustic cues and groundborne
vibration appear to be minimally important in the detection of
liveliness.

The worker termites are essentially unattracted by freshly
discharged spray, but they respond to aged secretion by defe-
cating upon it and encrusting it with soil. It is possible
that in nature they employ this behavior to bury enemies once
these are sprayed and incapacitated.

V.   DEFENSIVE USE OF SOUND AND ACOUSTIC APOSEMATISM

Many insects and other arthropods respond to disturbance
by producing stridulatory and other sounds (references in
Alexander 1967; Haskell 1961; Tuxen 1967). Although it had
long been suspected that such "disturbance" sounds have defensive value — Lesser as early as 1738 suggested that they
might "terrify...and repel (enemies)" — the view had remained essentially unsupported and had even been challenged
by Darwin (1874). But it is now know from several studies
that stridulatory sounds may indeed convey protection. Bauer
(1976) found phonic cicindellid beetles to be released more
frequently by sandpipers that control cicindellids that were
experimentally silenced, and Smith and Langley (1978) reported
grasshopper mice to take longer to kill squawking cicadas than
aphonic controls.

Particularly elegant experiments have been reported by
Masters (1979) who fed phonic insects and their aphonic controls to wolf spiders and field mice. Three types of insects
(mutillid wasps, *Dasymutilla* spp.; water scavenger beetles,
Tropisternus spp.; round sand beetles, *Omophron labiatum*) were
given to the spiders at night in the field under natural conditions. The silenced insects were more persistently attacked
than their normal phonic counterparts and were also more frequently killed. Tests with an artificial insect — a vibrat-
ing probe whose vibration accurately mimicked that of the
cuticle of a stridulating insect — clearly demonstrated the
intrinsic deterrent potential of stridulation: the spiders

FIGURE 9. *Chemical defense and stridulation operating in conjunction. The Australian tenebrionid beetle* Adelium por-catum *has a pair of eversible glands that produce quinonoid secretion. When disturbed, as by pinching of a leg (A), it everts the gland of the corresponding side. The stridulatory sound is produced by drawing two serrated ridges on the last abdominal tergum (arrow in B shows left ridge) across the elytral margins. C, enlarged view of ridge. (from Eisner et al., 1974).*

persisted longer in their attacks if the probe was silent. The tests with mice, which ordinarily forage at night, were staged in darkness in a soundproof room and observed under infrared illumination using an infrared-sensitive video monitoring system (Conner and Masters, 1978). They were offered female mutillid wasps, which again survived more frequently if they were unsilenced than if they were rendered aphonic. If deprived of their stings beforehand, both silenced and unsilenced mutillids were nearly always killed, but the mice took longer to attack and kill the unsilenced individuals.

Since stridulating arthropods are often also protected by other means [as by glandular discharge mechanisms (Fig. 9), systemic distasteful factors, or stings], it has been suggested that their sounds may serve as warning signals, operative in the manner of visual aposematism, but in the acoustic mode (Pocock 1896; Marshall 1902a, 1902b; Haskell 1961; Eisner 1970; Eisner *et al.*, 1974a). Masters (1979) presents an interesting discussion of how acoustic aposematism may function in the context of predation and of predator-prey coevolution. Acoustic aposematism is apparently at play in the interaction

of certain arctiid moths and bats. Arctiids are chemically
protected (Bisset *et al.*, 1960; Rothschild 1973), and they
include species that emit sounds, rich in ultrasound, in
response to the echolocating chirps of bats (Blest *et al.*,
1963). Bats turn away from the calls, presumably because
they have learned on the basis of previous experience with
moths that a prospective meal that protests audibly is distasteful (Dunning and Roeder 1965; Roeder 1967).

VI. DEFENSIVE STEROIDS OF FIREFLIES

Insectivorous birds, as I learned from a Swainson's thrush
called Phogel that was my pet for several years, can be fin-
icky gourmets. They treat different insects in different
ways, depending whether they like them very much, moderately,
or not at all. Phogel was distinctly thrushlike in her ways,
as I now know from having watched many thrushes. Insects that
she liked she took in her bill and swallowed outright, while
others that were chemically or in some alternative way protected she either rejected on first contact (intense dislike),
or pecked repeatedly and/or wiped in her plumage before either
rejecting or ingesting them (moderate dislike). Insects that
she disliked intensely she quickly learned to recognize and to
avoid on sight alone. I fed Phogel over 500 arthropods of
100 species one summer, including representatives of 12 in-
sectan orders. Among the items that she rated lowest were
several beetles belonging to families of known defensive chemistry (Meloidae, Cantharidae, Coccinellidae, Silphidae) and
fireflies (Eisner *et al.*, 1978b). Previous work had shown
fireflies to be rejected or ignored by predators, and had suggested, since fireflies reflex-bleed when disturbed, that they
might contain defensive chemicals in the blood (Lloyd 1973;
Blum and Sannasi 1974; Sydow and Lloyd 1975). Since Phogel's
behavior had provided us with the basis for a bioassay, we set
out to look for such substances. Hermit thrushes, tested in
numbers, shared Phogel's dislike of fireflies. They rejected
virtually all individuals of two common species (*Photinus ignitus* and *P. marginellus*) that were offered to them. The
single firefly that was swallowed (one of 135 presented to 9
thrushes) was promptly regurgitated. *Photinus* were then obtained in quantity, chemically fractionated, and the fractions
tested as topical additives of mealworms in feeding tests with
thrushes. Purification of active fractions led to the isolation of a series of novel steroid pyrones that we called lucibufagins (Fig. 10), which proved deterrent to birds at a
fraction of the dosages in which they occur in fireflies

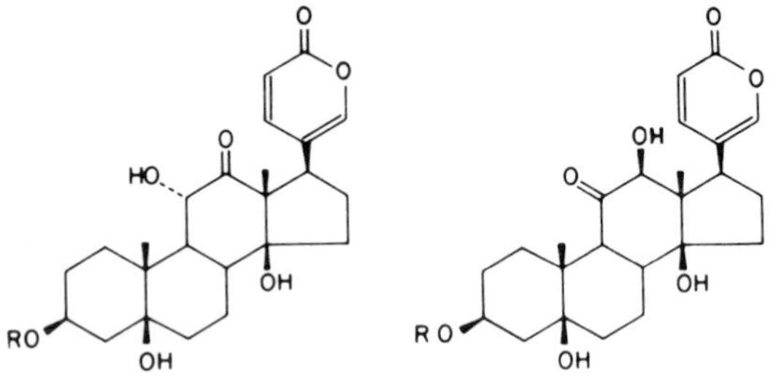

FIGURE 10. *Lucibufagins from* Photinus ignitus *and* P.
marginellus [R = H *or* COCH₃].

(Eisner *et al.*, 1978b; Goetz *et al.*, 1979; Meinwald *et al.*,
1979).
   The closest known relatives of lucibufagins are the familiar bufadienolides from certain toads and plants (Nakanishi
1974). Steroids as such, however, are not unknown as defensive agents in insects. A diversity of steroids is secreted
by dytiscid beetles (Weatherston and Percy, 1978), and cardenolides, produced either by the insects themselves or sequestered from ingested plant tissue, have been isolated from
danaid butterflies, grasshoppers, chrysomelid beetles, and
other insects (von Euw *et al.* 1967, 1971; Reichstein *et al.*,
1968; Rothschild *et al.*, 1970; Pasteels and Daloze 1977).
   Photinus are rejected by other predators as well, as for
example by ants and jumping spiders (Eisner, Hill, and Dodge,
unpublished), but they were known to have at least some enemies in nature. Among these, oddly enough, are the females
of certain other fireflies, belonging to the genus *Photuris*.
These females, appropriately named "femmes fatales" (Lloyd
1965, 1975; Carlson and Copeland 1978), feed on *Photinus*
males, which they lure at night by imitating the flash signal
of the *Photinus* female. We have learned that the "femmes fatales" derive more than mere nutritional benefit from the
Photinus they eat. *Photuris* are apparently unable to produce
lucibufagins themselves. They lack the compounds as larvae,
and also at the time of emergence from pupae. But they acquire and retain the compounds when fed *Photinus* in the laboratory, and as a consequence become unacceptable to predators
such as jumping spiders (Fig. 11). Furthermore, field-col-
lected *Photuris* females, which could be expected to differ in
age and dietary history, were found to contain lucibufagins in

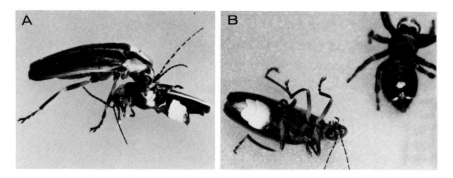

FIGURE 11. A Female of Photuris sp. (firefly "femme fatale") feeding on male of Photinus ignitus. B. Photuris female being rejected by a jumping spider (Phidippus audax). The rejection is attributable to the distasteful lucibufagins incorporated by the Photuris from the Photinus it ate.

amounts ranging from zero to levels commensurate with the quantities detected in Photinus-fed females in the laboratory (Eisner, Hill, Dodge, Goetz, and Meinwald, unpublished).

How Photinus itself comes upon possession of its lucibufagins remains unknown. Since insects seem generally incapable of producing steroids from non-steroidal precursors (Clayton 1970), it has been suggested that Photinus may derive the compounds from ingested cholesterol (Eisner et al., 1978b) a process already demonstrated to account for bufadienolide synthesis in toads (Porto and Gros, 1971).

VII. DIETARY ACQUISITION OF DEFENSIVE SUBSTANCES

It is becoming increasingly apparent that the strategy exemplified by the Photuris female — the acquisition of defensive material from a dietary source — is widespread among insects. Some pioneering papers on the subject are still classics (Brower and Brower 1964; Dethier 1954; Ehrlich and Raven 1965). Documented cases involve for the most part defensive appropriation of secondary metabolites from plants. Lepidoptera commonly incorporate distasteful or toxic materials from their larval host plants, and transmit these substances through the pupa to the adult. Danaid butterflies obtain cardenolides from milkweed plants in this fashion (Parsons, 1965; Brower et al., 1967; Brower and Glazier, 1975; Reichstein et al., 1968), certain swallowtail butterflies sequester aristolochic acids from Aristolochiaceae (von Euw et

al., 1969), and some arctiid moths incorporate pyrrolizidine
alkaloids from Compositae, Leguminosae and other plants (Aplin *et al.*, 1968; Rothschild, 1973). But sequestration is by
no means restricted to the Lepidoptera. Rothschild (1973)
lists a number of Neuroptera, Hemiptera, Coleoptera, Diptera,
and Orthoptera that are also known or believed to incorporate
toxins from their host plants.

Systemic incorporation of protective substances is obviously possible only if an insect is insensitive to the appropriated materials, but there are ways short of systemic incorporation by which plant metabolites can also be used for
defense. The larva of the sawfly *Neodiprion sertifer*, for
example, feeds on conifers and uses conifer resin for defense.
It never really ingests the resin. As it takes conifer tissue into the mouth, it manages somehow to channel the resin
into two diverticular pouches of the esophagus, while passing
the edible remainder of the morsels into the midgut for digestion and absorption. The diverticuli, like all parts of
the foregut, are lined with an impervious cuticular membrane
that prevents the resin from making actual contact with the
living tissues of the animal. When attacked, the larva discharges resin droplets from the mouth. By virtue of its contained monoterpenes, the fluid is repellent to predators
(Eisner *et al.*, 1974b). A similar defensive strategy is employed by Australian sawflies of the family Pergidae, which
feed on eucalyptus trees and use eucalypt oil for defense
(Fig. 12A) (Morrow *et al.*, 1976). Chromatographic traces of
extracts of the oil and of the larval effluent are virtually

FIGURE 12. A. Cluster of larvae of the Australian sawfly
Pseudoperga guerini, *responding to disturbance by emitting oil*
droplets from the mouth. B. Mature larva of Perga affinis,
beside an esophageal sac, replete with oil, isolated from one
such larva.(from Morrow et al., *1976).*

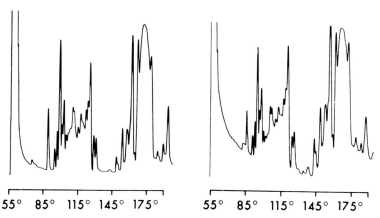

55° 85° 115° 145° 175°   55° 85° 115° 145° 175°

FIGURE 13. Gas-liquid chromatographic traces of leaf oil of Eucalyptus pauciflora *(left), and of oral fluid from a* Pseudoperga guerini *larva that fed on that eucalypt (right). (after Morrow et al., 1976).*

superimposable (Fig. 13). The quantity of oil sequestered and stored by a larva may constitute nearly 20% of body weight (Fig. 12B). Neither *Neodiprion* nor the Pergidae waste the sequestered fluid when they proceed to spin their cocoons. While the Pergidae incorporate the eucalypt oil into the wall of the cocoon, *Neodiprion* remains capable of protecting it- self by regurgitative emission from within the cocoon until it sheds the foregut and its resin content during the pupal molt. Many lepidopteran larvae also void enteric fluids through the mouth when they are disturbed (Eisner, 1970), and certain caterpillars have recently been noted to protect them- selves with plant oil that they store in an esophageal diver- ticulum (Common and Bellas, 1977).

Photuris are not the only insects known to appropriate defenses from animals rather than plants. We recently studied the caterpillar of *Laetilia coccidivora*, a pyralid species that feeds on scale insects, including the cochineal insect *Dactylopius confusus*. The red cochineal dye, carminic acid, extracted from *Dactylopius* and related scale insects, and used extensively in the fabric industry before the advent of ani- line dyes, is an anthraquinone (Fig. 14A). Tests with ants showed the compound to be a potent feeding deterrent (Fig. 14C). When a *Laetilia* larva is disturbed, it revolves the front end and regurgitates a droplet of intensely red fluid onto the offending agent. Attacking ants thus wetted promptly abandon the attack, and move away while attempting to wipe themselves clean of the contaminant (Fig. 14B). Analysis of the fluid showed it to contain unaltered carminic acid at con- centrations provently deterrent to ants. It is argued that

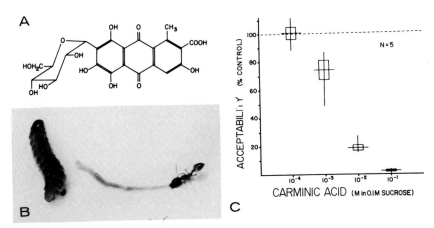

FIGURE 14. *A. Carminic acid, the red anthraquinonoid pigment from cochineal insects. B. Larva of* Laetilia coccidovora, *fed on its normal cochineal diet, repelling an ant (*Monomorium destructor*). The larva has dabbed a droplet of carminic acid-containing oral fluid on the ant, which is retreating, dragging its head and leaving a red streak in its wake. C. Acceptability of carminic acid solution to ants (*M. destructor*) expressed as percent of acceptability of control (*10^{-1}M *sucrose). Horizontal lines, vertical lines, and bars give means, ranges, and one standard error on each side of mean respectively. The concentration of carminic acid in the oral fluid of* Laetilia *approximates* 10^{-1}M. *(from Eisner* et al., *1980).*

carminic acid is to be viewed, in analogy with what holds true for so many secondary metabolites in plants, as a defensive material in the cochineal itself. What *Laetilia* has evolutionarily achieved is thus seen to be no different from what so many hervibores have achieved in parallel: it has crashed through the defensive chemical barrier of its host in a manner that does not preclude secondary utilization of the weaponry for defensive purposes of its own (Eisner *et al.*, 1980.

Even non-dietary materials may be appropriated for defense. The larva of the green lacewing *Chrysopa slossonae* lives in colonies of the wooly alder aphid, *Prociphilus tesselatus*, upon which it feeds. It is ordinarily virtually indistinguishable from its host (Fig. 15A), since it covers itself with a dense investiture of the aphid's wool — a long-chain keto-ester recently identified (Meinwald *et al.*, 1975) — which it plucks from the aphids with its mouthparts. Thus covered, the larvae are protected from assault by the ants that ordinarily shepherd the aphids (Fig. 15B). Larvae artificially deprived of their coating are seized by the ants and removed from the aphid colonies (Fig. 15C). A larva needs on

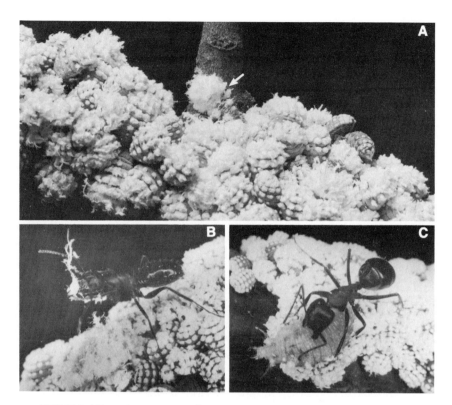

FIGURE 15. A. Larva of Chrysopa slossonae *(arrow) among its wooly-aphid prey (*Prociphilus tesselatus*). B. Aphid-guarding ant, backing off from the* Chrysopa *larva it has just bitten. The ant's mouthparts are contaminated with some of the waxy "wool" that the larva had plucked from aphids and applied to its back. C. Artificially denuded larva, under persistent attack by an ant.*

the average less than 20 min to invest itself with wool. A hungry denuded larva gives the coating procedure about the same behavioral priority as feeding (Eisner *et al.*, 1978a).

VIII. PLANT ALKALOIDS, DEFENSE, AND SEXUAL SELECTION IN LEPIDOPTERA

The process of utilization of ingested phytochemicals is carried beyond the purpose of defense in certain Lepidoptera.

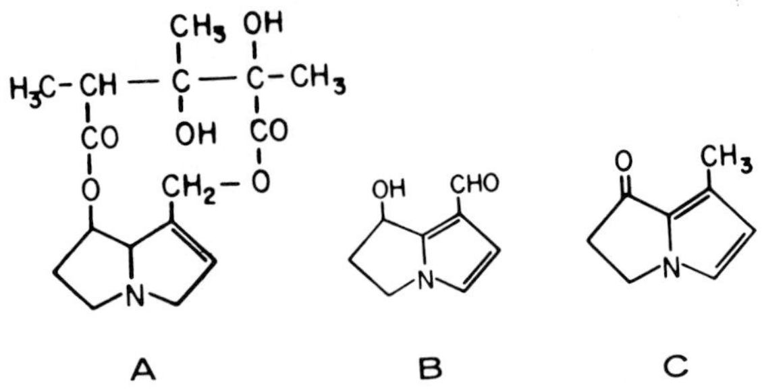

FIGURE 16. A. A pyrrolizidine alkaloid (monocrotaline). B. Corematal pheromone of Utetheisa ornatrix. C. Danaidone, the "hairpencil" pheromone of Danaus gilippus and several other danaid butterflies.

Species of two disparate evolutionary lineages within the order have recently been shown to utilize ingested plant alkaloids for production of pheromones that males employ in courtship.

One case is that of the arctiid moth *Utetheisa ornatrix*. Some years ago, while working on the defensive adaptations of moths *vis à vis* orb-weaving spiders (Eisner *et al.*, 1964), I discovered that *Utetheisa* is rejected by such spiders as *Nephila clavipes*, which cuts the moth from the web. Collaborative work has since shown that *Nephila* is unpalatable to spiders, as also to birds, by virtue of pyrrolizidine alkaloids (for example Fig. 16A) that it sequesters as a larva from its leguminous host plants (*Crotalaria* spp.). *Utetheisa* reared on alkaloid-free diet are eaten by the spiders, and the alkaloids themselves, when applied topically to palatable items such as mealworms, render these relatively unacceptable to spiders and birds (Eisner, Conner, and Hicks, unpublished). Courtship in *Utetheisa* involves conventional long-range attraction of males by the female, which broadcasts a pheromone downwind. The principal component of the pheromone has been shown to be an unsaturated hydrocarbon — Z,Z,Z-3,6,9-heneicosatriene — produced by the female whether or not she is raised on normal diet, and therefore probably biosynthesized by the female herself (Conner *et al.*, 1980). Once the male is within close range of the female he announces his presence by everting two tufts of glandular scales (coremata) from his abdomen (Fig. 17), while at the same time thrusting the abdomen against her. If she is prepared to accept him, she raises the wings slightly, exposes the abdominal tip, and couples with him (Conner, 1979). The major pheromonal component associated

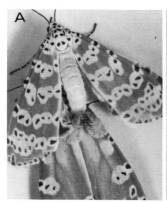

FIGURE 17. A. Male of Utetheisa ornatrix *brushing its everted coremata against a female during close-range court- ship interaction. B. Ventral view of abdominal tip of male* U. ornatrix, *showing retracted corema on right and everted corema on left.*

with the coremata has been identified and found to be of a structure obviously suggestive of derivation from pyrrolizi- dine alkaloids (Fig. 16B) (Conner, VanderMeer, Meinwald and Eisner, unpublished). Males reared on alkaloid-free diet lack the pheromone, and were shown in meticulous bioassays in which courtships were videotaped and analyzed by slow tape playback to have a reduced probability of gaining acceptance by the female. Moreover, the pheromone proved active in bio- assays in which the criterion was the wing-raising response of the female (Conner, 1979).

The question that arises is whether the derivation of a pheromone from a phytotoxin is to be viewed strictly as an economic expediency, or whether a more subtle adaptive justi- fication might be at play. I would like to suggest here, jointly with my former student William Conner, that the core- mata might be more than mere chemical "greeting cards." Since their pheromonal content could be a measure of the male's alkaloid load (and indirectly also of his potentially inherent alkaloid-sequestering ability), they could provide the female with information which, in the context of sexual selection, might be decisive. Although obvious questions need to be answered to substantiate the idea (for example: does the female appraise the pheromonal content of the male? Does pheromonal content vary in accord with systemic alkaloid con- tent? Is alkaloid-sequestering ability genetically con- trolled?) we advance the hypothesis here because we feel it might be applicable also to danaid butterflies, the second example of Lepidoptera known to derive pheromones from alkaloids.

Much has been learned and written lately about danaids. Suffice it to say that they too sequester pyrrolizidine alkaloids (Edgar *et al.*, 1973; 1976a; Schneider *et al.*, 1975), although they do so only as adults, to supplement, I would suggest, the cardenolides that their larval host plants (asclepiads) offer only in unreliable supply (Brower *et al.*, 1967). Danaid courtship (Pliske and Eisner, 1969; Seibt *et al.*, 1972) takes place by day, and is initiated on the wing, most probably by sight. But at close range there is again an interaction involving glandular brush eversion by the male (the brushes, called "hairpencils" are analogous rather than homologous to arctiid coremata). In almost all species where the hairpencils have been examined chemically (references in Conner, 1979), they were found to contain compounds obviously related to pyrrolizidine alkaloids (Fig. 16C). Dietary deprivation of alkaloid does indeed result in pheromone-deficient males (Edgar *et al.*, 1973; Schneider *et al.*, 1975), which are relatively unsuccessful in courtship unless artificially subsidized with pheromone (Pliske and Eisner, 1969). The similarity with *Utetheisa* is obvious, both in chemical and behavioral detail. Other Lepidoptera are also associated with pyrrolizidine alkaloid-containing plants (Edgar *et al.*, 1976b; Pliske *et al.*, 1976), and one wonders whether the parallel might not extend even further. In fact, if sequestering ability is indeed variable, genetically controlled, and chemically appraisable in the context of courtship, one could imagine totally different situations, involving perhaps even non-arthropods, where pheromonal advertisement of sequestering ability might be practiced.

ACKNOWLEDGMENTS

The contribution of my associates, and in particular their permission to cite results as yet unpublished, is gratefully noted.

REFERENCES

Alexander, R.D. (1967). Acoustical communication in arthropods. *Annual Rev. Entomol.* *12*, 495-526.

Aneshansley, D.J., Eisner, T., Widom, J.M. and Widom, B.
(1969). Biochemistry at 100°C: explosive secretory discharge
of bombardier beetles (*Brachinus*). *Science 165*, 61-63.

Aplin, R.T., Benn, M.H. and Rothschild, M. (1968). Poisonous alkaloids in the body tissues of the cinnabar moth (*Cal-
limorpha jacobaeae* L.). *Nature 219*, 747-748.

Bauer, T. (1976). Experimente zur Frage der biologischen
Bedeutung des Stridulationsverhaltens von Käfern. *Z. Tier-
psychol. 42*, 57-65.

Bettini, S. (1978), "Arthropod Venoms." *Handb. Exp. Pharm.
48.* Springer-Verlag, New York.

Bissett, G.W., Frazer, J.F.D., Rothschild, M. and Schach-
ter, M. (1960). A pharmacologically active choline ester and
other substances in the garden tiger moth, *Arctia caja* (L.).
Proc. Roy. Soc. (London) B152, 255-262.

Blest, A.D., Collett, T.S. and Pye, J.D. (1963). The
generation of ultrasonic signals by a New World arctiid moth.
Proc. Roy. Soc. (London) B158, 196-207.

Blum, M.S. and Sannasi, A. (1974). Reflex bleeding in the
lampyrid *Photinus pyralis*: defensive function. *J. Insect
Physiol. 20*, 451-460.

Brower, L.P. and Brower, J.V.Z. (1964). Birds, butterflies,
and plant poisons: A study in ecological chemistry. *Zoologica
49*, 137-159.

Brower, L.P. and Glazier, S.C. (1975). Localization of
heart poisons in the monarch butterfly. *Science 188*, 19-25.

Brower, L.P., Brower, J.V.Z. and Corvino, J.M. (1967).
Plant poisons in a terrestrial food chain. *Proc. Nat. Acad.
Sci. U.S.A. 57*, 893-898.

Carlson, A.D. and Copeland, J. (1978). Behavioral plasticity in the flash communication systems of fireflies. *Amer. Sci. 66*, 340-346.

Clayton, R.B. (1970). The chemistry of nonhormonal interactions: terpenoid compounds in ecology. *In* "Chemical Ecology" (Sondheimer, E. and Simeone, J.B., eds). pp. 235-280. Academic Press, New York.

Common, I.F.B. and Bellas, T.E. (1977). Regurgitation of host-plant oil from a foregut diverticulum in the larvae of *Myrascia megalocentra* and *M. bracteatella* (Lepidoptera: Oecophoridae). *J. Aust. Entomol. Soc. 16*, 141-147.

Conner, W.E. (1979). Chemical attraction and seduction: the courtship of *Utetheisa ornatrix* (Lepidoptera, Arctiidae). Ph.D. Thesis, Cornell University.

Conner, W.E., and Masters, W.M. (1978). Infrared video viewing. *Science 199*, 1004.

Conner, W.E., Eisner, T., VanderMeer, R.K., Guerrero, A., Ghiringelli, D. and Meinwald, J. (1980). Sex attractant of an arctiid moth (*Utetheisa ornatrix*): a pulsed chemical signal. *Behav. Ecol. Sociobiol.*, in press.

Darwin, C. (1874). "The Descent of Man and Selection in Relation to Sex." Appleton, New York.

Dean, J. (1979). Defensive reaction time of bombardier beetles. *J. Chem. Ecol. 5*, 691-701.

Dean, J. (1980a). Encounters between bombardier beetles and two species of toads (*Bufo americanus, B. marinus*): speed of prey-capture does not determine success. *J. Comp. Physiol. 135*, 41-50.

Dean, J. (1980b). Effect of thermal and chemical components of bombardier beetle chemical defense: glossopharyngeal response in two species of toads (*Bufo americanus, B. marinus*). *J. Comp. Physiol. 135*, 51-59.

Dethier, V.G. (1954). Evolution of feeding preferences in phytophagous insects. *Evolution 8*, 33-54.

Dunning, D.C. and Roeder, K.D. (1965). Moth sounds and the insect-catching behavior of bats. *Science 147*, 173-174.

Edgar, J.A., Culvenor, C.J. and Robinson, G.S. (1973). Hairpencil dihydropyrrolizidine derivatives of Danainae from the New Hebrides. *J. Aust. Entomol. Soc. 12*, 144-150.

Edgar, J.A., Cockrun, P.A. and Frahn, J.L. (1976a). Pyrrolizidine alkaloids in *Danaus plexippus* L. *and Danaus chrysippus* L. *Experientia 32*, 1535-1537.

Edgar, J.A., Culvenor, C.C.J. and Pliske, T.E. (1976b). Isolation of a lactone, structurally related to the esterifying acids of pyrrolizidine alkaloids, from the costal fringes of male Ithomiinae. *J. Chem. Ecol. 2*, 263-270.

Ehrlich, P.R. and Raven, P.H. (1965). Butterflies and plants: A study in coevolution. *Evolution 18*, 586-608.

Eisner, T. (1958). The protective role of the spray mechanism of the bombardier beetle, *Brachynus ballistarius* Lec. *J. Insect Physiol. 2*, 215-220.

Eisner, T. (1970). Chemical defense against predation in arthropods. *In* "Chemical Ecology" (Sondheimer, E. and Simeone, J.B., eds.), pp. 157-217. Academic Press, New York.

Eisner, T. and Dean, J. (1976). Ploy and counterploy in predator-prey interactions: orb-weaving spiders versus bombardier beetles. *Proc. Nat. Acad. Sci. U.S.A. 73*, 1365-1367.

Eisner, T., Alsop, R. and Ettershank, G. (1964). Adhesiveness of spider silk. *Science 146*, 1058-1061.

Eisner, T., Kluge, A.F., Carrell, J.E. and Meinwald, J. (1971). Defense of phalangid: liquid repellent administered by leg dabbing. *Science 173*, 650-652.

Eisner, T., Aneshansley, D., Eisner, M., Rutowski, R., Chong, B. and Meinwald, J. (1974a). Chemical defense and sound production in Australian tenebrionid beetles (*Adelium* spp.). *Psyche 81*, 189-208.

Eisner, T., Johnessee, J.S., Carrell, J., Hendry, L.B. and Meinwald, J. (1974b). Defensive use by an insect of a plant resin. *Science 184*, 996-999.

Eisner, T., Kriston, I. and Aneshansley, D.J. (1976). Defensive behavior of a termite (*Nasutitermes exitiosus*). *Behav. Ecol. Sociobiol. 1*, 83-125.

Eisner, T., Jones, T.H., Aneshansley, D.J., Tschinkel, W.R., Silberglied, R.E. and Meinwald, J. (1977). Chemistry of defensive secretions of bombardier beetles (Brachinini, Metriini, Ozaenini, Paussini). *J. Insect Physiol. 23*, 1383-1386.

Eisner, T., Hicks, K., Eisner, M and Robson, D.S. (1978a). "Wolf-in-sheep's-clothing" strategy of a predaceous insect larva. *Science 199*, 790-794.

Eisner, T., Wiemer, D.F., Hanes, L.W. and Meinwald, J. (1978b). Lucibufagins: defensive steroids from the fireflies *Photinus ignitus* and *P. marginellus* (Coleoptera: Lampyridae). *Proc. Nat. Acad. Sci. U.S.A. 75*, 905-908.

Eisner, T., Nowicki, S., Goetz, M. and Meinwald, J. (1980). Red cochineal dye (carminic acid): its "raison d'être." *Science*, in press.

Ernst, E. (1959). Beobachtungen beim Spritzakt der Nasutitermes-Soldaten. *Rev. Suisse Zool. 66*, 289-295.

Goetz, M., Wiemer, D.F., Haynes, L.W., Meinwald, J. and Eisner, T. (1979). Lucibufagines. Partie III. Oxo-11 et oxo-12-bufalines, steroides défensifs des lampyres *Photinus ignitus* et *P. marginellus* (Coleoptera: Lampyridae). *Helv. Chim. Acta 62*, 1396-1400.

Haskell, P.T. (1961), "Insect Sounds." Quadrangle Books, Chicago.

Hölldobler, B. (1977). Communication in social Hymenoptera. *In* "How Animals Communicate" (Sebeok, T.A., ed.), Ch. 19 pp. 418-471. Indiana Univ. Press, Bloomington, Indiana.

Kriston, I., Watson, J.A.L. and Eisner, T. (1977). Non-combative behavior of large soldiers of *Nasutitermes exitiosus* (Hill): an analytical study. *Insectes Sociaux 24*, 103-111.

Lasser, F.C. (1738), "Insectotheologia." Michael Blochburger, Frankfurt and Leipzip.

Lloyd, J.E. (1965). Aggressive mimicry in *Photuris:* firefly *femmes fatales*. *Science 149*, 653-654.

Lloyd, J.E. (1973). Firefly parasites and predators. *Coleopt. Bull. 27*, 91-106.

Lloyd, J.E. (1975). Aggressive mimicry in *Photuris* fire-flies: signal repertoires by *femmes fatales*. *Science 187*, 452-453.

Marshall, G.A.K. (1902a). Experimental evidence of terror caused by the squeak of *Acherontia atrops*. *Trans. R. Entomol. Soc. Lond.* 402.

Marshall, G.A.K. (1902b). Insect stridulation as a warning or intimidating character. *Trans. R. Entomol. Soc. Lond.* 404.

Maschwitz, U. and Mühlenberg, M. (1972). Chemische Gefahrenalarmierung bei einer Termite. *Naturwissenschaften 59*, 516-517.

Masters, W.M. (1979). Insect disturbance stridulation: its defensive role. *Behav. Ecol. Sociobiol. 5*, 187-200.

Meinwald, J., Smolanoff, J., Chibnall, A.C. and Eisner, T. (1975). Characterization and synthesis of waxes from homopterous insects. *J. Chem. Ecol. 1*, 269-274.

Meinwald, J., Wiemer, D.F. and Eisner, T. (1979). Lucibufagins. 2. Esters of 12-oxo-2β,5β,11α-trihydroxybufalin, the major defensive steroids of the firefly *Photinus pyralis* (Coleoptera: Lampyridae). *J. Amer. Chem. Soc. 101*, 3055-3060.

Moore, B.P. (1968). Studies on the chemical composition and function of the cephalic gland secretion in Australian termites. *J. Insect Physiol. 14*, 33-39.

Morrow, P.A., Bellas, T.E. and Eisner, T (1976). *Eucalyptus* oils in the defensive oral discharge of Australian saw-fly larvae (Hymenoptera: Pergidae). *Oecologia 24*, 193-206.

Nakanishi, K. (1974), "Natural Products Chemistry." Academic Press, New York.

Nutting, W.L., Blum, M.S. and Fales, H.M. (1974). Behavior of the North American termite *Tenuirostritermes tenuirostris*, with special reference to the soldier frontal gland secretion, its chemical composition, and use in defense. *Psyche 81*, 167-177.

Parsons, J.A. (1965). A digitalis-like toxin in the monarch butterfly, *Danaus plexippus* L. *J. Physiol., Lond. 178*, 290-304.

Pasteels, J.M. and Daloze, D. (1977). Cardiac glycosides in the defensive secretion of chrysomelid beetles: evidence for their production by the insects. *Science 197*, 70-72.

Pliske, T.E. and Eisner, T. (1969). Sex pheromone of the queen butterfly: biology. *Science 164*, 1170-1172.

Pliske, T.E., Edgar, J.A. and Culvenor, C.C.J. (1976). The chemical basis of attraction of Ithomiinae butterflies to plants containing pyrrolizidine alkaloids. *J. Chem. Ecol.* 2, 255-262.

Pocock, R.I. (1896). How and why scorpions hiss. *Nat. Sci. (Lond.) 9*, 17-25.

Porto, A.M. and Gros, E. (1971). Biosynthesis of the bufadienolide marginobufagin in toads *Bufo paracnemis* from cholesterol-20-^{14}C. *Experientia 27*, 506.

Prestwich, G.D. (1979). Chemical defense by termite soldiers. *J. Chem. Ecol. 5*, 459-480.

Prestwich, G.D., Tanis, S.P., Pilkiewicz, F.G., Miura, I. and Nakanishi, K. (1976a). Nasute termite soldier frontal gland secretions. 2. Structures of trinervitene congeners from *Trinervitermes* soldiers. *J. Amer. Chem. Soc. 98*, 6062-6065.

Prestwich, G.D., Tanis, S.P., Springer, J.P. and Clardy, J. (1976b). Nasute termite soldier frontal gland secretions. 1. Structure of Trinervi-2β,3α,9α-triol 9-0-acetate, a novel diterpene from *Trinervitermes* soldiers. *J. Amer. Chem. Soc. 98*, 6061-6062.

Reba, I. (1966). Applications of the coanda effect. *Sci. Amer. 214*, 84-92.

Reichstein, T., von Euw, J.V., Parsons, J.A. and Rothschild, M. (1968). Heart poisons in the monarch butterfly. *Science 161*, 861-866.

Remold, H. (1962). Über die biologische Bedentung der Duftdrüsen bei den Landwanzen (Geocorisae). *Z. Vergleich. Physiol. 45*, 636-694.

Roach, B., Dodge, K.R., Aneshansley, D.J., Wiemer, D., Meinwald, J. and Eisner, T. (1979). Chemistry of defensive secretions of ozaenine and paussine bombardier beetles (Coleoptera: Carabidae). *Coleopt. Bull. 33*, 17-20.

Roeder, K.D. (1967), "Nerve Cells and Insect Behavior." Harvard Univ. Press, Cambridge, Mass.

Rothschild, M. (1973). Secondary plant substances and warning colouration in insects. *In* "Insect/Plant Relationships." Symposia of the Roy. Entomol. Soc. Lond. (van Emden, H.F., ed.) Vol. 6, pp. 59-83. Blackwell Scientific Publ., London.

Rothschild, M., von Euw, J. and Reichstein, T. (1970). Cardiac glycosides in the oleander aphid, *Aphis nerii*. *J. Insect Physiol. 16*, 1141-1145.

Schildknecht, H. (1957). Zur Chemie des Bombardier Kaefers. *Angew. Chem. 69*, 62.

Schildknecht, H. and Holoubek, K. (1961) Die Bombardier Kaefer und ihre Explosionschemie. V. Mitteilung ueber Insekten-Abwehrstoffe. *Angew. Chem. 73*, 1-7.

Schildknecht, H., Maschwitz, E. and Maschwitz, U. (1968). Die Explosionschemie der Bombardier Kaefer (Coleoptera, Carabidae) III. Mitt.: Isolierung und Charakterisierung der Explosionskatalysatoren. *Z. Naturforsch.23B*, 1213-1218.

Schneider, D., Boppré, M., Schneider, H., Thompson, W.R., Boriak, C.J., Petty, R.L. and Meinwald, J. (1975). A pheromone precursor and its uptake in male *Danaus* butterflies. *J. Comp. Physiol. 97*, 245-256.

Smith, R.L. and Langley, W.M. (1978). Cicada stress sound: An assay of its effectiveness as a predator defense mechanism. *Southwest. Nat. 23*, 187-196.

Sydow, S.L. and Lloyd, J.E. (1975). Distasteful fireflies sometimes emetic, but not lethal. *Fla. Entomol. 58*, 312.

Tschinkel, W.R. (1975). A comparative study of the chemical defensive system of tenebrionid beetles. Defensive behavior and ancillary features. *Ann. Entomol. Soc. Amer. 68*, 439-453.

Tuxen, S.L. (1967), "Insektenstimmen." Springer Verlag, Berlin.

von Euw, J., Fishelson, J., Parsons, J.A., Reichstein, T. and Rothschild, M. (1967). Cardenolides (heart poisons) in a grasshopper feeding on milkweeds. *Nature 214*, 35-39.

von Euw, J., Reichstein, T. and Rothschild, M. (1969). Aristolochic acid-1 in the swallowtail butterfly *Pachlioptera aristolochiae* (Fabr.)(Papilionidae). *Israel J. Chem. 6*, 659-670.

von Euw, J., Reichstein, T. and Rothschild, M. (1971). Heart poisons (cardiac glycosides) in the lygaeid bugs *Caenocoris nerii* and *Spilostethus pandurus*. *Insect Biochem. 1*, 373-384.

Weatherston, J. and Percy, J.E. (1978). Venoms of Coleoptera. *In* "Arthropod Venoms. *Handbook of Experimental Pharmacology* (Bettini, S., ed.) Vol. 48, Ch. 19, pp. 489-509. Springer-Verlag, New York.

Wilson, E.O. (1971), "The Insect Societies." Harvard Univ. Press, Cambridge, Mass.

THE FUTURE FOR INSECTICIDES

Michael Elliott

Department of Insecticides and Fungicides
Rothamsted Experimental Station
Harpenden, Herts. U.K.

I. INTRODUCTION

In 1951, Sir Vincent Wigglesworth described the impact of insects on human affairs as follows: "Insects destroy man's growing crops and defoliate his forests; they are responsible for the spread of nearly all the great epidemic fevers of the tropics and subtropics, and for the infection of his livestock with some of their most fatal diseases. The structural timbers of his buildings are weakened and destroyed by insect attack; his household goods are ravaged by moths and beetles and a heavy toll is levied on his stored reserves of food, spices and tobacco." (Wigglesworth, 1976 *Insects and the Life of Man*, p.7). In 1980 this is still an apt introduction to a discussion of present and future needs for insecticides in insect pest control, for our problems have not lessened. Sir Vincent continued: "the opening up of the tropics has often encouraged the spread of insect-borne diseases. Improved cattle taken to tropical lands have rapidly succumbed to insect-borne infestations to which inferior native breeds have become tolerant. Intensive agriculture has created conditions favourable to the insect pests of crops and increased travel and commerce have led to the introduction of pests into new countries, where having left their native enemies behind, they have flourished exceedingly."

Sir Vincent was concerned with the action of insecticides, particularly in relation to insect physiology (1956b). In the Second World War, when he heard of the discovery of DDT, he was at first sceptical of the claims for its insecticidal properties. Later, the very powerful

879

action against many insects including body lice, malaria-
carrying mosquitoes and some veterinary and agricultural
pests was confirmed.   DDT was welcomed by many as the long
sought, residual contact insecticide, cheap and easy to
manufacture, to replace the natural insecticides derris and
pyrethrum, but as a biologist, Sir Vincent "had an almost
instinctive distrust of chemical control.. and a deep sense
of the complexity of living communities." (p. 12).   In
1976 (p. 2) he was to observe that we are coming back to the
ways of thinking which were general forty years ago, but had
been temporarily abandoned; to realise that disillusionment
with the over-enthusiasm for potent synthetic insecticides
is compelling a return to ecological modes of thought; and
to discover that the many sided attack, universal in the
past (fortified, of course, by greatly increased knowledge)
is now coming back under the banner of "integrated control"
or "pest management".

II. PRESENT SITUATION

    In 1980, the influence of insects on mankind is as power-
ful as ever. During several decades, industrial and academic
research has produced significant advances and developments
in compounds and procedures for insect control, but the problems with which insects confront us still become more serious
year by year as we must provide much more food for an expanding world population and increase other crops, for example
cotton, as synthetic fibres become more expensive. Numerous
analyses (for example, Graham-Bryce, 1976) have been made of
methods by which insects might be controlled. Corbett (1979)
concludes that there is no technique that could significantly
replace pesticides, although there are certainly specific
cases where non-chemical means will be used to limit pest
populations currently controlled chemically. However,
insecticides will be used more and more in conjunction with
other techniques in pest control programmes that are soundly
based biologically and economically. Pesticides will form
a key component of integrated control programmes (Metcalf,
1980).
    However, the efficiency with which we can control insects
with insecticides is very severely constrained in two ways:
by the necessity to use compounds which will not persist unduly and contaminate the environment and by the ability of
insects to develop resistance to insecticides. Therefore
insecticides with selective action and limited persistence
and compounds to which the susceptibility of insects can be

maintained by appropriate strategies are particularly desirable.   These two requirements may be inter-related, for
Sawicki (1979) considers that one of the most serious consequences of the widespread use of the persistent insecticide
DDT may have been selection of the *kdr* resistance mechanism
which is associated with nerve insensitivity and may be responsible for cross-resistance between pyrethroids and DDT in
several arthropod species.

   If synthetic compounds (apart from growth regulators,
juvenile hormone mimics, etc., which are considered elsewhere
in this volume) will continue to be essential for some years
to come, what developments with established or new products
can be anticipated?

III. FUTURE DEVELOPMENTS

A. *Natural Insecticides*

   Despite the existence of a number of natural insecticides
(Jacobson and Crosby, 1971; Casida, 1976) relatively few
have been used in practice and at present only nicotine, rotenone and pyrethrum survive as commercial products.   Only
the structures of the natural pyrethrins have provided a
basis for developing a range of practical insecticides
(Elliott *et al.*,1978; Elliott and Janes,1979). Many reports
of the insecticidal activity of natural products do not indicate the potency of the active compounds against economically
important insect species, and on further examination fail to
provide useful leads to development of practical insecticides,
either because of their low level of activity, or the
molecular complexity of the parent compound (Elliott, 1979).
However, in other fields many valuable toxicants have been
developed from the structures of natural products.   Therefore,
a further survey of plant materials, with the broad range of
test species and application techniques used by many agro-
chemical firms in their screens of synthetic compounds should
certainly discover a significant number of new active compounds.   The task of establishing new structures is rendered
much less formidable today by modern isolation and chromatographic techniques, spectroscopic methods and X-ray analysis.
Although the cost of collection, isolation and storage of
possibly unstable natural products is forbidding, the likelihood of finding a lead to a new group of insecticides based
on a natural product appears comparable to the chances of
discovering one by random screening.

   In the future the intrinsic potency and specificity of

commercial insecticides will become progressively more important as pressure mounts to lessen the risk of contaminating
the environment by diminished rates of application, especially of residual contact insecticides. The scope for increasing activity in various groups of insecticides will therefore
be considered first.

B. *Chlorinated Hydrocarbon Insecticides*

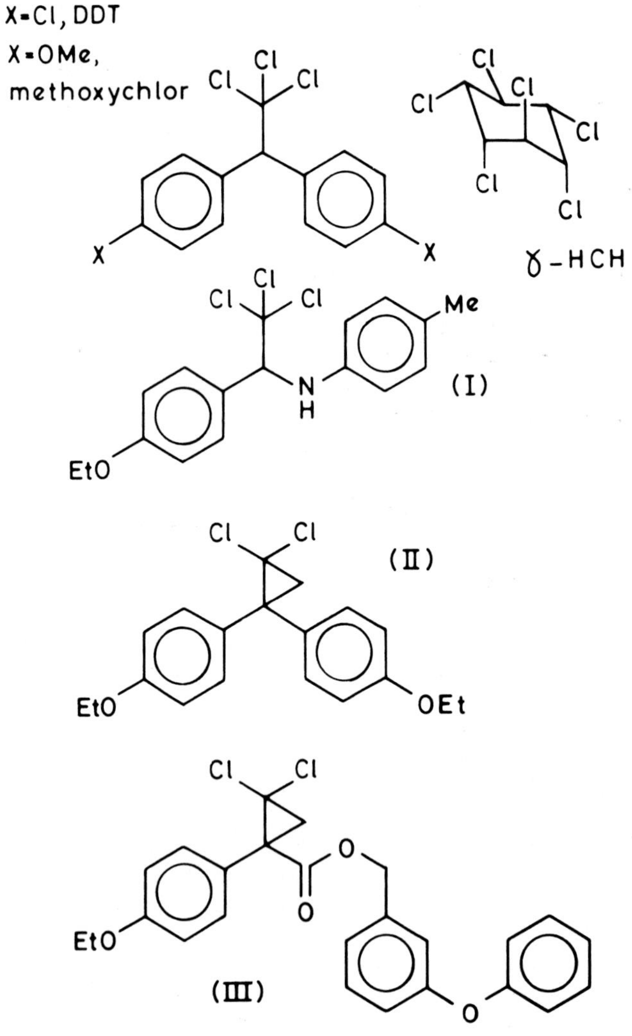

FIGURE 1. *DDT and analogues;* *gamma HCH.*

The first generally available residual contact insecticide was DDT (Fig. 1), but despite numerous attempts, few, if any, related compounds with greater activity have been discovered. Median lethal doses of DDT to insects are in the range 1-20 mg.kg^{-1}, and field application rates from 0.5-3.0 kg. ha^{-1} and for control of resistant insects, up to 100kg. ha^{-1} might be applied in one season.   More active compounds used at lower rates are obviously desirable. Although Metcalf (1976) and Holan et al. (1978) have made marked progress in developing related compounds less persistent than DDT, they are not significantly more active against commercially important pests than the original compounds and closely related products synthesised soon after the initial discovery of DDT.

The γ-isomer of hexachlorocyclohexane (gamma-HCH) (Fig. 1), introduced in the same era as DDT, is up to ten times more active than DDT against some insect pests (Elliott, 1979), but is relatively more expensive because other isomers, which taint food crops, must be removed. Compounds closely related to gamma-HCH are more difficult to synthesise than many of the analogues of DDT and so far no practical, more active, alternatives to the γ-isomer have been found.   Some of the halogenated cyclodienes (aldrin, dieldrin, endrin, endosulphan; Fig. 2) are somewhat more active than DDT; related compounds such as the nitrogen analogue of aldrin are more potent insecticides but at the expense of high mammalian toxicity.   The potency of these cyclodiene chlorinated hydrocarbons is indicated by field application rates (soil pests) of the order of 0.5 kg.ha^{-1};   heavier doses of less expensive,

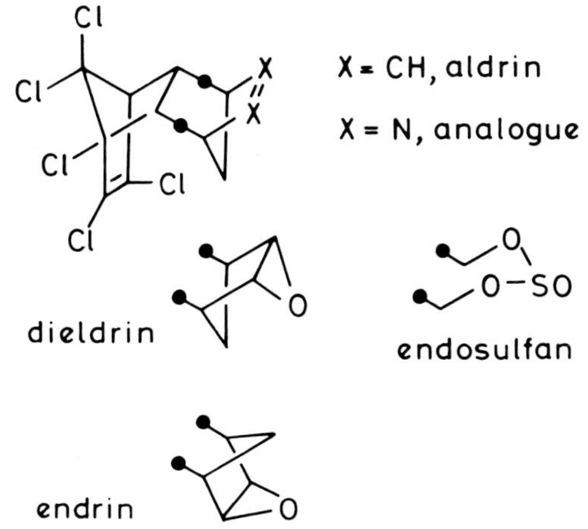

$X = CH$, aldrin

$X = N$, analogue

dieldrin

endosulfan

endrin

FIGURE 2.   Halogenated cyclodiene insecticides.

but also less active compounds such as camphechlor, are
necessary. Therefore, despite much investigation, the level
of activity of chlorinated hydrocarbon insecticides appears
to have reached a plateau, and unless more active compounds,
or less persistent analogues are developed, use of this class
of compound will diminish in the future, and indeed, some
chlorinated hydrocarbon insecticides are already prohibited
in many countries.

C. *Organophosphorus Insecticides*

The structural requirements for insecticidal activity in
organochlorine insecticides are so circumscribed that
few compounds with greater activity or diminished stability
to offset undue persistence have been developed.
In contrast, many different types of organophosphorus derivatives are insecticidal (Wigglesworth, 1954a); the diverse
structural variations provide compounds with a broad range
of properties and with valuable activity against many insect
species at varying stages of development and in differing
situations. The prototype parathion (Fig. 3) is still one
of the most active compounds in the class, although also
very toxic to mammals; malathion is much less toxic,
although also less active against most insect species. A
number of organophosphorus compounds (for example dimethoate
and acephate) are systemic and not unduly toxic to mammals;
others (dichlorvos) act in the vapour phase or in the soil
(chlorfenvinphos and chlorpyriphos). The detailed, biochemical mode of action of organophosphorus insecticides is
better understood than that of most other insecticides
(O'Brien, 1967; Aldridge, 1971; Corbett, 1974). The important
enzyme acetylcholinesterase is inhibited by phosphorylation
at an active site, with varying efficiency depending on the
nature of the leaving group (e.g. 4-nitrophenoxy in the case
of parathion). Design of organophosphorus insecticides
could therefore be approached more rationally than was possible with other groups (Albert, 1979) and many variations
were explored by industrial and academic workers. This
close attention suggests that the scope for increasing their
level of insecticidal activity must have been nearly completely exploited. Field application rates (about 0.6kg/
ha^{-1}) indicate that their potency does not differ greatly
from that of the more active organochlorine compounds and is
fully acceptable for compounds that are neither unduly persistent nor very toxic to mammals. The many structural
variations which are active insecticides suggest that the
potential of the group for providing insecticides for specific applications may not yet have been fully explored.

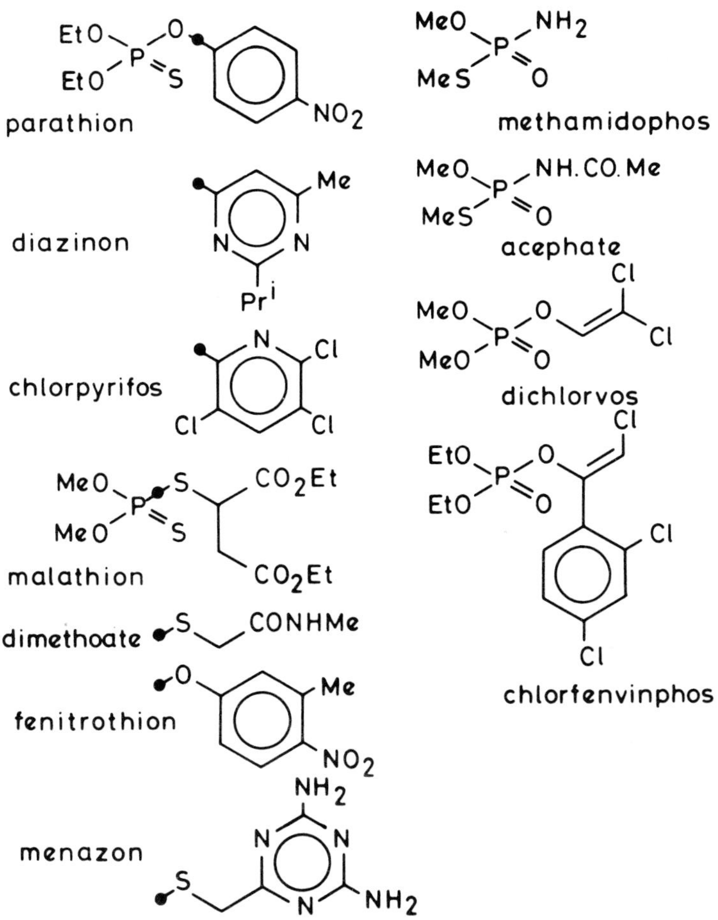

FIGURE 3.   Typical organophosphorus insecticides.

D. Carbamates

As with the organophosphorus compounds, a wide range of
N-methylcarbamates (Fig. 4) are insecticides.   Their mode
of action, inhibiting acetylcholinesterase by carbamoylation
of serine residues, is understood (O'Brien, 1967;   Corbett,
1974; Albert, 1979), so that rational progress has been
possible and the general structural features for greatest
activity in the group have probably been defined.   Carbaryl
is a broad spectrum, general purpose insecticide and propoxur
has contact action with rapid knockdown.   Compounds such
as carbofuran are active against soil pests and variations

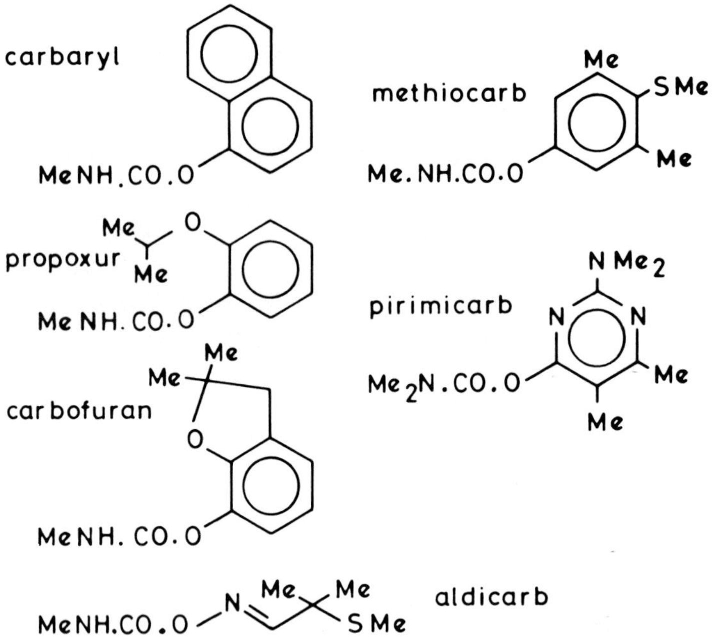

FIGURE 4.   Typical carbamate insecticides.

as in the oxime carbamates (e.g. aldicarb) provide valuable
nematicidal action; methiocarb is a powerful molluscicide
active at 0.2kg.ha^{-1} and pirimicarb a fast acting aphicide
with fumigant and translaminar properties does not affect
beneficial insects. The many possibilities for varying
structures within this group has provided scope for development. Field application rates in the region of 0.7kg.ha^{-1}
indicate adequate activity when the relatively simple structures of many of the members of the group are considered.

E. *Pyrethroids*

The greatest scope for increasing activity in insecticides
has been demonstrated only in the past decade with synthetic compounds related to pyrethrum (Crombie and Elliott,
1961; Elliott and Janes, 1973). Stepwise modification of
the structure of the most potent natural ester, pyrethrin I

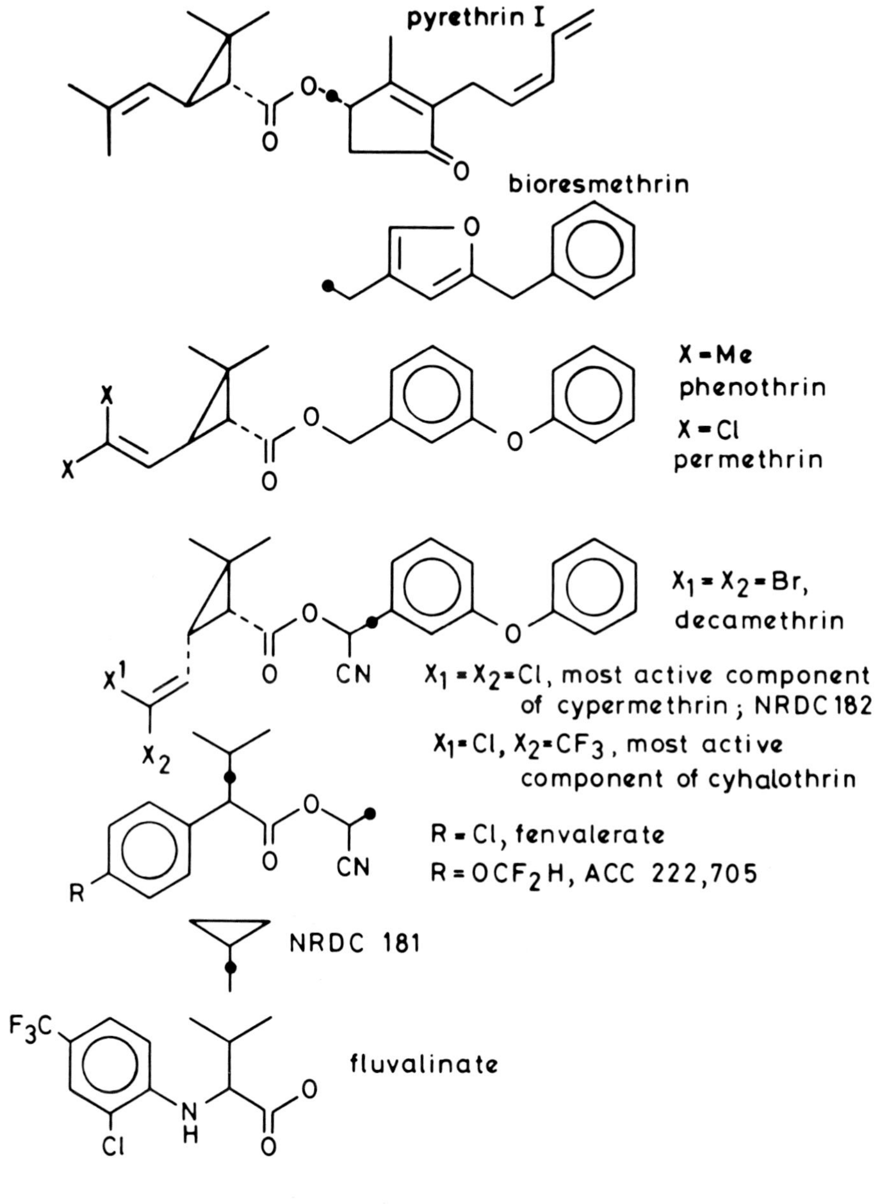

FIGURE 5.   Pyrethroid insecticides.

(Fig. 5) led to decamethrin* (Elliott *et al.*, 1974) and related compounds such as the dichloro (Elliott *et al.*, 1978) and chlorotrifluoromethyl (Huff, 1980) analogues (NRDC 182 and cyhalothrin, respectively). These have unprecedented insecticidal activity (median lethal doses to various insect species in the range 0.004-0.06mg.kg.$^{-1}$ by topical application) so that with decamethrin for example, field application rates of 7-50g. ha^{-1} are feasible (Elliott and Janes, 1978; Elliott *et al.*, 1978). The isosteric replacements involved in these modifications also eliminated centres of photo-instability in the molecules, rendering the new compounds suitable for controlling insects on agricultural crops. By a remarkable industrial application of chiral intermediates, (Martel, 1978) decamethrin, (Decis, K-Othrin), a compound fully resolved at three centres, is available commercially. The potential of the structure of the natural esters for development of practical field insecticides was further demonstrated in the outstanding potent and simple ester fenvalerate, of which the S,S-isomer is most potent (Nakayama *et al.*, 1978). Up to twenty research groups are now examining synthetic pyrethroids and further variations leading to active compounds are being discovered (e.g. Whitney and Wettstein, 1979; Henrick *et al.*, 1980). The very broad range of compounds having insecticidal and acaricidal activity indicates that other very active compounds will probably be discovered, possibly with valuable additional characteristics such as repellency and anti-feeding actions.

F. *Other Insecticides*

Despite much effort, few other families of insecticides have been developed. Compounds of which analogues are readily accessible by synthesis are Cartap, developed from the toxin in a marine annelid, chlordimeform (Hollingworth, 1976), diflubenzuron (Wellinga *et al.*, 1973), the nitro-methylene group (Soloway *et al.*, 1979) and most recently the 2,4-dinitrophenylhydrazone of hexafluoroacetone (Holan *et al.*, 1979). Only diflubenzuron and related compounds have so far been exploited.

---

* *Although this name, originally proposed for the compound, was not subsequently accepted by ISO, it has now been used so frequently that it is adopted here for convenience.*

IV. OTHER PROPERTIES INFLUENCING FUTURE DEVELOPMENT OF
    INSECTICIDES

A. *Stability and Persistence*

The enormous potential benefits for mankind of the in-
expensive contact insecticide DDT might have been realised
more completely if it had been much less stable and more
selectively toxic to pest species rather than to their
predators. With these different characteristics, fewer pests
might have developed resistance and control by natural enemies might have been significant. One approach to future
insecticides is therefore to examine how insecticides with
the merits of DDT and other chlorinated hydrocarbons but not
their deficiences might be found.

Compounds related to, and modifications derived from, DDT
(Fig. 1) (Metcalf, 1976) such as methoxychlor, N-4- methyl-
phenyl-trichlormethyl 4-ethoxybenzylamine (formula (I);
Hirwe *et al.*, 1972) and the 4-ethoxyphenyl-dichlorocyclopro-
pane (formulae (II) and (III); Holan, 1969, 1978, 1979) have
not yet been found to be effective substitutes, partly
because although more expensive to manufacture, they are not
significantly more active. However, the physical properties
of synthetic pyrethroids resemble those of the chlorinated
hydrocarbon insecticides, in their small solubilities in
water and lipophilic characteristics (Briggs *et al.*, 1976).
Lipoid solubility is probably essential for the action of
both groups of insecticides; no polar compounds related to
them are insecticidal and metabolic detoxification of pyret]
roids involves generating more polar derivatives.

Pyrethroids developed commercially in the past five yea
(permethrin, cypermethrin, decamethrin and fenvalerate) are
sufficiently stable to control insects on agricultural
crops, and therefore are appropriately considered as direct
substitutes for chlorinated hydrocarbon insecticides in son
applications. Adsorbed onto the waxy layers of plant
leaves they are accessible to kill insects, but in contact
with most types of soil are rapidly detoxified and convert
to more polar compounds by micro-organisms. The degradati
of the insecticides permethrin and cypermethrin to polar
products contrasts with the much slower metabolism of DDT
products as non-polar and as persistent in the environment
DDT itself. These pyrethroids are therefore stable enough
for insecticidal action, but their relatively low rates of
application and rapid detoxification in the soil greatly
diminish the risk of environmental contamination.

More polar insecticides, especially compounds acting sys-
temically, are essential for other applications, e.g. to control sap feeding insects (aphids). For these purposes, a
range of organophosphates and carbamates with appropriate
properties are available, as discussed above. Like pyrethroids, these insecticides contain a number of sites for
oxidative and esteratic degradation and only in rare instances
have proved unduly persistent (Hurtig, 1972).

B. *Toxicity to mammals*

The acute oral toxicity of DDT to mammals (LD50 about
120mg.kg.$^{-1}$ for rats) would not have precluded widespread
application if it had not also been lipophilic and not easily
degraded. These characteristics allowed bioconcentration of
DDT in the environment (Gunn, 1972; Bevenue, 1976).   The
scope for chemical modification to diminish mammalian
toxicity is demonstrated by comparing DDT with methoxychlor
(Fig. 1), fifty times less toxic to mammals, but few comparable alterations to transform other highly active but
toxic chlorohydrocarbons have been possible. However, the
principle is well established in organophosphorus insecticides (Albert, 1979) and carbamates (Fukuto, 1976) in compounds which exploit the different metabolic capabilities of
insects and mammals; for example acetylation of methamido-
phos to give acephate maintains insecticidal activity but
diminishes mammalian toxicity forty-five times. Other organophosphorus insecticides with lower mammalian toxicity are
malathion, fenitrothion, diazinon, menazon and dimethoate
(Fig. 3).
Pyrethroids, unlike the organochlorine insecticides, have
multiple sites for metabolic attack (Hutson, 1979) and even
more scope than organophosphates and carbamates for exploit-
ing the relative metabolising capabilities of insects and
mammals. The lipophilic character of pyrethroids promotes
rapid penetration to sensitive sites in the insect nervous
system, whereas in mammals, by normal routes of administration compounds must encounter powerful detoxifying enzymes
(esterases and monooxygenases) in the liver before sensitive
nervous centres are approached. This is confirmed by the
greater toxicity of pyrethroids administered to mammals in-
travenously rather than by mouth (Elliott and Janes, 1978).
For application near food and disinfestation of edible
crops immediately before harvest, which require the lowest
attainable mammalian toxicity, pyrethroids with appropriate
features in their structures can be selected viz. esters

(bioresmethrin and phenothrin, Fig. 5) of <u>trans</u>-substituted
cyclopropane acids with primary alcohols. In other compounds
(permethrin) susceptibility of the 3-phenoxybenzyl nucleus
to hydroxylation may be an adequate feature (Gaughan et al.,
1977) even when ester cleavage is suppressed by the presence
of an α-cyano group in the alcohol (α-cyano-3-phenoxy-
benzyl esters) or other hindering substituents.

TABLE

*Representative mammalian toxicities and field application
rates of insecticides*

	Oral toxicity[a]	Field rate[b]	Safety factor
Carbamates	45^c	0.7^g	64
Organophosphates	67^d	0.6^h	100
Organochlorines	230^e	0.5-3.0	up to 460
Pyrethroids	700^f	0.01-0.2	above 3500

*(a) to rat (mg.kg^{-1}) (b) kg.ha^{-1} Geometric means:
(c) for 11 compounds (d) for 83 compounds (e) for
21 compounds. (f) for agricultural pyrethroids
(g) for 12 compounds (h) for 45 compounds.*

Relative safety factors (quotients of application rates
and mammalian toxicities in this table) indicate the considerable potential for design of safer insecticides with
pyrethroids.

C. *Movement in Soil and Air*

Widespread application of insecticides (for example aerial
spraying of crops) may seriously contaminate the environment
if the compounds are translocated in air or soil.   Few
problems have developed with organophosphates and carbamates,
most of which are lipophilic and unstable, but the success
of the lipophilic and stable organochlorine insecticides in
many circumstances led to widespread dispersion of residues
by air movements and otherwise (Spencer and Cliath, 1975;
Metcalf, 1980). Where pyrethroids, which are less volatile
(decamethrin, for example has a vapour pressure of 1.5×10^{-8}mm

at 25°) are used instead of organochlorine compounds, comparable contamination should not occur, because their application rates and vapour pressures are lower. Pyrethroids are strongly adsorbed on most soils until decomposed and neither diffuse, nor are leached significantly, from the point of application (Elliott *et al.*, 1978).

D. *Synergists*

Sir Vincent (1956b) describes how the synergistic action of sesame oil for pyrethrum was discovered during the Second World War. Heavy oils were added to insecticide aerosols to lessen evaporation from small spray droplets and thus maintain an optimum size for contact with flying insects. Sesame oil was more effective than expected in achieving this and chemical investigation led to recognition of the constituent responsible, sesamin. Related synthetic compounds such as piperonyl butoxide considerably enhanced the insecticidal action of natural pyrethrum and ensured economic survival in competition with synthetic insecticides for a special range of applications (Casida, 1976). Few other commercial insecticide formulations contain synergists. Unless important new discoveries are made, (Wilkinson, 1976) synergists appear unlikely to influence greatly the development of insecticides in the future. The known synergists differ from most field insecticides in physical properties and photostabilities and combinations are therefore both difficult to formulate effectively and disproportionately more expensive to register than single toxicants.

E. *Selective action other than between insects and mammals*

Although critical timing and special application techniques may help to discriminate between pests and beneficial insects (predators, parasites or pollinators) the most valuable property of an insecticide, at present rare and elusive, is selective toxicity to the pest species. Regrettably, with new insecticides progressively more expensive to discover, develop and market, investment costs are most quickly recovered with broad spectrum products for major crop pests. An important issue to be faced in the future therefore is the means to provide support for development of selective insecticides, long ago advocated by Sir Vincent (1946c), which are needed for many special pest control operations and particularly in pest management (Metcalf, 1980).

Even more than in the search for new broad spectrum insecticides, development of selective products requires detailed knowledge of the behaviour, biochemistry, metabolism and interaction of both pests and beneficial insects, which must both therefore be reared or available otherwise. The selective compounds required are most likely to be found in families of insecticides within the framework of which subtle variations of structure and therefore of activity, penetration and susceptibility to metabolism are possible. At present only three such groups (carbamates, organophosphorus compounds and recently pyrethroids) have been investigated (Elliott, 1979) so further new types of insecticides are needed urgently. That there is scope for finding such compounds is illustrated, among other examples, by the selective aphicide, pirimicarb, which is safe to coccinellids (Baranyovits and Ghosh, 1969) and by the demonstration that synthetic pyrethroids were less toxic than other insecticides to parasites of the cotton pest *Heliothis spp* (Wilkinson *et al.,* 1979).

Although organochlorine insecticides may adversely affect some bird populations (Gunn, 1972), others tolerate enormous doses of the lipophilic pyrethroids (Elliott *et al.,* 1978). Although laboratory assays indicate that pyrethroids are very toxic to fish, whose gills strongly adsorb the compounds from very small concentrations in water, the practical hazard under field conditions has frequently proved much less serious than these results would suggest; soil and suspended organic matter adsorb the insecticide even more strongly. Potential progress in lowering intrinsic fish toxicity by structural modification is indicated in the cyclopropyl analogue of fenvalerate (Elliott and Janes, 1979).

F. *Beneficial side effects of pyrethroids*

Unanticipated, and as yet not fully explained, consequences of using the new photostable pyrethroids against cotton insect pests have been crop yields higher than obtained with organophosphates (Ruscoe, 1979; Highwood,1979). Some evidence indicates that pyrethroids may suppress plant diseases caused by viruses transmitted by aphids (e.g. *Myzus persicae,* yellow virus of beet and barley) through an irritant effect (Highwood, 1979, Hovellou and Evans, 1979). In other circumstances pyrethroids show repellent or antifeeding actions, if the structural features associated with these side effects can be identified, new insecticides with valuation additional behavioural characteristics may be developed.

IV. MODE OF ACTION OF INSECTICIDES

    In 1956 Sir Vincent (1956b) said "All these modern syn-
thetic insecticides have been discovered empirically in the
course of testing long series of chemicals. But once found
it is evident that they must intervene in some very special
way with the chemical metabolism of the insect. If we had
sufficient knowledge of insect biochemistry, it should have
been possible to predict the activity of these particular
substances; and given sufficient knowledge we should be able
to devise molecules which will disrupt the machine at
whatever point we desire.   Actually, it looks at the present
time as though the boot will be on the other leg, and that
it is the study of these insecticidal chemicals which will
reveal how the physiology of the insect proceeds".
    Nearly twenty-five years later we must reluctantly con-
clude that most insecticides are still developed empirically
from leads discovered by random synthesis and testing or by
examining structure activity relationships of natural products and related synthetic compounds. The study of insecticidal compounds has not yet revealed how the physiology of
the insect proceeds, nor except for some insight into poisoning by rotenone and by organophosphates and carbamates, is
the mechanism of action of any insecticide firmly established
at the molecular level. Nevertheless slow progress in
finding the new insecticides urgently needed serves only to
emphasise Sir Vincent's wisdom in requiring more knowledge
of insect physiology and biochemistry so that substantial
and well directed advances are possible in future. A salu-
tary reflection however, is that even in 1980 few biologically active molecules have been designed rationally from
knowledge of the structure of a receptor site in a living
organism (Albert, 1979). Even when such a site is identified, to assume that an active poison to complement it
structurally can then quickly be synthesised is unwise,
because the fatal lesion may involve both molecule and receptor adopting unique conformations in response to powerful
short range mutual attractions. Alternatively if a molecule
binds at several positions on its structure to a receptor,
its active conformation may be dominated by the "zipper"
principle (preliminary interaction at one position, with
subsequent contacts as the conformation becomes appropriate;
Burgen et al., 1975) and therefore differ completely from
any form deduced for the crystalline state, or for the
molecule in solution, or by minimum energy calculations.
In the field of insecticides, Holan has made significant
progress in designing active insecticides from the structure

of DDT, which has limited flexibility, by assuming that the
wedge shaped structure of the molecule complements the shape
of the membrane site with which it interacts (Holan, 1978,
and references cited there). The value of similar approaches
with more flexible molecules such as pyrethroids is less
certain (Elliott and Janes, 1976; Hopfinger and Battershell,
1979).

Much recent work on neurobiological aspects of insecticidal action was discussed at a meeting in September 1979,
and subsequently published (Symposium, 1980). Potter
emphasised the importance of such investigations at present,
because although the problems of environmental pollution by
pesticides had been largely overcome, no solution was in
sight to the problem of resistance. A united effort was
needed to find out more about the mode of action of currently
used chemicals and the resistance factors that have been
developed against them. Only finding fresh points of
attack in the physiological and biochemical systems of the
insect so that totally new insecticides could be developed
rationally offered any real hope of eventually coping with
the problem of resistance. Other speakers considered
possible insecticidal action associated with effects on
axonal transmissions, on the synapse, on the neuromuscular
junction, on the neuroendocrine and sensory systems and on
the whole organism by neuroactive agents. Osborne identified
glial cells as a possible target for insecticides and had
already shown that they are disrupted by gamma-HCH.
Similarities in action of DDT and pyrethroids were demonstrated by van der Bercken and Vijverberg in clamped myelin-
ated nerves, possibly associated with the cross resistance
patterns and negative temperature coefficients of action of
these classes of insecticides, but extension of these results to insect systems is dubious. Several new transmitters
at the synapses of the insect nervous system were proposed,
but their function was difficult to establish (Pitman).
Octopamine, one such transmitter, is probably involved in
the action of the formamidine group of insecticides (Murdock
and Hollingworth). Finlayson indicated that the absence
of glia around many neurosecretory cells may make them
especially vulnerable to insecticides and resultant interference with secretion of hormones could seriously disrupt
the internal functions of insects. The neurosecretory
neurons of *Rhodnius prolixus* and *Cariusius morosus* are exceptionally sensitive to pyrethroids (Orchard). Significant
advances were reported, at last, in the action of insecticides on isolated receptors, particularly in relation to
neurophysiological aspects of resistance to insecticides.

In *Musca domestica* and *Boophilus microplus* (Nicholson *et al.)*
and *Spodoptera littoralis* (Gammon and Holden) conventional
neurophysiology showed resistance to pyrethroids in nerves
from resistant arthropods.   The overall toxicity of permethrin to susceptible, *kdr* and super *kdr* houseflies was related
to the changes in susceptibility of peripheral nerve in
appropriate larvae: susceptible, 10^{-10}M; *kdr*, 10^{-7}M; super
kdr, 10^{-6}M.   Devonshire showed that the acetylcholinesterase
from houseflies resistant to organophosphates and carbamates
was less sensitive to these insecticides than enzyme from
normal strains, but that the presence of this mutation
seemed to confer no biological disadvantages.

The conference showed that despite significant advances,
most marked in the past five years, huge gaps remain in the
fundamental knowledge of the structure and function of the
insect nervous system.   Yet such information is essential
if, as Sir Vincent pointed out long ago, we are to improve
the understanding of its mode of action in order to design
more effective and selective insecticides.   Intense research
in this field by academic and industrial groups demonstrate
confidence in this belief, and the future of insecticides
and insect control depend heavily on adequate support for
such work.

VI. RESISTANCE

We have already developed, or should be able to discover,
insecticides powerful enough to control economically important
susceptible insects.   Insecticides such as decamethrin with
ED_{50} values in the region of 0.01mg.kg^{-1} indicate that
sufficient potency is attainable, as are probably other
desirable properties (adequate selectivity, low toxicity to
fish, controlled persistence in soil and elsewhere, etc.)
with diligent research.   If insects remained susceptible,
even the existing range of compounds might be adequate to
maintain, and even to improve upon, present standards of
control, and new discoveries, albeit now less frequent
(Corbett, 1979) could bring additional benefits and efficiency.
Such speculations are completely unrealistic, however,
because strains of at least 350 species of insects resist one
or more insecticides (Georghiou and Taylor, 1976;   Metcalf,
1980); houseflies immune to decamethrin (>10,000 times resistant) can be bred by appropriate laboratory techniques
(Farnham, 1980).   Resistance genes, although rare in normal
populations, may be rapidly selected by insecticides and we
cannot yet prevent this;   once present they persist

sufficiently even when the selecting insecticides are not used, to reappear and confer full resistance again on demand. Georghiou and Taylor (1976) list biological characteristics that define the propensity for resistance as the type of inheritance, dominance, level of resistance, relative fitness, genetic interactions, length and type of life-cycle, feeding habits and population movements. Each insecticide selects one or more mechanisms of resistance (delayed entry, increased detoxification, or decreased sensitivity of the site of action) which may combine to give multiple resistance in which each protects against a different group of insecticides or multiplicate resistance when more than one mechanism acts against the same group and this may affect the development of resistance to compounds of different groups many years later (Sawicki, 1975). An insect population that has been exposed to several groups of insecticides is thus formidably protected even against new types of poison, which may therefore be only transiently effective. However, few generalisations are possible, because even very closely related species of insects vary enormously in their ability to become resistant, some economically important pests (e.g. the locust) having remained susceptible to established insecticides. Unfortunately resistance has not yet developed sufficiently (Croft, 1978) among beneficial insects to counteract the adverse effects of resistant pests and sometimes apparently new types of resistance are found in areas where compounds had not been used before, (housefly and peach potato aphid populations in Great Britain; Farnham and Devonshire, 1980).

The most disquieting aspect of the phenomenon of insect resistance is that it manifests the essential mechanism by which living organisms have survived and evolved - adaptation under pressure from a changing environment. This explains the difficulty of finding effective solutions to the problems of resistance (Sawicki, 1979); mankind's attempts to control insects are part of the contest between the two most successful groups of organisms yet evolved. Where important pests do not yet resist any group of insecticides, maintenance of this state is very important. Most insect populations are at present susceptible to the synthetic pyrethroids, which should therefore in general not be used prophylatically but only in response to developing infestations. This is particularly important with the newer, more stable pyrethroids, unnecessary applications of which could select resistant strains of insects from populations which develop immunity readily (houseflies), emulating the damaging induction by DDT of kdr (nerve insensitivity) resistance mechanisms to pyrethroids. There can be no one solution to all problems associated with insect resistance; the subject is too complex.

For each ecosystem satisfactory control can only be achieved
by a thorough understanding of chemical and biological
influences on the pests and their enemies. These are the
fundamental requirements for developing sound control recom-
mendations to minimise risks involved in widespread application of insecticides. Strategies to delay the onset of
resistance and to control insects by all means which preserve
the effectiveness of insecticides are essential components of
our efforts to ensure survival.

VII. CONCLUSIONS

   Recent experience supports Sir Vincent's conclusion in
1951 (1976. *Insects and the Life of Man,* p.29) that "when
all these so-called cultural or naturalistic methods of
control have been developed, there remains a large residue
of pests for which insecticides must be used. Here again
more ecology is needed. We want to learn how to apply the
insecticide at such a time or in such a way as to touch the
pest and not its enemies. We want to choose insecticides
which discriminate between friend and foe. This is probably
where the future of insecticides lies - in the development
of materials with a selective action which will provide
unlimited scope for the ingenuity of biologists and chemists."
   Corbett (1978) lists applications for which no appropriate
insecticides are available, including control of soil insects
and disease vectors, and products at present defective
because of resistance, undue persistence or inadequate
selectivity between insect and insect and insects and mammals.
If the properties associated with the downward translocation
of insecticides following foliar application could be defined,
enormous scope for control of many pests and diseases would
be available (Graham-Bryce, 1976). Corbett (1979) gives
evidence that the pesticide industry is no longer in a phase
of rapid growth of technical innovations, but considers this
may be associated with non-technical factors such as
increased costs of research and development due to regulating
constraints. Graham-Bryce (1976) concludes from analysis
of established insecticides and their variations and the
possibilities of developing new structures based on more
intimate knowledge of the physiology and biochemistry of
insects that the prospects of finding new insecticides in the
future are good. The many outstanding problems of insect
control suggest that new insecticides are urgently needed -
more selective compounds are necessary and with an appropriate
balance of ecological properties. Before compounds are

introduced on a large scale as much investigation as possible
should ensure that they are used under conditions least likely
to induce resistance in insect pests or produce deleterious
side effects in the environment. The future for insecticides
therefore depends on identifying the properties required for
specific applications and ensuring that sufficient support is
provided to develop them and establish their safety in use.

ACKNOWLEDGMENTS

     I thank my colleagues P.E. Burt, N.F. Janes and R.M.
Sawicki for much help in preparing this article.

REFERENCES

Albert, A. (1979). "Selective Toxicity" (6th edition).
     Chapman and Hall, London.
Aldridge, W.N. (1971). The nature of the reaction of organo-
     phosphorus compounds and carbamates with esterases. *Bull.
     W.H.O. 44,* 25-30.
Baranyovits, F.L.C., and Ghosh, R. (1969). Pirimicarb
     (PP062): a new selective carbamate insecticide. *Chem.
     Ind. (London),* 1018-1019.
Bevenue, A. (1976). The "bioconcentration" aspects of DDT in
     the environment. *Residue Rev. 61,* 37-112.
Briggs, G.G., Elliott, M., Farnham, A.W., Janes, N.F.,
     Needham, P.H. Pulman, D.A., and Young, S.R. (1976)
     Relation of polarity with activity in pyrethroids.
     Pestic. Sci. 7, 236-240.
Burgen, A.S.V., Feeney, J., and Roberts, G.C.K. (1975).
     Binding of flexible ligands to macromolecules. *Nature
     (London) 253,* 753-755.
Casida, J.E. (1976). Prospects for new types of insecticides.
     In "The Future for Insecticides - Needs and Prospects"
     (R.L. Metcalf and J.J. McKelvey, Jr. eds.) pp. 349-369,
     Wiley, New York.
Corbett, J.R. (1974). "The Biochemical Mode of Action of
     Pesticides". Academic Press, London.
Corbett, J.R. (1978). The future of pesticides and other
     methods of pest control. *In* "Applied Biology", Vol III
     (T.H. Coaker, ed.), pp. 229-330. Academic Press, London.
Corbett, J.R. (1979). Technical considerations affecting the
     discovery of new pesticides. *Chem. Ind. (London)* 772-782.

Croft, B.A. (1978). Potentials for research and implementation of IPM on deciduous tree fruits. *In* "Pest control strategies". E.H. Smith and D. Pimentel (eds.) pp.105-115. Academic Press, New York.

Crombie, L., and Elliott, M. (1961). Chemistry of the natural pyrethrins. *Fortschr. Chem. Org. Naturst. 19*, 120-164.

Elliott, M. (1979). Progress in the design of insecticides. *Chem. Ind.(London)* 757-768.

Elliott, M., and Janes, N.F. (1973). Chemistry of the natural pyrethrins. *In* "Pyrethrum - the Natural Insecticide" (J.E. Casida, ed.) pp. 56-100. Academic Press, New York.

Elliott, M., and Janes, N.F. (1977). Preferred conformations of pyrethroids. *In* "Synthetic Pyrethroids" (M. Elliott, ed.) pp. 29-36. American Chemical Society, Washington.

Elliott, M., and Janes, N.F. (1979). Synthetic pyrethroids - a new class of insecticide. *Chem. Soc. Rev. 7*, 473-505.

Elliott, M., and Janes, N.F. (1979). Recent Structure-activity correlations in synthetic pyrethroids. *International Congress of Pesticide Chemistry, 4th, Zurich 1978- Advances in Pesticide Science* 166-173.

Elliott, M., Farnham, A.W., Janes, N.F., Needham, P.H., and Pulman, D.A. (1974). Synthetic insecticide with a new order of activity, *Nature (London), 248*, 710-711.

Elliott, M., Farnham, A.W., Janes, N.F., and Soderlund, D.M. (1978). Relative potencies of isomeric cyano-substituted 3-phenoxybenzyl esters. *Pestic. Sci. 9*, 112-116.

Elliott, M., Janes, N.F., and Potter, C. (1978). The future of pyrethroids in insect control. *Annu. Rev. Entomol. 23*, 443-469.

Farnham, A.W. (1980). Personal communication.

Farnham, A.W., and Devonshire, A.L. (1980). Report of Insecticides and Fungicides Department. *Ann. Rep. Rothamsted Exp. Stn. for 1979*.

Fukuto, T.R. (1976). Carbamate insecticides. *In* "The Future for Insecticides - Needs and Prospects" (R.L. Metcalf and J.J. McKelvey, Jr., eds). pp. 313-346. Wiley, New York.

Gaughan, L.C., Unai, T., and Casida, J.E. (1977). Permethrin metabolism in rats *J. Agr.Food Chem. 25*, 9-17.

Georghiou, G.P. and Taylor, C.E. (1976). Pesticide resistance as an evolutionary phenomenon. *15th International Congress of Entomology*, 759-785.

Graham-Bryce, I.J. (1976). Crop Protection : present achievement and future challenge. *Chem. Ind.(London)*, 545-553.

Gunn, D.L. (1972). Dilemmas in conservation for applied biologists. *Ann. Appl. Biol. 72*, 105-127.

Henrick, C.A., Garcia, B.A., Staal, G.B., Cerf, D.C.,
    Anderson, R.J., Gill, K., Chinn, H.R., Labovitz, J.N.,
    Leippe, M.M., Woo, S.L., Carney, R.L., Gordon, D.C., and
    Kohn, G.K. (1980). 3-Methyl-2-phenylaminobutanoates and
    2-(2-isoindolinyl)-3-methylbutanoates, two novel groups
    of synthetic pyrethroid esters not containing a cyclo-
    propane ring. *Pestic. Sci., 11,* in press.

Highwood, D.P. (1979). Some indirect benefits of the use of
    pyrethroid insecticides. *Proc.tenth Brit. Insectic.Fungic.
    Conf. (Brighton),* 361-9.

Hirwe, A.S., Metcalf, R.L., and Kapoor, I.P. (1972). -Tri-
    chloromethylbenzylanilines and -Trichloromethylbenzyl
    Phenyl Ethers with DDT-like Insecticidal Action. *J.Agr.
    Food Chem. 20,* 818-824.

Holan, G. (1969). New halocyclopropane insecticides and the
    mode of action of DDT. *Nature (London), 221,* 1025-1029.

Holan, G., O'Keefe, D.F., Virgona, C. and Walser, R. (1978).
    Structural and biological link between pyrethroids and
    DDT in new insecticides. *Nature (London), 272,* 734-736.

Holan, G. (1979). Phenylhydrazones, their use in insecticidal
    compositions and methods for their preparation. *European
    Patent Application,* 1019.

Holan, G., O'Keefe, D.F., Riks, K., Walser, R., and Virgona,
    C.T. (1979). New insecticides. Combined DDT isosteres and
    pyrethroid structures. *International Congress of Pesti-
    cide Chemistry, 4th, Zurich 1978- Advances in Pesticide
    Science,* 201-205.

Hollingworth, R.M. (1976). Chemistry, biological activity
    and uses of formamidine pesticides. *Environmental Health
    Perspectives 14,* 57-69.

Hopfinger, A.J., and Battershell, R.D. (1979). Conformational
    studies of phenothrin analogs and implications on insec-
    ticidal activity. *International Congress of Pesticide
    Chemistry, 4th, Zurich 1978- Advances in Pesticide
    Science* 196-200.

Hovellou, A., and Evans, D.D. (1979). Control of barley
    yellows dwarf virus with permethrin on winter barley in
    France. *Proc.tenth Brit.Insectic.Fungic.Conf.(Brighton),*
    9-15.

Huff, R.K. (1980). Highly halogenated chrysanthemic acid
    analogues. *Pestic. Sci., 11,* in press.

Hurtig, H. (1972). Long-distance transport of pesticides. *In*
    "Environmental toxicology of pesticides" (F. Matsumura,
    G.M. Boush and T. Misato, eds.) pp. 257-280. Academic
    press, New York.

Hutson, D.H. (1979). The metabolic fate of pyrethroid
    insecticides in mammals. *Progr. Drug Metabolism. 3,*
    215-52.

Jacobson, M., and Crosby, D.G. (1971). "Naturally Occurring
    Insecticides". Marcel Dekker, New York.
Martel, J. (1978). Definitions chimiques des pyrethrinoides
    photostables. *Phytiat.Phytopharm., 27,* 5-14.
Metcalf, R.L. (1976). Organochlorine insecticides, survey
    and prospects. *In* "The Future for Insecticides - Needs
    and Prospects" (R.L. Metcalf and J.J. McKelvey, Jr.,
    eds.) pp. 223-285. Wiley, New York.
Metcalf, R.L. (1980). Changing role of insecticides in crop
    protection. *Annu. Rev. Entomol. 25,* 219-256.
Nakayama, I., Ohno, N., Aketa, K., Suzuki, Y., Kato, T., and
    Yoshioka, H. (1978). Chemistry, absolute structures and
    biological aspect of the most active isomers of fenvaler-
    ate and other recent pyrethroids. *International Congress
    of Pesticide Chemistry, 4th, Zurich 1978- Advances in
    Pesticide Science,* 178-181.
O'Brien, R.D. (1967). "Insecticides - Action and Metabolism"
    Academic Press, New York.
Ruscoe, C.N.E. (1979). The impact of photostable pyrethroids
    as agricultural insecticides. *Proc.tenth Brit.Insectic.
    Fungic.Conf.(Brighton),* 803-814.
Sawicki, R.M. (1975). Effects of sequential resistance on
    pesticide management. *Proc.eighth Brit.Insectic.Fungic.
    Conf.(Brighton),*799-811.
Sawicki, R.M. (1979). Cross-resistance. *In* "Monograph on
    Resistance" (G.P. Georghiou and H.T. Reynolds, eds.) in
    preparation, F.A.O., Rome.
Soloway, S.B., Henry, A.C., Kollmeyer, W.D., Padgett, W.M.,
    Powell, J.E., Roman, S.A., Tieman, C.H., Corey, R.A., and
    Horne, C.A. (1979). Nitromethylene insecticides. *Inter-
    national Congress of Pesticide Chemistry, 4th, Zurich
    1978- Advances in Pesticide Science,* 206-217.
Spencer, W.F., and Cliath, M.M. (1975). Vaporisation of
    chemicals. *In* "Environmental Dynamics of Pesticides"
    (R. Hague and V.H. Freed, eds.) pp. 61-78. Plenum Press,
    New York.
Symposium: "Insect neurobiology and pesticide action (Neuro-
    tox 79)" (1980). 517 pp. Society of Chemical Industry,
    London.
Wellinga, K., Mulder, R., and van Daalen, J.J. (1973). Syn-
    thesis and laboratory evaluation of 1-(2,6-disubstituted
    benzoyl)-3-phenylureas, a new class of insecticides. II.
    Influence of the acyl moiety on insecticidal activity. *J.
    Agric. Food Chem. 21,* 993-998.
Whitney, W.K., and Wettstein, K. (1979). AC 222,705, a new
    pyrethroid insecticide-performance against crop pests.
    Proc.tenth Brit.Insectic.Fungic.Conf.(Brighton). 387-394.

Wilkinson, C.F. (1976). Insecticide synergism. *In* "The Future for Insecticides - Needs and Prospects" (R.L. Metcalf and J.J. McKelvey, Jr., eds.) pp. 195-222. Wiley, New York.

Wilkinson, J.D., Biever, K.D., and Ignoffo, C.M. (1979). Synthetic pyrethroid and organophosphate insecticides against the parasitoid *Apanteles marginiventrix* and the predators *Geocoris punctipes, Hippodamia convergens,* and *Podisus maculiventris*. *J. Econ. Entomol. 72,* 473-475.

THE FUTURE OF TSETSE BIOLOGY[*]

E. Bursell

Overseas Development Administration And
University of Bristol
Tsetse Research Laboratory
Department of Veterinary Medicine
Langford, Bristol

I. INTRODUCTION

The history of tsetse research stretches back to the early years of the century when field studies were begun in different parts of Africa. At this time the tsetse literature was dominated by ecological publications, but the study of tsetse physiology was initiated in 1929 with Wigglesworth's work on digestion (Wigglesworth, 1929d) and by the 1950's physiology had come to rival ecology as a field of research.

With the successful establishment of self-sustaining laboratory colonies in different parts of the world during the 1960's, the pace of physiological research was greatly increased, and an extension of work became possible into the relatively unexplored field of tsetse genetics. Unfortunately, these developments coincided with a cut-back in expenditure on field studies in many parts of Africa, and a serious imbalance has now become evident between the sophisticated laboratory work of recent times and the less advanced field studies of earlier years.

Since the development of effective methods of control has always been a major objective of tsetse research it is also

This article has been written against the background of the author's experience which is limited to East and Central Africa and therefore relates mainly to the savanna species of tsetse fly, i.e. Glossina morsitans Westw., G. swynnertoni Aust. and G. pallidipes Aust.

disturbing that achievements in the field of control have
remained unimpressive. The information about tsetse biology
that has built up during the century has admittedly served as
a basis for the development of a variety of control techniques,
and some of these have proved successful on a limited scale.
But if a comparison is made between earlier maps of the distribution of tsetse flies in Africa (e.g. Potts, 1953-1954)
and the more recent set prepared by Ford and Katando (1977)
there is no indication that control activities have had an
impact on the problem in any way commensurate with the
enormous amount of time and money that has, directly or indirectly, been spent on it. Despite all our efforts, the
tsetse fly continues to flourish.

II. POPULATION DYNAMICS

   Our failure to achieve large-scale control of tsetse flies
could be due to the absence of suitable control methods, or to
the inefficiency with which control programmes are executed.
What is required to identify the cause of our failure is a
thorough understanding of the population dynamics of the
tsetse fly, since success in control must depend on our
ability to interfere in the balance between birth and death
so that it swings in favour of death. To manipulate that
balance we need to know about the birth rate and the death
rate in natural populations of tsetse, and about the biotic
and abiotic factors which influence these rates. Our
ultimate concern must therefore be to produce reliable
estimates of the rate of birth and the rate of death, and to
establish the extent to which control operations are capable
of interfering appropriately in the balance between the two.

A. *The Rate of Birth*

   As far as the birth rate is concerned, which may here be
defined as the rate at which individuals are added to the
adult population, we are in a reasonable position because
reproductive physiology is one of the best documented aspects
of tsetse biology (see reviews by Saunders, 1970; Tobe and
Langley, 1978). Temperature exercises a controlling influence
on birth rate through its effect on developmental velocity;
the relation between the two has been carefully established
(see Glasgow, 1963) and good correspondence has been established between laboratory and field results in respect of
pupal development (Jackson and Phelps, 1967; Phelps and
Burrows, 1969a). The rate of birth would also be affected by
mortality in larval and pupal stages, and possible causes of

death have been extensively investigated. These include
nutritional stresses acting on the pregnant female, which may
cause the abortion of larval stages (Madubunyi, 1978); attacks
on the pupal stage by parasites and predators (reviewed by
Nash, 1970); extremes of temperature in pupal sites (Phelps
and Burrows, 1969b); and pupal desiccation (Bursell, 1958).
Under natural conditions the average burden of mortality
attributable to these effects does not appear to be substantial, and reasonable estimates of the birth rate in the
natural habitat can therefore be made on the basis of results
obtained from laboratory studies.

B. *The Rate of Death*

Unfortunately this is far from being the case as far as
the death rate is concerned, because here the results of
laboratory studies are of limited relevance to the natural
situation. Figure 1 shows that the age structure of a laboratory population is completely different from that of a field
population. The average longevity of laboratory females is
over 120 days and the death rate in mature insects is strongly
age-dependent; in the field, female life expectancy averages
no more than 35 days and, because the insects tend to die
before they begin to senesce, the rate of death in mature
females is largely independent of age. Similar differences
apply in the case of male populations, but here a detailed
comparison of age structures cannot be made, because
techniques have yet to be developed which will enable the age
of field flies to be accurately determined. The method
recently described by Schlein (1979) holds out some promise
in this direction, and it is to be hoped that its potential
will be fully explored. The fact remains, however, that the
pattern of mortality in laboratory and field populations is
markedly different, which means that the information that we
need about mortality must be derived entirely from field
work. It is when we move to field studies of the adult fly
in its natural environment that formidable technical difficulties are encountered, the magnitude and importance of
which are only now becoming fully apparent. They relate
basically to the seeming impossibility of getting an unbiased
sample of the adult population.

III. SAMPLING ERRORS

A. *The Fly Round*

Most of the early information about tsetse ecology relied

on a standard sampling technique referred to as the fly-
round (Ford *et al.*, 1959; Glasgow, 1970). This was used to
get an indication of the relation between the tsetse fly and
its habitat, and to monitor seasonal and long-term changes
in population density. The technique is based on the tendency
of tsetse flies to follow a walking man, and to settle on or
near him when he stops, thus enabling the insects to be
caught with small hand-nets. Fly-round transects were
generally marked out to sample different vegetation types
within an area inhabited by tsetse flies, and they were
traversed by a standard party of catchers at regular intervals.
The catches were predominantly of adult males, indicating a
marked bias in relation to sex. Further, the catch varied
with time of day, indicating that it reflected not only the
density of the population, but also the "availability" of
the population to the catching party, a function which would
change not only with time of day but also with season, with
host abundance and with differences in vegetation type.

As a sampling technique designed to explore the population dynamics of the tsetse fly, this left much to be desired,
but at that time there seemed to be no suitable alternative.
Most of the extensive ecological literature of this era,
which is based on fly-round sampling, is consequently of very
limited value, and the results obtained in carefully
conducted field investigations cannot be interpreted except
in the most general terms. Indeed, it could be argued that
the widespread adoption of such a fatally flawed sampling
technique prevented ecologists from making any significant
contribution to knowledge of the tsetse fly for several
decades. Its use led to the development of many false
concepts concerning, for instance, the importance of vision
in host location, or the regular movement of flies between
different parts of the habitat, and once such concepts had
gained general acceptance they tended to block progress towards a better understanding. Nor was this a matter of
merely academic importance, for the development of discrimina-
tive clearing as a method of tsetse control, which proved a
particularly costly failure, can be attributed directly to
the use of the fly-round as a sampling technique. It is
therefore disturbing to note that despite the dangers involved in the use of this technique, which have become
increasingly fully exposed, it continues to be used to this
day, not just to obtain a general impression of a tsetse
situation, but as the basis for detailed and weighty
analyses of population dynamics (e.g. Lambrecht, 1972;
Laveissière, 1977), analyses which the technique is totally
incapable of sustaining.

It was to escape the weaknesses of the fly-round as a

source of information about the tsetse that C.H.N. Jackson,
in the 1940's embarked on an extensive and meticulously
executed series of investigations based on the marking, release and recapture of tsetse flies (Jackson, 1941, 1944 and
1948). By focussing attention on the proportion of marked
flies in the fly-round catch, rather than on the actual
magnitude of the catch, the existence of a serious bias was
overcome, and it became possible to obtain an estimate of
population density, instead of an index of population size
bearing an unknown and inconstant relation to actual density.
At the same time the rates of birth and emigration, and of
death and immigration, could be calculated, providing for the
first time an indication of mortality levels in the natural
habitat, and of the nature and extent of dispersal.

Formidable technical difficulties were associated with
these early studies, partly because of the extremely low
availability of females to fly-round sampling, and partly
because the rates of recapture were very low. The estimates
which Jackson was able to make of population density were
therefore subject to substantial error, the magnitude of
which could not at that time be determined; but in fact his
estimates of death rate correspond extremely closely to recent
values obtained by Phelps and Vale (1978) using a wide range
of sampling systems and attaining recapture levels in excess
of 20% They indicate that in the hot, dry season the average
life span of *Glossina morsitans* males is no more than 2 weeks
while females live approximately twice that long (see Fig. 1).

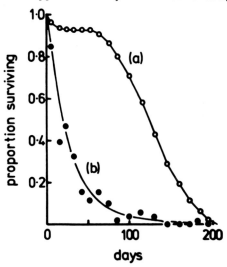

*FIGURE 1. The survival of female G. morsitans in the la-
boratory (a) and in the field (b). Data from Phelps and Vale
(1978) and from Jordan and Curtis (1972) respectively.*

In his consideration of dispersal, Jackson was greatly influenced by the fly-round tradition which had earlier led him to develop the "feeding ground" hypothesis (Jackson, 1930, 1933). This incorporated the concept of an "ambit" within which tsetse flies moved between different parts of the habitat, and he allowed his interpretation of the marking, release and recapture results to be coloured by that hypothesis. It has since been suggested that the available information on dispersal can more convincingly be interpreted on the basis of random movement (Bursell, 1970), but it remains a tribute to the quality of Jackson's investigations that to this day his results merit detailed re-analysis in the light of the more recently formulated models of tsetse dispersal (Rogers, 1977; Hargrove, in press).

C. Bait Oxen

The introduction of marking, release and recapture techniques represented a major advance in the field of tsetse ecology, but their usefulness was limited by the heavy demands that the technique made on skilled manpower. Simple fly-round catches therefore continued to provide the basis of most ecological investigations in spite of the biases associated with them, not only in terms of sex, but also of age and of nutritional state (Bursell, 1961a), and it was not until the middle sixties that other sampling systems began to be routinely used in certain parts of Africa. One system involved the use of mobile or stationary bait oxen and the results obtained represented a challenge to some of the concepts which had been developed on the basis of fly-round techniques. One of these was the notion of a cool and shady riverine refuge to which the tsetse population retreated during the hot, dry season. The idea was based on the observation that at that time of year it was only in the riverine vegetation that substantial catches of flies could be made with standard fly-round parties, while the surrounding and generally leafless woodland appeared to be devoid of flies. However, if catches were made from a stationary bait ox, which attracted females as well as males, then the catch rate in the leafless woodland did not differ greatly from that in the riverine fringe (Pilson and Pilson, 1967). Further studies indicated that there was little interchange between populations in different, though closely adjacent, vegetation types since they could be distinguished in terms of nutritional state (Bursell, 1966). The results made it clear that populations were capable of subsisting throughout the dry season in regions which had previously been considered totally inhospitable. This may account for the general failure of discrimination clearing as a control measure, since the method

is based on the clearing of vegetation that has been identified as favourable to the tsetse population on the evidence
of fly-round catches. This is not to say that the real
density of tsetse flies, as opposed to the "apparent" fly-
round density, may not differ in different parts of the habitat; but such differences should perhaps be interpreted on the
basis of selective effects rather than of directed movement.
Certain vegetation types may provide a greater abundance of
hosts and of suitable microhabitats during inclement seasons,
and may therefore be capable of supporting higher densities
of tsetse fly. But the densities would be high because flies
tend to live longer or disperse less in such vegetation types,
and not because they have been sought out by flies from less
favourable areas.

D. Electric Capture Systems

At about this time indications became available that
tsetse flies attempting to obtain a bloodmeal from man were
in a much poorer nutritional state than those attacking a
bait ox (Ford, 1969, 1970, 1972) recalling a suggestion
originally made in respect of females by Nash (1933) that man
might not be a satisfactory host for the tsetse fly, and indicating that much of the trouble with fly-round data might
reflect the use of man as a bait. An alternative capture
system was needed as a basis for further investigation and one
was devised by Vale (1974a) using electric nets capable of
stunning or killing tsetse flies that collided with them.
With this system he was able to study the attraction of flies
to artificial and natural baits and to determine the effect
of the presence of man (Vale, 1974b). Not only did this work
demonstrate the paramount importance of smell in the attraction of tsetse flies to their hosts, but it showed that man
was repellent to the tsetse (Fig. 2). In the light of these
findings one gains some impression of the singularly equivocal
nature of the stimulus provided by a standard catching party
on a fly-round; at one and the same time attractive, because
it is moving, and repellent, because it is human. There
would be a delicate sorting out of hunger stages, ages,
species and sex in the vicinity of such a party, with
different flies held at different points in the balance between attraction and repulsion. For the newly emerged fly,
with its scant fat reserves (Bursell, 1960; Phelps, 1973)
the need for food is paramount and their determined attack
on the catching party ensures gross over-representation of
this component of the population in the catch (Vale and
Phelps, 1978). Males of G. morsitans in the intermediate
"sexually appetitive" stage of the hunger cycle approach
to mate with attacking tenerals, but earlier and later stages

(a)

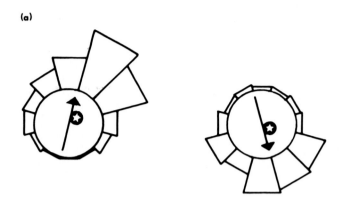

(b)

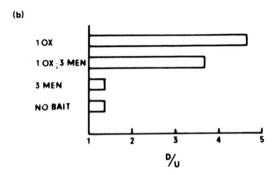

FIGURE 2.   *The responses of tsetse flies to stationary hosts.   a) The distribution of catches of G. morsitans and G. pallidipes on 12 electric panels surrounding a bait ox. Average wind direction is shown by an arrow and average position of the ox by a star.   The length of histograms extending from the central circle indicates the magnitude of the catch on each panel.   It is maximal on downwind panels indicating that tsetse flies respond to host odour by an upwind anemotaxis.   b) The response of females of G. pallidipes to host odours.   The ratio of catches on upwind and downwind halves of the ring of electric panels is used as a measure of the effectiveness of the olfactory stimulus.   The ratio is maximal when only the ox is present; it is reduced when the ox is accompanied by 3 men; and when the 3 men are on their own the response does not differ from base levels, in the absence of a host.   (Data from Vale, 1974b).*

of the hunger cycle are poorly represented. Females are held
back by a stronger repulsion, and though they are present in
the vicinity, they seldom get within range of the hand-nets
and are therefore greatly under-represented, as are both
sexes of *G. pallidipes* which are strongly repelled (Vale,
1974a). But the precise strength of the resulting biases will
depend on the strength of attack by hungry flies, which in
turn will be affected by the nutritional state of the population, the abundance of hosts and the time of day; and the
catch will therefore bear an indefinable relation to the
actual density of the different components of the population.

These considerations should dispose, once and for all, of
the fly-round as a sampling technique capable of yielding
reliable information about the state of a tsetse population,
but there are still no simple alternatives. A variety of
techniques have been devised and tested during recent years
including various traps (Hargrove, 1977), natural refuges
and resting sites (Pilson and Pilson, 1967), artificial
refuges (Vale, 1971) and ox-baited pits (Vale, 1974b) in
addition to mobile and stationary baits. But an assessment
of the performance of some of these sampling techniques in
relation to a mixed population of *G. morsitans* and *G.
pallidipes* of known composition has indicated that each has
its own type of bias.

As would be expected, the composition of the catch on the
fly-round equivalent (Table 1) is completely misleading. The
catches from ox-baited pits, which attract flies in search of
a bloodmeal, are fairly satisfactory except that they comprise
mainly flies in the late phases of the hunger cycle. This
method has the advantage of providing very high catch-levels,
but the fixed location and the need to dig large pits to
house the host animals militates against its widespread
adoption until such time as an artificial odour-source can be
developed. The catch from a mobile ox suffers to some degree
from the same bias as the fly-round, but this can be reduced
by maintaining the ox stationary (Pilson and Pilson, 1967) so
that in terms of the level of bias, of convenience and of
ability to attract substantial numbers of tsetse, this would
probably constitute the best compromise at present.

TABLE I. The Composition of Samples Obtained with Different Sampling Techniques Compared to the Composition of the Population from which the Samples were Drawn. Data from Vale and Phelps (1978)

	Species (G. pallidipes, both sexes) %	Composition Sex (G. morsitans) % females	Composition Age (both species, both sexes) % tenerals	Composition Nutrition (G. morsitans males) % fed
Population parameters	90	65	5	23*
Samples				
Mobile screens, handnets (=fly-round)	15	5	30	9
Mobile ox, handnets	75	20	15	15
Refuges	85	60	5	45
Ox-baited pits	90	60	5	10

aGiven that average meal size for G. morsitans males is 7.36 mg dry mass (Taylor, 1976) and average hunger cycle is 3 days (Bursell and Taylor, 1980); that the fatless dry mass of the starved abdomen is 1.00 mg and of the thorax is 4.43 mg (Bursell, 1973); that digestion is a logarithmic function of time (Randolph and Rogers, 1973) and is 74% complete in 29 hours and 95% complete in 48 hours (Langley, 1966) it can be calculated that the average male will pass beyond the criterion for a fed fly adopted by Vale and Phelps (1978) in 17 hours.

This is 23% of the hunger cycle and therefore 23% of males would be in this category.

Accepting that a perfect sampling technique may be an unattainable ideal, an attractive alternative would be to devise a method for assessing the nature and magnitude of the bias, so that the actual population composition could be derived by appropriate correction. Rogers and Randolph (1979) have indicated that by careful analysis of the nutritional state of flies in a sample it may be possible to provide a basis for such correction. If predictions made in this way could be shown to conform to the characteristics of a population from which the sample was drawn, this would clearly constitute an important development. Even then, the procedures involved in the analysis of nutritional state are demanding and time consuming, and the method could only hope to find widespread application among tsetse ecologists if a central facility could be established for the automated analysis of samples submitted from the field.

Major advances in the theory and practice of tsetse ecology have clearly been made during the last decade, which have brought us nearer to the answers that we seek. For one thing, they have enabled more representative samples to be obtained of an adult tsetse population, on the basis of which more accurate estimates of the rate of death have been made (Phelps and Vale, 1978), but the causes of death remain to be elucidated.

IV. CAUSES OF ADULT DEATH

Early indications that starvation may be an important agent of mortality in adult tsetse flies (Bursell and Glasgow, 1960; Bursell, 1961b) have received support from the later work of Phelps and Clarke (1974). These authors showed that during immature stages of adult life there was a powerful selection against smaller flies, which are known to be characterised by relatively scant food reserves. The heavy mortality imposed at this stage of the life cycle, which is itself distinguished from the mature stages by low levels of food reserve, has now been confirmed by recent work on population dynamics (Phelps and Vale, 1978; Taylor, 1980). These results are difficult to interpret except on the basis that starvation is a major cause of death, and if that is the case then the interactions between the tsetse fly and its hosts assumes great importance in the context of the species' population dynamics.

A. *Host Preferences*

A good foundation for a consideration of this aspect of
tsetse ecology has been laid by earlier work on the host preference of *Glossina* (reviewed by Weitz, 1970). Different
species show their own particular feeding patterns, with *G.
swynnertoni*, for example, feeding mainly on suids; *G.
morsitans* mainly on suids and bovids; and *G. pallidipes* mainly
on bovids, though there may be considerable flexibility in
point of detail, relating to the local situation. Despite
the obvious importance of these findings there was no early
attempt to explore their implications, and the basis of these
apparent feeding preferences have remained obscure. That they
are of great practical importance is suggested by the success
which has attended attempts to control *G. morsitans* by selective elimination of host animals. Excellent results have
been achieved in a programme which involved hunting of the
four favoured hosts, warthog, bushpig, kudu and bushbuck
(Cockbill, 1967), and this was followed up by an experiment
designed to test whether removal of the most favoured host
only would suffice to swing the balance of population dynamics
sufficiently in favour of death to ensure the collapse of a
tsetse population. It involved the simultaneous study of
warthog and tsetse ecology, followed by the removal, by
capture, of warthog from an area of 11 km^2. The results provided evidence that removal of the favoured host had indeed
put the tsetse population under substantial stress (Vale and
Cumming, 1976), but the flies switched their attention to
their second favourite, the kudu, and the density of this
species was adequate to prevent a population collapse. However, the results of the investigation clearly indicate that
the host/fly interrelation constitutes a weak link in the
life cycle of the species and that, for this reason, it deserves the closest attention.
  The development of electric sampling systems has opened
the way to a much more direct study of the interaction between fly and host than has hitherto been possible, and the
results obtained by Vale (1977) underline the great potential
of this technique. The responses of tsetse flies to a variety
of stationary hosts surrounded by an incomplete ring of
electric nets was studied in a way which made it possible to
determine not only the relative intensity of attraction to
different hosts, but also the proportion of flies which were
able to obtain a bloodmeal from the host. Results confirmed
earlier work (Vale, 1974b) in showing that the degree of
attraction increases with increasing body size of the host,
and also showed that the probability of successful feeding
varied widely between extremes of 0.00 for the impala and
0.51 for the donkey. This variation was related to differences

in complacency under attack from biting flies; the flies
which were attracted to the impala, for instance, were quite
incapable of obtaining a bloodmeal because of the animal's
intolerant behaviour, manifested in the shuddering skin, the
twitching ears, lashing tail and the restless grooming. This
impression was confirmed by showing that chemical sedation of
animals was capable of causing a substantial increase in the
proportion of successful feeds.

B. *Host tolerance*

This work was carried out in an area that supported a
mixed population of *G. morsitans* and *G. pallidipes* with the
latter species making up the bulk of the catch (see Phelps
and Vale, 1978). It is of interest, therefore, to examine
the extent to which the results might serve as a basis for
interpretation of the apparent feeding preferences of *G.
pallidipes* in this area. Available information is set out
in Table II, which shows estimates of the relative density of
the host animals tested by Vale, the average mass of each
species and the probability of feeding success. Accepting
that attractiveness is proportional to body mass, the distribution of feeds between the different species should be
given by the product of these three functions which is set
out in column 5 and expressed as a percentage of the total
in column 6. The calculated distribution is seen to compare
quite favourably with the distribution found by analysis of
bloodmeals from *G. pallidipes* collected in the same area.
This indicates that the apparent feeding preference of this
species of tsetse can be broadly interpreted in terms of the
availability, mass and tolerance of potential hosts, and that
it may not involve any positive selection or preference on
the part of the insect. It should be noted, however, that
when an attempt was made to analyse similar data for *G.
morsitans* (from Vale and Cumming, 1976) the correspondence
was poor, because warthogs accounted for a much higher
percentage of feeds than would be expected on the basis of
their availability, mass and tolerance. Since it has not
been possible to demonstrate a specially close relation between the habitats or the habits of warthog and *G. morsitans*
the basis of what appears to be an element of positive
selection would clearly merit investigation.

The concept of host tolerance has an important bearing
on the general problem of starvation, because it indicates
that it is not enough for a tsetse fly to locate a host at
the end of each hunger cycle; if the odour trail which it
follows leads to an intolerant species its chances of
obtaining a bloodmeal may be negligible, in which case it
would have to embark on a new search. The indications are

TABLE II.   *The feeding pattern of G. pallidipes in the*
            Zambezi valley compared with predicted feeding
            frequencies calculated on the basis of the
            relative abundance, mass and tolerance to
            attack of their hosts

Species	Relative abundance n	Mass (Kg) m	Tolerance		% Distribution	
			f	nmf	predicted	observed
Warthog	21	45	0.19	180)	18.0	22.1
Bushpig	1	54	0.08	4)		
Kudu	13	136	0.41	725	70.7	61.9
Buffalo	5	450	0.05	113	11.0	12.8
Bushbuck	5	30	0.02	3	0.3	0.0
Impala	32	40	0.00	0	0.0	3.2

Data on abundance from Cockbill (1969), on body mass from
Coe et al. (1976), on tolerance, expressed as the proportion
of attracted flies that succeed in getting a bloodmeal, from
Vale (1977) and on bloodmeal distribution from Phelps and
Vale (1978). For further explanation see text.

that on average as many as 10 hosts would need to be located
before a bloodmeal can be obtained, and the drain of host
location on the food reserves of a starving tsetse fly will
therefore be very much greater than we had imagined. What
is even more important is that the host tolerance is closely
dependent on the intensity of attack. By adjusting the extent
of coverage by electric nets surrounding the host animal, or
by boosting the attractiveness of the bait with supplementary
host odour, Vale was able to vary attack intensity and to show
that on a given host the proportion of successful feeds decreases markedly as the density of attacking flies increases.
What this implies is that death by starvation will be density
dependent and thus capable of exercising a regulating
influence on population density.

The evidence now seems compelling that starvation is an
important cause of death in adult tsetse flies and that it may
play a major role as a regulating influence in population
dynamics. This is not to say that there may not be other
density-dependent mortality effects, but convincing evidence
is lacking. Pathogens and parasites have rarely been implicated as important agents of mortality, but a variety of
predators have been described including birds, asilids and
spiders (see Nash, 1970). Rogers (1974) has demonstrated
that predation of tethered tsetse flies by birds shows

elements of density dependence, but the relevance of this to
the natural situation is questionable. High priority should
clearly be accorded, however, to the quantitative investigation of the effects of predation under natural conditions.

V. THE BEHAVIOUR OF TSETSE FLIES

     In discussing the ecology of tsetse flies reference has
repeatedly been made to different aspects of tsetse behaviour,
because a thorough knowledge of behaviour is an indispensible
prerequisite to an understanding of ecology. For the study
of insect behaviour the laboratory worker is usually considered to have the advantage over his counterpart in the
field because of the control that he can exercise over the
experimental situation and the precision with which his observations can be made, but reservations often need to be made
concerning the relevance of laboratory studies to the field
situation. Much important information has nevertheless become available from laboratory work, ranging from the results
of the pioneering studies of Jack and Williams (1937) on the
effect of temperature on scototactic responses to the recent
work at Silwood Park on rhythms of activity (Brady, 1972,
1975). The applicability of these studies to refuge-seeking
behaviour (Pilson and Pilson, 1967) and to diurnal rhythms
in the field (Brady and Crump, 1978), has been clearly demonstrated and the value of the work is unquestionable. But with
an insect like the tsetse, many of whose responses appear to
be made in free flight, formidable difficulties are involved
in setting up realistic laboratory experiments, and it would
be a great advantage if studies on some aspects of tsetse
behaviour could be undertaken in the natural habitat. Here
the technique of what might be called "proportionate sampling",
which has already been used to such good effect by Vale,
would appear to hold considerable promise. The use of incomplete rings of electrified nets enables the investigator
to monitor the number of flies moving in and out of a part
of the natural habitat, and the arrangement effectively forms
an arena in which known numbers of flies occur in a completely
natural situation. By determining how many of these respond
to a given stimulus, such as a trap, a refuge site or a host
animal, the strength of the behavioural response can be
accurately quantified in relative terms, as the proportion of
the known total that responds. Studies of this kind could
convincingly reinforce any knowledge gained on the basis of
laboratory work, and thereby lay the foundation for a better
understanding of the daily pattern of activity in a tsetse
population.

Ultimately, what one would like to know is the amount of time the average tsetse fly spends in different types of activity - how many hours at rest in refuges or in exposed resting sites, how many minutes in ranging or olfactorily directed flight - but progress in this area depends on the development of techniques that would enable the location and activity of individual tsetse flies to be continuously monitored. Appropriate technologies are undoubtedly already available, but the cost of applying them to this particular problem could be formidable.

VI. CONCLUSIONS

Recent theoretical and practical developments in tsetse ecology could serve as an effective basis for redressing the current imbalance between physiological and ecological studies. The need for the future will be to take advantage of superior sampling techniques for the investigation of a wide range of species in a wide variety of different habitats, and to determine the extent to which the concepts developed in relation to *G. morsitans* and *G. pallidipes* have general validity. A much more imaginative approach to ecology is now possible in the sense that ecologists can, to some extent, abandon their passive role as observers of the insect in its natural environment in favour of an active manipulation of the situation, thereby moving to the phase of what might be called experimental ecology. The potential here is enormous and, vigorously exploited, could form the basis for a very rapid advance in our understanding of tsetse ecology, especially to the extent that it is informed and supported by modern developments in the physiological and behavioural fields. What should be envisaged is a close and active interchange between the laboratory and the field, with a blurring of the distinction between the tsetse ecologist and the tsetse physiologist. The field however, remains the source of most of the information that we still need, and it is in the field that the future of tsetse biology must ultimately be shaped.

ACKNOWLEDGMENTS

My thanks are due to Dr. R.J. Phelps and Dr. G.A. Vale for helpful discussions and comments.

REFERENCES

Brady, J. (1972). Spontaneous, circadian components of tsetse
    fly activity. *J. Insect Physiol. 18,* 471-484.
Brady, J. (1975). Circadian changes in central excitability –
    the origin of behavioural rhythms in tsetse flies and
    other animals. *J. Entomol. Ser. A. 50,* 79-95.
Brady, J. and Crump, A.J. (1978). The control of circadian
    rhythms in tsetse flies: environment or physiological
    clock? *Physiol. Entomol. 3,* 177-190.
Bursell, E. (1958). The water balance of tsetse pupae. *Phil.
    Trans. Roy. Soc. London Ser. B. 241,* 179-210.
Bursell, E. (1960). The effect of temperature on the consump-
    tion of fat during pupal development in *Glossina. Bull.
    Entomol. Research 51,* 583-598.
Bursell, E. (1961a). The behaviour of tsetse flies (*Glossina
    swynnertoni* Austen) in relation to problems of sampling.
    Proc. Roy. Entomol. Soc. (London) Ser. A. 36, 1-20.
Bursell, E. (1961b). Starvation and desiccation in tsetse
    flies. *Entomol. Appl. Exptl. 4,* 301-310.
Bursell, E. (1966). The nutritional state of tsetse flies
    from different vegetation types in Rhodesia. *Bull. Entomol.
    Research 57,* 171-180.
Bursell, E. (1970). Dispersal and concentration of *Glossina.
    In* "The African Trypanosomiases" (H.W. Mulligan ed.),
    pp. 382-394. George Allen and Unwin, London.
Bursell, E. (1973). Development of mitochondria and contractile
    components of the flight muscle in adult tsetse flies,
    Glossina morsitans. J. Insect Physiol. 19, 1074-1086.
Bursell, E. and Glasgow, J.P. (1960). Further observations on
    lakeside and riverine communities of *Glossina palpalis
    fuscipes* Newstead. *Bull. Entomol. Research 51,* 47-56.
Bursell, E. and Taylor, P. (1980). An energy budget for
    Glossina. Bull. Entomol. Research. (In press).
Cockbill, G.F. (1967). The history and significance of
    trypanosomiasis problems in Rhodesia. *Proc. & Trans,
    Rhodesia Scientific Association 52,* 7-15.
Cockbill, G.F. (1969). Annual report for the year ended 30th
    September, 1968. *Report of the Tsetse and Trypanosomiasis
    Control Branch of the Department of Veterinary Services,
    Rhodesia.* 50 pp.
Coe, M.J., Cumming, D.H. and Phillipson, J. (1976). Biomass
    and production of large African herbivores in relation to
    rainfall and primary productivity. *Oecol.* (Berlin) *22,*
    341-354.
Ford, J. (1969). Feeding and other responses of tsetse to man
    and ox, and their epidemeological significance. *Acta Trop.
    26,* 249-269.

Ford, J. (1970). The search for food. *In* "The African
    Trypanosomiases" (H.W. Mulligan, ed.), pp. 298-304.
    George Allen and Unwin, London.
Ford, J. (1972). Observations on the behavioural responses of
    Glossina to man and ox. *Trans. Roy. Trop. Med. Hyg. 66*,
    314-315.
Ford, J. and Katondo, K.M. (1977). Maps of tsetse fly
    (*Glossina*) distribution in Africa, 1973, according to
    subgeneric groups on a scale of 1: 5 000 000. *Bull.
    Animal Health & Production 25*, 187-193.
Ford, J., Glasgow, J.P., Johns, D.L. and Welch, J.R. (1959).
    Transect fly-rounds in field studies of *Glossina. Bull.
    Entomol. Research 50*, 275-285.
Glasgow, J.P. (1970). Methods for the collecting and sampling
    of *Glossina*: Adults. *In* "The African Trypanosomiases"
    (H.W. Mulligan, ed.), pp. 400-415. George Allen and
    Unwin, London.
Hargrove, J.W. (1977). Some advances in the trapping of tsetse
    (*Glossina* spp.) and other flies. *Econ. Entomol. 2*,
    123-137.
Hargrove, J.W. Tsetse dispersal reconsidered. (In preparation).
Jack, R.W. and Williams, W.L. (1937). The effect of tempera-
    ture on the reaction of *Glossina morsitans* Westw. to
    light. A preliminary note. *Bull. Entomol. Research 28*,
    499-503.
Jackson, C.H.N. (1930). Contributions to the bionomics of
    Glossina morsitans. Bull. Entomol. Research 21, 491-527.
Jackson, C.H.N. (1933). The causes and implications of hunger
    in tsetse flies. *Bull. Entomol. Research 24*, 443-482.
Jackson, C.H.N. (1941). The analysis of a tsetse-fly popula-
    tion. *Ann. Eugenics, Cambridge 10*, 332-369.
Jackson, C.H.N. (1944). The analysis of a tsetse-fly popula-
    tion. II. *Ann. Eugenics, Cambridge 12*, 176-205.
Jackson, C.H.N. (1948). The analysis of a tsetse-fly popula-
    tion. III. *Ann. Eugenics, Cambridge 14*, 91-107.
Jackson, P.J. and Phelps, R.J. (1967). Temperature regimes in
    pupation sites of *Glossina morsitans orientalis*
    Vanderplank (Diptera). *Rhodesia Zambia Malawi J. Agric.
    Research 5*, 249-260.
Jordan, A.M. and Curtis, C.F. (1972). Productivity of
    Glossina morsitans morsitans Westwood maintained in the
    laboratory, with particular reference to the sterile-
    insect release method. *Bull. World Health Organization
    46*, 33-38.
Langley, P.A.L. (1966). The effect of environment and host
    type on the rate of digestion in the tsetse fly *Glossina
    morsitans* Westw. *Bull. Entomol. Research 57*, 39-48.

Lambrecht, F.L. (1972). Field studies of *Glossina morsitans* Westw. (Dipt. Glossinidae) in relation to Rhodesian sleeping sickness in N'gamiland, Botswana. *Bull. Entomol. Research 62*, 183-193.

Laveissière, C. (1977). Ecologie de *Glossina tachinoides* Westw. 1850 en savane humide d'Afrique de l'Ouest. III Etat alimentaire d'une population. *Cahiers ORSTROM, Série Entomologie Médicale et Parasitologie 15*, 331-337.

Madubunyi, L.C. (1978). Relative frequency of reproductive abnormalities in a natural population of *Glossina morsitans morsitans* Westwood (Diptera: Glossinidae) in Zambia. *Bull. Entomol. Research 68*, 437-442.

Nash, T.A.M. (1933). The ecology of *Glossina morsitans* Westw., and two possible methods for its destruction. I & II. *Bull. Entomol. Research 24*, 107-195.

Nash, T.A.M. (1970). Control by parasites and predators of *Glossina*. *In* "The African Trypanosomiases" (H.W. Mulligan, ed.), pp. 521-532. George Allen and Unwin, London.

Phelps, R.J. (1973). The effect of temperature on fat consumption during the puparial stages of *Glossina morsitans morsitans* Wests. (Diptera: Glossinidae) under laboratory conditions, and its implications in the field. *Bull. Entomol. Research 62*, 423-438.

Phelps, R.J. and Burrows, P. (1969a). Prediction of the pupal duration of *Glossina morsitans orientalis* Vanderplank under field conditions. *J. Appl. Ecol. 6*, 323-337.

Phelps, R.J. and Burrows, P.M. (1969b). Lethal temperatures for puparia of *Glossina morsitans orientalis* Vanderplank. *Entomol. Appl. Exptl. 12*, 23-32.

Phelps, R.J. and Clarke, G.P.Y. (1974). Seasonal elimination of some size classes in males of *Glossina morsitans morsitans* Westw. (Diptera: Glossinidae). *Bull. Entomol. Research 64*, 313-324.

Phelps, R.J. and Vale, G.A. (1978). Studies on populations of *Glossina morsitans morsitans* and *G. pallidipes* (Diptera: Glossinidae) in Rhodesia. *J. Appl. Ecol. 15*, 743-760.

Pilson, R.D. and Pilson, B.M. (1967). Behaviour studies of *Glossina morsitans* Westw. in the field. *Bull. Entomol. Research 57*, 227-257.

Potts, W.H. (1953-54). Distribution of tsetse species in Africa compiled from information collated by W.H. Potts, London, Directorate of Colonial Surveys.

Randolph, S.E. and Rogers, D. (1978). Feeding cycles and flight activity in field populations of tsetse (Diptera: Glossinidae). *Bull. Entomol. Research 68*, 655-671.

Rogers, D.J. (1977). Study of a natural population of *Glossina fuscipes fuscipes* Newstead and a model of fly movement. *J. Anim. Ecol. 46*, 281-307.

Rogers, D.J. (1974). Natural regulation and movement of tsetse fly populations. From "Les moyens de lutte contre les trypanosomes et leur vecteurs". *Symposium organised by L'Institut d'élevage et de médicine des pays tropiceaux*, Paris.

Rogers, D.J. and Randolph, S.E. (1979). Metabolic strategies of male and female tsetse (Diptera: Glossinidae) in the field. *Bull. Entomol. Research 68*, 639-654.

Saunders, D.S. (1970). Reproduction in *Glossina*. *In* "The African Trypanosomiases" (H.W. Mulligan, ed.), pp. 327-344. George Allen and Unwin, London.

Schlein, Y. (1979). Age grading of tsetse flies by the cuticular growth layers in the thoracic phragma. *Ann. Trop. Med. Parasit. 73*, 297-298.

Taylor, P. (1976). Blood-meal size of *Glossina morsitans* Westw. and *G. pallidipes* Austen (Diptera: Glossinidae) under field conditions. *Trans. Rhod. Sci. Ass. 57*, 29-34.

Taylor, P. (1980). The construction of a life-table for *Glossina morsitans morsitans* Westw. (Diptera:Glossinidae) from seasonal age measurement of a wild population. *Bull. Entomol. Research*. (In press).

Tobe, S. and Langley, P.A.L. (1978). Reproductive physiology of *Glossina*. *Ann. Rev. Entomol. 23*, 283-307.

Vale, G.A. (1971). Artificial refuges for tsetse flies (*Glossina* spp.). *Bull. Entomol. Research 61*, 331-350.

Vale, G.A. (1974a). New field methods for studying the responses of tsetse flies (Diptera: Glossinidae) to hosts. *Bull. Entomol. Research 64*, 199-208.

Vale, G.A. (1974b). The responses of tsetse flies to mobile and stationary baits. *Bull. Entomol. Research 64*, 545-588.

Vale, G.A. (1977). Feeding responses of tsetse flies (Diptera: Glossinidae) to stationary hosts. *Bull. Entomol. Research 67*, 635-649.

Vale, G.A. and Cumming, D.H.M. (1976). The effects of selective elimination of hosts on a population of tsetse flies (*Glossina morsitans morsitans* Westwood (Diptera: Glossinidae)). *Bull. Entomol. Research 66*, 713-729.

Vale, G.A. and Phelps, R.J. (1978). Sampling problems with tsetse flies (Diptera: Glossinidae). *J. Appl. Ecol. 15*, 715-726.

Weitz, B.G.F. (1970). Hosts of *Glossina*. *In* "The African Trypanosomiases" (H.W. Mulligan, ed.), pp. 317-326. George Allen and Unwin, London.

SCIENCE OF A PEST:
RESEARCH ON THE AFRICAN ARMYWORM AT THE
INTERNATIONAL CENTER OF INSECT PHYSIOLOGY
AND ECOLOGY, NAIROBI

J.W.S. Pringle

Department of Zoology
Oxford University
Oxford, England

I. INTRODUCTION. THE ORIGIN OF THE INTERNATIONAL CENTRE OF
INSECT PHYSIOLOGY AND ECOLOGY, NAIROBI

A. *Wigglesworth and the Export of Scientific Faith*

In a lecture which was published recently in a book form
(Wigglesworth, 1976. Insects and the Life of Man), Professor
Wigglesworth wrote "The prime contribution of pure science is
to make good the deficiency of knowledge." Again; "There is,
indeed, no hard and fast line between what I am calling
empiricism or direct experiment and what I am calling scientific research. Both are supported by the same implicit faith
in the constancy of natural laws - a faith so absolute that
few other religious faiths can equal it. The spread of this
faith among people of every kind is perhaps the greatest of
all the contributions of pure science to every day life."
Opportunity to give practical expression to his faith in
science came in 1969, when Wigglesworth was asked to advise
the Royal Society on the proposal to establish a new and
unusual research centre in Kenya.

B. *The Royal Society and the International Centre of Insect
Physiology and Ecology*

The International Centre of Insect Physiology and Ecology
in Nairobi, Kenya (ICIPE) owes its origin to the simultaneous
and independent initiative of Carl Djerassi, Professor of

925

Chemistry at Stanford University and Thomas R. Odhiambo, who
was then a senior lecturer in the Department of Zoology at
the University College of Nairobi, part of the University of
East Africa. In September 1967, Djerassi presented a paper
at the Pugwash conference in Ronneby, Sweden outlining a
possible pattern for research centres in developing countries.
He had been involved in the successful establishment of a
graduate school in the chemistry department of the University
of Mexico, where the profit from the exploitation of endemic
plant products had made it possible to finance an international research team and train many local scientists. The
published version of Djerassi's paper (Djerassi, 1968) has
the following summary:

"The question is raised whether a basic research center
of an internationally recognised standard of excellence can
be created in a country where scientific manpower is not yet
available. An affirmative answer is provided by proposing
a model which embodies the following three features: 1) an
international cadre of postdoctoral research fellows, 2)
overall scientific direction by a group of part-time directors
from major universities in different 'developed' countries,
and 3) selection of research areas with a possible ultimate
economic pay-off and a maximum multiplication factor."

In November 1967, Odhiambo published an article in Science
(Odhiambo, 1967) in which he summarized the difficulties of
research in Africa and the shortage of trained people. The
University was largely regarded as a teaching institution and
source of high-level manpower for government and private
enterprise, only an infinitesimal number of graduates staying
on to pursue post graduate work. Short-term investigations
for practical projects were performed by research establishments in various government departments, but external advice
was nearly always sought over major scientific issues. A
serious impediment to becoming a natural scientist was the
African's monistic view of nature, so that in his philosophy
there is no sharp distinction between the subjective and
objective worlds, a distinction that is basic to the whole
scientific philosophy. Appreciating that the most relevant
research fields for Africa were, for a long time, likely to be
in those related to agriculture and human and veterinary
medicine, Odhiambo suggested that the best long-term solution
to the problems of conducting effective research would be to
concentrate research effort in a very few large centres. "To
take one example" (he wrote) "for research in insect biology,
one could imagine the establishment of a large institute in a
locale where other ecological conditions are accessible. It
would have a small permanent staff, but would draw a large
number of post graduate students and other researchers from
many countries representing many disciplines (ecology,

taxonomy, physiology, biochemistry, toxicology and others).
The institute's program would be such that it would concentrate all its resources on a few particular problems over a
period, thus ensuring immediate returns from the funds invested in it. One can see the influence of such large 'centers
of excellence' reverberating throughout the countries where it
has been tried. At such centers expensive equipment can be
put to best advantage and the centers offer opportunities
for periodical renovation of one's scientific outlook. But
above all, they are powerhouses for the initiated and for
those wishing to be initiated in research."

Having read Djerassi's article, Odhiambo got in touch with
him and asked if he would be prepared to help launch a centre
of excellence in Nairobi on insect physiology and endocrinology. The idea was taken up by the American Academy of Arts
and Science and by the National Academy, who found considerable support among entomologists and chemists in U.S.A. and
Europe. After several preliminary meetings, an interim
organising group met in Nairobi in October 1969, at which the
Royal Society representatives argued successfully for basic
as opposed to empirical research and a pattern was laid down
for the proposed centre very much on the lines of Djerassi's
suggestions. In order to avoid over-optimism about quick
practical results from 'third-generation insecticides', the
last word in the title of the centre was changed from
'endocrinology' to 'ecology'. My involvement started when I
accepted an invitation to become one of the first Directors
of Research who would collaborate with Odhiambo in defining
and supervising the research programme.

In January 1970 the group met again in Wageningen,
Netherlands and the centre was formally incorporated with
Wigglesworth as one of its Board of Governors. Advice to
the Board would be received from an African Committee with
scientific representatives from African countries and an
International Committee, composed of representatives of
academies of science, to preserve the international character
and maintain high scientific standards. In his report which
led to the participation of the Royal Society of the enterprise, Wigglesworth wrote:

"The aim of the Centre will be to carry out research of
high quality in certain fields of insect physiology and
ecology. The fields selected have been defined by the
interests of an outstanding team of entomologists and chemists
from the United States and Europe who have declared their
readiness to take part. The topics to be studied include
insect 'hormones' controlling growth and reproduction, notably
in the tsetse fly and in locusts; insect 'pheromones'
(chemicals that control mating and other activities); insect

behaviour and ecology; mosquito genetics, including the study
of lethal genes; and the chemistry of plant products which can
act as insect hormones.

The research contemplated will be of fundamental nature;
but the topics chosen are such as may well yield results which
could transform current methods of insect control. To this
end it will be the policy of the Centre to foster close co-
operation with the many specialized institutes in East Africa
that are concerned in the control of insects harmful to man
and animals and to agricultural crops.

In addition to the advance of knowledge in these fields, a
primary aim of the Centre will be educational; to strengthen
the foundations of the University of East Africa by the
training of research students at the postgraduate level,
many of whom should in the future provide good recruits for
the existing institutes. This will be achieved through the
co-operation of the Directors of Research and of other friends
of ICIPE who will accept in their home laboratories the
African holders of ICIPE training grants and will supervise
research at the laboratories in Nairobi to be carried out
internationally mainly by expatriate post-doctoral research
workers, but with increasing co-operation from African
scientists.

The case for this somewhat novel pattern for a research
organization rests upon the coincidence of (1) world wide
interest in this field of study and its potential practical
importance; and (2) the existence of a suitable African
director. But the case for ICIPE is fortified by the educational element which is appropriate to present conditions in
East Africa and has appealed strongly to many of its
supporters. It will increase the provision for the training
of African research students in western laboratories and it
will afford a welcome increase in the opportunities for
western students to obtain some research experience under
rigorous conditions in the tropics."

As may be imagined, financial support for a new type of
centre was not readily obtained, but both research and
training were under way by 1972 through capital grants from
the Universities of Wageningen and Amsterdam and a number of
training fellowships. In that year the range of 'target
insects' was defined at meetings of the Directors of Research.
Support was obtained from the United Nations Development
Programme and a considerable number of aid agencies of
developed countries. The first permanent laboratory building
was financed by Sweden and was formally opened in June 1975.
Since then, development has been continuous, with increasing
cooperation with international agricultural research centres
in various parts of the world. Partly as a result of this
but mainly through financial pressure, the research programme

has become progressively more goal-oriented, but the objectives
are still to 'make good the deficiency of knowledge' rather
than to devise means of control. With the growth of confidence and competence among the African staff, the centre has
become more self-sufficient and in 1979 the system of
visiting Directors of Research was finally abolished and replaced with the more normal pattern of consultants. There has
undoubtedly been a weakening of the links with academies of
science and it remains to be seen whether the ICIPE Foundation,
which in 1977 replaced the original International Committee
as the formal channel for international collaboration, has a
real role to play. Perhaps most successful have been the
training programmes, through which Africans at all levels from
school to post-doctoral scientist are being imbued with 'an
implicit faith in the constancy of natural laws!" The main
lesson that has been learned by all those scientists and ad-
ministrators whose endeavours led to the establishment of
ICIPE has been that one cannot export western ideas about the
organisation of science to the Third World any more than one
can export social systems. What can, hopefully, be exported
is scientific faith, 'the greatest of all the contributions
of science to everyday life'.

II. ARMYWORM RESEARCH: ICIPE IN ACTION

A. *Introduction: The Position in 1972*

    The African armyworm, *Spodoptera exempta*, was one of the
six 'target insects' selected for research at ICIPE at the
time of its initiation. The preface to the First Annual
Report (Odhiambo, 1973) contains the following statement of
the position:
    "Now that the various locust species are under much
improved surveillance and suppression control in Africa, the
most serious hazard, actually or potentially, among the
migratory insect pests in Africa is the African armyworm. We
now have a system of forecasting outbreaks of armyworm moths
that works with reasonable accuracy in East Africa. We know
that the caterpillars restrict their choice of hosts to
graminaceous plants. We do not know the regulatory mechanisms
for this restricted host selection. Nor do we know much about
the behaviour of migratory and non-migratory moths, their
flight behaviour, their energy resources and flight metabolism,
and the way in which they congregate and set their migratory
direction. The ICIPE will be studying these problems, which
are basic to a rational design for the long-term control of
this important pest species."

The foundations of knowledge about this insect were laid
by a team headed by the late E.S. Brown which was based at
the laboratories of the East African Agriculture and Forestry
Organization (EAAFRO), Muguga, Kenya from 1960-68 (Brown and
Swaine, 1966; Brown *et al.*, 1969; Brown, 1970). The extent of
outbreaks varies greatly from year to year, sometimes being
absent altogether from the region, but a frequent pattern is
of a build-up in Tanzania in December, January or February,
followed by outbreaks in Kenya and Uganda between January and
May and in Ethiopia between April and July (Fig. 1). In bad

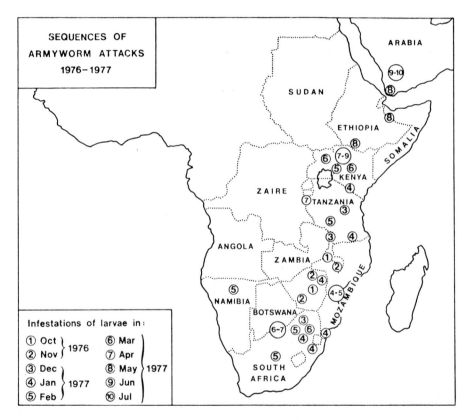

*FIGURE 1. Sequence of armyworm attacks: 1976-1977
(Rainey, 1979).*

years severe outbreaks may occur in southern Arabia between
June and August. This north-moving wave coincides with the

location of the intertropical front where the heaviest rains
occur due to the convergence of air masses and strongly
suggested that extensive migration of moths at night was
taking place. In order to monitor the populations an extensive network of ultra-violet light traps was set up, making it
possible for weekly forecasts to be issued of the areas at
risk (Odiyo, 1979). The reports from these traps confirmed
that for much of the year large areas were almost free of
moths. There was little evidence for a return southward
migration between August and September, though Brown *et al.*
(1969) regarded this as the most probable explanation of the
origin of outbreaks in November and December.

At the time the armyworm research programme at ICIPE was
being planned, E.S. Brown's team had been withdrawn and the
forecasting service was being operated by a reduced group at
EAFFRO, with no further research. Analysis of the light-trap
catches was, however, still being done at the Centre for
Overseas Pest Research in London, who remained interested in
this pest. By general agreement it was therefore decided
that ICIPE should concentrate on various aspects of behaviour,
with the long-term aim of improving the efficiency of the
warning service. A project grant was obtained from the
British Ministry of Overseas Development for equipment and
staff salaries and research started in 1973. The support of
the Royal Society, advised by The British National Committee
for ICIPE, chaired by Wigglesworth, was essential for the
initiation of this programme.

B. Discoveries Since 1973

The sections which follow summarise the more important
discoveries on armyworm biology made at ICIPE during the
period 1973-1978. In January 1975, a workshop was held in
Nairobi attended by most of the entomologists who had worked
on *Spodoptera* species in countries where they are pests and,
partly as a result of this, there has been increased effort
to understand their behaviour. In 1977 there were two major
developments. The Desert Locust Organization for Eastern
Africa (DLCOEA) officially extended its responsibilities to
include control measures against armyworm, and the Centre for
Overseas Pest Research (COPR) put a new and enlarged team to
work on this insect with governmental departments in Kenya and
Tanzania. The basic research at ICIPE, the more goal-oriented
work of national laboratories and COPR and the control plans
of DLCOEA are now coordinated to form a concerted effort to
mitigate the damage done to African agriculture.

III. FLIGHT CAPABILITY AND ORIENTATION

One of the first investigations carried out on the army-worm at ICIPE concerned the migratory capability of the moths (Aidley, 1974). The temporal succession of outbreaks, considered together with meteorological information, provided circumstantial evidence for moth migration over distances of 100-200 km in a downwind direction. By flying moths of both sexes on a flight mill and making allowance for the drag of the mill, Aidley showed that a true air speed of 5 km/hr could be maintained by some moths for the 12 hr period of darkness and that similar flight speeds could be attained during the next night if the moths were allowed to feed on sugar solution. Since night wind velocities of 10-15 km/hr are frequent near convergence zones, there was no physiological reason to doubt the estimates of migration distance.

Obviously the distance covered over the ground would be increased if the moths had some means of orienting their flight at night in a downwind direction. Evidence suggesting this had come from studies with ground-based radar (Schaefer, 1976). It was found that insects have side-view echoes 10-1000 times stronger than those seen end-view, that insects down to the size of small Noctuid moths can be 'seen' individually and that the echo amplitude is modulated at the wing-beat frequency. The ambiguity between the two orientations at 180° can be resolved by track analysis, knowing the wind-speed. Uniformity of orientation of flying insects, of many taxa (as judged by wing-beat frequency), was regularly observed in moonlight, starlight and on overcast nights; it was not seen in zones of strong wind-shift nor generally in very light winds.

It is difficult to imagine how an insect flying at night can obtain information about its orientation in relation to the wind direction except by reference to the ground; visual information is the most likely candidate among the possible senses and it was therefore decided to embark on a study of the visual system of *Spodoptera exempta*. Preliminary experiments showed that the visual threshold is very low and that strong optomotor reactions can be obtained to movement of the visual field (Langer, unpublished). In a further investigation of the fine structure and physiology of the visual receptors, Langer *et al.*, (1979) showed the presence of four different colour sensitivities in the retinula cells, with one cell sensitive in the red up to more than 700 nm. The presence of a very sensitive colour detector, with a high discrimination power, unusual in that it is sensitive also in the long wavelength part of the spectrum, may be of biological

importance for the moth to detect patterns in the visual field
for in-flight orientation during night migration or in connection with the selection of oviposition sites.

IV. REPRODUCTIVE BEHAVIOUR

In a migratory species, the period between emergence of
the female moth and oviposition limits the time and therefore
the geographical distance separating one generation of larvae
from the next. Brown and Swaine (1966) noted that only a
small proportional of females caught in light traps had been
fertilized, suggesting that the ability to fly strongly
develops in the adult before the ability to mate. Brown
et al. (1969) reported some observations made in external
cages at Muguga which showed a pre-oviposition period of 2-16
days depending on the temperature. Further studies of the
reproductive behaviour were obviously needed and these were
carried out at ICIPE from 1974 onwards (Khasimuddin, 1978).

Observations were made on moths both reared in a laboratory culture for 10 generations and hatched from prepupal
larvae and pupae collected at outbreaks. In both populations
all mating took place between 00.30 and 03.30 hrs. The
development of sexual maturity in the male was assayed by the
insect's alerting and courtship behaviour to a mature virgin
female, and was quantified into 10 recognizable stages and
given a numerical value. By scoring each individual male, a
single percentage figure could thus be given for the degree of
maturity of the population. Similarly, the development of
sexual maturity in the females could be measured by the
responses of fully mature males.

Laboratory-bred males required at least 48 hrs after
emergence before responding fully to females, while wild-
caught males matured in 24-36 hr. Laboratory-reared females
took 60 hr whereas wild-caught females were sexually
attractive 48 hr after emergence. Taken together with the
evidence that at some outbreaks a large number of moths fly
strongly on the night of emergence, this confirmed that
migration could occur before oviposition.

Towards the end of the period under review, synthetic
pheromones of *Spodoptera exempta* became available for field
trials (Beevor *et al.*, 1975). Pheromone traps exposed at
outbreak sites regularly caught only small numbers of moths
compared to the catches in light traps, confirming that a
considerable proportion of the insects at the site of
emergence are sexually immature.

V. POPULATION DIVERSITY

    A recognised way of determining the extent to which
mixing occurs throughout the population of a species is to
estimate the diversity of structure and other characteristics
between samples collected from different parts of the geographical range. Partially isolated parts of the population
may be expected to show genetic differences, but even purely
phenotypic variation can be an indicator of geographical
origin in a species like the armyworm in which larval development takes place in an environment different from that in
which migratory adults have been caught.
    Aidley and Lubega (1979) described the results of a study
of mean wing length in populations of moths caught at different times and different places. By statistical analysis of
the measurement on nearly 6,000 moths, they showed that there
is a significant increase in mean wing length at particular
stations later in the outbreak season and that in any one
month the wing lengths tend to be larger at the more northern
stations. In general this suggests that the moths are smaller
when the caterpillar has experienced lower temperatures.
There was no evidence for anything other than phenotypic
influences on this character, but there was evidence for more
than one source of the moths caught at a particular locality
over a period; the sample from one station in Tanzania on one
particular night differed significantly in wing length and sex
ratio from those caught there at other times. All the evidence was consistent with the idea that migrating moths are
concentrated at a meterological convergence zone.
    A search for the existence of true genetic diversity was
conducted by den Boer (1978), using as a measure the
frequency of six alleloenzymes that proved to be genetically
polymorphic. Samples of larvae were collected over a maximum
distance of 2,000 miles in Kenya, Tanzania and Rhodesia and
from different plants and were reared to maturity in the
laboratory. Polymorphism of the enzymes was determined by gel
electrophoresis and the allelic nature of the polymorphism
confirmed by single-pair matings. No heterogeneity among the
samples could be detected in any of the allele frequencies.
Comparison with published data on 17 other species of insect
showed that the average sample size used in this study was
amply sufficient to have revealed heterogeneity if it existed
and it was concluded that extensive mixing of populations by
migration must be occurring, not only in the north-moving
wave in East Africa but also between this population and the
insects which appear in the southern part of the range (see
Fig. 1).

   This work, by itself, indicates that extensive regional
cooperation is essential in any control policy.

VI. OFF-SEASON SURVIVAL

A. *Mechanisms for Survival*

   With increasingly strong evidence for the importance of
migration once dense populations of *Spodoptera exempta* have
become established, the most important question for the
planning of control programmes is the mechanism by which the
species is maintained in Eastern Africa during the off-season.
Research at ICIPE and, recently, by the scientists from COPR
has been increasingly directed towards the solution of various
aspects of this problem. There are three different but not
mutually exclusive possibilities:
   1) That somewhere in the region, possibly in Malawi,
Mozambique, Zambia or northern Rhodesia, there are hitherto
undetected concentrations which provide the source of the
migration waves (Rainey and Betts, 1979).
   2) That there is present throughout the year and over
widely dispersed regions in Eastern Africa a low density of
moths and caterpillars that increase in numbers when conditions
are favourable and get concentrated by atmospheric convergence
to the point when they become recognisable as outbreaks (Rose,
1979).
   3) That under some conditions and towards the end of the
outbreak season, a proportion of caterpillars or pupae enter
a diapause and so survive to emerge at the start of the next
season.
   The search for outbreaks in crops or grassland over a wide
area is not an appropriate subject for work at ICIPE, with its
orientation towards basic research. The other two possibilities do pose fundamental questions of insect biology.

B. *Low-density Populations*

   When present in high concentrations on grassland or
cereal crops, the caterpillars of *Spodoptera exempta* are
black, active and voracious and this form is the usual one in
laboratory cultures. When reared singly, however, the caterpillar is green and this "solitary" form is also found in the
field at low density. Wild populations usually contain a
proportion of 'non-black' caterpillars.
   After a severe outbreak, the moths often disappear
completely from the area. During April 1974, however, observations of moth behaviour at the time of emergence from out-

break sites showed that at some sites the catches in light traps were very low and moths which appeared in all respects to be ready for flight could not be induced to do so, settling immediately if disturbed and remaining on grass stems throughout the night (Khasimuddin, 1980).

It is not known whether the non-migratory form of the moth develops from the solitary green form of the caterpillar; in that case, there would be a true phase phenomenon similar in many respects to that of the desert locust. That the situation is more complicated than this was suggested by a study made in Rhodesia in January to May 1954 of three successive generations in the same area (Rose, 1975). The characteristics of these populations are shown in Table 1. The second generation of small moths, which were predominantly female, laid fertile eggs on the night of emergence and seemed not to migrate. It was suggested that although most of the moths of the first, high-density generation migrated, the smallest of them laid eggs locally to produce the caterpillars of the second, lower-density generation. Although there was a proportion of passive, non-black caterpillars in the third, apparently migratory generation, no fourth generation developed in this area.

TABLE 1. *Summary of Quality Differences Between Successive Generations of S. exempta (from Rose, 1975)*

Generation	Caterpillars		Moths		Pre-Oviposition period
	Size	Phase	Size	Sex Ratio	
?	—	—	Smallest	Mostly ♀♀	—
1	Large	Active	Large	Even	2 days
2	Small	Passive	Small	Mostly ♀♀	1 day
3	Largest	Active Passive	Largest	Even	2 days

Another case involving three successive generations in the same place was found in western Kenya in February to May 1975 by Khasimuddin (1979). Again the density of the second generation was lower than that of the first or third, though the total number of larvae was greater, but here both black and non-black caterpillars were present in each generation,

the proportion of black caterpillars being low in the second.
The sex ratio was not studied and there was a small, progressive increase in the average size of the moths over the
whole period. A fourth generation started, but the young
first- and second-instar larvae were observed dying due to
lack of food owing to lack of tender vegetative growth in the
absence of rain. The size of the caterpillars appeared to
be correlated with the state of the food plants, which was
optimal for the second generation.

It seems clear from these limited observations that low-
density populations can survive for several generations in the
same area under certain conditions, but much further work is
needed to elucidate the exact requirements for this to occur.
In both the cases described, the larval density was much less
in all generations than that found in true outbreaks, which
can reach 5,000 caterpillars per square metre. That even
lower densities occur is indicated by the occasional single
moths caught in light traps over a wide area outside the outbreak season, but the chances of finding green caterpillars,
which are likely to be feeding at the base of grasses, is very
small. Even quite a considerable build-up could occur on
range-land grasses without being reported.

There thus remains the possibility that outbreak densities
may originate by the concentration of moths from dispersed,
low-density populations. The study of these has revealed that
there is an interesting and complicated phase phenomenon in
this species and the physiological basis for this is something
that it would be valuable to understand from laboratory
studies.

C. Diapause

No evidence for diapause in *Spodoptera exempta* was forthcoming from the extensive field and laboratory studies of
Brown *et al.* (1969) and the only previous suggestion that it
may occur was found in Angola by Fonseca and Santos (1965).
The duration of larval and pupal life varies with the environmental temperature but the range of temperatures
experienced in East Africa during the year is too small for
this extension of the generation time to enable the species
to survive the five or six months of the year during which
plant growth is inadequate to support the larvae. During the
study period with which we are concerned, one case has been
described which is very difficult to account for except by the
occurrence of a facultative diapause (Khasimuddin, 1977).

During May and June 1974 extensive outbreaks occurred
throughout Kenya, and fully grown sixth instar larvae and
pupa were collected from many locations and allowed to develop

in the laboratory in Nairobi. The majority of pupae emerged
within two weeks, with an average pupal mortality of 27%,
which is normal. Those that did not emerge were left undisturbed and 4.6% of them produced healthy adult moths at
the beginning of January 1975. The insects showing this
apparent diapause came from five different localities in
Kenya and all of them had pupated 19-25th June 1974.

In spite of search, no further example has been found of
such an extreme extension of the generation time over the
period when there are no outbreaks in Kenya and attempts to
induce diapause by manipulation of the conditions for larval
development have so far been unsuccessful. It is obvious
that if even a small proportion of the population at the end
of one season can enter diapause and survive to emerge at the
beginning of the next favourable growth period, this would
provide a local reservoir, but the conditions required for it
to occur remain unknown.

VII. FOOD PREFERENCE OF THE CATERPILLAR

Among the species of *Spodoptera*, the migratory *exempta* of
Africa and *frugiperda* of America are limited in the field to
graminaceous and cyperaceous plants. *S. exigua*, which may be
migratory and *S. littoralis* which is not are omnivorous and
the larvae are normally found on other types of crop (Brown
and Dewhurst, 1975). A research programme was undertaken at
ICIPE to try to determine the basis for this food preference
in *S. exempta*.

Ma (1976a) investigated the oligophagy by comparing maize
and the non-graminaceous cassava (*Manihot esculenta*) as food
plants. Larvae were reared on semi-synthetic artificial diet
and used for experiments on the second day after the last
larval moult. Food intake in the last larval stage, measured
by the dry weight of frass excreted, was less and development
was slower on cassava, but 63% ultimately started feeding on
cassava and developed fully. If the diet-reared larvae were
allowed to feed on maize for 18 hrs before being transferred
to cassava, only 37% ultimately started feeding; there was
a relationship between the time spent feeding on maize and the
subsequent rejection of cassava. There is therefore some
innate food preference which is increased by experience of
the normal food plant.

Sensory ablation experiments were performed on larvae fed
for 18 hr on maize in order to reveal the basis for the rejection. Bilateral maxillectomy restored the percentage
accepting cassava to the level of larvae that had not fed on
maize (Fig. 2). Further experiments showed that the organ

that was essential for the rejection was the maxillary galea
(Fig. 3). This organ bears two styloconic sensilla, which
are thus the sense organs likely to be responsible for the
discrimination. The question then remained whether selection
was based on acceptable ingredients of the maize or on unacceptable ingredients of the cassava. The former was shown
to be the more probable, since larvae readily accepted cassava
if sandwiched between two discs of maize but under similar
conditions rejected castor (*Ricinus communis*), which belongs
to the same family as cassava but is known to contain feeding
inhibitors.

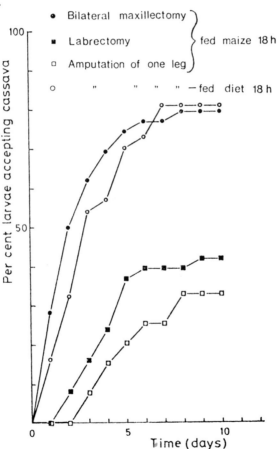

FIGURE 2. *Average cumulative acceptance of cassava within groups of diet-reared armyworm. Comparison between larvae
previously fed on artificial diet and those fed on maize and
subjected to various amputations (Ma, 1976a).*

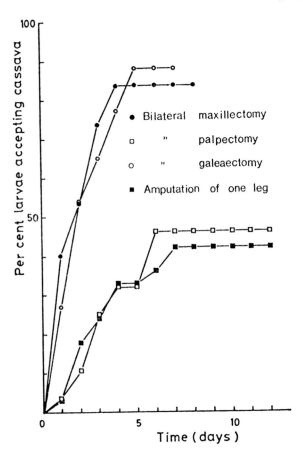

FIGURE 3. Average cumulative acceptance of cassava within groups of diet-reared armyworm larvae, fed on maize for 18 hr before being transferred to cassava and subjected to various amputations (Ma, 1976a).

Ma (1976b) described further behavioural experiments using artificial diet containing various sugars and other compounds and attempted to distinguish between biting, nibbling and continuous ingestion components of the overall feeding behaviour. The order of preference for sugars was shown to correspond to their occurrence in water extracts of species of wild and cultivated graminaceous plants that are the normal food for *S. exempta*, but no influence on feeding behaviour was found for inositol, which is present in the plants and to which there is chemosensitivity. Only minor differences in the order of preference for different sugars was found in experiments with larvae of *S. littoralis*, which is polyphagous.

Ma and Kubo (1977) analysed young maize plants for the presence of phagostimulant chemicals, and distinguished between the ether, hexane and aqueous extracts in their influence on the acceptability of styrofoam carriers with the extracts added. In tests with single fractions, only the aqueous extract induced feeding activity and only to about one third of the level induced by 100 mM sucrose. However, addition of the hexane extract raised the level of acceptance of 25 mM sucrose and addition of both the aqueous and hexane fractions to 25 mM sucrose restored acceptance to the level of 100 mM sucrose. The ether extract was always without effect. Further analysis of the larval behaviour showed that the hexane extract encouraged biting rather than ingestion, thus accounting for its effect when added to sucrose but lack of influence on food intake when tested alone.

More detailed analysis of the aqueous extract showed that, in addition to sucrose, this contained appreciable concentrations of adenosine. When tested by itself, pure adenosine had a phagostimulatory influence equivalent to that of 10 mM sucrose and the effects of adenosine and sucrose were additive. Adenine was less effective. However, since similar results were obtained with larvae of the polyphagous species, *Spodoptera litura*, the ingestion-stimulating components of the aqueous extract could not, by themselves, explain the different food preferences of the two species. The conclusion was that a combination of strong intolerance to chemical feeding inhibitors and a very strict requirement for a well-balance complex of feeding stimulants and biting incitants forms the basis of the oligophagy of *S. exempta*.

Ma (1977a) conducted electrophysiological experiments to determine the sensory capability of the two pairs of styloconic sensilla on the maxillae. In addition to a mechanoreceptor, the medial sensillum contains receptors for salt and for a range of sugars including meso-inositol. The lateral sensillum contains cells sensitive to mechanical stimuli, to salt, to adenosine and specifically to sucrose. Each sensillum has four receptor cells and chemsensitivity of seven of these is thus known. However, once again the range of sensitivity is similar in sensilla of larvae of *S. littoralis*, *S. litura* and also of *S. frugiperda*, so that the electrophysiological studies have not revealed the basis for the monophagy of *S. exempta*.

The problem is obviously extremely complicated and is unlikely to be solved except by a very detailed study of the influence of different sensory stimuli on the successive components of the overall feeding behaviour.

VIII. NATURALLY OCCURRING ANTI-FEEDANTS

An ancillary investigation with which the scientists of the armyworm group at ICIPE were concerned in collaboration with the chemistry laboratory was the mode of action of various chemical compounds found in the African plants. One of the most interesting of these is a group of related sesquiterpenoids (Nakanishi and Kubo, 1977) found in *Warburgia ugandense*. Warburganal is a dialdehyde that strongly suppresses the feeding response; maize leaves dipped in solutions containing 0.1 parts per million of warburganal are not eaten by larvae of *S. exempta* or *S. littoralis* (Meinwald *et al*., 1978). The influence of this compound on sugar sensitivity was investigated by Ma (1977b).

In behavioural tests using an agar-cellulose medium containing 0.1 M sucrose as a phagostimulant, 1 mM warburganal produces a 70% reduction of the feeding response; the threshold is at about 0.5 mM warburganal. This is 1000 times less sensitive than the response threshold using maize leaf discs and indicates that other receptors must be involved in the latter tests.

Electrophysiologically, it was shown that 1 mM warburganal, applied for longer than 1 min, produces irregular bursting discharges from the medial and lateral styloconic sensilla and that thereafter the nervous response to 10 mM sucrose (lateral sensillum) and meso-inositol (medial sensillum) is much reduced. Successive applications of warburganal enhance and prolong the reduction in sensitivity. The inhibitory effect is abolished by addition of cysteine and dithiothreitol, which contain free –SH groups, but not by other amino acids. This suggests that the inhibition is produced by reaction between the aldehyde groups of warburganal and –SH groups in the chemoreceptor membranes of the sensilla, an interpretation which is supported by the observation that other –SH blocking reagents such as p-chloro-mercuribenzoate and N-ethylmaleimide have an action similar to warburganal but at higher concentrations.

XI. CONCLUSION

The research work on the African armyworm described here is an example of the interesting scientific problems that arise from the study of an insect pest. The work so far done at ICIPE, while not yet providing the basis for effective control, has served to extend our knowledge of the biology of

this species and has stimulated other organizations to increase the effort devoted to this problem (Rose and Odiyo,
1979). At the same time, through the involvement of African
research assistants, students and technicians in the work,
the programme has contributed to the development of the
indigenous capacity for scientific research, without which
there is little chance that this part of the developing world
will be able to make its proper contribution to human enterprise.

REFERENCES

Aidley, D.J. (1974). Migratory capability of the African
armyworm moth, *Spodoptera exempta*. *E. Afr. agric. For. J.*
40, 202-205.

Aidley, D.J. (1976). Increase in respiratory rate during
feeding in larvae of the armyworm, *Spodoptera exempta*.
Physiological Entomology 1, 73-75.

Aidley, D.J. (1979). Variation in wing length of the African
armyworm, *Spodoptera exempta* in East Africa during 1973-74.
J. appl. Ecol. 16, 653-662.

Beevor, P.S., Hall, D.R., Lester, R., Poppi, R.G., Read, J.S.
and Nesbitt, Brenda F. (1975). Sex pheromones of the armyworm moth, *Spodoptera exempta* (Wlk.). *Experientia 31*,
22-23.

Brown, E.S. (1970). Control of the African armyworm,
Spodoptera exempta (Walk.) - an appreciation of the
problem. *E. Afr. agric. forest. J. 35*, 237-245.

Brown, E.S. and Swaine, G. (1966). New evidence on the migration of moths of the African armyworm, *Spodoptera exempta*
(Wlk.) (Lepidoptera, Noctuidae). *Bull. ent. Res. 56*,
671-684.

Brown, E.S., Betts, Elizabeth and Rainey, R.C. (1969).
Seasonal changes in distribution of the African armyworm,
Spodoptera exempta (Wlk.) (Lep., Noctuidae), with special
reference to Eastern Africa. *Bull. ent. Res. 58*, 661-728.

Brown, the late E.S. and Dewhurst, C.P. (1975). The genus
Spodoptera (Lepidoptera, Noctuidae) in Africa and the
Near East. *Bull. ent. Res. 65*, 221-262.

den Boer, M.H. (1978). Isoenzymes and migration in the African
armyworm *Spodoptera exempta* (Lepidoptera, Noctuidae).
J. Zool., Lond. 185, 539-553.

Djerassi, C. (1968). A high priority? Research centers in
developing nations. *Bull. atom. Scient. 24*, 22-27.

Fonseca Ferrao, A.P.S. and Santos, F.H. (1965). Estudos pre-
liminares sobre *Laphygma exempta* Wlk. *4ª Jornadas silvo-
agron. 2*, 173-197.

Khasimuddin, S. (1977). On the occurrence of an activating/ diapausing phenomenon in the African armyworm, *Spodoptera exempta* (Wlk.), (Lepidoptera: Noctuidae). *E. Afr. agric. For. J. 42*, 350.

Khasimuddin, S. (1978). Courtship and mating behaviour of the African armyworm, *Spodoptera exempta* (Walker) (Lepidoptera: Noctuidae). *Bull. ent. Res. 68*, 195–202.

Khasimuddin, S. (1980). Behavioural ecology of the African armyworm *Spodoptera exempta* (Walker) (Lepidoptera: Noctuidae); observations on population processes during a high density outbreak. *Insect. Sci. & appl.* (in press).

Khasimuddin, S. and Lubega, M.C. (1979). Behavioural ecology of the African armyworm, *Spodoptera exempta* (Walker) (Lepidoptera: Noctuidae); evidence of successive generations from Kenya. *Bull. ent. Res. 69*, 275–282.

Langer, H., Hamann, B. and Meinecke, C.C. (1979). Tetrachromatic visual system in the moth *Spodoptera exempta* (Insects: Noctuidae). *J. comp. Physiol. 129*, 235–239.

Ma, W-C. (1967a). Experimental observations of food-aversive responses in larvae of *Spodoptera exempta* (Wlk.) (Lepidoptera, Noctuidae). *Bull. ent. Res. 66*, 87–96.

Ma, W-C. (1976b). Mouth parts and receptors involved in feeding behaviour and sugar preception in the African armyworm, *Spodoptera exempta* (Lepidoptera, Noctuidae). *Symp. biol. Hung. 16*, 139–151.

Ma, W-C. (1977a). Electrophysiological evidence for chemosensitivity to adenosine, adenine and sugars in *Spodoptera exempta* and related species. *Experientia 33*, 356–357.

Ma, W-C. (1977b). Alterations of chemoreceptor function in armyworm larvae (*Spodoptera exempta*) by a plant-derived and sesquiterpenoid and by sulphydryl reagents. *Physiological Entomology 2*, 199–207.

Ma, W-C. and Kubo, I. (1977). Phagostimulants for *Spodoptera exempta*: identification of adenosine from *Zea mays*. *Ent. exp. & appl. 22*, 107–112.

Meinwald, J., Prestwich, G.D., Nakanishi, K. and Kubo, I. (1978). Chemical ecology: studies from East Africa. *Science 199*, 1167–1173.

Nakanishi, K. and Kubo, I. (1977). Studies on warburganal, muzigadial and related compounds. *Israel J. Chem. 16*, 28–31.

Odhiambo, T.R. (1967). East Africa: Science for development. *Science 158*, 876–881.

Odhiambo, T.R. (1973). *First Annual Report of the International Centre of Insect Physiology and Ecology*, p.1, Nairobi.

Odiyo, P.O. (1979). Forecasting infestations of a migrant pest: the African armyworm *Spodoptera exempta* (Walk.). *Phil. Trans, R. Soc. Lond. B 287*, 403–413.

Rainey, R.G. (1979). Control of the armyworm *Spodoptera exempta* in Eastern Africa and Southern Arabia. F.A.O. Report.

Rainey, R.G. and Betts, Elizabeth. (1979). Continuity in major populations of migrant pests: the Desert Locust and African armyworm. *Phil. Trans, R. Soc. Lond. B 287,* 359–374.

Rose, D.J.W. (1975). Field development and quality changes in successive generations of *Spodoptera exempta* Wlk., the African armyworm. *J. appl. Ecol. 12,* 727–739.

Rose, D.J.W. (1979). The significance of low density populations of the African armyworm, *Spodoptera exempta* (Walk.). *Phil. Trans, R. Soc. Lond. B 287,* 393–402.

Rose, D.J.W. and Odiyo, P.O. (1979). The African armyworm research project, 1977–79. *Phil. Trans. R. Soc. Lond. B 287,* 487–488.

Schaefer, G.W. (1976). Radar observations of insect flight. *Symp. roy. ent. Soc., Lond. 7,* 157–197.

THE SCIENTIFIC PAPERS
OF V.B. WIGGLESWORTH
FROM 1925 TO 1979

1. Wigglesworth, V.B., Woodrow, C.E., Smith, W. and Winter, L.B. (1923). On the effect of insulin on blood phosphate. *J. Physiol. 57*, 447–450.
2. Wigglesworth, V.B. and Woodrow, C.E. (1923). The relation between the phosphate in blood and urine. *Proc. Roy. Soc. B. 95*, 558–570.
3. Haldane, J.B.S., Wigglesworth, V.B. and Woodrow, C.E. (1924a). The effect of reaction changes on human inorganic metabolism. *Proc. Roy. Soc. B. 96*, 1–14.
4. Haldane, J.B.S., Wigglesworth, V.B. and Woodrow, C.E. (1924b). The effect of reaction changes on human carbohydrate and oxygen metabolism. *Proc. Roy. Soc. B. 96*, 15–28.
5. Wigglesworth, V.B. (1924a). Uric acid in the *Pieridae:* a quantitative study. *Proc. Roy. Soc. B. 97*, 149–155.
6. _____ (1924b). Studies on ketosis: I. The relation between alkalosis and ketosis. *Biochem. J. 18*, 1203–1216.
7. _____ (1924c). Studies on ketosis: II. The oxidation of ketone bodies by the isolated liver of the rat. *Biochem. J. 18*, 1217–1221.
8. Woodrow, C.E. and Wigglesworth, V.B. (1927). The production of lactic acid in frog's muscle *in vivo*. *Biochem. J. 21*, 812–814.
9. Wigglesworth, V.B. (1927a). Digestion in the cockroach. I. The hydrogen ion concentration in the alimentary canal. *Biochem. J. 21*, 791–796.
10. _____ (1927b). Digestion in the cockroach. II. The digestion of carbohydrates. *Biochem. J. 21*, 797–811.
11. _____ (1928a). A colorimetric method for the determination of pH of minute quantities of fluid. *Trans. Roy. Soc. Trop. Med. & Hyg. 21*, No. 4.
12. _____ (1928b). Digestion in the cockroach. III. The digestion of proteins and fats. *Biochem. J. 22*, 150–161.
13. _____ (1929a). Phthiriasis in the Primates: a sidelight on phylogeny. *Proc. Roy. Soc. Med. 22*, 829–830.
14. _____ (1929b). Delayed metamorphosis in a predaceous mosquito larva and a possible practical application. *Nature 123*, 17.
15. _____ (1929c). The early stages of some West African mosquitoes. *Bull. Ent. Res. 20*, 59–68.

16. Wigglesworth, V.B. (1929d). Digestion in the tsetse-fly: a study of structure and function. *Parasitology 21,* 288-321.

17. _____ (1929e). Observations on the *"Furau"* (Cicindelidae) of Northern Nigeria. *Bull. Ent. Res. 20,* 403-406.

18. _____ (1929f). A theory of tracheal respiration in insects. *Nature 124,* 986.

19. _____ (1930a). Some notes on the physiology of insects related to human disease. *Trans. Roy. Soc. Trop. Med. & Hyg. 23,* 553-570.

20. _____ (1930b). A theory of tracheal respiration in insects. *Proc. Roy. Soc. B. 106,* 229-250.

21. _____ (1930c). The formation of the peritrophic membrane in insects, with special reference to the larvae of mosquitoes. *Quart. J. Micr. Sci. 73,* 593-616.

22. _____ (1931a). Digestion in *Chrysops silacea* Aust. (Diptera, Tabanidae). *Parasitology 23,* 73-76.

23. _____ (1931b). Effect of desiccation on the bed-bug *(Cimex lectularius). Nature 127,* 307-308.

24. Sikes, E.K. and Wigglesworth, V.B. (1931). The hatching of insects from the egg, and the appearance of air in the tracheal system. *Quart. J. Micr. Sci. 74,* 165-192.

25. Wigglesworth, V.B. (1931c). The respiration of insects. *Biol. Revs. 6,* 181-220.

26. _____ (1931d). Excretion of uric acid. *Nature 128,* 116.

27. _____ (1931e). The physiology of excretion in a blood-sucking insect, *Rhodnius prolixus* (Hemiptera, Reduviidae). I. Composition of the urine. *J. Exp. Biol. 8,* 411-427.

28. _____ (1931f). The physiology of excretion in a blood-sucking insect, *Rhodnius prolixus* (Hemiptera, Reduviidae). II. Anatomy and histology of the excretory system. *J. Exp. Biol. 8,* 428-442.

29. _____ (1931g). The physiology of excretion in a blood-sucking insect, *Rhodnius prolixus* (Hemiptera, Reduviidae). III. The mechanics of uric acid excretion. *J. Exp. Biol. 8,* 443-451.

30. _____ (1931h). The extent of air in the tracheoles of some terrestrial insects. *Proc. Roy. Soc. B. 109,* 354-359.

31. _____ (1931i). Haematin in the tracheae of blood-sucking insects: an artefact. *Parasitology, 23,* 441-442.

32. _____ (1932a). On the function of the so-called 'rectal glands' of insects. *Quart. J. Micr. Sci. 75,* 131-150.

33. Gillett, J.D. and Wigglesworth, V.B. (1932). The climbing organ of an insect, *Rhodnius prolixus* (Hemiptera,Reduviidae). *Proc. Roy. Soc. B. 111*, 364-376.

34. Wigglesworth, V.B. (1932b). The hatching organ of *Lipeurus columbae* Linn. (Mallophaga), with a note on its phylogenetic significance. *Parasitology 24*, 365-367.

35. _____ (1933a). The effect of salts on the anal gills of the mosquito larva. *J. Exp. Biol. 10*, 1-15.

36. _____ (1933b). The function of the anal gills on the mosquito larva. *J. Exp. Biol. 10*, 16-26.

37. _____ (1933c). The adaptation of mosquito larvae to salt water. *J. Exp. Biol. 10*, 27-37.

38. _____ (1933d). The physiology of the cuticle and of ecdysis in *Rhodnius prolixus* (Triatomidae, Hemiptera); with special reference to the function of the oenocytes and of the dermal glands. *Quart. J. Micr. Sci. 76*, 269-318.

39. Wigglesworth, V.B. and Gillett, J.D. (1934a). The function of the antennae in *Rhodnius prolixus* (Hemiptera) and the mechanism of orientation to the host. *J. Exp. Biol. 11*, 120-139.

40. Wigglesworth, V.B. (1934a). Factors controlling moulting and 'metamorphosis' in an insect. *Nature 133*, 725.

41. Wigglesworth, V.B. and Gillett, J.D. (1934b). The function of the antennae in *Rhodnius prolixus*: confirmatory experiments. *J. Exp. Biol. 11*, 408.

42. Wigglesworth, V.B. (1934b). The physiology of ecdysis in *Rhodnius prolixus* (Hemiptera). II. Factors controlling moulting and 'metamorphosis'. *Quart. J. Micr. Sci. 77*, 191-222.

43. _____ (1935a). Functions of the corpus allatum of insects. *Nature 136*, 338.

44. _____ (1935b). The regulation of respiration in the flea, *Xenopsylla cheopsis*, Roths. (Publicidae). *Proc. Roy. Soc. B. 118*, 397-419.

45. _____ (1936a). The malaria epidemic in Ceylon 1934-1935. *Proc. Roy. Soc. Med. 29*, 20-23.

46. _____ (1936b). Symbiotic bacteria in a blood-sucking insect, *Rhodnius prolixus* Stal. (Hemiptera, Triatomidae). *Parasitology 28*, 284-289.

47. _____ (1936c). Maleria in Ceylon. *Asiatic Review* July 1936, 1-9.

48. _____ (1936d). The function of the corpus allatum in the growth and reproduction of *Rhodnius prolixus* (Hemiptera). *Quart. J. Micr. Sci. 79*, 91-121.

49. Wigglesworth, V.B. and Gillett, J.D. (1936). The loss of
    water during ecdysis in *Rhodnius prolixus* Stal.
    (Hemiptera). *Proc. R. Ent. Soc. Lond. (A) 11*,
    104-107.

50. Wigglesworth, V.B. (1937a). Wound healing in an insect
    (Rhodnius prolixus Hemiptera*)*. *J. Exp. Biol. 14*,
    364-381.

51. _____ (1937b). The chemical regulation of
    insect growth. *In* "Perspectives in Biochemistry"
    (Needham and Green, eds.), pp. 107-113. Cambridge.

52. _____ (1937c). A simple method of volumetric
    analysis for small quantities of fluid: estimation of
    chloride in 0.3ul. of tissue fluid. *Biochem. J. 31*,
    1719-1722.

53. _____ (1938a). The regulation of osmotic
    pressure and chloride concentration in the haemolymph
    of mosquito larvae. *J. Exp. Biol. 15*, 235-247.

54. _____ (1938b). The absorption of fluid from
    the tracheal system of mosquito larvae at hatching
    and moulting. *J. Exp. Biol. 15*, 248-254.

55. _____ (1939a). Hautung bei Imagines von
    Wanzen. *Naturwissenschaften 27*, 301.

56. _____ (1939b). Source of the moulting hormone
    in *Rhodnius* (Hemiptera). *Nature 144*, 753.

57. _____ (1939c). 'Visual adaptation' among
    Lepidoptera: observations and experiments by F.
    Suffert. *Proc. R. Ent. Soc. Lond. (A) 14*, 111-112.

58. _____ (1940a). Local and general factors in
    the development of "pattern" in *Rhodnius prolixus*
    (Hemiptera). *J. Exp. Biol. 17*, 180-200.

59. _____ (1940b). The determination of charac-
    ters at metamorphosis in *Rhodnius prolixus* (Hemiptera).
    J. Exp. Biol. 17, 201-222.

60. _____ (1941a). Permeability of insect cuticle.
    Nature 147, 116.

61. _____ (1941b). The effect of pyrethrum on the
    spiracular mechanism of insects. *Proc. R. Ent. Soc.
    Lond. (A) 16*, 11-14.

62. _____ (1941c). The sensory physiology of the
    human louse *Pediculus humanus corporis* De Geer
    (Anoplura). *Parasitology 33*, 67-109.

63. _____ (1941d). Malaria in war. *Nature 147*,
    436.

64. _____ (1942a). The significance of 'chromatic
    droplets' in the growth of insects. *Quart. J. Micr.
    Sci. 83*, 141-152.

65. Wigglesworth, V.B. (1942b). The storage of protein fat, glycogen and uric acid in the fat body and other tissues of mosquito larvae. *J. Exp. Biol. 19*, 56–77.

66. _____ (1942c). Some notes on the integument of insects in relation to the entry of contact insecticides. *Bull. Ent. Res. 33*, 205–218.

67. _____ (1943). The fate of haemoglobin in *Rhodnius prolixus* (Hemiptera) and other blood–sucking arthropods. *Proc. Roy. Soc. B. 131*, 313–339.

68. _____ (1944a). Preservation of insects attacking plants. *Proc. Roy. Ent. Soc. Lond. C 9*, 5–6.

69. _____ (1944b). Medical entomology. *Discovery* April 1944, 115–119.

70. _____ (1944c). Wordsworth and science. *Nature 153*, 367.

71. _____ (1944d). Action of inert dusts on insects. *Nature 153*, 493.

72. Brecher, G. and Wigglesworth, V.B. (1944). The transmission of *Actinomyces rhodnii* Erikson in *Rhodnius prolixus* Stal (Hemiptera) and its influence on the growth of the host. *Parasitology 35*, 220–224.

73. Wigglesworth, V.B. (1944e). Abrasion of soil insects. *Nature 154*, 333.

74. _____ (1945a). A case of DDT poisoning in man. *Brit. Med. J.* April 14th 1945, 517.

75. _____ (1945b). Growth and form in an insect. *In* "Essays on Growth and Form presented to D'Arcy Wentworth Thompson" pp. 23–40. Oxford.

76. _____ (1945c). Transpiration through the cuticle of insects. *J. Exp. Biol. 21*, 97–114.

77. _____ (1946a). Organs of equilibrium in flying insects. *Nature 157*, 655.

78. _____ (1946b). Water relations of insects. *Experientia II/6*, 1–14.

79. _____ (1946c). DDT and the balance of nature. *Atlantic Monthly*.

80. _____ (1947a). The epicuticle in an insect, *Rhodnius prolixus* (Hemiptera). *Proc. Roy. Soc. B. 134*, 163–181.

81. _____ (1947b). The corpus allatum and the control of metamorphosis in insects. *Nature 159*, 872.

82. _____ (1947c). The site of action of inert dusts on certain beetles infesting stored products. *Proc. R. Ent. Soc. Lond. A 22*, 65–69.

83. _____ (1948a). The functions of the corpus allatum in *Rhodnius prolixus* (Hemiptera). *J. Exp. Biol. 25*, 1–14.

84. Wigglesworth, V.B. (1948b). The structure and deposition
    of the cuticle in the adult mealworm, *Tenebrio
    molitor* L. (Coleoptera). *Quart. J. Micr. Sci. 89*,
    197-217.

85. _____ (1948c). The role of the cell in deter-
    mination. I. Growth changes in *Rhodnius prolixus*.
    Symposia Soc. Exp. Biol. II, Growth, 1-16.

86. _____ (1948d). Interaction of water and
    porous materials. The insect cuticle as a living
    system. *Disc. Faraday Soc., No. 3*, 172-182.

87. _____ (1948e). The insect as a medium for
    the study of physiology. *Proc. Roy. Soc. B 135*,
    430-446.

88. _____ (1948f). The insect cuticle. *Biol. Rev.
    23*. 408-451.

89. _____ (1948g). The insect epicuticle. *Eighth
    International Congress of Entomology*, Stockholm.

90. _____ (1949a). Insect biochemistry. *Ann. Rev.
    Biochem.* 595-614.

91. _____ (1949b). The utilization of reserve
    substances in *Drosophila* during flight. *J. Exp. Biol.
    26*, 150-163.

92. _____ (1949c). Augustus Daniel Imms 1880-
    1949. *Obituary Notices of the Royal Society 6*,
    463-470.

93. _____ (1949d). Les hormones et la regulation
    de la croissance chez un insecte. *Information
    Scientifique*, No. 5, 139-146.

94. _____ (1950a). The physiology of mosquitoes.
    Extract from Boyd's Malariology, 2nd Edn., 284-301.

95. Kramer, S. and Wigglesworth, V.B. (1950). The outer
    layers of the cuticle in the cockroach *Periplaneta
    americana* and the function of the oenocytes. *Quart.
    J. Micro. Sci 91*, 63-72.

96. Wigglesworth, V.B. (1950b). The science and practice of
    entomology. *Advanc. Sci.*, No. 26, 1-8.

97. _____ (1950c). A new method for injecting
    the tracheae and tracheoles of insects. *Quart. J.
    Micr. Sci. 91*, 217-224.

98. Wigglesworth, V.B. and Beament, J.W.L. (1950). The
    respiratory mechanisms of some insect eggs. *Quart. J.
    Micr. Sci. 91*, 429-452.

99. Wigglesworth, V.B. (1951a). Hormones and the metamorphosis
    of insects. *Endeavour 10*, 313-318.

100. _____ (1951b). Insects and human affairs.
    Essex Farmers' Journal 30, 25.

101. _____ (1951c). Metamorphosis in insects.
    Proc. R. Ent. Soc Lond. C. 15, 78-82.

102. Wigglesworth, V.B. (1951d). Source of moulting hormone
     in *Rhodnius*. *Nature 168*, 558.
103. _____ (1952a). The role of iron in histo-
     logical staining. *Quart. J. Micr. Sci. 93*, 105-118.
104. _____ (1952b). Symbiosis in blood-sucking
     insects. *Overged. Tijdschrift Ent. 95*, 63-68.
105. _____ (1952c). The thoracic gland in
     Rhodnius prolixus (Hemiptera) and its role in
     moulting. *J. Exp. Biol. 29*, 561-570.
106. _____ (1952d). Hormone balance and the
     control of metamorphosis in *Rhodnius prolixus*
     (Hemiptera). *J. Exp. Biol. 29*, 620-631.
107. _____ (1953a). Hormones and metamorphosis,
     with special reference to hemimetabolic insects.
     Trans. 9th Int. Congr. Ent. 2, 51-56.
108. _____ (1953b). The origin of sensory
     neurones in an insect, *Rhodnius prolixus* (Hemiptera).
     Quart. J. Micr. Sci. 94, 93-112.
109. _____ (1953c). Motility of insect
     tracheoles. *Nature 172*, 247.
110. _____ (1953d). Hormones and the development
     of hybrid Lepidoptera. *Entomologist's Record 65*,
     244-245.
111. _____ (1953e). Determination of cell
     function in an insect. *J. Embryol. Exp. Morph. 1*,
     269-277.
112. _____ (1953f). Surface forces in the
     tracheal system of insects. *Quart. J. Micr. Sci. 94*,
     507-522.
113. _____ (1954a). Organo-phosphorus insecti-
     cides. *Chemistry and Industry*, 477-478.
114. _____ (1954b). Growth and regeneration in
     the tracheal system of an insect, *Rhodnius prolixus*
     (Hemiptera). *Quart. J. Micr. Sci. 95*, 115-137.
115. _____ (1954c). Secretion of juvenile
     hormone by the corpus allatum of Calliphora. *Nature
     174*, 556.
116. _____ (1955a). The endocrine chain in an
     insect. *Nature 175*, 338.
117. _____ (1955b). The breathing mechanism of
     insects. *Discovery*, 110-113.
118. _____ (1955c). The mode of action of DDT.
     *Das Insektizid Dichlorphenyltrichlorathan und seine
     Bedeutung 1*, 93-111.
119. _____ (1955d). The contribution of pure
     science to applied biology. *Ann. Appl. Biol. 42*,
     34-44.

120. Wigglesworth, V.B. (1955e). The breakdown of the thoracic gland in the adult insect, *Rhodnius prolixus*. *J. Exp. Biol. 32*, 485-491.

121. _____ (1955f). The role of the haemocytes in the growth and moulting of an insect, *Rhodnius prolixus* (Hemiptera). *J. Exp. Biol. 32*, 649-663.

122. _____ (1955g). The control of metamorphosis in an insect. *Roy. Inst. Gt. Britain*, 7 pp.

123. _____ (1956a). The haemocytes and connective tissue formation in an insect, *Rhodnius prolixus* (Hemiptera). *Quart. J. Micr. Sci. 97*, 89-98.

124. _____ (1956b). Insect physiology in relation to insecticides. *J. Roy. Soc. Arts 104*, 426-438.

125. _____ (1956c). The functions of the amoebocytes during moulting in *Rhodnius*. *Ann. Des. Sci. Nat. Zool. 18*, 139-144.

126. _____ (1956d). Hormones and the metamorphosis of insects. *Scientia 50*, 4 pp.

127. _____ (1956e). Le role des hormones dans la metamorphose des insectes. *Scientia 50*, 4 pp.

128. _____ (1956f). La metamorfcsi degli insetti. *Rendiconti 3*, 3-7.

129. _____ (1956g). Patrick Alfred Buxton, 1892-1955. *Biographical Memoirs of Fellows of the Royal Society 2*, 69-84.

130. Zwicky, K. and Wigglesworth, V.B. (1956). The course of oxygen consumption during the moulting cycle of *Rhodnius prolixus* Stal (Hemiptera). *Proc. R. Ent. Soc. Lond. A. 31*, 153-160.

131. Wigglesworth, V.B. (1956h). Formation and involution of striated muscle fibres during the growth and moulting cycles of *Rhodnius prolixus* (Hemiptera). *Quart. J. Micr. Sci. 97*, 465-480.

132. _____ (1956i). Modo d'azione degli ormoni della crescita in *Rhodnius prolixus* Stal. *Boll. Zool. Agr. Bachic. 22*, 1-13.

133. _____ (1957a). The physiology of insect cuticle. *Ann. Rev. Ent. 2*, 37-54.

134. _____ (1957b). How an insect climbs up glass. *New Scientist*, April, 3 pp.

135. _____ (1957c). A simple method for staining mitochondria. *Nature 179*, 1033-1034.

136. _____ (1957d). The action of growth hormones in insects. *Symp. Soc. Exp. Biol. 11*, 204-227.

137. _____ (1957e). The use of osmium in the fixation and staining of tissues. *Proc. Roy. Soc. B 147*, 185-199.

138. Wigglesworth, V.B. (1957f). Insects and the farmer. (The fourth Middleton Memorial Lecture). *Agric. Progress 32*, 1-8.

139. _____ (1958a). Abrasion of the insect cuticle by aqueous suspensions of small particles. *Nature 181*, 779-780.

140. _____ (1958b). Some methods for assaying extracts of the juvenile hormone in insects. *J. Ins. Physiol. 2*, 73-84.

141. _____ (1958c). The integration of growth in *Rhodnius prolixus* Stal. *Proc. 10th Int. Congr. Ent. 1956 2*, 51-55.

142. _____ (1958d). The distribution of esterase in the nervous system and other tissues of the insect *Rhodnius prolixus*. *Quart. J. Micr. Sci. 99*, 441-450.

143. Smith, D.S. and Wigglesworth, V.B. (1959). Collagen in the perilemma of insect nerve. *Nature 183*, 127-128.

144. Wigglesworth, V.B. (1959a). Metamorphosis, polymorphism, differentiation. *Sci. Amer. 200*, 100-110.

145. _____ (1959b). The breathing tubes of insects. *New Scientist 5*, 567-569.

146. _____ (1959c). Insect blood cells. *Ann. Rev. Ent. 4*, 1-16.

147. _____ (1959d). The histology of the nervous system of an insect, *Rhodnius prolixus* (Hemiptera). I. The peripheral nervous system. *Quart. J. Micr. Sci. 100*, 285-298.

148. _____ (1959e). The histology of the nervous system of an insect, *Rhodnius prolixus* (Hemiptera). II. The central ganglia. *Quart. J. Micr. Sci. 100*, 299-313.

149. _____ (1959f). A simple method for cutting sections in the 0.5 to 1 µ range, and for sections of chitin. *Quart. J. Micr. Sci. 100*, 315-320.

150. _____ (1959g). The role of the epidermal cells in the 'migration' of tracheoles in *Rhodnius prolixus* (Hemiptera). *J. Exp. Biol. 36*, 632-640.

151. _____ (1960a). Nutrition and reproduction in insects. *Proc. Nutr. Soc. 19*, 18-23.

152. _____ (1960b). Metamorphosis and body form. *Harvey Lectures, 1958-1959*, 40-59.

153. _____ (1960c). The fauna of the orchard (Amos Memorial Lecture). *Ann. Rep. E. Malling Res. Sta. 1959*, 39-43.

154. _____ (1960d). Fuel and power in flying insects. *New Scientist 8*, 101-104.

155. Wigglesworth, V.B. and Beament, J.W.L. (1960). The
     respiratory structures in the eggs of higher
     Diptera. *J. Ins. Physiol. 4*, 184-189.
156. Wigglesworth, V.B. (1960e). Insektenmetamorphose und
     "Jugend-Hormon". *Umschau 60*, 389-391.
157. _____ (1960f). The nutrition of the central
     nervous system in the cockroach *Periplaneta americana*
     L. The role of perineurium and glial cells in the
     mobilization of reserves. *J. Exp. Biol. 37*, 500-512.
158. _____ (1960g). The epidermal cell and the
     metamorphosis of insects. *Nature 188*, 358-359.
159. _____ (1960h). Axon structure and the
     dictyosomes (Golgi bodies) in the neurones of the
     cockroach, *Periplaneta americana. Quart. J. Micr.
     Sci. 101*, 381-388.
160. _____ (1960i). The Tracheae and Tracheoles
     of insects. *XI Int. Cong. Entom. Wien*, 627-630.
161. _____ (1960j). Nutrition of the central
     nervous system of the cockroach, *Periplaneta
     americana* L. *XI Int. Cong. Entom. Wien*, 631.
162. _____ (1961a). Some histological studies on
     insect growth. *The Ontogeny of Insects. (Symposium
     in Prague 1959)*, 1961, 41-44.
163. _____ (1961b). The metamorphosis of insects.
     Notes Roy. Soc. Lond. 16, 81-84.
164. _____ (1961c). The epidermal cell. *The Cell
     and the Organism*, 127-143.
165. _____ (1961d). Some observations on the
     juvenile hormone effect of farnesol in *Rhodnius
     prolixus* Stal (Hemiptera). *J. Ins. Physiol. 7*, 73-78.
166. Schmialek, P. (1961e). (Appendix by V.B. Wigglesworth).
     Die Identifizierung zweier im Tenebriokot und in Hefe
     vorkommender Substanzen mit Juvenilhormonwirkung.
     Z. Naturfrisch 16b, 461-464.
167. Wigglesworth, V.B. (1961f). Insect Polymorphism - A
     tentative synthesis. *Insect Polymorphism*, 104-113.
168. _____ (1961g). Trachées et Trachéoles chez
     les Insectes. *Bull. Soc. Sci. Bret. 36*, 119-131.
169. _____ (1961h). La métamorphose des Insectes
     det l'Hormone juvenile (1). *Bull. Soc. Sci. Bret. 36*,
     113-118.
170. _____ (1962a). Insect forms and evolution.
     Discovery, 22-27.
171. _____ (1962b). Endocrine regulation during
     development 1. Hormones in relation to Metamorphosis.
     Gen. Comp. End. 1, 316-321.
172. Wigglesworth, V.B. and Salpeter, M.M. (1962a). Histology
     of the Malpighian tubules in *Rhodnius prolixus* Stal
     (Hemiptera). *J. Ins. Physiol. 8*, 299-307.

173. Wigglesworth, V.B. and Salpeter, M.M. (1962b). The aero-scopic chorion of the egg of *Calliphora erythrocephala* Meig. (Diptera) studied with the electron microscope. *J. Ins. Physiol. 8*, 635-641.

174. Wigglesworth, V.B. (1963a). Origin of wings in insects. *Nature 197*, 97-98.

175. _____ (1963b). The juvenile hormone effect of farnesol and some related compounds: quantitative experiments. *J. Ins. Physiol. 9*, 105-119.

176. _____ (1963c). The action of moulting hor-mone and juvenile hormone at the cellular level in *Rhodnius prolixus*. *J. Exp. Biol. 40*, 231-245.

177. _____ (1963d). A further function of the air sacs in some insects. *Nature 198*, 106.

178. _____ (1963e). The origin of flight in insects. *Proc. Roy. Ent. Soc. 28*, 23-32.

179. _____ (1963f). How insects survive extreme conditions. *Discovery*, 43-47.

180. _____ (1964a). The union of protein and nucleic acid in the living cells and its demonstra-tion by osmium staining. *Quart. J. Micr. Sci. 105*, 113-122.

181. _____ (1964b). The hormonal regulation of growth and reproduction in insects. *Advances in Insect Physiology 2*, 247-336.

182. _____ (1964c). Homeostasis in insect growth. *Symp. Soc. Exp. Biol. 18*, 265-281.

183. _____ (1965a). Insect Hormones. *Endeavour*, 21-26.

184. _____ (1965b). Biological control of pests. *Sci. J. 1*, 40-45.

185. _____ (1965c). The contributions of Sir John Lubbock (Lord Avebury) to insect physiology. Presi-dential Address: *R. Ent. Soc.*, 55-60.

186. _____ (1965d). Inaugural address: Fifty years of Insect Physiology. *XIIth Int. Cong. Entom.*, 40-45.

187. _____ (1965e). Proceedings of the Associa-tion of Applied Biologists. *Ann. appl. Biol. 56*, 315-350.

188. _____ (1965f). The juvenile hormone. *Nature 208*, 522-524.

189. _____ (1965g). Cell Associations and Organogenesis in the nervous system of insects. Re-printed from *Organogenesis* (R.L. DoHaan and H. Ursprung, eds.), pp. 199-217. Holt, Rinehart and Winston.

190. Wigglesworth, V.B. (1966a). Chairman's Introduction. *In* "Aspects of Insect Biochemistry" (T.W. Goodwin, ed.), xi. Academic Press, London and New York.

191. _____ (1966b). Hormones controlling growth and development in insects. *In* "Aspects of Insect Biochemistry" (T.W. Goodwin, ed.), pp. 79-82. Academic Press, London and New York.

192. _____ (1966c). Hormonal regulation of differentiation in insects. *In* "Cell differentiation and morphogenesis" (W. Beermann *et al*, eds.), pp. 180-209. North Holland Publ. Co., Amsterdam.

193. _____ (1966d). 'Catalysomes', or Enzyme Caps on Lipid Droplets: an Intracellular Organelle. *Nature 210*, 759.

194. _____ (1966e). Polyploidy and Nuclear Fusion. *Nature 212*, 1581.

195. _____ (1966f). Preformation and insect development. *Natuur-,Genees- en Heelkunde*, 3-26.

196. _____ (1967a). Summing up:Growth Hormones and the Gene System in the Insect *Rhodnius*. *Endocrine Genetics*, Memoirs of the Society for Endocrinology *15*, 77-85.

197. _____ (1967b). Cytological changes in the fat body of *Rhodnius* during starvation, feeding and oxygen want. *J. Cell Sci. 2*, 243-256.

198. _____ (1967c). The religion of science. *Ann. appl. Biol. 60*, 1-10.

199. _____ (1967d). The religious faith of the scientist. *Quaestiones entomologicae 4*, 245-247.

200. _____ (1967e). Polyploidy and Nuclear Fusion in the Fat Body of *Rhodnius* (Hemiptera). *J. Cell Sci. 2*, 603-616.

201. _____ (1969a). Chemical Structure and Juvenile Hormone Activity. *Nature 221*, 190-191.

202. _____ (1969b). Chemical structure and Juvenile Hormone Activity: comparative tests on *Rhodnius prolixus*. *J. Insect Physiol. 15*, 73-94.

203. _____ (1969c). Juvenile Hormone assays in insects, with special reference to metabolic breakdown. *Gen. comp. Endocr. 13*, 163.

204. _____ (1969d). The Insect Cuticle. *Memorie Soc. ent. ital. 48*, 167-178.

205. _____ (1970a). The pericardial cells of insects: analogue of the reticuloendothelial system. *J. Reticuloendothelial Soc. 7*, 208-216.

206. _____ (1970b). Structural lipids in the insect cuticle and the function of the oenocytes. *Tissue and Cell 2*, 155-179.

207. Wigglesworth, V.B. (1971a). Bound Lipid in the tissues of Mammal and Insect: a new histochemical method. *J. Cell Sci. 8*, 709-725.

208. _____ (1971b). Experimental Biology, pure and applied. *J. Exp. Biol. 55*, 1-12.

209. _____ (1971c). Boris Petrovitch Uvarov. 1889-1970. *Biographical Memoirs of Fellows of Royal Society 17*, 713-740.

210. _____ (1972). Insect Respiration. *Oxford Biology Readers*.

211. _____ (1973a). Assays on *Rhodnius* for Juvenile Hormone activity. *J. Insect Physiol. 19*, 205-211.

212. _____ (1973b). Haemocytes and basement membrane formation in *Rhodnius*. *J. Insect Physiol. 19*, 831-844.

213. _____ (1973c). Book Review: Insect Juvenile Hormones: Chemistry and Action. (J.J. Menn and M. Beroza, eds.). *Pesticide Biochemistry and Physiology 2*, 456-457.

214. _____ (1973d). The significance of "apolysis" in the moulting of insects. *J. Ent. (A) 47*, 141-149.

215. _____ (1973e). The role of the epidermal cells in moulding the surface pattern of the cuticle in *Rhodnius* (Hemiptera). *J. Cell Sci. 12*, 683-705.

216. _____ (1973f). History of Insect Physiology. (R.F. Smith, T.E. Mitten, and C.N. Smith, eds.), 517 pp. *Ann. Rev. Inc.*, Palo Alto.

217. _____ (1973g). Evolution of insect wings and flight. *Nature 246*, 127-129.

218. _____ (1973h). A Tribute to Sir Rickard Christophers on his 100th Birthday. *Trans. R. Soc. trop. Med. Hyg. 67*, 747-749.

219. _____ (1974a). Insect Hormones. (J.J. Head, ed.). *Oxford Biology Readers*, 1-16.

220. _____ (1974b). Insecta. *Encyclopaedia Britannica 15th Edn.*, 608-622.

221. _____ (1974c). Caste Determination. *Supplement to Bee World 55*, 148-150.

222. _____ (1975a). Lipid staining for the electron microscope: a new method. *J. Cell Sci. 19*, 425-437.

223. _____ (1975b). Distribution of lipid in the lamellate endocuticle of *Rhodnius prolixus*. *J. Cell Sci. 19*, 439-457.

224. Wigglesworth, V.B. (1975c). Incorporation of lipid into the epicuticle of *Rhodnius* (Hemiptera). *J. Cell Sci. 19*, 459–485.

225. _____ (1976a). The Evolution of Insect Flight. Insect Flight. *Symposia of the Roy. Ent. Soc. London* No. 7, 225–269.

226. _____ (1976b). Juvenile hormone and pattern formation. *Insect Development. 8th Symposium of the Roy. Ent. Soc. London,* 186–202.

227. _____ (1976c). The distribution of lipid in the cuticle of *Rhodnius*. *In* "The Insect Integument" (H.R. Hepburn, ed.), pp. 89–106. Elsevier, Amsterdam.

228. _____ (1976d). Préformation et croissance chex les insectes. *Bulletin de la Société Zoologique de France 101,* 771–780.

229. _____ (1977a). Structural changes in the epidermal cells of *Rhodnius* during tracheole capture. *J. Cell Sci. 26,* 161–174.

230. _____ (1977b). The waterproofing layer of the insect cuticle. *Symp. zool. Soc. Lond.* No. 39, 33–34.

231. _____ (1977c). J. Arthur Ramsay and Transport Physiology. *In* "Transport of ions and water in animals" (B.L. Gupta, R.B. Moreton, J.L. Oschman and B.J. Wall, eds.), pp. 1–8. Academic Press, London.

232. _____ (1977d). The control of form in the living body. *In* "The Encyclopaedia of Ignorance" (R. Duncan and M. Weston-Smith, eds.), Pergamon Press, Oxford,

233. _____ (1977e). The Juvenile Hormone as an agent for Pest Control. *In* "Produits Naturels et la Protection des Plantes", pp. 301–314. *Pontificiae Academia Scientiarvm Varia,* No. 41., 301–314

234. _____ (1979). Secretory activities of plasmatocytes and oenocytoids during the moulting cycle in an insect *(Rhodnius). Tissue and Cell 11,* 69–78.

THE BOOKS OF V.B. WIGGLESWORTH

Wigglesworth, V.B. (1934). "Insect Physiology." Methuen, London.

_____ (1956). "Insect Physiology." Methuen, London, 5th edition (revised).

_____ (1966). "Insect Physiology." Methuen, London, 6th edition (revised).

_____ (1974). "Insect Physiology." Chapman & Hall, London, 7th edition (revised).

Wigglesworth, V.B. (1937). "Insect Physiology." Chapman &
    Hall, London, Russian edition.
    _____ (1959). "Physiologie des Insectes." Dunod,
    Paris, French edition.
    _____ (1939). "The Principles of Insect
    Physiology." Methuen, London.
    _____ (1951). "The Principles of Insect
    Physiology." Methuen, London, 4th edition (revised).
    _____ (1953). "The Principles of Insect
    Physiology." Methuen, London, 5th edition (4th edition
    with addenda).
    _____ (1965). "The Principles of Insect
    Physiology." Methuen, London, 6th edition (revised).
    _____ (1972). "The Principles of Insect
    Physiology." Chapman & Hall, London, 7th edition (revised).
    _____ (1955). "Physiologie der Insekten." German
    translation by M. Lüscher. Birkhäuser, Basel.
    _____ (1954). "The Physiology of Insect
    Metamorphosis." Cambridge University Press.
    _____ (1959). "The Control of Growth and From."
    Cornell University Press, Ithaca.
    _____ (1964). "The Life of Insects." Weidenfeld
    & Nicolson, London.
    _____ (1970). "Insect Hormones." Oliver & Boyd,
    Edinburgh.
    _____ (1976). "Insects and the Life of Man."
    Chapman & Hall, London.

INDEX